Karl E. Case
Wellesley College

Ray C. Fair
Yale University

J. Frank Strain
Mount Allison University

Michael R. Veall
McMaster University

**First Canadian
Edition**

Principles of Microeconomics

**Prentice Hall Canada Inc.
Scarborough, Ontario**

Canadian Cataloguing in Publication Data

Principles of microeconomics

1st Canadian ed.
Includes index
ISBN 0-13-260407-8

1. Microeconomics.   I. Case, Karl E.

HB172.P74   1998   338.5   C97-931697-9

Prentice-Hall, Inc., Upper Saddle River, New Jersey
Prentice-Hall International (UK) Limited, London
Prentice-Hall of Australia, Pty. Limited, Sydney
Prentice-Hall Hispanoamericana, S.A., Mexico City
Prentice-Hall of India Private Limited, New Delhi
Prentice-Hall of Japan, Inc., Tokyo
Simon & Schuster Southeast Asia Private Limited, Singapore
Editora Prentice-Hall do Brasil, Ltda., Rio de Janeiro

ISBN 0-13-260407-8

Publisher: Pat Ferrier
Acquisitions Editor: Sarah Kimball
Developmental Editor: Maurice Esses
Senior Marketing Manager: Ann Byford
Copy Editor: Gail Copeland
Production Editor: Marjan Farahbaksh
Production Coordinator: Deborah Starks
Photo Research: Susan Wallace-Cox
Cover Design: David Cheung
Cover Image: Amwell/Tony Stone Images
Page Layout: Bill Renaud

Original edition published by Prentice-Hall, Inc., a division of Simon & Schuster, Upper Saddle River, New Jersey
Copyright © 1996 by Prentice-Hall Inc.

  2 3 4 5   RRD   01 00 99

Printed and bound in the United States

Visit the Prentice Hall Canada Web site! Send us your comments, browse our catalogues, and more.
www.phcanada.com Or reach us through e-mail at **phcinfo_pubcanada@prenhall.com**

Brief Table of Contents

Contents

INTRODUCTION

Global Coverage

Because the study of economics crosses national boundaries, this book includes international examples in almost every chapter. The following list is a summary of global examples and discussions in the text.

Preface

Economics is an important and exciting area of study. For those with purely intellectual interests, it offers one of the most elaborate constructions of sustained philosophical reasoning in existence. For the practically minded, it offers a unique way of thinking about problems that confront each of us every day, and it provides important insight into issues that dominate the front pages of our newspapers. Those with an interest in a business career will find much of direct relevance. So too will those interested in public policy.

A principles of economics course is, for many, the first serious introduction to economics. It is not an easy introduction, because students of economics must learn to think critically. They must be able to identify economic problems, acquire a firm grasp of basic economic principles and concepts, and, most importantly, develop their ability to apply the analytical tools of economics to economic problems. Simply reading a textbook and listening to lectures will not result in critical thinking. Students must learn by doing. Learning economics is an active process in which students continually apply new concepts to solve real problems.

Fortunately, there is an elaborate support network that can help students as they work through the basic principles of economics. The most important pillar in this support network is the instructor, who will both design and deliver the course. Your instructor's job is to make learning easier by introducing the principles and by showing how these principles can be used to yield insights into real probelms. Your instructor is also a motivator, a role model, and an indispensible resource. There is no substitute for the experience of seeing a live person setting up a problem and working it through.

The textbook is the second critical pillar of the support network. The text complements the lectures by providing an invaluable resource and reference. If a student misses an important point in a lecture, he or she must be able to revisit it in the textbook. But a textbook must be more than a reference tool. It should also supplement the lectures by offering a more comprehensive treatment of the principles. It should include numerous applications and real-world problems to help students appreciate the variety of issues that economics can illuminate. And it should help motivate students.

This textbook has been carefully designed to provide the best possible support for students attempting to master the principles of economics. It reflects the current state of knowledge about the way students learn. Content, organization, style, layout, the use of visual aids, and the presentation of real-world examples are all known to have an influence on student success. This book also incorporates the most current approaches to textbook design.

The Plan of *Principles of Microeconomics,* First Canadian Edition

The purpose of this volume is to introduce the discipline of economics and to provide a basic understanding of how economies function. This requires a blend of economic theory, institutional material, and real-world applications. We have tried to maintain a reasonable balance between these ingredients in every chapter in this book. We have also tried to present different theoretical views in an evenhanded way.

ORGANIZATION

The organization of the microeconomic material reflects our belief that the best way to understand how market economies operate—and the best way to understand basic economic theory—is to work through the perfectly competitive model first, including discussions of output *and* input markets and the connections between them, before turning to noncompetitive market structures. When students understand how a simple competitive system works, they can start thinking about how the pieces of the economy "fit together." We think this is a better approach to teaching economics than some of the more traditional approaches, which encourage students to think of economics as a series of disconnected alternative market models.

Doing competition first also allows students to see the power of the market system. It is impossible to discuss the things that markets do well until students have seen how a simple system determines the allocation of resources. This is our purpose in Chapters 6–11. Chapter 12 links the world of perfect competition with the imperfect world of noncompetitive markets, externalities, imperfect information, and poverty, all of which we discuss in Chapters 13–17. In Chapters 18–20 students use everything they've learned in Chapters 6–17 to take a closer look at some of the fields of applied microeconomics (the economics of taxation, labour economics, and the economics of health care and immigration). Finally, in Chapters 21–23, we examine some topics in international economics. Although we've chosen to place these chapters at the end of the book, instructors can integrate them into their course at any time they feel is appropriate.

COURSE DESIGNS

We also recognize that each instructor will want to leave his or her own stamp on the course. Moreover, time is always tight in the principles course and few instructors will try to cover all chapters in this text. Therefore, we have designed text to give instructors maximum flexibility in designing their own course.

A principles of microeconomics course that covers the standard core of material over one semester would likely include:

The Scope and Methods of Economics	Chapter 1
The Economic Problem: Scarcity and Choice	Chapter 2
The Structure of the Canadian Economy: The Private, Public, and International Sectors (This chapter is not analytically demanding and need not be covered in the lectures)	Chapter 3
Demand, Supply, and Market Equilibrium	Chapter 4
The Price System, Supply and Demand, and Elasticity	Chapter 5
Household Behaviour and Consumer Choice	Chapter 6
The Behaviour of Profit-Maximizing Firms and the Production Process	Chapter 7
Short-Run Costs and Output Decisions	Chapter 8
Costs and Output Decisions in the Long Run	Chapter 9
Input Demand: The Labour and Land Markets	Chapter 10
Monopoly	Chapter 13
Monopolistic Competition and Oligopoly	Chapter 14

The standard core shouldn't require more than 10 weeks to cover. Instructors interested in delivering a strong theory course may consider also covering:

The Capital Market and the Investment Decision	Chapter 11
General Equilibrium and the Efficiency of Perfect Competition	Chapter 12
Externalities, Public Goods, Imperfect Information, and Social Choice	Chapter 16
International Trade, Comparative Advantage, and Protectionism	Chapter 21

Those instructors who prefer a focus on policy and economic issues have a variety of options including:

Competition Policy and Regulation in Canada	Chapter 15
Income Distribution and Poverty	Chapter 17
Public Finance: The Economics of Taxation	Chapter 18
The Economics of Labour Markets and Labour Unions	Chapter 19
Current Topics in Applied Microeconomics: Health Care and Immigration	Chapter 20
Economic Growth in Developing Countries	Chapter 22
Economies in Transition and Alternative Economic Systems	Chapter 23

It is also possible for instructors to deviate significantly from the standard core by judicially covering basic theoretical concepts and four or five policy-oriented topics.

The Plan of *Principles of Macroeconomics*, First Canadian Edition

For professors who are teaching macroeconomics, a companion volume entitled *Principles of Macroeconomics* is also available.

This volume combines a study of economic theory, institutions, and real-world applications to provide a basic understanding of how the macroeconomy functions. We have tried to blend these ingredients in every chapter and have always remembered that the purpose of the graphs and the analysis is to help students understand actual economic events and policy debates.

ORGANIZATION

Many introductory economics programs are structured

so that one term is microeconomics and another term is macroeconomics. If the macroeconomics term comes first, then normally it will also include an overall introduction to economics corresponding to at least some of our Chapters 1 through 5, material that also begins *Principles of Microeconomics*. Chapters 2, 4, and an abbreviated Chapter 5 provide what most instructors will require before the study of macroeconomics can start: material on scarcity, opportunity cost, markets and supply and demand. Chapter 1 is an overall "introduction to economics" chapter (and includes an appendix on understanding graphs), while Chapter 3 is a brief description of the private, public, and international sectors.

Turning to macroeconomics proper, most instructors will want to convey some understanding of the basic Keynesian model of the economy and the basic theory of fiscal and monetary policy. These theories are presented in Chapters 9 to 12, the "core of the core." Unlike most other Canadian introductory textbooks, the role of the exchange rate is introduced explicitly when interest rates are discussed in Chapter 12. This recognizes that in a small, open economy such as Canada, the effects of monetary policy through the exchange rate are probably at least as important as the effects through interest rates. But allowing for the obvious openness of the Canadian economy and financial markets at this stage does not make the traditional analysis of monetary policy more complex. For example, we simply point out that an expansionary monetary policy may tend to increase aggregate demand *both* by reducing interest rates *and* by depreciating the exchange rate. Then the analysis proceeds in a very similar fashion to closed economy analysis. There is also some coverage of the important institutional aspects involved, including the government deficit and debt and the role of the Bank of Canada. Therefore, upon completion of these four chapters, the student should have a basic understanding of the types of macroeconomic policy and be prepared for an informed discussion of their use.

Chapter 13 is an optional chapter that focuses on the effects of interest rates and may be omitted without disrupting the overall flow of the book. Chapter 14 includes the aggregate supply/aggregate demand (AS/AD) model. Chapters 15 to 20 are all issues chapters providing more analysis on labour markets, government debt, consumption and investment behaviour, stabilization policy, major macroeconomic controversies, and growth. We should emphasize that the earlier chapters briefly cover all these topics, and the role of these additional chapters is to provide a fuller discussion.

The last four chapters in the book are issues chapters on the global economy. Chapter 22 is on international macroeconomics. While this is an important area, it is not as vital to cover this material as it may be with other introductory texts, since the basic role of the exchange rate has been incorporated much earlier. Chapters 21, 23, and 24 are common with the *Principles of Microeconomics* volume and cover the topics of "real" international trade, development, and comparative economic systems respectively. The preface to *Principles of Macroeconomics* includes a discussion of course design.

Highlights of the First Canadian Edition of *Principles of Microeconomics*

CANADIAN INSTITUTIONS, RECENT DATA, EXAMPLES, EVENTS, AND TOPICS

One important feature of this book is the way it combines discussion of theory with Canadian institutional detail. Charts, tables, and graphs in the book use the most recent data available. In addition, we have integrated topics that have recently generated a great deal of attention—the economics of information, environmental economics, privatization and deregulation, welfare reform, and the recent experiences of Russia and Poland, to name just a few.

COVERAGE OF INTERNATIONAL MATERIAL

Another important feature of this book is the extensive use of international material. We have covered international material in three ways. First, we have presented many "Global Perspective" boxes throughout the book. These boxes are designed to illustrate economic logic with global examples and to emphasize today's global economy. Second, we have integrated international examples directly into the text whenever appropriate. All international examples are listed in a table following the book's detailed table of contents. Third, the last part of the book, International Economics, treats international economics in detail. See the listing of Global Coverage directly following the Table of Contents.

STUDENT LEARNING AIDS

Each chapter begins with a brief overview of what the student has learned in the previous chapter and ends with a brief "look ahead" to the following chapter. To help students study, key terms have been printed in boldface and glossed in the margins. Each chapter ends with a point-by-point summary of the chapter, a list of review terms and concepts (cross-referenced to text page), and a problem set.

Because economics must be relevant to be interesting, we have created three types of boxes. *Global Perspective* boxes provide economic examples from around the world. *Application* boxes apply the theory learned in the text to real-world events and situations. *Issues and Controversies* boxes examine many of the economic issues currently under debate.

In addition, we have set the major principles of economics off from the text in such a way as to highlight their importance. These highlights flow logically from the preceding text and into the text that follows. Students will find these very useful in reviewing the key points in each chapter to prepare for exams.

PROBLEM SETS AND SOLUTIONS

Each chapter and appendix ends with a problem set that asks students to think about what they've learned in the chapter. These problems are not simple memorization questions. Rather, they ask students to perform graphical analysis or to apply economics to a real-world situation or policy decision. More challenging problems are indicated by an asterisk. The solutions to all even-numbered problems appear at the back of the book. The solutions to all odd-numbered problems, as well as additional problem sets, are available in the Instructor's Resource Manual.

CANADIAN CASE STUDIES

Each part in the Canadian edition ends with a *Canadian Case Study*, which concludes with questions for analytical thinking and is supplemented by a video. The cases are not simply additional problems; nor are they simple extensions of the text material. They are meant to be applications of some of the *ideas* that the part was designed to teach and they are intended to foster critical thinking and "thinking like an economist." They might be used as assignments or for class discussion.

ECONOMICS ON THE WEB

Technological change is affecting many academic disciplines. Economics is no exception. Online access to statistical data, industry and company information, government reports, and financial data can make finding information easier and faster, if you know where to look. But useless hits can waste valuable online searching time. To help students learn to access and use online information efficiently, we are providing three levels of help as part of the learning package:

1. We have included an appendix of URLs called Microeconomics on the Internet for useful sources of economic information.
2. We will provide up-to-date online linkages to relevant Web sites as part of the text's Companion Web Site, expected to be fully live in the spring of 1998. For more information on this and other online resources, go to **www.phcanada.com**.
3. We are making an online Syllabus Builder available to instructors. If you have ever wanted to start using the Internet or your school's network in your course but aren't sure where to start, Prentice Hall can help you. We can provide you with an authoring tool that will help you set up and use online resources in your course, on your network, for your students. If you are interested in taking advantage of this technology, please contact your Prentice Hall representative for further information and minimum requirements.

The Teaching Package

Each component of the teaching and learning package has been carefully crafted to ensure that the course is a rewarding experience for both instructors and students.

INSTRUCTOR'S RESOURCE MANUAL

An innovative instructor's resource manual is available for this text. The Instructor's Resource Manual (IRM) is the key integrative supplement in the teaching and learning package and has been designed with the *teaching* of economics in mind. Each chapter in the IRM corresponds to a chapter in the text and includes suggestions for integrating all of the elements of the teaching/learning package into the classroom. The manual also includes chapter outlines with key terminology; teaching notes and lecture suggestions that provide ideas for applying theory, reinforcing key concepts, overcoming student misconceptions, initiating classroom discussion, and integrating outside readings and global examples into the lecture; additional problems with solutions; solutions to all odd-numbered problems in the text; and answers for all the analytical thinking questions that accompany the book's Case Studies.

The IRM also includes a section called *Extended Applications for Teaching Economics*. This is a collection of instructors' favourite ideas, exercises, activities, experiments, and games that help economics come alive.

TEST ITEM FILE #1

The Case/Fair/Strain/Veall Test Item File is a comprehensive test bank. For each chapter, it provides approximately 100 multiple-choice questions, 10 true-false questions and 10 short-answer essay questions. The questions are classified into three levels of difficulty—easy, moderate, and difficult—and are page-referenced to the text. Problem sets (a series of questions based on a graph or scenario) can contain all three levels. Also included are challenging questions that require students to undertake several steps of reasoning, or to work backwards from effect to cause. The Test Item File is available in printed and electronic (word processing) formats.

PRENTICE HALL CUSTOM TEST

The Test Item File is designed for use with the Prentice Hall Custom Test, a computerized package that allows users to custom design, save, and generate classroom tests. The test program (which runs on Windows-based computers) permits instructors to edit and add or delete questions from the Test Item File, to edit existing graphics and create new graphics, and to export files to various word processing programs, including WordPerfect and Microsoft Word. Graphics capability ensures that all graphs included in the test item file can be printed next to the appropriate questions.

TEST ITEM FILE #2: REAL-WORLD PROBLEM SETS

This ancillary provides an additional 50 questions for each chapter. Created to provide the instructor with an additional testing resource, the Real-World Problem Sets can be used as quiz/testing tools or as homework problems.

Each problem set is based on current events and/or newspaper or magazine clippings. Students are asked to analyze a scenario or minicase, draw or interpret graphs, and answer questions. Solutions are provided for each problem.

TRANSPARENCY MASTERS

Transparency Masters of all the Figures and Tables in the text are available for classroom use.

POWERPOINT TRANSPARENCIES

Also available is a series of PowerPoint presentations that summarize concepts and theories, emphasize problem solving, provide visual support for lectures, and show the relevance of economics. The PowerPoint disk also includes additional sets of time-series data (not included in the textbook), drawn from a variety of sources. Lecture notes include a snapshot of each PowerPoint slide, provide lecture suggestions and discussion questions, and help instructors correlate the slides with the text and their classroom presentations.

CBC/PRENTICE HALL VIDEO LIBRARY FOR *PRINCIPLES OF MICROECONOMICS* AND *PRINCIPLES OF MACROECONOMICS*

CBC and Prentice Hall have combined their experience in academic publishing and global reporting to create a special video ancillary to the text. The library consists of 10 video segments from the CBC programs "The National Magazine" and "News in Review." Each of the segments has been chosen to supplement a Case Study in the text.

SIMON AND SCHUSTER'S COLLEGE NEWSLINK

College Newslink is a unique educational service that brings the leading newspapers of the world to the university campus via the World Wide Web. Stories, organized by academic disciplines and linked to other relevant Web sites, can help you keep up to date with world economic and political news. For a demonstration, go to **www.ssnewslink.com** or contact your local Prentice Hall representative. *Canadian Economics* is only one of the many news filters that you can select on this site.

The Learning Package

STUDY GUIDE

A comprehensive study guide has been prepared to reinforce the textbook and provide students with additional applications and exercises. Each chapter in the Study Guide corresponds to a chapter in the textbook and contains the following features:

• **Point-by-Point Objectives:** A list of learning goals for the chapter, along with a brief summary of the material, helpful study hints, tips, practice questions with solutions, and page references to the text.

● **Practice Tests:** A series of multiple-choice, short-answer, discussion, and application questions designed to test students' grasp of the material and help them prepare for exams.

● **Solutions:** Complete solutions—not just answers—to all questions in the Study Guide, complete with page references to the text.

In addition, the Study Guide contains a Graphing Tutorial (for text Appendix 1A) that guides students through graphing techniques. "Graphing Pointer" sections in selected chapters feature additional tips and insights for students as they learn the graphical material in that chapter.

COMPANION WEB SITE

The Companion Web Site, which will go live in the spring of 1998, offers links to Web sites that are useful in the study of economics, gives the students access to a powerful online study guide and CBC case updates, and provides a forum for student dialogue and questions on introductory economics. Please go to **www.prenticehall.ca** for more information.

ACKNOWLEDGMENTS

We are grateful to the many people who offered support, helpful suggestions, and recommendations for the Canadian edition. The list includes Neils Anthonisen, George DeBenedetti, John Houtsma, and Tara McCabe (all at Mount Allison University); Livio di Matteo (Lakehead University); and Don Dawson and Jim Williams (both of McMaster University). The contributions of Deb Fretz, also of McMaster, were especially valuable.

We would also particularly like to thank the following instructors who provided formal reviews on all or part of the manuscript:

Jeremiah Allen (University of Lethbridge)
Michael Bradfield (Dalhousie University)
Christopher J. Bruce (The University of Calgary)
Witold B. Jankowski (Lakehead University)
Marc Lavoie (University of Ottawa)
Scott Lynch (Memorial University of
    Newfoundland)
C.J. McKenna (University of Guelph)
Dan Otchere (Concordia University)
Don Pepper (British Columbia Institute of
    Technology)
Nicholas Rowe (Carleton University)
Jim Sentance (University of Prince Edward Island)

At Prentice Hall Canada, we are grateful to Sarah Kimball, Acquisitions Editor; Maurice Esses, Developmental Editor; Marjan Farahbaksh, Production Editor, and Gail Copeland, Copy Editor, for their help in developing and producing this book.

We welcome comments about the First Canadian Edition. Please write to us care of Acquisitions Editor, Economics, Prentice Hall Higher Education Division, 1870 Birchmount Road, Scarborough, Ontario M1P 2J7.

Frank Strain
Michael Veall

About the Authors

Karl E. Case

is the Marion Butler McLean Professor in the History of Ideas and Professor of Economics at Wellesley College. He also lectures on Economics and Tax Policy in the International Tax Program at Harvard Law School and is a Visiting Scholar at the Federal Reserve Bank of Boston. He received his B.A. from Miami University in 1968, spent three years in the army, and received his M.A. and Ph.D. from Harvard University. In 1980 and 1981 he was a Liberal Arts Fellow in Law and Economics at Harvard Law School.

Professor Case's research has been in the areas of public finance, taxation, and housing. He is the author or coauthor of four other books, including Economics and Tax Policy and Property Taxation: The Need for Reform, as well as numerous articles in professional journals.

For the past 20 years, he has taught at Wellesley, where he was Department Chair from 1982 to 1985. Before coming to Wellesley, he spent two years as Head Tutor (director of undergraduate studies) at Harvard, where he won the Allyn Young Teaching Prize. He has been a member of the AEA's Committee on Economic Education and was Associate Editor of the Journal of Economic Education, responsible for the section on innovations in teaching. He teaches at least one section of the principles course every year.

Ray C. Fair

is Professor of Economics at Yale University. He is a member of the Cowles Foundation at Yale and a Fellow of the Econometric Society. He received a B.A. in economics from Fresno State College in 1964 and a Ph.D. in economics from M.I.T. in 1968. He taught at Princeton University from 1968 to 1974 and has been at Yale since 1974.

Professor Fair's research has primarily been in the areas of macroeconomics and econometrics, with particular emphasis on macroeconometric model building. His publications include Specification, Estimation, and Analysis of Macroeconometric Models (Harvard Press, 1984) and Testing Macroeconometric Models (Harvard Press, 1994).

Professor Fair has taught introductory and intermediate economics at Yale. He has also taught graduate courses in macroeconomic theory and macroeconometrics.

About the Authors

J. Frank Strain is Associate Professor and Head of the Department of Economics at Mount Allison University in Sackville, New Brunswick, where he has taught since 1985. He received a B.A. from the University of Prince Edward Island, an M.A. from the University of New Brunswick, and a Ph.D. from the University of Manitoba.

Dr. Strain's research has been in the areas of regional economics, public finance, labour economics, and Canadian economic history. He is the author or coauthor of 20 articles in professional journals and edited volumes. As well, he is the author of one book—*Integration, Federalism, and Cohesion in the European Community*—and coauthor of another—*The Canadian Welfare State: Past, Present, and Future.*

Dr. Strain teaches a wide variety of undergraduate courses at Mount Allison. In 1997, he was awarded the Paul Pare Medal for Excellence in recognition of his contributions to teaching and research.

Michael R. Veall is Professor of Economics at McMaster University. He received a B.A. from McMaster in 1976, an M.A. from the University of Western Ontario in 1977, and a Ph.D. from M.I.T. in 1981. Aside from teaching at McMaster, Professor Veall has taught at The University of Western Ontario, Queen's University, the Australian National University, and the University at Mannheim in Germany. He has also been a von Humboldt fellow both at Mannheim and at the University of Munich, and has held honourary visiting positions at the University of York in England and at the University of Western Australia.

Professor Veall's research has been primarily in the area of applied econometrics. He is the author of a number of articles in professional journals including the *Canadian Journal of Economics, Canadian Public Policy, Econometrica,* the *International Economic Review,* the *Journal of Public Economics,* and the *Review of Economics and Statistics.* He has been a consultant to a number of public-sector organizations including Ontario Hydro and the federal Department of Finance.

His proudest professional accomplishment is helping almost 2000 students survive and, he hopes, enjoy courses in introductory economics. He also teaches senior and graduate econometrics at McMaster, and has taught graduate courses in public economics and international macroeconomics.

The Scope and Method of Economics

The study of economics should begin with a sense of wonder. Pause for a moment and consider a typical day in your life. For breakfast you might have bread made in a local bakery with flour produced in Manitoba from wheat grown in Saskatchewan and bacon from pigs raised in Quebec packaged in plastic made in Ontario. You spill coffee from Colombia on your shirt made in Malaysia from textiles shipped from the Philippines.

After class you drive with a friend in a Japanese car on a highway system that took 20 years and billions of dollars' worth of resources to build. You stop for gasoline refined in New Brunswick from Venezuelan crude oil brought to Canada on a supertanker that took three years to build at a shipyard in Nova Scotia.

At night you call your brother in Mexico City. The call travels over fibre-optic cable to a powerful antenna that sends it to a transponder on one of over 1000 communications satellites orbiting the earth.

You use or consume tens of thousands of things, both tangible and intangible, every day: buildings, the music of a rock band, the compact disc it is recorded on, telephone services, staples, paper, toothpaste, tweezers, soap, a digital watch, fire protection, antacid tablets, beer, banks, electricity, eggs, insurance, football fields, computers, buses, rugs, subways, health services, sidewalks, and so forth. Somebody made all these things. Somebody decided to organize men and women and materials to produce them and distribute them. Thousands of decisions went into their completion. Somehow they got to you.

Fourteen million people in Canada—almost half the total population—work at hundreds of thousands of different kinds of jobs producing nearly a trillion dollars' worth of goods and services every year. Some cannot find work; some choose not to work. Some are rich; others are poor.

Every year Canadians import billions of dollars' worth of tropical fruit, electronic equipment, Hollywood movies, and other goods and services produced in other countries. High-rise office buildings go up in central cities. Condominiums and homes are built in the suburbs.

Some countries are wealthy. Others are impoverished. Some are growing. Some are stagnating. Some businesses are doing well. Others are going bankrupt.

At any moment every society faces constraints imposed by nature and by previous generations. Some societies are handsomely endowed by nature with fertile land, water, sunshine, and natural resources. Others have deserts and few mineral resources. Some societies receive much from previous generations—art, music, technical knowledge, beautiful buildings, and productive factories. Others are left with overgrazed, eroded land, cities levelled by war, or polluted natural environments. All societies face limits.

economics *The study of how individuals and societies choose to use the scarce resources that nature and previous generations have provided.*

> **Economics** is the study of how individuals and societies choose to use the scarce resources that nature and previous generations have provided. The key word in this definition is *choose*. Economics is a behavioural science. In large measure it is the study of how people make choices. The choices that people make, when added up, translate into societal choices.

The purpose of this chapter and the next is to elaborate on this definition and to introduce the subject matter of economics. What is produced? How is it produced? Who gets it? Why? Is the result good or bad? Can it be improved?

Why Study Economics?

There are four main reasons to study economics: to learn a way of thinking, to understand society, to understand global affairs, and to be an informed voter.

To Learn a Way of Thinking

Probably the most important reason for studying economics is to learn a particular way of thinking. A good way to introduce economics is to review three of its most fundamental concepts: opportunity cost; marginalism; and information, incentives, and market coordination. If your study of economics is successful, you will find yourself using these concepts every day in making decisions.

■ **Opportunity Cost**   What happens in an economy is the outcome of thousands of individual decisions. Households must decide how to divide up their incomes over all the goods and services available in the marketplace. Individuals must decide whether to work, whether to go to school, and how much to save. Businesses must decide what to produce, how much to produce, how much to charge, and where to locate. It is not surprising that economic analysis focuses on the process of decision making.

Nearly all decisions involve trade-offs. There are advantages and disadvantages, costs and benefits, associated with every action and every choice. A key concept that recurs again and again in analyzing the decision-making process is the notion of opportunity cost. The full "cost" of making a specific choice includes what we give up by not making the alternative choice. That which we forgo, or give up, when we make a choice or a decision is called the **opportunity cost** of that decision.

opportunity cost *That which we forgo, or give up, when we make a choice or a decision.*

The concept applies to individuals, businesses, and entire societies. The opportunity cost of going to a movie is the value of the other things you could have done with the same money and time. If you decide to take time off in lieu of working, the opportunity cost of your leisure is the pay that you would have earned had you worked. Part of the cost of a university education is the income you could earn by working full time instead of going to school. If a firm purchases a new piece of equipment for $3000, it does so because it expects that equipment to generate more profit. There is an opportunity cost, however, since that $3000 could have been deposited in an interest-earning account. To a society, the opportunity cost of using resources for medical care is the value of the other goods that could be produced with the same resources.

The reason that opportunity costs arise is that resources are scarce. *Scarce* simply means *limited*. Consider one of our most important resources—time. There are only 24 hours in a day, and we must live our lives under this constraint. A farmer in rural Brazil must decide whether it is better to stay on the land and continue to farm or to go to the city and look for a job. A hockey player at the University of Toronto must decide whether she will play on the varsity team or spend more time improving her academic work.

■ **Marginalism and Sunk Costs** A second key concept used in analyzing choices is the notion of *marginalism*. In weighing the costs and benefits of a decision, it is important to weigh only the costs and benefits that are contingent upon the decision. Suppose, for example, that you lived in St. John's and that you were weighing the costs and benefits of visiting your mother in Vancouver. If business required that you travel to Winnipeg, the cost of visiting Mom would be only the additional, or *marginal*, time and money cost of getting to Vancouver from Winnipeg.

Consider the cost of producing this book. Assume that 10 000 copies are produced. The total cost of producing the copies includes the cost of the authors' time in writing the book, the cost of editing, the cost of making the plates for printing, and the cost of the paper and ink. If the total cost were $600 000, then the average cost of one copy would be $60, which is simply $600 000 divided by 10 000.

Although average cost is an important concept, a book publisher must know more than simply the average cost of a book. For example, suppose a second printing is being debated. That is, should another 10 000 copies be produced? In deciding whether to proceed, the costs of writing, editing, making plates, and so forth are irrelevant. Why? Because they have already been incurred—they are *sunk costs*. **Sunk costs** are costs that cannot be avoided, regardless of what is done in the future, because they have already been incurred. All that matters are the costs associated with the additional, or marginal, books to be printed. Technically, *marginal cost* is the cost of producing one more unit of output.

sunk costs *Costs that cannot be avoided, regardless of what is done in the future, because they have already been incurred.*

There are numerous examples in which the concept of marginal cost is useful. For an airplane that is about to take off with empty seats, the marginal cost of an extra passenger is essentially zero; the total cost of the trip is essentially unchanged by the addition of an extra passenger. Thus, setting aside a few seats to be sold at big discounts can be profitable even if the fare for those seats is far below the average cost per seat of making the trip. As long as the airline succeeds in filling seats that would otherwise have been empty, doing so is profitable—marginal revenue is greater than marginal cost.

■ **Information, Incentives, and Market Coordination** Suppose you have been hired to direct traffic at a highway toll plaza with four toll booths. How would you carry out your task? If your goal is to minimize the time drivers spend in a line-up, you will direct cars to the shortest line, and thus keep all the lines at approximately the same length. But is a traffic director really needed to ensure this result? Drivers will want to spend as little time as possible in a line-up, and so they have an *incentive* to choose the toll booth with the shortest line. As they approach the booths, the drivers will observe the length of the line at each booth and use this *information* to choose which line to enter. If one line is much shorter than the others, cars will quickly move into it until all the lines are equalized. Thus the "visible hand" of the traffic director is not really needed to *coordinate* the choices of the individual drivers to ensure that their time spent in line is minimized.

In *The Wealth of Nations*, one of the most important economics books ever published, Adam Smith, an eighteenth-century Scottish philosopher, argued that prices, wages, and profits in a market economy often provide the incentives and information needed to ensure the type of coordination observed at the toll booths. For example, if people suddenly want more live musical entertainment and less DJ dance music, an economic planner could act as a traffic director and order people to offer more live music and less DJ dance music. But a planner is not necessary. The change in people's tastes creates profit opportunities. Line-ups at live music venues will allow these venues to charge higher prices and earn higher profits while clubs supplying DJ dance music will face empty rooms and losses. In a process similar to what takes place at the toll booths—as the drivers move to the shortest line, eventually the length of wait at each line is the same—these profit opportunities will eventually be eliminated as venues try to increase profit by providing live music and avoid losses by supplying less DJ dance music.

A more dramatic real-life example is illustrated by the response to the OPEC oil price hikes of 1973. In that year OPEC (the Organization of Petroleum Exporting Countries) decided to reduce the supply of oil on world markets. The changes in prices and the new profit opportunities opened up by this decision provided the information and incentives required for Canadians to adjust to this important development. They responded to rising energy prices by increasing exploration for domestic oil and gas, searching for alternative energy sources, increasing purchases of home insulation, and using smaller and more fuel-efficient automobiles. The remarkable capacity of prices, wages, and profits in market economies to provide the information and incentives required to coordinate the decisions of individual decision makers is one of the most important insights explored in this introductory course in economics.

However, market solutions are not always desirable because individual pursuit of private goals is not always consistent with the public good. Many social and environmental problems (for example, poverty, too little protection for fragile ecosystems and endangered species, etc.) and many of the activities of governments in Canada are tied closely to problems with market institutions. As your knowledge of economics grows you will find yourself thinking critically about market institutions and identifying how they sometimes work well and how they sometimes falter.

> The study of economics teaches us a way of thinking and helps us make decisions.

To Understand Society

Another reason for studying economics is to understand society better. You cannot hope to understand how a society functions without a basic knowledge of its economy, and you cannot understand a society's economy without knowing its economic history. Clearly, past and present economic decisions have an enormous influence on the character of life in a society. The current state of the physical environment, the level of material well-being, and the nature and number of jobs are all products of the economic system.

To get a sense of the ways in which economic decisions have shaped our environment, imagine that you are looking out of a window on the top floor of a high-rise office building in any large city. The workday is about to begin. All around you are other tall glass and steel buildings full of workers. In the distance you see the smoke of factories. Looking down, you see thousands of commuters pouring off trains and buses, and cars backed up on highway exit ramps. You see trucks carrying goods from one place to another. You also see the face of urban poverty: just beyond the highway is a large low-rent housing development and, beyond that, a group of old factories, many boarded up and deteriorating.

What you see before you is the product of millions of economic decisions made over hundreds of years. People at some point decided to spend time and money building those buildings and factories. Somebody cleared the land, laid the tracks, built the roads, and produced the cars and buses.

Not only have economic decisions shaped the physical environment, they have determined the character of society as well. At no time has the impact of economic change on the character of a society been more evident than in England during the late eighteenth and early nineteenth centuries, a period that we now call the **Industrial Revolution.** Increases in the productivity of agriculture, new manufacturing technologies, and the development of more efficient forms of transportation led to a massive movement of the British population from the countryside to the city. At the beginning of the eighteenth century, approximately two out of three people in Great Britain were engaged in agriculture. By 1812, only one in three remained in agriculture, and by 1900 the figure was fewer than one in ten. People jammed into overcrowded cities and worked long hours in factories. The world had changed completely in two centuries—a period that, in the run of history, was nothing more than the blink of an eye.

It is not surprising that the discipline of economics began to take shape during this period. Social critics and philosophers looked around them and knew that their philosophies must expand to accommodate the changes. Adam Smith's *Wealth of Nations* appeared in 1776. It was followed by the writings of David Ricardo, Karl Marx, Thomas Malthus, and others. Each tried to make sense out of what was happening. Who was building the factories? Why? What determined the level of wages paid to workers or the price of food? What would happen in the future, and what should happen? The people who asked these questions were the first economists.

Similar changes continue to affect the character of life today. In 1996 the number of jobs in Canada increased by more than 117 000, but nearly 1.5 million people who wanted a job could not find one. While the economy was growing, the wages of many workers were falling relative to the cost of living. At the same time, baseball players, many of whom make in excess of $1 million dollars a year, threatened to go on strike. How does one make sense of all of this? Why do we have unemployment? What forces determine wages? Why is it that baseball players can command such high salaries?

> The study of economics is an essential part of the study of society.

Industrial Revolution *The period in England during the late eighteenth and early nineteenth centuries in which new manufacturing technologies and improved transportation gave rise to the modern factory system and a massive movement of the population from the countryside to the cities.*

To Understand Global Affairs

A third reason for studying economics is to understand global affairs. News headlines are filled with economic stories: a potential trade war between Canada and the United States, the struggle to prevent further collapse of the economies of Eastern Europe and the former Soviet Union, starvation and poverty in Africa.

All countries are part of a world economy, and understanding international

Many economists believe that Japan's recent economic troubles have weakened its ability to be a world leader. Worried about their future and the prices of their products, Japanese farmers demonstrate against global free trade.

relations begins with a basic knowledge of the economic links among countries. For centuries countries have attempted to protect their industries and workers from foreign competition by taxing imports and limiting the number of certain imports. Most economists argue, however, that unrestricted trade is in the long-run interest of all countries. Just after World War II many countries signed the General Agreement on Tariffs and Trade (GATT), in which they committed to lowering trade barriers. The process continues today, and not always smoothly, under the World Trade Organization (WTO), which replaced the GATT in 1995. Trade issues can be passionate, as Canadians demonstrated during the negotiations of the Canada–U.S. Free Trade Agreement and the subsequent North American Free Trade Agreement (NAFTA), which came into force in January 1994.

Canadians are investing heavily in industries in countries like Indonesia and China. During the 1980s the Japanese bought billions of dollars' worth of Canadian real estate, shares of corporate stocks, and government bonds. During the 1990s the Japanese, suffering economic problems at home, have pulled back, with important consequences for Canada. The end of the apartheid laws that legally separated the races in South Africa has created a new climate for international investment in that country.

The Iraqi invasion of Kuwait in 1990 and the resulting Persian Gulf War in 1991 sent world oil markets on a wild ride and in part led to *recession* (a period of decreasing output and rising unemployment). Meanwhile, the countries of Eastern Europe are struggling to create from the ground up economic and social institutions that took centuries to build in the West.

Another important issue in today's world is the widening gap between rich nations and poor nations. In 1995 world population was about 5.7 billion. Of that number, 4.3 billion lived in less-developed countries and 1.4 billion lived in more-developed countries. The 75% of the world's population that lives in the less-developed countries receives less than 20% of the world's income. In dozens of countries, per capita income is only a few hundred dollars a year.

An understanding of economics is essential to an understanding of global affairs.

TO BE AN INFORMED VOTER

For the last 25 years or so the Canadian economy has been on a roller coaster. In 1973–1974, the Organization of Petroleum Exporting Countries (OPEC) succeeded in raising the world price of oil by 400%. By 1974, prices in Canada were rising across the board at double-digit rates. Inflation again reached double-digit levels in 1980, at which time the economy plunged into recession. By December 1982, 12.8% of the workforce was unemployed. Then, in mid-1990, after a period of economic growth, the Canadian economy went into another recession. During the second, third, and fourth quarters of 1990, and the first quarter of 1991, gross domestic product (GDP, which is a measure of the total output of the Canadian economy) fell and unemployment increased sharply.

The recession of 1990–91 and the slow recovery that followed provided a backdrop to the 1997 federal election. During the campaign, polls consistently showed that economic issues—unemployment, the deficit, free trade with the United States, the GST (Goods and Services Tax)—were paramount in the minds of the voters. The political parties—led by Jean Charest (Progressive Conservatives), Jean Chrétien (Liberals), Gilles Duceppe (Bloc Québécois), Alexa McDonough (NDP), and Preston Manning (Reform)—reflected public concern and each offered an economic strategy which they promised to pursue if elected.

Canadian voters faced a choice between competing strategies. Voters without some knowledge of economics had to base their choice on extraneous factors such as party loyalty, attitudes toward the previous prime minister, candidates' television appearances, and the rhetorical skill of the party leaders. Only those with some knowledge of economics possessed the skills needed to assess critically the complex political platforms being offered.

> When we participate in the political process, we are voting on issues that require a basic understanding of economics.

The Scope of Economics

Most students taking economics for the first time are surprised by the breadth of what they study. Some think that economics will teach them about the stock market or what to do with their money. Others think that economics deals exclusively with problems like inflation and unemployment. In fact, it deals with all these subjects, but they are pieces of a much larger puzzle.

Economics has deep roots in, and close ties to, social philosophy. An issue of great importance to philosophers, for example, is distributional justice. Why are some people rich and others poor, and whatever the answer, is this fair? A number of nineteenth-century social philosophers wrestled with these questions, and out of their musings economics as a separate discipline was born.

The easiest way to get a feel for the breadth and depth of what you will be studying is to explore briefly the way economics is organized. First of all, there are two major divisions of economics: microeconomics and macroeconomics.

MICROECONOMICS AND MACROECONOMICS

Microeconomics deals with the functioning of individual industries and the behaviour of individual economic decision-making units: business firms and households. Microeconomics explores the decisions that individual businesses and consumers make. Firms' choices about what to produce and how much to charge and households' choices about what and how much to buy help to explain why the economy produces the things it does.

microeconomics *The branch of economics that examines the functioning of individual industries and the behaviour of individual decision-making units, that is, business firms and households.*

Another big question that microeconomics addresses is who gets the things that are produced. Wealthy households get more output than do poor households, and the forces that determine this distribution of output are the province of microeconomics. Why does poverty exist? Who is poor? Why do some jobs pay more than others?

Think again about all the things you consume in a day, and then think back to that view out over a big city. Somebody decided to build those factories. Somebody decided to construct the roads, build the housing, and produce the cars. Why? What is going on in all those buildings? It is easy to see that understanding individual micro decisions is very important to any understanding of society.

macroeconomics *The branch of economics that examines the economic behaviour of aggregates—income, employment, output, and so on—on a national scale.*

Macroeconomics looks at the economy as a whole. Instead of trying to understand what determines the output of a single firm or industry or the consumption patterns of a single household or group of households, macroeconomics examines the factors that determine the country's output or domestic product. Microeconomics is concerned with *household* income; macroeconomics deals with *national* income.

While microeconomics focuses on individual product prices and relative prices, macroeconomics looks at the overall price level and how quickly (or slowly) it is rising (or falling). Microeconomics questions how many people will be hired (or fired) this year in a particular industry or in a certain geographical area, and the factors that determine how much labour a firm or industry will hire. Macroeconomics deals with aggregate employment and unemployment: how many jobs exist in the economy as a whole, and how many people who are willing to work are not able to find work.

To summarize:

> Microeconomics looks at the individual unit—the household, the firm, the industry. It sees and examines the "trees." Macroeconomics looks at the whole, the aggregate. It sees and analyzes the "forest."

Table 1.1 summarizes these divisions and some of the subjects with which they are concerned.

THE DIVERSITY OF ECONOMICS

Individual economists focus their research and study in many diverse areas. Many of these specialized fields are reflected in the advanced courses offered at most colleges and universities. Some are concerned with economic history or the history of economic thought. Others focus on international economics or growth in less-developed countries. Still others study the economics of cities (urban economics) or the relationship between economics and law. (See the Application box on page 10 titled "The Fields of Economics" for more details.)

Economists also differ in the emphasis they place on theory. Some economists specialize in developing new theories, while others spend their time testing the theories of others. Some economists hope to expand the frontiers of knowledge, while others are more interested in applying what is already known to the formulation of public policies.

As you begin your study of economics, look through your school's course catalogue and talk to the faculty about their interests. You will discover that economics encompasses a broad range of inquiry and is linked to many other disciplines.

Table 1.1	Examples of Microeconomic and Macroeconomic Concerns			
DIVISION OF ECONOMICS	PRODUCTION	PRICES	INCOME	EMPLOYMENT
Microeconomics	*Production/Output in Individual Industries and Businesses*	*Price of Individual Goods and Services*	*Distribution of Income and Wealth*	*Employment by Individual Businesses and Industry*
	How much steel How much office space How many cars	Price of medical care Price of gasoline Food prices Apartment rents	Wages in the auto industry Minimum wage Executive salaries Poverty	Jobs in the steel industry Number of employees in a firm Number of accountants
Macroeconomics	*National Production/Output*	*Aggregate Price Level*	*National Income*	*Employment and Unemployment in the Economy*
	Total industrial output Gross domestic product Growth of output	Consumer prices Producer prices Rate of inflation	Total wages and salaries Total corporate profits	Total number of jobs Unemployment rate

The Method of Economics

Economics asks and attempts to answer two kinds of questions, positive and normative. **Positive economics** attempts to understand behaviour and the operation of economic systems *without making judgments* about whether the outcomes are good or bad. It strives to describe what exists and how it works. What determines the wage rate for unskilled workers? What would happen if we abolished the corporate income tax? Who would benefit? Who would lose? The answers to such questions are the subject of positive economics.

In contrast, **normative economics** looks at the outcomes of economic behaviour and asks if they are good or bad and whether they can be made better. Normative economics involves judgments and prescriptions for courses of action. Should the government be involved in regulating the price of gasoline? Should the income tax be changed to reduce or increase the burden on upper-income families? Should Ontario Hydro be broken up into a set of smaller companies? Should we protect Canadian agriculture from foreign competition? Normative economics is often called *policy economics*.

Of course most normative questions involve positive questions. To know whether the government *should* take a particular action, we must know first if it *can* and second what the consequences are likely to be. (For example, if Ontario Hydro is broken up, will there be more competition and lower prices?)

Some claim that positive, value-free economic analysis is impossible. They argue that analysts come to problems with biases that cannot help but influence their work. Furthermore, even in choosing what questions to ask or what problems to analyze, economists are influenced by political, ideological, and moral views.

While this argument has some merit, it is nevertheless important to distinguish between analyses that attempt to be positive and those that are intentionally and explicitly normative. Economists who ask explicitly normative questions should be forced to specify their grounds for judging one outcome superior to another. What does it mean to be better? The criteria for such evaluations must be clearly spelled out and thoroughly understood for conclusions to have meaning.

positive economics *An approach to economics that seeks to understand behaviour and the operation of systems without making judgments. It describes what exists and how it works.*

normative economics *An approach to economics that analyzes outcomes of economic behaviour, evaluates them as good or bad, and may prescribe courses of action. Also called* policy economics.

A good way to convey the diversity of economics is to describe some of its major fields of study and the issues that economists address.

■ INDUSTRIAL ORGANIZATION looks carefully at the structure and performance of industries and firms within an economy. How do businesses compete? Who gains and who loses?

■ URBAN AND REGIONAL ECONOMICS studies the spatial arrangement of economic activity. Why do we have cities? Why are manufacturing firms locating farther and farther from the centre of urban areas?

■ ECONOMETRICS applies statistical techniques and data to economic problems in an effort to test hypotheses and theories. Most schools require economics degree students to take at least one course in statistics or econometrics.

■ COMPARATIVE ECONOMIC SYSTEMS examines the ways alternative economic systems function. What are the advantages and disadvantages of different systems? What is the best way to convert the planned economies of the former Soviet Union to market systems?

■ ECONOMIC DEVELOPMENT focuses on the problems of poor countries. What can be done to promote development in these nations? Important concerns of development economists include population growth and control, provision for basic needs, and strategies for international trade.

■ LABOUR ECONOMICS deals with the factors that determine wage rates, employment, and unemployment. How do people decide whether to work, how much to work, and at what kind of job? How have the roles of unions and management changed in recent years?

Economics studies many important issues. Some social problems—such as unemployment—are addressed in many of the major fields of study in economics.

■ FINANCE examines the ways in which households and firms actually pay for, or finance, their purchases. It involves the study of capital markets (including the stock and bond markets), futures and options, capital budgeting, and asset valuation.

■ INTERNATIONAL ECONOMICS studies trade flows among countries and international financial institutions. What are the advantages and disadvantages for a country that allows its citizens to buy and sell freely in world markets? Why is the Canadian dollar strong or weak?

■ PUBLIC ECONOMICS examines the role of government in the economy. What are the economic functions of government, and what should they be? How should the government finance the services that it provides? What kinds of government programs should confront the problems of poverty, unemployment, and pollution?

■ ECONOMIC HISTORY traces the development of the modern economy. What economic and political events and scientific advances caused the Industrial Revolution that began in eighteenth-century Great Britain? What explains the tremendous growth and progress of post–World War II Japan? What caused the Great Depression of the 1930s?

■ LAW AND ECONOMICS analyzes the economic function of legal rules and institutions. How does the law change the behaviour of individuals and businesses? Do different liability rules make accidents and injuries more or less likely? What are the economic costs of crime?

■ THE HISTORY OF ECONOMIC THOUGHT, which is grounded in philosophy, studies the development of economic ideas and theories over time, from Adam Smith in the eighteenth century to the works of economists such as Thomas Malthus, Karl Marx, and John Maynard Keynes. Because economic theory is constantly developing and changing, studying the history of ideas helps give meaning to modern theory and puts it in perspective.

Positive economics is often divided into descriptive economics and economic theory. **Descriptive economics** is simply the compilation of data that describe phenomena and facts. Examples of such data appear in the *Canada Yearbook*, a large volume of data published by Statistics Canada every year that describes many features of the Canadian economy.

Where do all these data come from? Statistics Canada produces an enormous amount of raw data every year, as do the Bank of Canada and a number of federal government departments. The computer and the Internet now provide an invaluable means to access much of this economic information. However, keep in mind that information you might obtain from the Net is not always reliable or worthwhile. Nonetheless, there are some very good web sites. Table 1.2 lists some sites that are worth exploring. For a larger list, see the section near the end of the book entitled Microeconomics on the Internet.

Economic theory attempts to generalize about data and interpret them. An **economic theory** is a statement or set of related statements about cause and effect, action and reaction. One of the first theories you will encounter in this text is the *law of demand*, which was most clearly stated by Alfred Marshall in 1890: when the price of a product rises, people tend to buy less of it; when the price of a product falls, they tend to buy more.

descriptive economics *The compilation of data that describe phenomena and facts.*

economic theory *A statement or set of related statements about cause and effect, action and reaction.*

Table 1.2	Computers: Accessing Economic Information through the Internet
Statistics Canada	http://www.statcan.ca/ This site provides access to statistical information on Canada including major monthly and quarterly economic indicators. You will also find here a detailed description of the Canadian Socio-Economic Information System (CANSIM), the most important and comprehensive source of Canadian economic data. You should be able to get access to CANSIM through your school library.
Finance Canada	http://www.fin.gc.ca/ This site provides information on federal tax and expenditure policies as well as some links to the Internet sites of Canadian financial institutions and provincial governments.
Bank of Canada	http://bank-banque-canada.ca/ This site includes information on Canadian monetary policy, a variety of financial statistics, and a description of debt management policy.
Industry Canada	http://inc.gc.ca This site contains microeconomic analysis and statistical research information from Industry Canada. It provides links to a quarterly newsletter on microeconomic analysis, Industry Canada research publications, the Microeconomic Monitor, Provincial Industrial Overviews, and some online international trade data.
Resources for Economists on the Internet	http://econwpa.wustl.edu/econFAQ/econFAQ.html This document—which is written by Bill Goffe, Department of Economics and International Business, University of Southern Mississippi—is a comprehensive and regularly updated guide to information on the Internet of interest to people working in the discipline of economics.
Canadian Economics Association	http://economics.ca This site has links to most economics departments at Canadian universities and a variety of other useful sites.

inductive reasoning *The process of observing regular patterns from raw data and drawing generalizations from them.*

The process of observing regular patterns from raw data and drawing generalizations from them is called **inductive reasoning.** In all sciences, theories begin with inductive reasoning and observed regularities. For example, Aristotle believed that the speed at which objects fall toward the earth depends on their size as well as their weight. But in a series of experiments carried out between 1589 and 1591, Galileo was able to show that bodies of very different sizes seemed to fall at approximately the same speed when dropped from the Leaning Tower of Pisa. Over a century later, Galileo's data led Sir Isaac Newton to formulate the theory of gravity, which eventually became the basis of Albert Einstein's work.

Social scientists, including economists, study human behaviour. They develop and test theories of how human beings, institutions, and societies behave. The behaviour of human beings is by its nature not as regular or predictable as the behaviour of electrons, molecules, or planets, but there are patterns, regularities, and tendencies.

Theories do not always arise out of formal numerical data. All of us have been collecting observations of people's behaviour and their responses to economic stimuli for most of our lives. We may have observed our parents' reaction to a sudden increase—or decrease—in income or to the loss of a job or the acquisition of a new one. We all have seen people standing in line waiting for a bargain. And, of course, our own actions and reactions are another important source of data.

THEORIES AND MODELS

In many disciplines, including physics, chemistry, meteorology, political science, and economics, theorists build formal models of behaviour. A **model** is a formal statement of a theory. It is usually a mathematical statement of a presumed relationship between two or more variables.

A **variable** is a measure that can change from time to time or from observation to observation. Income is a variable—it has different values for different people, and different values for the same person at different times. The rental price of a movie on a videocassette is a variable; it has different values at different stores and at different times. There are countless other examples.

Because all models simplify reality by stripping part of it away, they are abstractions. Critics of economics often point to abstraction as a weakness. Most economists, however, see abstraction as a real strength.

The easiest way to see how abstraction can be helpful is to think of a map. A map is a representation of reality that is simplified and abstract. A city or province appears on a piece of paper as a series of lines and colours. The amount of reality that the map maker can strip away before the map loses something essential depends on what the map is going to be used for. If I want to drive from Fredericton to Sudbury, I need to know only the major highways and roads. I lose absolutely nothing and gain clarity by cutting out the local streets and roads. If, on the other hand, I need to get around in Montreal, I may need to see every street and alley.

Most maps are two-dimensional representations of a three-dimensional world; they show where roads and highways go but do not show hills and valleys along the way. Trail maps for hikers, however, have "contour lines" that represent changes in elevation. When you are in a car, changes in elevation matter very little; they would make a map needlessly complex and much more difficult to read. But if you are on foot carrying a 30-kilogram pack, a knowledge of elevation is crucial.

Like maps, economic models are abstractions that strip away detail to expose only those aspects of behaviour that are important to the question being asked. The principle that irrelevant detail should be cut away is called the principle of **Ockham's razor** after the fourteenth-century philosopher William of Ockham.

But be careful. Although abstraction is a powerful tool for exposing and

model *A formal statement of a theory. Usually a mathematical statement of a presumed relationship between two or more variables.*

variable *A measure that can change from time to time or from observation to observation.*

Ockham's razor *The principle that irrelevant detail should be cut away.*

analyzing specific aspects of behaviour, it is possible to oversimplify. Economic models often strip away a good deal of social and political reality to get at underlying concepts. When an economic theory is used to help formulate actual government or institutional policy, political and social reality must often be reintroduced if the policy is to have a chance of working.

The key here is that the appropriate amount of simplification and abstraction depends upon the use to which the model will be put. To return to the map example: you don't want to walk around Halifax with a map made for drivers—the hill rising from the waterfront is too steep!

■ **All Else Equal:** *ceteris paribus* It is almost always true that whatever you want to explain with a model depends on more than one factor. Suppose, for example, that you want to explain the total number of kilometres driven by automobile owners in Canada. The number of kilometres driven will change from year to year or month to month; it is a variable. The issue, if we want to understand and explain changes that occur, is what factors cause those changes.

Obviously, many things might have an impact on total kilometres driven. First, more or fewer people may be driving. This, in turn, can be affected by changes in the driving age, by population growth, or by changes in the law. Other factors might include the price of gasoline, the household's income, the number and age of children in the household, the distance from home to work, the location of shopping facilities, and the availability and quality of public transport. When any of these variables change, the members of the household may drive more or less. If changes in any of these variables affect large numbers of households across the country, the total number of kilometres driven will change.

Very often we need to isolate or separate out these effects. For example, suppose that we want to know the impact on driving of a higher tax on gasoline. This change would raise the price of gasoline at the pump, but would not (at least in the short run) affect income, workplace location, number of children, and so forth.

To isolate the impact of one single factor, we use the device of **ceteris paribus,** or **all else equal.** We ask: what is the impact of a change in gasoline price on driving behaviour, *ceteris paribus*, or assuming that nothing else changes? If gasoline prices rise by 10%, how much less driving will there be, assuming no simultaneous change in anything else—that is, assuming that income, number of children, population, laws, and so on all remain constant?

> **ceteris paribus** Literally, "all else equal." Used to analyze the relationship between two variables while the values of other variables are held unchanged.

> Using the device of *ceteris paribus* is one part of the process of abstraction. In formulating economic theory, the concept helps us simplify reality in order to focus on the relationships that we are interested in.

■ **Expressing Models in Words, Graphs, and Equations** Consider the following statements: "Lower airline ticket prices cause people to fly more frequently." "Higher interest rates slow the rate of home sales." "When firms produce more output, employment increases." "Higher gasoline prices cause people to drive less and to buy more fuel-efficient cars." "When the Canadian dollar falls in value against the value of foreign currencies, firms that export products produced in Canada find their sales increasing."

Each of these statements expresses a relationship between two variables that can be quantified. In each case there is a stimulus and a response, a cause and an effect. Quantitative relationships can be expressed in a variety of ways. Sometimes words are sufficient to express the essence of a theory, but often it is necessary to be more specific about the nature of a relationship or about the magnitude of a response. The most common method of expressing the quantitative relationship between two variables is *graphing* that relationship on a two-dimensional plane. In fact, we will use graphical analysis extensively in Chapter 2 and beyond. Because it is essential that you be familiar with the basics of graphing, a careful review of graphing techniques is presented in the appendix to this chapter.

Quantitative relationships between variables can also be presented through equations. For example, suppose we discovered that over time, Canadian households collectively spend, or consume, 90% of their income and save 10% of their income. We could then write:

$$C = 0.90Y \text{ and } S = 0.10Y$$

where C is consumption spending, Y is income, and S is saving. Writing explicit algebraic expressions like these helps us understand the nature of the underlying process of decision making. Understanding this process is what economics is all about.

■ **Cautions and Pitfalls** In formulating theories and models, it is especially important to avoid two pitfalls: the *post hoc* fallacy and the fallacy of composition.

The **Post Hoc** *Fallacy* Theories often make statements, or sets of statements, about cause and effect. It can be quite tempting to look at two events that happen in sequence and assume that the first caused the second to happen. Clearly, this is not always the case. This common error is called the **post hoc, ergo propter hoc** (or "after this, therefore because of this") fallacy.

There are thousands of examples. The Toronto Maple Leafs have won seven games in a row. Last night, I went to the game and they lost. I must have "jinxed" them. They lost *because* I went to the game.

Stock market analysts indulge in what is perhaps the most striking example of the *post hoc* fallacy in action. Every day the stock market goes up or down, and every day some analyst on some national news program singles out one or two of the day's events as the cause of some change in the market: "Today the TSE Index rose five points on heavy trading; analysts say that the increase was due to Finance Minister Paul Martin's latest budget." But did the Martin budget really cause the increase in the TSE Index? If the stock market had fallen, presumably some reason would have been found to "explain" that as well (perhaps the reason would also have been Paul Martin's budget). Overall, it is difficult to link many daily changes in the stock market to specific news events.

Very closely related to the *post hoc* fallacy is the often erroneous link between correlation and causation. Two variables are said to be *correlated* if one variable changes when the other variable changes. But correlation does not imply causation. Cities that have high crime rates also have lots of automobiles, so there is a very high degree of correlation between number of cars and crime rates. Can we argue, then, that cars *cause* crime? No. The reason for the correlation here may have nothing to do with cause and effect. Big cities have lots of people, lots of people have lots of cars, and therefore big cities have lots of cars. Big cities also have high crime rates for many reasons—crowding, poverty, anonymity, unequal distribution of wealth, and the ready availability of drugs, to mention only a few. But the presence of cars is not one of them.

The Fallacy of Composition To conclude that what is true for a part is necessarily true for the whole is to fall into the **fallacy of composition.** Often what holds for an individual does not hold for a group or for society as a whole. Suppose that a large group of cattle ranchers graze their cattle on the same range. To an individual rancher, more cattle and more grazing mean a higher income. But because its capacity is limited, the land can support only so many cattle. If every cattle

post hoc, ergo propter hoc Literally, "after this (in time), therefore because of this." A common error made in thinking about causation: if Event A happens before Event B happens, it is not necessarily true that A caused B.

fallacy of composition The belief that what is true for a part is necessarily true for the whole.

rancher increased the number of cattle sent out to graze, the land would become overgrazed and barren, and everyone's income would fall. In short:

> Theories that seem to work well when applied to individuals or households often break down when they are applied to the whole.

■ **Testing Theories and Models: Empirical Economics**   In science, a theory is rejected when it fails to explain what is observed or when another theory better explains what is observed. Prior to the sixteenth century almost everyone believed that the earth was the centre of the universe and that the sun and stars rotated around it. The astronomer Ptolemy (A.D. 127–151) built a model that explained and predicted the movements of the heavenly bodies in a geocentric (earth-centred) universe. Early in the sixteenth century, however, the Polish astronomer Nicholas Copernicus found himself dissatisfied with the Ptolemaic model and proposed an alternative theory or model, placing the sun at the centre of the known universe and relegating the earth to the status of one planet among many. The battle between the competing models was waged, at least in part, with data based on observations—actual measurements of the movements of the planets. The new model ultimately predicted much better than the old, and in time it came to be accepted.

In the seventeenth century, building on the works of Copernicus and others, Sir Isaac Newton constructed yet another body of theory that seemed to predict planetary motion with still more accuracy. Newtonian physics became the accepted body of theory, relied on for almost 300 years. Then Albert Einstein did his work. The theory of relativity replaced Newtonian physics because it predicted even better. Relativity was able to explain some things that earlier theories could not.

Economic theories are also confronted with new and often conflicting data from time to time. The collection and use of data to test economic theories is called **empirical economics.**

Numerous large data sets are available to facilitate economic research. For example, economists studying the labour market can now test behavioural theories against the actual working experiences of thousands of randomly selected people. Macroeconomists continuously monitoring and studying the behaviour of the national economy pass thousands of items of data, collected by both government agencies and private companies, back and forth on diskettes and over telephone lines. Housing market analysts analyze data tapes containing observations recorded in connection with millions of home sales.

All scientific research needs to isolate and measure the responsiveness of one variable to a change in another variable *ceteris paribus*. Physical scientists, such as physicists and geologists, can often impose the condition of *ceteris paribus* by conducting controlled experiments. They can, for example, measure the effect of one chemical on another while literally holding all else constant in an environment that they control completely. Social scientists, who study people, rarely have this luxury.

While controlled experiments are difficult in economics and other social sciences, they are not impossible. For example, some economists examine certain types of behaviour, such as risk-taking and willingness to cooperate, in controlled experiments involving individuals using techniques similar to those used in psychology laboratories. Other economists have been able to examine human behaviour in large-scale social experiments such as the Mincome experiment in Manitoba, where a number of citizens participated in an experiment designed to determine how a policy which guarantees a minimum income affects the amount of work people perform. However, social experiments are expensive and most questions in

empirical economics *The collection and use of data to test economic theories.*

economics are not easily answered in a psychology lab. As a consequence, economists typically use another technique in their research: they try to observe the behaviour of groups of similar people under different circumstances. For example, if one province increases gasoline taxes and another does not, it may be that a subsequent difference in the growth rate of gasoline consumption can be attributed to the difference in taxes. But one must be very careful using this technique since other changes (for example, a change in relative incomes in the two provinces) can contribute to the different consumption behaviours. Statistical models and the computer are frequently used to try to hold other things equal in empirical economic research.

ECONOMIC POLICY

Economic theory helps us understand how the world works, but the formulation of *economic policy* requires a second step. We must have objectives. What do we want to change? Why? What is good and what is bad about the way the system is operating? Can we make it better?

Such questions force us to be specific about the grounds for judging one outcome superior to another. What does it mean to be better? Four criteria are frequently applied in making these judgments:

Criteria for Judging Economic Outcomes:	1. Efficiency
	2. Equity
	3. Growth
	4. Stability

■ **Efficiency** In physics "efficiency" refers to the ratio of useful energy delivered by a system to the energy supplied to it. An efficient automobile engine, for example, is one that uses up a small amount of fuel per kilometre for a given level of power.

efficiency *In economics, allocative efficiency. An efficient economy is one that produces what people want and does so at the least possible cost.*

In economics, **efficiency** means *allocative efficiency*. An efficient economy is one that produces what people want and does so at the least possible cost. If the system allocates resources to the production of things that nobody wants, it is inefficient. If all members of a particular society were vegetarian and somehow half of all that society's resources were used to produce meat, the result would be inefficient. It is inefficient when steel beams lie in the rain and rust because somebody fouled up a shipping schedule. If a firm could produce its product using 25% less labour and energy without sacrificing quality, it too is inefficient.

The clearest example of an efficient change is a voluntary exchange. If you and I each want something that the other has and we agree to exchange, we are both better off, and no one loses. When a company reorganizes its production or adopts a new technology that enables it to produce more of its product with fewer resources, without sacrificing quality, it has made an efficient change. At least potentially, the resources saved could be used to produce more of something.

Inefficiencies can arise in numerous ways. Sometimes they are caused by government regulations or tax laws that distort otherwise sound economic decisions. Suppose that land in Prince Edward Island is best suited for potato production and that land in Manitoba is best suited for wheat production. Clearly, a law that requires Manitoba to produce only potatoes and P.E.I. to produce only wheat would be inefficient. If firms that cause environmental damage are in no way held accountable for their actions, the incentive to minimize those damages is lost, and the result is inefficient.

Since most changes that can be made in an economy will leave some people better off and others worse off, we must have a way of comparing the gains and losses that may result from any given change. Most often we simply compare their sizes in dollar terms. A change is efficient if the value of the resulting gains exceeds the value of the resulting losses. In this case the winners can potentially compensate the losers and still be better off.

■ **Equity** While efficiency has a fairly precise definition that can be applied with some degree of rigour, **equity** ("fairness") lies in the eye of the beholder. Few people agree on what is fair and what is unfair. To many, fairness implies a more equal distribution of income and wealth. Fairness may imply alleviating poverty, but the extent to which poverty should be reduced is the subject of enormous disagreement. For thousands of years philosophers have wrestled with the principles of justice that should guide social decisions. They will probably wrestle with such questions for thousands of years to come.

Despite the impossibility of defining equity or fairness universally, public policy makers judge the fairness of economic outcomes all the time. Rent control laws were passed because some legislators thought that landlords treated low-income tenants unfairly. Certainly most social welfare programs are created in the name of equity.

■ **Growth** As the result of technological change, the building of machinery, and the acquisition of knowledge, societies learn to produce new things and to produce old things better. In the early days of the Canadian economy, it took nearly half the population to produce the required food supply. Today less than 5% of the country's population is engaged in agriculture.

When we devise new and better ways of producing the things we use now and develop new products and services, the total amount of production in the economy increases. **Economic growth** is an increase in the total output of an economy. If output grows faster than the population, output per capita rises and standards of living increase. Presumably, when an economy grows there is more of what people want. Rural and agrarian societies become modern industrial societies as a result of economic growth and rising per capita output.

economic growth *An increase in the total output of an economy.*

Some policies discourage economic growth and others encourage it. Tax laws, for example, can be designed to encourage the development and application of new production techniques. Research and development in some societies are subsidized by the government. Building roads, highways, bridges, and transport systems in developing countries may speed up the process of economic growth. If businesses and wealthy people invest their wealth outside their country rather than in its own industries, growth in their home country may be slowed.

■ **Stability** Economic **stability** refers to the condition in which national output is steady or growing, with low inflation and full employment of resources. An economy may at times be unstable. During the 1960s, the Canadian economy experienced relatively steady growth and generally low rates of inflation and unemployment. Consumer prices never rose more than 4.5% in a single year and after 1961 the unemployment rate was less than 6% of the labour force. The 1970s and 1980s were much less stable. Canada experienced two periods of rapid inflation (over 10%) and a period of severe unemployment from 1982 through 1985. The beginning of the 1990s was another period of instability, with a recession occurring in 1990–1991. By 1997 there were signs of renewed economic growth and many hoped that a healthy rate of growth would be sustained into the next century. The causes of instability and the ways in which governments have attempted to stabilize the economy are the subject matter of macroeconomics.

stability *A condition in which output is steady or growing, with low inflation and full employment of resources.*

An Invitation

This chapter is meant to prepare you for what is to come. The first part of the chapter invited you into an exciting discipline that deals with important issues and questions. You cannot begin to understand how a society functions without knowing something about its economic history and its economic system.

The second part of the chapter introduced the method of reasoning that economics requires and some of the tools that economics uses. We believe that learning to think in this very powerful way will help you better understand the world.

As you proceed, it is important that you keep track of what you've learned in earlier chapters. This book has a plan; it proceeds step by step, each section building on the last. It would be a good idea to read through each chapter's table of contents and flip through each chapter before you read it to be sure you understand where it fits in the big picture.

Summary

1. *Economics* is the study of how individuals and societies choose to use the scarce resources that nature and previous generations have provided.

Why Study Economics?

2. There are many reasons to study economics, including (a) to learn a way of thinking, (b) to understand society, (c) to understand global affairs, and (d) to be an informed voter.

3. That which we forgo when we make a choice or a decision is the *opportunity cost* of that decision.

The Scope of Economics

4. *Microeconomics* deals with the functioning of individual markets and industries and with the behaviour of individual decision-making units: firms and households.

5. *Macroeconomics* looks at the economy as a whole. It deals with the economic behaviour of aggregates—national output, national income, the overall price level, and the general rate of inflation.

6. Economics is a broad and diverse discipline with many special fields of inquiry. These include economic history, international economics, and urban economics.

The Method of Economics

7. Economics asks and attempts to answer two kinds of questions: positive and normative. *Positive economics* attempts to understand behaviour and the operation of economies without making judgments about whether the outcomes are good or bad.

Normative economics looks at the results or outcomes of economic behaviour and asks if they are good or bad and whether they can be improved.

8. Positive economics is often divided into two parts. *Descriptive economics* involves the compilation of data that accurately describe economic facts and events. *Economic theory* attempts to generalize and explain what is observed. It involves statements of cause and effect—of action and reaction.

9. An economic *model* is a formal statement of an economic theory. Models simplify and abstract from reality.

10. It is often useful to isolate the effects of one variable or another while holding "all else constant." This is the device of *ceteris paribus*.

11. Models and theories can be expressed in many ways. The most common ways are in words, in graphs, and in equations.

12. Because one event happens before another, the second event does not necessarily happen as a result of the first event. To assume that "after" implies "because" is to commit the fallacy of *post hoc, ergo propter hoc*. The belief that what is true for a part is necessarily true for the whole is the *fallacy of composition*.

13. *Empirical economics* involves the collection and use of data to test economic theories. In principle, the best model is the one that yields the most accurate predictions.

14. To make policy, one must be careful to specify criteria for making judgments. Four specific criteria are used most often in economics: *efficiency, equity, growth,* and *stability*.

ceteris paribus 13

descriptive economics 11

economic growth 17

economic theory 11

economics 2

efficiency 16

empirical economics 15

equity 16

fallacy of composition 14

inductive reasoning 11

Industrial Revolution 5

macroeconomics 8

microeconomics 7

model 12

normative economics 9

Ockham's razor 12

opportunity cost 2

positive economics 9

post hoc, ergo propter hoc 14

stability 17

sunk costs 3

variable 12

Problem Set

1. One of the scarce resources that constrains our behaviour is time. Each of us has only 24 hours in a day. How do you go about allocating your time in a given day among competing alternatives? How do you go about weighing the alternatives? Once you choose a most important use of time, why do you not spend all your time on it? Use the notion of opportunity cost in your answer.

2. Which of the following statements might be made by someone studying positive economics? Briefly explain your answer.
   a. The North American Free Trade Agreement (NAFTA) is likely to lead to increased exports of Canadian-made automobiles to Mexico.
   b. NAFTA is likely to make the people of Canada better off.
   c. The 1995 federal budget reduced unemployment insurance payments. This legislation is likely to increase employment.
   d. The unemployment caused by deficit reduction is unfair.
   e. The introduction of a toll system to pay for the TransCanada Highway in Nova Scotia is unfair because it will impose larger burdens on lower-income households.
   f. Increasing the toll on the bridges in Halifax by $1 is likely to reduce congestion in the city.

3. Describe one of the major economic issues facing the government of your city or your province. (*Hint:* You might look at a local newspaper. Most issues that make it into the paper will have an impact on people's lives.) Who will be affected by the resolution of this issue? What alternative actions have been proposed? Who will be the winners? The losers?

4. Suppose that all of the 10 000 voting-age citizens of Lumpland are required to register to vote every year. Suppose also that the citizens of Lumpland are fully employed and that they each value their time at $10 per hour. In addition, assume that nonvoting high-school students in Lumpland are willing to work for $5 per hour. The government has two choices: (1) it can hire 200 students to work at registration locations for five hours per day for 10 days, or (2) it can hire 400 students for five hours per day for 10 days. If the government hires 200 students, each of the 10 000 citizens will have to wait in line for an hour to register. If the government hires 400 students, there will be no waiting time.

   Assume that the cost of paying the students is obtained by taxing each citizen equally. The current government is very conservative and has decided to hold taxes down by hiring only 200 students. Do you agree with this decision? Why or why not? Is it efficient? Is it fair?

5. Suppose that a city is considering building a bridge across a river. The bridge will be paid for out of tax dollars, and the city gets its revenues from a sales tax imposed on things sold in the city. The bridge would provide more direct access for commuters and shoppers and would alleviate the huge traffic jam that occurs every morning at the bridge down the river in another city.
   a. Who would gain if the bridge were built? Could those gains be measured? How?
   b. Who would be hurt? Could those costs be measured? How?
   c. How would you determine if it were efficient to build the bridge?

6. Define *equity*. How would you decide if building the bridge described in question 5 were fair/equitable?

7. For each of the following situations, identify the full cost (opportunity costs) involved:

   a. A worker earning an hourly wage of $8.50 decides to cut back to half time in order to attend classes at York University.

   b. Samarah decides to drive to Kingston from Toronto to visit her son, who attends Queen's University.

   c. Tom decides to go to a wild fraternity party and stays out all night before his physics exam.

   d. Tova spends $200 on a new dress.

   e. The Confab Company spends $1 million to build a new branch plant that will probably be in operation for at least 10 years.

   f. Alex's father owns a small grocery store in town. Alex works 40 hours a week in the store but receives no compensation.

Appendix to Chapter 1 — How to Read and Understand Graphs

Economics is the most quantitative of the social sciences. If you flip through the pages of this or any other economics text, you will see countless tables and graphs. These tables and graphs serve a number of purposes. First, they illustrate important economic relationships. Second, they make difficult problems easier to understand and analyze. Finally, patterns and regularities that may not be discernible in simple lists of numbers can often be seen when those numbers are laid out in a table or on a graph.

A **graph** is a two-dimensional representation of a set of numbers, or data. There are many ways that numbers can be illustrated by a graph.

Time Series Graphs

It is often useful to see how a single measure or variable changes over time. One way to present this information is to plot the values of the variable on a graph, with each value corresponding to a different time period. A graph of this kind is called a **time series graph.** On a time series graph, time is measured along the horizontal scale and the variable being graphed is measured along the vertical scale. Figures 1A.1 and 1A.2 are time series graphs that present the total income in the Canadian economy for each year between 1975 and 1996.* These graphs are based on the data found in Table 1A.1. By displaying these data graphically, we can see clearly that (1) total personal disposable income has been increasing steadily since 1975, and (2) during certain periods, disposable income was increasing at a faster rate than during other periods.

Graphs must be read very carefully. For example,

The measure of income presented in Table 1A.1 and in Figures 1A.1 and 1A.2 is disposable income in millions of dollars. It is an approximation of the total personal income received by all households in Canada added together minus the taxes that they pay.

look at Figure 1A.2, which plots the same data that are plotted in Figure 1A.1. The only difference between the two graphs is that the scales used on the horizontal axes are different. (The distance separating each year in Figure 1A.1 is twice as large as the distance separating each year in Figure 1A.2.) As a consequence, it looks like income is growing more rapidly in Figure 1A.2 than in Figure 1A.1. This is not true, of course; the same data are plotted in both graphs.

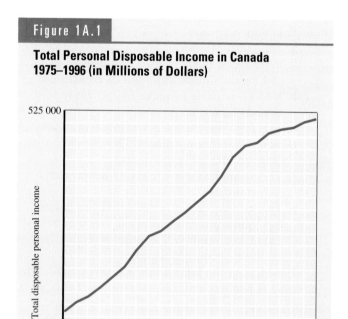

Figure 1A.1

Total Personal Disposable Income in Canada 1975–1996 (in Millions of Dollars)

Source: Statistics Canada, *National Income and Expenditure Accounts,* Cat. no. 13-001.

Figure 1A.2

Total Personal Disposable Income in Canada 1975–1996 (in Millions of Dollars)

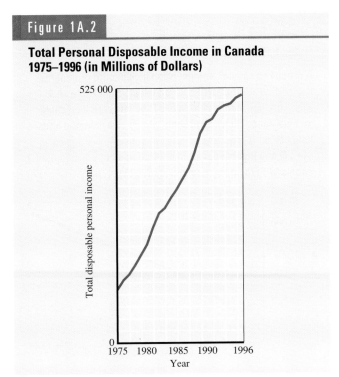

Source: Statistics Canada, *National Income and Expenditure Accounts*, Cat. no. 13-001.

Table 1A.1	Total Personal Disposable Income in Canada 1975–1996 (in Millions of Dollars)

YEAR	TOTAL PERSONAL DISPOSABLE INCOME
1975	113 321
1976	128 239
1977	141 374
1978	159 466
1979	179 852
1980	203 653
1981	237 682
1982	262 861
1983	276 013
1984	300 346
1985	321 337
1986	338 093
1987	361 435
1988	394 235
1989	432 135
1990	451 976
1991	465 943
1992	478 158
1993	488 462
1994	495 246
1995	508 247
1996	513 300

Source: Statistics Canada, *National Income and Expenditure Accounts*, Cat. no. 13-001.

Graphing Two Variables on a Cartesian Coordinate System

More important than simple graphs of one variable are graphs that contain information on two variables at the same time. The most common method of graphing two variables is the **Cartesian coordinate system.** This system is constructed by simply drawing two perpendicular lines: a horizontal line, or **X axis,** and a vertical line, or **Y axis.** The axes contain measurement scales that intersect at 0 (zero). This point is called the **origin.** On the vertical scale, positive numbers lie above the horizontal axis (that is, above the origin) and negative numbers lie below it. On the horizontal scale, positive numbers lie to the right of the vertical axis (to the right of the origin) and negative numbers lie to the left of it. The point at which the graph intersects the Y axis is called the **Y-intercept.**

When two variables are plotted on a single graph, each point represents a *pair* of numbers. The first number is measured on the X axis and the second number is measured on the Y axis. For example, the following points (X, Y) are plotted on the set of axes drawn in Figure 1A.3: (4, 2), (2, –1), (–3, 4), (–3, –2). Most, but not all, of the graphs in this book are plots of two variables where both values are positive numbers (such as [4, 2] in Figure 1A.3). On these graphs, only the upper right-hand quadrant of the coordinate system (i.e., the quadrant in which all X and Y values are positive) will be drawn.

Plotting Income and Consumption Data for Households

Table 1A.2 presents some data that were collected by Statistics Canada. In a survey of over 10 000 households, each household was asked to keep careful track of all its expenditures. The table shows average income and average spending for those households that were surveyed, ranked by income. For example the average income for the top fifth (20%) of the households was $96 647, and their average spending was $54 882.

Figure 1A.4 presents the numbers from Table 1A.2 graphically using the Cartesian coordinate system. Along the horizontal scale, the X axis, we measure average income. Along the vertical scale, the Y axis, we measure average consumption spending. Each of the five pairs of numbers from the table is represented by a point on the graph. Since all numbers are positive numbers, we need to show only the upper right quadrant of the coordinate system.

To help you read this graph, we have drawn a dashed line connecting all the points where consumption and income would be equal. *This 45° line does not represent any data.* Rather, it represents the line along which all variables on the X axis correspond exactly to the

A Cartesian Coordinate System

A Cartesian coordinate system is constructed by drawing two perpendicular lines: a vertical axis (the *Y* axis) and a horizontal axis (the *X* axis). Each axis is a measuring scale.

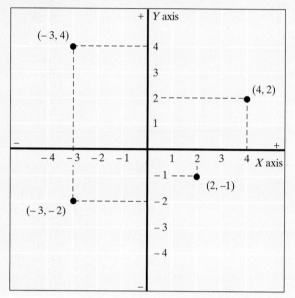

Household Consumption and Income

A graph is a simple two-dimensional geometric representation of data. This graph displays the data from Table 1A.2. Along the horizontal scale (*X* axis), we measure household income. Along the vertical scale (*Y* axis), we measure household consumption. Note: at point A, consumption equals $14 442 and income equals $12 104; at point B, consumption equals $23 178 and income equals $25 131.

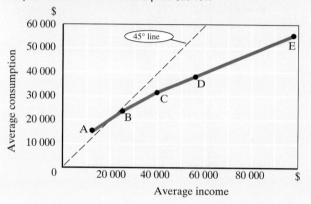

Source: Statistics Canada, *National Income and Expenditure Accounts,* Cat. no. 13-001.

variables on the *Y* axis (for example, [1, 1], [2, 2], [3.7, 3.7], etc.). The heavy blue line traces out the data; the dashed line is only to help you read the graph.

There are several things to look for when reading

a graph. The first thing you should notice is whether the line slopes upward or downward as you move from left to right. The blue line in Figure 1A.4 slopes upward, indicating that there seems to be a **positive relationship** between income and spending: the higher a household's income, the more a household tends to consume. If we had graphed the percentage of each group receiving welfare payments along the *Y* axis, the line would presumably slope downward, indicating that welfare payments are lower at higher income levels. The income level/welfare payment relationship is thus a **negative** one.

Slope

The **slope** of a line or curve is a measure that indicates whether the relationship between the variables is positive or negative and how much of a response there is in *Y* (the variable on the vertical axis) when *X* (the variable on the horizontal axis) changes. The slope of a line between two points is the change in the quantity being measured on the *Y* axis divided by the change in the quantity being measured on the *X* axis. We will normally use Δ (the Greek letter delta) to refer to a change in a variable. In Figure 1A.5, the slope of the line between points *A* and *B* is Δ*Y* divided by Δ*X*. Sometimes it's easy to remember slope as "the rise over the run," indicating the vertical change over the horizontal change.

Table 1A.2	Consumption Expenditures and Income, 1992*	
	AVERAGE INCOME	AVERAGE CONSUMPTION EXPENDITURES
Bottom fifth	$12 104	$14 442
2nd fifth	25 131	23 178
3rd fifth	39 111	30 790
4th fifth	55 859	38 789
Top fifth	96 647	54 882

*Income and consumption data are for households. A household is a person or group of persons occupying a dwelling unit. A dwelling is defined as any structurally separate set of living premises with a private entrance from outside the building or from a common hallway or stairway inside.

Source: Statistics Canada, *Family Expenditures in Canada,* Cat. no. 62-555.

A Curve with a Positive Slope (a) and a Curve with a Negative Slope (b)

A positive slope indicates that increases in *X* are associated with increases in *Y* and that decreases in *X* are associated with decreases in *Y*. A negative slope indicates the opposite—when *X* increases, *Y* decreases and when *X* decreases, *Y* increases.

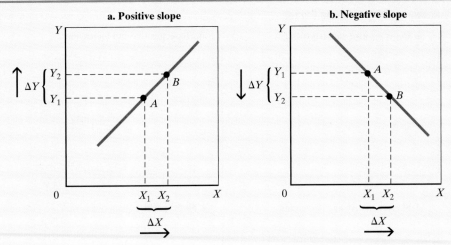

To be precise, ΔX between two points on a graph is simply X_2 minus X_1, where X_2 is the X value for the second point and X_1 is the X value for the first point. Similarly, ΔY is defined as Y_2 minus Y_1, where Y_2 is the Y value for the second point and Y_1 is the Y value for the first point. Slope is equal to

$$\frac{\Delta Y}{\Delta X} = \frac{Y_2 - Y_1}{X_2 - X_1}.$$

As we move from A to B in Figure 1A.5a, both X and Y increase; the slope is thus a positive number. On the other hand, as we move from A to B in Figure 1A.5b, X increases [$(X_2 - X_1)$ is a positive number], but Y decreases [$(Y_2 - Y_1)$ is a negative number]. The slope in Figure 1A.5b is thus a negative number, since a negative number divided by a positive number gives a negative quotient.

To calculate the numerical value of the slope between points A and B in Figure 1A.4, we need to calculate ΔY and ΔX. Since consumption is measured on the Y axis, ΔY is 8736 [$(Y_2 - Y_1) = (23\ 178 - 14\ 442)$]. Since income is measured along the X axis, ΔX is 13 027 [$(X_2 - X_1) = (25\ 131 - 12\ 104)$]. The slope between A and B is $\Delta Y/\Delta X = 8736/13\ 027 = +.6706$.

Another interesting thing to note about the data graphed in Figure 1A.4 is that all the points lie roughly along a straight line. (If you look very closely, however, you can see that the slope declines as one moves from left to right; the line becomes slightly less steep.) A straight line has a constant slope. That is, if you pick any two points along it and calculate the slope, you will always get the same number. A horizontal line has a zero slope (ΔY is zero); a vertical line has an "infinite" slope, since ΔY is too big to be measured.

Unlike the slope of a straight line, the slope of a *curve* is continually changing. Consider, for example, the curves in Figure 1A.6. Figure 1A.6a shows a curve with a positive slope that decreases as you move from left to right. The easiest way to think about the concept of increasing or decreasing slope is to imagine what it is like walking up a hill from left to right. If the hill is steep (as it is in the first part of Figure 1A.6a), you are moving a lot in the Y direction for each step you take in the X direction. If the hill is less steep (as it is further along in Figure 1A.6a), you are moving less in the Y direction for every step you take in the X direction. Thus, when the hill is steep, slope ($\Delta Y/\Delta X$) is a larger number than it is when the hill is flatter. The curve in Figure 1A.6b has a positive slope, but its slope *increases* as you move from left to right.

The same analogy holds for curves that have a negative slope. Figure 1A.6c shows a curve with a negative slope that increases (in absolute value)* as you move from left to right. This time think about skiing down a hill. At first, the descent in Figure 1A.6c is gradual (low slope), but as you proceed down the hill (to the right), you descend more quickly (high slope). Figure 1A.6d shows a curve with a negative slope that *decreases* in absolute value as you move from left to right.

In Figure 1A.6e, the slope goes from positive to negative as X increases. In 1A.6f, the slope goes from negative to positive. At point A in both, the slope is zero. (Remember, slope is defined as $\Delta Y/\Delta X$. At point A, Y is not changing [$\Delta Y = 0$]. Therefore slope at point A is zero.)

---

*The absolute value *of a number is its value disregarding its sign, that is, disregarding whether it is positive or negative:* -7 *is bigger in absolute value than* -4; -9 *is bigger in absolute value than* $+8$.

Changing Slopes along Curves

a. Slope: positive and decreasing

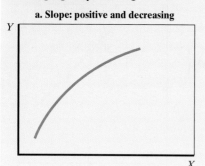

b. Slope: positive and increasing

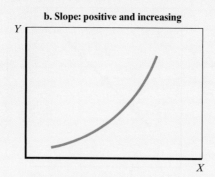

c. Slope: negative and increasing

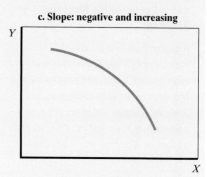

d. Slope: negative and decreasing

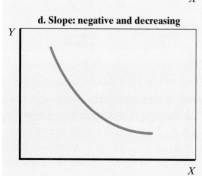

e. Slope: positive, then negative

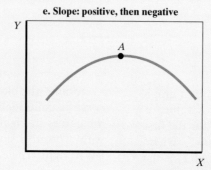

f. Slope: negative, then positive

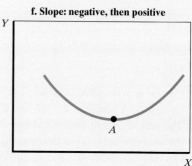

Some Precautions

When you read a graph, it is important to think carefully about what the points in the space defined by the axes represent. Table 1A.3 and Figure 1A.7 present a graph of consumption and income that is very different from the one in Table 1A.2 and Figure 1A.4. First, each point in Figure 1A.7 represents a different year; in Figure 1A.4, each point represented a different group of

National Income and Consumption

It is important to think carefully about what is represented by points in the space defined by the axes of a graph. In this graph, we have income graphed with consumption, as was the case in Figure 1A.4, but here each observation point is national income and aggregate consumption in different years, measured in billions of dollars.

Table 1A.3	Aggregate Income and Consumption for Canada, 1965–1995 (in Billions of Dollars)	
	AGGREGATE NATIONAL INCOME	AGGREGATE CONSUMPTION
1965	57.5	34.7
1970	89.1	51.9
1975	171.5	97.6
1980	309.8	172.4
1985	478.0	274.5
1990	669.5	399.3
1995	776.3	466.0

Source: Statistics Canada, *Canadian Economic Observer, Historical Statistical Supplement, 1994–95,* Cat. no. 11-210, Table 1.

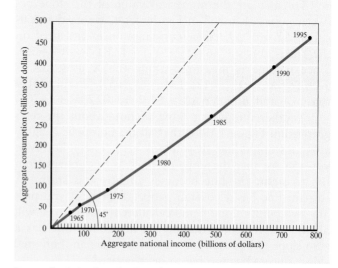

Source: Statistics Canada, *Canadian Economic Observer, Historical Statistical Supplement, 1994–95,* Cat. no. 11-210, Table 1.

households at the *same* point in time (1992). Second, the points in Figure 1A.7 represent *aggregate* consumption and income for the whole nation measured in *billions* of dollars; in Figure 1A.4, the points represented average *household* income and consumption measured in dollars.

It is interesting to compare these two graphs. All points on the aggregate consumption curve in Figure 1A.7 lie below the 45-degree line, which means that aggregate consumption is always less than aggregate income. On the other hand, the graph of average household income and consumption in Figure 1A.4 crosses the 45-degree line, implying that for some households consumption is larger than income.

Summary

1. A *graph* is a two-dimensional representation of a set of numbers, or data. A *time series graph* illustrates how a single variable changes over time.

2. The most common method of graphing two variables on one graph is the *Cartesian coordinate system,* which includes an X (horizontal) *axis* and a Y (vertical) *axis.* The points at which the two axes intersect is called the *origin.* The point at which a graph intersects the Y axis is called the *Y-intercept.*

3. The *slope* of a line or curve indicates whether the relationship between the two variables graphed on a Cartesian coordinate system is positive or negative and how much of a response there is in Y (the variable on the vertical axis) when X (the variable on the horizontal axis) changes. The slope of a line between two points is the change in the quantity being measured on the Y axis divided by the change in the quantity being measured on the X axis.

Review Terms and Concepts

Cartesian coordinate system A common method of graphing two variables that makes use of two perpendicular lines against which the variables are plotted. 21

graph A two-dimensional representation of a set of numbers, or data. 20

negative relationship A relationship between two variables, X and Y, in which a decrease in X is associated with an increase in Y, and an increase in X is associated with a decrease in Y. 22

origin On a Cartesian coordinate system, the point at which the horizontal and vertical axes intersect. 21

positive relationship A relationship between two variables, X and Y, in which a decrease in X is associated with a decrease in Y, and an increase in X is associated with an increase in Y. 22

slope A measurement that indicates whether the relationship between variables is positive or negative and how much of a response there is in Y (the variable on the vertical axis) when X (the variable on the horizontal axis) changes. 22

times series graph A graph illustrating how a variable changes over time. 20

X axis On a Cartesian coordinate system, the horizontal line against which a variable is plotted. 21

Y axis On a Cartesian coordinate system, the vertical line against which a variable is plotted. 21

Y-intercept The point at which a graph intersects the Y axis. 21

1. Graph each of the following sets of numbers. Draw a line through the points and calculate the slope of each line.

1		2		3		4		5		6	
X	Y	X	Y	X	Y	X	Y	X	Y	X	Y
1	5	1	25	0	0	0	40	0	0	0.1	100
2	10	2	20	10	10	10	30	10	10	0.2	75
3	15	3	15	20	20	20	20	20	20	0.3	50
4	20	4	10	30	30	30	10	30	10	0.4	25
5	25	5	5	40	40	40	0	40	0	0.5	0

2. For each of the following equations graph the line and calculate its slope.
   a. $P = 10 - 2q_D$ (Put q_D on the X axis)
   b. $P = 100 - 4q_D$ (Put q_D on the X axis)
   c. $P = 50 + 6q_S$ (Put q_S on the X axis)
   d. $I = 10\ 000 - 500r$ (Put I on the X axis)

3. For each of the graphs in Figure 1 below, say whether the curve has a positive or negative slope. Give an intuitive explanation for the slope of each curve.

Figure 1

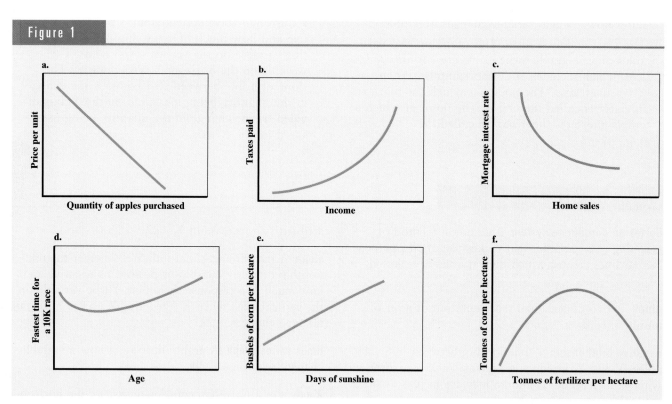

The Economic Problem: Scarcity and Choice

Chapter 1 began with a broad definition of economics. As you saw there, every society has some system or mechanism that transforms what nature and previous generations provide into useful form. Economics is the study of that process and its outcomes. Economists attempt to answer the questions: What gets produced? How is it produced? Who gets it? Why? Is it good or bad? Can it be improved?

This chapter explores these questions further. In a sense, this entire chapter *is* the definition of economics. It lays out the central problems addressed by the discipline and provides the framework that will guide you through the rest of the book.

Human wants are unlimited, but resources are not. Limited, or scarce, resources force individuals and societies to choose. The central function of any economy, no matter how simple or how complex, is to transform resources into useful form in accordance with those choices. The process by which this transformation takes place is called **production.**

The term **resources** is very broad. Some resources are the product of nature: land, wildlife, minerals, timber, energy, even the rain and the wind. At any given time, the resources, or **inputs,** available to a society also include those things that have been produced by previous generations, such as buildings and equipment. Things that are produced and then used to produce other valuable goods or services later on are called *capital resources*, or simply **capital.** Buildings, machinery, equipment, tables, roads, bridges, desks, and so forth are part of the country's capital stock. *Human resources*—labour, skills, and knowledge—are also an important part of a country's resources.

production *The process by which resources are transformed into useful forms.*

resources or **inputs** *Anything provided by nature or previous generations that can be used directly or indirectly to satisfy human wants.*

capital *Things that have already been produced that are in turn used to produce other goods and services.*

producers *Those people or groups of people, whether private or public, who transform resources into usable products.*

outputs *Usable products.*

Producers are those who take resources and transform them into usable products, or **outputs.** Private manufacturing firms purchase resources and produce products for the market. Governments do so as well. National defence, the justice system, police and fire protection, and sewer services—all are examples of outputs produced by the government, which is sometimes called the *public sector.*

Individual households often produce products for themselves. A household that owns its own home is in essence using land and a structure (capital) to produce "housing services" that it consumes itself. A symphony orchestra is no less a producer than General Motors. An orchestra takes capital resources—a building, musical instruments, lighting fixtures, musical scores, and so on—and combines them with land and highly skilled labour to produce performances.

Scarcity, Choice, and Opportunity Cost

In the second half of this chapter, we discuss the global economic landscape. But before you can understand the different types of economic systems, it is important to understand the basic economic concepts of scarcity, choice, and opportunity cost.

THE THREE BASIC QUESTIONS

three basic questions *The questions that all societies must answer: (1) What will be produced? (2) How will it be produced? (3) Who will get what is produced?*

All societies must answer **three basic questions:**

> 1. What will be produced?
> 2. How will it be produced?
> 3. Who will get what is produced?

Stated a slightly different way, the economic system must determine the *allocation of scarce resources* among producers, the *mix of output,* and the *distribution of that output* (Figure 2.1).

■ **Scarcity and Choice in a One-Person Economy** The simplest economy is one in which a single person lives alone on an island where no one has ever been before. Consider Ivan, the survivor of a plane crash, who finds himself cast ashore in such a place. Here, individual and society are one; there is no distinction between social and private. *Nonetheless, nearly all of the basic decisions that characterize complex economies must be made.* That is, although Ivan himself will get whatever he produces, he still must decide how to allocate the resources of the island, what to produce, and how and when to produce it.

FIGURE 2.1

The Three Basic Questions

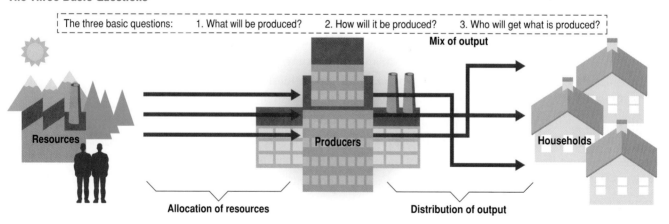

The three basic questions: 1. What will be produced? 2. How will it be produced? 3. Who will get what is produced?

Mix of output

Resources   Producers   Households

Allocation of resources   Distribution of output

First, Ivan must decide *what* he wants to produce. Notice that the word *needs* does not appear here. Needs are absolute requirements, but beyond just enough water, basic nutrition, and shelter to survive, they are very difficult to define. What is an "absolute necessity" for one person may not be for another. In any case, Ivan must put his wants in some order of priority and make some choices.

Next he must look at the *possibilities*. What can he do to satisfy his wants, given the limits of the island? In every society, no matter how simple or complex, people are constrained in what they can do. In this society of one, Ivan is constrained by time, his physical condition, his knowledge, his skills, and the resources and climate of the island.

Given that resources are limited, or scarce, Ivan must decide *how* to use them best to satisfy his hierarchy of wants. Food would probably come close to the top of his list. Should he spend his time simply gathering fruits and berries? Should he hunt for game? Should he clear a field and plant seeds? Clearly, the answers to these questions depend on the character of the island, its climate, its flora and fauna (*are* there any fruits and berries?), the extent of his skills and knowledge (does he know anything about farming?), and his preferences (he may be a vegetarian).

■ **Opportunity Cost**   The concepts of *constrained choice* and *scarcity* are central to the discipline of economics. They can be applied when discussing the behaviour of individuals like Ivan and when analyzing the behaviour of large groups of people in complex societies.

Given the scarcity of time and resources, Ivan has less time to gather fruits and berries if he chooses to hunt—he trades more meat for less fruit. There is a trade-off between food and shelter, too. If Ivan likes to be comfortable, he may work on building a nice place to live, but that may require giving up the food he might have produced. As we noted in Chapter 1, that which we forgo when we make a choice is the **opportunity cost** of that choice.

Ivan may occasionally decide to rest, to lie on the beach and enjoy the sun. In one sense, that benefit is free—he doesn't have to pay for the privilege. In reality, however, it does have a cost, an opportunity cost. Lying in the sun means using time that otherwise could have been spent doing something else. The true cost of that leisure is the value to Ivan of the other things he could have produced, but did not, during the time he spent on the beach.

In the 1960s, the United States decided to put a human being on the moon. To put a human being on the moon required devoting enormous resources to the space program, resources that could have been used to produce other things. The opportunity cost of placing a man on the moon was the total value of all the other things that those resources could have produced. Among other possibilities, taxes might have been lower. That would have meant more income for the population to spend on goods and services. Those same resources could also have been used for medical research, to improve education, to repair roads and bridges, to aid the poor, or to support the arts.

In making everyday decisions it is often helpful to think about opportunity costs. Should I go to a residence party or not? First, it costs $4 to get in. When I pay out money for anything, I give up the other things that I could have bought with that money. Second, it costs two or three hours. Clearly, time is a valuable commodity for a student. I have exams next week and I need to study. I could go to a movie instead of the party. I could go to another party. I could sleep. Just as Ivan must weigh the value of sunning on the beach against more food or better housing, so I must weigh the value of the fun I may have at the residence party against everything else I might otherwise do with the time and money.

opportunity cost *That which we forgo, or give up, when we make a choice or a decision.*

■ Scarcity and Choice in an Economy of Two or More   Now suppose that another survivor of the crash, Colleen, appears on the island. Now that Ivan is not alone things are more complex, and some new decisions must be made. Ivan's and Colleen's preferences about what things to produce are likely to be different. They will probably not have the same knowledge or skills. Perhaps Colleen is very good at tracking animals, while Ivan has a knack for building things. How should they split the work that needs to be done? Once things are produced, they must decide how to divide them. How should their products be distributed?

The mechanism for answering these fundamental questions is clear when Ivan is alone on the island. The "central plan" is his; he simply decides what he wants and what to do about it. The minute someone else appears, however, a number of decision-making arrangements immediately become possible. One or the other may take charge, in which case that person will decide for both of them. The two may agree to cooperate, with each having an equal say, and come up with a joint plan. Or they may agree to split the planning, as well as the production duties. Finally, they may go off to live alone at opposite ends of the island. Even if they live apart, however, they may take advantage of each other's presence by specializing and trading.

> Modern industrial societies must answer exactly the same questions that Colleen and Ivan must answer, but the mechanics of larger economies are naturally more complex. Instead of two people living together, Canada has over 30 million. Still, decisions must be made about what to produce, how to produce it, and who gets it.

■ Specialization, Exchange, and Comparative Advantage   The idea that members of society benefit by specializing in what they do best has a long history and is one of the most important and powerful ideas in all of economics. David Ricardo, a major nineteenth-century British economist, formalized the point precisely. According to Ricardo's **theory of comparative advantage,** specialization and free trade will benefit all trading parties, even when some are "absolutely" more efficient producers than others. Ricardo's basic point applies just as much to Colleen and Ivan as it does to different countries.

To keep things simple, suppose that Colleen and Ivan have only two tasks to accomplish each week: gathering food to eat and cutting logs to be used in constructing a house. If Colleen could cut more logs than Ivan in one day, and Ivan could gather more nuts and berries than Colleen could, specialization would clearly lead to more total production. Both Ivan and Colleen would benefit if Colleen only cuts logs and Ivan only gathers nuts and berries. But suppose that Ivan is slow and somewhat clumsy in his nut-gathering and that Colleen is better at both cutting logs *and* gathering food. Ricardo's point is that it still pays for them to specialize and exchange.

Suppose that Colleen can cut 10 logs per day and that Ivan can cut only five. Also suppose that Colleen can gather 10 baskets of food per day and that Ivan can gather only eight (see table embedded in Figure 2.2). Assume also that Ivan and Colleen value baskets of food and logs equally. How then can the two gain from specialization and exchange? Think of opportunity costs. When Colleen gives up a day of food production to work on the house, she cuts 10 logs and sacrifices 10 baskets of food. The opportunity cost of 10 logs is thus 10 baskets of food if Colleen switches from food to logs. But because Ivan can cut only five logs in a day, he has to work for two days to cut 10 logs. In two days, Ivan could have produced 16 baskets of food (2 days × 8 baskets per day). The opportunity cost of 10 logs is thus 16 baskets of food if Ivan switches from food to logs.

theory of comparative advantage *Ricardo's theory that specialization and free trade will benefit all trading parties, even those that may be absolutely more efficient producers.*

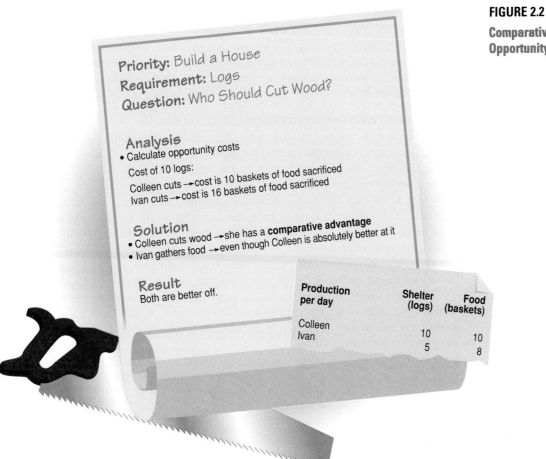

FIGURE 2.2

Comparative Advantage and Opportunity Costs

Priority: Build a House
Requirement: Logs
Question: Who Should Cut Wood?

Analysis
- Calculate opportunity costs

Cost of 10 logs:
Colleen cuts → cost is 10 baskets of food sacrificed
Ivan cuts → cost is 16 baskets of food sacrificed

Solution
- Colleen cuts wood → she has a **comparative advantage**
- Ivan gathers food → even though Colleen is absolutely better at it

Result
Both are better off.

Production per day	Shelter (logs)	Food (baskets)
Colleen	10	10
Ivan	5	8

As Figure 2.2 makes clear, even though Colleen is *absolutely* more efficient at food production than Ivan, she should specialize in logs and let Ivan specialize in food. This way, the maximum number of logs and baskets of food are produced. A person or a country is said to have a comparative advantage in producing a good or service if it is *relatively* more efficient than a trading partner at doing so. Colleen is relatively more efficient at log production because the opportunity cost of switching from food to logs is lower for her than it is for Ivan.

Looking at the same problem from the standpoint of food production leads to exactly the same conclusion. If Colleen were to switch from cutting logs to gathering food, she would sacrifice 10 logs to produce only 10 baskets of food. But if Ivan were to switch from cutting logs to gathering food, he would sacrifice 10 logs to produce a full 16 baskets! Even though Colleen has an *absolute advantage* in both cutting logs and producing food, Ivan has a *comparative advantage* producing food because for the same sacrifice of logs, Ivan produces much more food.

The theory of comparative advantage shows that trade and specialization work to raise productivity. But specialization may also lead to the development of skills that enhance productivity even further. By specializing in log cutting, Colleen will get even stronger shoulders. By spending more time at gathering food, Ivan will refine his food-finding skills. The same applies to countries that engage in international trade. A country that specializes in producing textiles will refine its skills in textile making, while a country that specializes in growing corn will increase its corn-growing skills.

The degree of specialization in modern industrial societies is breathtaking. Once again let your mind wander over the range of products and services available or under development today. As knowledge expands, specialization becomes a necessity. This is true not only for scientists and doctors but also in every career from tree surgeon to divorce lawyer. Understanding specialization and trade will help you to explain much of what goes on in today's global economy.

■ **Weighing Present and Expected Future Costs and Benefits**   Very often we find ourselves weighing benefits available today against benefits available tomorrow. Here too the notion of opportunity cost is helpful.

While alone on the island, Ivan had to choose between cultivating a field and just gathering wild nuts and berries. Gathering nuts and berries provides food now; gathering seeds and clearing a field for planting will yield food tomorrow, if all goes well. Using today's time to farm may well be worth the effort if doing so will yield more food than Ivan would otherwise have in the future. By planting, Ivan is trading present value for future values. Working to gather seeds and clear a field has an opportunity cost—the present leisure he might consume and the value of the berries he might gather if he did not work the field.

The simplest example of trading present for future benefits is the act of saving. When I put income aside today for use in the future, I give up some things that I could have had today in exchange for something tomorrow. The saver must weigh the value of what that income can buy today against what it might be expected to buy later. Since nothing is certain, some judgment about future events and expected values must be made. What are interest rates likely to be? What will my income be in 10 years? How long am I likely to live?

We trade off present and future benefits in small ways all the time. If you decide to study rather than go to the residence party, you are trading present fun for the expected future benefits of higher grades. If you decide to go outside on a very cold day and run eight kilometres, you are trading discomfort in the present for being in better shape later on.

■ **Capital Goods and Consumer Goods**   A society trades present for expected future benefits when it devotes a portion of its resources to research and development or to investment in capital. As we said earlier in this chapter, *capital* in its broadest definition is anything that is produced that will be used to produce other valuable goods or services over time.

Building capital means trading present benefits for future ones. Ivan and Colleen might trade gathering berries or lying in the sun for cutting logs to build a nicer house in the future. In a modern society, resources used to produce capital goods could have been used to produce **consumer goods**—that is, goods for present consumption. Heavy industrial machinery does not directly satisfy the wants of anyone, but producing it requires resources that could instead have gone into producing things that do satisfy wants directly—food, clothing, toys, or golf clubs.

consumer goods *Goods produced for present consumption.*

Capital is everywhere. A road is capital. Once built, we can drive on it or transport goods and services over it for many years to come. The benefits of producing it will be realized over many years. A house is also capital. When it is built, the builder presumes that it will provide shelter and valuable services for a long time. Before a new manufacturing firm can start up, it must put some capital in place. The buildings, equipment, and inventories that it owns are its capital. As it contributes to the production process, this capital yields valuable services through time.

In Chapter 1 we talked about the enormous amount of capital—buildings, roads, factories, housing, cars, trucks, telephone lines, and so forth—that you might see from a window high in an office tower. Much of it was put in place by previous generations, yet it continues to provide valuable services today; it is part of this generation's endowment of resources. In order to build every building, every road, every factory, every house, every car or truck, society must forgo using resources to produce consumer goods today. To get an education, I pay tuition and put off joining the workforce for a while.

Capital need not be tangible. When you spend time and resources developing skills or getting an education, you are investing in human capital—your own human capital—that will continue to exist and yield benefits to you for years to come. A computer program produced by a software company may come on a tangible disk that costs 75¢ to make, but its true intangible value comes from the ideas embodied in the program itself, which will drive computers to do valuable tasks over time. It too is capital.

The process of using resources to produce new capital is called **investment.** (In everyday language, the term *investment* is often used to refer to the act of buying a share of stock or a bond, as in "I invested in some Treasury bills." In economics, however, investment always refers to the creation of capital: the purchase or putting in place of buildings, equipment, roads, houses, and the like.) A wise investment in capital is one that yields future benefits that are more valuable than the present cost. When you spend money for a house, for example, presumably you value its future benefits. That is, you expect to gain more from living in it than you would from the things you could buy today with the same money.

Capital is able to generate future benefits in excess of cost by increasing the productivity of labour. A person who has to dig a hole can dig a bigger hole with a shovel than without a shovel. A computer can do in several seconds what it took hundreds of bookkeepers hours to do 15 years ago. This increased productivity makes it less costly to produce products.

> Because resources are scarce, the opportunity cost of every investment in capital is forgone present consumption.

investment *The process of using resources to produce new capital.*

THE PRODUCTION POSSIBILITY FRONTIER

A simple graphical device called the **production possibility frontier (ppf)** illustrates the principle of constrained choice and scarcity. The ppf is a graph that shows all the combinations of goods and services that can be produced if all of society's resources are used efficiently. Figure 2.3 shows a ppf for a hypothetical economy.

On the *Y* axis we measure the quantity of capital goods produced, and on the *X* axis, the quantity of consumption goods. All points below and to the left of the curve (the shaded area) represent combinations of capital and consumption goods that are possible for the society given the resources available and existing technology. Points above and to the right of the curve, such as point *G*, represent combinations that cannot be reached. If an economy were to end up at point *A* on the graph, it would be producing no consumption goods at all; all resources would be used for the production of capital. If an economy were to end up at point *B*, it would be devoting all of its resources to the production of consumer goods and none of its resources to the formation of capital.

While all economies produce some of each kind of good, different economies emphasize different things. About 18% of gross output in Canada in 1993 was new capital. In the United States, capital accounted for about 16% of gross output in 1993, while in Uruguay the figure was 14%. By contrast, in Japan, capital accounted for about 30% of gross output. Japan is closer to point *A* on its ppf, Uruguay closer to *B*, and the United States and Canada are somewhere in between.

Points that are actually on the production possibility frontier can be thought of as points of both full resource employment and production efficiency. (Recall

production possibility frontier (ppf) *A graph that shows all the combinations of goods and services that can be produced if all of society's resources are used efficiently.*

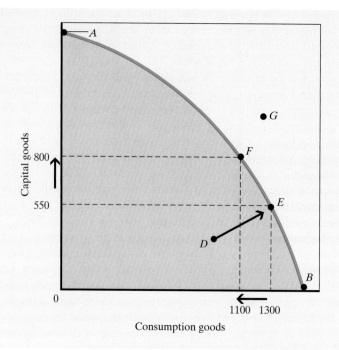

FIGURE 2.3

Production Possibility Frontier

The production possibility frontier illustrates a number of economic concepts. One of the most important is opportunity cost. The opportunity cost of producing more capital goods is that fewer consumption goods can be produced. Moving from E to F, the number of capital goods increases from 550 to 800. To produce more capital goods, resources must be transferred from the production of consumer goods. Moving from E to F, the number of consumer goods decreases from 1300 to 1100.

from Chapter 1 that an efficient economy is one that produces the things that people want at least cost. *Production efficiency* is a state in which a given mix of outputs is produced at least cost.) Resources are not going unused, and there is no waste. Points that lie within the shaded area, but that are not on the frontier, represent either unemployment of resources or production inefficiency. An economy producing at point *D* in Figure 2.3 can produce more capital goods and more consumption goods, for example, by moving to point *E*. This is possible only if resources were initially not fully employed or if resources were not being used efficiently.

■ **Unemployment** During the Great Depression of the 1930s, the Canadian economy experienced prolonged unemployment. Hundreds of thousands of workers who were willing to work found themselves without jobs. In 1933, nearly 20% of the civilian labour force was unemployed. Unemployment remained high until World War II, when increased defence spending created new jobs. In the mid 1970s, early 1980s, and through much of the 1990s the economy experienced high levels of unemployment. In 1976, the annual unemployment rate reached a postwar high of 7.2%. By 1983 the rate had climbed to 11.9%, with 1.5 million people looking for work. In 1992, 1.6 million were unemployed.

In addition to the hardship that falls on the unemployed themselves, unemployment of labour means unemployment of capital. During the downturn of 1982, manufacturing plants in Canada were running at less than 73% of their total capacity. That meant that a considerable fraction of the country's industrial capital was sitting idle and, in effect, being wasted. Clearly, when there is unemployment we are not producing all that we can.

Periods of unemployment correspond to points inside the production possibility frontier, points like *D* in Figure 2.3. Moving onto the frontier from a point like *D* means moving up and to the right, achieving full employment of resources and increasing production of both capital goods and consumer goods.

■ **Inefficiency** Production inefficiency is one way an economy can fail to be efficient. An economy is also inefficient when it is producing at the wrong point on the ppf—that is, when it is producing a combination of goods and services that does not match the wants of its people.

Certainly, a badly managed economy will not produce up to potential and will be inside the ppf. Suppose, for example, that the land and climate in Prince Edward Island are best suited for potato production and that the land and climate in Saskatchewan are best suited for wheat production. If Parliament passes a law forcing farmers in P.E.I. to plant 50% of their land in wheat and farmers in Saskatchewan to plant 50% in potatoes, neither potato nor wheat production will be up to potential. The economy will be at a point like *A* in Figure 2.4—inside the production possibility frontier. Allowing each province to specialize in producing the crop that it produces best increases the production of both potatoes and wheat and moves the economy to a point like *B* in Figure 2.4.

In extreme cases, a wrong output mix is obvious. Suppose, for example, that a society uses all of its resources to produce beef efficiently, but that everyone in the society is a vegetarian. The result is a total waste of resources (assuming that the society cannot trade beef for vegetables with another society).

A wrong mix of output can be less obvious, however. Beef production is a highly competitive industry in Canada. Thousands of farmers sell millions of cattle each year to hundreds of meat packing firms. Most grocery stores have plentiful stocks at reasonable prices because there are many suppliers competing for business.

Suppose that the government were to grant the sole right to produce beef (that is, a *monopoly*) to a single company. Even if all resources remained fully and efficiently employed, the monopoly would push the economy to a less desirable point on the ppf—that is, a point at which beef is underproduced and other goods are overproduced, a point such as *D* instead of *C* in Figure 2.5. This is because without competition monopolists will restrict output and raise their prices. In the absence of the monopoly, the society can move back to point *C*, which more closely matches the preferences of its people.

■ **Negative Slope and Opportunity Cost** As we've seen, points that lie on the production possibility frontier represent points of full resource employment and production efficiency. But society can choose only one point on the curve. Because a

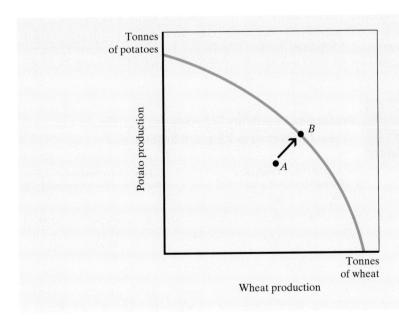

FIGURE 2.4

Inefficiency from Misallocation of Land in Farming

Society can end up inside its production possibility frontier at a point like *A* by using its resources inefficiently. If, for example, P.E.I.'s climate and soil were best suited for potato production and those of Saskatchewan were best suited for wheat production, a law that forced Saskatchewan farmers to produce potatoes and P.E.I. farmers to produce wheat would result in less of both. In such a case, society might be at point *A* rather than point *B*.

FIGURE 2.5

Inefficient Mix of Output Resulting from a Monopoly

Even if resources are combined efficiently in production, the result is inefficient if the economy is not producing the combination of goods and services that people want. This can occur if a monopoly controls an industry.

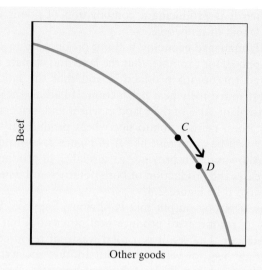

society's choices are constrained by available resources and existing technology, when those resources are fully and efficiently employed it can produce more capital goods only by reducing production of consumption goods. The opportunity cost of the additional capital is the forgone production of consumption goods.

The fact that scarcity exists is illustrated by the negative slope of the production possibility frontier. In moving from point *E* to point *F* in Figure 2.3, capital production *increases* by $800 - 550 = 250$ units (a positive change), but that increase in capital can be achieved only by shifting resources out of the production of consumption goods. Thus, in moving from point *E* to point *F* in Figure 2.3, consumption goods production *decreases* by $1300 - 1100 = 200$ units of the consumption good (a negative change). The slope of the curve, the ratio of the change in capital goods to the change in consumption goods, is negative.[1]

■ **The Law of Increasing Opportunity Costs** We have noted that the slope of the ppf indicates the trade-off that a society faces between two goods that it produces. We can learn something further about the shape of the frontier and the nature of this trade-off by considering potato and wheat production in P.E.I. and Saskatchewan. Suppose that in a recent year, P.E.I. and Saskatchewan together produced 900 000 tonnes of potatoes and 20 million tonnes of wheat. Table 2.1 presents these two numbers plus some hypothetical combinations of potato and wheat production that

Table 2.1	Production Possibility Schedule for Total Potato and Wheat Production in P.E.I. and Saskatchewan	
Point on ppf	**Total Potato Production** (thousands of tonnes per year)	**Total Wheat Production** (thousands of tonnes per year)
A	1 300	6 000
B	1 100	15 000
C	900	20 000
D	700	24 000
E	500	26 500

[1]*The value of the slope of a society's production possibility frontier is called the* marginal rate of transformation *(MRT). In Figure 2.3, the MRT between point E and point F is simply the ratio of the change in capital goods (a positive number) to the change in consumption goods (a negative number).*

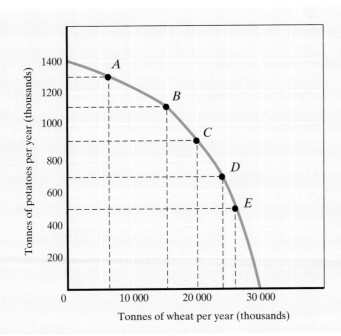

FIGURE 2.6

Potato and Wheat Production
in P.E.I. and Saskatchewan

The ppf illustrates that the opportunity cost of potato production increases as we shift resources
from wheat production to potato
production. Moving from *E* to *D*,
we get an additional 200 000
tonnes of potatoes at a cost of 2.5
million tonnes of wheat. Moving
from *B* to *A*, we get only 200 000
tonnes of potatoes at a cost of 9.0
million tonnes of wheat. The cost
per tonne of potatoes—measured
in lost or forgone wheat—has increased over three times.

might exist for P.E.I. and Saskatchewan together. Figure 2.6 graphs the data from Table 2.1.

Suppose that the demand for potatoes dramatically increases. If this happens, farmers would probably shift some of their land from wheat production to potato production. Such a shift is represented by a move from point C (where potatoes = 900, and wheat = 20 000) up and to the left along the ppf toward points A and B in Figure 2.6. As this happens it becomes more and more difficult to produce additional potatoes. The best land for potato production (potatoes like the cool and moist growing season found on P.E.I.) was presumably already in potatoes, and the best land for wheat production (where summers are hot and relatively dry), already in wheat. As we try to produce more potatoes, the land is less and less suited to that crop. And as we take more and more land out of wheat production, we will be taking increasingly better wheat-producing land. All of this is to say that the opportunity cost of more potatoes, measured in terms of wheat, increases.

Moving from E to D, we can get 200 000 tonnes of potatoes (700 − 500) by sacrificing 2 500 000 tonnes of wheat (26 500 − 24 000)—that is, each additional tonne of potatoes costs 12.5 tonnes of wheat (i.e., 2500/200 = 12.5 tonnes of wheat per tonne of potatoes). However, when we are already taxing the ability of the land to produce potatoes, it becomes more difficult to produce more potatoes, and the opportunity cost goes up. Moving from B to A (which involves growing potatoes in the most arid parts of Saskatchewan wheat country), to get an additional 200 000 tonnes of potatoes (1300 − 1100), we have to sacrifice 9 000 000 tonnes of wheat (15 000 − 6000). In this case the cost of an additional tonne of potatoes is 45 tonnes of wheat (i.e., 9000/200 = 45 tonnes of wheat per tonne of potatoes). Using the same reasoning, we can see that if the demand for wheat were to increase substantially and we were to move down and to the right along the production possibility frontier, then it would become increasingly difficult to produce wheat, and the opportunity cost of wheat in terms of potatoes would rise.

It is important to remember that the ppf represents choices available within the constraints imposed by the current state of agricultural technology. In the long run, technology may improve, and when that happens we have *growth*.

economic growth *An increase in the total output of an economy. It occurs when a society acquires new resources or when it learns to produce more using existing resources.*

■ **Economic Growth** **Economic growth** is characterized by an increase in the total output of an economy. It occurs when a society acquires new resources or when society learns to produce more with existing resources. New resources may mean a larger labour force or an increased capital stock. The production and use of new machinery and equipment (capital) increases the productivity of workers. Improved productivity also comes from technological change and *innovation,* the discovery and application of new, efficient techniques of production.

There have been dramatic increases in the productivity of Canadian agriculture over the past 40 years. Based on data compiled by Statistics Canada, Table 2.2 shows that the yield per acre in potato production has increased by almost 75% since 1956. Productivity in wheat production has also increased. Between 1956 and 1995 wheat output per acre increased by over 35%. These increases are the result of more efficient farming techniques, more and better capital (tractors, combines, and other equipment), and advances in scientific knowledge and technological change (hybrid seeds, fertilizers, and so forth). As you can see in Figure 2.7, increases such as these shift the ppf up and to the right.

Sources of Growth and the Dilemma of the Poor Countries Economic growth arises from many sources, the two most important of which, over the years, have been the accumulation of capital and technological advances. For poor countries, capital is essential; they must build the communication networks and transportation systems necessary to develop industries that function efficiently. They also need capital goods to develop their agricultural sectors.

Recall that capital goods are produced only at a sacrifice of consumption goods if the economy is fully employed (i.e., on the ppf). The same can be said for technological advances. Technological advances come from research and development that use resources, and thus they too must be paid for. The resources used to produce capital goods—to build a road, a tractor, or a manufacturing plant—*and* to develop new technologies could have been used to produce consumption goods.

When a large part of a country's population is very poor, taking resources out of the production of consumption goods such as food and clothing is very difficult. In addition, in some countries those wealthy enough to invest in domestic industries may choose instead to invest abroad because of political turmoil at home. As a result, it often falls to the governments of poor countries to generate revenues for capital production and research out of tax collections.

Table 2.2	Increasing Productivity in Potato and Wheat Production: Canada, 1956–1995	
	POTATOES YIELD IN TONNES PER HECTARE	**WHEAT YIELD IN TONNES PER HECTARE**
1956	15.1	62.3
1966	19.3	68.9
1976	21.7	77.1
1986	25.0	82.3
1995	26.2	84.5

Sources: 1956–1966: Statistics Canada, *Handbook of Agricultural Statistics,* Part I Field Crops, 1921–1974. Cat. no. 21-516; 1975–1990: Statistics Canada, *Canada Yearbook* (various years), Cat. no. 11-402E; 1995 wheat: Statistics Canada, *Grain Trade of Canada,* Cat. no. 22-201–XPB; 1995 potatoes: Statistics Canada, *Fruit and Vegetable Production,* Cat. no. 22-003-XPB.

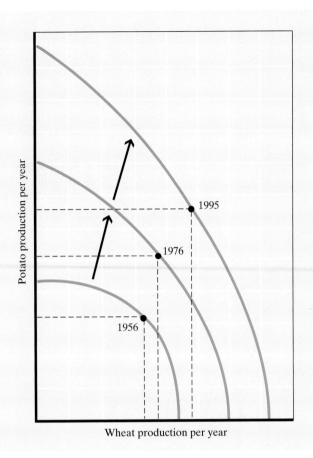

FIGURE 2.7

Economic Growth Shifts the ppf Up and to the Right

Productivity increases have enhanced the ability of Canada to produce both potatoes and wheat. As Table 2.2 shows, productivity increases were more dramatic for potatoes than for wheat. The shifts in the ppf were thus not parallel.

Note: The ppf also shifts if the amount of land or labour in potato and wheat production changes. Although we emphasize productivity increases here, the actual shifts between years were in part due to land and labour changes.

All these factors have contributed to the growing gap between poor and rich countries. Figure 2.8 graphs the result, using production possibility frontiers. On the left, the rich country devotes a larger portion of its production to capital, while the poor country produces mostly consumption goods. On the right, you see the result: the ppf of the rich country shifts up and out farther and faster.

> Although it exists only as an abstraction, the production possibility frontier illustrates a number of very important concepts that we shall use throughout the rest of this book: scarcity, unemployment, inefficiency, opportunity cost, the law of increasing opportunity cost, and economic growth.

THE ECONOMIC PROBLEM

Recall that the three basic questions facing all economic systems are: (1) What will be produced? (2) How will it be produced? and (3) Who will get it?

When Ivan was alone on the island, the mechanism for answering these questions was simple. He thought about his own wants and preferences, looked at the constraints and limits imposed by the resources of the island and his own skills and time, and made his decisions. As he set about his work, he allocated available resources quite simply, more or less by dividing up his available time. Distribution of the output was irrelevant. Because Ivan was the society, he got it all.

Introducing even one more person into the economy—in this case, Colleen—changed all that. With Colleen on the island, resource allocation involves deciding

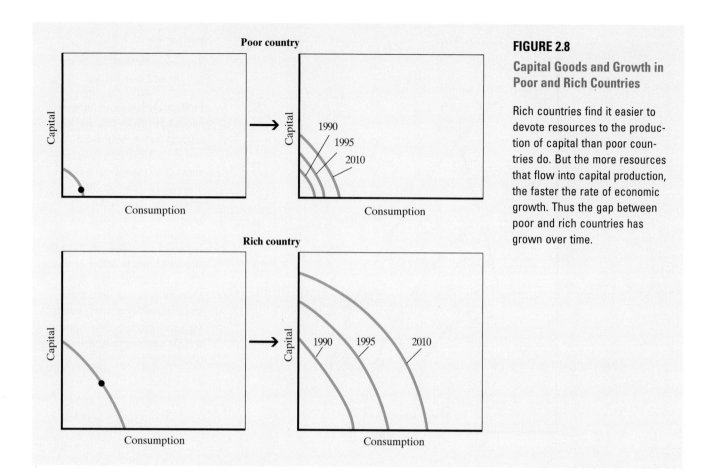

Poor country

Capital / Consumption

1990
1995
2010

Rich country

Capital / Consumption

1990 1995 2010

FIGURE 2.8

Capital Goods and Growth in Poor and Rich Countries

Rich countries find it easier to devote resources to the production of capital than poor countries do. But the more resources that flow into capital production, the faster the rate of economic growth. Thus the gap between poor and rich countries has grown over time.

not only how each person spends time but also who does what. Labour must be allocated to the various tasks. And now there are two sets of wants and preferences. And even after two people decide what to produce, they have to decide how to divide it. If Ivan and Colleen go off on their own and form two completely separate, self-sufficient economies, there will be lost potential. Clearly, two people can do many more things together than one person can do alone. They may use their comparative advantages in different skills to specialize. Cooperation and coordination may give rise to gains that would otherwise not be possible.

When a society consists of millions of people, the problem of coordination and cooperation becomes enormous, but so does the potential for gain. In large, complex economies, specialization can go wild, with people working in jobs as different in their detail as an impressionist painting is from a blank page. The range of products available in a modern industrial society is beyond anything that could have been imagined a hundred years ago, and so is the range of jobs.

The amount of coordination and cooperation in a modern industrial society is almost impossible to imagine. Yet something seems to drive economic systems, if sometimes clumsily and inefficiently, toward producing the things that people want. Given scarce resources, how, exactly, do large, complex societies go about answering the three basic economic questions? This is the **economic problem,** and this is what this text is about.

economic problem *Given scarce resources, how, exactly, do large, complex societies go about answering the three basic economic questions?*

Economic Systems

Now that you understand the economic problem, we can explore how different economic systems go about answering the three basic questions.

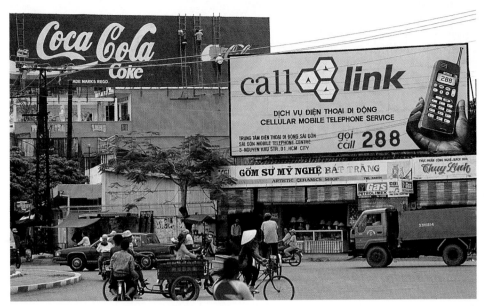

One of the routes to economic growth is investment in capital. Despite low per capita income, Hanoi (Vietnam) is ordering cellular phones by the thousands, as well as more than 300 000 fibre-optic phone lines per year.

Command Economies

In some modern societies government plays a big role in answering the basic economic questions. In pure **command economies,** a central authority or agency generally draws up a plan that establishes what will be produced and when, sets production goals, and makes rules for distribution. Planners in command economies use complex computer programs to determine the materials, labour, and energy inputs required to produce a variety of output targets. The final output targets are then set with an eye toward the same constraint that the single manager of a one-person economy faces—limited resources. Centrally determined income policies then establish how much compensation workers and managers receive for their labours.

command economy *An economy in which a central authority or agency draws up a plan that establishes what will be produced and when, sets production goals, and makes rules for distribution.*

Even in pure planned economies, people do exercise some choice. Commodities are sold at prices set by the government, and to the extent that they are able to pay those prices people are free to buy what is available. Sometimes more is demanded than is produced; sometimes goods are left on the shelves. These signals are used in the next plan to adjust output targets.

It is an understatement to say that the planned economies have not fared well over the last decade. In fact, the planned economies of Eastern Europe and the former Soviet Union—including the Russian Republic—have completely collapsed. (Another former command economy, that of Poland, has done better. For more details, see the Global Perspective box on page 42 titled "Poland and the Russian Republic: An Update.") China remains committed to many of the principles of a planned economy, but reforms have moved it sharply away from pure central planning.

Laissez-Faire Economies: The Free Market

At the opposite end of the spectrum from the command economy is the **laissez-faire economy.** The term *laissez faire,* which, translated literally from French, means "allow [them] to do," implies a complete lack of government involvement in the economy. In this type of economy, individual people and firms pursue their own self-interest without any central direction or regulation; the sum total of millions

laissez-faire economy *Literally from the French: "allow [them] to do." An economy in which individual people and firms pursue their own self-interests without any central direction or regulation.*

In the late 1980s the command economies of Eastern Europe collapsed like a string of dominoes. The process began when the Berlin Wall, which had separated the Communist East from the capitalist West for nearly 30 years, was torn down in November 1989. Finally, in 1991, the once mighty Soviet Union disintegrated, ending 75 years of communism and nearly half a century of Cold War with the West.

What lies ahead for the economies of the newly independent countries of the former Soviet Union and for the economies of the other Eastern European nations? One fear is that complete economic collapse will lead to chaos and ethnic warfare, and the events of 1993 and 1994 in Bosnia and Serbia attest to this danger. There is, however, one country where the transition from central planning and government control to the free market showed some early signs of working: Poland.

An economic success story is taking shape in Poland, three years after the country became the first in Eastern Europe to risk the rigors of "shock therapy" . . . . [rapid decontrol of prices and privatization of government enterprises]. . . .

Industrial production, which declined a precipitous 39 percent in 1990 and 1991, is on the rise, and Poland is on track this year to become the first among former Communist nations to record annual economic growth. . . .

Polish policy makers were supported in 1990 by an overwhelming public consensus for radical change, and have been encouraged since then to stay the course by an explosion of pent-up entrepre-

People who visit planned economies frequently comment on the lack of variety in consumer goods. This problem has substantially decreased in Poland, which began its transition to a free market economy in the early 1990s.

neurial spirit and by a relatively productive agricultural sector that was already largely in private hands. . . .

"I think they've made it," said Jeffrey Sachs, the Harvard economist who helped shape Poland's economic program. . . . "They have definitely turned the corner. The panic is over. The reforms are secure."

Russia has moved much more slowly, and the political turmoil there was even greater than in Poland. Markets have not instantaneously improved standards of living and many doubt that they will have this effect. Nonetheless, by the summer of 1994 Russia's huge economy was beginning to show signs of life:

This August [1994], there is an eerie stability. Monthly inflation is down to 6 percent compared with 26 percent a year ago. Salaries are worth more with the ruble stronger, and con-

sumer spending is up. There is consensus on economic policy under Prime Minister Viktor S. Chernomyrdin, who has adopted the tight-money policies he criticized in January. . . .

On a trip this week down the Volga River, talking to ordinary Russians, Mr. Yeltsin had a new announcement: "I see that in many regions the economic slide has stopped."

Poland's economy has continued to grow, and the 1997 growth rate was expected to be about 6%. In Russia, inflation has been reduced further, and economic growth in 1997 was expected to be positive for the first time since reforms began.

Sources: Stephen Engelberg, "21 Months of 'Shock Therapy' Resuscitates Polish Economy," *The New York Times*, December 17, 1992, p. 1; Steven Erlanger, "End of Russia's Economic Slide Brings Eerie Calm," *The New York Times*, August 22, 1994, p. 1.

of individual decisions ultimately determines all basic economic outcomes. The central institution through which a laissez-faire system answers the basic questions is the **market,** a term that is used in economics to signify an institution through which buyers and sellers interact and engage in exchange.

The interactions between buyers and sellers in any market range from simple to complex. Early explorers of Canada who wished to exchange with Native Peoples did so simply by bringing their goods to a central place and trading them. Today, a jewellery maker in Quebec may sell gold necklaces to a buyer through the Internet, which shows the product as an image on a computer screen—customers send in orders by e-mail and pay with a credit card. Ultimately, funds are transferred through a complicated chain of financial transactions. The result is that a buyer in Vancouver buys a necklace from an unseen jewellery producer in Quebec.

In short:

> Some markets are simple and others are complex, but they all involve buyers and sellers engaging in exchange. The behaviour of buyers and sellers in a laissez-faire economy determines what gets produced, how it is produced, and who gets it.

The following chapters explore market systems in great depth. A quick preview is worthwhile here, however.

■ **Consumer Sovereignty** In an unregulated market, goods and services are produced and sold only if the supplier can make a profit. In simple terms, making a profit means selling goods or services for more than it costs to produce them. Clearly, you can't make a profit unless someone wants the product that you are selling. This logic leads to the notion of **consumer sovereignty:** the mix of output found in any free market system is dictated ultimately by the tastes and preferences of consumers who "vote" by buying or not buying. Businesses rise and fall in response to consumer demands; no central directive or plan is necessary.

In a market economy, producers may be small or large. One person who hand paints eggshells may start to sell them as a business; a woman who has been showing her poodle may start handling other people's dogs in the show ring. On a larger scale, a group of furniture designers may put together a large portfolio of sketches, several million dollars, and start a bigger business. At the extreme are huge corporations like IBM, Mitsubishi, and Exxon, each of which sells tens of billions of dollars' worth of products every year.

■ **Individual Production Decisions: Free Enterprise** Under a market system, individual producers must also figure out how to organize and coordinate the actual production of their products or services. The owner of a small shoe repair shop must buy the equipment and tools that she needs, hang signs, and set prices by herself. In a big corporation, so many people are involved in planning the production process that in many ways corporate planning resembles the planning in a command economy. Whether the firms are large or small, however, production decisions in a market economy are made by separate private organizations acting in what they perceive to be their own interests.

Individuals seeking profits also start new businesses. Since new businesses require capital investment before they can begin operation, starting a new business involves risk. Every day new businesses are born and others fail. A well-run business that produces a product for which demand exists will succeed; a poorly run business or one that produces a product for which little demand exists is likely to fail.

Proponents of market systems argue that free enterprise leads to more efficient production and better response to diverse and changing consumer preferences. If a producer produces inefficiently, competitors will come along, fight for the business, and eventually take it away. Thus in a competitive market economy, competition forces producers to use efficient techniques of production. It is competition, then, that ultimately dictates how outputs are produced.

■ **Distribution of Output**   In a market system, the distribution of output—who gets what—is also determined in a decentralized way. The amount that any one household gets depends on its income and wealth. *Income* is the amount that a household earns each year. It comes in a number of forms: wages, salaries, interest, and the like. *Wealth* is the amount that households have accumulated out of past income through saving or inheritance.

To the extent that income comes from working for a wage, it is at least in part determined by individual choice. You will work for the wages available in the market only if these wages (and the things they can buy) are sufficient to compensate you for what you give up by working. Your leisure certainly has a value also. You may discover that you can increase your income by getting more education or training. You *can't* increase your income, however, if you acquire a skill that no one wants.

Although your income determines how much of society's output you can buy and consume, not all income comes from working. Individuals may also earn income by owning all or part of a business for which they do not work. Those who risk their wealth by buying shares in companies or by lending it out to be used for business investments earn a return on their wealth. Returns may come directly, as profit, or indirectly, as interest or dividends on stock. (We discuss these options in detail in Chapter 3.) In a market economy, people make independent decisions about what to do with their wealth.

In sum:

> In a market system, the basic economic questions are answered without the help of a central government plan or directives. This is what the "free" in free enterprise means—the system is left to operate on its own, with no outside interference. Individuals pursuing their own self-interest will go into business and produce the products and services that people want; others will decide whether to acquire skills or not, whether to work or not, and whether to buy, sell, invest, or save the income that they earn.

price *The amount that a product sells for per unit. It reflects what society is willing to pay.*

■ **Price Theory**   The basic coordinating mechanism in a market system is price. A **price** is the amount that a product sells for per unit, and it reflects what society is willing to pay. Prices of inputs—labour, land, capital—determine how much it costs to produce a product. Prices of various kinds of labour, or *wage rates*, determine the rewards for working in different jobs and professions. Many of the independent decisions made in a market economy involve the weighing of prices and costs, so it is not surprising that much of economic theory focuses on the factors that influence and determine prices. This is why microeconomic theory is often simply called *price theory.*

MIXED SYSTEMS, MARKETS, AND GOVERNMENTS

The differences between command economies and laissez-faire economies in their pure forms are enormous. But in fact these pure forms do not exist in the world;

all real systems are in some sense "mixed." That is, individual enterprise exists and independent choice is exercised even in economies in which the government plays the major role.

Conversely, no market economies exist without government involvement and government regulation. Canada certainly has features of a market economy, but government also plays a critical role. The government directly produces many goods and services, it employs workers, and raises revenue through taxation. The government also redistributes income by means of taxation and social welfare expenditures, and it regulates many economic activities.

One of the major themes in this book, and indeed in economics, is the tension between the advantages of unregulated markets and the need for government involvement in the economy. Advocates of markets argue that markets work best when left to themselves. They produce only what people want; without buyers, sellers go out of business. Competition forces firms to adopt efficient production techniques. Wage differentials lead people to acquire needed skills. Competition also leads to innovation in both production techniques and products. The result is quality and variety. But market systems have problems too.

> Even staunch defenders of the free enterprise system recognize that market systems are not perfect. First, they do not always produce what people want at lowest cost—there are inefficiencies. Second, rewards (income) may be unevenly distributed, and some groups may be left out. Third, periods of unemployment and inflation recur with some regularity.

Many people point to these problems as reasons for government involvement. Indeed, for some problems government involvement may be the only solution. But government decisions are made by people who presumably, like the rest of us, act in their own self-interest. While governments may indeed be called upon to improve the functioning of the economy, there is no guarantee that they will do so. Just as markets may fail to produce an allocation of resources that is perfectly efficient and fair, governments may fail to improve matters.

■ **Inefficiencies** Markets may not produce all the goods that people want and are willing to pay for. There are some goods and services whose benefits are social, or collective, such as national defence, open park areas, a justice system, and police protection. These are called **public, or social, goods.** The fact that the benefits of such goods are collective presents the private market with a problem. Once a public good is produced, everyone gets to enjoy its benefits, whether they have paid for it or not. If police protection lowers a city's crime rate, all citizens of that city are safer.

public, or social, goods *Goods and services whose benefits are social, or collective.*

How, then, can a private business firm make a profit "selling" such a service to individual consumers? In most cases, it cannot. A private firm selling an automobile won't give it to you unless you pay for it. A producer of a public good doesn't have that option. Thus, if there is a public good that citizens decide they want, they must collectively arrange for its production. Traditionally, societies have funded public goods through governments, which are granted taxing authority.

Government intervention may also be necessary because private decision makers in search of profits can make bad decisions from society's point of view. The market system provides an incentive to produce a product if, and only if, people are willing to pay more for it than the cost of the resources needed to produce it. This works to society's advantage as long as the resource costs reflect the *full* cost to society of producing the product. For example, if the environment is damaged during the production process and producers do not factor in these costs, profit-producing activities may not balance out to society's advantage. Governments involve themselves in markets to make sure that decision makers consider all the benefits and costs of their decisions.

Markets work best when they are competitive. Competition forces producers to choose the most efficient methods of production. Inefficient producers are driven out of business by the forces of competition. Competition also leads to innovation and new products. However, powerful firms in a market system can gain control of their markets and block competition. A firm that gains control of a market may stifle innovation, charge higher prices than necessary, and cause a general misallocation of resources.

■ **Redistribution of Income**   Governments may also get involved in a market system because the final distribution of income (and thus of output) is considered inequitable. Market systems are based on the principle of individual self-interest and enterprise. Our rewards are supposed to be commensurate with how well we compete. But some people are not well equipped to compete—some are physically unable to work; some are mentally unable to hold a job. Whatever the cause, thousands of people find that they cannot get along economically. Sometimes this is their fault, but often it is not. In all cases, however, society must decide what, if anything, to do about it.

Every government redistributes income to a certain extent. In Canada, social assistance, employment insurance, and a host of other programs have been designed to assist people who are poor or are temporarily without work.

Income redistribution is a subject of endless debate. Some claim that taxes on the rich and programs for the poor destroy the incentives that the market provides for hard work, enterprise, and risk taking. Others argue that because many of the poor, particularly children, are in the position they are in through no fault of their own, cuts in income redistribution programs are cruel and unfair.

■ **Stabilization**   Macroeconomics explores the causes and consequences of unemployment and price inflation. In market economies, the level of unemployment is not planned, and prices are set freely by the forces of supply and demand. But governments may, through taxing and spending policies and by regulating the banking system, exert a stabilizing influence over prices and over the general level of output and employment. Like income redistribution, the desirability and the character of government involvement in the macroeconomy are hotly debated.

Looking Ahead

This chapter has described the economic problem in broad terms. We have outlined the questions that all economic systems must answer. We also discussed very broadly the two kinds of economic systems and some of the advantages and disadvantages of each. In the next chapter we turn from the general to the specific. There we discuss in some detail the institutions of Canadian capitalism: how the private sector is organized, what the government actually does, and how the international sector operates. Chapters 4 and 5 then begin the task of analyzing the way market systems work.

Summary

1. Every society has some system or mechanism for transforming what nature and previous generations have provided into useful form. Economics is the study of that process and its outcomes.

2. *Producers* are those who take resources and transform them into usable products, or *outputs*. Private firms, households, and governments all produce something.

Scarcity, Choice, and Opportunity Cost

3. All societies must answer *three basic questions*: What will be produced? How will it be produced? Who will get what is produced? These three questions make up the *economic problem*.

4. One person alone on an island must make the same basic decisions that complex societies make. When society consists of more than one person, questions of distribution, cooperation, and specialization arise.

5. Because resources are scarce relative to human wants in all societies, using resources to produce one good or service implies *not* using them to produce something else. This concept of *opportunity cost* is central to an understanding of economics.

6. Using resources to produce *capital* that will in turn produce benefits in the future implies *not* using those resources to produce consumer goods in the present.

7. Even if one individual or country is absolutely more efficient at producing goods than another, all parties will gain if they specialize in producing goods in which they have a *comparative advantage*.

8. A *production possibility frontier* (ppf) is a graph that shows all the combinations of goods and services that can be produced if all of society's resources are used efficiently. The production possibility frontier illustrates a number of important economic concepts: scarcity, unemployment, inefficiency, increasing opportunity cost, and economic growth.

9. *Economic growth* occurs when society produces more, either by acquiring more resources or by learning to produce more with existing resources. Improved productivity may come from additional capital, or from the discovery and application of new, more efficient techniques of production.

Economic Systems

10. In some modern societies, government plays a big role in answering the three basic questions. In pure *command economies*, a central authority generally draws up a plan that determines what will be produced, how it will be produced, and who will get it.

11. A *laissez-faire economy* is one in which individuals independently pursuing their own self-interest, without any central direction or regulation, ultimately determine all basic economic outcomes.

12. A *market* is an institution through which buyers and sellers interact and engage in exchange. Some markets involve simple face-to-face exchange; others involve a complex series of transactions, often over great distance or electronically.

13. There are no purely planned economies and no pure laissez-faire economies; all economies are mixed. Individual enterprise, independent choice, and relatively free markets exist in centrally planned economies, and there is significant government involvement in market economies such as that of Canada.

14. One of the great debates in economics revolves around the tension between the advantages of unregulated markets and the need for government involvement in the economy. Markets produce what people want, and competition forces firms to adopt efficient production techniques. The need for government intervention arises because markets are characterized by inefficiencies and an unequal distribution of income, and they experience regular periods of inflation and unemployment.

capital 27

command economy 40

consumer goods 32

consumer sovereignty 43

economic growth 38

economic problem 40

investment 33

laissez-faire economy 41

market 43

opportunity cost 29

outputs 28

price 44

producers 28

production 27

production possibility frontier (ppf) 33

public, or social, goods 45

resources or inputs 27

theory of comparative advantage 30

three basic questions 28

Problem Set

1. Kristen and Anna live in the Cavendish area of P.E.I. They own a small business in which they make wristbands and potholders and sell them to people on the beach. Kristen can make 15 wristbands per hour, but only three potholders. Anna is a bit slower and can make only 12 wristbands or two potholders in an hour.

| | OUTPUT PER HOUR | |
	KRISTEN	ANNA
Wristbands	15	12
Potholders	3	2

   a. For Kristen, what is the opportunity cost of a potholder? For Anna? Who has a comparative advantage in the production of potholders? Explain.

   b. Who has a comparative advantage in the production of wristbands? Explain.

   c. Assume that Kristen works 20 hours per week in the business. If Kristen were in business on her own, graph the possible combinations of potholders and wristbands that she could produce in a week. Do the same for Anna.

   d. If Kristen devoted half of her time (10 out of 20 hours) to wristbands and half of her time to potholders, how many of each would she produce in a week? If Anna did the same thing, how many of each would she produce? How many wristbands and potholders would be produced in total?

   e. Suppose that Anna spent all 20 hours of her time on wristbands and Kristen spent 17 hours on potholders and three hours on wristbands. How many of each would be produced?

   f. Suppose that Kristen and Anna can sell all their wristbands for $1 each and all their potholders for $5.50 each. If each of them worked 20 hours per week, how should they split their time between wristbands and potholders? What is their maximum joint revenue?

2. Define *capital*. What distinguishes land from capital? Is a tree capital?

3. "Studying economics instead of going to town and partying is like building a boat instead of lying on the beach." Explain this statement carefully using the concepts of capital and opportunity cost.

4. Suppose that a simple society has an economy with only one resource, labour. Labour can be used to produce only two commodities—X, a necessity good (food), and Y, a luxury good (music and merriment). Suppose that the labour force consists of 100 workers. One labourer can produce either five units of necessity per month (by hunting and gathering) or 10 units of luxury per month (by writing songs, playing the guitar, dancing, and so on).

   a. On a graph, draw the economy's production possibility frontier. Where does the ppf intersect the Y axis? Where does it intersect the X axis? What meaning do those points have?

   b. Suppose the economy ended up producing at a point *inside* the ppf. Give at least two reasons why this could occur. What could be done to move the economy to a point *on* the ppf?

   c. Suppose you succeeded in lifting your economy to a point on its ppf. What point would you choose? How might your small society decide the point at which it wanted to be?

   d. Once you have chosen a point on the ppf, you still need to decide how your society's product will be divided up. If you were a dictator, how would you decide? What would happen if you left product distribution to the market?

5. One of the justifications for government involvement in a market economy is that the market system is unlikely to produce "public goods" in sufficient quantity.

   a. Define a *public good.*

   b. Why does the private market have a difficult time allocating resources to the production of public goods?

   c. Give five examples of goods provided by federal, provincial, or municipal governments that may yield public benefits.

   d. Assume that the production of public good X requires a certain amount of land, labour, and capital that the government will have to procure. How would you measure the full costs of this good's provision? (*Hint:* recall opportunity costs.)

   e. If you were a benevolent dictator, how would you go about determining if the production of a particular public good were worth it? How would you measure its benefits?

6. What progress has been made in recent years in Eastern Europe? Which countries are growing? Which are in decline? What factors seem to have contributed to the differences in success across countries?

3

The Structure of the Canadian Economy: The Private, Public, and International Sectors

private sector *Includes all independently owned profit-making firms, nonprofit organizations, and households; all the decision-making units in the economy that are not part of the government.*

public sector *Includes all agencies at all levels of government—federal, provincial, and local.*

The previous chapter described the economic problem. All societies are endowed by nature and by previous generations with scarce resources. A process called "production" combines and transforms these resources into goods and services that are demanded by the members of society.

At the end of Chapter 2, we briefly described the economic systems that exist in the world today. This chapter describes the basic institutional structure of the Canadian economy in more detail. Because most production is undertaken by private individuals and organizations, we first look at the private sector. The **private sector** is made up of independently owned firms that exist to make a profit, nonprofit organizations, and individual households. It includes Chrysler Canada, the Catholic Church, fishers in Newfoundland, the corner drugstore, and the babysitter down the street. The private sector is defined by independent ownership and control. In essence, it includes all the decision-making units within the economy that are not part of the government.

Next, we turn to a discussion of the public sector. The **public sector** is the government and its agencies at all levels—federal, provincial, and local. Government employees—tax assessors, public school teachers, post office workers, colonels in the army, Supreme Court justices, and the Prime Minister—work in the public sector. Just as the Ford Motor Company uses land, labour, and capital to produce automobiles, the public sector uses land, labour, and capital to produce goods and services such as police and fire protection, education, and national defence. The public sector in Canada also produces some things that are simultaneously produced by the private sector. Canada Post provides overnight express-mail service that competes directly with similar services provided by private firms such as FedEx and UPS.

Finally, we provide a brief introduction to the **international sector** and discuss the importance of imports and exports to the Canadian economy. From any one country's perspective, the international sector consists of the economies of the rest of the world. The Canadian economy has always been heavily influenced by events abroad. Economic changes in China and Eastern Europe, the election of a new president in the United States, the end of a recession in Japan, and other global events all have important implications for the functioning of the Canadian economy. In a very real sense there is only one economy: the world economy.

Recall the distinction drawn in Chapter 1 between descriptive economics and economic theory, and then notice what this chapter is not. We do not analyze behaviour in this chapter. Here we describe institutions only as they exist. We also try very hard to avoid any normative distinctions. We do not talk about proper or improper roles of government in the economy, for example, or the things that governments might do to make the economy more efficient or fair.

In Chapter 4, we begin to analyze behaviour. Before we begin the analysis in Chapter 4, however, it is important to have some sense of the institutional landscape. One purpose for studying economics is to understand the world and what people actually do. This chapter provides some important facts that describe the realities of the Canadian economy.

international sector From any one country's perspective, the economies of the rest of the world.

The Private Sector: Business and Industrial Organization in Canada

How is business organized in Canada? Let us see first how the law permits *individual firms* to be organized. Then we can talk about the different ways that *industries* are structured. An individual firm's behaviour depends on both its own legal structure and its relationship to other firms in its industry.

THE LEGAL ORGANIZATION OF FIRMS

Most private sector activity takes place within business firms that exist to make a profit. Some other private sector organizations that exist for reasons other than profit—clubs, cooperatives, and nonprofit organizations, for example—do produce goods or services. Because these organizations represent a small fraction of private sector activity, however, we focus here on profit-making firms.

> A business set up to make profits may be organized in one of three basic legal forms: (1) a proprietorship, (2) a partnership, or (3) a corporation. A single business may pass through more than one of these forms of organization during its development.

■ **The Proprietorship** The least complex and most common form a business can take is the simple **proprietorship.** There is no legal process involved in starting a proprietorship. You simply start operating. You must, however, keep records of revenues and costs and pay personal income taxes on your profit.

A professor who does consulting on the side, for example, receives fees and has costs (computer expenses, research materials, and so forth). This consulting business is a proprietorship, even though the proprietor is the only employee and the business is very limited. A large restaurant that employs hundreds of people may also be a proprietorship if it is owned by a single person. Many doctors and lawyers in private practice report their incomes and expenses as proprietors.

proprietorship A form of business organization in which a person simply sets up to provide goods or services at a profit. In a proprietorship, the proprietor (or owner) is the firm. The assets and liabilities of the firm are the owner's assets and liabilities.

In a proprietorship, one person owns the firm. In a sense, that person *is* the firm. If the firm owes money, the proprietor owes the money; if the firm earns a profit, the proprietor earns a profit. There is no limit to the proprietor's responsibility; if the business gets into financial trouble, the proprietor alone is liable. That is, if a business does poorly or ends up in debt, those debts are the proprietor's personal responsibility. There is no wall of protection between a proprietor and her business, as is the case between corporations and their owners.

partnership *A form of business organization in which there is more than one proprietor. The owners are responsible jointly and separately for the firm's obligations.*

■ **The Partnership**   A **partnership** is a proprietorship with more than one proprietor. When two or more people agree to share the responsibility for a business, they form a partnership. While no formal legal process is required to start this kind of business, most partnerships are based on agreements, signed by all the partners, that detail who pays what part of the costs and how profits shall be divided. Because profits from partnerships are taxable, accurate records of receipts and expenditures must be kept and each party's profits must be reported to Revenue Canada.

In a partnership, as in a proprietorship, there is no limit to the liability of the owners (that is, the partners) for the firm's debts. But with a partnership it can be worse because each partner is both jointly and separately liable for all the debts of the partnership. If you own one-third of a partnership that goes out of business with a debt of $300 000, you owe your creditors $100 000, and so does each of your partners. But if your partners skip town, you owe the entire $300 000.

corporation *A form of business organization resting on a legal charter that establishes the corporation as an entity separate from its owners. Owners hold shares and are liable for the firm's debts only up to the limit of their investment, or share, in the firm.*

share of stock *A certificate of partial ownership of a corporation that entitles the holder to a portion of the corporation's profits.*

■ **The Corporation**   A **corporation** is a formally established legal entity that exists separately from those who establish it and those who own it. To establish a corporation, a corporate charter must be obtained. This is quite easily accomplished. A lawyer simply fills out the appropriate paperwork and files it with the right government office, along with certain fees. When a corporation is formed, **shares of stock** (certificates of partial ownership) are issued and either sold or assigned. A corporation is owned by its shareholders, who are in a sense partners in the firm's success or failure. Each share of stock entitles the holder to a portion of the corporation's profits. Shareholders differ from simple partners, however, in two important ways. First, the liability of shareholders is limited to the amount they paid for the stock. If the company goes out of business or bankrupt, the shareholders may lose what they have invested, but no more than that. They are *not* liable for the debts of the corporation beyond the amount they invested. Second, the federal government levies special taxes on corporations. The federal government does not levy special taxes on proprietors and partners.

net income *The profits of a firm.*

The federal corporate income tax is a tax on the **net income,** or profits, of corporations. The tax is approximately 28% of net income with a special rate of 12% available to small corporations. Each province also levies a corporate tax. Net income after taxes can be distributed to shareholders of the corporation as **dividends**—that is, the share of profits they receive from the corporation. Because dividends are also subject to taxation the Canadian tax system includes an adjustment to reduce the degree of "double taxation" that owners of corporations face.

dividends *The portion of a corporation's profits that the firm pays out each period to shareholders. Also called* distributed profits.

The special privilege granted to corporations limiting their liability is often called a *franchise.* Some view the corporate tax as a payment to the government in exchange for this grant of limited liability status.

retained earnings *The profits that a corporation keeps, usually for the purchase of capital assets. Also called* undistributed profits.

Corporate net income is usually divided into three parts. Some of it is paid to the federal and provincial governments in the form of taxes. Some of it is paid out to shareholders as dividends (sometimes called *distributed profits*). And some of it usually stays within the corporation to be used for the purchase of capital assets. This part of corporate profits is called **retained earnings,** or *undistributed profits.*

In 1995, corporations in Canada earned total profits at an annual rate of

$59.3 billion. Out of this, $20.0 billion in taxes was paid, leaving $39.3 billion in after-tax profits. Of this amount, $15.5 billion was paid out to shareholders and the rest, $23.8 billion, was retained. In percentage terms, taxes accounted for 33.7%, while shareholders directly received 26.1% of total profits (Table 3.1).

Many corporations are very large. Each year the *Financial Post* magazine publishes a list of the 500 largest industrial corporations in Canada. The top 10—ranked by total revenue—are listed in Table 3.2. BCE Inc. tops the list with just over $28 billion in revenues. BCE Inc., the major player in the telecommunications industry in Canada, is also the largest corporate employer with over 121 000 employees. The big three auto manufacturing companies rank just behind BCE Inc.

The internal organization of a firm, whether it is a proprietorship, a partnership, or a corporation, affects its behaviour and the behaviour of potential investors. For example, because they are protected by a corporation's limited liability status, potential investors may be more likely to back high-risk but potentially high-payoff corporate ventures.

While a firm's internal structure is important, it is less important to an understanding of a firm's behaviour than is the organization of the industry or the market in which the firm competes. For example, whether it is a proprietorship or a corporation, a firm with little or no competition is likely to behave differently from a firm facing stiff competition from many rivals. With this in mind, we now expand our focus from the individual firm to the industry.

The Organization of Industries

The term **industry** is used loosely to refer to groups of firms that produce similar products. Industries can be defined narrowly or broadly, depending on the issue being discussed. For example, a company that produces and packages cheese is a part of the cheese industry, the dairy products industry, the food products industry, and the agricultural products industry.[1]

Whether we define industries broadly or narrowly, how firms within any industry behave depends on how that industry is organized. When we speak of **market organization** we refer to the way an industry is structured: how many firms there are in an industry, whether products are virtually the same or differentiated, whether or not firms in the industry can control prices or wages, whether or not competing firms can freely enter and leave the industry, and so forth. The kind of industry—or *market*—in which a firm operates determines, in large part, how it will behave.

industry *All the firms that produce a similar product. The boundaries of a "product" can be drawn very widely ("agricultural products"), less widely ("dairy products"), or very narrowly ("cheese"). The term* industry *can be used interchangeably with the term* market.

market organization *The way an industry is structured. Structure is defined by how many firms there are in an industry, whether products are differentiated or are virtually the same, whether or not firms in the industry can control prices or wages, and whether or not competing firms can enter and leave the industry freely.*

Table 3.1	The Distribution of Corporate Profits in 1995		
		Billions of Dollars	Percent of Before-Tax Profit
Profits before tax		59.3	100.0
Minus profits tax		−20.0	−33.7
Profits after tax		39.3	66.3
Minus dividends paid		−15.5	−26.1
Undistributed profits		23.8	40.2

Source: Statistics Canada, *National Income and Expenditure Accounts, Annual Estimates*, Cat. no. 13-201-XBP.

---

[1] *Statistics Canada uses a code system, the Standard Industrial Classification (S.I.C.) System, which defines industries at various levels of detail.*

Table 3.2	Ten Largest Corporations in Canada by Revenue, 1996		
Rank	Company	Revenue ($ thousands)	No. of employees
1	BCE Inc.	28 167 000	121 000
2	General Motors of Canada Ltd.	28 079 058	32 701
3.	Ford Motor Company of Canada Ltd.	25 536 617`	25 818
4	Chrysler Canada Ltd.	17 060 000	14 000
5	Seagram Co. Ltd.	16 396 859	30 000
6	George Weston Ltd.	12 709 000	75 000
7	TransCanada Pipelines Ltd.	10 790 600	2 663
8	Thompson Corp.	10 531 083	50 000
9	Alcan Aluminum Ltd.	10 382 450	33 000
10	Noranda Inc.	9 515 000	33 000

Source: "The Financial Post 500," *Financial Post Magazine,* 1997.

In the discussion that follows, we analyze industries as if their structures fit their definitions precisely. In reality, however, industries are not always easy to categorize. Some industries have some characteristics generally associated with one form of organization and other characteristics associated with a different form of organization. Nonetheless, these categories provide a useful and convenient framework for thinking about the organization of industries in the Canadian economy.

■ **Perfect Competition** At one end of the market-organization spectrum is the competitive industry in which many relatively small firms produce nearly identical products. **Perfect competition** is a very precisely defined form of industry structure. (The word *perfect* here does not refer to virtue. It simply means "total," or "complete.") In a perfectly competitive industry, no single firm has any control over prices. That is, no single firm is large enough to affect the market price of its product or the prices of the inputs that it buys. This crucial observation follows from two characteristics of competitive industries. First, a competitive industry is composed of many firms, each small relative to the size of the industry. Second, every firm in a perfectly competitive industry produces exactly the same product; the output of one firm cannot be distinguished from the output of the others. Products in a perfectly competitive industry are said to be **homogeneous.**

These characteristics limit the decisions open to competitive firms and simplify the analysis of competitive behaviour. Because all firms in a perfectly competitive industry produce virtually identical products, and because each firm is small relative to the market, perfectly competitive firms have no control over the prices at which they sell their output. Taking prices as a given, then, each firm can decide only how much output to produce and how to produce it.

Consider agriculture, the classic example of a perfectly competitive industry. A beef rancher in Alberta has absolutely no control over the price of beef. Prices are determined not by the individual ranchers but rather by the interaction of many suppliers and many demanders. The only decisions left to the beef ranchers are how many cows to raise and when and how to sell the matured cattle.

Another mark of perfectly competitive industries is ease of entry. *Ease of entry* means that new firms can easily enter a market and compete for profits. No barriers exist to prevent new firms from competing. New firms can, and do, frequently enter such industries in search of profits, while others go out of business when they suffer losses. For example, most young children get their first exposure to the world of business by selling lemonade on a hot summer day. One of the first lessons these young entrepreneurs learn is that if business is good a "friend" or

perfect competition *An industry structure (or market organization) in which there are many firms, each small relative to the industry, producing virtually identical products and in which no firm is large enough to have any control over prices. In perfectly competitive industries, new competitors can freely enter and exit the market.*

homogeneous products *Undifferentiated outputs: products that are identical to, or indistinguishable from, one another.*

When entry is easy, it is hard to earn "high" profits for long. These young entrepreneurs will learn this lesson early in their careers.

neighbour will set up her/his own lemonade stand. If entry is easy firms do not earn "high" profits for very long.

When a firm *exits* an industry, it simply stops producing a product. Sometimes an exiting firm goes out of business altogether. During the last 10 years, for example, thousands of small farmers have gone out of business, sold off their assets, paid what bills they could, and disappeared.

To summarize:

> Perfectly competitive industries are made up of many firms, each small relative to the size of the total market. In these industries, individual firms do not distinguish or differentiate their products from those of their competitors. Product prices are determined by market forces and are virtually unaffected by decisions of any single firm. Entry into and exit from the market are relatively easy.

■ **Monopoly**   At the other end of the spectrum is **monopoly**, a market or industry in which only one firm produces a product for which there are no close substitutes.

When there is only one firm in a market, that firm sets the price of its product. This does not mean, however, that monopolies can set any price they please. Even monopolies face the constraint of the market. Even if a firm produces a good that everyone likes, the firm gains nothing if it charges a price so high that no one buys it. The price a monopolist chooses determines the quantity it will be able to sell. It will sell more at lower prices and less at higher prices. Thus, even a monopolist is subject to discipline imposed by the market.

For a monopoly to remain a monopoly, it must find some way to keep other firms from entering its market and competing for profits. Often governments erect such **barriers to entry.** Sometimes they grant an exclusive licence to one producer. In Taiwan, for example, the national government licensed only one company to produce beer and prohibited beer imports until 1987. In Canada, public utilities—

monopoly *An industry structure (or market organization) in which there is only one large firm that produces a product for which there are no close substitutes. Monopolists can set prices but are subject to market discipline. For a monopoly to continue to exist, something must prevent potential competitors from entering the industry and competing for profits.*

barrier to entry *Something that prevents new firms from entering and competing in an industry.*

electric power and gas companies, for example—have traditionally been shielded by the government from competition. For many years Bell Canada dominated the market for long distance telephone services. However, dramatic changes in the telecommunications industry in the last few years have made that market much more competitive.

Sometimes monopolies are specific to a particular time and location. University residence operations frequently involve exclusive vendor agreements with food service companies such as Marriott, Versa, and Beaver Foods. Since most residence meal plans cover only food purchased in residence cafeterias, the vendor is providing a service for which there is no close substitute, and entry is blocked. Do you think monopoly privileges influence the price or quality of food service in university cafeterias?

In sum:

> A monopoly is a one-firm industry that produces a product for which there are no close substitutes. Such a firm can set price, but its pricing behaviour is constrained by its market: it can sell a product only if people are willing to buy it. A monopolist is protected from competition by barriers to entry.

■ Monopolistic Competition Somewhere between monopoly and competition, but much closer to competition, is a very common hybrid market organization called **monopolistic competition.** In a monopolistically competitive industry, many firms compete for essentially the same customers, but each firm produces a slightly different product. If these firms can *differentiate* their products successfully, they establish a *brand loyalty* that allows them to enjoy the benefits of a monopoly. Procter & Gamble is the only producer of Ivory Soap—it "monopolizes" the market for Ivory—but the soap business is still very competitive because many close substitutes are available. Prentice Hall Canada is the only company that can sell this book, but there are many other economics texts.

While individual firms in perfectly competitive markets have no control over price, monopolistic competitors do exercise some price-setting power. That control is quite limited, however, because of the many close substitutes available. Monopolistically competitive firms are thus subject to a great deal of "market discipline."

A good example of monopolistic competition can be found in the music industry. Every rock band has a unique style; each has its own name. Entry is relatively inexpensive; all you need are musicians, instruments, amplifiers, and a P.A. system. Thinking of each band as a small firm, management differentiates the product in an attempt to compete, and the competition is fierce. Very successful rock bands are more like monopolies, however; there are no "close" substitutes for The Tragically Hip, Spirit of the West, U2, or the Rolling Stones.

In monopolistically competitive industries, there is both price and quality competition. Firms often enter these industries because they have an idea for a new product that represents a slight variation or improvement on an old one. Perhaps the purest example of a monopolistically competitive market is the restaurant industry. Every major city in the world contains hundreds and hundreds of restaurants, each producing a slightly differentiated product in a highly competitive way. The cosmetics and clothing industries are also monopolistically competitive. Firms in such industries must decide on output, price, and quality of product.

Free, or at least relatively easy, entry and exit characterize monopolistic competition. When a firm enjoys success in one of its product lines, its profits invite new firms to come into its market with new brands or styles. Many new restaurants are born every year and many unsuccessful ones quietly expire.

monopolistic competition *An industry structure (or market organization) in which many firms compete, producing similar but slightly differentiated products. There are close substitutes for the product of any given firm. Monopolistic competitors have some control over price. Price and quality competition follow from product differentiation. Entry and exit are relatively easy, and success invites new competitors.*

To summarize:

> Monopolistically competitive firms contain large numbers of relatively small firms. Unlike firms in perfectly competitive industries, firms in monopolistically competitive industries differentiate their products. Individual firms produce unique products and thus, despite their small size, exercise some control over price. Entry and exit are relatively easy.

■ **Oligopoly** An industry in which there are only a small number of firms is called an **oligopoly**. The automobile industry in Canada, for example, has only three major Canadian competitors and a few smaller ones. A total of eight firms produce 100% of all tobacco, and four large firms control 75% of the petroleum product industry. Except for the fact that each contains only a few competitors, however, oligopolistic industries have little in common. In some, products are highly differentiated (automobiles, for example); in others, they are not (the steel industry, for example). In some, the industry is dominated by one very large firm; in others, the participating firms are of roughly equal size and have roughly equal power.

Oligopolies behave somewhat unpredictably. In markets where two or three large rivals compete head-on, the competing firms often execute strategies that anticipate counterstrategies. In setting price, for example, one firm must take into account how its competitors in the oligopoly are likely to react. One firm's action usually triggers a reaction from another, which in turn triggers still another reaction, and so on. The strategies and counterstrategies employed by these firms determine who gets the sales. As a result, oligopolies are characterized by a great deal of uncertainty, and it is difficult to generalize about their behaviour.

Entry into an oligopolistic industry is usually possible, but difficult. Because firms in oligopolies are generally large, a large initial investment is usually required to break in.

In sum:

> Oligopolies are industries with a few large firms, but beyond that it is hard to generalize. In some oligopolies, firms differentiate their products; in others, they do not. Individual firms do exercise control over prices and generally behave "strategically" with respect to one another.

The four main kinds of market organization in Canada are summarized in Figure 3.1.

oligopoly *An industry structure (or market organization) with a small number of (usually) large firms producing products that range from highly differentiated (automobiles) to standardized (steel). In general, entry of new firms into an oligopolistic industry is difficult but possible.*

FIGURE 3.1

Characteristics of Different Market Organizations

	Number of firms	Products differentiated or homogeneous	Firms have price-setting power	Free entry	Distinguishing characteristics	Examples
Perfect competition	Many	Homogeneous	No	Yes	Price competition only	Beef rancher Coffee shop
Monopolistic competition	Many	Differentiated	Yes, but limited	Yes	Price and quality competition	Restaurants Music industry
Oligopoly	Few	Either	Yes	Limited	Strategic behaviour	Automobile manufacturer Tobacco producer
Monopoly	One	A unique, single product	Yes	No	Still constrained by market demand	Public utility Food services in a university residence

How Competitive Is the Canadian Economy?

In a paper published as part of the Royal Commission on the Economic Union and Development Prospects for Canada, R.S. Khemani provides evidence on the extent of competition in the Canadian economy in 1980.[2] Khemani found that more than two-fifths (44%) of Canadian output was generated in sectors or industries that can be described as *effectively competitive*, almost one-fifth (18%) originated under *oligopolistic* conditions, and more than one-third (38%) of economic activity in Canada was *government-supervised or -regulated*.

The classification *effectively competitive* signifies more than just perfect competition. It also includes all of what we described as monopolistic competition. The *oligopolistic* classification roughly corresponds to the oligopoly structure described in the previous section. Finally, sectors that are *government-supervised or -regulated* include sectors dominated by large monopoly firms such as telephone and electrical power companies and sectors dominated by small single proprietorships as in agriculture and the fisheries, which are governed by marketing boards and strict licensing regulations.

Although the data on competitiveness for the economy as a whole are revealing, they hide significant variation across sectors of the economy. Table 3.3 presents data on broadly defined sectors for 1980. The table indicates that some sectors of the Canadian economy were very competitive in 1980 (construction, for example) while others were dominated by a small number of firms (mining, for example).

In comparison with the United States, our major trading partner, Canada has had a low degree of effective competition. One study of competition in the U.S. economy in the early 1980s found that almost four-fifths of total U.S. output was generated by effectively competitive sectors.[3] This represents double the proportion found for Canada at about the same time.

Table 3.3	Competition in the Canadian Economy, 1980		
Industry/Sector	*Oligopolistic*	*Government-Supervised or -Regulated*	*Effectively Competitive*
Agriculture, forestry, fishing, and trapping	0%	47%	53%
Mining	70%	23%	7%
Manufacturing	28%	0%	72%
Construction	0%	0%	100%
Transportation and communications, and utilities	0%	82%	18%
Trade	44%	2%	54%
Finance, insurance, and real estate	17%	49%	34%
Services (community, business, and personal)	1%	57%	42%
Public administration and defence	0%	100%	0%
Total (all sectors)	18%	38%	44%

Source: R.S. Khemani, "The Extent and Evolution of Competition in the Canadian Economy," in D.G. McFetridge (ed.), *Canadian Industry in Transition*, Collected Research Studies of the Royal Commission on the Economic Union and Development Prospects for Canada, vol. 2 (Toronto: University of Toronto Press, 1986), pp. 140–141.

---

[2] R.S. Khemani, "The Extent and Evolution of Competition in the Canadian Economy," in D.G. McFetridge (ed.), Canadian Industry in Transition, Collected Research Studies of the Royal Commission on the Economic Union and Development Prospects for Canada, vol. 2 (Toronto: University of Toronto Press, 1986), pp. 135–176.

[3] William G. Shepherd, "Causes of Increased Competition in the U.S. Economy, 1939–1980," Review of Economics and Statistics LXIV (November 1982): pp. 613–626.

Nonetheless, a number of developments over the past 20 years may have increased the effective competition in the Canadian economy. The most important is the elimination of many restrictions on trade across national and provincial borders. The Canada–U.S. Free Trade Agreement, which came into effect in 1989; the North American Free Trade Agreement (NAFTA), a free trade agreement among Canada, the U.S., and Mexico; and new rules governing trade among member countries of the World Trade Organization (which includes Canada) opened up the Canadian market to firms from other countries, thereby increasing effective competition and constraining the ability of government to regulate certain sectors. Canadian governments have also unilaterally reduced the degree of supervision and regulation in many sectors through a process known as deregulation. Finally, improvements in transport and telecommunication—the emergence of the World Wide Web and the Internet has been especially important in this respect—have made it possible for Canadians to shop all over the world.

STRUCTURAL CHANGES IN THE CANADIAN ECONOMY

Table 3.4 gives a breakdown of national income by major industry. The data point to a number of major changes in the structure of the economy over the past 125 years. First, the primary sector (agriculture, logging, fishing and trapping, and mining) has declined steadily in relative importance over the period. For much of the nineteenth century the Canadian economy was based on the production of primary products for export. Fur, fish, timber, and wheat were especially important. Production of these products—called *staples* by one of Canada's most famous economists, Harold A. Innis—directly involved large numbers of Canadians. It also indirectly involved many others, including those who produced inputs required in staple production, those who transported these goods to market, those who processed the staples into finished products, and those who provided goods and

Table 3.4	Percentage Share of National Income by Major Sector, 1870, 1926, 1956, 1976, 1996				
	1870	*1926*	*1956*	*1976*	*1996*
Primary Sector	46.2	23.4	13.1	8.5	7.3
Agriculture, logging, fishing, and trapping	45.3	20.2	8.8	4.3	2.8
Mining, quarrying, oil wells	0.9	3.2	4.3	4.2	4.5
Secondary Sector	22.6	38.7	47.3	39.2	35.7
Manufacturing	NA	21.7	28.5	20.9	18.8
Construction	NA	4.1	6.5	7.3	4.9
Transportation and communications	NA	12.9*	9.9	8.1	8.9
Electric power, water, and other utilities	NA	*	2.4	2.9	3.1
Service Sector	31.2	37.9	39.7	51.3	56.9
Wholesale and retail trade	NA	11.6	12.5	11.9	12.2
Finance, insurance, and real estate	NA	10.0	10.1	12.0	16.2
Community, business, and personal services	NA	12.9	10.9	20.5	22.3
Public administration	NA	3.4	6.2	7.9	6.2

NA = not available
* Transportation and communications, and Electric power, water, and other utilities are combined

Sources: M.C. Urquhart and K.A.H. Buckley, *Historical Statistics of Canada*, first edition (Toronto: Macmillan, 1965); M.C. Urquhart and K.A.H. Buckley, *Historical Statistics of Canada*, second edition (Ottawa: Statistics Canada, 1983); and Statistics Canada, *National Income and Expenditure Accounts*, Cat. no. 31-201.

services to those in the staple trades. The importance of staple products in early Canadian economic history led many to consider Canada a staple-producing country and Canadians as "hewers of wood and drawers of water."

But in the twentieth century the relative importance of the primary sector declined and that of the manufacturing sector and service sectors grew. By 1956 only 13.1% (i.e., 8.8% and 4.3%) of Canadian income was directly generated in the primary sector while 28.5% of Canada's national income originated in the manufacturing sector. Some of this manufacturing activity was still tied to the processing of natural resources but an increasing share resulted from the production of sophisticated consumer and producer goods (equipment and machinery).

Although many Canadians still believe that natural resource products are the linchpin of the Canadian economy, the data on structure indicate otherwise. In an attempt to illustrate the dramatic changes in the Canadian economy, economists like to ask people to name the most important Canadian export. Do you know what it is? People are generally amazed to discover that Canada's most important export is automobiles and automobile parts and they are still more amazed to learn that in 1995 the value of automotive exports was greater than the sum of exports of all agricultural products, all fish products, oil and natural gas, hydroelectricity, and lumber and other saw mill products. Today we are far from the staple-producing economy of the early nineteenth century.

Although Canada has a large and dynamic manufacturing sector, even this sector is in relative decline. By 1996 the relative share of the manufacturing sector had declined to 18.8% of total output. In contrast, the service sector has continued to grow in relative importance over the past 30 years. Indeed, service sector growth is one of the most striking features of recent Canadian economic history.

The growth of the service sector has sparked concern that "good" jobs are being lost and replaced by "bad" ones. Manufacturing has traditionally been thought of as a high-wage sector while the service sector is considered a low-wage sector. However, like the belief that Canadians are "hewers of wood and drawers of water," this view needs to be reconsidered. Doctors, lawyers, teachers, computer technicians and software designers, bankers, stockbrokers, budding rock musicians, and hamburger flippers at the local fast-food joint are all service producers. Thus, some service providers earn high incomes, some earn low incomes. Simple generalizations about the nature of service jobs can be misleading.

While some people are deeply concerned about the structural changes occurring in the Canadian economy, others see them as a natural consequence of continued economic growth and progress. For example, the decline in the relative importance of agriculture occurred as farmers learned more and more productive farming methods. As the need for farm labour declined so too did food prices. With lower food prices, people could spend their money on other things—manufactured goods and services. Because agriculture needed fewer workers, labour was available for employment in the new expanding sectors. Thus as the Canadian economy grew and developed, some sectors, such as agriculture, shrank in relative importance and others, such as manufacturing and services, grew in relative importance.

Modern economies are in a continuous state of change. Resources are always moving. Literally thousands of new firms are started every year and old, tired firms—not to mention young and inefficient ones—go out of business every day. Some firms grow rapidly in size, while others shrink. The purpose of this book is to help you understand this process. Why are new firms formed? Why do others go out of business? Why are some sectors expanding while others are contracting?

The Public Sector: Taxes and Government Spending in Canada

Thus far we have talked only about the sets of decisions facing private firms. But this is only part of the story. The Canadian economy is best characterized as a mixed economy because there is a large public sector that plays a major role in determining the allocation of resources, the mix of output, and the distribution of rewards. To understand the workings of the Canadian economy, it is necessary to understand the role of government.

The public sector in Canada operates on many levels—there is a national government in Ottawa, there are 10 provincial and two territorial governments, there are thousands of municipal governments (cities, towns, and villages), and there are thousands more local school and hospital boards. Each of these public sector levels contributes in its own way to economic activity in this country. How big is the public sector? What do the different levels of government do? How do these governments finance their activities?

THE SIZE OF THE PUBLIC SECTOR

An economy's **gross domestic product,** or **GDP,** is the total value of all final goods and services produced in the economy in a given period of time, say, a year. The concept of GDP is used extensively in macroeconomics. Here it is enough to say that GDP is used as a measure of a country's total annual "output." As you can see from Figure 3.2, public expenditure at all levels, as a percentage of GDP, increased from 21.3% in 1950 to 47.6% in 1995. Thus growth in the public sector over the past 45 years has been substantial.

Government spending can be divided into three major categories: *purchases of goods and services, transfer payments* to households, and *interest payments* on the national debt. **Purchases of goods and services** make up that proportion of national output that government actually uses or "consumes" directly. They include new highways, the services of teachers and doctors, and all other goods and services purchased by the public sector. The wages and salaries of government employees are included in this category. **Transfer payments** are cash payments made directly to households—employment insurance benefits, social assistance, old age security, Canada and Quebec Pension Plan benefits, and the like. The government

gross domestic product (GDP) *The total value of all final goods and services produced by a national economy within a given time period.*

government purchases of goods and services *A category of government spending that includes the portion of national output that the government uses, or "consumes," directly—ships for the navy, memo pads for the RCMP, salaries for government employees.*

government transfer payments *Cash payments made by the government directly to households for which no current services are received. They include old age security benefits, employment insurance, and welfare payments.*

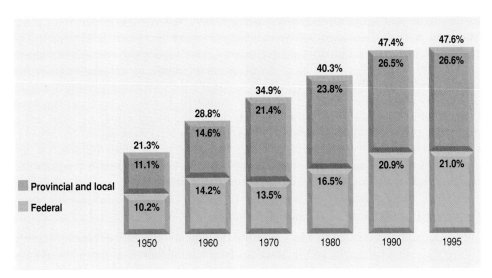

FIGURE 3.2

Total Government Expenditure as a Percentage of GDP, 1950–1995

Total government expenditures grew from 21.3% of GDP in 1950 to 47.6% in 1995. The sum of provincial and local government expenditure grew somewhat more rapidly than federal government expenditure.

Source: David B. Perry, "Fiscal Figures: Changes in Government Spending Patterns," *Canadian Tax Journal* vol. 44, no. 2 (1996): p. 586, Table 6.

■ Provincial and local
■ Federal

	1950	1960	1970	1980	1990	1995
Total	21.3%	28.8%	34.9%	40.3%	47.4%	47.6%
Provincial and local	11.1%	14.6%	21.4%	23.8%	26.5%	26.6%
Federal	10.2%	14.2%	13.5%	16.5%	20.9%	21.0%

Table 3.5	The Size of the Canadian Public Sector, 1950–1995

	GOVERNMENT EXPENDITURES AS A PERCENTAGE OF GDP (EXCLUDING INTERGOVERNMENTAL TRANSFERS)					
	1950	1960	1970	1980	1990	1995
Purchases of goods and services	9.0	12.2	17.1	17.7	18.8	17.9
Transfer payments to persons	5.3	7.8	7.8	9.0	12.3	13.9
Interest payments on debt	2.8	2.8	3.6	5.4	9.5	9.8
Other	4.2	6.0	6.4	7.6	6.8	6.0
Total	21.3	28.8	34.9	40.3	47.4	47.6

Source: David B. Perry, "Fiscal Figures: Changes in Government Spending Patterns," *Canadian Tax Journal* vol. 44, no. 2 (1996): Tables 5, 6, 9, and 10.

government interest payments
Cash payments made by the government to those who own government bonds.

receives no current services in exchange for these payments. **Interest payments** on the public debt are also cash payments, but they are paid to those who own government bonds. Table 3.5 reveals how the government spending has changed in these three major categories since 1950. Notice that transfer payments and interest on the public debt account for most of the increase in the relative size of the public sector since 1970.

The rise in transfer payments reflects higher unemployment rates (which increase the use of transfer programs) and increases in spending on other programs, such as programs for the elderly. In fact, the Canada and Quebec Pension Plans alone account for two percentage points of the increase in government expenditure relative to GDP. Since 1970 interest charges tripled because of the large deficits over much of the period illustrated in Table 3.5. When governments spend more than they raise in revenue, they must borrow. They do so by issuing bonds on which they must pay interest. Two major recessions (periods in which economic activity declines, tax revenues fall, and spending on social programs increases) and high interest rates played an important role in the rise in government debt in Canada and in the growth in interest charges. Control of debt is one of the major public sector issues today.

How big is the public sector in Canada relative to the public sectors of other countries? Good statistics are not easy to find, but Figure 3.3 presents some international comparisons based on taxes collected. Taxes support public sector activities and tax data are easy to find. Nonetheless, the tax data must be interpreted carefully. For example, Canadians and the citizens of many other countries pay for medical care and hospital insurance through taxes, whereas people in the United States do not. Ideally if data were available we would base comparisons on information on both taxes and what people receive in return for their taxes. The figure shows total taxes collected by all levels of government as a percentage of gross domestic product (GDP).

In 1975, tax collections in Canada amounted to 33.0% of GDP. This placed Canada in ninth place among the 19 countries in the comparison. Between 1975 and 1991 taxes as a percentage of GDP increased in all 19 countries. In Canada, taxes rose from 33.0% to 37.3% of GDP. However, in the United States, the increase was virtually negligible—from 29.6% to 29.8%. How would you account for the relatively small size of the increase in the United States?

GOVERNMENT STRUCTURE AND EXPENDITURE

When Canada was created in 1867 a critical document—the British North America (BNA) Act—divided public sector functions between the federal and provincial governments. A popular view of Canadian federalism suggests that most functions en-

FIGURE 3.3

Taxes as a Percentage of Gross Domestic Product, 1975 and 1991

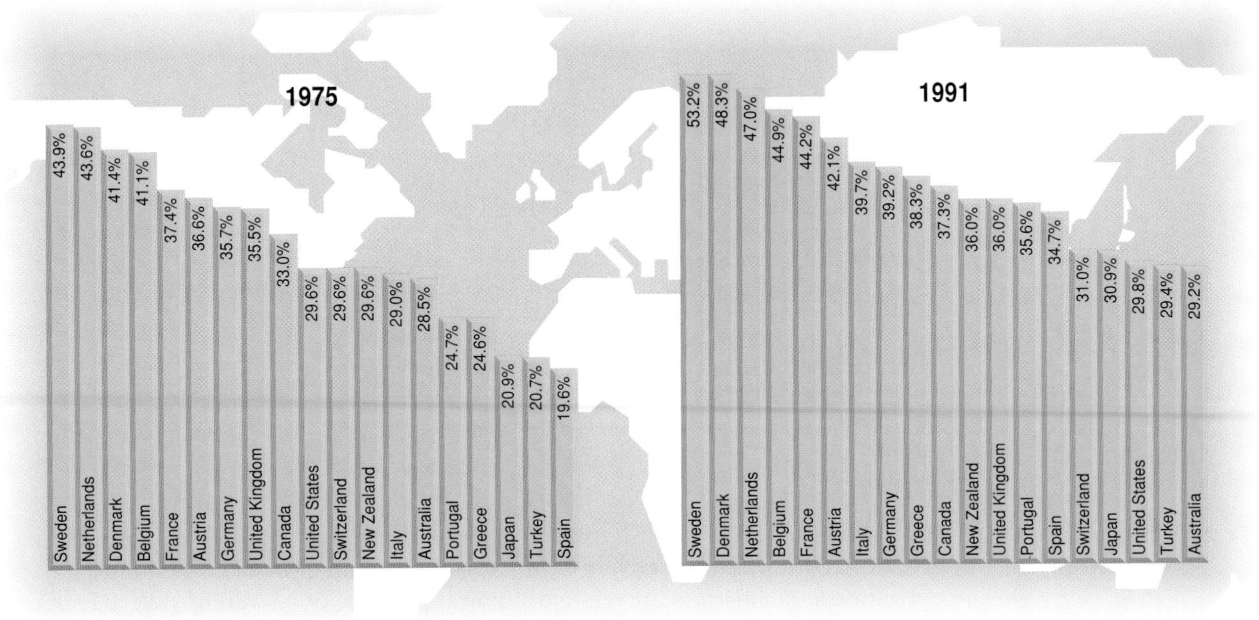

1975

Country	Percentage
Sweden	43.9%
Netherlands	43.6%
Denmark	41.4%
Belgium	41.1%
France	37.4%
Austria	36.6%
Germany	35.7%
United Kingdom	35.5%
Canada	33.0%
United States	29.6%
Switzerland	29.6%
New Zealand	29.6%
Italy	29.0%
Australia	28.5%
Portugal	24.7%
Greece	24.6%
Japan	20.9%
Turkey	20.7%
Spain	19.6%

1991

Country	Percentage
Sweden	53.2%
Denmark	48.3%
Netherlands	47.0%
Belgium	44.9%
France	44.2%
Austria	42.1%
Italy	39.7%
Germany	39.2%
Greece	38.3%
Canada	37.3%
New Zealand	36.0%
United Kingdom	36.0%
Portugal	35.6%
Spain	34.7%
Switzerland	31.0%
Japan	30.9%
United States	29.8%
Turkey	29.4%
Australia	29.2%

Source: Statistical Abstract of the United States, 1994, p. 867.

trusted to the national government dealt with matters in which all Canadians had a common stake. Of these, national defence and an integrated Canadian economy were most important. The provinces, on the other hand, were given responsibility for local and cultural matters such as education, health, and social welfare, thereby limiting potential areas of conflict. Moreover, the provinces were given ultimate authority over municipal government, school boards, and hospital boards.

The British North America Act provided a constitutional framework for the development of the Canadian public sector. But it could not anticipate the many economic and social changes that were to occur after 1867. For example, while the BNA Act assigned the largest revenue *sources* to the federal government, it left the provincial governments responsible for *services* for which it has since turned out they are ill equipped to fund from their own resources, services that include the now critically important areas of health, education, and social welfare. In principle, the distribution of legislative powers in the BNA Act should have precluded the development of the welfare state since provincial governments lacked the resources to support expansion of such a system and the national government lacked the authority to establish it in the first place. However, Canadian politicians proved remarkably innovative. The federal government was able to assume a key role in the welfare state through constitutional amendment (for example, a constitutional amendment gave the federal government the authority needed to implement a national unemployment insurance program), through fiscal transfers to provinces (in 1995, the federal government gave provincial governments over $28 billion to spend in areas in provincial jurisdiction), and through use of its so-called spending power (which allows the federal government to attach conditions—such as the conditions established in the Canada Health Act—to its transfers to the provinces). The result is an extremely complex system of government that involves conflict and cooperation, specialization and overlap, and, most important, continual change and adaptation. Indeed, change is as important a characteristic of the public sector as it is of the private sector.

Table 3.6

Activities of Different Levels of Government in Canada, 1950–1995

	Government Expenditures as a Percentage of GDP					
	1950	1960	1970	1980	1990	1995
Purchases of goods and services						
Federal government	4.5	5.9	4.8	4.2	4.3	3.9
Provincial/local/hospital sector	4.5	6.3	12.2	13.5	14.5	14.0
Transfer payments to persons						
Federal government	3.2	5.0	4.6	5.3	6.3	7.0
Provincial/local/hospital sector	2.1	2.8	3.2	3.7	4.4	4.9
Interest payments on debt						
Federal government	2.2	1.9	2.1	3.2	6.2	5.9
Provincial/local/hospital sector	0.6	0.9	1.6	2.2	3.2	3.8
Other						
Federal government	1.2	1.8	2.0	3.8	4.1	4.2
Provincial/local/hospital sector	3.0	4.2	4.4	4.4	4.4	3.8

Source: David B. Perry, "Fiscal Figures: Changes in Government Spending Patterns," *Canadian Tax Journal* vol. 44, no. 2 (1996): Table 10.

Table 3.6 divides total government expenditure as a percentage of GDP into two categories: federal government expenditure and provincial/local/hospital expenditures, to illustrate the relative importance of the two levels of government that enjoy constitutional status. The provincial/local/hospital sector (or the PLH sector) is not subdivided here because the distribution of responsibilities among these three levels differs widely from province to province.

Table 3.6 illustrates three important features of the structure of the Canadian public sector. First, the provincial/local/hospital sector is a much more important provider of goods and services than the federal government. This is not surprising given the provincial governments have primary responsibility for health, education, roads, and social services. Moreover, the activity of the PLH sector in this area has grown dramatically since 1950 in contrast to that of the federal government, whose goods and services expenditure accounts for a smaller proportion of GDP than it did in 1950. Second, the federal government is more active in directly transferring income than the provincial/local/hospital sector. Finally, debt charges are most significant at the federal level.

SOURCES OF GOVERNMENT REVENUE

A breakdown of sources of government revenue in Canada in 1976/77 and 1995/96 is provided in Table 3.7. The biggest single source of revenue for governments in Canada in 1995/96 is the *personal income tax*, which accounted for 45.1% of federal government revenue and 20.4% of provincial government revenue. All personal income tax is collected by the federal government in all provinces except Quebec, which is responsible for its own provincial personal income tax collection. Personal income tax is withheld from most people's pay each week by their employers, who send it to Revenue Canada. Revenue Canada then distributes the provincial share to each of the provinces. Self-employed persons are responsible for sending Revenue Canada their own estimated taxes four times each year. Each year we add up our total income, subtract the items we are allowed to exclude or deduct, claim our tax credits, and figure out the tax we should have paid for the year. If we owe more than we paid, we must send the difference to Revenue Canada by April 30. If we paid more than we owe, we get a refund.

corporate income taxes *Taxes levied on the net incomes of corporations.*

Corporations must pay a special **corporate income tax.** (Profits from other

Table 3.7 — Sources of Public Sector Revenue

	Federal Revenues (% distribution)		Provincial/Local/Hospital Revenues (% distribution)	
	1976/77	1995/96	1976/77	1995/96
Personal income tax	42.0	45.1	16.0	20.4
Corporate income tax	15.0	9.8	5.0	3.3
General sales taxes	11.0	15.2	10.0	10.7
Excise taxes	6.0	5.4	5.0	4.6
Health and social insurance levies	7.0	13.4	5.0	5.2
Customs duties	6.0	2.2	0	0
Property taxes	0	0	14.0	17.0
Transfers from other levels of government	0	0	21.0	15.6
Other*	13.0	8.0	23.0	23.6

*Other includes licences, sale of goods and services, natural resource revenues, return on investments.

Sources: Statistics Canada, *Public Sector Finance, 1995–96*, Cat. no. 68-212; and Statistics Canada, *Public Finance Historical Data 1965/66–1991/92*, Cat. no. 68-512.

forms of business organizations—single proprietorships and partnerships—are taxed directly as ordinary personal income of the owners.) While personal income tax collections have been rising as a percentage of government revenue over the past 20 years, corporate income taxes have been falling in relative importance (see Table 3.7). The decline in the relative importance of the corporate tax has been a source of concern for many. However, it is important to distinguish between who is legally responsible for writing a cheque to the government and who actually pays the tax by experiencing a loss in general well-being. This distinction, which in economics is known as the distinction between the *legal and economic incidence of a tax,* is critically important in debates about the corporate tax. Corporations are owned by individuals and it is individuals who ultimately must pay the tax. Moreover, a corporation may be able to pass on the tax by charging consumers higher prices or paying workers less than they would receive in the absence of the corporate tax. For example, if corporations can pass on the corporate tax to consumers or workers in low income brackets then the relatively poor in our society may end up bearing a disproportionate share of the tax. We will return to the difference between legal and economic tax incidence in later chapters.

Sales taxes are another growing source of government revenue. The Goods and Services (GST) and provincial sales taxes (currently in place in all provinces except Alberta) are known together as *general sales taxes* since they are levied on a wide variety of goods and services. The federal government currently collects more than 15% of its total revenue from general sales taxes, and the PLH sector collects almost 11% of its revenue from this source. In addition, both levels of government collect revenue from taxes levied on the sales of specific products, such as cigarettes, alcoholic beverages, and gasoline. These taxes are known as **excise taxes**.

A fourth important source of government revenue is the **payroll taxes** used to finance social insurance programs like Employment Insurance and the Canada/Quebec Pension Plans. Payroll taxes, which are based on wages and salaries paid, are paid by both employers and employees. They are presented as Health and Social Insurance Levies in Table 3.7. In 1995/96 almost 14% of federal government revenue was collected through payroll taxes and about 5% of provincial revenue came from this source.

excise taxes *Taxes on specific commodities.*

payroll taxes *Taxes levied at a flat rate on wages and salaries. Proceeds support various government-administered social-benefit programs, including the social insurance system and the unemployment benefits system.*

Financial institutions play an important role in allocating savings in the private, public, and international sectors of the economy.

Some revenue sources are unique to a particular level of government. Only the federal government levies *customs duties*; customs duties are taxes imposed on goods and services produced in other countries. Only provincial and local governments levy property taxes; property taxes are determined as a percentage of the estimated or "assessed" value of commercial, industrial, and residential property. *Property taxes* are an important source of revenue for provincial and local governments. They accounted for 17% of PLH revenue in 1995/96.

The PLH sector also relies heavily on grants of money from higher levels of government. For example, the federal government estimates that it transfers over $30 billion to the provinces each year. In 1995/96 these transfers accounted for over 15% of PLH revenue. These government *transfer payments*—which include Equalization (a program designed to help the poorer provinces) and the Canada Health and Social Transfer (a grant intended to help provinces provide medicare, hospital insurance, post-secondary education, and provincial social assistance)—play a critical role in the Canadian federation.

Finally, governments collect revenue from a variety of other sources including profits from government enterprises such as lotteries, user fees imposed on users of public services, and royalties collected from firms selling natural resources owned by government.

Like all aspects of the Canadian economy, public sector revenue sources have changed dramatically over time. At Confederation, customs duties were the dominant revenue source. Today they are insignificant. The federal income tax was introduced in 1917 to generate a small amount of additional revenue to help pay for the costs incurred during World War I. Today it is the largest single source of revenue for the public sector.

The International Sector: Imports and Exports in Canada

From almost the first moment Europeans arrived in Canada, Canadians have been engaged in trade with the rest of the world. We sell goods and services we produce to people residing in other countries, and they sell goods and services they produce to us. Indeed, international trade has been more important to Canada throughout its history than it has been to almost any other country in the world.

From 1750 to 1850 our economic history was dominated by England. We were part of the British Empire, and the Industrial Revolution in England generated a rapidly growing demand for natural resource products that could be produced in Canada. Meanwhile, the growing Canadian economy generated a demand for manufactured goods produced in England. Moreover, a significant proportion of the capital needed in the growing Canadian economy was financed by the English. Borrowing from the rest of the world has been an important aspect of the Canadian economy ever since.

Over time the patterns of trade changed, but the importance of trade to the Canadian economy did not. After 1850, the United States became increasingly important as a trading partner and as a source of foreign capital investment.

Because trade is so important to the Canadian economy, Canadians have always been sensitive to developments in the international economy. Three developments in recent years are particularly important in increasing the relative importance of trade. First, the rapid economic growth of Japan and other Southeast Asian states (such as Korea, Singapore, Taiwan, Hong Kong, China, and Malaysia) has increased the absolute importance of Pacific trade. Second, the emergence of regional trading blocs has influenced trade patterns. We are an integral partner in an emerging North American trading area currently involving the U.S., Mexico, and Chile; many countries in Europe are members of the EU (European Union); and there is talk of the formation of a Pacific Rim trading area. The key feature of a trading bloc is that its participants are not subject to trading restrictions imposed on nonmembers. Finally, dramatic improvements in communications and other technologies have helped foster a general tendency known as globalization, meaning that goods, services, and capital are able to move across national boundaries much more easily than ever before.

Currently, Canadian exports equal about 38% of GDP, a very large share of total Canadian production. Imports are about 35% of GDP, a very large share of total expenditures of Canadian consumers, firms, and governments. The size and importance of the international sector of the Canadian economy is examined in more detail in Chapter 21.

From Institutions to Theory

This chapter has sketched the institutional structure of the Canadian economy. As we turn to economic theory, both positive and normative, you should reflect on the basic realities of economic life in Canada presented here. Why is the service sector expanding and the manufacturing sector contracting? Why is the public sector as large as it is? What economic functions does it perform? What determines the level of imports and exports? What effects do cheap foreign products have on the Canadian economy?

One of the most important questions in economics concerns the relative merits of public sector involvement in the economy. Should the government be involved in the economy, or should the market be left to its own devices? Before we can confront these and other important issues, we need to establish a theoretical framework. Our study of the economy and its operation begins in Chapter 4 with the behaviour of suppliers and demanders in private markets.

Summary

1. The *private sector* is made up of privately owned firms that exist to make a profit, nonprofit organizations, and individual households. The *public sector* is the government and its agencies at all levels—federal, provincial, and local. The *international sector* is the global economy. From any one country's perspective, the international sector consists of the economies of the rest of the world.

The Private Sector: Business and Industrial Organization in Canada

2. A *proprietorship* is a firm with a single owner. A *partnership* has two or more owners. Proprietors and partners are fully liable for all the debts of the business. A *corporation* is a formally established legal entity that limits the liability of its owners. The owners are not responsible for the debts of the firm beyond what they invest.

3. The term *industry* is used loosely to refer to groups of firms that produce similar products. Industries can be broadly or narrowly defined. A company

that produces cheese belongs to the cheese industry, the dairy industry, the food products industry, and the agricultural products industry.

4. In *perfect competition,* no single firm has any control over prices. This follows from two characteristics of this industry structure: (1) perfectly competitive industries are composed of many firms, each small relative to the size of the industry, and (2) each firm in a perfectly competitive industry produces exactly the same product—that is, products are *homogeneous.*

5. A *monopoly* is a *market organization,* or industry structure, in which there is only one firm producing a product for which there are no close substitutes. To remain a monopoly in a profitable industry, a firm must be able to block the entry of competing firms.

6. *Monopolistic competition* is an industry structure in which many firms compete, but in which each firm produces a slightly different product. Although each firm's product is unique, however, there are many close substitutes. Entry and exit

into monopolistically competitive industries are relatively easy.

7. An *oligopoly* is an industry with a small number of firms. In general, entry of new firms into an oligopolistic industry is difficult but possible.

The Public Sector: Taxes and Government Spending in Canada

8. The importance of the public sector in Canada has grown dramatically since World War II. Public expenditures at all levels increased from 21.3% of GDP in 1950 to 47.6% of GDP in 1995.

9. The Canadian public sector is organized on a federal basis with many levels of government. The federal and provincial governments enjoy a special constitutional status. Provincial governments have ultimate responsibility for medical and hospital care, social welfare assistance, and education. The federal government has jurisdiction over national defence and an integrated economy. As well, the federal government is responsible for a number of income security programs such as Employment Insurance, Old Age Security, and the Canada Pension Plan.

10. Since 1950, expenditures on areas within provincial jurisdiction have grown faster than expenditures in areas falling within the jurisdiction of the federal government. Almost all the growth in federal government expenditure in this period can be attributed to increasing transfer payments (to persons and provincial governments) and to rising interest payments on the national debt.

11. The biggest single source of revenue for governments in Canada is the personal income tax. It accounts for over 45% of federal government revenue and over 20% of provincial government revenue. Sales taxes are now the second most important source of revenue for both levels of government.

The International Sector: Imports and Exports in Canada

12. Thousands of transactions between Canadians and virtually every other country in the world take place daily. Canada is and has always been a country that relies heavily on international trade. The United States is Canada's most important trading partner, and automobiles are Canada's most important export.

Review Terms and Concepts

barrier to entry 55

corporate income taxes 64

corporation 52

dividends 52

excise taxes 65

government interest
    payments 62

government purchases of goods and
    services 61

government transfer
    payments 61

gross domestic product
    (GDP) 61

homogeneous products 54

industry 53

international sector 51

market organization 53

monopolistic competition 56

monopoly 55

net income 52

oligopoly 57

partnership 52

payroll taxes 65

perfect competition 54

private sector 50

proprietorship 51

public sector 50

retained earnings 52

share of stock 52

1. Health care continues to be a major issue in the 1990s. Look up the latest figures on health care expenditures as a percentage of GDP. In your province what share of total government expenditure (federal, provincial, and local) is devoted to health care?

2. **a.** How many separate governments make decisions affecting your life?
   b. What are the five biggest functions of local government?
   c. What is the logic for assigning these functions to local government as opposed to provincial or federal government?

3. Do a short research project on one of the following large government services. What does the service accomplish or hope to accomplish? What is the basic logic for government involvement? How much was spent on the service in 1995 compared to 1980?
   a. Canada Council
   b. Canada Pension Plan
   c. Employment Insurance
   d. Parks Canada
   e. Canada Student Loan Program
   f. Trans-Canada Highway

4. NAFTA was much debated prior to coming into force on January 1, 1994. What groups were opposed to it? Why? What are the basic arguments in favour of NAFTA?

5. Use the Internet to collect the most recent data on federal government expenditures and revenues and on international trade. Does the most recent data indicate major changes?

6. The chapter contains evidence on growth of both the public sector and the service sector. How are these two developments related?

7. What are the differences between a proprietorship and a corporation? If you were going to start a small business, which form of organization would you choose? What are the advantages and disadvantages of the two forms of organization?

8. "Most firms are corporations, but they account for a relatively small portion of total output in Canada." Do you agree or disagree with this statement? Explain your answer.

9. In 1995 shareholders directly received only 26.1% of total corporate profits. What happened to the rest?

10. Perfectly competitive industries are made up of large numbers of firms, each small relative to the size of the industry and each producing homogeneous products. What does this imply about an individual firm's ability to influence price? Explain your answer.

11. How is a monopolistically competitive industry like a monopoly? In what ways is it like a perfectly competitive industry?

12. How is it possible for government spending to increase as a percentage of GDP while taxes and government employment are both decreasing?

13. Why is the federal government spending much more on interest payments now than it was a decade ago? Explain.

Demand, Supply, and Market Equilibrium

4

Chapters 1 and 2 introduced the discipline, methodology, and subject matter of economics. Chapter 3 described the institutional landscape of the Canadian economy—its private, public, and international sectors. We now begin the task of analyzing how a market economy actually works. This chapter and the next present an overview of the way individual markets work. They introduce some of the concepts needed to understand both microeconomics and macroeconomics.

As we proceed to define terms and make assumptions, it is important to keep in mind what we are doing. In Chapter 1 we were very careful to explain what economic theory attempts to do. Theories are abstract representations of reality, like a map that represents a city. We believe that the models presented here will help you understand the workings of the economy just as a map helps you get where you want to go in a city. But just as a map presents one view of the world, so too does any given theory of the economy. Alternatives exist to the theory that we present. We believe, however, that the basic model presented here, while sometimes abstract, is useful in gaining an understanding of how the economy works.

In the simple island society discussed in Chapter 2, the economic problem was solved directly. Colleen and Ivan allocated their time and used the resources of the island to satisfy their wants. Ivan might be a farmer, Colleen a hunter and carpenter. He might be a civil engineer, she a doctor. Exchange occurred, but complex markets were not necessary.

In societies of many people, however, production must satisfy wide-ranging tastes and preferences. Producers therefore specialize. Farmers produce more food than they can eat in order to sell it to buy manufactured goods. Physicians are paid for specialized services, as are lawyers, construction workers, and editors. When there is specialization, there must be exchange, and exchange takes place in markets.

This chapter begins to explore the basic forces at work in market systems. The purpose of our discussion is to explain how the individual decisions of households and firms together, without any central planning or direction, answer the three basic questions: what will be produced, how will it be produced, and who will get what is produced? We begin with some definitions.

Firms and Households: The Basic Decision-Making Units

Throughout this book, we discuss and analyze the behaviour of two fundamental decision-making units: *firms*—the primary producing units in an economy—and *households*—the consuming units in an economy. Both are made up of people performing different functions and playing different roles. In essence, then, what we are developing is a theory of human behaviour.

A **firm** exists when a person or a group of people decides to produce a product or products by transforming *inputs* (that is, resources in the broadest sense) into *outputs* (the products that are sold in the market). Some firms produce goods; others produce services. Some are large, some are small, and some are in between. But all firms exist to transform resources into things that people want. The Toronto Symphony Orchestra takes labour, land, a building, musically talented people, electricity, and other inputs and combines them to produce concerts. The production process can be extremely complicated. The first flutist in the orchestra, for example, uses training, talent, previous performance experience, a score, an instrument, the conductor's interpretation, and her own feelings about the music to produce just one contribution to an overall performance.

Most firms exist to make a profit for their owners, but some do not. Your university, for example, fits the description of a firm. It takes inputs in the form of labour, land, skills, books, and buildings and produces a service that we call education. Although it sells that service for a price, it does not exist to make a profit, but rather to provide education of the highest quality possible.

Still, most firms exist to make a profit. They engage in production because they can sell their product for more than it costs to produce it. The analysis of firm behaviour that follows rests on the assumption that *firms make decisions in order to maximize profits.*

An **entrepreneur** is one who organizes, manages, and assumes the risks of a firm. It is the entrepreneur who takes a new idea or a new product and turns it into a successful business. All firms have implicit in them some element of entrepreneurship. When a new firm is created—whether a proprietorship, a partnership, or a corporation—someone must organize the new firm, arrange financing, hire employees, and take risks. That person is an entrepreneur. Sometimes existing companies introduce new products, and sometimes new firms develop or improve on an old idea, but at the root of it all is entrepreneurship, which some see as the core of the free enterprise system.

At the root of the debate about the potential of free enterprise in formerly socialist Eastern Europe is the question of entrepreneurship. Does an entrepreneurial spirit exist in that part of the world? If not, can it be developed? Without it the free enterprise system breaks down.

The consuming units in an economy are **households**. A household may consist of any number of people: a single person living alone, a married couple with

firm *An organization that transforms resources (inputs) into products (outputs). Firms are the primary producing units in a market economy.*

entrepreneur *A person who organizes, manages, and assumes the risks of a firm, taking a new idea or a new product and turning it into a successful business.*

households *The consuming units in an economy.*

The Toronto Symphony Orchestra is a firm. It combines inputs (land, labour, a concert hall, musically talented people, and electricity) and uses them to produce outputs (musical performance).

four children, or 15 unrelated people sharing a house. Household decisions are presumably based on the individual tastes and preferences of the consuming unit. The household buys what it wants and can afford. In a large, heterogeneous, and open society such as Canada, wildly different tastes find expression in the marketplace. A six-block walk in any direction on any street in Montreal or a drive from Yonge and Bloor streets north into rural Ontario should be enough to convince anyone that it is difficult to generalize about what people like and do not like.

Even though households have wide-ranging preferences, they also have some things in common. All—even the very rich—have ultimately limited incomes, and all must pay in some way for the things they consume. While households may have some control over their incomes—they can work more or less—they are also constrained by the availability of jobs, current wages, their own abilities, and their accumulated and inherited wealth (or lack thereof).

Input Markets and Output Markets: The Circular Flow

Households and firms interact in two basic kinds of markets: product or output markets and input or factor markets. Goods and services that are intended for use by households are exchanged in **product** or **output markets**. In output markets, competing firms *supply* and households *demand*.

To produce goods and services, firms must buy resources in **input** or **factor markets**. Firms buy inputs from households, which supply these inputs. When a firm decides how much to produce (supply) in output markets, it must simultaneously decide how much of each input it needs to produce the desired level of output. To produce automobiles, Chrysler Canada must use many inputs, including tires, steel, complicated machinery, and many different kinds of skilled labour.

product or **output markets** *The markets in which goods and services are exchanged.*

input or **factor markets** *The markets in which the resources used to produce products are exchanged.*

Figure 4.1 shows the *circular flow* of economic activity through a simple market economy. Note that the flow reflects the direction in which goods and services flow through input and output markets. For example, goods and services flow from firms to households through output markets. Labour services flow from households to firms through input markets. Payment (most often in money form) for goods and services flows in the opposite direction. Payment for goods and services flows from households to firms, and payment for labour services flows from firms to households.

In input markets, households *supply* resources. Most households earn their incomes by working—they supply their labour in the **labour market** to firms that demand labour and pay workers for their time and skills. Households may also lend their accumulated or inherited savings to firms for interest or exchange those savings for claims to future profits, as when a household buys shares of stock in a corporation. In the **capital market,** households supply the funds that firms use to buy capital goods. In exchange, these households receive interest or claims to future profits. Households may also supply land or other real property in exchange for rent in the **land market.**

Inputs into the production process are also called **factors of production.** Land, labour, and capital are the three key factors of production. Throughout this text, we use the terms *input* and *factor of production* interchangeably. Thus, input markets and factor markets mean the same thing.

Early economics texts included entrepreneurship as a type of input, just like land, labour, and capital. Treating entrepreneurship as a separate factor of production has fallen out of favour, however, partially because it is unmeasurable. Most economists today implicitly assume that it is in plentiful supply. That is, if profit opportunities exist, it is likely that entrepreneurs will crop up to take advantage of them. This assumption has turned out to be a good predictor of actual economic behaviour and performance.

The supply of inputs and their prices ultimately determine households' income. The amount of income a household earns thus depends on the decisions it makes concerning what types of inputs it chooses to supply. Whether to stay in school, how much and what kind of training to get, whether to start a business, how many hours to work, whether to work at all, and how to invest savings are all household decisions that affect income.

As you can see, then:

> Input and output markets are connected through the behaviour of both firms and households. Firms determine the quantities and character of outputs produced and the types and quantities of inputs demanded. Households determine the types and quantities of products demanded and the quantities and types of inputs supplied.[1]

labour market *The input/factor market in which households supply work for wages to firms that demand labour.*

capital market *The input/factor market in which households supply their savings, for interest or for claims to future profits, to firms that demand funds in order to buy capital goods.*

land market *The input/factor market in which households supply land or other real property in exchange for rent.*

factors of production *The inputs into the production process. Land, labour, and capital are the three key factors of production.*

---

[1]*Our description of markets begins with the behaviour of firms and households. Modern orthodox economic theory essentially combines two distinct but closely related theories of behaviour. The "theory of household behaviour," or "consumer behaviour," has its roots in the works of nineteenth-century utilitarians such as Jeremy Bentham, William Jevons, Carl Menger, Leon Walras, Vilfredo Pareto, and F.Y. Edgeworth. The "theory of the firm" developed out of the earlier classical political economy of Adam Smith, David Ricardo, and Thomas Malthus. In 1890 Alfred Marshall published the first of many editions of his* Principles of Economics. *That volume pulled together the main themes of both the classical economists and the utilitarians into what is now called "neoclassical economics." While there have been many changes over the years, the basic structure of the model that we build can be found in Marshall's work.*

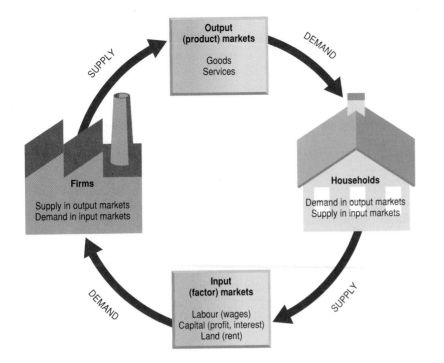

FIGURE 4.1

The Circular Flow of Economic Activity

Diagrams like this one show the circular flow of economic activity, hence the name *circular flow diagram*. Here, goods and services flow clockwise: labour services supplied by households flow to firms, and goods and services produced by firms flow to households. Money (not pictured here) flows in the opposite (counterclockwise) direction: payment for goods and services flows from households to firms, and payment for labour services flows from firms to households.

Demand in Product/Output Markets

In real life, households make many decisions at the same time. To see how the forces of demand and supply work, however, let us focus first on the amount of a single product that an individual household decides to consume within some given period of time, such as a month or a year.

> A household's decision about what quantity of a particular output, or product, to demand depends upon a number of factors:
>
> - The *price of the product* in question.
> - The *income available* to the household.
> - The household's *amount of accumulated wealth*.
> - The *prices of other products* available to the household.
> - The household's *tastes and preferences*.
> - The household's *expectations* about future income, wealth, and prices.

Colour Guide

Note that in Figure 4.1 households are depicted in *blue* and firms are depicted in *red*. From now on all diagrams relating to the behaviour of households will be in blue or shades of blue, and all diagrams relating to the behaviour of firms will be in red or shades of red.

Quantity demanded is the amount (number of units) of a product that a household would buy in a given period *if it could buy all it wanted at the current market price.*

Of course, the amount of a product that households finally purchase depends on the amount of product actually available in the market. But the quantity demanded at any moment may exceed or fall short of the quantity supplied. These differences between the quantity demanded and the quantity supplied are very important. The phrase *if it could buy all it wanted* is critical to the definition of quantity demanded because it allows for the possibility that quantity supplied and quantity demanded are unequal.

quantity demanded *The amount (number of units) of a product that a household would buy in a given period if it could buy all it wanted at the current market price.*

Our analysis of demand and supply is leading up to a theory of how market prices are determined. Prices are determined by interaction between demanders and suppliers. To understand this interaction, we first need to know how product prices influence the behaviour of suppliers and demanders *separately*. We therefore begin our discussion of output markets by focusing exclusively on this relationship.

■ **Changes in Quantity Demanded versus Changes in Demand** The most important relationship in individual markets is that between market price and quantity demanded. For this reason, we need to begin our discussion by analyzing the likely response of households to changes in price using the device of *ceteris paribus*, or "all else equal." That is, we will attempt to derive a relationship between the quantity demanded of a good per time period and the price of that good, holding income, wealth, other prices, tastes, and expectations constant.

It is very important to distinguish between price changes, which affect the quantity of a good demanded, and changes in other factors (such as income), which change the entire relationship between price and quantity. For example, if a family begins earning a higher income, it might buy more of a good at every possible price. To be sure that we distinguish between changes in price and other changes that affect demand, we will throughout the rest of the text be very precise about terminology. Specifically:

> Changes in the price of a product affect the *quantity demanded* per period. Changes in any other factor, such as income or preferences, affect *demand*. Thus we say that an increase in the price of Coca-Cola is likely to cause a decrease in the *quantity of Coca-Cola demanded*. Similarly, we say that an increase in income is likely to cause an increase in the *demand* for most goods.

demand schedule *A table showing how much of a given product a household would be willing to buy at different prices.*

demand curve *A graph illustrating how much of a given product a household would be willing to buy at different prices.*

PRICE AND QUANTITY DEMANDED: THE LAW OF DEMAND

A **demand schedule** shows the quantities of a product that a household would be willing to buy at different prices. Table 4.1 presents a hypothetical demand schedule for Anna, a student who went off to university to study economics while her boyfriend went to art school. If telephone calls were free (a price of zero), Anna would call her boyfriend every day, or 30 times a month. At a price of $.50 per call, she makes 25 calls a month. When the price hits $3.50, she cuts back to seven calls a month. This same information presented graphically is called a **demand curve**. Anna's demand curve is presented in Figure 4.2.[2]

You will note in Figure 4.2 that *quantity* is measured along the horizontal axis, and *price* is measured along the vertical axis. This is the convention we follow throughout this book.

■ **Demand Curves Slope Downward** The data in Table 4.1 show that at lower prices, Anna calls her boyfriend more frequently; at higher prices, she calls less

Table 4.1

Anna's Demand Schedule for Telephone Calls

Price (per Call)	Quantity Demanded (Calls per Month)
$ 0	30
0.50	25
3.50	7
7.00	3
10.00	1
15.00	0

[2]*Drawing a smooth curve, as we do in Figure 4.2, suggests that Anna can make a quarter of a phone call or half of a phone call. For example, according to the graph, at a price of $12 per call, Anna would make half a call and at $8 per call, about a call and a half. While fractional purchases are for goods that are divisible, such as phone calls—you might talk for one minute instead of two minutes—and products sold by weight, they are impossible for large purchases, such as automobiles. We use the term* lumpy *to describe goods that cannot be divided. You would not draw a smooth, downward sloping curve of a household's demand for automobiles, for example, because there might be only one (or at most two) points, and any points in between would be meaningless. Whenever we draw a smooth demand curve, we are assuming divisibility.*

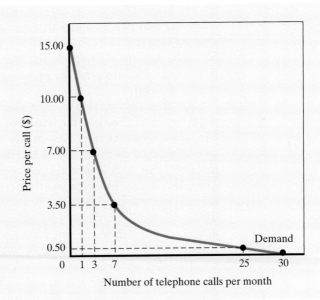

FIGURE 4.2

Anna's Demand Curve

The relationship between price and quantity demanded presented graphically is called a *demand curve*. Demand curves have a negative slope, indicating that lower prices cause quantity demanded to increase. Note that Anna's demand curve is blue; demand in product markets is determined by household choice.

frequently. There is thus a *negative, or inverse, relationship between quantity demanded and price.* When price rises, quantity demanded falls, and when price falls, quantity demanded rises. Thus demand curves always slope downward. This negative relationship between price and quantity demanded is often referred to as the **law of demand,** a term first used by economist Alfred Marshall in his 1890 textbook.

Some people are put off by the abstractness of demand curves. Of course, we don't actually draw our own demand curves for products. When we want to make a purchase, we usually face only a single price, and how much we would buy at other prices is irrelevant. But demand curves help analysts understand the kind of behaviour that households are *likely* to exhibit if they are actually faced with a higher or lower price. We know, for example, that if the price of a good rises enough, the quantity demanded must ultimately drop to zero. The demand curve is thus a tool that helps us explain economic behaviour and predict reactions to possible price changes.

Marshall's definition of a social "law" captures the idea:

> The term "law" means nothing more than a general proposition or statement of tendencies, more or less certain, more or less definite . . . a *social law* is a statement of social tendencies; that is, that a certain course of action may be expected from the members of a social group under certain conditions.[3]

It seems reasonable to expect that consumers will demand more of a product at a lower price and less of it at a higher price. Households must divide their incomes over a wide range of goods and services. If the price of a kilogram of beef rises while income and the prices of all other products remain the same, the household must sacrifice more of something else in order to buy each kilogram of beef. If I spend $9 for a kilogram of prime beef, I am sacrificing the other things that I might have bought with that $9. If the price of prime beef were to jump to $11 per kilogram, while chicken breasts remained at $5.99 (remember *ceteris paribus*—

law of demand *The negative relationship between price and quantity demanded. As price rises, quantity demanded decreases. As price falls, quantity demanded increases.*

---

[3]*Alfred Marshall,* Principles of Economics, *8th ed. (New York: Macmillan, 1948), p. 33. (The first edition was published in 1890.)*

we are holding all else constant), I would have to give up more chicken and/or other items in order to buy that kilogram of beef. So I would probably eat more chicken and less beef. Anna calls her boyfriend three times when phone calls cost $7 each. A fourth call would mean sacrificing $7 worth of other purchases. At a price of $3.50, however, the opportunity cost of each call is lower, and she calls more frequently.

Another explanation behind the fact that demand curves are very likely to slope downward rests on the notion of *utility*. Economists use utility as a measure of happiness or satisfaction. Presumably we consume goods and services because they give us utility. But as we consume more of a product within a given period of time, it is likely that each additional unit consumed will yield successively less satisfaction. The utility I gain from a second ice cream cone is likely to be less than the utility I gained from the first; the third is worth even less, and so forth. This *law of diminishing marginal utility* is an important concept in economics. If each successive unit of a good is worth less to me, I am not going to be willing to pay as much for it. It is thus reasonable to expect a downward slope in the demand curve for that good.

The idea of diminishing marginal utility also helps to explain Anna's behaviour. The demand curve is a way of representing what she is willing to pay per phone call. At a price of $7, she calls her boyfriend three times per month. A fourth call, however, is worth less than the third—that is, the fourth call is worth less than $7 to her, so she stops at three. If the price were only $3.50, however, she would keep right on calling. But even at $3.50, she would stop at seven calls per month. This behaviour reveals that the eighth call has less value to Anna than the seventh.

Thinking about the ways that people are affected by price changes also helps us see what is behind the law of demand. Consider this example: Craig lives and works in British Columbia. His elderly mother lives in Newfoundland. Last year, the airlines got into a price war, and the price of flying between Vancouver and St. John's dropped from $1500 to $750. How might Craig's behaviour change?

First, he is better off. Last year he flew home to Newfoundland three times at a total cost of $4500. This year he can fly to Newfoundland the same number of times, buy exactly the same combination of other goods and services that he bought last year, and have $2250 left over! Because he is better off—his income can buy more—he may fly home more frequently. Second, the opportunity cost of flying home has changed. Before the price war Craig had to sacrifice $1500 worth of other goods and services each time he flew to St. John's. After the price war he must sacrifice only $750 worth of other goods and services for each trip. The trade-off has changed. Both of these effects are likely to lead to a higher quantity demanded in response to the lower price.[4]

In sum:

> It is reasonable to expect quantity demanded to fall when price rises, *ceteris paribus*, and to expect quantity demanded to rise when price falls, *ceteris paribus*. Demand curves have a negative slope.

■ **Other Properties of Demand Curves** Two additional things are notable about Anna's demand curve. First, it intersects the Y, or price, axis. This means that there is a price above which no calls will be made. In this case, Anna simply stops calling when the price reaches $15 per call.

---

[4]*These separate effects are called the "income" and "substitution" effects of the price change. They will be formally defined and discussed in later chapters.*

As long as households have limited incomes and wealth, all demand curves will intersect the price axis. For any commodity, there is always a price above which a household will not, or cannot, pay. Even if the good or service is very important, all households are ultimately "constrained," or limited, by income and wealth.

Second, Anna's demand curve intersects the X, or quantity, axis. Even at a zero price, there is a limit to the number of phone calls Anna will make. If telephone calls were free, she would call 30 times a month, but not more.

That demand curves intersect the quantity axis is a matter of common sense. Demands for most goods are limited, if only by time, even at a zero price.

OTHER DETERMINANTS OF HOUSEHOLD DEMAND

Of the many factors likely to influence a household's demand for a specific product, we have considered only the price of the product itself. Other determining factors include household income and wealth, the prices of other goods and services, tastes and preferences, and expectations.

■ **Income and Wealth** Before we proceed, we need to define two terms that are often confused, *income* and *wealth*. A household's **income** is the sum of all the wages, salaries, profits, interest payments, rents, and other forms of earnings received by the household *in a given period of time*. Income is thus a *flow* measure: we must specify a time period for it—income *per month* or *per year*. You can spend or consume more or less than your income in any given period. If you consume less than the amount of your income, you save. To consume more than your income in a period, you must either borrow or draw on savings accumulated from previous periods.

Wealth is the total value of what a household owns less what it owes. Another word for wealth is **net worth**—the amount a household would have left if it sold off all its possessions and paid off all its debts. Wealth is a *stock* measure: it is measured at a given moment, or point, in time. If, in a given period, you spend less than your income, you save; the amount that you save is added to your wealth. Saving is the flow that affects the stock of wealth. When you spend more than your income, you *dissave*—you reduce your wealth.

Clearly, households with higher incomes and higher accumulated savings or inherited wealth can afford to buy more things. In general, then, we would expect higher demand at higher levels of income/wealth and lower demand at lower levels of income/wealth. Goods for which demand goes up when income is higher and for which demand goes down when income is lower are called **normal goods.** Movie tickets, restaurant meals, telephone calls, and shirts are all normal goods.

But generalization in economics can be hazardous. Sometimes demand for a good falls when household income rises. Consider, for example, the various qualities of meat available. When a household's income rises, it is likely to buy higher quality meats—its demand for filet mignon is likely to rise—but its demand for lower quality meats—chuck steak, for example—is likely to fall. Transportation is another example. At higher incomes, people can afford to fly. People who can afford to fly are less likely to take the bus long distances. Thus higher income may reduce the number of times someone takes a bus. Goods for which demand falls when income rises are called **inferior goods.**

■ **Prices of Other Goods and Services** No consumer decides in isolation on the amount of any one commodity to buy. Rather, each decision is part of a larger set

income *The sum of all a household's wages, salaries, profits, interest payments, rents, and other forms of earnings in a given period of time. It is a flow measure.*

wealth or **net worth** *The total value of what a household owns minus what it owes. It is a stock measure.*

normal goods *Goods for which demand goes up when income is higher and for which demand goes down when income is lower.*

inferior goods *Goods for which demand falls when income rises.*

of decisions that are made simultaneously. Obviously, households must apportion their incomes over many different goods and services. As a result, the price of any one good can and does affect the demand for other goods.

This is most obviously the case when goods are substitutes for each other. To return to our lonesome first-year student: if the price of a telephone call rises to $10, Anna will call her boyfriend only once a month (see Table 4.1). But of course she can get in touch with him in other ways. Presumably she substitutes some other, less costly, form of communication, such as writing more letters or sending e-mail messages.

Consider another example. There is currently much discussion about the relative merits of cars produced in North America and cars produced in Japan. Recently, North American consumers have faced a sharp rise in the price of Japanese cars. As a result, we would expect to see consumers substitute North American-made cars for Japanese-made cars. The demand for North American cars should rise and the quantity of Japanese cars demanded should fall.

When an *increase* in the price of one good causes demand for another good to *increase* (a positive relationship), we say that the goods are **substitutes.** A *fall* in the price of a good causes a *decline* in demand for its substitutes. Substitutes are goods that can serve as replacements for one another.

To be substitutes, two products need not be identical. Identical products are called **perfect substitutes.** Japanese cars are not identical to Canadian cars. Nonetheless, all have four wheels, are capable of carrying people, and run on gasoline. Thus, significant changes in the price of one country's cars can be expected to influence demand for the other country's cars. Compact discs are substitutes for records and tapes, restaurant meals are substitutes for meals eaten at home, and flying from Toronto to Montreal is a substitute for taking the train.

Often, two products "go together"—that is, they complement each other. Our lonesome letter writer, for example, will find her demand for stamps and stationery rising as she writes more letters. Bacon and eggs are **complementary goods,** as are cars and gasoline, and cameras and film. During a price war among the airlines in the summer of 1994 when travel became less expensive, the demand for taxi service to and from airports and for luggage increased. When two goods are complements, a *decrease* in the price of one results in *increase* in demand for the other, and vice versa.

Because any one good may have many potential substitutes and complements at the same time, a single price change may affect a household's demands for many goods simultaneously; the demand for some of these products may rise while the demand for others may fall. For example, a relatively new technology for personal computers is the CD-ROM. Massive amounts of data can now be stored digitally on compact discs that can be read by personal computers with a CD-ROM drive. When these drives first came on the market they were quite expensive, selling for several hundreds of dollars each. Now they are much less expensive, and most new computers have them built in. As a result, the demand for the CD-ROM discs (complementary goods) is soaring. Many computer manufacturers now include a CD-ROM encyclopedia when you purchase one of their machines. As more and more people adopt the CD technology and the price of CDs and CD hardware falls, fewer people will be buying encyclopedias printed on paper (substitute goods).

■ **Tastes and Preferences**   Income, wealth, and the prices of things available are the three factors that determine the combinations of things that a household is *able* to buy. You know that you cannot afford to rent an apartment at $1200 per month if your monthly income is only $400. But within these constraints, you are more or less free to choose what to buy. Your final choice depends on your individual tastes and preferences.

substitutes *Goods that can serve as replacements for one another; when the price of one increases, demand for the other goes up.*

perfect substitutes *Identical products.*

complements, complementary goods *Goods that "go together"; a decrease in the price of one results in an increase in demand for the other, and vice versa.*

Changes in preferences can and do manifest themselves in market behaviour. As the medical consequences of smoking have become more and more clear, for example, more and more people have stopped smoking. As a result, the demand for cigarettes has dropped significantly. Fifteen years ago the major big-city marathons drew only a few hundred runners. Now tens of thousands enter and run. The demand for running shoes, running suits, stopwatches, and other running items has greatly increased.

Within the constraints of prices and incomes, it is preference that shapes the demand curve. But it is difficult to generalize about tastes and preferences. First of all, they are volatile. Five years ago, more people smoked cigarettes and fewer people had VCRs. Second, they are idiosyncratic. Some people like to talk on the telephone, while others prefer the written word; some people prefer dogs, while others are crazy about cats; some people like chicken wings, while others prefer legs. The diversity of individual demands is almost infinite.

■ **Expectations** What you decide to buy today certainly depends on today's prices and your current income and wealth. But you also have expectations about what your position will be in the future. You may have expectations about future changes in prices, too, and these may affect your decisions today.

Examples of the ways expectations affect demand abound. When people buy a house or a car, they often must borrow part of the purchase price and pay it back over a number of years. In deciding what kind of house or car to buy, they presumably must think about their income today, as well as what their income is likely to be in the future.

As another example, consider a student in her final year of medical school living on a scholarship and summer earnings totalling $14 000. Compare her with another person earning $7 an hour at a full-time job, with no expectation of a significant change in income in the future. The two have virtually identical incomes. But even if they had the same tastes, the medical student is likely to demand different things, simply because she expects a major increase in income later on.

Increasingly, economic theory has come to recognize the importance of expectations. We will devote a good deal of time to discussing how expectations affect more than just demand. For the time being, however, it is important to understand that demand depends on more than just *current* incomes, prices, and tastes.

SHIFT OF DEMAND VERSUS MOVEMENT ALONG A DEMAND CURVE

Recall that a demand curve shows the relationship between quantity demanded and the price of a good. Such demand curves are derived while holding income, tastes, and other prices constant. If this condition of *ceteris paribus* were relaxed, we would have to derive an entirely new relationship between price and quantity.

Let us return once again to Anna (Table 4.1 and Figure 4.2). Suppose that when we derived the demand schedule in Table 4.1, Anna had a part-time job that paid $200 per month. Now suppose that her parents inherit some money and begin sending her an additional $200 per month. Assuming that she keeps her job, Anna's income is now $400 per month.[5]

With her higher income, Anna would probably call her boyfriend more frequently, regardless of the price of a call. Table 4.2 and Figure 4.3 present Anna's

---

[5]*The income from home may affect the amount of time Anna spends working. In the extreme, she may quit her job and her income will remain at $200. In essence, she would be spending the entire $200 on leisure. Here we assume that she keeps the job and that her income is higher. The point is that since labour-supply decisions affect income, they are closely tied to output-demand decisions. In a sense, the two decisions are made simultaneously.*

Table 4.2	Shift of Anna's Demand Schedule Due to Increase in Income	
Price (per Call)	SCHEDULE D_1 Quantity Demanded (Calls per Month at an Income of $200 per Month)	SCHEDULE D_2 Quantity Demanded (Calls per Month at an Income of $400 per Month)
$ 0	30	35
0.50	25	33
3.50	7	18
7.00	3	12
10.00	1	7
15.00	0	2
20.00	0	0

original-income schedule (D_1) and increased-income demand schedule (D_2). At $.50 per call, the frequency of her calls (or the quantity she demands) increases from 25 to 33 calls per month; at $3.50 per call, frequency increases from seven to 18 calls per month; at $10 per call, frequency increases from one to seven calls per month. (Note in Figure 4.3 that even if calls are free, Anna's income matters; at zero price, her demand increases. With a higher income, she may visit her boyfriend more, for example, and more visits might mean more phone calls to organize and plan.)

The conditions that were in place at the time the original demand curve was derived have now changed. In other words, a factor that affects Anna's demand for telephone calls (in this case, her income) has changed, and there is now a new relationship between price and quantity demanded. Such a change is referred to as a **shift of the demand curve.**

It is very important to distinguish between a change in quantity demanded—that is, some movement *along* a demand curve—and a shift of demand. Demand schedules and demand curves show the relationship between the price of a good or service and the quantity demanded per period, *ceteris paribus.* If price changes, quantity demanded will change—this is a **movement along the demand curve.** When any of the other factors that influence demand change, however, a new relationship between price and quantity demanded is established—this is a *shift of the demand curve.* The result, then, is a *new* demand curve. Changes in income, preferences, or prices of other goods cause the demand curve to shift:

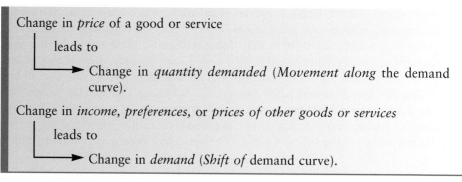

Change in *price* of a good or service

  leads to

  → Change in *quantity demanded* (*Movement along* the demand curve).

Change in *income, preferences,* or *prices of other goods or services*

  leads to

  → Change in *demand* (*Shift of* demand curve).

Figure 4.4 illustrates this point. In Figure 4.4a, an increase in household income causes demand for hamburger (an inferior good) to decline, or shift to the left from D_1 to D_2. (Because quantity is measured on the horizontal axis, a decrease

shift of a demand curve *The change that takes place in a demand curve when a new relationship between quantity demanded of a good and the price of that good is brought about by a change in the original conditions.*

movement along a demand curve *What happens when a change in price causes quantity demanded to change.*

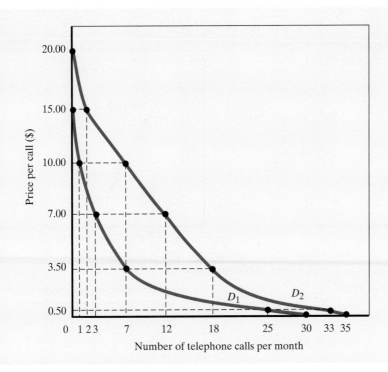

FIGURE 4.3

Shift of a Demand Curve Following a Rise in Income

When the price of a good changes, we move *along* the demand curve for that good. When any other factor that influences demand changes (income, tastes, etc.), the relationship between price and quantity is different; there is a *shift* of the demand curve, in this case from D_1 to D_2.

means a move to the left.) Demand for steak (a normal good), on the other hand, increases, or shifts to the right, when income rises.

In Figure 4.4b, an increase in the price of hamburger from $4.49 to $6.50 a kilogram causes a household to buy less hamburger each month. In other words, the higher price causes the *quantity demanded* to decline from five kilograms to three kilograms per month. This change represents a movement *along* the demand curve for hamburger. In place of hamburger, the household buys more chicken. The household's demand for chicken (a substitute for hamburger) rises—the demand curve shifts to the right. At the same time, the demand for ketchup (a good that complements hamburger) declines—its demand curve shifts to the left.

FROM HOUSEHOLD DEMAND TO MARKET DEMAND

Market demand is simply the sum of all the quantities of a good or service demanded per period by all the households buying in the market for that good or service. Figure 4.5 on page 85 shows the derivation of a market demand curve from three individual demand curves. (Although this market demand curve is derived from the behaviour of only three people, most markets have thousands or even millions of demanders.) As the table in Figure 4.5 shows, when the price of a kilogram of coffee is $8.50, both A and C would purchase two kilograms per month, while B would buy none; at that price, presumably, B drinks tea. Market demand at $8.50 would thus be a total of two plus two, or four kilograms. At a price of $5.50 per kilogram, however, A would purchase three kilograms per month, B one kilogram, and C four kilograms. Thus, at $5.50 per kilogram, market demand would be three plus one plus four, or eight kilograms of coffee per month.

The total quantity demanded in the marketplace at a given price, then, is simply the sum of all the quantities demanded by all the individual households shopping in the market *at that price*. A market demand curve shows the total amount of a product that would be sold at each price if households could buy all they wanted at that

market demand *The sum of all the quantities of a good or service demanded per period by all the households buying in the market for that good or service.*

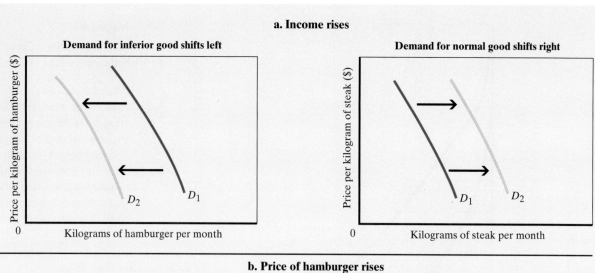

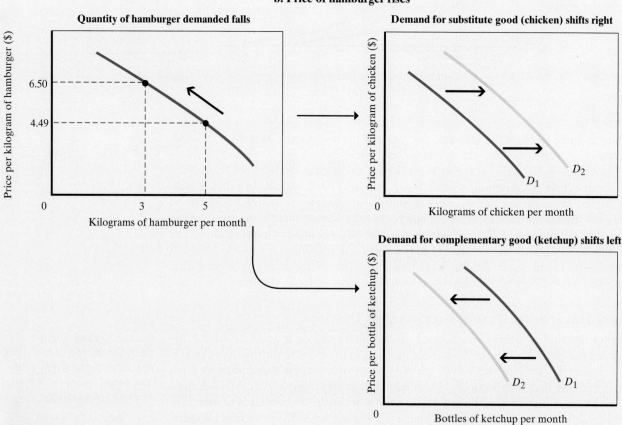

FIGURE 4.4

Shifts versus Movement along a Demand Curve

a. When income increases, the demand for inferior goods *shifts to the left* and the demand for normal goods *shifts to the right*.
b. If the price of hamburger rises, the quantity of hamburger demanded declines—this is a movement along the demand curve. The same price would shift the demand for chicken (a substitute for hamburger) to the right and the demand for ketchup (a complement to hamburger) to the left.

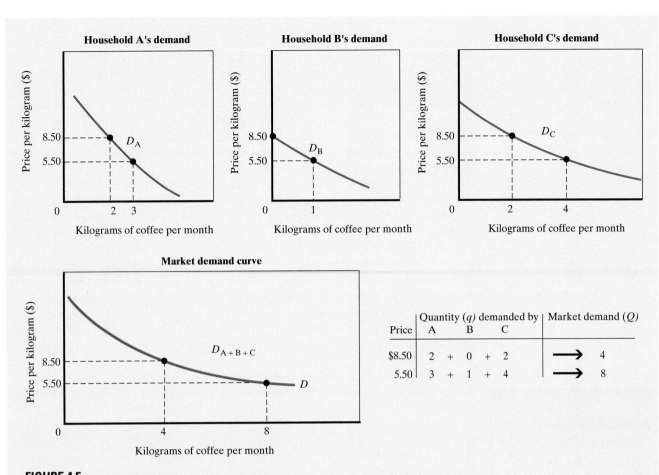

FIGURE 4.5

Deriving Market Demand from Individual Household Demand Curves

Total demand in the marketplace is simply the sum of the demands of all the households shopping in a particular market. It is the sum of all the individual demand curves—that is, the sum of all the individual quantities demanded at each price.

price. As Figure 4.5 shows, the market demand curve is the sum of all the individual demand curves—that is, the sum of all the individual quantities demanded at each price. The market demand curve thus takes its shape and position from the shapes, positions, and number of individual demand curves. If more people decide to shop in a market, more demand curves must be added, and the market demand curve will shift to the right. Market demand curves may also shift as a result of preference changes, income changes, or changes in the number of demanders.

As a general rule throughout this book, capital letters refer to the entire market and lowercase letters refer to individual households or firms. Thus, in Figure 4.5, Q refers to total quantity demanded in the market, while q refers to the quantity demanded by individual households.

Supply in Product/Output Markets

In addition to dealing with households' demands for outputs, economic theory also deals with the behaviour of business firms, which supply in output markets and demand in input markets (see again Figure 4.1). Firms engage in production, and we assume that they do so for profit. Successful firms make profits because they are able to sell their products for more than it costs to produce them.

Supply decisions can thus be expected to depend on profit potential. Because **profit** is the simple difference between revenues and costs, supply is likely to react to changes in revenues and changes in production costs. The amount of revenue that a firm earns depends on the price of its product in the market and on how much it sells. Costs of production depend on many factors, the most important of which are (1) the kinds of inputs needed to produce the product, (2) the amount of each input required, and (3) the prices of inputs.

The supply decision is just one of several decisions that firms make in order to maximize profit. There are usually a number of ways to produce any given product. A golf course can be built by hundreds of workers with shovels and grass seed or by a few workers with heavy earth-moving equipment and sod blankets. Hamburgers can be individually fried by a short-order cook or grilled by the hundreds on a mechanized moving grill. Firms must choose the production technique most appropriate to their products and projected levels of production. The best method of production is the one that minimizes cost, thus maximizing profit.

Which production technique is best, in turn, depends on the prices of inputs. Where labour is cheap and machinery is expensive and difficult to transport, firms are likely to choose production techniques that use a great deal of labour. Where machines are available and labour is scarce or expensive, they are likely to choose more capital-intensive methods. Obviously, the technique ultimately chosen determines input requirements. Thus, by choosing an output supply target and the most appropriate technology, firms determine which inputs to demand.

To summarize:

> Assuming that its objective is to maximize profits, a firm's decision about what quantity of output, or product, to supply depends on
> 1. The price of the good or service
> 2. The cost of producing the product, which in turn depends on
>   ■ The price of required inputs (labour, capital, and land), and
>   ■ The technologies that can be used to produce the product
> 3. The prices of related products

With the caution that no decision exists in a vacuum, let us begin our examination of firm behaviour by focusing on the output supply decision and the relationship between quantity supplied and output price, *ceteris paribus*.

PRICE AND QUANTITY SUPPLIED: THE LAW OF SUPPLY

Quantity supplied is the amount of a particular product that a firm would be willing and able to offer for sale at a particular price during a given time period. A **supply schedule** shows how much of a product a firm will supply at alternative prices. Table 4.3 itemizes the quantities of soybeans that an individual farmer such as Clarence Brown might supply at various prices. If the market paid $75 or less for a tonne of soybeans, Brown would not supply any soybeans. For one thing, it costs more than $75 to produce a tonne of soybeans; for another, Brown can use his land more profitably to produce something else. At $85 per tonne, however, at least some soybean production takes place on Brown's farm, and a price increase from $85 to $115 per tonne causes the quantity supplied by Brown to increase from 400 to 600 tonnes per year. The higher price may justify shifting land from wheat to soybean production or putting previously fallow land into soybeans. Or

profit *The difference between revenues and costs.*

Table 4.3

Clarence Brown's Supply Schedule for Soybeans

Price (per Tonne)	Quantity Supplied (Tonnes per Year)
$ 75	0
85	400
115	600
150	800
200	1200
250	1200

quantity supplied *The amount of a particular product that a firm would be willing and able to offer for sale at a particular price during a given time period.*

supply schedule *A table showing how much of a product firms will supply at different prices.*

it may lead to more intensive farming of land already in soybeans, using expensive fertilizer or equipment that was not cost-justified at the lower price.

Generalizing from Farmer Brown's experience, we can reasonably expect an increase in market price to lead to an increase in quantity supplied. In other words, there is a positive relationship between the quantity of a good supplied and price. This statement sums up the **law of supply.**

The information in a supply schedule presented graphically is called a **supply curve.** Supply curves slope upward. The upward, or positive, slope of Brown's curve in Figure 4.6, for example, reflects this positive relationship between price and quantity supplied.

Note in Brown's supply schedule, however, that when price rises above $200 to $250, quantity supplied no longer increases. Often an individual firm's ability to respond to an increase in price is constrained by its existing scale of operations, or capacity, in the short run. For example, Brown's ability to produce more soybeans depends on the size of his farm, the fertility of his soil, and the types of equipment he has. The fact that output stays constant at 1200 tonnes per year suggests that he is running up against the limits imposed by the size of his farm and his existing technology.

In the longer run, however, Brown may acquire more land, or technology may change, allowing for more soybean production. The terms *short run* and *long run* have very precise meanings in economics; we will discuss them in detail later. Here it is important only to understand that time plays a critical role in supply decisions. When prices change, firms' immediate response may be different from what they are able to do after a month or a year. Short-run and long-run supply curves are often different.

OTHER DETERMINANTS OF FIRM SUPPLY

Of the factors listed above that are likely to affect the quantity of output supplied

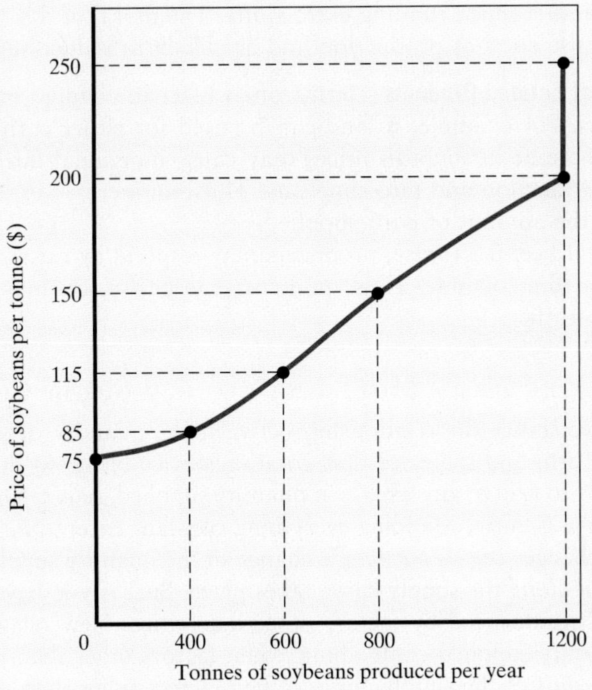

law of supply *The positive relationship between price and quantity of a good supplied. An increase in market price will lead to an increase in quantity supplied, and a decrease in market price will lead to a decrease in quantity supplied.*

supply curve *A graph illustrating how much of a product a firm will supply at different prices.*

FIGURE 4.6

Clarence Brown's Individual Supply Curve

A producer will supply more when the price of output is higher. The slope of a supply curve is positive. Note that the supply curve is red. Supply is determined by choices made by firms.

by a given firm, we have thus far discussed only the price of output. Other factors that affect supply include the cost of producing the product and the prices of related products.

■ **The Cost of Production**   Regardless of the price that a firm can command for its product, price must exceed the cost of producing the output for the firm to make a profit. Thus, the supply decision is likely to change in response to changes in the cost of production. Cost of production depends on a number of factors, including the available technologies and the price of the inputs (labour, land, capital, energy, and so forth) that the firm needs.

Technological change can have an enormous impact on the cost of production over time. Consider agriculture. The introduction of fertilizers, the development of complex farm machinery, and the use of bioengineering to increase the yield of individual crops all have powerfully affected the cost of producing agricultural commodities. Farm productivity in Canada has increased dramatically over the years, as was seen in Table 2.2 in Chapter 2. In 1925, wheat yields in Saskatchewan averaged 1265 kilograms per hectare and in 1996, they averaged 2270 kilograms per hectare. Over the same period, barley yields in Alberta went from 1400 kilograms per hectare to 3340 kilograms per hectare.

When a technological advance lowers the cost of production, output is likely to increase. When yield per hectare increases, individual farmers can and do produce more. The output of the Ford Motor Company increased substantially after the introduction of assembly-line techniques. The production of electronic calculators, and later personal computers, boomed with the development of inexpensive techniques to produce microprocessors.

Cost of production is also affected directly by the price of the factors of production. When the price of oil rose so dramatically beginning in 1973, this affected the costs of production in many sectors of the economy. As a result, cab drivers faced higher gasoline prices, airlines faced higher fuel costs, and manufacturing firms faced higher heating bills. The result: cab drivers probably spent less time driving around looking for fares, airlines cut a few low-profit routes, and some manufacturing plants stopped running extra shifts. The moral of this story: increases in input prices raise costs of production and are likely to reduce supply.

■ **The Prices of Related Products**   Firms often react to changes in the prices of related products. For example, if land can be used for either corn or soybean production, an increase in soybean prices may cause individual farmers to shift land out of corn production and into soybeans. Thus, an increase in soybean prices actually affects the amount of corn supplied.

Similarly, if beef prices rise, producers may respond by raising more cattle. But leather comes from cowhide. Thus, an increase in beef prices may actually increase the supply of leather.

SHIFT OF SUPPLY VERSUS MOVEMENT ALONG A SUPPLY CURVE

A supply curve shows the relationship between the quantity of a good or service supplied by a firm and the price that good or service brings in the market. Higher prices are likely to lead to an increase in quantity supplied, *ceteris paribus*. Remember: the supply curve is derived holding everything constant except price. When the price of a product changes *ceteris paribus*, a change in the quantity supplied follows—that is, a *movement along* the supply curve takes place. But, as you have seen, supply decisions are also influenced by factors other than price. New relationships between price and quantity supplied come about when factors other than price change, and the result is a *shift* of the supply curve. When factors other than price cause supply curves to shift, we say that there has been a *change in supply*.

Recall that the cost of production depends upon the price of inputs and the technologies of production available. Now suppose that a major breakthrough in the production of soybeans has occurred; genetic engineering has produced a superstrain of disease- and pest-resistant seed. Such a technological change would enable individual farmers to supply more soybeans at *any* market price. Table 4.4 and Figure 4.7 describe this change. At \$150 a tonne, farmers would have produced 800 tonnes from the old seed (schedule S_1 in Table 4.4); with the lower cost of production and higher yield resulting from the new seed, they produce 1100 tonnes (schedule S_2 in Table 4.4). At \$85 per tonne, they would have produced 400 tonnes from the old seed; but with the lower costs and higher yields, output rises to 625 tonnes.

Increases in input prices may also cause supply curves to shift. What impact would an increase in the price of oil have on farmers? Since fertilizers are made in part from petrochemicals and since tractors run on gasoline, Farmer Brown would have faced higher costs than he did before the oil price increase. Such increases in production cost shift the supply curve to the left—that is, less is produced at any given market price. If Brown's soybean supply curve shifted far enough to the left, it would intersect the price axis at a higher point, meaning that it would take a higher market price to induce Brown to produce any soybeans at all.

As with demand, it is very important to distinguish between *movements along* supply curves (changes in quantity supplied) and *shifts in* supply curves (changes in supply):

Change in *price* of a good or service

     leads to

         → Change in *quantity supplied* (*Movement along* a supply curve).

Change in *costs, input prices, technology,* or *prices of related goods and services*

     leads to

         → Change in *supply* (*Shift of* supply curve).

FROM INDIVIDUAL FIRM SUPPLY TO MARKET SUPPLY

Market supply is determined in the same fashion as market demand. It is simply the sum of all that is supplied each period by all producers of a single product.

market supply *The sum of all that is supplied each period by all producers of a single product.*

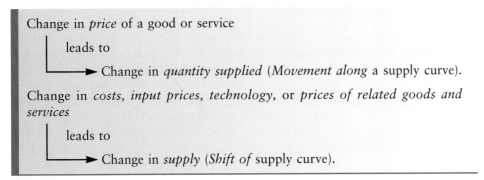

Table 4.4	Shift of Supply Schedule for Soybeans Following Development of a New Disease-Resistant Seed Strain	
	SCHEDULE S_1	**SCHEDULE S_2**
Price (per Tonne)	Quantity Supplied (Tonnes per Year Using Old Seed)	Quantity Supplied (Tonnes per Year Using New Seed)
\$ 75	0	150
85	400	625
115	600	900
150	800	1100
200	1200	1500
250	1200	1500

FIGURE 4.7

Shift of Supply Curve for Soybeans Following Development of a New Seed Strain

When the price of a product changes, we move *along* the supply curve for that product; the quantity supplied rises or falls. When any other factor affecting supply changes, the supply curve *shifts*.

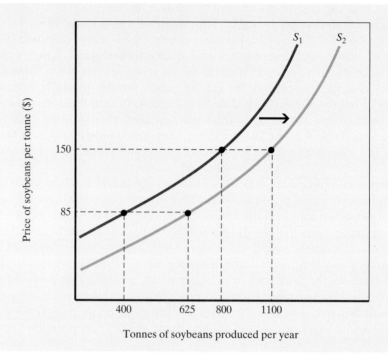

Figure 4.8 derives a market supply curve from the supply curves of three individual firms. (In a market with more firms, total market supply would be the sum of the amounts produced by each of the firms in that market.) As the table in Figure 4.8 shows, at a price of $150 farm A supplies 3000 tonnes of soybeans, farm B supplies 1000 tonnes, and farm C supplies 2500 tonnes. At this price, the total amount supplied in the market is 3000 plus 1000 plus 2500, or 6500 tonnes. At a price of $85, however, the total amount supplied is only 2500 tonnes (1000 plus 500 plus 1000). The market supply curve is thus the simple addition of the individual supply curves of all the firms in a particular market—that is, the sum of all the individual quantities supplied at each price.

The position and shape of the market supply curve depends on the positions and shapes of the individual firms' supply curves from which it is derived. But it also depends on the number of firms that produce in that market. If firms that produce for a particular market are earning high profits, other firms may be tempted to go into that business. When the technology to produce computers for home use became available, literally hundreds of new firms got into the act. The popularity and profitability of the Internet has led to the formation of new Net service providers. When new firms enter an industry, the supply curve shifts to the right. When firms go out of business, or "exit" the market, the supply curve shifts to the left.

Market Equilibrium

So far we have identified a number of factors that influence the amount that households demand and firms supply in product (output) markets. The discussion has emphasized the role of market price as a determinant both of quantity demanded and quantity supplied. We are now ready to see how supply and demand in the market interact to determine the final market price.

We have been very careful in our discussions thus far to separate household decisions about how much to demand from firm decisions about how much to supply. The operation of the market, however, clearly depends on the interaction

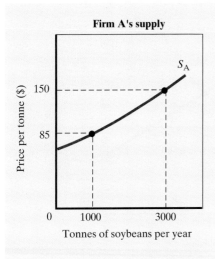

Firm A's supply

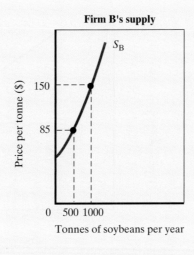

Firm B's supply

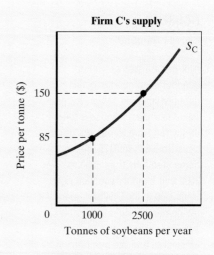

Firm C's supply

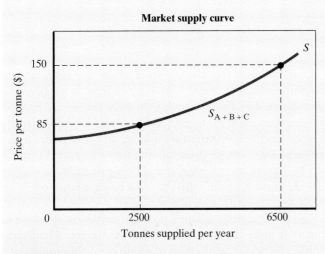

Market supply curve

	Quantity (q) supplied by			Market supply (Q)
Price	A	B	C	
$150	3000 +	1000 +	2500	→ 6500
$85	1000 +	500 +	1000	→ 2500

FIGURE 4.8

Deriving Market Supply from Individual Firm Supply Curves

Total supply in the marketplace is the sum of all the amounts supplied by all the firms selling in the market; it is the sum of all the individual quantities supplied at each price.

between suppliers and demanders. At any moment, one of three conditions prevails in every market: (1) the quantity demanded exceeds the quantity supplied at the current price, a situation called *excess demand*; (2) the quantity supplied exceeds the quantity demanded at the current price, a situation called *excess supply*; or (3) the quantity supplied equals the quantity demanded at the current price, a situation called **equilibrium.** At equilibrium, no tendency for price to change exists.

EXCESS DEMAND

Excess demand exists when quantity demanded is greater than quantity supplied at the current price. Figure 4.9, which plots both a supply curve and a demand curve on the same graph, illustrates such a situation. As you can see, market demand at $85 per tonne (5000 tonnes) exceeds the amount that farmers are currently supplying (2500 tonnes).

equilibrium *The condition that exists when quantity supplied and quantity demanded are equal. At equilibrium, there is no tendency for price to change.*

excess demand *The condition that exists when quantity demanded exceeds quantity supplied at the current price.*

FIGURE 4.9

Excess Demand

At a price of $85 per tonne, quantity demanded exceeds quantity supplied. When *excess demand* arises, there is a tendency for price to rise. As price rises from $85 to $125, quantity demanded falls from 5000 to 3500 and quantity supplied rises from 2500 to 3500. When quantity demanded equals quantity supplied, excess demand is eliminated and the market is in equilibrium. Here, the equilibrium price is $125, and the equilibrium quantity is 3500 tonnes.

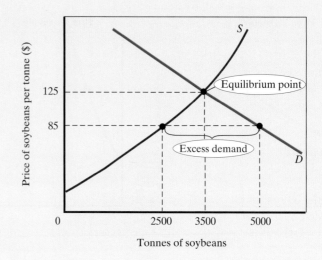

When excess demand occurs in an unregulated market, there is a tendency for price to rise as demanders compete against each other for the limited supply. The adjustment mechanisms may differ, but the outcome is always the same. For example, consider the mechanism of an auction. In an auction, items are sold directly to the highest bidder. When the auctioneer starts the bidding at a low price, many people bid for the item. At first there is excess demand: quantity demanded exceeds quantity supplied. As would-be buyers offer higher and higher prices, bidders drop out, until the one who offers the most ends up with the item being auctioned. Price rises until quantity demanded and quantity supplied are equal.

At a price of $85 (see Figure 4.9 again), farmers produce soybeans at a rate of 2500 tonnes per year, but at that price the demand is for 5000 tonnes. Most farm products are sold to local dealers who in turn sell large quantities in major market centres, where bidding would push prices up if quantity demanded exceeded quantity supplied. As price rises above $85, two things happen: (1) the quantity demanded falls as buyers drop out of the market and perhaps choose a substitute, and (2) the quantity supplied increases as farmers find themselves receiving a higher price for their product and shift additional acres into soybean production.[6]

This process continues until the excess demand is eliminated. In Figure 4.9, this occurs at $125, where quantity demanded has fallen from 5000 to 3500 tonnes per year and quantity supplied has increased from 2500 to 3500 tonnes per year. When quantity demanded and quantity supplied are equal and there is no further bidding, the process has achieved an equilibrium, a situation in which *there is no natural tendency for further adjustment*. Graphically, the point of equilibrium is the point at which the supply curve and the demand curve intersect.

---

[6]*Once farmers have produced in any given season, they cannot change their minds and produce more, of course. When we derived Clarence Brown's supply schedule in Table 4.3, we imagined him reacting to prices that existed at the time he decided how much land to plant in soybeans. In Figure 4.9, the upward slope shows that higher prices justify shifting land from other crops. Final price may not be determined until final production figures are in. For our purposes here, however, we have ignored this timing problem. Perhaps the best way to think about it is that demand and supply are flows, or rates, of production—that is, we are talking about the number of tonnes produced per production period. Adjustments in the rate of production may take place over a number of production periods.*

The process through which excess demand leads to higher prices is different in different markets. Consider the market for houses in the hypothetical town of Boomville with a population of 25 000 people, most of whom live in single-family homes. Normally about 75 homes are sold in the Boomville market each year. But last year, a major business opened a plant in town, creating 1500 new jobs that pay good wages. This attracted new residents to the area, and real estate agents now have more buyers than there are properties for sale. Quantity demanded now exceeds quantity supplied. In other words, there is excess demand.

Auctions are not unheard of in the housing market, but they are rare. This market usually works more subtly, but the outcome is the same. Properties are sold very quickly and housing prices begin to rise. Boomville sellers soon learn that there are more buyers than usual, and they begin to "hold out" for higher offers. As prices for houses in Boomville rise, quantity demanded eventually drops off and quantity supplied increases. Quantity supplied increases in at least two ways: (1) encouraged by the high prices, builders begin constructing new houses, and (2) some people, attracted by the higher prices their homes will fetch, put their houses on the market. Discouraged by higher prices, however, some potential buyers (demanders) may begin to look for housing in neighbouring towns and settle on commuting. Eventually, equilibrium will be reestablished, with the quantity of houses demanded just equal to the quantity of houses supplied.

While the mechanics of price adjustment in the housing market differ from the mechanics of an auction, the outcome is exactly the same:

> When quantity demanded exceeds quantity supplied, price tends to rise. When the price in a market rises, quantity demanded falls and quantity supplied rises until an equilibrium is reached at which quantity demanded and quantity supplied are equal.

This process is called *price rationing*. When excess demand exists, some people will be satisfied and some will not. When the market operates without interference, price increases will distribute what is available to those who are willing and able to pay the most. As long as there is a way for buyers and sellers to interact, those who are willing to pay more will make that fact known somehow. (We discuss the nature of the price system as a rationing device in great detail in Chapter 5.)

Excess Supply

Excess supply exists when the quantity supplied exceeds the quantity demanded at the current price. As with excess demand, the mechanics of price adjustment in the face of excess supply can differ from market to market. If automobile dealers find themselves with unsold cars in the fall when the new models are coming in, for example, you can expect to see price cuts. Sometimes dealers offer discounts to encourage buyers; sometimes buyers themselves simply offer less than the price initially asked. In any event, products do no one any good sitting in dealers' lots or on warehouse shelves. The auction metaphor introduced earlier can also be applied here. If the initial asking price is too high, no one bids, and the auctioneer tries a lower price. It's almost always true that certain items do not sell as well as anticipated during the Christmas holidays. After Christmas most stores have big sales during which they lower the prices of overstocked items. Quantities supplied exceeded quantities demanded at the current prices, so stores cut prices.

Across the province from Boomville is Bustville, where last year a drug manufacturer shut down its operations and 1500 people found themselves out of

excess supply *The condition that exists when quantity supplied exceeds quantity demanded at the current price.*

work. With no other prospects for work, many residents decided to pack up and move. They put their houses up for sale, but there were few buyers. The result was an excess supply of houses: the quantity of houses supplied exceeded the quantity demanded at the current prices.

As houses sit unsold on the market for months, sellers start to cut their asking prices. Potential buyers begin offering considerably less than sellers are asking. As prices fall, two things are likely to happen. First, the low housing prices may attract new buyers. People who might have bought in a neighbouring town see that there are housing bargains to be had in Bustville, and quantity demanded rises in response to price decline. Second, some of those who put their houses on the market may be discouraged by the lower prices and decide to stay in Bustville. Developers are certainly not likely to be building new housing in town. Lower prices thus lead to a decline in quantity supplied as potential sellers pull their houses from the market.

Figure 4.10 illustrates another excess supply situation. At a price of $150 per tonne, farmers are supplying soybeans at a rate of 4000 tonnes per year, but buyers demand only 2000. With 2000 (4000 minus 2000) tonnes of soybeans going unsold, the market price falls. As price falls from $150 to $125, quantity supplied decreases from 4000 tonnes per year to 3500. The lower price causes quantity demanded to rise from 2000 to 3500. At $125, quantity demanded and quantity supplied are equal. For the data shown here, then, $125 and 3500 tonnes are the equilibrium price and quantity.

Early in 1994, crude oil production worldwide exceeded the quantity demanded, and prices fell significantly as competing producer countries tried to maintain their share of world markets. Although the mechanism by which price is adjusted is different for automobiles, housing, soybeans, and crude oil, the outcome is the same:

> When quantity supplied exceeds quantity demanded at the current price, the price tends to fall. When price falls, quantity supplied is likely to decrease and quantity demanded is likely to increase until an equilibrium price is reached where quantity supplied and quantity demanded are equal.

FIGURE 4.10

Excess Supply

At a price of $150, quantity supplied exceeds quantity demanded by 2000 tonnes. This excess supply will cause price to fall.

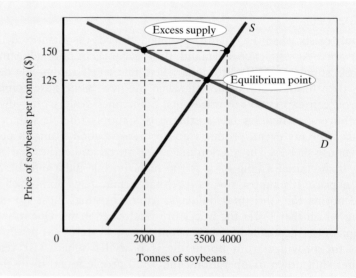

CHANGES IN EQUILIBRIUM

When supply and demand curves shift, the equilibrium price and quantity change. The following example will help to illustrate this point.

South America is a major producer of coffee beans. A cold snap there can reduce the coffee harvest enough to affect the world price of coffee beans. In the summer of 1994, a major freeze hit Brazil and Colombia and drove up the price of coffee on world markets to a record $7.30 per kilogram.

Figure 4.11 illustrates how the freeze pushed up coffee prices. Initially, the market was in equilibrium at a price of $3.65. At that price, the quantity demanded was equal to quantity supplied (six billion kilograms). At a price of $3.65 and a quantity of six billion kilograms, the demand curve (labelled D) intersected the initial supply curve (labelled S_1). (Remember that equilibrium exists when quantity demanded equals quantity supplied—the point at which the supply and demand curves intersect.)

The freeze caused a decrease in the supply of coffee beans. That is, it caused the supply curve to shift to the left. In Figure 4.11, the new supply curve (the supply curve that shows the relationship between price and quantity supplied after the freeze) is labelled S_2.

At the initial equilibrium price, $3.65, there is now an excess demand for coffee. If the price were to remain at $3.65, quantity demanded would not change; it would remain at six billion kilograms. But at that price, quantity supplied would drop to three billion kilograms. At a price of $3.65, quantity demanded is greater than quantity supplied.

When excess demand exists in a market, price can be expected to rise, and rise it did. As the figure shows, price rose to a new equilibrium at $7.30. At $7.30, quantity demanded is again equal to quantity supplied, this time at 4.5 billion kilograms—the point at which the new supply curve (S_2) intersects the demand curve.

Notice that as the price of coffee rose from $3.65 to $7.30, two things happened. First, the quantity demanded declined (a movement along the demand

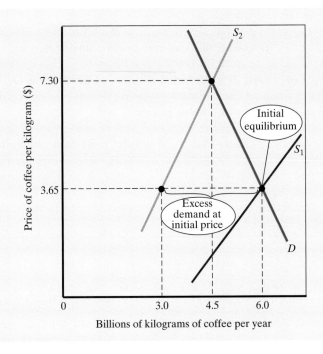

FIGURE 4.11

The Coffee Market: A Shift of Supply and Subsequent Price Adjustment

Before the freeze, the coffee market was in equilibrium at a price of $3.65. At that price, quantity demanded equalled quantity supplied. The freeze shifted the supply curve to the left (from S_1 to S_2), increasing equilibrium price to $7.30.

curve) as people shifted to substitutes such as tea and hot cocoa. Second, the quantity supplied began to rise, but within the limits imposed by the damage from the freeze. (It might also be that some countries or areas with high costs of production, previously unprofitable, came into production and shipped to the world market at the higher price.) That is, the quantity supplied increased in response to the higher price *along* the new supply curve, which lies to the left of the old supply curve. The final result was a higher price ($7.30), a smaller quantity finally exchanged in the market (4.5 billion kilograms), and coffee bought only by those willing to pay $7.30 per kilogram.

Figure 4.12 presents 10 examples of supply and demand shifts and the resulting changes in equilibrium price and quantity. Be sure to go through each graph carefully and ensure that you understand each.

Demand and Supply in Product Markets: A Review

As you continue your study of economics, you will discover that it is a discipline full of controversy and debate. There is, however, little disagreement about the basic way that the forces of supply and demand operate in free markets. If you hear that a freeze in Florida has destroyed a good portion of the citrus crop, you can bet that the price of oranges will rise.[7] If you read that the weather on the Prairies has been good and a record wheat crop is expected, you can bet that wheat prices will fall. If fishers in British Columbia are not allowed to fish, you can bet that the price of fish will go up. (For additional examples of how the forces of supply and demand work, see the Application box on page 99 titled "Supply and Demand in the News.")

Here are some important points to remember about the mechanics of supply and demand in product markets:

1. A demand curve shows how much of a product a household would buy if it could buy all it wanted at the given price. A supply curve shows how much of a product a firm would supply if it could sell all it wanted at the given price.
2. Quantity demanded and quantity supplied are always per time period—that is, per day, per month, or per year.
3. The demand for a good is determined by household income and wealth, the prices of other goods and services, tastes and preferences, and expectations.
4. The supply of a good is determined by costs of production and the prices of related products. Costs of production are determined by available technologies of production and input prices.
5. Be careful to distinguish between movements along supply and demand curves and shifts of these curves. When the price of a good changes, the quantity of that good demanded or supplied changes—that is, a movement occurs along the curve. When any other factor changes, the curves shift, or change position.
6. Market equilibrium exists only when quantity supplied equals quantity demanded at the current price.

---

[7]*In economics you have to think twice, however, even about a "safe" bet. If you bet that the price of frozen orange juice will rise after a freeze, you will lose your money. It turns out that much of the crop that is damaged by a freeze can be used, but for only one thing—to make frozen orange juice. Thus, a freeze actually* increases *the supply of frozen juice on the market. Following the last two hard freezes in Florida, the price of oranges shot up, but the price of frozen orange juice fell sharply!*

A. DEMAND SHIFTS

1. Increase in income: X is a normal good

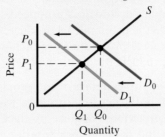

2. Increase in income: X is an inferior good

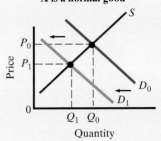

3. Decrease in income: X is a normal good

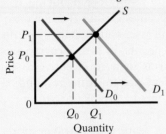

4. Decrease in income: X is an inferior good

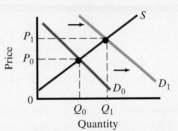

5. Increase in the price of a substitute for X

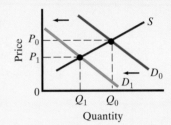

6. Increase in the price of a complement for X

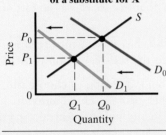

7. Decrease in the price of a substitute for X

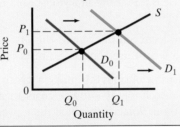

8. Decrease in the price of a complement for X

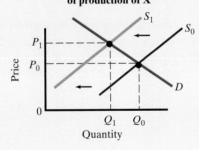

B. SUPPLY SHIFTS

9. Increase in the cost of production of X

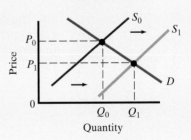

10. Decrease in the cost of production of X

FIGURE 4.12

Examples of Supply and Demand Shifts for Product X

Looking Ahead: Markets and the Allocation of Resources

You can already begin to see how markets answer the basic economic questions of what is produced, how it is produced, and who gets what is produced. A firm will produce what is profitable to produce. If it can sell a product at a price that is sufficient to leave a profit after production costs are paid, it will in all likelihood produce that product. Resources will flow in the direction of profit opportunities.

■ Demand curves reflect what people are willing and able to pay for products; they are influenced by incomes, wealth, preferences, the prices of other goods, and expectations. Because product prices are determined by the interaction of supply and demand, prices reflect what people are willing to pay. If people's preferences or incomes change, resources will be allocated differently. Consider, for example, an increase in demand—a shift in the market demand curve. Beginning at an equilibrium, households simply begin buying more. At the equilibrium price, quantity demanded becomes greater than quantity supplied. When there is excess demand, prices will rise, and higher prices mean higher profits for firms in the industry. Higher profits, in turn, provide existing firms with an incentive to expand and new firms with an incentive to enter the industry. Thus, the decisions of independent private firms responding to prices and profit opportunities determine *what* will be produced. No central direction is necessary.

Adam Smith saw this self-regulating feature of markets more than 200 years ago:

> Every individual . . . by pursuing his own interest . . . promotes that of society. He is led . . . by an invisible hand to promote an end which was no part of his intention.[8]

The term Smith coined, the *invisible hand,* has passed into common parlance and is still used by economists to refer to the self-regulation of markets.

■ Firms in business to make a profit have a good reason to choose the best available technology—lower costs mean higher profits. Thus, individual firms determine *how* to produce their products, again with no central direction.

■ So far we have barely touched on the question of distribution—*who* gets what is produced? But you can see part of the answer in the simple supply and demand diagrams. When a good is in short supply, price rises. As it does, those who are willing and able to continue buying do so; others stop buying.

The next chapter begins with a more detailed discussion of these topics. How, exactly, is the final allocation of resources (the mix of output and the distribution of output) determined in a market system?

---

[8]*Adam Smith,* The Wealth of Nations, *p. 456.*

The basic forces of supply and demand are at work throughout the world, as the following news articles illustrate. As an exercise, draw and label demand and supply diagrams for each situation.

1. Two consecutive leftward shifts of supply, causing a dramatic increase in prices:

[June 29, 1994] Coffee prices surged more than 25 percent yesterday, the largest one-day rise in more than seven years, as a damaging frost struck much of the coffee-growing areas of Brazil.

"We are going to see this market skyrocket," said Judith Ganes, coffee analyst for Merrill Lynch. "Consumers are likely to feel it at the retail level."

Coffee for July delivery jumped 33.8 cents, to US$1.5975 a pound—after peaking earlier at US$1.80—its highest price since November 1986.

[July 11, 1994] A second killing frost in key coffee-growing regions of Brazil sent coffee futures soaring 25% to their highest level in eight years. Including the toll from last month's freeze, the damage could wipe out 50% or more of next year's crop.

In hectic trading on New York's Coffee, Sugar and Cocoa Exchange yesterday, coffee for September delivery rose 46.45 cents to US$2.3375 a pound, a new contract high.

2. Supply shifts to the right, causing prices to fall:

[July 17, 1995] Deregulation of Canada's natural gas industry in 1986 unleashed reserves equal to 25 years of production, previously locked in the ground by government decree. Markets flooded, prices plunged. When the supply bubble bursts, desperate producers reasoned, robust prices will ensue. But so far no good. A price run up that started two years ago collapsed this winter. Pessimists think a stable rebound may elude Alberta's gasmen until well past 2000. Ironically the latest threat is deregulation of the American electricity business.

3. Demand may shift to right, leading to higher prices (if, in the example, the electricity industry shifts to gas-fired plants):

[July 17, 1995] The effect of electricity deregulation is harder to gauge. At a recent Calgary conference, American gas lawyer John Jimison pointed out that competition is finally being forced into the monopolistic electricity industry. He argued that a drive to cut costs is inevitable in a deregulated power sector, and will lead to more efficient use of existing generating capacity. In that case, new gas-gobbling power generating capacity may not be needed for years. Many in the gas industry had hoped that electricity deregulation would trigger the construction of dozens of gas-fired plants, which are cheaper to build and maintain than plants using oil, coal, or nuclear power.

4. Demand shifts to right, causing prices to rise:

[May 12, 1995] Should you be sitting in your little ol' home, wondering if you will ever be

An increase in the supply of natural gas due to deregulation resulted in a lower price for Alberta gas producers.

able to sell it at a price anywhere near what you paid for it, I have some crumbs of comfort.....Keep in mind that immigration has been swelling Ontario's population growth, predominantly people in the 35 and younger group who will add to housing demand.... The next piece of the jigsaw that needs to fall into place is for mortgage rates to go down as they have been in recent weeks.

Sources: Leonard Sloane, "Coffee Futures Soar 25%, Biggest Daily Rise in 7 Years," *The New York Times*, June 29, 1994; Suzanne McGee, "Second Cold Snap Harms Brazil's Coffee Crop Sending Prices to Highest Level in Eight Years," *The Wall Street Journal*, July 11, 1994; "The Bubble from Hell: Natural Gas Prices are Down and Could Easily Stay There," *Alberta and Western Report* vol. 10, no. 26 (July 17, 1995): pp. 19–20; "It Doesn't Take Much to Push Up Home Prices," *Financial Post Daily* vol. 8, no. 57 (May 12, 1995): p. 16.

1. In societies with many people, production must satisfy wide-ranging tastes and preferences, and producers must therefore specialize.

Firms and Households: The Basic Decision-Making Units

2. A *firm* exists when a person or a group of people decides to produce a product or products by transforming resources, or *inputs*, into *outputs*—the products that are sold in the market. Firms are the primary producing units in a market economy. We assume firms make decisions to maximize profits.

3. *Households* are the primary consuming units in an economy. All households' incomes are subject to constraints.

Input Markets and Output Markets: The Circular Flow

4. Households and firms interact in two basic kinds of markets: *product or output markets* and *input or factor markets*. Goods and services intended for use by households are exchanged in output markets. In output markets, competing firms supply and competing households demand. In input markets, competing firms demand and competing households supply.

5. Ultimately, firms determine the quantities and character of outputs produced, the types and quantities of inputs demanded, and the technologies used in production. Households determine the types and quantities of products demanded and the types and quantities of inputs supplied.

Demand in Product/Output Markets

6. The quantity demanded of an individual product by an individual household depends on (1) income, (2) wealth, (3) the price of the product, (4) the prices of other products, (5) tastes and preferences, and (6) expectations about the future.

7. *Quantity demanded* is the amount of a product that an individual household would buy in a given period if it could buy all it wanted at the current price.

8. A *demand schedule* shows the quantities of a product that a household would buy at different prices. The same information presented graphically is called a *demand curve*.

9. The *law of demand* states that there is a negative relationship between price and quantity demanded.

As price rises, quantity demanded decreases, and vice versa. Demand curves slope downward.

10. All demand curves eventually intersect the price axis because there is always a price above which a household cannot, or will not, pay. All demand curves also eventually intersect the quantity axis because demand for most goods is limited, if only by time, even at a zero price.

11. When an increase in income causes demand for a good to rise, that good is a *normal good*. When an increase in income causes demand for a good to fall, that good is an *inferior good*.

12. If a rise in the price of good X causes demand for good Y to increase, the goods are substitutes. If a rise in the price of X causes demand for Y to fall, the goods are complements.

13. *Market demand* is simply the sum of all the quantities of a good or service demanded per period by all the households buying in the market for that good or service. It is the sum of all the individual quantities demanded at each price.

Supply in Product/Output Markets

14. *Quantity supplied* by a firm depends on (1) the price of the good or service, (2) the cost of producing the product, which includes the prices of required inputs and the technologies that can be used to produce the product, and (3) the prices of related products.

15. *Market supply* is the sum of all that is supplied each period by all producers of a single product. It is the sum of all the individual quantities supplied at each price.

16. It is very important to distinguish between *movements* along demand and supply curves and *shifts* of demand and supply curves. The demand curve shows the relationship between price and quantity demanded. The *supply curve* shows the relationship between price and quantity supplied. A change in price is a movement along the curve. Changes in tastes, income, wealth, expectations, or prices of other goods and services cause demand curves to shift; changes in costs, input prices, technology, or prices of related goods and services cause supply curves to shift.

Market Equilibrium

17. When quantity demanded exceeds quantity supplied at the current price, *excess demand* exists and the

price tends to rise. When prices in a market rise, quantity demanded falls and quantity supplied rises until an *equilibrium* is reached at which quantity supplied and quantity demanded are equal. At equilibrium, there is no further tendency for price to change.

18. When quantity supplied exceeds quantity demanded at the current price, *excess supply* exists and the price tends to fall. When price falls, quantity supplied decreases and quantity demanded increases until an equilibrium price is reached where quantity supplied and quantity demanded are equal.

Review Terms and Concepts

capital market 74

complements, complementary goods 80

demand curve 76

demand schedule 76

entrepreneur 72

equilibrium 91

excess demand 91

excess supply 93

factors of production 74

firm 72

households 72

income 79

inferior goods 79

input or factor markets 73

labour market 74

land market 74

law of demand 77

law of supply 87

market demand 83

market supply 89

movement along a demand curve 82

normal goods 79

perfect substitutes 80

product or output markets 73

profit 86

quantity demanded 75

quantity supplied 86

shift of a demand curve 82

substitutes 80

supply curve 87

supply schedule 86

wealth or net worth 79

Problem Set

1. Illustrate the following with supply and demand curves:
   a. Between 1994 and 1995, employment and income in Quebec fell, creating a decline in the demand for housing and lowering home prices.
   b. In 1994, the Canadian dollar fell in value on foreign currency markets. One result was that Canadian exports looked less expensive to foreign buyers. As a result, the quantity demanded of Canadian-produced wheat increased.
   c. Before economic reforms were implemented in Poland, the price of meat was held substantially below equilibrium by law. When reforms were implemented, prices rose dramatically, the quantity demanded fell, and the quantity supplied rose.
   d. The government imposes a regulation that sharply decreases the number of trees available for lumber production in Canada to protect two endangered species. Illustrate the effects on the lumber market and on the housing market.

2. Housing prices in Toronto and Vancouver have been on a roller-coaster ride. Illustrate each of the following situations with supply and demand curves:
   a. In both cities an increase in income combined with expectations of a strong market shifted demand and caused prices to rise rapidly during the mid- to late 1980s.
   b. By 1990, the construction industry boomed as more and more developers started new residential projects. But those new projects expanded the supply of housing just as demand was shifting as a result of falling incomes and expectations during the 1990–1991 recession.

3. There has been a great debate among housing policy analysts over the best way to increase the number of housing units available to low-income households. One strategy is to provide people with housing "vouchers," paid for by the government, that can be used to "rent" housing supplied by the private market. A second strategy is to have the government subsidize housing suppliers or simply to build public housing.
   a. Illustrate both supply- and demand-side strategies using supply and demand curves. Which strategy will result in higher rents?
   b. Critics of housing vouchers (the demand-side

strategy) argue that because the supply of housing to low-income households is limited and will not respond at all to higher rents, demand vouchers will serve only to drive up rents and make landlords better off. Illustrate their point with supply and demand curves.

4. The following two sets of statements contain common errors. Identify and explain each.
   a. Demand increases. This causes prices to rise. Higher prices cause demand to fall. Therefore prices fall back to their original levels.
   b. The supply of meat in Russia increases. This causes meat prices to fall. Lower prices mean that Russian households spend more on meat.

5. In August of 1993, the Toronto Blue Jays were battling it out with the Boston Red Sox for first place in the American League East. On August 2, the Blue Jays played the Red Sox in Boston. All tickets to the Blue Jays game were sold out a month in advance, and many people who wanted to get tickets could not. The following week the Sox travelled to Ohio to play the Cleveland Indians (a team in last place). The Cleveland game broke records for low attendance. In fact, only 1600 went to that game in a stadium that seats 80 000! Fenway Park in Boston holds 36 000 people. Cleveland Stadium holds 80 000. Assume for simplicity that tickets to all regular season games are priced at $20.
   a. Draw supply and demand curves for tickets to each of the two games. You have enough information to identify a point on each demand and supply curve. Use the laws of demand to complete the demand curve and note that supply is fixed and does not change with price as you complete the supply curve.
   b. Is there a pricing policy that would have filled the ballpark for the Cleveland game?
   c. The price system was not allowed to work to ration the Blue Jays tickets. How do you know? How do you suppose the tickets were rationed?

6. Consider the effects of the following two programs that influence the cigarette market in Canada: (1) Health Canada administers an advertising program designed to discourage cigarette smoking, particularly by the young. (2) In Ontario, where most Canadian tobacco is grown, there is a marketing board system which effectively restricts the amount of land on which tobacco can be grown.

   Show on a graph how the advertising program (if successful) and the marketing board restrictions are likely to affect the price and quantity of cigarettes consumed.

7. In 1999, a rare disease hits the Canadian cattle herd, causing a 20% decrease in Canadian beef production. As a result chicken prices rise. Illustrate this situation with supply and demand curves (draw diagrams for both markets).

*8. Consider the market for pizza. Suppose that the market demand for pizza is given by the equation $Q_d = 300 - 20P$ and the market supply for pizza is given by the equation $Q_s = 20P - 100$, where Q_d = quantity demanded, Q_s = quantity supplied, P = price (per pizza).
   a. Graph the supply and demand schedules for pizza using $5 through $15 as the value of P.
   b. In equilibrium, how many pizzas would be sold and at what price?
   c. What would happen if suppliers set the price of pizza at $15? Explain the market adjustment process.
   d. Suppose that the price of hamburgers, a substitute for pizza, doubles. Assume that this leads to a doubling of the demand for pizza (that is, at each price consumers demand twice as much pizza as before). Write the equation for the new market demand for pizza.
   e. Find the new equilibrium price and quantity of pizza.

---

*Note: Problems marked with an asterisk are more challenging.

The Price System, Supply and Demand, and Elasticity

Every society has a system of institutions that determines what is produced, how it is produced, and who gets what is produced. Although in some societies these decisions are made centrally, through planning agencies or by government directive, in every society many decisions are made in a decentralized way, through the operation of markets.

Markets exist in all societies, and Chapter 4 provided a bare-bones description of how markets operate. In this chapter, we continue our examination of supply, demand, and the price system.

The Price System: Rationing and Allocating Resources

The market system, also called the *price system*, performs two important and closely related functions in a society with unregulated markets. First, it provides an automatic mechanism for distributing scarce goods and services. That is, it serves as a **price rationing** device for allocating goods and services to consumers when the quantity demanded exceeds the quantity supplied. Second, the price system ultimately determines both the allocation of resources among producers and the final mix of outputs.

PRICE RATIONING

Consider first the simple process by which the price system eliminates excess demand. Figure 5.1 shows hypothetical supply and demand curves for lobsters caught off the coast of Atlantic Canada.

Lobsters are considered a delicacy. They are served in the finest

price rationing *The process by which the market system allocates goods and services to consumers when quantity demanded exceeds quantity supplied.*

restaurants, and people cook them at home on special occasions. As Figure 5.1 shows, the equilibrium price of live lobsters was $10 per kilogram in 1997. At this price, lobster boats brought in lobsters at a rate of 20 million kilograms per year— an amount that was just enough to satisfy demand.

Market equilibrium existed at $10 per kilogram, because at that price quantity demanded was equal to quantity supplied. (Remember that equilibrium occurs at the point where the supply and demand curves intersect. In Figure 5.1, this occurs at point C.)

Now suppose that in 1998 the waters off a section of the Atlantic coast become contaminated with a poisonous parasite. As a result, the Department of Fisheries and Oceans is forced to close 50 000 square kilometres of the most productive lobstering areas. Even though many of the lobster boats shift their trapping activities to other waters, there is a sharp reduction in the quantity of lobster supplied. The supply curve shifts to the left, from S_{1997} to S_{1998}. This shift in the supply curve creates a situation of excess demand at $10. At that price, the quantity demanded is 20 million kilograms and the quantity supplied is 10 million kilograms. Quantity demanded exceeds quantity supplied by 10 million kilograms (20 million minus 10 million).

The reduced supply causes the price of lobster to rise sharply. As the price rises, the available supply is "rationed." Who gets it? Those who are willing and able to pay the most.

You can see the market's price rationing function clearly in Figure 5.1. As the price rises from $10, the quantity demanded declines along the demand curve, moving from point C (20 million kilograms) toward point B (16 million kilograms). The higher prices mean that restaurants must charge much more for lobster rolls and stuffed lobsters. As a result, many people simply decide to stop buying lobster or order it less frequently when they dine out. Some restaurants drop it from the menu entirely, and some shoppers at the fish counter turn to lobster substitutes such as swordfish and salmon.

As the price rises, lobster trappers (suppliers) also change their behaviour. They stay out longer than they did when the price was $10 per kilogram. Quantity supplied

FIGURE 5.1

The Market for Lobsters

Suppose that in 1998, 50 000 square kilometres of lobstering waters off the coast of Atlantic Canada are closed. The supply curve shifts to the left. Before the waters are closed, the lobster market is in equilibrium at the price of $10 and a quantity of 20 million kilograms. The decreased supply of lobster leads to higher prices, and a new equilibrium is reached at $13.75 and 16 million kilograms.

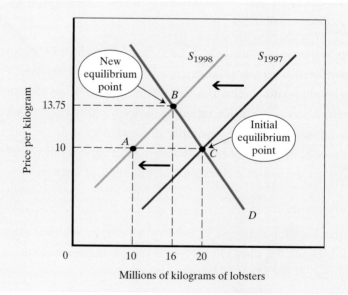

increases from 10 million kilograms to 16 million kilograms. This increase in price brings about a movement along the 1998 supply curve from point *A* to point *B*.

Finally, a new equilibrium is established at a price of $13.75 per kilogram and a total output of 16 million kilograms. At the new equilibrium, total production is 16 million kilograms per year, and the market has determined who gets the lobsters. *The lower total supply is rationed to those who are willing and able to pay the higher price.*

This idea of "willingness to pay" is central to the distribution of available supply, and willingness depends on both desire (preferences) and income/wealth. Willingness to pay does not necessarily mean that only the very rich will continue to buy lobsters when the price increases. Lower-income people may continue to buy some lobster, but they will have to be willing to sacrifice more of other goods in order to do so.

In sum:

> The adjustment of price is the rationing mechanism in free markets. Price rationing means that whenever there is a need to ration a good—that is, when excess demand exists—in a free market, the price of the good will rise until quantity supplied equals quantity demanded—that is, until the market clears.

There is some price that will clear any market you can think of. Consider the market for a famous painting such as Van Gogh's *Portrait of Dr. Gachet*. Figure 5.2 illustrates the operation of such a market. At a low price, there would be an enormous excess demand for such an important painting. The price would be bid up until there was only one remaining demander. The demander who gets the painting would be the one who is willing and able to pay the most. Presumably, that price would be very high. In fact, Van Gogh's *Portrait of Dr. Gachet* sold for a record US $82.5 million in 1990. If the product is in strictly scarce supply, as a single painting is, its price is said to be *demand determined*; that is, its price is determined solely and exclusively by the amount that the highest bidder or bidders are willing to pay.

One might interpret the statement that "there is some price that will clear any market" to mean "everything has its price." But that is not exactly what it means.

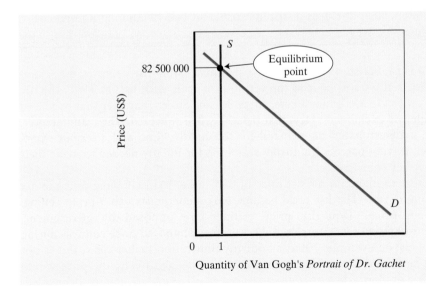

FIGURE 5.2

Market for a Rare Painting

There is some price that will clear any market, even if supply is strictly limited. In an auction for a unique painting, the price (bid) will rise to eliminate excess demand until there is only one bidder willing to purchase the single available painting.

Suppose you own a small silver bracelet that has been in your family for many generations. It is quite possible that you wouldn't sell it for *any* amount of money. Does this mean that the market is not working, or that quantity supplied and quantity demanded are not equal? Not at all. It means simply that *you* are the highest bidder. By turning down all bids, you are setting your own price, revealing that the bracelet is worth more to you than to those who bid on it. To keep the bracelet, you must be willing to forgo what anybody offers for it.

CONSTRAINTS ON THE MARKET AND ALTERNATIVE RATIONING MECHANISMS

On occasion, both governments and private firms decide to use some mechanism other than the market system to ration an item for which there is excess demand at the current price. (This was often the case in the former Soviet Union and other Communist nations like Cuba. See the Global Perspective box on page 108 titled "The Market Comes to Cuba" for more details.) Policies designed to stop price rationing are commonly justified in a number of ways.

The rationale most often used is fairness. It is not "fair" to let landlords charge high rents, not "fair" for oil companies to run up the price of gasoline, not "fair" for insurance companies to charge enormous premiums, and so on. After all, the argument goes, we have no choice but to pay—housing and insurance are necessary, and one needs gasoline to get to work. While it is not precisely true that price rationing allocates goods and services solely on the basis of income and wealth, income and wealth do constrain our wants. Why should all the gasoline or all the tickets to the World Series go just to the rich? it is asked.

Various schemes to keep price from rising to equilibrium are based on several perceptions of injustice, among them (1) that price-gouging is bad, (2) that income is unfairly distributed, and (3) that some items are necessities, and everyone should be able to buy them at a "reasonable" price. Regardless of the rationale, the following examples will make two things clear:

> 1. Attempts to bypass price rationing in the market and to use alternative rationing devices are much more difficult and costly than they would seem at first glance.
>
> 2. Very often, such attempts distribute costs and benefits among households in unintended ways.

■ **Tickle Me Elmo, Christmas 1996** Every Christmas, some toy captures the imagination of children who place it at the very top of their wish list. In 1996, the toy of choice was Tickle Me Elmo, a cute, fuzzy Sesame Street character that produced a short giggle and exclaimed "Hey, that tickles" when squeezed. The manufacturer, Tyco Toys, underestimated the demand for the cuddly Elmo and a serious shortage emerged, leaving parents frantically searching for the toy needed to make their children's wishes come true.

price ceiling *A maximum price that sellers may charge for a good, usually set by government.*

Tyco chose to maintain the list price of $35 rather than allowing prices to act as a rationing device. The list price became what economists call a **price ceiling**, or maximum price. Typically price ceilings are imposed by government. (Government-imposed rent controls and government-imposed price controls during wartime are classic examples.) But, as our toy illustration makes clear, this is not always the case. Had the market been allowed to operate freely, the price would have increased dramatically until quantity supplied was equal to quantity demanded.

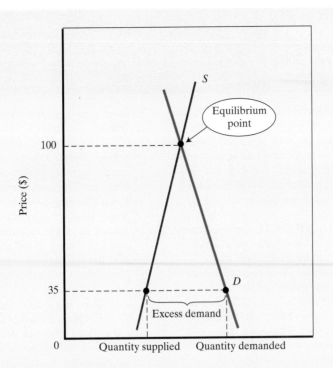

FIGURE 5.3

Excess Demand Created by a Price Ceiling of $35

If the price had been set by the interaction of supply and demand, the price of a Tickle Me Elmo doll would have been approximately $100. At $35, the quantity demanded exceeded the quantity supplied. Since the price system was not allowed to function, an alternative rationing system had to be found to distribute the available supply of the toy.

Those willing and able to pay a high price would have been the ones to get the available Tickle Me Elmos.

You can see the effects of the price ceiling by looking carefully at Figure 5.3. If the price had been set by the intersection of supply and demand it would have increased to approximately $100. But, at a price of $35, quantity demanded exceeded quantity supplied and a state of excess demand existed. Because Tyco and almost all retailers selling the toy opted to maintain the list price, other rationing devices were needed.

A number of rationing devices were used to allocate the scarce dolls. The most common nonprice rationing system is **queuing,** a term that simply means waiting in line. Desperate parents returned again and again to stores (a real cost to the parents) in search of the elusive toy. In Fredericton, New Brunswick, a Wal-Mart store advertised an Elmo special for one hour, beginning at 3 A.M. (yes, in the morning!). Three hundred shoppers showed up to compete for 48 Elmos. An unsuspecting employee suffered two cracked ribs and a concussion when the shoppers stampeded. Under this system Elmos went to those who were willing to get up at 3 A.M. and fight for the scarce product.

A second nonprice rationing device used was that of **favoured customers.** Some retailers simply reserved their limited stock of Elmos for friends, relatives, and favoured customers. Not surprisingly many customers tried to become "favoured" by offering side payments to store managers.

With so many people desperate for the Tickle Me Elmo toy, scalpers emerged. Some scalpers were able to find customers willing to pay over $500. In this case, resale was legal since the price ceiling was imposed by the producer and the retailers. However, if the ceiling had been imposed by government, resale at a higher

queuing *A nonprice rationing mechanism that uses waiting in line as a means of distributing goods and services.*

favoured customers *Those who receive special treatment from dealers during crises.*

Price rationing allocates goods and services to those who are willing and able to pay for them. One of the central premises of communism is that price rationing for basic necessities, such as food, is unfair; everyone should be able to afford such items as food and shelter. But regulating prices to "fair" levels below equilibrium means that quantity supplied will be less than quantity demanded.

In addition, preventing the price mechanism from operating requires that some device other than price be used to ration the available goods. Before the collapse of communism in the Soviet Union and Eastern Europe, people waited in long lines at state stores, which could not meet the citizens' demands. The stores were not well stocked in part because farmers could get a much better price for their goods on the illegal black market.

Although Cuba has remained committed to communist principles,

in 1994 the door opened for the first time to market-oriented reforms. Farmers are now allowed to sell some of their products in an open market. The hope is that higher prices will result in greater quantities of agricultural goods supplied:

SAN NICOLÁS, Cuba—This might have been called a market town when there was still anything much to buy. But as farmers rumbled into it this weekend on loaded-down tractors and their customers came however they could, San Nicolás seemed almost in the midst of a new discovery.

A marketplace of sorts was set up on the long concrete platform that had housed the local "free farmers' market" until 1986, when the ruling Communist Party abolished it and others as a dangerous devi-

ation from the revolutionary course . . . .

[The marketplace was established as] a step to halt the economic free fall that began in 1989 with the collapse of Cuba's trading partners in the Soviet bloc. . . After meeting quotas for the state, farmers will be allowed to sell their surplus produce in public markets at whatever price they can get . . . .

"This is a start," said Elvira Núñez, a slight 73-year-old woman who was delicately packing a few squashes into a shopping bag made from an old sugar sack. "Because people have to eat in order to live."

Source: Tim Golden, "Cubans Get a Taste of Capitalism," *The New York Times,* September 26, 1994, p. A1.

---

black market *A market in which illegal trading takes place at market-determined prices.*

ration coupons *Tickets or coupons that entitle individual persons to purchase a certain amount of a given product per month.*

price would have been illegal. But even when governments impose price ceilings and do their best to enforce them, new markets often emerge. These illegal or **black markets** generate prices determined by supply and demand. (For more details on the black market, see the Issues and Controversies box on page 110 titled "Tickets? Supply Meets Demand on the Sidewalk.")

While it is unlikely to be used for dolls, we should note a fourth nonprice rationing device: **ration coupons.** Ration coupons were employed in Canada in the 1940s when the government imposed wartime price ceilings on meat, sugar, gasoline, and many other items. The ration coupon entitled a family to a specific quantity of the product per month. The ration coupon was supposed to ensure that everyone received the same amount, regardless of income.

When ration coupons are used with no prohibition against trading them, however, the result is very similar to a system of price rationing. Those who are willing and able to pay the most simply buy up the coupons and use them to purchase gasoline, chocolate, fresh eggs, or anything else that is sold at a restricted price.[1] This means that the price of the restricted good will effectively rise to the market clearing price. For instance, suppose that you decide not to sell your ration coupon.

---

[1]Of course, if you are assigned a number of coupons and sell them, you are better off than you would be with price rationing. Ration coupons thus serve as a way of redistributing income.

You are then forgoing what you would have received by selling the coupon. Thus the real price of the good you purchase will be higher (if only in opportunity cost) than the restricted price. Even when trade in coupons is declared illegal, it is virtually impossible to stop black markets from developing.

■ **The World Cup, 1994** Another way to understand the rationing function of the price system is to look at the ways in which tickets to popular sporting events and concerts are sold and distributed. One of the most interesting recent examples is the 1994 World Cup soccer tournament.

In the summer of 1994, the World Cup came to the United States. The matches took place in nine cities, including Boston, Washington, Chicago, and Los Angeles. A total of 52 games were played among qualifying teams representing 24 countries. The final game between Italy and Brazil was played on July 17 in the Rose Bowl in Pasadena, California. (Brazil won.)

Regarding supply, a total of 3.6 million tickets were available for the games. Demand for soccer tickets was very high. Soccer is without question the most popular sport in the world, and it is literally true that wars have been fought because of the outcome of matches. With national pride at stake, tens of thousands of people flocked to the United States. In addition, the sport's growing popularity in the United States led to high ticket demand by U.S. residents. Rather than charging market-clearing prices, the event's organizers decided to charge "fair" prices and set the average ticket price at about US$58.

This price was below equilibrium, and there was excess demand for the tickets almost from the time that they went on sale. Interestingly, organizers of similar high-interest sporting events (like the Super Bowl, the NBA playoffs, and the World Series) almost always price tickets below the level that would just fill the stadiums. Why? In their words, to do otherwise would be "unfair"; only the "rich" would be able to attend if prices were set too high. As Alan Rothenberg, Chairman of World Cup USA, put it: "We definitely could have charged more. . . . Obviously we wanted to price the tickets high enough so we can pay for the event. . . . but at the same time not be unfair to the public."

We have seen, however, that if the price system is not going to be used to allocate the tickets among demanders, another method must be found. One method gives the tickets to certain favoured customers. *The Washington Post* (December 25, 1993) reported that 25% to 30% of the seats at RFK Stadium in Washington, D.C. were committed to "corporate sponsors, city officials, members of Congress, and other dignitaries." Another 15% were held for soccer's world governing body, and yet another 15% were held for the "U.S. soccer community"—coaches, officials, and players. The remaining tickets were sold through a mail lottery and, in some cities, by queuing.

The distribution of tickets was not really over until the final match was played. Consider the demand for tickets to the final match that were distributed to fans months earlier. The organizing body did charge

When soccer mania hit the United States in 1994, the demand for tickets for the World Cup final games was very high. Rather than charging market-clearing prices for tickets, the event's organizers decided to charge "fair" prices. As a result, a lucrative underground market for the tickets developed. Many people showed that they were willing and able to pay in excess of US$3000 per ticket.

Whenever a limit is placed on price, there is the opportunity for profit. "Scalpers" make their living by obtaining tickets (either by standing in line or by buying them from those willing to sell) and then reselling those tickets to those willing to pay more. In most provinces, scalping is illegal. The point of restricting prices, whether done by private promoters or the government, is to make the tickets available at affordable prices. Remember, however, that if that price is set below equilibrium, some nonprice rationing mechanism—such as standing in line, a lottery, or favoured customers—must be used to distribute the tickets.

Is scalping good or bad for society? A recent decision by a Toronto judge to throw out a scalping conviction against a ticket broker has raised the question of whether scalping should be illegal. The same question has been raised in New York City.

Ticket scalping has been very good to Kevin Thomas, and he makes no apologies. He sees himself as a classic American entrepreneur: a high-school dropout from the Bronx who taught himself a trade, works seven nights a week, earns $40 000 a year, and at age 26 has $75 000 in savings, all by providing a public service outside New York's theaters and sports arenas.

He has just one complaint. "I've been busted about 30 times in the last year," he said one recent evening, just after making $280 at a Knicks game. "You learn to deal with it—I give the cops a fake name, and I pay the fines when I have to, but I don't think it's fair. I look at scalping like working as a stockbroker, buying low and selling high. If people are willing to pay me the money, what kind of problem is that?"

It is a significant problem to public officials in New York and New Jersey, who are cracking down on street scalpers like Mr. Thomas and on licensed ticket brokers. Undercover officers are enforcing new restrictions on reselling tickets at marked-up prices, and the attorneys general of the two states are pressing well-publicized cases against more than a dozen ticket brokers.

But economists tend to see scalping from Mr. Thomas's perspective. To them, the governments' crusade makes about as much sense as the old campaigns by Communist authorities against "profiteering." Economists argue that the restrictions inconvenience the public, reduce the audience for cultural and sports events, waste the police's time, deprive New York City of tens of millions of dollars of tax revenue, and actually drive up the cost of many tickets.

Think carefully about the arguments presented. What side are you on?

Sources: "Judge Throws out Scalping Conviction," *Canadian Press Newswire*, September 22, 1995; John Tierney, "Tickets? Supply Meets Demand on the Sidewalk," *The New York Times*, December 26, 1992.

more for final game tickets—the price of the cheapest ticket was US$180 and the most expensive US$475, with the average around US$300. But consider the potential demand! As *Worth* magazine (May 1994) put it, "Foreign fans will be waving huge wads of bills near game day." Because the Rose Bowl holds only 91 794 people, by some estimates the equilibrium ticket price was in the vicinity of US$3000!

Figure 5.4 illustrates the situation. The supply curve is vertical at 91 794 tickets—the fixed number of seats available. As the demand curve shows, some people were willing to pay prices far in excess of US$3000—and many did. The *Los Angeles Times* reported that one man paid US$250 000 for a set (unspecified number) of tickets. Even before tickets were issued, an extensive and complicated black market had begun operating. Ticket agents and scalpers ran advertisements in newspapers offering thousands of dollars for good seats in order to resell them at a profit.

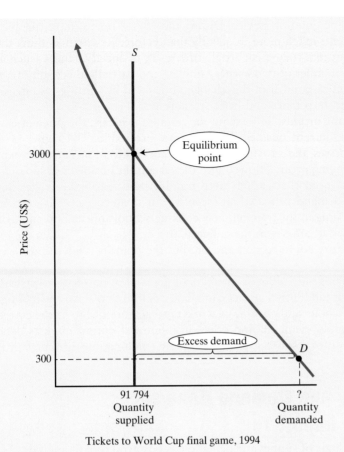

Price (US$)

3000 - - - - - - - - - - - - - - - ◯ Equilibrium point

S

300 - - - - - - - - - ◯ Excess demand - - - - - - D

91 794
Quantity
supplied

?
Quantity
demanded

Tickets to World Cup final game, 1994

FIGURE 5.4

Supply of and Demand for World Cup Final Game Tickets, Brazil versus Italy, July 17, 1994

World Cup 1994 final game tickets were initially sold for an average face price of about US$300. The Rose Bowl in Pasadena holds 91 794 people. Thus, the supply curve is vertical at 91 794 tickets. At US$300, the quantity demanded far exceeded the quantity supplied. The result was enormous excess demand.

Now consider someone who paid US$180 for a final game ticket and went to the game. What price did she really pay to go to the game? The answer: a lot more than US$180, since she could easily have sold her ticket for 15 times what she paid for it. All of a sudden the opportunity cost of going to the game changed. To attend the final game she had to give up the opportunity to sell her ticket at a great profit. By not selling her ticket, she revealed that going to the game was worth more to her than all the other things that US$3000 or US$4000 could buy.

What, then, can we conclude about alternatives to the price rationing system?

No matter how good the intentions of private organizations and governments, it is very difficult to prevent the price system from operating and to stop willingness to pay from asserting itself. Every time an alternative is tried, the price system seems to sneak in the back door. With favoured customers and black markets, the final distribution may be even more unfair than that which would result from simple price rationing.

PRICES AND THE ALLOCATION OF RESOURCES

Thinking of the market system as a mechanism for allocating scarce goods and services among competing demanders is very revealing. But the market determines much more than just the distribution of final outputs. It also determines what gets produced and how resources are allocated among competing uses.

Consider a change in consumer preferences that leads to an increase in demand for a specific good or service. During the 1970s, for example, people began going to restaurants much more frequently than before. Researchers think that this trend, which continues today, is partially the result of social changes (such as a dramatic rise in the number of two-earner families) and partially the result of rising incomes. The market responded to this change in demand by shifting resources, both capital and labour, into more and better restaurants.

With the increase in demand for restaurant meals, the price of eating out rose, and the restaurant business became more profitable. The higher profits attracted new businesses and provided old restaurants with an incentive to expand. As new capital, seeking profits, flowed into the restaurant business, so too did labour. New restaurants need chefs. Chefs need training, and the higher wages that came with increased demand provided an incentive for them to get it. In response to the increase in demand for training, new cooking schools opened up and existing schools began to offer courses in the culinary arts.

This story could run on and on, but the point is clear:

> Price changes resulting from shifts of demand in output markets cause profits to rise or fall. Profits attract capital; losses lead to disinvestment. Higher wages attract labour and encourage workers to acquire skills. At the core of the system, supply, demand, and prices in input and output markets determine the allocation of resources and the ultimate combinations of things produced.

Supply and Demand Analysis: An Oil Import Tax

The basic logic of supply and demand is a powerful tool of analysis. As an extended example of the power of this logic we will consider a recent policy proposed in the United States to tax imports of oil into that country. This policy proposal—which is designed to protect U.S. producers from foreign competition (including competition from Canadians)—is similar to the proposals affecting durum wheat, potatoes, and softwood lumber which were instrumental in provoking Canada to pursue the Free Trade Agreement (FTA) with the U.S. in 1987. Despite the FTA and the subsequent NAFTA agreement, the U.S. Congress still contemplates protectionist measures on occasion.

Consider the following background information. Between 1985 and 1989, the United States increased its dependence on oil imports dramatically. In 1989, total U.S. demand for crude oil was 13.6 million barrels per day. Of that amount, only 7.7 million barrels per day (57%) were supplied by U.S. producers, with the remaining 5.9 million barrels per day (43%) imported. Approximately 750 000 barrels of Canadian-produced oil were shipped to the U.S. each day in 1989. The price of oil on world markets that year averaged US$18.

A stiff tax on oil imports was recommended by policy analysts, members of Congress, environmentalists, and industry representatives. A number of arguments in support of the tax were advanced. First, some argued that the tax would enhance national security by reducing dependence on foreign energy sources and increasing national production. Second, some claimed the tax would reduce oil consumption and improve air quality by reducing automobile use. Third, politicians saw the tax as a new source of revenue to help reduce a government deficit running at over $200 billion per year. Finally, the industry noted that the tax would increase incomes and possibly employment of those working within the energy oil sector.

Simple supply and demand analysis makes the arguments in support of the import fee easier to understand. The two diagrams in Figure 5.5 on page 113 show the

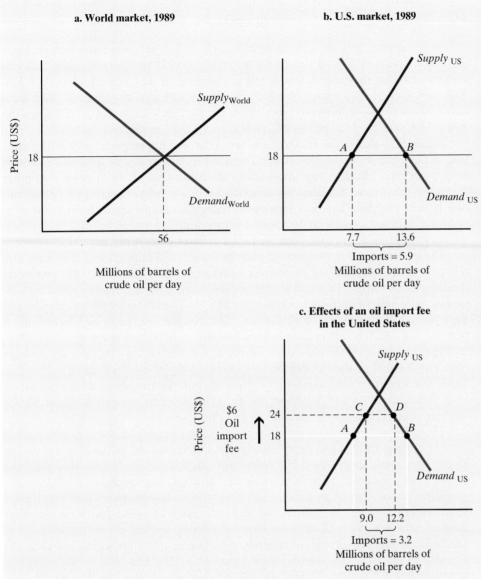

a. World market, 1989

Price (US$)

$Supply_{World}$

18

$Demand_{World}$

56

Millions of barrels of
crude oil per day

b. U.S. market, 1989

$Supply_{US}$

18   A   B

$Demand_{US}$

7.7   13.6

Imports = 5.9

Millions of barrels of
crude oil per day

**c. Effects of an oil import fee
in the United States**

Price (US$)

$Supply_{US}$

$6
Oil
import
fee   24   C   D
             18   A   B

$Demand_{US}$

9.0   12.2

Imports = 3.2

Millions of barrels of
crude oil per day

FIGURE 5.5

**The World and U.S. Markets
for Crude Oil, 1989**

At a world price of US$18, pro-
duction in the United States is
7.7 million barrels per day and
the total quantity of oil demanded in the United States is
13.6 million barrels per day. The
difference is total imports (5.9
million barrels per day). If the
government levies a 33% tax on
imports, the price of a barrel of
oil rises to US$24. The quantity
demanded falls to 12.2 million
barrels per day. At the same
time, the quantity supplied by
U.S. producers increases to 9.0
million barrels per day, and the
quantity imported falls to 3.2 million barrels per day.

world market for crude oil and the U.S. market for crude oil in 1989. World production was about 56 million barrels per day in 1989, and the average world price
was (as we saw above) about US$18. These amounts are shown as the equilibrium
price and quantity in Figure 5.5a.

Figure 5.5b shows the U.S. market. Assume that the United States can buy all
the oil that it wants at the world price of US$18. This means that U.S. producers
cannot get away with charging any more than US$18 per barrel. (Why would any-
one pay more than $18 for a barrel of U.S.-produced oil when they can get as
much foreign oil as they want for $18 per barrel?) The curve labelled $Supply_{US}$
shows the amount that U.S. suppliers will produce at each price level. At a price
of $18, U.S. production is 7.7 million barrels. Stated somewhat differently, U.S.
producers will produce at point *A* on the supply curve. The total quantity of oil
demanded in the United States in 1989 was 13.6 million barrels per day. This can
also be seen in Figure 5.5b. At a price of $18, the quantity demanded in the United
States is point *B* on the demand curve.

The difference between the total quantity demanded (13.6 million barrels per day) and U.S. production (7.7 million barrels per day) is total imports (5.9 million barrels per day).

Now suppose that the government levies a tax of 33% on imported oil. Since the import price is $18, a tax of $6 (or 0.33 × $18) per barrel means that importers of oil in the United States will pay a total of $24 per barrel ($18 + $6). This new higher price means that U.S. producers can also charge up to $24 for a barrel of crude. Note, however, that the tax is paid only on imported oil. Thus the entire $24 paid for U.S.-produced crude goes to U.S. producers.

Figure 5.5c shows the result of the tax. First, the higher price leads to a reduction in the quantity of oil demanded. The quantity demanded drops to 12.2 million barrels per day. This is a movement *along* the demand curve from point *B* to point *D*. At the same time, the quantity supplied by U.S. producers increases to 9.0 million barrels per day. This is a movement *along* the supply curve from point *A* to point *C*. With an increase in domestic quantity supplied and a decrease in domestic quantity demanded, imports decrease to 3.2 million barrels per day (12.2 − 9.0).[2]

The increase in U.S. production and the decrease in imports to 3.2 million barrels per day go a long way to address national security concerns. U.S. producers should also be happy. In a world without the tax the total revenue earned by U.S. producers is $50.589 billion per year (i.e., $18 × 7.7 million barrels per day × 365 days per year). In a world with the tax, their revenue increases to $78.84 billion per year (i.e., $24 × 9.0 million barrels per day × 365 days per year).

The tax also generates revenues for the U.S. government. The total tax revenue collected is equal to the tax per barrel ($6) times the number of imported barrels. Since the quantity imported is 3.2 million barrels per day, total revenue is $6 × 3.2 million, or $19.2 million *per day*. This amount is equal to about $7 billion per year ($19.2 million per day × 365 days per year).

The increased revenue enjoyed by the U.S. producers and the U.S. government must be coming from somewhere. Clearly, the U.S. consumers of gasoline are the big losers. They spend more on oil in a world with the tax and get less oil. (Calculate the difference in consumer expenditure using the information provided.)

What about Canadian producers? The reduction in imports into the United States initially inconveniences Canadian producers who must now look for other markets, which may entail new distribution systems. But the impact on revenues of Canadian producers ultimately depends on what happens on world markets. Oil not sold to the U.S. can always be sold elsewhere. The U.S. import tax results in an additional 2.7 million barrels per day for sale outside the U.S. The world market price will adjust to assure the market clears. If price falls, Canadian producers will lose revenue.

Elasticity

The principles of supply and demand enable us to make certain predictions about how households and firms are likely to behave in both national and international markets. When the price of a good rises, for example, households are likely to purchase less of it and firms are likely to supply more of it. When costs of production fall, firms are likely to supply more—supply will increase, or shift to the right. When the price of a good falls, households are likely to buy fewer substitutes—demand for substitutes is likely to decrease, or shift to the left.

---

[2]*These figures were not chosen randomly. It is interesting to note that in 1985 the world price of crude oil averaged about US$24 a barrel. U.S. production was 9.0 million barrels per day, and U.S. consumption was 12.2 million barrels per day, with imports of only 3.2 million. The drop in price between 1985 and 1989 increased imports to 5.9 million, an 84% increase.*

The size, or magnitude, of these reactions can be very important. In the early 1970s, the Organization of Petroleum Exporting Countries (OPEC) succeeded in increasing the world price of crude oil substantially. Because this strategy raised revenues to the oil-producing countries, we might expect this strategy to work for everyone. But if the banana-exporting countries, which we will call OBEC, had done the same thing, the strategy would not have worked.

Why? Suppose the banana-exporting countries decide to cut production by 30% in order to drive up the world price of bananas. At first, when the quantity of bananas supplied declines, the quantity demanded is greater than the quantity supplied and the world price rises. The issue for OBEC, however, is *how much* the world price will rise. That is, how much will people be willing to pay in order to continue consuming bananas? Unless the percentage *increase* in price is greater than the percentage *decrease* in output, the OBEC countries will lose revenues. And a little research shows us that the news is not good for OBEC. There are many reasonable substitutes for bananas. As the price of bananas rises, people simply eat fewer bananas and eat more pineapples or oranges. Many people are simply not willing to pay a higher price for bananas. The quantity of bananas demanded declines 30%—to the new quantity supplied—after only a modest price rise, and OBEC fails in its mission; its revenues decrease instead of increase.

The quantity of oil demanded is not nearly as responsive to a change in price as is the quantity of bananas demanded because no substitutes for oil are readily available. Oil products are used to run automobiles, heat homes, and run industrial equipment. When OPEC cut production, the price of oil rose sharply. Quantity demanded fell somewhat, but the world price increased by 400 percent. What makes the cases of OPEC and OBEC different is the *magnitude* of the response in the quantity demanded to a change of price.

The importance of actual measurement can hardly be overstated. Without the ability to measure and predict how much people are likely to respond to economic changes, all the economic theory in the world would be of little help to policy makers. In fact, most of the research being done in economics today involves the collection and analysis of quantitative data that measure behaviour. This is a dramatic change in the discipline of economics that has taken place only in the last 30 years.

Economists commonly measure responsiveness using the concept of **elasticity.** Elasticity is a general concept that can be used to quantify the response in one variable when another variable changes. If some variable, A, changes in response to changes in another variable, B, the elasticity of A with respect to B is equal to the percentage change in A divided by the percentage change in B:

elasticity *A general concept that can be used to quantify the response in one variable when another variable changes.*

$$\text{elasticity of } A \text{ with respect to } B = \frac{\%\Delta A}{\%\Delta B}$$

We may speak of the elasticity of demand or supply with respect to price, of the elasticity of investment with respect to the interest rate, or of the elasticity of tax payments with respect to income. We begin with a discussion of price elasticity of demand.

PRICE ELASTICITY OF DEMAND

You have already been exposed to the law of demand. Recall that, *ceteris paribus,* when prices rise, quantity demanded can be expected to decline, and when prices fall, quantity demanded can be expected to rise. The normal negative relationship between price and quantity demanded is reflected in the downward slope of demand curves.

■ **Slope and Elasticity**   The slope of a demand curve may in a rough way reveal the responsiveness of the quantity demanded to price changes, but slope can be quite misleading. In fact, it is not a good formal measure of responsiveness.

Consider a thirsty consumer who must decide how many 355-millilitre cans of pop to consume each week. Her choices are represented by the two identical demand curves in Figure 5.6. The only difference between the two is that quantity demanded is measured in cans in the graph on the left and in millilitres in the graph on the right. When we calculate the numerical value of each slope, however, we get very different answers. The curve on the left has a slope of $-1/10$, and the curve on the right has a slope of $-1/3550$, yet the two curves represent the *exact same behaviour.* If we had changed dollars to cents on the Y axis, the two slopes would be -10 and $-2/71$ respectively. (Review the Appendix to Chapter 1 if you don't understand how these numbers are calculated.)

The problem is that the numerical value of the slope of a line or curve depends on the units used to measure the variables on the axes. To correct this problem, we convert the changes in price and quantity to percentages. The price increase in Figure 5.6 leads to a decline of five cans, or 1775 millilitres, in the quantity of pop demanded—a decline of 50% from the initial 10 cans, or 3550 millilitres, whether we measure the pop in cans or millilitres.

We define **price elasticity of demand,** then, simply as the ratio of the percentage change in quantity demanded to the percentage change in price. Stated mathematically:

price elasticity of demand $= \dfrac{\%\ \text{change in quantity demanded}}{\%\ \text{change in price}}$

Percentage changes should always carry the sign (plus or minus) of the change. Positive changes, or increases, take a $(+)$. Negative changes, or decreases, take a $(-)$. The law of demand implies that price elasticity of demand is nearly always a negative number. Price increases $(+)$ will lead to decreases in quantity demanded $(-)$, and price decreases $(-)$ will lead to increases in quantity demanded $(+)$. Thus, the numerator and denominator should have opposite signs, resulting in a negative ratio.

■ **Types of Elasticity**   Table 5.1 gives the hypothetical responses of demanders to a 10% price increase in four markets. Insulin is absolutely necessary to an insulin-dependent diabetic, and the quantity demanded is unlikely to respond to an increase in price. When the quantity demanded does not respond at all to a price change, the percentage change in quantity demanded is zero, and the elasticity is zero. In this case, we say that the demand for the product is **perfectly inelastic.** Figure 5.7a on page 118 illustrates the perfectly inelastic demand for insulin. Because quantity demanded does not change *at all* when price changes, the demand curve is simply a vertical line.

Unlike insulin, basic telephone service is generally considered a necessity but not an absolute necessity. If a 10% increase in telephone rates results in a 1% decline in the quantity of service demanded, demand elasticity is $(-1 \div 10) = -0.1$.

When the percentage change in quantity demanded is smaller in absolute size than the percentage change in price, as is the case with telephone service, then elasticity is less than one in absolute size.[3] When a product has an elasticity between zero and minus (negative) one, we say that demand is **inelastic.** The demand for

---

[3]*The term* absolute size *or* absolute value *means ignoring the sign. The absolute value of –4 is 4; the absolute value of –3.8 is greater than the absolute value of 2.*

price elasticity of demand *The ratio of the percentage change in quantity demanded to the percentage change in price.*

perfectly inelastic demand *Demand in which quantity demanded does not respond at all to a change in price.*

inelastic demand *Demand that responds somewhat, but not a great deal, to changes in price. Inelastic demand always has a numerical value between zero and minus one.*

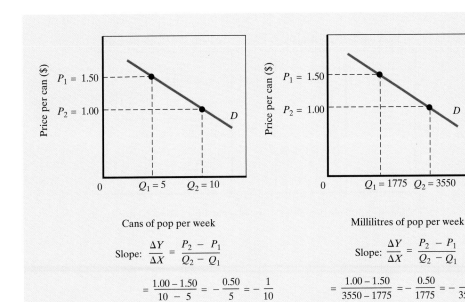

FIGURE 5.6

Slope Is Not a Useful Measure of Responsiveness of Demand

Changing the unit of measure from cans to millilitres changes the measured slope of the demand curve dramatically. But the behaviour of buyers in the two diagrams is identical. Since slope depends on the unit of measure on both X and Y axes, it is a poor measure of responsiveness.

basic telephone service is inelastic at -0.1. Stated simply, inelastic demand means that there is some responsiveness of demand, but not a great deal, to a change in price.

A warning: You must be very careful about signs. Because it is generally understood that demand elasticities are negative (demand curves have a negative slope), they are often reported and discussed without the negative sign. For example, a technical paper might report that the demand for housing "appears to be inelastic with respect to price, or less than one (0.6)." What the writer means is that the estimated elasticity is -0.6, which is between zero and minus one. Its absolute value is less than one.

Returning to Table 5.1, we see that a 10% increase in beef prices drives down the quantity of beef demanded by 10%. Demand elasticity is thus $(-10 \div 10) = -1$. When the percentage change in quantity of product demanded is the same as the percentage change in price in absolute value, we say that the demand for that product has **unitary elasticity.** The elasticity of a unitarily elastic product is always minus one (-1). As Table 5.1 shows, the demand for beef has unitary elasticity.

When the percentage decrease in quantity demanded is larger than the percentage increase in price in absolute size, we say that demand is **elastic.** The demand for bananas, for example, is likely to be quite elastic because there are many substitutes for bananas (other fruits, for instance). If a 10% increase in the price

unitary elasticity *A demand relationship in which the percentage change in quantity of a product demanded is the same as the percentage change in price in absolute value (a demand elasticity of minus one).*

elastic demand *A demand relationship in which the percentage change in quantity demanded is larger in absolute value than the percentage change in price (a demand elasticity with an absolute value greater than one).*

Table 5.1	Hypothetical Demand Elasticities for Four Products		
Product	**% Change in Price (%ΔP)**	**% Change in Quantity Demanded (%ΔQ_D)**	**Elasticity (%ΔQ_D / %ΔP)**
Insulin	+10%	0%	0 ⟶ Perfectly inelastic
Basic telephone service	+10%	−1%	−0.1 ⟶ Inelastic
Beef	+10%	−10%	−1.0 ⟶ Unitarily elastic
Bananas	+10%	−30%	−3.0 ⟶ Elastic

FIGURE 5.7

Perfectly Elastic and Perfectly Inelastic Demand Curves

Figure 5.7a shows a perfectly inelastic demand curve for insulin. Price elasticity of demand is zero. Quantity demanded is fixed; it does not change at all when price changes. Figure 5.7b shows a perfectly elastic demand curve for crude oil. A tiny price increase drives the quantity demanded to zero. In essence, perfectly elastic demand implies that individual producers can sell all they want at the going market price but cannot charge a higher price.

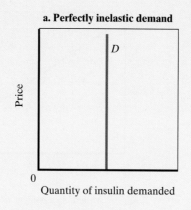

a. Perfectly inelastic demand

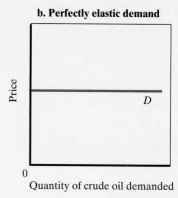

b. Perfectly elastic demand

perfectly elastic demand
Demand in which quantity demanded drops to zero at the slightest increase in price.

of bananas leads to a 30% decrease in the quantity of bananas demanded, the price elasticity of demand for bananas is $(-30 \div 10) = -3$. When the absolute value of elasticity exceeds one, demand is elastic.

Finally, if a small increase in the price of a product causes the quantity demanded to drop immediately to zero, demand for that product is said to be **perfectly elastic.** Suppose, for example, that you produce a product that can be sold only at a predetermined, fixed price. If you charged even one penny more, no one would buy your product because people would simply buy from another producer who hadn't raised the price. This is very close to reality for domestic oil producers, who cannot charge more than the world price for crude oil, and for farmers, who cannot charge more than the current market price for their crops.

A perfectly elastic demand curve is illustrated in Figure 5.7b. Because the quantity demanded drops to zero above a certain price, the demand curve for a perfectly elastic good is a horizontal line. Perfect elasticity implies that individual producers can sell all they want at a fixed price but cannot charge a higher price.

CALCULATING ELASTICITIES

Elasticities must be calculated cautiously. Return for a moment to the demand curves in Figure 5.6. The fact that these two identical demand curves have dramatically different slopes should be enough to convince you that slope is a poor measure of responsiveness.

The concept of elasticity circumvents the measurement problem posed by the graphs in Figure 5.6 by converting the changes in price and quantity into percentage changes. Recall that elasticity of demand is the *percentage* change in quantity demanded divided by the *percentage* change in price.

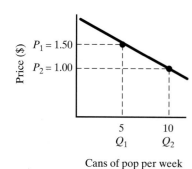

■ **Calculating Percentage Changes** Because we need to know percentage changes to calculate elasticity, let's begin our example by calculating the percentage change in quantity demanded. Figure 5.6a, reproduced in the margin, shows that the quantity of pop demanded increases from 5 cans (Q_1) to 10 cans (Q_2) when price drops from \$1.50 to \$1.00 per can. Thus, the change in quantity demanded is equal to $Q_2 - Q_1$, or 5 cans.

To convert this change into a percentage change, we must decide on a *base* against which to calculate the percentage. It is often convenient to use the initial value of quantity demanded (Q_1) as the base—that is, to calculate the change as a percentage of the initial value of quantity demanded.

To calculate percentage change in quantity demanded using the initial value as the base, the following formula is used:

$$\% \text{ change in quantity demanded} = \frac{\text{change in quantity demanded}}{Q_1} \times 100$$

$$= \frac{Q_2 - Q_1}{Q_1} \times 100.$$

In Figure 5.6, $Q_2 = 10$ and $Q_1 = 5$. Thus:

$$\% \text{ change in quantity demanded} = \frac{10 - 5}{5} \times 100 = \frac{5}{5} \times 100 = 100\%.$$

Expressing this equation verbally, we can say that an increase in quantity demanded from 5 cans to 10 cans is a 100% increase from 5 cans. Note that you arrive at exactly the same result if you use the diagram in Figure 5.6b, in which quantity demanded is measured in millilitres. An increase from Q_1 (1775 millilitres) to Q_2 (3550 millilitres) is a 100% increase.

We can calculate the percentage change in price in a similar way. Once again, let's use the initial value of P (that is, P_1) as the base for calculating the percentage. Using P_1 as the base, the formula for calculating the percentage change in P is simply:

$$\% \text{ change in price} = \frac{\text{change in price}}{P_1} \times 100$$

$$= \frac{P_2 - P_1}{P_1} \times 100.$$

In Figure 5.6a, P_2 equals 1.00, and P_1 equals 1.50. Thus, the change in P, or ΔP, is a negative number: $P_2 - P_1 = 1.00 - 1.50 = -0.50$. This is true because the change is a decrease in price. Plugging the values of P_1 and P_2 into the equation above, we get:

$$\% \text{ change in price} = \frac{1.00 - 1.50}{1.50} \times 100 = \frac{-0.50}{1.50} \times 100 = -33.3\%.$$

In other words, decreasing price from \$1.50 to \$1.00 is a 33.3% decline.

■ **Elasticity Is a Ratio of Percentages**   Once all the changes in quantity demanded and price have been converted into percentages, calculating elasticity is a matter of simple division. Recall that the formal definition of elasticity is:

$$\text{price elasticity of demand} = \frac{\% \text{ change in quantity demanded}}{\% \text{ change in price}}$$

If demand is elastic, the ratio of percentage change in quantity demanded to percentage change in price will have an absolute value greater than one. If demand is inelastic, the ratio will have an absolute value less than one. If the two percentages are exactly equal, so that a given percentage change in price causes an equal percentage change in quantity demanded, elasticity is equal to minus one; this is unitary elasticity.

Substituting the percentages calculated above, we see that a 33.3% decrease in price leads to a 100% increase in quantity demanded; thus:

$$\text{price elasticity of demand} = \frac{+100\%}{-33.3\%} = -3.0.$$

According to these calculations, the demand for pop is elastic.

■ **The Midpoint Formula** Although simple, the use of the initial values of P and Q as the bases for calculating percentage changes can be misleading. Let's return to the example of demand for pop in Figure 5.6a, where we have a change in quantity demanded of 5 cans. Using the initial value Q_1 as the base, we calculated that this change represents a 100% increase over the base. Now suppose that the price of pop rises back to $1.50, causing the quantity demanded to drop back to 5 cans. How much of a percentage decrease in quantity demanded is this? We now have $Q_1 = 10$ and $Q_2 = 5$. Using the same formula we used above, we get:

$$\begin{aligned}\% \text{ change in quantity demanded} &= \frac{\text{change in quantity demanded}}{Q_1} \times 100 \\ &= \frac{Q_2 - Q_1}{Q_1} \times 100 \\ &= \frac{5 - 10}{10} \times 100 = -50\%.\end{aligned}$$

Thus, an increase from 5 cans to 10 cans is a 100% increase (since the initial value used is 5), while a decrease from 10 cans to 5 cans is only a 50% decrease (since the initial value used is 10). This does not make much sense because in both cases we are calculating elasticity on the same interval on the demand curve. Changing "direction" of the calculation should not change the elasticity.

To describe percentage changes more accurately, a simple convention has been adopted. Instead of using the initial values of Q and P as the bases for calculating percentages, we use these values' *midpoints* as the bases. That is, we use the value halfway between P_1 and P_2 for the base in calculating the percentage change in price, and the value halfway between Q_1 and Q_2 as the base for calculating percentage change in quantity demanded.

midpoint formula *A more precise way of calculating percentages using the value halfway between P_1 and P_2 for the base in calculating the percentage change in price, and the value halfway been Q_1 and Q_2 as the base for calculating the percentage change in quantity demanded.*

Thus, the **midpoint formula** for calculating the percentage change in quantity demanded becomes:

$$\begin{aligned}\% \text{ change in quantity demanded} &= \frac{\text{change in quantity demanded}}{Q_1} \times 100 \\ &= \frac{Q_2 - Q_1}{(Q_1 + Q_2)/2} \times 100.\end{aligned}$$

Substituting the numbers from the original Figure 5.6a we get:

$$\% \text{ change in quantity demanded} = \frac{10 - 5}{(10 + 5)/2} \times 100 = \frac{5}{7.5} \times 100 = 66.6\%.$$

Using the point halfway between P_1 and P_2 as the base for calculating the percentage change in price, we get:

$$\% \text{ change in price} = \frac{\text{change in price}}{(P_1 + P_2)/2} \times 100$$

$$= \frac{P_2 - P_1}{(P_1 + P_2)/2} \times 100.$$

Substituting the numbers from the original Figure 5.6a yields:

$$\% \text{ change in price} = \frac{1.00 - 1.50}{(1.00 + 1.50)/2} \times 100 = \frac{-0.50}{1.25} \times 100 = -40.0\%.$$

We can thus say that a change from a quantity of 5 to a quantity of 10 is a +66.6% change using the midpoint formula, and a change in price from $1.50 to $1.00 is a −40% change using the midpoint formula.

Using these percentages to calculate elasticity yields:

$$\text{price elasticity of demand} = \frac{\% \text{ change in quantity demanded}}{\% \text{ change in price}} = \frac{66.6\%}{-40.0\%} = -1.67.$$

Using the midpoint formula in this case gives a lower demand elasticity, but the demand remains elastic because the percentage change in quantity demanded is still greater than the percentage change in price in absolute size.

The calculations based on the midpoint approach are summarized in Table 5.2.

■ **Elasticity Changes along a Straight-Line Demand Curve** An interesting and important point is that elasticity changes from point to point along a demand curve even if the slope of that demand curve does not change—that is, even along a straight-line demand curve. Indeed, the differences in elasticity along a demand curve can be quite large.

Consider the demand schedule shown in Table 5.3 and the demand curve in Figure 5.8. Henri works about 22 days per month in a downtown Vancouver office tower. On the top floor of the building is a nice dining room. If lunch in the dining room costs $10, Henri would eat there only twice a month. If the price of lunch falls to $9, he would eat there four times a month. (Henri would bring his lunch to work on other days.) If lunch were only a dollar, he would eat there 20 times a month.

Let's calculate price elasticity of demand between points *A* and *B* on the demand curve in Figure 5.8. Moving from *A* to *B*, the price of a lunch drops from

Table 5.3

Demand Schedule for Office Dining Room Lunches

Price (per Lunch)	Quantity Demanded (Lunches per Month)
$11	0
10	2
9	4
8	6
7	8
6	10
5	12
4	14
3	16
2	18
1	20
0	22

Table 5.2   **Calculating Price Elasticity**

First, calculate percentage change in quantity demanded (%ΔQ_D):

$$\% \text{ change in quantity demanded} = \frac{\text{change in quantity demanded}}{(Q_1 + Q_2)/2} \times 100 = \frac{Q_2 - Q_1}{(Q_1 + Q_2)/2} \times 100$$

Substituting the numbers from Figure 5.6:

$$\% \text{ change in quantity demanded} = \frac{10 - 5}{(10 + 5)/2} \times 100 = \frac{5}{7.5} \times 100 = 66.6\%$$

Next, calculate percentage change in price (%ΔP):

$$\% \text{ change in price} = \frac{\text{change in price}}{(P_1 + P_2)/2} \times 100 = \frac{P_2 - P_1}{(P_1 + P_2)/2} \times 100$$

Substituting the numbers from Figure 5.6:

$$\% \text{ change in price} = \frac{1.00 - 1.50}{(1.00 + 1.50)/2} \times 100 = \frac{-0.50}{1.25} \times 100 - 40.0\%$$

Price elasticity compares the percentage change in quantity demanded and the percentage change in price:

$$\frac{\% \Delta Q_D}{\% \Delta P} = \frac{66.6\%}{-40.0\%}$$

$$= -1.67$$

$$= \textit{Price elasticity of demand}$$

FIGURE 5.8

Demand Curve for Lunch at the Office Dining Room

Between points *A* and *B*, demand is quite elastic at −6.4. Between points *C* and *D*, demand is quite inelastic at −0.294.

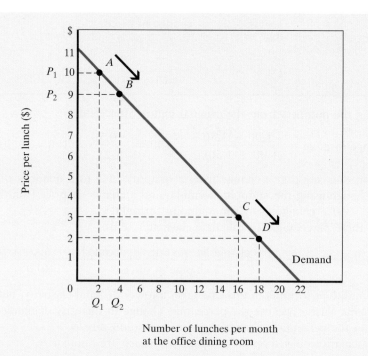

Price per lunch ($)

Number of lunches per month at the office dining room

$10 to $9 (a decrease of $1) and the number of dining room lunches that Henri eats per month increases from two to four (an increase of two). We will use the midpoint approach.

First, we calculate the percentage change in quantity demanded:

$$\% \text{ change in quantity demanded} = \frac{Q_2 - Q_1}{(Q_1 + Q_2)/2} \times 100.$$

Substituting the numbers from Figure 5.8, we get:

$$\% \text{ change in quantity demanded} = \frac{4 - 2}{(4 + 2)/2} \times 100 = \frac{2}{3} \times 100 = 66.7\%.$$

Next, we calculate the percentage change in price:

$$\% \text{ change in price} = \frac{P_2 - P_1}{(P_1 + P_2)/2} \times 100.$$

Substituting the numbers from Figure 5.8:

$$\% \text{ change in price} = \frac{9 - 10}{(9 + 10)/2} \times 100 = \frac{-1}{9.5} \times 100 = -10.5\%.$$

Finally, we calculate elasticity by comparing the two ratios as:

$$\text{elasticity of demand} = \frac{\% \text{ change in quantity demanded}}{\% \text{ change in price}}$$

$$= \frac{66.7\%}{-10.5\%} = -6.4.$$

The percentage change in quantity demanded is 6.4 times larger than the percentage change in price. In other words, Henri's demand between points *A* and *B* is quite responsive; his demand between points *A* and *B* is elastic.

Now consider a different movement along the same demand curve in Figure 5.8. Moving from point C to point D, the graph indicates that at a price of $3, Henri eats in the office dining room 16 times per month; if the price drops to $2, he eats there 18 times per month. These changes expressed in numerical terms are exactly the same as the price and quantity changes between points A and B in the figure—price falls $1, and quantity demanded increases by two meals. Expressed in percentage terms, however, these changes are very different.

Using the midpoints as the base, the $1 price decline is only a 10.5% reduction when price is up around $9.50, between points A and B. The same $1 price decline is a 40% reduction when price is down around $2.50, between points C and D. The two-meal increase in quantity demanded is a 66.7% increase when Henri averages only three meals per month, but it is only an 11.76% increase when he averages 17 meals per month. The elasticity of demand between points C and D is thus 11.76% divided by −40%, or −0.294. (Work these numbers out for yourself by using the midpoint formula.)

The percentage changes between A and B are very different from those between C and D, and so are the elasticities. Henri's demand is quite elastic (−6.4) between points A and B; a 10.5% reduction in price caused a 66.7% increase in quantity demanded. But his demand is inelastic (−0.294) between points C and D; a 40% decrease in price caused only an 11.8% increase in quantity demanded. In general, the elasticity of demand with a linear demand curve always varies as one moves along the demand curve. As an exercise try calculating the elasticity at different points on this demand curve to see how elasticity varies. Moreover, there will always be a point on a linear demand curve where the demand for the product has a unitary elasticity. In Figure 5.8 this occurs over the price range $6 to $5.

■ **Elasticity and Total Revenue**   We mentioned that OPEC was successful in the early 1970s in increasing its revenues by restricting supply and pushing up the market price of crude oil. We also argued that a similar strategy by OBEC, the Organization of Banana Exporting Countries, would probably fail. Why? The quantity of oil demanded is not as responsive to a change in price as is the quantity of bananas demanded. In other words, the demand for oil is more inelastic than is the demand for bananas.

We can now use the more formal definition of elasticity to make our argument that OPEC would succeed and OBEC would fail more precise. In any market, $P \times Q$ is total revenue (TR) received by producers:

$$TR = P \times Q$$
$$\text{total revenue} = \text{price} \times \text{quantity}$$

OPEC's total revenue is the price per barrel of oil (P) times the number of barrels its participant countries sell (Q). To wheat producers, total revenue is the price per tonne times the number of tonnes sold.

When price increases in a market, quantity demanded declines. As we've seen, when price (P) declines, quantity demanded (Q_D) increases. The two factors move in opposite directions:

Effects of price changes on quantity demanded
$$P \uparrow \longrightarrow Q_D \downarrow$$
and
$$P \downarrow \longrightarrow Q_D \uparrow .$$

Because total revenue is the product of P and Q, whether TR rises or falls in response to a price increase depends on which is bigger, the percentage increase in price or the percentage decrease in quantity demanded. If the percentage decrease in quantity demanded is smaller than the percentage increase in price, total revenue will rise. This is what occurs when demand is *inelastic*. In this case, the percentage price rise simply outweighs the percentage quantity decline, and $P \times Q = TR$ rises:

> Effect of price increase on a product with inelastic demand: $\uparrow P \times Q_D \downarrow = TR \uparrow$.

If, however, the percentage decline in quantity demanded following a price increase is larger than the percentage increase in price, total revenue will fall. This occurs when demand is *elastic*. The percentage price increase is outweighed by the percentage quantity decline:

> Effect of price increase on a product with elastic demand: $\uparrow P \times Q_D \downarrow = TR \downarrow$.

The opposite is true for a price cut. When demand is elastic, a cut in price increases total revenues:

> Effect of price cut on a product with elastic demand: $\downarrow P \times Q_D \uparrow = TR \uparrow$.

When demand is inelastic, a cut in price reduces total revenues:

> Effect of price cut on a product with inelastic demand: $\downarrow P \times Q_D \uparrow = TR \downarrow$.

Review the logic of these equations to make sure you understand the reasoning thoroughly.

With this knowledge, we can now easily see why the OPEC cartel was so effective. The demand for oil is inelastic. Restricting the quantity of oil available led to a huge increase in the price of oil—the percentage increase in the price of oil was larger in absolute value than the percentage decrease in the quantity of oil demanded. Hence, OPEC's total revenues went up. On the other hand, an OBEC cartel would not be effective because the demand for bananas is elastic. A small increase in the price of bananas results in a large decrease in the quantity of bananas demanded and thus causes total revenues to fall. For some details on the elasticity experiences of some other businesses, see the Application box on page 127 titled "London Newspapers and New York Restaurants Learn about Elasticity."

■ **Elasticity, Total Revenue, and the Linear Demand Curve** Figure 5.9 shows the relationship between the elasticity of demand and total revenue when the demand curve is linear. The top part of this figure shows the same demand curve as Figure 5.8. When we examined this demand curve earlier we found that demand for lunch in the office dining room was elastic over the price range from $10 to $9 (point *A* to point *B*), unitary elastic over the range $6 to $5 (point *C* to point *D*), and inelastic over the price range from $3 to $2 (point *E* to point *F*).

The relationship between total revenue and the elasticity of demand is illustrated in the bottom panel of Figure 5.9. When the price is $10 (point *A* in the top part of the figure), 2 units are sold for a total revenue of $20 (point *A'*). When the price is $9 (point *B* in the top part of the figure), 4 units are sold for a total revenue of $36 (point *B'*). As long as demand is elastic, reductions in price result in higher revenue. When price is $6 (point *C* in the top part of the figure), 10 units are sold for a total revenue of $60 (point *C'*). If price is $5 (point *D*), 12 units are sold and

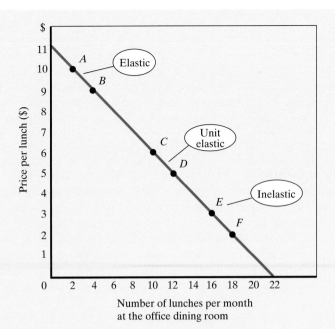

FIGURE 5.9

Relationship between Elasticity and Total Revenue

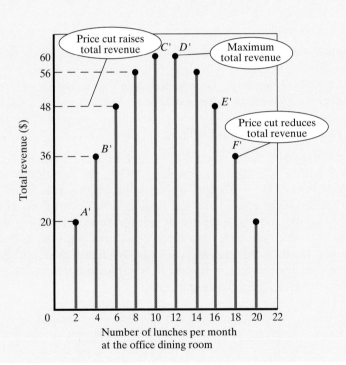

revenue is still $60 (point D'). Thus when demand is unitary elastic, changing price has no impact on total revenue. But if demand is inelastic, reducing price results in lower revenue. At a price of $3 (point E in the top part of the figure), 16 units are sold for a total revenue of $48 (point E'). When price is $2 (point F in the top part of the figure), 18 units are sold but total revenue is only $36 (point F').

Notice that total revenue is at a maximum when demand is unit elastic. This does not, however, imply that profits are maximized at this point. Profits depend on both costs and revenues and it is impossible to make definitive statements based only on revenue information.

THE DETERMINANTS OF DEMAND ELASTICITY

Elasticity of demand is a way of measuring the responsiveness of consumers' demand to changes in price. As a measure of behaviour, it can be applied to individual households or to market demand as a whole. I love peaches and I would hate to give them up. My demand for peaches is therefore inelastic. But not everyone is crazy about peaches, and, in fact, the market demand for peaches is relatively elastic. Because no two people have exactly the same preferences, reactions to price changes will be different for different people, and this makes generalizations hazardous. Nonetheless, a few principles do seem to hold.

■ **Availability of Substitutes**   Perhaps the most obvious factor affecting demand elasticity is the availability of substitutes. When substitute products are easily obtained, the quantity demanded is likely to respond quite readily to changes in price. Consider a number of farm stands lined up along a country road. If every stand sells fresh corn of roughly the same quality, Mom's Green Thumb will find it very difficult to charge a price much higher than the competition charges because a nearly perfect substitute is available just down the road. The demand for Mom's corn is thus likely to be very elastic. An increase in price will lead to a rapid decline in the quantity demanded of Mom's corn.

When substitutes are not readily available, demand is likely to be less elastic. In Table 5.1, we considered two products that have no readily available substitutes, local telephone service and insulin for diabetics, and there are many others. Demand for these products is likely to be perfectly inelastic.

■ **The Importance of Being Unimportant**   When an item represents a relatively small part of our total budget, we tend to pay little attention to its price. For example, if I pick up a pack of mints once in a while when I go to the supermarket, I might not even notice an increase in price from 25¢ to 35¢, yet that is a 40% increase in price. In cases such as these, we are not likely to respond very much to changes in price, and demand is likely to be inelastic.

■ **The Time Dimension**   When the OPEC countries cut output and succeeded in pushing up the price of crude oil in the early 1970s, few substitutes were immediately available. Demand was relatively inelastic, and prices rose substantially. During the last 25 years, however, we have had time to adjust our behaviour in response to the higher price, and the quantity of oil demanded has fallen dramatically. Automobiles manufactured today get more kilometres per litre, and some drivers have cut down on their driving. Millions have insulated their homes, most have turned down their thermostats, and some have explored alternative energy sources.

All this illustrates a very important point:

> The elasticity of demand in the short run may be very different from the elasticity of demand in the long run. In the longer run, demand is likely to become more elastic, or responsive, simply because households make adjustments over time and producers develop substitute goods.

OTHER IMPORTANT ELASTICITIES

So far we have been discussing price elasticity of demand, which measures the responsiveness of quantity demanded to changes in price. However, as we noted earlier, elasticity is a perfectly general concept. If B causes a change in A and we can measure the change in both, we can calculate the elasticity of A with respect to B. Let us look briefly at three other important types of elasticity: (1) income elasticity of demand, (2) cross-price elasticity, and (3) elasticity of supply.

Businesses must carefully consider the demand elasticity for their products when adjusting prices. Consider these two examples:

1. The London *Independent* During the summer of 1994, the *Independent*, a daily newspaper printed in London, announced a price cut to 30 pence from 50 pence. As a result, daily circulation increased from 240 000 copies to 280 000 copies. At first glance, the price cut might seem successful, but look closely at the result.

A price cut from 50 pence to 30 pence is a 60% reduction (50% using the midpoint formula). The increase in circulation each day is only 16.6% (15.4% using the midpoint formula). Thus, demand is *inelastic*:

$$\text{Elasticity} = \frac{+15.4\%}{-50.0\%} = -0.31$$

When demand is inelastic, a cut in price leads to a reduction in daily revenues.

Before: 50 pence × 240 000 copies = 12 000 000 pence (£120 000) in revenue

After: 30 pence × 280 000 copies = 8 400 000 pence (£84 000) in revenue

2. Restaurants in New York City In 1992, New York City was experiencing economic hard times. Unemployment was up, incomes were down, and there was great uncer-

tainty about the future. Like other businesses, restaurants were suffering. Fewer people were dining out, and those who were avoided the most expensive restaurants.

The 1992 Democratic National Convention in July brought thousands of visiting delegates and journalists to the city. But many feared the out-of-town visitors would suffer "sticker shock" and avoid the city's most expensive restaurants. (Prices in New York are much higher than in most other parts of the United States.) And so a plan was hatched. A group of 100 restaurants got together and offered lunch for US$19.92, and a number of them added special dinner menus with meals priced at US$24.92. These prices may sound high to you, but they were a substantial reduction for most of the participating restaurants!

The result: revenues were up during the convention. But what happened after the delegates left? Many restaurants decided to keep their prices down and got a real surprise: local demand was elastic.

How do you know that demand for meals at San Domenico is elastic? Can you infer from the numbers in the article approximately what the elasticity of demand is?

"We have been able to bring in new traffic," said Tony May, owner of San Domenico, on Central Park South, where the promotion has been continued.

Owners of New York's expensive restaurants have found that the demand for meals there can be quite elastic. When they lowered prices in 1992, demand increased enough to increase total revenues.

"I was very stubborn about lowering prices, but I learned a lesson. Besides, once they come into the restaurant, they don't all order the prix fixe menu." Mr. May added that while his average check has decreased about 20 percent during the promotion, his gross sales have grown about 30 percent.

Source: The New York Times, December 10, 1992, p. 1.

■ Income Elasticity of Demand **Income elasticity of demand,** which measures the responsiveness of demand with respect to changes in income, is defined as:

$$\text{income elasticity of demand} = \frac{\%\ \text{change in quantity demanded}}{\%\ \text{change in income}}$$

income elasticity of demand
Measures the responsiveness of demand with respect to changes in income.

Estimating income elasticities is important for many reasons. For example, income elasticities are useful in predicting how anticipated changes in income will change consumption of heavily taxed commodities such as alcohol, gasoline, and tobacco. This can help the government forecast its tax revenues. A study by A. Alley from the B.C. Ministry of Finance and Corporate Relations, and D. Ferguson and K. Stewart at the University of Victoria, estimated income elasticities for a variety of alcoholic beverages in British Columbia as ranging from about .29 for imported wines to .26 for spirits, to .06 for beer. So a 1% increase in income is estimated to increase B.C. imported wine consumption by only .3%. The change in beer consumption is even smaller.[4]

cross-price elasticity of demand *A measure of the response of the quantity of one good demanded to a change in the price of another good.*

■ **Cross-Price Elasticity of Demand**   **Cross-price elasticity of demand,** which measures the response of the quantity of one good demanded to a change in the price of another good, is defined as:

$$\text{cross-price elasticity of demand} = \frac{\% \text{ change in quantity of } Y \text{ demanded}}{\% \text{ change in price of } X}$$

Like income elasticity, cross-price elasticity can be either positive or negative. A *positive* cross-price elasticity indicates that an increase in the price of X causes the demand for Y to rise. This implies that the goods are substitutes. If cross-price elasticity turns out to be *negative,* an increase in the price of X causes a decrease in the demand for Y. This implies that the goods are complements.

elasticity of supply *A measure of the response of the quantity of a good supplied to a change in the price of that good. Likely to be positive in output markets.*

■ **Elasticity of Supply**   **Elasticity of supply,** which measures the response of the quantity of a good supplied to a change in price of that good, is defined as:

$$\text{elasticity of supply} = \frac{\% \text{ change in quantity supplied}}{\% \text{ change in price}}$$

In output markets, the elasticity of supply is likely to be a positive number— that is, a higher price leads to an increase in the quantity supplied, *ceteris paribus.* (Recall our discussion of upward-sloping supply curves in this chapter and the last.)

elasticity of labour supply *A measure of the response of labour supplied to a change in the price of labour. Can be positive or negative.*

In input markets, however, some interesting problems crop up. Perhaps the most studied elasticity of all is the **elasticity of labour supply,** which measures the response of labour supplied to a change in the price of labour. Economists have examined household labour supply responses to such government programs as welfare, social insurance, the income tax system, need-based student aid, and employment insurance, among others.

In simple terms, the elasticity of labour supply is defined as:

$$\text{elasticity of labour supply} = \frac{\% \text{ change in quantity of labour supplied}}{\% \text{ change in the wage rate}}$$

It seems reasonable at first glance to assume that an increase in wages increases the quantity of labour supplied. That would imply an upward-sloping supply curve and a positive labour supply elasticity. But this is not necessarily so. An increase in wages makes workers better off. They can work the same amount and have higher incomes. One of the things that they might like to "buy" with that higher income is more leisure time. "Buying" leisure simply means working fewer hours, and the "price" of leisure is the lost wages. Thus it is quite possible that an increase in wages to some groups will lead to a reduction in the quantity of labour supplied.

---

[4]*Alley, A., D. Ferguson, and K. Stewart, "An Almost Ideal Demand System for Alcoholic Beverages in British Columbia,"* Empirical Economics *vol. 17 (1992): 401–418.*

Looking Ahead

We have now examined the basic forces of supply and demand and discussed the nature of the market/price system and some other important concepts. These basic concepts will serve as building blocks for what comes next. Whether you are studying microeconomics or macroeconomics, you will be studying the function of markets and the behaviour of market participants in more detail in the following chapters.

Since the concepts presented in the first five chapters are so important to your understanding of what is to come, this might be a good point for a brief review of Part One.

Summary

The Price System: Rationing and Allocating Resources

1. In a market economy, the market system (or price system) serves two functions. It determines the allocation of resources among producers and the final mix of outputs. It also distributes goods and services on the basis of willingness and ability to pay. In this sense, it serves as a *price rationing* device.

2. Governments, as well as private firms, sometimes decide not to use the market system to ration an item for which there is an excess demand at current prices. Examples of nonprice rationing systems include *queuing, favoured customers,* and *ration coupons.* The most common rationale for policies or practices designed to avoid price rationing is "fairness."

3. Attempts to bypass the market and use alternative nonprice rationing devices are much more difficult and costly than it would seem at first glance. Schemes that open up opportunities for favoured customers, *black markets,* and side payments often end up less "fair" than the free market.

Supply and Demand Analysis: An Oil Import Tax

4. The basic logic of supply and demand is a powerful tool for analysis. For example, supply and demand analysis shows that an oil import tax will reduce quantity of oil demanded, increase domestic production, and generate revenues for the government.

Elasticity

5. *Elasticity* is a perfectly general measure of responsiveness that can be used to quantify many different relationships. If one variable, *A*, changes in response to changes in another variable, *B*, the elasticity of *A* with respect to *B* is equal to the percentage change in *A* divided by the percentage change in *B*.

6. The slope of a demand curve is an inadequate measure of responsiveness, because its value depends on the units of measurement used. For this reason, elasticities are calculated using percentages.

7. *Price elasticity of demand* is the ratio of the percentage change in quantity demanded of a good to the percentage change in price of that good. *Perfectly inelastic* demand is demand whose quantity demanded does not respond at all to changes in price; its numerical value is zero. *Inelastic* demand is demand whose quantity demanded responds somewhat, but not a great deal, to changes in price; its numerical value is between zero and negative one. *Elastic* demand is demand in which the percentage change in quantity demanded is larger in absolute value than the percentage change in price. Its absolute value is greater than one. *Unitary elasticity* of demand describes a relationship in which the percentage change in the quantity of a product demanded is the same as the percentage change in price; unitary elasticity has a numerical value of negative one. *Perfectly elastic* demand describes a relationship in which a small increase in the price of a product causes the quantity demanded for that product to drop to zero.

8. If demand is elastic, a price increase will reduce the quantity demanded by a larger percentage than the percentage increase in price, and total revenue ($P \times Q$) will fall. If demand is inelastic, a price increase will increase total revenue.

9. If demand is elastic, a price cut will cause quantity demanded to increase by a greater percentage than the percentage decrease in price, and total revenue

will rise. If demand is inelastic, a price cut will cause quantity demanded to increase by a smaller percentage than the percentage decrease in price, and total revenue will fall.

10. The elasticity of demand depends on (1) the availability of substitutes, (2) the importance of the item in individual budgets, and (3) the time frame in question.

11. There are several important elasticities. *Income elasticity of demand* measures the responsiveness of the quantity demanded with respect to changes in income. *Cross-price elasticity of demand* measures the response of the quantity of one good demanded to a change in the price of another good. *Elasticity of supply* measures the response of the quantity of a good supplied to a change in the price of that good. The *elasticity of labour supply* measures the response of the quantity of labour supplied to a change in the price of labour.

Review Terms and Concepts

black market 108

cross-price elasticity of demand 128

elastic demand 117

elasticity 115

elasticity of labour supply 128

elasticity of supply 128

favoured customers 107

income elasticity of demand 127

inelastic demand 116

midpoint formula 120

perfectly elastic demand 118

perfectly inelastic demand 116

price ceiling 106

price elasticity of demand 116

price rationing 103

queuing 107

ration coupons 108

unitary elasticity 117

Problem Set

1. Illustrate the following with supply and/or demand curves:
   a. A perfectly elastic demand curve.
   b. A labour supply curve along which elasticity of labour supply is positive.
   c. A situation of excess labour supply (unemployment) caused by a "minimum wage" law.
   d. The effect of a sharp increase in heating oil prices on the demand for insulation material.

2. The box on page 110 makes the argument that scalping, which is illegal in most provinces, may in fact serve a useful function. Do you agree or disagree? Write an essay explaining your answer.

3. A sporting goods store has estimated the demand curve for Brand A running shoes as a function of price. Use the following diagram to answer the questions below:
   a. Calculate demand elasticity using the midpoint formula between points *A* and *B*, between points *C* and *D*, and between points *E* and *F*.
   b. If the store currently charges a price of $50, then increases this price to $60, what happens to total revenue from shoe sales ($P \times Q$)? Repeat the exercise for initial prices of $30 and $10.

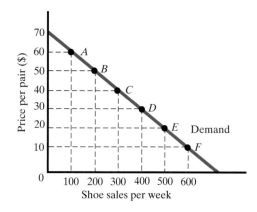

c. Explain why the answers to a. can be used to predict the answers to b.

4. In an effort to "support" the price of some agricultural goods, Agriculture Canada has at times paid farmers a subsidy for the land they leave unplanted. The rationale is that the subsidy increases the "cost" of planting and that it will reduce supply and increase the price of competitively produced agricultural goods. Critics argue that because the subsidy is a payment to farmers, it will reduce costs and lead to lower prices. Which argument is correct? Explain.

5. Illustrate the following with supply and/or demand curves:

    a. The federal government "supports" the price of wheat by paying farmers not to plant wheat on some of their land.

    b. As the economy has begun to recover from the recession of 1990-1992, incomes are rising and expectations about the future are becoming more positive. As a result, home prices in many parts of the country are rising.

    c. The impact of an increase in the price of chicken on the price of hamburger.

    d. In a bill to be presented to the Legislature, the MPPs of Ontario will be asked to vote on whether to abolish rent control. Under rent control, rents are held by law to levels below equilibrium. If rent control is discontinued, there will be an impact on housing demand and supply.

    e. Incomes rise, shifting the demand for gasoline. Crude oil prices rise, shifting the supply of gasoline. At the new equilibrium, the quantity of gasoline sold is less than it was before. (Crude oil is used to produce gasoline.)

6. "The price of blue jeans has risen substantially in recent years. Demand for blue jeans has also been rising. This is hard to explain because the law of demand says that higher prices should lead to lower demand." Do you agree?

7. Taxicab fares in most cities are regulated. Several years ago, taxicab drivers in a North American city obtained permission to raise their fares 10%, and they anticipated that revenues would increase by about 10% as a result. They were disappointed, however. When the commissioner granted the 10% increase, revenues increased by only about 5%.

    What can you infer about the elasticity of demand for taxicab rides? What were taxicab drivers assuming about the elasticity of demand?

8. Studies have fixed the short-run price elasticity of demand for gasoline at the pump at 0.20. Suppose that renewed conflict in the Persian Gulf leads to a sudden cutoff of crude oil supplies. As a result, U.S. supplies of refined gasoline drop 10%.

    a. If gasoline was selling for US$1.40 per gallon before the cutoff, how much of a price increase would you expect to see in the U.S. in the coming months?

    b. Suppose that the U.S. government imposes a price ceiling on gas at $1.40 per gallon. How would the relationship between consumers and gas station owners change?

9. For each of the following, say whether you agree or disagree and explain your answer.

    a. The demand curve pictured below is elastic.

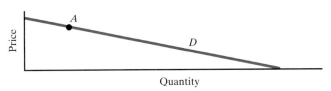

    b. If supply were to increase somewhat in the diagram below, prices would fall and firms would earn less revenue.

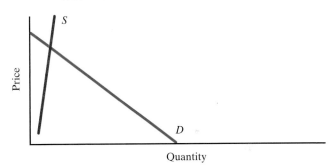

The Price System and the Community of Elliot Lake

Until the early 1950s, Elliot Lake was just another piece of northern Ontario wilderness. In many ways its development as a community was the product of the Cold War and a natural deposit of uranium. The existence of this deposit was known prior to the 1950s but there were few uses for this mineral at that time. With very little demand, the price of uranium remained low, which meant that there was no inducement for a profit-maximizing firm to mine the deposit.

The story of Elliot Lake's history after 1950 is easily told with the help of the simple but powerful demand and supply model. As an exercise try to follow the story by actually following events using the model. Initially demand and supply are equal at a low price and with very limited uranium production and consumption.

With the development of the first atomic weapon during World War II interest in uranium (which is used in the manufacture of atomic weapons) increased. As the U.S. and the Soviet Union embarked on an arms race in the early 1950s demand for uranium grew rapidly (a shift in the uranium demand curve). Rising uranium demand had a predictable effect on uranium prices: they rose. As prices rose, mining the deposit at Elliot Lake became attractive to a developer (which can be shown as a movement along the uranium supply curve).

But the mine developer faced a problem: there were no miners in Elliot Lake; it was simply a wilderness area. By offering a high wage and attractive fringe benefits (the

price of labour) the developer was able to attract the needed labour force. Why was a relatively high wage necessary? Because workers believed that there were opportunity costs associated with living in Elliot Lake: it was isolated relative to most communities, winters were cold, and black flies were a serious problem. But a high wage more than compensated for these costs and so workers were willing to locate to the community in return for this compensation.

As long as demand was strong and uranium prices high the mine at Elliot Lake and the surrounding community prospered. Houses were erected, a good hospital was built, and a network of businesses emerged to service the community, etc. But when the demand for uranium fell (a shift in the demand

curve) in response to the end of the Cold War uranium prices also fell. Mining at Elliot Lake became less attractive and production and employment fell (a movement along the supply curve). Workers looked elsewhere for employment and many left the community.

The collapse of the uranium price threatened the very existence of the Elliot Lake community. But in the end it did not destroy the community. Why? Because the mining industry had built a large stock of housing at Elliot Lake. With the exodus of workers due to cutbacks at the mine many homes were put up for sale (an increase in the supply of homes on the real estate market). But there was no work at the mine and thus no new workers interested in buying the homes (a decrease in demand). The impact on

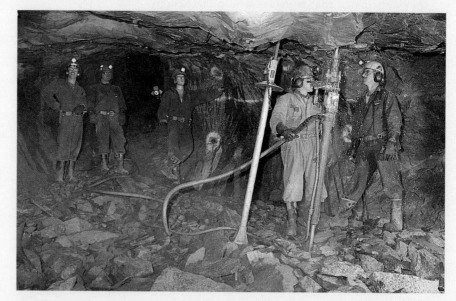

Elliot Lake developed around a single industry: uranium mining. But when uranium prices fell and mining stopped, the economic base of the community disappeared.

house prices was predictable: they fell dramatically.

The price of a home could, in principle, have fallen to zero and the wilderness could have eventually reclaimed the ghost town. For home owners the housing was a sunk cost. The expenditure they had made on their home in the past could not be undone in the present. But fortunately for these home owners the demand for housing in Elliot Lake was not perfectly price inelastic. When prices fell quantity demanded rose.

But who would demand a house in Elliot Lake? Without employment in the mine the opportunity cost of moving to Elliot Lake now included lost wages as well as the isolation, cold winters, and black flies. A free $100 000 house doesn't look that attractive if it means giving up a $35 000-a-year income each year for the rest of your life. However, if you do not have to give up your income to get a free house, the free house can look very attractive.

Who in our society is in a position to move to a place where there is no work without this having an effect on their income? Those who have retired are, since they receive a pension and other income from savings. Thus one might predict that retired people would be most likely to be interested in moving to Elliot Lake to take advantage of the low housing prices. In fact, this is exactly what happened. The influx of retired people assured housing prices did not fall to zero.

The adjustments at Elliot Lake are a remarkable testimony to the

Mining activity created a community with well developed community services in a location with many natural attractions. These assets, combined with low housing prices, attracted a new type of resident—retired people—who gave the community new life.

power of markets. Rather than becoming a ghost town, Elliot Lake became a vibrant retirement community.

Questions for Analytical Thinking

1. The influx of retired people to Elliot Lake was a result of low housing prices and a modern hospital. Explain, using basic economic principles, why the hospital might be an important attraction.

2. Which of the following two retired couples would be more likely to be interested in moving to Elliot Lake? The first couple lives in the Toronto suburb of Scarborough in a house that they purchased in 1952. Today the market value of that house is $220 000. The second couple

lives in Perth, Ontario, where they own a house that has a market value of $50 000. It was also purchased in 1952. Focus on opportunity cost in your answer.

3. Why is the supply of housing on the Elliot Lake real estate market unlikely to be perfectly inelastic?

4. What impact would a fall in housing prices in Toronto have on the demand for housing in Elliot Lake? Why?

5. Suppose a new use for uranium is invented and that the demand for uranium increases. How might this affect the community of Elliot Lake?

Video Resource: "Grey Acres," *The National Magazine*, May 21, 1996

6

Part Two

Foundations of
Microeconomics

Household Behaviour
and Consumer Choice

**Household Choice in Output
Markets**

The Determinants of Household
Demand

The Budget Constraint

The Basis of Choice: Utility

Diminishing Marginal Utility

Allocating Income to Maximize Utility

The Utility-Maximizing Rule

Diminishing Marginal Utility and
Downward-Sloping Demand

Income and Substitution Effects

Consumer Surplus

**Household Choice in Input
Markets**

The Labour Supply Decision

The Price of Leisure

Income and Substitution Effects of a
Wage Change

Saving and Borrowing: Present versus
Future Consumption

**A Review: Households in Output
and Input Markets**

Appendix: Indifference Curves

ow that we have discussed the basic forces of supply and demand,
we can explore the underlying behaviour of the two fundamental
decision-making units in the economy, households and firms.

Figure 6.1 presents a diagram of a simple competitive economy. The
figure is an expanded version of the circular flow diagram first presented
in Figure 4.1. It is designed to guide you through Part Two (Chapters
6–12) of this book. You will see the "big picture" much more clearly if
you follow this diagram closely as you work your way through this part
of the book. (For your convenience, the diagram will be repeated several
times in the next few chapters.)

Recall that households and firms interact in two kinds of markets: output (product) markets, shown at the top of Figure 6.1, and input (factor)
markets, shown at the bottom. Households *demand* outputs and *supply* inputs. In contrast, firms *supply* outputs and *demand* inputs. This chapter
explores the behaviour of households, focusing first on household demand
for outputs and then on household supply in labour and capital markets.

The remaining chapters in Part Two focus on firms and the interaction between firms and households. Chapters 7 through 9 analyze the behaviour of firms in output markets in both the short run and the long run.
Chapter 10 focuses on the behaviour of firms in input markets in general,
especially the labour and land markets. Chapter 11 discusses the capital
market in more detail. Chapter 12 puts all the pieces together and analyzes the functioning of a complete market system. Following Chapter 12,
Part Three of the book relaxes many assumptions and begins to analyze
market imperfections and the potential for and pitfalls of government

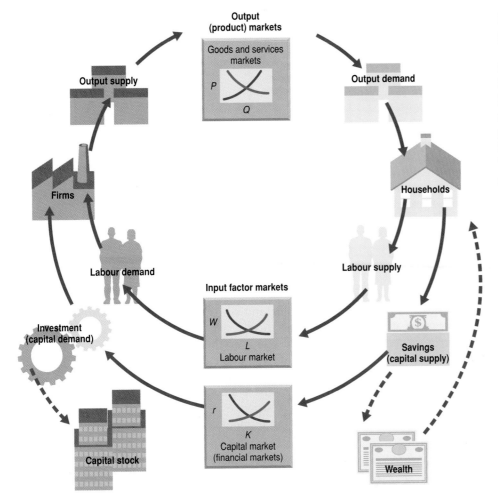

FIGURE 6.1

Firm and Household Decisions

Households demand in output markets and supply labour and capital in input markets. To simplify our analysis, we have not included the government and international sectors in this circular flow diagram. These topics will be discussed in detail later.

involvement in the economy. The plan for Chapters 6 through 17 is outlined in Figure 6.2.

Recall that throughout this book, all diagrams that describe the behaviour of households are drawn or highlighted in *blue*. All diagrams that describe the behaviour of firms are drawn or highlighted in *red*. Look carefully at the supply and demand diagrams in Figure 6.1, and notice that in both the labour and capital markets, the supply curves are blue. This is because labour and capital are supplied by households. The demand curves for labour and capital are red because firms demand these inputs for production.

■ **Assumptions**   Before we proceed with our discussion of household choice, we need to make a few basic assumptions. The key assumption that we make in Chapters 6 through 12 is that all markets are perfectly competitive. Recall from Chapter 3 that a *perfectly competitive* market is one in which no single firm is large enough to have any control over the price of its products or the prices of the inputs that it buys. Similarly, no single household in a perfectly competitive market has any control over the prices of the products that it buys or the prices of the inputs (labour and capital) that it sells.

FIGURE 6.2

Understanding the Micro-
economy and the Role of
Government

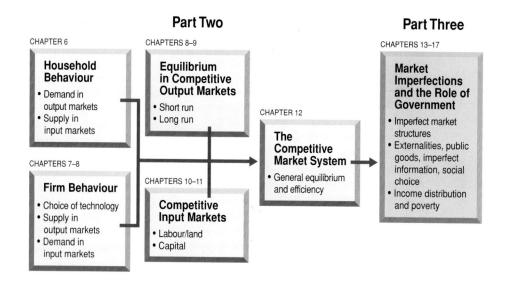

We also assume that households and firms possess all the information they need to make market choices. Specifically, we assume that households possess knowledge of the qualities and prices of everything available in the market. Firms know all that there is to know about wage rates, capital costs, and output prices. This is often referred to as the assumption of **perfect knowledge.**

By the end of Chapter 12 we will have a complete picture of an economy, but it will be based on this set of fairly restrictive assumptions. At first, this may seem unrealistic to you. Keep the following in mind, however:

> Much of the economic analysis in the chapters that follow applies to all forms of market structure. Indeed, much of the power of economic reasoning is that it is quite general. When we turn to imperfect markets in Part Three, we will discover that much of the decision-making logic described in Chapters 6 through 12 for both households and firms applies there as well. Since monopolists, oligopolists, monopolistic competitors, and perfect competitors share the objective of maximizing profits, it should not be surprising that their behaviour is in many ways similar. We focus here on perfect competition because many of these basic principles are easier to learn in the simplest of cases first.

perfect knowledge *The assumption that households possess a knowledge of the qualities and prices of everything available in the market and that firms have all available information regarding wage rates, capital costs, and output prices.*

Household Choice in Output Markets

Every household must make three basic decisions:

1. How much of each product, or output, to demand;
2. How much labour to supply; and
3. How much to spend today and how much to save for the future.[1]

In the pages that follow, we examine each of these decisions.

As we begin our fairly lengthy look at demand in output markets, you must keep in mind that the choices underlying the demand curve are only part of the larger household-choice problem. Closely related decisions about how much to

---

[1] *As you will see in Chapters 10 and 11, this decision is of primary importance in the capital market.*

work and how much to save are equally important and must be made simultaneously with output-demand decisions.

The Determinants of Household Demand

As we saw in Chapter 4,

> Several factors influence the quantity of a given good or service demanded by a single household:
> - The price of the product
> - The income available to the household
> - The household's amount of accumulated wealth
> - The prices of other products available to the household
> - The household's tastes and preferences, and
> - The household's expectations about future income, wealth, and prices

Demand schedules and demand curves express the relationship between quantity demanded and price, *ceteris paribus*. A change in price leads to a movement along a demand curve. Changes in income, in other prices, or in preferences shift demand curves to the left or right. We refer to these shifts as "changes in demand." But the interrelationship among these variables is more complex than the simple exposition in Chapter 4 might lead you to believe.

The Budget Constraint

Before we examine the household choice process, we need to discuss exactly what choices are open or not open to households. If you look carefully at the list of items that influence household demand, you will see that the first four actually define the set of options available:

> Information on a household's income and wealth, together with information on product prices, make it possible to distinguish those combinations of goods and services that are affordable from those that are not.[2]

Income, wealth, and prices thus define what we call a household's **budget constraint.** The budget constraint facing any household results primarily from limits imposed externally by one or more markets. In competitive markets, for example, households cannot control prices; they must buy goods and services at market-determined prices. A household has some control over its income. Its members can choose to work or not, and they can sometimes decide how many hours to work and how many jobs to hold. But constraints exist in the labour market, too. The amount that household members are paid is limited by current market wage rates; whether they can get a job is determined by the availability of jobs.

While income does in fact depend, at least in part, on the choices that households make, we will treat it as a given for now. Later on in this chapter we will relax this assumption and explore labour supply choices in more detail.

The income, wealth, and price constraints that surround the exercise of choice are best illustrated with an example. Consider Elisha, a recent graduate of the University of Lethbridge, who takes a job as an account manager at a

budget constraint *The limits imposed on household choices by income, wealth, and product prices.*

---

[2]*Remember that we drew the distinction between income and wealth in Chapter 4. Income is the sum of a household's earnings within a given period; it is a flow variable. Wealth, in contrast, is a stock variable; briefly, it is what a household owns minus what it owes at a given point in time.*

public relations firm. Let's assume that she receives a salary of $1000 per month (after taxes), and that she has no wealth and no credit. Elisha's monthly expenditures are limited to her flow of income. Table 6.1 summarizes some of the choices open to her.

A careful search of the housing market reveals four vacant apartments. The least expensive is a one-room studio with a small kitchenette that rents for $400 per month, including utilities. If she lived there, Elisha could afford to spend $250 per month on food and still have $350 left over for other things.

About four blocks away is a one-bedroom apartment with wall-to-wall carpeting and a larger kitchen. It has much more space, but it is 50% more expensive. The rent is $600, including utilities. If Elisha took this apartment, she might cut her food expenditures by $50 per month and have only $200 per month left for everything else.

In the same building as the one-bedroom apartment is an identical unit on the top floor of the building with a balcony facing west toward the sunset. The balcony and view add $100 to the monthly rent. To live there, Elisha would be left with only $300 to split between food and other expenses.

Just because she was curious, Elisha took a look at a townhouse in the suburbs that was renting for $1000 per month. Obviously, unless she could get along without eating or doing anything else that costs money, she could not afford it. The combination of the townhouse and any amount of food is outside her budget constraint.

Notice that we have used the information that we have on income and prices to identify different combinations of housing, food, and other items that are available to a single-person household with an income of $1000 per month. We have said nothing about the process of choosing. Rather, we have carved out what is called a **choice set** or **opportunity set,** the set of options that is defined and limited by Elisha's budget constraint.

choice set or opportunity set
The set of options that is defined and limited by a budget constraint.

■ **Preferences, Tastes, Trade-Offs, and Opportunity Cost**   So far, we have identified only the combinations of goods and services that are available to Elisha and those that are not. Within the constraints imposed by limited incomes and fixed prices, however, households are free to choose what they will buy and what they will not buy. Their ultimate choices are governed by their individual preferences and tastes.

It will help you to think of the household-choice process as a process of allocating income over a large number of available goods and services. A household's final demand for any single product is just one of many outcomes that result from the decision-making process. Think, for example, of a demand curve that shows a household's reaction to a drop in the price of air travel. There are certain periods every year when people travel less frequently. During these periods, special fares flood the market and many people decide to take trips that they otherwise would

Table 6.1	Possible Budget Choices of a Person Earning $1000 per Month after Taxes				
Bundle	Monthly Rent	Food	Other Expenses	Total	Available?
A	$400	$250	$350	$1000	Yes
B	600	200	200	1000	Yes
C	700	150	150	1000	Yes
D	1000	100	100	1200	No

Personal preferences play an important role in consumers' decision-making processes. Some beer drinkers prefer ales over lagers. Some like dark beers, others prefer light beers. The variety of types of beer on the market reflects differences in taste among beer drinkers.

not have taken. The decision to travel is a decision not to do or buy something else. If I live in Toronto and decide to spend $229 to visit my mother in Thunder Bay, that is $229 that I will not be spending on new clothes, dinners at a restaurant, or a new set of tires.

As you can see, then, a change in the price of a single good changes the constraints within which households choose, and this may change the entire allocation of income. Demand for some goods and services may rise while demand for others may fall. A complicated set of trade-offs lies behind the shape and position of a household's demand curve for a single good. Whenever a household makes a choice, it is really weighing the good or service it chooses against all the other things that the same money could buy.

Consider again our young account manager and her options as listed in Table 6.1. Elisha's choice of an apartment from among the three alternatives that lie within her budget constraint depends on her own tastes and preferences. She must make a personal judgment about the relative values that she places on housing, food, and other things. If she hates to cook, likes to eat at restaurants, and goes out three nights a week, she will probably trade off some housing for dinners out and money to spend on clothes and other things. She will probably rent the studio for $400. But she may love to spend long evenings at home reading, listening to classical music, and sipping tea while watching the sunset. In that case, she will probably trade off some restaurant meals, evenings out, and travel expenses for the added comfort of the larger apartment with the balcony and the view.

Thinking of constraints in this way highlights a very important point:

> As long as a household faces a limited budget—and all households ultimately do—the real cost of any good or service is the value of the other goods and services that could have been purchased with the same amount of money. The real cost of a good or service is its opportunity cost, and opportunity cost is determined by relative prices and income.

■ The Budget Constraint More Formally Trudee and Mark are struggling graduate students of economics. Their tuition is completely paid by graduate fellowships. They live as advisers in an undergraduate residence, in return for which they receive an apartment and meals. Their fellowships also give them $200 each month to cover all their other expenses. To simplify things, let's assume that Trudee and Mark spend their money on only two things: meals at the local Thai restaurant and nights at the local jazz club, The Hungry Ear. Thai meals go for a fixed price of $20 per couple. Two tickets to the jazz club, including espresso, are $10.

As Figure 6.3 shows, we can graphically depict the choices that are available to our dynamic duo. The axes measure the *quantities* of the two goods that Trudee and Mark buy. The horizontal axis measures the number of Thai meals consumed per month, and the vertical axis measures the number of trips to The Hungry Ear. (Note that price is not on the vertical axis here.) Every point in the space between the axes represents some combination of Thai meals and nights at the jazz club. The question is: which of these points can Trudee and Mark purchase with a fixed budget of $200 per month? That is, which points are in the opportunity set and which are not?

One possibility is that the kids in the residence are driving Trudee and Mark crazy. The two grad students want to avoid the dining hall at all costs. Thus they might decide to spend all their money on Thai food and none of it on jazz. This decision would be represented by a point *on* the horizontal (X) axis because all the points on that axis are points at which Trudee and Mark make no jazz club visits. How many meals can Trudee and Mark afford? The answer is simple. If income is $200 and the price of Thai meals is $20, they can afford $200 ÷ $20 = 10 meals. This point is labelled A on the budget constraint in Figure 6.3.

Another possibility is that general exams are coming up and Trudee and Mark decide to chill out at The Hungry Ear to relieve stress. Suppose that they choose to spend all their money on jazz and espresso and none of it on Thai food. This decision would be represented by a point *on* the vertical (Y) axis because all the points on this axis are points at which Trudee and Mark eat no Thai meals. How many jazz club visits can they afford? Again, the answer is simple. With an income

FIGURE 6.3

Budget Constraint and Opportunity Set for Trudee and Mark

A budget constraint separates those combinations of goods and services that are available, given limited income, from those that are not. Those combinations that are available make up the opportunity set.

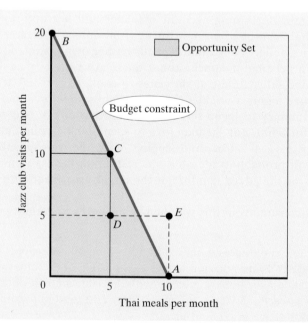

of $200 and with the price of jazz/espresso at $10, they can go to The Hungry Ear $200 ÷ $10 = 20 times. This is the point labelled *B* in Figure 6.3. The line connecting points *A* and *B* is Trudee and Mark's budget constraint.

What about all the points between *A* and *B* on the budget constraint? Think about the trade-off between Thai meals and trips to the Ear. Starting from point *B*, suppose Trudee and Mark give up trips to the jazz club to buy more Thai meals. Since trips to the jazz club are priced at $10 and Thai meals are priced at $20, each additional Thai meal "costs" two trips to The Hungry Ear. The opportunity cost of a Thai meal is two jazz club trips.

Point *C* on the budget constraint represents a compromise. Here Trudee and Mark go to the club ten times and eat at the Thai restaurant five times. To verify that point *C* is on the budget constraint, price it out. Ten jazz club trips cost a total of $10 × 10 = $100, and five Thai meals cost a total of $20 × 5 = $100. The total is thus $100 + $100 = $200.[3]

The budget constraint divides all the points between the axes into two groups: those that can be purchased for $200 or less (the opportunity set) and those that are unavailable. Point *D* on the diagram costs less than $200; point *E* costs more than $200. (Verify that this is true.) The opportunity set is the shaded area in Figure 6.3.

■ **Budget Constraints Change when Prices Rise or Fall**   Now suppose that the Thai restaurant is offering "two-for-one certificates" good during the month of November. In effect, this means that the price of Thai meals drops to $10 for Trudee and Mark. How would the budget constraint in Figure 6.3 change?

First, point *B* would not change. If Trudee and Mark spend all their money on jazz, the price of Thai meals is irrelevant. Trudee and Mark can still afford only 20 trips to the jazz club. What has changed is point *A*, which moves to point *A'* in Figure 6.4. At the new lower price of $10, if Trudee and Mark spent all their

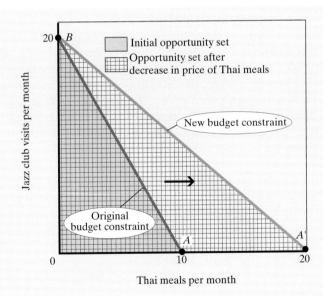

FIGURE 6.4

The Effect of a Decrease in Price on Trudee and Mark's Budget Constraint

When the price of a good decreases, the budget constraint swivels to the right, increasing the opportunities available and expanding choice.

---

[3]*The budget constraint can be written $20X + $10Y = $200, which is the equation of the line in Figure 6.3. This equation simply tells you to multiply the number of units of X consumed by $20, then multiply the number of units of Y consumed by $10; the sum of these two products should equal $200. More generally, the budget constraint in a two-good world is given by* $P_X X + P_Y Y = I$, *where* P_X *is the price of X,* P_Y *is the price of Y, and I is income.*

money on Thai meals, they could buy twice as many Thai meals, $200 ÷ $10 = 20. The budget constraint *swivels*, as shown in Figure 6.4.

The new, flatter budget constraint reflects the new trade-off between Thai meals and Hungry Ear visits. Now, after the price of Thai meals drops to $10, the opportunity cost of a Thai meal is only one jazz club visit. Trudee and Mark need to sacrifice only one club visit for each meal. The opportunity set has expanded because at the lower price more combinations of Thai meals and jazz are available.

Figure 6.4 thus illustrates a very important point. When the price of a single good changes, more than just the quantity of that good demanded may be affected. The household now faces an entirely different choice problem—the opportunity set has expanded. At their same income of $200, the new lower price means that Trudee and Mark might choose more Thai meals, more jazz club visits, or more of both! They are clearly better off.

To summarize:

> The budget constraint is defined by income, wealth, and prices. Within those limits, households are free to choose, and the household's ultimate choice depends on its own likes and dislikes.

The range of goods and services available in a modern society is as vast as consumer tastes are variable, and this makes any generalization about the household choice process hazardous. Nonetheless, the theory of household behaviour that follows is an attempt to derive some logical propositions about the way households make choices.

The Basis of Choice: Utility

Somehow, from the millions of things that are available, each of us manages to sort out a set of goods and services to buy. When we make our choices, we make specific judgments about the relative worth of things that are very different.

utility *The basis of choice. The satisfaction, or reward, a product yields relative to its alternatives.*

During the nineteenth century, this notion of the subjective weighing of values was formalized into a concept called utility. Whether one item is preferable to another depends upon how much **utility,** or satisfaction, it yields relative to its alternatives. What is it that enables us to decide on the relative worth of a new puppy or a stereo? A trip to the Rockies or a weekend in Montreal? Working or not working? As we make our choices, we are effectively weighing the utilities we would receive from all the possible available goods.

Certain problems are implicit in the concept of utility. First, it is impossible to measure utility completely and accurately. Second, it is impossible to compare the utilities of different people—that is, one cannot say whether person A or person B has a higher level of utility. Despite these problems, however, the idea of utility helps us understand the process of choice better.

DIMINISHING MARGINAL UTILITY

In making their choices, most people spread their incomes over many different kinds of goods. One reason people prefer variety is that consuming more and more of any one good reduces the marginal, or extra, satisfaction we get from further consumption of the same good. Formally, **marginal utility (MU)** is the

marginal utility (MU) *The additional satisfaction gained by the consumption or use of one more unit of something.*

additional satisfaction gained by the consumption or use of *one more* unit of something.

It is important to distinguish marginal utility from total utility. **Total utility** is the total amount of satisfaction obtained from consumption of a good or service. Marginal utility comes only from the *last unit* consumed; total utility comes from *all* units consumed.

Suppose that you live next to a store that sells homemade ice cream that you are crazy about. But even though you get a great deal of pleasure from eating ice cream, you don't spend your entire income on it. The first cone of the day tastes heavenly. The second is merely delicious. The third is still very good, but it's clear that the glow is fading. Why? Because the more of any one good we consume in a given period, the less satisfaction, or utility, we get out of each additional, or marginal, unit. In 1890 Alfred Marshall called this "familiar and fundamental tendency of human nature" the **law of diminishing marginal utility.**[4]

Consider this simple example. Frank loves rock music, and a rock band is playing seven nights a week at a club near his house. Table 6.2 shows how the utility he derives from the band might change as he goes to the club more and more frequently. The first visit generates 12 "utils," or units of utility. If Frank goes again another night he enjoys it, but not quite as much as the first night. The second night by itself yields 10 additional utils. *Marginal utility* is 10, while the *total utility* derived from two nights at the club is 22. Three nights per week at the club provide 28 total utils; the marginal utility of the third night is 6, since total utility rose from 22 to 28. Figure 6.5 on page 145 graphs total and marginal utility using the data in Table 6.2. Total utility increases up through Frank's fifth trip to the club, but levels off on the sixth night. Marginal utility, which has declined from the beginning, is now at zero.

ALLOCATING INCOME TO MAXIMIZE UTILITY

How many times in one week would Frank go to the club to hear his favourite band? The answer depends on three things: Frank's income, the price of admission to the club, and the alternatives available. If the price of admission were zero and no alternatives existed, he would probably go to the club five nights a week. (Remember, the sixth does not increase his utility, so why should he bother to go?) But Frank is also a basketball fan. His city has many good high school teams, and he can go to games six nights a week if he wants to.

Let us say for now that admission to both the music club and the basketball games is free—that is, there is no price/income constraint. There is a time constraint, however, because there are only seven nights in a week. Table 6.3 lists Frank's total and marginal utilities from attending basketball games and going to music clubs. From column 3 of the table we can conclude that on the first night Frank will go to a basketball game. The game is worth far more to him (21 utils) than a trip to the club (12 utils).

On the second night, Frank's decision is not so easy. As he has been to one basketball game this week, the second is worth less (12 utils, as compared to 21 for the first basketball game). In fact, it is worth exactly the same as a first trip to the club, so he is indifferent to whether he goes to the game or the club. So he splits the next two nights. One night he sees basketball game number two (12 utils), the other he spends at the club (12 utils). At this point, Frank has been

---
[4]*Alfred Marshall*, Principles of Economics, *8th ed. (New York: Macmillan, 1948), p. 93 (1st ed., 1890).*

total utility *The total amount of satisfaction obtained from consumption of a good or service.*

law of diminishing marginal utility *The more of any one good consumed in a given period, the less satisfaction (utility) is generated by consuming each additional (marginal) unit of the same good.*

Table 6.2

Total Utility and Marginal Utility of Trips to the Club per Week

Trips to Club	Total Utility	Marginal Utility
1	12	12
2	22	10
3	28	6
4	32	4
5	34	2
6	34	0

(1) Trips to Club per Week	(2) Total Utility	(3) Marginal Utility (MU)	(4) Price (P)	(5) Marginal Utility per Dollar (MU/P)
1	12	12	$3.00	4.0
2	22	10	3.00	3.3
3	28	6	3.00	2.0
4	32	4	3.00	1.3
5	34	2	3.00	0.7
6	34	0	3.00	0

(1) Basketball Games per Week	(2) Total Utility	(3) Marginal Utility (MU)	(4) Price (P)	(5) Marginal Utility per Dollar (MU/P)
1	21	21	$6.00	3.5
2	33	12	6.00	2.0
3	42	9	6.00	1.5
4	48	6	6.00	1.0
5	51	3	6.00	0.5
6	51	0	6.00	0

to two basketball games and spent one night at the club. Where will Frank go on evening four? To the club again, because the marginal utility from a second trip to the club (10 utils) is greater than the marginal utility from attending a third basketball game (9 utils).

Frank is splitting his time among the two activities in order to maximize total utility. At each successive step, he chooses the activity that yields the most marginal utility. Continuing with this logic, you can see that spending three nights at the club and four nights watching basketball produces total utility of 76 utils each week (28 plus 48). No other combination of games and club trips can produce as much utility.

So far, the only cost of a night of listening to music is a forgone basketball game, and the only cost of a basketball game is a forgone night of music. Now let's suppose that it costs $3 to get into the club and $6 to go to a basketball game. Suppose further that after paying rent and taking care of other expenses Frank has only $21 left over to spend on entertainment. Typically, consumers allocate limited incomes, or budgets, over a large set of goods and services. Here we have a limited income ($21) being allocated between only two goods, but the principle is the same. Income ($21) and prices ($3 and $6) define Frank's budget constraint. Within that constraint, Frank chooses in order to maximize utility.

Because the two activities now cost different amounts, we need to find the *marginal utility per dollar* spent on each activity. If Frank is to spend his money on the combination of activities lying within his budget constraint that gives him the most total utility, each night he must choose the activity that gives him the *most utility per dollar spent*. As you can see from column 5 in Table 6.3, Frank gets 4 utils per dollar on the first night he goes to the club (12 utils ÷ $3 = 4 utils per dollar). On night two he goes to a game and gets 3.5 utils per dollar (21 utils ÷ $6 = 3.5 utils per dollar). On night three it's back to the club. Then what happens? When all is said and done—work this out for yourself—Frank ends up going to two games and spending three nights at the club. No other combination of activities that $21 will buy yields more utility.

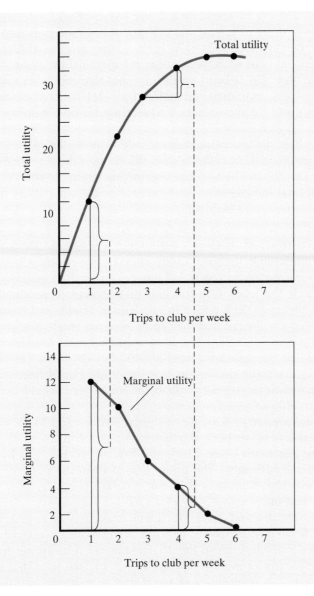

FIGURE 6.5

Graphs of Frank's Total and Marginal Utility

Marginal utility is the additional utility gained by consuming one additional unit of a commodity—in this case, trips to the club. When marginal utility is zero, total utility stops rising.

THE UTILITY-MAXIMIZING RULE

In general, a utility-maximizing consumer spreads out his or her expenditures until the following condition holds:

$$\text{Utility-Maximizing Rule: } \frac{MU_X}{P_X} = \frac{MU_Y}{P_Y} \text{ for all pairs of goods}$$

where MU_X is the marginal utility derived from the last unit of X consumed, MU_Y is the marginal utility derived from the last unit of Y consumed, P_X is the price per unit of X, and P_Y is the price per unit of Y.

To see why this utility-maximizing rule is true, think for a moment about what would happen if it were *not* true. For example, suppose MU_X/P_X were greater than MU_Y/P_Y; that is, suppose that a consumer purchased a bundle of goods so that the marginal utility from the last dollar spent on X were greater than the marginal utility from the last dollar spent on Y. This would mean that the consumer could increase her or his utility by spending a dollar less on Y and a dollar more on X. But as a consumer shifts to buying more X and less Y, she runs into diminishing marginal utility. Buying more units of X *decreases* the marginal utility derived from consuming additional units of X. As a result, the marginal utility of another dollar spent on X falls. Now *less* is being spent on Y and that means its marginal utility *increases*. This process continues until $MU_X/P_X = MU_Y/P_Y$. When this condition holds, there is no way for the consumer to increase his or her utility by changing the bundle of goods purchased.

You can see how the utility-maximizing rule works in Frank's choice between rock music and basketball. At each stage, Frank chooses the activity that gives him the most utility per dollar. If he goes to a game, the utility he will derive from the next game—marginal utility—falls. If he goes to the club, the utility he will derive from his next visit falls, and so forth.

DIMINISHING MARGINAL UTILITY AND DOWNWARD-SLOPING DEMAND

The concept of diminishing marginal utility offers us one reason why people spread their incomes over a variety of goods and services rather than spending them all on one or two items. It also leads us to conclude that demand curves slope downward.

To see why this is so, let's return to our friends Trudee and Mark, the struggling graduate students. Recall that they chose between meals at a Thai restaurant and trips to a jazz club. Now think about their demand curve for Thai meals shown in Figure 6.6. When the price of a meal is $40, they decide not to buy any Thai meals. What they are really deciding is that the utility gained from even that first scrumptious meal each month isn't worth the utility that would come from the other things that $40 can buy.

Now consider a price of $25. At this price, Trudee and Mark buy five Thai meals. Clearly the first, second, third, fourth, and fifth meal each generates enough utility to justify the price. Mark and Trudee "reveal" this by buying five meals. But after the fifth meal, the utility gained from the next meal (the sixth meal) is not worth $25. That is, it does not generate as much utility as the other things that $25 can buy.

Ultimately, every demand curve hits the quantity axis as a result of diminishing marginal utility—in other words, demand curves slope downward. How many times will Trudee and Mark go to the Thai restaurant if meals are free? Twenty-five times. After 25 times a month, they are so sick of Thai food that they will not eat any more even if it is given away free! That is, marginal utility—the utility gained from the last meal—has dropped to zero. If you think this is unrealistic, ask yourself how much water you drank today.

The concept of utility as we have discussed it here is abstract. It may seem artificial, first because utility cannot be measured, and second because comparisons cannot be made among individuals. While the idea of utility is, we believe, a helpful way of thinking about the choice process, there is an explanation for downward-sloping demand curves that does not rely on the concept of utility or the assumption of diminishing marginal utility. This explanation centres on income and substitution effects.

Income and Substitution Effects

Another way of thinking about household choices avoids any direct use of the concept of utility. It also leads us to the conclusion that a negative, or downward-sloping, relationship is very likely to exist between quantity demanded and price.

Keeping in mind that consumers face constrained choices, consider the probable response of a household to a decline in the price of some heavily used product,

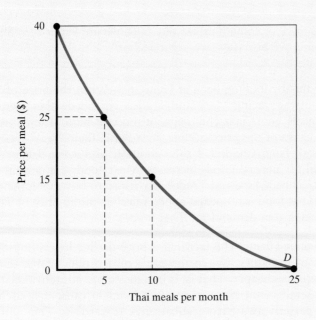

FIGURE 6.6

Diminishing Marginal Utility and Downward-Sloping Demand

At a price of $40, the utility gained from even the first Thai meal is not worth the price. However, a lower price of $25 lures Trudee and Mark into the Thai restaurant five times a month. (The utility from the sixth meal is not worth $25.) If the price is $15, Trudee and Mark will eat Thai meals 10 times a month—until the marginal utility of a Thai meal drops below the utility they could gain from spending $15 on other goods. At 25 meals a month, they cannot tolerate the thought of another Thai meal even if it is free!

ceteris paribus. How might a household currently consuming many goods be likely to respond to a fall in the price of one of those goods if its income, its preferences, and all other prices remained unchanged? Clearly, the household would face a new budget constraint, and its final choice of all goods and services might change. A decline in the price of gasoline, for example, may affect not only how much gasoline you purchase but also the kind of car you buy, when and how much you travel, where you go, and (not so directly) how many movies you see this month and how many projects around the house you get done.

■ **The Income Effect** Price changes affect households in two ways. First, if we assume that households confine their choices to products that improve their well-being, then a decline in the price of any product, *ceteris paribus,* makes the household unequivocally better off. In other words, if a household continues to buy the exact same amount of every good and service after the price decrease, it will have income left over. That extra income may be spent on the product whose price has declined, hereafter called good X, or on other products. The change in consumption of X due to this improvement in well-being is called the **income effect of a price change.**

Suppose that I live in Toronto and that three times a year I fly to Thunder Bay to visit my mother. Suppose further that last year a round-trip ticket to Thunder Bay cost $229. This year, however, increased competition among the airlines has led one airline to offer round-trip tickets to Thunder Bay for $129. Assuming that the price remains at $129 all year, I am better off this year than I was last year. I can now fly home exactly the same number of times, and I will have spent $300 less for airline tickets than I did last year. Now that I'm better off, I have additional opportunities. I could fly home a fourth time this year, leaving $171 ($300 minus $129) to spend on other things, or I could fly home the same number of times (three) and spend all of the extra $300 on other things.

The key idea here is simple:

> When the price of something we buy falls, we are *better off*. When the price of something we buy rises, we are *worse off*.

You can see this by looking back at Figure 6.4. When the price of Thai meals fell, the opportunity set facing Mark and Trudee expanded—they were able to afford more Thai meals, more jazz club trips, or more of both. They were unequivocally better off because of the price decline. In a sense, their "real" income was higher.

Now recall from Chapter 4 the definition of a *normal good*. When income rises, demand for normal goods increases. Most goods are normal goods. Because of the price decline, Mark and Trudee can afford to buy more; their "real" income is higher. If Thai food is a normal good, a decline in the price of Thai food should lead to an increase in demand for Thai food.

■ **The Substitution Effect** The fact that a price decline leaves households better off is only part of the story. When the price of a product falls, that product also becomes *relatively* cheaper. That is, it becomes more attractive relative to potential substitutes. A fall in the price of product X might cause a household to shift its purchasing pattern away from substitutes toward X. This shift is called the **substitution effect of a price change.**

Earlier, we made the point that the "real" cost or price of a good is what one must sacrifice in order to consume it. This opportunity cost is determined by relative prices.

To see why this is so, consider again the choice that I face when a round-trip ticket to Thunder Bay costs $229. Each trip that I take requires a sacrifice of $229 worth of other goods and services. When the price drops to $129, the opportunity cost of a ticket has dropped by $100. In other words, after the price decline, I have to sacrifice only $129 (rather than $229) worth of other goods and services to visit Mom.

To clarify in your mind the distinction between the income and substitution effects, imagine how I would be affected if two things happened to me simultaneously. First, the price of round-trip air travel between Toronto and Thunder Bay drops from $229 to $129. Second, my income is reduced by $300. Although I am now faced with new relative prices and a lower income, I can still fly home three times this year, and I can still consume exactly the same amount of other goods and services. But will I continue to consume the same amount of air travel and other goods and services?

Not necessarily. I may be able to make gains in well-being by taking more trips home. How? The opportunity cost of a trip home is now lower, *ceteris paribus* (that is, assuming no change in the prices of other goods and services). Thus, a trip to Thunder Bay now requires a sacrifice of only $129 worth of other goods and services, not the $229 worth that it did before. I will substitute away from other goods toward trips to see my mother if the value I place on an additional trip to see her exceeds the new opportunity cost.

Everything works in the opposite direction when a price rises, *ceteris paribus*. A price increase makes households worse off. If income and other prices don't change, spending the same amount of money buys less, and households will be forced to buy less. They may purchase less X or cut spending on other things. This is the income effect. In addition, when the price of a product rises, that item becomes more expensive relative to potential substitutes, and the household is likely

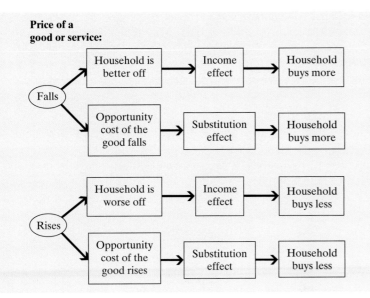

Price of a good or service:

Falls → Household is better off → Income effect → Household buys more

Falls → Opportunity cost of the good falls → Substitution effect → Household buys more

Rises → Household is worse off → Income effect → Household buys less

Rises → Opportunity cost of the good rises → Substitution effect → Household buys less

FIGURE 6.7

Income and Substitution Effects Explain Why Demand Curves Slope Downward

For normal goods, the income and substitution effects work in the same direction. Higher prices lead to a lower quantity demanded, and lower prices lead to a higher quantity demanded.

to substitute other goods for it. This is the substitution effect. (For two other examples of the substitution and income effects, see the Application box on page 150 titled "The Substitution and Income Effects of Drug Patent Legislation and NAFTA.")

What do the income and substitution effects tell us about the demand curve? Quite simply:

> Both the income and substitution effects imply a negative relationship between price and quantity demanded—in other words, downward-sloping demand. When the price of something falls, *ceteris paribus*, we are better off, and we are likely to buy more of that good and other goods (income effect). And because lower price also means "less expensive relative to substitutes," we are likely to buy more of the good (substitution effect). When the price of something rises, we are worse off, and we will buy less of it (income effect). Higher price also means "more expensive relative to substitutes," and we are likely to buy less of it and more of other goods (substitution effect).[5]

Figure 6.7 summarizes the income and substitution effects for a normal good.

---

[5]*Careful thought should convince you that for some goods the income and substitution effects work in opposite directions. When our income rises, we may buy less of some goods. In Chapter 4, we called such goods inferior goods.*

When the price of an inferior good rises, it is, like any other good, more expensive relative to substitutes, and we are likely to buy less of it as we replace it with lower-priced substitutes. However, the price increase leaves us worse off, and when we are worse off we increase our demand for inferior goods. Thus, the income effect could lead us to buy more of the good, partially offsetting the substitution effect.

Even if a good is "very inferior," demand curves will slope downward as long as the substitution effect is larger than the income effect. But it is possible, at least in theory, for the income effect to be larger. In such a case, a price increase would actually lead to an increase in quantity demanded. This possibility was pointed out by Alfred Marshall in Principles of Economics. Marshall attributes the notion of an upward-sloping demand curve to Sir Robert Giffen, and for this reason the notion is often referred to as Giffen's paradox. Fortunately or unfortunately, no one has ever demonstrated that a Giffen good has ever existed.

The distinction between substitution and income effects helps us analyze the impact of various government policies. Here let us consider two separate examples.

DRUG PATENT LEGISLATION

In 1993, the House of Commons passed Bill C-91, a law giving brand-name drug manufacturers patent protection of up to 20 years for each new drug they develop. Bill C-91 was introduced to protect companies developing new pharmaceutical products from competition from so-called generic firms who copy the new drugs and offer them for sale on the market. The brand-name manufacturers successfully lobbied the Canadian government for protection, arguing that competition from generic firms would result in market prices that would fail to take into account the costs of research and development, which are substantial for a new product. Generic drug manufacturers incur no such costs. Faced with competition from generic firms, companies developing new drugs argued that they would have little incentive to continue investing in research and development. They further claimed that reduced pharmaceutical research would hurt all Canadians by decreasing the number of new, effective drugs that would be developed in future years.

As part of their lobbying effort the brand-name drug manufacturers promised to create thousands of re-

Research and development activity is extremely important in the pharmaceutical industry. Bill C-91 was introduced to create employment for pharmaceutical researchers.

search and development jobs in Canada if the government granted patent protection. Most of these jobs would be created in Quebec, Ontario, Alberta, and British Columbia. One question that arose in the debate over Bill C-91 was: what impact would this legislation have on employment outside Quebec, Ontario, Alberta, and B.C.?

To answer this question, we begin by assuming that patent protection would result in a lower supply of new drugs than would be the case if generic firms had the freedom to copy and market the products. Hence, the

price of new drugs would rise. What would the impact of this price increase be?

Here, let us distinguish between the substitution effect and the income effect of the price change. First, the substitution effect of a price increase depends on the substitutes available. Because there are relatively few substitutes in the pharmaceutical industry the substitution effect here will be small. Both doctors and patients want "the best" product available. And where health is concerned few people will question a doctor's judgment and ask for a cheaper and potentially less

Consumer Surplus

The argument, made several times already, that the market forces us to reveal a great deal about our personal preferences, is an extremely important one, and it bears repeating at least once more here. If you are free to choose within the constraints imposed by prices and your income and you decide to buy, say, a hamburger for $2.50, you have "revealed" that a hamburger is worth at least $2.50 to you.

effective alternative. Second, the income effect of a price increase depends on the income elasticity of demand. Because most people will want to buy the prescribed drugs no matter what their income, the income effect will also be small. Provincial drug plans for the poor and the elderly and the existence of private drug insurance programs will further reduce the size of the income effect. Thus, because of the small substitution and income effects, we predict that higher prices are unlikely to have much effect on the consumption of prescribed pharmaceutical products. In other words, demand here is highly inelastic.

If demand is not affected by the higher prices then a larger proportion of the consumer's budget will be allocated to pharmaceutical purchases under Bill C-91 than would be the case if competition from generic producers were allowed. Consequently, consumers will have less income left after purchasing pharmaceutical products to purchase other things. To predict the impact of Bill C-91 outside Quebec, Ontario, Alberta, and B.C. we would need to predict which "other things" are affected. An economist would suggest that goods with a high income elasticity of demand (especially luxury products) would be most affected.

This example illustrates that a piece of legislation directly affecting one sector of the economy (in this case, pharmaceuticals) can have pre-dictable indirect implications for sectors that at first glance may appear unrelated to the policy initiative (in this case, luxury products). Lower spending on sectors providing goods and services with high income elasticities of demand will result in lower incomes and possibly unemployment in these sectors.

NAFTA

The North American Free Trade Agreement (NAFTA), an agreement among Canada, the U.S., and Mexico, came into force January 1, 1994. One consequence of NAFTA was lower prices in all three countries for traded goods and services that were previously subject to tariffs. In some markets Canadian firms were unable to compete with competitors from the U.S. and Mexico, whose costs were lower. As a result, in Canada there were a number of highly visible and much publicized plant closures and large-scale layoffs. We can attribute these closures and layoffs to the substitution effect because Canadian consumers substituted lower-cost foreign goods and services for higher-cost Canadian-made goods and services.

Let us now consider the income effect. Because Canadian consumers used less income to purchase products they were buying prior to the free trade agreement, they had money left over. What do they do with this "left over income"? Economists predict that consumers will purchase products with a high income elasticity of demand. Many of these products are not traded at all—such as restaurant meals and personal fitness services. The increased demand for goods and services generated by the price reductions in the traded goods sectors translates into higher employment in sectors that face a high income elasticity of demand.

Because this increase in employment is an indirect result of NAFTA and because it is not very visible it is often ignored by the press and the general public. Knowledge of the distinction between income and substitution effects allows economists to identify a source of employment gains that would otherwise go unnoticed.

The indirect effects of policies like Bill C-91 and NAFTA are, however, extremely difficult to measure. To identify these indirect effects empirically one needs to "hold other things equal." But economists are rarely able to "hold other things equal." For example, the implementation of Bill C-91, the Canada–U.S. Free Trade Agreement, and NAFTA coincided with a major recession, the "downsizing" of many firms that were taking advantage of new computer and information technologies, and significant reductions in government spending in the economy. All of these developments will affect the distribution of employment and it is all but impossible to separate out the impact of each.

A simple market demand curve such as the one in Figure 6.8a on page 152 illustrates this point quite clearly. At the current market price of $2.50, consumers will purchase 7 million hamburgers per month. There is only one price in the market, and the demand curve tells us how many hamburgers households would buy if they could purchase all they wanted at the posted price of $2.50. Anyone who values a hamburger at $2.50 or more will buy it; anyone who does not value it that highly will not.

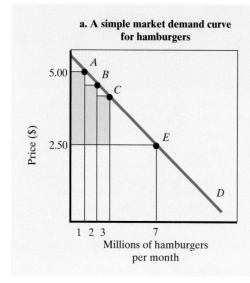

a. A simple market demand curve for hamburgers

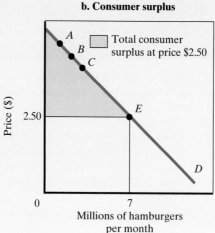

b. Consumer surplus

FIGURE 6.8

Market Demand, Revealed Preference, and Consumer Surplus

The difference between the maximum amount that a person is willing to pay for a good and its current market price is the person's consumer surplus. The total consumer surplus suggested by the data in Figure 6.8a is represented by the shaded area in Figure 6.8b.

consumer surplus *The difference between the maximum amount a person is willing to pay for a good and its current market price.*

Some people, however, value hamburgers at more than $2.50. As Figure 6.8a shows, even if the price were at $5.00, consumers would still buy one million hamburgers. If these people were able to buy the good at a price of $2.50, they would earn what is called a **consumer surplus.** Consumer surplus is the difference between the maximum amount a person is willing to pay for a good and its current market price. The consumer surplus earned by the people willing to pay $5.00 for a hamburger is approximately equal to the shaded area between point *A* and the price, $2.50.

The second million hamburgers in Figure 6.8a are valued at more than the market price as well, although the consumer surplus gained is slightly less. Point *B* on the simple market demand curve shows the maximum amount that consumers would be willing to pay for the second million hamburgers. The consumer surplus earned by these people is equal to the shaded area between *B* and the price, $2.50. Similarly, for the third million hamburgers, maximum willingness to pay is given by point *C*; consumer surplus is a bit lower than it is at points *A* and *B*, but it is still significant.

The total value of the consumer surplus suggested by the data in Figure 6.8a is roughly equal to the area of the shaded triangle in Figure 6.8b. To understand why this is so, think about offering hamburgers to consumers at successively lower prices. If the good were actually sold for $2.50, those near point *A* on the demand curve would get a large surplus; those at point *B* would get a smaller surplus. Those at point *E* would get none.

The idea of consumer surplus helps to explain an old paradox that dates back to Plato. Adam Smith wrote about it in 1776:

> The things which have the greatest value in use have frequently little or no value in exchange; and on the contrary, those which have the greatest value in exchange have frequently little or no value in use. Nothing is more useful than water: but it will purchase scarce any thing; scarce anything can be had in exchange for it. A diamond, on the contrary, has scarce any value in use; but a very great quantity of other goods may frequently be had in exchange for it.[6]

_____
[6]*Adam Smith*, The Wealth of Nations, *Modern Library Edition (New York: Random House, 1937), p. 28 (1st ed. 1776). The cheapness of water is referred to by Plato in* Euthydem., 304B.

Although diamonds have arguably more than "scarce any value in use" today (they are used to cut glass, for example), Smith's **diamond/water paradox** is still instructive, at least where water is concerned.

The low price of water owes much to the fact that it is in plentiful supply. Even at a price of zero we do not consume an infinite amount of water. We consume up to the point where *marginal* utility drops to zero. The *marginal* value of water is zero. Each of us enjoys an enormous consumer surplus when we consume nearly free water. We tend to take water for granted, but imagine what would happen to its price if there were simply not enough for everyone. If water were in very short supply, it would command a high price indeed. As the figure in the margin shows, at a price of zero, the "value" of water is the entire shaded area.

Consumer surplus measurement is a key element in **cost-benefit analysis**, the formal technique by which the benefits of a public project are weighed against its costs. To decide whether to build a new electrical power plant, we need to know the value, to consumers, of the electricity that it will produce. Just as the value of water to consumers is not just its price times the quantity that people consume, the value of electricity generated is not just the price of electricity times the quantity the new plant will produce. The total value that should be weighed against the costs of the plant includes the consumer surplus that electricity users will enjoy if the plant is built.

diamond/water paradox *A paradox stating that (1) the things with the greatest value in use frequently have little or no value in exchange, and (2) the things with the greatest value in exchange frequently have little or no value in use.*

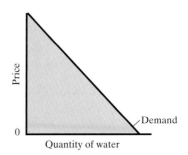

cost-benefit analysis *The formal technique by which the benefits of a public project are weighed against its costs.*

Household Choice in Input Markets

So far, we have focused on the decision-making process that lies behind output demand curves. Households with limited incomes allocate those incomes across various combinations of goods and services that are available and affordable. In looking at the factors affecting choices in the output market, we assumed that income was fixed, or given. We noted at the outset, however, that income is in fact partially determined by choices that households make in input markets (look back at Figure 6.1). We now turn to a discussion of the two decisions households make in input markets: the labour supply decision and the saving decision.

THE LABOUR SUPPLY DECISION

Most income in Canada is wage and salary income paid in compensation for labour. Household members supply labour in exchange for wages or salaries. As in output markets, households face constrained choices in input markets. They must decide:

1. Whether to work,
2. How much to work, and
3. What kind of job to work at.

In essence, household members must decide how much labour to supply. The choices they make are affected by:

1. The availability of jobs,
2. Market wage rates, and
3. The skills they possess.

As with decisions in output markets, the labour supply decision involves a set of trade-offs. There are basically two alternatives to working for a wage: (1) not working, and (2) unpaid work. If I don't work, I sacrifice income for the benefits of staying at home and reading, watching TV, going swimming, or sleeping. Another option is to work and produce, but not for a money wage. In this case, I sacrifice money income for the benefits of growing my own food in my garden, bringing up my children, or taking care of my house.

As with the trade-offs in output markets, my final choice depends on how I value the alternatives available. If I work, I earn a wage that I can use to buy things. Thus, the trade-off is between the value of the goods and services I can buy in the market with the wages I earn versus the value of things I can produce at home (home-grown food, well-raised children, clean clothes, and so on) or the value I place on leisure. This choice is illustrated in Figure 6.9. In general, then:

> The wage rate can be thought of as the price—or the opportunity cost—of either the benefits of unpaid work or of leisure.

THE PRICE OF LEISURE

In our analysis in the early part of this chapter, households had to allocate a limited budget across a set of goods and services. Now they must choose among goods, services, and *leisure*.

When we add leisure to the picture, we do so with one important distinction. Trading off one good for another involves buying less of one and more of another, so households simply reallocate *money* from one good to the other. "Buying" more leisure, however, means reallocating *time* between work and nonwork activities.

If we assume that jobs are available, that households have the option of part-time work, that households receive no nonwage income (such as interest, dividends, or gifts from family members), and that there are no taxes, we can draw the budget constraint facing a typical household. Figure 6.10 shows an opportunity set that includes leisure. The quantity of leisure consumed appears on the *X* axis; on the *Y* axis is the amount of daily income. Assuming that the primary motive for work-

FIGURE 6.9

The Trade-Off Facing Households

The decision to enter the workforce involves a trade-off between wages (and the goods and services that wages will buy) on the one hand, and leisure and the value of nonmarket production on the other.

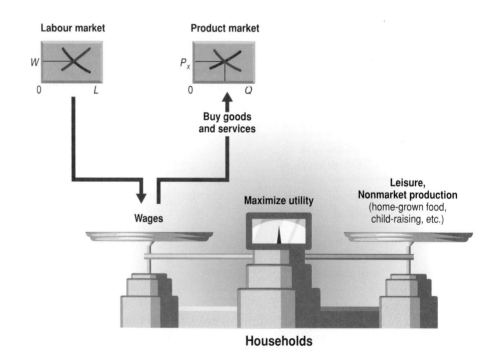

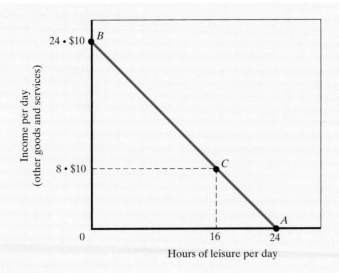

FIGURE 6.10

The Labour–Leisure Choice

By plotting income on the Y axis and hours of leisure on the X axis, the graph shows all combinations of daily income and leisure available to someone who can choose how many hours to work at a given wage rate of $10. If he chose not to work, he would consume 24 hours of leisure and earn no income. If he worked all the time, he would earn 24 × $10 = $240 per day and have no leisure at all.

ing is to obtain the things that wages will buy, we can think of the Y axis as a measure of all other goods. Since there is no nonwage income, the only way to get goods and services is by working to earn wages.

If I decide to use all my time for leisure activities, I will earn no income and consume no other goods, the situation indicated by point A on the budget constraint. If I decide to work every hour of the day and night for a wage of $10 per hour, I will earn 24 × $10 = $240 per day and be at point B on the budget constraint. If I take a regular job and work eight hours per day, I will earn 8 × $10 = $80 per day and consume 16 hours of leisure, point C on the budget constraint. For each hour of leisure that I decide to consume, I give up one hour's wages. Thus the wage rate is the *price of leisure*.

Conditions in the labour market determine the budget constraints and final opportunity sets that face households. The availability of jobs and these jobs' wage rates determine the final combinations of goods and services that a household can afford. The final choice within these constraints depends on each household's unique tastes and preferences. Some people place very little value on leisure, while others place a high value on things like playing tennis or lying on the beach—but everyone needs to put food on the table.

INCOME AND SUBSTITUTION EFFECTS OF A WAGE CHANGE

A **labour supply curve** shows the quantity of labour supplied as a function of the wage rate. The shape of the labour supply curve depends on how households react to changes in the wage rate.

Consider an increase in wages. First of all, an increase in wages makes households better off. If they work the same number of hours—that is, if they supply the same amount of labour—they will earn higher incomes and be able to buy more goods and services. But they can also buy more leisure. If leisure is a normal good (that is, a good for which demand increases as income increases), an increase in income will lead to a higher demand for leisure and a lower labour supply. This is the *income effect of a wage increase*.

There is also, however, a potential *substitution effect of a wage increase*. A higher wage rate means that leisure is more expensive. If you think of the wage rate as the price of leisure, each individual hour of leisure consumed at a higher wage

labour supply curve *A diagram that shows the quantity of labour supplied as a function of the wage rate. Its shape depends on how households react to changes in the wage rate.*

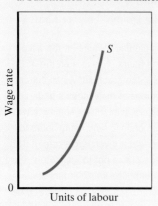

a. Substitution effect dominates

Wage rate

0   Units of labour

S

b. Income effect dominates

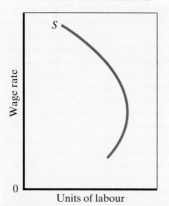

Wage rate

0   Units of labour

S

FIGURE 6.11

Two Labour Supply Curves

If we think of leisure as a normal good, an increase in wages that increases income may lead via the income effect to more leisure and less work. When the income effect outweighs the substitution effect, the result may be a "backward-bending" labour supply curve: lower labour supply at higher wages.

costs more in forgone wages. As a result, we would expect households to substitute other goods for leisure. This means working more, or a lower demand for leisure and a higher labour supply.

Note that in the labour market the income and substitution effects work in *opposite* directions when leisure is a normal good. The income effect of a wage increase implies buying more leisure and working less; the substitution effect implies buying less leisure and working more. Whether households will supply more labour overall or less labour overall when wages rise depends on the relative strength of both the income and the substitution effects.

If the substitution effect is greater than the income effect, the wage increase will increase labour supply. This suggests that the labour supply curve slopes upward, or has a positive slope, like the one in Figure 6.11a. If the income effect outweighs the substitution effect, however, a higher wage will lead to added consumption of leisure, and labour supply will decrease. This implies that the labour supply curve "bends back," as the one in Figure 6.11b does.

During the early years of the Industrial Revolution in late eighteenth-century Great Britain, the textile industry operated under what was called the "putting-out" system. Spinning and weaving were done in small cottages to supplement the family farm income, hence the term "cottage industry." During that period, wages and household incomes rose considerably. Some economic historians claim that this higher income actually led many households to take more leisure and work fewer hours; the empirical evidence suggests a backward-bending labour supply curve.

Just as income and substitution effects helped us understand household choices in output markets, they now help us understand household choices in input markets. The point here is simple:

> When leisure is added to the choice set, the line between input and output market decisions becomes blurred. In fact, households decide simultaneously how much of each good to consume and how much leisure to consume.

SAVING AND BORROWING: PRESENT VERSUS FUTURE CONSUMPTION

We began this chapter by looking behind the demand curve to examine the way households allocate a fixed income over a large number of available goods and services. We then pointed out that, at least in part, choices made by households determine income levels. Within the constraints imposed by the market, households decide whether to work and how much to work.

So far, however, we have talked about only the current period—the allocation of current income among alternative uses and the work/leisure choice today. But households can also (1) use present income to finance future spending—they can *save*—or (2) use future income to finance present spending—they can *borrow*.

When a household decides not to spend part of its current income but rather to save it, it is using current income to finance future consumption. That future consumption may come in 3 years, when you use your savings to buy a car; in 10 years, when you sell stock to put a deposit on a house; or in 45 years, when you retire and begin to receive money from your pension plan. But most people cannot finance large purchases—a house or condominium, for example—out of current income and savings. They almost always borrow money and sign a mortgage. When a household borrows, it is, in essence, financing a current purchase with future income. It pays back the loan out of future income.

Even in simple economies such as the two-person, desert-island economy of Colleen and Ivan (see Chapter 2), people must make decisions about *present versus future consumption*. Colleen and Ivan had a number of options. They could

(1) produce goods for today's consumption by hunting and gathering, (2) consume leisure by sleeping on the beach, or (3) work on projects to enhance future consumption opportunities. Building a house or a boat over a five-year period is trading present consumption for future consumption.

When a household saves, it usually puts the money into something that will generate income. There is no sense in putting money under your mattress when you can make it work in so many ways: savings accounts, mutual funds, stocks, corporate bonds, and so forth—some of which are virtually risk free. When you put your money in any of these places, you are actually lending it out, and the borrower pays you a fee for its use. This fee usually takes the form of *interest*.

Just as changes in wage rates affect household behaviour in the labour market, so do changes in interest rates affect household behaviour in capital markets. When interest rates change, they affect both the cost of borrowing *and* the return to saving. Higher interest rates mean that borrowing is more expensive—required monthly payments on a newly purchased house or car will be higher. But higher interest rates also mean that saving will earn a higher return: $1000 invested in a 5% GIC (guaranteed investment certificate) or bond yields $50 per year, but if rates rise to 10%, the annual interest rises to $100.

But what impact do interest rates have on saving behaviour? As with the effect of wage changes on labour supply behaviour, the effect of changes in interest rates on saving behaviour can best be understood in terms of income and substitution effects. Suppose, for example, that I have been saving for a number of years for retirement. Will an increase in interest rates lead to an increase or a decrease in my saving? The answer is not obvious. First, because each dollar saved will earn a higher rate of return, the "price" of spending today in terms of forgone future spending is higher. That is, each dollar that I spend today (instead of saving) costs me more in terms of future consumption because my saving will now earn a higher return. On this score I will be led to save *more*, and this is the substitution effect at work.

But note that I will also earn more on all the saving that I have done to date, and in this sense I am better off. I will not need to save as much for retirement or future consumption as I did before. Consequently, I will be led to save *less*, and this is the income effect at work. The final impact of a change in interest rates depends on the relative size of the income and substitution effects. Most empirical evidence indicates that saving tends to increase as the interest rate rises. In other words, the substitution effect is larger than the income effect.

Saving and investment decisions involve a huge and complex set of institutions, the **financial capital market**, in which the suppliers of capital (households that save) and the demand for capital (business firms that want to invest) interact. The amount of capital investment in a full-employment economy is constrained in the long run by the saving rate of that economy.[7] You can think of household *saving*, then, as the economy's supply of capital. When a firm borrows to finance a capital acquisition, it is almost as if households have supplied the capital for the fee we call interest. We treat capital markets in detail in Chapter 11.

financial capital market *The complex set of institutions in which suppliers of capital (households that save) and the demand for capital (business firms wanting to invest) interact.*

---

[7]*Here we are looking at a country as if it were isolated from the rest of the world—as if it were a closed economy. Very often, however, capital investment is financed by funds loaned or provided by foreign citizens or governments. For example, a substantial amount of U.S. savings finds its way into Canada each year to buy stocks, bonds, and other financial instruments. In part, these flows finance capital investment. Also, Canada and other countries that contribute funds to the World Bank and the International Monetary Fund have provided billions in outright grants and loans to help developing countries produce capital.*

A Review: Households in Output and Input Markets

In probing the behaviour of households in both input and output markets and examining the nature of constrained choice, we went behind the household output demand curve, using the simplifying assumption that income was fixed and given. Income, wealth, and prices set the limits, or *constraints,* within which households must make their choices in output markets. Within those limits, households make their choices on the basis of personal tastes and preferences.

The notion of *utility* helps to explain the process of choice. The law of *diminishing marginal utility* partly explains why people seem to spread their incomes over many different goods and services and why demand curves have a negative slope. Another important explanation behind the negative relationship between price and quantity demanded lies in *income effects* and *substitution effects.*

As we turned to input markets, we relaxed the assumption that income was fixed and given. In the labour market, households are forced to weigh the value of leisure against the value of goods and services that can be bought with wage income. Once again, we found household preferences for goods and leisure operating within a set of constraints imposed by the market. Households also face the problem of allocating income and consumption over more than one period of time. They can finance spending in the future with today's income by saving and earning interest, or they can spend tomorrow's income today by borrowing.

We now have a rough sketch of the factors that determine output demand and input supply. (You can review these in Figure 6.1.) In the next three chapters, we turn to firm behaviour and explore in detail the factors that affect output supply and input demand.

Summary

1. In perfectly competitive markets, prices are determined by the forces of supply and demand, and no single household or firm has any control over them. The assumption of a perfectly competitive market underlies all of our discussions through Chapter 12. Much of what we say in these chapters, however, can be generalized to the other forms of market structure. We also assume that households possess *perfect knowledge* of the qualities and prices of everything available in the market.

Household Choice in Output Markets

2. Every household must make three basic decisions: (1) how much of each product, or output, to demand, (2) how much labour to supply, and (3) how much to spend today and how much to save for the future.

3. Income, wealth, and prices define a household's *budget constraint.* The budget constraint separates those combinations of goods and services that are available from those that are not. All the points below and to the left of a graph of a household's budget constraint make up its *choice set,* or *opportunity set.*

4. It is best to think of the household choice problem as one of allocating income over a large number of goods and services. A change in the price of one good may change the entire allocation. Demand for some goods may rise while demand for others may fall.

5. As long as a household faces a limited income, the real cost of any single good or service is the value of the *other* goods and services that could have been purchased with the same amount of money.

6. Within the constraints of prices, income, and wealth, household decisions ultimately depend on preferences—likes, dislikes, and tastes.

The Basis of Choice: Utility

7. The idea of subjective weighing of values was formalized in the nineteenth century into the concept of *utility.* Whether one item is preferable to another depends on how much utility, or satisfaction, it yields relative to its alternatives.

8. The *law of diminishing marginal utility* says that the more of any good we consume in a given period of time, the less satisfaction, or utility, we get out of each additional, or marginal, unit of that good.

9. Households allocate income among goods and services in order to maximize utility. This implies choosing activities that yield the highest marginal utility per dollar. In a two-good world, households will choose so as to equate the marginal utility per dollar spent on X with the marginal utility per dollar spent on Y. This is the *utility-maximizing rule*.

Income and Substitution Effects

10. The fact that demand curves slope downward, or have a negative slope, can be explained in two ways: (1) marginal utility for all goods diminishes, and (2) for most normal goods both the *income and substitution effects* of a price decline lead to more consumption of the good.

Consumer Surplus

11. When any good is sold at a fixed price, households must "reveal" whether that good is worth the price being asked. For many people who buy in a given market, the product is worth more than its current price. Those people receive a *consumer surplus*.

Household Choice in Input Markets

12. In the labour market, a trade-off exists between the value of the goods and services that can be bought in the market or produced at home and the value that one places on leisure. The opportunity cost of paid work is leisure and unpaid work. The wage rate is the price, or opportunity cost, of either the benefits of unpaid work or of leisure.

13. The income and substitution effects of a change in the wage rate work in opposite directions. Higher wages mean that (1) leisure is more expensive (likely response: people work *more*—substitution effect), and (2) more income is earned in a given number of hours so some time may be spent on leisure (likely response: people work less—income effect).

14. In addition to deciding how to allocate its present income among goods and services, a household may also decide to save or borrow. When a household decides to save part of its current income, it is using current income to finance future spending. When a household borrows, it finances current purchases with future income.

15. A change in interest rates has a positive effect on saving if the substitution effect dominates the income effect, and a negative effect if the income effect dominates the substitution effect. Most empirical evidence shows that the substitution effect dominates here.

Review Terms and Concepts

budget constraint 137

choice set or opportunity set 138

consumer surplus 152

cost-benefit analysis 153

diamond/water paradox 153

financial capital market 157

income effect of a price change 147

labour supply curve 155

law of diminishing marginal utility 143

marginal utility (*MU*) 142

perfect knowledge 136

substitution effect of a price change 148

total utility 143

utility 142

utility-maximizing rule 145

1. Sketch the following budget constraints:

	P_X	P_Y	INCOME
a.	$20	$50	$1000
b.	40	50	1000
c.	20	100	1000
d.	20	50	2000
e.	0.25	0.25	7.00
f.	0.25	0.50	7.00
g.	0.50	0.25	7.00

2. On January 1, Professor Smith made a resolution to lose some weight and save some money. He decided that he would strictly budget $100 for lunches each month. For lunch he has only two choices: the faculty club, where the price of a lunch is $5, and Alice's Restaurant, where the price of a lunch is $10. Every day that he doesn't eat lunch, he runs eight kilometres.

 a. Assuming that Professor Smith spends the entire $100 each month at either Alice's or the club, sketch his budget constraint. Show actual numbers on the axes.

 b. Last month Professor Smith chose to eat at the club 10 times and at Alice's five times. Does this choice fit within his budget constraint?

 c. Last month, Alice ran a half-price lunch special all month. All lunches were reduced to $5. Show the effect on Professor Smith's budget constraint.

 d. During the sale, Professor Smith continued to eat at Alice's only five times but ate at the club 15 times. This implies that Alice's meals are "inferior goods." Explain why. (*Hint:* Use income and substitution effects.)

3. Reform of the Canadian welfare system has been a goal of many provincial governments. The major thrust of welfare reform proposals over the last two decades has been to restore the incentive to work. Because welfare programs are for low income families, those who earn income lose their eligibility for welfare. This acts as a stiff "tax" on working.

 A number of provinces have significantly reduced social assistance payments per person. Cutting benefits makes living on welfare less attractive, it is argued, and should lead to an expansion in the labour supply.

Consider the following scenario: Welfare recipients' benefits are reduced by $0.50 for every dollar earned. For example, someone who earns $200 per month loses $100 in welfare benefits; thus the net gain from working is only $100. Then, the system is reformed so that benefits are reduced by $0.80 for every dollar earned. Thus if the individual earns $200, $160 is now lost in welfare benefits.

Using income and substitution effects, explain why the reformed system could lead to either an increase or a decrease in labour supply.

4. Assume that Mei has $100 per month to divide between dinners at a Chinese restaurant and nights at Zanzibar, a local pub. Assume that going to Zanzibar costs $20 and eating at the Chinese restaurant costs $10. Suppose that Mei spends two nights at Zanzibar and eats six times at the Chinese restaurant.

 a. Draw Mei's budget constraint and show that she can afford six meals and two nights at Zanzibar.

 b. Assume that Mei comes into some money and can now spend $200 per month. Draw her new budget constraint.

 c. As a result of the increase in income, Mei decides to spend eight nights at Zanzibar and eat at the Chinese restaurant four times. What kind of a good is Chinese food? What kind of a good is a night at Zanzibar?

 d. What part of the increase in Zanzibar trips is due to the income effect, and what part is due to the substitution effect? Explain your answer.

5. Sketch the income/leisure budget constraint facing a person with

 a. a 24-hour endowment of time daily,

 b. $50 in property income per day (received regardless of work effort),

 c. a job that requires a minimum of eight hours of work per day and that pays a wage of $10 per hour, plus time-and-a-half for all work over eight hours per day ($1.5 \times \$10$), and

 d. no other work opportunities.

Note: All these should be embodied in a *single* income/leisure budget constraint.

6. For each of the following events, consider how you might react. What things might you consume more of? What things might you consume less of? Would you work more or less? Would you increase or decrease your saving? Are your responses consistent with the discussion of household behaviour in this chapter?

    a. Tuition at your university is raised 25%.

    b. You receive an award that pays you $300 per month for the next five years.

    c. The price of food doubles. (If you are on a meal plan, assume that your board charges double.)

    d. A new business opens up nearby offering part-time jobs at $20 per hour.

7. Assume that as a result of two recent hijackings and bombings, people's desire to fly diminishes significantly. Describe and graph (using supply and demand curves) how you might expect the air travel market to react. What might happen to the price of airline tickets? Explain consumers' reactions to any price changes in terms of income and substitution effects.

8. Is it possible for a unit of a good to have a negative marginal utility? Can you think of an example? How would consumption of this unit affect total utility? Why would it make no sense to purchase knowingly a good with negative utility?

Appendix to Chapter 6   Indifference Curves

Early in this chapter, you saw how a consumer choosing between two goods is constrained by the prices of those goods and by his or her income. This appendix returns to that example and analyzes the process of choice more formally. (Before we proceed, review carefully the text under the heading "The Budget Constraint More Formally" on page 140.)

Assumptions

We base the following analysis on four assumptions:

1. We assume that this analysis is restricted to goods that yield positive marginal utility, or, more simply, that "more is better." One way to justify this assumption is to say that if more of something actually makes you worse off, you can simply throw it away at no cost. This is the assumption of free disposal.

2. The **marginal rate of substitution** is defined as MU_X/MU_Y, or the ratio at which a household is willing to substitute Y for X. When MU_X/MU_Y is equal to four, for example, I would be willing to trade four units of Y for one additional unit of X.

We assume a diminishing marginal rate of substitution. That is, as more of X and less of Y is consumed, MU_X/MU_Y declines. As you consume more of X and less of Y, X becomes less valuable in terms of units of Y, or Y becomes more valuable in terms of X. This is almost, but not precisely, equivalent to assuming diminishing marginal utility.

3. We assume that consumers have the ability to choose among the combinations of goods and services available. Confronted with the choice between two alternative combinations of goods and services, A and B, a consumer will respond in one of three ways: (1) she prefers A over B, (2) she prefers B over A, or (3) she is indifferent between A and B.

4. We assume that consumer choices are consistent with a simple postulate of rationality. If a consumer shows that he prefers A to B and subsequently shows that he prefers B to a third alternative, C, he should prefer A to C if confronted with a choice between the two.

Deriving Indifference Curves

If we accept these four assumptions, we can construct a "map" of a consumer's preferences. These preference maps are made up of indifference curves. An **indifference curve** is a set of points, each point representing a combination of goods X and Y, all of which yield the same total utility.

Figure 6A.1 on page 162 shows how we might go about deriving an indifference curve for a hypothetical consumer. Each point in the diagram represents some amount of X and some amount of Y. Point A in the diagram, for example, represents X_A units of X and Y_A units of Y. Now suppose that we take some amount of Y away from our hypothetical consumer, moving him to A'. At A' he has the same amount of X—that is, X_A units—but less Y; he now has only Y_C units of Y. Since "more is better," our consumer is unequivocally worse off at A' than he was at A.

To compensate for the loss of Y, we now begin giving our consumer some more X. If we give him just a little, he will still be worse off than he was at A; if we give him lots of X, he will be better off. But there must be some quantity of X that will just compensate for the loss of Y. By giving him that amount, we will have put together a bundle, Y_C and X_C, which yields the exact

An Indifference Curve

An indifference curve is a set of points, each representing a combination of some amount of good X and some amount of good Y, that all yield the same amount of total utility. The consumer depicted here is indifferent between bundles A and B, B and C, and A and C.

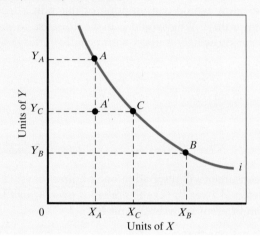

those shown on the diagram; in fact, their number is infinite. Notice that as you move up and to the right, utility increases.

The shapes of the indifference curves depend upon the preferences of the consumer, and the whole set of indifference curves is called a **preference map**. Each consumer has a unique preference map.

Properties of Indifference Curves

The indifference curves shown in Figure 6A.2 are drawn bowing in toward the origin, or zero point, on the axes. In other words, the absolute value of the slope of the indifference curves decreases, or the curves get flatter, as we move to the right. Thus, we say that indifference curves are convex toward the origin. This shape follows directly from the assumption of diminishing marginal rate of substitution and makes sense if you remember the law of diminishing marginal utility.

To understand the convex shape, compare the segment of curve i_1 between A and B with the segment of the same curve between C and D. Moving from A to B, the consumer is willing to give up a substantial amount of Y to get a small amount of X. (Remember that total utility is constant along an indifference curve; the consumer is therefore indifferent between A and B.) Moving from C and D, however, the consumer is willing to give up only a small amount of Y to get more X.

same total utility as bundle A. If confronted with a choice between bundles A and C, our consumer will say "Either one; I don't care." In other words, he is *indifferent* between A and C. When confronted with a choice between bundles C and B (which represents X_B and Y_B units of X and Y), he is also indifferent. The points along the curve labelled i in Figure 6A.1 represent all the combinations of X and Y that yield the same total utility to our consumer. That curve is thus an indifference curve.

Obviously, each consumer has a whole set of indifference curves. Return for a moment to Figure 6A.1. Starting at point A again, imagine that we give the consumer a tiny bit more X *and* a tiny bit more Y. Because more is better, we know that the new bundle will yield a higher level of total utility, and the consumer will be better off. Now, just as we constructed the first indifference curve, we can construct a second one. What we get is an indifference curve that parallels the first, but that is *higher* and to the *right* of it. Because utility along an indifference curve is constant at all points, every point along the new curve represents a higher level of total utility than every point along the first.

Figure 6A.2 shows a set of four indifference curves. The curve labelled i_4 represents the combinations of X and Y that yield the highest level of total utility among the four. Many other indifference curves exist between

A Preference Map: A Family of Indifference Curves

Each consumer has a unique family of indifference curves called a preference map. Higher indifference curves represent higher levels of total utility.

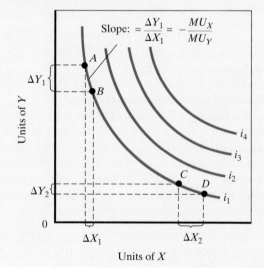

This changing trade-off makes complete sense when you remember the law of diminishing marginal utility. Notice that between A and B, a lot of Y is consumed, and the marginal utility derived from a unit of Y is likely to be small. At the same time, though, only a little bit of X is being consumed, so the marginal utility derived from consuming a unit of X is likely to be high.

Suppose, for example, that X is pizza and Y is cans of pop. Near A and B, a thirsty, hungry football player who has 10 cans of pop in front of him but only one slice of pizza will trade several cans of pop for another slice. Down around C and D, however, he has 20 slices of pizza and only a single can of pop. Now he will trade several slices of pizza to get an additional can of pop.

We can show how the trade-off changes more formally by deriving an expression for the slope of an indifference curve. Let's look at the arc (i.e., the section of the curve) between A and B. We know that in moving from A to B, total utility remains constant. That means that the utility lost as a result of consuming less Y must be matched by the utility gained from consuming more X. We can approximate the loss of utility by multiplying the marginal utility of Y (MU_Y) by the number of units by which consumption of Y is curtailed (ΔY). Similarly, we can approximate the utility gained from consuming more X by multiplying the marginal utility of X (MU_X) by the number of additional units of X consumed (ΔX). Remember, since the consumer is indifferent between points A and B, total utility is the same at both points. Thus, these two must be equal in magnitude—that is, the gain in utility from consuming more X must equal the loss in utility from consuming less Y. Since ΔY is a negative number (because consumption of Y decreases from A to B), it follows that:

$$MU_X \bullet \Delta X = - (MU_Y \bullet \Delta Y).$$

If we divide both sides by MU_Y and by ΔX, we obtain:

$$\Delta Y/\Delta X = - \left(\frac{MU_X}{MU_Y} \right).$$

Recall that the slope of any line is calculated by dividing the change in Y (that is, ΔY) by the change in X (that is, ΔX). This leads us to conclude that:

The slope of an indifference curve is the ratio of the marginal utility of X to the marginal utility of Y, and it is negative.

Now let's return to our pizza (X) and pop (Y) example. As we move down from the A:B area to the C:D area, our football player is consuming less pop and more pizza. The marginal utility of pizza (MU_X) is falling and the marginal utility of pop (MU_Y) is rising. That means

that MU_X/MU_Y (the **marginal rate of substitution**) is falling, and the absolute value of the slope of the indifference curve is declining. And, indeed, it does get flatter.

Consumer Choice

As you recall, demand depends upon income, the prices of goods and services, and preferences or tastes. We are now ready to see how preferences as embodied in indifference curves interact with budget constraints to determine how the final quantities of X and Y will be chosen.

In Figure 6A.3, a set of indifference curves is superimposed on a consumer's budget constraint. Recall that the budget constraint separates those combinations of X and Y that are available to our consumer from those that are not. The constraint simply shows those combinations that can be purchased with an income of I at prices P_X and P_Y. The budget constraint crosses the X axis at I/P_X, or the number of units of X that can be purchased with I if nothing is spent on Y. Similarly, the budget constraint crosses the Y axis at I/P_Y, or the number of units of Y that can be purchased with an income of I if nothing is spent on X. The shaded area is the consumer's opportunity set. The slope of a budget constraint is $-P_X/P_Y$.

Figure 6A.3

Consumer Utility-Maximizing Equilibrium

Consumers will choose that combination of X and Y that maximizes total utility. Graphically, the consumer will move along the budget constraint until the highest possible indifference curve is reached. At that point, the budget constraint and the indifference curve are tangent. This occurs at X* and Y* (point B).

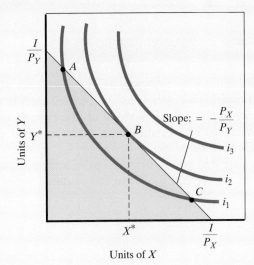

Consumers will choose from among available combinations of X and Y the one that maximizes utility. In graphic terms, the consumer will move along the budget constraint until he or she is on the highest possible indifference curve. Utility rises by moving from points such as A or C (which lie on i_1) toward B (which lies on i_2). Any movement away from point B moves the consumer to a lower indifference curve—a lower level of utility. In this case, utility is maximized when our consumer buys X^* units of X and Y^* units of Y. At point B, the budget constraint is just tangent to (that is, just touches) indifference curve i_2.

As long as indifference curves are convex to the origin, utility maximization will take place at that point at which the indifference curve is just tangent to the budget constraint.

The tangency condition has important implications. Where two curves are tangent, they have the same slope, which implies that the slope of the indifference curve is exactly equal to the slope of the budget constraint at the point of tangency:

$$-\frac{MU_X}{MU_Y} = -\frac{P_X}{P_Y}.$$

slope of indifference curve = slope of budget constraint

By multiplying both sides by MU_Y and dividing both sides by P_Y, we can rewrite this utility-maximizing rule as:

$$\frac{MU_X}{P_X} = \frac{MU_Y}{P_Y}.$$

This is the same rule derived in our earlier discussion without using indifference curves. We can describe this rule intuitively by saying that consumers maximize their total utility by equating the marginal utility per dollar spent on X with the marginal utility per dollar spent on Y. If this rule did not hold, utility could be increased by shifting money from one good to the other.

Deriving a Demand Curve from Indifference Curves and Budget Constraints

We now turn to the task of deriving a simple demand curve from indifference curves and budget constraints. A demand curve shows the quantity of a single good, X in this case, that a consumer will demand at various prices. To derive the demand curve, we need to confront our consumer with several alternative prices for X while keeping other prices, income, and preferences constant.

Figure 6A.4 on page 165 shows the derivation. We begin with price P_X^1. At that price, the utility-maximizing point is A, where the consumer demands X_1 units of X. Therefore, in the right-hand diagram, we plot P_X^1 against X_1. This is the first point on our demand curve.

Now we lower the price of X to P_X^2. Lowering the price expands the opportunity set, and the budget constraint shifts to the right. Because the price of X has fallen, if our consumer spends all of his income on X, he can buy more of it. He is also better off, since he can move to a higher indifference curve. The new utility-maximizing point is B, where the consumer demands X_2 units of X. Because the consumer demands X_2 units of X at a price of P_X^2 we plot P_X^2 against X_2 in the right-hand diagram. A second price cut to P_X^3 moves our consumer to point C, where he demands X_3 units of X, and so on. Thus, we see how the demand curve can be derived from a consumer's preference map and budget constraint.

Summary

1. An *indifference curve* is a set of points, each point representing a combination of goods X and Y, all of which yield the same total utility. A particular consumer's set of indifference curves is called a *preference map*.
2. The slope of an indifference curve is the ratio of the marginal utility of X to the marginal utility of

Y, and it is negative.

3. As long as indifference curves are convex to the origin, utility maximization will take place at that point at which the indifference curve is just tangent to (that is, just touches) the budget constraint. The utility-maximizing rule can also be written as $MU_X/P_X = MU_Y/P_Y$.

Deriving a Demand Curve from Indifference Curves and Budget Constraint

In Figure 6A.4, indifference curves are labelled i_1, i_2, and i_3; budget constraints are shown by the three diagonal lines from $\dfrac{I}{P_Y}$ to $\dfrac{I}{P_X^1}$, $\dfrac{I}{P_X^2}$, and $\dfrac{I}{P_X^3}$. Lowering the price of X from P_X^1 to P_X^2 and then to P_X^3 shifts the budget constraint to the right. At each price there is a different utility-maximizing combination of X and Y. Utility is maximized at point A on i_1, point B on i_2, and point C on i_3. Plotting the three prices against the quantities of X chosen results in a standard downward-sloping demand curve.

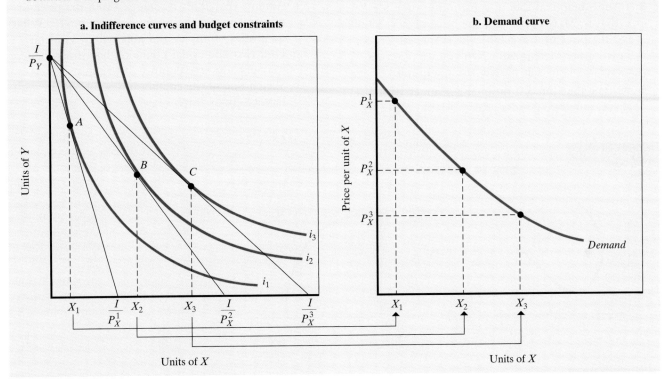

a. Indifference curves and budget constraints

b. Demand curve

indifference curve A set of points, each point representing a combination of goods X and Y, all of which yield the same total utility. 161

marginal rate of substitution MU_X/MU_Y; the ratio at which a household is willing to substitute good Y for good X. 161

preference map A consumer's set of indifference curves. 162

1. Which of the four assumptions that were made at the beginning of the appendix are violated by the indifference curves in Figure 1? Explain.

2. Assume that a household receives a weekly income of $100. If Figure 2 represents that household's choices as the price of X changes, plot three points on the household's demand curve.

*3. If Ann's marginal rate of substitution of Y for X is 5 (that is, $MU_X/MU_Y = 5$), the price of X is $9.00, and the price of Y is $2.00, she is spending too much of her income on Y. Do you agree or disagree? Explain your answer using a graph.

*4. Assume that Jim is a rational consumer who consumes only two goods, apples (A) and nuts (N).

Assume that his marginal rate of substitution of apples for nuts is given by the following formula:

$$MRS = MU_N/MU_A = A/N$$

That is, Jim's MRS is simply equal to the ratio of the number of apples consumed to the number of nuts consumed.

a. Assume that Jim's income is $100, the price of nuts is $5, and the price of apples is $10. What quantities of apples and nuts will he consume?

b. Find two additional points on his demand curve for nuts ($P_N = 10 and $P_N = 2).

c. Sketch one of the equilibrium points on an indifference curve graph.

Figure 1

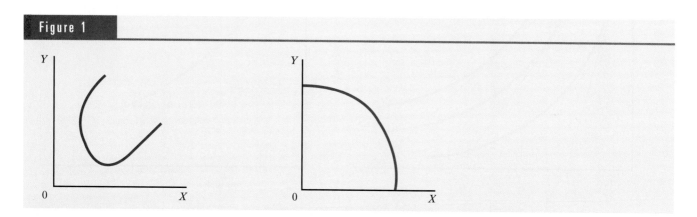

Figure 2

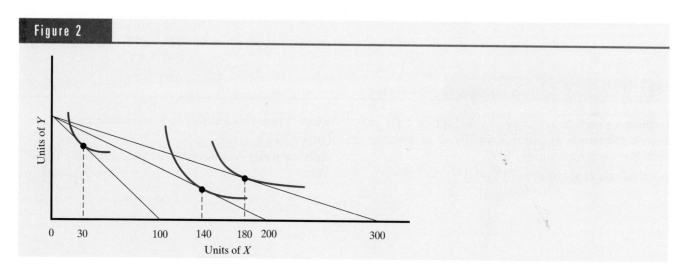

The Behaviour of Profit-Maximizing Firms and the Production Process

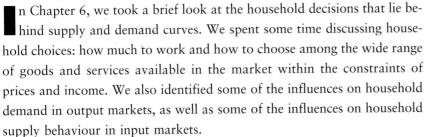

The Behaviour of Profit-Maximizing Firms

Profits and Economic Costs

Short-Run versus Long-Run Decisions

The Bases of Decisions: Market Price of Output, Available Technology, and Input Prices

The Production Process

Production Functions: Total Product, Marginal Product, and Average Product

Production Functions with Two Variable Factors of Production

Choice of Technology

Appendix: From Technology and Factor Prices to Cost: Isoquants and Isocosts

In Chapter 6, we took a brief look at the household decisions that lie behind supply and demand curves. We spent some time discussing household choices: how much to work and how to choose among the wide range of goods and services available in the market within the constraints of prices and income. We also identified some of the influences on household demand in output markets, as well as some of the influences on household supply behaviour in input markets.

We now turn to the other side of the system and examine the behaviour of firms. Business firms purchase inputs in order to produce and sell outputs. In other words, they *demand* factors of production in input markets and *supply* goods and services in output markets. Figure 7.1 on page 168 repeats the now familiar circular flow diagram you first encountered in Chapter 6. Here in Chapter 7 we look inside the firm at the production process that actually transforms inputs into outputs. Chapters 8 and 9 use information on input prices and production technology to discuss cost curves, from which we derive firms' output supply curves. In Chapters 10 and 11, we discuss input markets (specifically, labour, land, and capital markets) and derive firms' input demand curves. Chapter 12 puts all the pieces of the system together and analyzes how the system as a whole functions. In Chapters 13 through 17, we relax some of our assumptions—including the assumption of perfect competition—and examine the role of government in a market economy.

FIGURE 7.1

Firm and Household Decisions

Firms supply output and demand labour and capital in input markets. This chapter and the next four chapters focus on the left side of this diagram—everything that is highlighted in red.

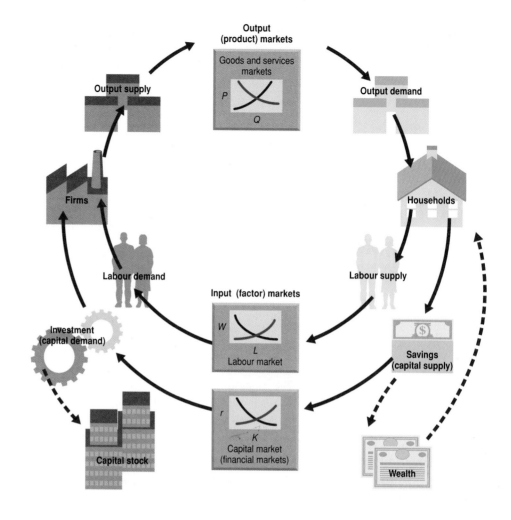

While Chapters 7 through 12 describe the behaviour of perfectly competitive firms, much of what we say in these chapters applies to firms that are not perfectly competitive as well. For example, when we turn to monopoly in Chapter 13, we will be describing firms that are similar to competitive firms in many ways. All firms, whether competitive or not, demand inputs, engage in production, and produce outputs. All firms have an incentive to maximize profits and thus to minimize costs.

production *The process by which inputs are combined, transformed, and turned into outputs.*

Central to our analysis is **production,** the process by which inputs are combined, transformed, and turned into outputs. Firms vary in size and internal organization, but they all take inputs and transform them into things for which there is some demand. An independent accountant, for example, combines labour, paper, telephone service, time, learning, and a personal computer to provide help to confused taxpayers. A rock band combines talent, energy, instruments, costumes, amplifiers, lighting, and labour to produce music. An automobile plant uses steel, labour, plastic, electricity, machines, and countless other inputs to produce cars. Before we begin our discussion of the production process, however, we need to clarify some of the assumptions on which our analysis is based.

■ **Production Is Not Limited to Firms** While our discussions in the next several chapters focus on profit-making business firms, it is important to understand that production and productive activity are not confined to private business firms. Households also engage in transforming factors of production (labour, capital, energy, natural resources, etc.) into useful things. When I work in my garden, I am combining land, labour, fertilizer, seeds, and tools (capital) into the vegetables I eat and the flowers I enjoy. The child-rearing activities of parents transform their young into productive human beings. The government also combines land, labour, and capital to produce public services for which demand exists: national defence, police and fire protection, and education, to name a few.

Private business firms are set apart from other producers, such as households and government, by their purpose. A **firm** exists when a person or a group of people decides to produce a good or service to meet a perceived demand. In most cases, firms exist to make a profit. They engage in production (that is, they transform inputs into outputs) because they can sell their products for more than it costs to produce them.

Even among firms that exist to make a profit, however, there are many important differences. A firm's behaviour is likely to depend upon how it is organized internally and upon its relationship to the firms with which it competes. How many competitors are there? How large are they? How do they compete?

In Chapter 3 we discussed the different ways that businesses can organize—as proprietorships, as partnerships, or as corporations. We also discussed the different forms of industry in the Canadian economy—perfect competition, monopolistic competition, oligopoly, and monopoly. Before we finish with microeconomics, we will analyze the behaviour of all four of these industry types. But it is logical to start with the simplest. Thus, the next three chapters will deal exclusively with the behaviour of firms in perfectly competitive industries.

firm *An organization that comes into being when a person or a group of people decides to produce a good or service to meet a perceived demand. Most firms exist to make a profit.*

■ **Perfect Competition** As you learned in Chapter 3, **perfect competition** exists in an industry that contains many relatively small firms producing identical products. The most important characteristic of a perfectly competitive industry is that no single firm has any control over prices. In other words, an individual firm cannot affect the market price of its product or the prices of the inputs that it buys. This important characteristic follows from two assumptions. First, a competitive industry is composed of many firms, each small relative to the size of the industry. Second, every firm in a perfectly competitive industry produces **homogeneous products,** which means that the output of one firm cannot be distinguished from the output of the others.

These assumptions limit the decisions open to competitive firms and simplify the analysis of competitive behaviour. Firms in perfectly competitive industries do not differentiate their products, nor do they make decisions about price. Rather, each firm takes prices as given—that is, as determined in the market by the laws of supply and demand—and decides only how much to produce and how to produce it.

The idea that competitive firms are "price-takers" is central to our discussion. Of course, we do not mean by this that firms cannot affix price tags to their merchandise; all firms have this ability. We simply mean that, given the availability of perfect substitutes, any product priced over the market price will not be sold. Thus, to sell any goods, competitive firms must adhere to the market price.

These assumptions also imply that the demand for the product of a competitive firm is perfectly elastic (see Chapter 5). Take, for example, the P.E.I. potato farmer whose situation is shown in Figure 7.2 on page 170. The left side of the diagram represents the current conditions in the market. Potatoes are currently

perfect competition *An industry structure (or market organization) in which there are many firms, each small relative to the industry, producing virtually identical products and in which no firm is large enough to have any control over prices. In perfectly competitive industries, new competitors can freely enter and exit the market.*

homogeneous products *Undifferentiated products; products that are identical to, or indistinguishable from, one another.*

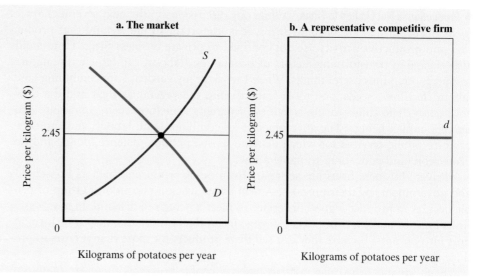

FIGURE 7.2

Demand Facing a Single Firm in a Perfectly Competitive Market

If a representative firm in a perfectly competitive market raises the price of its output above $2.45, the quantity demanded of *that firm's* output will drop to zero. Each firm faces a perfectly elastic demand curve, *d*.

a. The market

b. A representative competitive firm

Price per kilogram ($)

Kilograms of potatoes per year

2.45

S

D

0

Price per kilogram ($)

Kilograms of potatoes per year

2.45

d

0

free entry *The condition that exists when there are no barriers to prevent new firms from competing for profits in a profitable industry.*

free exit *The condition that exists when firms can simply stop producing their product and leave a market. Firms incur no additional costs by exiting the industry.*

selling for $2.45 per kilogram.[1] The right side of the diagram shows the demand for potatoes as the farmer sees it. If she were to raise her price, she would sell no potatoes at all; because there are perfect substitutes available, the quantity demanded of her potatoes would drop to zero. To lower her price would be silly because she can sell all she wants at the current price. (Remember, each farmer's production is very small relative to the entire potato market.)

In perfect competition we also assume that firms can freely enter and exit the industry. The assumption of **free entry** implies that if firms in an industry are earning high profits, new firms that seek to do the same thing are likely to spring up. There are no barriers that prevent a new firm from competing. Fast-food restaurants are quick to spring up when a new shopping centre opens, and new gas stations appear when a housing development or a new highway is built. Where profit opportunities present themselves, we assume that firms will enter and compete for them.

Free exit is possible when firms can simply stop producing their product and leave a market. Firms incur no additional costs by exiting the industry, hence the term *free exit*. In the 1950s, for example, two major industries in Quebec were textiles and furniture. As time went on and conditions changed, fewer and fewer of those firms remained in business. Generally speaking, a firm closes down because it is suffering losses or because profits are insufficient. Quebec textile and furniture producers found themselves facing increasing foreign competition with lower production costs. While some firms packed up and moved, others simply left the business altogether.

As you saw in Chapter 3, the best examples of perfect competition are probably found in agriculture. In that industry, products are absolutely homogeneous— it is impossible to distinguish one farmer's wheat from another's—and prices are set by the forces of supply and demand in a huge national market.

---

[1]*Recall that capital letters refer to the entire market and lower-case letters refer to representative firms. For example, in Figure 7.2, the market demand curve is labelled D and the demand curve facing the firm is labelled d.*

The Behaviour of Profit-Maximizing Firms

All types of firms must make several basic decisions to achieve what we assume to be their primary objective—maximum profits. Perfectly competitive firms have three basic decisions to make. Actually, *all* firms must make these three decisions, but (as we will see later) noncompetitive firms have other decisions to make as well. The three basic decisions (Figure 7.3) are:

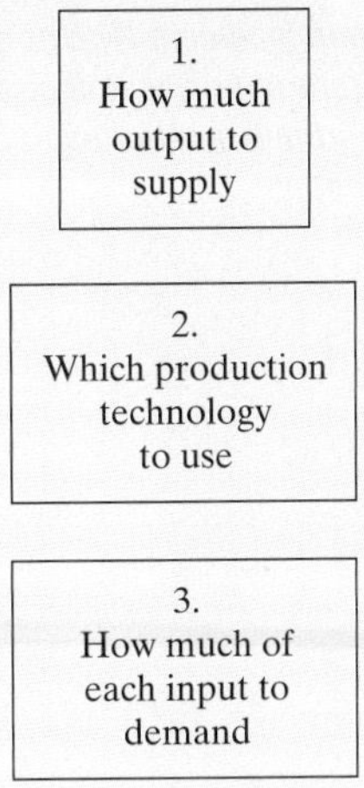

> The Three Decisions That All Firms Must Make:
> 1. How much output to supply (quantity of product);
> 2. How to produce that output (which production technique/technology to use); and
> 3. How much of each input to demand.

FIGURE 7.3

The Three Decisions That All Firms Must Make

1. How much output to supply

2. Which production technology to use

3. How much of each input to demand

The first and last choices are linked by the second choice. Once a firm has decided how much to produce, the choice of a production method determines the firm's input requirements. If a sweater company decides to produce 5000 sweaters this month, it knows how many production workers it will need, how much electricity it will use, how much raw yarn to purchase, and how many sewing machines to run. A grower who sets out to produce and ship 3000 kilograms of apples knows how many pickers to hire, how many baskets to have on hand, and so forth.

Similarly, given a technique of production, any set of input quantities determines the amount of output that can be produced. Certainly the number of machines and workers employed in a sweater mill determines how many sweaters can be produced, and the number of trees and pickers determines the number of kilograms of apples a grower can ship.

Changing the *technology* of production will change the relationship between input and output quantities. An apple orchard that uses expensive equipment to raise pickers up into the trees will harvest more fruit with fewer workers in a given period of time than an orchard in which pickers use simple ladders. It is also possible that two different technologies can produce the same quantity of output. For example, a fully computerized textile mill with only a few workers running the machines may produce the same number of sweaters as a mill with no sophisticated machines but many workers. A profit-maximizing firm chooses the technology that minimizes its costs for a given level of output.

Remember as we proceed that we are discussing and analyzing the behaviour of *perfectly competitive* firms. Thus, we will say nothing about price-setting behaviour, product quality, and other characteristics of the product, or choices that lead to product differentiation. In perfect competition, both input and output prices are beyond a firm's control—they are determined in the market and are not the decisions of any individual firm. And remember that all firms in a given industry produce the exact same product. When we analyze the behaviour of firms in other kinds of markets (in Chapters 13 and 14), the three basic decisions will be expanded to include the setting of prices and the determination of product quality.

PROFITS AND ECONOMIC COSTS

As noted earlier, we assume that firms are in business to make a profit and that the behaviour of firms is guided by the goal of maximizing profits. But what is profit? In simplest terms, **profit** is the difference between total revenues and total costs:

> Profit = Total revenue − Total cost

profit *The difference between total revenues and total costs.*

revenue or **total revenue**
*Receipts from the sale of a product
($P \times q$).*

economic costs *The full costs of
production including (1) a normal
rate of return on investment and (2)
the opportunity cost of each factor
of production.*

Revenues are simply receipts from the sale of the product. **Total revenue** is equal to the number of units produced and sold (q) times the price received per unit (P). Costs, however, are more complicated. In economics, the definition of total costs includes more than simple out-of-pocket costs. **Economic costs** (which economists use to mean "total costs") are the *full* costs of production and include (1) a normal rate of return and (2) the opportunity cost of each factor of production.

■ **Normal Rate of Return** When someone decides to start a firm, he or she must commit resources. To operate a manufacturing firm, you need a plant and some equipment. To start a restaurant, you need to buy grills, ovens, tables, chairs, and so forth. In other words, you must invest in capital. Such investment requires resources that stay tied up in the firm as long as it operates. Even firms that have been around a long time must continue to invest. Plant and equipment wear out and must be replaced. Firms that decide to expand must put new capital in place. This is as true of proprietorships, where the resources come directly from the proprietor, as it is of corporations, where the resources needed to make investments come from shareholders.

Whenever resources are used to invest in a business, there is an opportunity cost. Instead of opening a candy store, I could put my funds into an alternative use such as a term deposit or a government bond and earn interest. Instead of using its retained earnings to build a new plant, a firm could simply earn interest on those funds or pay them out to shareholders.

Why do firms put their funds into the business rather than into the bank or into some other alternative use? When people decide to invest resources in a business, we assume that the decision is based on the expectation of profit. But a firm isn't profitable in a meaningful sense unless it earns more for its investors than what they forgo by not buying a bond or a term deposit. Using resources to invest in a firm thus has an opportunity cost.

normal rate of profit or **normal
rate of return** *A rate of profit that
is just sufficient to keep owners
and investors satisfied. For
relatively risk-free firms, it should
be nearly the same as the interest
rate on risk-free government bonds.*

A **normal rate of profit** (also called a **normal rate of return**) is the rate that is just sufficient to keep owners or investors satisfied. From the standpoint of a manager, the normal rate of return is the opportunity cost of investment. In other words, it is the rate of profit just equal to the profit rate the firm could make by investing its resources elsewhere. If the rate of return were to fall below normal, it would be difficult or impossible for managers to raise resources needed to purchase new capital. Owners of the firm would be receiving profits that were lower than they could receive elsewhere in the economy.

If the firm has fairly steady revenues and the future looks secure, the normal profit rate should be very close to the interest rate on risk-free government bonds. I certainly won't keep investors interested in my firm if I don't pay them a rate of return at least as high as they can get from a risk-free government or corporate bond. If my firm is rock solid and the economy is steady, I may not have to pay a much higher rate. But if my firm is in a very speculative industry and the future of the economy is shaky, I may have to pay substantially more to keep my shareholders happy. In exchange for taking such a risk, they will expect a higher return.

A normal profit rate is added as part of costs in calculating the full economic costs of a business enterprise. Adding a normal profit rate to costs means that when a firm earns exactly a normal rate of return or profit, it actually earns zero economic profits. **Economic profits**, or **excess profits** as they are sometimes called, are profits over and above normal. In other words, profits are considered economic profits only if they are greater than the opportunity cost of investing in the industry.

economic profits or **excess
profits** *Profits over and above the
normal rate of return on investment.*

A simple example will illustrate the concepts of a normal profit as part of cost and economic profit as "profit over and above a normal return to capital." Suppose that Michelle and Laura decide to start a small business selling belts in the Calgary airport. To get into the business they need to invest in a fancy pushcart. The price of the pushcart is $20 000 with all the displays and attachments built in. Suppose that Michelle and Laura estimate that they will sell 3000 belts each year for $10 each. Further, assume that each belt costs $5 from the supplier. Finally, the cart must be staffed by one clerk who works for an annual wage of $14 000. Is this business going to make a profit?

To answer this question, we must determine total revenue and total cost. First, annual revenues are simply $30 000 (3000 belts × $10). Total costs include the costs of the belts—$15 000 (3000 belts × $5)—plus the labour cost of $14 000, for a total cost of $29 000. Thus, on the basis of the annual revenue and cost flows, the firm *seems* to be making a profit of $1000 ($30 000 − $29 000).

But what about the $20 000 initial investment in the pushcart? This investment is *not* a direct part of the cost of Michelle and Laura's firm. If we assume that the cart maintains its value over time, *the only thing that Michelle and Laura are giving up is the interest that they might have earned had they not tied up their funds in the pushcart.* That is, the only real "cost" is the opportunity cost of the investment, which is the forgone interest on the $20 000.

Now suppose that Michelle and Laura want a minimum return equal to 10%—which is, say, the rate of interest that they could have gotten by purchasing corporate bonds. This implies a normal return of 10%, or $2000 annually (= $20 000 × .10) on the $20 000 investment. But, as we determined above, Michelle and Laura will earn only $1000 annually. This is only a 5% return on their investment. Thus, they are really earning a below normal return. Recall that the opportunity cost of capital must be added to cost in calculating economic profit. Thus, full economic costs in this case are $31 000 ($29 000 + $2000 in forgone interest on the investment). Economic profits are negative: $30 000 minus $31 000 equals −$1000. These calculations are summarized in Table 7.1. Because economic profits are negative, Michelle and Laura are actually earning an *economic loss* on their belt business.

When a firm earns *positive* economic profits, it is earning profit at a rate more than sufficient to retain the interest of investors. In fact, economic profits are likely to attract new firms into an industry and cause existing firms to expand.

When a firm suffers *negative* economic profits—that is, when it incurs economic losses—it is earning at a rate below that required to keep investors happy. Such economic losses may or may not be losses as an accountant would measure them. Even if I earn a positive profit of 10% on my assets, I am earning below normal profits, or economic losses, if a normal return for my industry is 15%. In this

Table 7.1	Calculating Total Revenue, Total Cost, and Profit	
Initial investment:		$20 000
Interest rate:		10%
Total revenues (3000 belts x $10 each):		$30 000
Costs:		
Belts from supplier (3000 belts × $5 each)		$15 000
Labour cost		14 000
Normal return/Opportunity cost of capital ($20 000 × 0.10)		+ 2 000
Total costs:		$31 000
Profit = Total revenues − Total costs =		−$ 1 000
•There is an economic loss of $1000.		

case, I have a net economic loss of 5% per year, and my investors will be looking to bail out. Economic losses may cause some firms to exit the industry; others will contract in size. Certainly new investment will not flow into such an industry.

■ **Opportunity Costs of All Inputs** Economic costs include the opportunity costs of all inputs, not just out-of-pocket costs. If you open a restaurant and work 40 hours a week helping to run it, the cost of running the restaurant includes the cost of your time, even if you do not pay yourself a formal wage. (If you don't pay yourself a wage, your time does not show up on the restaurant's books.) If you could be earning $15 per hour working full-time at a local factory, the opportunity cost of your time helping to run the restaurant is $600 per week (40 hours × $15). In analyzing costs, it is important to include both direct out-of-pocket costs *and* opportunity costs.

SHORT-RUN VERSUS LONG-RUN DECISIONS

The decisions made by a firm—how much to produce, how to produce it, and what inputs to demand—all take time into account. If a firm decides that it wants to double or triple its output, it may need time to arrange financing, hire architects and contractors, and build a new plant. Planning for a major expansion can take years. In the meantime, the firm must decide how much to produce within the constraint of its existing plant. If a firm decides that it wants to get out of a particular business, it may take time to arrange an orderly exit. There may be contract obligations to fulfil, equipment to sell, and so forth. Once again, the firm must decide what to do in the meantime.

A firm's immediate response to a change in the economic environment may also differ from its response over time. Consider, for example, a small restaurant with 20 tables that becomes very popular. The immediate problem is getting the most profit within the constraint of the existing restaurant. The owner might consider adding a few tables or speeding up service to squeeze in a few more customers. Some popular restaurants do not take reservations, forcing people to wait at the bar, which increases drink revenues and keeps tables full at all times. At the same time, the owner may be thinking of expanding his current facility, moving to a larger facility, or opening a second restaurant. In the future, he might buy the store next door and double his capacity. Such decisions might require him to negotiate a lease, buy new equipment, and hire more staff. It takes time to make and implement these decisions.

Because the character of immediate response differs from long-run adjustment, it is useful to define two time periods: the short run and the long run. Two assumptions define the **short run**: (1) a fixed scale (or a fixed factor of production) and (2) no entry into or exit from the industry. First, the short run is defined as that period during which existing firms have some *fixed factor of production*—that is, during which some factor locks them into their current scale of operations. Second, new firms cannot enter, and existing firms cannot exit, an industry in the short run. Firms may curtail operations, but they are still locked into some costs, even though they may be in the process of going out of business.

Just which factor or factors of production are fixed in the short run differs from industry to industry. For a manufacturing firm, the size of the actual physical plant is often the greatest limitation. A factory is built with a given production rate in mind. While that rate can be increased, output cannot increase beyond a certain limit in the short run. For a private physician, the limit may be her own capacity to see patients; the day has only so many hours. In the long run, she may invite others to join her practice and expand, but for now, in the short run, she *is* the firm, and her capacity is the firm's capacity. For a farmer, the fixed factor may be land.

short run *The period of time for which two conditions hold: the firm is operating under a fixed scale (fixed factor) of production and firms can neither enter nor exit an industry.*

In a public transit system, the rails and trains can be thought of as fixed capital in the short run. Unfortunately, demand for service is concentrated around peak commuting hours and not spread out evenly over the day. Thus, for most hours in the day excess capacity exists, while at rush hour the system's capacity is barely adequate to meet demand. In Japan, "subway pushers" are hired to literally push people into jammed subway cars at rush hour.

The capacity of a small farm is limited by the number of hectares being cultivated.

In the **long run,** there are no fixed factors of production. Firms can plan for any output level they find desirable. They can double or triple output, for example. In addition, new firms can start up operations (enter the industry), and existing firms can go out of business (exit the industry).

No hard-and-fast rule specifies how long the short run is. The point is simply that firms make two basic kinds of decisions: those that govern the day-to-day operations of the firm and those that involve longer-term strategic planning. Sometimes major decisions can be implemented in weeks; often, however, the process takes years.

long run *That period of time for which there are no fixed factors of production. Firms can increase or decrease scale of operation, and new firms can enter and existing firms can exit the industry.*

THE BASES OF DECISIONS: MARKET PRICE OF OUTPUT, AVAILABLE TECHNOLOGY, AND INPUT PRICES

As we said earlier, the three fundamental decisions of firms are made with the objective of maximizing profits. Since profits equal total revenues minus total costs, each firm needs to know how much it costs to produce its product and how much its product can be sold for.

To know how much it costs to produce a good or service, I need to know something about the production techniques that are available and about the prices of the inputs required. To estimate how much it will cost me to operate a gas station, for instance, I need to know what equipment I need, how many workers, what kind of a building, and so forth. I also need to know the going wage rates for mechanics and unskilled labourers, the cost of gas pumps, interest rates, rents per square metre of land on high-traffic corners, and the wholesale price of gasoline. And, of course, I need to know how much I can sell gasoline and repair services for.

In the language of economics, I need to know three things:

The Bases of Decision Making:	1. The market price of output; 2. The techniques of production that are available; and 3. The prices of inputs.

Output price determines potential revenues. The techniques available tell me how much of each input I need, and input prices tell me how much they will cost. Together, the available production techniques and the prices of inputs determine costs.

The rest of this chapter and the whole next chapter focus on costs of production. We begin at the heart of the firm, with the process of production itself. Faced with a set of input prices, firms must decide on the best, or optimal, method of production (Figure 7.4). The **optimal method of production** is the one that minimizes cost. With cost determined and the market price of output known, a firm will make a final judgment about the quantity of its product to produce and the quantity of each input to demand.

optimal method of production *The production method that minimizes cost.*

The Production Process

Recall that production is the process through which inputs are combined and transformed into outputs. **Production technology** relates inputs to outputs. Specific quantities of inputs are needed to produce any given service or good. A loaf of bread requires certain amounts of water, flour, and yeast, some kneading and patting, as well as an oven, gas, or electricity. A trip from downtown Toronto to suburban Scarborough can be produced with a taxicab, 45 minutes of a driver's labour, some gasoline, and so forth.

production technology *The relationship between inputs and outputs.*

Most outputs can be produced by a number of different techniques. You can tear down an old building and clear a lot to create a park in several ways, for example. Five hundred men and women with small hammers could descend upon it and carry the pieces away by hand; this would be a **labour-intensive technology.** The same park could be produced by two people with a wrecking crane, a steam shovel, a backhoe, and a dump truck; this would be a **capital-intensive technology.** Similarly, different inputs can be combined to transport people from suburban

labour-intensive technology *Technology that relies heavily on human labour rather than capital.*

capital-intensive technology *Technology that relies heavily on capital rather than human labour.*

FIGURE 7.4

Determining the Optimal Method of Production to Maximize Profits

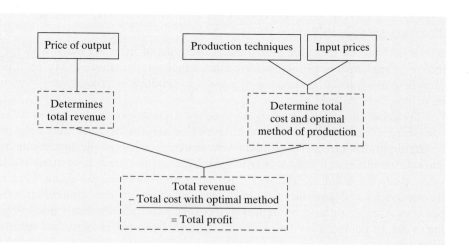

North York to downtown Toronto. The subway carries thousands of people simultaneously and uses a massive amount of capital relative to labour. Cab rides to Toronto require much more labour relative to capital; a driver is needed for every couple of passengers.

An insurance company needs office space to produce its product, but office space can be assembled in a variety of ways. In suburban locations, office parks are often spacious, with trees and grass and buildings of two or three stories. In central cities, offices are stacked on top of one another in glass towers. Thus in central cities, a small amount of land is combined with a great deal of capital to produce insurance services. In suburban office parks, the same services are produced with more land.

In choosing the most appropriate technology, firms choose the one that minimizes the cost of production. For a firm in an economy with a plentiful supply of inexpensive labour but not much capital, the optimal method of production will involve labour-intensive techniques. In contrast, firms in an economy with high wages and high labour costs have an incentive to substitute away from labour and to use more capital-intensive, or labour-saving, techniques. Suburban office parks use more land and have more open space in part because land in the suburbs is more plentiful and less expensive than land in the middle of a big city. Spreading out is cheaper than building a high-rise office tower.

PRODUCTION FUNCTIONS: TOTAL PRODUCT, MARGINAL PRODUCT, AND AVERAGE PRODUCT

The relationship between inputs and outputs (that is, the technology of production) expressed numerically or mathematically is called a **production function** (or **total product function**). A production function shows units of total product as a function of units of inputs.

Imagine, for example, a small sandwich shop. All the sandwiches made in the shop are grilled, and the shop owns only one grill, which can accommodate only two people comfortably. As columns 1 and 2 of the production function in Table 7.2 on page 178 show, one person working alone can produce only 10 sandwiches per hour. He has to answer the phone, wait on customers, keep the tables clean, and so on. The second worker can stay at the grill full time and not worry about anything except making sandwiches. She can produce 15 sandwiches per hour. A third person trying to use the grill produces crowding, but, with careful use of space, more sandwiches can be produced. The third worker adds 10 sandwiches per hour. Note that the added output from hiring a third worker is less because of the capital constraint, *not* because the third worker is somehow less efficient or hard working. We assume that all workers are equally capable.

The fourth and fifth workers can work at the grill only while the first three are putting the pickles, onions, and wrapping on the sandwiches they have made. But then the first three must wait to get back to the grill. Worker four adds a net of five sandwiches per hour to the total, and worker five adds just two. Adding a sixth worker adds no output at all. The current maximum capacity of the shop is 42 sandwiches per hour.

Figure 7.5a graphs the total product data from Table 7.2.

■ **Marginal Product and the Law of Diminishing Returns** **Marginal product** is the additional output that can be produced by hiring one more unit of a specific input, holding all other inputs constant. As column 3 of Table 7.2 shows, the marginal product of the first unit of labour in the sandwich shop is 10 sandwiches; the marginal product of the second is 15; the third, 10; and so forth. The marginal product of the sixth worker is 0. Figure 7.5b graphs the marginal product of labour curve from the data in Table 7.2.

production function or **total product function** A numerical or mathematical expression of a relationship between inputs and outputs. It shows units of total product as a function of units of inputs.

marginal product The additional output that can be produced by adding one more unit of a specific input, ceteris paribus.

Table 7.2   **Production Function**

(1) Labour Units (Employees)	(2) Total Product (Sandwiches per Hour)	(3) Marginal Product of Labour	(4) Average Product of Labour (Total Product ÷ Labour Units)
0	0	—	—
1	10	10	10.0
2	25	15	12.5
3	35	10	11.7
4	40	5	10.0
5	42	2	8.4
6	42	0	7.0

law of diminishing returns
When additional units of a variable input are added to fixed inputs after a certain point, the marginal product of the variable input declines.

The **law of diminishing returns** states that *after a certain point, when additional units of a variable input are added to fixed inputs* (in this case, the building and grill), *the marginal product of the variable input declines*. The British economist David Ricardo first formulated the law of diminishing returns on the basis of his observations of agriculture in nineteenth-century England. Within a given area of land, he noted, successive "doses" of labour and capital yielded smaller and smaller increases in crop output. The law of diminishing returns is true in agriculture because only so much more can be produced by farming the same land more intensely. In manufacturing, diminishing returns set in when a firm begins to strain the capacity of its existing plant.

At our sandwich shop, diminishing returns set in when the third worker is

FIGURE 7.5

Production Function for Sandwiches

A *production function* is a mathematical representation of the relationship between inputs and outputs. In Figure 7.5a, total product (sandwiches) is graphed as a function of labour inputs. The *marginal product* of labour is the additional output that one additional unit of labour produces. Figure 7.5b shows that the marginal product of the second unit of labour at the sandwich shop is 15 units of output; the marginal product of the fourth unit of labour is 5 units of output.

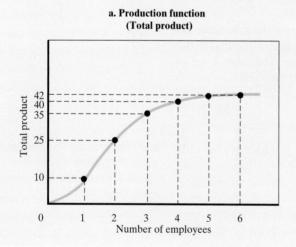

a. Production function
(Total product)

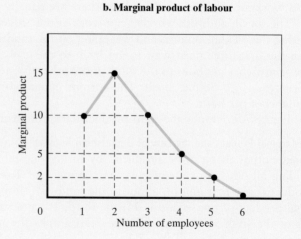

b. Marginal product of labour

added. The marginal product of the second worker is actually higher than the first (see Figure 7.5b). The first worker takes care of the phone and the tables, which frees the second worker to concentrate exclusively on sandwich making. But from that point on, the grill gets crowded.

Diminishing returns characterize many productive activities. Consider, for example, an independent accountant who works primarily for private citizens preparing their tax returns. As he adds more and more clients, he must work later and later into the evening. An hour spent working at 1 A.M. after a long day is likely to be less productive than an hour spent working at 10 A.M. Here the fixed factor of production is the accountant himself. Ultimately, the capacity of his mind and body limit his production, much like the walls of a plant limit production in a factory.

Diminishing returns, or *diminishing marginal product*, begin to show up when more and more units of a variable input are added to a fixed input, such as scale of plant. Recall that we defined the short run as that period in which some fixed factor of production constrains the firm. It follows, then, that:

> Diminishing returns always apply in the short run, and in the short run every firm will face diminishing returns. This means that every firm finds it progressively more difficult to increase its output as it approaches capacity production.

■ **Marginal Product versus Average Product** **Average product** is the average amount produced by each unit of a variable factor of production. At our sandwich shop with one grill, that variable factor is labour. In Table 7.2, you saw that the first two workers together produce 25 sandwiches per hour. Their average product is therefore 12.5 (25 ÷ 2). The third worker adds only 10 sandwiches per hour to the total. These 10 sandwiches are the *marginal* product of labour. (Recall that marginal product is the product of only the last unit of labour.) The *average product* of the first three units of labour, however, is 11.7 (the average of 10, 15, and 10). Stated in equation form, the average product of labour is the *total* output divided by total units of labour:

average product *The average amount produced by each unit of a variable factor of production.*

$$\text{Average product of labour} = \frac{\text{Total product}}{\text{Total units of labour}}$$

Average product "follows" marginal product, but it does not change as quickly. If marginal product is above average, the average rises; if marginal product is below average, the average falls. Suppose, for example, that you have had six exams and that your average is 86. If you score 75 on the next exam, your average score will fall, but not all the way to 75. In fact, it will fall only to 84.4. If you score a 95 instead, your average will rise to 87.3. As columns 3 and 4 of Table 7.2 show, marginal product at the sandwich shop declines continuously after the third worker is hired. Average product also decreases, but more slowly.

Figure 7.6 on page 180 shows a typical production function and the marginal and average product curves derived from it. The marginal product curve is a graph of the slope of the total product curve—that is, of the production function. Average product and marginal product start out equal, as they do in Table 7.2. As marginal product climbs, the graph of average product follows it, but more slowly, up to L_1 (point A).

Notice that marginal product starts out increasing. (Remember that it did so in the sandwich shop as well.) Most production processes are designed to be run well by more than one worker. Take an assembly line, for example. To work efficiently, an assembly line needs a worker at every station; it's a cooperative process.

FIGURE 7.6

Typical Production Function

Marginal and average product curves can be derived from total product curves. The marginal product of labour is the slope of the total product curve. Average product follows marginal product; it rises when marginal product is above it and falls when marginal product is below it.

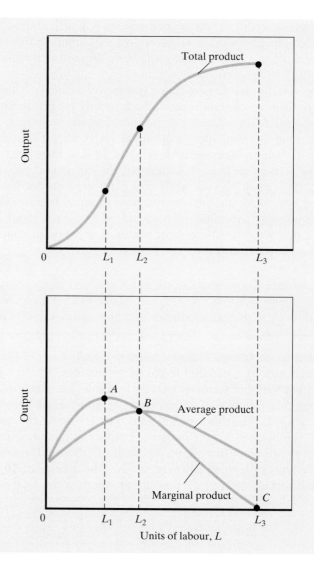

The marginal product of the first workers is low or zero. But as workers are added, the process starts to run and marginal product rises.

At point A (L_1 units of labour), marginal product begins to fall. Because every plant has a finite capacity, efforts to increase production will always run into the limits of that capacity. At point B (L_2 units of labour), marginal product has fallen to equal the average product, which has been increasing. Between point B and point C (between L_2 and L_3 units of labour), marginal product falls below average product, and thus average product begins to follow it *down*. Average product is at its maximum at point B, where it is equal to marginal product.

At L_3 more labour yields no more output, and marginal product is zero—the assembly line has no more positions, the grill is jammed, and the accountant is so tired that he can't see another client.[2] (If you have trouble understanding the relationships among the three curves in Figure 7.6, review the calculations in Table 7.2 and review the appendix on graphing in Chapter 1.)

---

[2]*In theory the total product curve could turn downward beyond* L_3. *This would imply that more workers would actually get in the way and that output would fall. If this were to happen, marginal product would actually be negative beyond* L_3.

PRODUCTION FUNCTIONS WITH TWO VARIABLE FACTORS OF PRODUCTION

So far we have considered production functions with only one variable factor of production. But inputs work together in production. In general, additional capital increases the productivity of labour. Because capital—buildings, machines, and so on—is of no use without people to operate it, we say that capital and labour are *complementary inputs*.

A simple example will clarify this point. Consider again the sandwich shop. If the demand for sandwiches began to exceed the capacity of the shop to produce them, the shop's owner might decide to expand capacity. This would mean opening up more space and purchasing more capital in the form of a new grill.

A second grill would essentially double the shop's productive capacity. Table 7.3 shows the effect of a new grill on the marginal product of labour in the shop. With only one grill, the first worker produces 10 sandwiches per hour and the second produces 15. Diminishing returns set in with the third worker, who can crank out only 10 sandwiches. Returns continue to diminish with the fourth worker, who can make only 5 sandwiches. But with two grills, diminishing returns don't set in until there are two workers at *each* grill. The second, third, and fourth workers produce 15 sandwiches each per hour. Remember, employee one is handling the phone and the tables, so employees two, three, and four can go full speed on the two grills.

With two grills, the fifth worker is the one that begins to crowd. The fifth worker is the third sandwich maker on the first grill; she can produce only 10 sandwiches an hour. The sixth worker is the third worker on the second grill; he can also produce 10 sandwiches an hour. It is not until seven people are working on the grills that marginal product drops to 5. (Look back at Table 7.3.) The productivity of labour has been enhanced by adding capital to the production process. Just as the new grill enhances the productivity of workers in the sandwich shop, new businesses and the capital that they put in place raise the productivity of workers in developing countries like Malaysia, India, and Kenya.

Figure 7.7 shows graphically how the increase in capital enhances the productivity of labour and shifts the marginal product curve to the right. This simple relationship lies at the heart of worries about productivity at the national and international levels. Building new, modern plants and equipment enhances a country's productivity. Since the 1950s, for example, Japan has accumulated capital (i.e., built plant and equipment) faster than any other country in the world. The result is a very high average quantity of output per worker in Japan.

Table 7.3	**Marginal Product of Labour in Sandwich Production with Two Grills**			
	ONE GRILL		**TWO GRILLS**	
Units of Labour	Total Product	Marginal Product	Total Product	Marginal Product
0	0	0	0	0
1	10	10	10	10
2	25	15	25	15
3	35	10	40	15
4	40	5	55	15
5	42	2	65	10
6	42	0	75	10
7	42	0	80	5

FIGURE 7.7

Shift of a Marginal Product of Labour Curve Resulting from an Increase in Capital

When more capital is added in the form of a new grill, the productivity of labour is enhanced. The added capital shifts the marginal product of labour curve to the right. (Although Table 7.3 provides data on the marginal product of only seven workers, you should be able to figure out the marginal product of labour of the eighth and ninth workers when there are two grills.)

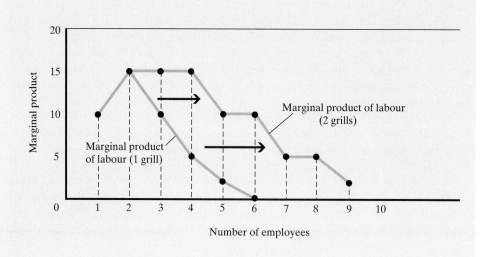

Choice of Technology

As our sandwich shop example shows, inputs (factors of production) are complementary. Capital enhances the productivity of labour. Workers in the sandwich shop are more productive when they are not crowded on a single grill. Similarly, labour enhances the productivity of capital. When more workers are hired at a plant that is operating at 50% of capacity, previously idle machines suddenly become productive.

But inputs can also be substituted for one another. If labour becomes expensive, firms can adopt labour-saving technologies; that is, they can substitute capital for labour. Assembly lines can be automated by replacing human beings with machines, and capital can be substituted for land when land is scarce. (See the Global Perspective box on page 184 titled "Production Technologies: Robots in Canada, Skyscrapers in India.") If capital becomes relatively expensive, firms can substitute labour for capital. In short, most goods and services can be produced in a number of ways, using alternative technologies. One of the key decisions that all firms must make is which technology to use.

Consider the choices available to the diaper manufacturer in Table 7.4. Five different techniques of producing 100 diapers are available. Technology *A* is the

Table 7.4	Inputs Required to Produce 100 Diapers Using Alternative Technologies	
Technology	**Units of Capital (K)**	**Units of Labour (L)**
A	2	10
B	3	6
C	4	4
D	6	3
E	10	2

Table 7.5		Cost-Minimizing Choice among Alternative Technologies (100 Diapers)			
			$COST = (L \times P_L) + (K \times P_K)$		
			IF		IF
Technology	Units of Capital (K)	Units of Labour (L)	$P_L = \$1$ $P_K = \$1$		$P_L = \$5$ $P_K = \$1$
A	2	10	$12		$52
B	3	6	$ 9		$33
C	4	4	$ 8		$24
D	6	3	$ 9		$21
E	10	2	$12		$20

most labour intensive, requiring 10 hours of labour and 2 units of capital to produce 100 diapers. (You can think of units of capital as machine hours.) Technology E is the most capital intensive, requiring only 2 hours of labour but 10 hours of machine time.

To choose a production technique, the firm must look to input markets to find out the current market prices of labour and capital. What is the wage rate (P_L), and what is the cost per hour of capital (P_K)?

Suppose that labour and capital are both available at a price of $1 per unit. Column 4 of Table 7.5 presents the calculations required to determine which technology is the best. The winner is technology C. Assuming that the firm's objective is to maximize profits, it will choose the least-cost technology. Using technology C, the firm can produce 100 diapers for $8. All four of the other technologies produce 100 diapers at a higher cost.

Now suppose that the wage rate (P_L) were to rise sharply, from $1 to $5. You might guess that this increase would lead the firm to substitute labour-saving capital for workers, and you'd be right. As column 5 of Table 7.5 shows, the increase in the wage rate means that technology E is now the cost-minimizing choice for the firm. Using 10 units of capital and only 2 units of labour, the firm can produce 100 diapers for $20. All other technologies are now more costly.

To summarize:

Two things determine the cost of production: (1) the technologies that are available and (2) input prices. Profit-maximizing firms will choose the technology that minimizes the cost of production given current market input prices.

So far, we have looked only at a *single* level of output. That is, we have determined how much it will cost to produce 100 diapers using the best available technology when $P_L = \$1$ or $5 and $P_K = \$1$. But the best technique for producing 1000 diapers or 10 000 diapers may be entirely different. The next chapter explores the relationship between cost and the level of output in some detail. One of our main objectives in that chapter will be to determine the amount that a competitive firm will choose to supply during a given time period.

As we saw in the text, most products can be produced with different combinations of inputs; the choice of technique depends on the prices of land, labour, and capital, which can change over time and differ from location to location. The following examples illustrate the importance of technological choice.

Substitution of Capital for Labour: Robotics in Manufacturing

The ultimate substitution of capital for labour is robotics. Twenty-five years ago, robots were confined to the world of science fiction. Today robots are common and Canadian firms are very active in this emerging industry. For example, CRS Robotics Corporation, a Burlington, Ontario-based company, started by entrepreneur Ray Simmons, is succeeding in this highly competitive industry.[1]

> "There isn't a country in Western Europe where we don't have a robot installed in one industry or another," Simmons says. "We are now exporting to 22 countries in Europe and Asia, as well as the U.S." From loading grenades at a NATO

The ultimate substitution of capital for labour is robotics. Rather than replacing workers in droves, robots are used to perform tasks that are boring, repetitive, or otherwise ill-suited to humans.

site in Norway, to mixing ingredients at a pizzeria in Pittsburgh, to aiding advanced AIDS research in medical labs around the world, the all-Canadian robots provide a strong testament to this country's ability to produce cutting-edge technology to tackle a broad range of tasks that are far too hazardous, impractical, or mundane to be done by humans....

It is also a technology which is in very hot demand in

the all-important U.S. market, which according to a recent Frost and Sullivan market research study is now growing at double-digit rates and will be worth over US$1.2 billion by the year 2000. That kind of burgeoning demand is reflected in CRS Robotics' own track record of robust growth in recent years, which culminated in the shipment of the company's 1000th robot earlier this year [1996]....

To Simmons' pleasant surprise a good chunk of that growth is now being fuelled by Canadian-based companies, reversing an earlier trend when exports accounted for 95% of the company's business. "About 20% of our business is in Canada now," Simmons says, "which is fantastic." Simmons credits an improving domestic economy for this turnaround in Canadian sales, as well as a better understanding by Canadian companies about how robotic technology can improve their manufacturing productivity.

Summary

1. Firms vary in size and internal organization, but they all take inputs and transform them into outputs through a process called *production*.

2. In *perfect competition*, no single firm has any control over prices. This follows from two assumptions: (1) perfectly competitive industries are composed of many firms, each small relative to the size of the industry, and (2) each firm in a perfectly competitive industry produces *homogeneous products*.

3. The demand curve facing a competitive firm is perfectly elastic. If a single firm raises its price above the market price, it will sell nothing. Because it can sell all it produces at the market price, a firm has no incentive to reduce price.

The Behaviour of Profit-Maximizing Firms

4. Profit-maximizing firms in all industries must make three choices: (1) how much output to supply,

"The automotive industry has proven that robotics are a good investment, even though there were some teething pains originally," he explains. *"Now that other industries have witnessed the success the Big Three automakers had with robots in meeting high quality, productivity, and costing requirements, they are also starting to view it as a strategic technology."* Whereas five years ago, the company's customer base consisted almost exclusively of automotive companies, its clients now include various food processing and electronics manufacturing companies, as well as a rapidly growing list of analytical and clinical laboratories, which now account for about 30% of the business.

Substitution of Capital for Land: Office Towers in Bombay

As you travel into any major city in the world from a distance of 50 kilometres out, the density of development increases and buildings tend to get taller and taller. Building a tall

Skyscrapers are simply the substitution of capital for land in production. When land in desirable locations is expensive, as it is in the centre of most cities, skyscrapers start appearing. This is precisely what began happening in Bombay, India, in 1994.

building is simply the substitution of capital for land in production, and it occurs most frequently where land prices are very high. When available land is scarce and the demand for it is increasing, land prices rise and tall buildings appear. This was happening in Bombay, India, during 1994:[2]

Prices of commercial property in Bombay have risen by around 50% since the beginning of the year. Space-seekers have been

driven to the suburbs, inconveniently far from the business district, but even there prices are rocketing. In a government-promoted development of offices spread over 80 hectares . . . in the suburb of Bandra, prices have risen faster even than on Nariman Point. . . . Between the overcrowding of Nariman Point and the far-flung suburbs are the city's older industrial areas. Developers have got their eyes on a 180-hectare site occupied by 54 textile mills and 120 000 mill-workers. The value of this land is estimated at 75 billion rupees (US$2.4 billion). Some mill-owners have developed bits of land, and gleaming new skyscrapers tower over the mill-workers' grimy settlements.

Sources: [1]"Canadian Robots World Class Workers," *Plant* vol. 54, no. 5 (March 6, 1996): pp. 1, 8. [2]*The Economist*, July 30–August 5, 1994, p. 34.

(2) how to produce that output, and (3) how much of each input to demand.

5. Profit equals *total revenue* minus total cost. *Economic cost* includes (1) a normal return, or profit, to the owners, and (2) the opportunity cost (rather than the money cost) of each factor of production and out-of-pocket cost.

6. A *normal rate of return* to capital is included in economic cost because tying up resources in the capital stock of a firm has an opportunity cost. If you start a business or buy a share of stock in a corporation, you do so because you expect a profit. Investors will not invest their money in a business unless they are guaranteed a rate of return similar to or above the rate they can obtain by purchasing risk-free government bonds.

7. *Economic profits* are profits over and above a normal rate of return. A firm earning zero economic profits is a firm earning just exactly a normal rate of return. A firm does not show economic profits unless it is earning above a normal return for its owners. A firm actually earning a profit as an accountant measures it is suffering a loss from the perspective of economics if the profit rate is below normal.

8. Two assumptions define the *short run*: (1) a fixed scale or fixed factor of production and (2) no entry to or exit from the industry. In the *long run*, firms can choose any scale of operations they want, and new firms can enter and leave the industry.

9. To make decisions, firms need to know three things: (1) the market price of their output, (2) the techniques of production that are available, and (3) the price of inputs.

The Production Process

10. The relationship between inputs and outputs (the *production technology* expressed numerically or mathematically) is called a *production function* or *total product function*.

11. The *marginal product* of a variable input is the additional output that an added unit of that input will produce if all other inputs are held constant. The *law of diminishing returns* states that when additional units of a variable input are added to fixed inputs after a certain point, the marginal product of the variable input will decline.

12. *Average product* is the average amount of product produced by each unit of a variable factor of production. If marginal product is above average product, the average product rises; if marginal product is below average product, the average product falls.

13. Capital and labour are at the same time complementary and substitutable inputs. Capital enhances the productivity of labour, but it can also be substituted for labour.

Choice of Technology

14. One of the key decisions that all firms must make is which technology to use. Profit-maximizing firms will choose that combination of inputs that minimizes costs and therefore maximizes profits.

Review Terms and Concepts

average product 179

capital-intensive technology 176

economic costs 172

economic profits or excess profits 172

firm 169

free entry 170

free exit 170

homogeneous products 169

labour-intensive technology 176

law of diminishing returns 178

long run 175

marginal product 177

normal rate of profit or normal rate of return 172

optimal method of production 176

perfect competition 169

production 168

production function or total product function 177

production technology 176

profit 171

revenue or total revenue 172

short run 174

Equations:

1. Profit = Total revenue − Total cost

2. Average product of labour = $\dfrac{\text{Total product}}{\text{Total units of labour}}$

Problem Set

1. The graph below gives the current situation in the perfectly competitive market for apples in Canada.

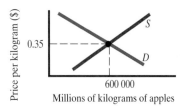

a. Graph the demand curve facing a single representative apple farmer in Canada.

b. Explain the shape of the individual farmer's demand curve carefully. What specific assumptions lie behind its shape?

2. Suppose that next year you become president of a small nonprofit theatre company. Your playhouse has 120 seats and a small stage. The actors have national reputations, and demand for tickets is enormous relative to the number of seats available; every performance is sold out months in advance. You are elected because you have demonstrated an ability to raise funds successfully. Describe some of

the decisions that you must make in the short run. What might you consider to be your "fixed factor"? What alternative decisions might you be able to make in the long run? Explain.

3. Ted Baxter runs a small newspaper company in southern New Brunswick. The paper has been in business for 25 years. The total value of the firm's capital stock is $1 000 000, which Ted owns outright. This year the firm earned a total of $250 000 after out-of-pocket expenses. Without taking the opportunity cost of capital into account, this means that Ted is earning a 25% return on his capital. Suppose that risk-free bonds are currently paying a rate of 10% to those who buy them.
   a. What is meant by the "opportunity cost of capital"?
   b. Explain why opportunity costs are "real" costs even though they do not necessarily involve out-of-pocket expenses.
   c. What is the opportunity cost of Ted's capital?
   d. How much economic profit is Ted earning?

4. The following table gives total output or total product as a function of labour units used:

LABOUR	TOTAL OUTPUT
0	0
1	5
2	9
3	12
4	14
5	15

   a. Define diminishing returns.
   b. Does the table indicate a situation of diminishing returns? Explain your answer.

5. Suppose that whirligigs can be produced using two different production techniques, A and B. The following table provides the total input requirements for each of five different total output levels:

	Q = 1		Q = 2		Q = 3		Q = 4		Q = 5	
TECH.	K	L	K	L	K	L	K	L	K	L
A	2	5	1	10	5	14	6	18	8	20
B	5	2	8	3	11	4	14	5	16	6

   a. Assuming that the price of labour (P_L) is $1 and the price of capital (P_K) is $2, calculate the total cost of production for each of the five levels of output using the optimal (least-cost) technology at each level.
   b. How many labour hours (units of labour) would be employed at each level of output? How many machine hours (units of capital)?
   c. Graph total cost of production as a function of output. (Put cost on the Y axis and output, Q, on the X axis.) Again, assume that the optimal technology is used.
   d. Repeat a. through c. under the assumption that the price of labour (P_L) rises from $1 to $3 while the price of capital (P_K) remains at $2.

6. During the early phases of industrialization, the number of persons engaged in agriculture usually drops sharply, even as agricultural output is growing. Given what you know about production technology and production functions, can you explain this seeming inconsistency?

7. Since the end of World War II, manufacturing firms in Canada, the United States, and Europe have been moving farther and farther outside of central cities. At the same time, firms in finance, insurance, and other parts of the service sector have been locating near the downtown areas in tall buildings. One major reason seems to be that manufacturing firms find it difficult to substitute capital for land, while service-sector firms that use office space do not.
   a. What kinds of buildings represent substitution of capital for land?
   b. Why do you think that manufacturing firms might find it difficult to substitute capital for land?
   c. Why is it relatively easier for a law firm or an insurance company to substitute capital for land?
   d. Why is the demand for land likely to be very high near the centre of a city?
   *e. One of the reasons for substituting capital for land near the centre of a city is that land is more expensive near the centre. What is true about the relative supply of land near the centre of a city? (*Hint:* What is the formula for the area of a circle?)

From Technology and Factor Prices to Cost: Isoquants and Isocosts

This chapter has shown that the cost structure facing a firm depends on two key pieces of information: (1) input (factor) prices and (2) technology. This appendix presents a more formal analysis of technology and factor prices and their relationship to cost.

A New Look at Technology: Isoquants

Table 7A.1 is expanded from Table 7.4 to show the various combinations of capital (K) and labour (L) that can be used to produce three different levels of output (q). For example, 100 units of X can be produced with two units of capital and ten units of labour, or with three units of K and six units of L, or with four units of K and four units of L, and so forth. Similarly, 150 units of X can be produced with three units of K and ten units of L, or with four units of K and seven units of L, and so forth.

A graph that shows all the combinations of capital and labour that can be used to produce a given amount of output is called an **isoquant**. Figure 7A.1 graphs three isoquants, one each for $q_x = 50$, $q_x = 100$, and $q_x = 150$, based on the data in Table 7A.1. Notice that all the points on the graph have been connected, indicating that there are an infinite number of combinations of labour and capital that can produce each level of output. For example, 100 units of output can also be produced with 3.50 units of labour and 4.75 units of capital. (Verify that this point is on the isoquant labelled $q_x = 100$.)

Figure 7A.1 shows only three isoquants, but there are many more not shown. For example, there are separate isoquants for $q_x = 101$, $q_x = 102$, and so on. If we assume that producing fractions of a unit of output is possible, there must be an isoquant for $q_x = 134.57$, for $q_x = 124.82$, and so on. One could imagine an infinite number of isoquants in Figure 7A.1. The higher the level

Isoquants Showing All Combinations of Capital and Labour That Can Be Used to Produce 50, 100, and 150 Units of Output

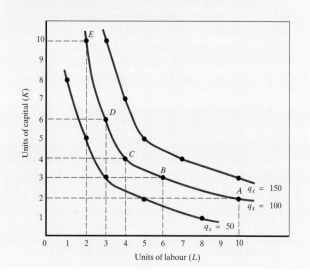

of output, the farther up and to the right the isoquant will lie.

Figure 7A.2 derives the slope of an isoquant. Because points A and B are both on the $q_x = 100$ isoquant, the two points represent two different combinations of K and L that can be used to produce 100 units of output. In moving from point A to point B along the curve, less capital is employed but more labour is used. An approximation of the amount of output lost by using less capital is ΔK times the marginal product of capital (MP_K). The *marginal product of capital* is the number of units of output produced by a single marginal unit of capital. Thus, $\Delta K \bullet MP_K$ is the total output lost by using less capital.

But for output to remain constant (as it must, because A and B are on the same isoquant), the loss of output from using less capital must be exactly matched by the added output produced by using more labour. This amount can be approximated by ΔL times the marginal product of labour (MP_L). Since the two must be equal, it follows that:

$$\Delta K \bullet MP_K = -\Delta L \bullet MP_L.\text{[1]}$$

---

[1]*We need to add the negative sign to ΔL because in moving from point A to point B, ΔK is a negative number and ΔL is a positive number. The minus sign is needed to balance the equation.*

Alternative Combinations of Capital (K) and Labour (L) Required to Produce 50, 100, and 150 Units of Output

	$q_x = 50$		$q_x = 100$		$q_x = 150$	
	K	L	K	L	K	L
A	1	8	2	10	3	10
B	2	5	3	6	4	7
C	3	3	4	4	5	5
D	5	2	6	3	7	4
E	8	1	10	2	10	3

The Slope of an Isoquant is Equal to the Ratio of MP_L to MP_K

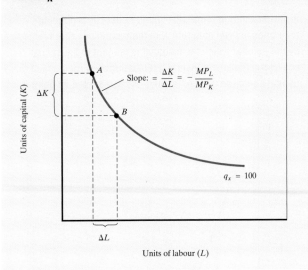

Isocost Lines Showing the Combinations of Capital and Labour Available for $5, $6, and $7

An isocost line shows all the combinations of capital and labour that are available for a given total cost.

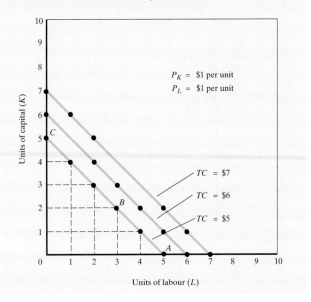

If we then divide both sides of this equation by ΔL and then by MP_K, we arrive at the following expression for the slope of the isoquant:

$$\text{Slope of isoquant:} \quad \frac{\Delta K}{\Delta L} = -\frac{MP_L}{MP_K}$$

The ratio of MP_L to MP_K is called the **marginal rate of technical substitution**. It is the rate at which a firm can substitute capital for labour and hold output constant.

Factor Prices and Input Combinations: Isocosts

A graph that shows all the combinations of capital and labour that are available for a given total cost is called an **isocost line**. (Recall that total cost includes opportunity costs and a normal rate of return.) Just as there are an infinite number of isoquants (one for every possible level of output), there are an infinite number of isocost lines, one for every possible level of total cost.

Figure 7A.3 shows three simple isocost lines assuming that the price of labour (P_L) is $1 per unit and that the price of capital (P_K) is $1 per unit.[2] The lowest isocost line shows all the combinations of K and L that can be purchased for $5. For example, $5 will buy five units of labour and no capital (point A), or three units of

labour and two units of capital (point B), or no units of labour and five units of capital (point C).

All these points lie along a straight line. The equation of that straight line is:

$$(P_K \bullet K) + (P_L \bullet L) = TC.$$

Substituting our data for the lowest isocost line into this general equation, we get:

$$(\$1 \bullet K) + (\$1 \bullet L) = \$5, \text{ or } K + L = 5.$$

Remember that the X and Y scales are units of labour and units of capital, not dollars.

On the same graph are two additional isocosts showing the various combinations of K and L available for a total cost of $6 and $7. These are only three of an infinite number of isocosts. At any total cost, there is an isocost that shows all the combinations of K and L available for that amount.

Figure 7A.4 on page 190 shows another isocost line. This isocost assumes a different set of factor prices, $P_L = \$5$ and $P_K = \$1$. The diagram shows all the combinations of K and L that can be bought for $25. One way to draw the line is to determine the endpoints. For example, if the entire $25 were spent on labour, how much labour could be purchased? The answer is, of

---

[2]*The opportunity costs of the owner's labour time are included in the wage bill and the normal rate of return is included in the price of capital (the owner is assumed to pay herself for the capital she supplies to the firm).*

Isocost Line Showing All Combinations of Capital and Labour Available for $25

One way to draw an isocost line is to determine the endpoints of that line and draw a line connecting them.

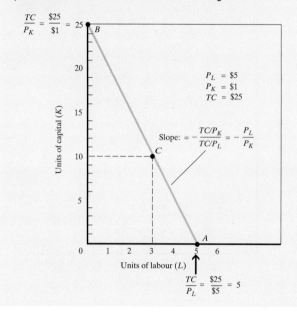

Finding the Least-Cost Combination of Capital and Labour to Produce 50 Units of Output

Profit-maximizing firms will minimize costs by producing their chosen level of output with the technology represented by the point at which the isoquant is tangent to an isocost line. Here, the cost-minimizing technology—three units of capital and three units of labour—is represented by point A.

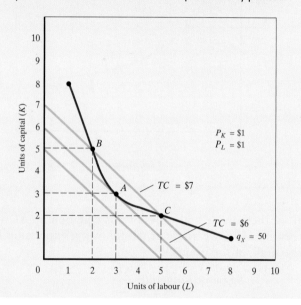

course, five units ($25 divided by $5 per unit). Thus, point A, which represents five units of labour and no capital, is on the isocost line. Similarly, if all of the $25 were spent on capital, how much capital could be purchased? The answer is 25 units ($25 divided by $1 per unit). Thus, point B, which represents 25 units of capital and no labour, is also on the isocost line. Another point on this particular isocost is three units of labour and 10 units of capital, point C.

The slope of an isocost line can be calculated easily if you first find the endpoints of the line. In Figure 7A.4, we can calculate the slope of the isocost line by taking $\Delta K/\Delta L$ between points B and A. Thus,

$$\text{Slope of isocost line: } \frac{\Delta K}{\Delta L} = -\frac{TC/P_K}{TC/P_L} = -\frac{P_L}{P_K}.$$

Plugging in the endpoints from our example, we get:

$$\text{Slope of line } AB = -\frac{\$5}{\$1} = -5.$$

Finding the Least-Cost Technology with Isoquants and Isocosts

Figure 7A.5 superimposes the isoquant for $q_x = 50$ on the isocost lines in Figure 7A.3, which assume that $P_K = \$1$ and $P_L = \$1$. The question now becomes one of choosing among the combinations of K and L that can be used to produce 50 units of output. Recall that each point on the isoquant (labelled $q_x = 50$ in Figure 7A.5) represents a different technology—a different combination of K and L.

We assume that our firm is a competitive, profit-maximizing firm that will choose the particular combination that minimizes cost. Because every point on the isoquant lies on some particular isocost line, we can determine the total cost for each combination along the isoquant. For example, point B (five units of capital and two units of labour) lies along the isocost for a total cost of $7. Notice that five units of capital and two units of labour cost a total of $7. (Remember, $P_K = \$1$ and $P_L = \$1$.) But the same amount of output (50 units) can be produced at lower cost. Specifically, by using three units of labour and three units of capital (point A), total cost is reduced to $6. *No other combination of* K *and* L *along isoquant* $q_x = 50$ *is on a lower isocost line.* In seeking to maximize profits, then,

> The firm will choose the combination of inputs that is least costly. The least costly way to produce any given level of output is indicated by the point of tangency between an isocost line and the isoquant corresponding to that level of output.[3]

In Figure 7A.5, the least-cost technology of producing 50 units of output is represented by point *A*, the point at which the $q_x = 50$ isoquant is just tangent to (that is, just touches) the isocost line.

Figure 7A.6 adds the other two isoquants from Figure 7A.1 to Figure 7A.5. Assuming that $P_K = \$1$ and $P_L = \$1$, the firm will move along each of the three isoquants until it finds the least-cost combination of *K* and *L* that can be used to produce that particular level of output. The result is plotted in Figure 7A.7. The minimum cost of producing 50 units of *X* is \$6; the minimum cost of producing 100 units of *X* is \$8; and the minimum cost of producing 150 units of *X* is \$10.

Figure 7A.6

Minimizing Cost of Production for $q_x = 50$, $q_x = 100$, and $q_x = 150$

Plotting a series of cost-minimizing combinations of inputs—shown in this graph as points A, B, and C—on a separate graph results in a cost curve like the one shown in Figure 7A.7.

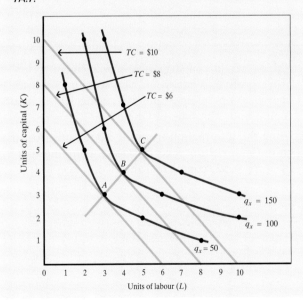

----

[3]*This assumes that the isoquants are continuous and convex (bowed) toward the origin.*

Figure 7A.7

A Cost Curve Shows the *Minimum* Cost of Producing Each Level of Output

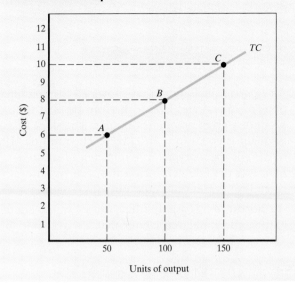

The Cost-Minimizing Equilibrium Condition

At the point where a line is just tangent to a curve, the two have the same slope. (We have already derived expressions for the slope of an isocost and the slope of an isoquant.) At each point of tangency (such as at points *A*, *B*, and *C* in Figure 7A.6), then, the following must be true:

$$\text{Slope of isoquant} = -\frac{MP_L}{MP_K} = \text{Slope of isocost} = -\frac{P_L}{P_K}$$

Thus:

$$\frac{MP_L}{MP_K} = \frac{P_L}{P_K}$$

Dividing both sides by P_L and multiplying both sides by MP_K, we get:

$$\frac{MP_L}{P_L} = \frac{MP_K}{P_K}$$

This is the firm's cost-minimizing equilibrium condition.

This expression makes sense if you think about what it says. The left side of the equation is the marginal product of labour divided by the price of a unit of labour. Thus, it is the product derived from the last dollar spent on labour. The right-hand side of the equation is the product derived from the last dollar spent on capital. If the product derived from the last dollar spent on labour were not equal to the product derived from the last dollar spent on capital, the firm could decrease costs by using more labour and less capital or by using more capital and less labour.

Look back to Chapter 6 and see if you can find a similar expression and some similar logic in our discussion of household behaviour. In fact, there is great symmetry between the theory of the firm and the theory of household behaviour.

Summary

1. An *isoquant* is a graph that shows all the combinations of capital and labour that can be used to produce a given amount of output. The slope of an isoquant is equal to $-MP_L/MP_K$. The ratio of MP_L to MP_K is the *marginal rate of technical substitution*. It is the rate at which a firm can substitute capital for labour and hold output constant.

2. An *isocost line* is a graph that shows all the combinations of capital and labour that are available for a given total cost. The slope of an isocost line is equal to $-P_L/P_K$.

3. The least-cost method of producing a given amount of output is found graphically at the point at which an isocost line is just tangent to (that is, just touches) the isoquant corresponding to that level of production. The firm's cost-minimizing equilibrium condition is $MP_L/P_L = MP_K/P_K$.

Review Terms and Concepts

isocost line A graph that shows all the combinations of capital and labour available for a given total cost. 189

isoquant A graph that shows all the combinations of capital and labour that can be used to produce a given amount of output. 188

marginal rate of technical substitution The rate at which a firm can substitute capital for labour and hold output constant. 189

Equations:

1. Slope of isoquant: $\dfrac{\Delta K}{\Delta L} = -\dfrac{MP_L}{MP_K}$

2. Slope of isocost line: $\dfrac{\Delta K}{\Delta L} = -\dfrac{TC/P_K}{TC/P_L} = -\dfrac{P_L}{P_K}$

Problem Set

1. Assume that $MP_L = 5$ and $MP_K = 10$. Assume also that $P_L = \$2$ and $P_K = \$5$. This implies that the firm should substitute labour for capital. Explain why.

2. In the isoquant/isocost diagram (Figure 1 on page 193), suppose that the firm is producing 1000 units of output at point *A* using 100 units of labour and 200 units of capital. As an outside consultant, what actions would you suggest to management to improve profits? What would you recommend if the firm were operating at point *B*, using 100 units of capital and 200 units of labour?

3. Using the information from the isoquant/isocost diagram (Figure 2 on page 193), and assuming that $P_L = P_K = \$2$, complete Table 1 on page 193.

Figure 1

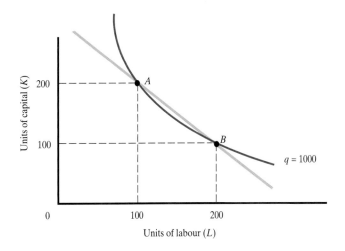

Figure 2

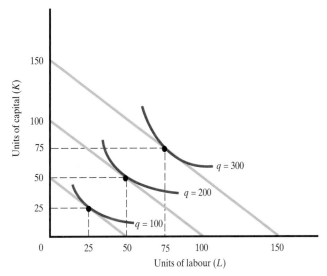

Table 1

OUTPUT UNITS	TOTAL COST OF OUTPUT	UNITS OF LABOUR DEMANDED	UNITS OF CAPITAL DEMANDED
100			
200			
300			

8

Short-Run Costs and Output Decisions

This chapter continues our examination of the decisions that firms make in their quest for profits. You have seen that firms in perfectly competitive industries make three very specific decisions (Figure 8.1, page 195). These decisions are:

1. How much output to supply;
2. How to produce that output (that is, which production technique/ technology to use); and
3. What quantity of each input to demand.

Remember though that *all* types of firms make these decisions, not just those in perfectly competitive industries. We continue to use perfectly competitive firms as a teaching device, but much of the material in this chapter applies to firms in noncompetitive industries as well.

We have assumed so far that firms are in business to earn profits and that they make choices to maximize those profits. (Remember that *profit* is the difference between revenues and costs.) Because firms in perfectly competitive markets are price takers in both input and output markets, many decisions depend upon prices over which firms have no control. Like households, firms also face market constraints.

In the last chapter, we focused on the production process. This chapter focuses on the *costs* of production. To calculate costs, a firm must know two things: the quantity and combination of inputs it needs to produce its product and how much those inputs cost. (Don't forget that economic costs include a normal return to capital—the opportunity cost of capital.) As we begin to examine how technology and input prices determine costs, we focus first on input markets. By the end of the chapter, we

FIGURE 8.1

Decisions Facing Firms

DECISIONS	are based on	INFORMATION
1. The quantity of output to *supply*		1. The price of output
2. How to produce that output (which technique to use)		2. Techniques of production available*
3. The quantity of each input to *demand*		3. The price of inputs*
		*determines production costs

will have enough information to figure out how much of its product a firm is likely to supply (that is, how much output to produce) at each possible price. In other words, we will have derived the supply curve of a competitive firm in the short run.

Take a moment and look back at the circular flow diagram, Figure 7.1 on page 168. There you can see exactly where we are in our study of the competitive market system. The goal of this chapter is to look behind the supply curve in output markets. It is important to understand, however, that producing output implies demanding inputs at the same time. You can also see in Figure 7.1 two of the information sources that firms use in their output supply and input demand decisions: firms look to output markets for the price of output and to input markets for the prices of capital and labour.

Costs in the Short Run

Our emphasis in this chapter is on costs *in the short run only*. Recall that the short run is that period during which two conditions hold: (1) existing firms face limits imposed by some fixed factor of production, and (2) new firms cannot enter, and existing firms cannot exit, an industry.

In the short run, all firms (competitive and noncompetitive) have costs that they must bear regardless of their output. Some costs, in fact, must be paid even if the firm stops producing (that is, even if output is zero). These kinds of costs are called **fixed costs,** and the important thing to remember about them is that firms can do nothing in the short run to avoid them or to change them. In the long run, a firm has no fixed costs, because it can expand, contract, or exit the industry.

Firms do have certain costs in the short run that depend on the level of output they have chosen. These kinds of costs are called **variable costs.** Fixed costs and variable costs together make up **total costs:**

$$TC = TFC + TVC$$

where *TC* denotes total costs, *TFC* denotes total fixed costs, and *TVC* denotes total variable costs. We will return to this equation after discussing fixed costs and variable costs in detail.

FIXED COSTS

In discussing fixed costs, we must distinguish between total fixed costs and average fixed costs.

fixed cost *Any cost that a firm bears in the short run that does not depend on its level of output. These costs are incurred even if the firm is producing nothing. There are no fixed costs in the long run.*

variable cost *Any cost that a firm bears that depends on the level of production chosen.*

total cost (TC) *Fixed costs plus variable costs.*

■ **Total Fixed Cost (*TFC*)** Total fixed cost is sometimes referred to as *overhead*. If you operate a factory, you must heat the building to keep the pipes from freezing in the winter. Even if no production is taking place, you may have to keep the roof from leaking, pay a guard to protect the building from vandals, and make payments on a long-term lease. There may also be insurance premiums, taxes, and city fees to pay, as well as contract obligations to workers.

Fixed costs represent a larger portion of total costs for some firms than for others. Electric companies, for instance, maintain generating plants, thousands of kilometres of distribution wires, poles, transformers, and so forth. Usually, such plants are financed by issuing bonds to the public (that is, by borrowing). The interest that must be paid on these bonds represents a substantial part of the utilities' operating cost and is a fixed cost in the short run, no matter how much (if any) electricity is being produced.

For the purposes of our discussion in this chapter, we will assume that firms use only two inputs: labour and capital.[1] Recall that capital is both produced and yields services over time in the production of other goods and services. It is the plant and equipment of a manufacturing firm; the computers, desks, chairs, doors, and walls of a law office; and the boat that Ivan and Colleen built on their desert island. It is sometimes assumed that capital is a fixed input in the short run and that labour is the only variable input. To be a bit more realistic, however, we will assume that capital has both a fixed *and* a variable component. After all, some capital can be purchased in the short run.

Consider a small consulting firm that employs several economists, research assistants, and secretaries. It rents space in an office building and has a five-year lease. The rent it pays on the office space can be thought of as a fixed cost in the short run. The monthly electric and heating bills are also essentially fixed (although the amounts may vary slightly from month to month). So are the salaries of the basic administrative staff. Payments on some capital equipment—a large copying machine, for instance, and the main word processing system—can also be thought of as fixed.

The same firm also has costs that vary with output. When there is a lot of work, the firm hires more employees at both the professional and research assistant level. The capital used by the consulting firm may also vary, even in the short run. Payments on the computer system do not change, but the firm may rent additional computer time when necessary. It can buy additional personal computers, word processing terminals, or databases quickly, if need be. It must pay for the copy machine, but the machine costs more when it is running than when it is not.

Total fixed costs (*TFC*) are those costs that do not change with output, even if output is zero. Column 2 of Table 8.1 presents data on the fixed costs of a hypothetical firm. Fixed costs are $1000 at all levels of output (*q*). Figure 8.2a on the next page shows total fixed costs as a function of output. Since *TFC* does not change with output, the graph is simply a straight horizontal line at $1000. The important thing to remember here is that:

Firms have no control over fixed costs in the short run.

■ **Average Fixed Cost (*AFC*)** Average fixed cost (*AFC*) is total fixed cost (*TFC*) divided by the number of units of output (*q*):

$$AFC = \frac{TFC}{q}$$

[1] *While this may seem unrealistic, virtually everything that we will say about firms using these two factors can easily be generalized to firms that use many factors of production.*

total fixed costs (*TFC*) or overhead *The total of all costs that do not change with output, even if output is zero.*

average fixed cost (*AFC*) *Total fixed cost divided by the number of units of output; a per unit measure of fixed costs.*

Table 8.1
Short-Run Fixed Cost (Total and Average) of a Hypothetical Firm

(1)	(2)	(3)
q	*TFC*	*AFC* (*TFC/q*)
0	$1000	$ —
1	1000	1000
2	1000	500
3	1000	333
4	1000	250
5	1000	200

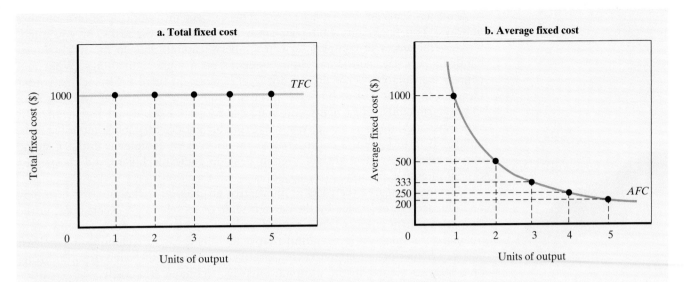

a. Total fixed cost

Total fixed cost ($)

1000 •••••

0   1   2   3   4   5

Units of output

TFC

b. Average fixed cost

Average fixed cost ($)

1000 •
500 •
333 •
250 •
200 •

0   1   2   3   4   5

Units of output

AFC

FIGURE 8.2

Short-Run Fixed Cost (Total and Average) of a Hypothetical Firm

Average fixed cost is simply total fixed cost divided by the quantity of output. As output increases, average fixed cost declines because we are dividing a fixed number ($1000) by a larger and larger quantity.

For example, if the firm in Figure 8.2 produced three units of output, average fixed costs would be $333 (i.e., $1000 divided by three). If the same firm produced five units of output, average fixed cost would be $200 (i.e., $1000 divided by five). *Average fixed cost falls as output rises*, because the same total is being spread over, or divided by, a larger number of units (see column 3 of Table 8.1). This phenomenon is sometimes called **spreading overhead**.

Graphs of average fixed cost, like that in Figure 8.2b (which presents the average fixed cost data from Table 8.1), are downward-sloping curves. Notice that *AFC* approaches zero as the quantity of output increases. If output were 100 000 units, average fixed cost would equal only one cent per unit in our example ($1000 ÷ 100 000 = $0.01). *AFC* never actually reaches zero.

spreading overhead *The process of dividing total fixed costs by more units of output. Average fixed cost declines as q rises.*

Variable Costs

Variable costs can be classified into three categories: total variable cost, marginal cost, and average variable cost.

■ **Total Variable Cost (*TVC*)** Total variable costs (*TVC*) are those costs that depend on or vary with the level of output in the short run. To produce more output, a firm uses more inputs. The cost of additional output depends directly on the additional inputs that are required and how much they cost.

As you saw in Chapter 7, input requirements are determined by technology. Firms generally have a number of production techniques available to them, and the option they choose is assumed to be the one that produces the desired level of output at the least cost. To find out which technology involves the least cost, a firm must compare the total variable costs of producing that level of output using different production techniques.

This is as true of small businesses as it is of large manufacturing firms. Suppose, for example, that you are a small farmer. A certain amount of work has to be done

total variable cost (*TVC*) *The total of all costs that depend on or vary with output in the short run.*

to plant and harvest your 60 hectares. You can get this work done in a number of ways. You might hire four farmhands and divide up the tasks, or you might buy several pieces of complex farm machinery (capital) and do the work single-handedly. Clearly, your final choice depends on a number of things. What machinery is available? What does it do? Will it work on small fields such as yours? How much will it cost to buy each piece of equipment? What wage will you have to pay farmhands? How many will you need to get the job done? If machinery is expensive and labour is cheap, you will probably choose the labour-intensive technology. If farm labour is expensive and the local farm equipment dealer is going out of business, you might get a good deal on some machinery and choose the capital-intensive method.

Having compared the costs of alternative production techniques, the firm may be influenced in its choice by the current scale of its operation. Remember, in the short run a firm is locked into a *fixed* scale of operations. A firm currently producing on a small scale may find that a labour-intensive technique is the least costly, whether or not labour is comparatively expensive; the same firm producing on a larger scale might find a capital-intensive technique less costly.

The **total variable cost curve** is a graph that shows the relationship between total variable cost and the level of a firm's output (q). At any given level of output, total variable cost depends on (1) the techniques of production that are available and (2) the prices of the inputs required by each technology. To examine this relationship in more detail, let us look at some hypothetical production figures.

Table 8.2 on page 199 presents an analysis that might lie behind three points on the total variable cost curve of a typical firm. In this case, there are two production techniques available, one somewhat more capital intensive than the other. We will assume that the price of labour is $1 per unit and the price of capital is $2 per unit. For the purposes of this example, we focus on *variable capital*—that is, on capital that can be changed in the short run. In practice, some capital (such as buildings and large, specialized machines) is fixed in the short run. In our example, we will use K to denote variable capital. Remember, however, that the firm has other capital, capital that is fixed in the short run.

Analysis reveals that to produce one unit of output, the labour-intensive technique is least costly. Technique A requires four units of both capital and labour, which would cost a total of $12. Technique B requires six units of labour but only two units of capital for a total cost of only $10. To maximize profits, the firm would use technique B to produce one unit. The total variable cost of producing one unit of output would thus be $10.

The relatively labour-intensive technique B is also the best method of production for two units of output. Using B, the firm can produce two units for $18. If the firm decides to produce three units of output, however, technique A is cheaper. Using the least-cost technology (A), the total variable cost of production is $24. The firm will use nine units of capital at $2 each and six units of labour at $1 each.

Figure 8.3 graphs the relationship between variable costs and output based on the data in Table 8.2, assuming the firm chooses, for each output, the least-cost technology.

The important point to remember here is that:

> The total variable cost curve embodies information about both factor, or input, prices and technology. It shows the cost of production using the best available technique at each output level, given current factor prices.

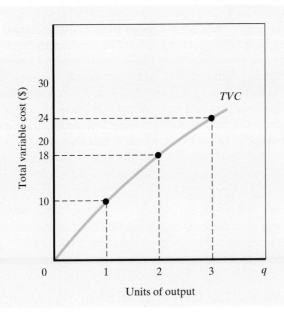

FIGURE 8.3

Total Variable Cost Curve

In Table 8.2, total variable cost
is derived from production requirements and input prices. A
total variable cost curve expresses the relationship between *TVC* and total output.

■ **Marginal Cost (*MC*)** The most important of all cost concepts is that of **marginal cost (*MC*)**, the increase in total cost that results from the production of one more unit of output. Let us say, for example, that a firm is producing 1000 units of output and decides to raise output to 1001. Producing the extra unit raises costs, and the increase (that is, the cost of producing the 1001st unit) is the marginal cost. Focusing on the "margin" is one way of looking at variable costs: marginal costs reflect changes in variable costs because they vary when output changes. Fixed costs do not change when output changes.

Table 8.3 shows how marginal cost is derived from total variable cost by simple subtraction. The total variable cost of producing the first unit of output is $10. Raising production from one unit to two units increases total variable cost from $10 to $18; the difference is the marginal cost of the second unit, or $8. Raising output from two to three units increases total variable cost from $18 to $24. The marginal cost of the third unit, therefore, is $6.

It is important to think for a moment about the nature of marginal cost. Specifically, marginal cost is the cost of the added inputs, or resources, needed to

marginal cost (*MC*) *The increase in total cost that results from producing one more unit of output. Marginal costs reflect changes in variable costs.*

Table 8.2	Derivation of Total Variable Cost Schedule from Technology and Factor Prices			
PRODUCE	USING TECHNIQUE	UNITS OF INPUT REQUIRED (PRODUCTION FUNCTION) K	L	TOTAL VARIABLE COST ASSUMING $P_K = \$2, P_L = \$1$ $TVC = (K \times P_K) + (L \times P_L)$
1 Unit of output	A	4	4	(4 × $2) + (4 × $1) = $12
	B	2	6	(2 × $2) + (6 × $1) = $10
2 Units of output	A	7	6	(7 × $2) + (6 × $1) = $20
	B	4	10	(4 × $2) + (10 × $1) = $18
3 Units of output	A	9	6	(9 × $2) + (6 × $1) = $24
	B	6	14	(6 × $2) + (14 × $1) = $26

Table 8.3
Derivation of Marginal Cost from Total Variable Cost

Units of output	Total variable costs ($)	Marginal costs ($)
0	0	0
1	10	10
2	18	8
3	24	6

produce one additional unit of output. Look back at Table 8.2, and think about the additional capital and labour needed to go from one unit to two units. In other words, think about the added resources needed to produce the second unit of output. Producing one unit of output with technique *B* requires two units of capital and six units of labour; producing two units of output using the same technique requires four units of capital and ten units of labour. Thus, the second unit requires two *additional* units of capital and four *additional* units of labour. What then is the added, or marginal, cost of the second unit? Two units of capital cost $2 each ($4 total) and four units of labour cost $1 each (another $4), for a total marginal cost of $8 (which is exactly the number we derived in Table 8.3).

> While the easiest way to derive marginal cost is to look at total variable cost and subtract, don't lose sight of the fact that when a firm increases its output level, it hires or demands more inputs. *Marginal cost* measures the *additional* cost of inputs required to produce each successive unit of output.

■ **The Shape of the Marginal Cost Curve in the Short Run**   The assumption of a fixed factor of production in the short run means that a firm is stuck at its current scale of operation (in our example, the size of the plant). As a firm tries to increase its output, it will eventually find itself trapped by that scale. Thus, our definition of the short run also implies that *marginal cost eventually rises with output*. The firm can hire more labour and use more materials—that is, it can add variable inputs—but diminishing returns eventually set in.

Recall the sandwich shop, with one grill and too many workers trying to prepare sandwiches on it, from Chapter 7. With a fixed grill capacity, more labourers could make more sandwiches, but the marginal product of each successive cook declined as more people tried to use the grill. If each additional unit of labour adds less and less to total output, *it follows that it requires more labour to produce each additional unit of output*. Thus, each additional unit of output costs more to produce. In other words, *diminishing returns, or decreasing marginal product, implies increasing marginal cost* (Figure 8.4).

Recall too the accountant who makes a living by helping people file their tax returns. He has an office in his home and works alone. His fixed factor of production is his own time. There are only so many hours in a day, and he has only so much stamina. In the long run, he may decide to hire and train an associate, but in the meantime (the short run) he has to decide how much to produce, and that decision is constrained by his current scale of operations. The fact that he has no trained associate and that each day contains only 24 hours constrains the number of clients that he can take on. The biggest component of the accountant's cost is time. When he works, he gives up leisure and other things that he

Perhaps the biggest constraint on an entrepreneur is time; there are only 24 hours in a day. Eventually time constraints produce diminishing returns. The more one works, the less one sleeps and the less productive one becomes.

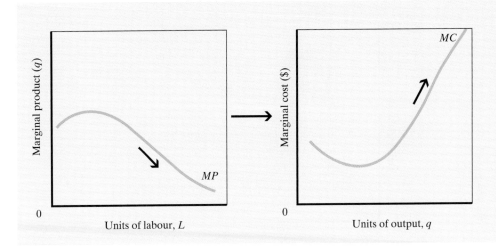

FIGURE 8.4

Declining Marginal Product Implies that Marginal Cost Will Eventually Rise with Output

In the short run, every firm is constrained by some fixed factor of production. Having a fixed input implies diminishing returns (declining marginal product) and a limited capacity to produce. As that limit is approached, marginal costs rise.

could do with his time. With more and more clients, he works later and later into the night; as he does so, he becomes less and less productive, and his hours become more and more valuable for sleep and relaxation. In other words, the marginal cost of doing each successive tax return rises.

To reiterate:

> In the short run, every firm is constrained by some fixed input that leads to diminishing returns to variable inputs and that limits its capacity to produce. As a firm approaches that capacity, it becomes increasingly costly to produce successively higher levels of output. Marginal costs ultimately increase with output in the short run.

■ **Graphing Total Variable Costs and Marginal Costs**   Figure 8.5 shows how the total variable cost curve and the marginal cost curve of a typical firm might look. Notice first that the shape of the marginal cost curve is consistent with short-run diminishing returns. At first *MC* declines, but eventually the fixed factor of production begins to constrain the firm, and marginal cost rises. Up to 100 units of output, producing each successive unit of output costs slightly less than producing the one before. Beyond 100 units, however, the cost of each successive unit is greater than the one before.

Clearly, more output costs more in total than less output. Total variable costs (*TVC*), therefore, *always increase* when output increases. Even though the cost of each additional unit changes, *total* variable cost rises when output rises. Thus the *total* variable cost curve always has a positive slope.

You might think of the total variable cost curve as a staircase. Each step takes you out along the quantity axis by a single unit, and the height of each step is the increase in total variable cost. As you climb the stairs, you are always going up, but the steps have different heights. At first, the stairway is steep, but as you continue to climb, the steps get smaller (marginal cost declines). The 100th stair is the smallest. As you continue to walk out beyond 100 units, the steps begin to get larger; the staircase gets steeper (marginal cost increases).

Remember that the numerical value of the slope of a line is equal to the change in the unit measured on the *Y* axis divided by the change in the unit measured on the *X* axis. The slope of a total variable cost curve is thus the change in total variable cost divided by the change in output ($\Delta TVC/\Delta q$). Since marginal

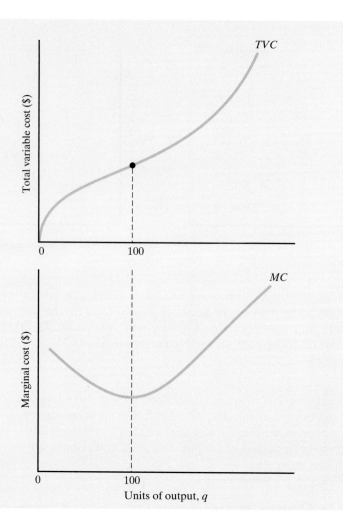

FIGURE 8.5

Total Variable Cost and Marginal Cost for a Typical Firm

Total variable costs always increase with output. Marginal cost is the cost of producing each additional unit. Thus, the marginal cost curve shows how total variable cost changes with single unit increases in total output.

cost is by definition the change in total variable cost resulting from an increase in output of one unit ($\Delta q = 1$), *marginal cost actually is the slope of the total variable cost curve:*

$$\text{Slope of } TVC = \frac{\Delta TVC}{\Delta q} = \frac{\Delta TVC}{1} = \Delta TVC = MC.$$

Notice that up to 100 units, marginal cost decreases and the variable cost curve becomes flatter. The slope of the total variable cost curve is declining; that is, total variable cost increases, but at a *decreasing rate*. Beyond 100 units of output, marginal cost increases and the total variable cost curve gets steeper; total variable costs continue to increase, but at an *increasing rate*.

■ **Average Variable Cost (*AVC*)**   A more complete picture of the costs of a hypothetical firm appears in Table 8.4. Column 2 shows total variable costs—derived from information on input prices and technology. Column 3 derives marginal cost by simple subtraction. For example, raising output from three units to four units increases variable costs from $24 to $32, making the marginal cost of the fourth unit $8 ($32 – $24). The marginal cost of the fifth unit is $10, the difference between $32 (*TVC*) for four units and $42 (*TVC*) for five units.

Average variable cost (*AVC*) is total variable cost divided by the number of units of output (*q*):

$$AVC = \frac{TVC}{q}$$

average variable cost (*AVC*)
Total variable cost divided by the number of units of output.

In Table 8.4, we calculate *AVC* in column 4 by dividing the numbers in column 2 (*TVC*) by the numbers in column 1 (*q*). For example, if the total variable cost of producing five units of output is $42, then the average variable cost is $42 divided by five units, or $8.40.

The important distinction to remember here is as follows:

Marginal cost is the cost of *one additional unit*. Average variable cost is the average variable cost per unit of *all the units* being produced.

■ **The Relationship between Average Variable Cost and Marginal Cost**   Average variable cost and marginal cost are related in a very specific way. When marginal cost is *below* average, average variable cost declines toward it. (Think again of the test score analogy introduced in Chapter 7. If you have an average score of 85 on three exams, and you then receive a 75, your average will fall.) In Table 8.4, the average variable cost of producing two units is $9 (*TVC/q* = $18 ÷ 2). The marginal cost of the third is $6, an amount lower than the marginal cost of the second unit. The average variable cost thus falls to $8 (24 ÷ 3).

Similarly, when marginal cost is *above* average variable cost, average variable cost increases toward it. If you had received a 95 on your last test instead of a 75, your average would have risen. In Table 8.4 the average variable cost of four units is $8. The marginal cost of the fifth unit is $10, and the average rises to $8.40. It follows, then, that:

Average variable cost always moves toward marginal cost.

Table 8.4		**Short-Run Costs of a Hypothetical Firm**						
(1)	*(2)*	*(3)* **MC** (ΔTVC)	*(4)* **AVC** (TVC/q)	*(5)*	*(6)* **TC** (TVC + TFC)	*(7)* **AFC** (TFC/q)	*(8)* **ATC** (TC/q or AFC + AVC)
q	**TVC**			**TFC**			
0	$0	$—	$—	$1000	$1000	$ —	$ —
1	10	10	10	1000	1010	1000	1010
2	18	8	9	1000	1018	500	509
3	24	6	8	1000	1024	333	341
4	32	8	8	1000	1032	250	258
5	42	10	8.4	1000	1042	200	208.4
—	—	—	—	—	—	—	—
—	—	—	—	—	—	—	—
—	—	—	—	—	—	—	—
500	8000	20	16	1000	9000	2	18

FIGURE 8.6

More Short-Run Costs

The relationship between marginal cost and average variable cost is important. When marginal cost is *below* average cost, average cost is declining. When marginal cost is *above* average cost, average cost is increasing. Rising marginal cost intersects average variable cost at the minimum point of *AVC*.

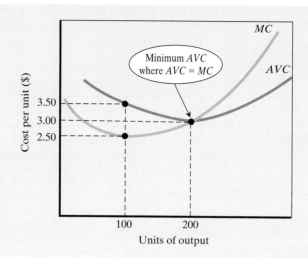

■ **Graphing Average Variable Costs and Marginal Costs** The relationship between average variable cost and marginal cost can be illustrated graphically. Figure 8.6 duplicates the lower diagram for a typical firm in Figure 8.5 but adds average variable cost. As the graph shows, average variable cost *follows* marginal cost, but lags behind because it is the average of all previous units.

As we move from left to right, we are looking at higher and higher levels of output per period. As we increase production, marginal cost—which at low levels of production is above $3.50 per unit—falls as coordination and cooperation begin to play a role. At 100 units of output, marginal cost has fallen to $2.50. Notice that average variable cost falls as well, but not as rapidly as marginal cost.

After 100 units of output, we begin to see diminishing returns take hold. Marginal cost begins to increase as higher and higher levels of output are produced. But notice that average cost is still falling until 200 units because marginal cost remains below it. At 100 units of output, marginal cost is $2.50 per unit but the *average* variable cost of production is $3.50. Thus even though marginal cost is rising after 100 units, it is still pulling the average of $3.50 downward.

At 200 units, however, marginal cost has risen to $3.00 and average cost has fallen to $3.00; marginal and average costs are equal. At this point marginal cost continues to rise with higher output. But from 200 units upward, *MC* is *above* *AVC*, and thus exerts an *upward* pull on the average variable cost curve. At levels of output below 200 units, marginal cost is below average variable cost, and average variable cost decreases as output increases. At levels of output above 200 units, marginal cost is above average variable cost, and average variable cost increases as output increases.

If you follow this logic you will see that:

> Marginal cost intersects average variable cost at the lowest, or minimum, point of *AVC*.

Another example using test scores should help you to understand why this is so. Consider the following sequence of test scores: 95, 85, 92, 88. The average of these four is 90. Now suppose you get an 80 on your fifth test. This score will drag down your average to 88. Now suppose that you get an 85 on your sixth test. This score is higher than 80, but it's still *below* your 88 average. As a result, your average continues to fall (from 88 to 87.5), even though your marginal test score rose. But if instead of an 85 you get an 89—just one point over your average—you've turned your average around; it is now rising.

TOTAL COSTS

We are now ready to complete the cost picture by adding total fixed costs to total variable costs. Recall that

$$TC = TFC + TVC$$

Total cost is graphed in Figure 8.7, where the same vertical distance (equal to *TFC*, which is constant) is simply added to *TVC* at every level of output. In Table 8.4 on page 203, column 6 adds the total fixed cost of $1000 to total variable cost to arrive at total cost.

■ **Average Total Cost (*ATC*)** Average total cost (*ATC*) is total cost divided by the number of units of output (*q*):

average total cost (*ATC*) *Total cost divided by the number of units of output.*

$$ATC = \frac{TC}{q}$$

Column 8 in Table 8.4 shows the result of dividing the costs in column 6 by the quantities in column 1. For example, at five units of output, *total* cost is $1042; *average* total cost is $1042 divided by five, or $208.40. The average total cost of producing 500 units of output is only $18—that is, $9000 divided by 500.

Another, more revealing, way of deriving average total cost is to add average fixed cost and average variable cost together:

$$ATC = AFC + AVC$$

For example, column 8 in Table 8.4 is the sum of column 4 (*AVC*) and column 7 (*AFC*).

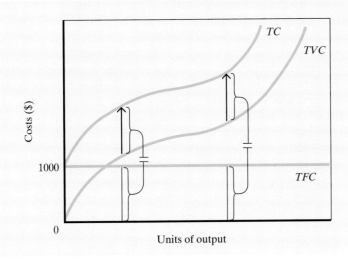

FIGURE 8.7

Total Cost Equals Total Fixed Cost Plus Total Variable Cost

Adding total fixed cost to total variable cost means adding the same amount of total fixed cost to every level of total variable cost. Thus, the total cost curve has the same shape as the total variable cost curve; it is simply higher by an amount equal to *TFC*.

Figure 8.8 on page 207 derives average total cost graphically for a typical firm. The bottom part of the figure graphs average fixed cost. At 100 units of output, average fixed cost is $ATC/q = \$1000 \div 100 = \$10$. At 400 units of output, $AFC = \$1000 \div 400 = \$2.50$. The top part shows the declining average fixed cost added to average variable cost at each level of output. Because AFC gets smaller and smaller, ATC gets closer and closer to AVC as output increases, but the two lines never cross.

■ **The Relationship between Average Total Cost and Marginal Cost** The relationship between average *total* cost and marginal cost is exactly the same as the relationship between average *variable* cost and marginal cost. The average total cost curve follows the marginal cost curve, but lags behind because it is an average over all units of output. The average total cost curve lags behind the marginal cost curve even more than the average variable cost curve does, because the cost of each added unit of production is now averaged not only with the variable cost of all previous units produced, but with fixed costs as well.

Fixed costs equal $1000 and are incurred even when the output level is zero. Thus, the first unit of output in the example in Table 8.4 on page 203 costs $10 in variable cost to produce. The second unit costs only $8 in variable cost to produce. The total cost of two units is $1018; average total cost of the two is ($1010 + $8)/2, or $509. The marginal cost of the third unit is only $6. The total cost of three units is thus $1024, or $1018 + $6, and the average total cost of three units is ($1010 + $8 + $6)/3, or $341.

As you saw with the test scores example, marginal cost is what drives changes in average total cost:

> If marginal cost is *below* average total cost, average total cost will *decline* toward marginal cost; if marginal cost is *above* average total cost, average total cost will *increase*. As a result, marginal cost intersects average *total* cost at ATC's minimum point, for the same reason that it intersects the average *variable* cost curve at its minimum point.

SHORT-RUN COSTS: A REVIEW

Let us now pause for a moment to review what we have learned about the behaviour of firms. We know that firms make three basic choices: how much product or output to produce or supply, how to produce that output, and how much of each input to demand in order to produce what they intend to supply. We assume that these choices are made to maximize profits. Profits are equal to the difference between a firm's revenue from the sale of its product and the costs of producing that product: profit = total revenue minus total cost.

So far, we have looked only at costs, but costs are only one part of the profit equation. To complete the picture, we must turn to the output market and see how these costs compare with the price that a product commands in the market. Before we do so, however, it is important to consolidate what we have said about costs.

Before a firm does anything else, it needs to know the different methods that it can use to produce its product. The technologies available determine the combinations of inputs that are needed to produce each level of output. Firms choose the technique that produces the desired level of output at least cost. The cost curves that result from the analysis of all this information show the cost of producing each level of output using the best available technology.

Remember that so far we have talked only about short-run costs. The curves we have drawn are therefore *short-run cost curves*. The shape of these curves is determined in large measure by the assumptions that we make about the short run, especially the assumption that some fixed factor of production leads to diminish-

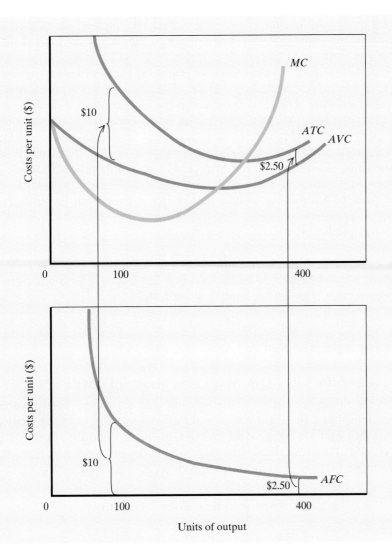

To get average total cost, we add average fixed and average variable costs at all levels of output. Since average fixed cost falls with output, an ever-declining amount is added to *AVC*. Thus, *AVC* and *ATC* get closer together as output increases, but the two lines never cross.

ing returns. Given this assumption, marginal costs eventually rise, and average cost curves are likely to be U-shaped.

After gaining a complete knowledge of how to produce a product and how much it will cost to produce it at each level of output, the firm turns to the market to find out what it can sell its product for. It is to the output market that we now turn our attention.

Output Decisions: Revenues, Costs, and Profit Maximization

To calculate potential profits, firms must combine their cost analyses with information on potential revenues from sales. After all, if a firm can't sell its product for more than it costs to produce it, it won't be in business long. In contrast, if the market gives the firm a price that is significantly greater than the cost it incurs to produce a unit of its product, the firm may have an incentive to expand output. Large profits might also attract new competitors to the market.

Let us now examine in detail how a firm goes about determining how much output to produce. For the sake of simplicity, we will continue to examine the decisions of a perfectly competitive firm. A perfectly competitive industry, you will recall, has many firms that are small relative to the size of the market. In such an environment, firms have no control over the market price of their products. Product price is determined by the interaction of many suppliers and many demanders.

Figure 8.9 (which is similar to Figure 7.2) shows a typical firm in a perfectly competitive industry. Price is determined in the market at $P^* = \$5$. The individual firm can charge any price that it wants for its product, but if it charges above $5, the quantity demanded falls to zero, and the firm won't sell anything. Many other firms are producing exactly the same product, so why should consumers pay more than the going market price? The firm could also sell its product for less than $5, but there is no reason to do so. If the firm can sell all it wants to sell at the going market price of $5, and we assume that it can, it would not be sensible to sell it for less.

All this implies that:

> In the short run a competitive firm faces a demand curve that is simply a horizontal line at the market equilibrium price. In other words, competitive firms face perfectly elastic demand in the short run.

In Figure 8.9, market equilibrium price is $P^* = \$5$ and the firm's perfectly elastic demand curve is labelled d.

Total Revenue (TR) and Marginal Revenue (MR)

total revenue (TR) *The total amount that a firm takes in from the sale of its product: The price per unit times the quantity of output the firm decides to produce (P × q).*

Profit is the difference between total revenue and total cost. **Total revenue** is the total amount that a firm takes in from the sale of its product. A perfectly competitive firm sells each unit of product for the same price, regardless of the output level it has chosen. Therefore, total revenue is simply the price per unit times the quantity of output that the firm decides to produce:

> Total revenue = Price × Quantity
>
> $$TR = P \times q$$

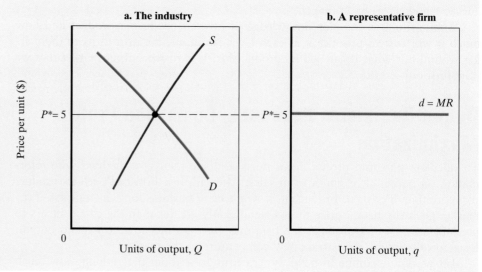

FIGURE 8.9

Demand Facing a Typical Firm in a Perfectly Competitive Market

Because perfectly competitive firms are very small relative to the market, they have no control over price. A firm can sell all it wants at the market price but would sell nothing if it charged a higher price. Thus, the demand curve facing a perfectly competitive firm is simply a horizontal line at the market equilibrium price, P^*.

Recall that price is assumed to be fixed in a competitive industry. Our firm is so small relative to the industry that changes in its output do not affect the market price. Thus, the only way a firm can affect the amount of revenue that it takes in is by adjusting output.

Marginal revenue (MR) is the added revenue that a firm takes in when it increases output by one additional unit. If a firm producing 10 521 units of output per month increases that output to 10 522 units per month, it will take in an additional amount of revenue each month. The revenue associated with the 10 522nd unit is simply the amount that the firm sells that one unit for. Thus, for a competitive firm, marginal revenue is simply equal to the current market price of each additional unit sold. In Figure 8.9, for example, the market price is $5. Thus, if the representative firm raises its output from 10 521 units to 10 522 units, its revenue will increase by $5.

A firm's *marginal revenue curve* is a curve that shows how much revenue the firm will gain by raising output by one unit at every level of output. The *marginal revenue curve and the demand curve facing a competitive firm are identical.* The horizontal line in Figure 8.9b can be thought of as both the demand curve facing the firm and its marginal revenue curve.

marginal revenue (MR) *The additional revenue that a firm takes in when it increases output by one additional unit. In perfect competition,* P = MR.

COMPARING COSTS AND REVENUES TO MAXIMIZE PROFIT

The discussion in the next few paragraphs conveys one of the most important concepts in all of microeconomics. As we pursue our analysis, remember that we are working under two assumptions: (1) that the industry we are examining is perfectly competitive and (2) that firms choose the level of output that yields the maximum, total profit.

■ **The Profit-Maximizing Level of Output** Look carefully at the diagrams in Figure 8.10. Once again we have the whole market, or industry, on the left and a single, typical small firm on the right. And again the current market price is P^*.

First, the firm observes market price (Figure 8.10a) and knows that it can sell all that it wants to for $P^* = \$5$ per unit. Next, it must decide how much to produce. It might seem reasonable to pick the output level where marginal cost is at its minimum point—in this case, at an output of 100 units. Here the difference between marginal revenue, $5, and marginal cost, $2.50, is the greatest.

But remember that a firm wants to maximize the difference between *total* revenue and *total* cost, not the difference between *marginal* revenue and *marginal* cost. The fact that marginal revenue is greater than marginal cost actually indicates that profit is *not* being maximized! Think about the 101st unit. Adding that single unit to production each period adds $5 to revenues but adds only about $2.50 to cost. Profits would be higher by about $2.50. Thus, the optimal (profit-maximizing) level of output is clearly higher than 100 units.

Now look at an output level of 250 units. Here, once again, raising output increases profit. The revenue gained from producing the 251st unit (marginal revenue) is still $5, and the cost of the 251st unit (marginal cost) is only about $4.

This process leads to the conclusion that:

> As long as marginal revenue is greater than marginal cost, even though the difference between the two is getting smaller, added output means added profit. Whenever marginal revenue exceeds marginal cost, the revenue gained by increasing output by one unit per period exceeds the cost incurred by doing so.

The logic leads us to 300 units of output. At 300 units, marginal cost has risen to $5. At 300 units of output, $P^* = MR = MC = \$5$.

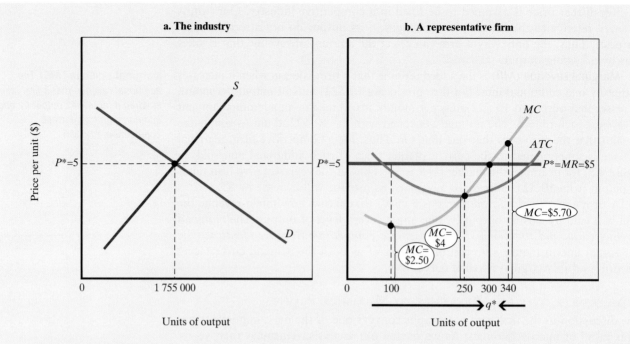

a. The industry

b. A representative firm

FIGURE 8.10

The Profit-Maximizing Level of Output for a Perfectly Competitive Firm

If price is above marginal cost, as it is at 100 and 250 units of output, profits can be increased by raising output; each additional unit increases revenues by more than it costs to produce the additional output. Beyond $q^* = 300$, however, added output will reduce profits. At 340 units of output, an additional unit of output costs more to produce than it will bring in revenue when sold on the market. Profit-maximizing output is thus q^*, the point at which $P^* = MC$.

Notice that if the firm were to produce *more* than 300 units, marginal cost rises above marginal revenue. At 340 units of output, for example, the cost of the 341st unit is about $5.70 while that added unit of output still brings in only $5 in revenue, thus reducing profit. It simply does not pay to increase output above the point where marginal cost rises above marginal revenue because such increases will *reduce* profit.

The inevitable conclusion, then, is that:

> The profit-maximizing perfectly competitive firm will produce up to the point where the price of its output is just equal to short-run marginal cost—the level of output at which $P^* = MC$.[2]

Thus, in Figure 8.10, the profit-maximizing level of output, q^*, is 300 units.

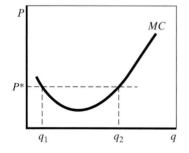

[2]To be very precise, it is possible for price to be equal to marginal cost at two points, one where marginal cost is declining and another where marginal cost is increasing (see graph to the left). Profit is maximized where marginal cost crosses price on its way up (q_2). The marginal costs of the first few units of production are high, because at such a low level of output the firm is not using its plant very efficiently. It would never make sense to produce at these low levels. In fact, to stop at the first point where P = MC (q_1) would be to minimize profits. Can you figure out why?

Keep in mind, though, that all types of firms (not just those in perfectly competitive industries) are profit maximizers. Thus,

> The profit-maximizing output level for *all* firms is the output level where $MR = MC$.

(Make sure you understand why this is so.) In perfect competition, however, $MR = P$, as shown above. Hence, for perfectly competitive firms we can rewrite our profit-maximizing condition as $P = MC$.

■ **A Numerical Example** Table 8.5 presents some data for another hypothetical firm. Let's assume that the market has set a $15 unit price for the firm's product. Total revenue in column 6 is the simple product of $P \times q$ (the numbers in column 1 times $15). The table derives total, marginal, and average costs exactly as Table 8.4 did. Here, however, we have included revenues, and we can calculate the profit, which is shown in column 8.

Column 8 shows that a profit-maximizing firm would choose to produce four units of output. At this level, profits are $20; at all other output levels, they are lower. Now let's see if "marginal" reasoning leads us to the same conclusion.

First, should the firm produce at all? If it produces nothing, it suffers losses equal to $10. If it increases output to one unit, marginal revenue is $15 (remember that it sells each unit for $15), and marginal cost is $10. Thus, it gains $5 on that unit, reducing its loss each period from $10 to $5.

Should the firm increase output to two units? The marginal revenue from the second unit is again $15, but the marginal cost is only $5. Thus, by producing the second unit the firm gains $10 ($15 − $5) and turns a $5 loss into a $5 profit. The third unit adds $10 to profits. Again, marginal revenue is $15 and marginal cost is $5, an increase in profit of $10, for a total profit of $15.

The fourth unit offers still more profit. Price is still above marginal cost, which means that producing that fourth unit will increase profits. Price, or marginal revenue, is $15, and marginal cost is just $10. Thus, the fourth unit adds $5 to profit. At unit number five, however, diminishing returns push marginal cost up above price. The marginal revenue from producing the fifth unit is $15, while marginal cost is now $20. As a result, profit per period drops by $5, to $15 per period. Clearly, the firm will not produce the fifth unit.

The profit-maximizing level of output is thus four units. The firm produces as long as price (marginal revenue) is greater than marginal cost. (For an in-depth example of profit maximization see the Application box on pages 212–213 titled "Case Study in Marginal Analysis: An Ice Cream Store.")

Table 8.5		Profit Analysis for a Simple Firm					
(1)	(2)	(3)	(4)	(5)	(6) TR	(7) TC	(8) PROFIT
q	TFC	TVC	MC	P = MR	(P × q)	(TFC + TVC)	(TR − TC)
0	$10	$ 0	$—	$15	$ 0	$10	$−10
1	10	10	10	15	15	20	−5
2	10	15	5	15	30	25	5
3	10	20	5	15	45	30	15
4	10	30	10	15	60	40	20
5	10	50	20	15	75	60	15
6	10	80	30	15	90	90	0

The following is a description of the decisions made by the owner of a small ice cream parlour. After being in business for one year, this entrepreneur had to ask herself, should I stay in business?

The cost figures on which she based her decisions are presented below. These numbers do not include one important item: the managerial labour provided by the owner. In her calculations, the entrepreneur did not include a wage for herself, but we will assume an opportunity cost of $30 000 per year ($2500 per month).

FIXED COSTS

The fixed components of the store's monthly costs include the following:

Rent (200 square metres)	$2012.50
Electricity	325.00
Debt service (loan payment)	737.50
Maintenance	295.00
Telephone	65.00
Total	$3435.00

Not all of the items on this list are strictly fixed, however. Electricity costs, for example, would be slightly higher if the store produced more ice cream and stayed open longer, but the added cost would be minimal.

VARIABLE COSTS

The ice cream store's variable costs include two components: (1) behind-the-counter labour costs, and (2) the cost of making ice cream. The store employs high school students at a wage of $5.65 per hour. Including the employer's share of Employment Insurance and Canada Pension Plan contributions, the gross cost of each hour of labour is $6.00 per hour. There are two employees working in the store at all times. The full cost of producing ice cream is $0.80 per litre. Each litre contains approximately four servings. Customers can add toppings

Marginal analysis is as important to the owner of a small ice cream store as it is to the managers of a million-dollar manufacturing operation.

free of charge, and the average cost of the toppings taken by a customer is about $0.05:

Gross labour costs	$6.00/hour
Costs of producing one litre of ice cream (four servings per litre)	$0.80
Average cost of added toppings per serving	$0.05

REVENUES

The store sells ice cream cones, sundaes, and floats. The average price of a purchase at the store is $1.45.

The store is open eight hours per day, 26 days a month, and serves an average of 240 customers per day:

Average purchase	$1.45
Days open per month	26
Average number of customers per day	240

From the information given above, it is possible to calculate the store's average monthly profit. Total revenue is equal to 240 customers × $1.45 per customer × 26 open days in an average month: $TR = \$9048$ per month.

PROFITS

The store sells 240 servings per day. Because there are four servings of ice cream per litre, the store uses exactly 60 litres per day (240 servings divided by 4). Total costs are $0.80 × 60, or $48, per day for ice cream and $12 per day for toppings (240 × $0.05). The cost of variable labour is $6 × 8 hours × 2 workers, or $96 per day. Total variable costs are therefore $156 ($48 + $12 + $96) per day. Since the store is open 26 days a month, the total variable cost per month is $4056 ($156 × 26).

Adding fixed costs of $3435 to variable costs of $4056, we get total cost of operation of $7491 per month. Thus, the firm is averaging a profit of $1557 per month ($9048 − 7491). *But this is not an "economic profit" because we haven't accounted for the opportunity cost of the owner's time and efforts.* In fact, when we factor in an implicit wage of $2500 per month for the owner, we see that the store is suffering *losses* of $943 per month ($1557 − $2500).

Total Revenue (*TR*)	$9048
Total Fixed Cost (*TFC*)	3435
+ Total Variable Cost (*TVC*)	4056
Total Costs (*TC*)	7491

Total Profit (*TR* − *TC*)	1557
Adjustment for Implicit Wage	2500
Economic Profit	− 943

Should the entrepreneur stay in business? If she wants to make $2500 per month and she thinks that nothing about her business will change, she must shut down in the long run. But two things keep her going: (1) a decision to stay open longer and (2) hope for more customers in the future.

OPENING LONGER HOURS: MARGINAL COSTS AND MARGINAL REVENUES

The store's normal hours of operation are noon until 8 P.M. On an experimental basis, the owner extends its hours until 11 P.M. for one month. The following table shows the average number of additional customers for each of the added hours:

Hour	Customers
8–9 P.M.	41
9–10 P.M.	20
10–11 P.M.	8

Assuming that the late customers spend an average of $1.45, we can calculate the marginal revenue and the marginal cost of staying open longer. The marginal cost of one serving of ice cream is $0.80 divided by 4 = $0.20 + 0.05 (for topping) = $0.25. (See table below.)

Marginal analysis tells us that the store should stay open for two additional hours. Each day that the store stays open from 8–9 P.M. it will make an added profit of $59.45 − $22.25, or $37.20. Staying open from 9–10 P.M. adds $29.00 − $17.00, or $12.00, to profit. Staying open the third hour, however, *decreases* profits because the marginal revenue generated by staying open from 10 – 11 P.M. is less than the marginal cost. The entrepreneur decides to stay open for two additional hours per day. This adds $49.20 ($37.20 + 12.00) to profits each day, a total of $1279.20 per month.

By adding the two hours, the store turns an economic loss of $943 per month into a $336.20 profit after accounting for the owner's implicit wage of $2500 per month.

The owner decides to stay in business and open the two additional hours per day. She earns over $4000 more per year than she would have earned at her old job.

Hour	Marginal Revenue (*MR*)	Marginal Cost (*MC*)		Added Profit per Hour (*MR* − *MC*)
8–9 P.M.	$1.45 × 41 = $59.45	Ice Cream: 0.25 × 41 = Labour: 2 × 6.00 = Total	$10.25 12.00 $22.25	$37.20
9–10 P.M.	$1.45 × 20 = $29.00	Ice Cream: 0.25 × 20 = Labour: 2 × 6.00 = Total	$5.00 12.00 $17.00	$12.00
10–11 P.M.	$1.45 × 8 = $11.69	Ice Cream: 0.25 × 8 = Labour: 2 × 6.00 = Total	$ 2.00 12.00 $14.00	$ − 2.31

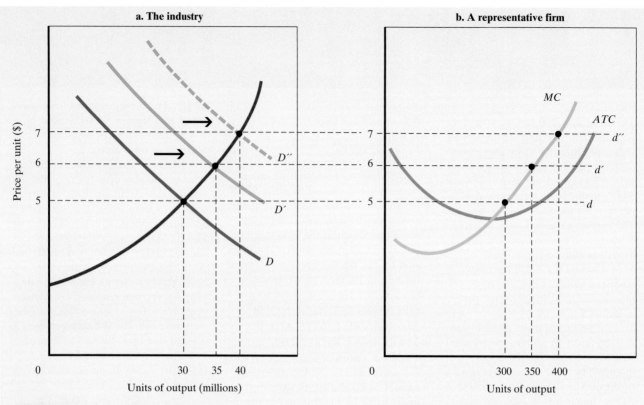

a. The industry

b. A representative firm

FIGURE 8.11

Marginal Cost Is the Supply Curve of a Perfectly Competitive Firm

At any market price* the marginal cost curve shows the output level that maximizes profit. Thus, the marginal cost curve of a perfectly competitive profit-maximizing firm is the firm's short-run supply curve.

This is true except when price is so low that it pays a firm to shut down—a point that will be discussed in Chapter 9.

THE SHORT-RUN SUPPLY CURVE

Consider how the typical firm described in Figure 8.10 would behave in response to an increase in price. In Figure 8.11a, assume that something happens that causes demand to increase (shift to the right), driving price from $5 to $6 and finally to $7. When price is $5, a profit-maximizing firm will choose output level 300 in Figure 8.11b. To produce any less, or to raise output above that level, would lead to a lower level of profit. At $6 the same firm would increase output to 350, but it would stop there. Similarly, at $7, the firm would raise output to 400 units of output.

The *MC* curve in Figure 8.11b relates price and quantity supplied. At any market price, the marginal cost curve shows the output level that maximizes profit. A curve that shows how much output a profit-maximizing firm will produce at every price also fits the definition of a supply curve. (Review Chapter 4 if this point is not clear to you.) It therefore follows that:

> The marginal cost curve of a competitive firm is the firm's short-run supply curve.

As you will see, there is some price level below which the firm will shut down its operations and simply bear losses equal to fixed costs even if price is above marginal cost. This important point is discussed in the next chapter.

Looking Ahead

At the beginning of this chapter we set out to combine information on technology, factor prices, and output prices to derive the supply curve of a competitive firm. We have now accomplished that goal.

Because marginal cost is such an important concept in microeconomics, you should carefully review any sections of this chapter that were unclear to you. Above all, keep in mind that the *marginal cost curve* carries information about both *input prices* and *technology*. The firm looks to output markets for information on potential revenues, and the current market price defines the firm's marginal revenue curve. The point where price (which is equal to marginal revenue in perfect competition) is just equal to marginal cost is the perfectly competitive firm's profit-maximizing level of output. Thus, the marginal cost curve *is* the perfectly competitive firm's supply curve in the short run.

In the next chapter, we turn to the long run. What happens when firms are free to choose their scale of operations without being limited by a fixed factor of production? Without diminishing returns that set in as a result of a fixed scale of production, what determines the shape of cost curves? What happens when new firms can enter industries in which profits are being earned? How do industries adjust when losses are being incurred? How does the structure of an industry evolve over long periods of time?

Summary

1. Profit-maximizing firms make decisions in order to maximize profit (total revenue minus total cost).

2. To calculate production costs, firms must know two things: the quantity and combination of inputs they need to produce their product and how much those inputs cost.

Costs in the Short Run

3. *Fixed costs* are costs that do not change with the output of a firm. In the short run, firms cannot avoid them or change them, even if production is zero.

4. *Variable costs* are those costs that depend on, or vary with, the level of output chosen. Fixed costs plus variable costs equal *total costs* ($TC = TFC + TVC$).

5. *Average fixed cost (AFC)* is total fixed cost divided by the quantity of output. As output rises, average fixed cost declines steadily because the same total is being spread over a larger and larger quantity of output. This phenomenon is called *spreading overhead*.

6. Numerous combinations of inputs can be used to produce a given level of output. *Total variable cost*

(TVC) is the total of all costs that depend on or vary with output in the short run.

7. *Marginal cost (MC)* is the increase in total cost that results from the production of one more unit of output. If a firm is producing 1000 units, the additional cost of increasing output to 1001 units is marginal cost. Marginal cost measures the cost of the additional inputs required to produce each successive unit of output. Because fixed costs do not change when output changes, marginal costs reflect changes in variable costs.

8. In the short run, a firm is limited by a fixed factor of production, or a fixed scale of plant. As a firm increases output, it will eventually find itself trapped by that scale. Because of the fixed scale, marginal cost eventually rises with output.

9. Marginal cost is the slope of the total variable cost curve. The total variable cost curve always has a positive slope, because total costs always rise with output. But increasing marginal cost means that total costs ultimately rise at an increasing rate.

10. *Average variable cost (AVC)* is equal to total variable cost divided by the quantity of output.

11. When marginal cost is above average variable cost, average variable cost is *increasing*. When marginal cost is below average variable cost, average variable cost is *declining*. Marginal cost intersects average variable cost at *AVC*'s minimum point.

12. *Average total cost (ATC)* is equal to total cost divided by the quantity of output. It is also equal to the sum of average fixed cost and average variable cost.

13. If marginal cost is below average total cost, average total cost will decline toward marginal cost. If marginal cost is above average total cost, average total cost will increase. Marginal cost intersects average total cost at *ATC*'s minimum point.

Output Decisions: Revenues, Costs, and Profit Maximization

14. In the short run, a perfectly competitive firm faces a demand curve that is a horizontal line (in other words, perfectly elastic demand).

15. *Total revenue (TR)* is simply price times the quantity of output that a firm decides to produce and sell. *Marginal revenue (MR)* is the additional revenue that a firm takes in when it increases output by one unit.

16. For a perfectly competitive firm, marginal revenue is equal to the current market price of its product.

17. A profit-maximizing firm in a perfectly competitive industry will produce up to the point at which the price of its output is just equal to short-run marginal cost: $P = MC$. The more general profit-maximizing formula is $MR = MC$ ($P = MR$ in perfect competition). The marginal cost curve of a perfectly competitive firm is the firm's short-run supply curve.

Review Terms and Concepts

average fixed cost (*AFC*) 196
average total cost (*ATC*) 205
average variable cost (*AVC*) 203
fixed cost 195
marginal cost (*MC*) 199

marginal revenue (*MR*) 209
spreading overhead 197
total cost (*TC*) 195
total fixed costs (*TFC*) or overhead 196

total revenue (*TR*) 208
total variable cost (*TVC*) 197
total variable cost curve 198
variable cost 195

Equations:

1. $TC = TFC + TVC$
2. $AFC = TFC/q$
3. slope of $TVC = MC$
4. $AVC = TVC/q$

5. $ATC = TC/q = AFC + AVC$
6. $TR = P \times q$
7. Profit-maximizing level of output for all firms: $MR = MC$

8. Profit-maximizing level of output for perfectly competitive firms: $P = MC$

1. The following table gives capital and labour requirements for 10 different levels of production:

q	K	L
0	0	0
1	2	5
2	4	9
3	6	12
4	8	15
5	10	19
6	12	24
7	14	30
8	16	37
9	18	45
10	20	54

a. Assuming that the price of labour (P_L) is $5 per unit and the price of capital (P_K) is $10 per unit, compute and graph the total variable cost curve, the marginal cost curve, and the average variable cost curve for the firm.

b. Do the curves have the shapes that you might expect? Explain.

c. Using the numbers here, explain the relationship between marginal cost and average variable cost.

d. Using the numbers here, explain the meaning of "marginal cost" in terms of additional inputs needed to produce a marginal unit of output.

e. If output price was $57, how many units of output would the firm produce? Explain.

2. Do you agree or disagree with each of the following statements? Give your reasons.

a. If marginal cost is rising, average cost must also be rising.

b. A profit-maximizing firm must minimize cost. Thus firms will always produce the level of output at which average total cost is minimized.

c. Average fixed cost does not change as output changes.

3. A firm's cost curves are given by the following table:

q	TC	TFC	VC	AVC	ATC	MC
0	$100	$100				
1	130	100				
2	150	100				
3	160	100				
4	172	100				
5	185	100				
6	210	100				
7	240	100				
8	280	100				
9	330	100				
10	390	100				

a. Complete the table.

b. Graph AVC, ATC, and MC on the same graph. What is the relationship between the MC curve and ATC? Between MC and AVC?

c. Suppose that market price is $30. How much will the firm produce in the short run? How much are total profits? Show them on the graph.

d. Suppose that market price is $50. How much will the firm produce in the short run? What are total profits? Show them on the graph.

e. Suppose that market price is $10. How much would the firm produce in the short run? What are total profits? Show them on the graph.

4. A 1997 University of Windsor graduate inherited her mother's printing company. The capital stock of the firm consists of three machines of various vintages, all in excellent condition. All machines can be running at the same time:

	Cost of Printing and Binding per Book	Maximum Total Capacity per Month
Machine 1	$1.00	100 books
Machine 2	$2.00	200 books
Machine 3	$3.00	500 books

a. Assume that "cost of printing and binding per book" includes *all* labour and materials, including the owner's own wages. Assume further that Mom signed a long-term contract (50 years) with a service company to keep the machines in good repair for a fixed fee of $100 per month.
(i) Derive the firm's marginal cost curve.
(ii) Derive the firm's total cost curve.

b. At a price of $2.50, how many books would

the company produce? What would total revenues be? Total costs? Total profits?

5. The following curve is a production function for a firm that uses just one variable factor of production, labour. It shows total output, or product, for every level of inputs:

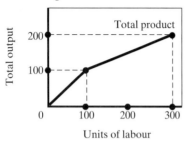

a. Derive and graph the marginal product curve.
b. Suppose that the wage rate is $4. Derive and graph the firm's marginal cost curve.
c. If output sells for $6, what is the profit-maximizing level of output? How much labour will the firm hire?

6. Elena and Emmanuel live on the Black Sea in Bulgaria and own a small fishing boat. A crew of four is required to take the boat out fishing. The current wage paid to the four crew members is a total of 5000 levs per day (a lev is the Bulgarian unit of currency). Assume that the cost of operating and maintaining the boat is 1000 levs per day when fishing, and zero otherwise. The following schedule gives the appropriate catch for each period during the year:

Period	Catch per Day
Prime fishing: 180 days	100 kilograms
Month 7: 30 days	80 kilograms
Month 8: 30 days	60 kilograms
Rest of the year	40 kilograms

The price of fish in Bulgaria is no longer regulated by the government, and is now determined in competitive markets. Suppose that the price has been stable all year at 80 levs per kilogram.

a. What is the marginal product of a day's worth of fishing during prime fishing season? During month 7? During month 8?
b. What is the marginal cost of a kilogram of fish during prime fishing season? During month 7? During month 8? During the rest of the year?
c. If you were Elena and Emmanuel, how many months per year would you hire the crew and go out fishing? Explain your answer using marginal logic.

Costs and Output Decisions in the Long Run

The last two chapters presented a theory of the behaviour of profit-maximizing competitive firms in the short run. Recall that all firms must make three fundamental decisions: (1) how much output to produce or supply, (2) how to produce that output, and (3) how much of each input to demand.

Firms use information on input prices, output prices, and technology to make the decisions that will lead to the most profit. Since profits equal revenues minus costs, firms must know how much their products will sell for and how much production will cost, using the most efficient technology.

In Chapter 8 we saw in detail how cost curves can be derived from production functions and input prices. Once a firm has a clear picture of its short-run costs, the price at which it sells its output determines the quantity of output that will maximize profit. Specifically, we saw that a profit-maximizing perfectly competitive firm will supply output up to the point that price (marginal revenue) equals marginal cost. The marginal cost curve of such a firm is thus the same thing as its supply curve.

In this chapter, we turn from the short run to the long run. The condition in which firms find themselves in the short run (are they making profits? are they incurring losses?) determines what is likely to happen in the long run. Remember that output (supply) decisions in the long run are less constrained than they are in the short run, for two reasons. First, in the long run, the firm has no fixed factor of production that confines its production to a given scale. Second, firms are free to enter industries in order to seek profits and to leave industries in order to avoid losses.

The long run has important implications for the shape of cost curves. As we saw, in the short run the assumption of a fixed factor of production eventually causes marginal cost to increase along with output. This is not the case in the long run, however. With no fixed scale, the shape of cost curves becomes more complex and less easy to generalize about. The shape of long-run cost curves has important implications for the way an industry's structure is likely to evolve over time.

We begin our discussion of the long run by looking at firms in three short-run circumstances: (1) firms earning economic profits, (2) firms suffering economic losses but continuing to operate to reduce or minimize those losses, and (3) firms that find it in their interest to shut down and bear losses just equal to fixed costs. We then examine how these firms will alter their cost and production decisions in response to their short-run conditions.

Although we continue to focus on perfectly competitive firms, it should be stressed that *all* firms are subject to the spectrum of short-run profit or loss situations, regardless of market structure. Assuming perfect competition allows us to simplify our analysis and provides us with a strong background for understanding the discussions of imperfectly competitive behaviour in later chapters.

Short-Run Conditions and Long-Run Directions

Before we begin our examination of firm behaviour, let us review the concept of profit that we are using here. Recall that a normal rate of profit is included in costs as we measure them in economics. Thus, when we say that a firm is earning profits, we mean that it is earning a profit over and above a normal rate of return to capital. A *normal rate of return* is a profit rate that is just sufficient to keep current investors interested in the industry. Thus, when we speak of profits, we really mean profits above normal. Sometimes, for emphasis, these extranormal profits are called *economic profits* (see Chapter 7).

When we use the term "profit," then, we are simply taking into account the opportunity cost of capital. By investing in a firm, its owners or lenders are forgoing what they could earn by investing elsewhere. This is why the normal rate of return must be at least equal to the interest rate on "safe" investments (government bonds, for example). Only when investors earn profits above the normal level are they earning economic profits. And only when they are earning economic profits are new investors likely to be attracted to the industry.

When we say that a firm is suffering *losses,* we mean that it is earning a profit rate for its investors that is below normal. Such a firm may be suffering losses as an accountant would measure them or simply be earning at a very low (that is, below normal) profit rate. Investors in a firm are not going to be happy if they earn a return of only 2% when they can get 5% on Canada Savings Bonds. A firm that is **breaking even,** or earning zero economic profits, is one that is earning exactly a normal profit rate. New investors are not attracted, but current ones are not running away, either.

breaking even *The situation in which a firm is earning exactly a normal profit rate.*

With this in mind, then, we can say that for any firm one of three conditions holds at any given moment: (1) the firm is making economic profits, (2) the firm is suffering economic losses, or (3) the firm is just breaking even. Profitable firms will, of course, want to maximize their profits in the short run, while firms suffering losses will want to minimize those losses in the short run.

MAXIMIZING PROFITS

The best way to understand the behaviour of a firm that is currently earning profits is by way of example.

■ **Example: The Blue Velvet Car Wash**   When a firm earns revenues in excess of costs (including a normal profit rate), it is earning economic profits. Let us take as an example the Blue Velvet Car Wash. Suppose that investors have put up $500 000 to construct a building and purchase all the equipment required to wash cars. Let's also suppose that investors expect to earn a minimum return of 10% on their investment. If the money to set up the business had been borrowed from the bank instead, the car wash owners would have paid a 10% interest rate. In either case, the firm earns an economic profit only *after* it has paid its investors, or the bank, 10% of $500 000, or $50 000 every year. This normal profit of $50 000 is part of the firm's annual costs.

The car wash is open 50 weeks per year and is capable of washing up to 500 cars per week. Whether it is open and operating or not, the car wash has fixed costs. Those costs include $1000 per week to investors (that is, the $50 000 per year normal profit rate) and $1000 per week in other fixed costs (a basic maintenance contract on the equipment, a long-term lease, and so forth).

When the car wash is operating, there are also variable costs. Workers must be paid, and materials such as soap and wax must be purchased. The wage bill is $1000 per week. Materials, electricity, and so forth run $600 if the car wash is run at full capacity. If the car wash is not in operation, there are no variable costs. Table 9.1 summarizes the costs of the Blue Velvet Car Wash.

This car wash business is quite competitive. There are many car washes of equal quality in the area, and they offer their service at $8. If Blue Velvet wants customers, it cannot charge a price for car washes above $8. (Recall the perfectly elastic demand curve facing perfectly competitive firms; review Chapter 8 if necessary.) If we assume that Blue Velvet washes 500 cars each week, it takes in revenues of $4000 from operating (500 cars × $8). Is this total revenue enough to make an economic profit?

The answer is yes. Revenues of $4000 are sufficient to cover both fixed costs of $2000 and variable costs of $1600, leaving an economic profit of $400 per week. If Blue Velvet shut down (that is, if it stopped operating the car wash), it would suffer losses equal to fixed costs of $2000. It is clearly in the firm's interest to continue operating.

■ **Graphic Presentation**   Figure 9.1 graphs the performance of a firm that is earning economic profits in the short run. Figure 9.1a illustrates the industry, or the market, and Figure 9.1b illustrates a representative firm. At present, the market is clearing at a price of $5. Thus, we assume that the individual firm can sell all it wants at a price of $P^* = \$5$, but that it is constrained by its capacity; its marginal cost curve rises in the short run because of the assumption of a fixed factor. You already know that a perfectly competitive profit-maximizing firm produces up to the point that price equals marginal cost. As long as price (marginal revenue) exceeds marginal cost, firms can push up profits by increasing short-run output. The firm in the diagram, then, will produce, or supply, $q^* = 300$ units of output (point A, where $P = MC$).

Both revenues and costs are shown graphically. *Total revenue (TR)* is simply the product of price and quantity: $P^* \times q^* = \$5 \times 300 = \$1500$. On the diagram, total revenue is equal to the area of the rectangle P^*Aq^*0 (the area of a rectangle is equal to its length times its width). At output q^*, average total cost is $4.20

Table 9.1

Blue Velvet Car Wash Weekly Costs

TOTAL FIXED COSTS (TFC):

1. Normal return (profit) to investors	$1000
2. Other fixed costs (maintenance contract, lease, etc.)	1000
	$2000

TOTAL VARIABLE COSTS (TVC) (500 WASHES):

1. Labour	$1000
2. Materials	600
	$1600

TOTAL COSTS (TC = TFC + TVC): **$3600**

Total Revenue (TR) at P = $8 (i.e., 500 × $8)	$4000
Profit (TR − TC)	$400

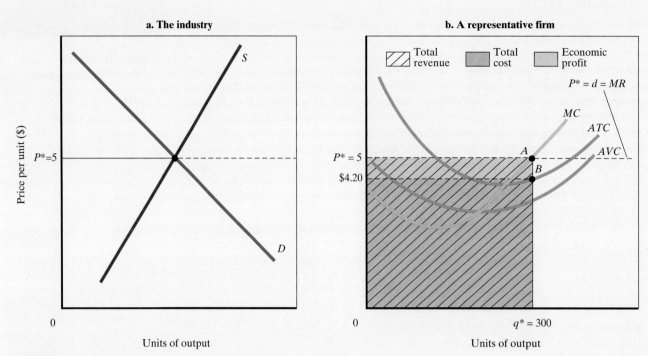

FIGURE 9.1

Firm Earning Economic (Excess) Profits in the Short Run

A profit-maximizing perfectly competitive firm will produce up to the point where $P^* = MC$. Profits are the difference between total revenue and total costs. At $q^* = 300$, total revenue is $5 \times 300 = \$1500$, total cost is $\$4.20 \times 300 = \$1260$, and total profit = $\$1500 - \$1260 = \$240$.

(point B). Numerically, it is equal to the length of line segment q^*B. Since average total cost is derived by dividing total cost by q, we can get back to total cost by *multiplying* average total cost by q. That is,

$$ATC = \frac{TC}{q}$$

and

$$TC = ATC \times q.$$

Total cost (TC), then, is $\$4.20 \times 300 = \$1260$, the area shaded purple in the diagram. *Total economic profit* is simply the difference between total revenue (*TR*) and total cost (*TC*), or $\$240$. This is the area that is shaded pink in the diagram. This firm is earning positive economic profits.

As we will see later in the chapter, a firm that is earning economic profits in the short run and expects to continue to do so has an incentive to expand its scale of operation in the long run. Those profits also give new firms an incentive to enter and compete in the market.

Minimizing Losses

A firm that is not earning economic profit or breaking even is suffering a loss. Firms suffering losses fall into two categories: (1) those that find it advantageous to shut down operations immediately and bear losses equal to fixed costs, and (2) those that continue to operate in the short run to minimize their losses. The most important thing to remember here is that firms cannot exit the industry in the short run. The firm can shut down, but it cannot get rid of its fixed costs by going out of business. We assume that fixed costs must be paid in the short run no matter what the firm does.

Whether a firm suffering losses decides to produce or not to produce in the short run depends on the advantages and disadvantages of continuing production. If a firm shuts down, it earns no revenues and has no variable costs to bear. If it continues to produce, it both earns revenues and incurs variable costs. Because a firm must bear fixed costs *whether or not* it shuts down, its decision depends *solely on whether revenues from operating are sufficient to cover variable costs*. **Operating profit (or loss)** (sometimes called **net operating revenue**) is defined as total revenue (TR) minus total variable cost (TVC). In general:

operating profit (or loss) or **net operating revenue** *Total revenue minus total variable cost* ($TR - TVC$).

> If revenues exceed variable costs, operating profit is positive and can be used to offset fixed costs and reduce losses, and it will pay the firm to keep operating.
>
> If revenues are smaller than variable costs, the firm suffers operating losses that push total losses above fixed costs. In this case, the firm can minimize its losses by shutting down.

■ **Producing at a Loss to Offset Fixed Costs: The Blue Velvet Revisited** To return to the car wash example, suppose that competitive pressure pushed the price per wash down to $6. Total revenues for Blue Velvet would fall to $3000 per week (500 cars × $6). If variable costs remained at $1600, total costs would be $3600 ($1600 + $2000 fixed costs), a figure higher than total revenues. The firm would then be suffering economic losses of $600.

In the long run, Blue Velvet may want to go out of business, but in the short run it is stuck, and it must decide what to do.

The car wash has two options: operate or shut down. If it shuts down, it has no variable costs, but it also earns no revenues, and its losses will be equal to its fixed costs of $2000 (Table 9.2, Case 1). If it decides to stay open (Table 9.2, Case 2), it will make operating profits. Revenues will be $3000, more than sufficient to

Table 9.2	A Firm Will Operate if Total Revenue Covers Total Variable Cost		

CASE 1: SHUT DOWN		CASE 2: OPERATE AT PRICE = $6	
Total Revenue ($q = 0$):	$0	Total Revenue ($6 × 500):	$3000
Fixed costs	$2000	Fixed costs	$2000
Variable costs	+ 0	Variable costs	+1600
Total costs	$2000	Total costs	$3600
Profit/Loss ($TR - TC$):	− $2000	Operating Profit/Loss ($TR - TVC$):	$1400
		Total Profit/Loss ($TR - TC$):	− $ 600

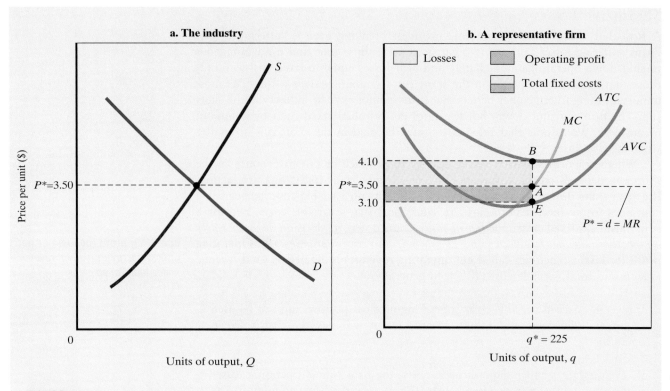

a. The industry

b. A representative firm

FIGURE 9.2

Firm Suffering Economic Losses but Showing an Operating Profit in the Short Run

When price is sufficient to cover average variable costs, firms suffering short-run losses will continue to operate rather than shut down. Total revenues ($P^* \times q^*$) cover variable costs, leaving an operating profit of $90 to cover part of fixed costs and reduce losses to $135.

cover variable costs of $1600. By operating, the firm gains $1400 per week operating profits that it can use to offset its fixed costs. By operating, then, the firm reduces its losses from $2000 to $600.

■ **Graphic Presentation** Figure 9.2 graphs a firm suffering economic losses. The market price, set by the forces of supply and demand, is $P^* = \$3.50$. If the firm decides to operate, it will do best by producing up to the point where price (marginal revenue) is equal to marginal cost—in this case, at an output of $q^* = 225$ units.

Once again, total revenue (TR) is simply the product of price and quantity ($P^* \times q^*$) = \$3.50 \times 225 = \$787.50$, or the area of rectangle P^*Aq^*0. Average total cost at $q^* = 225$ is $4.10, and it is equal to the length of q^*B. Total cost is the product of average total cost and q^* ($ATC \times q^*$), or $4.10 \times 225 = \$922.50$. Because total cost is greater than total revenue, the firm is suffering economic losses of $135, shown on the graph by the area of the grey shaded rectangle.

Operating profit—the difference between total revenue and total *variable* cost—can also be identified. On the graph, total revenue (as we said) is $787.50. *Average* variable cost at q^* is the length of q^*E. Total variable cost is the product of average variable cost and q^* and is therefore equal to $3.10 \times 225 = \$697.50$. Profit on operation is thus $787.50 − \$697.50 = \$90$, the area of the pink shaded rectangle.

Remember that average total cost is equal to average fixed cost plus average variable cost. This means that at every level of output average fixed cost is the difference between average total and average variable cost:

$$ATC = AFC + AVC$$

or

$$AFC = ATV - AVC = \$4.10 - \$3.10 = \$1.00$$

In Figure 9.2, therefore, average fixed cost is equal to the length of BE (the difference between ATC and AVC at q^* or \$1.00). Since total fixed cost is simply average fixed cost (\$1.00) times $q^* = \$225$, total fixed cost is equal to \$225, the entire grey and pink shaded rectangle. Thus, if the firm had shut down, its losses would be equal to \$225. By operating, the firm earns an operating profit equal to the pink shaded area (\$90) covering some fixed costs and reducing losses to the grey shaded area (\$135).

If we think only in averages, it seems logical that a firm in this position will continue to operate:

As long as price (which is equal to average revenue per unit) is sufficient to cover average variable costs, the firm stands to gain by operating rather than by shutting down.

■ **Shutting Down to Minimize Loss**   When revenues are insufficient to cover even variable costs, firms suffering losses find it advantageous to shut down, even in the short run.

Suppose, for example, that competition and the availability of sophisticated new machinery pushed the price of a car wash all the way down to \$3.00. Washing 500 cars per week would then yield revenues of only \$1500 (Table 9.3). With variable costs at \$1600, operating would mean losing an additional \$100 *over and above* fixed costs of \$2000. This means that total losses would amount to \$2100. Clearly, a profit-maximizing/loss-minimizing car wash would reduce its losses from \$2100 to \$2000 by shutting down, even in the short run.

Table 9.3	A Firm Will Shut Down if Total Revenue Is Less than Total Variable Cost

CASE 1: SHUT DOWN		CASE 2: OPERATE AT PRICE = \$3	
Total Revenue ($q = 0$):	\$0	Total Revenue (\$3 × 500):	\$1500
Fixed costs	\$2000	Fixed costs	\$2000
Variable costs	+ 0	Variable costs	+1600
Total costs	\$2000	Total costs	\$3600
Profit/Loss ($TR - TC$):	−\$2000	Operating Profit/Loss ($TR - TVC$):	−\$100
		Total Profit/Loss ($TR - TC$):	−\$2100

From this example, we can generalize that:

> Any time that price (average revenue) is below the minimum point on the average variable cost curve, total revenue will be less than total variable cost, and operating profit will be negative (that is, there will be a loss on operation). In other words, when price is below all points on the average variable cost curve, the firm will suffer operating losses at any possible output level the firm could choose. When this is the case, the firm will stop producing ($q = 0$) and bear losses equal to fixed costs. This is why the bottom of the average variable cost curve is called the **shut-down point.** At all prices above it, the *MC* curve shows the profit-maximizing level of output. At all prices below it, optimal short-run output is zero.

shut-down point *The lowest point on the average variable cost curve. When price falls below the minimum point on AVC, total revenue is insufficient to cover variable costs and the firm will shut down and bear losses equal to fixed costs.*

We can now refine our earlier statement that a perfectly competitive firm's marginal cost curve is actually its short-run supply curve. Recall that a profit-maximizing perfectly competitive firm will produce up to the point at which $P = MC$. As we have just seen, though, a firm will shut down when P is less than the minimum point on the *AVC* curve. Also recall that the marginal cost curve intersects the *AVC* curve at *AVC*'s lowest point. It therefore follows that:

> The short-run supply curve of a competitive firm is that portion of its marginal cost curve that lies above its average variable cost curve (Figure 9.3).

THE SHORT-RUN INDUSTRY SUPPLY CURVE

Supply in a competitive industry is simply the sum of the quantity supplied by the individual firms in the industry at each price level. The **short-run industry supply curve** is the sum of the individual firm supply curves—that is, the marginal cost curves (above *AVC*) of all the firms in the industry. Because quantities are being added (that is, because we are finding the total quantity supplied in the industry at each price level), the curves are added horizontally.

short-run industry supply curve *The sum of marginal cost curves (above AVC) of all the firms in an industry.*

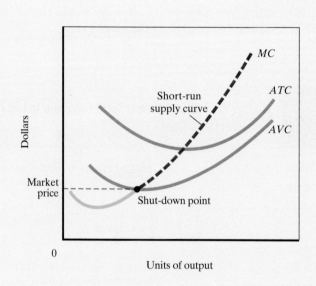

FIGURE 9.3

Short-Run Supply Curve of a Perfectly Competitive Firm

At prices below average variable cost, it pays a firm to shut down rather than to continue operating. Thus, the short-run supply curve of a competitive firm is the part of its marginal cost curve that lies *above* its average variable cost curve.

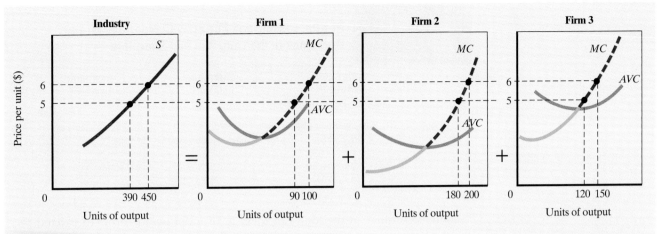

FIGURE 9.4

The Industry Supply Curve in the Short Run Is the Horizontal Sum of the Marginal Cost Curves (*above AVC*) of All the Firms in an Industry

If there are only three firms in the industry, the industry supply curve is simply the sum of all the products supplied by the three firms at each price. For example, at $6, firm 1 supplies 100 units, firm 2 supplies 200 units, and firm 3 supplies 150 units, for a total industry supply of 450.

Figure 9.4 shows the supply curve for an industry with just three firms.[1] At a price of $6, firm 1 produces 100 units, the output where $P = MC$. Firm 2 produces 200 units, and firm 3 produces 150 units. The total amount supplied on the market at a price of $6 is thus 450 (100 + 200 + 150). At a price of $5, firm 1 produces 90 units, firm 2 produces 180 units, and firm 3 produces 120 units. At a price of $5, the industry thus supplies 390 units (90 + 180 + 120).

Two things can cause the industry supply curve to shift. In the short run, the industry supply curve shifts if something—an increase in the price of some input, for instance—shifts the marginal cost curves of all the individual firms simultaneously. For example, when the cost of producing components of home computers decreased, the marginal cost curves of all computer manufacturers shifted downward. Such a shift amounted to the same thing as an outward shift in their supply curves. Each firm was willing to supply more computers at each price level because computers were now cheaper to produce.

In the long run, an increase or decrease in the number of firms—and, therefore, in the number of individual firms' supply curves—shifts the total industry supply curve. If new firms enter the industry, the industry supply curve moves to the right; if firms exit the industry, the industry supply curve moves to the left.

We return to shifts in industry supply curves and discuss them further when we take up long-run adjustments later in this chapter.

LONG-RUN DIRECTIONS: A REVIEW

Table 9.4 summarizes the different circumstances that perfectly competitive firms may face as they plan for the long run. Profit-making firms will produce up to the point where price and marginal cost are equal in the short run. (Remember, for perfectly competitive firms, marginal revenue is equal to price.) Since "profit" means

---

[1]*Perfectly competitive industries are assumed to have "many firms." Many is, of course, more than three. We use three firms here simply for the purposes of illustration.*

Table 9.4		Profits, Losses, and Perfectly Competitive Firms' Decisions in the Long Run and Short Run	
	SHORT-RUN CONDITION	**SHORT-RUN DECISION**	**LONG-RUN DECISION**
Profits		$P = MC$: operate	Expand: new firms enter
Losses	1. With operating profit ($TR \geq TVC$)	$P = MC$: operate (losses < fixed costs)	Contract: firms exit
	2. With operating losses ($TR < TVC$)	Shut down: losses = fixed costs	Contract: firms exit

"economic profit," in the long run there is an incentive for firms to expand their scales of plant, and for new firms to enter the industry.

Firms suffering losses will produce if, and only if, revenues are sufficient to cover variable costs. If a firm can earn a profit on operations, it can reduce the losses it would suffer if it shut down. Such firms, like profitable firms, will also produce up to the point where $P = MC$. If firms suffering losses cannot cover variable costs by operating, they will shut down and bear losses equal to fixed costs. Whether or not a firm that is suffering losses decides to shut down in the short run, it has an incentive to contract in the long run. The simple fact is that when firms are suffering economic losses, they will generally exit the industry in the long run.

In the short run, a firm's decision about how much to produce depends upon the market price of its product and the shapes of its cost curves. Remember that the short-run cost curves show costs that are determined by the *current* scale of plant. In the long run, however, firms have to choose among many *potential* scales of plant.

The long-run decisions of individual firms depend on what their costs are likely to be at different scales of operation. Just as firms have to analyze different technologies to arrive at a cost structure in the short run, they must also compare their costs at different scales of plant to arrive at long-run costs. Perhaps a larger scale of operations will reduce production costs and provide an even greater incentive for a profit-making firm to expand. Or perhaps large firms will run into problems that constrain growth. The analysis of long-run possibilities is even more complex than the short-run analysis, because more things are variable—scale of plant is not fixed, for example, and there are no fixed costs because firms can exit their industry in the long run. In theory, firms may choose *any* scale of operation, and so they must analyze many possible options.

Now let us turn to an analysis of cost curves in the long run.

Long-Run Costs: Economies and Diseconomies of Scale

As you already know, the shapes of short-run cost curves follow directly from the assumption of a fixed factor of production. As output increases beyond a certain point, the fixed factor (which we usually think of as fixed scale of plant) causes diminishing returns to other factors and thus increasing marginal costs. In the long run, however, there is no fixed factor of production. Firms can choose any scale of production. They can double or triple output or go out of business completely.

The shape of a firm's long-run average cost curve depends on how costs vary with scale of operations. For some firms, increased scale, or size, reduces costs; for others, increased scale leads to inefficiency and waste. When an increase in a firm's scale of production leads to lower average costs, we say there are **increasing returns to scale,** or **economies of scale.** When average costs do not change with the scale of production, we say that there are **constant returns to scale.** Finally, when an increase in a firm's scale of production leads to higher average costs, we say that there are **decreasing returns to scale,** or **diseconomies of scale.** Because these economies of scale all are found within the individual firm, they are considered *internal* economies of scale. In the appendix to this chapter, we talk about *external* economies of scale, which describe economies or diseconomies of scale on an industrywide basis.

INCREASING RETURNS TO SCALE

Technically, the phrase *increasing returns to scale* refers to the relationship between inputs and outputs. When we say that a production function exhibits increasing returns, we mean that a given percentage increase in the production of output requires a smaller percentage increase in the inputs. For example, if a firm were to double output, it would need less than twice as much of each input to produce that output. Stated the other way around, if a firm doubled or tripled inputs, it would more than double or triple output.

When firms can count on fixed input prices—that is, when the prices of inputs do not change with output levels—increasing returns to scale also means that as output rises, average cost of production falls. The term "economies of scale" refers directly to this reduction in cost per unit of output that follows from larger-scale production. For an example of economies of scale in Canadian farming, see the Application box on the next page.

■ **The Sources of Economies of Scale** Most of the economies of scale that immediately come to mind are technological in nature. Automobile production, for example, would be much more costly per unit if a firm were to produce 100 cars per year by hand. Early in this century, Henry Ford introduced standardized production techniques that increased output volume, reduced costs per car, and made the automobile available to almost everyone.

Some economies of scale do not result from technology but from sheer size. Very large companies, for instance, can buy inputs in volume at discounted prices. Large firms may also produce some of their own inputs at considerable savings. And they can certainly save in transport costs when items are shipped in bulk.

Economies of scale can be seen all around us. A bus that carries 100 people between Vancouver and Seattle uses less labour, capital, and gasoline than do 100 people driving 100 different automobiles. The cost per passenger (average cost) is lower on the bus. Roommates who share an apartment are taking advantage of economies of scale. Costs per person for heat, electricity, and space are lower when an apartment is shared than they would be if each person rented a separate apartment.

■ **Graphic Presentation** A firm's **long-run average cost curve (LRAC)** shows the different scales on which it can choose to operate in the long run. In other words, a firm's *LRAC* curve traces out the position of all its possible short-run curves, each corresponding to a different scale. At any time, the existing scale of plant determines the position and shape of the firm's short-run cost curve. But the firm must consider in its long-run strategic planning whether to build a plant of a *different* scale. The long-run average cost curve simply shows the positions of the different sets of short-run curves among which the firm must choose. The long-run average cost curve is the "envelope" of a series of short-run curves; in other words, it "wraps around" the set of all possible short-run curves like an envelope. (Later in this chapter, page 238,

increasing returns to scale or **economies of scale** *An increase in a firm's scale of production leads to lower average costs per unit produced.*

constant returns to scale *An increase in a firm's scale of production has no effect on average costs per unit produced.*

decreasing returns to scale or **diseconomies of scale** *An increase in a firm's scale of production leads to higher average costs per unit produced.*

long-run average cost curve (LRAC) *A graph that shows the different scales on which a firm can choose to operate in the long run.*

Application

Why Small Farmers Have Trouble Competing: Economies of Scale in Agriculture and Hog Raising

Economies of scale, or increasing returns to scale, exist when larger firms have lower average costs than smaller firms. If economies of scale exist in agriculture one would expect the average size of farms to increase over time as smaller operations find themselves unable to compete. Indeed, this is exactly what we observe in Canadian agriculture.

As an example consider the results of a study of the Ontario hog industry by Mike von Massow, Alfons Weersink, and Calum Turvey, three agricultural economists at the University of Guelph. They have observed that "the number of hog producers has declined steadily from over 30 000 in 1970 to approximately 10 000 in 1990....This decline coincided with growth in the number of hogs marketed over the same period of about two million." More output from fewer farms implies a larger average size of farm. These Guelph economists have also developed an economic model that predicts that "there will be approximately 60% fewer hog producers in Ontario by the turn of the century than at the beginning of 1990."

Similar trends exist in other provinces. The emergence of new "super farms"—especially in Manitoba, Saskatchewan, and Alberta—may result in even more dramatic changes in the hog sector than predicted by von Massow, Weersink, and Turvey. For example, a new "super farm" operation (called Lean N Low) was recently proposed by Gary Shaw and Jim Gowans in Red Willow, Alberta.

Messrs. Shaw and Gowans are courting financial backers for their proposed four acre, state-of-the-art, low cost pig barn, which they say will produce 27 000 hogs every year. If their plan succeeds, Lean N Low operations will be one of the biggest hog operations in

As a result of economies of scale in agriculture, family-owned farms are increasingly being replaced by large-scale agribusinesses. Economies of scale are present not only in sugar beet and other produce farming (top), but also in hog and other livestock farming (bottom).

the province and the only one owned by shareholders.

. . . Mr. Shaw, a hog nutritionist from Red Deer, expects to save $12 per hog in production costs by doing things big. "Building for 27 000 hogs helps us capitalize on economies of scale", he says, "and makes us so cost-effective that we can withstand any kind of competitive pressure."

He expects Lean N Low to turn a profit after one year of operation. If all goes well, a second, identical barn will be

added to take the plant's capacity to 54 000 hogs yearly. Mr. Shaw says Alberta pork producers are going to have to get bigger or die, adding that at least 12 similarly large-scale hog farms are at work in Saskatchewan and Manitoba.

Sources: M. von Massow, A. Weersink, and C.G. Turvey, "Dynamics of Structural Change in the Ontario Hog Industry," *Canadian Journal of Agricultural Economics* 40 (1992): 93–107; "Is that Money I Smell? Two Entrepreneurs Start A Mega-Hog Farm Near Stettler," *Western Report* vol. 10, no.29 (August 7, 1995): p. 15.

the Issues and Controversies box titled "The Long-Run Average Cost Curve: Flat or U-Shaped?" describes the debate on how the *LRAC* is constructed.)

Figure 9.5 shows short-run and long-run average cost curves for a firm that realizes economies of scale up to about 100 000 units of production and roughly constant returns to scale after that. The diagram shows three potential scales of operation, each with its own set of short-run cost curves. Each point on the *LRAC* curve represents the minimum cost at which the associated output level can be produced.

Once the firm chooses a scale on which to produce, it becomes locked into one set of cost curves in the short run. If the firm were to settle on Scale 1, it would not realize the major cost advantages of producing on a larger scale. By roughly doubling its scale of operations from 50 000 to 100 000 units (Scale 2), the firm reduces average costs per unit significantly.

Figure 9.5 shows that at every moment firms face two different cost constraints. In the long run, firms can change their scale of operation, and costs may be different as a result. But at any *given* moment, a particular scale of operation exists, acting as a binding constraint on the firm's capacity to produce in the short run. Remember that in the short run, a fixed factor of production leads to diminishing returns. That is why we see both short- and long-run curves in the same diagram. The owner of a small restaurant must decide what to do within the walls of her current establishment in the short run; at the same time, she must consider whether or not to expand her capacity in the long run.

CONSTANT RETURNS TO SCALE

Technically, the term *constant returns* means that the quantitative relationship between input and output stays constant, or the same, when output is increased. If a firm doubles inputs, it doubles output; if it triples inputs, it triples output; and so forth. Furthermore, if input prices are fixed, constant returns implies that average cost of production does not change with scale. In other words, constant returns to scale means that the firm's long-run average cost curve remains flat.

The firm in Figure 9.5 exhibits roughly constant returns to scale between Scale 2 and Scale 3. The average cost of production is about the same in each. If the firm

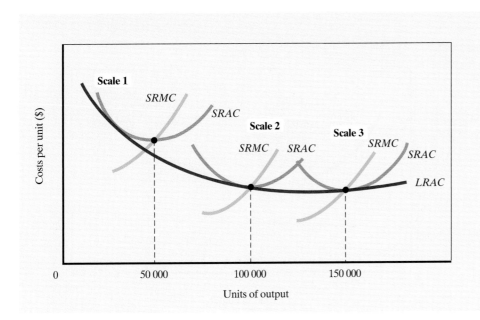

FIGURE 9.5

A Firm Exhibiting Economies of Scale

The long-run average cost curve of a firm shows the different scales on which the firm can choose to operate in the long run. Each scale of operation defines a different short run. Here the firm exhibits economies of scale when moving from Scale 1 to Scale 2 (average cost declines). And the firm exhibits roughly constant returns to scale when moving from Scale 2 to Scale 3 (average cost remains about the same).

exhibited constant returns at higher levels, the *LRAC* would continue as a flat, straight line.

Economists have studied cost data extensively over the years to estimate the extent to which economies of scale exist. Evidence suggests that in most industries firms don't have to be gigantic to realize cost savings from scale economies. For example, automobile production is accomplished in thousands of separate assembly operations, each with its own economies of scale. Perhaps the best example of efficient production on a small scale is the manufacturing sector in Taiwan. Taiwan has enjoyed very rapid growth based on manufacturing firms that employ fewer than 100 workers!

One simple theoretical argument supports the empirical result that most industries seem to exhibit constant returns to scale (a flat *LRAC*) after some level of output. Competition always pushes firms to adopt the least-cost technology and scale. If cost advantages result with larger scale operations, the firms that shift to that scale will drive the smaller, less efficient firms out of business. A firm that wants to grow when it has reached its "optimal" size can do so by building another identical plant. It thus seems logical to conclude that most firms face constant returns to scale *as long as* they can replicate their existing plants. Thus, when you look at developed industries, you can expect to see firms of different sizes operating with similar costs. These firms produce using roughly the same scale of plant, but larger firms simply have more plants.

DECREASING RETURNS TO SCALE

When average cost increases with scale of production, a firm faces *decreasing returns to scale*, or *diseconomies of scale*. The most often cited example of a diseconomy of scale is bureaucratic inefficiency. As size increases beyond a certain point, operations tend to become more difficult to manage. You can easily imagine what happens when a firm grows top-heavy with managers who have accumulated seniority and high salaries. The coordination function is more complex for larger firms than for smaller ones, and the chances that it will break down are greater.

A large firm is also more likely than a small firm to find itself facing problems with organized labour. Unions can demand higher wages and more benefits, go on strike, force firms to incur legal expenses, and take other actions that increase pro-

FIGURE 9.6

A Firm Exhibiting Economies and Diseconomies of Scale

Economies of scale push this firm's costs down to q^*. Beyond q^*, the firm experiences diseconomies of scale. q^* is the level of production at lowest average cost, using optimal scale.

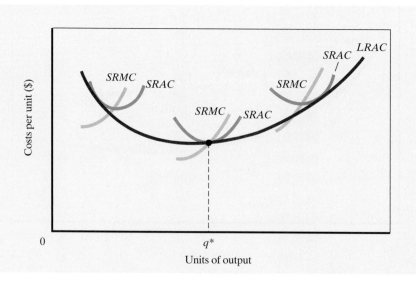

duction costs. (This does not mean that unions are "bad," but rather that their activities often increase costs. A more detailed discussion of unions and labour appears in Chapter 19.)

Figure 9.6 describes a firm that exhibits both economies of scale and diseconomies of scale. Average costs decrease with scale of plant up to q^* and increase with scale after that. This long-run average cost curve looks very much like the short-run average cost curves we have examined in the last two chapters. But do not confuse the two:

> All short-run average cost curves are U-shaped, because we assume a fixed scale of plant that constrains production and drives marginal cost upward as a result of diminishing returns. In the long run, we make no such assumption; rather, we assume that scale of plant can be changed.

The shape of a firm's long-run average cost curve depends on how costs react to changes in scale. Some firms do see economies of scale, and their long-run average cost curves slope downward. Most firms seem to have flat long-run average cost curves. Still others encounter diseconomies, and their long-run average costs slope upward. Thus, the same firm can face diminishing returns—a short-run concept—and still have a long-run cost curve that exhibits economies of scale.

It is important to note that economic efficiency requires taking advantage of economies of scale (if they exist) and avoiding diseconomies of scale. The **optimal scale of plant** is the one that minimizes cost. In fact, as we will see next, competition forces firms to use the optimal scale.

optimal scale of plant *The scale of plant that minimizes cost.*

Long-Run Adjustments to Short-Run Conditions

We began this chapter by discussing the different short-run positions in which firms may find themselves. Firms can be operating at a profit or suffering economic losses; they can be shut down or producing. We say that the industry is not in equilibrium if firms have an incentive to enter or exit in the long run. Thus, when firms are earning economic profits (profits above normal) or are suffering economic losses (profits below normal, or negative), the industry is not at an equilibrium, and firms will change their behaviour. What they are likely to do depends in part on costs in the long run. This is why we spent a good deal of time discussing economies and diseconomies of scale.

We can now put these two ideas together and discuss the actual long-run adjustments that are likely to take place in response to short-run profits and losses.

SHORT-RUN PROFITS: EXPANSION TO EQUILIBRIUM

We begin our analysis of long-run adjustments with a perfectly competitive industry in which firms are earning economic profits. We assume that all firms in the industry are producing with the same technology of production, and that each firm has a long-run average cost curve that is U-shaped. A U-shaped long-run average cost curve implies that there are some economies of scale to be realized in the industry, and that all firms ultimately begin to run into diseconomies at some scale of operation.

Figure 9.7 on the next page shows a representative perfectly competitive firm initially producing at Scale 1. Market price is $P_1 = \$12$, and individual firms are enjoying economic profits. Total revenue at our representative firm, which is producing 1000 units of output per period, exceeds total cost. Our firm's profit per period is equal to the shaded pink rectangle. (Make sure you understand why the

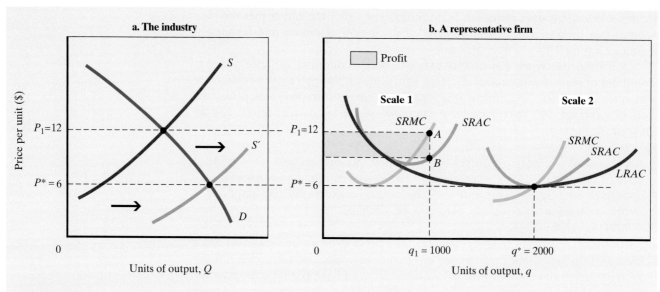

FIGURE 9.7

Firms Expand in the Long Run when Increasing Returns to Scale Are Available

When there are economies of scale to be realized, firms have an incentive to expand. Thus firms will be pushed by competition to produce at their optimal scales. Price will be driven to the minimum point on the *LRAC* curve.

pink rectangle represents profits. Remember that perfectly competitive firms maximize profit by producing at $P = MC$, that is, at point A in Figure 9.7.)

At this point, our representative firm has not realized all the economies of scale available to it. By expanding to Scale 2, it will reduce average costs significantly, and unless price drops it will increase profits. As long as firms are enjoying profits and economies of scale exist, firms will expand. Thus, we assume that the firm in Figure 9.7 shifts to Scale 2.

At the same time, the existence of economic profits will attract new entrants to the industry. Both the entrance of new firms and the expansion of existing firms have the same effect on the short-run industry supply curve (Figure 9.7a). Both cause the short-run supply curve to shift to the right, from S to S'. Remember that the short-run industry supply curve is the sum of all the marginal cost curves (above the minimum point of AVC) of all the firms in the industry. Here, it will shift to the right, for two reasons. First, since all firms in the industry are expanding to a larger scale, their individual short-run marginal cost curves shift to the right. Second, with new firms entering the industry, there are more firms and thus more marginal cost curves to add up.

As capital flows into the industry, the supply curve in Figure 9.7a shifts to the right and price falls. The question is, where will the process stop? In general:

> Firms will continue to expand as long as there are economies of scale to be realized, and new firms will continue to enter as long as economic profits are being earned.

In Figure 9.7a, final equilibrium is achieved only when price falls to $P^* = \$6$ and firms have exhausted all the economies of scale available in the industry. At

$P^* = \$6$, no economic profits are being earned and none can be earned by changing the level of output.

Look carefully at the final equilibrium in Figure 9.7. Each firm will choose the scale of plant that produces its product at minimum long-run average cost. Competition drives firms to adopt not just the most efficient technology in the *short* run, but also the most efficient scale of operation in the *long* run.

> In the long run, equilibrium price (P^*) is equal to long-run average cost, short-run marginal cost, and short-run average cost. Economic profits are driven to zero:
>
> $$P^* = SRMC = SRAC = LRAC,$$
>
> where *SRMC* denotes short-run marginal cost, *SRAC* denotes short-run average cost, and *LRAC* denotes long-run average cost. No other price is an equilibrium. Any price above P^* means that there are profits to be made in the industry, and new firms will continue to enter. Any price below P^* means that firms are suffering economic losses, and firms will exit the industry. Only at P^* will economic profits be just equal to zero, and only at P^* will the industry be in equilibrium.

SHORT-RUN LOSSES: CONTRACTION TO EQUILIBRIUM

Firms that suffer short-run losses have an incentive to leave the industry in the long run, but cannot do so in the short run. As we have seen, some firms incurring losses will choose to shut down and bear losses equal to fixed costs. Others will continue to produce in the short run in an effort to minimize their losses.

Figure 9.8 on page 236 depicts a firm that will continue to produce $q_1 = 1000$ units of output in the short run, despite its losses. (We are assuming here that the firm is earning losses that are smaller than the firm's fixed costs.) With losses, the long-run picture will change. Firms have an incentive to get out of the industry, and as they exit, the short-run supply curve of the industry shifts to the left. As it shifts, the equilibrium price rises, from $8 to $9.

Once again the question is: how long will this adjustment process continue? In general:

> As long as losses are being sustained in an industry, firms will shut down and leave the industry, thus reducing supply—shifting the supply curve to the left. As this happens, price rises. This gradual price rise reduces losses for firms remaining in the industry until those losses are ultimately eliminated.

In Figure 9.8, equilibrium occurs when price rises to $P^* = \$9$. At that point, remaining firms will maximize profits by producing $q^* = 1160$ units of output. Price is just sufficient to cover average costs, and economic profits and losses are zero.

All of this leads us to conclude that:

> Whether we begin with an industry in which firms are earning profits or suffering losses, the final long-run competitive equilibrium condition is the same:
>
> $$P = SRMC = SRAC = LRAC,$$
>
> and economic profits are zero. At this point, individual firms are operating at the most efficient scale of plant—that is, at the minimum point on their *LRAC* curve.

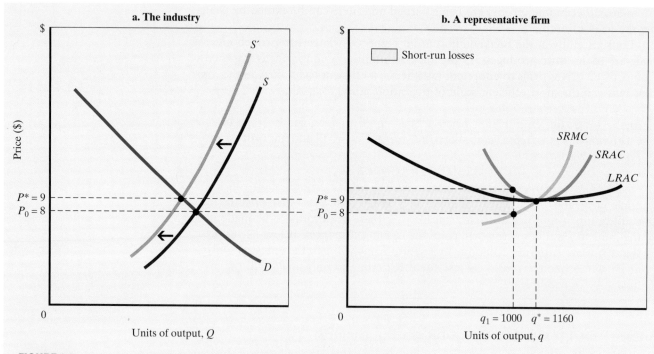

a. The industry

$P^* = 9$
$P_0 = 8$

Units of output, Q

b. A representative firm

Short-run losses

SRMC
SRAC
LRAC

$P^* = 9$
$P_0 = 8$

$q_1 = 1000$ $q^* = 1160$

Units of output, q

FIGURE 9.8

Long-Run Contraction and Exit in an Industry Suffering Short-Run Losses

When firms in an industry suffer losses, there is an incentive for them to exit. As firms exit, the supply curve shifts from S to S', driving price up to P^*. As price rises, losses are gradually eliminated and the industry returns to equilibrium.

THE LONG-RUN ADJUSTMENT MECHANISM: INVESTMENT FLOWS TOWARD PROFIT OPPORTUNITIES

The central idea in our discussion of entry, exit, expansion, and contraction is this:

> In competitive markets, investment capital flows toward profit opportunities. The actual process is complex and varies from industry to industry.

The logic of competitive markets is that as profit opportunities develop they are quickly eliminated. In Chapter 1 we described driving up to a toll booth and suggested that shorter-than-average lines are quickly eliminated as cars shift into them. So, too, are profits in competitive industries eliminated as new competing firms move into open slots, or perceived opportunities, in the industry.

In practice, the entry and exit of firms in response to profit opportunities usually involves the financial capital market. In capital markets, people are constantly looking for profits. When firms in an industry do well, capital is likely to flow into that industry in a variety of forms. Entrepreneurs start new firms, and firms producing entirely different products may join the competition in order to break into new markets. It happens all around us. The tremendous success of premium coffee shops such as The Second Cup and Starbucks spawned dozens of competitors. In one Ontario university town, a coffee bar opened to rave reviews, long lines, and high prices and economic profits. Soon there were three more coffee bars in the neighbourhood, no lines, and lower prices. Magic? No: just the natural functioning of competition.

When there is promise of extraordinary profits, investments are made and output expands. When firms end up suffering losses, firms contract, and some go out of business. It can take quite a while, however, for an industry to achieve **long-run competitive equilibrium,** the point at which $P = SRMC = SRAC = LRAC$ and economic profits are zero. In fact, because costs and tastes are in a constant state of flux, very few industries ever really get there. The economy is always changing. There are always some firms making profits and some firms suffering losses.

long-run competitive equilibrium *When P = SRMC = SRAC = LRAC and economic profits are zero.*

This, then, is a story about tendencies:

> Investment, in the form of new firms and expanding old firms, will, over time, tend to favour those industries in which profits are being made. At the same time, industries in which firms are suffering losses will gradually contract from disinvestment.

Output Markets: A Final Word

In the last four chapters, we have been building a model of a simple market system under the assumption of perfect competition. Let us provide just one more example to review the actual response of a competitive system to a change in consumer preferences.

Over the past decade, Canadians have developed a taste for fine wine. We know that household demand is constrained by income, wealth, and prices, and that income is (at least in part) determined by the choices that households make. Within these constraints, households choose, and increasingly they choose—or demand—wine. The demand curve for wine has shifted to the right, causing excess demand followed by an increase in price.

With higher prices, wine producers find themselves earning economic profits. *This increase in price and consequent rise in profits is the basic signal that leads to a reallocation of society's resources.* In the short run, wine producers are constrained by their current scales of operation. The Niagara Peninsula has only a limited number of vineyards and only a limited amount of vat capacity, for example.

In the long run, however, we would expect to see resources flow in to compete for these economic profits, and this is exactly what happens. New firms enter the wine-producing business. New vines are planted and new vats and production equipment are purchased and put in place. Vineyard owners move into new provinces—British Columbia, Nova Scotia, and Prince Edward Island—and established growers increase production. Overall, more wine is produced to meet the new consumer demand. At the same time, competition is forcing firms to operate using the most efficient technology available.

What starts as a shift in preferences thus ends up as a shift in resources. Land is reallocated and labour moves into wine production. All this is accomplished without any central planning or direction.

You have now seen what lies behind the demand curves and supply curves in competitive output markets. The next two chapters take up competitive *input* markets and complete the picture.

The Canadian firm Bombardier launched an extremely successful product: the Sea Doo. Their success—and, in particular, the attractive profits—encouraged the entry of new producers offering similar products.

The long-run average cost curve has been a source of controversy in economics for many years. A long-run average cost curve was first drawn as the "envelope" of a series of short-run curves in a classic article written by the Canadian economist Jacob Viner in 1931.[1] In preparing that article, Viner gave his draftsman the task of drawing the long-run curve through the minimum points of all the short-run average cost curves.

In a supplementary note written in 1950, Viner commented:

. . . the error in Chart IV is left uncorrected so that future teachers and students may share the pleasure of many of their predecessors of pointing out that if I had known what an envelope was, I would not have given my excellent draftsman the technically impossible and economically inappropriate task of drawing an AC curve which would pass through the lowest cost points of all the AC curves yet not rise above any AC curve at any point. . . .[2]

While this story is an interesting part of the lore of economics, a more recent debate concentrates on the economic content of this controversy. In 1986, Professor Herbert Simon of Carnegie-Mellon University stated bluntly:

I think the textbooks are a scandal . . . the most widely used textbooks use the old long-run and short-run cost curves to illustrate the theory of the firm. . . . [the U-shaped long-run cost curve] postulated that in the long run the size of the firm would increase to a scale associated with the minimum cost on the long-run curve. It was supposed to predict something about the size distribution of firms in the industry. It doesn't do that and there

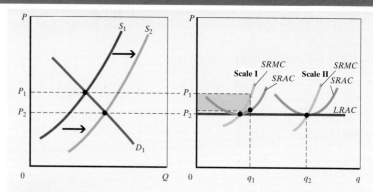

FIGURE 1

Long-Run Expansion in an Industry with Constant Returns to Scale

are other problems. Most serious is the fact that most empirical studies show the firm's cost curves not to be U-shaped, but in fact to slope down to the right and then level off, without a clearly defined minimum point.[3]

Professor Simon makes an important point. Suppose that we were to redraw Figure 9.7b with a flat long-run average cost curve. Figure 1 shows a firm earning short-run economic profits using Scale I, but there are no economies of scale to be realized.

Despite the lack of economies of scale, expansion of such an industry would likely take place in much the same way as we described in the text. First, existing firms have an incentive to expand because they are making profits. At current prices, a firm that doubles its scale would earn twice the economic profits even if cost did not fall with expansion. Of course, as long as economic profits persist, new firms have an incentive to enter the industry. Both of these events will shift the short-run industry supply curve to the right, from S_1 to S_2, and price will fall, from P_1 to P_2. Expansion and entry will stop only when price has fallen to $LRAC$. Only then will economic profits be eliminated. At equilibrium, $P = SRMC = SRAC = LRAC$.

This model does not predict the final firm size or the structure of the industry. When the long-run AC curve is U-shaped, firms stop expanding at the minimum point on $LRAC$ since further expansion means higher costs; thus, optimal firm size is determined technologically. If the $LRAC$ curve is flat, however, small firms and large firms have identical average costs.

If this is true, and it seems to be in many industries, the structure of the industry in the long run will depend on whether existing firms expand faster than new firms enter. If new firms enter quickly in response to profit opportunities, the industry will end up with large numbers of small firms. But if existing firms expand more rapidly than new firms enter, the industry may end up with only a few very large firms. There is thus an element of randomness in the way industries expand. In fact, most industries contain some large firms and some small firms, which is exactly what Simon's flat $LRAC$ model predicts.

Sources: [1]Jacob Viner, "Cost Curves and Supply Curves," *Zeitschrift fur Nationalokonomie* vol. 3 (1–1931): pp. 23–46. [2]George J. Stigler and Kenneth E. Boulding, eds., *AEA Readings in Price Theory* vol. 6 (Chicago: Richard D. Irwin, 1952), p. 227. [3]Interview with Herbert A. Simon, "The Failure of Armchair Economics," *Challenge*, November–December 1986, pp. 23–24.

Summary

1. For any firm, one of three conditions holds at any given moment: (1) the firm is earning economic profits, (2) the firm is suffering losses, or (3) the firm is just breaking even—that is, earning a normal rate of return and zero economic profits.

Short-Run Conditions and Long-Run Directions

2. A firm that is earning economic profits in the short run and expects to continue to do so has an incentive to expand in the long run. Profits also provide an incentive for new firms to enter the industry.

3. In the short run, firms suffering losses are stuck in the industry. They can shut down operations ($q = 0$), but they must still bear fixed costs. In the long run, firms suffering losses can exit the industry.

4. A firm's decision about whether to shut down in the short run depends solely on whether its revenues from operating are sufficient to cover its variable costs. If revenues exceed variable costs, the *operating profits* can be used to pay some fixed costs and thus reduce losses.

5. Any time that price is below the minimum point on the average variable cost curve, total revenue will be less than total variable cost, operating profit will be negative, and the firm will shut down. The minimum point on the average variable cost curve (which is also the point where marginal cost and average variable cost intersect) is called the *shut-down point*. At all prices above the shut-down point, the *MC* curve shows the profit-maximizing level of output. At all prices below it, optimal short-run output is zero.

6. The *short-run supply curve* of a firm in a perfectly competitive industry is the portion of its marginal cost curve that lies above its average variable cost curve.

7. Two things can cause the industry supply curve to shift: (1) in the short run, anything that causes marginal costs to change across the industry, such as an increase in the price of a particular input; and (2) in the long run, entry or exit of firms.

Long-Run Costs: Economies and Diseconomies of Scale

8. When an increase in a firm's scale of production leads to lower average costs, the firm exhibits *increasing returns to scale*, or *economies of scale*. When average costs do not change with the scale of production, the firm exhibits *constant returns to scale*. When an increase in a firm's scale of production leads to higher average costs, the firm exhibits *diseconomies of scale*.

9. A firm's *long-run average cost curve* (*LRAC*) shows the costs associated with different scales on which the firm can choose to operate in the long run.

Long-Run Adjustments to Short-Run Conditions

10. When short-run profits exist in an industry, firms will enter and existing firms will expand. These events cause the industry supply curve to shift to the right. When this happens, price falls and ultimately profits are eliminated.

11. When short-run losses are suffered in an industry, some firms exit and some firms reduce scale. These events cause the industry supply curve to shift to the left, raising price and eliminating losses.

12. *Long-run competitive equilibrium* is reached when $P = SRMC = SRAC = LRAC$ and economic profits are zero.

13. In efficient markets investment capital flows toward profit opportunities.

Review Terms and Concepts

breaking even 220

constant returns to scale 229

decreasing returns to scale or diseconomies of scale 229

increasing returns to scale or economies of scale 229

long-run average cost curve (**LRAC**) 229

long-run competitive equilibrium 237

operating profit (or loss) or net operating revenue 223

optimal scale of plant 233

short-run industry supply curve 226

shut-down point 226

Equation:

Long-run competitive equilibrium:
$P = SRMC = SRAC = LRAC$

1. Explain why it is possible that a firm with a production function that exhibits increasing returns to scale can run into diminishing returns at the same time.

2. Which of the following industries do you think are likely to exhibit large economies of scale? Explain why in each case.
   a. Home building
   b. Electric power generation
   c. Vegetable farming
   d. Software development
   e. Aircraft manufacturing
   f. Higher education
   g. Accounting services

3. For Cases A through F below, would you (1) operate or shut down in the short run, and (2) expand your plant or exit the industry in the long run?

	A	B	C	D	E	F
Total revenue	1500	2000	2000	5000	5000	5000
Total cost	1500	1500	2500	6000	7000	4000
Total fixed cost	500	500	200	1500	1500	1500

4. Assume that you are hired as an analyst at a major Toronto consulting firm. Your first assignment is to do an industry analysis of the tribble industry. After extensive research and two all-nighters, you have obtained the following information.

   Long-Run Costs:
   Capital costs: $5 per unit of output
   Labour costs: $2 per unit of output

   No economies or diseconomies of scale.

   Industry currently earning a normal return to capital (economic profit is zero).

   The industry is perfectly competitive. Each firm produces the same amount of output, and there are 100 firms.

   Total industry output: 1.2 million tribbles

   Demand for tribbles is expected to grow rapidly over the next few years to a level twice as high as it is now, but (due to short-run diminishing returns) each of the 100 existing firms is likely to be producing only 50% more.
   a. Sketch the long-run cost curve of a representative firm.
   b. Show the current conditions by drawing

   two diagrams, one showing the industry and one showing a representative firm.
   c. Sketch the increase in demand and show how the industry is likely to respond in the short run and in the long run.

5. Consider Adam, a baker of apple pies. To make one pie, Adam uses one hour of labour and one kilogram of apples. He bakes the pies in an oven that he leases for $100 per day. A (short-run) contract requires him to pay the lease even if he bakes no pies. The hourly wage that Adam pays is $5, and each kilogram of apples costs $2. Assume that Adam has only one oven available, and that he can bake a maximum of 50 apple pies in one day.
   a. What are Adam's fixed costs (per day)? Variable costs? Total costs? (Express these as a function of q, the number of apple pies.)
   b. Determine and graph average variable cost, average fixed cost, average total cost, and marginal cost.
   c. Suppose that the market for apple pies is perfectly competitive. Adam can therefore sell all the pies he wants in one day for $8 each. How many apple pies should Adam produce per day in the short run? What will his profits or losses be?
   d. At a price of $8, how many pies (per day) should Adam produce in the long run? Explain your answer.
   e. What is the minimum price necessary for Adam to operate in the short run? In the long run?

6. Do you agree or disagree with the following statements? Explain why in a sentence or two.
   a. A firm will never sell its product for less than it costs to produce it.
   b. If the short-run marginal cost curve is U-shaped, the long-run average cost curve is likely to be U-shaped as well.

7. The Smythe chicken farm produces 25 000 chickens per month. Total cost of production at the Smythe farm is $28 000. Down the road are two other farms. The Faubus Farm produces 55 000 chickens a month and total cost is $50 050. Mega Farm produces 100 000 chickens per month at a total cost of $91 000. These data suggest that there are significant economies of scale in chicken production. Do you agree or disagree with this statement? Explain your answer.

External Economies and Diseconomies and the Long-Run Industry Supply Curve

External Economies and Diseconomies

Sometimes average costs increase or decrease with the size of the industry, in addition to responding to changes in the size of the firm itself. When long-run average costs decrease as a result of industry growth, we say that there are **external economies.** When average costs increase as a result of industry growth, we say that there are **external diseconomies.** (Remember the distinction between internal and external economies: *internal* economies of scale are found within firms, while *external* economies occur on an industry-wide basis.)

In the late 1970s and early 1980s the computer hardware and software industries grew phenomenally. In the United States the computer industry was centred in relatively specific geographical locations: the Silicon Valley of California; around Austin, Texas; in Boston, Massachusetts; and in North Carolina. One of the advantages of locating businesses in the same industry in the same geographic area is potential external economies. As the industry grows, local schools train students for jobs in the industry, reducing training expenses for the firms. People in the industry have easy access to and learn from one another.

In Canada, Kanata and the Ottawa-Carleton region of Ontario emerged as the "Silicon Valley North." A mix of large and small hardware and software firms such as Corel, Nortel, Mitel, Digital Equipment, Cognos, SHL Systemhouse (to name just a few) are now located in the region to take advantage of the external

economies. Similarly, an agglomeration of call-centre operations emerged around Moncton, New Brunswick, in the early 1990s. And the growing biotechnology industry seems likely to follow this pattern as well. Currently, over 30% of Canada's core agricultural biotechnology companies are found in Saskatoon.[1]

While these are examples of industries in which external economies are a possibility, the construction industry is one in which external diseconomies seem to exist. Between 1966 and 1969 Canada experienced one of the most dramatic booms in residential construction activity in our history. The number of residential building permits issued grew by 22.0% in 1967, by 19.2% in 1968, and by 6.8% in 1969. As illustrated in Table 9A.1 the increased demand for lumber and other sawmill products increased lumber prices dramatically. Between 1966 and 1969 lumber prices increased by 41.3%, a much larger increase than recorded for consumer goods in general (12.8%).[2]

In the residential construction industry, a change in the scale of any individual firm's operations has no impact on the price of lumber, because no firm has any control over price. The increase in lumber prices in the late 1960s resulted in part from expansion of the *industry*, which led to an external diseconomy.

The Long-Run Industry Supply Curve

Recall that long-run competitive equilibrium is achieved when entering firms responding to profits or exiting firms fleeing from losses drive price to a level that just covers long-run average costs. Economic profits are zero, and $P = LRAC = SRAC = SRMC$. At this point, individual firms are operating at the most efficient scale of plant—that is, at the minimum point on their $LRAC$ curve.

[1]*BICON Consulting Associates,* Opportunities for Biotechnology-Based Business in Atlantic Canada, *A Study Prepared for the Atlantic Agriproducts Competitiveness Council and the Atlantic Canada Opportunities Agency, January 1997, p. 22.*

[2]*The cumulative percentage increase between 1966 and 1969 is not found by simply adding the increases in individual years. Instead one proceeds as follows: (1) $1.00 worth of lumber in 1966 costs $1.126 (i.e., $1 × 1.126) in 1967 since prices rose by 12.6%; (2) in 1968 the same lumber cost $1.3512 (i.e., $1.126 × 1.2) since prices rose by 20%; and (3) in 1969 the lumber would have cost $1.413352 (i.e., $1.35512 × 1.046) since prices rose by 4.6%. The cumulative increase is [($1.413352 − $1)/$1] × 100 or 41.33%.*

Table 9A.1

Construction Activity and the Price of Lumber Products, 1966–1969

	New Housing Permits	Percentage Increase in Housing Permits	Percentage Increase in Lumber Prices	Percentage Increase in Consumer Prices
1966	134 474	—	—	—
1967	164 123	22.0%	12.6%	3.8%
1968	196 878	19.2%	20.0%	4.0%
1969	210 415	6.8%	4.6%	4.5%

Sources: Statistics Canada, *Construction Price Statistics,* Cat. no. 62-007; Statistics Canada, *Prices and Price Indices,* Cat. no. 68-002.

As we saw in the text, long-run equilibrium is not easily achieved. But even if a firm or an industry does achieve long-run equilibrium, it will not remain at that point indefinitely. Economies are dynamic. As population and the stock of capital grow, and as preferences and technology change, some sectors will expand and some will contract. How do industries adjust to long-term changes? The answer depends on both internal and external factors.

The extent of *internal* economies (or diseconomies) determines the shape of a firm's long-run average cost curve (*LRAC*). If a firm changes its scale and either expands or contracts, its average costs will increase, decrease, or stay the same *along* the *LRAC* curve. Recall that the *LRAC* curve shows the relationship between a firm's output (q) and average total cost (*ATC*). A firm enjoying internal economies will see costs decreasing as it expands its scale; a firm facing internal diseconomies will see costs increasing as it expands its scale.

But external economies and diseconomies have nothing to do with the size of *individual* firms in a competitive market. Since individual firms in perfectly competitive industries are very small relative to the market, other firms are affected only minimally when an individual firm changes its output or scale of operation. *External* economies and diseconomies arise from industry expansions; that is, they arise when many firms increase their output simultaneously or when new firms enter an industry. If industry expansion causes costs to increase (external diseconomies), the *LRAC* curves facing individual firms shift upward; costs increase regardless of the level of output finally chosen by the firm. Similarly, if industry expansion causes costs to decrease (external economies), the *LRAC* curves facing individual firms shift downward; costs decrease at all potential levels of output.

An example of an expanding industry facing external economies is illustrated in Figure 9A.1. Initially, the industry and the representative firm are in long-run competitive equilibrium at the price P_1 determined by the intersection of the initial demand curve D_1 and the initial supply curve S_1. P_1 is the long-run equilibrium price; it intersects the initial long-run average cost curve ($LRAC_1$) at its minimum point. At this point, economic profits are zero.

Let us assume that as time passes, demand increases—that is, the demand curve shifts to the right

---

Figure 9A.1

A Decreasing-Cost Industry: External Economies

In a decreasing-cost industry, average cost declines as the industry expands. As demand expands from D_1 to D_2, price rises from P_1 to P_2. As new firms enter and existing firms expand, supply shifts from S_1 to S_2, driving price down. If costs decline as a result of the expansion to $LRAC_2$, the final price will be below P_1 at P_3. The long-run industry supply curve (*LRIS*) slopes downward in a decreasing-cost industry.

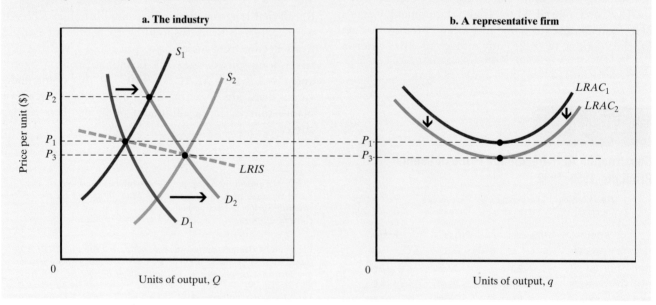

An Increasing-Cost Industry: External Diseconomies

In an increasing-cost industry, average cost increases as the industry expands. As demand shifts from D_1 to D_2, price rises from P_1 to P_2. As new firms enter and existing firms expand output, supply shifts from S_1 to S_2, driving price down. If long-run average costs rise as a result to $LRAC_2$, the final price will be P_3—above P_1. The long-run industry supply curve ($LRIS$) slopes up in an increasing-cost industry.

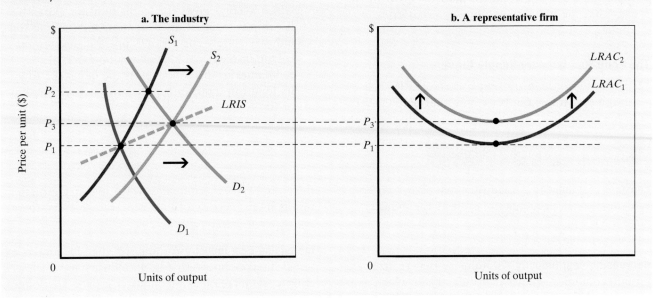

from D_1 to D_2. This increase in demand will push price all the way to P_2. Without drawing the short-run cost curves, we know that economic profits now exist and that firms are likely to enter the industry to compete for them. In the absence of external economies or diseconomies, firms would enter the industry, shifting the supply curve to the right and driving price back to the bottom of the long-run average cost curve, where profits are zero. But the industry in Figure 9A.1 enjoys external economies. As firms enter and the industry expands, costs decrease. And as the supply curve shifts to the right from S_1 toward S_2, the long-run average cost curve shifts downward to $LRAC_2$. Thus, to reach the new long-run equilibrium level of price and output, the supply curve must shift all the way to S_2. Only when the supply curve reaches S_2 is price driven down to the new equilibrium price of P_3, the minimum point on the *new* long-run average cost curve.

Presumably, further expansion would lead to even greater savings because the industry encounters external economies. The dashed light-red line in Figure 9A.1a, which traces out price and total output over time as the industry expands, is called the **long-run industry supply**

curve (**LRIS**). When an industry enjoys external economies, its long-run supply curve slows down. Such an industry is called a **decreasing-cost industry.**

In figure 9A.2, we derive the long-run industry supply curve for an industry that faces external *diseconomies*. (These were suffered in the construction industry, you will recall, when increased house-building activity drove up lumber prices.) As demand expands from D_1 to D_2, price is driven up from P_1 to P_2. In response to the resulting higher profits, firms enter, shifting the short-run supply curve to the right and driving price down. But this time, as the industry expands, the long-run average cost curve shifts up to $LRAC_2$ as a result of external diseconomies. Now, price has to fall back only to P_3 (the minimum point on $LRAC_2$), not all the way to P_1, to eliminate economic profits. This type of industry, whose long-run industry supply curve slopes up to the right, is called an **increasing-cost industry.**

It should not surprise you to know that industries in which there are no external economies or diseconomies of scale have flat, or horizontal, long-run industry supply curves. These industries are called **constant-cost industries.**

Summary

External Economies and Diseconomies

1. When long-run average costs decrease as a result of industry growth, we say that the industry exhibits *external economies*. When long-run average costs increase as a result of industry growth, we say that the industry exhibits *external diseconomies*.

The Long-Run Industry Supply Curve

2. The *long-run industry supply curve* (LRIS) is a graph that traces out price and total output over time as an industry expands. A *decreasing-cost industry* is one in which average costs fall as the industry expands. It exhibits external economies, and its long-run industry supply curve slopes downward. An *increasing-cost industry* is one in which average costs rise as the industry expands. It exhibits external diseconomies, and its long-run industry supply curve slopes upward. A *constant-cost industry* is one that shows no external economies or diseconomies as the industry grows. Its long-run industry supply curve is horizontal, or flat.

Review Terms and Concepts

constant-cost industry An industry that shows no economies or diseconomies of scale as the industry grows. Such industries have flat, or horizontal, long-run supply curves. 243

decreasing-cost industry An industry that realizes external economies—that is, an industry in which average costs decrease as the industry grows. The long-run supply curve for such an industry has a negative slope. 243

external economies and **diseconomies** When industry growth results in a decrease of long-run average costs, there are *external economies*; when industry growth results in an increase of long-run average costs, there are *external diseconomies*. 241

increasing-cost industry An industry that encounters external diseconomies—that is, an industry in which average costs increase as the industry grows. The long-run supply curve for such an industry has a positive slope. 243

long-run industry supply curve (*LRIS*) A graph that traces out price and total output over time as an industry expands. 243

Problem Set

1. In deriving the short-run industry supply curve (the sum of firms' marginal cost curves), we assumed that input prices are constant because competitive firms are price takers. This same assumption holds in the derivation of the long-run industry supply curve. Do you agree or disagree? Explain.

2. Consider an industry that exhibits external diseconomies of scale. Suppose that over the next 10 years, demand for that industry's product increases rapidly. Describe in detail the adjustments likely to follow. Use diagrams in your answer.

3. A representative firm producing cloth is earning a short-run profit at a price of $10 per metre. Draw a supply and demand diagram showing equilibrium at this price. Assuming that the industry is a constant-cost industry, use the diagram to show the long-term adjustment of the industry as demand grows over time. Explain the adjustment mechanism.

Input Demand: The Labour and Land Markets

As we have seen, all business firms must make three fundamental decisions: (1) how much to produce and supply in output markets; (2) how to produce that output, that is, which technology to use; and (3) how much of each input to demand. So far, our discussion of firm behaviour has focused on the first two questions. In Chapters 7–9, we explained how profit-maximizing firms choose among alternative technologies and decide how much to supply in output markets.

We now turn to the behaviour of firms in perfectly competitive input markets (highlighted in Figure 10.1 on the next page), going behind input demand curves in much the same way that we went behind output supply curves in the previous two chapters. When we look behind input demand curves, we discover the exact same set of decisions that we saw when we analyzed output supply curves. In a very real sense, we have already talked about everything covered in this chapter. It is the perspective that is new.

The three main inputs are labour, land, and capital. Transactions in the labour and land markets are fairly straightforward. In the labour market, households sell labour directly to firms in exchange for wages. In the land market, landowners sell or rent land directly to others. The capital market is more complex. To buy a capital asset—a machine, for example—a firm must use funds that it obtains from households. In a sense, then, households supply capital, just as they supply labour. This chapter discusses input markets in general, while the next chapter focuses on the capital market in some detail.

FIGURE 10.1

Firm and Household Decisions

Firms and households interact in both input and output markets. This chapter highlights firm choices in input markets.

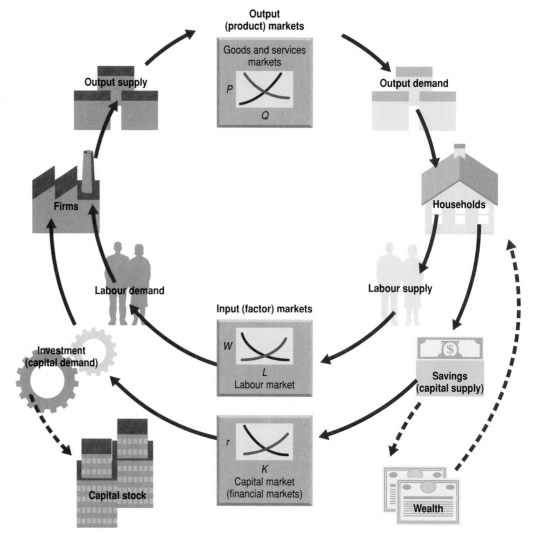

Output
(product) markets

Goods and services markets

Output supply

P

Q

Output demand

Firms

Households

Labour demand

Labour supply

Input (factor) markets

W

L
Labour market

Investment
(capital demand)

Savings
(capital supply)

r

K
Capital market
(financial markets)

Capital stock

Wealth

Input Markets: Basic Concepts

Before we begin our discussion of input markets, it will be helpful to establish some basic concepts: derived demand, complementary and substitutable inputs, diminishing returns, and marginal revenue product.

derived demand *The demand for resources (inputs) that is dependent on the demand for the outputs those resources can be used to produce.*

■ **Demand for Inputs: A Derived Demand**   A firm cannot make a profit unless there is a demand for its product. Households must be willing to pay for the firm's output. The quantity of output that a firm produces in both the long run and the short run thus depends on the value that the market places on the firm's product. This means that demand for inputs depends on the demand for outputs. In other words, input demand is **derived** from output demand.

productivity of an input *The amount of output produced per unit of that input.*

The value attached to a product and the inputs needed to produce that product define the input's productivity. Formally, the **productivity of an input** is the amount of output produced per unit of that input. When a large amount of output is produced per unit of an input, the input is said to be *highly productive*. When only a small amount of output is produced per unit of the input, the input is said to exhibit *low productivity*.

Prices in competitive input markets depend on firms' demand for inputs, households' supply of inputs, and the interaction between the two. In the labour market, for example, households must decide whether to work and how much to work. In Chapter 6 we saw that the opportunity cost of working for a wage is either leisure or the value derived from unpaid labour—working in the garden, for instance, or raising children. In general, firms will demand workers as long as the value of what those workers produce exceeds what they must be paid. Households will supply labour as long as the wage they receive exceeds the value of leisure or the value that they derive from nonpaid work.

■ **Inputs: Complementary and Substitutable** Inputs can be **complementary** or **substitutable**. Two inputs used together may enhance, or complement, each other. For example, a new machine that raises the productivity of labour is useless without someone to run it. But machines can also be substituted for labour, or—less often perhaps—labour can be substituted for machines.

complementary inputs *Factors of production that can be used together to enhance each other.*

substitutable inputs *Factors of production that can be used in place of each other.*

All this means that a firm's input demands are tightly linked to one another. An increase or decrease in wages naturally causes the demand for labour to change, but it may also have an effect on the demand for capital or land. If we are to understand the demand for inputs, therefore, we must understand the connections among labour, capital, and land.

■ **Diminishing Returns** Recall that we defined the short run as that period during which some fixed factor of production limits a firm's capacity to expand. Under these conditions, the firm that decides to increase output will eventually encounter diminishing returns. Stated more formally, a fixed scale of plant means that the marginal product of variable inputs eventually declines.

Recall also that **marginal product of labour (MP_L)** is the additional output that is produced if a firm hires one additional unit of labour. For example, if a firm pays for 400 hours of labour per week—10 workers working 40 hours each—and asks one worker to stay an extra hour, the product of the 401st hour is the marginal product of labour for that firm.

marginal product of labour (MP_L) *The additional output produced by one additional unit of labour.*

In Chapter 7, we talked at some length about declining marginal product at a sandwich shop. The first two columns of Table 10.1 on the next page reproduce some of the production data from that shop. You may remember that the shop has only one grill, at which only two or three people can work comfortably. In this example, the grill is the fixed factor of production in the short run and labour is the variable factor. The first worker can produce 10 sandwiches per hour, and the second can produce 15 (see column 3 of Table 10.1). The second worker can produce more because the first is busy answering the phone and taking care of customers, as well as making sandwiches. After the second worker, however, marginal product declines; the third worker adds only 10 sandwiches per hour, because the grill gets crowded. The fourth worker can squeeze in quickly while the others are serving or wrapping, but adds only five additional sandwiches each hour, and so forth.[1]

In this case, the capacity of the grill ultimately limits output. To see how the firm might make a rational choice about how many workers to hire, we need to know more about the value of the firm's product and the cost of labour.

■ **Marginal Revenue Product** The **marginal revenue product (MRP)** of a variable input is the additional revenue a firm earns by employing one additional unit of that input, *ceteris paribus*. If labour is the variable factor, for example, hiring an

marginal revenue product (MRP) *The additional revenue a firm earns by employing one additional unit of input, ceteris paribus.*

---

[1]*As we said in Chapter 7, we assume that all workers are equally skilled and motivated. The third worker is no less hard working or skilled than the first two. Rather, the grill is getting crowded. Put another way, the capital constraint is binding.*

(1) Total Labour Units (Employees)	(2) Total Product (Sandwiches per Hour)	(3) Marginal Product of Labour (MP$_L$) (Sandwiches per Hour)	(4) Price (P$_X$) (Value Added per Sandwich)*	(5) Marginal Revenue Product (MP$_L$ × P$_X$) (per Hour)
0	0	–	–	–
1	10	10	$0.50	$5.00
2	25	15	0.50	7.50
3	35	10	0.50	5.00
4	40	5	0.50	2.50
5	42	2	0.50	1.00
6	42	0	0.50	0

*The "price" is essentially profit per sandwich; see discussion in text.

additional unit will lead to added output (the *marginal product* of labour). The sale of that added output will yield revenue. *Marginal revenue product* is the revenue that is produced by selling the good or service that is produced by the marginal unit of labour. In a competitive firm, marginal revenue product is the value of a factor's marginal product.

Using labour as our variable factor, we can state this proposition more formally by saying that if MP_L is the marginal product of labour and P_X is the price of output, then the marginal revenue product of labour is:

$$MRP_L = MP_L \times P_X$$

When calculating marginal revenue product, we need to be very precise about what is being produced. A sandwich shop, to be sure, sells sandwiches, but it does not produce the bread, meat, cheese, mustard, and mayo that go into the sandwiches. What the shop is producing is "sandwich cooking and assembly services." The shop is "adding value" to the meat, bread, and other ingredients by preparing and putting it all together in ready-to-eat form. With this in mind, let's assume that each finished sandwich in our shop sells for $0.50 over and above the costs of its ingredients. Thus, the *price of the service* the shop is selling is $0.50 per sandwich, and the only variable cost of providing that service is that of the labour used to put the sandwiches together. Thus, if X is the product of our shop, $P_X = \$0.50$.

Table 10.1, column 5, calculates the marginal revenue product of each worker if the shop charges $0.50 per sandwich over and above the costs of its ingredients. The first worker produces 10 sandwiches per hour which, at $0.50 each, generates revenues of $5 per hour. The addition of a second worker yields $7.50 an hour in revenues. After the second worker, diminishing returns drive MRP_L down. The marginal revenue product of the third worker is $5 per hour; for the fourth worker, only $2.50, and so forth.

Figure 10.2 graphs the data from Table 10.1. Notice that the marginal revenue product curve has the same downward slope as the marginal product curve, but that MRP is measured in dollars, not units of output. The MRP curve shows the dollar value of labour's marginal product.

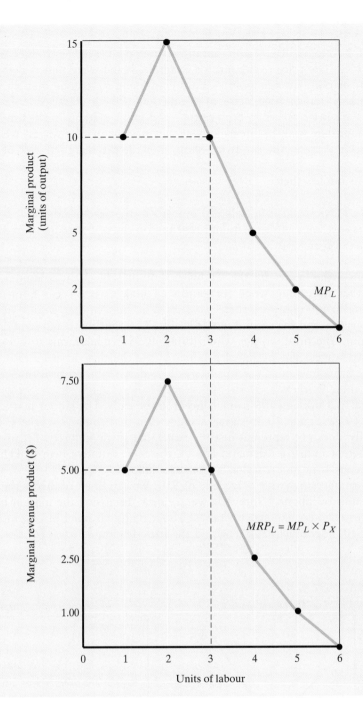

FIGURE 10.2

Deriving a Marginal Revenue Product Curve from Marginal Product

The marginal revenue product of labour is the price of output, P_X, times the marginal product of labour, MP_L. In competition, MRP_L is the market value of labour's marginal product. As long as output price is constant, the MRP_L curve has the same downward slope as the MP_L curve.

Labour and Land Markets

Let's begin our discussion of input markets simply, by discussing a firm that uses only one variable factor of production.

A Firm Using Only One Variable Factor of Production: Labour

Demand for an input depends on that input's marginal revenue product and its unit cost, or price. The price of labour, for example, is the wage that is determined in the labour market. (At this point we are continuing to assume that the sandwich shop uses only one variable factor of production—labour. Remember that competitive firms are price takers in both output and input markets. Such firms can hire all the labour they want to hire as long as they pay the market wage.) We can think of the hourly wage at the sandwich shop, then, as the marginal cost of a unit of labour.

All this implies that:

> A profit-maximizing firm will add inputs—in the case of labour, it will hire workers—as long as the marginal revenue product of that input exceeds its market price.

Look again at the figures for the sandwich shop in Table 10.1, column 5, and then suppose that the going wage for sandwich makers is $4 per hour. A profit-maximizing firm would hire three workers. The first worker would yield $5 per hour in revenue and the second would yield $7.50, but they each would cost only $4 per hour. The third worker would bring in $5 per hour, but still cost only $4 in marginal wages. The marginal product of the fourth worker ($2.50), however, would not bring in enough revenue to pay his salary. Total profit is thus maximized by hiring three workers.

Figure 10.3 presents this same concept graphically. The labour market appears in Figure 10.3a; Figure 10.3b shows a single firm that employs workers. This firm, incidentally, does not represent just the firms in a single industry. Because firms in many different industries demand labour, the representative firm in Figure 10.3b represents any firm in any industry that uses labour.

The firm faces a market wage rate of $10. We can think of this as the marginal cost of a unit of labour. (Note that we are now discussing the margin in units of *labour*; in previous chapters, we talked about marginal units of *output*.) Given a wage of $10, how much labour would the firm demand?

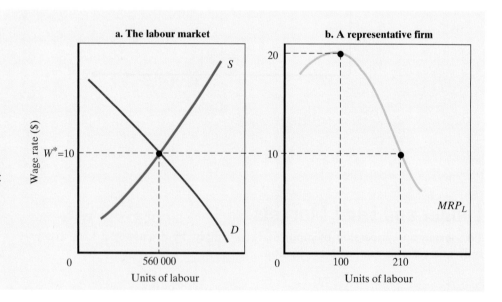

FIGURE 10.3

Marginal Revenue Product and Factor Demand for a Firm Using One Variable Input (Labour)

A competitive firm using only one variable factor of production will use that factor as long as its marginal revenue product exceeds its unit cost. A perfectly competitive firm will hire labour as long as MRP_L is greater than the going wage, W^*. The hypothetical firm will demand 210 units of labour.

One might think that 100 units would be hired, the point at which the difference between marginal revenue product and wage rate is greatest. But the firm is interested in maximizing total profit, not marginal profit. Hiring the 101st unit of labour generates $20 in revenue at a cost of only $10. Because MRP_L is greater than the cost of the input required to produce it, hiring one more unit of labour adds to profit. This will continue to be true as long as MRP_L remains above $10, which is all the way to 210 units. At that point, the wage rate is equal to the marginal revenue product of labour, or

$$W^* = MRP_L = 10.$$

The firm will not demand labour beyond 210 units, because the cost of hiring the 211th unit of labour would be greater than the value of what that unit produces. (Recall that the fourth sandwich maker can produce only an extra $2.50 an hour in sandwiches, while his salary is $4 per hour.)

Thus the curve in Figure 10.3b tells us how much labour a firm that uses only one variable factor of production will hire at each potential market wage rate. If the market wage falls, the quantity of labour demanded will rise; if the market wage rises, the quantity of labour demanded will fall. This description should sound familiar to you—it is, in fact, the description of a demand curve. Therefore we can now say that:

> When a firm uses only one variable factor of production, that factor's marginal revenue product curve is the firm's demand curve for that factor in the short run.

For another example of the relevance of marginal revenue product, see the Application box on page 254 titled "Millionaire Baseball Players and Their Marginal Revenue Product."

■ **Comparing Marginal Revenue Product and Marginal Cost to Maximize Profits** In Chapter 8, we saw that a competitive firm's marginal cost curve is the same as its supply curve. That is, at any output price, the marginal cost curve determines how much output a profit-maximizing firm will produce. We came to this conclusion by comparing the marginal revenue that a firm would earn by producing one more unit of output with the marginal cost of producing that unit of output.

There is no difference between the reasoning in Chapter 8 and the reasoning in this chapter. The only difference is that what is being measured at the margin has changed. In Chapter 8, the firm was comparing the marginal revenues and costs of producing another unit of output. Here, the firm is comparing the marginal revenues and costs of employing another unit of input. To see this similarity, look at Figure 10.4 on the next page. If the only variable factor of production is labour, the condition $W^* = MRP_L$ is the same condition as $P = MC$. The two statements say exactly the same thing.

In both cases, the firm is comparing the cost of production with potential revenues from the sale of product *at the margin*. In Chapter 8, the firm compared the price of output (P, which is equal to MR in perfect competition) directly with cost of production (MC), where cost was derived from information on factor prices and technology. (Review the derivation of cost curves in Chapter 8 if this is unclear.) Here, information on output price and technology is contained in the marginal revenue product curve, which is compared with information on input price to determine the optimal level of input to demand.

The assumption of one variable factor of production makes the trade-off facing firms easy to see. Figure 10.5 shows that in essence firms weigh the value of

FIGURE 10.4

The Two Profit-Maximizing Conditions Are Simply Two Views of the Same Choice Process

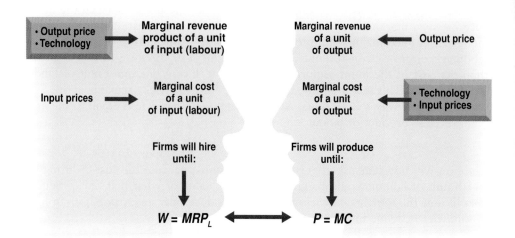

labour as reflected in the market wage against the value of the product of labour as reflected in the price of output:

> Assuming that labour is the only variable input, if society values a good more than it costs firms to hire the workers to produce that good, the good will be produced. In general, the same logic also holds for more than one input. Firms weigh the value of outputs as reflected in output price against the value of inputs as reflected in marginal costs.

■ **Deriving Input Demands** For the small sandwich shop, calculating the marginal product of a variable input (labour) and marginal revenue product was easy. Although it may be more complex, the decision process is essentially the same both for big corporations and for small proprietorships.

When an airline hires more flight attendants, for example, it increases the quality of its service to attract more passengers and thus sell more of its product. Flight attendants must be paid a wage, however. In deciding how many to hire, the airline must figure out how much new revenue the added flight attendants are likely to generate relative to their wages.

At the sandwich shop, diminishing returns set in at a certain point. The same holds true for an airplane. Once a sufficient number of attendants are on a plane, additional attendants add little to the quality of service, and the marginal product of each additional attendant diminishes. Like the grill, the airplane has a fixed physical capacity, and the addition of a variable factor beyond a certain level might even give rise to negative marginal product. Too many attendants could bother the passengers and make it difficult to get to the restrooms.

In making your own decisions, you too compare marginal gains with input costs in the presence of diminishing returns. Suppose you grow vegetables in your yard. You do this for a number of reasons. First, you save money at the grocery store—vegetables are an output with a measurable monetary value. Second, you can plant what you like, and the vegetables taste better fresh from the garden. Third, you simply like to work in the garden—you get sun, exercise, and fresh air.

Like the sandwich shop and the airline, you also face diminishing returns. You have only 70 square metres of garden to work with, and with land as a fixed factor in the short run, your marginal product will certainly decline. You can work all day every day, but your limited space will produce only so many string beans. The first few hours you spend each week watering, fertilizing, and dealing with major

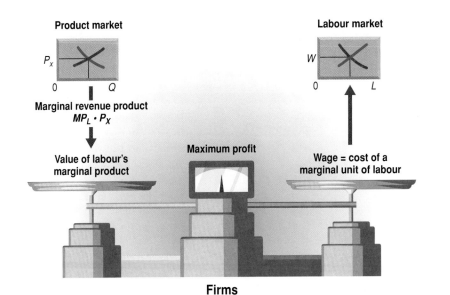

Product market

P_x

0   Q

Marginal revenue product
$MP_L \cdot P_X$

Value of labour's
marginal product

Maximum profit

Labour market

W

0   L

Wage = cost of a
marginal unit of labour

Firms

FIGURE 10.5

The Trade-Off Facing Firms

Firms weigh the cost of labour as reflected in wage rates against the value of labour's marginal product. Assuming labour is the only variable factor of production, if society values a good more than it costs firms to hire the workers to produce that good, the good will be produced.

weed and bug infestations probably have a high marginal product. But after five or six hours, there is little else you can do to increase yield. Diminishing returns also apply to your sense of satisfaction. The farmers' markets are now full of cheap fresh produce that tastes nearly as good as yours. And once you have been out in the garden for a few hours, the hot sun and hard work start to lose their charm and the earth under your fingernails gives way to the less gritty pleasure of watching a baseball game on TV.

Although your gardening does not involve a salary (unlike the sandwich shop and the airline, which pay out wages), the labour you supply has a value that must be weighed, even if the cost of a unit of your labour is only the value you could derive by using that time doing something else, such as watching TV. When the returns from gardening diminish beyond a certain point, you must weigh the value of additional gardening time against leisure and the other options available to you.

It is as true for the sandwich shop as for you that less labour is likely to be employed as the cost of labour rises. If the comparative labour market pushed the daily wage to $6 per hour, the sandwich shop would hire only two workers instead of three (see Table 10.1). If you suddenly became very busy at school, your time would become more valuable and you would probably devote fewer hours to gardening.

A FIRM EMPLOYING TWO VARIABLE FACTORS OF PRODUCTION

When a firm employs more than one factor of production, the analysis of input demand becomes more complicated, but the principles stay the same. We shall now consider a firm that employs variable capital (K) and labour (L) inputs, and thus faces factor prices P_K and P_L.[2] (Recall that *capital* refers to plant, equipment, and inventory used in production. We assume that some portion of the firm's capital stock is fixed in the short run, but that some of it is variable—for example, some machinery and equipment can be installed quickly.) Our analysis can be applied to any two factors of production and can easily be generalized to three or more. It can also be applied to the long run, when all factors of production are variable.

---

[2]*The price of labour, P_L, is the same as the wage rate, W. We will often use the term P_L instead of W to stress the symmetry between labour and capital.*

Consider the following article, which appeared in *The New York Times* on January 8, 1993:

Barry Bonds and his agent, Dennis Gilbert, might not like it, but Cecil Fielder [then of the Detroit Tigers] became, in reality if not in pure numbers, the highest-paid player in baseball yesterday.

Fielder and his agent, Jim Bronner, reached agreement with the Detroit Tigers on a five-year contract worth $36 million. The package includes an eye-popping $10 million signing bonus, the largest ever given a baseball player. Just a month ago, the Kansas City Royals gave David Cone, a free agent pitcher, a $9 million signing bonus.

Fielder, a burly 29-year-old first baseman who earned $4.5 million in 1992, could have been a free agent after next season. He will receive salaries of $2.2 million in each of the first two years and $7.2 million in each of the next three.[1]

While the baseball strike of 1994–1995 stopped contract talks short, the question remains: how in the world could anyone be worth $7.2 million per year? Why would owners be willing to pay millions of dollars a year to a single player? As we've seen in this chapter, profit-maximizing employers will hire work-

Before the 1994–1995 strike, Cecil Fielder, then of the Detroit Tigers, became the highest-paid player in baseball history at a salary of $30 million for a five-year contract. Could it be that Fielder's marginal revenue product is greater than $6 million per year?

ers only as long as their marginal revenue product (MRP_L) is greater than or equal to their wage. Could it then be possible that Cecil Fielder is "worth it"?

Gerald W. Scully, Professor of Management at the University of Texas at Dallas, has made a statistical estimate of the contribution that

ballplayers made to the revenues of their teams during the 1980s. The results may surprise you:

[In 1984]. . . an extra victory was worth $195,653. Now consider the effect on revenues of adding a hitter like Andre Dawson, the National League MVP of 1987, or a pitcher like Roger Clemens, the Cy Young Award winner in the American League in 1986. Dawson had a slugging average of .568 over 621 at bats. Chicago had a team slugging average of .432 over 5,583 at bats. Dawson contributed 11.1 percent of the at-bats and 0.63 of the team's slugging average. Given the relationship between slugging average and wins, those 63 points were conservatively worth 11 games. The marginal revenue [product] of those 11 games was about $2.2 million. Roger Clemens posted a 24–4 record in Boston in 1986. Assuming that Clemens was the source of the margin of victory in those net 20 games, his performance was worth $3.9 million [in 1986]. . . By such economic standards such players are not overpaid.[2]

Sources: [1]Murray Chass, "Fielder Cracks Tigers' Vault," *The New York Times*, January 8, 1993, p. B7. [2]Gerald W. Scully, *The Business of Major League Baseball* (Chicago: University of Chicago Press, 1989), pp. 155–156.

You have seen that inputs can be complementary or substitutable. Land, labour, and capital are used *together* to produce outputs. The worker who uses a shovel digs a bigger hole than one with no shovel; add a steam shovel and that worker becomes even more productive. When an expanding firm adds to its stock of capital, it raises the productivity of its labour, and vice versa. Thus, each factor

Table 10.2

Table 10.2 **Response of a Firm to an Increasing Wage Rate**

Technology	Input Requirements per Unit of Output		Unit Cost If $P_L = \$1$ $P_K = \$1$ $(P_L \times L) + (P_K \times K)$	Unit Cost If $P_L = \$2$ $P_K = \$1$ $(P_L \times L) + (P_K \times K)$
	K	L		
A (capital intensive)	10	5	$15	$20
B (labour intensive)	3	10	$13	$23

complements the other. At the same time though, land, labour, and capital can also be substituted for one another. If labour becomes expensive, some labour-saving technology (robotics, for example) may take its place.

In firms employing just one variable factor of production, a change in the price of that factor affects only the demand for the factor itself. When more than one factor can vary, however, we must consider the impact of a change in one factor price on the demand for other factors as well.

■ **Substitution and Output Effects of a Change in Factor Price**   Table 10.2 presents data on a hypothetical firm that employs variable capital and labour. Suppose that the firm faces a choice between two available technologies of production—technique A, which is capital intensive, and technique B, which is labour intensive. When the market price of labour is $1 per unit and the market price of capital is $1 per unit, the labour-intensive method of producing output is less costly. Each unit costs only $13 to produce using technique B, while the unit cost of producing using technique A is $15. If the price of labour rises to $2, however, technique B is no longer less costly. Labour has become more expensive relative to capital. The unit cost rises to $23 for labour-intensive technique B, but to only $20 for capital-intensive technique A.

Table 10.3 on the next page shows the impact of such an increase in the price of labour on both capital and labour demand when a firm produces 100 units of output. When each input factor costs $1 per unit, the firm chooses technique B and demands 300 units of capital and 1000 units of labour. Total variable cost is $1300. An increase in the price of labour to $2 causes the firm to switch from technique B to technique A. In doing so, it substitutes capital for labour. The amount of labour demanded drops from 1000 to 500 units; the amount of capital demanded increases from 300 to 1000 units, while total variable cost increases to $2000.

The tendency of firms to substitute away from a factor whose relative price has risen and toward a factor whose relative price has fallen is called the **factor substitution effect.** The factor substitution effect is part of the reason that *input demand curves slope downward.* When an input, or factor of production, becomes less expensive, firms tend to substitute it for other factors and thus buy *more* of it. When a particular input becomes more expensive, firms tend to substitute other factors and buy *less* of it. When energy prices in Canada rose in the 1970s, for example, people took an interest in conservation. For some consumers, this meant the purchase of new insulation for their homes and smaller cars. Firms, as well as private citizens, tried to substitute capital for energy wherever they could.

The firm described in Tables 10.2 and 10.3 continued to produce 100 units of output after the wage rate doubled. An *increase* in the price of a production factor, however, also means an increase in the costs of production. Notice that total

factor substitution effect *The tendency of firms to substitute away from a factor whose price has risen and toward a factor whose price has fallen.*

Table 10.3	The Substitution Effect of an Increase in Wages on a Firm Producing 100 Units of Output			

	To Produce 100 Units of Output:		
	Total Capital Demanded	Total Labour Demanded	Total Variable Cost
When P_L = $1, P_K = $1, firm uses technology B.	300	1000	$1300
When P_L = $2, P_K = $1, firm uses technology A.	1000	500	$2000

variable cost increased from $1300 to $2000. When a firm faces higher costs, it is likely to produce less in the short run. When a firm decides to cut output, its demand for all factors declines—including, of course, the factor whose price increased in the first place. This is called the **output effect of a factor price increase.**[3]

A *decrease* in the price of a factor of production, in contrast, means lower costs of production. If their output price remains unchanged, firms will increase output. This, in turn, means the demand for all factors of production will increase. This is the **output effect of a factor price decrease.**

The output effect helps explain why input demand curves slope downward. Output effects and factor substitution effects work in the same direction. Consider, for example, a decline in the wage rate. Lower wages mean that a firm will substitute labour for capital and other inputs. Stated somewhat differently, the factor substitution effect leads to an increase in demand for labour. Lower wages mean lower costs, and lower costs lead to more output. This increase in output means that the firm will hire more of all factors of production, including labour itself. This is the output effect of a factor price decrease. Notice that both effects lead to an increase in the demand for labour when the wage rate falls.

■ Deriving an Input Demand Curve when Two Factors of Production Are Variable

Deriving a firm's input demand curve is more complicated when two factors of production are variable than it is when just one factor varies. Let's return to our example of the sandwich shop once again. Table 10.1 listed the shop's marginal product and marginal revenue product schedules, assuming a fixed grill capacity. If the market wage for sandwich makers were $4 per hour, the shop would hire three workers, each of whom would generate more than $4 per hour in revenues. Only if the market wage rate fell below $2.50 per hour and labour were the only variable factor of production would the firm increase the amount of labour demanded from three to four units. (The marginal revenue product of the fourth worker, $2.50 per hour, would then exceed the new market wage.)

But now let's assume that grill capacity is also variable in the short run.[4] Suppose that a decline in wages reduces cost enough to warrant an expansion. The purchase of a second grill will raise the productivity of labour and shift the marginal revenue product curve out to the right. Earlier, when we discussed marginal revenue product as the additional revenue earned by hiring one additional unit of labour at the margin, *ceteris paribus*, we assumed that all other inputs (specifically,

---

[3]*It is certainly possible that a cut in output involving a major switch in the optimal technique of production will increase the demand for some input factor. When this happens, the factor in demand is called an inferior factor. For purposes of our discussion, however, we will assume that increases in output increase the demand for all factors, and that decreases in production decrease the demand for all factors.*
[4]*We continue to assume that we are in the short run and that the capacity of the shop is fixed. But within that fixed capacity, the firm must choose whether to install a new grill or not.*

(1) Total Labour Units	(2) Total Product (Sandwiches per Hour)	(3) Marginal Product of Labour (MP_L) (Sandwiches per Hour)	(4) Price (P_X) (Value Added per Sandwich)	(5) Marginal Revenue Product ($MP_L \times PX$) (per Hour)
0	0	–	—	–
1	10	10	$0.50	$5.00
2	25	15	0.50	7.50
3	40	15	0.50	7.50
4	55	15	0.50	7.50
5	65	10	0.50	5.00
6	75	10	0.50	5.00
7	80	5	0.50	2.50
8	85	5	0.50	2.50
9	87	2	0.50	1.00
10	89	2	0.50	1.00
11	89	0	0.50	0

the grill capacity at the sandwich shop) remained constant. If we now change grill capacity, we get a new MRP_L schedule.

Consider the productivity of labour with two grills. Table 10.4 shows the marginal product and marginal revenue product of labour at a sandwich shop that has two grills. We know that two workers can fit comfortably at each grill. As column 3 shows, the first worker can produce 10 sandwiches per hour and the next three workers can each produce 15. When there was only one grill, the marginal product of the fifth worker was just two sandwiches (see Table 10.1), but when there is a second grill her productivity increases to 10 sandwiches. She is now the third worker on one of the grills (that is, the fifth or sixth worker hired).

Marginal revenue product also increases with the addition of a second grill. As column 5 of Table 10.4 shows, the MRP_L of the second, third, and fourth worker is now $7.50 per hour each. The fifth adds revenues of $5 per hour instead of just $1, and so on down the line. Figure 10.6 on the next page shows how the addition of new capital shifts the marginal revenue product curve of labour to the right. With the new grill in place, a wage rate of $4 per hour means that the shop can hire six workers instead of just three. The marginal revenue product of the sixth worker is $5 per hour, still above that worker's price of $4 per hour. The shop will draw the line at the seventh worker, whose MRP_L is only $2.50.

Figure 10.7 on page 259 shows the typical response of a firm to a decline in the market wage. At the outset, the market is in equilibrium, with supply and demand equal at wage rate W_0 and the firm operating with a capital stock K_1. At the initial wage, the firm will hire as long as the marginal revenue product of labour exceeds the wage rate. The profit-maximizing level of labour demand is l_0 (the point at which $W_0 = MRP_L$).

Given these conditions, let us now assume that a sudden influx of "guest workers" from a neighbouring region increases the supply of labour from S_0 to S_1 and drives down the wage rate in the labour market. The new lower wage, W_1, reduces the firm's costs. In response, the firm increases output and decides to purchase more variable capital. Just as the new grill did for the sandwich shop, the new capital increases the productivity of labour and shifts the marginal revenue product curve out to the right.

The new marginal revenue product curve is labelled MRP_L (at K_2) in

FIGURE 10.6

Effect of Increase in Capital on Labour Productivity in Sandwich Production

Expanding capacity by purchasing additional capital (a grill) increases the productivity of labour. The fifth worker added only $1 per hour to revenues with one grill. With two grills, the fifth worker brings in $5 per hour in revenue.

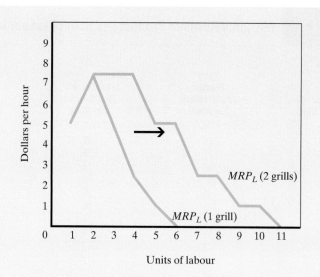

Units of labour

Figure 10.7b. With the new capital in place, the firm now hires labour up to l_1. At that point, the new wage is equal to the new MRP_L. At a wage of W_0, the quantity of labour demanded is l_0; at a wage of W_1, the quantity of labour demanded is l_1. Continuing with this logic, we can conclude that:

> The demand-for-labour curve (D_L) is the line connecting all points such as A and B in Figure 10.7b. A competitive profit-maximizing firm will hire labour until $W = MRP_L$.

This discussion is meant to illuminate two important points:

> First, demand for any factor of production in a competitive industry depends on its productivity and on how its product is valued in the marketplace. Second, the productivity of any factor depends critically on the amount of other factors employed with it. The productivity of labour, for example, is enhanced when additional capital is used in the production process.

LAND MARKETS AND PURE RENT

Unlike labour and capital, land has a special feature that we have not yet considered: it is in strictly fixed (perfectly inelastic) supply in total. The only real questions about land thus centre around how much it is worth and to what use it will be put.

Because land is fixed in supply, we say that its price is **demand determined.** In other words, the price of land is determined exclusively by what households and firms are willing to pay for it. The return to any factor of production in fixed supply is called a **pure rent.**

Thinking of the price of land as demand determined can be confusing because all land is not the same. Some land is clearly more valuable than other land. The value of a plot of land in an attractive part of Winnipeg near the Assiniboine River is worth much more than the same size plot bordering the railyards. The price of a hectare of prime Toronto real estate is likely to be several hundred times that of a hectare of land north of Thunder Bay on the Canadian Shield.

demand determined price *The price of a good that is in fixed supply; it is determined exclusively by what firms and households are willing to pay for the good.*

pure rent *The return to any factor of production that is in fixed supply.*

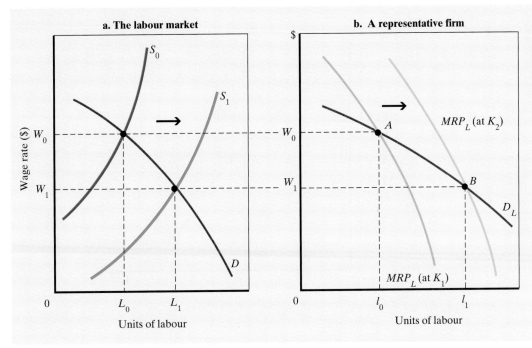

a. The labour market

S_0

Wage rate ($)

W_0

W_1

S_1

D

0

L_0 L_1

Units of labour

b. A representative firm

$

W_0

A

W_1

B

MRP_L (at K_2)

D_L

MRP_L (at K_1)

0

l_0 l_1

Units of labour

What lies behind these differences in land values? As with any other factor of production, land will presumably be sold or rented to the user who is willing to pay the most for it. The value of land to a potential user may depend upon the characteristics of the land itself or upon its location. For example, more fertile land should produce more farm products per hectare and thus command a higher price than less fertile land. A piece of property located at the intersection of two highways may be of great value as a site for a gas station because of the amount of traffic that passes the intersection daily.

A numerical example may help to clarify our discussion. Consider the potential uses of a corner lot in a suburb of Regina. Alan wants to build a clothing store on the lot. He anticipates that he can earn economic profits of $10 000 per year there because of the land's excellent location. Bella, another person interested in buying the corner lot, believes that she can earn $35 000 per year in economic profit if she builds a drugstore there. Clearly, Bella will be able to outbid Alan, and the landowner will sell (or rent) to the highest bidder.

Because location is often the key to profits, landowners are frequently able to "squeeze" their renters. One of the most popular locations in the Halifax area, for example, is Spring Garden Road. There are dozens of restaurants in and around the area and most of them are full most of the time. Despite this seeming success, most of the restaurant owners are not getting rich. Why? Because they must pay very high rents on the location of their restaurants. A substantial portion of each restaurant's revenues goes to rent the land that (by virtue of its scarcity) is the key to unlocking those same revenues.

Although Figure 10.8 shows that the supply of land is perfectly inelastic (a vertical line), the supply of land in a *given use* may not be perfectly inelastic or fixed. Think, for example, about farmland and land available for housing developments. As a city's population grows, housing developers find themselves willing to pay more and more for land. As land becomes more valuable for development, some farmers sell out, and the supply of land available for development increases. This

FIGURE 10.8

The Rent on Land is Demand Determined

Because the land in general (and each parcel in particular) is in fixed supply, its price is demand determined.

Graphically, a fixed supply is represented by a vertical, perfectly inelastic supply curve. Rent, R_0, depends exclusively on demand—what people are willing to pay.

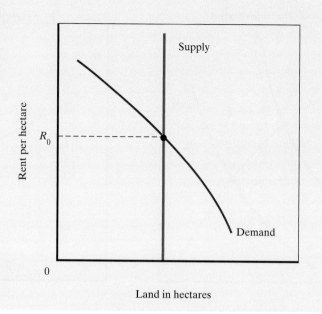

analysis would lead us to draw an upward-sloping supply curve (not a perfectly inelastic supply curve) for land in the land-for-development category.

Nonetheless, our major point—that land earns a pure rent—is still valid:

> The supply of land of a *given quality* at a *given location* is truly fixed in supply; its value is determined exclusively by the amount that the highest bidder is willing to pay for it. Since land cannot be reproduced, supply is perfectly inelastic.

■ **Rent and the Value of Output Produced on Land** Because the price of land is demand determined, rent depends on what the potential users of the land are willing to pay for it. As we've seen, land will end up being used by whoever is willing to pay the most for it. But what determines willingness to pay? Let us now connect our discussion of land markets with our earlier discussions of factor markets in general.

As our example of two potential users bidding for a plot of land shows, the bids depend on the land's potential for profit. Alan's plan would generate $10 000 a year; Bella's would generate $35 000 a year. But these profits do not just materialize. Rather, they come from producing and selling an output that is valuable to households. Land in a popular downtown location is expensive because of what can be produced on it. Note that land is needed as an input into the production of nearly all goods and services. A restaurant located next to a popular theatre can charge a premium price because it has a relatively captive clientele. Clearly, the restaurant must produce a quality product to stay in business, but the location alone provides a substantial profit opportunity.

It should come as no surprise to you that the demand for land follows the same rules as the demand for inputs in general. Recall that a profit-maximizing firm will employ an additional factor of production as long as its marginal revenue product exceeds its market price. For example, a profit-maximizing firm will hire labour as long as the revenue earned from selling labour's product is sufficient to cover the cost of hiring additional labour—which for perfectly competitive firms equals the wage rate. The same thing is true for land:

> A firm will pay for and use land as long as the revenue earned from selling the product produced on the land is sufficient to cover the price of the land. Stated in equation form, this means that the firm will use land up to the point at which $MRP_H = P_H$, where H is land (hectares).

Just as the demand curve for labour reflects the value of labour's product as determined in output markets, so does the demand for land depend on the value of land's product in output markets. The profitability of the restaurant located next to the theatre results from the fact that the meals produced there command a price in the marketplace.

The allocation of a given plot of land among competing uses thus depends on the trade-off between competing products that can be produced on that plot of land. Agricultural land becomes developed when its value in producing housing or manufactured goods or providing space for a shopping mall exceeds its value in producing crops. A corner lot in Regina becomes the site of a drugstore rather than a clothing store because the people in that neighbourhood have a greater need for a drugstore.

One final word about land. Because land cannot be moved physically, the value of any one parcel depends to a large extent upon the uses to which adjoining parcels are put. A factory belching acrid smoke will probably reduce the value of adjoining land, while a new highway that increases accessibility may enhance it.

THE FIRM'S PROFIT-MAXIMIZATION CONDITION IN INPUT MARKETS

Thus far we have discussed the labour and land markets in some detail. Although we will put off a detailed discussion of capital until the next chapter, it is now possible to generalize about competitive demand for factors of production. As we've seen, every firm has an incentive to use variable inputs as long as the revenue generated by those inputs covers the costs of those inputs at the margin. More formally, firms will employ each input up to the point that its price equals its marginal revenue product. This condition holds for all factors at all levels of output:

> Profit-Maximizing Condition for the Perfectly Competitive Firm:
>
> $$P_L = MRP_L = (MP_L \times P_X)$$
> $$P_K = MRP_K = (MP_K \times P_X)$$
> $$P_H = MRP_H = (MP_H \times P_X)$$
>
> where L is labour, K is capital, H is land (hectares), X is output, and P_X is the price of that output.

When all these conditions are met, the firm will be using the optimal, or least costly, combination of inputs. If all these conditions hold at the same time, it is possible to rewrite them in another way:

$$\frac{MP_L}{P_L} = \frac{MP_K}{P_K} = \frac{MP_H}{P_H}$$

Your intuition tells you much the same thing that these equations do: the marginal product of the last dollar spent on labour must be equal to the marginal product of the last dollar spent on capital, which must be equal to the marginal product of the last dollar spent on land, and so forth. If this were not the case, the firm could produce more with less and reduce cost. Suppose, for example, that $MP_L/P_L > MP_K/P_K$. In this situation, the firm can produce more output by shifting dollars out of capital and into labour.

Hiring more labour drives down the marginal product of labour, and using less capital increases the marginal product of capital. This means that the ratios come back to equality as the firm shifts out of capital and into labour.

So far we have used very general terms to discuss the nature of input demand by firms in competitive markets, where input prices and output prices are taken as given. The most important point here is that demand for a factor depends on the value that the market places on its marginal product.[5] The rest of this chapter explores the forces that determine the shapes and positions of input demand curves.

Input Demand Curves

When we discussed supply and demand in Chapter 5, we spent a good deal of time talking about the factors that influence the responsiveness, or elasticity, of output demand curves. We have not talked about *input* demand curves in any detail, however, and we now need to say more about what lies behind them.

SHIFTS IN FACTOR DEMAND CURVES

Factor (input) demand curves are derived from information on technology (that is, production functions) and output price (see Figure 10.4). A change in the demand for outputs, a change in the demand for complementary and substitutable inputs, changes in the prices of other inputs, and technological change all can cause factor demand curves to shift. These shifts in demand are important because they directly affect the allocation of resources among alternative uses, as well as the level and distribution of income.

■ **The Demand for Outputs**   By now you know that a firm will demand an input as long as its marginal revenue product exceeds its market price. Marginal revenue product, which in perfect competition is equal to a factor's marginal product times the price of output, is the value of the factor's marginal product:

$$MRP_L = MP_L \times P_X.$$

The amount that a firm is willing to pay for a factor of production, then, depends directly on the value of the things that the firm produces. It follows that:

> If product demand increases, product price will rise and marginal revenue product (factor demand) will increase—the *MRP* curve will shift to the right. If product demand declines, product price will fall and marginal revenue product (factor demand) will decrease—the *MRP* curve will shift to the left.

Go back and raise the price of sandwiches from $0.50 to $1 in the sandwich shop example examined in Table 10.1 or Table 10.4 to see that this is so.

To the extent that any input is used intensively in the production of some product, changes in the demand for that product cause factor demand curves to shift and the prices of those inputs to change. Land prices are a good example. Forty years ago land along the coastline of Atlantic Canada was used for agriculture, small woodlots, or not at all. The price of this coastal land was low because it had

---

[5]*If you worked through the appendix in Chapter 7, you saw this same condition derived graphically from an isocost/isoquant diagram. Note:* $MP_L/P_L = MP_K/P_K \rightarrow MP_L/MP_K = P_L/P_K.$

a low marginal revenue product—largely due to the low prices of the products produced on this land.

Wood and agricultural products are only two of the products that can be produced on coastal land. As Canadians became more affluent, increasing numbers of us became interested in using coastal land in another way: as a place to spend our vacations. Entrepreneurs responded by establishing campgrounds, rental cabins, and cottage developments. This, in turn, bid up the price of land in locations that offered vacationers the types of amenities they desired (beautiful scenery, opportunities for recreational activities, seclusion, etc.). The rise in land prices, in this case, simply reflects the high value (price) people are willing to pay for vacation land and thus the higher marginal revenue product of that land.

■ **The Demand for Complementary and Substitutable Inputs** In our discussion thus far, we have kept coming back to the fact that factors of production complement each other. The productivity of, and thus the demand for, any one factor of production depends upon the quality and quantity of the other factors with which it works. This was certainly the case at the sandwich shop, where the simple addition of the second grill raised the productivity of labour and increased the shop's demand for labour.

The effect of capital accumulation on wages is one of the most important themes in all of economics. In general:

> The production and use of capital enhances the productivity of labour, and normally increases the demand for labour and drives up wages.

Take as an example transportation. In a poor country like Bangladesh, one person with an ox cart can move a small load over bad roads very slowly. By contrast, the stock of capital used by workers in the transportation industry in Canada is enormous. A truck driver in Canada works with a substantial amount of capital. The typical 18-wheel tractor trailer, for example, is a piece of capital worth over $130 000. The roads themselves are capital that was put in place by the government. The amount of material that a single driver can now move between distant points in a short time is staggering relative to what it was just 25 years ago. This increase in productivity has resulted directly from the addition of new capital to the industry and is reflected in the wages and incomes of truck drivers.

The infusion of capital into an industry raises the productivity of other inputs in that industry. However, it may also sometimes serve as a substitute for labour and thus cause the demand for labour to fall. Nowhere has this been more evident than in agriculture, where the shift to modern capital-intensive methods of production has greatly enhanced the productivity of land but has substantially reduced the demand for labour.

■ **The Prices of Other Inputs** When a firm has a choice among alternative technologies, the choice it makes will depend to some extent on relative input prices. You saw in Tables 10.2 and 10.3 that an increase in the price of labour substantially increased the demand for capital as the firm switched to a more capital-intensive production technique.

During the 1970s, the large increase in energy prices relative to prices of other factors of production had a number of effects on the demand for those other inputs. Insulation of new buildings, installation of more efficient heating plants, and similar efforts substantially raised the demand for capital as capital was substituted for energy in production. But it has also been argued that the energy crisis led to an increase in demand for labour. If capital and energy are complementary inputs—that is, if technologies that are capital intensive are also energy intensive—the argument goes, the higher energy prices tended to push firms away from capital-intensive techniques and toward more labour-intensive techniques.[6] A new highly automated technique, for example, might need fewer workers, but it would also require a vast amount of electricity to operate. High electricity prices could lead a firm to reject the new techniques and stick with an old, more labour-intensive method of production.

■ **Technological Change** Closely related to the impact of capital accumulation on factor demand is the potential impact of **technological change**—that is, the introduction of new methods of production or new products. A new technique of production is nearly always developed to reduce production costs. New technologies usually introduce ways to produce outputs with fewer inputs by increasing the productivity of existing inputs or by raising marginal products. Because marginal revenue product reflects productivity, increases in productivity directly shift input demand curves. If the marginal product of labour rises, for example, the demand for labour shifts to the right (increases).

technological change *The introduction of new methods of production or new products intended to increase the productivity of existing inputs or to raise marginal products.*

Think for a moment about the dramatic impact of modern technology on the production of automobiles. Early in this century, the invention of assembly lines gave new meaning to the concept of mass production and raised the productivity of labour substantially. Today the word in automotive technology is robotics. Many of the tasks once performed along assembly lines by human workers are now handled by highly automated robots. These robots are clear substitutes for labour, but they also increase the productivity of those human beings remaining on the job. Robots are being introduced in industry at a rapid pace. See the Global Perspective box in Chapter 7 titled "Production Technologies: Robots in Canada, Skyscrapers in India," on page 184.

The 1980s and 1990s were the decades of the computer; many experts are predicting that the first decade of the twenty-first century will be the decade of virtual reality (VR). VR lets users interact with computer-generated worlds through sight, sound, and touch. The applications are almost limitless; here, an architect uses a VR program to design the interior of a building.

New products born of technological advance also influence factor demands. The computer age has made many skills obsolete, but it has created a demand for many more. In 1965, people who could repair expensive mechanical calculators were in demand. But as the price of calculators declined drastically, the demand for repair people dried up; today, when a calculator breaks, people simply throw it away and buy a new one. As for the descendant of the old calculator, most Canadians now work with a computer and many have a computer at home. An enormous industry that did not even exist 20 years ago now employs thousands of people in thousands of companies producing software to make those machines work.

In sum:

> Technological change can and does have a powerful influence on factor demands. As new products and new techniques of production are born, so are demands for new inputs and new skills. As old products become obsolete, so too do the labour skills and other inputs needed to produce them.

Resource Allocation and the Mix of Output in Competitive Markets

We now have a complete, but simplified, picture of household and firm decision making. (Review Figure 10.1 one more time to see how both households and firms

---

[6]*This argument was made in a series of papers by Professor Dale Jorgenson of Harvard University.*

interact in two arenas, output markets and input markets.) We have also examined some of the basic forces that determine the allocation of resources and the mix of output in perfectly competitive markets.

In this competitive environment, profit-maximizing firms make three fundamental decisions: (1) how much to produce and supply in output markets, (2) how to produce (which technology to use), and (3) how much of each input to demand. Chapters 7–9 looked at these three decisions from the perspective of the output market. We derived the supply curve of a competitive firm in the short run and discussed output market adjustment in the long run. Deriving cost curves, we learned, involves evaluating and choosing among alternative technologies. Finally, we saw how a firm's decision about how much product to supply in output markets implicitly determines input demands. Input demands, we argued, are also derived demands. That is, they are ultimately linked to the demand for output.

To show the connection between output and input markets, this chapter took these same three decisions and examined them from the perspective of input markets. Firms hire up to the point at which each input's marginal revenue product is equal to its price.

■ **Trade-Offs Facing Firms and Households** Looking at output and input markets together sheds light on why firms and households choose as they do. Firms are in business to make a profit, and they must sell their output for more than it costs them to produce it. Output price reflects what households are willing to pay for consumer goods. *A firm will hire an input only if it can be used to produce a product that someone is willing to pay for.* Furthermore, a firm will hire an input, or factor of production, as long as the value of what it produces—its marginal revenue product—exceeds the price the firm has to pay for that factor.

Factor prices are determined by the interaction of supply and demand in input markets. A factor supply curve shows the prices required to attract the factor from its alternative use. The alternative to supplying labour, for example, is either leisure or unpaid work. The alternative to supplying financial resources for capital formation is present consumption. Because land is fixed in supply, its supply curve is vertical.

Thus, firms weigh the values of products against the values of resources. With their goal of maximizing profits, firms weigh what households reveal they are willing to pay in output markets against the wages that households require to supply resources. The firm provides the technology for transforming the resources into useful form.

Households also weigh the values of products supplied to the market against the values of the resources at their disposal. A household can consume leisure or it can work and use the income derived from work to buy goods.

■ **The Distribution of Income** In the last few chapters, we have been focusing primarily on the firm. But throughout our study of microeconomics, we have also been building a theory that explains the distribution of income among households. We can now put the pieces of this puzzle together.

As we saw in this chapter, income is earned by households as payment for the factors of production that household members supply in input markets. Workers receive wages in exchange for their labour, owners of capital receive profits and interest in exchange for supplying capital (saving), and landowners receive rents in exchange for the use of their land. The incomes of capital owners depend on the market price of capital (the amount households are paid for the use of their savings). And the incomes of landowners depend on the rental values of their land.

If markets are competitive, the equilibrium price of each input is equal to its marginal revenue product ($W = MRP_L$, and so forth). In other words, at equilibrium, each factor ends up receiving rewards determined by its productivity as

marginal productivity theory of income distribution *At equilibrium, all factors of production end up receiving rewards determined by their productivity as measured by marginal revenue product.*

measured by marginal revenue product. This is referred to as the **marginal productivity theory of income distribution.** We will turn to a more complete analysis of income distribution in Chapter 17.

Looking Ahead

We have now completed our discussion of competitive labour and land markets. (More on the labour market and labour unions can be found in Chapter 19.) The next chapter takes up the complexity of what we have been loosely calling the "capital market." There we discuss the relationship between the market for physical capital and financial capital markets and look at some of the ways that firms make investment decisions. Once we examine the nature of overall competitive equilibrium in Chapter 12, we can finally begin the process of relaxing some of the assumptions that have restricted the scope of our inquiry—most importantly, the assumption of perfect competition in input and output markets.

Summary

1. The exact same set of decisions that lies behind output supply curves also lies behind input demand curves. It is only the perspective that is different.

Input Markets: Basic Concepts

2. Demand for inputs depends on demand for the outputs that they produce; input demand is thus a *derived demand. Productivity* is a measure of the amount of output produced per unit of input.

3. In general, firms will demand workers as long as the value of what those workers produce exceeds what they must be paid. Households will supply labour as long as the wage exceeds the value of leisure or the value that they derive from nonpaid work.

4. Inputs are at the same time *complementary* and *substitutable.* For example, capital raises the productivity of labour, and thus it complements labour; at the same time, capital may be substituted for labour.

5. In the short run, some factor of production is fixed. This means that all firms encounter diminishing returns in the short run. Stated somewhat differently, diminishing returns means that all firms encounter declining marginal product in the short run.

6. The *marginal revenue product (MRP)* of a variable input is the additional revenue a firm earns by employing one additional unit of the input, *ceteris paribus. MRP* is equal to the input's marginal product times the price of output.

Labour and Land Markets

7. Demand for an input depends on that input's marginal revenue product. Profit-maximizing perfectly competitive firms will buy an input (e.g., hire labour) up to the point where the input's marginal revenue product equals its price. For a firm employing only one variable factor of production, the *MRP* curve is the firm's demand curve for that factor in the short run.

8. For a perfectly competitive firm employing one variable factor of production, labour, the condition $W = MRPL$ is exactly the same as the condition $P = MC$. Firms weigh the value of outputs as reflected in output price against the value of inputs as reflected in marginal costs.

9. When a firm employs two variable factors of production, a change in factor price has both a *factor substitution effect* and an *output effect.*

10. A wage increase may lead a firm to substitute capital for labour and thus cause the demand for labour to decline. This is the *factor substitution effect of the wage increase.*

11. A wage increase increases cost, and higher cost may lead to lower output and less demand for all inputs, including labour. This is the *output effect of the wage increase.* The effect is the opposite for a wage decrease.

12. Because land is in strictly fixed supply, its price is *demand determined*—that is, its price is determined exclusively by what households and firms are willing to pay for it. The return to any factor of production in fixed supply is called a *pure rent.* A

firm will pay for and use land as long as the revenue earned from selling the product produced on that land is sufficient to cover the price of the land. The firm will use land up to the point at which $MRP_H = P_H$ where H is land (hectares).

13. Every firm has an incentive to use variable inputs as long as the revenue generated by those inputs covers the costs of those inputs at the margin. Therefore, firms will employ each input up to the point that its price equals its marginal revenue product. This profit-maximizing condition holds for all factors at all levels of output.

Input Demand Curves

14. A shift in a firm's demand curve for a factor of production can be influenced by the demand for the firm's product, the amount and productivity of other inputs used, the prices of other inputs, and changes in technology.

Resource Allocation and the Mix of Output in Competitive Markets

15. Because the price of a factor at equilibrium in competitive markets is equal to its marginal revenue product, the distribution of income among households depends in part on the relative productivity of factors. This is the *marginal productivity theory of income distribution*.

Review Terms and Concepts

complementary inputs 247

demand determined price 258

derived demand 246

factor substitution effect 255

marginal product of labour
   (MP_L) 247

marginal productivity theory of income distribution 266

marginal revenue product (*MRP*) 247

output effect of a factor price increase/decrease 256

productivity of an input 246

pure rent 258

substitutable inputs 247

technological change 264

Equations:
$MRP_L = MP_L \times P_X$
$W^* = MRP_L$

Problem Set

1. Assume that a firm that manufactures widgets can produce them with one of three processes, used alone or in combination. The following table indicates the amounts of capital and labour required by each of the three processes to produce one widget.

	UNITS OF LABOUR	UNITS OF CAPITAL
Process 1	4	1
Process 2	2	2
Process 3	1	3

   a. Assuming that capital costs $3 per unit and labour cost $1 per unit, which process will be employed?

   b. Plot the three points on the firm's *TVC* curve corresponding to $q = 10$, $q = 30$, and $q = 50$.

   c. At each of the three output levels, how much K and L will be demanded?

   d. Repeat parts a.–c., assuming the price of capital is $3 per unit and that the price of labour has risen to $4 per unit.

2. The following schedule shows the technology of production at the Delicious Apple Orchard for 1998:

WORKERS	TOTAL KILOGRAMS OF APPLES PER DAY
0	0
1	40
2	70
3	90
4	100
5	105
6	102

If apples sell for $2 per kilogram and workers can be hired in a competitive labour market for $30 per day, how many workers should be hired? What if workers unionized and the wage rose to $50? (*Hint:* Create marginal product and marginal revenue product columns for the table.) Explain your answers clearly.

3. The following graph is the production function for a firm using only one variable factor of production, labour:

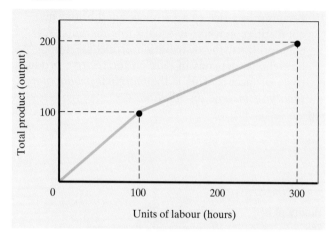

a. Graph the marginal product of labour for the firm as a function of the number of labour units hired.

b. Assuming that the price of output, P_X, is equal to $6, graph the firm's marginal revenue product schedule as a function of the number of labour units hired.

c. If the current equilibrium wage rate is $4 per hour, how many hours of labour would you hire? How much output will you produce?

4. Describe how each of the following events would affect (1) the demand for construction workers and (2) construction wages in Victoria, B.C. Illustrate with supply and demand curves.

a. A sharp increase in interest rates on new-home mortgages reduces the demand for new houses substantially.

b. The economy of Victoria booms. Office rents rise, creating demand for new office space.

c. An influx of elderly people come to take advantage of Victoria's favourable climate.

5. The demand for land is a derived demand. Think of a popular location near your campus. What determines the demand for land in that area? What outputs are sold by businesses located there? Discuss the relationship between land prices and the prices of those products.

6. Governments sometimes provide firms with an "investment tax credit" that effectively reduces the price of capital. In theory, these credits are designed to stimulate new investment and thus create jobs. Critics have argued that if there are strong factor substitution effects, these subsidies could actually reduce employment. Explain their arguments.

7. a. Define marginal revenue product.

b. At equilibrium in a competitive industry, $W = MRP_L$. Briefly explain why.

c. Suppose that the competitive zump industry employs 50% of the highly trained zump makers in the country. Suppose also that demand for zumps shifts, driving the price of zumps up by 50%. The wages of people who make zumps are likely to rise. Show why using a graph.

The Capital Market and the Investment Decision

We saw in Chapter 10 that perfectly competitive firms hire factors of production (inputs) up to the point at which the marginal revenue product of each factor is equal to the price of that factor. The three main factors of production are land, labour, and capital. We also saw that factor prices are determined by the interaction of supply and demand in the factor markets. The wage rate is determined in the labour market, the price of land is determined in the land market, and the price of capital is determined in the capital market.

In Chapter 10, we explored the labour and land markets in some detail. In this chapter we consider the demand for capital and the capital market more fully. Transactions between households and firms in the labour and land markets are direct. In the labour market, households offer their labour directly to firms in exchange for wages, and in the land market landowners rent or sell their land directly to firms in exchange for rent or an agreed-upon price. In the capital market, though, households often indirectly supply the financial resources necessary for firms to purchase capital. When households save and add funds to their bank accounts, for example, firms can borrow these funds from the bank to finance their capital purchases.

Earlier, in Chapter 9, we discussed the incentives of new firms to enter industries in which profit opportunities exist and the incentives that existing firms have to leave industries in which they are suffering economic losses. We also described the conditions under which existing firms have an incentive either to expand or to reduce their scales of operation. That chapter was in a preliminary way describing the process of capital allocation. When new firms enter an industry or an existing firm expands, someone pays to put capital (plant, equipment, and inventory) in place. Since the future is uncertain, capital investment decisions always involve risk. The essential feature of market capitalist systems is that the decision to put capital to use in a particular enterprise is made by private citizens putting their savings at risk in search of private gain. This chapter describes the set of institutions through which such transactions take place.

Capital, Investment, and Depreciation

Before we proceed with our analysis of the capital market, we need to review some basic economic principles and introduce some related concepts.

CAPITAL

One of the most important concepts in all of economics is the concept of **capital.** Recall that:

> Capital goods are those goods produced by the economic system that are used as inputs to produce other goods and services in the future. Capital goods thus yield valuable productive services over time.

■ Tangible Capital   When we think of capital, we generally think of the physical capital employed by business firms. The major categories of **physical,** or **tangible, capital** are (1) nonresidential structures (office buildings, power plants, factories, shopping centres, warehouses, and docks, for example); (2) durable equipment (machines, trucks, sandwich grills, automobiles, and so on); (3) residential structures; and (4) inventories of inputs and outputs that firms have in stock.

Most firms need tangible capital, along with labour and land, to produce their products. A restaurant's capital requirements include a kitchen, ovens and grills, tables and chairs, silverware, dishes, and light fixtures. These items must be purchased up front and maintained if the restaurant is to function properly. A manufacturing firm must have a plant, specialized machinery, trucks, and inventories of parts. A winery needs casks, vats, piping, temperature-control equipment, and cooking and bottling machinery.

In addition to its shelves and display cases, the capital stock of a retail drugstore is made up mostly of inventories. Drugstores do not produce the aspirin, vitamins, and toothbrushes that they sell. Those things are bought from manufacturers and put on display. The product actually produced and sold by a drugstore is convenience. Like any other product, convenience is produced with labour and capital in the form of a store with lots of products, or inventory, displayed on the sales floor and kept in storerooms. The inventories of inputs and outputs that manufacturing firms maintain are also capital. To function smoothly and meet the demands of buyers, for example, the Ford Motor Company maintains inventories of both auto parts (tires, windshields, etc.) and completed cars.

An apartment building is also capital. Produced by the economic system, it yields valuable services over time, and it is used as an input to produce housing services, which are rented out.

■ Social Capital: Infrastructure   Some physical or tangible capital is owned by the public rather than by private firms. **Social capital,** sometimes called **infrastructure,** is capital that provides services to the public. Most social capital takes the form of public works like highways, roads, bridges, mass transit systems, and sewer and

capital *Those goods produced by the economic system that are used as inputs in the production of future goods and services.*

physical, or **tangible, capital** *Material things used as inputs in the production of future goods and services. The major categories of physical capital are nonresidential structures, durable equipment, residential structures, and inventories.*

social capital, or **infrastructure** *Capital that provides services to the public. Most social capital takes the form of public works (roads and bridges) and public services (police and fire protection).*

water systems. Police stations, fire stations, city halls, courthouses, and police cars are forms of social capital that are used as inputs to produce the services that government provides.

All firms use some forms of social capital in producing their outputs. Manufacturing firms transport their raw materials and products over highways and secondary roads. Even insurance companies in office towers use water pumped through publicly owned pipes and receive police and fire protection services that are produced with social capital.

Recent economic research has shown that a country's infrastructure plays a very important role in helping private firms produce their products efficiently. When public capital is not properly cared for—for example, when roads deteriorate or when airports are not modernized to accommodate increasing traffic—private firms that depend on efficient transportation networks suffer. When the Liberal Party was elected in 1993, it launched an infrastructure investment program, which increased spending on public capital—road and bridge repair, new water and sewage systems, and a variety of other projects.

■ **Intangible Capital** Not all capital is physical. Some things that are intangible (nonmaterial) satisfy every part of our definition of capital. When a business firm invests in advertising to establish a brand name, it is producing a form of **intangible capital** called goodwill. This goodwill yields valuable services to the firm over time.

intangible capital *Nonmaterial things that contribute to the output of future goods and services.*

When a firm establishes a training program for employees, it is investing in the skills of its workers. One can think of such an investment as the production of an intangible form of capital called **human capital.** It is produced with labour (instructors) and capital (classrooms, computers, projectors, and books). Human capital in the form of new or augmented skills is an input—it will yield valuable productive services for the firm in the future.

human capital *A form of intangible capital that includes the skills and other knowledge that workers have or acquire through education and training and that yields valuable services to a firm over time.*

When research produces valuable results, such as a new production process that reduces costs or a new formula that creates a new product, the new technology itself can be thought of as capital. Furthermore, even ideas can be patented and the rights to them can be sold.

■ **The Time Dimension** The most important dimension of capital is that it exists through time. Labour services are used at the time they are provided. Households consume services and nondurable goods[1] almost immediately after purchase. But capital exists now and into the future. Therefore,

> The value of capital is only as great as the value of the services it will render over time.[2]

■ **Measuring Capital** Labour is measured in hours, and land is measured in square metres or hectares. But because capital comes in so many forms, it is virtually impossible to measure it directly in physical terms. The indirect measure generally used is *current market value.* The measure of a firm's **capital stock** is the current market value of its plant, equipment, inventories, and intangible assets. Using value

capital stock *The current market value of a firm's plant, equipment, inventories, and intangible assets.*

---

[1]*Consumer goods are generally divided into three categories: durables, semidurables, and nondurables. Technically, durable goods are goods that are expected to last for more than one year. Nondurable goods are goods that are expected to last less than one year. Semidurables are those goods that fall between durables and nondurables (e.g., clothing and footwear).*

[2]*Conceptually, consumer durable goods, such as automobiles, washing machines, and the like, are capital. They are produced, they yield services over time, and households use them as inputs to produce services such as transportation and clean laundry.*

as a measuring stick, business managers, accountants, and economists can, in a sense, add buildings, barges, and bulldozers into a measure of total capital.

Capital is measured as a stock value. That is, it is measured at a point in time. The capital stock of the XYZ Corporation on July 31 is $3 453 231. Or at the beginning of 1995, the gross nonresidential fixed capital stock (buildings and equipment) of all private industries (including farms) in Canada was $1.7 trillion, including $1.27 trillion in structures and $0.43 trillion in equipment.[3]

Although it is measured in terms of money, or value, it is very important to think of the actual capital stock itself:

> When we speak of capital, we refer not to money or to financial assets such as bonds or stocks, but rather to the firm's physical plant, equipment, inventory, and intangible assets.

INVESTMENT AND DEPRECIATION

Recall the difference between stock and flow measures discussed in earlier chapters. *Stock measures* are valued at a particular point in time, while *flow measures* are valued over a period of time. The easiest way to think of the difference between a stock measure and a flow measure is to think about a tub of water. The volume of water in the tub is measured at a point in time and is a stock. The amount of water that flows into the tub *per hour* and the amount of water that evaporates out of the tub *per day* are flow measures. Flow measures have meaning only when the time dimension is added. Clearly, water flowing into the tub at a rate of 20 litres per hour is very different than a rate of 20 litres per year.

Stocks of capital are affected over time by two flows: investment and depreciation. When a firm produces or puts in place new capital—a new piece of equipment, for example—it has invested. **Investment** is a flow that increases the stock of capital. Because it has a time dimension, we speak of investment per period (by the month, quarter, or year).

As you proceed, be careful to keep in mind that the term *investing* is not used in economics to describe the act of buying a share of stock or a bond. Although people commonly use the term this way ("I invested in some BCE stock" or "he invested in Canada Savings Bonds"), the term *investment* when used correctly refers *only to the creation of new capital.*

Table 11.1 on the next page presents data on investment in the Canadian economy in 1995. About one-third of the total was new durable equipment. Almost all the rest was investment in structures, both residential (apartment buildings, condominiums, houses, and so forth) and nonresidential (factories, shopping malls, and so forth). Inventory investment was small.

Depreciation is the decline in an asset's economic value over time. If you have ever owned a car, you are aware that its resale value falls with age. Suppose you bought a new Pontiac in 1994 for $20 500 and you decide to sell it two years and 40 000 kilometres later. Checking the newspaper and talking to several dealers, you find out that, given its condition and the mileage, you can expect to get $12 000 for it. It has depreciated $8500 ($20 500–$12 000). Table 11.1 shows that in 1995 depreciation in the Canadian economy was $96.2 billion.

A capital asset can depreciate because it wears out physically or because it becomes obsolete. Take, for example, a computer control system in a factory. If a new, technologically superior system is developed that does the same job for half the

investment New capital additions to a firm's capital stock. Although capital is measured at a given point in time (a stock), investment is measured over a period of time (a flow). The flow of investment increases the stock of capital.

depreciation The decline in an asset's economic value over time.

---

[3]*Statistics Canada*, Fixed Capital Flows and Stocks, 1961–94, *Cat. no. 13–568, Table 1.*

Table 11.1	Investment in the Canadian Economy, 1995		
	Billions of Current Dollars	**As a Percentage of Total Gross Investment**	**As a Percentage of GDP**
Nonresidential structures	46.5	32.9	6.0
Durable equipment	49.7	35.2	6.4
Inventories	7.0	5.0	0.1
Residential structures	38.0	26.9	4.9
Total gross private investment	141.2	100.0	17.4
− Depreciation	−96.2	−68.1	−12.3
Net investment = (gross investment minus depreciation)	45.0	31.9	5.1

Source: Statistics Canada, National Income and Expenditure Accounts, *Annual Estimates, 1995,* Cat. no. 13–201-XPB.

price, the old system may be replaced even if it still functions well. The Pontiac depreciated because of wear and tear *and* because new models had become available.

The Capital Market

Where does capital come from? How and why is it produced? How much and what kinds of capital are produced? Who pays for it? These questions are answered in the complex set of institutional structures in which households supply their savings to firms that demand funds in order to buy capital goods. Collectively, these institutions are called the **capital market.**

Although governments and households make some capital investment decisions, most decisions to produce new capital goods—that is, to invest—are made by firms. A firm cannot invest, however, unless it has the funds to do so. Although firms can invest in many ways, it is always the case that:

capital market *The market in which households supply their savings to firms that demand funds in order to buy capital goods.*

The funds that firms use to buy capital goods come, directly or indirectly, from households. When a household decides not to consume a portion of its income, it saves. Investment by firms is the *demand for capital*; saving by households is the *supply of capital*. Various financial institutions then facilitate the transfer of households' savings to firms that use them for capital investment.

Let us use a simple example to see how the system works. Suppose that some firm wants to purchase a machine that costs $1000 and that some household decides at the same time that it wants to save $1000 from its income. Figure 11.1 shows one way that the household's decision to save might connect with the firm's decision to invest.

Either directly or through a financial intermediary (such as a bank), the household agrees to lend its savings to the firm. In exchange, the firm contracts to pay the household interest at some agreed-upon rate each period. If the household lends directly to the firm, the firm gives the household a *bond*, which is nothing more than a contract that promises to repay the loan at some specific time in the future. The bond also specifies the flow of interest to be paid in the meantime.

The new saving adds to the household's stock of wealth. The household's net worth has increased by the $1000, which it holds in the form of a bond.[4] The bond

---

[4]Note that it is the act of saving *that increases the household's wealth, not the act of buying the bond. Buying the bond simply transforms one financial asset (money) into another (a bond). The household could simply have held on to the money.*

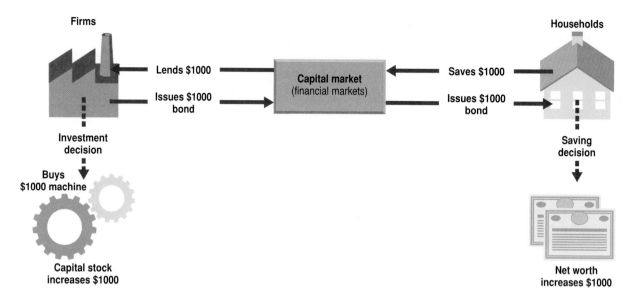

FIGURE 11.1

$1000 in Savings Becomes $1000 of Investment

is an asset to the household because it represents the firm's promise to repay the $1000 at some future date with interest. The firm uses the $1000 to buy a new $1000 machine, which it adds to its stock of capital. In essence, the household has supplied the capital demanded by the firm. It's almost as if the household bought the machine and rented it to the firm for an annual fee. Presumably, this investment will generate added profits that will facilitate the payment of interest to the household.

> In general, projects are undertaken as long as the profits likely to be realized from the investment are sufficient to cover the interest payments to the household.

Sometimes the transfer of household savings through the capital market into investment occurs without a financial intermediary. Recall from Chapter 4 that an *entrepreneur* is one who organizes, manages, and assumes the risk of a firm. When an entrepreneur starts a new business by buying capital with his own savings, he is both demanding capital and supplying the resources (i.e., his savings) needed to purchase that capital; no third party is involved in the transaction. Most investment, however, is accomplished with the help of financial intermediaries (third parties such as banks, insurance companies, and pension funds) that stand between the supplier (saver) and the demander (investing firm). The part of the capital market in which savers and investors interact through intermediaries is often referred to as the **financial capital market.**

financial capital market *The part of the capital market in which savers and investors interact through intermediaries.*

CAPITAL INCOME: INTEREST AND PROFITS

It should now be clear to you how capital markets fit into the circular flow. They facilitate the movement of household savings into the most productive investment projects. When households allow their savings to be used to purchase capital, they receive payments, and these payments (along with wages and salaries) are part of household incomes. Income that is earned on savings that have been put to use through financial capital markets is called **capital income.** Capital income is received by households in many forms, the two most important of which are *interest* and *profits*.

■ **Interest** The most common form of capital income received by households is interest. In simplest terms, **interest** is the payment made for the use of money. Banks pay interest to depositors, whose deposits are lent out to businesses or individuals who want to make investments.[5] Banks also *charge* interest to those who borrow money. Corporations pay interest to households that buy their bonds. The government borrows money by issuing bonds, and the buyers of those bonds receive interest payments.

Interest is almost always expressed as an annual rate. The *interest rate* is the agreed-upon annual interest payment expressed as a percentage of the loan or deposit. For example, a $1000 bond (representing a $1000 loan from a household to a firm) that carries a fixed 10% interest rate will pay the household $100 per year ($1000 × 0.10) in interest. A savings account that carries a 5% annual interest rate will pay $50 annually on a balance of $1000.

The interest rate is usually agreed to at the time a loan or deposit is made. Sometimes borrowers and lenders agree to adjust periodically the level of interest payments depending on market conditions. These types of loans are called *adjustable* or *floating rate loans*. (*Fixed-rate loans* are loans in which the interest rate never varies.) In recent years there have even been adjustable rates of interest on term deposits.

A loan's interest rate depends on a number of factors. A loan that involves more risk will generally pay a higher interest rate than a loan with less risk. For example, consider two entrepreneurs approaching a bank for a loan. One of the entrepreneurs wants to build several cabins at an increasingly popular tourist location where there is a limited supply of accommodations. The other wants to build the same cabins at a much less popular location that has not traditionally attracted visitors but that has features that might attract some tourists. A bank loans officer is unlikely to treat these loan applications equivalently. Since one project has a greater chance of success than the other, the loans officer will want a higher interest rate on the loan to the higher-risk project to protect the bank from the greater risk of default (that is, not repaying) or, as is more likely, the bank will reject the loan application. If the loan application is rejected, the entrepreneur will have to look elsewhere for financing and will face a higher interest rate.

It is generally agreed that the safest borrower is the Canadian government, even though its debt is now over half a trillion dollars and continues to rise. Most people believe that there is little risk of the Canadian government defaulting on its loans since it has the ability to collect more taxes, it has many assets (crown lands, national parks, etc.) that it could sell, and it ultimately has the power to repay through the creation of new money. As a consequence, the Canadian government can borrow money at a lower interest rate than any other borrower.

■ **Profits** As the term is commonly used, **profit** means any excess of revenues over cost in a given period. Profits can be earned by all forms of business enterprise: proprietorships, partnerships, and corporations. Profits are part of the incomes of proprietors and partners. Corporations, in contrast, often do not pay out all of their profits to shareholders. As you saw in Chapter 3, corporate profits are

capital income *Income earned on savings that have been put to use through financial capital markets.*

interest *The payments made for the use of money. Almost always expressed as an annual rate.*

profit *The excess of revenues over cost in a given period.*

---

[5]*Although we are focusing on investment by businesses, households can and do make investments also. The most important form of household investment is the construction of a new house, usually financed by borrowing in the form of a mortgage. A household may also borrow to finance the purchase of an existing house, but when it does so, no new investment is taking place.*

divided into three categories: dividends (profits distributed to shareholders), retained earnings (profits not distributed to shareholders), and profit taxes.

Recall that the term "profits," as used in economics, refers to *economic*, or *excess*, profits—that is, profits over and above a normal return. Economic profit is defined this way because true economic cost includes the opportunity cost of capital. Suppose, for example, that I decide to open a candy store that requires an initial investment of $100 000. Clearly, if I borrow the $100 000 from a bank, I am not making a profit until I cover the interest payments on my loan.

Even if I use my own savings or raise the funds I need by selling shares in my business, I am not making a profit until I cover the opportunity cost of using those funds to start my business. Because I always have the option of lending my funds at the current market interest rate, I earn an economic profit only when I earn a rate of return that is higher than the market interest rate. For example, if the market interest rate is 11%, the annual profits my candy store earns would not be considered economic profits unless they are greater than $11 000 a year. The first $11 000 of my profits is actually part of the cost of capital—it is the normal return on a $100 000 investment when the interest rate is 11% ($100 000 × 0.11 = $11 000).

As another example, suppose that the Maple Leaf Lamp Company was started in 1995, and that 100% of the $1 million needed to start up the company (to buy the plant and equipment) was raised by selling shares of stock. Now suppose that the company earns a total profit of $200 000 per year, all of which is paid out to shareholders. Since $200 000 is 20% of the company's total capital stock, we could say that the firm is enjoying a 20% rate of profit and that shareholders are earning profits of $200 000. But only a part of that $200 000 is *economic* profit. If the market interest rate is 10%, then 10% of $1 million ($100 000) is really part of the cost of capital. Not until the firm earns *over* a 10% rate of return on its investment is it earning economic profits.

■ **Functions of Interest and Profit** Capital income serves several functions. First, interest and profit may function as incentives to postpone gratification. When you save, you pass up the chance to buy things that you want right now. Rather than spending and consuming something today, you decide to spend and consume something in the future, using what you hope will be increased funds. One view of interest and profit is that they are the rewards for postponing consumption.

Second, interest and profit also serve as rewards for innovation and risk taking. The entrepreneur's goal is to reap rewards in the form of profits from the new enterprise. When a new firm makes it big, the rewards can be enormous. Successful entrepreneurs have accumulated huge fortunes. K.C. Irving, a New Brunswick entrepreneur, made millions. Every year the *Financial Post* magazine publishes the names of the richest people in Canada, and virtually every major fortune listed there is traceable to the founding of some business enterprise that "made it big." In 1996 the top 10 included newspaper publishing

Economic profits sometimes reward entrepreneurs for taking risks. Bill Gates, founder and CEO of Microsoft, may be one of the wealthiest people in the world.

(Ken Thomson, $8.2 billion), retail stores (the Eaton family, $1.76 billion), communications (Ted Rogers, $1.4 billion), and telephone switch making (Terry Matthews, $864 million).

Many argue that rewards for innovation and risk taking are the essence of the Canadian free enterprise system. The potential for big financial rewards is one factor that motivates innovation, and innovation is good for much of society. Ideas lead to new products and new ways of producing things. Innovation is at the core of economic growth and progress. More efficient production techniques mean that the resources saved can be used to produce new things. There is another side to this story, however. Critics of the free enterprise system claim that such large rewards are not justified and that accumulations of great wealth and power are not in society's best interests.

FINANCIAL MARKETS IN ACTION

As you have seen, when a firm issues a fixed-interest-rate bond, it borrows funds and pays interest at an agreed-upon rate to the person or institution that buys the bond. Many other mechanisms, four of which are illustrated below (Figure 11.2), also channel household savings into investment projects. The Global Perspective box titled "Rural Credit in Bangladesh and Indonesia" offers additional examples.

■ **Case A: Business Loans**   As I look around my home town, I see several ice cream stores doing very well, but I think that I can make better ice cream than they do. To go into the business, I need capital: ice cream–making equipment, tables, chairs, freezers, signs, and a store. Because I put up my house as collateral, I am not a big risk, and the bank grants me a loan at a fairly reasonable interest rate. Banks have these funds to lend only because households deposit their savings there.

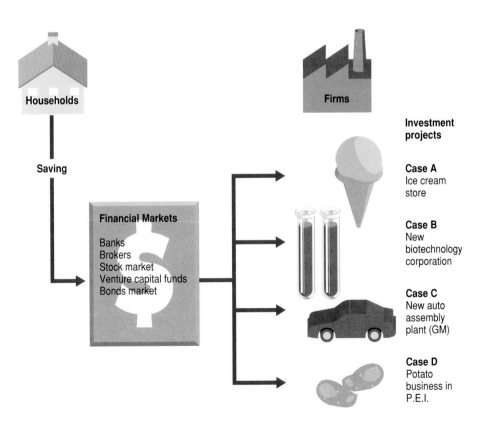

FIGURE 11.2

Financial Markets Link Household Saving and Investment by Firms

Global Perspective

Rural Credit in Bangladesh and Indonesia

Low-income people interested in establishing a business in Canada often face considerable difficulties when they approach a bank or other financial institution in hopes of securing a loan. Commercial banks believe the risk is too high.

This problem is not unique to Canada; other countries have experimented with innovative policies. One successful policy is the Grameen ("Village") Bank in Bangladesh.

The Grameen Bank was founded in 1977 by a U.S.-trained economist named Mohammed Yunus. The project was supported by the Bangladesh Bank and seven other government-owned commercial banks. Within four years, the Grameen Bank had extended its operations to 433 villages. By 1995, it had lent money to 1.6 million people in 32 000 villages. The average loan is about US$100 and the maximum loan is US$1200. A small farmer might borrow money to buy a cow, or a fisherman might borrow to buy materials for a fishing net. The most amazing thing about the Grameen Bank is that 96% of its loans have been paid back in full.

One of the bank's interesting innovations is that it lends to groups. Loans are made to groups of five people of roughly equal socioeconomic status. These groups elect their own leaders and discipline is maintained through peer pressure. The groups must meet weekly and make weekly instalment payments:

> Lending to small groups formed by potential borrowers who are collectively responsible for repayment serves several purposes. Small groups . . . generate a sense of belonging and a clear perception that each individual's performance is crucial to the group's overall success or failure. Motivated group members tend to monitor their more

The Grameen Bank of Bangladesh makes small loans to village-centred groups. Most of the bank's clients have been fishermen or farmers. To date, 96% of the bank's loans have been repaid in full. Pictured here is a jute harvest in Bangladesh.

> lax peers, for no group member can receive further credit until the entire group's debts are repaid.[1]

The Grameen Bank's function is exactly the same as the function of other financial intermediaries: to collect household saving and make it available to businesses, which pay a fee to use it for the purchase or creation of capital.

A number of small funds supported by foundations have opened in North America on the Grameen model. Most seem to have very low default rates on loans to very small enterprises in rural or central city areas. But to date, the scale is nothing like it is in Bangladesh.

An institution similar to the Grameen Bank is the Unit Desa ("Village Unit") of the Bank Rakyat Indonesia, which supplies credit and collects saving in rural Indonesia. A recent report describes two typical loans.[2]

> One loan of 1.2 million rupiah (about $700) was made to a couple to buy a grinding and milling machine to be used for

grinding coffee and milling corn and rice. Before taking the loan, the family was making a living in petty trading. After the loan, the family operated a processing service for the surrounding area and had three full-time employees outside the immediate family. It paid the loan back in full.

> Another loan of 3 million rupiah (about $1800) was made to two partners to buy a steam furnace for a bean-curd processing factory. At the time the loan was made, the factory employed four workers and supplied about 15 bean-curd peddlers a day. With the steam processor, the output of the factory doubled and four additional full-time workers were hired.

Sources: [1]Jacob Yaron, "Successful Rural Finance Institutions," *Finance and Development*, March 1994, p. 34. [2]Richard Patton and Jay Rosengard, *Progress with Profits: The Development of Rural Banking in Indonesia* (Cambridge, MA: Harvard Institute for International Development, 1990).

■ **Case B: Venture Capital** A scientist at a leading university develops an inexpensive method of producing a very important family of virus-fighting drugs, using microorganisms created through gene splicing. This is a new process and a new business, and no one really knows whether it will be profitable or not. The business could very well fail within 12 months, but if it succeeds, the potential for profit is huge.

Our scientist goes to a *venture capital fund* for financing. Such funds take household savings and put them into high-risk ventures in exchange for a share of the profits if the new businesses succeed. By investing in many different projects, the funds reduce the risk of going broke. Once again, household funds make it possible for firms to undertake investments. If a venture succeeds, those owning shares in the venture capital fund receive substantial profits.

■ **Case C: Retained Earnings** General Motors decides that it wants to build a new assembly plant in Oshawa, and it discovers that it has enough funds to pay for the new facility. The new investment is thus paid for through internal funds, or *retained earnings.*

The result is exactly the same as if the firm had gone to households via some financial intermediary and borrowed the funds to pay for the new plant. General Motors is owned by its shareholders. When it earns a profit, that profit really belongs to the shareholders. If GM uses its profits to buy new capital, it does so only with the shareholders' implicit consent. When a firm takes its own profit and uses it to buy capital assets instead of paying it out to its shareholders, the total value of the firm goes up, as does the value of the shares held by stockholders. As in the other examples, GM's capital stock increases, and so does the net worth of households.

When a household owns a share of stock that *appreciates,* or increases in value, the appreciation is part of the household's income. Unless the household sells the stock and consumes the gain, that gain is part of saving. In essence, when a firm retains earnings for investment purposes, it is actually saving on behalf of its shareholders.

■ **Case D: The Stock Market** A former high-ranking government official decides to start a new potato processing business in P.E.I., and he also decides to raise the funds needed by issuing shares of stock. Households buy the shares with income that they decide not to spend. In exchange, they are entitled to a share of the potato firm's profits.

The shares of stock become part of households' net worth. The proceeds from stock sales are used to buy plant equipment and inventory. Savings flow into investment, and the firm's capital stock goes up by the same amount as household net worth.

CAPITAL ACCUMULATION AND ALLOCATION

You can see from the preceding examples that various, and sometimes complex, connections between households and firms facilitate the movement of saving into productive investment. The methods may differ, but the results are the same.

Think again about Colleen and Ivan, whom we discussed in Chapter 2. They found themselves alone on a deserted island. They had to make choices about how to allocate available resources, including their time. One important choice was how much energy to devote to producing goods and services for present consumption and how much to devote to investment that will bring future enjoyment. By spending long hours working on a house or a boat Colleen and Ivan are saving and investing. First, they are using resources that could be used to produce more immediate rewards—they could gather more food or simply lie in the sun and relax. Second, they are applying those resources to the production of capital and capital accumulation.

Industrialized or agrarian, small or large, simple or complex, all societies exist through time and must allocate resources over time. In simple societies, investment and saving decisions are made by the same people. Colleen and Ivan decide whether to forgo present pleasures (consumption) and whether to produce capital goods (a house, a boat). However:

> In modern industrial societies, investment decisions (capital production decisions) are made primarily by firms. Households decide how much to save, and in the long run saving limits or constrains the amount of investment that firms can undertake. The capital market exists in between to direct savings into profitable investment projects.

The Demand for New Capital and the Investment Decision

We saw in Chapter 9 that firms have an incentive to expand in industries that earn economic profits (that is, profits over and above the normal rate of return) and in industries in which economies of scale lead to lower average costs at higher levels of output. We also saw that economic profits in an industry stimulate the entry of new firms into that industry. The expansion of existing firms and the creation of new firms both involve investment in new capital.

Even when there are no economic profits in an industry, however, firms must still do some investing. First, equipment wears out and must be replaced if the firm is to stay in business. Second, firms are constantly changing; a new technology may become available, sales patterns may shift, or the firm may expand or contract its product line.

With these points in mind, we now turn to a discussion of the investment decision process within the individual firm. In the end we will see (just as we did in Chapter 10) that a perfectly competitive firm invests in capital up to the point at which the marginal revenue product of capital is equal to the price of capital. (Because we based much of our discussion in Chapter 10 on the assumption of perfect competition, it makes sense to continue doing so here. Keep in mind, though, that much of what we say here also applies to firms that are not perfectly competitive. In Chapter 13, we begin relaxing the assumptions of perfect competition.)

Forming Expectations

We have already said that the most important dimension of capital is that of time. Capital produces useful services over *some period of time*. In building an office tower, a developer makes an investment that will be around for decades. In deciding where to build a branch plant, a manufacturing firm commits a large amount of resources to purchase capital that will be in place for a long time.

It is important to remember, though, that capital goods do not begin to yield benefits until they are *used*. Often the decision to build a building or purchase a piece of equipment must be made years before the actual project is completed. While the acquisition of a small business computer may take only days, the planning process for downtown development projects in big Canadian cities has been known to take decades.

■ **The Expected Benefits of Investments** Decision makers must have expectations about what is going to happen in the future. A new plant will be very valuable—that is, it will produce much profit—if the market for a firm's product grows and the price of that product remains high. The same plant will be worth little if the economy goes into a slump or consumers grow tired of the firm's product. An office tower may turn out to be an excellent investment if all the space gets rented at market rents that are as high as, or higher than, rents in other office towers, but it may be a poor investment if many new office buildings go up at the same time, flooding the office space market, pushing up the vacancy rate, and driving down rents—which is exactly what happened to Olympia and York's development at Canary Wharf in London, England, in the early 1990s. It follows, then, that:

> The investment process requires that the potential investor evaluate the expected flow of future productive services that an investment project will yield.

Remember that households, business firms, and governments all undertake investments. A household must evaluate the future services that a new roof will yield. A firm must evaluate the flow of future revenues that a new plant will generate. Governments must estimate how much benefit society will derive from a new bridge or a war memorial.

An official of General Electric once described the difficulty involved in making such predictions. GE subscribes to a number of different economic forecasting services. In 1982, those services provided the firm with 10-year predictions of new housing construction in the U.S. that ranged from a low of 400 000 new units per year to a high of 4 million new units per year. Because General Electric sells millions of household appliances to contractors building new houses, condominiums, and apartments, the forecast was critical. If GE decided that the high number was more accurate, it would need to spend literally billions of dollars on new plant and equipment to prepare for the extra demand. If GE decided that the low number was more accurate, it would need to begin closing several of its larger plants and disinvesting. In fact, GE took the middle road. It assumed that housing production would be between 1.5 and 2 million units—which, in fact, it turned out to be.

General Electric is not an exception. All firms must rely on forecasts to make sensible investment and production decisions, but forecasting is an inexact science because so much depends on events that cannot be foreseen.

■ **The Expected Costs of Investments**   The benefits of any investment project take the form of future profits. These profits must be forecast. But costs must also be evaluated. Like households, firms have access to financial markets, both as borrowers and as lenders. If a firm borrows, it must *pay* interest over time; if it lends, it will *earn* interest. If the firm borrows to finance a project, the interest on the loan is part of the cost of the project.

Even if a project is financed with the firm's own funds, rather than by borrowing, there is an opportunity cost involved. A thousand dollars put into a capital investment project will generate an expected flow of future profit; the same $1000 put into the financial market (in essence, lent to another firm) will yield a flow of interest payments. The project will not be undertaken unless it is expected to yield more than the market interest rate will yield. The cost of an investment project may thus be direct or indirect because:

> The ability to lend at the market rate of interest means that there is an *opportunity cost* associated with every investment project. The evaluation process thus involves not only estimating future benefits, but also comparing them with the possible alternative uses of the funds required to undertake the project. At a minimum, those funds could earn interest in financial markets.

Table 11.2		Potential Investment Projects and Expected Rates of Return for a Hypothetical Firm, Based on Forecasts of Future Profits Attributable to the Investment	

	Project	(1) Total Investment (Dollars)	(2) Expected Rate of Return (Percentage)
A.	New computer network	400 000	25
B.	New branch plant	2 600 000	20
C.	Sales office in another province	1 500 000	15
D.	New automated billing system	100 000	12
E.	Ten new delivery trucks	400 000	10
F.	Advertising campaign	1 000 000	7
G.	Employee cafeteria	100 000	5

expected rate of return *The annual rate of return that a firm expects to obtain through a capital investment.*

COMPARING COSTS AND EXPECTED RETURN

Once expectations have been formed, firms must quantify them—that is, they must assign some dollars-and-cents value to them. One way to quantify expectations is to calculate an **expected rate of return** on the investment project. For example, if a new computer network that costs $400 000 is likely to save $100 000 per year in data processing costs forever after, the expected rate of return on that investment is 25% per year. Each year the firm will save $100 000 as a result of the $400 000 investment. The expected rate of return will be less than 25% if the computer network wears out or becomes obsolete after a while and the cost savings cease. For example, if the network lasts only ten years (with cost savings of $100 000 in each of the 10 years), after which time it is worthless and the savings cease, the expected rate of return will be only 21.4%.[6] The expected rate of return will be even less if the network depreciates gradually during the 10 years, resulting in cost savings of less than $100 000 in years 2 through 10. In short:

The expected rate of return on an investment project depends on the price of the investment, the expected length of time that the project provides additional cost savings or revenue, and the expected amount of revenue attributable each year to the project.

Table 11.2 presents a menu of investment choices and expected rates of return that face a hypothetical firm. Because expected rates of return are based on forecasts of future profits attributable to the investments, any change in expectations would change all the numbers in column 2.

Figure 11.3 on the next page graphs the total amount of investment in millions of dollars that the firm would undertake at various interest rates. If the interest rate were 24%, the firm would fund only Project A, the new computer network. It can borrow at 24% and invest in a computer that is expected to yield 25%. At 24%, then, the firm's total investment is $400 000. (At such a high interest rate, of course, only very profitable projects would be funded if we were talking about the real world and not the hypothetical world of the table and figure.) The first vertical orange line in Figure 11.3 shows that at any interest rate above 20% and below 25%, only $400 000 worth of investment (that is, Project A) will be undertaken.

If the interest rate were 18%, the firm would fund projects A and B, and its

---

[6]*This 21.4% figure can be computed using the present-value analysis discussed in the appendix to this chapter.*

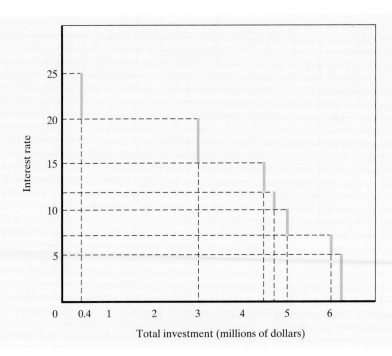

FIGURE 11.3

Total Investment as a Function of the Market Interest Rate

The demand for new capital depends on the interest rate. When the interest rate is low, firms are more likely to invest in new plant and equipment than when the interest rate is high. This is because the interest rate determines the direct cost (interest on a loan) or the opportunity cost (alternative investment) of each project.

total investment would rise to $3 million ($400 000 + $2 600 000). If the firm could borrow at 18%, the flow of additional profits generated by the new computer and the new plant would more than cover the costs of borrowing, but none of the other projects would be justified. At an interest rate of 14%, the firm would undertake projects A, B, and C, at a total cost of $4.5 million. Only if the interest rate fell below 5% would the firm fund all seven investment projects.

The investment schedule in Table 11.2 and its graphic depiction in Figure 11.3 describe the firm's demand for new capital, expressed as a function of the market interest rate. If we add the total investment undertaken by *all* firms at every interest rate, we arrive at the demand for new capital in the economy as a whole. In other words, the market demand curve for new capital is simply the sum of all the individual demand curves for new capital in the economy (Figure 11.4 on page 284). In a sense, the investment demand schedule is a ranking of all the investment opportunities in the economy in order of expected yield.

> Only those investment projects in the economy that are expected to yield a rate of return higher than the market interest rate will be funded. At lower market interest rates, more investment projects are undertaken.

The most important thing to remember about the investment demand curve is that its shape and position depend critically on the *expectations* of those making the investment decisions. Because many influences affect these expectations, they are usually volatile and subject to frequent change. Thus, while lower interest rates tend to stimulate investment, and higher interest rates tend to slow it, many other hard-to-measure and hard-to-predict factors also affect the level of investment spending. These might include government policy changes, election results, global affairs, inflation, and changes in currency exchange rates.

■ **The Expected Rate of Return and the Marginal Revenue Product of Capital**   The concept of the expected rate of return on investment projects is analogous to the concept of

FIGURE 11.4

Investment Demand

Lower interest rates are likely to stimulate investment in the economy as a whole, while higher interest rates are likely to slow investment.

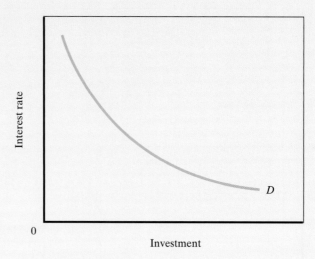

the marginal revenue product of capital (MRP_K). Recall that we defined the marginal revenue product of an input as the additional revenue a firm earns by employing one additional unit of an input, *ceteris paribus*. Also recall our earlier discussion of labour demand in a sandwich shop in Chapter 7. If an additional worker can produce 15 sandwiches in one hour (the marginal product of labour: $MP_L = 15$) and each sandwich brings in $0.50 (the price of the service produced by the sandwich shop: $P_X = \$0.50$), the marginal revenue product of labour is equal to $7.50 ($MRP_L = MP_L \times P_X = 15 \times \$0.50 = \$7.50$).

Now think carefully about the return to an additional unit of new capital (the marginal revenue product of capital). Suppose that the rate of return on an investment in a new machine is 15%. This means that the investment project yields the same return as a bond yielding 15%. If the current interest rate is less than 15%, the investment project will be undertaken because:

> A perfectly competitive profit-maximizing firm will keep investing in new capital up to the point at which the expected rate of return is equal to the interest rate. This is analogous to saying that the firm will continue investing up to the point at which the marginal revenue product of capital is equal to the price of capital, or $MRP_K = P_K$, which is what we learned in Chapter 10.

A Final Word on Capital

The concept of capital is one of the central ideas in economics. Capital is produced by the economic system itself. Capital generates services over time, and it is used as an input in the production of goods and services.

The enormous productivity of modern industrial societies is due in part to the tremendous amount of capital that they have accumulated over the years. It may surprise you to know that the average worker in Canada works with over $130 000 worth of capital. There is no question that the economic success of modern Japan resulted first and foremost from the very high rates of investment that began in that country after World War II and have continued for nearly 45 years.

The bulk of this chapter described the institutions and processes that determine the amount and types of capital produced in a market economy. Existing firms in search of increased profits, potential new entrants to the markets, and entrepreneurs with new ideas all are continuously evaluating potential investment projects. At the same time, households are saving. Each year households save some portion of their after-tax incomes. This new saving becomes part of their net worth, and they want to earn a return on it. Each year a good portion of the saving finds its way into the hands of firms who use it to buy new capital goods.

Between households and firms is the financial capital market. Millions of people participate in financial markets every day. There are literally thousands of financial managers, pension funds, mutual funds, brokerage houses, options traders, and banks whose sole purpose is to earn the highest possible rate of return on people's saving.

Brokers, bankers, and financial managers are continuously scanning the financial horizons for profitable investments. What businesses are doing well? What businesses are doing poorly? Should we lend to an expanding firm? All the analysis done by financial managers seeking to earn a high yield for clients, by managers of firms seeking to earn high profits for their stockholders, and by entrepreneurs seeking profits from innovation serves to channel capital into its most productive uses. Within firms, the evaluation of individual investment projects involves forecasting costs and benefits and valuing streams of potential income that will be earned only in future years.

We have now completed our discussion of competitive input and output markets. We have looked at household and firm choices in output markets, labour markets, land markets, and capital markets.

We now turn to a discussion of the allocative process that we have described. How do all the parts of the economy fit together? Is the result good or bad? Can we improve on it? All this is the subject of Chapter 12.

Summary

Capital, Investment, and Depreciation

1. The central feature of market capitalist systems is that the decision to put capital to use in a particular enterprise is made by private citizens putting their savings at risk in search of private gain. The set of institutions through which such transactions occur is called the *capital market*.

2. *Capital goods* are those goods produced by the economic system that are used as inputs to produce other goods and services in the future. Capital goods thus yield valuable productive services over time.

3. The major categories of *physical*, or *tangible*, *capital* are nonresidential structures, durable equiment, residential structures, and inventories. *Social capital* is capital that provides services to the public. *Intangible (nonmaterial) capital* includes *human capital* and goodwill.

4. The most important dimension of capital is that it exists through time. Therefore, its value is only as great as the value of the services it will render over time.

5. The most common measure of a firm's *capital stock* is the current market value of its plant, equipment, inventories, and intangible assets. However, in thinking about capital it is important to think of the actual capital stock rather than its simple monetary value.

6. In economics, the term *investment* refers to the creation of new capital, not to the purchase of a share of stock or a bond. Investment is a flow that increases the stock of capital.

7. *Depreciation* is the decline in an asset's economic value over time. A capital asset can depreciate because it wears out physically or because it becomes obsolete.

The Capital Market

8. Income that is earned on savings that have been put to use through *financial capital markets* is called *capital income*. The two most important forms of capital income are *interest* and *profits*. Interest is the fee paid by a borrower to a lender. Interest and profits reward households and entrepreneurs for innovation, risk taking, and postponing gratification.

9. In modern industrial societies, investment decisions (capital production decisions) are made primarily by firms. Households decide how much to save; and in the long run, saving limits the amount of investment that firms can undertake. The capital market exists in between to direct savings into profitable investment projects.

The Demand for New Capital and the Investment Decision

10. Before investing, investors must evaluate the expected flow of future productive services that an investment project will yield.

11. The availability of interest to lenders means that there is an opportunity cost associated with every investment project. This cost must be weighed against the stream of earnings that a project is expected to yield.

12. A firm will decide whether to undertake an investment project by comparing costs with expected returns. The *expected rate of return* on an investment project depends on the price of the investment, the expected length of time that the project provides additional cost savings or revenue, and the expected amount of revenue attributable each year to the project.

13. The investment demand curve shows the demand for capital in the economy as a function of the market interest rate. Only those investment projects that are expected to yield a rate of return higher than the market interest rate will be funded. Lower interest rates should stimulate investment.

14. A perfectly competitive profit-maximizing firm will keep investing in new capital up to the point at which the expected rate of return is equal to the interest rate. This is equivalent to saying that the firm will continue investing up to the point at which the marginal revenue product of capital is equal to the price of capital, or $MRP_K = P_K$.

Review Terms and Concepts

capital 270

capital income 275

capital market 273

capital stock 271

depreciation 272

expected rate of return 282

financial capital market 274

human capital 271

intangible capital 271

interest 275

investment 272

physical, or tangible, capital 270

profit 275

social capital, or infrastructure 270

Problem Set

1. During 1994 and 1995, the Bank of Canada took action to increase interest rates. How might this action affect the future productive capacity of the economy?

2. You and 99 other partners are offered the chance to buy a gas station. Each partner would put up $10 000. The revenues from the operation of the station have been steady at $420 000 per year for several years and are projected to remain steady into the future. The costs (not including opportunity costs) of operating the station (including maintenance and repair, depreciation, salaries, and so forth) have also been steady at $360 000 per year. Currently five-year Government of Canada bonds are yielding 7.5% interest. Would you go in on the deal?

3. The board of directors of the Quando Company in Singapore is presented with the following list of investment projects for implementation next year:

PROJECT	TOTAL COST SINGAPORE DOLLARS	ESTIMATED RATE OF RETURN
Factory in Kuala Lumpur	17 356 400	13%
Factory in Bangkok	15 964 200	15
A new company aircraft	10 000 000	12
A factory outlet store	3 500 000	18
A new computer network	2 000 000	20
A cafeteria for workers	1 534 000	7

Sketch total investment as a function of the interest rate (with the interest rate on the *Y* axis). Currently, the interest rate in Singapore is 8%. How much investment would you recommend to Quando's board?

4. In each of the following, identify who is saving and who is investing. There need not be both actions in every example.
   a. Frank sells some GM stock to Laura and uses the proceeds to buy 10 shares of BCE stock from Stefan.
   b. Sarah's income is $20 000 this year. She spent $19 000 and put the rest into BCE stock.
   c. A Toronto developer borrows $350 million from a group of banks and builds an office tower.
   d. Sarah's grandmother earns no income this year. Grandma supports herself by selling $5000 worth of bonds to a bond dealer.

   e. Tom's income this year was $100 000. He spent $90 000 and put the rest into Mexican government bonds. The Mexican government used the proceeds to help build a power plant.

5. "Lower interest rates are discouraging to households, and they are likely to invest less." Do you agree or disagree with this statement? Explain your answer.

6. Give at least three examples of how savings can be channelled into productive investment. Why is investment so important for an economy? What do you sacrifice when you invest today?

7. Explain what we mean when we say that "households supply capital and firms demand capital."

8. Suppose that I decide to start a small business. To raise start-up funds, I sell 1000 shares of stock for $100 each. For the next five years, I take in annual revenues of $50 000. My total annual costs of operating the business are $20 000. If all of my profits are paid out as dividends to shareholders, how much of my total annual profit can be considered economic profit? Assume that the current interest rate is 10%.

9. Describe the capital stock of your college or university. How would you go about measuring its value? Has your school made any major investments in recent years? If so, describe them. What does your school hope to gain from these investments?

Appendix to Chapter 11   Calculating Present Value

We have seen in this chapter that a firm's major goal in making investment decisions is to evaluate revenue streams that will not materialize until the future. One way for the firm to decide whether or not to undertake an investment project is to compare the expected rate of return from the investment with the current interest rate available in the financial market. This procedure was discussed in the text, although the way in which the expected rate of return is calculated was touched upon only briefly.

The purpose of this appendix is to present an alternative method of evaluating future revenue streams through present-value analysis.

Present Value

Consider the expected flow of profits from the investment shown in Table 11A.1 on page 288. If such a project cost $1200 to put in place, would the firm undertake it? At first glance, you might answer yes. After all, the total flow of profit is $1600. But this flow of profit is fully realized only after five years have passed. The same $1200 could be put into a government bond, where it would earn interest and perhaps produce a higher yield than if it were invested in the project. You can easily see that the desirability of the investment project will depend on the interest rate that is available in the market.

Table 11A.1

Expected Profits from a $1200 Investment Project

Year 1	$100
Year 2	100
Year 3	400
Year 4	500
Year 5	500
All later years	0
Total	$1600

Table 11A.2

Calculation of Total Present Value of a Hypothetical Investment Project (Assuming $r = 10\%$)

End Of . . .	(R)	Divided By $(1 + r)^t$	Present Value ($)
Year 1	100	(1.1)	90.91
Year 2	100	$(1.1)^2$	82.65
Year 3	400	$(1.1)^3$	300.53
Year 4	500	$(1.1)^4$	341.51
Year 5	500	$(1.1)^5$	310.46
Total present value:			1126.06

One way of thinking about interest is to say that it *allows us to buy and sell claims to future dollars.* Future dollars have prices in the present. That is, a contract for $1 to be delivered in one year, two years, or 10 years can be purchased today. How? By simply depositing a certain amount in an interest-bearing certificate or account. Using the *present prices* of future dollars gives us a way to compare values that will be realized in the future with present costs. This method allows us to evaluate investment projects that will yield benefits into the future.

It is not difficult to figure the "price" today of $1 to be delivered in one year. You must now pay an amount (X) such that when you get X back in one year with interest you will have $1. If r is the interest rate available in the market, r times X, or rX, is the amount of interest that X will earn for you in one year. Thus, at the end of a year you will have $X + rX$, or $X(1 + r)$, and you want this to be equal to $1. Solving for X algebraically:

$$\$1 = X(1 + r), \text{ so } X = \frac{\$1}{1 + r}$$

We say that X is the **present value (PV)**, or **present discounted value,** of $1 one year from now. Actually, X is the current market price of $1 to be delivered in one year. It is the amount you have to put aside now if you want to end up with $1 a year from now.

Now let's go more than one year into the future and consider more than a single dollar. For example, what is the present value of a claim on $100 in two years? Using the same logic as above, let X be the present value, or current market price, of $100 payable in two years. Thus, X plus the interest it would earn compounded for two years is equal to $100.[1] After one year, you would have $X + rX$, or $X(1 + r)$. After two years, you would have this amount plus another year's interest on the whole amount:

$$X(1 + r) + r[X(1 + r)]$$
or
$$X(1 + r)(1 + r), \text{ which is } X(1 + r)^2$$

Again solving algebraically for X:

$$\$100 = X(1 + r)^2, \text{ so } X = \frac{\$100}{(1 + r)^2}$$

If the market interest rate were 10%, or 0.10, then the present value of $100 in two years would be

$$X = \frac{\$100}{(1.1)^2} = \$82.65.$$

If you put $82.65 in a certificate earning 10% per year, you would earn $8.26 in interest after one year, giving you $90.91. Interest in the second year would be $9.09, leaving you with exactly $100 at the end of two years.

In general, the present value, or present discounted value, of R dollars t years from now is

$$PV = \frac{R}{(1 + r)^t}$$

Table 11A.2 calculates the present value of the income stream in Table 11A.1 at an interest rate of 10%. The

[1]*Thus far, all our examples have involved* simple interest—*interest that is computed on principal alone, not on principal plus interest. In the real world, however, many loans involve* compound interest—*interest that is computed on the basis of principal plus interest. If you deposit funds into an interest-compounding account at a bank and do not withdraw the interest payments as they are added to your account, you will earn interest on your previously earned interest.*

total present value turns out to be $1126.06. This tells the firm that it can simply go to the financial market today and buy a contract that pays $100 one year from now, another that pays $100 two years from now, still another that pays $400 three years from now, and so forth, all for the low price of $1126.06. To put this another way, it could lend out or deposit $1126.06 in an account paying a 10% interest rate, withdraw $100 next year, withdraw $100 in the following year, take another $400 at the end of three years, and so forth. When it takes its last $500 at the end of the fifth year, the account will be empty—the balance in the account will be exactly zero. Thus, *at current market interest rates*, the firm has exactly duplicated the income stream that the investment project would have yielded for a total present price of $1126.06. Why then would it pay out $1200 to undertake this investment? The answer, of course, is that it would not.

We can restate the point this way:

> If the present value of the income stream associated with an investment is less than the full cost of the investment project, the investment should not be undertaken.

It is important to remember here that we are discussing the *demand for new capital*. Business firms must evaluate potential investments in order to decide whether they are worth undertaking. This involves predicting the flow of potential future profits arising from each project and comparing those future profits with the return available in the financial market at the current interest rate. The present-value method allows firms to calculate how much it would *cost today* to purchase or contract for the exact same flow of earnings in the financial market.

Lower Interest Rates, Higher Present Values

Now suppose that interest rates fall from 10% to 5%. With a lower interest rate, the firm will have to *pay more* now to purchase the same number of future dollars. Take, for example, the present value of $100 in two years. You saw that if the firm puts aside $82.65 at 10% interest, it will have exactly $100 in two years; at a 10% interest rate, the present discounted value, or current market price, of $100 in two years is $82.65. But $82.65 put aside at a 5% interest rate would generate only $4.13 in interest in the first year and $4.34 in the sec-

Table 11A.3

Calculation of Total Present Value of a Hypothetical Investment Project (Assuming *r* = 5%)

End Of ...	$(R)	Divided By $(1 + r)^t$	Present Value ($)
Year 1	100	(1.05)	95.24
Year 2	100	$(1.05)^2$	90.70
Year 3	400	$(1.05)^3$	345.54
Year 4	500	$(1.05)^4$	411.35
Year 5	500	$(1.05)^5$	391.76
Total present value:			1334.59

ond year, for a total balance of $91.12 after two years. In order to get $100 in two years, the firm needs to put aside more than $82.65 now. Solving for X as we did before,

$$X = \frac{\$100}{(1 + r)^2} = \frac{\$100}{(1.05)^2} = \$90.70.$$

When the interest rate falls from 10% to 5%, the present value of $100 in two years rises by $8.05 ($90.70 − $82.65).

Table 11A.3 recalculates the present value of the full stream at the lower interest rate; it shows that a decrease in the interest rate from 10% to 5% causes the total present value to rise to $1334.59. Because the investment project will yield the same stream of earnings for a present price of only $1200, it is now a better deal than the financial markets. Under these conditions, a profit-maximizing firm will make the investment. (As discussed earlier, a lower interest rate leads to more investment.)

The basic rule is:

> If the present value of an expected stream of earnings from an investment exceeds the cost of the investment necessary to undertake it, then the investment should be undertaken. But if the present value of an expected stream of earnings falls short of the cost of the investment, then the financial market can generate the same stream of income for a smaller initial investment, and the investment should not be undertaken. When the interest rate or the rate of return offered by the market exceeds the rate of return on a project, the investment is not justified at the current interest rate.

Present Value

1. The present value (*PV*) of *R* dollars to be paid *t* years in the future is the amount you need to pay today, at current interest rates, to ensure that you end up with *R* dollars *t* years from now. It is the current market value of receiving *R* dollars in *t* years.

Lower Interest Rates, Higher Present Values

2. If the present value of the income stream associated with an investment is less than the full cost of the investment project, the investment project should not be undertaken. If the present value of an expected stream of income exceeds the cost of the investment necessary to undertake it, then the investment should be undertaken.

Review Terms and Concepts

present value (*PV*) or **present discounted value** The present discounted value of *R* dollars to be paid *t* years in the future is the amount you need to pay today, at current interest rates, to ensure that you end up with *R* dollars *t* years from now. It is the current market value of receiving *R* dollars in *t* years. 288

Equation:

$$PV = \frac{R}{(1 + r)^t}$$

Problem Set

1. Your Uncle Joe has just died and left $10 000 payable to you when you turn 30 years old. You are now 20. Currently, the annual rate of interest one can obtain by buying 10-year bonds is 6.5%. Your brother offers you $6000 cash right now to sign over your inheritance. Would you do it?

2. A special task force has determined that the present discounted value of the benefits from a bridge project comes to $23 786 000. The total construction cost of the bridge is $25 000 000. This implies that the bridge should be built. Do you agree with this conclusion? Explain your answer. What impact could a substantial decline in interest rates have on your answer?

3. Calculate the present value of the income streams A–E, in Table 1 at right, at an 8% interest rate and again at a 10% rate.

Suppose that the investment behind the flow of income in E is a machine that cost $1235 at the beginning of year 1. Would you buy the machine if the interest rate were 8%? If the interest rate were 10%?

Table 1

End Of Year	A	B	C	D	E
1	$80	$80	$100	$100	$500
2	80	80	100	100	300
3	80	80	1100	100	400
4	80	80	0	100	300
5	1080	80	0	100	0
6	0	80	0	1100	0
7	0	1080	0	0	0

General Equilibrium and the Efficiency of Perfect Competition

I n the last seven chapters, we have built a model of a simple perfectly competitive economy. Our discussion has revolved around the two fundamental decision-making units, *households* and *firms,* which interact in two basic market arenas, *input markets* and *output markets.* (Look again at the circular flow diagram, shown in Figure 12.1 on page 292.) By limiting our discussion to perfectly competitive firms, we have been able to examine in detail how the basic decision-making units interact in the two basic market arenas.

Households make constrained choices in both input and output markets. In Chapter 5 we discussed an individual household demand curve for a single good or service. Then in Chapter 6 we went behind the demand curve and saw how income, wealth, and prices define the budget constraints within which households exercise their tastes and preferences. We soon discovered, however, that we could not look at household decisions in output markets without thinking about the decisions that are made simultaneously in input markets. Household income, for example, depends on choices made in input markets: whether to work, how much to work, what skills to acquire, and so forth. Input market choices are constrained by such factors as current wage rates, the availability of jobs, and interest rates.

Firms are the primary producing units in a market economy. Profit-maximizing firms, to which we have limited our discussion, earn their profits by selling products and services for more than it costs to produce them. With firms, as with households, output markets and input markets cannot be analyzed separately. All firms make three specific decisions

FIGURE 12.1

Firm and Household Decisions

Firms and households interact in both input and output markets.

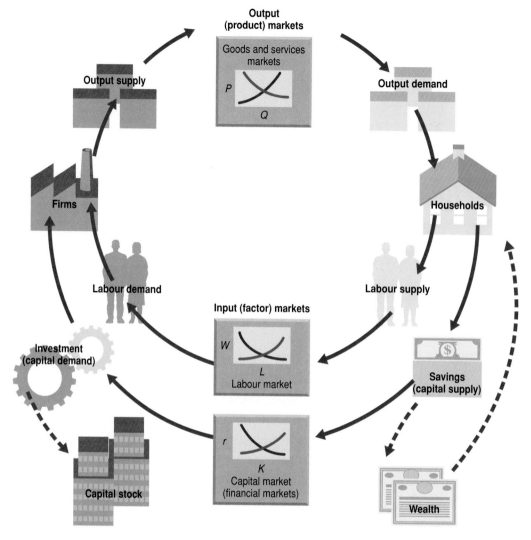

Output (product) markets

Goods and services markets

P

Q

Output supply

Output demand

Firms

Households

Labour demand

Labour supply

Input (factor) markets

W

L

Labour market

Investment (capital demand)

Savings (capital supply)

r

K

Capital market (financial markets)

Capital stock

Wealth

simultaneously: (1) how much output to supply, (2) how to produce that output (that is, which technology to use), and (3) how much of each input to demand.

In Chapters 7–9, we explored these three decisions from the viewpoint of output markets. We saw that the portion of the marginal cost curve that lies above a firm's average variable cost curve is the supply curve of a perfectly competitive firm in the short run. Implicit in the marginal cost curve is a choice of technology and a set of input demands. In Chapters 10 and 11, we looked at the perfectly competitive firm's three basic decisions from the viewpoint of input markets.

Output and input markets are connected because firms and households make simultaneous choices in both arenas. But there are other connections among markets as well. Firms buy in both capital and labour markets, for example, and they can substitute capital for labour and vice versa. A change in the price of one factor can easily change the demand for other factors. Buying more *capital*, for instance, usually changes the marginal revenue product of *labour* and shifts the labour demand curve. Similarly, a change in the price of a single good or service usually affects household demand for other goods and services, as when a price decrease makes one good more attractive than other close substitutes. The same change also makes households better off when they find that the same amount of income will buy more. Such additional "real income" can be spent on any of the other goods and services that the household buys.

The point here is simple:

> Input and output markets cannot be considered separately or as if they operated independently. While it is important to understand the decisions of individual firms and households and the functioning of individual markets, we now need to "add it all up," to look at the operation of the system as a whole.

You have seen the concept of equilibrium applied both to markets and to individual decision-making units. In individual markets, supply and demand determine an equilibrium price. Perfectly competitive firms are in short-run equilibrium when price and marginal cost are equal ($P = MC$). In the long run, however, equilibrium in a competitive market is achieved only when economic profits are eliminated. Households are in equilibrium when they have equated the marginal utility per dollar spent on each good to the marginal utility per dollar spent on every *other* good. This process of examining the equilibrium conditions in individual markets and for individual households and firms separately is called **partial equilibrium analysis.**

A **general equilibrium** exists when all markets in an economy are in simultaneous equilibrium. An event that disturbs the equilibrium in one market may disturb the equilibrium in many other markets as well. The ultimate impact of the event depends upon the way *all* markets adjust to it. Thus, partial equilibrium analysis, which looks at adjustments in one isolated market, may be misleading.

Thinking in terms of a general equilibrium leads to some important questions. Is it possible for all households and firms and all markets to be in equilibrium simultaneously? Are the equilibrium conditions that we have discussed separately compatible with one another? Why is an event that disturbs an equilibrium in one market likely to disturb many others simultaneously?

In talking about general equilibrium, the first concept we explore in this chapter, we continue our exercise in *positive economics*—that is, we seek to understand how systems operate without making value judgments about outcomes. Later in the chapter, we turn from positive economics to *normative economics* as we begin to judge the economic system. Are its results good or bad? Can we make them better?

In judging the performance of any economic system, you will recall, it is essential first to establish specific criteria to judge by. In this chapter, we use two such criteria: *efficiency* and *equity* (fairness). First we demonstrate that the allocation of resources is **efficient**—that is, the system produces what people want and does so at the least possible cost—if all the assumptions that we have made thus far hold. When we begin to relax some of our assumptions, however, it will become apparent that free markets may *not* be efficient. Several sources of inefficiency naturally occur within an unregulated market system. In the final part of this chapter, we introduce the potential role of government in correcting market inefficiencies and achieving fairness.

partial equilibrium analysis *The process of examining the equilibrium conditions in individual markets and for households and firms separately.*

general equilibrium *The condition that exists when all markets in an economy are in simultaneous equilibrium.*

efficiency *The condition in which the economy is producing what people want at least possible cost.*

General Equilibrium Analysis

Two examples will help us illustrate some of the insights that we can gain when we move from partial to general equilibrium analysis. In this section, we will consider the impact on the economy of (1) a major technological advance and (2) a shift in consumer preferences. This chapter's Global Perspective box, "Growth and Change in Global Markets," provides some other examples. As you read, remember

Global Perspective

Growth and Change in Global Markets

As the world moved into 1997, different sectors and different regions of the Canadian economy were experiencing different rates of growth and change. So too were different countries around the world growing and changing in different ways. The following excerpts from the *Financial Post* describe some of these changes. Each illustrates important links between markets. They show how changes in product demand, for example, can have an impact on labour and capital markets, and how labour and capital markets can affect product markets.

1. Demand for products produced in Japan affects the demand for steel produced in Japan, which affects the demand for coal produced in British Columbia:[1]

The demand for lumber, construction labourers, cement, and other inputs in the residential construction industry is influenced by developments in other markets. The interest rate in the capital market has an especially significant impact on the residential construction industry.

> The picturesque B.C. town [of Tumbler Ridge], home to coal miners working at the Bullmoose and Quinette mines, is breathing easier after last week's agreement between Japanese buyers and mine owner Teck Corp.....
>
> The Bullmoose and Quinette mines were developed in response to Japanese demands for coal to fuel Japan's booming steel industry, says Jim Wood, director of communications for the Calgary-based

> Coal Association of Canada. In the late 1970s, Japan expected to have phenomenal growth and believed more and more coal would be needed to fuel that growth. They also wanted to diversify their energy sources away from oil.
>
> In the early 1980s they latched onto northeastern B.C. with a deal that involved mining companies, the B.C. government and Ottawa. Two mines were developed: the Bullmoose open-pit coal mine, now owned

> 61% by Teck in partnership with Rio Algom and Nissho Iwai Canada Ltd., and the Quinette mine, 60 km south of the Bullmoose mine, now owned 45% by Teck and managed by the company.
>
> To service the new mines, a new town was carved out of the wilderness at Tumbler Ridge, roads were built, rail lines were upgraded, a new power line was built, and new coal-handling capabilities were added to Prince Rupert's Ridley

that we are looking for the connections between markets, particularly between input and output markets.

A Technological Advance: The Electronic Calculator

Graduate students working in quantitative fields of study in the late 1960s, and even as late as the early 1970s, recall classrooms filled with noisy mechanical calculators. At that time, a calculator weighed about 18 kilograms and was only able

Island. Ten new coal trains, of 100 cars each plus locomotives, were ordered....

Over time, however, the Japanese realized the economic growth they had expected wouldn't materialize. They didn't need all the coal being produced and didn't want to pay for it.... The price and volume were negotiated downward in the 1980s, but the next few years were secure.

With the new contracts [1997] "the mines will continue to produce and the town will exist into the next century," Wood says.

2. Growth in business and tourist travel increases demand for hotel rooms, which increases the price of hotel accommodation and the prices of hotels.[2]

Canadians making hotel reservations often find the rooms filled earlier and the prices higher than in recent years. That may not be good news for travellers, but it is welcome news to the hotel industry and its investors.

Capital investment in the Canadian lodging industry was $500 million last year, up 22% from the year before, according to a report by the hotel division of brokerage firm Colliers Macaulay Nicolls Inc. Hotels are no longer the debt-laden distress properties that fell to the banks in the debt and liquidity crisis of the early 1990s. Real estate is attractive again because of "improved operating performance, low interest rates and the formation of large capital pools, particularly in the U.S.," the report says.

Hotel sales have dropped off somewhat this year since the prices they are commanding are much higher than in the past few years and some owners have chosen to hang on hopes of a greater upside, say industry watchers.

But as long as it's cheaper to buy a hotel than build one, room rates and occupancy should continue to increase. New construction doesn't usually begin until occupancy climbs above 75%. In 1995, the average Canadian hotel occupancy rate was 61.4%, says the Collier report.

3. Interest rates decrease in the capital market, increasing demand for new and existing housing. (That is, more people look to buy existing houses and the number of new housing projects increases.) Higher housing demand stimulates sectors producing inputs and complementary products like lumber and carpets.[3]

Housing starts are expected to increase 13.7% this year and show further gains in 1998, Canada Mortgage and Housing Corp. said Friday. In its regular housing outlook, the government agency predicted housing starts will rise to 141 800 in 1997 and 150 700 in 1998, compared with 124 713 in 1996.

New housing activity is expected to be spurred by low mortgage rates, a strong increase in jobs, and improving consumer confidence. "So far in this recovery, housing activity has been riding the coattails of lower mortgage rates," said CMHC economist Michel Laurence.

Over the next two years, further momentum in housing will come from stronger private job creation, as consumer spending finally joins exports in boosting employment levels to new highs.

Sources: [1]Johanna Powell, "Coal Sector Gets Boost from Japan's Steel Industry [Bullmoose and Quinette Mines]," *The Financial Post*, (May 10/12, 1997): p. 39. [2]Barbara Shecter, "Low Rates, Restructurings, Bring Hotels Back to Life," *The Financial Post* (September 14/16, 1996): p. 55. [3]"Housing Starts Expected To Increase 13.7% in 1997," *The Financial Post* (February 8/10, 1997): p. 4; Dow Jones.

to add, subtract, multiply, and divide. These machines had no memory, and they took 20 to 25 seconds to do one multiplication problem.

Major corporations had rooms full of accountants with such calculators on their desks, and the sound when 30 or 40 of them were running was deafening. During the 1950s and 1960s, most firms had these machines, but few people had a calculator in their homes because the cost of a single machine was several hundred dollars. Some high schools had calculators for accounting classes, but most schoolchildren in Canada had never seen one.

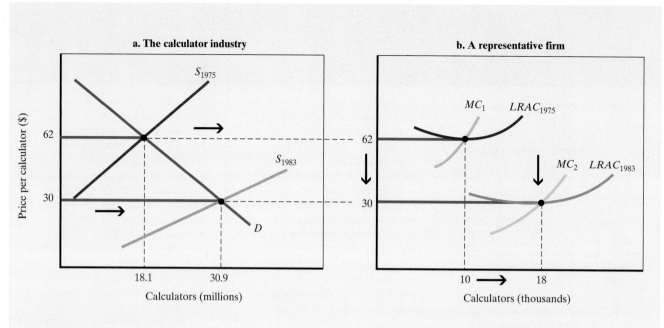

a. The calculator industry

b. A representative firm

FIGURE 12.2

Cost-Saving Technological Change in the Calculator Industry

The 1970s and 1980s brought major technological changes to the calculator industry. In 1975, 18.1 million calculators were sold at an average price of $62. As technology made it possible to produce at lower costs, cost curves shifted downward. As new firms entered the industry and existing firms expanded, output rose and market price dropped. In 1983, 30.9 million calculators were produced and sold at an average price of $30.

In the 1960s, Wang Laboratories developed an electronic calculator. Bigger than a modern personal computer, it had several keyboards attached to a single main processor. It could add, subtract, multiply, and divide, but it also had a memory. Its main virtue was speed and quietness. It did calculations instantaneously without any noise. The Wang machine sold for around $2800.

The beginning of the 1970s saw rapid developments in the industry. First, calculators shrank in size. The Bomar Corporation made one of the earliest hand-held calculators, the Bomar Brain. These early versions could do nothing more than add, subtract, multiply, and divide, they had no memory, and they still sold for several hundred dollars. Then, in the early 1970s, a number of technological breakthroughs made it possible to mass produce very small electronic circuits (silicon chips). This, in turn, made calculators very inexpensive to produce, and it is here that we begin our general equilibrium story. Costs in the calculator industry shifted downward dramatically (Figure 12.2b). As costs fell, profits increased. Attracted by economic profits, new firms rapidly entered the market. Instead of one or two firms producing state-of-the-art machines, dozens of firms began cranking them out by the thousands. As a result, the industry supply curve shifted out to the right, driving down prices toward the new lower costs (see Figure 12.2a).

As the price of electronic calculators fell, the market for the old mechanical calculators died a quiet death. With no more demand for their product, producers found themselves suffering losses and got out of the business. As the price of electronic calculators kept falling, thousands of people who had never had a calculator began to buy them. By 1973, calculators were available at discount appliance stores for under $100, and by 1975, 18.1 million were produced annually and sold at an average price of $62. The average price fell to under $30 by 1983. You can now buy a basic calculator for less than $5, or get one free with a magazine subscription.

The rapid decline in the cost of producing calculators led to a rapid expansion of supply and a decline in price. (See Figure 12.2a.) The lower prices increased the quantity demanded to such an extent that most homes now have at least one calculator, and thousands of people walk around with calculators in their pockets.

This is only a partial equilibrium story, however. The events we described above also had effects on many other markets. In other words, they disturbed the general equilibrium. When mechanical calculators became obsolete, many people who had over the years developed the skills required to produce and repair those complex machines found themselves unemployed. At the same time, demand for workers in the production, distribution, and sales of the new electronic calculators boomed. New skills were required, and the expansion of the industry led to an increase in demand for the kinds of labour needed. The new technology thus caused a reallocation of labour across the labour market.

Capital was also reallocated. New firms invested in the plant and equipment needed to produce electronic calculators. Old capital owned by the firms that previously made mechanical calculators became obsolete and depreciated, and it ended up on the scrapheap. The mechanical calculators themselves, once an integral part of the capital stocks of accounting firms, banks, and so forth, were scrapped as they became obsolete and were replaced by the cheaper, more efficient new models.

When a new billion-dollar industry suddenly appears, it earns billions of dollars in revenues that might have been spent on other things. Even though the effects of this success on any one other industry were probably small, general equilibrium analysis tells us that in the absence of the new industry and the demand for its product, households will demand other goods and services, and other industries will produce more. In this case, society has benefited a great deal. Everyone can now buy a very useful product at a low price. The new calculators have raised the productivity of certain kinds of labour and reduced costs in many industries.

The point here is clear:

> A significant—if not sweeping—technological change in a single industry affects many markets. Households face a different structure of prices and must adjust their consumption of many products. Labour reacts to new skill requirements and is reallocated across markets. Capital is also reallocated.

A SHIFT IN CONSUMER PREFERENCES: THE WINE INDUSTRY IN THE 1970S

For a more formal view of the general equilibrium effects of a change in one market on other markets, consider an economy with just two sectors, X and Y. For purposes of our discussion, let us say that the wine business in Canada is industry X and everything else is industry Y. Let us also assume that the wine industry is perfectly competitive.

During the 1970s, Canadian consumer preferences in alcoholic beverages shifted significantly in favour of wine. Table 12.1 on the next page provides some data. Domestic wine production increased by 254% between 1965 and 1980. In addition, in 1980 Canada imported almost nine times as much wine as it had in 1965. Overall demand increased 430%. Part of this increase was due to increased population, part was probably due to a change in the age distribution of the population, and part was due to a simple change in preferences. Per capita consumption of wine rose 319%.

Figure 12.3 shows the initial equilibrium in sectors X and Y. We assume that both sectors are initially in long-run competitive equilibrium. Total output in sector X is Q_X^0, the product is selling for a price of P_X^0, and each firm in the industry produces up to where P_X^0 is equal to marginal cost—q_X^0. At that point, price is just equal to average cost, and economic profits are zero. The same condition holds initially in sector Y. The market is in zero profit equilibrium at a price of P_Y^0.

Now assume that a change in consumer preferences (or in the age distribution of the population, or in something else) shifts the demand for X out to the right from D_X^0 to D_X^1. That shift drives price up to P_X^1. If households decide to buy more X, without an increase in income they must buy *less* of something else. Since everything else is represented by Y in this example, the demand for Y must decline, and the demand curve for Y shifts to the left from D_Y^0 to D_Y^1.

With the shift in demand for X, price rises to P_X^1 and profit-maximizing firms immediately increase output to q_X^1 (the point where $P_X^1 = MC_X$). But now there are economic profits in X, profits over and above a normal rate of return. With the downward shift of demand in Y, price falls to P_Y^1. Firms in sector Y cut back to q_Y^1 (the point where $P_Y^1 = MC_Y$), and the lower price causes firms producing Y to suffer economic losses.

In the short run, adjustment is simple. Firms in both industries are constrained by their current scales of plant. Firms can neither enter nor exit their respective industries. Each firm in industry X raises output somewhat, from q_X^0 to q_X^1. Firms in industry Y cut back from q_Y^0 to q_Y^1.

In response to the existence of economic profit in sector X, the capital market begins to take notice. In Chapter 9 we said that new firms are likely to enter an industry in which there are economic profits to be earned. Financial analysts see the economic profits as a signal of future healthy growth, and entrepreneurs may become interested in moving into the industry.

Adding all this together, we would expect to see investment begin to favour sector X. This is indeed the case. Capital begins to flow into sector X. As new firms enter, the short-run supply curve in the industry shifts to the right and continues to do so until all economic profits are eliminated. In the top left diagram in Figure 12.3, the supply curve shifts out from S_X^0 to S_X^1, a shift that drives the price back down to P_X^0.

We would also expect to see a movement out of sector Y because of the existence of economic losses. Some firms will exit the industry. In the bottom left

	Table 12.1	**Production and Consumption of Wine in Canada, 1965–1980**		
Year	*Canadian Production (Thousands of litres)*	*Imports (Thousands of litres)*	*Total (Thousands of litres)*	*Consumption per Capita (litres)*
1965	6 589	3 369	9 958	0.51
1970	10 468	6 647	17 115	0.80
1975	16 771	12 265	29 036	1.40
1980	23 375	29 370	52 745	2.14
Percent change, 1965–1980	+254	+771	+430	+319

Source: Statistics Canada, *The Control and Sale of Alcoholic Beverages in Canada,* Cat. no. 63-202.

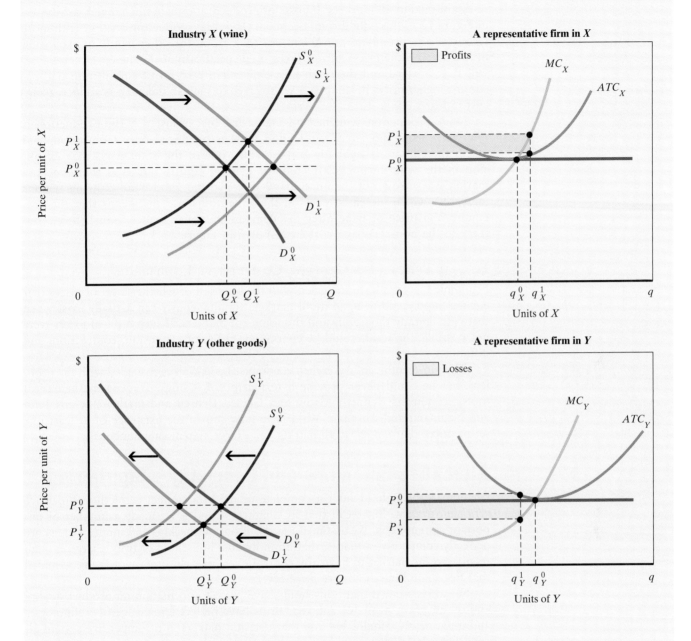

FIGURE 12.3

Adjustment in an Economy with Two Sectors

Initially, demand for X shifts from D_X^0 to D_X^1. This shift pushes the price of X up to P_X^1, creating economic profits. Demand for Y shifts down from D_Y^0 to D_Y^1, pushing the price of Y down to P_Y^1, and creating economic losses. Firms have an incentive to leave sector Y and an incentive to enter sector X. Exiting sector Y shifts supply in that industry to S_Y^1, raising price and eliminating losses. Entry and expansion shift supply in X to S_Y^1, thus reducing price and eliminating profits.

diagram in Figure 12.3, the supply curve shifts back from S_Y^0 to S_Y^1, a shift that drives the price back up to P_Y^0. At this point all economic losses are eliminated.

Note that a new general equilibrium is not reached until equilibrium is re-established in all markets. If costs of production remain unchanged, as they do in Figure 12.3, this equilibrium occurs at the initial product prices, but with more resources and production in X and less in Y. If, on the other hand, an expansion in X drives up the prices of resources used specifically in X, the cost curves in X will shift upward and the final, post-expansion, zero-profit equilibrium will occur at a higher price. In Chapter 9 we referred to such an industry as an increasing-cost industry.

Wine production is in fact an increasing-cost industry. Wine production is relatively "land intensive," and good wine is produced only from good land where the climate is right for grapes. Thus, one of the other ways that expansion in the wine business affected the general equilibrium was that the land market was thrown off balance. Land prices in the good wine-growing regions increased, which increased costs in the wine industry. This means that the new equilibrium price of wine after the demand shift was higher than before, contrary to the nonincreasing cost case shown in Figure 12.3.

FORMAL PROOF OF A GENERAL COMPETITIVE EQUILIBRIUM

Economic theorists have struggled with the question of whether a set of prices that equates supply and demand in all markets simultaneously can actually exist when there are literally thousands and thousands of markets. If such a set of prices were not possible, the result could be continuous cycles of expansion, contraction, and instability.

The nineteenth-century French economist Leon Walras struggled with the problem, but he could never provide a formal proof. Using advanced mathematical tools, economists Kenneth Arrow and Gerard Debreu and mathematicians John von Neumann and Abraham Wald have now shown the existence of at least one set of prices that *will* clear all markets in a large system simultaneously.

Allocative Efficiency and Competitive Equilibrium

Chapters 4 through 11 built a complete model of a simple, perfectly competitive economic system. But recall that in Chapters 4 and 5 we made a number of important assumptions. We assumed that both output markets and input markets are perfectly competitive—that is, that no individual household or firm is large enough relative to the market to have any control over price. In other words, we assumed that firms and households are *price takers*.

We also assumed that households have perfect information on product quality and on all prices available and that firms have perfect knowledge of technologies and input prices. Finally, we said that decision makers in a competitive system always consider all the costs and benefits of their decisions, that there are no "external" costs.

If all these assumptions hold, the economy will produce an efficient allocation of resources. As we relax these assumptions one by one, however, you will discover that the allocation of resources is no longer efficient and that a number of sources of inefficiency occur naturally.

PARETO EFFICIENCY

In Chapter 1 we introduced several specific criteria used by economists to judge the performance of economic systems and to evaluate alternative economic policies.

These criteria are (1) efficiency, (2) equity, (3) growth, and (4) stability. In Chapter 1 you also learned that an *efficient* economy is one that produces the things that people want and does so at least cost. The idea behind the efficiency criterion is that the economic system exists to serve the wants and needs of the people in a society. If resources can be somehow reallocated to make the people "better off," then they should be. We want to use the resources at our disposal to produce maximum well-being; the trick is defining "maximum well-being."

For many years, social philosophers wrestled with the problem of "aggregation." When we say "maximum well-being" we mean "maximum" *for society*. Societies are made up of many people, however, and the problem has always been how to maximize satisfaction, or well-being, for all members of society. What has emerged is the now widely accepted concept of *allocative efficiency*, first developed by the Italian economist Vilfredo Pareto in the nineteenth century. Pareto's very precise definition of efficiency is often referred to as **Pareto efficiency** or **Pareto optimality.**

Specifically, a change is said to be efficient if it at least potentially makes some members of society better off without making other members of society worse off. An efficient, or *Pareto optimal*, system is one in which no such changes are possible. An example of a change that makes some people better off and nobody worse off is a simple voluntary exchange. I have apples; you have nuts. I like nuts; you like apples. We trade. We both gain, and no one loses.

For such a definition to have any real meaning, we must answer two questions: (1) what do we mean by "better off"? and (2) how do we account for changes that make some people better off and others worse off?

The answer to the first question is simple. People themselves decide what "better off" and "worse off" mean. I am the only one who knows whether I'm better off after a change. If you and I exchange one item for another because I like what you have and you like what I have, we both "reveal" that we are better off after the exchange because we agreed to it voluntarily. If everyone in the neighbourhood wants a park and they all contribute to a fund to build one, they have consciously changed the allocation of resources, and they all are better off for it.

The answer to the second question is more complex. Nearly every change that one can imagine leaves some people better off and some people worse off. If some gain and some lose as the result of a change, and it can be demonstrated that the value of the gains exceeds the value of the losses, then the change is said to be *potentially efficient*. In practice, however, the distinction between a *potential* and an *actual* efficient change is often ignored, and all such changes are simply called *efficient*.

Pareto efficiency or **Pareto optimality** *A condition in which no change is possible that will make some members of society better off without making some other members of society worse off.*

■ **Example: Budget Cuts and Motor Vehicle Registration** In recent years governments have cut spending in an effort to deal with large government deficits. Almost every area of government has been affected, including motor vehicle registration offices. This has meant, among other things, reductions in the number of clerks in motor vehicle registration offices. As a consequence, motor vehicle owners have found themselves waiting in longer lines when they want to register their vehicles or get a driver's licence.

Clearly, drivers and car owners began paying a price: standing in line, which uses time and energy that could otherwise be used more productively. But before we can make sensible efficiency judgments, we must be able to measure, or at least approximate, the value of both the gains and the losses produced by the budget cut. To approximate the losses to car owners and drivers, we might ask how much people would be willing to pay to avoid standing in those long lines.

Consider an office where 500 people stood in line every day for about one hour each. If each person were willing to pay just $2 to avoid standing in line, the damage incurred would be $1000 (500 × $2) per day. If the registry were open 250 days per year, the reduction in labour force at that office alone would create a cost to car owners, conservatively estimated, of $250 000 (250 × $1000) per year.

Suppose that taxpayers saved about $80 000 per year by having fewer clerks at that office. If the clerks were reinstated, there would be some gains and some losses. Car owners and drivers would gain, and taxpayers would lose. But since we can show that the value of the gains would substantially exceed the value of the losses, it can be argued that reinstating the clerks would be an efficient change. Note that the only *net* losers would be those taxpayers who don't own a car and don't hold driver's licences.[1]

THE EFFICIENCY OF PERFECT COMPETITION

In Chapter 2 we discussed the "economic problem" of dividing up scarce resources among alternative uses. We also discussed the three basic questions that all societies must answer, and we set out to explain how these three questions are answered in a competitive economy:

> The Three Basic Questions
>
> 1. *What will be produced?* What determines the final mix of output?
> 2. *How will it be produced?* How do capital, labour, and land get divided up among firms? In other words, what is the allocation of resources among producers?
> 3. *Who will get what is produced?* What determines which households get how much? What is the distribution of output among consuming households?

The following discussion of efficiency uses these three questions and their answers as the bases for an informal "proof" of the efficiency of competition. To demonstrate that the perfectly competitive system leads to an efficient, or Pareto optimal, allocation of resources, we need to show that no changes are possible that will make some people better off without making others worse off. Specifically, we will show that under perfect competition (1) resources are allocated among firms efficiently, (2) final products are distributed among households efficiently, and (3) the system produces the things that people want.

■ **Efficient Allocation of Resources among Firms** The simple definition of efficiency holds that firms must produce their products using the best available—that is, lowest cost—technology. Clearly, if more output could be produced with the same amount of inputs, it would be possible to make some people better off without making others worse off.

The competitive model we have been using rests on several assumptions that assure us that resources in such a system would indeed be efficiently allocated among firms. Most important of these is the assumption that individual firms maximize profits. To maximize profit, a firm must minimize the cost of producing its chosen level of output. With a full knowledge of existing

---

[1]*But, you might ask, aren't there other gainers and losers? What about the clerks themselves? In analyses like this one, it is usually assumed that the citizens who pay lower taxes now spend their added income on other things. The producers of those other things need to expand to meet the new demand, and they hire more labour. Thus, a contraction of 100 jobs in the public sector will open up 100 jobs in the private sector. If the economy is fully employed, the transfer of labour to the private sector is assumed to create no net gains or losses to the workers themselves.*

technologies, firms will choose the technology that produces the output it wants at least cost.

There is more to this story than meets the eye, however. Inputs must be allocated *across* firms in the best possible way. If we find that it is possible, for example, to take capital from firm A and swap it for labour from firm B and produce more product in both firms, then the original allocation was inefficient. Recall our example from Chapter 2. Farmers in Saskatchewan and P.E.I. both produce wheat and potatoes. The climate and soil in most of Saskatchewan are best suited to wheat production; the climate and soil in P.E.I. are best suited to potato production. Clearly, Saskatchewan should produce most of the wheat and P.E.I. should produce most of the potatoes. A law that forces Saskatchewan land into potato production and P.E.I. land into wheat production would result in less of both—an inefficient allocation of resources. But if markets are free and open, Saskatchewan farmers will naturally find a higher return by planting wheat, and P.E.I. farmers will find a higher return in potatoes. The free market, then, should lead to an efficient allocation of resources among firms.

The same argument can be made more general. Misallocation of resources among firms is unlikely as long as every single firm faces the same set of prices and trade-offs in input markets. Recall from Chapter 10 that perfectly competitive firms will hire additional factors of production as long as their marginal revenue product exceeds their market price. As long as all firms have access to the *same* factor markets and the *same* factor prices, the last unit of a factor hired will produce the same value in each firm. Certainly firms will use different technologies and factor combinations, but at the margin, no single profit-maximizing firm can get more value out of a factor than that factor's current market price. If, for example, workers can be hired in the labour market at a wage of $6.50, *all* firms will hire workers as long as the marginal revenue product produced by the marginal worker (labour's marginal revenue product—MRP_L) remains above $6.50. *No* firms will hire labour beyond the point at which MRP_L falls below $6.50. Thus, at equilibrium, additional workers are not worth more than $6.50 to any firm, and switching labour from one firm to another will not produce output of any greater value to society. Each firm has hired the profit-maximizing amount of labour. In short:

> The assumptions that factor markets are competitive and open, that all firms pay the same prices for inputs, and that all firms maximize profits lead to the conclusion that the allocation of resources among firms is efficient.

■ **Efficient Distribution of Outputs among Households** Even if the system is producing the right things, and is doing so efficiently, these things still have to get to the right people. The Joneses shouldn't end up with the things that the Smiths like, and the Smiths shouldn't end up with the things that the Joneses like. Just as open, competitive factor markets ensure that firms don't end up with the wrong inputs, open, competitive output markets ensure that households don't end up with the wrong goods and services.

Within the constraints imposed by income and wealth, households are free to choose among all the goods and services available in output markets. A household will buy a good as long as that good generates utility, or subjective value, greater than its market price. Utility value is revealed in market behaviour. You don't go out and buy something unless you are willing to pay *at least* the market price.

Remember that the value you place on any one good depends on what you must give up to have that good. The trade-offs available to you depend on your budget constraint. The trade-offs that are desirable depend on your preferences. If you buy a $400 CD player for your residence room, you may be giving up a trip home. If I buy it, I may be giving up four new tires for my car. But we've both revealed that the CD player is worth at least as much to us as all the other things that $400 can buy. As long as we are free to choose among all the things that $400 can buy, we will not end up with the wrong things; it's not possible to find a trade that will make us both better off.

This argument is really quite intuitive:

> We all know that people have different tastes and preferences, and that they will buy very different things in very different combinations. But as long as everyone shops freely in the same markets, no redistribution of final outputs among people will make them better off. If you and I buy in the same markets and pay the same prices, and I buy what I want and you buy what you want, neither of us can possibly end up with the wrong combination of things.

■ **Producing What People Want: The Efficient Mix of Output** It does no good to produce things efficiently or to distribute them efficiently if the system produces the wrong things. Will competitive markets produce the things that people want?

If the system is producing the wrong mix of output, we should be able to show that producing more of one good and less of another will make people better off. To show that perfectly competitive markets are efficient, then, we must demonstrate that no such changes in the final mix of output are possible.

The condition that ensures that the right things are produced is $P = MC$. That is, in both the long run and the short run, a perfectly competitive firm will produce at the point where the price of its output is equal to the marginal cost of production. The logic is this: when a firm weighs price and marginal cost, it weighs the

The value placed on good X by society through the market, or the social value of a marginal unit of X

If $P_X > MC_X$, society gains value by producing *more X*.
If $P_X < MC_X$, society gains value by producing *less X*.

Market-determined value of resources needed to produce a marginal unit of X. MC_X is equal to the opportunity cost of those resources: lost production of other goods or the value of the resources left unemployed (leisure, vacant land, etc.)

FIGURE 12.4

The Key Efficiency Condition: Price Equals Marginal Cost

Society will produce the efficient mix of output if all firms equate price and marginal cost.

value of its product to society *at the margin* against the value of the things that could otherwise be produced with the same resources. If product Y is worth more to people than what otherwise could be produced with the same resources, then competition ensures that product Y will be produced instead of those other things. Figure 12.4 summarizes this logic.

But this is true *only if price is a good measure of the value that society places on a good and only if marginal cost is a good measure of the value of the things that might otherwise be produced with the same resources.* Indeed, price is sometimes a good measure of the worth of a marginal unit of a good or service to society.[2] Anyone who subjectively values a good or service at more than its market price buys that good or service; anyone who values it less than the market price does not buy it. Thus, when a *marginal* unit of product is produced, the person or household that ends up with that marginal unit is that person or household that values it just at the market price.

To establish that marginal cost is a good measure of the societal cost, or opportunity cost, of additional production of a good, let's turn back to input markets. Resources are required to produce an added unit of output. These resources come from one of two sources: either they were previously unused (or unemployed), or they were used (or employed) but in the production of some other good or service.

Consider labour as an example of a factor that would otherwise have been employed producing something else. Recall that workers are paid a wage just equal to the marginal revenue product of labour ($W = MRP_L = P_X \times MP_L$). Thus, if a certain amount of labour is drawn out of the production of good X, society loses an amount of product X equal in value to the value of the labour withdrawn.

At equilibrium, with many firms each buying labour up to the point at which $W = MRP_L$, a unit of labour will be attracted from one firm to another only when the *product* of that unit of labour is valued more highly in the second firm. If all resources are valued in competitive markets, the marginal cost of a unit of output is just equal to the value of the goods that otherwise would have been produced with the same inputs.

Using labour as an example once again, consider what happens when resources that would otherwise have been unemployed are used in production. If each firm equates the equilibrium wage to the value of labour's marginal product, and a person chooses not to be in the labour force, that person reveals that either leisure or the value of nonpaid labour is worth more to him or her than the value that society places on his or her potential product in the market. It is therefore efficient *not* to work. Thus, if you go from being voluntarily unemployed to holding a job in which you produce goods or services for the market, you are giving up leisure that is *less* valuable to you than the wage you are paid. Those who value leisure more highly will not take a job; those who place an even lower value on leisure are already working. Remember that the "price," or opportunity cost, of each hour of leisure is the wage you could have earned by working that additional hour.

Marginal cost, then, is a good measure of what society gives up by using resources to produce more of a good or service. If the resources needed to produce something are taken away from the production of something else, *MC* measures the value of the *product* given up; if those resources were previously unused, *MC* measures the value of *leisure* that is given up.

---

[2]*Price is only a good measure of value when the current distribution of income is considered desirable. If income is distributed differently, demand for various products will be different, and so will equilibrium prices.*

In sum:

> Because competitive firms will produce as long as the price of their product is greater than the marginal cost of production, they will produce as long as a gain for society is possible. That is, if society values good *X* more than it values good *Y* or what otherwise would be produced with the same resources needed to produce *X*, then more *X* will indeed be produced. The market guarantees that the right things are produced, and competitive markets therefore yield an efficient mix of output.[3] By this same reasoning, however, if the price of some good ends up above the marginal cost of production at equilibrium, additional production will provide benefits in excess of the real costs to society. This means that the good is being underproduced and that the outcome is inefficient.

Figure 12.5 shows how a simple competitive market system leads individual households and firms to make efficient choices in input and output markets. For simplicity, the figure assumes only one factor of production, labour. Households weigh the market wage against the value of leisure and time spent in unpaid household production. But the wage is a measure of labour's potential product because firms weigh labour cost (wages) against the value of the product produced and hire up to the point at which $W = MRP_L$. Households use wages to buy market-produced goods. Thus, households implicitly weigh the value of market-produced goods against the value of leisure and household production.

When a firm's scale is balanced, it is earning maximum profit; when a household's scale is balanced, it is maximizing utility. Under these conditions, no changes can improve social welfare.

Perfect Competition versus Real Markets

So far, we have built a model of a perfectly competitive market system that produces an efficient allocation of resources, an efficient mix of output, and an efficient distribution of output. But the perfectly competitive model is built on a set of assumptions, all of which must hold for our conclusions to be fully valid. We have assumed that all firms and households are price takers in input and output markets, that firms and households have perfect information, that all firms maximize profits, and so forth.

But these assumptions do not always hold in real-world markets. When this is the case, the conclusion that free, unregulated markets will produce an efficient outcome breaks down. The remainder of this chapter discusses some inefficiencies that occur naturally in markets and some of the strengths, as well as the weaknesses, of the market mechanism. We also discuss the usefulness of the competitive model for understanding the real economy.

The Sources of Market Failure

In suggesting some of the problems encountered in real markets and some of the possible solutions to these problems, the rest of this chapter previews the next part of this book, which focuses on the economics of market failure and the role of government in the economy.

---

[3]*It is important to understand that firms do not act consciously to balance social costs and benefits. In fact, the usual assumption is that firms are self-interested, private profit-maximizers. It just works out that in perfectly competitive markets, when firms are weighing private benefits against private costs, they are actually (perhaps without knowing it) weighing the benefits and costs to society as well.*

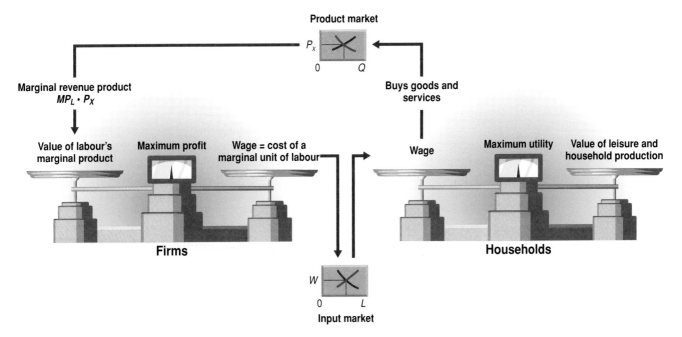

FIGURE 12.5

Efficiency in Perfect Competition Follows from a Weighing of Values by Both Households and Firms

For simplicity, assume that there is just one variable factor of production, labour. Households are presumed to weigh the value of market-produced goods against the value of leisure and household production. To buy products, households must earn income from wages. But because firms weigh the cost of labour, as reflected in wages, against the value of labour's product, households are actually weighing the value of leisure and home production against the value of what they would produce ($W = MP_L \times P_X$) if they entered the labour force. The result is an efficient balance in both output and input markets.

Market failure occurs when resources are misallocated, or allocated inefficiently. The result is waste or lost value. In this section, we briefly describe four important sources of market failure: (1) *imperfect market structure,* or noncompetitive behaviour, (2) the existence of *public goods,* (3) the presence of *external costs and benefits,* and (4) *imperfect information.* Each condition results from the failure of one of the assumptions basic to the perfectly competitive model, and each is discussed in more detail in later chapters. Each also points to a potential role for government in the economy. The desirability and extent of actual government involvement in the economy is a hotly debated subject.

> **market failure** *Occurs when resources are misallocated, or allocated inefficiently. The result is waste or lost value.*

IMPERFECT MARKETS

Until now we have operated on the assumption that the number of buyers and sellers in each market is large. When each buyer and each seller is only one of a great many in the market, no individual buyer or seller can independently influence price. Thus, all economic decision makers are by virtue of their relatively small size forced to take input prices and output prices as given. When this assumption does not hold—that is, when single firms have some control over price and potential competition—the result is **imperfect competition** and an inefficient allocation of resources.

> **imperfect competition** *An industry in which single firms have some control over price and competition. Imperfectly competitive industries give rise to an inefficient allocation of resources.*

A Saskatchewan wheat farmer is probably a "price taker," but Xerox and Chrysler Canada most certainly are not. Many firms in many industries do have some control over price. The degree of control that is possible depends on the character of competition in the industry itself.

An industry that is comprised of just one firm producing a product for which there are no close substitutes is called a **monopoly**. Although a monopoly has no other firms to compete with, it is still constrained by market demand. To be successful, the firm still has to produce something that people want. Essentially, a monopoly must choose both price and quantity of output simultaneously because the amount that it will be able to sell depends on the price it sets. If the price is too high, it will sell nothing. Presumably a monopolist sets price in order to maximize profit. That price is generally significantly above average costs, and such a firm usually earns economic profits.

In competition, economic profits will attract the entry of new firms into the industry. A rational monopolist who is not restrained by the government does everything possible to block any such entry in order to preserve economic profits in the long run. As a result, society loses the benefits of more product and lower prices. A number of barriers to entry can be raised. Sometimes a monopoly is actually licensed by government, and entry into its market is prohibited by law. Taiwan has only one beer company; most areas in Canada have only one local telephone company. Ownership of a natural resource can also be the source of monopoly power. If I buy up all the coal mines in Canada and I persuade Parliament to restrict coal imports, no one can enter the coal industry and compete with me.

Between monopoly and perfect competition are a number of other imperfectly competitive market structures. *Oligopolistic industries* are made up of a small number of firms, each with a degree of price-setting power. *Monopolistically competitive industries* are made up of a large number of firms that acquire price-setting power by differentiating their products or by establishing a brand name. Only General Mills can produce Wheaties, for example, and only Miles Laboratories can produce Alka-Seltzer.

> In all imperfectly competitive industries, output is lower—the product is underproduced—and price is higher than it would be under perfect competition. The equilibrium condition $P = MC$ does not hold, and the system does not produce the most efficient product mix.

In Canada, many forms of noncompetitive behaviour are covered under a piece of legislation called the Competition Act. The purpose of this act is "to maintain and encourage competition in Canada in order to promote the efficiency and adaptability of the Canadian economy, in order to expand opportunities for Canadian participation in world markets while at the same time recognizing the role of foreign competition in Canada, in order to ensure that small and medium-size enterprises have an equitable opportunity to participate in the Canadian economy, and in order to provide consumers with competitive prices and product choices." (Competition policy is discussed in more detail in Chapters 13, 14, and 15.)

PUBLIC GOODS

A second major source of inefficiency lies in the fact that private producers simply do not find it in their best interest to produce everything that members of society want. More specifically, there is a whole class of goods called **public**, or

monopoly *An industry comprised of only one firm that produces a product for which there are no close substitutes and in which significant barriers exist to prevent new firms from entering the industry.*

public, or social, goods *Goods or services that bestow collective benefits on members of society; they are, in a sense, collectively consumed. Generally, no one can be excluded from enjoying their benefits. The classic example is national defence.*

social, goods that will be underproduced or not produced at all in a completely unregulated market economy.[4]

Public goods are goods or services that bestow collective benefits on society; they are, in a sense, collectively consumed. The classic example is national defence, but there are countless others—police protection, preservation of wilderness lands, and public health, to name a few. These things are "produced" using land, labour, and capital just like any other good. Some public goods, such as national defence, benefit the whole country. Others, such as clean air, may be limited to smaller areas—the air may be clean in a small Newfoundland outport but dirty in a southern Ontario city.

Public goods are consumed by everyone, not just by those who pay for them. Once the good is produced, no one can be excluded from enjoying its benefits. Producers of **private goods,** like hamburgers, can make a profit because they don't hand over the product to you until you pay for it. (Chapters 4–11 centred on the production of private goods.)

private goods *Products produced by firms for sale to individual households.*

If the provision of public goods were left to private, profit-seeking producers with no power to force payment, a serious problem would arise. Suppose, for example, that I value some public good, X. If there were a functioning market for X, I would be willing to pay for it. But suppose that I am asked to contribute voluntarily to the production of X. Should I contribute? Perhaps I should on moral grounds, but not on the basis of pure self-interest.

At least two problems can get in the way. First, since I cannot be excluded from using X for not paying, I get the good whether I pay or not. Why should I pay if I don't have to? Second, since public goods that provide collective benefits to large numbers of people are expensive to produce, any one person's contribution is not likely to make much difference to the amount of the good ultimately produced. Would the national defence suffer, for example, if you didn't pay your share of the bill? Probably not. Thus, nothing happens if you don't pay; the output of the good doesn't change much, and you get it whether you pay or not.

For these reasons:

> Private provision of public goods fails. A completely laissez-faire market system will not produce everything that all members of a society might want. Citizens must band together to ensure that desired public goods are produced, and this is generally accomplished through government spending financed by taxes. The purpose of government provision of public goods is to correct for a naturally occurring failure of the market to produce everything that consumers want.

Public goods are the subject of Chapter 16.

EXTERNALITIES

A third major source of inefficiency in the market is the existence of external costs and benefits. An **externality** is a cost or benefit imposed or bestowed on an individual or group that is outside, or external to, the transaction—in other words, something that affects a third party. In a city, external costs are pervasive. The classic example is pollution, but there are thousands of others, such as noise, congestion, and painting your house a colour that the neighbours think is ugly.

Not all externalities are negative, however. Housing investment, for example,

externality *A cost or benefit resulting from some activity or transaction that is imposed or bestowed upon parties outside the activity or transaction.*

---

[4]*While they are normally referred to as public goods, many of the things we are talking about are services.*

may yield benefits for neighbours. A farm located near a city provides residents in the area with nice views, fresher air, and a less congested environment.

Externalities are a problem only if decision makers do not take them into account. The logic of efficiency presented earlier in this chapter required that firms weigh social benefits against social costs. If a firm in a competitive environment produces a good, it is because the value of that good to society exceeds the social cost of producing it—this is the logic of $P = MC$. If social costs or benefits are overlooked or left out of the calculations, inefficient decisions result.

The market itself has no automatic mechanism that provides decision makers with an incentive to consider external effects. Through government, however, society has established over the years a number of different institutions for dealing with externalities. Tort law, for example, is a body of legal rules that deals with third-party effects. Under certain circumstances, those who impose costs are held strictly liable for them; in other circumstances, liability is assessed only if the cost results from "negligent" behaviour. Tort law deals with small problems as well as larger ones. If a neighbour sprays her lawn with a powerful chemical and kills your prize shrub, you can take her to court and force her to pay for it. Huge damages were caused when a large oil tanker ran aground in the Shetland Islands off Scotland in early 1993. Most damage claims resulting from the accident will be settled in court.

The effects of externalities can be enormous. A recent example of an externality with potentially horrifying results is toxic waste dumping. For years, companies piled chemical wastes indiscriminately into dump sites near water supplies and residential areas. In some locations, those wastes seeped into the ground and contaminated the drinking water. During 1992 and 1993, several medical journals published reports linking "second-hand" smoke to lung disease and other health problems. In response to the evidence that smoking damages not only the smoker but others as well, governments have increased prohibitions against smoking on airplanes and in public places.

For years, economists have suggested that a carefully designed set of taxes and subsidies could help to "internalize" external effects. For example, if a paper mill that pollutes the air and waterways were taxed in proportion to the damage caused by that pollution, it would consider those costs in its decisions.

Sometimes, interaction among and between parties can lead to the proper consideration of externality without government involvement. If someone plays her radio loudly on the fourth floor of your university residence, that person imposes an externality on the other residents of the building. The residents, however, can get together and negotiate a set of mutually acceptable rules to govern radio playing.

Calculating damages from externalities in dollar terms is a difficult, but often necessary, task. Judges in liability cases are forced to make judgments of this sort all the time. Public policies that attempt to deal with problems like acid rain will hurt one sector at the expense of another. If the costs of acid rain are as large as some suggest, for example, taxing the industrial firms that cause acid rain will make it very difficult for many of them to survive. If a power plant is forced by government mandate to install every possible measure to reduce pollution, electric bills will rise sharply. Unless absolute rights are involved, gains and losses must be weighed. There are no easy answers.

The key point here is that:

> The market does not always force consideration of all the costs and benefits of decisions. Yet for an economy to achieve an efficient allocation of resources, all costs and benefits must be weighed.

We discuss externalities in detail in Chapter 16.

IMPERFECT INFORMATION

The fourth major source of inefficiency is **imperfect information** on the part of buyers and sellers:

> The conclusion that markets work efficiently rests heavily on the assumption that consumers and producers have full knowledge of product characteristics, available prices, and so forth. The absence of full information can lead to transactions that are ultimately disadvantageous.

imperfect information *The absence of full knowledge regarding product characteristics, available prices, and so forth.*

Some products are so complex that consumers find it difficult to judge the potential benefits and costs of purchase. Certainly demanders in the market for medical care do not fully understand what they buy. Buyers of life insurance have a very difficult time sorting out the terms of the more complex policies and determining the true "price" of the product. Consumers of almost any service that requires expertise, such as plumbing or TV repair, have a hard time evaluating what is needed, much less how well it is done. It is difficult for a used car buyer to find out the true "quality" of the cars in Big Jim's Car Emporium.

Some forms of misinformation can be corrected with simple rules such as "truth-in-advertising" regulations. In some cases, the government provides information to citizens; job centres and consumer information services exist for this purpose. In some industries, such as medical care, there is no clear-cut solution to the problem of noninformation or misinformation. We discuss all these topics in detail in Chapter 16.

Evaluating the Market Mechanism

Is the market system good or bad? Should the government be involved in the economy, or should it leave the allocation of resources to the free market? So far, our information is mixed and incomplete. To the extent that the perfectly competitive model reflects the way markets really operate, there seem to be some clear advantages to the market system. But when we relax the assumptions and expand our discussion to include noncompetitive behaviour, public goods, externalities, and the possibility of imperfect information, we see at least a potential role for government.

The market system does seem to provide most participants with the incentive to weigh costs and benefits and to operate efficiently. Firms can make profits only if a demand for their products exists. If there are no externalities, or if such costs or benefits are properly internalized, firms *will* weigh social benefits and costs in their production decisions. Under these circumstances, the profit motive should provide competitive firms with an incentive to minimize cost and to produce their products using the most efficient technologies. Likewise, competitive input markets should provide households with the incentive to weigh the value of their time against the social value of what they can produce in the labour force.

But markets are far from perfect. Freely functioning markets in the real world do not always produce an efficient allocation of resources, and this provides a potential role for government in the economy. Many have called for government involvement in the economy to correct for market failure—that is, to help markets function more efficiently. As you will see, however, some feel that government involvement in the economy creates more inefficiency than it cures.

In addition, we have thus far discussed only the criterion of efficiency, and economic systems and economic policies must be judged by many other criteria, not the least of which is *equity*, or fairness. Indeed, some contend that the outcome of any free market is ultimately unfair, because some become rich while others remain very poor.

Part 3, which follows, explores the issue of market imperfections and government involvement in the economy in greater depth. In Chapter 13, we begin with a discussion of output and pricing decisions in monopoly markets. In Chapter 14, we move on to a discussion of output and pricing decisions in monopolistically competitive industries and oligopolistic industries. Chapters 15, 16, and 17 are concerned with the potential role of the government in regulating industry, controlling externalities, and redistributing income.

Looking Ahead

In this chapter we have wrapped up the perfectly competitive model described in detail in the last seven chapters. In discussing the idea of "general equilibrium," we saw how the markets described separately in earlier chapters are all interrelated and how adjustments in any one market can cause subsequent adjustments in many or all of the others. To understand the way an economic system functions and to think properly about public policy issues, it is essential that we consider these interconnections. Partial equilibrium analysis can lead to wrong answers.

We also turned for the first time to normative economics. We began by reviewing the concept of efficiency. Next, we took a look at the efficiency of the perfectly competitive system. If all the assumptions of perfect competition hold, the result is efficient. No changes could be made in the allocation of resources among firms, in the mix of output, or in the distribution of output among members of society that would even potentially make some better off without making some worse off.

But the assumptions of perfect competition simply do not hold in the real world. When we relax them in order to describe the world more accurately, we see some of the problems that the unconstrained market does not solve for itself.

Summary

General Equilibrium Analysis

1. Both firms and households make simultaneous choices in both input and output markets. For example, input prices determine output costs and affect firms' output supply decisions; wages in the labour market affect labour supply decisions, income, and ultimately how much output households can and do purchase.

2. A *general equilibrium* exists when all markets in an economy are in simultaneous equilibrium. An event that disturbs the equilibrium in one market may disturb the equilibrium in many other markets as well. *Partial equilibrium* analysis can be misleading, because it looks only at adjustments in one isolated market.

Allocative Efficiency and Competitive Equilibrium

3. An *efficient* economy is one that produces the goods and services that people want and does so at least possible cost. A change is said to be efficient if it at least potentially makes some members of society better off without making others worse off. An efficient, or *Pareto optimal*, system is one in which no such changes are possible.

4. If a change makes some people better off and some people worse off, but it can be shown that the value of the gains exceeds the value of the losses, the change is said to be *potentially efficient*.

5. If all the assumptions of perfect competition hold, the result is an efficient, or Pareto optimal, allocation of resources. To prove this statement, it is necessary to show that resources are allocated efficiently among firms, that final products are distributed efficiently among households, and that the system produces what people want.

6. The assumptions that factor markets are competitive and open, that all firms pay the same prices for inputs, and that all firms maximize profits lead to the conclusion that the allocation of resources among firms is efficient.

7. People have different tastes and preferences, and they buy very different things in very different combinations. But as long as everyone shops freely in the same markets, no redistribution of outputs

among people will make them better off. This leads to the conclusion that final products are distributed efficiently among households.

8. Because perfectly competitive firms will produce as long as the price of their product is greater than the marginal cost of production, they will continue to produce as long as a gain for society is possible. The market thus guarantees that the right things are produced. In other words, the perfectly competitive system produces what people want.

The Sources of Market Failure

9. When the assumptions of perfect competition do not hold, the conclusion that free, unregulated markets will produce an efficient allocation of resources breaks down.

10. An imperfectly competitive industry is one in which single firms have some control over price and competition. Forms of *imperfect competition* include monopoly, monopolistic competition, and oligopoly. In all imperfectly competitive industries, output is lower and price is higher than it would be in competition. Imperfect competition is a major source of market inefficiency.

11. *Public*, or *social*, *goods* bestow collective benefits on members of society. Because the benefits of so-cial goods are collective, people cannot in most cases be excluded from enjoying them. Thus, private firms usually do not find it profitable to produce public goods. The need for public goods is thus another source of inefficiency.

12. An *externality* is a cost or benefit that is imposed or bestowed on an individual or group that is outside, or external to, the transaction—in other words, something that affects a third party. If such social costs or benefits are overlooked, the decisions of households or firms are likely to be wrong, or inefficient.

13. Market efficiency depends on the assumption that buyers have perfect information on product quality and price and that firms have perfect information on input quality and price. *Imperfect information* can lead to wrong choices and inefficiency.

Evaluating the Market Mechanism

14. Sources of market failure—such as imperfect markets, social goods, externalities, and imperfect information—are considered by many to justify the existence of government and governmental policies that seek to redistribute costs and income on the basis of efficiency, equity, or both.

Review Terms and Concepts

efficiency 293
externality 309
general equilibrium 293
imperfect competition 307
imperfect information 311

market failure 307
monopoly 308
Pareto efficiency or **Pareto optimality 301**
partial equilibrium analysis 293

private goods 309
public, or social, goods 308
Equation:
Key efficiency condition in perfect competition: $P_X = MC_X$

Problem Set

1. In 1992 and 1993 the prices of forest products increased dramatically. One part of the reason for this increase in price was the reduced supply of timber due to environmental regulations limiting logging. Another part of the explanation has to do with an increase in demand.
   a. What sectors in Canada are likely to use large amounts of timber products? Under what circumstances do these sectors see an increase in the demand for their products?
   b. Go to the library and find data on the number of housing starts in Canada in 1991, 1992, and 1993. What pattern do you see in the numbers? Can you offer an explanation?

2. A medium-sized bakery has just opened in Slovakia. A loaf of bread is currently selling for 14 koruna (the Slovakian currency) over and above the cost of intermediate goods (flour, etc.). Assuming that labour is the only variable factor of production, the following table gives the production schedule for bread:

WORKERS	LOAVES OF BREAD
0	0
1	15
2	30
3	42
4	52
5	60
6	66
7	70

a. Suppose that the current wage rate in Slovakia is 119 koruna per hour. How many workers will the bakery employ?

b. Suppose that the economy of Slovakia begins to grow, incomes rise, and the price of a loaf of bread is pushed up to 20 koruna. Assuming no increase in the price of labour, how many workers will the bakery hire?

c. An increase in the demand for labour pushes up wages to 125 koruna per hour. What impact will this increase in cost have on employment and output in the bakery at the 20-koruna price of bread?

d. If all firms behaved like our bakery, would the allocation of resources in Slovakia be efficient? Explain your answer.

3. Do you agree or disagree with each of the following statements? Explain your answer.

a. "Housing is a 'public good' and should be produced by the public sector because private markets will fail to produce it efficiently."

b. "Monopoly power is inefficient, since large firms will produce too much product, dumping it on the market at artificially low prices."

c. "Medical care is an example of a potentially inefficient market because consumers do not have perfect information about the product."

4. A major source of chicken feed in Canada is anchovies, small fish that can be scooped up out of the ocean at low cost. Every seven years, the anchovies disappear to spawn, and producers must turn to grain, which is more expensive, to feed their chickens. What is likely to happen to the cost of chicken when the anchovies disappear? What are substitutes for chicken? How are the markets for these substitutes affected? Name some complements to chicken. How are the markets for these complements affected? How might the allocation of farmland be changed as a result of the anchovies' disappearance?

5. Suppose two passengers both end up with a reservation for the last seat on a train from Montreal to Toronto. Two alternatives are proposed:
a. Toss a coin.
b. Sell the ticket to the highest bidder.
Compare the two from the standpoint of efficiency and equity.

6. Assume that there are two sectors in an economy: goods (G) and services (S). Both sectors are perfectly competitive, with large numbers of firms and constant returns to scale. As income rises, households spend a larger portion of their incomes on S and a smaller portion on G. Using supply and demand curves for both sectors and a diagram showing a representative firm in each sector, explain what would happen to output and prices in the short run and the long run in response to an increase in income. (Assume that the increase in income causes demand for G to shift left and demand for S to shift right.) In the long run what would happen to employment in the goods sector? In the service sector? (*Hint:* See Figure 12.3.)

The Changing Canadian Pork Industry

Both the Canadian and U.S. pork industries have traditionally consisted of thousands of small, family-run hog farms that sell live hogs to the processors. (There are about 10 000 hog farms in Canada.) The processing stage of the industry is more concentrated than the farming stage; a single packing plant may process 8000 hogs a day. Names of major Canadian packers—Maple Leaf, Schneiders, Gainers—are widely known, but the names of individual producers are not.

Historically, the individual pork producers had little command over price. These farmers faced similar costs for their inputs and used similar methods of production. Packing plants were willing to purchase as many swine as an individual farmer wished to sell, so the farmer had no incentive to lower the selling price. Moreover, hogs are virtually identical; the product is homogeneous. Thus the live hog production industry had been perfectly competitive.

The primary determinant of changes in pork prices has traditionally been changes in supply. New entrants, changing costs (fuel and feed prices, in particular), new breeds that mature rapidly, and new production techniques (including use of new information on the relationship between feed regime and weight gain) have been the primary determinants of changes in supply. The individual hog farmer has had to struggle to stay up with the best practice of the industry to remain in business.

Moreover, the industry is unforgiving. An increase in supply going to the processors can send prices plummeting. This is particularly problematic for individual hog farmers attempting to protect their

The Canadian pork industry is almost perfectly competitive. Traditionally, hog farmers have faced similar costs and had little control over prices. The product is homogeneous: one hog is very much like another.

cash flow when faced with increases in fuel or feed prices.

In recent years the individual hog farmer has faced a new challenge. Large-scale hog production factories, often integrated with both feed suppliers and final processors, have appeared. The unit cost of operating these large-scale facilities is relatively low. There is real concern that these new operations will destroy the traditional family-based hog operation.

Questions for Analytical Thinking

1. If an increase in supply sends "prices plummeting," what can we say about the elasticity of demand for pork? What is the relationship between the elasticity of demand and the stability of prices in this industry?

2. If a farmer temporarily keeps hogs from market, what is likely to happen to the average weight of hogs sold (once they are sent to market)? How will this affect the price per kilogram received by farmers?

3. Why might the new large-scale integrated hog farms enjoy economies of scale?

4. Why would these large-scale producers be a threat to the small, family-run hog farm?

5. Do the large-scale integrated farms produce the same product as the family-run hog farm? Do customers care about the differences? Should they?

6. How might an advertising cam-

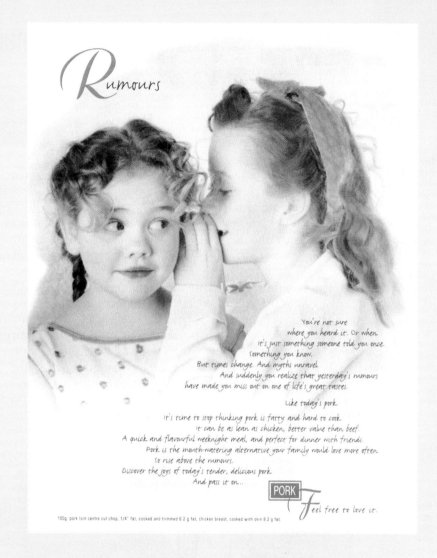

In an attempt to increase demand for their product, Canadian pork producers attempt to differentiate their product from that of other meat producers. The next step may be for pork producers to differentiate their product on the basis of the size of their production facility, with small producers arguing that their product is higher quality.

paign by small producers aimed at differentiating the family farmer's product from that produced in the integrated factory help the family hog farmers?

Video Resource: "The Smell of Money," Parts 1 and 2, *Country Canada*, March 3, 1996

Part Three

**Market Imperfections and
the Role of Government**

Monopoly

Imperfect Competition and Market Power: Core Concepts
Defining Industry Boundaries
Barriers to Entry
Price: The Fourth Decision Variable

Price and Output Decisions in Pure Monopoly Markets
Demand in Monopoly Markets
Perfect Competition and Monopoly Compared
Collusion and Monopoly Compared

The Social Costs of Monopoly
Inefficiency and Consumer Loss
Rent-Seeking Behaviour
Remedies of Monopoly

Natural Monopoly
Identifying a Natural Monopoly
Regulating a Natural Monopoly

(Optional Material) **Market Power in Input Markets: Monopsony**

Imperfect Markets: A Review and a Look Ahead

In Chapters 6 through 12, we devoted most of our attention to building a model of a perfectly competitive economy. To do so, we needed to make some fairly restrictive assumptions. In Chapter 12 we began to see what happens when we relax some of them.

A number of very important assumptions, you will recall, underlie the logic of perfect competition. One is that a large number of firms and households interact in each individual output market. Another is that firms in a given market produce undifferentiated, or homogeneous, products. Together, these two conditions limit firms' choices. With many firms in each market, no single firm has any control over market prices. Single firms may decide how much to produce and how to produce, but the market determines output price. The assumption that new firms are free to enter industries and to compete for profits led us to conclude that opportunities for economic profit are eliminated in the long run as competition drives price to a level equal to the average cost of production.

In the next two chapters, we explore the important implications of relaxing these basic assumptions. In this chapter, we focus on the case of a single firm in an industry—a monopoly.

Imperfect Competition and Market Power: Core Concepts

imperfectly competitive industry *An industry in which single firms have some control over the price of their output.*

market power *an imperfectly competitive firm's ability to raise price without losing all demand for its product.*

A market, or industry, in which individual firms have some control over the price of their output in **imperfectly competitive**. All firms in an imperfectly competitive market have one thing in common: they exercise market power, the ability to raise price without losing all demand for their product. Imperfect competition and market power are major sources of inefficiency.

Imperfect competition does not mean that *no* competition exists in the market. In fact, in some imperfectly competitive markets competition takes place in even *more* arenas than perfectly competitive markets. Firms can differentiate their products, advertise, improve quality, market aggressively, cut prices, and so forth.

For a firm to exercise control over the price of its product, it must be able to *limit competition* by erecting barriers to entry. If your firm produces T-shirts, and if other firms can enter freely into the industry and produce exactly the same T-shirts that you produce, the result will be the outcome that you would expect in a perfectly competitive industry: the supply will increase, the price of T-shirts will be driven down to their average cost, and economic profits will be eliminated.

But note that T-shirts having the official National Hockey League team logo are more expensive than generic T-shirts. If your firm can prevent other firms from producing exactly the same product, or if it can prevent other firms from entering the market, then it has a chance of preserving its economic profits. Only the NHL's licensees are allowed to use the official logo.

DEFINING INDUSTRY BOUNDARIES

A *monopoly*, you will recall, is an industry with a single firm in which the entry of new firms is blocked. An *oligopoly* is an industry in which there is a small number of firms, each of which is large enough to have an impact on the market price of its outputs. Firms that differentiate their products in industries that have many producers and free entry are called *monopolistic competitors* (review Figure 3.1). But where do we set the boundary of an industry? For example, although Procter & Gamble is the only firm that can produce Ivory soap, there are many other brands of soap. In general:

The ease with which consumers can substitute for a product limits the extent to which a monopolist can exercise market power. The more broadly a market is defined the more difficult it becomes to find substitutes.

Consider hamburger, for example. A firm that produces Brand X hamburger faces stiff competition from other hamburger sellers, even though it is the only producer of Brand X. The Brand X firm has little market power because near-perfect substitutes for its hamburger are available. But if a firm were the *only* producer of hamburger (or, better yet, the only producer of beef), it would have more market power, because fewer (or no) alternatives would be available. When fewer substitutes exist, a monopolist has more power to raise price because demand for its product is less elastic, as Figure 13.1 on the next page shows. A monopolist that produces all the food in an economy would exercise enormous market power because there are no substitutes at all for food as a category.

To be meaningful, therefore, our definition of a monopolistic industry must be

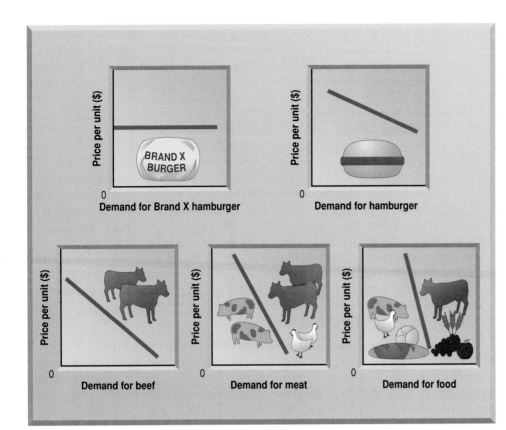

FIGURE 13.1

The Boundary of a Market and Elasticity

We can define an industry as broadly or as narrowly as we like. The more broadly we define the industry, the fewer substitutes there are, and the less elastic demand for that industry's product is likely to be. A monopoly is an industry with one firm that produces a product for which there are *no close substitutes.* The producer of Brand X hamburger cannot properly be called a monopolist because this producer has no control over market price and there are many substitutes for Brand X hamburger.

Labels within figure:

Price per unit ($) — Demand for Brand X hamburger

Price per unit ($) — Demand for hamburger

Price per unit ($) — Demand for beef

Price per unit ($) — Demand for meat

Price per unit ($) — Demand for food

more precise. We define **pure monopoly** as an industry with a single firm (1) that produces a product for which there are no close substitutes and (2) in which significant barriers to entry prevent other firms from entering the industry to compete for profits.

BARRIERS TO ENTRY

Firms that already have market power an maintain that power either by preventing other firms from producing an exact duplicate of their product or by preventing firms from entering the industry. A number of **barriers to entry** can be erected.

■ **Government Franchises** Many firms are monopolies by virtue of government directive. Local telephone-operating companies, for example, are often granted exclusive licences by provinces to provide "local exchange service." No other firms are permitted to offer telephone service within specific local areas. Provincial governments also grant electric companies the sole right to supply power within given areas. The usual defence of this kind of monopoly power by **government franchise** is that it is more efficient for a single firm to produce the particular product (usually a service) than it is for many firms to produce the same product. If very large economies of scale are possible, it makes no sense to have many small firms producing the same thing at much higher costs. (We discuss these so-called "natural monopolies" more formally later in this chapter.)

Governments usually regulate monopolies to which they have granted exclusive licences. Utility boards in each province watch over electric companies and local telephone companies. Indeed, one of government's major responsibilities is to regulate the prices charged by these utilities to ensure that they don't abuse their monopoly power.

Fairness, or equity, is another frequently cited defence of government-regulated

pure monopoly *An industry with a single firm that produces a product for which there are no close substitutes and in which significant barriers to entry prevent other firms from entering the industry to compete for profits.*

barrier to entry *Something that prevents new firms from entering and competing in imperfectly competitive industries.*

government franchise *A monopoly by virtue of government directive.*

monopoly. Technological progress in the telecommunications industry has reduced the advantages that come from size, for example, but clearly, neither the federal government nor the provinces are ready to open local exchange service to competition. The reason is that governments want to ensure that everyone has access to a telephone at affordable rates. In Canada, many private households are provided with telephone service at a price below the cost of producing it; local telephone companies earn the bulk of their profits from business users, who are charged a price above cost. Deregulating local service would thus mean higher telephone bills for these households, a change that many would consider "unfair."

Large economies of scale and equity are not the only justifications that governments give for granting monopoly licences, however. Sometimes government wants to maintain control of an industry, and a monopoly is easier to control than a competitive industry. For example, most provincial governments permit liquor to be sold only through provincially-controlled and -managed liquor stores. However, when large economies of scale do not exist in an industry, or when equity is not a concern, the argument is that the province wants to prevent private parties from encouraging and profiting from "sin." Another is that government monopolies are a convenient source of revenues. How can anyone criticize the provincially licensed, implicit taxation of drinking or gambling?

patent *A barrier to entry that grants exclusive use of the patented product or process to the inventor.*

■ **Patents** Another legal barrier that prevents entry into an industry is a **patent**, which grants exclusive use of the patented product or process to the inventor. Patents provide an incentive for invention and innovation. New products and new processes are developed through research undertaken by individual inventors and by firms. Research requires resources and time, which have opportunity costs. Without the protection that a patent provides, the results of research would become available to the general public very quickly. If research did not lead to expanded profits, corporations claim very little research would be done. On the negative side, though, patents do serve as a barrier to competition, and they do keep the benefits of research from flowing through the market to consumers.

To understand a patent's effects on profits, suppose that the industry producing blank videocassettes is competitive and that the full economic cost (including normal profit) of producing videocassettes is $5 each. In a perfectly competitive market, price will be driven to average cost, and consumers will pay $5 per tape.

Now suppose that the BASF company develops a new type of tape material that makes it possible to produce tapes of equal quality for $3. If no patent protection existed, every company in the industry would quickly analyze the new tape material and begin producing tapes at a cost of $3. Soon competition would drive the price of tapes to $3, and consumers would enjoy the full benefits of the new technology. But this would eliminate BASF's incentive to do research on new materials.

If, however, BASF can protect its new material with a patent, it can produce tapes for $3, charge a price closer to $5, and make significant economic profits. These profits reward the developers of the new material, but they also keep the benefits from consumers.[1]

---

[1]*Another alternative is* licensing. *Suppose BASF licenses the use of its material for $1 per tape produced. If other firms use the new material, costs will fall to $4 ($3 per tape plus the licence fee). The price of tapes will fall to $4 and BASF will get a royalty of $1 for every tape produced using the new material. Here the new technology is used by all producers, and the inventor splits the benefits with consumers. Because forcing the non-patent-holding producers to use an inefficient technology results in waste, some analysts have proposed adding mandatory licensing to the current patent system.*

Finite terms for patent protection represent an attempt to balance the benefits of firms and the benefits of households. On the one hand, it is important to stimulate invention and innovation; on the other hand, invention and innovation do society no good unless their benefits eventually flow to the public.

In recent years, public attention has been focused on the high price of health care. One factor contributing to these costs is the very high price of many prescription drugs. Equipped with newly developed tools of bioengineering, the pharmaceutical industry has been granted thousands of patents for new drugs. When a new drug that is necessary for the treatment of a disease is developed, the patent wards are justified by high research and development costs; other argue that these profits are simply the result of a monopoly position protected by the patent system.

■ **Economies of Scale and Other Cost Advantages** Some products can be produced efficiently only in big, expensive production facilities. For example, it is estimated that an oil refinery large enough to achieve maximum-scale economies in the production of gasoline would cost more than $500 million to build. No matter how high his or her spirits are running, a small entrepreneur is not going to jump into the refining business in search of economic profit. The need to raise an initial investment of half a billion dollars certainly limits the pool of potential entrants, a situation that is compounded by the riskiness of the business. Hence, large capital requirements are often a barrier to entry.

Sometimes large economies of scale are not production related. Breakfast cereal can be produced efficiently on a very small scale, for example; large-scale production does not reduce costs. But the breakfast cereal market is dominated by heavily advertised brand names. To compete successfully, a new firm would have to mount an advertising campaign costing millions of dollars, an enormous investment in the intangible capital called goodwill. The large front-end investment requirement in the presence of risk is certainly likely to deter would-be entrants to the cereal market.

■ **Ownership of a Scarce Factor of Production** You can't enter the diamond-producing business unless you own a diamond mine. There are not many diamond mines in the world, and most are already owned by a single firm, the DeBeers Company of South Africa. Once, the Aluminum Company of America (now Alcoa) owned or controlled virtually 100% of the bauxite deposits in the world and until the 1940s monopolized the production and distribution of aluminum. Obviously, if

The DeBeers Company of South Africa controls approximately 80% of the world market for uncut diamonds. Yet DeBeers' decades-old monopoly is being threatened by a recent spate of prospectors digging for diamonds in the Angolan Cuango River.

the production of a product requires a particular input, and one firm owns the entire supply of that input, that firm will control the industry. The fact of ownership alone serves as a barrier to entry.

PRICE: THE FOURTH DECISION VARIABLE

To review what we've said so far: a firm has market power when it has some control over the price of its product—that is, when it can raise the price of its product without losing all demand. The exercise of market power requires that the firm be able to limit competition in some way. It does this either by erecting barriers to the entry of new firms or by preventing other firms from producing the exact same product.

Regardless of the source of market power, output price is not taken as given by the firm. Rather,

> Price is a decision variable for imperfectly competitive firms. Firms with market power must therefore decide not only (1) how much to produce, (2) how to produce it, and (3) how much to demand in each input market (see Figure 7.3), but also (4) *what price to charge for their output.*

This does not mean that "market power" allows a firm to charge any price it likes, however. The market demand curve constrains the behaviour even of a pure monopolist. To sell its product successfully, a firm must produce something that people want to sell it at a price they are willing to pay.

Price and Output Decisions in Pure Monopoly Markets

For purposes of analyzing monopoly behaviour, we make two basic assumptions: (1) that entry to the market is strictly blocked, and (2) that firms act to maximize profits.

Initially, we also assume that our pure monopolist buys in competitive input markets. Even though the firm is the only one producing for its product market, it is only one among many firms buying factors of production in input markets. The telephone company, for example, must hire labour like any other firm. To attract workers it must pay the market wage; to buy fibre-optic cable, it must pay the going price. In these input markets, therefore, the monopolistic firm is a price taker.

On the cost side of the profit equation, then, a pure monopolist does not differ one bit from a perfect competitor. Both choose the technology that minimizes the cost of production. The cost curve of each represents the minimum cost of producing each level of output. The difference arises on the revenue, or demand, side of the equation, and this is where we begin our analysis.

DEMAND IN MONOPOLY MARKETS

A competitive firm, you will recall, faces a fixed, market-determined price, and we assume that it can sell all that it wants to sell at that price; it is constrained only by its current capacity in the short run. The demand curve facing a competitive firm is thus a horizontal line (Figure 13.2 on the next page). Raising the price of its product means losing all demand, because perfect substitutes are available. The competitive firm has no incentive to charge a lower price either.

Because a competitive firm can charge only one price, regardless of the output level chosen, its *marginal revenue*—the additional revenue that it earns by raising output by one unit—is simply the price of the output, or $P^* = \$5$ in Figure 13.2. Remember that marginal revenue is important because a profit-maximizing firm will increase output as long as marginal revenue exceeds marginal costs.

The most important distinction between competition and monopoly is that:

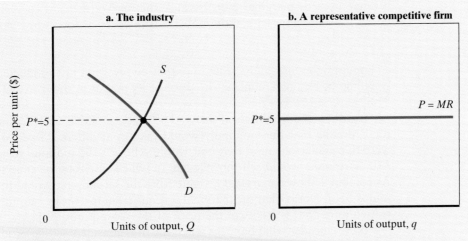

a. The industry

b. A representative competitive firm

Price per unit ($)

$P*=5$

S

D

0

Units of output, Q

$P*=5$

$P = MR$

0

Units of output, q

FIGURE 13.2

The Demand Curve Facing a Perfectly Competitive Firm Is Perfectly Elastic; in a Monopoly, the Market Demand Curve Is the Demand Curve Facing the Firm

Perfectly competitive firms are price takers; they are small relative to the size of the market and thus cannot influence market price. The implication is that the demand curve facing a perfectly competitive firm is perfectly elastic. If the firm raises its price, it sells nothing, and there is no reason for the firm to lower its price if it can sell all it wants at $P*$ = $5. In a monopoly, the firm is the industry. Thus the market demand curve is the demand curve facing the monopoly, and the total quantity supplied in the market is what the monopoly decides to produce.

> With only one firm in a monopoly market, there is no distinction between the firm and the industry. In a monopoly, the firm *is* the industry. The market demand curve is thus the demand curve facing the firm, and the total quantity supplied in the market is what the firm decides to produce (Figure 13.2a).

Before we proceed any further, we need to make a few more basic assumptions. First, we assume that a monopolistic firm cannot price discriminate. That is, it sells its product to all demanders at the same price. (*Price discrimination* means selling to different consumers or groups of consumers at different prices.)

We also assume that the monopoly faces a known demand curve. That is, we assume that the firm has enough information to predict how households will react to different prices. (In actuality, many firms use sophisticated statistical methods to estimate the elasticity of demand for their products. Other firms may use less formal methods, including trial and error, sometimes called "price searching." All firms with market power must have some sense of how consumers are likely to react to various prices, however.) Knowing the demand curve it faces, the firm must *simultaneously* choose both the quantity of output to supply and the price of that output. Once the firm chooses a price, the market determines how much will be sold. Stated somewhat differently, the monopoly chooses the single point on the market demand curve where it wants to be.

■ **Marginal Revenue and Market Demand** Just like a competitor, a profit-maximizing monopolist will continue to produce output as long as marginal revenue exceeds marginal cost. Because the market demand curve is the demand curve for a monopoly, a monopolistic firm faces a downward-sloping demand curve. Thus,

> For a monopolist, an increase in output involves not just producing more and selling it, but also reducing the price of its output in order to sell it.

Consider the hypothetical demand schedule in Table 13.1. Column 3 lists the total revenue that the monopoly would take in at different levels of output. If it were to produce one unit, that unit would sell for $10, and total revenue would be $10. Two units would sell for $9 each, in which case total revenue would be $18. As column 4 shows, marginal revenue from the second unit would thus be $8 ($18 minus $10). Notice that the marginal revenue from increasing output from one unit to two units ($8) is *less* than the price of the second unit ($9).

Now consider what happens when the firm considers setting production at four units rather than three. The fourth unit would sell for $7, but because the firm can't price discriminate, it must sell all four units for $7 each. Had the firm chosen to produce only three units, it could have sold those three units for $8 each. Thus, offsetting the revenue gain of $7 is a revenue loss of $3—that is, $1 for each of the three units that would have sold at the higher price. The marginal revenue of the fourth unit is thus $7 minus $3, or $4, which is considerably below the price of $7. (Remember, unlike a monopolistic firm, a perfectly competitive firm does not have to charge a lower price to sell more; thus $P = MR$ in competition.)

Marginal revenue can also be derived simply by looking at the change in total revenue. At three units of output, total revenue is $24; at four units of output, total revenue is $28. Marginal revenue is the difference, or $4.

Moving from six units of output to seven units of output actually reduces total revenue for the firm. At seven units of output, marginal revenue is negative. While it is true that the seventh unit will sell for a positive price ($4), the firm must sell all seven units for $4 each (for a total revenue of $28). If output had been restricted to six units, each would have sold for $5. Thus, offsetting the revenue gain of $4 is a revenue loss of $6—that is, $1 for each of the six units that the firm would have sold at the higher price. Increasing output from six to seven units actually decreases revenue by $2. Figure 13.3 on the next page graphs the marginal revenue schedule derived in Table 13.1. Notice that at every level of output except one unit, marginal revenue is *below* price. Marginal revenue turns from positive to

Table 13.1	Marginal Revenue Facing a Monopolist		
(1) Quantity	(2) Price	(3) Total Revenue	(4) Marginal Revenue
0	$11	$ 0	$—
1	10	10	10
2	9	18	8
3	8	24	6
4	7	28	4
5	6	30	2
6	5	30	0
7	4	28	−2
8	3	24	−4
9	2	18	−6
10	1	10	−18

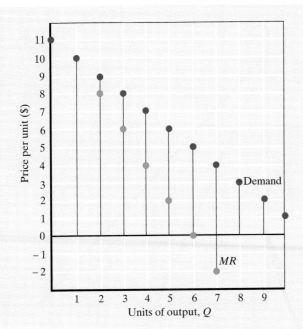

FIGURE 13.3

Marginal Revenue Curve Facing a Monopolist

At every level of output except one unit, a monopolist's marginal revenue is below price. This is so because (1) we assume that the monopolist must sell all its product at a single price (no price discrimination), and (2) to raise output and sell it, the firm must lower the price it charges. Selling the additional output will raise revenue, but this increase is offset somewhat by the lower price charged for all units sold. Therefore, the increase in revenue from increasing output by one (the marginal revenue) is less than price.

negative after six units of output. When the demand curve is a straight line, the marginal revenue curve bisects the quantity axis between the origin and the point where the demand curve hits the quantity axis (Figure 13.4).

Look carefully at Figure 13.4. What you can see in the diagram is that:

> A monopoly's marginal revenue curve shows the change in total revenue that results as a firm moves along the segment of the demand curve that lies directly above it.

Consider starting at an output of zero units per period in the top panel of Figure 13.4. At zero units, of course, total revenue (shown in the bottom panel) is zero because nothing is sold. To begin selling, the firm must lower the product's price. Marginal revenue is positive, and total revenue begins to increase. To sell increasing quantities of the good, the firm must lower its price more and more. As output increases between zero and Q^* and the firm moves down its demand curve from point A to point B, marginal revenue remains positive and total revenue continues to increase. The quantity of output (Q) is rising, which tends to push total revenue ($P \times Q$) *up*. At the same time, the price of output (P) is falling, which tends to push total revenue ($P \times Q$) *down*. Up to point B, the effect of increasing Q dominates the effect of falling P, and total revenue rises; marginal revenue is positive (above the quantity axis).[2]

But what happens as we move further along the quantity axis above Q^*—that is, further down the demand curve from point B toward point C? We are still lowering P to sell more output, but above (to the right of) Q^*, marginal revenue is negative and total revenue in the bottom panel starts to fall. Beyond Q^*, the effect

---

[2]*Recall from Chapter 5 that if the percentage change in Q is greater than the percentage change in P as you move along a demand curve, the absolute value of elasticity of demand is greater than one. Thus, as we move along the demand curve in Figure 13.4 between point A and point B, demand is elastic.*

FIGURE 13.4

Marginal Revenue and Total Revenue

A monopoly's marginal revenue curve bisects the quantity axis between the origin and the point where the demand curve hits the quantity axis. A monopoly's *MR* curve shows the change in total revenue that results as a firm moves along the segment of the demand curve that lies exactly above it.

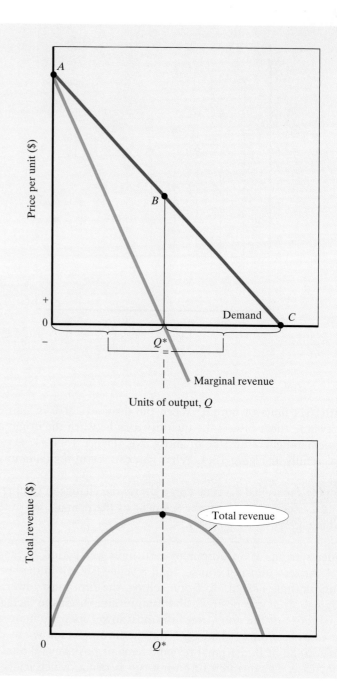

of cutting price on total revenue is larger than the effect of increasing quantity. As a result, total revenue ($P = Q$) falls. AT point C, revenue once again is at zero, this time because price has dropped to zero![3]

■ **The Monopolist's Profit-Maximizing Price and Output**   We have spent much time in defining and explaining marginal revenue because it is an important factor in the

---

[3]*Beyond Q^*, between points B and C on the demand curve in Figure 13.4, the decline in price must be bigger in percentage terms than the increase in quantity. Thus the absolute value of elasticity beyond point B is less than one: demand is inelastic. At point B, marginal revenue is zero; the decrease in P exactly offsets the decrease in price, and elasticity is unitary or equal to minus one.*

monopolist's choice of profit-maximizing price and output. Figure 13.5 on page 328 superimposes a demand curve and the marginal revenue curve derived from it over a set of cost curves. In determining price and output, a monopolistic firm must go through the same basic decision process that a competitive firm goes through. As you know, any profit-maximizing firm will raise its production as long as the added revenue from the increase outweighs the added cost. In more specific terms, we can say that:

> All firms, including monopolies, find it profitable to raise output as long as marginal revenue is greater than marginal cost. Any positive difference between marginal revenue and marginal cost can be thought of as marginal profit.

The optional price/output combination for the monopolist in Figure 13.5 is $P_m = \$4.00$ and $Q_m = 4000$, the quantity at which the marginal revenue curve and the marginal cost curve intersect. At any output below 4000, marginal revenue is greater than marginal cost. At any output above 400, increasing output would reduce profits, because marginal cost exceeds marginal revenue. This leads us to conclude that:

> The profit-maximizing level of output for a monopolist is the one at which marginal revenue equals marginal cost: $MR = MC$.

Because marginal revenue for a monopoly lies below the demand curve, the final price chosen by the monopolist will be above marginal cost ($P_m = \$4.00$ is greater than $MC = \$1.50$). At 4000 units of output, price will be fixed at \$4 (point A on the demand curve), and total revenue will be $P_m \times Q_m = \$4 \times 4000 = 16\ 000$ (area P_mAQ_m0). Total cost is the product of average total cost and units of output, $\$3 \times 400 = \$12\ 000$ (area CBQ_m0). Total profit is the difference between total revenue and total cost, $\$16\ 000 - \$12\ 000 = \$4000$. In Figure 13.5, total profit is equal to the area of the pink rectangle P_mABC.

Among competitive firms, the presence of economic profits provides an incentive for new firms to enter the industry, thus shifting supply to the right, driving down price, and eliminating profits. Remember, however, that for monopolies we assume that barriers to entry have been erected and that profits are protected.

■ **The Absence of a Supply Curve in Monopoly** In perfect competition, the supply curve of a firm in the short run is the same as the portion of the firm's marginal cost curve that lies above the average variable cost curve. As the price of the good produced by the firm changes, the perfectly competitive firm simply moves up or down its marginal cost curve in choosing how much output to produce.

As you can see, however, Figure 13.5 contains nothing that we can point to and call a supply curve. The amount of output that a monopolist produces depends on its marginal cost curve *and* on the shape of the demand curve that it faces. In other words, the amount of output that a monopolist supplies is not independent of the shape of the demand curve. Thus,

> A monopoly firm has no supply curve that is independent of the demand curve for its product.

To see why this is so, consider what a firm's supply curve means. A supply curve shows the quantity of output the firm is willing to supply at each price. If we ask a monopolist how much output she is willing to supply at a given price, the monopolist will say that her supply behaviour depends not just on marginal cost but also on the marginal revenue associated with that price. And, to know what

FIGURE 13.5

Price and Output Choice for a Profit-Maximizing Monopolist

A profit-maximizing monopolist will raise output as long as marginal revenue exceeds marginal cost. Maximum profit is achieved at an output of 4000 units per period and a price of $4. Above 4000 units of output, marginal cost is greater than marginal revenue; increasing output beyond 4000 units would reduce profit.

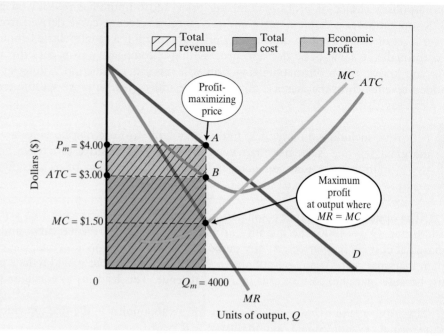

that marginal revenue would be, the monopolist must know what her demand curve looks like.

In sum: in perfect competition, we can draw a firm's supply curve without knowing anything more than the firm's marginal cost curve. The situation for a monopolist is more complicated:

> A monopolist sets both price and quantity, and the amount of output that it supplies depends on both its marginal cost curve and the demand curve that it faces.

■ **Monopoly in the Long and Short Run**   One of the key distinctions we made in our analysis of perfectly competitive markets was the distinction between the long run and the short run. In the short run, you will recall, all firms face some fixed factor of production, and no entry into or exit from the industry is possible. The assumption of a fixed factor of production is the primary reason that marginal cost increases with output in the short run. That is, the short-run marginal cost curve of a typical competitive firm slopes upward and to the right because of the limitations imposed by the fixed factor. In the long run, however, firms can enter and exit the industry. Long-run equilibrium is established when the entry and exit of firms drives economic profits in the industry to zero.

The destination between the long and short runs is somewhat less important in monopoly markets. In the short run, monopolists are limited by a fixed factor of production, just as competitive firms are. The cost curves in Figure 13.5 reflect the diminishing returns to the monopoly's fixed factor of production (for example, plant size).

What will happen to the monopoly in the long run? If the monopoly is earning economic profits (profits over and above a normal return to capital), nothing will happen. In competition, profits lead to expansion and entry, but in monopoly, entry is blocked. In addition, because we assume that the monopoly is a profit-maximizing firm, it will operate at the most efficient scale of production, and it will neither expand nor contract in the long run. Thus, Figure 13.5 will not change in the long run.

It is possible for a monopoly to find itself suffering economic losses (profits below normal). A monopoly that finds itself unable to cover total costs is illustrated in Figure 13.6. The best that the firm can do is produce Q_m = 10 000 units of output (the point at which $MR = MC$) and charge P_m = \$4 for its output (point E on the demand curve). But at 10 000 units of output per period, total revenue of \$40 000 ($P_m \times Q_m$, where P_m = \$4 and Q_m = 10 000), which is equal to the area P_mEQ_m0, is not sufficient to cover total costs of \$50 000 ($ATC \times Q_m$, where ATC = \$5 and Q_m = 10 000), which is equal to the area FDQ_m0. The firm thus suffers losses equal to \$10 000, the shaded area (rectangle $FDEP_m$). Notice, however, that total revenue is sufficient to cover the level of *variable* costs, which equals \$25 000 ($AVC \times Q_m$, where AVC = \$2.50 and Q_m = 10 000). Thus, operating in the short run generates a profit on operation (total revenue minus total variable costs is greater than zero) that can be used to cover some of the firm's short-run fixed costs. The basis of the monopolist's decision is thus exactly the same as that for a competitive firm:

> If a firm can reduce its losses by operating in the short run, it will do so.

Similarly, in the long run, a firm that cannot generate enough revenue to cover total costs will go out of business, whether it is competitive or monopolistic. Since the demand curve in Figure 13.6 lies completely below the average total cost curve, the monopoly will go out of business in the long run, and its product will not be produced because it is simply not worth the cost of production to buyers.

PERFECT COMPETITION AND MONOPOLY COMPARED

One way to understand monopoly is to compare equilibrium output and price in a perfectly competitive industry with the output and price that would be chosen if the same industry were organized as a monopoly. To make this comparison meaningful, let us exclude from consideration any technological advantage that a single large firm might enjoy.

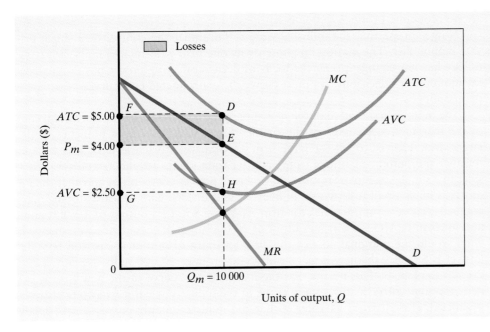

FIGURE 13.6

Price and Output Choice for a Monopolist Suffering Losses in the Short Run

It is possible for a profit-maximizing monopolist to suffer short-run losses. AT 10 000 units of output (the point at which $MR = MC$), total revenue is sufficient to cover variable cost but not to cover total cost. Thus, the firm will operate in the short run but go out of business in the long run.

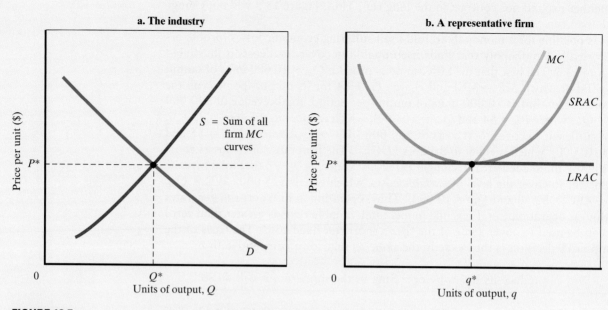

a. The industry

Price per unit ($)

$P*$

S = Sum of all firm MC curves

D

0        $Q*$

Units of output, Q

b. A representative firm

Price per unit ($)

MC

$SRAC$

$P*$

$LRAC$

0        $q*$

Units of output, q

FIGURE 13.7

A Perfectly Competitive Industry in Long-Run Equilibrium

In a perfectly competitive industry in the long run, price will be equal to long-run average cost. The market supply curve is the sum of all the short-run marginal cost curves of the firms in the industry. Here we assume that firms are using a technology that exhibits constant returns to scale: $LRAC$ is flat. Big firms enjoy no cost advantage.

We begin our comparisons, then, with a competitive industry made up of a large number of firms operating with a production technology that exhibits constant returns to scale in the long run. (Recall that *constant returns to scale* means that average cost is the same whether the firm operates one large plant or many small plants.) Figure 13.7 shows a perfectly competitive industry at long-run equilibrium, a condition in which price is equal to long-run average costs and in which there are no economic profits.

Now suppose that the industry were to fall under the control of a single private monopolist. The monopolist now owns one firm with many plants. But technology has not changed; only the locus of decision-making power has. To analyze the monopolist's decisions, we must derive the consolidated cost curves now facing the monopoly.

The marginal cost curve of the new monopoly will simply be the horizontal sum of the marginal cost curves of the smaller firms, which are now branches of the larger firm. That is, to get the large firm's MC curve, at each level of MC we add together the output quantities from each separate plant. To understand why, consider this simple example. Suppose that there is perfect competition and that the industry is made up of just two small firms, A and B, each with upward-sloping marginal cost curves. Suppose that for firm A, MC = $5 at an output of 10 000 units and for firm B, MC = $5 at an output of 20 000 units. If these firms were merged, what would the marginal cost of the 30 000th unit of output per period be? The answer is $5 since the new larger firm would produce 10 000 units in plant A and 20 000 in plant B. This means that the marginal cost curve of the new firm is *exactly the same curve* as the supply curve in the industry when it was competitively organized. (Recall from Chapter 9 that the industry supply curve in a perfectly competitive industry is the sum of the marginal cost curves [above average variable cost] of all the individual firms in that industry.)[4]

Figure 13.8 on page 332 illustrates the cost curve, marginal revenue curve, and demand curve of the consolidated monopoly industry. If the industry were competitively organized, total industry output would have been $Q_c = 4000$ and price would have been $P_c = \$3$. These price and output decision are determine by the intersection of the competitive supply curve, S_c, and the market demand curve.

No longer faced with a price that it cannot influence, however, the monopolist can choose any price/quantity combination along the demand curve. The output level that maximizes profits to the monopolist is $Q_m = 2500$—the point at which marginal revenue intersects marginal cost. Output will be priced at $P_m = \$4$. To increase output beyond 2500 units or to charge a price below $4 (which represents the amount consumers are willing to pay) would reduce profit. The final result is that:

> Relative to a competitively organized industry, a monopolist restricts output, charges higher prices, and earns economic profits.

And remember, all we did was to transfer decision-making power from the individual small firms to a consolidated owner. The new firm gains nothing at all technologically from being big.

COLLUSION AND MONOPOLY COMPARED

Suppose now that the industry discussed above did not become a monopoly. Instead, suppose the individual firm owners simply decide to work together in an effort to limit competition and increase joint profits, a behaviour called **collusion.** In this case, the outcome would be exactly the same as the outcome of a monopoly in the industry. Firms certainly have an incentive to collude. When they act independently, they compete away whatever profits they can find. But, as we saw in Figure 13.8, when price increases to $4 across the industry, the monopolistic firm earns economic profits.

Despite the fact that collusion is illegal, it has taken place in some industries. In a recent case, a number of Quebec City-area concrete manufacturers were successfully prosecuted for meeting secretly to fix prices and divide up markets. Fines totalled over $5.8 million. More recently, an unusual and illegal price-fixing arrangement was discovered among Italian bread bakeries in New York. (See the Application box on page 335 titled "Rent-Seeking Behaviour in the Italian Bread Market.")

collusion *The act of working with other producers in an effort to limit competition and increase joint profits.*

The Social Costs of Monopoly

So far we have seen that a monopoly produces less output and charges a higher price than a competitively organized industry, if no large economies of scale exist for the monopoly. You are probably thinking at this point that producing less and charging more to earn economic profits is not likely to be in the best interests of consumers, and you are right.

INEFFICIENCY AND CONSUMER LOSS

In Chapter 12, we argued that price must equal marginal cost ($P = MC$) for markets to produce what people want. This argument rests on two propositions:

---

[4]*The same logic will show that the average cost curve of the consolidated firm is simply the sum of the average cost curves of the individual plants.*

FIGURE 13.8

In the newly organized monopoly, the marginal cost curve is exactly the same as the supply curve that represented the behaviour of all the independent firms when the industry was organized competitively. This enables us to compare the monopoly outcome with the competitive outcome. Quantity produced by the monopoly will be less than the competitive level of output, and the monopoly price will be higher than the price under perfect competition.

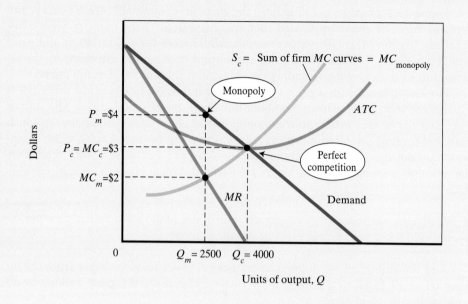

(1) that price provides a good approximation of the social value of a unit of output, and (2) that marginal cost, in the absence of externalities (costs or benefits to external parties not weighed by firms), provides a good approximation of the product's social opportunity cost. In pure monopoly, price ends up above product's marginal cost. When this happens, the firm is underproducing from society's point of view; society would be better off if the firm produced more and charged a lower price. We can therefore conclude that:

> Monopoly leads to an inefficient mix of output.

A slightly simplified version of the monopoly diagram appears in Figure 13.9 on the next page, which shows how we might make a rough estimate of the size of the loss to social welfare that arises from monopoly. (For the sake of clarity here, we will ignore the short-run cost curves and assume constant returns to scale in the long run.) Under competitive conditions, firms would produce output up to $Q_c = 4000$ units per period, and price would ultimately settle at $P_c = \$2$, equal to long-run average cost. Any price above \$2 will mean economic profits, which would be eliminated by the entry of new competing firms in the long run. (You should remember all this from Chapter 9.)

A monopoly firm in the same industry, however, would produce only $Q_m = 2000$ units per period and charge a price of $P_m = \$4$, since $MR = MC$ at $Q_m = 2000$ units. The monopoly would make a profit equal to total revenue minus total cost, or $P_m \times Q_m$ minus $P_c \times Q_m$. Profit to the monopoly is thus equal to the area $P_m A C P_c$, or \$4000. ([\$4 × 2000] - [\$2 × 2000] = \$8000 − \$4000 = \$4000. Remember $P_c = AC$ in this example.)

Now consider the gains and losses associated with increasing price from \$2 to \$4 and cutting output from 4000 units to 2000 units. You might guess that the winner will be the monopolist and the loser will be the consumer, but let us see how it works out.

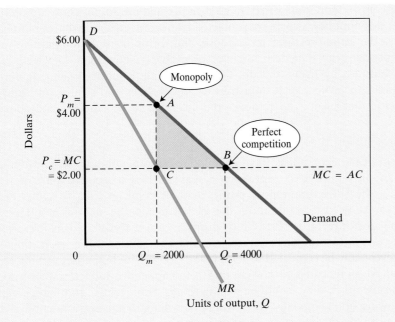

FIGURE 13.9

Welfare Loss from Monopoly

A demand curve shows the amounts that people are willing to pay at each potential level of output. Thus the demand curve can be used to approximate the benefits to the consumer of raising output above 2000 units. *MC* reflects the marginal cost of the resources needed. The triangle ABC roughly measures the net social gain of moving from 2000 units to 4000 units per period (or the loss that results when monopoly decreases output from 4000 units to 2000 units per period).

At $P_c = \$2$, the price that would be charged under perfect competition, there are no economic profits. Consumers are paying a price of $2, but the demand curve shows that many are willing to pay more than that. For example, a substantial number of people would pay $4. Those people willing to pay more than $2 are receiving what we earlier called a *consumer surplus*. The demand curve shows approximately how much households are willing to pay at each level of output, and thus the area of triangle DBP_c gives us a rough measure of the "consumer surplus" being enjoyed by households when the price is $2. Consumers willing to pay exactly $4 get a surplus equal to $2. Those who place the highest value on this good—that is, those who are willing to pay the most—get a surplus equal to DP_c or $4.

Now the industry is reorganized as a monopoly that cuts output to 2000 units and raises price to $4. The big winner is the monopolist, who ends up earning economic profits equal to $4000 each period.

The big losers are the consumers. Their "surplus" now shirnks from the area of triangle DAB_c to the area of triangle DAP_m. Part of that loss (which is equal to DBP_c minus DAP_m, or the area P_mABP_c) is covered by the monopolist's gain of P_mACP_c, but not all of it. The loss to consumers exceeds the gain to the monopoly by the area of triangle ABC (P_mABP_c minus P_mACP_c), which roughly measures the net loss in social welfare associated with monopoly power in this industry. Since the area of a triangle is half its base times its height, the welfare loss is $1/2 \times 2000 \times \$2 = \$2000$ per period. If we could push price back down to the competitive level and increase output up to 4000 units per period, consumers would gain more than the monopolist would lose, and the gain in social welfare would approximate the area of ABC, or $2000.

In this example, the presence of a monopoly also causes an important change in the distribution of real income. In Figure 13.9, area P_mACP_c is economic profit of $4000 flowing every period to the monopolist. If price were pushed down to $2 by competition or regulation, those excess profits would pass to consumers in the form of lower prices. Society may value this resource transfer on equity grounds in addition to efficiency grounds.

Of course, monopolies may have social costs that do not show up on these diagrams. Monopolies, which are protected from competition by barriers to entry, do not face the same pressures to cut costs and to innovate as competitive firms do. A competitive firm that does not use the most efficient technology will be driven out of business by firms that do. One of the significant arguments against tariffs and quotas to protect such industries as automobiles and steel from foreign competition is that protection removes the incentive to be efficient and competitive.

RENT-SEEKING BEHAVIOUR

In recent years, economists have encountered another serious worry. While triangles ABC in Figure 13.9 represents a real net loss to society, part of rectangle P_mACP_c (the $4000 monopoly profit) may also end up lost. To understand why this is so, we need to think about the incentives facing potential monopolists.

The area of rectangle P_mACP_c is profit over and above a normal return to capital. If entry into the market were free and competition were open, these profits would eventually be competed to zero. Clearly, owners of businesses earning economic profits have an incentive to prevent this from happening. In fact, the diagram shows exactly how much they would be willing to pay to prevent it from happening. A rational owner of a competitive firm would be willing to pay any amount less than the entire rectangle. Any portion of profits left over after expenses is better than zero, which would be the case if free competition eliminated all profits.

There are many things that a potential monopolist can do to protect his or her profits. One obvious approach is to push the government to impose restrictions on competition. A classic example is the behaviour of taxicab drivers. To operate a cab legally in many Canadian cities, you need a licence. The cities tightly control the number of licences available. If entry into the taxi business were open, competition would hold down cab fares to the cost of operating cabs. But cab drivers have become a powerful lobbying force and have succeeded in restricting the number of licences issued. This restriction keeps fares high and preserves monopoly profits.

There are countless other examples. Business groups spend large sums of money lobbying Members of Parliament to get favourable legislation. Some experts claim that regulation of Canadian rail and trucking industries by the now defunct Canadian Transport Commission (CTC) was heavily influenced by the industry's efforts to restrict competition and preserve profits.

rent-seeking behaviour *Actions taken by households or firms to preserve extranormal profits.*

This kind of behaviour, in which households or firms take action to preserve extranormal profits, is called **rent-seeking behaviour**.[5] Recall from Chapter 10 that rent is the return to a factor of production in strictly limited supply. Rent-seeking behaviour has two important implications.

First it consumes resources. Lobbying and building barriers to entry are not costless activities. Lobbyists' wages, expenses of the regulatory bureaucracy, and the like must be paid. Indeed, extranormal profits may be completely consumed through rent-seeking behaviour that produces nothing of social value; all it does is help to preserve the current distribution of income.

Second, the frequency of rent-seeking behaviour leads us to another view of government. So far we have considered only the role that government might play in helping to achieve an efficient allocation of resources in the face of market failure—in this case, failures that arise from imperfect market structure. Later in this

---

[5]*The term "rent-seeking behaviour" was coined by Anne Krueger in an important article published in 1974. Much of the theory dates to earlier work by Gordon Tullock. See Anne O. Krueger, "The Political Economy of the Rent-Seeking Society."* American Economic Review 64 (1974): pp. 291–303; *and J. Buchanan, R. Tollison, and G. Tullock (eds.),* Toward a Theory of the Rent-Seeking Society *(College Station, TX: Texas A & M University Press, 1980).*

Application

Rent-Seeking Behaviour in the Italian Bread Market

Rent-seeking behaviour refers to actions taken by households or firms to create and protect extranormal profits. The following article from *The New York Times* speaks for itself:

For years, law-enforcement officials heard complaints about a small group of unscrupulous bakers trying to corner the Italian-bread market in much of New York City. Using threats of violence, the authorities were told, the cartel controlled the distribution of fresh Italian bread to small grocery stores in Brooklyn and Staten Island, inflating prices and eliminating competition.

But investors found that bakers and store owners were reluctant to cooperate. The only way to get to the heart of the Italian-bread racket, they decided, was to open a bakery themselves.

So a team of a half dozen undercover detectives opened a storefront at 327 West 11th Street in Greenwich Village in early 1993 and called it Louis Basile's. Wearing bakers' whites, they pretended to bake several dozen loaves of bread each day, taking turns getting up at 3 A.M. to drive to New Jersey to buy the real stuff, and wrapping the loaves in the customized white paper sleeves that are the signature of authentic, fresh Italian bread.

It was not long after the investigators began trying to sell the bread to neighborhood grocery stories in Manhattan and Brooklyn that they heard from the Association of Independent Bakers and Distributors of Italian Bread. Over drinks at the White Horse Tavern on Hudson Street, investigators

As a result of rent-seeking behaviour, the price of a loaf of Italian bread in New York City was raised 10 cents and held at that level. The 1990 price increase cost consumers millions of dollars.

say, a detective posing as a baker was told by two members of the association that violence could come to Basile's and its employees if they did not play by association rules.

The rules involved fixed prices for bread and a system of distribution that forced a store to buy from a single baker, said the Manhattan District Attorney, Robert M. Morgenthau. . . .

Daniel J. Castleman, head of investigations in Mr. Morgenthau's office, said association members included about 50 bakeries that supplied Italian bread to over 1,000 small grocery stores and delicatessens in the city.

Mr. Castleman said the office was unable to estimate what percentage of the city's bread sales were affected by the association's practices, in part because sales in larger supermarkets were not involved. But he said the association controlled virtually all of Staten Island and most neighborhoods in

Brooklyn where Italian bread was popular and was expanding into Manhattan, Queens and Westchester and Nassau counties. . . .

As an example of the association's activity, Mr. Morgenthau cited a decision in 1990 to raise the retail price of bread from 75 to 85 cents. Five cents of the increase went to the bakers and the other five was divided between the bread deliverers and the store owners, he said.

"Because the association had a lock on the market, consumers had no choice but to pay the increase," Mr. Morgenthau said. . . .

While Mr. Morgenthau said he could not estimate how much the association and its members profited from illegal operations, Mr. Castleman said the 1990 price increase cost consumers millions of dollars.

Source: Seth Faison, "Price-Fixing Plan Is Charged in New York Italian Bakeries," *The New York Times*, July 14, 1994, p. A1.

chapter and in Chapter 15 we survey the measures government might take to ensure that resources are efficiently allocated when monopoly power arises. But the idea of rent-seeking behaviour introduces the important notion of **government failure**, in which the government becomes the tool of the rent seeker, and the allocation of resources is made even less efficient than before.

The idea of government failure is at the centre of **public choice theory**, which holds that governments are made up of people, just as business firms are. These people—politicians and bureaucrats—can be expected to act in their own self-interest, just as owners of firms can be expected to. We turn to the economics of public choice in Chapter 16.

government failure *Occurs when the government becomes the tool of the rent seeker and the allocation of resources is made even less efficiently by the intervention of government.*

public choice theory *An economic theory that proceeds on the assumption that the public officials who set economic policies and regulate the players act in their own self-interest, just as firms do.*

REMEDIES FOR MONOPOLY

It is recognized that monopoly power is not in the public interest, and numerous antimonopoly laws have been enacted. As we will see in Chapter 15, the government has taken two basic approaches to limiting monopoly power: (1) breaking up the monopoly into a number of smaller competing firms (restructuring the industry), and (2) allowing the firm to operate as a monopoly, but under strict regulations. One way the government can control monopoly is by setting the price of its output at competitive levels.

Under some circumstances, breaking up a monopoly would *not* be in the public interest. Some monopolies are better left intact. It is to these "natural monopolies" that we now turn our attention.

Natural Monopoly

In comparing monopoly and competition, we assumed that the efficient scale of operation was small. When this is the case, there is no technological reason to have big firms instead of small firms. In some industries, however, there are technological economies of scale so large that it makes sense to have just one firm. Examples are rare, but public utilities—the electric company or the telephone company, for example—are among them. A firm that realizes such large economies of scale is called a **natural monopoly**.

natural monopoly *An industry that realizes such large economies of scale in producing its product that single-firm production of that good or service is most efficient.*

Although Figure 13.10 on the next page presents an exaggerated picture, it does serve to illustrate our point. One large-scale plant (Scale 2) can produce 500 000 units of output at an average unit cost of $1. If the industry were restructured into five firms, each producing on a smaller scale (Scale 1), the industry could produce the same amount, but average unit cost would be five times as high ($5). Consumers thus see a considerable gain when economies of scale are realized.

The critical point here is that:

> Economies of scale must be realized at a scale that is close to total demand in the market.

Notice in Figure 13.10 that the long-run average cost curve continues to decline almost until it hits the market demand curve. If at a price of $1 market demand is *5 million* units of output, there would be no reason to have only one firm in the industry. Ten firms could each produce 500 000 units, and each could reap the full benefits of the available economies of scale.

IDENTIFYING A NATURAL MONOPOLY

Empirical studies suggest that very few true natural monopolies exist. The most often-cited example has always been the telephone system. Would it make any sense

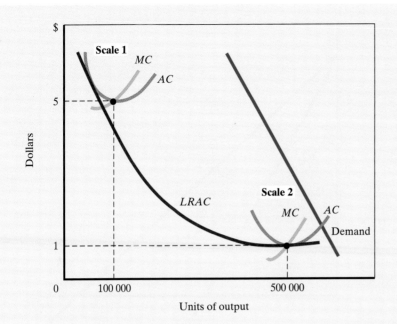

FIGURE 13.10

A Natural Monopoly

A natural monopoly is a firm in which the most efficient scale is very large. Here average cost declines until a single firm is producing nearly the entire amount demanded in the market. With one firm producing 500 000 units, average cost is $1 per unit. With five firms each producing 100 000 units, average cost is $5 per unit.

to have two or more telephone cables running down each street? Providing local exchange service requires an enormous initial investment in switching equipment, wires, trenches, poles, and the like. Thus, fixed costs are very high, while marginal costs are very low. This means that average costs will continuously decline—one of the conditions that defines a natural monopoly.

Lately, however, this conventional wisdom has come under fire as modern technology opens up new ways of doing business in the telephone industry. For example, more and more telephone traffic is being transmitted through the air by microwave. Microwave transmitters can now be installed at relatively low cost, and no poles or connected wires are needed. Small firms are also stringing newly developed fibre-optic cable from location to location at relatively low cost.

These developments have led many analysts to conclude that the monopoly power granted to telephone companies to provide local services can no longer be justified on the basis of large economies of scale. Nonetheless, such monopoly power is still granted. The current argument in favour of maintaining the local monopoly status is to ensure universal access to the telephone system at low cost. Public utility boards, through their mandate to control basic service, can see that this happens.

Even though the argument for maintaining monopolies in local telephone service has shifted from one of efficiency to one of equity, the basic natural monopoly argument based on large efficient scale still seems valid where power companies are concerned. Electric power is still transmitted only over wires, and given this technology, huge economies of scale undeniably exist.

REGULATING A NATURAL MONOPOLY

A more complete diagram of the cost structure of a natural monopoly appears in Figure 13.11 on page 338. For simplicity, let us assume that the firm has very large initial fixed costs and very low constant marginal costs. Demand is fully exhausted while average cost is still in the process of declining. Like the business shown in Figure 13.10, operating this business on a small scale would make no sense because production costs would rapidly rise if firm size were reduced.

If an exclusive government licence were issued to this firm, which would then

FIGURE 13.11

The Problem of Regulating a Natural Monopoly

An unregulated monopolist would produce only up to the point at which *marginal cost* and *marginal revenue* are equal—400 000 units of output. If price were set at the efficient level, $PE = MC = \$0.35$, the firm would always suffer losses, because that price is insufficient to cover average costs. A compromise is for regulators to set price at $PA = \$0.75$, which is just sufficient to cover costs including a normal profit rate.

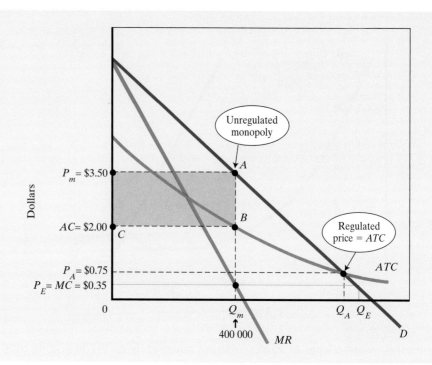

be allowed to choose price and quantity freely, the firm would price at $P_m = \$3.50$, produce 400 000 units of output, and earn economic profits of P_mABC.[6] Such a firm, if left unregulated, would take all the benefits from the economies of scale away from consumers. All of this is simply to say that:

> Acknowledging a single firm as a natural monopoly and allowing it to operate under the protection of a government franchise essentially requires that the government become involved in regulating the firm.

One regulation possibility is for the government to set the price of the monopoly's output equal to marginal cost of production—that is, at $P_E = MC$, in this case $\$0.35$. This would be the price of the output if it were produced competitively and efficiently. Notice, however, that marginal cost is *always* below average cost. Thus, if the government were to set price at $P_E = MC$, no level of output would produce enough revenue to cover total costs. If average revenue per unit (which, you will recall, equals price) is always below average cost per unit, there can be no profit. The firm would therefore suffer losses and go out of business in the long run.

Two other solutions to this regulatory dilemma are possible. The efficient solution would be to enforce a **price ceiling**—that is, a maximum price per unit above which the producer may not legally charge—at marginal cost and to subsidize the monopoly to keep it in business. Because this requires the use of tax dollars, however, it is rarely used.

By far the most common regulatory practice is to control price in a way that allows the owners of the public utility to earn a fair rate of return. The government regulator's "fair rate of return" is very much like the economist's "normal

price ceiling *A maximum price per unit above which the producer of a good or service may not legally charge.*

---

[6]*You should by this point be able to figure out why economic profits are equal to rectangle P_mABC. Remember: Economic profits = total revenue minus total costs. In this case, $P_mAQ_m0 - CBQ_m0 = P_mABC$. You should verify that profits are $600 000.*

rate of return." Because a normal return to capital is included in economic costs, a price that allows a firm to earn a normal return (which we assume is the same as the regulator's "fair return") would be a price just sufficient to cover average total costs (*ATC*). In Figure 13.11, a price ceiling set at $P_A = \$0.75$ would leave the firm earning zero profits and just a normal rate of return.

While **average-cost pricing**—that is, setting price to cover average cost per unit including a fair return—will lower cost to consumers, transfer profits from monopolists, and reduce the net loss of social welfare, it does *not* produce efficient results. (Remember, economic efficiency requires production levels at which price equals marginal cost.) It is a compromise whose chief virtue is that it requires no tax revenues to subsidize utilities.

average-cost pricing *Setting price to cover average cost per unit including a fair return.*

OPTIONAL MATERIAL

Market Power in Input Markets: Monopsony

Up to this point, we have been talking about market power in terms of output, or product, markets. Even monopolies, we assumed, were price takers in input markets. But it is also possible for a firm to exercise control over prices in input markets. Consider, for example, a firm that is the *only buyer* in a market, the company that hires labour in a "company town." A market with only one buyer is called a **monopsony**.[7]

monopsony *A market in which there is only one buyer for a good or service.*

We have said time and time again that competitive firms are price takers in input markets as well as output markets. The wage rate, for example, is set by the supply and demand that result when many firms demand labour and many households supply it. An individual competitive firm takes an externally determined wage rate as a given and will demand an input as long as the marginal revenue product of that input exceeds its price. The marginal revenue product of labour, for example, is the added revenue that the firm earns by hiring one additional unit of labour. The unit of labour produces some product—its marginal product—which, when sold, brings in revenue. In making input decisions, the competitive firm compares the marginal gains from hiring each unit of labour (that is, what the product of that unit sells for) against the "marginal cost" of that unit (that is, the wage rate). (If this sounds unfamiliar, you might want to review Chapter 10.)

When a firm hires labour competitively, it hires all the labour it needs at the current market wage. But suppose that the firm is the *only* buyer of labourers with some particular skill. This means that the firm now faces a market supply curve rather than a market-determined equilibrium wage. The wage rate thus becomes a decision variable for the firm. If the market supply curve of labour slopes upward, and the monopsony firm needs more labour, it must offer a higher wage to get that labour. The marginal cost of an additional unit of labour is no longer just equal to the wage rate. This leads us to the concept of **marginal factor cost (*MFC*)**, the additional cost of using one additional unit of a factor of production at the margin.

marginal factor cost (*MFC*) *The additional cost of using one more unit of a given factor of production.*

Using the supply schedule in Table 13.2 on page 340, suppose that the monopsony firm wants to increase its use of labour from three units to four. The fourth unit of labour will work for a wage of $8 per hour, but because our firm cannot price discriminate, it must pay all workers the higher wage. When the monopsony employed three workers, it had to pay them only $6 per hour each. When the fourth unit of labour is added, those three will each earn an additional $2 per hour.

---

[7]The terms "monopoly" and "monopsony" both derive from Greek root words. In both cases *mon(o)* means "sole" or "single." "Monopoly" adds a form of the Greek verb *polein*, "to sell." "Monopsony" adds a form of the Greek verb *opsonein*, "to buy food."

	Table 13.2		Deriving Marginal Resource Cost for a Monopsonist	
	(1) Units of Labour Supplied	**(2)** Wage	**(3)** Total Factor Cost (TFC)	**(4)** Marginal Factor Cost (MFC)
	0	$0	$—	$—
	1	2	2	—
	2	4	8	6
	3	6	18	10
	4	8	32	14
	5	10	50	18
	6	12	72	22
	7	14	98	26

The total cost of increasing labour from three to four units, therefore, is the $8 that goes to the fourth worker plus the $2 to each of the other three. The marginal factor cost is thus $14. In other words, increasing the use of labour by one unit will cost the firm $14. The marginal factor cost is higher than the wage rate at every level of labour demand except one, because the higher wage needed to attract any additional labour supply goes to all workers, not just to the marginal worker.

Figure 13.12 shows a typical marginal factor cost schedule that is above the labour supply schedule facing a monopsonist in a labour market. It is superimposed on the firm's marginal revenue product of labour schedule. Using our now-familiar marginal logic, we can conclude that:

A profit-maximizing firm hires labour as long as its marginal revenue product exceeds is marginal factor cost. Therefore, the profit-maximizing amount of labour for the monopsonist occurs at the point where $MRP_L = MFC$.

FIGURE 13.12

A Monopsonist Will Hold Wages below Marginal Revenue Product and Hire Less Labour than a Perfect Competitor

For a monopsonist, the marginal cost of hiring one additional unit of labour is higher than the wage rate, because the firm must increase the wage of all workers to attract the new worker into the labour force. The monopsonist will hire only up to 400 000 hours of labour and pay a wage of $8 per hour.

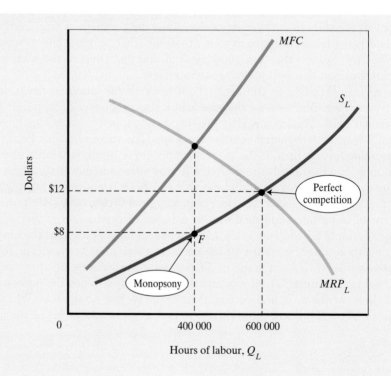

Note that this condition is true for all firms, not just monopsonists. In perfectly competitive labour markets, the wage equals the marginal factor cost. Thus the profit-maximizing amount of labour for a perfectly competitive firm can be written as $MRP_L = W$, which is what we learned in Chapter 10.

The monopsonist in Figure 13.12 would hire labour up to 400 000 hours (the point at which MFC and MRP_L intersect) and thus set a wage equal to $8 per hour (point F on the supply curve). In competition, the wage would be $12 per hour, the point at which quantity supplied and quantity demanded (marginal revenue product) are equal, and 600 000 hours of labour would be hired. (Review Chapter 10 if this reasoning is unclear to you.) Thus, much like a monopolist who curtails production and charges a price above the level set by competition, a monopsonist cuts back on the hours of labour hired and pays a wage below the level set by competition.

As you saw in Chapter 12, the condition $W = MRP_L$ ensures that households supply, and that firms hire, the efficient amount of labour. This condition implies that the market wage facing households and affecting their labour-supply behaviour reflects the value of the product of labour. With monopsony, the wage rate is held considerably below MRP_L at competitive equilibrium. Because marginal revenue product is the value of labour's product, keeping the wage lower keeps people out of the workforce who would otherwise be producing output that has a value to society. Thus, monopsony is inefficient.

Imperfect Markets: A Review and a Look Ahead

A firm has *market power* when it exercises some control over the price of its output or the prices of the inputs that it uses. The extreme case of a firm with market power is the pure monopolist. In pure monopoly, a single firm produces a product for which there are no close substitutes in an industry in which all new competitors are barred from entry.

Our focus in this chapter on pure monopoly (which occurs only rarely) has served a number of purposes. First, the monopoly model does indeed describe a number of industries quite well. Second, the monopoly case clearly illustrates the observation that imperfect competition leads to an inefficient allocation of resources. Finally, the analysis of pure monopoly offers a number of important insights into the more commonly encountered market models of monopolistic competition and oligopoly, which we discussed briefly in this chapter and will discuss in detail in the next chapter.

Summary

1. A number of important assumptions underlie the logic of pure competition. Among them are: (1) a large number of firms and households are interacting in each market; (2) firms in a given market produce undifferentiated, or homogeneous, products; and (3) new firms are free to enter industries and to compete for profits. The first two assumptions imply that firms have no control over input prices or output prices; the third implies that opportunities for economic profit are eliminated in the long run.

Imperfect Competition and Market Power: Core Concepts

2. A market in which individual firms have some control over price is imperfectly competitive. Such firms exercise *market power*. The three forms of *imperfect competition* are monopoly, oligopoly, and monopolistic competition.

3. A *pure monopoly* is an industry with a single firm that produces a product for which there are no close substitutes and in which there are significant *barriers to entry*.

4. There are many barriers to entry, including government franchises and licences, patents, economies of scale, and ownership of scarce factors of production.

5. Market power means that firms must make four decisions instead of three: (1) how much to produce, (2) how to produce it, (3) how much to demand in each input market, and (4) *what price to charge for their output.*

6. Market power does not imply that a monopolist can charge any price it wants. Monopolies are constrained by market demand. They can sell only what people will buy and only at a price that people are willing to pay.

Price and Output Decisions in Pure Monopoly Markets

7. In perfect competition, many firms supply homogeneous products. With only one firm in a monopoly market, however, there is no distinction between the firm and the industry—the firm *is* the industry. The market demand curve is thus the firm's demand curve, and the total quantity supplied in the market is what the monopoly firm decides to produce.

8. For a monopolist, an increase in output involves not just producing more and selling it but also reducing the price of its output in order to sell it. Thus marginal revenue, to a monopolist, is not equal to product price, as it is in competition. Rather, marginal revenue is lower than price because to raise output one unit *and to be able to sell* that one unit, the firm must lower the price it charges to all buyers.

9. A profit-maximizing monopolist will produce up to the point at which marginal revenue is equal to marginal cost ($MR = MC$).

10. Monopolies have no identifiable supply curves. They simply choose a point on the market demand curve. That is, they choose a price and quantity to produce, which depend on both marginal cost and the shape of the demand curve.

11. In the short run, monopolists are limited by a fixed factor of production, just as competitive firms are. Monopolies that do not generate enough revenue to cover costs will go out of business in the long run.

12. Compared to a competitively organized industry, a monopolist restricts output, charges higher prices, and earns economic profits. Because MR always lies below the demand curve for a monopoly, monopolists will always charge a price higher than MC (the price that would be set by perfect competition).

The Social Cost of Monopoly

13. When firms price above marginal cost, the result is an inefficient mix of output. The decrease in consumer surplus is larger than the monopolist's profit, thus causing a net loss in social welfare.

14. Actions that firms take to preserve excess economic profits, such as lobbying for restrictions on competition, are called rent seeking. *Rent-seeking behaviour* consumes resources and adds to social cost, thus reducing social welfare even further.

Natural Monopoly

15. When a firm exhibits economies of scale so large that average costs continuously decline with output, it may be efficient to have only one firm in an industry. Such an industry is called a *natural monopoly.*

16. The most common method of regulating a natural monopoly is to control the monopoly's price in a way that allows the owners of the monopoly to earn a fair rate of return. This method, called *average-cost pricing*, will lower costs to consumers, but it does not produce efficient results.

(Optional) Market Power in Input Markets: Monopsony

17. A market with only one buyer is a *monopsony*. The problems of firms that exercise market power in input markets are similar to the problems of monopoly.

18. *Marginal factor cost* is the additional cost of using one more unit of a given factor of production. A profit-maximizing firm will hire labour as long as its marginal revenue product exceeds its marginal factor cost.

average-cost pricing 339

barrier to entry 319

collusion 331

government failure 336

government franchise 319

imperfectly competitive industry 318

marginal factor cost (*MFC*) 339

market power 318

monopsony 339

natural monopoly 336

patent 320

price ceiling 338

public choice theory 336

pure monopsony 319

rent-seeking behaviour 334

Problem Set

1. Do you agree or disagree with each of the following statements? Explain your reasoning.
   a. For a monopoly, price is equal to marginal revenue because a monopoly has the power to control price.
   b. A natural monopoly will produce at an efficient level of output if its price is simply set by the regulatory agency at marginal cost.
   c. Because a monopoly is the only firm in an industry, it can charge virtually any price for its product.

2. Explain why the marginal revenue curve facing a competitive firm differs from the marginal revenue curve facing a monopolist.

3. Assume that the potato chip industry in Canada in 1997 was competitively structured and in long-run competitive equilibrium; firms were earning a normal rate of return. In 1998 two smart lawyers quietly bought up all the firms and began operations as a monopoly called "Wonks." To operate efficiently, Wonks hired a management consulting firm, which estimated long-run costs and demand. These results are presented in the following figure:

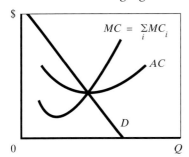

($\sum_i MC_i$ = the horizontal sum of the marginal cost curves of the individual branches/firms)
   a. Indicate 1997 output and price on the diagram.
   b. Assuming that the monopolist is a profit-maximizer, indicate on the graph total revenue, total cost, and total profit after the consolidation.

   c. Compare the perfectly competitive outcome with the monopoly outcome.
   d. In 1998, an old buddy from law school files a complaint with the Bureau of Competition Policy claiming that Wonks has monopolized the potato chip industry. Suppose you work for the Bureau and you are asked to prepare a brief memo (two or three paragraphs) outlining the issues. In your response, be sure to include
      i the economic justification for action
      ii a proposal to achieve an efficient market outcome.

4. Consider the following monopoly that produces paperback books:
   $$\text{Fixed costs} = \$1000$$
   $$\text{Marginal cost} = \$1 \text{ (and is constant)}.$$
   a. Draw the average total cost curve and the marginal cost curve on the same graph.
   b. Assume that all households have the same demand schedule, given by the following relationship:

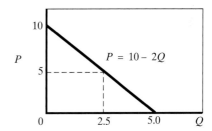

If there are 400 households in the economy, draw the market demand curve and the marginal revenue schedule facing the monopolist.
   c. What is the monopolist's profit-maximizing output? What is the monopolist's price?
   d. What is the "efficient price," assuming no externalities?
   e. Suppose that the government "imposed" the efficient price by setting a ceiling on price at the efficient level. What is the long-run output of the monopoly?

f. Can you suggest an alternative approach for achieving an efficient outcome?

5. Consider the following labour supply schedule and production data:

WAGE RATE	QUANTITY OF LABOUR SUPPLIED	UNITS OF LABOUR	MARGINAL REVENUE PRODUCT LABOUR
$4	1	1	$10
5	2	2	9
6	3	3	8
7	4	4	7
8	5	5	6
9	6	6	5
10	7	7	4

a. Calculate marginal factor cost at each level of labour supply.

b. If the firm whose marginal revenue product schedule is given is a monopsonist, how much labour will be demanded? What wage will be paid? Explain your answer.

c. If the *MRP* schedule of labour were the industry demand schedule in a competitive industry, what would the wage rate be? How many units of labour would be employed?

Monopolistic Competition and Oligopoly

Monopolistic Competition
Product Differentiation, Advertising, and Social Welfare
Price and Output Determination in Monopolistic Competition
Economic Efficiency and Resource Allocation

Oligopoly
Oligopoly Models
Oligopoly and Economic Performance
Industrial Concentration and Technological Change

A Role for Government?

We have now examined two "pure" market structures. At one extreme is *perfect competition,* a market structure in which many firms, each small relative to the size of the market, produce undifferentiated products and have no market power at all. Each competitive firm takes price as given and faces a perfectly elastic demand for its product. At the other extreme is *pure monopoly,* a market structure in which only one firm is the industry. The monopoly holds the power to set price and is protected against competition by barriers to entry. Its market power would be complete if it did not face the discipline of the market demand curve. Even a monopoly, however, must produce a product that people want and are willing to pay for.

Most industries in Canada fall somewhere between these two extremes. In this chapter, we focus on two types of industries in which firms exercise some market power but at the same time face competition. The first type, *monopolistic competition,* differs from perfect competition only in that firms can differentiate their products. Entry to a monopolistically competitive industry is free, and each industry is made up of many firms.

The second type, *oligopoly,* is an extremely broad category that covers many different kinds of firm behaviour and industry structure. An oligopoly is an industry with a small number of competitors. Each firm in an oligopoly is large enough to have some control over market price, but beyond that the character of competition varies greatly from industry to industry. An oligopoly may have 2 firms or 20, and those firms may produce differentiated or undifferentiated products.

Before we go on, it is useful to outline the approach that we will take to studying and analyzing monopolistic competition and oligopoly. We will start with a description of the structure of each kind of industry. How many firms are there? What portion of the industry's total sales is accounted for by the largest firms in the industry? Are there barriers to entry? If so, how do they operate? Do firms produce homogeneous or differentiated products? Are there economies of scale?

After examining structure, we analyze the behaviour of firms in the industry. How are prices set? Does a dominant firm in effect set price for other, smaller firms? Do firms advertise? How much research do the firms do? How often are new product lines introduced?

Finally, we discuss the performance of each type of industry and how efficiently the firms in that industry operate. Do the industry's behaviour and structure lead to inefficiency? Does the industry enhance or retard economic growth? What impact do the industry's structure and behaviour have on the distribution of income?

Monopolistic Competition

monopolistic competition *A common form of industry (market) structure in Canada, characterized by a large number of firms, none of which can influence market price by virtue of size alone. Some degree of market power is achieved by firms producing differentiated products. New firms can enter and established firms can exit such an industry with ease.*

A **monopolistically competitive industry** has the following characteristics:

1. a large number of firms;
2. no barriers to entry;
3. product differentiation.

While pure monopoly and perfect competition are rare, monopolistic competition is very common in Canada. Take, for example, the restaurant business. The Vancouver Yellow Pages devote 27 pages to listing over 1700 different restaurants in the area. Each of these restaurants produces a slightly different product and makes an attempt to distinguish itself in consumers' minds. Entry to the market is certainly not blocked. Although many restaurants fail, small firms can nonetheless compete and survive because there are no economies of scale in the restaurant business.

The feature that distinguishes monopolistic competition from monopoly and oligopoly is that firms cannot influence market price by virtue of their size. No one restaurant is big enough to affect the market price of a prime rib dinner, for example, even though all restaurants can certainly control their *own* prices. Rather, firms gain control over price in monopolistic competition by differentiating their products. You make it in the restaurant business by producing a product that people want and that others are not producing, and/or by establishing a reputation for good food and good service. By producing a unique product or establishing a particular reputation, a firm becomes, in a sense, a "monopolist"—that is, no one else can produce the exact same good.

The feature that distinguishes monopolistic competition from pure monopoly is that good substitutes are available in a monopolistically competitive industry. With 1700 restaurants in the Vancouver area, there are dozens of reasonably good Italian, Chinese, and French restaurants. Vancouver's Chinatown, for example, has about 50 small Chinese restaurants, with over a dozen packed into a single block. The menus are nearly identical, and they all charge virtually the same prices. At the other end of the spectrum are those restaurants, with very well established names and prices far above the cost of production, that are always booked. That, of course, is the goal of every restaurateur who ever put a stockpot on the range.

Table 14.1	Concentration Ratios in Selected Industries, 1988	

	PERCENTAGE OF REVENUE CONTROLLED BY LEADING ENTERPRISES	
Industry	CR4	CR8
Construction	2.2	3.5
Agriculture, forestry, fishing	2.6	4.4
Services	4.5	6.9
Clothing industries	6.6	9.9
Wholesale trade	7.4	12.5
Furniture industries	7.6	13.4
Retail trade	9.7	14.8
Machinery	11.3	18.6
Knitting mills	11.4	18.1
Wood industries	17.8	25.2
Leather products	16.9	26.2

Source: Statistics Canada, *Annual Report of the Minister of Industry, Science, and Technology under the Corporation and Labour Unions Returns Act (CALURA), Part 1, Corporations, 1988* (Ottawa: Minister of Industry, Science, and Technology, 1991).

Tables 14.1 and 14.2 present some data on industries that have the characteristics of monopolistic competition. Table 14.1 provides data based on concentration ratios. A concentration ratio is the percentage of total industry sales accounted for by the largest four (CR4) or eight (CR8) firms. The reported concentration ratios show that industries like retail trade, wholesale trade, furniture, and services are not dominated by a small number of firms. Table 14.2 provides a finer breakdown of industries. Once we look at wooden household furniture as opposed to wood industries in general, the concentration is higher. In the wooden household furniture industry, for example, there are 422 establishments (production sites such as plants or mills) and the largest four enterprises (firms) account for only 11 of these establishments and 20.8% of all shipments. The noncommercial trailer industry appears more concentrated, with the four largest enterprises accounting for over two-thirds of shipments. But even in this industry there are a significant number of enterprises (62) and entry is relatively easy.

Table 14.2	Percentage of Value of Shipments Accounted for by the Largest Enterprises in Selected Industries, 1992			

	SIC Number	Number of Enterprises	Top 4 Establishments (% of Shipments)	Top 8 Establishments (% of Shipments)
Noncommercial trailer industry	3243	62	66.5%	88.15%
Book publishing	2831	186	61.5%	68.9 %
Sweater industry	2491	63	54.0%	88.1 %
Business printing and forms	2811	202	49.0%	61.8 %
Bed spring and mattress	2681	82	42.6%	54.65%
Men's and boy's shirts and underwear	2434	101	33.6%	51.4 %
Pharmaceutical and medicine	3741	117	29.5%	50.7 %
Women's dresses	2443	95	NA	42.2 %
Wooden household furniture	2111	422	20.8%	30.5 %
Sign and display	3971	529	12.9%	18.1 %

Source: Industry Canada, http://strategis.ic.gc.ca/sc_ecnmy/sio/classic.html.

To review:

> Firms in a monopolistically competitive industry are small relative to the total market. New firms can enter the industry in pursuit of profit, and relatively good substitutes for the firms' products are available. Firms in monopolistically competitive industries try to achieve a degree of market power by differentiating their products—by producing something new, different, or better, or by creating a unique identity in the minds of consumers.

Before we go on to discuss the behaviour of such firms, a few words about advertising and product differentiation are in order.

PRODUCT DIFFERENTIATION, ADVERTISING, AND SOCIAL WELFARE

product differentiation *A strategy that firms use to achieve market power. Accomplished by producing products that have distinct positive identities in consumers' minds.*

Monopolistically competitive firms achieve whatever degree of market power they command through **product differentiation**. To be chosen over competitors, products must have distinct positive identities in consumers' minds. This differentiation is often accomplished through advertising.

In 1995 firms spent over $7.5 billion on advertising in Canada, as Table 14.3 shows. Advertising reaches us through every medium of communication. Table 14.4 shows advertising expenditures by major industrial category. Retail trade leads the pack with expenditures of over $0.8 billion in advertising in 1995. In 1995, 30 seconds of prime commercial advertising time during the Super Bowl cost US$1 000 000. A 30-second spot on the last episode of *Cheers* in 1993 and during NBC's showing of *Jurassic Park* in 1995 each cost US$650 000.

The effects of product differentiation in general and advertising in particular on the allocation of resources have been hotly debated for years. Advocates claim that these forces give the market system its vitality and power. Critics argue that they cause waste and inefficiency. Before we proceed to the formal models of monopolistic competition and oligopoly, the major points of this debate are worth reviewing.

■ **The Case for Product Differentiation and Advertising** The most important advantage of open product competition is that it provides us with the variety inherent in a steady stream of new products while ensuring that the quality of those products remains high. We have said before that one of the most important characteristics of a modern economy is the tremendous variety of tastes and preferences that it can satisfy. A walk through several neighbourhoods of a big city, or even an hour in a modern department store or mall, should be enough to convince you that one thing we can say for certain about human wants is that they are almost infinite in their variety.

Free and open competition with differentiated products may be the only way to satisfy all of us. Think of the variety of music we listen to—bluegrass, heavy metal, country, folk, rap, classical, grunge. Business firms engage in constant market research to satisfy these wants. What do consumers want? What colours? What cuts? What sizes? The only firms that succeed are the ones that answer these questions correctly and thereby satisfy an existing demand.

In recent years, quite a few of us have taken up the sport of running. The market has responded in a very big way. Now there are numerous running magazines; hundreds of orthotic shoes designed specifically for runners with particular running styles; running suits of every imaginable colour, cloth, and style; weights for the hands, ankles, and shoe laces; tiny radios to slip into your sweatbands; and so

Table 14.3

Advertising Expenditures, 1995

	Dollars (millions)
Newspapers	$1900
Television	1844
Direct mail	911
Other	788
Yellow Pages	864
Radio	754
Periodicals	440
Total	$7501

Source: Estimates jointly prepared by Statistics Canada, Canadian Newspaper Association, Television Bureau of Canada, Tele-Direct Publications, Radio Marketing Bureau, Canadian Community Newspaper Association, Magazines Canada, and MediaCom. Reported in *Marketing Magazine,* September 16, 1996, p. 4.

forth. Even physicians have differentiated their products: sports medicine clinics have diets for runners, therapies for runners, and doctors specializing in shin splints or Morton's toe. There is even a running shoe with a small computer built into the heel to monitor a runner's time, distance, and calories expended.

The products that satisfy a real demand survive, but the market shows no mercy to products that no one wants. They sit on store shelves, are sold at heavy discount prices or not at all, and eventually disappear. Firms making products that don't sell go out of business, the victims of an economic Darwinism in which only the products that can thrive in a competitive environment survive.

The standard of living rises when the technology of production improves—that is, when we learn to produce more with fewer resources. But the standard of living also rises when we have product *innovation*, when new and better products come on the market. Just think of all the things that we have and use today that didn't exist 10 or 15 years ago. Compact disc players, microwave ovens, VCRs, mountain bikes, and personal computers have all been developed in the last two decades.

Variety is also important to us psychologically. The astonishing range of products available exists not just because your tastes differ from mine. Human beings get bored easily. We grow tired of things, and diminishing marginal utility sets in. I don't go only to French restaurants; it's nice to eat Greek or Chinese food once in a while too. To satisfy many people with different preferences that change over time, the market must be free to respond with new products.

People who visit planned economies always comment on the lack of variety. Indeed, before the Berlin Wall came down in 1989 and East and West Germany were reunited in 1990, the classic story was one of driving from colourful and exciting West Berlin into dull and grey East Berlin; variety seemed to vanish. As the Wall came down, thousands of Germans from the East descended on the department stores of the West. Visitors to China since the economic reforms of the mid-1980s claim that the biggest visible sign of change is the increase in the selection of products available to the population.

Proponents of product differentiation also argue that it leads to efficiency. If my product is of higher quality than my competition's, my product will sell more and my firm will do better. If I can produce something of high quality more cheaply—that is, more efficiently—than my competition can, I will force them to do likewise or go out of business. Creating a brand name through advertising also helps to ensure quality. Firms that have spent millions to establish a brand name or a reputation for quality have something of value to protect.

For product differentiation to be successful, of course, consumers must know about product quality and availability. In perfect competition, where all products are alike, we assume that consumers have perfect information; without it, the market fails to produce an efficient allocation of resources. Complete information is even more important when we allow for product differentiation. How do consumers get this information? The answer is, at least in part, through advertising. The basic function of advertising, according to its proponents, is to assist consumers in making informed, rational choices.

Supporters of product differentiation and advertising also claim that these techniques promote competition. New products can compete with old, established brands only if they can get their messages through to consumers. When consumers are informed about a wide variety of potential substitutes, they can more effectively resist the power of monopolies.

Table 14.4		
Advertising Expenditure by Sector, 1995		
		Dollars (Millions)
Retail Trade		891.1
Automobiles		514.4
Food		395.7
Business equipment and services		395.0
Entertainment		300.9
Financial and insurance services		213.7
Restaurants/night clubs		186.9
Travel and transportation		182.1
Local automotive dealers		137.7
Cosmetics and toiletries		126.9
Total		3344.4

Source: A.C. Neilson Annual Survey of Advertising Expenditures in Canada. Reported in *Marketing Magazine*, October 28, 1996, p. 24.

Those who favour product differentiation argue that it is the only way to satisfy the enormous range of tastes and preferences. Differentiation allows the Whirlpool company to produce refrigerators in standard sizes and colours for Canadian customers, but in different sizes and colours for its Asian customers. The reason for these different colours? Asians often put their refrigerators in their living rooms.

To sum up:

> The advocates of free and open competition believe that differentiated products and advertising give the market system its vitality and are the basis of its power. They are the only ways to begin to satisfy the enormous range of tastes and preferences in a modern economy. Product differentiation also helps to ensure high quality and efficient production, and advertising provides consumers with the valuable information on product availability, quality, and price that they need to make efficient choices in the marketplace.

■ **The Case against Product Differentiation and Advertising** Critics of product differentiation and advertising argue that these practices waste society's scarce resources. The argument is that enormous sums of money are spent to create minute, meaningless differences among products.

Drugs, both prescription and nonprescription, are a prime example. Companies spend millions and millions of dollars to "hype" brand-name drugs that contain exactly the same compounds as those available under their generic names. The antibiotics erythromycin and erythrocin have the same ingredients; yet the latter is half as expensive as the former. Aspirin is aspirin, yet we pay twice the price for an advertised brand, because the manufacturer has convinced us that there is a tangible—or intangible—difference.

Those who argue against product differentiation believe that it wastes valuable resources that could be put to better use. There are few marketing rivalries as strong as that between Coke and Pepsi. Each company spends millions of dollars per year on advertising and giveaways. But are the two products really that different?

Do we really need 50 different kinds of soap, all of whose prices are inflated substantially by the cost of advertising? For a firm producing a differentiated product, advertising is part of the everyday cost of doing business; its price is built into the average cost curve and thus into the price of the product in the short run and the long run. Thus, consumers pay to finance advertising.

In a way, advertising and product differentiation turn the market system completely around. We have been talking about an economic system designed to meet the needs and satisfy the desires of members of society—that is, as a means to an end, which is the social good. Advertising is intended to change people's preferences and to create wants that otherwise would not have existed. From the advertiser's viewpoint, people exist to satisfy the needs of the economy. In other words, the *goal* of the economic system has been lost, and the *means* has become the end.[1]

Critics also argue that the information content of advertising is minimal at best and deliberately deceptive at worst. It is meant to change our minds, to persuade us, and to create brand "images." Try to determine how much real information there is in the next 10 advertisements you see on television. To the extent that no information is conveyed, critics argue, advertising creates no real value, and thus a substantial portion of the $7.5 billion worth of resources that we devote to advertising is wasted.

Competitive advertising can also easily turn into unproductive warfare. Suppose there are five firms in an industry and that one of these firms begins to advertise heavily. In order to survive, the others respond in kind. If one firm drops out of the race, it will certainly lose out. Advertising of this sort may not increase demand

---

[1] *This point was made by John Kenneth Galbraith in* The Affluent Society *(Boston: Houghton Mifflin, 1958).*

for the product or improve profitability for the industry at all. Instead, it is all too often a "zero sum game"—a game that, on balance, no one wins.

Advertising may reduce competition by creating a barrier to the entry of new firms into an industry. One famous case study taught at the Harvard Business School calculates the cost of entering the breakfast cereal market. To be successful, a potential entrant would have to start with millions of dollars in an extensive advertising campaign to establish a brand name recognized by consumers. Entry to the breakfast cereal game is not completely blocked, but such financial requirements make it much more difficult.

Finally, some argue that advertising by its very nature imposes a cost on society. We are continuously bombarded by bothersome jingles and obtrusive images. Driving home from work, we pass 50 billboards and listen to 15 minutes of news and 20 minutes of advertising on the radio. When we get home, we open and throw away 10 pieces of unsolicited junk mail, glance at a magazine containing 50 pages of writing and 75 pages of advertisements, and perhaps watch a television show that is interrupted every 10 minutes for a "message."

In sum:

> The bottom line, critics of product differentiation and advertising argue, is waste and inefficiency. Enormous sums are spent to create minute, meaningless, and possibly nonexistent differences among products. Advertising raises the cost of products and frequently contains very little information. Often, it is merely an annoyance. Product differentiation and advertising have turned the system upside down: people exist to satisfy the needs of the economy, not vice versa. Advertising can lead to unproductive warfare and may serve as a barrier to entry, thus reducing real competition.

■ **No Right Answer** One of the things that you will see over and over as you study economics is that many questions have no right answers. There are strong arguments on both sides of the advertising debate, and even the empirical evidence leads to conflicting conclusions. Some studies show that advertising leads to concentration and excess profits; others, that advertising improves the functioning of the market.[2]

PRICE AND OUTPUT DETERMINATION IN MONOPOLISTIC COMPETITION

Recall that monopolistically competitive industries are made up of a large number of firms, each small relative to the size of the total market. Thus, no one firm can affect market price by virtue of its size alone. Firms do differentiate their products, however. By doing so, they gain some control over price.

■ **Product Differentiation and Demand Elasticity** Purely competitive firms face a perfectly elastic demand for their product: all firms in a perfectly competitive industry produce exactly the same product. If Firm A tried to raise price, buyers would simply go elsewhere and Firm A would sell nothing. When a firm can distinguish its product from all others in the minds of consumers, as we assume it can under monopolistic competition, it probably can raise price without losing all demand. Figure 14.1 on page 352 shows how product differentiation might make demand somewhat less elastic for a hypothetical firm.

---

[2]*The most widely quoted study showing that advertising restricts competition is William S. Comoner and Thomas A. Wilson,* Advertising and Market Power *(Cambridge, Mass.: Harvard University Press, 1974). As one example of the opposing argument, see John M. Scheidell,* Advertising, Prices, and Consumer Reaction: A Dynamic Analysis *(Washington, D.C.: American Enterprise Institute, 1978).*

FIGURE 14.1

Product Differentiation Reduces the Elasticity of Demand Facing a Firm

The demand curve faced by a monopolistic competitor is likely to be less elastic than the demand curve faced by a perfectly competitive firm, but more elastic than the demand curve faced by a monopolist because close substitutes for the products of a monopolistic competitor are available.

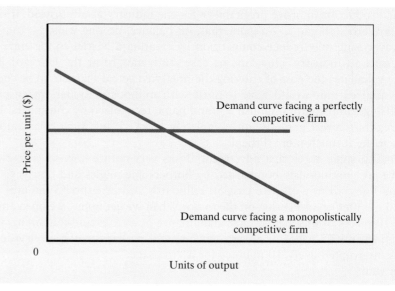

A monopoly is an industry with a single firm that produces a good for which there are no close substitutes. A monopolistically competitive firm is like a monopoly in that it is the only producer of its unique product. Only one firm can produce Cheerios, Heinz Ketchup, Labatt Blue, and Oreo cookies. But unlike the product in a monopoly market, the product of a monopolistically competitive firm has many close substitutes competing for the consumer's favour. Thus,

> While the demand curve faced by a monopolistic competitor is likely to be less elastic than the demand curve faced by a perfectly competitive firm, it is likely to be more elastic than the demand curve faced by a monopoly.

■ **Price/Output Determination in the Short Run** Under conditions of monopolistic competition, a profit-maximizing firm behaves very much like a monopolist in the short run. First, marginal revenue is not equal to price, because the monopolistically competitive firm has some control over output price. Like a monopolistic firm, a monopolistically competitive firm must lower price in order to increase output and sell it. The monopolistic competitor's marginal revenue curve thus lies *below* its demand curve, intersecting the quantity axis midway between the origin and the point at which the demand curve intersects it. (If necessary, review Chapter 13 to get a grip on this idea.)

The firm then chooses that combination of output and price that maximizes profit.

> To maximize profit, the monopolistically competitive firm will increase production until the marginal revenue from increasing output and selling it no longer exceeds the marginal cost of producing it. This occurs at the point at which marginal revenue equals marginal cost: $MR = MC$.

In Figure 14.2a on the next page, the profit-maximizing output is $q_0 = 2000$, the point at which marginal revenue equals marginal cost. To sell 2000 units of product, the firm must charge \$6. Total revenue is $P_0 \times q_0 = \$12\ 000$, or

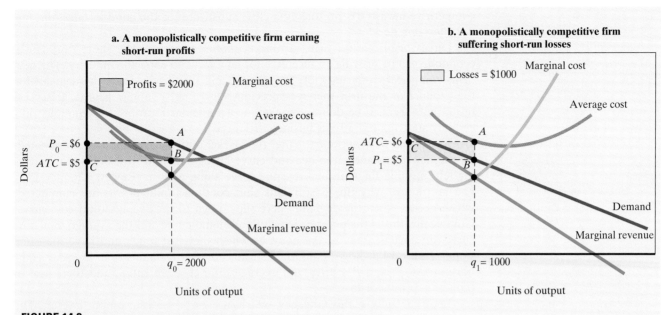

FIGURE 14.2

Monopolistic Competition in the Short Run

In the short run, a monopolistically competitive firm will produce up to the point at which $MR = MC$. At $q_0 = 2000$ in panel a, the firm is earning economic profits equal to $P_0 ABC = \$2000$. In panel b, another monopolistically competitive firm with a similar cost structure is shown facing a weaker demand and suffering short-run losses at $q_1 = 1000$ equal to $CABP_1 = \$1000$.

the area of $P_0 Aq_00$. Total cost is equal to average total cost times q_0, which is \$10 000 or CBq_00. Total profit is equal to the difference, \$2000 (the pink shaded area $P_0 ABC$).

Nothing guarantees that a firm in a monopolistically competitive industry will earn economic profits in the short run. Figure 14.2b shows what happens when a firm with the same cost curves faces a weaker market demand. Even though the firm does have some control over price, market demand is insufficient to make the firm profitable.

As in pure competition, such a firm minimizes its losses by producing up to the point where marginal revenue is equal to marginal cost. Of course, as in competition, the price that the firm charges must be sufficient to cover variable costs. Otherwise, the firm will shut down and suffer losses equal to total fixed costs, rather than increase losses by producing more. In other words, the firm must make a profit on operation. In Figure 14.2b, the loss-minimizing level of output is $q_1 = 1000$ at a price of \$5. Total revenue is $P_1 \times q_1 = \$5000$, or $P_1 Bq_10$. Total cost is $ATC \times q_1 = \$6000$, or CAq_10. Because total cost is greater than revenue, the firm suffers a loss of \$1000 equal to the grey shaded area, $CABP_1$.

■ **Price/Output Determination in the Long Run** In analyzing monopolistic competition, our key assumption is that entry and exit are free in the long run. Firms can enter an industry when there are profits to be made, and firms suffering losses can fold up and go out of business. But entry into an industry of this sort is somewhat different from entry into pure competition, because products are differentiated in monopolistic competition. A firm that enters a monopolistically competitive industry is producing a close substitute for the good in question, *but not the same good.*

Let us begin with a firm earning economic profits in the short run. Those economic profits provide an incentive for new firms to enter the industry. The new firms compete by offering close substitutes, and this drives down the demand for the product of the firm that was previously earning economic profits. If several restaurants seem to be doing very well in a particular location, for example, others may start up and attract business from them.

New firms will continue to enter the market until excess profits are eliminated. As the new firms enter, the demand curve facing each old firm begins to shift to the left, pushing the marginal revenue curve along with it. (Review Chapter 13 if you are unsure why this is so.) This shift continues until profits are eliminated, which occurs when the demand curve slips down to the average total cost curve. Graphically, this is the point at which the demand curve and the average total cost curve are tangent (that is, the point at which they just touch and have the same slope). Figure 14.3 shows a monopolistically competitive industry in long-run equilibrium. At q^* and P^*, price and average total cost are equal, and there are no economic profits or losses.

Look carefully at this tangency, which in Figure 14.3 is at output level q^*. The tangency occurs at the profit-maximizing level of output. At this point, marginal cost is equal to marginal revenue. At any level of output other than q^*, ATC lies above the demand curve. This means that at any other level of output, ATC is greater than the price that the firm can charge. (Recall that the demand curve shows the price that can be charged at every level of output.) Hence, price equals average cost at q^* and economic profits equal zero.

This final equilibrium must occur at the point at which the demand curve is *just tangent* to the average total cost curve. If the demand curve cut across the average cost curve, thus intersecting it at two points, the demand curve would be *above* the average cost curve at some levels of output. Producing at those levels of output would mean economic profits. Economic profits would attract entrants, thus shifting the market demand curve to the left, and thus lowering profits. If the demand curve were always *below* the average cost curve, all levels of output would produce losses for the firm. This would cause firms to exit the industry, thus shifting

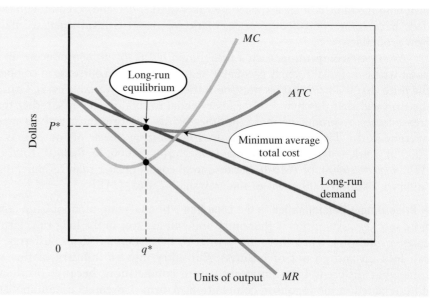

FIGURE 14.3

Monopolistically Competitive Firm at Long-Run Equilibrium

As new firms enter a monopolistically competitive industry in search of profits, the demand curves of profit-making existing firms begin to shift to the left, pushing marginal revenue with them as consumers switch to the new close substitutes. This process continues until profits are eliminated, which occurs for a firm when its demand curve is just tangent to its average cost curve.

the market demand curve to the right, and thus increasing profits (or reducing losses) for those firms still in the industry. Thus:

> The firm's demand curve must end up tangent to its average total cost curve for economic profits to equal zero. This is the condition for long-run equilibrium in a monopolistically competitive industry.

Even if a monopolistically competitive firm starts with losses, it will arrive at the same long-run equilibrium. (Look back at Figure 14.2b, which shows a firm suffering losses.) Suppose that too many restaurants open up in a given small area, for example, and that none of the restaurants is able to make a profit. This situation cannot persist and there will be a "shake-out" sometime in the near future—that is, one or more of the firms suffering losses will decide to drop out of the industry.

When this happens, the firms remaining in the industry will get a larger share of the total business, and their demand curves will shift to the right. Thus firms that were suffering losses find those losses reduced by the additional demand. The demand curves of the remaining monopolistic competitors will continue to shift until losses are eliminated. Thus, we end up with the same long-run equilibrium as we did when we started out with a firm earning profits. At equilibrium, demand is tangent to average total cost, and there are no economic profits or losses.

ECONOMIC EFFICIENCY AND RESOURCE ALLOCATION

We have already noted some of the similarities between monopolistic competition and pure competition. Because entry is free and economic profits are eliminated in the long run, we might conclude that the result of monopolistic competition is efficient. There are two problems, however.

First, once a firm achieves any degree of market power by differentiating its product (as is the case in monopolistic competition), its profit-maximizing strategy is to hold down production and charge a price above marginal cost, as you saw in Figures 14.2 and 14.3. Remember from Chapter 12 that price is the value that society places on a good, and marginal cost is the value that society places on the resources needed to produce that good. Thus, by holding production down and price above marginal cost, monopolistically competitive firms prevent the efficient use of resources. More product could be produced at a resource cost below the value that consumers place on the product.

Second, as Figure 14.3 shows, the final equilibrium in a monopolistically competitive firm is necessarily to the left of the low point on its average total cost curve. Thus, a typical firm in a monopolistically competitive industry will not realize all the economies of scale available. (In pure competition, you will recall, firms are pushed to the bottom of their long-run average cost curves, and the result is an efficient allocation of resources.)

Suppose, for example, that a number of firms enter an industry and build plants on the basis of initially profitable positions. But as more and more firms compete for those profits, individual firms find themselves with smaller and smaller market shares, and they end up eventually with "excess capacity." The firm in Figure 14.3 is not fully utilizing its existing capacity because competition drove its demand curve to the left. Thus, in monopolistic competition we end up with many firms, each producing a slightly different product at a scale that is less than optimal. Would it not be more efficient to have a smaller number of firms, each producing on a slightly larger scale?

The costs of less-than-optimal production, however, need to be balanced against the gains that can accrue from aggressive competition among products. If, as we said earlier, product differentiation leads to the introduction of new products, improvements in old products, and greater variety, then an important gain in economic welfare may counteract (and perhaps outweigh) the loss of efficiency from pricing above marginal cost or not fully realizing all economies of scale.

Most industries that comfortably fit the model of monopolistic competition are very competitive. Price competition coexists with product competition, and firms do not earn incredible profits. Nor do they violate any of the competition laws that we discuss in detail in the next chapter.

Monopolistically competitive firms have not been a subject of great concern among economic policy makers. Their behaviour appears to be sufficiently controlled by competitive forces, and no serious attempt has been made to regulate or control them.

Oligopoly

oligopoly *A form of industry (market) structure characterized by a few firms, each large enough to influence market price. Products may be homogeneous or differentiated. The behaviour of any one firm in an oligopoly depends to a great extent on the behaviour of others.*

An **oligopoly** is an industry dominated by a few firms that, by virtue of their individual sizes, are large enough to influence the market price. Oligopolies exist in many forms. In some oligopoly markets, products are differentiated—the classic example is the automobile industry. In others, products are nearly homogeneous (such as primary metal). Some oligopolies have a very small number of firms, each large enough to influence price. Others have many firms, of which only a few control market price.

An industry that has a relatively small number of firms that dominate the market is called a *concentrated industry*. Oligopolies are concentrated industries. Table 14.5 contains some data on nine industries that are relatively concentrated.

The complex interdependence that usually exists among firms in these industries makes oligopoly very difficult to analyze. The behaviour of any one firm depends on the reactions it expects of all the other firms in the industry. Because individual firms make so many decisions—how much output to produce, what price to charge, how much advertising to do, whether and when to introduce new product lines, and so forth—industrial strategies are usually complex and difficult to generalize about.

Table 14.5	Concentration Ratios in Selected Industries, 1988	
	Percentage of Revenue Controlled by Leading Enterprises	
Industry	**CR4**	**CR8**
Tobacco products	98.9	100.0
Petroleum and coal products	74.5	90.8
Storage	71.7	79.0
Beverages	59.2	77.6
Primary metals	63.3	76.6
Communications	64.8	76.4
Rubber products	51.2	74.5
Transport equipment	68.4	74.4
Metal mining	58.9	73.9

Source: Statistics Canada, *Annual Report of the Minister of Industry, Science, and Technology under the Corporation and Labour Unions Returns Act (CALURA), Part 1, Corporations, 1988* (Ottawa: Minister of Industry, Science, and Technology, 1991).

OLIGOPOLY MODELS

Because many different types of oligopolies exist, a number of different oligopoly models have been developed. A complete survey would exceed our purposes, but the discussion that follows provides a good sample of the alternative approaches to the behaviour (or conduct) of oligopolistic firms. As you will see, all kinds of oligopoly have one thing in common:

> The behaviour of any given oligopolistic firm depends on the behaviour of the other firms in the industry.

■ **The Collusion Model** In Chapter 13, we examined what happens when a perfectly competitive industry falls under the control of a single profit-maximizing firm. In that analysis, we assumed neither technological nor cost advantages to having one firm rather than many. We saw that when many competing firms act independently, they produce more, charge a lower price, and earn less profit than they would have if they had acted as a single unit. If these firms get together and agree to cut production and increase price—that is, if firms can agree *not* to price compete—they will have a bigger total-profit pie to carve up. When a group of profit-maximizing oligopolists colludes on price and output, the result is exactly the same as it would be if a monopolist controlled the entire industry:

> The colluding oligopoly will face market demand and produce only up to the point at which marginal revenue and marginal cost are equal ($MR = MC$), and price will be set above marginal cost.

Review the section of Chapter 13 titled "Collusion and Monopoly Compared" if you are unsure why this is so.

A group of firms that gets together and makes price and output decisions jointly is called a **cartel**. Perhaps the most familiar example of a cartel today is the Organization of Petroleum Exporting Countries (OPEC). As early as 1970, the OPEC cartel began to cut petroleum production. Its decisions in this matter led to a 400% increase in the price of crude oil on world markets during 1973 and 1974.

cartel *A group of firms that gets together and makes joint price and output decisions in order to maximize joint profits.*

Price fixing is not controlled internationally, but it is illegal in Canada. Nonetheless, the incentive to fix prices can be irresistible, and industries are caught in the act from time to time. In 1996, for example, a group of Japanese companies selling thermal fax paper in Canada were convicted of price fixing. They faced fines of about $600 000.

For a cartel to work, a number of conditions must be present. First, demand for the cartel's product must be inelastic. If many substitutes are readily available, the cartel's price increases may become self-defeating as buyers switch to substitutes. Second, the members of the cartel must play by the rules. If a cartel is holding up prices by restricting output, there is a big incentive for members to cheat by increasing output. Breaking ranks can mean very large profits.

Both of these problems have plagued the OPEC cartel in recent years. The demand for oil has turned out to be much more elastic in the long run than it was in the short run. The high prices of the early 1980s led to sharp decreases in the demand for oil during that decade. In addition, the amount of oil produced by non-OPEC countries (including Canada) has increased significantly. Finally, at least some OPEC countries exceeded their quotas. For example, evidence exists that during the 1980s Kuwait was producing more than its OPEC quota of oil. These events caused oil prices to fall during much of the 1980s.

tacit collusion *Collusion occurs when price- and quantity-fixing agreements among producers are explicit. Tacit collusion occurs when such agreements are implicit.*

Cournot model *A model of a two-firm industry (duopoly) in which a series of output-adjustment decisions leads to a final level of output that is between that which would prevail if the market were organized competitively and that which would be set by a monopoly.*

Collusion occurs when price- and quantity-fixing agreements are explicit. **Tacit collusion** occurs when firms end up fixing price without a specific agreement, or when such agreements are implicit. A small number of firms with market power may fall into the practice of setting similar prices or following the lead of one firm without ever meeting or setting down formal agreements.

■ **The Cournot Model** Perhaps the oldest model of oligopoly behaviour was put forward by Augustin Cournot almost 150 years ago. The **Cournot model** is based on three assumptions: (1) that there are just two firms in an industry—a situation called a *duopoly;* (2) that each firm takes the output of the other as given; and (3) that both firms maximize profits.

The story begins with a new firm producing nothing and the existing firm producing everything. That is, the existing firm simply takes the market demand curve as its own, acting like a monopolist. When the new firm starts operating, it assumes that the existing firm will continue to produce the same level of output and charge the same price as before. The market demand of the new firm, then, is simply market demand less the amount that the existing firm is currently selling. In essence, the new firm assumes that its demand curve is everything on the market demand curve below the price charged by the older firm.

When the new firm starts operation, the existing firm discovers that its demand has eroded because some output is now sold by the new firm. The old firm now assumes that the new firm's output will remain constant, subtracts the new firm's demand from market demand, and produces a new, lower level of output. But that throws the ball back to the new firm, which now finds that the competition is producing *less.*

These adjustments get smaller and smaller, with the new firm raising output in small steps and the initial firm lowering output in small steps until the two firms split the market and charge the same price. Like the collusion model:

> The Cournot model of oligopoly results in a quantity of output somewhere between that which would prevail if the market were organized competitively and that which would be set by a monopoly.

While the Cournot model illustrates the interdependence of decisions in oligopoly, its assumptions about strategic reactions are quite naive. The two firms in the model react only after the fact and never anticipate the competition's moves.

kinked demand curve model *A model of oligopoly in which the demand curve facing each individual firm has a "kink" in it. The kink follows from the assumption that competitive firms will follow suit if a single firm cuts price but will not follow suit if a single firm raises price.*

■ **The Kinked Demand Curve Model** Another common model of oligopolistic behaviour assumes that firms believe that rivals will follow suit if they *cut* prices but not if they *raise* prices. This **kinked demand curve model** assumes that the elasticity of demand in response to an increase in price is different from the elasticity of demand in response to a price cut. The result is a "kink" in the demand for a single firm's product.

You can see some of these reactions by examining the demand curve in Figure 14.4 on the next page. If the initial price of Firm B's product is P^*, raising its price above P^* would cause Firm B to face an elastic demand curve if its rivals did not also raise their prices (segment d_1 of the demand curve). That is, in response to the price increase, demand for Firm B's product would fall off quickly. The reaction to a price *decrease* would not be as great, however, because rivals would decrease price too. Firm B would lose some of its market share by increasing price, but it would not gain a larger share by decreasing price (segment d_2 of the demand curve).

Recall the very important point that a firm's marginal revenue curve reflects the changes in demand occurring along the demand curve *directly above it.*

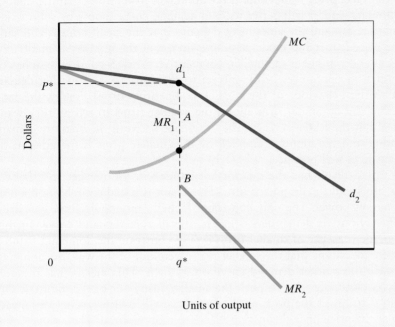

FIGURE 14.4

A Kinked Demand Curve Oligopoly Model

The kinked demand model assumes that competing firms follow price cuts but not price increases. Thus, if Firm B increases its price, the competition will not, and quantity demanded of Firm B's product will fall off quickly. But if Firm B cuts price, other firms will also cut price and the price cut will not gain as much quantity demanded for Firm B as it would if other firms did not follow. At prices above P^* demand is relatively elastic. Below P^* demand is less elastic.

(Review the derivation of the marginal revenue curve in Chapter 13 if this is not fresh in your mind.) This being the case, MR_1 reflects the changes in P and q along demand curve segment d_1. MR_2 reflects changes in P and q along demand curve segment d_2. Since the demand curve is discontinuous at q^*, the marginal revenue curve is also discontinuous, jumping from point A all the way down to point B.

As always, profit-maximizing firms will produce as long as marginal revenue is greater than marginal cost. If, as in Figure 14.4, the marginal cost curve passes through q^* at any point between A and B, the optimal price is P^* and the optimal output is q^*. To the left of q^*, marginal revenue is greater than marginal cost. To maximize profits, then, the firm should increase output. To the right of q^*, marginal cost is greater than marginal revenue. In this case the firm should not increase output, because producing above q^* will reduce profits.

Notice that this model predicts that price in oligopolistic industries is likely to be more stable than costs. In Figure 14.4, the marginal cost curve can shift up or down by a substantial amount before it becomes advantageous for the firm to change price at all. A number of attempts have been made to test whether oligopolistic prices are indeed more stable than costs. While the results do not support the hypothesis of stable prices, the evidence is far from conclusive.[3]

The kinked demand curve model has been criticized on a number of grounds. First, it fails to explain why price is at P^* to begin with. Second, the assumption that competing firms will follow price cuts but not price increases is overly simple. Real-world oligopolistic pricing strategies are much more complex.

■ **The Price-Leadership Model** In another form of oligopoly, one firm dominates an industry and all the smaller firms follow the leader's pricing policy—hence the

---

[3]*See, for example, Julian Simon, "A Further Test of the Kinky Oligopoly Demand Curve," American Economic Review (December 1969); and George Stigler, "The Kinky Oligopoly Demand Curve and Rigid Prices," Journal of Political Economy 55 (1947).*

price leadership *A form of oligopoly in which one dominant firm sets prices and all the smaller firms in the industry follow its pricing policy.*

descriptive term **price leadership.** If the dominant firm knows that the smaller firms will follow its lead, it will derive its own demand curve simply by subtracting from total market demand the amount of demand that the smaller firms will satisfy.

The price-leadership model assumes, first, that the industry is made up of one large firm and a number of smaller, competitive firms. Second, it assumes that the dominant firm maximizes profit subject to the constraint of market demand *and* subject to the behaviour of the smaller, competitive firms. Finally, the model assumes that the dominant firm allows the smaller firms to sell all they want to at the price that the leader has set. The difference between the quantity demanded in the market and the amount supplied by the smaller firms is the amount that the dominant firm will produce.

The final result has the quantity demanded in the market split between the smaller firms and the dominant firm. This result is based entirely on the dominant firm's market power. The only constraint facing a monopoly firm, you will recall, is the behaviour of demanders—that is, the market demand curve. In this case, however, the presence of smaller firms acts to constrain the dominant firm's power. If we were to assume that the smaller firms were out of the way, the dominant firm would face the market demand curve on its own. This means that the dominant firm has a clear incentive to push the smaller firms out of the industry. One way to do so is to lower the price until all of the smaller firms go out of business and then raise the price once the market has been monopolized. The practice of a large, powerful firm driving smaller firms out of the market by temporarily selling at an artificially low price is called *predatory pricing*. As we will see in the next chapter, such behaviour, common during the nineteenth century, became illegal with the passage of combines legislation.

In sum:

> As in the other oligopoly models, an oligopoly with a dominant price leader will produce a level of output between that which would prevail under competition and that which a monopolist would choose in the same industry. It will also set a price between the monopoly price and the competitive price. Some competition is usually more efficient than none at all.

■ **Game Theory** The firms in Cournot's model do not anticipate the moves of the competition. Yet in choosing strategies in an oligopolistic market, real-world firms can and do try to guess what the opposition will do in response.

In 1944, John von Neumann and Oskar Morgenstern published a path-breaking work in which they analyzed a set of problems, or *games,* in which two or more people or organizations pursue their own interests and in which no one of them can dictate the outcome.[4] During the last few years, game theory has become an increasingly popular field of study and a fertile area for research. The notions of game theory have been applied to analyses of firm behaviour, politics, international relations, and foreign policy. In 1994 the Nobel Prize in Economic Science was awarded jointly to three early game theorists: John F. Nash of Princeton, John C. Harsanyi of Berkeley, and Reinhard Selten of the University of Bonn.

game theory *Analyzes oligopolistic behaviour as a complex series of strategic moves and reactive countermoves among rival firms. In game theory, firms are assumed to anticipate rival reactions.*

Game theory goes something like this. In all conflict situations, and thus all games, there are decision makers (or players), rules of the game, and payoffs (or prizes). Players choose strategies without knowing with certainty what strategy the opposition will use. At the same time, though, some information that indicates how their opposition may be "leaning" may be available to the players.

---

[4]*See J. von Neumann and O. Morgenstern,* Theory of Games and Economic Behavior *(Princeton, N.J.: Princeton University Press, 1944).*

Figure 14.5 illustrates what is called a payoff matrix for a very simple game. Each of two firms, A and B, must decide whether to mount an expensive advertising campaign. If neither firm decides to advertise, each will earn a profit of $50 000. But if one firm advertises and the other does not, the firm that does will increase its profit by 50% (to $75 000), while driving the competition into the loss column. If both firms decide to advertise, they will each earn profits of $10 000. They may generate a bit more demand by advertising, but that demand is completely wiped out by the expense of the advertising itself.

If Firms A and B could collude (and we assume that they cannot), their optimal strategy would be to agree not to advertise. That solution maximizes the joint profits to both firms. If neither firm advertises, joint profits are $100 000. If both firms advertise, joint profits are only $20 000. If only one of the firms advertises, joint profits are $50 000.

The strategy that Firm A will actually choose depends on (1) the information available concerning B's likely strategy, and (2) A's preferences for risk. In this case, it is possible to predict behaviour. Consider A's choice of strategy. Regardless of what B does, it pays A to advertise. If B does not advertise, A makes $25 000 more by advertising than by not advertising. Thus, A will advertise. If B does advertise, A must advertise to avoid a loss. The same logic holds for B. Regardless of the strategy pursued by A, it pays B to advertise. A **dominant strategy** is one that is best no matter what the opposition does. In this game, both players have a dominant strategy, and it is likely that both will advertise.

The result of the game in Figure 14.5 is an example of what is called a prisoners' dilemma. The term comes from a game in which two prisoners (call them Ginger and Rocky) are accused of robbing the local convenience store together, but the evidence is shaky. If they both confess, they each get five years in prison for armed robbery. If neither confesses, they get convicted of a lesser charge, shoplifting, and get one year in prison each. The problem is that the Crown attorney has offered each of them a deal independently. If Ginger confesses and Rocky doesn't, Ginger goes free and Rocky gets seven years. If Rocky confesses and Ginger doesn't, Rocky goes free and Ginger gets seven years. The payoff matrix for the prisoners' dilemma is given in Figure 14.6.

Looking carefully at the payoffs, you may notice that both Ginger and Rocky have dominant strategies: to confess. That is, Ginger is better off confessing regardless of what Rocky does, and Rocky is better off confessing regardless of what Ginger does. The likely outcome is thus that both will confess, even though they would be better off if they both kept their mouths shut!

dominant strategy *In game theory, a strategy that is best no matter what the opposition does.*

FIGURE 14.5

Payoff Matrix for Advertising Game

A's STRATEGY	B's STRATEGY	
	Don't advertise	Advertise
Don't advertise	A's profit = $50 000 B's profit = $50 000	A's loss = $25 000 B's profit = $75 000
Advertise	A's profit = $75 000 B's loss = $25 000	A's profit = $10 000 B's profit = $10 000

FIGURE 14.6

The Prisoners' Dilemma

	ROCKY	
GINGER	**Don't confess**	**Confess**
Don't confess	Ginger: 1 year Rocky: 1 year	Ginger: 7 years Rocky: free
Confess	Ginger: free Rocky: 7 years	Ginger: 5 years Rocky: 5 years

Is there any way out of this dilemma? There may be under circumstances in which the game is played over and over. Look back at the game in Figure 14.5. Clearly, the best outcome for both firms is for neither to advertise. Suppose that Firm A decided not to advertise for one period to see how Firm B would respond. If Firm B continued to advertise, A would have to resume advertising to survive. But suppose that B's strategy was to play tit for tat. That is, suppose that B decided to simply match A's strategy. In this case, both firms might—with no explicit collusion—end up not advertising after A figures out what B is doing. (For an example of the prisoners' dilemma at work in the airline industry, see the Application box on page 364 titled "A Prisoners' Dilemma and the Canadian Airlines.")

There are many games in which one player does not have a dominant strategy but in which the outcome is predictable. Consider the game in Figure 14.7a on the next page, in which C does not have a dominant strategy. If D plays the left strategy, C will play the top strategy. If D plays the right strategy, C will play the bottom strategy. But the question remains: what strategy will D choose to play? If C knows the options, she will see that D has a dominant strategy and is likely to play it. D does better playing the right-hand strategy regardless of what C does; he can guarantee himself a $100 win by choosing right and is guaranteed to win nothing by playing left. Since D's behaviour is predictable (he will play the right-hand strategy) C will play bottom. When all players are playing their best strategy given what their competitors are doing, the result is called a **Nash equilibrium.**

Nash equilibrium *In game theory, the result of all players playing their best strategy given what their competitors are doing.*

Now suppose that the game in Figure 14.7 were changed. Suppose that all the payoffs are the same except that if D chooses left and C chooses bottom, C loses $10 000 (Figure 14.7b). While D still has a dominant strategy (playing right), C now stands to lose a great deal by choosing bottom on the off chance that D chooses left instead. When uncertainty and risk are introduced, the game changes. C is likely to play top and guarantee herself a $100 profit rather than to risk losing $10 000 to win $200, even if there is just a small chance of D's choosing left. A **maximin strategy** is one chosen by a player to maximize the minimum gain that it can earn. In essence, one who plays a maximin strategy assumes that the opposition will play the strategy that does the most damage.

maximin strategy *In game theory, a strategy chosen to maximize the minimum gain that can be earned.*

When game theory first appeared in the late 1940s, it seemed that it would in time be able to explain the behaviour of oligopolistic firms in great detail. However, when we move from two potential strategies to three or four, and particularly when

FIGURE 14.7

Payoff Matrixes for Left/Right–Top/Bottom Strategies

a. Original Game

C's STRATEGY	D's STRATEGY	
	Left	**Right**
Top	C wins $100 D wins $0	C wins $100 D wins $100
Bottom	C loses $100 D wins $0	C wins $200 D wins $100

b. New Game

C's STRATEGY	D's STRATEGY	
	Left	**Right**
Top	C wins $100 D wins $0	C wins $100 D wins $100
Bottom	C loses $10 000 D wins $0	C wins $200 D wins $100

we move to more than two players, the number of potential outcomes and the properties of the strategy pairings become enormously complex. As a result, it becomes very difficult to predict the strategy (or the combination of strategies) that a firm might choose in any given circumstance.

In the end, game theory leaves us with a greater understanding of the problem of oligopoly but with an incomplete and inconclusive set of propositions about the likely behaviour of oligopolistic firms. Some very interesting conclusions emerge about a fairly small number of specific game circumstances, but game theory doesn't provide much help with an industry of five firms, each simultaneously choosing product, pricing, output, and advertising strategies.

About all we are left with is the certainty of interdependence:

> The strategy that an oligopolistic firm chooses is likely to depend on that firm's perception of competing firms' likely responses.

■ **Contestable Markets** Before we discuss the performance of oligopolies, we should note one relatively new theory of behaviour that has limited applications but some important implications for understanding imperfectly competitive market behaviour.

A market is **perfectly contestable** if entry to it *and* exit from it are costless. That is, a market is perfectly contestable if a firm can move into it in search of excess profits but lose nothing if it fails. To be part of a perfectly contestable market, a firm must have capital that is both mobile and easily transferable from one market to another.

Take, for example, a bus company that is the only company serving a route between a small town and a large city. Other bus companies can enter easily if monopoly profits are earned. A similar situation may occur when a new industrial complex is built at a fairly remote site and a number of trucking companies offer their services. Because the trucking companies' capital stock is mobile, they can move their trucks somewhere else at no great cost if business is not profitable.

Because entry is cheap, participants in a contestable market are continuously faced with competition or the threat of competition. Even if there are only a few firms competing, the openness of the market forces all these firms to produce efficiently or be driven out of business. This threat of potential competition remains high simply because new firms face little risk in going after a new market. If things don't work out in a crowded market, they don't lose their

perfectly contestable market *A market in which entry and exit are costless.*

One of the most important economic events of 1996 was the near bankruptcy of Canadian Airlines International. Industry analysts estimate that Canadian lost $1.4 billion between 1988 and 1996, leaving the airline with a staggering debt load. These losses were incurred despite the use of more efficient planes, fuel prices considerably lower than at their peak in the late 1970s, and rapidly growing demand for international travel.

Some economists have argued that part of the explanation may lie in game theory. Consider the following simple example (the numbers are hypothetical). Suppose that Air Canada and Canadian Airlines are competing for a lucrative route between Toronto and Vancouver. Each airline may choose independently to cut price (hold a "seat sale") or charge a high price. The profits from the route depend on the strategies chosen by both firms and are given in the four small boxes.

Notice that if the game is played a single time, each firm has a dominant strategy. That is, Air Canada will choose to cut fares regardless of what Canadian does and Canadian will cut fares regardless of what Air Canada does. Each loses despite the fact that high prices result in more

		Air Canada (AC)	
		Price High	Cut Fares
Canadian Airlines International (CAI)	Price High	AC's profit = $100 CAI's profit = $120	AC's profit = $140 CAI's profit = −$200
	Cut Fares	AC's profit = −$200 CAI's profit = $150	AC's profit = −$100 CAI's profit = −$100

profits for both. This is a classic prisoners' dilemma and it may explain the aggressive seat sales, with price reductions of 50% or more, adopted by Air Canada and Canadian in the mid-1990s.

Recall from the text that one solution to the prisoners' dilemma might be to try a "tit for tat" strategy in repeated trials in the hopes of signalling the opposition that if it charges a high price you will too. Airlines in the United States appear to have followed this strategy and they were charged with price fixing. The following excerpt from *The New York Times* describes part of the settlement made by the airlines:

> Major airlines agreed to pay $40 million in discounts to state and local governments to settle a price-fixing lawsuit, a group of 10 state attorneys general said yesterday.
>
> The airlines settled a separate class-action suit last year brought by passengers by agreeing to pay out $458 million in discounts. The airlines earlier this year resolved a Federal antitrust suit by agreeing not to announce price changes in advance . . .
>
> The price-fixing claims centered on an airline practice of announcing price changes in advance through the reservation systems. If competitors did not go along with the price change, it could be rescinded before it was to take effect.

Source: The Associated Press, "Suit Settled by Airlines," *The New York Times,* October 12, 1994, p. D8.

investment. They can simply transfer their capital to a different place or different use.

> In contestable markets, even large oligopolistic firms end up behaving like perfectly competitive firms. Prices are pushed to long-run average cost by competition, and economic profits do not persist.

■ **Summary**   To recap: oligopoly is a market structure that is consistent with a variety of behaviours.

The only necessary condition of oligopoly is that firms are large enough to have some control over price. Oligopolies are concentrated industries. At one extreme is the cartel, in which a few firms get together and jointly maximize profits—thus, in essence, acting as a monopolist. At the other extreme, the firms within the oligopoly vigorously compete for small contestable markets by moving capital quickly in response to observed economic profits. In between the two are a number of alternative models, all of which stress the interdependence of oligopolistic firms.

OLIGOPOLY AND ECONOMIC PERFORMANCE

How well do oligopolies perform? Should they be regulated or changed? Are they efficient, or do they lead to an inefficient use of resources? On balance, are they good or bad?

With the exception of the contestable-markets model, all the models of oligopoly we have examined lead us to conclude that concentration in a market leads to pricing above marginal cost and output below the efficient level. When price is above marginal cost at equilibrium, consumers are paying more for the good than it costs to produce that good in terms of products forgone in other industries. To increase output would be to create value that exceeds the social cost of the good, but profit-maximizing oligopolists have an incentive not to increase output.

Entry barriers in many oligopolistic industries also prevent new capital and other resources from responding to profit signals. Under competitive conditions or in contestable markets, excess profits would attract new firms and thus increase production. But this does not happen in most oligopolistic industries. The problem is most severe when entry barriers exist and firms explicitly or tacitly collude. The results of collusion are essentially identical to the results of a monopoly. Firms jointly maximize profits by fixing prices at a high level and splitting up the profits.

Product differentiation under oligopoly presents us with the same dilemma that we encountered in monopolistic competition. On the one hand, vigorous product competition among oligopolistic competitors produces variety and leads to innovation in response to the wide variety of consumer tastes and preferences. It can thus be argued that vigorous product competition is efficient. On the other hand, product differentiation may lead to waste and inefficiency. Product differentiation accomplished through advertising may have nothing to do with product quality, and advertising itself may have little or no information content. If it serves as an entry barrier that blocks competition, product differentiation can cause the market allocation mechanism to fail.

To sum up:

Oligopolistic, or concentrated, industries are likely to be inefficient for several reasons. First, profit-maximizing oligopolists are likely to price above marginal cost. When price is above marginal cost, there is underproduction from society's point of view—in other words, society could get more for less, but it doesn't. Second, strategic behaviour can lead to outcomes that are not in society's best interest. Specifically, strategically competitive firms can force themselves into deadlocks that waste resources. Finally, to the extent that oligopolies differentiate their products and advertise, there is the promise of new and exciting products. At the same time, however, there remains a real danger of waste and inefficiency.

Some economists argue that most technical changes are introduced by large firms, such as Northern Telecom, which have the profits needed to support research and development expenditures. But others argue small firms are more dynamic since they encourage creativity in a way impossible in large, bureaucratic organizations.

INDUSTRIAL CONCENTRATION AND TECHNOLOGICAL CHANGE

One of the major sources of economic growth and progress throughout history has been technological advance. Innovation, both in methods of production and in the creation of new and better products, is one of the engines of economic progress. Much innovation starts with research and development efforts undertaken by firms in search of profit.

Several economists, most notably Joseph Schumpeter and John Kenneth Galbraith, argued in works now considered classics that industrial concentration actually increases the rate of technological advance. As Schumpeter put it in 1942:

> As soon as we . . . inquire into the individual items in which progress was most conspicuous, the trail leads not to the doors of those firms that work under conditions of comparatively free competition but precisely to the doors of the large concerns . . . and a shocking suspicion dawns upon us that big business may have had more to do with creating that standard of life than keeping it down.[5]

The Schumpeterian hypothesis caused the economics profession to pause and take stock of its theories. The conventional wisdom had always been that concentration and barriers to entry insulate firms from competition and lead to sluggish performance and slow growth.

The evidence regarding where innovation comes from is mixed. Certainly, most small businesses do not engage in research and development, and most large firms do. When R&D expenditures are considered as a percentage of sales, firms in industries with high concentration ratios spend more on research and development than firms in industries with low concentration ratios.

[5]A. *Schumpeter,* Capitalism, Socialism and Democracy *(New York: Harper, 1942); and J.K. Galbraith,* American Capitalism *(Boston: Houghton Mifflin, 1952).*

Oligopolistic companies in the telecommunications sector are noted for research. It has been estimated that Bell Labs conducted 10% of *all* basic research in the United States in the 1970s. Nortel is one of the leading industrial research organizations in Canada. IBM, which despite its recent problems set the industry standard in personal computers, has certainly introduced as much new technology to the computer industry as any other firm.

However, the "high-tech revolution" grew out of many tiny start-up operations. Companies such as Apple Computer, Lotus Development Corporation, Intel, and many others barely existed only a generation ago. The new biotechnology firms that are just beginning to work miracles with genetic engineering are still tiny operations that started with research done by individual scientists in university laboratories.

As with the debate about product differentiation and advertising, significant ambiguity on this subject remains. Indeed, there may be no right answer. Technological change seems to come in fits and starts, sometimes from small firms and sometimes from large ones.

A Role for Government?

Certainly there is much to guard against in the behaviour of large, concentrated industries. Barriers to entry, large size, and product differentiation all lead to market power and to potential inefficiency. Barriers to entry and collusive behaviour stop the market from working toward an efficient allocation of resources.

For several reasons, however, economists no longer attack industry concentration with quite the same fervour that they once did. First, the theory of contestable markets shows that even firms in highly concentrated industries can be pushed to produce efficiently under certain market circumstances. Second, the benefits of product differentiation and product competition are real, at least in part. After all, a constant stream of new products and new variations of old products does come to the market almost daily. Third, the effects of concentration on the rate of research and development spending are, at worst, mixed. It is certainly true that large firms do a substantial amount of the total research in Canada. Finally, in some industries, substantial economies of scale simply preclude a completely competitive structure.

In addition to the debate over the desirability of industrial concentration, there is a never-ending debate regarding the role of government in regulating markets. One view is that high levels of concentration lead to inefficiency and that government should act to improve the allocation of resources—to help the market work more efficiently. This logic has been used to justify the laws and other regulations aimed at moderating noncompetitive behaviour.

An opposing view holds that the clearest examples of effective barriers to entry are those actually created by government. This view holds that government regulation in past years has been ultimately anticompetitive and has made the allocation of resources less efficient than it would have been with no government involvement. Recall from our discussion in Chapter 13 that those who earn economic profits have an incentive to spend resources to protect themselves and their profits from competitors. This *rent-seeking* behaviour may include using the power of government.

In the next chapter, we look carefully at the potential role of government in correcting the market failure brought about by imperfectly competitive markets. We then turn to a discussion of the government's role in providing social goods and correcting externalities (Chapter 16) and an examination of the government's role in income redistribution (Chapter 17).

Monopolistic Competition

1. A monopolistically competitive industry has the following structural characteristics: (1) a large number of firms, (2) no barriers to entry, and (3) *product differentiation*. Relatively good substitutes for a monopolistic competitor's products are available. Thus monopolistic competitors try to achieve a degree of market power by differentiating their products.

2. Advocates of free and open competition believe that differentiated products and advertising give the market system its vitality and are the basis of its power. Critics argue that product differentiation and advertising are wasteful and inefficient.

3. By differentiating their products, firms hope to be able to raise price without losing all demand. The demand curve facing a monopolistic competitor is less elastic than the demand curve faced by a perfectly competitive firm but more elastic than the demand curve faced by a monopoly.

4. To maximize profit in the short run, a monopolistically competitive firm will produce as long as the marginal revenue from increasing output and selling it exceeds the marginal cost of producing it. This occurs at the point at which $MR = MC$.

5. When firms enter a monopolistically competitive industry, they introduce close substitutes for the goods being produced. This attracts demand away from the firms already in the industry. Demand faced by each firm shifts left, and profits are ultimately eliminated in the long run. This long-run equilibrium occurs at the point where the demand curve is just tangent to the average total cost curve.

6. Monopolistically competitive firms end up pricing above marginal cost. This is inefficient, as is the fact that monopolistically competitive firms will not realize all economies of scale available.

Oligopoly

7. An *oligopoly* is an industry dominated by a few firms that, by virtue of their individual sizes, are large enough to influence market price. The behaviour of a single oligopolistic firm depends on the reactions it expects of all the other firms in the industry. Industrial strategies usually are very complicated and difficult to generalize about.

8. When firms collude, either explicitly or tacitly, they jointly maximize profits by charging an agreed-upon price or by setting output limits and splitting profits. The result is exactly the same as it would be if one firm monopolized the industry: the firm will produce up to the point at which $MR = MC$, and price will be set above marginal cost.

9. The *Cournot model* of oligopoly is based on three assumptions: (1) that there are just two firms in an industry—a situation called *duopoly*; (2) that each firm takes the output of the other as a given; and (3) that both firms maximize profits. The model holds that a series of output-adjustment decisions in the duopoly leads to a final level of output between that which would prevail under perfect competition and that which would be set by a monopoly.

10. A firm faces a kinked demand curve if competitors follow price cuts but fail to respond to price increases. The *kinked demand curve* model predicts that in oligopolistic industries price is likely to be more stable than costs.

11. The *price-leadership* model of oligopoly leads to a similar but not identical result as the collusion model. In this organization, the dominant firm in the industry sets a price and allows competing firms to supply all they want at that price. An oligopoly with a dominant price leader will produce a level of output between that which would prevail under competition and that which a monopolist would choose in the same industry. It will also set a price between the monopoly price and the competitive price.

12. *Game theory* analyzes the behaviour of firms as if their behaviour were a series of strategic moves and countermoves. It helps us understand the problem of oligopoly but leaves us with an incomplete and inconclusive set of propositions about the likely behaviour of individual oligopolistic firms.

13. A market is *perfectly contestable* if entry to it and exit from it are costless—that is, if a firm can move into a market in search of excess profits but lose nothing if it fails. Firms in such industries must have mobile capital. In contestable markets, even large oligopolistic firms end up behaving like perfect competitors: prices are pushed to long-run average cost by competition, and economic profits do not persist.

14. The behaviour of oligopolistic firms is likely to lead to an inefficient allocation of resources.

Problem Set

1. For each of the following state whether you agree or disagree. Explain your answer carefully.

   a. Successful product differentiation has the effect of increasing the elasticity of demand facing a monopolistically competitive firm.

   b. Long-run equilibrium in a monopolistically competitive industry is virtually identical to long-run equilibrium in monopoly.

   c. In monopolistically competitive industries, firms are able to exert market power (control prices) by virtue of their size relative to the market.

2. All over the world in the 1990s, people were singing. In Japan, Karaoke bars drew millions of patrons who wanted to sing popular songs accompanied by recorded videos and a prompter lighting up the words. In Taiwan, literally tens of thousands of Karaoke (KTV) establishments have opened since the mid-1980s, where groups of people can go into small private rooms and sing to each other while being prompted on a video screen. Each establishment is a bit different from the next. Some are upscale and expensive; others are less expensive, have a smaller selection of songs to choose from, and are not as well maintained. Ten years ago the industry did not exist.

   a. Into what industry category does the Taiwanese Karaoke business seem to fall?

   b. The first Karaoke establishments in Taiwan in business made lots of money. What do you think has happened to the price of admission and the profits of most KTV establishments in recent years? Use a graph to explain your answer.

3. Which of the following markets are likely to be perfectly contestable? Explain your answers.

   a. Shipbuilding

   b. Trucking

   c. Housecleaning services

   d. Wine production

4. The matrix in Figure 1 shows payoffs based on the strategies chosen by two firms. If they collude and hold prices at $10, each will earn profits of $5 million. If A cheats on the agreement, lowering its price, but B does not, A will get 75% of the business and earn profits of $8 million and B will lose $2 million. Similarly, if B cheats and A does not, B will earn $8 million and A will lose $2 million. If both cut prices, they will end up with $2 million each in profits.

   Which strategy minimizes the maximum potential loss for A? For B? If you were A, which strategy would you choose? Why? If A cheats, what will B do? If B cheats, what will A do? What is the most likely outcome of such a game? Explain.

5. Assume that you are in the business of building houses. You have analyzed the market carefully,

FIGURE 1		B's STRATEGY	
		STAND BY AGREEMENT	CHEAT
A's STRATEGY	STAND BY AGREEMENT	A's profit = $5 million B's profit = $5 million	A's profit = −$2 million B's profit = $8 million
	CHEAT	A's profit = $8 million B's profit = −$2 million	A's profit = $2 million B's profit = $2 million

and you know that at a price of $120 000 you will sell 800 houses per year. In addition, you know that at any price above $120 000 no one will buy your houses because the government provides equal quality houses to anyone who wants one at $120 000. You also know that when you lower your price by $20 000, the quantity that you can sell increases by 200 units. For example, at a price of $100 000 you can sell 1000 houses, at a price of $80 000 you can sell 1200 houses, and so forth.

  a. Sketch the demand curve facing your firm.
  b. Sketch the effective marginal revenue curve facing your firm.
  c. If the marginal cost of building a house is $100 000, how many will you build, and what price will you charge? What if $MC = $85 000$?

6. Examine the short-run graph in Figure 2 for a monopolistically competitive firm.
  a. What is the profit-maximizing level of output?
  b. What price will be charged in the short run?
  c. How much is short-run total revenue? Total cost? Total profit?
  d. Describe what will happen to this firm in the long run.

7. Write a position paper on industrial concentration for the prime minister. Is this a problem in Canada? What are some of the possible advantages and disadvantages of government actions against concentrated industries?

8. The payoff matrixes in Figure 3 show the payoffs for two games. The payoffs are given in parentheses.

The figure on the left refers to the payoff to A, the figure on the right to the payoff to B. Hence (2, 25) means a $2 payoff to A and a $25 payoff to B.

  a. Is there a dominant strategy in each game for each player?
  b. If Game 1 were repeated a large number of times, and you were A and you could change your strategy, what might you do?
  c. Which strategy would you play in Game 2? Why?

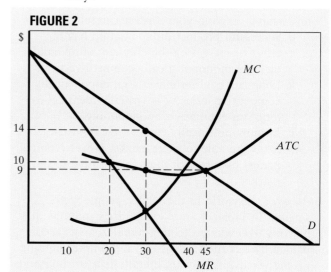

FIGURE 2

FIGURE 3

GAME 1: PRICING

		FIRM B	
		PRICE HIGH	PRICE LOW
FIRM A	PRICE HIGH	(15, 15)	(2, 25)
	PRICE LOW	(25, 2)	(5, 5)

GAME 2: CHICKEN

		BOB (B)	
		SWERVE	DON'T SWERVE
ANN (A)	SWERVE	(5, 5)	(3, 10)
	DON'T SWERVE	(10, 3)	(−10, −10)

Competition Policy and Regulation in Canada

If all the assumptions of perfect competition hold, the allocations of resources in an economy is efficient—the system produces the goods and services people want, and it does so at least cost. This was a message originally articulated by Adam Smith, whose pioneering work *An Inquiry into the Nature and Causes of the Wealth of Nations* (1776) provided the first systematic treatment of the advantages of organizing an economy on market capitalist principles. A modern treatment of this argument was presented in Chapter 12, where we saw that no shuffling of resources in a perfectly competitive economy can improve the welfare of some without reducing the welfare of others.

Competition plays a critical role in ensuring that the pursuit of private profit generates desirable social outcomes. But as shown in Chapters 13 and 14, businesses can potentially secure and keep economic profits by restricting competition. Moreover, we saw that if firms are able to achieve some degree of control over their products' price, they are likely to end up charging more than the socially optimal price and producing less than the socially optimal output.

Concern with the tendency for businesspeople to restrict competition was clearly articulated by Adam Smith when he argued that "to narrow competition is always the interest of the dealers" and that "people of the same trade seldom meet together, even for merriment or diversion, but the conversation ends in a conspiracy against the public, or some contrivance to raise prices."[1] Governments have introduced laws, broadly known as competition policy, to try to keep this tendency in check.

---

[1] *Adam Smith*, An Inquiry into the Nature and Causes of the Wealth of Nations *(Oxford: Clarendon Press, 1976), pp. 267, 145.*

There are also situations where governments will either create a crown, or government-run, corporation or allow imperfect competition. This achieves two things simultaneously: consumers get the benefits of economies of scale, and the governments can regulate prices to keep them close to the socially optimal level.

When unregulated markets fail to produce efficiently, governments can and do act to improve the allocation of resources. However, some government action can lead to a less efficient allocation of resources. This chapter discusses in some detail the history and theory of government involvement in imperfectly competitive markets.

Historical Background

The period immediately following Confederation was one of rapid growth and change in Canada. Improvements in transportation, population growth, and the introduction of new manufacturing techniques combined to transform the frontier Canadian society. The construction of the Intercolonial Railway (linking Nova Scotia, New Brunswick, and P.E.I. to Quebec and Ontario), the Canadian Pacific Railway (linking central Canada and the west), and their numerous branch lines were particularly significant. Prior to the construction of the transcontinental rail system, most firms were small and their markets local. The high cost of transportation confined access to local markets, and production technologies were efficient only on a small scale. But the railroads opened up the country, and firms began to compete for national markets. Many of the new technologies that emerged exhibited economies of scale; real advantages to size in some industries soon became apparent.

In 1879 the Conservative government introduced the National Policy, which included a system of tariffs (a tax applied only to goods from outside the country). The tariffs effectively insulated Canadian producers from foreign competition. Because the Canadian market was relatively small, only a few firms in industries with potential economies of scale would be able to survive.

Communications technology also changed dramatically during the same period. The telegraph made an appearance as early as 1846 and the telephone was invented by Alexander Graham Bell of Brantford, Ontario; telephone networks expanded steadily.[2] Improved communications allowed markets to expand and reduced the obstacles of geography.

As all of these forces drew Canada together, the character of the economy changed. Small firms selling to local markets faced three options. They could expand to take advantage of scale economies by selling to regional and national markets; they could remain small and try to survive in a world with large firms producing products very cheaply; or they could sell out to larger firms or merge with competitors. It was a difficult time for business as most business owners struggled to earn what historian Michael Bliss has called "a living profit."[3]

Competition was fierce and often brutal. In the struggle to survive, firms cut prices to drive competitors out of business. Many cartels and producer groups formed in an attempt to fix prices and control output. Thousands of small businesses

---

[2]This section draws on I. Drummond, Progress Without Planning: The Economic History of Ontario from Confederation to the Second World War (Toronto: University of Toronto Press, 1987), pp. 259-263.

[3]Michael Bliss, Northern Enterprise: Five Centuries of Canadian Business (Toronto: McClelland and Stewart, 1987), p. 362. For a general discussion of the problem faced by Canadian business in this period see Michael Bliss, A Living Profit: Studies in the Social History of Canadian Business (Toronto: McClelland and Stewart, 1974).

were gobbled up by bigger ones. The adjustment was a painful one and when it was complete, firms were larger and markets less competitive.

It wasn't long before people saw that something was wrong with the system that had emerged. With size came power, and with power came hunger for more power. Small independent farmers, facing large, powerful railroads, monopsonistic buyers, and declining agricultural prices, began to organize. So too did worker groups, to oppose powerful employers, child labour, long hours, and meagre wages. These groups felt that big business was responsible for many of society's ills. The popular image of big business at the time is probably best captured in cartoons of grotesquely fat men with big cigars and diamond stickpins, crushing workers and farmers underfoot. Politicians faced mounting pressure to respond.

The federal government responded in two ways. First, in 1888, the government began to regulate railway rates. Starting a railway system, especially a railway system such as that which extended across Canada in the 1880s, involves an extremely large capital investment. As a consequence the total fixed cost of running a railway is a large proportion of total cost and the average total costs fall continuously as use of the railway increases. The Canadian politicians of the 1880s realized that the economies of scale enjoyed by the Canadian Pacific Railway potentially offered Canadians the lowest possible freight rates. But these economies of scale also left the CPR as a monopoly with the ability to charge prices well above the minimum unit cost. To control such activity, the Railway Committee of the Privy Council was established to set railway fares and freight rates. This was a pragmatic response to deal with monopoly power while allowing a single firm to exploit large economies of scale. (The policy of rate regulation was gradually extended to other natural monopolies such as electric power, telephone service, air transport, radio, and television in the first eight decades of the twentieth century. However, since the early 1980s governments have been deregulating many of these industries.)

The second response to public pressure came in 1889. In that year the Canadian government introduced its first competition policy in a piece of legislation titled An Act for the Prevention and Suppression of Combinations in Restraint of Trade. This law, which became section 520 of the Criminal Code in 1892, was not (for reasons discussed below) very effective.

Direct government involvement in running firms has an even longer history than government regulation in Canada. But the government did not assume this role enthusiastically. Indeed, in the nineteenth century governments only ended up with control when private firms that delivered essential services (such as canals) went bankrupt. But at the beginning of the twentieth century things changed.

Electrification and the expansion of telephone service involved a mix of private and community activity. Private firms were reluctant to expand into rural areas or to relatively small towns and cities because of the cost. To fill the void some communities opted to service themselves. For example, the people of Freetown, Prince Edward Island, established their own cooperative power company in 1896. Other communities turned to their municipal governments to organize power and telephone service.

Ontario Hydro, one of the first provincial crown corporations, was created in the early twentieth century as a result of a battle fought between proponents of public power and the early leaders of the private electrical generation and distribution industry. The proponents of public power believed that a government-run system of electrical distribution was needed to keep power rates down, and that cheap power was needed to spur development of the economy as a whole and the manufacturing sector in particular. In the end their arguments carried the day, setting a precedent for future use of crown corporations to deal with situations of natural monopoly. (The CBC in radio and television, Air Canada in air transport, the

Canadian National Railway, NB Power, and Hydro-Québec are all organizations that began life as crown corporations.)

The number of federal government crown corporations expanded most rapidly during World War II. This expansion owes much to C.D. Howe, then minister of munitions and supply. "Government-owned business became a favourite technique of Howe and his officials for filling gaps in the private sector. To coax a new company to life (even with the promises of government contracts) would take time— too much time. However a stroke of the pen could create a crown corporation, and necessity caused Howe to use his pen often."[4] Howe's example was followed in the postwar period as more and more crown corporations were established. But, as with regulation, crown corporations also came under attack in the early 1980s, and since that time government has moved to privatize many of these organizations.

Canadian Competition Policy

There are four important aspects to the analysis of competition policy. First, the possible goals must be identified. Second, it is necessary to identify business practices that keep the goals from being achieved without government action. Third, the legal provisions must be analyzed to see if they are actually consistent with the specified goals. Fourth, it is important to examine the record of enforcement to determine if the goals are being achieved.

GOALS OF COMPETITION POLICY

There are two possible goals of competition policy, one economic, the other political. The economic goal of competition policy is to ensure an efficient and equitable allocation of scarce resources. If this is the only goal of competition policy, encouraging competition is a means to achieve a desirable end, not an end in itself. The political goal of competition policy is to discourage the concentration of economic and political power in the hands of a few. Discouraging the formation of large firms, cartels, and other forms of collusion might contribute to the achievement of this goal, but only indirectly. Concern with the concentration of political power is more a concern with the concentration of wealth or ownership than with industrial structure.

The current Canadian competition policy, which is largely governed by the 1986 Competition Act, gives the economic goal primacy. The 1986 Competition Act states explicitly that its purpose is "to maintain and encourage competition in Canada in order to promote the efficiency and adaptability of the Canadian economy, in order to expand opportunities for Canadian participation in world markets while at the same time recognizing the role of foreign competition in Canada, in order to ensure small and medium-sized enterprises have an equitable opportunity to participate in the Canadian economy, and in order to provide consumers with competitive prices and product choices." Indeed, in response to concerns about the impact of increases in newspaper industry concentration on editorial diversity, the civil servant in charge of competition policy argued that the concerns should be addressed through social policy rather than competition policy.[5]

---

[4]*Kenneth Norrie and Douglas Owram,* A History of the Canadian Economy, *second edition (Toronto: Harcourt Brace Canada, 1996), p. 385.*
[5]*"Competition Bureau Keeps Watch on Newspaper Deals,"* Financial Post Daily *vol. 9, no. 54 (May 8, 1996): p. 6.*

ANTICOMPETITIVE PRACTICES

One contribution of economists to the design of and debate around competition policy is to identify business practices that reduce economic welfare. The following list identifies some of these practices (all of these are potentially illegal under the Competition Act):

- mergers
- cartels
- predatory pricing
- price discrimination
- resale price maintenance
- exclusive dealing and tied selling
- refusal to supply
- abuse of dominant position
- misleading advertising and deceptive marketing practices

The practice that typically appears at the top of the list is **mergers** of existing firms that result in monopoly or a serious reduction in competition. One of the first things economists note in discussion of mergers is that industries with substantial economies of scale can produce at lower unit costs when there are a small number of firms in the industry. Thus concentration can improve economic welfare. Second, economists note that concentration alone is a poor indicator of the state of price competition in an industry. The extent of foreign competition, the availability of substitutes, a history of highly competitive practice, and a variety of other factors have a significant effect on the power of firms in an industry to raise price above marginal cost. Thus monopoly and mergers should not be considered bad per se. However, they can, in certain circumstances, reduce economic welfare. Thus economists would argue that monopolies and mergers should be individually examined to determine their impact on economic welfare.

merger *The combining of two or more companies into a single company.*

A second business practice of concern is the formation of trusts, **cartels,** and producer groups to restrict output, fix prices, and/or rig bids. Firms use price fixing and collusion to help protect themselves from competition and earn monopoly profits.

cartel *A group of firms that acts together as if it were a monopoly.*

The third practice is an anticompetitive practice known as **predatory pricing.** Predatory pricing involves a firm selling products at prices below cost to lessen or eliminate competition. Predatory pricing is always a short-term strategy whereby a firm sells at prices lower than unit cost to deter a new entrant or eliminate a competitor. In the long term the firm will raise prices above unit cost.

predatory pricing *A strategy whereby a firm sells at a price below cost to drive competitors out of business. The goal is to absorb losses in the short run to reduce competition, thereby opening up an opportunity to make economic profits in the long run.*

Price discrimination (charging different customers different prices), when it has no rationale except to reduce competition, is the fourth business practice identified as problematic. For example, suppose several companies buy rolled steel to make filing cabinets. The largest producer, by virtue of its size and bargaining power, may be able to obtain a very low price from the steel producers, a price not justified by cost saving due to large volume. The bargaining power thus gives the largest producer an advantage over its smaller competitors. This can lead to monopoly power in the long run. But there are other rationales for price discrimination. For example, firms often offer quantity discounts since transaction costs are lowered. This type of price discrimination can increase economic welfare.

price discrimination *A pricing policy that involves charging different customers different prices even though the cost of production is the same.*

The fifth practice on the list is **resale price maintenance,** a practice that involves a producer fixing the price a retailer charges (producers can set a suggested retail price, but they cannot force the retailer to charge it). A fixed resale price hurts consumers since retailers are unable to offer discounts as part of their competitive

resale price maintenance *A policy of forcing retailers to sell a product at a price fixed by the manufacturer.*

strategy. However, some economists argue that resale price maintenance is efficient. They argue that a product is more than a physical object. For example, when someone buys a new computer, she acquires not only the computer but also the salesperson's knowledge about and experience with the product. This knowledge is part of what is sold and its cost is reflected in the suggested selling price. If a customer can go to one (high-priced) store and get advice about the computer and then go to another (low-price) store, which does not offer advice, to purchase the computer, the high-price stores will quickly stop giving advice. This, it is argued, would lower economic welfare.

exclusive dealing *A policy of supplying a product only if the purchaser agrees not to buy similar products from competitors.*

Restrictive trade practices, such as **exclusive dealing** and **tied selling**, constitute the sixth potentially anticompetitive business practice. These practices involve a product that is supplied subject to the condition that the purchaser must buy from only one supplier (exclusive dealing) or to the condition that the purchaser must buy other products from the supplier (tied selling).

tied selling *A policy of supplying a product only if the purchaser agrees to buy other products from the supplier.*

The seventh practice is known as **refusal to supply.** This is a practice whereby a firm refuses to sell a product to another firm and in which the refusal limits the ability of the buyer to carry on his or her business.

refusal to supply *A policy of not selling a product to another firm as part of a strategy to increase market share by eliminating that firm as a competitor.*

A firm that enjoys significant market power could **abuse its dominant position.** There are a large number of business practices that could be considered abuse of dominant position. These include introducing new brands selectively and on a temporary basis to eliminate a competitor; a vertically integrated supplier's squeezing of the margin available to an unintegrated customer who competes with the supplier, to impede or prevent the customer's expansion in a market; and buying up products to prevent the erosion of existing price levels.

abuse of dominant position *Any policy pursued by the dominant firm in an industry to limit competition.*

Finally, a firm could gain an advantage over other firms through false or misleading advertising and other deceptive marketing practices. For a market economy to work, consumers must have valid information on product availability, quality, and price. **Misleading advertising** and **deceptive marketing practices** are used to capture customers by providing inaccurate information. A significant number of misleading advertising cases are prosecuted in Canada each year. (We discuss this topic in more detail in Chapter 16.)

misleading advertising and **deceptive marketing practices** *Occur when firms attempt to capture customers by providing inaccurate information about product availability, quality, and price.*

LEGAL LANGUAGE

The 1889 anticombines legislation provides a useful starting point for a brief discussion of legal language and enforcement. The 1889 legislation stated:

> Everyone is guilty of an indictable offence who conspires, combines, agrees or arranges with any other person or with any railway, steamship, steamboat or transportation company, *unlawfully*
>
> (a) to *unduly* limit the facilities for transporting, producing, manufacturing, supplying, or dealing in any article or commodity which may be a subject of trade or commerce; or
>
> (b) to restrain or injure trade or commerce in relation to any such article or commodity; or
>
> (c) to *unduly* prevent, limit, or lessen the manufacture or production of any such article or commodity, or to *unreasonably* enhance the price thereof; or
>
> (d) to *unduly* prevent or lessen competition in the production, manufacture, purchase, barter, sale, transportation, or supply of any such article or commodity, or in the price of insurance upon person or property.

The use of words such as *unduly* and *unreasonably* in the original legislation indicates that the objective was to take action when business practices in some sense reduced economic welfare. But because the actual words used could be subject to a variety of interpretations (how would you define the words "unduly lessen competition"?), the legislation provided the courts with very little guidance for its application. In particular, the legislation did not state explicitly which business practices were considered to limit competition unduly.

The legislation's absence of reference to specific anticompetitive practices also had implications for enforcement. On the one hand, no guidance was provided to persons interested in identifying and prosecuting illegal practices. As a consequence, few cases were prosecuted and there were no convictions. On the other hand, almost any business practice could be declared uncompetitive and illegal provided prosecutors could convince the courts the practice contravened the law. This flexibility was valuable given how innovative firms could be in the ways they attempted to restrict competition in order to attain economic profits.

The 1889 act was included in the Criminal Code in 1892, and thus the Crown had to prove its cases beyond "reasonable doubt." This was a very stringent requirement given the highly technical nature of the arguments that might arise in such cases. One would expect fewer successful prosecutions under criminal law than under civil law, where a case must be proved on a reasonable balancing of probabilities.

Finally, the 1889 legislation did not include provision for investigative and enforcement machinery. The absence of an independent law enforcement body made it relatively easy for business to avoid prosecution.

ENFORCEMENT

Given its imprecise wording, inclusion in the Criminal Code, and the absence of enforcement machinery, it should not be surprising to find that Canada's first competition law was ineffective. If one also notes that the legislation included reference to *unlawfully* without defining what was unlawful, the absence of convictions is perfectly understandable. Historian Michael Bliss argues that "the 1889 law was pious antimonopoly posturing that had no effect on anything."[6]

In a 1900 amendment to the law the word *unlawfully* was deleted. Despite this significant change, between 1909 and 1912 a wave of mergers resulted in an increase in concentration in some industries. Public concern at the time prompted the introduction of new legislation in 1910. The Combines Investigations Act improved enforcement procedures by (1) allowing the minister of labour to appoint ad hoc boards of investigation with the power to subpoena witnesses and documents, and (2) allowing any six persons to apply to a judge for an order directing an investigation into an alleged combine. The 1910 legislation also made the goal of competition policy more explicit by stating that a combination, merger, trust, or monopoly was illegal only if *it operated or was likely to operate to the detriment of the public.*

Between 1910 and 1986 the Combines Investigation Act and related provisions in the Criminal Code evolved to strengthen investigative and enforcement machinery and to incorporate new forms of anticompetitive behaviour. In 1935 predatory pricing and some forms of price discrimination were explicitly identified and made illegal. Amendments in 1952 made resale price maintenance an offence. In 1960 new provisions were introduced to more clearly define mergers and monopolies.

---

[6]*Michael Bliss*, Northern Enterprise: Five Centuries of Canadian Business *(Toronto: McClelland and Stewart, 1987), p. 362.*

Section 91 of the 1986 Competition Act defines a merger as "the acquisition or establishment, direct or indirect, by one or more persons, whether by sale or lease of shares or assets, by amalgamation or by combination or otherwise, of control over or significant interest in the whole or part of a business of a competitor, supplier, customer, or other person." The Director of Investigation and Research of the Bureau of Competition Policy is directed by the legislation to examine all mergers in which the parties to the merger have revenues or assets in excess of $400 million or in which the business being acquired has revenue or assets in excess of $35 million. If the director believes the merger will substantially lessen competition, the case is taken before the Competition Tribunal for judgment.

The act explicitly states that the tribunal cannot conclude that competition has been substantially lessened solely on the basis of market share or concentration. It must consider all relevant factors. Moreover, the act states that the tribunal should try to identify all efficiency gains from a merger, and if potential gains exceed potential losses, the merger should be allowed to proceed.

The following article describes one case that has come before the tribunal. Like all merger cases, it raises complex and difficult issues. Examine this case carefully and form your own judgment.

Canadian Pacific Ltd. was sideswiped Friday by the federal Bureau of Competition Policy, which began proceedings to try to force CP Ships to sell off Cast North America Inc. The Bureau asked the Competition Tribunal, a quasi-judicial court, to compel CP Ships to divest itself of Cast, a container ship-ping line bought by CP in March 1995 when Cast was insolvent....

In its application, the Bureau alleges the merger will, or is likely to, substantially hurt competition in the North American shipping business between Montreal and Europe. "The Port of Montreal, as the gateway for billions of dollars in international trade, is an important part of [Canada's transportation] network. Preserving competition in this sector will ensure consumers, shippers and businesses will not face the prospect of paying higher prices for goods and services," said Francine Matte, acting director of investigation and research for the Bureau.

At the heart of the issue is the fact that CP Ships also owns and operates container line Canada Maritime. CP says running Cast and Canada Maritime as sister companies has meant "substantial improvements in operational efficiency." CP Ships says it will "vigorously oppose" the Bureau's application. If the Tribunal rules against CP, it could be compelled to divest itself of Cast.[1]

The following information is relevant when thinking about this case.

CP bought Cast for a reported $70 million. The acquisition gave CP two container shipping companies—Cast and Canada Maritime Ltd.—with a total of 18 container ships. The two companies have a dominant position at the Port of Montreal, handling 80% of the port's container business, much of which travels between Europe and the U.S. Midwest.

Winnie Siu, an analyst at

Transportation plays a critical role in the Canadian economy, and the Bureau of Competition Policy will take action if it believes the benefits of competition are threatened in this, or any other, sector.

Salman Partners Inc. in Vancouver, said yesterday the loss of Cast would be a significant blow to CP—if divestiture is eventually forced by the tribunal. "They really turned Cast around, and increased their market share," Siu said. "It would be pretty significant." CP does not release results for Cast, but said in its 1995 annual report that it has "restored profits" to the carrier after five years of steep losses.

Some industry observers have suggested CP's eastern rail freight system—operated by the St. Lawrence & Hudson Railway Co. Ltd.—might suffer if CP were forced to sell Cast. The railway is the chief carrier of Cast's containers between Montreal and the U.S. Midwest. If another rail carrier—potentially Canadian National—took the Cast business, the already troubled St. Lawrence & Hudson Railway would lose precious revenue.[2]

Sources: [1]"CP Pushed To Divest: Bureau of Competition Policy Begins Proceedings To Try To Force CP Ships to Sell Container Shipping Line," *Financial Post* vol. 90, no. 51 (December 21/23, 1996): p. 3. [2]"CN Tracks Challenge to CP's Purchase of Cast," *Financial Post Daily* vol. 9, no. 185 (December 24, 1996): p. 5.

Still, the record of enforcement of Canada's competition policy between 1910 and 1986 was, at best, mixed. The Crown successfully pursued numerous cases involving price fixing, resale price maintenance, misleading advertising, and exclusive dealing and tied selling. However, it was much less successful in its pursuit of convictions in situations involving price discrimination, predatory pricing, and monopolies and mergers.

The only case prior to 1945 involving a merger—R. vs. *Western Fruits and Vegetables*—resulted in an acquittal. Cases against Canadian Breweries and the Western Sugar Company in 1959 also ended in acquittals, as did a case (in the appeals courts) launched in response to K.C. Irving's acquisition of all English-language daily newspapers in New Brunswick. Given the ramifications of corporate takeovers and mergers (there are several hundred mergers per year in Canada, some involving significant change in industrial concentration), the inability to secure convictions became a major source of concern. The problem was made especially obvious given the much better record achieved by authorities in the United States.

The Crown's difficulty in successful prosecution of merger cases stemmed from the courts' decision that the Crown must prove beyond reasonable doubt not only that a merger lessened competition, but also that the lessening was detrimental to the public. The inability to secure convictions was examined by the Economic Council of Canada in the late 1960s. The Economic Council recommended a new approach to dealing with mergers. This new approach had three features. First, the Economic Council argued for the creation of a quasi-judicial tribunal made up of persons of experience and expertise. The tribunal would be responsible for determining whether a business practice (merger, price discrimination, etc.) was in the public interest. This would remove proceedings from the criminal system and thereby address the problems introduced by having to prove one's case beyond reasonable doubt. Second, the Economic Council argued that this tribunal should have the power to prohibit or dissolve mergers that it felt were not in the public interest. Third, the Economic Council argued that the overriding goal of competition policy should be to maximize economic efficiency.

The Economic Council produced its report in 1969, but it took almost 20 years for its recommendations to appear in new legislation. Two pieces of legislation, the Competition Act and the Competition Tribunal Act, both passed in 1986, now govern Canadian competition policy. Under the new regime, action against potentially anticompetitive practices can be initiated in three ways. First, parties to mergers involving more than $400 million in assets or gross revenues from sales must notify the Director of Investigation and Research of the Bureau of Competition Policy. These mergers are then investigated by the Bureau of Competition Policy, which can bring the case before the Competition Tribunal if the Bureau feels that the proposed merger is in violation of the Act. Second, the director can initiate an investigation if she believes some business activity violates the Act. Finally, the minister of industry can initiate an investigation on the application of six Canadian residents.

The Competition Tribunal is a quasi-judicial body with the power to request attendance at hearings, swear in witnesses, inspect documents, and enforce judgments. Judgments of the Competition Tribunal are based on civil rather than criminal law, thus allowing the tribunal to weigh costs and benefits when rendering judgment. Remedies and sanctions available to the tribunal include fines, imprisonment, the breakup of a firm that has reached a dominant position through anticompetitive practices, and, in the case of mergers, either not allowing the merger or ordering the divestiture of some parts of the merged firms.

Few merger cases have come before the Competition Tribunal since 1986 and, as a consequence, there is a very small body of precedents on the application of the new competition policy. However, a relatively large number of cases have been investigated by the Bureau of Competition Policy, most of which have been resolved in the office of the director with the parties to the contestable merger either not proceeding or reorganizing to the satisfaction of the director. Moreover, some believe the legislation has had a significant "deterrence" effect by discouraging firms from pursuing mergers that might be subject to an investigation.

The Canadian Business and Current Affairs (CBCA) database provides access to most Canadian newspaper and magazine articles on business and political topics, all searchable by full text. Try using this resource (which is likely to be available at your library or on your campus computer network) to find information on recent cases considered by the Bureau of Competition Policy. (Also see the Issues and Controversies box on page 378 titled "The Enforcement of Canadian Competition Policy" for a discussion of one recent case.) It should not come as a surprise to find that competition policy is unpopular in the world of big business. Substantial resources have been invested in political lobbying by business in an attempt to limit the scope of competition policy. The strength of the business lobby accounts, in part, for the 20-year lag between the Economic Council of Canada's original recommendations and the 1986 legislation.

DEBATE OVER CANADIAN COMPETITION POLICY

Canadian competition policy is not without critics. Some critics argue that competition policy is too stringent. Others argue that it is not stringent enough.

■ **International Competition** One argument against competition policy is simply that it is unnecessary in today's global economy. International competition, it is argued, is fierce enough to ensure low prices and economic efficiency. If a Canadian firm attempts to charge monopoly prices, it will quickly face competition from foreign firms. On the other hand, those in favour of competition argue that, if anything, globalization has made things worse, since many global markets are dominated by a small number of huge firms. Consequently, they argue that a global competition policy is now needed to deal with this problem.

■ **Efficient Capital Flows and Relatively Contestable Markets** The critics of competition policy also argue that barriers to entry are not as formidable as they once were. Capital markets have become more efficient; investors are always looking for profitable ventures and are now able to mobilize the large sums necessary to enter almost any industry if there are economic profits to be earned. The efficiency of capital markets serves to make more and more markets contestable. Critics of competition policy argue that both actual entry and the threat of entry make market power less of a problem.

■ **Distrust of Government** Even if it can be shown that competition policy is a good idea in theory, many people do not want to put more power in the hands of government. They feel that government intervention creates more problems than it solves. They claim bureaucracy is slow and wasteful.

■ **Distrust of Private Power** Others argue that competition policy should focus more on political goals. Concentrations of power can undermine democracy, and competition policy should protect democratic institutions even if it does so with some loss in economic welfare.

Regulation

Government plays two basic roles that seem contradictory: (1) it promotes competition and restricts market power, and (2) it restricts competition by simultaneously regulating and protecting certain industries. So far, we have looked exclusively at the way the government protects competition. Now we turn to government activities that end up protecting monopoly power.

The government regulates many areas of the economy that have nothing to do with market structure. Some of these areas (environmental protection, for example) are discussed in later chapters. In the section that follows, however, we examine only the regulation of natural monopolies.

REGULATION OF NATURAL MONOPOLY

In Chapter 13 we introduced you to some of the ways the market fails when market power is unrestrained. Firms that can control price and bar the entry of new firms find it advantageous to overprice and underproduce relative to what is best for society. A number of solutions to this problem are possible, at least in theory. One solution is to restructure the industry to make it more competitive. A second is to impose some sort of price regulation—a price ceiling at marginal cost, for example. Yet another is public or government ownership and operation.

Competition policy, which we examined above, is based on the proposition that competition, not regulation or public ownership, is the best way to achieve efficiency in an economy. Nonetheless, it has always been understood that not all markets can be, or should be, competitively structured. Most important among these exceptions are firms or industries that can take advantage of very large economies of scale—the natural monopolies described in Chapter 13.

Figure 15.1 on page 382 illustrates a natural monopoly. Notice that average total cost is still declining when the demand curve intersects it. To break such a firm into smaller pieces, each producing some fraction of total demand, would mean that each of the small firms would have to produce at a much higher average cost. (All of this is implied by the existence of large economies of scale. If this is not clear to you, review Chapter 13.)

Most natural monopolies have very high fixed costs and low marginal costs. Take, for example, an electric utility. Building a power generation plant and putting up poles and wires is costly. Once they are in place, the cost of generating and distributing one additional kilowatt of electricity is low. Part of the reasoning behind the protection of such industries is that having more than one firm undertake the very large initial investment is a waste of resources.

One solution to the natural monopoly problem is to let the firm continue to exist as a monopoly but to regulate the price of its product and its rate of return. If the natural monopoly in Figure 15.1 went unregulated, it would produce Q^* units of output (the point at which $MR = MC$) and charge price P^*, far above marginal costs. But imposing a simple price ceiling at $P = MC$ would not work, because at that price marginal cost is below average cost, and the firm could not make even a normal profit. Remember that price is equal to average revenue, and if average revenue is less than average cost, total revenue will be less than total cost. This implies a loss.

Theory suggests three options for regulation: (1) set the *efficient price* ($P = MC$) and provide a subsidy out of general government revenues to the monopoly; (2) set price equal to average cost (P_A), which would allow firms to charge a price that covers all costs, including a normal return on invested capital; or

FIGURE 15.1

Regulating a Natural Monopoly

A natural monopoly exists when a firm exhibits very large economies of scale. Here long-run average costs facing the firm continue to decline with output even when a single firm is producing all the output demanded in the market. With no regulation, the firm would produce at Q^* and price at P^*. Regulating price to be equal to marginal cost results in losses. Setting price at P_A means that average cost is covered and that investors earn a normal rate of return.

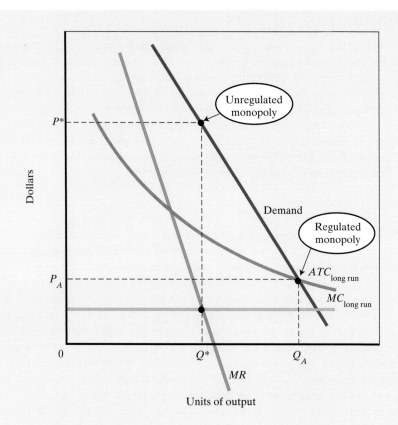

(3) impose a fee on each user of the monopoly's product—a basic service charge as a lump sum and a price for usage equal to marginal cost.

THE PROBLEMS OF REGULATION

The theory of natural monopoly sounds fairly simple: regulatory agencies are charged with setting prices that allow regulated monopolies to earn a normal rate of return. A number of problems are inherent in regulation, however, and these will probably always perplex the regulator to some degree.

■ **Gathering and Analyzing the Necessary Data** Regulation requires analyzing a great deal of information. The first problem is calculating the base—presumably some measure of the "value" of the firm's capital investment—on which a fair return should be allowed. Debate over the value of a public utility can go on and on, for example.

The regulatory agency must also analyze costs. Should all costs be allowed in setting price? Which costs are reasonable? Regulatory agencies have developed methods for analyzing all the information necessary, but analysis is a difficult process, subject to differences of opinion and to error.

Furthermore, the political process that attends rate regulation is time-consuming and cumbersome. Regulatory agencies are empowered to act in the "public interest." Whenever decisions are made, the public must be consulted. These consultations take the form of public hearings and open sessions. And the final decisions made by regulatory agencies can be reviewed in the courts. Interested parties have not been shy about filing suits after an unfavourable or unpopular decision. When a private firm makes a pricing mistake, it can act quickly to change its price. When a regulatory agency makes a mistake, however, correcting it may take a long time.

■ **Lack of Incentives To Be Efficient** Because the return to a regulated natural monopoly is set by the agency, the monopoly may lack the incentive to use efficient production techniques. For example, if a regulatory agency fixes the return by setting a rate expressed as a percentage of the utility's assets, the dollar amount of profit depends only on the total value of those assets. Thus, firms may actually have an incentive to overinvest in capital if the allowed return exceeds the cost of capital. This tendency is called the **Averch-Johnson effect,** after the scholars who noted the proclivity of regulated firms to build more capital capacity than they need.[7]

In general, then, we can say that when regulated firms are guaranteed a standard rate of return, they have no incentive to keep costs at a minimum. When profits are not linked to some measure of performance, there is no reason for the firm to perform well and no severe penalty for weak performance.

Averch-Johnson effect *The tendency for regulated monopolies to build more capital than they need. Usually occurs when allowed rates of return are set by a regulatory agency at some percentage of fixed capital stocks.*

■ **Excessive Nonprice Competition** Regulated monopolies generally do not have a problem with nonprice competition, because they don't have competition. In regulated industries where several firms compete directly with each other while being required to charge the same price, however, product differentiation can become excessive.

The marketing zeal of the airlines in the early 1970s is the example most often cited of this effect. During that time, airlines offered frequent flights, excellent meals, free drinks, and all kinds of other little frills that are hard to imagine today, in an effort to increase ticket sales. As a result of deregulation, competition now drives airlines to produce the service that people want at least cost and thus at a lower price.

REGULATION IN CANADA

Regulation of natural monopolies in Canada has a long history. Initially governments restricted their attention to railways, but as technology changed and new natural monopolies emerged, regulatory activity was extended into other industries. Regulation of the telecommunications industry began in 1906 when the federal government decided to play an active role in setting rates for telephone services. The regulation of electrical power rates in Ontario began in the same year. Later, regulation was extended to cover radio and television, air transport, and oil and gas.

Although small in number, the industries that faced direct regulation were critically important to the health of the economy and governments believed that it was important to closely monitor these industries to ensure they performed their role as effectively as possible. As a consequence, specialized regulatory agencies were created to both monitor and regulate. The Canadian Radio-Television and Telecommunications Commission (the CRTC) was created to regulate the telecommunications industry, including most telephone companies. The National Transportation Agency's (NTA) coverage includes rail, airline, and interprovincial trucking. The National Energy Board (NEB) regulates oil and gas. Provincial public utility boards generally cover industries that constitutionally fall within provincial jurisdiction.

In recent years significant steps have been taken to deregulate many of the

---

[7]*Harvey Averch and Leland Johnson, "Behavior of the Firm under Regulatory Constraint,"* American Economic Review *LII (December 1962): pp. 1052–1069.*

One of the most radical experiments in privatization took place in Britain in the 1980s. During the postwar period, Britain had established crown corporations to produce coal, steel, electricity, water, air transport, rail, telephone services, and a variety of other products. When the Conservatives were elected in 1979, the new prime minister, Margaret Thatcher, decided to privatize these corporations. Mrs. Thatcher strongly believed that the government should stay out of business if the private sector could do the job. Thus she advocated privatizing all firms that were not natural monopolies. Moreover, she believed natural monopolies should be returned to the private sector and then subjected to regulation.

During the 1980s Britain privatized all four of its utilities (water, gas, electricity, and telecommunications) by selling them off to private investors. Regulatory agencies were established to regulate the new firms by setting a maximum price. It was hoped that firms would respond by reducing costs since profits could be increased by operating more efficiently. The regulators were also directed to encourage competition and to avoid any action that would discourage competition.

The following excerpt from *The Economist* briefly describes some results of the British experience:

Since Britain pioneered the privatisation of state-owned firms in the 1980s, hardly a country in the world has failed to follow in its footsteps. Now, governments around the world are starting to look closely at a policy that went hand-in-hand with Britain's big sell-offs: regulation.

A clutch of watchdogs with names such as Oftel (the telecoms regulator) and Ofgas (for gas) now oversee Britain's privatised monopolies, with two objectives: to set maximum prices and to promote competition. Now Latin American and Asian countries, in which the privatisation of utilities is well under way, are showing great interest in this method of regulation. . . .

As for promoting competition, the regulators seem to have been relatively successful. The telecoms market is becoming highly competitive. New entrants are looming in the gas industry. A host of new generators have taken on the privatised electricity companies. Yet here, too, there are legitimate quibbles.

Source: The Economist, August 13, 1994, p. 64.

industries traditionally covered by regulation. But in the heyday of regulation the regulatory agencies played an extremely important role in each of the sectors covered. Moreover, the regulators were directed by government not only to ensure that prices were not too high, but also to ensure that industries operated in a way that satisfied certain other national objectives. For example, regulatory agencies have attempted to ensure that electricity rates and telephone rates faced by customers in urban and rural areas are approximately the same, that radio and television programming contains a certain minimum Canadian content, and that small communities have adequate transport services. They have also enforced extremely low prices on certain activities, such as the transportation of grain from the Prairies. In each of these situations the regulators forced private firms to absorb a loss on some part of their operations. To compensate, the regulatory agencies allowed the firms to make excess profits on some other part of their operations.

■ **Cross-Subsidization and Cream Skimming** A firm that uses excess profits from one part of its operation to cover losses in another part of its operation is engaged in an activity known as *cross-subsidization*. A firm will not cross-subsidize indefinitely since cross-subsidization eventually reduces profits. Indeed, even if a firm does not operate as a profit maximizer and is willing to give up profits to achieve another objective, it will not be able to cross-subsidize in the long run. Entrepreneurs will observe the profits earned in the profitable side of a firm's operation and will enter as a competitor in that part of the business. Any excess profits are eliminated and the original firm is forced to jettison the unprofitable part of its operation. This type of selective competition is known as *cream skimming* since it involves a competitor focusing only on the most profitable part of the business.

Regulatory agencies that tried to enforce cross-subsidization were forced also to restrict competition. Thus, in air transport, carriers were kept out of highly profitable routes involving Montreal, Toronto, and Vancouver to ensure that citizens in smaller and more isolated communities had air service at a reasonable cost. In television, competitors were kept out to ensure that profits were made to be put back into Canadian programming. Users of long distance telephone service paid prices in excess of production costs to cross-subsidize local service—urban residents subsidized rural residents.

DEREGULATION

In the late 1970s and early 1980s pressures mounted on government to deregulate industries. One source of pressure was critics of regulation, who argued that the firms being regulated had "captured" the regulatory agencies and that the regulatory agencies were now acting in the interests of the regulated rather than in the "public interest." For example, when competition between the railway and trucking industries increased, the regulators tried to protect the railway industry by keeping freight rates high. Recall the theory of rent-seeking behaviour discussed in Chapter 13: if a firm finds that it is possible to earn economic profits and protect those profits by preventing competition, it will expend resources to do so. These expenditures include lobbying for regulatory protection.

The critics of regulation also argued that the public would be better served by deregulation and increased competition. Moreover, they argued that cross-subsidization was no longer necessary or appropriate, pointing out that new technologies were reducing the importance of distance; Canadian culture was mature and no longer needed protection; and income redistribution should be from rich to poor individuals, not from urban to rural residents.

A second source of pressure arose from technological and institutional changes in the economy. These changes introduced new substitutes (which significantly reduced the market power of natural monopolies) and made it increasingly difficult to keep competition at bay.

The coming of the age of satellite communication technologies, fibre-optic cables, and computerized switching had a huge effect on both the television industry and the long distance telephone service industry. The cost of delivering long distance calls fell and new firms emerged to take advantage of a potentially profitable market. Satellite receivers made it all but impossible for the CRTC to limit the access of American television stations to the Canadian market. Meanwhile the Americans had already begun to deregulate and Canadians were increasingly relying on the U.S. infrastructure as a way of saving money. A person travelling from Saint John, New Brunswick, to Vancouver would travel to Bangor, Maine, fly to Seattle on an American airline, and then go to Vancouver. Long distance calls were also routed through the U.S. because it was much cheaper. Thus regulators found it almost impossible to restrict entry. Regulated firms faced lower demand and increased financial problems.

The Canadian airline industry was deregulated with the introduction of the 1987 National Transportation Act. The National Transportation Agency no longer sets air or rail rates and is officially committed to allowing competition across transport modes to ensure resources in the transportation sector. The CRTC has allowed competition in the long distance telephone market.

Satellite communication technologies, fibre-optic cables, and computerized switching helped generate competition in the long distance telephone market.

The deregulation debate in the late 1990s will focus on provincial electric utilities. The electric utility is the classic natural monopoly with large fixed costs, no close substitutes, and an "essential" product. But it may no longer fit the definition very well. While large economies of scale may still exist in power distribution, power generation can be done on a relatively small scale at scattered sites. Small plants can efficiently produce power and feed it into the power "grid." It is possible for even this industry to be quite competitive.

CROWN CORPORATIONS

crown corporation *A corporation owned and operated by government.*

A final solution to the natural monopoly problem is government (or crown) ownership and operation of the business. Canada Post, Ontario Hydro, SaskTel, the CBC, Canadian National Railway, Petro-Canada, and Air Canada are all companies that are or have been **crown corporations.** Because the crown corporations are not in business to maximize the return to shareholders, they can, in principle, operate in a way that produces higher levels of economic welfare than their privately run counterparts. However, there are many people who are concerned that governments are not very efficient business operators.

privatization *The transfer of government business to the private sector.*

One of the most popular trends of the 1980s was **privatization,** or the transfer of government businesses to the private sector. Canadian National Railway, Petro-Canada, and Air Canada were all privatized. In Japan, the Japan National Railway was sold to the public and Britain and France have sold stock in state-owned banks, energy companies, and telecommunications firms. (For more details on Great Britain's activities in this area, see the Global Perspective box titled "Privatization, Regulation, and Competition in British Public Utilities" on page 384.) Canadian governments are currently debating the merits of privatizing garbage collection, electric power generation and distribution, prisons, and even water treatment.

Why the rush to privatize? The basic logic is simple. The incentive to be efficient is greater when one's own money is at risk. Given that governments are often willing to bail out crown corporations, the incentives for these firms to be efficient can be very weak indeed. Also, political pressures can result in unwise investment decisions, and management of crown corporations have less flexibility than their private counterparts, since decisions are reviewed by the political process. Privatization, on the other hand, affords managers the opportunity (and freedom) to make decisions solely in the best interests of the firm and its shareholders (i.e., to make efficient decisions).

Defenders of crown corporations, in contrast, argue that crown corporations are very responsive to public needs. Indeed, many were created during World War II by C.D. Howe because the stakes were high and the private sector could not be relied on to deliver the goods. They also argue that crown corporations are efficient. The French government, for example, operates one of the most efficient and innovative railroads in the world, and comparisons of Canadian National Railway (when it was still a crown corporation) and CP Rail (private) have revealed very little difference in efficiency.

THE POLICY MAKERS' DILEMMA

One of the lessons we hope you take from this course (and from your entire university education) is that complicated questions have no simple answers. There are strong arguments for government involvement in the economy through competition policy, regulation, and crown corporations. Unchecked monopoly power, collusion, and price fixing can be enormously expensive to a society.

It is equally clear, unfortunately, that government policy can and does impose costs on society. Information needed to design optimal policy may not be available and policy makers do not usually bear as much of the cost of mistakes as do decision makers in the private sector. Policies can be captured by those whom the policies were originally designed to control. Politicians can use policies to try to influence voters rather than to ensure efficiency.

> The role of a policy maker is to understand the arguments, weigh the evidence, and proceed in one direction or the other. While policy decisions must be made without knowledge of the outcome, enlightened uncertainty is better than ignorance.

Summary

1. Governments have assumed two basic roles with respect to imperfectly competitive industries: (1) they *promote* competition and restrict market power, primarily through competition policy, and (2) they *restrict* competition by regulating industries. In addition, governments may become directly involved in business by creating crown corporations.

Historical Background

2. Competition policy and regulation have a long history in Canada. The first piece of legislation designed to encourage competition was passed in 1889. Regulation has a still longer history, and it dates to 1888 when the federal government assumed power to set rail rates.

3. Government-owned and -run *crown corporations* were established to provide essential services such as electric power, rail, and radio and television. In addition, a number of crown corporations were formed during World War II to supply goods and services that the private sector was unable to deliver quickly and efficiently.

Canadian Competition Policy

4. Competition policy can be used to pursue two goals, one economic, the other political. First, the twin economic objectives of equity and efficiency in the use of scarce resources are the focus of Canadian competition policy. Competition policy may also be used to ensure that no business firm acquires too much political power, thus potentially undermining our democratic system of government.

5. Canadian competition policy is designed to stop *price fixing, predatory pricing, price discrimination, mis-*

leading advertising, resale price maintenance, exclusive dealing and *tied selling, refusal to supply,* and *abuse of a dominant position* in a market. In addition, it attempts to prevent *mergers* that might reduce economic welfare.

6. Responsibility for enforcement of Canada's Competition Act (1986) falls on the Bureau of Competition Policy. The bureau is required to assess all large mergers and to bring any merger that it believes will reduce economic welfare before the Competition Tribunal. The Competition Tribunal, a quasi-judicial body made up of knowledgeable individuals, has the power to disallow a merger if it judges that the merger will reduce economic welfare.

7. The case for government intervention in imperfectly competitive industries is well established: unchecked monopoly power, price discrimination, collusion, and price fixing can be enormously expensive to society. Proponents of competition policy point out that most of the real gains arise because competition policy deters anticompetitive behaviour. Without such laws, the temptation to fix prices, collude, and engage in deceptive advertising would be irresistible.

8. The basic argument against competition policy is that it uses resources unnecessarily. International competition and efficient capital markets will ensure that monopoly profits do not last for long.

Regulation

9. When an industry demonstrates very large economies of scale, it may be efficient to have only one large firm in that industry. Such a firm is called a

natural monopoly. If a single-firm industry is protected on the grounds that it is a natural monopoly, it must be regulated to prevent exploitation of its monopoly power.

10. In past years, the government has been involved in regulating industries that are not natural monopolies. In the last decade, however, a number of these industries (including trucking, airlines, and telecommunications) have been totally or partially deregulated.

11. There are a number of problems associated with regulation. First, it is difficult to collect and analyze all the data necessary to regulate an industry. Second, firms that are guaranteed a certain rate of return lack incentives to be efficient. This may give rise to the *Averch-Johnson effect,* in which a monopoly tends to build more capital than it needs. Finally, regulation may give rise to excessive non-price competition.

12. The proper role of government in the world of business is hard to define. Doing nothing about noncompetitive industries inevitably results in significant social losses. The competition laws have strengths and weaknesses, but most economists feel they deter behaviour that might otherwise cost society too much. Where very large economies of scale make it logical to preserve monopoly structure in an industry, regulation may be the only reasonable course of action.

Review Terms and Concepts

abuse of dominant position 376
Averch-Johnson effect 383
cartel 375
crown corporation 386
exclusive dealing 376

merger 375
misleading advertising and deceptive marketing practices 376
predatory pricing 375
price discrimination 375

privatization 386
refusal to supply 376
resale price maintenance 375
tied selling 376

Problem Set

1. Legal language is a critical factor in the development of any policy. Write a brief essay describing the type of information you would need to make a case against a firm you think has *unduly* restricted competition against the *public interest.* Assume you must make your case in the criminal justice system where your case must be proven *beyond reasonable doubt.*

2. How would one distinguish predatory pricing from an aggressive competitive strategy that benefits consumers by lowering prices?

3. Write a short essay exploring the case for and against the following statement: Free trade is the best competition policy of all.

4. A small town 80 kilometres from a bigger city has had two grocery stores for almost 100 years; but recently the owners of the stores decided to merge their operations. Would this be allowed under Canadian competition policy?

5. Perhaps the strongest critic of competition policy is Professor Robert H. Bork. Professor Bork argues that there is little justification for interfering with the natural operation of a free market system. Sometimes called "economic Darwinism," Bork's philosophy is that monopoly or market power are of little concern because they "will be eroded if not based on superior efficiency." Write a brief essay either supporting or challenging Professor Bork's position. (For elaboration, see Robert Bork, *The Antitrust Paradox,* New York: Basic Books, 1978.)

6. As head of the Plutonia Public Utility Commission, you must make a recommendation concerning electric rates in the town of Plutonia, where power is provided by a private electric company that en-

joys a monopoly. Currently the price of electricity is regulated at $0.105 per kilowatt hour (kW·h). Total usage is 89.3 million kW·h. Assume that variable costs amount to $0.048 per kW·h, fixed costs of maintaining the power plant total $1.5 million annually, and demand elasticity is zero. The commission has established that a fair return on invested capital to the owners of the electric company is 10%. If total invested capital in the plant was $45 million, would you recommend a rate hike or a cut? By how much?

7. Explain why restructuring fails as a remedy in the case of a natural monopoly. Illustrate your answer with a graph. What alternatives are there to restructuring in the case of a natural monopoly?

8. Explain, using graphs, why restructuring a monopoly into a number of competing firms is likely to lead to a more efficient allocation of resources.

9. One of the objectives of deregulation of telephone services is to bring lower prices to consumers through competition. Long distance rates have indeed fallen since deregulation, but the price of local service has gone up. Does this mean that restructuring and deregulation have failed? Explain.

10. University students want low tuition fees and student organizations such as the Canadian Federation of Students often lobby government in hopes of securing greater regulation of tuition fees. What arguments could be made in support of regulation? Against?

16

Externalities, Public Goods, Imperfect Information, and Social Choice

market failure *Occurs when resources are misallocated, or allocated inefficiently.*

In Chapters 6 through 12, we built a complete model of a perfectly competitive economy under a set of fairly restrictive assumptions. By Chapter 12, we had demonstrated that the allocation of resources under perfect competition is efficient. At the end of that chapter, we began to relax some of the assumptions on which the competitive model is based. We introduced the idea of **market failure,** and in Chapters 13 and 14 we talked about three kinds of imperfect markets: monopoly, oligopoly, and monopolistic competition. In Chapter 15 we discussed some of the ways government has responded to the inefficiencies of imperfect markets and to the development of market power.

As we continue our examination of market failure, we look first at *externalities* as a source of inefficiency. Often when we engage in transactions or make economic decisions, second or third parties suffer consequences that decision makers have no incentive to consider. For example, for many years manufacturing firms and power plants had no reason to worry about the impact of smoke from their operations on the quality of the air we breathe. Now we know that air pollution harms people, and it has become one of the most often-cited examples of an externality.

Next, we consider a second type of market failure that involves a class of products that private firms find it unprofitable to produce even if members of society want them. These products are called *public goods* or *social goods*. Public goods yield collective benefits, and in most societies, governments either produce them or arrange for their provision. The process of choosing what social goods to produce is very different from the process of private choice.

A third source of market failure is *imperfect information*. In Chapters 6 through 12, we assumed that households and firms make choices in the presence of perfect information—that households know all that there is to know about product availability, quality, and price and that firms know all there is to know about factor availability, quality, and price. When information is imperfect, a misallocation of resources may result.

Finally, while the existence of public goods, externalities, and imperfect information are examples of market failure, it is not necessarily true that government involvement will always improve matters. Just as markets can fail, so too can governments. In fact, when we look carefully at the incentives facing government decision makers, we find several reasons behind government failure.

Externalities and Environmental Economics

An **externality** exists when the actions or decisions of one person or group impose a cost or bestow a benefit on some second or third parties. Externalities are sometimes called *spillovers* or *neighbourhood effects*. Inefficient decisions result when decision makers fail to consider social costs and benefits.

externality *A cost or benefit resulting from some activity or transaction that is imposed or bestowed upon parties outside the activity or transaction. Sometimes called spillovers or neighbourhood effects.*

The presence of externalities is a significant phenomenon in modern life. Examples are everywhere: air, water, land, sight, and sound pollution; traffic congestion; automobile accidents; abandoned housing; nuclear accidents; and secondhand cigarette smoke are only a few of them. Because so many externalities affect the environment, the study of externalities is a major concern of *environmental economics*.

The opening of Eastern Europe in 1989 and 1990 revealed that environmental externalities are not limited to free market economies. Part of the logic of a planned economy is that when economic decisions are made socially (by the government, presumably acting on behalf of the people) rather than privately, planners can and will take all costs—private and social—into account. This has not been the case, however. When East and West Germany were reunited and the borders of Europe were opened, many were shocked by the disastrous condition of the environment in virtually all of Eastern Europe. (For more details, see Figure 16.1 on the next page and the Global Perspective box on page 394 titled "Transitional Economies and Environmental Issues.")

As societies become more and more urbanized, externalities become more and more important. The reason is clear: when we live closer together, our actions are more likely to affect others.

Marginal Social Cost and Marginal-Cost Pricing

Profit-maximizing perfectly competitive firms will produce output up to the point at which price is equal to marginal cost ($P = MC$). Let us take a moment here to review why this condition is essential to the proposition that competitive markets produce what people want (that is, an efficient mix of output).

When a firm weighs price and marginal cost and no externalities exist, it is in fact weighing the full benefits to society of additional production against the full costs to society of that production. Those who benefit from the production of a product are the people or households who end up consuming it. The price of a product is a good measure of what an additional unit of that product is "worth," since those who value it more highly already buy it. People who value it less than the current price are not buying it. If marginal cost includes all costs—that is, all costs *to society*—of producing a marginal unit of a good, then additional production is efficient, provided that P is greater than MC. Up to the point where $P = MC$, each unit of production yields benefits in excess of cost.

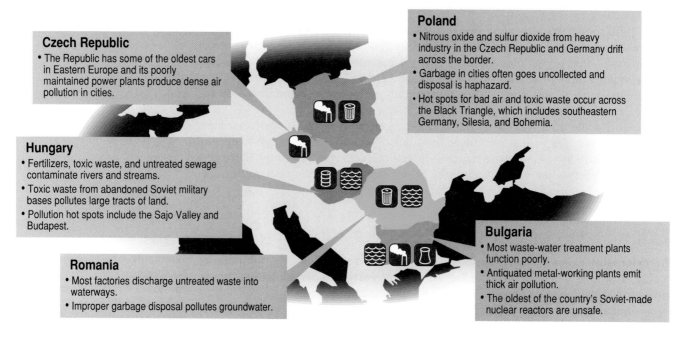

FIGURE 16.1

Environmental Problems in Eastern Europe

Source: Marlise Simons, "East Europe Sniffs Freedom's Air, and Gasps," *The New York Times,* November 3, 1994, p. A1.

Consider a firm in the business of producing laundry detergent. As long as the price per unit that consumers pay for that detergent exceeds the cost of the resources needed to produce one marginal unit of it, the firm will continue to produce. Producing up to the point where $P = MC$ is efficient, because for every unit of detergent produced, consumers derive benefits that exceed the cost of the resources needed to produce it. Producing at a point where $MC > P$ is inefficient, because marginal cost will rise above the unit price of the detergent. For every unit produced beyond the level at which $P = MC$, society uses up resources that have a value in excess of the benefits that consumers place on detergent. Figure 16.2a on the next page shows a firm and an industry in which no externalities exist.

But suppose that the production of the firm's product imposes external costs on society as well. If it does not factor those additional costs into its decisions, the firm is likely to overproduce. In Figure 16.2b, a certain measure of external costs is added to the firm's marginal cost curve. We see these external costs in the diagram, but the firm is ignoring them. The curve labelled *MSC,* which stands for **marginal social cost (MSC),** is the simple sum of the marginal costs of producing the product plus the correctly measured damage costs imposed in the process of production.

marginal social cost (MSC) *The total cost to society of producing an additional unit of a good or service. MSC is equal to the sum of the marginal costs of producing the product and the correctly measured damage costs involved in the process of production.*

If the firm does not have to pay for these damage costs, it will produce exactly the same level of output (q^*) as before, and price (P^*) will continue to reflect only the costs that the firm actually pays to produce its product. The firms in this industry will continue to produce, and consumers will continue to consume their product, but the market price takes into account only part of the full cost of producing the good. At equilibrium (q^*), marginal social costs are considerably greater than *price.* (Recall that *price* is a measure of the full value to consumers of a unit of the product at the margin.)

Let us say that our detergent plant freely dumps untreated toxic waste into a river. The waste imposes a number of specific costs on people who live down-

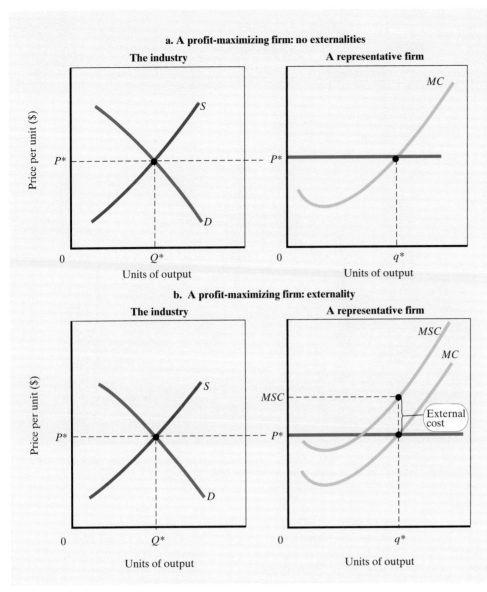

a. A profit-maximizing firm: no externalities

The industry

A representative firm

Price per unit ($)

P^*

0 Q^*

Units of output

S

D

P^*

MC

0 q^*

Units of output

b. A profit-maximizing firm: externality

The industry

A representative firm

Price per unit ($)

P^*

0 Q^*

Units of output

S

D

MSC

P^*

MSC

MC

External cost

0 q^*

Units of output

FIGURE 16.2

Profit-Maximizing Competitive Firms Will Produce up to the Point That Price Equals Marginal Cost ($P = MC$)

If we assume that the current price reflects what consumers are willing to pay for a product at the margin, firms that create external costs without weighing them in their decisions are likely to produce too much. At q^*, marginal social cost exceeds the price paid by consumers.

stream: it kills the fish in the river, it makes the river ugly to look at and rotten to smell, and it destroys the river for recreational use. There may also be serious health hazards, depending on what chemicals the firm is dumping. Obviously, the plant's product also provides certain benefits. Its soap is valuable to consumers, who are willing and able to pay for it. The firm employs people and capital, and its revenues are sufficient to cover all costs. The issue, however, is how the *net benefits* produced by the plant compare with the damage that it does. You don't need a sophisticated economic model to know that *someone* should consider the costs of those damages.

■ **Acid Rain** The case of acid rain is an excellent example of an externality and of the issues and conflicts involved in dealing with externalities. Manufacturing firms and power plants in the midwestern United States burn coal with a high sulfur content. When the smoke from those plants mixes with moisture in the atmosphere, the result is a dilute acid that is blown by the prevailing winds north

Global Perspective

Transitional Economies and Environmental Issues

In theory, socialist economies are supposed to pay attention to externalities and social costs better than free market economies, where private firms must often be prodded to consider external effects. The radical changes that have taken place in Eastern Europe over the last few years certainly challenge this once-conventional wisdom, as the following excerpt describes:

> PRAGUE— . . . . almost five years after the collapse of Communism, the region's environment continues to decay. Chemical works, smelters, coal mines and power plants are still infusing air and water with waste far surpassing international standards and causing severe health problems. Toxic dumps go on poisoning ground water and cities keep on spewing their raw sewage into rivers.

Pollution and deforestation have been problems in Eastern Europe for decades, but only since the fall of Communism have such problems come to the world's attention.

What's more, capitalism is bringing its own problems—more traffic pollution, less public transport, more plastic foam, more clashes between environmentalists and the peddlers of consumerism.

There have been some gains. Factory emissions have dropped, perversely the result of a sputtering economy in which many plants have closed or slowed production. But the enormous task of installing filters, scrubbers and treatment plants has barely begun. And energy still comes largely from highly polluting brown coal . . .

In theory, Communism with its strict central planning had more power than free-wheeling capitalism to avoid or prevent damaging nature. Yet, with its squandering of raw materials and energy, the economic artifice made in Moscow produced exceptional levels of pollution that maimed the lives of many of its citizens.

In the end, it was this poisoning that provided a rare platform for challenging the state when other forms of protest were not tolerated. The environmental devastation became a powerful catalyst as citizens' groups formed throughout the East, spurring broader protests before the fall of Communism. Almost inevitably, in 1989, the new leaders had to commit themselves to an urgent clean-up. . . .

On the cold and high plateaus where the German, Czech and Polish borders meet and tree stumps look as if ravaged by fire, foresters have been planting new and hardy seedlings. Yet few young firs are surviving. In the valleys below, a phalanx of power plants and industries driven by brown coal are still spewing sulfur and soot, as they have done for more than three decades. This region, dubbed the Black Triangle, is one of the world's biggest makers of acid rain.

Source: Marlise Simons, "East Europe Sniffs Freedom's Air, and Gasps," *The New York Times*, November 3, 1994, p. A1.

to Canada, where it falls to earth in the rain. The subject of a major conflict between the Canadian and U.S. governments and between industry and environmental groups, this acid rain is imposing enormous costs where it falls. Estimates of damage from fish kills, building deterioration, and deforestation range into the billions of dollars.

Decision makers at the manufacturing firms and public utilities using high-sulfur coal should weigh these costs, of course. But there is another side to this story. Burning cheap coal and not worrying about the acid rain that may be falling on someone else means jobs and cheap power for residents of the United States. Forcing coal-burning plants to pay for past damages from acid rain or even requiring them to begin weighing the costs that they are presently imposing will undoubtedly raise electricity prices and production costs.[1] There is also little doubt that some firms will be driven out of business and that jobs will be lost. However, if the electricity and other products produced in the United States are worth the full costs imposed by acid rain, plants would not shut down; consumers would simply pay higher prices. If those goods are not worth the full cost, they should not be produced, at least not in current quantities or using current production methods.

The case of acid rain highlights the fact that efficiency analysis ignores the *distribution* of gains and losses. That is, to establish efficiency we need only to demonstrate that the total value of the gains exceeds the total value of the losses. If U.S. producers and the consumers of their products were forced to pay an amount equal to the damages they cause, the gains from reduced damage in Canada would be at least as great as costs in the United States. The beneficiaries of forcing firms to consider these costs would be the households and firms in Canada. After many years of debate and significant lobbying by the government of Canada, the U.S. Congress passed and President Bush signed the Clean Air Act of 1990. Included in the law are strict emissions standards aimed, in part, at controlling the production and distribution of acid rain.

■ **Other Externalities** Other examples of external effects are all around us. When I drive my car into the centre of the city at rush hour, I contribute to the congestion and impose costs (in the form of lost time and auto emissions) on others. In fact, one focus of a 1992 world environmental conference called the Earth Summit was the possibility of worldwide climate warming as a result of so-called "greenhouse emissions" (like carbon dioxide) from industrial plants and automobiles. While potential costs are high, great uncertainty, both in the scientific evidence and in the magnitude of the potential costs, surrounds the issue.

In addition, secondhand cigarette smoke has become a matter of public concern. Smoking has been banned on domestic air carriers, and many municipalities have passed laws severely restricting smoking in public places.

Despite these problems, it is important to keep in mind that not all externalities are negative. For example: an abandoned house in an urban neighbourhood that is restored and occupied makes the neighbourhood better and adds value to the neighbours' homes.

PRIVATE CHOICES AND EXTERNAL EFFECTS

To help us understand externalities better, let us use a simple two-person example. Harry lives in a residence at a large university in Ontario, where he is a first-year

---

[1]*Look back at Figure 16.2. If the firm is suddenly forced to pay the full cost of production, it will reduce output. The gains from this output reduction are greater than the value of the goods given up because marginal social cost is above price.*

student. When he graduated from high school, his family gave him an expensive stereo system. Unfortunately, when Harry's residence was built, the university's capital budget was tight, and the walls are made of quarter-inch sheetrock over three-inch aluminum studs. You can hear people sleeping four rooms away. Harry likes bluegrass music of the particularly "twangy" kind. Because of a hearing loss after an accident some years ago, he often does not notice the volume at which he plays his music.

Jake, who lives next door to Harry, isn't much of a music lover, but when he does listen, he listens to Brahms concerti and occasionally to Mozart. Needless to say, Harry's music bothers Jake.

Let's assume for a moment that there are no further external costs or benefits to anyone other than Harry and Jake. Figure 16.3 diagrams the decision process that the two students face. The downward-sloping curve labelled *MB* represents the value of the marginal benefits that Harry derives from listening to his music. Of course, Harry doesn't sit down to draw this curve, any more than anyone else (other than an economics student) sits down to draw actual demand curves. Curves like this are simply abstract representations of the way people behave. But if you think carefully about it, such a curve must exist. To ask how much an hour of listening to music is worth to you is to ask how much you would be willing to pay to have it. Start at $0.01 and raise the "price" slowly in your mind. Presumably, you must stop at some point; where you stop depends on your taste for music and your income.

You can think, then, about the benefits that Harry derives from listening to bluegrass as the maximum amount of money that he would be willing to pay to listen to his music for an hour. For the first hour, let us say, the figure for *MB* is $0.50. We assume diminishing marginal utility, of course. The more hours Harry listens, the lower the additional benefits from each successive hour. As the diagram shows, the *MB* curve falls below $0.05 per hour after eight hours of listening time.

We call the costs that Harry must pay for each additional hour of listening to music **marginal private costs**, labelled *MPC* in Figure 16.3. These include the cost of electricity and so forth. These costs are constant at $0.05 per hour.

Then there is Jake. Although Harry's music doesn't poison Jake, give him lung cancer, or even cause him to lose money, it damages him nonetheless. He gets a headache, loses sleep, and can't concentrate on his work. Jake is harmed, and it is possible (at least conceptually) to measure that harm in terms of the maximum amount that he would be willing to pay to avoid it. The damage, or cost, imposed on Jake is represented in Figure 16.3 by the curve labelled *MDC*. Formally, **marginal damage cost (*MDC*)** is the additional harm done by increasing the level of an externality-producing activity by one unit. Assuming that Jake would be willing to pay some amount of money to avoid the music, it is also reasonable to assume that the amount increases with each successive hour. His headache gets worse with each additional hour of being forced to listen to bluegrass.

In the simple two-person society of Jake and Harry, it's easy to add up social benefits and costs. At every level of output (stereo playing time), total social cost is simply the sum of the private costs borne by Harry and the damage costs borne by Jake. In Figure 16.3, *MPC* (which is constant at $0.05 per hour) is added to *MDC* to get *MSC*.

Consider now what would happen if Harry simply ignored Jake.[2] If Harry decides to play the stereo, Jake will be damaged. As long as Harry gains more in

marginal private cost (*MPC*)
The amount that a consumer pays to consume an additional unit of a particular good.

marginal damage cost (*MDC*)
The additional harm done by increasing the level of an externality-producing activity by one unit. If producing product X pollutes the water in a river, MDC is the additional cost imposed by the added pollution that results from increasing output by one unit of X per period.

---

[2]*It may actually be easier for people to ignore the social costs imposed by their actions when those costs fall on large numbers of other people whom they do not have to look in the eye or whom they do not know personally. For the moment, however, we simply assume that Harry takes no account of Jake.*

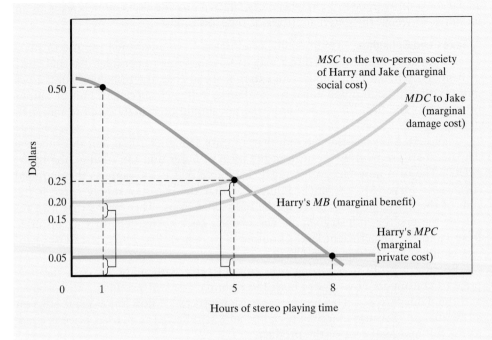

FIGURE 16.3

Externalities in a University Residence

The marginal benefits to Harry exceed the marginal costs he must bear to play his stereo for a period of up to eight hours. But when the stereo is playing, a cost is being imposed on Jake. When we add the costs borne by Harry to the damage costs imposed on Jake we get the full cost of the stereo to the two-person society made up of Harry and Jake. Playing the stereo more than five hours is inefficient because the benefits to Harry are less than the social cost for every hour above five. If Harry considers only his private costs, he will play the stereo for too long a time from society's point of view.

personal benefits from an additional hour of listening to music than he incurs in costs, the stereo will stay on. He will play it for eight hours (the point where Harry's $MB = MPC$). This result is inefficient; for every hour of play beyond five, the marginal social cost borne by society (in this case, a society made up of Harry and Jake) exceeds the benefits to Harry (that is, $MSC >$ Harry's MB).

It is generally true, then, that:

> When economic decisions ignore external costs, whether those costs are borne by one person or by society as a whole, those decisions are likely to be inefficient.

We will return shortly to Harry and Jake to see how they deal with their problem. First, however, we need to discuss the general problem of correcting for externalities.

INTERNALIZING EXTERNALITIES

A number of mechanisms are available to provide decision makers with incentives to weigh the external costs and benefits of their decisions, a process called *internalization*. In some cases, externalities are internalized through bargaining and negotiation without government involvement. In other cases, private bargains fail and the only alternative may be government action of some kind.

Five basic approaches have been taken to solving the problem of externalities: (1) government-imposed taxes and subsidies, (2) private bargaining and negotiation, (3) legal rules and procedures, (4) the sale or auctioning of rights to impose externalities, and (5) direct government regulation. While each approach is best suited for a different set of circumstances, all five provide decision makers with an incentive to weigh the external effects of their decisions.

■ **Taxes and Subsidies**   Traditionally, economists have advocated the use of marginal taxes and subsidies as a direct way of forcing firms to consider external costs or benefits. When a firm imposes an external social cost, the reasoning goes, a per unit tax should be imposed equal to the damages of each successive unit of output produced by the firm. In other words, the tax should be *exactly equal* to marginal damage costs.[3]

Figure 16.4 repeats the diagram that appears as Figure 16.2b, but this time the damage costs are paid by the firm in the form of a per unit tax (that is, the tax = MDC). The firm now faces a marginal cost curve that is the same as the marginal social cost curve ($MC' = MSC$). Remember that the industry supply curve is the sum of the marginal cost curves of the individual firms. This means that as a result of the tax the industry supply curve shifts back to the left, driving up price from P_0 to P_1. The efficient level of output is q_1, where $P = MC'$. (Recall our general equilibrium analysis from Chapter 12.)

Because a profit-maximizing firm equates price with marginal cost, the new price to consumers now covers both the resource costs of producing the product and the damage costs. The consumer-decision process is now once again efficient at the margin, because marginal social benefit as reflected in market price is equal to the full marginal cost of the product.

Measuring Damages   The biggest problem with this approach is that damages must be estimated in financial terms. For the detergent plant polluting the nearby river to be properly taxed, the government must evaluate the damages done to residents downstream in money terms. This is a difficult, but not impossible, task. When legal remedies are pursued, judges are forced to make such estimates as they decide on compensation to be paid. Surveys of "willingness to pay," studies of property values in affected versus nonaffected areas, and sometimes the market value of recreational activities can provide basic data.

The monetary value of damages to health and loss of life is, naturally, much more difficult to estimate, and any measurement of such losses is certainly controversial. But even here, policy makers frequently make judgments that implicitly set values on life and health. Thousands of deaths and tens of thousands of serious injuries result from traffic accidents in Canada every year, yet Canadians are unwilling to give up driving or to reduce the highway speed limit to 90 kilometres per hour—the costs of either course of action would be too high. Indeed, in response to public demand, New Brunswick passed legislation increasing the speed limit to 110 kilometres per hour on some highways. If most Canadians are willing to increase the risk of death in exchange for shorter driving times, the value we place on life clearly has its limits.

It is important to note that taxing externality-producing activities may not eliminate damages. Taxes on these activities are not designed to eliminate externalities; they are simply meant to force decision makers to consider the full costs of their decisions. Even if we assume that a tax correctly measures all the damage done, the decision maker may find it advantageous to continue causing the damage. For example, the detergent manufacturer may find it most profitable simply to pay the tax and go on polluting the river. That is, it may find that it can continue

---

[3]*As we discuss later in this chapter, damage costs are difficult to measure. It is often assumed that they are proportional to the volume of pollutants discharged into the air or water. Instead of taxes, governments often impose* effluent charges, *which make the cost to polluters proportional to the amount of pollution caused. We will use the term "tax" to refer both to taxes and effluent charges.*

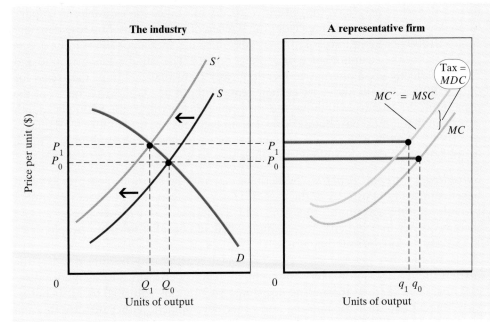

The industry

A representative firm

FIGURE 16.4

Tax Imposed on a Firm Equal to Marginal Damage Cost

If a per unit tax exactly equal to marginal damage costs is imposed on a firm, the firm will weigh the tax, and thus the damage costs, in its decisions. At the new equilibrium price, P_1, consumers will be paying an amount sufficient to cover full resource costs as well as the cost of damage imposed. The efficient level of output for the firm is q_1.

to pollute because the revenues from selling its product are sufficient to cover the cost of resources used *and to compensate the damaged parties fully*. In such a case, producing the product in spite of the pollution is "worth it" to society. It would be inefficient for the firm to stop polluting. Only if damage costs were very high would it make sense to stop. Thus, you can see the importance of proper measurement of damage costs.

Reducing Damages to an Efficient Level Taxes also provide firms with an incentive to use the most efficient technology for dealing with damage. If a tax reflects true damages, and if it is reduced when damages are reduced, firms may choose to avoid or reduce the tax by using a different technology that causes less damage. Suppose, for example, that our soap manufacturer is taxed $10 000 per month for polluting the river. If the soap plant can ship its waste to a disposal site elsewhere at a cost of $7000 per month and thereby avoid the tax, it will do so. If a plant belching sulfides into the air can install "smoke scrubbers" that eliminate emissions for an amount less than the tax imposed for polluting the air, it certainly will do so.

The Incentive to Take Care and to Avoid Harm It is important to note that all externalities involve at least two parties and that it is not always clear which party is "causing" the damage. Take our friends Harry and Jake. Harry enjoys music; Jake enjoys quiet. If Harry plays his music, he imposes a cost on Jake. If Jake can force Harry to stop listening to music, he imposes a cost on Harry.

Often, the best solution to an externality problem may not involve stopping the externality-generating activity. Suppose, for example, that Jake and Harry's residence has a third resident, Raoul. Raoul hates silence and loves bluegrass music. The resident adviser on Harry's floor arranges for Raoul and Jake to switch rooms. What was once an external cost has been transformed into an external benefit. Everyone is better off. Harry and Raoul get to listen to music, and Jake gets the silence he craves.

Sometimes, then, the most efficient solution to an externality problem is for the damaged party to avoid the damage. But if full compensation is paid by the damager, damaged parties may have no incentive to do so. Take, for example, a laundry located next to the exhaust fans from the kitchen of a restaurant. Suppose damages run to $1000 per month because the laundry must use special air filters in its dryers so that the clothes will not smell of cooking odours. The laundry looks around and finds a perfectly good alternative location away from the restaurant that rents for only $500 per month above its current rent. Without any compensation from the restaurant, the laundry will move and the total damage will be the $500 per month extra rent that it must pay. But if the restaurant compensates the laundry for damages of $1000 a month, why should the laundry move? Under these conditions, a move is unlikely, even though it would be efficient.

Subsidizing External Benefits   Sometimes activities or decisions generate external benefits instead of costs, as in the case of Harry and Raoul. Real estate investment provides another example. Investors who revitalize a downtown area—an old theatre district in a big city, for example—provide benefits to many people, both in the city and in surrounding areas.

Activities that provide such external social benefits may be subsidized at the margin to give decision makers an incentive to consider them. Just as ignoring social costs can lead to inefficient decisions, so too can ignoring social benefits. Government subsidies for housing and other development, either directly through specific expenditure programs or indirectly through tax exemptions and abatements, have been justified on such grounds.

■ **Bargaining and Negotiation**   In a notable article written in 1960, Ronald Coase pointed out that the government need not be involved in every case of externality.[4] Taxes and subsidies would be irrelevant in the case of Harry and Jake, for example. Coase argued that private bargains and negotiations are likely to lead to an efficient solution in many social damage cases without any government involvement at all. This argument is referred to as the **Coase theorem**.

Coase theorem *Under certain conditions, when externalities are present, private parties can arrive at the efficient solution without government involvement.*

For Coase's solution to work, three conditions must be satisfied. First, the basic rights at issue must be clearly understood. Either Harry has the right to play his stereo or Jake has the right to silence. These rights will probably be spelled out in residence rules. Second, there must be no impediments to bargaining. Parties must be willing and able to discuss the issues openly and without cost. Third, only a few people can be involved. Serious problems can develop when one of the parties to a bargain is a large group of people, such as all the residents of a large town.

For the sake of our example, let us say that all three of these conditions hold for Harry and Jake and that no room swap with someone like Raoul is possible. The residence rules establish basic rights in this case by specifying that during certain hours of the day, Harry has the right to play his stereo as loudly as he pleases. Returning to Figure 16.3 and our earlier discussion, suppose that under the rules Harry is free to choose any number of music-playing hours between zero and eight.

Because Harry is under no legal constraint to pay any attention to Jake's wishes, you might be tempted to think that he will ignore Jake and play his stereo for eight hours. (Recall that up to eight hours, the marginal benefits to Harry exceed the marginal costs that he must pay.) However, Jake is willing to pay Harry to play his stereo less than eight hours. For the first hour of play, the marginal damage to Jake is $0.15, so Jake would be willing to pay Harry $0.15 in the first hour to have Harry turn off his stereo. The opportunity cost to Harry of playing the first hour is thus $0.15 plus the (constant) marginal private cost of $0.05, or $0.20. Since the marginal gain to Harry in the first hour is $0.50, Harry would not accept the bribe. Likewise, for hours two through five the marginal benefit to Harry

---

[4]*See Ronald Coase, "The Problem of Social Cost,"* Journal of Law and Economics *(1960).*

exceeds the bribe that Jake would be willing to pay plus the marginal private cost.

After five hours, however, Jake is willing to pay $0.25 per hour to have Harry turn off his stereo. This means that the opportunity cost to Harry is $0.30. But after five hours the marginal benefit to Harry of another hour of listening to his stereo falls below $0.25. Harry will thus accept the bribe not to listen to his music in the sixth hour. Similarly, a bribe of $0.25 per hour is sufficient to have Harry not play the stereo in the seventh and eighth hours, and Jake would be willing to pay such a bribe. Five hours is thus the efficient amount of playing time. More hours or fewer hours reduces net total benefits to Harry and Jake.

Coase also pointed out that bargaining will bring the contending parties to the right solution regardless of where rights are initially assigned. For example, suppose that the residence rules state that Jake has the right to silence. This being the case, Jake can go to the residence administrators and have them enforce the rule. Now when Harry plays the stereo and Jake asks him to turn it off, Harry must comply.

Now the tables are turned. Accepting the rules (as he must), Harry knocks on Jake's door. Jake's damages from the first hour are only $0.15. This means that if he were compensated by more than $0.15, he would allow the music to be played. Now the stage is set for bargaining. Harry gets $0.45 in net benefit from the first hour of playing the stereo ($0.50 minus private cost of $0.05). Thus, he is willing to pay up to $0.45 for the privilege. If there are no impediments to bargaining, money will change hands. Harry will pay Jake some amount between $0.15 and $0.45 and, just as before, the stereo will continue to play. Jake has, in effect, sold his right to have silence to Harry. As before, bargaining between the two parties will lead to five hours of stereo playing. At exactly five hours, Jake will stop taking compensation and tell Harry to turn the stereo off. (Look again at Figure 16.3 to see that this is true.)

Note that in both cases the offer of compensation might be made in some form other than cash. Jake may offer Harry goodwill, a favour or two, or the use of his Harley Davidson for an hour.

Coase's critics are quick to point out that the conditions required for bargaining to produce the efficient result are not always present. The biggest problem with Coase's system is also a common problem. Very often one party to a bargain is a large group of people, and our reasoning may be subject to a fallacy of composition.

Suppose, for example, that a power company in a major city is polluting the air. The damaged parties are the thousands of people who live near the plant. For the sake of argument, let's assume that the plant has the right to pollute. The Coase theorem predicts that the people who are damaged by the smoke will get together and offer a bribe (just as Jake offered a bribe to Harry). If the bribe is sufficient to induce the power plant to stop polluting or reduce the pollutants with air scrubbers, then it will accept the bribe and cut down on the pollution. If it is not, the pollution will continue, but the firm will have weighed all the costs (just as Harry did when he continued to play the stereo) and the result will be efficient.

But not everyone will contribute to the bribe fund. First, each contribution is so small relative to the whole that no single contribution makes much of a difference. Thus, making a contribution may seem unimportant or unnecessary to some. Second, everyone gets to breathe the cleaner air, whether he or she contributes to the bribe or not. Many people will not participate simply because they are not compelled to, and the private bargain breaks down—the bribe that the group comes up with will be less than the full damages unless everyone participates. (We discuss these two problems—the "drop-in-the-bucket" and the "free rider"—fully later in this chapter.) Thus, when the number of damaged parties is large, government taxes or regulation may be the only avenue to a remedy.

■ Legal Rules and Procedures For bargaining to result in an efficient outcome, the initial assignment of rights must be clear to both parties. When rights are established by law, more often than not some mechanism to protect those rights is also built into the law. In some cases where a nuisance exists, for example, there may be injunctive remedies. In such cases, the victim can go to court and ask for an **injunction** that forbids the damage-producing behaviour from continuing. If the residence rules specifically give Jake the right to silence, Jake's getting the resident adviser to speak to Harry is something like getting an injunction.

Injunctive remedies are irrelevant when the damage has already been done. Consider accidents. If your leg has already been broken as the result of an automobile accident, enjoining the driver of the other car from drinking and driving won't work—it's already too late. In these cases, rights must be protected by **liability rules,** rules that require A to compensate B for damages imposed. In theory, such rules are designed to do exactly the same thing that taxing a polluter is designed to do: provide decision makers with an incentive to weigh all the consequences, actual and potential, of their decisions. Just as taxes do not stop all pollution, liability rules do not stop all accidents.

However, the threat of liability actions does induce people to take more care than they might otherwise take. Product liability is a good case in point. If a person is damaged in some way because a product is defective, the producing company is in most cases held strictly liable for the damages, even if the company took reasonable care in producing the product. Thus producers have a powerful incentive to be careful. If consumers know they will be generously compensated for any damages, however, they may not have as powerful an incentive to be careful when using the product.

■ Selling or Auctioning Pollution Rights We have already established that not all externality-generating activities should be banned. Around the world, the private automobile has become the clearest example of an externality-generating activity whose benefits (many believe) outweigh its costs.

Many externalities are imposed when we drive our cars. First, congestion is an externality. When many of us decide to drive into the city at rush hour, each of us imposes costs on the rest of us. Even though the marginal "harm" imposed by any one driver is small, the sum total is a serious cost to all who spend hours in traffic jams. Second, most of the air pollution in North America comes from automobiles. The problem is most evident in Los Angeles, where smog loaded with harmful emissions (mostly from cars) blankets the city virtually every day. Finally, driving increases the likelihood of accidents, raising insurance costs to all.

While we do not ignore these costs from the standpoint of public policy, we certainly have not banned driving. This is also true for many other forms of pollution. In many cases we have consciously opted to allow ocean dumping, river pollution, and air pollution within limits.

There is no question that the right to impose environmental externalities is beneficial to the parties causing the damage. In a sense, the right to dump in a river or pollute the air or the ocean can be thought of as a resource. Thinking of the privilege to dump in this way suggests an alternative mechanism for controlling pollution: selling or auctioning the pollution rights to the highest bidder. Canada's Green Plan advocates increased use of this type of economic instrument. To minimize the cost of compliance and to distribute the burden fairly, each firm in a marketable pollution permit program is issued tradeable pollution rights. These rights can be sold at auction to firms that face high compliance costs. (For an example, see the Global Perspective box on page 404 entitled "The Clean Air Act, Pollution Auctions, and Mexican Power Plants.")

injunction *A court order forbidding the continuation of behaviour that leads to damages.*

liability rules *Laws that require A to compensate B for damages imposed.*

Another example of the selling of externality rights takes place in Singapore, where the right to buy a car is auctioned off each year. Despite very high taxes and the need for special permits to drive in downtown areas, the roads in Singapore have become quite congested. The government decided to limit the number of new cars on the road because the external costs associated with them (congestion and pollution) have become very high. With these limits imposed, the decision was made to distribute car-ownership rights to those who place the highest value on them. It seems likely that taxi drivers, trucking companies, bus lines, and travelling salespeople will buy the licences, while families who drive for convenience instead of taking public transportation will find them too expensive.

Congestion and pollution are not the only externalities that Singapore's government takes seriously. In 1994, the fine for littering was $625, for failing to flush a public toilet $94, and for eating on a subway $312. In addition, 514 people were convicted in 1992 of illegally smoking in public.

■ **Direct Regulation of Externalities** Taxes, subsidies, legal rules, and public auction are all methods of indirect regulation designed to induce firms and households to weigh the social costs of their actions against the benefits. The actual size of the external cost/benefit depends on the reaction of households and firms to the incentives provided by the taxes, subsidies, and rules.

However, for obvious reasons, many externalities are too important to be regulated indirectly. These externalities must be regulated directly. For example, dumping cancer-causing chemicals into the ground near a public water supply is simply illegal, and those who do it can be prosecuted and sent to jail.

Direct regulation of externalities takes place at the federal, provincial, and local level. Environment Canada, a federal department, is responsible for a number of pieces of legislation that set specific standards for permissible discharges into the air and water. Each province also has a department

Singapore is known for its many laws designed to reduce negative externalities. Littering, chewing gum in public, eating on a subway car, failing to flush a public toilet, and vandalizing public property are all considered serious offences that are punishable by imprisonment, fines, and/or public chastisement.

(or ministry) charged with regulating activities that are likely to harm the environment.

Many criminal penalties and sanctions for violating environmental regulations are like the taxes imposed on polluters. Not all violations and crimes are stopped, but violators and criminals face "costs." For the outcome to be efficient, the penalties they can expect to pay should reflect the damage their actions impose on society.

Public (Social) Goods

Another source of market failure lies in the existence of **public goods,** often called **social,** or **collective, goods.** These kinds of goods represent a market failure because they have characteristics that make it difficult for the private sector to produce them profitably:

> In an unregulated market economy with no government to see that they are produced, public goods would at best be produced in insufficient quantity and at worst not produced at all.

public goods (social, or **collective, goods)** *Goods or services that bestow collective benefits on members of society. Such goods are both nonrival in consumption and their benefits are nonexcludable.*

Global Perspective

The Clean Air Act, Pollution Auctions, and Mexican Power Plants

The Clean Air Act, passed in the United States in 1990, imposed strict limits on the amount of pollution that the United States' largest power plants can generate. Instead of regulating each plant separately, the act sets aggregate limits and allocates to each plant a set of pollution "rights" that can be sold to other plants at auction. The polluters who find it most costly to clean up their emissions simply buy the right to pollute from plants that can more easily reduce emissions. Allowing the market to distribute the rights, some argue, will lead to a more efficient distribution of the costs of cleanup. The following excerpt describes the United States' first-ever pollution auction:

The Environmental Protection Agency's first auction of rights to pollute the air attracted more participants than had been expected and reaped $21 million. . . .

At stake were more than 275,000 pollution allowances, each permitting a utility to emit a ton of sulfur dioxide, the chemical that causes acid rain. Under the 1990 Clean Air Act, the E.P.A. set strict "spot" emissions limits to take effect in 1995, covering 110 of the nation's largest, dirtiest power plants. Even stricter "advance" limits, applicable to about 800 plants, will take effect by the year 2000. . . .

The act allows utilities that can reduce emissions below the permitted levels to sell the allowances they do not need to others that are having trouble meeting the limits. In theory, market forces will encourage utilities that can cut pollution the most for the least investment in scrubbers or fuel

changes to lead the way. That would allow the nation to shave billions of dollars off the cost of meeting pollution-reduction goals. . . .[1]

By 1995 it was clear that the act was working well. The cost of sulfur dioxide emissions had fallen sharply and many plants had reduced their emissions more than the act called for during its early years.

But the Clean Air Act applies only to U.S. firms, and increasing attention has focused on pollution sources outside of the United States. Of particular concern has been Mexico, where environmental issues were a major stumbling block in the final negotiations that led to the North American Free Trade Agreement (NAFTA) in 1994.

Sulfur dioxide became a particularly sore point in 1995, when Mexico was in the process of building a very large power plant just 16 kilometres south of Eagle Pass, Texas. The new plant and another one nearby will produce a total of 200 000 tonnes of sulfur dioxide per year, and a lot of it will find its way across the border into the United States.

As the following excerpt from a *New York Times* article by economist Peter M. Emerson and law professor Sanford E. Gaines points out, resolving such an issue is difficult:

For the many Mexicans who are seeking a better life, a reliable supply of low-cost electricity is essential. Mexicans enjoy clean air and beautiful vistas as much as anyone else, but their lower incomes and need for economic development may make them unable or unwilling to spend as much on the environment as Americans would like. . . .

For many Americans, pollution is the issue—and economic power is a way to stop it. For instance, some people are proposing that the Texas Public Utility Commission ban the sale in Texas of northern Mexican electricity. The threatened loss of such a large market, the theory goes, will force Mexico to curb pollution from its plants.

Then comes the finger-pointing. While no one knows whose pollution contributes exactly how much to the problem, many Americans focus on the 200 000 tonnes of sulfur dioxide from the two Mexican plants. For their part, many Mexicans emphasize that the United States is the continent's biggest producer of the pollutant.

The result: no progress. Air pollution over the whole region worsens and the cost of its correction rises.[2]

Emerson and Gaines argue that the solution to this problem might be found if the pollution-rights trading program were expanded to include Mexico and Canada. They also suggest that U.S. entrepreneurs might finance better anti-pollution equipment at Mexican power plants in exchange for more pollution allowances, and go on to argue that such a program would reduce the danger of NAFTA's breaking down because of lack of cooperation on environmental matters.

Sources: [1]Barnaby J. Feder, "Sold: $21 Million of Air Pollution," *The New York Times*, March 30, 1983. [2]Peter M. Emerson and Sanford E. Gaines, "Why Not Trade Pollution, Too?" *The New York Times*, January 1, 1995, p. F9.

THE CHARACTERISTICS OF PUBLIC GOODS

Public goods are defined by two closely related characteristics: they are nonrival in consumption and/or their benefits are nonexcludable.

A good is **nonrival in consumption** when A's consumption of it does not interfere with B's consumption of it. This means that the benefits of the goods are collective—they accrue to everyone. National defence, for instance, benefits us all. The fact that I am protected in no way detracts from the fact that you are protected; every citizen is protected just as much as every other citizen. If the air is cleaned up, my breathing that air does not interfere with your breathing it, nor (under ordinary circumstances) is that air used up as more people breathe it. Private goods in contrast are *rival in consumption*. If I eat a hamburger, you cannot eat it too.

Goods can sometimes generate collective benefits and still be rival in consumption. This happens when crowding occurs. For example, a park or a pool can accommodate many people at the same time, generating collective benefits for everyone. But when too many people crowd in on a hot summer day, they begin to interfere with each other's enjoyment. Beyond a certain level of use, the park or the pool becomes rival in consumption.

Most public goods are also **nonexcludable.** This means that once the good is produced, people cannot be excluded for any reason from enjoying its benefits. Once a national defence system is established, it protects everyone. When the police department sets up a successful crime-prevention program, everyone in town is less likely to be the victim of a crime.

For a private profit-making firm to produce a good and make a profit, it must be able to withhold that good from those who do not pay. McDonald's can make money selling chicken sandwiches only because you don't get the chicken sandwich unless you pay for it first. If payment were voluntary, McDonald's would probably not be in business for long.

Let us consider a clever entrepreneur who decides to offer better police protection to the city of Metropolis. Careful (and we will assume correct) market research reveals that the citizens of Metropolis do indeed want high-quality protection and that they are willing to pay for it. Not everyone is willing to pay the same amount. Some can afford more, others can afford less, and people have different preferences and different feelings about risk. Our entrepreneur nevertheless hires a sales force and begins to sell his service. Soon, however, he encounters a problem. Because his is a private company, payment is strictly voluntary. He can't force anyone to pay. Payment for a hamburger is voluntary too, but a hamburger can be withheld for nonpayment. The good that our new firm is selling, however, is by nature a public good.

As a potential consumer of a public good, I face a dilemma. I want more police protection, and, let's say, I'm even willing to pay $50 a month for it. But nothing is contingent upon my payment. First, if the good is produced, the crime rate falls and all residents benefit. I get that benefit whether I pay for it or not. In other words, I get a free ride, and that is why this dilemma is called the **free-rider problem.** Second, my payment is very small relative to the amount that must be collected to provide the service. Thus, the amount of police protection actually produced will not be significantly affected by the amount that I contribute, or whether I contribute at all. This is the **drop-in-the-bucket problem.**

The outcome is clear:

> A consumer acting in his or her own self-interest has no incentive to contribute voluntarily to the production of public goods. Some will feel a moral responsibility or social pressure to contribute, and those people indeed may do so. But the economic incentive is missing, and most people do not find room in their budgets for many voluntary payments.

nonrival in consumption *A characteristic of public goods; one person's enjoyment of the benefits of a public good does not interfere with another's consumption of it.*

nonexcludable *A characteristic of most public goods; once a good is produced, no one can be excluded from enjoying its benefits.*

free-rider problem *A problem intrinsic to public goods; because people can enjoy the benefits of public goods whether they pay for them or not, they are usually unwilling to pay for them.*

drop-in-the-bucket problem *A problem intrinsic to public goods; the good or service is usually so costly that its provision generally does not depend on whether or not any single person pays.*

INCOME DISTRIBUTION AS A PUBLIC GOOD?

In the next chapter, we add the issues of justice and equity to the matters of economic efficiency that we are considering here. There we explain that the government may wish to change the distribution of income that results from the operation of the unregulated market on the grounds that the distribution is not fair. Before we do so, however, we need to note that some economists have argued for redistribution of income on grounds that it generates public benefits.

For example, let us say that many members of Canadian society want to eliminate hunger in Canada. Suppose that you are willing to give $200 per year in exchange for the knowledge that people are not going to bed hungry. Many private charities in Canada use the money they raise to feed the poor. If you want to contribute to this activity, you can certainly do so privately, through charity. So why do we need government involvement?

To answer this question, we must first consider the benefits of eliminating hunger. First, it generates collective psychological benefits; simply knowing that people are not starving helps us sleep better. Second, eliminating hunger may reduce disease, and this in turn has a number of beneficial effects. People who are fit and strong are more likely to stay in school and to get and keep jobs. This reduces welfare claims and contributes positively to the economy. If people are less likely to get sick, insurance premiums for everyone will go down. Robberies may decline because fewer people are desperate for money. This means that all of us are less likely to be victims of crime, both now and in the future.

These are goals that members of society may very well want to achieve. But just as there is no economic incentive to contribute voluntarily to national defence, so there is no economic incentive to contribute to private causes. If hunger is eliminated, you benefit whether you contributed or not—the free-rider problem again. At the same time, poverty is a huge problem and your contribution cannot possibly have any influence on the amount of national hunger—the drop-in-the-bucket problem again. Thus, the goals of income redistribution may be more like national defence than like a chicken sandwich from McDonald's.

> If we accept the idea that redistributing income generates a public good, private endeavours may fail to do what we want them to do, and government involvement may be called for.

PUBLIC PROVISION OF PUBLIC GOODS

All societies, past and present, have had to face the problem of providing public goods. When members of society get together to form a government, they do so to provide themselves with goods and services that will not be provided if they act separately. Like any other good or service, a body of laws (or system of justice) is produced with labour, capital, and other inputs. Law and the courts yield social benefits, and they must be set up and administered by some sort of collective, cooperative effort.

Notice that we are talking about public *provision*, not public *production*. Once the government decides what service it wants to provide, it often contracts with the private sector to produce the good. Much of the material used in the public education system is produced by private sector firms. Highways, government offices, data processing services, and so forth are usually produced by private firms.

One of the immediate problems of public provision is that it frequently leads to public dissatisfaction. It is easy to be angry at government. Part, but certainly not all, of the reason for this dissatisfaction lies in the nature of the goods that government provides. Firms that produce or sell private goods post a price—we can choose to buy any quantity we want, or we can walk away without any. It makes no sense to get mad at a shoe store, because no one can force you to shop there.

You cannot shop for collectively beneficial public goods. When it comes to national defence, the government must choose one and only one kind and quantity of (collective) output to produce. Because none of us can choose how much should be spent or on what, we are all dissatisfied. Even if the government does its job with reasonable efficiency, at any given time about half of us think that we have too much national defence and about half of us think that we have too little.

OPTIMAL PROVISION OF PUBLIC GOODS

In a famous article first published in the early 1950s, Paul Samuelson demonstrated that there exists an *optimal,* or *most efficient,* level of output for every public good.[5] The discussion of the Samuelson solution that follows leads us straight to the thorny problem of how societies, as opposed to individuals, make choices.

■ **Samuelson's Theory** An efficient economy is one that produces what people want. Private producers, whether competitors or monopolists, are constrained by the market demand for their products. If they can't sell their products for more than it costs to produce them, they are out of business. But because private goods permit exclusion, firms can withhold their products until households pay. This contingency of delivery upon payment forces households to reveal something about their preferences. No one is forced to buy or not to buy, but if you want a product you must pay for it. Buying a product at a posted price reveals that it is "worth" at least that amount to you and to everyone who buys it.

Market demand for a private good is simply the sum of the quantities that each household decides to buy (as measured on the horizontal axis). The diagrams in Figure 16.5 on the next page review the derivation of a market demand curve. Assume that society consists of two people, A and B. At a price of $1, A demands 9 units of the private good and B demands 13. Thus, market demand at a price of $1 is 22 units. If price were to rise to $3, A's demand would drop to 2 units and B's would drop to 9 units; market demand at a price of $3 is thus $2 + 9 = 11$ units. The point here is that:

> The price mechanism forces people to reveal what they want, and it forces firms to produce only what people are willing to pay for, but it works this way only because exclusion is possible.

People's preferences and demands for public goods are conceptually no different than their preferences and demands for private goods. One may want fire protection and be willing to pay for it in the same way that one wants to listen to a CD. To demonstrate that an efficient level of production exists, Samuelson assumes that we know people's preferences. Figure 16.6 on page 409 shows demand curves for buyers A and B. If the public good were available in the private market at a price of $6, A would buy X_1 units. Or, put another way, A is willing to pay $6 per unit to obtain X_1 units of the public good. B, on the other hand, is willing to pay only $3 per unit to obtain X_1 units of the public good.

Remember, however, that public goods are nonrival—that benefits accrue simultaneously to everyone. One, and only one, quantity can be produced, and that

---

[5]Paul A. Samuelson, *"Diagrammatic Exposition of a Theory of Public Expenditure,"* Review of Economics and Statistics *XXXVII (1955).*

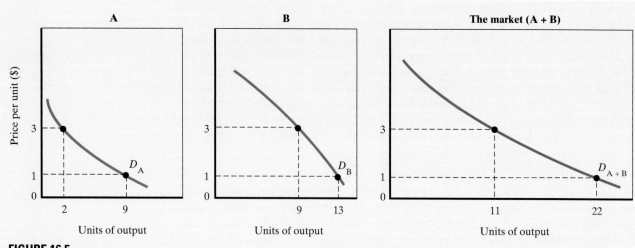

FIGURE 16.5

With Private Goods, Consumers Decide What Quantity to Buy; Market Demand Is the Sum of Those Quantities at Each Price

At a price of $3, A buys 2 units and B buys 9 for a total of 11. At a price of $1, A buys 9 units and B buys 13 for a total of 22. We all buy the quantity of each private good that we want. Market demand is the horizontal sum of all individual demand curves.

is the amount that everyone gets. If X_1 units are produced, A gets X_1 and B gets X_1. If X_2 units are produced, A gets X_2 and B gets X_2.

To arrive at market demand for public goods, then, we do not sum quantities. Rather, *we add up the amounts that individual households are willing to pay for each potential level of output.* In Figure 16.6 A is willing to pay $6 per unit for X_1 units and B is willing to pay $3 per unit for X_1 units. Thus, if society consists only of A and B, society is willing to pay $9 per unit for X_1 units of public good X. For X_2 units of output, society is willing to pay a total of $4 per unit.

In sum:

> For private goods, market demand is the horizontal sum of individual demand curves—we add the different *quantities* that households consume (as measured on the *horizontal* axis). For public goods, market demand is the vertical sum of individual demand curves—we add the different *amounts* that households are willing to pay to obtain each level of output (as measured on the *vertical* axis).

Samuelson argued that once we know how much society is willing to pay for a public good, we need only compare that amount to the cost of its production. Figure 16.7 on page 410 reproduces A's and B's demand curves and the total demand curve for the public good. As long as society (in this case, A and B) is willing to pay more than the marginal cost of production, the good should be produced. If A is willing to pay $6 per unit of public good and B is willing to pay $3 per unit, society is willing to pay $9.

The efficient level of output here is X^* units. If at that level A is charged a fee of $6 per unit of X produced and B is charged a fee of $3 per unit of X, everyone should be happy. Resources are being drawn from the production of other goods

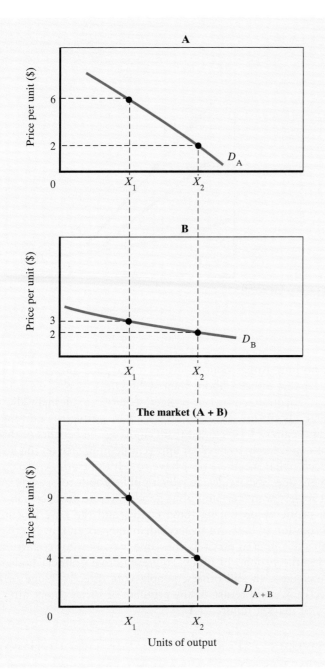

A

B

The market (A + B)

Units of output

FIGURE 16.6

With Public Goods, There Is Only One Level of Output, and Consumers Are Willing to Pay Different Amounts for Each Level

A is willing to pay $6 per unit for X_1 units of the public good. B is willing to pay only $3 for X_1 units. Society—in this case A and B—is willing to pay a total of $9 for X_1 units of the good. Since only one level of output can be chosen for a public good, we must add A's contribution to B's to determine market demand. This means adding demand curves vertically.

and services only to the extent that people want the public good and are willing to pay for it. We have thus arrived at the **optimal level of provision for public goods.**

> At the optimal level, society's total willingness to pay per unit is equal to the marginal cost of producing the good.

■ **The Problems of Optimal Provision**   One major problem exists, however. To produce the optimal amount of each public good, the government must know something that it cannot possibly know—everyone's preferences. Because exclusion is

optimal level of provision for public goods *The level at which resources are drawn from the production of other goods and services only to the extent that people want the public good and are willing to pay for it. At this level, society's willingness to pay per unit is equal to the marginal cost of producing the good.*

FIGURE 16.7

Optimal Production of a Public Good

Optimal production of a public good means producing as long as society's total willingness to pay per unit (D_A + $_B$) is greater than the marginal cost of producing the good.

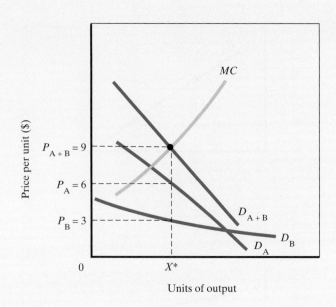

impossible, nothing forces households to reveal their preferences. Furthermore, if we ask households directly about their willingness to pay, we run up against the same problem encountered by our protection-services salesman above. If my actual payment depends on my answer, I have an incentive to hide my true feelings. Knowing that I cannot be excluded from enjoying the benefits of the good and that my payment is not likely to have an appreciable influence on the level of output finally produced, what incentive do I have to tell the truth—or to contribute?

How, then, does society decide which public goods to provide? We assume that members of society want certain public goods. Private producers in the market cannot make a profit by producing these goods, and the government cannot obtain enough information to measure society's demands accurately. No two societies have dealt with this dilemma in precisely the same way. In some countries, dictators simply decide for the people. In others, representative political bodies speak for the people's preferences. In still others, people vote directly. None of these solutions works perfectly. We will return to the problem of social choice after discussing one more source of market failure.

LOCAL PROVISION OF PUBLIC GOODS: THE TIEBOUT HYPOTHESIS

In 1956 Charles Tiebout made an important point: to the extent that local governments are responsible for providing public goods, an efficient market-choice mechanism may in fact exist. Consider a set of towns that are identical except for police protection. Towns that choose to spend a lot of money on police are likely to have a lower crime rate. A lower crime rate will attract households who are risk averse and are willing to pay higher taxes for lower risk of being a crime victim. Those who are willing to bear greater risk may choose to live in the low-tax/high-crime towns. Also, if some town is very efficient at crime prevention, it will attract residents. Given that each town has limited space, property values will be bid up in that town. The higher home price in that town is the "price" of the lower crime rate.

According to the **Tiebout hypothesis,** an efficient mix of public goods is produced when local prices (in the form of taxes or higher housing costs) come to reflect consumer preferences just as they do in the market for private goods. What is

Tiebout hypothesis *An efficient mix of public goods is produced when local land/housing prices and taxes come to reflect consumer preferences just as they do in the market for private goods.*

different in the Tiebout world is that people exercise consumer sovereignty not by "buying" different combinations of goods in a market, but by "voting with their feet" (choosing among bundles of public goods and tax rates produced by different towns and participating in local government).

Imperfect Information

In Chapters 6 through 12, we assumed that households and firms possess complete information on products and inputs. To make informed choices among various goods and services available in the market, households must have full information on product quality, availability, and price. Similarly, to make sound judgments about what inputs to use, firms must have full information on input availability, quality, and price.

The absence of full information can cause households and firms to make mistakes. A voluntary exchange is almost always evidence that both parties benefit. Thus most voluntary exchanges are efficient. But in the presence of imperfect information, not all exchanges are efficient. The most obvious example is fraud. Perry sells a bottle of coloured water to Ed claiming that it will grow hair on Ed's bald head. Clearly, if Ed had known what was really in the bottle, he would not have purchased it.

Firms as well as consumers can be the victims of incomplete or inaccurate information. Recall that a profit-maximizing competitive firm will hire workers as long as the marginal revenue product of labour (MRP_L) is greater than the wage rate. But how can a firm judge the *productivity* of a potential hire? Also, suppose that a worker steals from the firm. Clearly, the cost of employing that worker is greater than just the wage that he or she is paid.

ADVERSE SELECTION

The problem of **adverse selection** can occur when a buyer or seller enters into an exchange with another party who has more information. Suppose, for example, that there are only two types of workers: lazy workers and hard workers. Each worker knows which she is, but employers cannot tell. If there is only one wage rate, lazy workers will be overpaid relative to their productivity and hard workers will be underpaid. Recall that workers weigh the value of leisure and nonmarket production against the wage in deciding whether to enter the labour force. Since hard workers will end up underpaid relative to their productivity, fewer hard workers than is optimal will be attracted into the labour force. Similarly, since lazy workers are overpaid relative to their productivity, more of them will be attracted into the labour force than is optimal. Hence, the market has selected among workers adversely.

adverse selection *Can occur when a buyer or seller enters into an exchange with another party who has more information.*

The classic case of adverse selection is the used car market. Suppose that owners (potential sellers) of used cars have all the information about the real quality of their cars. To simplify matters, suppose further that half of all used cars are "lemons" (bad cars) and that half are "cherries" (good cars). Suppose further that consumers (potential used-car buyers) are willing to pay $6000 for a cherry but only $2000 for a lemon.

If half the cars for sale were lemons and half were cherries, the market price of a car would be about $4000, and consumers would have a 50–50 chance of getting a lemon. But there is an adverse selection problem because of unequal information. Used car *sellers* know whether they have a lemon or a cherry while used car *buyers* do not. Lemon owners know that they are making out like bandits by selling at $4000, while cherry owners know that they are not getting what their car

The theory of imperfect information makes it clear that your chances of buying a "lemon" on a used car lot are quite high.

is really worth. Thus, more lemon owners are attracted into selling their cars than are cherry owners.

Over time, buyers come to understand that the probability of getting a lemon is greater than the probability of getting a cherry, and the price of used cars drops. This, of course, makes matters worse because it provides even less incentive for cherry owners to sell their cars. This process will continue until only lemons are left in the market. Once again, the unequal information leads to an adverse selection.[6]

Adverse selection is also a problem in insurance markets. Insurance companies insure people against risks like health problems or accidents. Individuals know more about their own health than anyone else, even with required medical exams. If medical insurance rates are set at the same level for everyone, then medical insurance is a better deal for those who are unhealthy than for those who are healthy and likely never to have a claim. This means that more unhealthy people will buy insurance, which forces insurance companies to raise premiums. As with used cars, fewer healthy people and more unhealthy people will end up with insurance.

MORAL HAZARD

moral hazard Arises when one party to a contract passes the cost of his or her behaviour on to the other party to the contract.

Another information problem that arises frequently in insurance markets is *moral hazard*. Often, people enter into contracts in which the result of the contract at least in part depends upon one of the parties' future behaviour. A **moral hazard** problem arises when one party to a contract passes the cost of his or her behaviour on to the other party to the contract. For example, accident insurance policies are contracts that agree to pay for repairs to your car if it is damaged in an accident. Whether you have an accident or not in part depends on whether you drive cautiously. Similarly, apartment leases may specify that the landlord perform routine maintenance around the apartment. If you decide to kick the door every time you come into the house or punch the wall every time you get angry, your landlord ultimately pays the repair bill.

Such contracts can lead to inefficient behaviour. The problem is very much like the externality problem in which firms and households have no incentive to consider the full costs of their behaviour. If my car is fully insured against theft, why should I lock it? If visits to the dentist are free under my dental insurance plan, why not get my teeth cleaned six times a year?

Like adverse selection, the moral hazard problem is an information problem. Contracting parties cannot always determine the future behaviour of the person with whom they are contracting. If all future behaviour could be predicted, contracts could be written to try to eliminate undesirable behaviour. Sometimes this is possible. Life insurance companies do not pay off in the case of suicide. Fire insurance companies will not write a policy unless you have smoke detectors. If you cause unreasonable damage to an apartment, your landlord can retain your security deposit.

Nonetheless:

> It is impossible to know everything about behaviour and intentions. If a contract absolves one party of the consequences of his or her action, and people act in their own self-interest, the result is inefficient.

---

[6]This discussion is based on a classic article by George Akerlof, "The Market for 'Lemons': Quality, Uncertainty, and the Market Mechanism," Quarterly Journal of Economics 84 (August 1970): pp. 488–500.

MARKET SOLUTIONS

Imperfect information violates one of the assumptions of perfect competition, but not all information problems are market failures. In fact, information is itself valuable, and there is an incentive for competitive producers to produce it. As with any other good, there is an efficient quantity of information production.

Often, information is produced by consumers and producers themselves. The information-gathering process is called *market search*. When we go shopping for a "good buy" or for the "right" sweater, we are collecting the information that we need to make an informed choice. Just as products are produced as long as the marginal benefit from additional output exceeds the marginal cost of production, consumers have an incentive to continue searching out information until the expected marginal benefit from an additional hour of search is equal to the cost of that additional hour. After I've looked in 11 different stores that sell sweaters, I know a great deal about the quality and prices available. Continuing to look takes up valuable time and effort that could be used doing other things. In shopping for a house or a car, I may spend much more time and effort searching out information than I might for a sweater since the potential benefits (or losses) are much greater.

Firms also spend time and resources searching for information. Potential employers ask for letters of reference, resumes, and interviews before offering employment. Market research helps firms respond to consumer preferences. It should come as no surprise to you that the general rule is:

> Like consumers, profit-maximizing firms will gather information as long as the marginal benefits from continued search are greater than the marginal costs of engaging in it.

Many firms produce information for consumers and businesses. *Consumer Reports* is a magazine that tests consumer products and sells the results in the form of a periodical. Credit bureaus keep track of people's credit histories and sell credit reports to firms who need them to evaluate potential credit customers. "Headhunting" firms collect information and search out applicants for jobs.

The point of all this is simple. Because the market handles many information problems efficiently, we don't need to assume perfect information to arrive at an efficient allocation of resources. However, some information problems are not handled well by the market.

GOVERNMENT SOLUTIONS

One of the most important characteristics of information is that it is essentially a public good. If a set of test results on the safety of various products is produced, my having access to that information in no way reduces the value of that information to others. In other words, information is nonrival in consumption. When information is very costly for individuals to collect and disperse, it may be cheaper for government to produce it once for everybody.

In many cases, the government has set up special administrative agencies to ensure that accurate information reaches the public. The Canadian Competition Act, discussed in Chapter 15, prohibits misleading advertising. The federal Department of Industry identifies, controls, and prevents product misrepresentation in the marketplace by enforcing legislation covering measuring devices used in commercial trade, labelling, packaging, and quality control. The department also sets standards for potentially hazardous products. Health and Welfare Canada regulates the content of food and drugs that are permitted on the market. It is illegal to sell a drug that has not been demonstrated to be effective. In addition, many provinces have consumer protection laws.

Social Choice

social choice *The problem of deciding what society wants; the process of adding up individual preferences to make a choice for society as a whole.*

One view of government, or the public sector, holds that it exists to provide things that "society wants." A society is a collection of individuals, and each individual has a unique set of preferences. Defining what society wants, therefore, becomes a problem of **social choice**—of somehow adding up, or aggregating, individual preferences.

It is also important to understand, however, that government is made up of individuals—politicians and government workers—whose *own* objectives in part determine what government does. To understand government, then, we must understand the incentives facing politicians and public servants, as well as the difficulties of aggregating the preferences of the members of a society.

THE VOTING PARADOX

Democratic societies use ballot procedures to determine aggregate preferences and to make the social decisions that follow from them. If all votes could be unanimous, efficient decisions would be guaranteed. Unfortunately, unanimity is virtually impossible to achieve when millions of people, each with his or her own different preferences, are involved.

impossibility theorem
A proposition demonstrated by Kenneth Arrow showing that no system of aggregating individual preferences into social decisions will always yield consistent, nonarbitrary results.

The most common social decision-making mechanism is majority rule. But this system is far from perfect. In a well-known work published in 1951, Kenneth Arrow proved what has come to be called the **impossibility theorem**.[7] Arrow has shown that it is impossible to devise a voting scheme that respects individual preferences and gives consistent, nonarbitrary results.

One example of a seemingly irrational result emerging from majority-rule voting is the voting paradox. Suppose that, faced with a decision about the future of the institution, the president of a major university opts to let her three top administrators vote on the following options: should the university (A) increase the number of students and hire more faculty, (B) maintain the current size of the faculty and student body, or (C) cut back on faculty and reduce the student body? Figure 16.8 represents the preferences of the three administrators diagrammatically.

The vice president for finance (VP1) wants growth. He prefers A to B and B to C. The vice president for development (VP2), however, doesn't want to rock the boat. She prefers maintaining the current size of the institution, option B, to either of the others. If the status quo is out of the question, she would prefer option C. The dean believes in change; he wants to shake the place up, and he doesn't care whether that means increase or decrease. He prefers C to A and A to B.

Table 16.1 shows the results of the vote. When the three vote on A versus B, they vote in favor of A—that is, to increase the size of the university rather than keep it the same size. VP1 and the dean outvote VP2. Voting on B and C produces a victory for option B; two of the three would rather hold the line than decrease the size of the institution. After two votes we have the result that A (increase) is preferred to B (no change) and that B (no change) is preferred to C (decrease).

voting paradox *A simple demonstration of how majority-rule voting can lead to seemingly contradictory and inconsistent results. A commonly cited illustration of the kind of inconsistency described in the impossibility theorem.*

The problem arises when we then have the three vote on A against C. Both VP2 and the dean vote for C, giving it the victory; C is actually preferred to A. But if A beats B, and B beats C, how can C beat A? The results are inconsistent.

The **voting paradox** illustrates several points. Most important is the fact that when preferences for public goods differ across individuals, any system for adding up, or aggregating, those preferences can lead to inconsistencies. In addition, it illustrates just how much influence the person who sets the agenda has. If a vote had been taken on A and C first, the first two votes might never have occurred. This is

---

[7]Kenneth Arrow, Social Choice and Individual Values *(New York: John Wiley, 1951).*

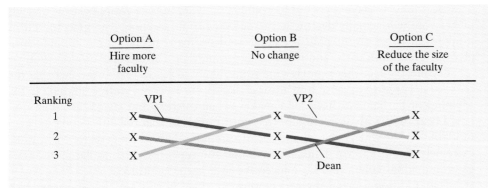

	Option A Hire more faculty	Option B No change	Option C Reduce the size of the faculty

FIGURE 16.8

Preferences of Three Top University Officials

VP1 prefers A to B and B to C. VP2 prefers B to C and C to A. The dean prefers C to A and A to B.

why the person setting the agenda for a meeting has enormous power; she establishes the rules under which and the order in which the items of business will be considered.

Another problem with majority-rule voting is that it leads to logrolling. **Logrolling** occurs when elected representatives or those attending a meeting trade votes—D helps get a majority in favour of an issue E wants to pursue, and in exchange E helps D get a majority on her issue. It is not clear whether logrolling is, on balance, a good thing or a bad thing from the standpoint of efficiency. On the one hand, a program that benefits one region or constituency might generate enormous net social gains, but because the group of beneficiaries is fairly small, it will not command a majority of delegates. If another bill that is likely to generate large benefits to another area is also awaiting a vote, a trade of support between the two sponsors of the bills should result in the passage of two good pieces of efficient legislation. On the other hand, logrolling can also turn out unjustified, inefficient outcomes with too much government spending.

logrolling *Occurs when elected representatives trade votes, agreeing to help each other get certain pieces of legislation passed.*

Concern that logrolling generates too much government spending is frequently expressed in the United States, where the practice is an accepted part of the political process. In Canada, where Members of Parliament almost always vote with their parties, logrolling has not been a major issue. Still, some "behind-the-scenes" logrolling does occur in Canada.

A number of other problems also follow from voting as a mechanism for public choice. For one thing, voters do not have much of an incentive to become well informed. When you go out to buy a car or, on a smaller scale, a CD player, you are the one who suffers the full consequences of a bad choice. Similarly, you are the beneficiary of the gains from a good choice. Not so in voting. One person's vote is not likely to determine whether a bad choice or a good choice is made. Although many

Table 16.1	Results of Voting on University's Plans: The Voting Paradox

	VOTES OF:			
VOTE	VP1	VP2	DEAN	RESULT*
A versus B	A	B	A	A wins: A > B
B versus C	B	B	C	B wins: B > C
C versus A	A	C	C	C wins: C > A

*A > B is read "A is preferred to B."

of us feel that we have a civic responsibility to vote, no one really believes that his or her vote will actually determine the outcome of an election. The time and effort it takes just to get to the polls is enough to deter many people. Becoming informed involves even more costs, and it is not surprising that many people do not do it.

Beyond the fact that a single vote is not likely to be decisive is the fact that the costs and benefits of wise and unwise social choices are widely shared. If the Member of Parliament that I elect makes a bad mistake and wastes a billion dollars, I bear only a small fraction of that cost. It may be that the direct consequences of a vote are so widely shared and seem so remote that voters perceive them to be extremely small or zero. Thus, even though the sums involved are large in aggregate, individual voters find little incentive to become informed.

Two additional problems with voting are that choices are almost always limited to *bundles* of publicly provided goods, and we vote infrequently. There are five political parties at the federal level: the Bloc Québécois, the Liberals, the NDP, the Progressive Conservatives, and Reform. We vote for a government only every four or five years. In private markets, we can look at each item separately and decide how much of each we want. We also can shop daily. In the public sector, though, we vote for a platform or a party that takes a particular position on a whole range of issues. In the public sector it is very difficult, or impossible, for voters to unbundle issues.

There is, of course, a reason why bundling occurs in the sphere of public choice. It is difficult enough to convince people to go to the polls for a general election. If we voted separately on every bill, we would spend our lives at the polls. This is in fact one reason for representative democracy. We elect officials who we hope will become informed and represent our interests and preferences.

GOVERNMENT INEFFICIENCY

Recent work in economics has focused not just on the government as an extension of individual preferences but also on government officials as people with their own agendas and objectives. That is, government officials are assumed to maximize their own utility, not the social good. To understand the way government functions, we need to look not only at the preferences of individual members of society but also at the incentive structures that exist around public officials.

One group of officials that we seem to worry about constantly are the civil servants who work for government agencies. What incentive do these people have to produce a good product and to be efficient? Might such incentives be lacking?

In the private sector, where firms compete for profits, only efficient firms producing goods that consumers will buy survive. If a firm is inefficient—if it is producing at a higher-than-necessary cost—the competition will drive it out of business. This is not necessarily so in the public sector. If a government bureau is producing a necessary service, or one mandated by law, it does not need to worry about customers. No matter how bad the service is at the registry of motor vehicles, everyone with a car must buy its product.

The efficiency of a government agency's internal structure depends on the way incentives facing workers and agency heads are structured. If the budget allocation of an agency is based on the last period's spending alone, for example, agency heads have a clear incentive to spend more money, however inefficiently. This point is not lost on government officials, who have experimented with many ways of rewarding agency heads and employees for cost-saving suggestions.

But critics point out that such efforts to reward productivity and punish inefficiency are rarely successful. It is difficult to punish, let alone dismiss, a government employee. Elected officials are subject to recall, but it usually takes gross negligence to rouse voters into instituting such a measure. And elected officials are rarely associated with problems of bureaucratic mismanagement, which they decry on a daily basis.

Critics of "the bureaucracy" argue that no set of internal incentives can ever match the discipline of the market, and they point to studies of private versus public garbage collection, airline operations, fire protection, mail service, and so forth, all of which suggest that there may be lower costs in the private sector. Indeed, one of the major policy initiatives in the public sector in recent years has been "privatization." Supporters of privatization argue that if the private sector can possibly provide a service, it is likely to do so more efficiently. When this is the case, the public sector should allow the private sector to take over.

One concern regarding wholesale privatization is the potential effect it may have on distribution. Some advocates of privatization have suggested governments sell their entire stock of public housing to the private sector. But would the private sector continue to provide housing to poor people? The worry is that it would not, because it might not be profitable to do so.

Like voters, public officials suffer from a lack of incentive to become fully informed and to make tough choices. Consider, for example, an elected official. If the real objective of an elected official is to get reelected, then his or her real incentive must be to provide visible goods for his or her constituency while hiding the costs or spreading them thin. Self-interest may thus easily lead to poor decisions and public irresponsibility.

RENT SEEKING REVISITED

Another problem with public choice is that special-interest groups can and do spend resources to influence the legislative process. As we said before, individual voters have little incentive to become well informed and to participate fully in the legislative process. But favour-seeking special-interest groups have a great deal of incentive to participate in political decision making. We saw in Chapter 13 that a monopolist would be willing to pay a substantial amount to prevent competition from eroding its economic profits. Many—if not all—industries lobby for favourable treatment, softer regulation, or Competition Act exemption. This behaviour, as you recall, is called *rent seeking*.

In fact, rent seeking extends far beyond those industries that lobby for government help in preserving monopoly powers. Any group that benefits from a government policy has an incentive to use its resources to lobby for that policy. Farmers lobby for supply management, oil producers lobby for exploration incentives, tobacco manufacturers lobby against restrictions on advertising their products, and so forth.

In the absence of well-informed and active voters, special-interest groups assume an important and perhaps a critical role. But there is another side to this story. Some have argued that favourable legislation is, in effect, for sale in the marketplace. Those willing and able to pay the most are more successful in accomplishing their goals than those with fewer resources.

When firms spend money and effort to influence government policy or to block foreign competition, they are engaging in rent-seeking behaviour. Although most farmers behave as nearly perfect competitors, many have worked hard politically to influence government subsidies and regulations that affect their profits.

■ **Government Failure** The point of the preceding sections is simple:

> Theory may well suggest that unregulated markets fail to produce an efficient allocation of resources. But this should not lead you to the conclusion that government involvement necessarily leads to efficiency. There are good reasons to believe that government attempts to produce the right goods and services in the right quantities efficiently may also fail.

Government and the Market

There is no question that government must be involved in both the provision of public goods and the control of externalities. While the argument is less clear-cut, a strong case can also be made for government actions to increase the flow of information. No society has ever existed in which citizens did not get together to protect themselves from the abuses of an unrestrained market and to provide for themselves certain goods and services that the market did not provide. The question is not *whether* we need government involvement. The question is *how much* and *what kind* of government involvement we should have.

Critics of government involvement correctly point out that the existence of an "optimal" level of public-goods production does not guarantee that governments will achieve it. In fact, it is easy to show that governments will generally fail to achieve the most efficient level. Nor is there any reason to believe that governments are capable of achieving the "correct" amount of control over externalities or dispersing the proper information to all those who need it. Markets do indeed fail to produce an efficient allocation of resources, but governments also fail for a number of reasons.

1. Measurement of social damages and benefits is difficult and imprecise. For example, estimates of the costs of acid rain range from practically nothing to incalculably high amounts.

2. There is no precise mechanism through which citizens' preferences for public goods can be correctly determined. All voting systems lead to inconsistent results. Samuelson's optimal solution works only if each individual in a society pays in accordance with his or her own preferences. Since this is impossible under our system, we all must be taxed to pay for the mix of public goods that the imperfect voting mechanism grants us.

3. Because government agencies are not subject to the discipline of the market, we have little reason to expect that they will be efficient producers. The amount of waste, corruption, and inefficiency in government is a hotly debated issue. Although government is not subjected to the discipline of the market, it must, however, submit to the discipline of the press, tight budgets, and the opinion of the voters.

4. Both elected and appointed officials have needs and preferences of their own, and it is naive to expect them to act selflessly for the good of society (even if they know what would be best for society). Bureaucrats in the Department of National Defence, for example, have a clear incentive to increase the size of their budgets, and elected officials rely heavily on those same bureaucrats for information.

Just as critics of government involvement concede that the market fails to achieve full efficiency, defenders of government must acknowledge government's failures. Nonetheless, defenders of government involvement respond that we get closer to an efficient allocation of resources by trying to control externalities and by doing our best to produce the public goods (including information) that people want with the imperfect tools we have than we would by leaving everything to the market.

Summary

Externalities and Environmental Economics

1. Often when we engage in transactions or make economic decisions, second or third parties suffer consequences that decision makers have no incentive to consider. These are called *externalities*. A classic example of an external cost is pollution.

2. When external costs are not considered in economic decisions, we may engage in activities or produce products that are not "worth it." When external benefits are not considered, we may fail to do things that are indeed "worth it." The result is an inefficient allocation of resources.

3. A number of alternative mechanisms have been used to control externalities: (1) government-imposed taxes and subsidies, (2) private bargaining and negotiation, (3) legal remedies such as *injunctions* and *liability rules*, (4) the sale or auctioning of rights to impose externalities, and (5) direct regulation.

Public (Social) Goods

4. In a free market, certain goods and services that people want will not be produced in adequate amounts. These *public goods* have characteristics that make it difficult or impossible for the private sector to produce them profitably.

5. Public goods are *nonrival in consumption;* their benefits fall collectively on members of society or on groups of members. Public goods are also *nonexcludable.* It is generally impossible to exclude people who have not paid from enjoying the benefits of public goods. An important example of a public good is national defence.

6. One of the major problems of public provision is that it leads to public dissatisfaction. We can choose any quantity of private goods that we want, or we can walk away without buying any. When it comes to public goods such as national defence, however, the government must choose one and only one kind and quantity of (collective) output to produce.

7. Theoretically, there exists an *optimal level of provision* for each public good. At this level, society's willingness to pay per unit equals the marginal cost of producing the good. To discover such a level, however, we would need to know the preferences of each individual citizen.

8. According to the *Tiebout hypothesis,* an efficient mix of public goods is produced when local land/housing prices and taxes come to reflect consumer preferences just as they do in the market for private goods.

Imperfect Information

9. Choices made in the presence of imperfect information may not be efficient. In the face of incomplete information, consumers and firms may encounter the problem of *adverse selection.* When buyers or sellers enter into market exchanges with other parties who have more information, low-quality goods are exchanged in greater numbers than high-quality goods. *Moral hazard* arises when one party to a contract passes the cost of his or her behaviour on to the other party to the contract. If a contract absolves one party of the consequences of his or her actions, and people act in their own self-interest, the result is inefficient.

10. In many cases, the market provides solutions to information problems. Profit-maximizing firms will continue to gather information as long as the marginal benefits from continued search are greater than the marginal costs of engaging in it. Consumers will follow a similar process: more time is afforded to the information search for larger decisions. In other cases, government must be called on to collect and disperse information to the public.

Social Choice

11. Because there is no way to know everyone's preferences about public goods, we are forced to rely on imperfect *social choice* mechanisms, such as majority rule.

12. The theory that suggests that free markets do not achieve an efficient allocation of resources

should not lead one to conclude that government involvement necessarily leads to efficiency. Governments also fail demonstrably.

Government and the Market

13. Defenders of government involvement in the economy acknowledge its failures but believe that we get closer to an efficient allocation of resources with government than we would without it. By trying to control externalities and by doing our best to provide the public goods that society wants, we do better than we would if we left everything to the market.

Review Terms and Concepts

adverse selection 411

Coase theorem 400

drop-in-the-bucket problem 405

externality 391

free-rider problem 405

impossibility theorem 414

injunction 402

liability rules 402

logrolling 415

marginal damage cost (*MDC*) 396

marginal private cost (*MPC*) 396

marginal social cost (*MSC*) 392

market failure 390

moral hazard 412

nonexcludable 405

nonrival in consumption 405

optimal level of provision for public goods 409

public goods (social, or collective, goods) 403

social choice 414

Tiebout hypothesis 410

voting paradox 414

Problem Set

1. "If government imposes on the firms in a polluting industry penalties (taxes) that exceed the actual value of the damages done by the pollution, the result is an inefficient and unfair imposition of costs on those firms and on the consumers of their products." Discuss. Use a diagram to show how consumers are harmed.

2. The 1993 federal election saw incumbents lose in record numbers, and the Conservatives went from being the governing party to holding just two seats. Voters were clearly not happy with what they saw happening in Ottawa. Three economic theories may help explain their anger:

    a. *Public goods theory:* Since public goods are collective, the government is constrained to pick a single level of output for all of us. National defence is an example. The government must pick one level of defence expenditure, and some of us will think it's too much, some will think it's too little, and no one is happy.

    b. *Problems of social choice:* It is simply impossible to choose collectively in a rational way that satisfies voters/consumers of public goods.

    c. *Public choice and public officials:* Once elected or appointed, public officials tend to act in accordance with their own preferences and not out of concern for the public.

Briefly explain each theory and how it may be a source of voter anger. Which of the three do you find the most persuasive?

3. Two areas of great concern to government in recent years have been education and health care. Using the concepts of public goods and imperfect information, write a brief essay justifying or criticizing government involvement in these two areas.

4. It has been argued that the following are examples of "mixed goods." They are essentially private but partly public. For each, describe the private and public components and discuss briefly why the government should or should not be involved in their provision.

    a. Elementary and secondary education

    b. Higher education

    c. Medical care

    d. Air traffic control

5. A paper factory dumps polluting chemicals into the Snake River. Thousands of citizens live along the river, and they bring suit claiming damages. You are asked by the judge to testify at the trial as an impartial expert. The court is considering four possible solutions, and you are asked to comment on the potential efficiency and equity of each. Your testimony should be brief.

    a. Deny the merits of the case and simply affirm

the polluter's right to dump. The parties will achieve the optimal solution without government.

b. Find in favour of the plaintiff. The polluters will be held liable for damages and must fully compensate citizens for all past and future damages imposed.

c. Order an immediate end to the dumping. No damages awarded.

d. Refer the matter to Environment Canada, which will impose a tax on the factory equal to the marginal damage costs. Proceeds will not be paid to the damaged parties.

6. Explain why you agree or disagree with each of the following statements:

a. The government should be involved in providing housing for the poor because housing is a "public good."

b. From the standpoint of economic efficiency, an unregulated market economy tends to overproduce public goods.

7. Society is made up of two individuals whose demands for public good X are given in Figure 1. Assuming that the public good can be produced at a constant marginal cost of $6, what is the optimal level of output? How much would you charge A? B?

8. Government involvement in general scientific research has been justified on the grounds that advances in knowledge are public goods—once produced, information can be shared at virtually no cost. A new production technology in an industry could be made available to all firms, reducing costs of production, driving down price, and benefiting the public. The patent system, however, allows private producers of "new knowledge" to exclude others from enjoying the benefits of that knowledge. Inventors would have little incentive to produce new knowledge if there were no possibility of profiting from their inventions. If one company holds exclusive rights to an advanced production process, it produces at lower cost but can use the exclusion to acquire monopoly power and hold price up.

a. On balance, is the patent system a good or a bad thing?

b. Is government involvement in scientific research a good idea? Discuss.

9. "The Coase theorem implies that we never need to worry about regulating externalities because the private individuals involved will reach the efficient outcome through negotiations." Is this statement true or false? Justify your answer and use examples.

10. Explain how imperfect information problems such as adverse selection or moral hazard might affect the following markets or situations:

a. Workers applying for disability benefits from a company

b. The market for used computers

c. The market for customized telephone systems for university offices and residence rooms

d. The market for automobile collision insurance

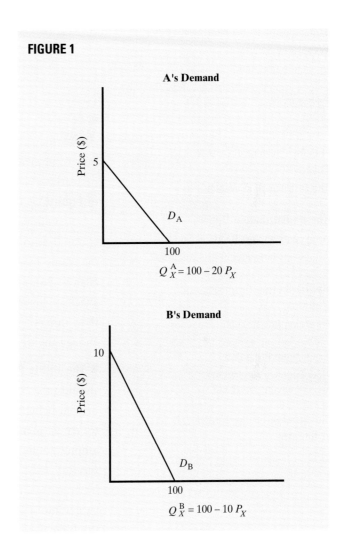

FIGURE 1

A's Demand

$Q_X^A = 100 - 20\,P_X$

B's Demand

$Q_X^B = 100 - 10\,P_X$

Income Distribution and Poverty

What role should government play in the economy? Thus far, we have focused only on actions the government might be called upon to take to improve market efficiency. But even if we achieved markets that are perfectly efficient, would the result be fair? We now turn to the question of **equity,** or fairness.

Somehow, the goods and services produced in every society get distributed among its citizens. Some of those citizens end up with palatial mansions in neighbourhoods such as Rosedale in Toronto, weekend ski trips to Banff or Whistler; others end up without enough to eat and live in shacks. This chapter focuses on distribution. Why do some people get more than others? What are the sources of inequality? Should the government change the distribution generated by the market?

■ **The Utility Possibilities Frontier**   Ideally, in discussing distribution, we should talk not about the distribution of things but about the distribution of well-being. In the nineteenth century, philosophers used the concept of *utility* as a measure of well-being. As they saw it, people make choices among goods and services on the basis of the utility that those goods and services yield. People act so as to maximize utility. If a person prefers a night at the symphony to a rock concert, it is because that person expects to get more utility from the symphony performance. If we extend this thinking, we might argue that if household A gets more total utility than household B, A is better off than B.

Utility is not directly observable or measurable. But thinking about it as if it were can help us understand some of the ideas that underlie debates about distribution. Suppose, for example, that society consisted of only

equity *Fairness.*

two people, "I" and "J." Next suppose that the line PP' in Figure 17.1 represents all the combinations of I's utility and J's utility that are possible, given the resources and technology available in their society. (Note that this is an extension of the production possibilities frontier discussed in Chapter 2.)

Any point inside PP', or the **utility possibilities frontier,** is inefficient because both I and J could be better off. A is one such point. B is one of many possible points along PP' that society should prefer to A, because both members are better off at B than they are at A.

While point B is clearly preferable to point A from everyone's point of view, how does point B compare with point C? Both B and C are efficient; I cannot be made better off without making J worse off, and vice versa. Indeed, all the points along PP' are efficient, but they may not be equally desirable. If all the assumptions of competitive market theory held, the market system would lead to one of the points along PP'. The actual point reached would depend upon I's and J's initial endowments of wealth, skills, and so forth.

In practice, however, the market solution leaves some people out. The rewards of a market system are linked to productivity, and some people in every society are simply not capable of being very productive. All societies make some provision for the very poor. Most often, public expenditures on behalf of the poor are financed with taxes collected from the rest of society. Society thus makes a judgment that those who are better off should give up some of their rewards so that those at the bottom can have more than the market system would allocate to them. In a democratic state, such redistribution is presumably undertaken because a majority of the members of that society think that it is fair, or just.

Early economists drew analogies between social choices among alternative outcomes and consumer choices among alternative outcomes. A consumer chooses on the basis of his or her own unique utility function, or measure of his or her own well-being; a society, they said, chooses on the basis of a social welfare function that embodies the society's ethics.

Such theoretical discussions of fairness and equity focus on the distribution and redistribution of utility. But because utility is neither observable nor measurable,

utility possibilities frontier *A graphical representation of a two-person world that shows all points at which A's utility can be increased only if B's utility is decreased.*

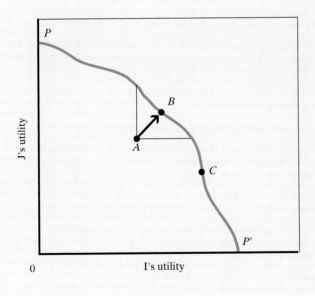

FIGURE 17.1

Utility Possibilities Frontier

If society were made up of just two people, I and J, and all of the assumptions of perfect competition held, the market system would lead to some point along PP'. Every point along PP' is efficient; it is impossible to make I better off without making J worse off, and vice versa. But which point is best? Is B better than C?

most discussions of social policy centre on the *distribution of income* or the *distribution of wealth* as indirect measures of well-being. It is important that you remember throughout this chapter, however, that income and wealth are imperfect measures of well-being. Someone with a profound love of the outdoors may choose to work in a national park for a low wage rather than to work for a consulting firm in a big city for a high wage. The choice reveals that she is better off, even though her measured income is lower. As another example, think about five people with $1 each. Now suppose that one of those people has a magnificent voice, and that the other four give up their dollars to hear her sing. The exchange leads to inequality of measured wealth—the singer has $5 and no one else has any, but all are better off than they were before.

While income and wealth are imperfect measures of utility, they have no observable substitutes and are therefore the measures we use throughout this chapter. First, we review the factors that determine the distribution of income in a market setting. Second, we look at the data on income distribution, wealth distribution, and poverty in Canada. Third, we talk briefly about some theories of economic justice. Finally, we describe a number of current redistributional programs, including social assistance (or welfare), employment insurance, the child tax benefit, and public housing.

The Sources of Household Income

Why do some people and some families have more income than others? Before we turn to data on the distribution of income, let us review what we already know about the sources of inequality:

> Households derive their incomes from three basic sources: (1) from wages or salaries received in exchange for labour; (2) from property (that is, capital, land, and so forth); and (3) from government.

WAGES AND SALARIES

About 63% of personal income in Canada in 1995 was received in the form of wages and salaries. Hundreds of different wage rates are paid to employees for their labour in thousands of different labour markets. As you saw in Chapter 10, competitive market theory predicts that all factors of production (including labour) are paid a return equal to their marginal revenue products—that is, the market value of what they produce at the margin. There are a number of reasons why one type of labour might be more productive than another and why some households have higher incomes than others.

■ **Required Skills, Human Capital, and Working Conditions**   Clearly, some people are simply born with attributes that translate into valuable skills. Patrick Ewing, David Robinson, and Shaquille O'Neal are great basketball players, partly because they happen to be over seven feet tall. They didn't decide to go out and invest in height; they were born with the right genes. Some people have perfect pitch and beautiful voices; others are tone deaf. Some people have quick mathematical minds; others cannot add two and two.

The rewards of a skill that is in strictly limited supply depend upon the demand for that skill. Men's professional basketball is extremely popular, and the top NBA players make millions of dollars per year. There are some great female basketball players, too, but because women's professional basketball has not become popular in Canada or the United States, these women's skills go comparatively unrewarded.

In tennis, however, people want to see women play, and women therefore earn prize money similar to the money earned by men. (For more on the relative earning power of men and women, see the Issues and Controversies box on pages 426–427 titled "The Controversy over Pay Equity.")

Some people with rare skills can make enormous salaries in a free market economy. Luciano Pavarotti has a voice that millions of people are willing to pay to hear in person and on tapes and CDs. Céline Dion sells a million copies of every album she makes. Before Pablo Picasso died, he could sell small sketches for vast sums of money. Were they worth it? They were worth exactly what the highest bidder was willing to pay.

Not all skills are inborn, however. Some people have invested in training and schooling to improve their knowledge and skills, and therein lies another source of inequality in wages. When we go to school, we are investing in **human capital** that we expect to yield dividends, partly in the form of higher wages, later on. Human capital is also produced through on-the-job training. People learn their jobs and acquire "firm-specific" skills when they are on the job. Thus, in most occupations there is a reward for experience. Pay scale often reflects numbers of years on the job, and those with more experience earn higher wages than those in similar jobs with less experience.

Some jobs are more desirable than others. Entry-level positions in "glamour" industries such as publishing and television tend to be low-paying. Since talented people are willing to take entry-level jobs in these industries at salaries below what they could earn in other occupations, there must be other, nonwage rewards. It may be that the job itself is more personally rewarding, or that a low-paying apprenticeship is the only way to acquire the human capital necessary to advance. In contrast, less desirable jobs often pay wages that include **compensating differentials.** Of two jobs requiring roughly equal levels of experience and skills that compete for the same workers, the job with the poorer working conditions usually has to pay a slightly higher wage to attract workers away from the job with the better working conditions.

Compensating differentials are also required when a job is very dangerous. Those who take great risks are usually rewarded with high wages. High-beam workers on skyscrapers and bridges command premium wages. Fire fighters in cities that have many old, run-down buildings are usually paid more than those in relatively tranquil rural or suburban areas.

■ Multiple Income Households Another source of wage inequality among households lies in the fact that many households have more than one earner in the labour force. Second, and even third, incomes are becoming more the rule than the exception for Canadian families. In 1961 about 29.3% of women over the age of 15 were in the labour force. By 1978 the figure had increased to 48.5%, and it continued to climb slowly but steadily to a level of 57.7% by 1995.

Comparing two-earner and one-earner households highlights another problem of using money income as a measure of well-being. Consider, for example, a family of four with both parents working and an identical family with only one wage earner. The two-earner family will have a significantly higher money income, but the comparison ignores the value of what the non-wage-earning spouse produces. When one parent stays home, he or she normally provides services that would otherwise have to be purchased. The children are cared for, the house is maintained, food may be grown in the garden. When both parents work, there are expenses for day care, housecleaning, yard work, home repairs, and so forth.

When one parent stays home voluntarily, that family has revealed that it values

human capital *The stock of knowledge, skills, and talents that people possess; it can be inborn or acquired through education and training.*

Mining is a very dangerous occupation. For this reason, miners are typically paid a compensating differential that raises their wages above those of the average Canadian worker.

compensating differentials *Differences in wages that result from differences in working conditions. Risky jobs usually pay higher wages; highly desirable jobs usually pay lower wages.*

Women appear to face discrimination in the labour market on two fronts. First, on average, women earn significantly less than men. Women in full-time employment earn, on average, about 70% of the income of the typical male with full-time employment. But the gap narrows significantly if other things are held equal (on average, women are younger and have less experience). Indeed, two years after graduation female university graduates are earning slightly more than their male counterparts. But most studies of the differences between male and female wages find that men earn slightly more, even after controlling for all other factors, including occupation.

Second, there is an undeniable occupational segregation between men and women. Most nurses are women. So too are most teachers, secretaries, and social workers. On the other hand, most auto mechanics are men. So are most construction workers.

There are two views about why these differences exist. One view holds that most wage differentials can be attributed to choices women make about what jobs to take, how many hours to work, and when to enter and leave the labour force. The argument is that labour markets are efficient and that wages reflect productivity. Women earn lower wages because they have chosen to enter occupations that require little training and have low productivity, or because they avoid dangerous occupations and seek those that allow free movement into and out of the labour force.

This view also argues that the gap between women's and men's wages will close when women obtain the same amount of training as men, when they enter the same professions, and when they remain on the job without taking time off to raise families.

The second view holds that women's choices are not free and that wage differentials cannot be explained by differences in productivity. This view maintains that women are channeled into certain occupations by custom, tradition, and discrimination and that wages in those occupations are kept artificially low. It is argued that

jobs requiring similar skills, contributing similar amounts to employer earnings, and having similar working conditions are likely to be paid low wages when they are traditionally filled by women.

Those who espouse this second view argue that the wage gap can be closed in a number of ways. First, employers could be persuaded or forced to accept women into jobs that were held previously only by men. Second, wages across occupations of "comparable worth" could be equalized:

Under this approach, expert panels would evaluate the intellectual and physical demands of jobs within a particular company or controlled by a single employer (such as a state or local government). The panel would assign points to each job based on its working conditions, responsibility, and other characteristics, and would weigh each of these factors. The result would be a composite score, or index, that, it is claimed, would measure the

the home-produced services more than the income it would otherwise earn. It is better off than it would be if both parents were working, even though it has a lower money income. Again, this means that we must exercise caution when discussing the fairness of the distribution of money income.

■ **Unemployment**   Before turning to property income, it is important to mention another major cause of inequality in Canada that is the subject of much discussion in macroeconomics: *unemployment.*

People earn wages only when they have jobs. In recent years, Canada has been through two severe recessions (economic downturns). In 1976, the unemployment rate hit 7.2%, and over three-quarters of a million people were unable to find work; in 1983, the unemployment rate was 11.9%, and over 1.5 million were jobless. More recently, a slow recovery from the recession of 1990–1991 kept the *"worth" of each job. People holding jobs of comparable worth as measured by these scores would receive equal pay.**

In 1977, the federal government added a provision to its human rights legislation requiring it and any federally regulated companies to provide equal pay for work of equal or comparable worth. In 1990, Prince Edward Island became the last province to introduce legislation mandating equal pay for work of equal value in the public sector. Ontario, under the NDP government of Bob Rae, implemented legislation requiring equal pay for work of equal value in the private sector, the only province to do so. This piece of legislation was repealed by the Conservative government led by Mike Harris.

The NDP government in Ontario had hoped to replicate the success of a similar plan introduced in Australia in the mid-1970s. The Australian plan resulted in the base pay for women rising from 65% of men's to 94% between 1970 and 1980.

Critics of the comparable worth

Although men and women now work side by side in most industries, on average, women still earn significantly less than men.

approach argue that such laws will end up hurting women. Raising wages above their equilibrium levels, it is argued, will cause employers to hire fewer women. Those who end up with jobs will earn higher wages, but some will be left out. There is mixed evidence on this score from the Australian experience. One study found that pay equalization slowed the growth of women's employment by one-third and increased women's unemployment by half a percentage

point. Other studies found virtually no effect.

Critics also claim that the job evaluation process is hopelessly complex. They argue that the only reliable indicator of a job's worth is the wage rate that an employer must pay to fill it.

Source: Henry Aaron and Cameran Lougy, *The Comparable Worth Controversy* (Washington, D.C.: The Brookings Institution, 1986).
*Aaron and Lougy, *The Comparable Worth Controversy*, p. 2.

number of unemployed high (1.4 million people were unemployed in 1995 for an unemployment rate of 9.5%).

Unemployment hurts primarily those who are laid off, and thus its costs are narrowly distributed. For some workers, the costs of unemployment are lowered by employment insurance benefits paid out of a fund accumulated with receipts from a tax on payrolls.

INCOME FROM PROPERTY

Another important source of income inequality is that some people have **property income**—that is, income from the ownership of real property and financial holdings—while many others do not. Some people own a great deal of wealth, and some have no assets at all. Overall, about 12.7% of personal income in Canada in 1995 came from ownership of property. In general:

property income *Income from the ownership of real property and financial holdings. It takes the form of profits, interest, dividends, and rents.*

> The amount of property income that a household earns depends upon (1) how much property it owns and (2) what kinds of assets it owns. Such income generally takes the form of profits, interest, dividends, and rents.

Households come to own assets through saving and through inheritance. Many of today's large fortunes were inherited from previous generations. The Thomsons, the Irvings, and the Bronfmans, to name a few, still have large holdings of property originally accumulated by previous generations. Thousands of families receive smaller inheritances each year from their parents. But most families receive little through inheritance, and most of their wealth or property comes from saving.

Often vast fortunes are accumulated in a single generation when a business becomes successful. Paul Desmarais built a personal fortune estimated at over $1 billion from his Power Corporation. *Fortune* magazine estimates that Bill Gates, founder and chief executive officer of Microsoft, is worth over US$7 billion. Masatoshi Ito made US$5 billion running a supermarket chain in Japan.

Another important component of wealth today is real estate. For most people, the biggest asset they will ever own is their home, and the value accumulated in owner-occupied houses is a major source of inequality. A house earns a return just like any other asset, a return that comes in the form of "housing services"—the owner of the house lives in it rent free. In addition to these returns, houses can *appreciate,* or increase in value. During the 1980s, the real estate market had some dramatic impacts on the distribution of income as the prices of single-family housing boomed in a number of metropolitan areas. In Toronto and Vancouver average housing prices increased by more than 50% in real terms between 1985 and 1989.

Those who owned houses when prices rose ended up with substantial accumulations of value in their houses. But those who did not own found themselves much worse off. Not only did their rents increase, but many families found themselves unable to make the leap from renting to home ownership because of the dramatically higher prices. The average price of an existing single-family house in Canada in 1996 was about $150 000. To purchase this house required a minimum of $15 000 cash down payment (10%) and a monthly mortgage payment of about $650.

But the early 1990s demonstrated that real estate values can fall as dramatically as they rise. The average residential house price in Ontario fell by 4.7% in 1990, 1.2% in 1991, 6.3% in 1992, and 3.2% in 1993 (a reduction of almost $20 000 over the four years).

INCOME FROM THE GOVERNMENT: TRANSFER PAYMENTS

About 17% of personal income in 1995 came from governments in the form of **transfer payments.** Transfer payments are payments made by government to people who do not supply goods or services in exchange. Some, but not all, transfer payments (such as social assistance and employment insurance) are made to people with low incomes, precisely because they have low incomes. Transfer payments thus reduce the amount of inequality in the distribution of income.

Not all transfer income goes to the poor. For example, one of the biggest programs at the federal level, Old Age Security, is not designed to direct income only to the poor. In general, however:

> Transfer programs are by and large designed to provide income to those in need. They are part of the government's attempts to offset some of the problems of inequality and poverty.

transfer payments *Payments by government to people who do not supply goods or services in exchange.*

The Distribution of Income

Despite the many problems with using income as a measure of well-being, it is useful to know something about how income is actually distributed. Before we examine the data, however, we should pin down precisely what the data represent.

There are two possible definitions of income. The first is **economic income**, which is defined as the amount of money that a household can spend during a given period of time without increasing or decreasing its net assets. Economic income includes anything that enhances your ability to spend—wages and salaries, dividends, interest received, incomes from unincorporated business, transfers from the government (including transfers "in kind" such as subsidized education services, health care, etc.), rents, etc. In addition, if you own an asset (such as a share of stock) that increases in value, that gain is part of your economic income, whether you sell the asset to "realize the gain" or not.

The second definition is **money income.** Money income excludes noncash transfer payments, capital gains income, lottery and other gambling winnings, inheritances, gifts, and fringe benefits. Money income is less inclusive than economic income and will be distributed more equally due to the concentration of capital gains, gifts, lottery winnings, and inheritances. Because economic income is very difficult to measure in statistical surveys, income distribution data produced by Statistics Canada involves money income only. Money income is typically reported before tax, with taxes considered a use of income.

Another important consideration is the definition of the income earning unit. Income distribution data in Canada are prepared for families, unattached individuals, and family units (families and unattached individuals together). The economic family is defined as a group of individuals related by blood, marriage, or adoption who share a common dwelling. Thus the family involves two or more people. Unattached individuals are people living on their own outside a family. Because unattached individuals are often either relatively young or relatively old we should expect to find that average incomes of unattached individuals are well below those recorded for families.

Definitions are extremely important when examining the distribution of income. For example, in 1995, Statistics Canada estimated that about 63% of personal income came from wages and salaries, and that about 19% of personal income (as defined in the System of National Income and Expenditure Accounts) came from investment income and net incomes from unincorporated businesses. In contrast, the money income measure used in the income distribution data produced by Statistics Canada suggests that over 70% of income came from wages and salaries and that only 4% of income came from investment income.

INCOME INEQUALITY IN CANADA

Table 17.1 presents estimates of the distribution of money income across families, unattached individuals, and unattached individuals and families for 1995. The data are presented in "quintiles," that is, the income earning units are first ranked by income and then split into five groups of equal size. Thus, the richest 20% of families received 40.2% of all money income received by families, the poorest 20% of unattached individuals received 5.4% of all money income earned by unattached individuals, and the middle 20% of families and unattached individuals received 16.4% of all money income earned by families and unattached individuals.

Table 17.2 breaks down money income received by families and unattached individuals in 1995 into components. Wage and salary income (i.e., labour income) is not as evenly distributed as total money income (refer to Table 17.1 for total money income data). The bottom fifth only received 1.7% of wage and salary

economic income *The amount of money a household can spend during a given time period without increasing or decreasing its net assets. Wages, salaries, dividends, interest income, transfer payments, rents, and so forth are sources of economic income.*

money income *The measure of income used by Statistics Canada. Because it excludes capital gains, noncash transfer payments, and many fringe benefits, it is less inclusive than economic income.*

Table 17.1	Distribution of Money Income in Canada, 1995 (Percentages)		
Quintile	Families	Unattached Individuals	Families and Unattached Individuals
Bottom fifth	6.4	5.4	4.7
Second fifth	12.0	10.6	10.2
Third fifth	17.4	15.5	16.4
Fourth fifth	23.9	24.0	24.5
Top fifth	40.2	44.6	44.1

Source: Statistics Canada, *Income Distributions By Size, 1995*, Cat. no. 13-207.

income as opposed to 4.7% of total money income. The top fifth received 49.5% of labour income as opposed to 44.1% of all money income.

The top 20% receive a still larger share of income from self-employment and from investments. Income from investments comes from owning things: land earns rent, bonds and deposit accounts earn interest, stocks earn dividends, and so forth.

Transfer payments include social assistance payments, employment insurance benefits, transfers to the elderly, and child tax benefits. Transfer payments flow to low-income households, but not exclusively to them. Old Age Security payments, for example, flow to everyone who has reached a certain age, regardless of income. In a similar fashion, employment insurance benefits go to anyone (regardless of income) who is unemployed and who has met the minimum qualifying conditions. Nonetheless, transfers represent a much more important income component at the bottom of the distribution than at the top.

■ **Changes in the Distribution of Income** Table 17.3 presents the distribution of money income among Canadian families and unattached individuals for selected years. As you can see, income distribution has remained relatively stable over a long period of time. There is evidence of small increases in the share of total money income going to the top and bottom quintiles of the distribution and of a small reduction in the share going to the second and third quintiles, but these changes are remarkably small given the social, technological, and cultural changes that have occurred in Canada over the past 50 years. Moreover, there is no evidence to support the view that government has played Robin Hood, taking massive shares of income from the rich and giving them to the poor.

■ **The Lorenz Curve and the Gini Coefficient** The distribution of income can be

Table 17.2	Distribution of Money Income by Components, 1995 (Percentages): Families and Unattached Individuals				
Quintile	Wages and Salaries	Income from Self-Employment	Transfer Payments	Investment Income	Other
Bottom fifth	1.7	1.5	22.2	3.4	4.1
Second fifth	6.4	8.2	28.5	10.6	15.2
Third fifth	15.2	16.0	20.7	15.2	22.4
Fourth fifth	27.2	17.9	16.2	18.4	23.6
Top fifth	49.5	56.4	12.4	52.4	34.7

Source: Statistics Canada, *Income Distributions By Size, 1995*, Cat. no. 13-207.

Table 17.3	Distribution of Money Income, 1951–1995 (Percentages): Families and Unattached Individuals					
Quintile	1951	1961	1971	1981	1985	1995
Bottom fifth	4.4	4.2	3.6	4.6	4.6	4.7
Second fifth	11.2	11.9	10.6	10.9	10.4	10.2
Third fifth	18.3	18.3	17.6	17.6	17.0	16.4
Fourth fifth	23.3	24.5	24.9	25.2	24.9	24.5
Top fifth	42.8	41.1	43.3	41.8	43.0	44.1

Source: 1951 and 1961: Statistics Canada, *Incomes, Liquid Assets, and Indebtedness of Nonfarm Families in Canada, Selected Years, 1951–1965,* Cat. no. 13-508; 1971: Statistics Canada, *Income Distributions By Size in Canada, 1971,* Cat. no. 13-544; 1981–1995: Statistics Canada, *Income Distributions by Size, 1995,* Cat. no. 13-207.

Lorenz Curve *A widely used graph of the distribution of income, with cumulative percentage of families plotted along the horizontal axis and cumulative percentage of income plotted along the vertical axis.*

Gini coefficient *A commonly used measure of inequality of income derived from a Lorenz Curve. It can range from zero to a maximum of one.*

graphed in several ways. The most widely used graph is the **Lorenz Curve,** shown in Figure 17.2. Plotted along the horizontal axis is the percentage of families, and along the vertical axis is the cumulative percentage of income. The curve shown here represents the year 1995 using data for families from Table 17.1.

During that year, the bottom 20% of families earned only 6.4% of total money income. The bottom 40% earned 18.4% (6.4% plus 12.0%), and so forth. If income were distributed equally—that is, if the bottom 20% earned 20% of the income, the bottom 40% earned 40% of the income, and so forth—the Lorenz Curve would be a 45° line between zero and 100%. More unequal distributions produce Lorenz Curves that are farther from the 45° line.

The **Gini coefficient** is a commonly used measure of the degree of inequality

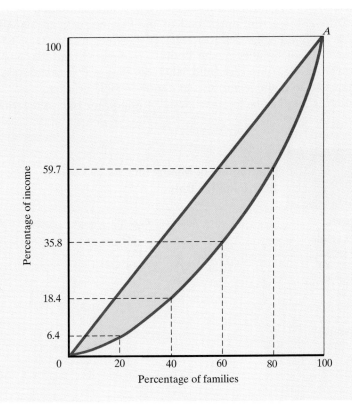

FIGURE 17.2

Lorenz Curve for Canada, 1995

The Lorenz Curve is the most common way of presenting income distribution graphically. The larger the shaded area, the more unequal the distribution. If distribution were equal, the Lorenz Curve would be the 45° line 0A.

in a distribution. It is the ratio of the shaded area in Figure 17.2 to the total triangular area below and to the right of the diagonal line 0A.

If income is equally distributed, there is no shaded area (because the Lorenz Curve and the 45° line are the same), and the Gini coefficient is zero. The Lorenz Curves for distributions with more inequality are further down and to the right, their shaded areas are larger, and their Gini coefficients are higher. The maximum Gini coefficient is one. As the Lorenz Curve shifts down to the right, the shaded area becomes a larger portion of the total triangular area below 0A. If one family earned all the income (with no one else receiving anything), the shaded area and the triangle would be the same, and the ratio would equal one.

■ **Regional Differences in Incomes and the Role of Education in Income Distribution** So far we have been looking at income distribution among all families and unattached individuals in Canada. But looking just at families and unattached individuals without differentiating them in any way hides some important distinctions. For example, one might want to compare the distribution of total money income earned by Francophone Canadians with the distribution of income among Anglophone Canadians. Or one might want to compare the distribution of income in different age groups. Information provided by Statistics Canada allows one to look at income distribution in a variety of ways.

Table 17.4 presents data on the distribution of money income in different regions of Canada for families only for 1995. It should not be surprising to find that the poorest region of Canada, Atlantic Canada (Newfoundland, Nova Scotia, Prince Edward Island, and New Brunswick), has the highest proportion of people in the lower income classes (just over one-third of Atlantic Canadian families earn less than $30 000). In contrast, only one-fifth of families in Ontario earn less than $30 000. Differences at the upper end of the income scale are equally striking. Almost 12% of families in Ontario received incomes in excess of $100 000 in 1995. Only 7.4% of families in the Prairie provinces (Manitoba, Saskatchewan, and Alberta) exceeded this threshold, and less than 4.0% of Atlantic Canadian families managed to make it into the six-figure income bracket.

Education is another factor that plays an important role in determining one's

Table 17.4	Distribution of Money Income by Region, 1995: Families Only				
Income Class	**Atlantic**	**Quebec**	**Ontario**	**Prairies**	**B.C.**
Less than $10 000	2.9	1.9	1.5	2.1	2.4
$10 000–$20 000	14.8	12.1	8.0	8.9	7.6
$20 000–$30 000	17.4	15.8	11.5	14.9	12.2
$30 000–$40 000	16.0	15.5	13.1	14.0	13.1
$40 000–$50 000	14.0	13.4	12.2	13.8	13.1
$50 000–$60 000	10.4	11.6	11.6	11.9	13.1
$60 000–$70 000	8.4	9.1	10.3	10.2	10.8
$70 000–$80 000	5.7	6.8	8.5	7.9	11.2
$80 000–$90 000	4.1	4.0	7.1	5.6	8.4
$90 000–$100 000	2.3	3.1	4.4	3.5	4.0
Over $100 000	3.7	6.6	11.9	7.4	11.0

Source: Statistics Canada, *Income Distributions By Size, 1995*, Cat. no. 13-207-XPB.

Table 17.5	Educational Attainment and the Distribution of Income, 1995 (Percentages)			
	High School or Less	*Beyond High School*	*Total*	*University*
Lowest quintile	63.8	36.2	100%	6.5
Second quintile	58.7	41.3	100%	8.7
Third quintile	50.3	49.7	100%	11.8
Fourth quintile	41.1	58.9	100%	17.8
Highest quintile	30.7	69.3	100%	34.7
Total	48.9	51.1	100%	15.9

Source: Statistics Canada, *Income Distributions By Size, 1995,* Cat. no. 13-207-XPB.

position in the distribution of income. This is not surprising given that higher levels of education open up opportunities to secure higher paying jobs. Table 17.5 presents information on the educational attainment of the head of families in each quintile. Only 6.5% of the lowest quintile of families had a university education, which stands in stark contrast to 34.7% in the highest quintile. Those with high school or less education, on the other hand, are overrepresented in the lowest quintile and underrepresented in the highest quintile.

POVERTY

Most of the government's concern with income distribution and redistribution has focused on poverty. "Poverty" is a very complicated word to define, however. In simplest terms, it means the condition of people who have very low incomes. The dictionary defines the term simply as "lack of money or material possessions." But how low does your income have to be before you are classified as poor?

■ **The Problem of Definition** Philosophers and social policy makers have long debated the meaning of "poverty." One school of thought argues that poverty should be measured by determining how much it costs to buy the "basic necessities of life." This approach involves identifying the costs of specific "bundles" of food, clothing, and housing that are supposed to represent the minimum standard of living. In Canada, work by Christopher Sarlo takes this approach to the measurement of poverty.[1]

Some critics argue that defining bundles of necessities is a hopeless task. While it might be possible to define a minimally adequate diet, what is a "minimum" housing unit? Is a car necessary? What about dental care? Other critics argue that poverty is culturally defined and is therefore a relative concept, not an absolute one. Poverty in Bangladesh, for example, is very different from poverty in Canada. Even in Canada, urban poverty is different from rural poverty. If poverty is a relative concept, the definition of it might change significantly as a society accumulates wealth and achieves higher living standards. The Canadian Council on Social Development uses a poverty measure that is explicitly relative: they classify anyone earning less than half of the Canadian average income as poor.

There are other candidates as well. One might argue that anyone earning less than what they could earn on social assistance (welfare) is poor. Social assistance rates are chosen by democratically elected governments to combat poverty. Thus it is possible to argue that they reflect the views of poverty that are held by the

[1]See Christopher Sarlo, Poverty in Canada, *second edition (Vancouver: Fraser Institute, 1996).*

Canadian people at large. However, public opinion polls often show that Canadians believe that governments provide too little assistance to the poor.

Although it is difficult to define precisely, the word "poverty" is one that we all understand intuitively to some degree. It conveys images of run-down, overcrowded, rat-infested housing, homeless people, etc. But if we are to keep statistics and administer public programs, we need more than an intuitive sense of poverty.

There is no official poverty line in Canada and Statistics Canada does not produce statistics on poverty. However, a set of **low income cutoffs** are produced by Statistics Canada and these are the most widely quoted measure of low income in this country. These low income cutoffs are selected on the basis that families below these limits usually spend 54.7% or more of their income on food, shelter, and clothing. Different low income cutoffs are produced for different family sizes and for different regions to reflect variation in needs.

■ **Low Incomes in Canada**   Data on the incidence of low incomes among Canadians reveal significant variation in experience across age groups, regions, and type of family. Some of this information is reported in Table 17.6. As Table 17.6 illustrates, age has a significant effect on the incidence of low incomes. Over 43% of Canadian families headed by an individual under 24 years of age had incomes less than the low income cutoff and over 65% of unattached individuals under the age of 24 had low incomes. For many of these individuals low income is a temporary condition. Some are enrolled in an educational institution (such as a university) and are not working full time. Others are searching for a good job. Still others have found their good job but are earning relatively low incomes in the present with the hope that their incomes will steadily improve over their lifetimes.

The importance of age in low income, and the temporary nature of these low incomes for the young, clearly indicate the importance of life cycle considerations in the analysis of low income and the distribution of income generally. The typical life cycle experience involves low incomes when young, rising incomes through middle age, and finally, low incomes after retirement. As a consequence, many economists argue that incomes over an entire lifetime should ideally be taken into account in the measurement of poverty and income inequality.

Table 17.6 also illustrates the importance of family type in poverty. Lone parent families experience a much higher incidence of low income than families generally. Lone parent families headed by women are especially likely to have low income, with 56.8% of such families receiving less than the low income cutoff.

In combination, age and family type have a particularly important effect on poverty among children. Indeed, the incidence of low income among Canadian children under the age of 16 has grown over the past 15 years. Table 17.7 documents changes in the incidence of low income among children and the elderly since 1981. The experience of the elderly stands in stark contrast to that of children. A decreasing proportion of the elderly are experiencing low incomes, thanks in part to government transfer programs such Old Age Security and the Canada/Quebec Pension Plan. Not surprisingly, child poverty has become an important political issue in Canada.

THE DISTRIBUTION OF WEALTH

Data on the distribution of wealth are not as readily available as data on the distribution of income. One estimate of the distribution of Canadian wealth, defined as what one owns minus what one owes, is presented in Table 17.8. In these estimates for 1980 the richest 1% of Canadians owned 18.8% of Canadian wealth; the richest 20% of Canadians owned 73.3% of Canadian wealth. The top 60% owned 99.2%, leaving the bottom 40% with only 0.8%.

Table 17.6

Incidence of Low Income in Canada, 1995

	Families	Unattached Individuals
All	14.2	39.3
Age		
Under 24	43.5	65.9
24–34	18.7	26.3
35–44	15.1	29.4
45–54	10.5	34.3
55–64	12.8	43.7
Over 65	7.8	45.1
Region		
Atlantic	15.6	42.0
Quebec	16.7	46.8
Ontario	12.6	35.7
Prairies	14.2	36.3
B.C.	13.0	35.9
Family type		
Lone parent, male head, children under 18	30.7	
Lone parent, female head, children under 18	56.8	

Source: Statistics Canada, *Income Distributions By Size, 1995,* Cat. no. 13-207-XPB.

Table 17.7	Incidence of Low Income among Children and the Elderly		
	1981	*1986*	*1991*
Children, under 16	15.2	17.0	18.3
Elderly, 65 and over	33.0	24.9	20.0
All others	12.7	14.2	14.3

Source: Statistics Canada, *Canada Year Book, 1994,* Table 6.19.

Clearly, the distribution of wealth is significantly more unequal than the distribution of income. Part of the reason is that wealth is passed from generation to generation and thus accumulates. Large fortunes also accumulate when small businesses become successful large businesses. Some argue that an unequal distribution of wealth is the natural and inevitable consequence of risk taking in a market economy; it provides the incentive structure necessary to motivate entrepreneurs and investors. Others believe that too much inequality can undermine democracy and lead to social conflict. Many of the arguments for and against income redistribution, discussed in the next section, apply equally well to wealth distribution.

The Redistribution Debate

Debates about the role of government in correcting for inequity in the distribution of income revolve around two kinds of issues, philosophical and practical. Philosophical issues are those dealing with the "ideal." What should the distribution of income be if we could give it any shape we desired? What is "fair"? What is "just"? Practical issues deal with what is, and what is not, possible. Suppose we wanted to eliminate poverty altogether. How much would it cost, and what would we sacrifice to do so? When we take wealth or income away from higher-income people and give it to lower-income people, do we destroy incentives? What are the effects of this kind of redistribution?

Clearly, policy makers must deal with both kinds of issues, but it seems logical to confront the philosophical issues first. If you do not know where you want to go, you cannot talk very well about how to get there or how much it costs to get there. Indeed, you may find that you do not want to go anywhere at all. Many respected economists and philosophers do, in fact, argue quite convincingly that the government should not redistribute income.

ARGUMENTS AGAINST REDISTRIBUTION

Those who argue against government redistribution believe that the market, when left to operate on its own, is fair. This argument rests on the proposition that "one is entitled to the fruits of one's efforts."[2] Remember that if market theory is correct, rewards paid in the market are linked to productivity. In other words, labour and capital are paid in accordance with the value of what they produce.

This view also holds that property income—that is, income from land or capital—is no less justified than labour income. All factors of production have marginal products. Capital owners receive profits or interest because the capital that they own is productive.

The argument against redistribution also rests on the principles behind "freedom of contract" and the protection of property rights. When I enter into an agreement either to sell my labour or to commit my capital to use, I do so freely. In

[2]*Powerful support for this notion of "entitlement" can be found in the works of the seventeenth-century English philosophers Thomas Hobbes and John Locke.*

Table 17.8

Estimated Distribution of Wealth among Canadian Adults, 1980

	Cumulative Share of Wealth
Top 1%	18.8%
Top 5%	42.9%
Top 10%	57.1%
Top 20%	73.3%
Top 60%	99.9%

Source: Lars Osberg, *Economic Inequality in Canada* (Toronto: Butterworths, 1981), p. 37.

return I contract to receive payment, which becomes my "property." When a government taxes me and gives my income to someone else, that action violates these two basic rights.

The more common arguments against redistribution are not philosophical. Rather, they point to more practical problems. First, it is said that taxation and transfer programs interfere with the basic incentives provided by the market. Taxing higher-income people reduces their incentive to work, save, and invest. Taxing the "winners" of the economic game also discourages risk taking. Furthermore, providing transfers to those at the bottom reduces their incentive to work as well. All of this leads to a reduction in total output that is the "cost" of redistribution.

Another practical argument against redistribution is that it does not work. Some critics point to the rise in the poverty rate during the early 1980s and again in the early 1990s as an indication that antipoverty programs simply drain money without really helping the poor out of poverty. Whether or not these programs actually help people break out of poverty, the charge of bureaucratic inefficiency in administration always exists. Social programs must be administered by people who must be paid. Some degree of waste and inefficiency is inevitable in any sizeable bureaucracy.

ARGUMENTS IN FAVOUR OF REDISTRIBUTION

The argument most often used in favour of redistribution is that a society as wealthy as Canada has a moral obligation to provide all its members with the basic necessities of life. The Canadian Constitution does, after all, commit Canadian governments to "promoting equal opportunity for the well-being of all Canadians."[3]

Many people, often through no fault of their own, find themselves left out. Some are born with mental or physical problems that severely limit their ability to "produce." Then, of course, there are children. Even if some parents can be held accountable for their low incomes, do we want to punish innocent children for the faults of their parents and thus perpetuate the cycle of poverty? The elderly, without redistribution of income, would have to rely exclusively on savings to survive once they retire, and many conditions can lead to inadequate savings. Should the victims of bad luck be doomed to inevitable poverty? Illness is perhaps the best example. Without the redistribution of resources through publicly provided health care, the accumulated savings of very few can withstand the drain of extraordinary medical bills and the exorbitant cost of nursing home care.

Proponents of redistribution refute "practical" arguments against it by pointing to empirical studies that show little negative effect on the incentives of those who benefit from transfer programs. For many of those people—children, the elderly, the mentally ill—incentives are irrelevant, they say, and providing a basic income to most of the unemployed does not discourage them from working when they have the opportunity to do so.[4] We now turn briefly to several more formal arguments.

■ **Utilitarian Justice** First put forth by the Englishmen Jeremy Bentham and John Stuart Mill in the late eighteenth and early nineteenth centuries, the essence of the utilitarian argument in favour of redistribution is that "a dollar in the hand of a rich person is worth less than a dollar in the hand of a poor person." The rich spend their marginal dollars on luxury goods. It is very easy, for example, to spend over $100 per person for a meal in a good restaurant in Halifax or Vancouver. The

---

[3]*Constitution Act, 1982 [en. by the Canada Act 1982 (U.K.), c.11, s.1], s. 36(1)(a).*
[4]*For a discussion of the empirical evidence on the effects of transfer programs and taxation on incentives, see Chapter 19.*

poor, in contrast, spend their marginal dollars on necessities—food, clothing, and shelter. If the marginal utility of income declines as income rises, the value of a dollar's worth of luxury goods is worth less than a dollar's worth of necessity. Thus, redistributing from the rich to the poor increases total utility. To put this notion of **utilitarian justice** in everyday language: through income redistribution, the rich sacrifice a little and the poor gain a lot.

The utilitarian position is not without its problems, of course. People have very different tastes and preferences. Who is to say that you value a dollar more or less than I do? Because utility is unobservable and unmeasurable, comparisons between individuals cannot be easily made. Nonetheless, many people find the basic logic of the utilitarians persuasive.

■ **Social Contract Theory—Rawlsian Justice** The work of Harvard University philosopher John Rawls has generated a great deal of recent discussion, both within the discipline of economics and between economists and philosophers.[5] In the tradition of Hobbes, Locke, and Rousseau, Rawls argues that, as members of society, we have a contract with one another. In the theoretical world that Rawls imagines, an original *social contract* is drawn up, and all parties agree to it without knowledge of who they are or who they will be in society. This condition is called the "original position" or the "state of nature." With no vested interests to protect, members of society are able to make disinterested choices.

As we approach the contract, everyone has a chance to end up very rich or homeless. On the assumption that we are all "risk averse," Rawls believes that people will attach great importance to the position of the least fortunate members of society because anyone could end up there. **Rawlsian justice,** then, is argued from the assumption of risk aversion. Rawls concludes that any contract emerging from the original position would call for an income distribution that would "maximize the well-being of the worst-off member of society."

Any society bound by such a contract would allow for inequality, but only if that inequality had the effect of improving the lot of the very poor. If inequality provided an incentive for people to work hard and innovate, for example, those inequalities should be tolerated as long as some of the benefits went to those at the bottom.

■ **The Works of Karl Marx** For many decades, a major rivalry existed between the two superpowers, the United States and the Soviet Union. At the heart of this rivalry was a fundamental philosophical difference of opinion about how economic systems work and how they should be managed. At the centre of the debate were the writings of Karl Marx.

Marx did not write very much about socialism or communism. His major work, *Das Kapital* (published in the nineteenth century), was a three-volume analysis and critique of the capitalist system that he saw at work in the world around him. We know what Marx thought was wrong with capitalism, but he was not very clear about what would replace it. In one essay, written late in his life, he put forward the oft-quoted line "from each according to his ability, to each according to his needs,"[6] but he was not specific about the applications of this principle.

Marx's view of capital income, however, does have important implications for income distribution. In the preceding chapters, we discussed profit as a return to a productive factor. The owners of capital receive the return because they own the capital, not because they are productive. Marx observed that in a capitalist society

utilitarian justice *The idea that "a dollar in the hand of a rich person buys less than a dollar in the hand of a poor person." If the marginal utility of income declines with income, transferring income from the rich to the poor will increase total utility.*

Rawlsian justice *A theory of distributional justice that concludes that the social contract emerging from the "original position" would call for an income distribution that would maximize the well-being of the worst-off member of society.*

[5]*See John Rawls,* A Theory of Justice *(Cambridge, Mass.: Harvard University Press, 1972).*
[6]*Karl Marx, "Critique of the Gotha Program" (May 1875), in* The Marx-Engels Reader, *Robert Tucker (ed.) (New York: W. W. Norton), p. 388.*

some people own capital while most people do not. According to Marx, this special inequality shapes the relationships among people and has a profound impact on the history of any capitalist society. Moreover, Marx argued that if one looks back at the history of the process via which capital goods are produced and accumulated one must conclude that capital was ultimately produced by the working classes, who did not get to claim it.

Because capital is ultimately produced by workers but accumulates in the hands of capital owners, it is sometimes argued that profit is an illegitimate expropriation by capitalists of the fruits of labour's efforts. It follows, then, that Marxists see the property income component as the primary source of inequality in capitalist societies. If capital were owned by workers, the distribution of income would be much more equal and class conflict between workers and capitalists would be eliminated.

Despite the fact that the Soviet Union no longer exists, China, Cuba, and a number of other countries remain Communist, and a number of economists still argue that the Marxist critique of capitalism is valid even though one version of an alternative has failed.

■ **Income Distribution as a Public Good**   Those who argue that the unfettered market produces a just income distribution certainly do not believe that private charity should be forbidden. Voluntary redistribution does not involve any violation of property rights by the state.

In Chapter 16, however, you saw that there may be a problem with private charity. Suppose that people really do want to end the hunger problem, for example. As they write out their cheques to charity, they encounter the classic public-goods problem. First, there are free riders. If hunger and starvation are eliminated, the benefits—even the merely psychological benefits—flow to everyone, whether they contributed or not. Second, any contribution is a drop in the bucket. One individual contribution is so small that it can have no real effect.

With private charity, as with national defence, nothing depends upon whether I pay or not. Thus, private charity may fail for the same reason that the private sector is likely to fail to produce national defence and other public goods. People will find it in their interest not to contribute. Thus, we turn to government to provide things that we want that will not be provided adequately if we act separately—in this case, help for the poor and hungry.

Redistribution Programs and Policies

The role of government in changing the *distribution of income* is a hotly debated issue. The debate involves not only what government programs are appropriate to fight poverty but the character of the tax system as well. Unfortunately, the quality of the public debate on the subject is low. Usually it consists of a series of claims and counterclaims about what social programs do to incentives rather than a serious inquiry into what our distributional goal should be.

In this section, we talk about the tools of redistributional policy in Canada. As we do so, you will have a chance to assess for yourself some of the evidence about their effects.

Financing Redistribution Programs: Taxes

Redistribution always involves two parties or groups: those who end up with less and those who end up with more. Because redistribution programs are financed by tax dollars, it is important to know who the donors and recipients are—that is, who pays the taxes and who receives the benefits of those taxes.

The mainstay of the Canadian tax system is the personal income tax. The income tax is progressive. This means that those with higher incomes pay a higher percentage of their income in taxes. Even though the tax is subject to many exemptions, deductions, and so forth that allow some taxpayers to reduce their tax burdens, almost all studies of the income tax show that its burden as a percentage of income rises as income rises.

But the personal income tax is only one of many taxes. Canadians face a wide variety of taxes, including general sales taxes (provincial sales taxes and the federal Goods and Services Tax [GST], for example), excise taxes, property taxes, and payroll taxes. What is important to the individual taxpayer is the overall burden of taxation, including all federal, provincial, and municipal taxes. Most studies of the effect of taxes on the distribution of income suggest that the overall burden is either proportional or only slightly progressive.

Table 17.9 presents one set of estimates of effective tax rates for 1988. While some progressivity is visible, it is very slight. Those earning less than $20 000 a year face a tax rate of about 30%, those earning income in the $20 000–$300 000 range face an effective tax rate of about 34%, and those earning more than $300 000 face a rate of 35%. Table 17.10 on page 440 shows the impact of taxes on the cumulative distribution of income in 1994. Again a slight progression is evident, but in general we can conclude that the tax side of the equation produces very little change in the distribution of income.

A number of economists have advocated a negative income tax system as an effective means of redistributing income. Indeed, Canada tried a limited negative income tax experiment in Manitoba in the 1970s. The principle of a negative tax system is relatively simple. When people fill out their income tax form they calculate their level of income. If their income is above a certain threshold level they must pay tax as is the case in the current personal income tax system. But if they earn less than the threshold, the government will write them a cheque (a negative tax), with the size of the negative tax depending on how far the taxpayer is from the threshold. (Those close to but below the threshold receive a small negative tax, those far below receive a larger cheque, and those with no income at all receive the largest possible transfer. The transfer received by those who earn no income is sometimes called a guaranteed annual income.)

A key feature of a negative income tax is that the transfers are **income tested,** that is, the size of the transfer depends on one's income. Because a negative income tax gives the largest transfers to the poorest in society and takes the most revenue from the most affluent in society, it will always reduce inequality. Although Canada has never implemented a negative income tax system, an increasing number of programs in this country are based on the principle of income testing.

income tested transfer
A transfer that changes continuously as income changes.

Table 17.9	Estimated Effective Tax Rates, 1988

Income	*Percentage of Income*
Less than $20 000	30.0
$20 000–$300 000	34.0
Over $300 000	35.0

Source: Frank Vermaeten, W. Irwin Gillespie, and Arndt Vermaeten, "Tax Incidence in Canada," *Canadian Tax Journal* vol. 42, no. 2 (1994): pp. 348–416.

Table 17.10	Distribution of Family Income Before and After Taxes, 1994	
	Before Taxes	*After Taxes*
Bottom quintile	6.4	7.7
Second quintile	12.2	13.4
Third quintile	18.3	17.7
Fourth quintile	24.1	23.8
Top quintile	39.6	36.8

Source: Statistics Canada, *Income Distributions By Size, 1994*, Cat. no. 13-207-XPB and Statistics Canada, *Income After Tax, Distributions By Size, 1994*, Cat. no. 13-210.

EXPENDITURE PROGRAMS

Some programs designed to redistribute income or to aid the poor provide cash income to recipients. Others provide benefits in the form of health care, subsidized housing, or child care. Still others provide training or help workers find jobs.

■ **Transfers to the Elderly**   Canada has a large and complex system to transfer income to the elderly. The incidence of low income among the elderly has fallen steadily over time. This is a concrete indicator of the success of the Canadian system of transfers to those over 65 (see Table 17.7).

The transfer system designed to assist the elderly involves three different programs: Old Age Security, Guaranteed Income Supplement, and Canada/Quebec Pension Plan payments. The *Old Age Security (OAS)* benefit is a **demogrant,** meaning it basically goes to all Canadians, regardless of income, who have a particular demographic characteristic. In 1995, everyone over the age of 65 in Canada received a payment of about $400 per month. The OAS benefit is taxable; the affluent have to pay back a larger portion of this transfer in the form of taxes than do the poor.[7] The *Guaranteed Income Supplement (GIS)* is an additional income tested benefit available to the elderly. In 1995, it provided a maximum benefit of about $475 per month. The GIS benefit declines rapidly as income increases, thus it goes exclusively to poor Canadians over the age of 65. In the fiscal year 1995–96, the government of Canada paid out over $15 billion in OAS benefits and almost $5 billion in GIS benefits. In the 1996 budget, the federal government proposed a new "Seniors Benefit" to replace both the OAS and GIS by the year 2001. The Seniors Benefit will be "income tested."

The third major program designed for the elderly is the *Canada/Quebec Pension Plan (CPP/QPP).*[8] This pension plan is complex. In some respects it is designed to operate in ways similar to private pension plans. With a private pension plan, members make contributions during their working lives in the expectation that they will receive a pension upon retirement. In this respect pension plans are similar to savings plans in which a certain amount is saved each month and then the accumulated savings are withdrawn little by little after retirement. However, a pension is a very special savings plan since it involves insurance. Individual pension plan members do not know when they will die. In a savings plan, those who die young leave their savings to their heirs; those who live a long time may outlive their accumulated savings. In a pension plan, everyone contributes to a common pool of

demogrant *A transfer payment that depends only on a demographic characteristic (such as age) and that does not change as income changes.*

---

[7]*There is also special provision for a "clawback," which imposes a high tax rate on OAS payments to high-income individuals.*
[8]*Quebec runs its own pension plan, which is almost identical to the Canada Pension Plan.*

saving. The heirs of those who die young do not get any benefits and those who live a long time will continue to receive benefits. Because it is possible to predict how long the members of a pension plan will live on average but it is not possible to predict how long individual members of the plan will live, subscribing to a pension plan can be advantageous to all. Each member is guaranteed that he or she will not outlive his or her saving and one's monthly contribution to ensure this outcome will be much lower than is the case if the individual were to try to secure this guarantee through personal saving. The reason monthly contributions are lower is that a transfer occurs in a private pension plan whereby those members who die young leave money to those members who live a long time.

The Canada Pension Plan involves similar principles, but it is not fully funded (the payouts expected based on what we know about life expectancy exceed the accumulated contributions made by those who are members of the plan). As a consequence, some general tax revenue must go to cover the unfunded portion of the Canada/Quebec Pension Plan. Thus the Canada Pension Plan involves two types of transfers: one from recipients of the plan who die young to those who live a long time, and another from current taxpayers (those not yet eligible to draw on the plan) to those individuals—seniors—who are drawing the Canada or Quebec Pension. Currently both the Canada and Quebec pension plans are very close to breaking even, but we know that increasing amounts of general tax revenue will have to be devoted to these plans in the future. Adjusting contribution rates and benefits is an important policy issue in Canada today.

■ **Child Tax Benefit**   The child tax benefit transfers about $5 billion a year to poor families with children. The child tax benefit is very similar to a negative income tax with a guaranteed annual income targeted to families with children. The size of the child tax benefit is based on the number and ages of children and on the amount of family net income reported on one's tax form. As a concrete example of how the program works consider a number of families with two children (both of whom are under the age of seven), earning different incomes. The first family earns $20 000 per year and qualifies for the maximum benefit of $2466 since its income is less than $26 000 (every family earning less than approximately $26 000 qualifies for the maximum benefit). The second family earns $30 000 per year. Its benefit is reduced by $0.05 for every dollar earned above approximately $26 000 and so they receive a child tax benefit of $2266. The third family earns $50 000 and receives no benefit (no family earning above $50 000 is eligible to receive the child tax benefit).

■ **Employment Insurance**   The Canadian Employment Insurance Program is another important transfer program. Like the Canada/Quebec Pension Plan, the *Employment Insurance Program (EI)* involves an element of insurance. Individuals do not know if they will lose their job, and employment insurance provides a means to contribute when you have a job, to guarantee an income in the event that you lose a job. Thus it involves a transfer from those who are employed to those who are unemployed. It is not explicitly income tested but instead is based on a work test: if you (1) lose your job and (2) meet the minimum qualifying requirements, you are eligible to receive the EI benefit. But like the Canada/Quebec Pension Plan, EI is not a pure insurance program. Participation is compulsory. Benefits are subject to a maximum (which means that high-income earners who lose their jobs suffer a substantial loss in income). Contributions are not tied to the risk of unemployment (workers in unstable jobs pay lower premiums than they would under a pure insurance plan; workers in stable jobs pay more).

Although employment insurance benefits are not aimed at the poor alone, many of the unemployed are poor. Thus the Employment Insurance Program is

One of the most vigorously debated topics in recent years has been workfare, a policy of forcing those receiving social assistance to either work or enrol in an education/training program in exchange for their welfare benefits. Critics of workfare argue that this policy violates the rights of the poor and amounts to a policy of "blaming the victim." Moreover, they argue that workfare programs have unintended consequences such as creating unemployment among those currently employed and reducing volunteerism in society. Proponents, on the other hand, see workfare as a way to limit the social loss that occurs when people are unemployed and not contributing to society's output, and as an opportunity to give social assistance recipients experience and on-the-job training. They also hold that workfare reduces government expenditures in the long term.

In 1995, David Tsubouchi, Ontario's Minister of Community and Social Services, planned to implement a reform of welfare that would require all able-bodied men and women to work or to be retrained in return for their benefits.

"The Tories' Common Sense Revolution calls for cuts to [Ontario's] welfare, now the highest in Canada, and [for investment of] $500 million in plans such as workfare and learnfare. The aim is to reduce the number of people on welfare by 5% per year over 3 years.

When it comes to the workfare end of the reform, Tsubouchi will have several examples to consider, not the least of which is Alberta, where good chunks of Harris's Common Sense Revolution came from. Under Alberta's workfare program, about 2000 people are doing such things as working at day-care centres, senior citizens homes or planting trees along roadsides. The cost of the program is covered by savings from other changes to the welfare system including reducing caseloads and lowering benefits.... Overall, the province's caseload has dropped to about 51 500 from 96 300 at the beginning of 1993.

But Tsubouchi may also want to look at another example of a workfare/welfare program where the caseload size is closer to that of Ontario. Quebec has had a workfare program in place for six years, but 10 days ago the province's Minister of Income Security, Jeanne Blackburn, pulled the plug as part of a major overhaul of the entire welfare system.

Until 1989, Quebecers over the age of 30 did not have to work or train to receive their cheques. But, spurred by taxpayer resentment that thousands of Quebecers were getting government money for doing nothing in return, the law was changed. Most welfare recipients, excluding single mothers of young children, the handicapped, and the sick were told their benefits would be cut sharply unless they completed

extremely important to many of Canada's working poor. Expenditures on Employment Insurance in 1995 exceeded $15 billion. The revenue was raised through an earmarked payroll tax.

■ **Provincial Social Assistance**   Social assistance, or welfare, in Canada is within the jurisdiction of the provinces. The 12 different social assistance programs in Canada, one for each province and territory, generated over $15 billion in expenditures in 1995. Given that municipalities in Nova Scotia, Ontario, and Manitoba have some control over program design, it is possible to argue that there are actually hundreds of different social assistance programs in this country. Social assistance benefits, eligibility criteria, and appeal procedure vary significantly as one crosses the country.

Nonetheless, all social assistance programs have some common features as a result of the way these programs are funded. Between 1966 and 1996 a federal government program known as the *Canada Assistance Plan (CAP)* covered high school, worked on community programs, or signed up for on the job training programs. It also offered to pay part of the salary for recipients hired by companies to do regular jobs.

Blackburn, who established a task force to come up with ways to reform the system, declared "right now it's not working" in part because workfare has become an administrative nightmare. But more than that, the aims of the program have failed: the plan has not saved taxpayers money, nor helped significant numbers of welfare recipients find steady work.

"You may find some success at the micro level," says Alain Noel, associate professor of Political Science at the Université de Montréal, and a member of Blackburn's task force. "But if you look at the big picture in terms of how many people are on welfare, it's not going to make a huge difference." Noel also says another

conclusion of the volumes of studies done in other parts of North America is that while workfare may help satisfy the admirable goal of having as many people contribute to the wealth of society as a whole, it also costs money. "Workfare means more than just sending a cheque. You have to provide training and counselling, some form of jobs that have to be subsidized in some way or another. I'd say that it is an essential dilemma of workfare in a liberal society like ours: people want to reduce public spending but at the same time for workfare to work you need to spend more."

...The National Anti-Poverty Organization, which has studied Quebec's workfare experience closely, points to another particular program, known as Extra, which places recipients with companies and provides the employer with a $100-a-month subsidy per new employee for six months.

Rather than result in full-time hiring, however, a whopping 97% of recipients in Extra find themselves back on job waiting lists. Moreover, NAPO says, 50 000 or so unemployed Quebecers in various workfare programs have provided employers with what amounts to a large pool of cheap labour. The temptation to replace one's own employees with cheaper workers is often great. "We have a lot of concern when suddenly free labour is available for employers like that," says Francois Dumaine, assistant director of the Ottawa-based group. "What we've seen is that workers have been replaced by welfare recipients."

Source: James Walker, "Quebec's Six-Year Experiment With Workfare Hasn't Paid Off: Welfare Recipients Haven't Found Steady Work," *Financial Post* vol. 89, no. 26 (July 1/3, 1995): p. 15.

approximately one-half of all provincial assistance expenditures in Canada. To qualify for this federal transfer, the provinces had to meet some general standards including requirements that assistance benefits be calculated using a "needs test." This test involves comparing the budgetary needs of an applicant with the assets and income of the household. In 1996, the Canada Assistance Plan was replaced by the *Canada Health and Social Transfer (CHST)*, which provides a lump sum grant to the province to support provincial social assistance programs, health care (medicare and hospital insurance), and post-secondary education. The CHST does not involve as many restrictions as the CAP. It is likely that the social assistance system in the future will exhibit even more diversity than it does today.

One of the most controversial provincial government policy initiatives in recent years has been a series of experiments with workfare—a policy of forcing recipients of social assistance to work in exchange for their benefits. The Issues and Controversies box titled "Workfare" explores some aspects of this policy.

■ **Other Programs** The public education system, which ensures children a free education, is an important redistributive program. Although free public education is available to rich and poor alike, it contributes to an equalization of opportunities. Subsidization of universities and our system of student loans and bursaries has a similar effect by keeping access to university open to those with low incomes. Given that success in education also depends on resources available in the home (access to books, a well-balanced diet, etc., and increasingly a home computer), government involvement in the education system does not alone ensure equal opportunities for success. But without such involvement, those born into low-income families would have little chance to succeed in a labour market that places a high value on educational credentials.

The Canadian medicare system, which provides free medical care, also has a significant effect on the distribution of well-being. Like public education, medicare is available to both rich and poor, with those who make high use of the health care system receiving income from those whose health care needs are not as great. The medicare system ensures that Canadians do not end up in poverty as a result of costly medical bills. Moreover, illness is not entirely a random event as there is evidence that the poor are more likely to suffer illness than the rich.[9]

Canadian governments also support a number of other programs that address the needs of the poor. These include the Goods and Services Tax Credit, which refunds at least part of the GST paid by those with low incomes; social housing programs, which meet a proportion of the housing needs of the poor; special subsidies to cover child care expenses incurred by the working poor; programs to support Aboriginal peoples, etc. When viewed as a whole the Canadian income security system is remarkably comprehensive, yet few would argue that it has eliminated poverty, and the evidence suggests that it has had relatively small effect on income distribution.

■ **International Comparisons** Many Canadian employers and employees complain about the taxes they have to pay to cover the cost of our redistributive programs. However, it is important to recognize that Canadian expenditures on income support as a percent of GDP are only marginally higher than those by governments in the United States and are significantly lower than expenditures by most European governments. Indeed, Canadian expenditures as a proportion of GDP are half those of Germany and France.

HOW EFFECTIVE ARE INCOME REDISTRIBUTION PROGRAMS?

Are government income redistribution programs effective? The data suggest that the distribution of income has changed little despite the growth of redistribution programs. Moreover, poverty among children is growing and a source of concern. Only the elderly have experienced significant improvements over time. The relatively small impact of redistribution programs has been at the centre of a debate over the effectiveness of government programs.

One view holds that economic growth is the best way to cure poverty. Poverty programs are expensive and must be paid for with tax revenues. The high rates of taxation required to support these programs, critics say, have eroded the incentive to work, save, and invest, thus slowing the rate of economic growth. Moreover, the transfer programs themselves breed dependency. In addition, the rise in child poverty is cited as evidence that antipoverty programs don't work.

The opposite view is that poverty would be much more widespread without antipoverty programs. According to this view the impact of antipoverty programs

---

[9]See: Robert G. Evans, Morris L. Barer, and Theodore Marmor, Why Some People Are Healthy and Others Are Not: The Determinants of Health of Populations (New York: Aldine De Grutyer, 1994).

on work, saving, and investment is quite small. The incidence of low incomes has increased not because of antipoverty programs themselves but because the economy has failed to create adequate jobs.

Some also consider income redistribution programs to be a major factor in the rise of Canadian government debt. They argue that we simply can't afford our current system of transfers, even if it is effective. But others note that social spending as a proportion of GDP has not increased by much over the past 20 years and that slow growth in tax revenues combined with high interest rates account for almost all of the growth in government debt. They argue that with lower interest rates, faster economic growth, and more employment, debt will fall and the governments will enjoy fiscal room to expand income redistribution programs without tax increases.

Government or the Market? A Review

Part 2 of this book (Chapters 6–12) introduced you to the behaviour of households and firms in input and output markets. There you learned that if all the assumptions of perfect competition held in the real world, the outcome would be perfectly efficient.

But as we began to relax the assumptions of perfect competition in Part 3 (Chapters 13–17), we began to see a potential role for government in the economy. Some firms acquire market power and tend to underproduce and overprice. Unregulated markets give private decision makers no incentives to weigh the social costs of externalities. Goods that provide collective benefits may not be produced in sufficient quantities without government involvement. And, as we saw in this chapter, the final distribution of well-being determined by the free market may not be considered equitable by society.

Remember, however, that government is not a cure for all economic woes. There is nothing to guarantee that public sector involvement will improve matters. In fact, many argue that government involvement may bring about even more inequity and inefficiency because bureaucrats are often driven by self-interest, not public interest.

You now have a strong foundation in microeconomic theory. Part 4 of this book—Chapters 18–20—presents several topics in applied economics: public finance, labour economics, the economics of health care reform, and the economics of immigration. These chapters are meant to provide you with an overview of how the discipline addresses some of the most pressing problems of our time. They also represent a preview of what you will encounter in more advanced courses in economics.

Summary

1. Even if all markets were perfectly efficient, the result might not be fair. Even in relatively free market economies, governments redistribute income and wealth, usually in the name of fairness, or *equity*.

2. Because utility is neither directly observable nor measurable, most policy discussions deal with the distributions of income and wealth as imperfect substitutes for the concept of "the distribution of well-being."

The Sources of Household Income

3. Households derive their incomes from three basic sources: (1) from wages or salaries received in exchange for labour (about 63%); (2) from property such as capital and land (about 12.7%); and (3) from government (about 17%).

4. Differences in wage and salary incomes across households result from differences in the characteristics of workers (skills, training, education,

experience, and so on) and from differences in jobs (dangerous, exciting, glamorous, difficult, and so forth). Household income also varies with the number of household members in the labour force, and it can decline sharply if members become unemployed.

5. The amount of *property income* that a household earns depends on the amount and kinds of property it owns. Transfer income from governments flows substantially, but not exclusively, to lower-income households. *Transfer payments* are by and large designed to provide income to those in need.

The Distribution of Income

6. The 20% of families at the top of the income distribution received 40.2% of the total income in Canada in 1995, while the bottom 20% earned just 6.4%. Income distribution in Canada has remained basically stable over a long period of time.

7. The *Lorenz Curve* is a commonly used graphic device for describing the distribution of income. The *Gini coefficient* is an index of income inequality that ranges from zero for perfect equality to one for total inequality.

8. Statistics Canada uses a *low income cutoff* to identify people with low incomes. Approximately 14% of families and 39% of unattached individuals in Canada were considered to be low-income earners in 1995.

9. Low incomes among the elderly in Canada has fallen significantly over the past 30 years. But low incomes among children, especially children in families headed by a lone female parent, has grown. Over 56% of families headed by a lone female parent had low incomes in 1995.

10. Data on the distribution of wealth are not as readily available as data on the distribution of income. The distribution of wealth in Canada is more

unequal than the distribution of income. The wealthiest 10% of households owned nearly 60% of all household assets, while the wealthiest 1% owned nearly 20% of all household assets in 1980.

The Redistribution Debate

11. The basic philosophical argument against government redistribution rests on the proposition that one is entitled to the fruits of one's efforts. It also rests on the principles of freedom of contract and protection of property rights. More common arguments focus on the negative effects of redistribution on incentives to work, save, and invest.

12. The basic philosophical argument in favour of redistribution is that a society as rich as Canada has a moral obligation to provide all its members with the basic necessities of life. More formal arguments can be found in the works of the utilitarians, Rawls, and Marx.

Redistribution Programs and Policies

13. In Canada, redistribution is accomplished through taxation and through a number of government transfer programs. The largest of these are transfers to the elderly, social assistance, the child tax benefit, employment insurance, medicare, and various housing subsidy programs, including public housing.

14. There is currently much debate over the effectiveness of antipoverty programs. One view holds that the best way to cure poverty is with economic growth. Poverty programs are expensive and must be paid for with tax revenues. The high rates of taxation required to support these programs have eroded the incentive to work, save, and invest, thus slowing the rate of economic growth. In addition, the rise in child poverty is cited as evidence that antipoverty programs do not work. The opposite view holds that without antipoverty programs, poverty would be much worse.

Review Terms and Concepts

compensating differentials 425

demogrant 440

economic income 429

equity 422

Gini coefficient 431

human capital 425

income tested transfer 439

Lorenz Curve 431

low income cutoffs 434

money income 429

property income 427

Rawlsian justice 437

transfer payments 428

utilitarian justice 437

utility possibilities frontier 423

1. Redistributive programs can be based on an income test where the size of transfer is based solely on income, or they can be based on some other characteristic of the individual such as age, employment status, presence of a disability, etc. The Old Age Security (OAS) benefit is distributed to all Canadians over the age of 65. Do you think this program should be income tested? Suppose that the OAS is taxable under the income tax, would your answer change? Defend your positions.

2. Some people in Canadian society are very rich. Is this situation justifiable? Why? Why not?

3. List the factors you believe account for the poverty experienced by individual Canadians. Indicate whether the factors are or are not under the control of the individual. Rank the factors, based on your opinion, from the most important cause of poverty to the least important.

4. New Ph.D.s in economics entering the job market find that academic jobs (jobs teaching at colleges and universities) pay about 30% less than nonacademic jobs such as working at a bank or a consulting firm. Those who take academic jobs are clearly worse off than those who take nonacademic jobs. Do you agree? Explain your answer.

5. Statistics Canada normally does not collect data by racial group for statistics such as income or unemployment. However, data are collected in this way in the United States. Table 1 gives U.S. figures for income distribution among blacks and whites, as well as for the country as a whole.

Using the data in Table 1, create two graphs. The first graph should plot the Lorenz Curves for black families and white families. The second graph should plot the Lorenz Curve for the 1980 "all" data and the Lorenz Curve for the 1992 "all" data.

In each graph, which has the higher Gini coefficient? How do you interpret the result?

TABLE 1

			PERCENTAGE OF INCOME	
	BLACK	**WHITE**	**1992 ALL**	**1980 ALL**
Lower fifth	3.0	4.9	4.4	5.1
Second fifth	8.2	10.9	10.5	11.6
Third fifth	15.0	16.7	16.5	17.5
Fourth fifth	25.0	23.7	24.0	24.3
Highest fifth	48.8	43.8	44.6	41.6

6. Should welfare benefits be higher in Toronto and Vancouver than they are in rural Newfoundland? Defend your answer.

7. The incidence of low income among the elderly has been sharply reduced in the last 30 years. How has this been accomplished?

8. Write a memo to your MP urging either an increase or a decrease in federal spending on public housing. Defend your position carefully, using both philosophical and practical arguments.

9. "Income inequality is evidence that our economic system is working well, not poorly." What arguments might this speaker use to support his opinion of income redistribution policies? How might he respond when regional disparities are brought to his attention?

Canadian Case Study Three | The Future of Work

Technological change can leave workers without jobs. The introduction of automatic teller machines (ATMs) has had a visible impact on employment in the banking industry.

Many in our society are concerned that the introduction of computer and telecommunications technologies is creating a permanent and growing class of unemployed. Economists, however, are generally optimists, believing that any unemployment will be temporary and that in the long run workers will benefit from the introduction of new technology through higher wages and improved standards of living.

The optimism common among economists is based on two observations. First, a market system has, in theory, a remarkable capacity. Market prices automatically respond to changes in technology in a way that facilitates proper adjustment to the change. Second, economists know that there have been revolutionary technological changes in the past (the steam engine, electric power, the automobile) and that these did not create permanent and rising unemployment. Indeed, they created the basis for dramatic improvements in our standard of living.

How does the market facilitate adjustment? The initial introduction of new technology can create unemployment. However, market prices in all markets will adjust in response. Indeed, the prices will change in a way that increases employment, thus offsetting the initial decrease in employment. The ability of the market model to "self-correct" is known as negative feedback since the initial move in one direction (higher unemployment) generates a reaction in the opposite direction (less unemploy-

ment). Consider the following concrete reactions to a change in technology:

1. *Technological change and re-engineering reduce costs and create unemployment.* But in a competitive economy the lower costs will result in lower prices, an increase in the quantity demanded for the lower-priced product, and a partially offsetting increase in employment.

2. *Lower prices would also be expected to have an income effect, increasing demand in all normal-good producing sectors and increasing labour demand.*

3. *If the new technology increases profits we will see more people investing in new business, thus creating employment.*

4. *If new technology increases profits, the demand for new technology will rise.* This new

technology has to be produced by someone. Thus, the demand for new technology creates employment in the new technology sector.

5. *If there are still workers unemployed, at least in the long run, wages will fall, making workers more attractive and increasing employment.* Lower wages not only reduce costs and prices still further, but also induce firms to increase their use of labour relative to capital.

These are, in theory, powerful forces. Moreover, actual historical experience suggests that they are at work in the real world.

Nonetheless, all economists recognize that firms are "downsizing" by laying off workers whose jobs were made redundant by re-engineering (re-engineering is a term often used to describe a radical transformation of the workplace to take full advantage of computer technology). Bank tellers are being replaced by automated teller machines; autoworkers are being replaced by robots; accountants are being replaced by integrated business software systems. These traumatic adjustments involve real hardship for those affected.

Questions for Analytical Thinking

1. Technological change typically results in a change in the skills demanded by firms. How might the market facilitate adjustment to a change in needed skills?

2. The market adjustment to technological change is not instantaneous. It takes time. During the transition period the people affected will experience a significant drop in income. Revisit arguments for and against redistribution and try to justify a position for or against a policy of redistributing income to those who lose as a result of technological change.

3. Most dynamic systems— whether an economic system, an ecological system, or a physical system—exhibit positive and negative feedback mechanisms. Positive feedback reinforces the original change. Negative feedback works in the opposite direction to the original change. Try to explain how an economic system would react to technological change if there were no negative feedback mechanism (i.e., when prices and wages are fixed and people who become unemployed no longer have income needed to purchase goods and services).

4. Economists who believe that the self-correcting tendencies of a market economy are weak argue that high and potentially permanent unemployment is a possible outcome when we experience a major technological change. Explain why this would be true.

5. Go to the library and find data on Canadian and U.S. unemployment rates between 1966 and today. Do you think the data support the position of the optimists or the pessimists? Why?

Video Resource: "The Future of Work," Parts 1 and 2, *The National Magazine*, September 5, 1996

Public Finance: The Economics of Taxation

An introductory course in economics has several goals, one of which is to introduce a body of theory about how economies work. The first 17 chapters of this book contain what amounts to the core of microeconomic theory.

Another purpose of an introductory course in economics is to survey the major subfields of the discipline. In Chapter 1 we briefly described a number of these subfields. This chapter is the first of several that expand on those brief descriptions. Because the discipline is so varied, we cannot possibly survey all the areas of economic inquiry. We therefore limit our discussion to four of the most widely debated economic issues of the day: public finance (Chapter 18), labour economics (Chapter 19), and the economics of health care and immigration (Chapter 20).

The Economics of Taxation

The five chapters in Part 3 analyzed the potential role of government in the economy. Taken together, those chapters discuss much of the field of *public economics*. From there, it is an easy transition to the field of *public finance*, with which we begin our survey of applied economics. No matter what functions we end up assigning to government, in order to do anything at all government must first raise revenues. The primary vehicle that the government uses to finance itself is taxation.[1]

---

[1]*Before we proceed, you may want to review the discussion of the public sector in Chapter 3. There we describe the basic sources of revenue for federal, provincial, and local governments, as well as the things those revenues are spent on. You will often hear the taxing and spending policies of federal or provincial governments referred to as "fiscal policies." The word* fiscal *comes from* fisc, *another word for a government treasury.*

The most important thing to remember about taxes is that ultimately they are paid by people, or by households:

> Taxes may be imposed on transactions, institutions, property, meals, and all kinds of other things, but in the final analysis they are paid by individuals or households.

TAXES: BASIC CONCEPTS

Before we begin our analysis of the Canadian tax system, we need to clarify some terms. There are many different kinds of taxes, and tax analysts use a very specific language to describe them. Every tax has two parts: a *base* and a *rate structure*. The **tax base** is the measure or value upon which the tax is levied. In Canada, taxes are levied on a variety of different bases, including income, sales, property, and corporate profits. The **tax rate structure** determines the portion of the tax base that must be paid in taxes. A tax rate of 25% on income, for example, means that I pay a tax equal to 25% of my income.

■ **Taxes on Stocks versus Taxes on Flows**   Tax bases may be either stock measures or flow measures. The local property tax is a tax on the value of residential, commercial, or industrial property. For instance, home owners are taxed on the current assessed value of their homes. Current value is a stock variable—that is, it is measured or estimated at a point in time.

Other taxes are levied on flows. (Review Chapter 4 if the difference between stock and flow variables is unclear to you.) Income is a flow. Most people are paid on a weekly, biweekly, or monthly basis, and they have taxes deducted from every paycheque. Retail sales take place continuously, and a retail sales tax takes a portion of that flow.

■ **Proportional, Progressive, and Regressive Taxes**   All taxes are ultimately paid out of income. A tax whose burden is a constant proportion of income for all households is called a **proportional tax.** A comprehensive tax of 20% on all forms of income, with no deductions or exclusions, is an example of a proportional tax.

A tax that exacts a higher proportion of income from higher-income households than it does from lower-income households is a **progressive tax.** Because its rate structure increases with income, the Canadian personal income tax is a progressive tax. At current federal and provincial rates of taxation, for example, someone with a taxable income of $30 000 would pay a tax of roughly 25%, while someone with an income of $60 000 would fall into the 43% bracket.

A tax that exacts a lower proportion of income from higher-income earners than it does from lower-income earners is a **regressive tax.** *Excise taxes* (taxes on specific commodities) are regressive. The retail sales tax is also a regressive tax. Suppose the retail sales tax in your province is 5%. You might assume that it is a proportional tax because everyone pays 5%. But all people do not spend the same fraction of their income on taxable goods and services. In fact, higher-income households save a larger fraction of their incomes. Thus, even though they spend more money on more expensive things and may pay more taxes in *dollars* than lower-income families do, they end up paying a smaller *proportion* of their incomes in sales tax.

Table 18.1 on the next page shows this principle at work in three families. The lowest-income family saves 20% of its $10 000 income, leaving $8000 for consumption. With a 5% sales tax, the household pays $400, or 4% of total income, in tax. The $50 000 family saves 50% of its income, or $25 000, leaving

tax base *The measure or value upon which a tax is levied.*

tax rate structure *The percentage of a tax base that must be paid in taxes—25% of income, for example.*

proportional tax *A tax whose burden is the same proportion of income for all households.*

progressive tax *A tax whose burden, expressed as a percentage of income, increases as income increases.*

regressive tax *A tax whose burden, expressed as a percentage of income, falls as income increases.*

Table 18.1

The Burden of a Hypothetical 5% Sales Tax Imposed on Three Households with Different Incomes

Household	Income	Saving Rate, %	Saving	Consumption	5% Tax on Consumption	Tax as a % of Income
A	$ 10 000	20	$ 2000	$ 000	$ 400	4.0
B	20 000	40	8000	12 000	600	3.0
C	50 000	50	25 000	25 000	1250	2.5

$25 000 for consumption. With the 5% sales tax, the household pays $1250, only 2.5% of its total income, in tax.

■ **Marginal versus Average Tax Rates** When discussing a specific tax or taxes in general, it is often useful to distinguish between average tax rates and marginal tax rates. Your *average tax rate* is the total amount of tax you pay divided by your total income. For example, if you earned a total income of $15 000 and paid income taxes of $1500, your average income tax rate would be 10% ($1500 divided by $15 000). If you paid $3000 in taxes, your average rate would be 20% ($3000 divided by $15 000).

Your *marginal tax rate* is the tax rate that you pay on any additional income that you earn. If you take a part-time job and pay an additional $280 in tax on the extra $1000 you've earned, your marginal tax rate is 28% ($280 divided by $1000). Marginal and average tax rates are usually different.

> Marginal tax rates have the most influence on behaviour. Decisions about how much to work depend on how much of the added income you get to take home. Similarly, a firm's decision about how much to invest depends in part on the additional, or marginal, profits that the investment project would yield after tax.

The Canadian personal income tax provides an excellent example of how and why marginal tax rates can differ. Each year, you must file a tax return with Revenue Canada on or before April 30. On that form you first figure out the total tax that you are responsible for paying. Next, you determine how much was withheld from your income and sent to Revenue Canada by your employer. If too much was withheld, you get a refund. If not enough was withheld, you have to write a cheque to the government for the difference.

Calculating the amount of tax that you are responsible for paying involves at least five steps:

1. Determine your total income from all sources.

2. Identify all deductions you are entitled to claim. You may deduct a portion of your contributions to registered pension plans (RPPs) and registered retirement savings plans (RRSPs), union and professional dues, and child care expenses from your total income to arrive at your taxable income.

3. Apply the appropriate tax rate to your taxable income to yield the federal income tax that you owe. Table 18.2 presents the tax rates for federal tax in 1997.

4. Calculate your tax credits. Items included in the calculation of your tax credits include a basic personal amount of $6456, an amount for one's spouse, contributions to Employment Insurance and the Canada Pension Plan, tuition fees, and charitable donations.

Table 18.2

Federal Personal Income Tax Rates

Income Earned	Tax Rate
0–$29 590	17%
$29 591–$59 180	26%
$59 181 or more	29%

5. Calculate your net tax payable. To do this, you take 17% of the credit items and subtract this amount from the federal income tax you calculated in step 3.

As an illustration of the federal tax calculation, suppose you are a single taxpayer who earned $70 000 in 1996. You put $5000 in an RRSP but have no other deductions. Thus your taxable income is $65 000. The first $29 590 is taxed at a rate of 17%. Income from $29 591 to $59 180 is taxed at a rate of 26%. The final $5819 is taxed at a rate of 29%. Therefore, total federal income tax is: $5030.30 + $7693.14 + $1687.51 = $14 410.95. Your credit is calculated based on a Canada Pension Plan contribution of $806, an Employment Insurance contribution of $1000, and the personal amount of $6456. Adding these together and multiplying by 0.17 yields a credit of $1404.54. Subtracting the credit from federal income tax yields the actual amount of federal tax you owe: $13 006.41.

You can now see the difference between average and marginal rates. Your average tax rate is $13 006.41 as a percent of $70 000, or 19%. But any additional income you earn over $70 000 would be taxed at 29%. These calculations are summarized in Table 18.3.

Provincial governments, with the exception of Quebec, allow the federal government to collect taxes on their behalf using the same tax form. Each province sets a rate, expressed as a percentage of federal tax payable, which yields the total tax payable to the provincial government. Table 18.4 on page 454 shows the 1996 provincial tax rates. If you were a resident of Newfoundland earning $70 000 as in the above example, you would pay $13 006.41 to the federal government and an additional $8975, which the federal government collects and gives to the government of Newfoundland. The average combined federal–provincial effective tax rate is then 31.4% and the combined marginal tax rate is 49%.

To complicate things further the federal government and all the provinces have introduced surtaxes. The federal government surtaxes (a tax on a tax) involve (1) taking 3% of the federal tax owed and adding this onto the final tax bill; and

Table 18.3	Tax Calculations for a Single Taxpayer Earning $70 000 in 1997	
A. Total income		$70 000
− Deductions		5 000
B. = Taxable income		$65 000
Tax Calculation		
$0–$29 590 (i.e., $29 590 × 0.17)		$5 030.30
$29 591–$59 180 (i.e., [$59 180 − $29 591] = $29 589 × 0.26)		$7 693.14
$59 181–$65 000 (i.e., [$65 000 − $59 181] = $5819 × 0.29)		$1 687.51
C. Federal tax =		$14 410.95
Tax Credit Calculation		
Basic personal amount		$6 456.00
CPP contributions		$806.00
EI contributions		$1 000.00
Total eligible for credit		$8 262.00
D. Credit (17% of eligible amount)		$1 404.54
Federal tax owed (C − D)		$13 006.41
Average tax rate = $13 006.41/$70 000		19.0%
Marginal tax rate		29.0%

Table 18.4

Provincial Tax Rates, 1996

Province	Basic Rate (as a % of federal tax payable)
Newfoundland	69.0%
Prince Edward Island	59.5%
Nova Scotia	59.5%
New Brunswick	64.0%
Ontario	56.0%
Manitoba	52.0%
Saskatchewan	50.0%
Alberta	45.5%
British Columbia	52.0%

Quebec administers its own tax system. The rate structure for 1996 was as follows:

Taxable Income	Tax Rate
0–$7000	16.0%
$7001–$14 000	19.0%
$14 001–$23 000	21.0%
$23 001–$50 000	23.0%
Over $50 000	24.0%

Source: Revenue Canada

benefits-received principle *A theory of fairness that holds that taxpayers should contribute to government (in the form of taxes) in proportion to the benefits that they receive from public expenditures.*

ability-to-pay principle *A theory of taxation that holds that citizens should bear tax burdens in line with their ability to pay taxes.*

(2) if federal tax before the addition of the surtax exceeds $12 500 an additional 5% surtax is applied to the basic federal tax in excess of $12 500. If you earned $70 000, as in our example, you face a surtax of 3% on your tax payable of $13 006.41 ($390.19) plus a tax of 5% on the $506.41 in excess of $12 500 ($25.32) for a total surtax of $415.51. An estimate of the marginal tax rates facing those paying the highest marginal rate in each province is presented in Table 18.5. The calculations in this table assume a single taxpayer earning only wage and salary income with only personal, CPP, and EI tax credits.

TAX EQUITY

One of the criteria for evaluating the economy that we defined in Chapter 1 (and returned to in Chapter 17) was fairness, or *equity*. Everyone agrees that tax burdens should be distributed fairly, that all of us should pay our "fair share" of taxes, but there is endless debate about what constitutes a fair tax system.

One theory of fairness is called the **benefits-received principle.** Dating back to the eighteenth-century economist Adam Smith and earlier writers, the benefits-received principle holds that taxpayers should contribute to government according to the benefits that they derive from public expenditures. This principle ties the tax side of the fiscal equation to the expenditure side. For example, automobile users pay gasoline excise taxes, and the tax revenue is in turn used to build and maintain highway systems. The beneficiaries of public highways are thus taxed in rough proportion to their use of those highways.

The difficulty with applying the benefits principle is that the bulk of public expenditures are for public goods—national defence, for example. The benefits of public goods fall collectively on all members of society, and there is no way to determine what value individual taxpayers receive from them.

A different principle, and one that has dominated the formulation of tax policy in Canada for decades, is the **ability-to-pay principle.** This principle holds that taxpayers should bear tax burdens in line with their ability to pay. Here the tax side of the fiscal equation is viewed separately from the expenditure side. Under this system, the problem of attributing the benefits of public expenditures to specific taxpayers or groups of taxpayers is avoided.

■ **Horizontal and Vertical Equity** If we accept the idea that ability to pay should be the basis for the distribution of tax burdens, two principles follow. First, the principle of *horizontal equity* holds that those with equal ability to pay should bear

Table 18.5

Highest Marginal Income Tax Rates: Combined Federal and Provincial Taxes, 1996

Province	Combined Marginal Rate	Approximate Income Level at Which Highest Rate Is Reached
Newfoundland	53.3%	$63 000
Prince Edward Island	50.3%	$93 000
Nova Scotia	50.3%	$78 000
New Brunswick	51.3%	$93 000
Ontario	52.6%	$67 000
Manitoba	50.4%	$63 000
Saskatchewan	52.0%	$63 000
Alberta	46.0%	$63 000
British Columbia	54.0%	$80 000

Source: Authors' Calculations

equal tax burdens. Second, the principle of *vertical equity* holds that those with greater ability to pay should pay more.

Although these notions seem appealing, we must have answers to two interdependent questions before they can be meaningful. First, how is ability to pay measured? What is the "best" tax base? Second, if A has a greater ability to pay than B, *how much* more should A contribute?

WHAT IS THE "BEST" TAX BASE?

The three leading candidates for best tax base are *income, consumption,* and *wealth.* Before we debate the merits of each as a basis for taxation, however, let us review the meanings of these terms.

Income—or, to be precise, *economic income*—is anything that enhances one's ability to command resources. The most used technical definition of economic income is the value of what one consumes plus any change in the value of what one owns:

> Economic Income = Consumption + Change in Net Worth

This broad definition includes many items that are not counted by Revenue Canada in its definition of "income." For example, the broad definition includes the value of benefits not received in money form, such as medical benefits, employer pension plan contributions, paid country club memberships, and so forth. Increases or decreases in the value of stocks or bonds, whether or not they are "realized" through sale, are part of economic income. For income tax purposes, capital gains count as income only when they are realized, but for purposes of defining economic income, all increases in asset values count, whether they are realized or not.

A few other items that we do not usually think of as income are included in a comprehensive definition of income. If I own my house outright and live in it rent free, income flows from my house just as interest flows from a bond or profit from a share of stock. By owning the house, I enjoy valuable housing benefits that I would otherwise have to pay rent for. I am my own landlord and I am, in essence, earning my own rent. Other components of economic income include any gifts and bequests received and food grown at home.

The point here is that:

> In economic terms, income is income, regardless of source and regardless of use.

Consumption is the total value of things that a household consumes in a given period. It is equal to income minus saving, or:

> Consumption = Income − Saving (change in net worth)

Wealth, or *net worth,* is simply the value of all the things that one owns after one's liabilities are subtracted. If you were to sell off today everything of value that you own—stocks, bonds, houses, cars, and so forth—at their current market prices and pay off all your debts—loans, mortgages, and so forth—you would end up with your net worth. In other words:

> Net Worth = Assets − Liabilities

Remember, income and consumption are flow measures. We must speak of income per month or per year. Wealth and net worth are stock measures taken at a point in time.

For years, conventional wisdom among economists held that income was the best measure of ability to pay taxes. Many who feel that consumption is a better measure have recently challenged that assumption. The following arguments are not just arguments about fairness and ability to pay; they are also arguments about the best base for taxation.

Be careful to remember as you proceed that the issue under debate is which *base* is the best base, not which *tax* is the best tax or whether taxes ought to be progressive or regressive. While sales taxes are regressive, it is possible to have a personal consumption tax that is progressive. Under such a system, individuals would simply report their income as they do now, but all documented saving would be deductible. The difference between income and saving is a measure of personal consumption that could be taxed with progressive rates.

■ **Consumption as the Best Tax Base** The view favouring consumption as the best tax base dates back at least to the seventeenth-century English philosopher Thomas Hobbes, who argued that people should pay taxes in accordance with "what they actually take out of the common pot, not what they leave in." The standard of living, the argument goes, depends not on income but on how much income is spent. If we want to redistribute well-being, therefore, the tax base should be consumption, because consumption is the best measure of well-being.

A second argument with a distinguished history dates back to work done by Irving Fisher in the early part of this century. Fisher and many others have argued that a tax on income discourages saving by taxing savings twice. A story told originally by Fisher illustrates this theory quite nicely.[2]

Suppose that Alex builds a house for Frank. For this service, Alex is paid $10 000 and given an orchard containing 100 apple trees. Alex spends the $10 000 today, but he saves the orchard, and presumably he will consume or sell the fruit it bears every year in the future. Suppose that at year's end the province levies a 10% tax on Alex's total income, which includes the $10 000 and the orchard. First, the government takes 10% of the $10 000, which is 10% of Alex's consumption. Second, it takes 10% of the orchard—10 trees—which is 10% of Alex's saving. If this is all the government did, there would be no double taxation of saving. If, however, the income tax is also levied in the following year, Alex will be taxed on the income generated by the 90 trees that he still owns. If the income tax is levied in the year after that, Alex will again be taxed on the income generated by his orchard, and so on. The income tax is thus taxing Alex's saving more than once. It taxes the initial saving *plus* all the future income generated from the saving. To avoid the double taxation of saving, either the original saving of 100 trees should not be taxed or the income generated from the after-tax number of trees (90) should not be taxed.

The same logic can be applied to cash saving. Suppose that the income tax rate is 25% and that you earn $20 000. Out of the $20 000 you consume $16 000 and save $4000. At the end of the year, you owe the government 25% of your total income, or $5000. You can think of this as a tax of 25% on consumption ($4000) and 25% on savings ($1000). Why, then, do we say that the income tax is a double tax on saving? To understand the argument you have to think about the $4000 that is saved.

[2]*Irving Fisher and Herbert Fisher,* Constructive Income Taxation: A Proposal for Reform *(New York: Harper, 1942), Ch. 8, p. 56.*

If you save $4000, you will no doubt put it to some use. Safe possibilities include putting it in an interest-bearing account or buying a bond with it. If you do either of these, you will earn interest that you can consume in future years. In fact, when we save and earn interest we are spreading some of our present earnings over future years of consumption. Just as the orchard yields future fruit, so the bond yields future interest, which is considered income in the year it is earned and is taxed as such. The only way that you can earn that future interest income is if you leave your money tied up in the bond or the account. You can consume the $4000 today *or* you can have the future flow of interest; you can't have both. Yet both are taxed.

Suppose that the interest rate is 10%. If you save $4000 and put that money into a long-term bond that pays 10% annual interest, you have converted your $4000 into an additional income flow of $400 per year. That flow will be taxed at 25%, or $100 per year. Thus, your saving is taxed both when you earn it *and* as you consume it in the future. Many people think this is unfair.

It is also inefficient. As you will see in more detail later, a tax that distorts economic choices creates *excess burdens*. By double taxing saving, an income tax distorts the choice between consumption and saving, which is really the choice between present consumption and future consumption. Double taxing may also tend to reduce the saving rate and the rate of investment—and ultimately the rate of economic growth.

■ **Income as the Best Tax Base**   Your ability to pay is your ability to command resources, and many argue that your income is the best measure of your capacity to command resources today. According to proponents of income as a tax base, you should be taxed not on what you actually draw out of the common pot, but rather on the basis of your *ability* to draw from that pot. In other words, your decision to save or consume is no different from your decision to buy apples, to go out for dinner, or to give money to your mother. It is your *income* that enables you to do all these things, and it is income that should be taxed, regardless of its sources and regardless of how you use it. Saving is just another use of income.

If income is the best measure of ability to pay, the double taxation argument doesn't hold water. An income tax taxes savings twice only if consumption is the measure used to gauge a person's ability to pay. It does not do so if income is the measure used. Acquisition of the orchard enhances your ability to pay today; a bountiful crop of fruit enhances your ability to pay when it is produced. Interest income is no different than any other form of income; it too enhances your ability to pay. Taxing both is thus fair.

■ **Wealth as the Best Tax Base**   Still others argue that the real power to command resources comes not from any single year's income but from accumulated wealth. Aggregate net worth in Canada is many times larger than aggregate income.

If two people have identical annual incomes of $10 000, but one also has an accumulated net worth of $1 million, is it reasonable to argue that these two people have the same ability to pay, or that they should pay equal taxes? Most people would answer no. Those who favour income taxation, however, argue that net wealth comes from after-tax income that has been saved. An income tax taxes consumption and saving correctly, they say. To subsequently take part of what has been saved would be an unfair second hit—*real* double taxation.

Those who favour wealth as the best tax base argue that a person's real power to command resources comes from accumulated wealth, not any single year's income. Those who oppose it argue that a tax based on accumulated wealth would result in double taxation.

■ **No Simple Answer** As you can see, the "best-base" debate has a number of sides. Before the 1970s, most tax economists favoured a comprehensive income base. Today, many economists favour a comprehensive personal consumption tax. Part of the reason for the increasing popularity of consumption taxes is a growing concern with the falling saving rate in Canada in recent years. There have been concerns about productivity growth in Canada, as in many other countries, and many point to the inadequacy of saving as the culprit. As we saw in earlier chapters, household saving provides resources for firms to invest in capital that raises the productivity of labour.

The Canadian tax system reflects the debate between the advocates of a consumption base and an income base. Although the most important tax in the Canadian tax system—personal income tax—suggests, by name at least, that it is an income tax, the tax base is actually a hybrid of consumption and income. Certain types of saving are given special treatment in the Canadian income tax system. If a proportion of income (up to a maximum specified in the tax legislation) is placed in a Registered Retirement Savings Plan (RRSP), it is exempt from tax. One can also exempt a proportion of income by saving through a Registered Education Savings Plan (RESP). Income is not income, regardless of use, in the Canadian tax system. Income that is saved gets special treatment, but not all saving is exempt from tax as is the case under a consumption tax base.

The expansion of the federal sales tax in 1991 (renamed the Goods and Services Tax [GST] at that time), also reflects increasing interest in taxing consumption rather than income. Higher income tax rates might have been an alternative, but the Canadian government chose to increase consumption taxation instead.

Tax Incidence: Who Pays?

When a government levies a tax, it writes a law assigning responsibility for payment to specific people or specific organizations. To understand a tax, however, we must look beyond those named in the law as the initial taxpayers.

First, remember the cardinal principle of tax analysis: the burden of a tax is ultimately borne by individuals or households; institutions have no real taxpaying capacity. Second, the burden of a tax is not always borne by those initially responsible for paying it. Directly or indirectly, tax burdens are often *shifted* to others. When we speak of the **incidence of a tax,** we are referring to the ultimate distribution of its burden.

tax incidence *The ultimate distribution of a tax's burden.*

The simultaneous reactions of many households and/or firms to the presence of a tax may cause relative prices to change, and price changes affect households' well-being. Households may feel the impact of a tax on the sources side or on the uses side of the income equation. (We use the term *income equation* because the amount of income from all *sources* must be exactly equal to the amount of income allocated to all *uses*—including saving—in a given period.) On the **sources side,** a household is hurt if the net wages or profits that it receives fall; on the **uses side,** a household is hurt if the prices of the things that it buys rise. If your wages remain the same but the price of every item that you buy doubles, you are in the same position you would have been in if your wages had been cut by 50% and prices hadn't changed. In short:

sources side/uses side *The impact of a tax may be felt on one or the other or on both sides of the income equation. A tax may cause net income to fall (damage on the sources side), or it may cause prices of goods and services to rise so that income buys less (damage on the uses side).*

> The imposition of a tax or a change in a tax can change behaviour. Changes in behaviour can affect supply and demand in markets and cause prices to change. When prices change in input or output markets, some households are made better off and some are made worse off. These final changes determine the ultimate burden of the tax.

Tax shifting takes place when households can alter their behaviour and do something to avoid paying a tax. This is especially easily accomplished when only certain items are singled out for taxation. For example, suppose a heavy tax were levied on bananas. Initially the tax would make the price of bananas much higher, but there are many potential substitutes for bananas. Consumers can avoid the tax by not buying bananas, and that is exactly what many of them will do. But, as demand drops, the market price of bananas falls and banana growers lose money. Thus, the tax shifts from consumers to the growers, at least in the short run.

A tax such as the retail sales tax, which is levied at the same rate on *all* consumer goods, is harder to avoid. The only thing that consumers can do to avoid such a tax is to consume less of everything. If consumers do so, saving will increase, but otherwise there are few opportunities for tax avoidance and therefore for tax shifting. The general principle here is that:

> Broad-based taxes are less likely to be shifted and more likely to "stick" where they are levied than "partial taxes" are.

tax shifting *Occurs when households can alter their behaviour and do something to avoid paying a tax.*

THE INCIDENCE OF PAYROLL TAXES

In 1995 over 15% of federal revenues came from social insurance taxes, also called "payroll taxes." The revenues from the various payroll taxes go to support the Canada Pension Plan, Employment Insurance, and other health and disability benefits for workers. Some of these taxes are levied on employers as a percentage of payroll, and some are levied on workers as a percentage of wages or salaries earned.

To analyze the payroll tax, let us take a tax of $\$T$ per unit of labour levied on employers and briefly sketch the reactions that are likely to follow. When the tax is first levied, firms find that the price of labour is higher. Before the tax was levied, they paid $\$W$ per hour; now they must pay $\$W + \$T$. Firms may react in two ways. First, they may substitute capital for the now more expensive labour. Second, higher costs and lower profits may lead to a cut in production. Both reactions mean a lower demand for labour. Lower demand for labour, in turn, reduces wages, and part of the tax is thus passed on (or *shifted to*) the workers, who end up earning less. The extent to which the tax is shifted to workers depends on how workers react to the lower wages.

We can develop a more formal analysis of this situation with a picture of the market before the tax is levied. Figure 18.1 on page 460 shows equilibrium in a hypothetical labour market with no payroll tax. Before we proceed, however, we should review the factors that determine the shapes of the supply and demand curves.

■ Labour Supply and Labour Demand Curves in Perfect Competition: A Review
Recall that the demand for labour in competitive markets depends on its productivity. As you saw in Chapter 10, a competitive, profit-maximizing firm will hire labour up to the point at which the market wage is equal to labour's marginal revenue product. The shape of the demand curve for labour shows how responsive *firms* are to changes in wages. Several factors determine a firm's reactions to changes in wage rates: how easy it is to substitute capital for labour, whether labour costs are large or small relative to total costs, and how elastic the demand for the firm's product is.[3]

The shape of the labour supply curve shows how responsive *workers* are to changes in wages. As you saw in Chapter 6, lower wages may affect workers' be-

---

[3]*If demand for output is highly inelastic, increases in costs from a rise in wages generally flow through to consumers in the form of higher prices.*

FIGURE 18.1

Equilibrium in a Competitive Labour Market—No Taxes

With no taxes on wages, the wage that firms pay is the same as the wage that workers take home. At a wage of W_0, the quantity of labour supplied and the quantity of labour demanded are equal.

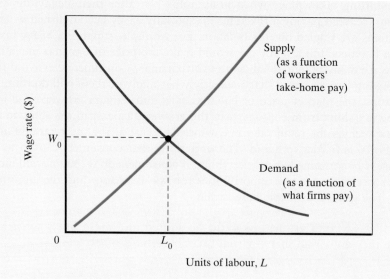

haviour in two ways. First, lower wages mean that workers will earn less income for the same amount of effort. They will therefore be able to buy fewer goods and services. They will also buy less leisure by working more. This is the *income effect* of a decrease in wages.

Second, a lower wage means that leisure is less expensive relative to other goods—an additional hour of leisure means an hour of lost wages, and wages are now lower. Workers "substitute" leisure for other goods by working less and buying less of other goods with the lower income. This is the *substitution effect* of a decrease in wages. An upward-sloping labour supply curve means that, on balance, the substitution effect is stronger than the income effect, and that lower wages lead to less work effort. If the opposite were true, the labour supply curve would bend back.[4]

In either case, the labour supply curve represents the reaction of workers to changes in the wage rate. Their behaviour depends on the *after-tax* wage that they actually take home per hour of work. In contrast, labour demand is a function of the full amount that firms must pay per unit of labour, an amount that may include a tax if it is levied directly on payroll, as it is in our example. Such a tax, when present, drives a "wedge" between the price of labour that firms face and take-home wages.

■ **Imposing a Payroll Tax: Who Pays?** In Figure 18.1, there were no taxes, and the wage that firms paid was the same as the wage that workers took home. At a wage of W_0, quantity of labour supplied and quantity of labour demanded were equal, and the labour market was in equilibrium.[5]

But now suppose that employers must pay a tax of $T per unit of labour. Figure 18.2 on page 462 shows a new supply curve that is parallel to the old supply curve but above it by a distance, T. The new curve, S', shows labour supply as a function of what firms pay. Regardless of how the ultimate burden of the tax is

---

[4]*Evidence regarding the relative size of the income and substitution effects is presented in Chapter 19. For more on the backward-bending supply curve, see Figure 6.11 and the accompanying discussion.*
[5]*Although the supply curve has a positive slope, that slope implies nothing about the actual shape of the labour supply curve in Canada. Empirical estimates of supply elasticities are treated more fully in Chapter 19.*

shared, there is a difference between what firms pay and what workers take home.

If the initial wage is W_0 per hour, firms will face a price of $W_0 + T$ per unit of labour immediately after the tax is levied. Workers still receive only W_0, however. The higher wage rate—that is, the higher price of labour that firms now face—reduces the quantity of labour demanded from L_0 to L_d, and the firms lay off workers. Workers initially still receive W_0, so that amount of labour supplied does not change, and the result is an excess supply of labour equal to $(L_0 - L_d)$.

The excess supply applies downward pressure to the market wage, and wages fall, thus shifting some of the tax burden on to workers. The issue, of course, is: how far will wages fall? Figure 18.2 shows that a new equilibrium is achieved at W_1, with firms paying $W_1 + T$. When workers take home W_1, they will supply L_1 units of labour; if firms must pay $W_1 + T$, they will demand L_1 units of labour, and the market clears.

In this case, then, the burden of the payroll tax is shared by employers and employees. Initially, firms paid W_0; after the tax, they pay $W_1 + T$. Initially, workers received W_0; after the tax, they end up with the lower wage W_1. Total tax collections by the government are equal to $T \times L_1$; geometrically, they are equal to the entire shaded area in Figure 18.2. The workers' share of the tax burden is the lower portion, $(W_0 - W_1) \times L_1$. The firms' share is the upper portion, $[(W_1 + T) - W_0] \times L_1$.

The relative sizes of the firms' share and the workers' share of the total tax burden depend on the shapes of the demand and supply curves. Look at Figure 18.2 and try to imagine what would happen to the size of the workers' shaded rectangle if the supply curve became steeper (more vertical). A more vertical supply curve means that the quantity of labour supplied is relatively inelastic—it does not change very much when net wages change. A more vertical supply curve would mean that the lower shaded rectangle (the workers' share) would be larger and the upper shaded rectangle (the firms' share) would be smaller. A more elastic (horizontal) supply curve would mean that the lower shaded rectangle (workers' share) would be smaller and the upper shaded rectangle (firms' share) would be larger.

Thus:

Workers bear the bulk of the burden of a payroll tax if labour supply is relatively inelastic, and firms bear the bulk of the burden of a payroll tax if labour supply is relatively elastic.

Empirical studies of labour supply behaviour in Canada suggest that for most of the workforce, the elasticity of labour supply is close to zero. This leads to the conclusion that:

Most of the payroll tax in Canada is probably borne by workers.

The result would be exactly the same if the tax were initially levied on workers rather than on firms. Suppose we go back to the equilibrium in Figure 18.2, with wages at W_0. But now assume the tax of $\$T$ per hour is levied on workers rather than firms. The burden will end up being shared by firms and workers in the *exact same proportions*. Initially, take-home wages will fall to $W_0 - T$. Workers will supply less labour, creating excess demand and pushing market wages up. That shifts part of the burden back to employers. The "story" is different, but the result is the same.

Table 18.6 on page 462 presents an estimate of the incidence of payroll taxes in Canada in 1988. This estimate assumes that both the employers' share and employees' share of the payroll taxes are ultimately *borne by employees.*

FIGURE 18.2

Incidence of a Per Unit Payroll Tax in a Competitive Labour Market

With a tax on firms of $T per unit of labour hired, the market will adjust, shifting the tax partially to workers. When the tax is levied, firms must at first pay $W_0 + T$. This reduces labour demand to L_d. The result is excess supply, which pushes wages down to W_1 and passes some of the burden of the tax on to workers.

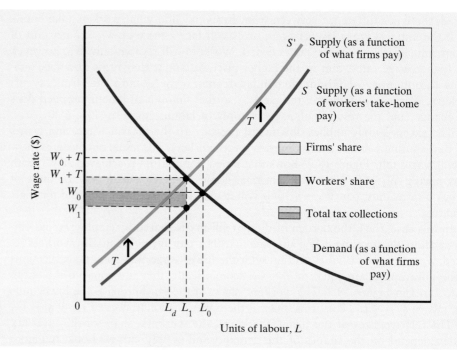

Table 18.6

Estimated Incidence of Payroll Taxes in Canada, 1988

Income	Tax as a % of Income
Less than $10 000	2.0
$10 000–$20 000	3.8
$20 000–$30 000	5.0
$30 000–$40 000	6.0
$40 000–$50 000	6.2
$50 000–$60 000	6.4
$60 000–$70 000	6.1
$70 000–$80 000	6.0
$80 000–$90 000	5.9
$90 000–$100 000	5.7
$100 000–$150 000	5.0
$150 000–$300 000	2.5
Over $300 000	1.0

Source: Frank Vermaeten, W. Irwin Gillespie, and Arndt Vermaeten, "Tax Incidence in Canada," *Canadian Tax Journal* vol. 42, no. 2 (1994): pp. 348–416.

The payroll tax is regressive for two reasons. First, both CPP and EI contributions are made on earnings only, up to a specified maximum. Second, wages and salaries fall as a percentage of total income as we move up the income scale. Those with higher incomes earn a larger portion of their incomes from profits, dividends, rents, and so forth, and these kinds of income are not subject to the payroll tax.

Some economists dispute the conclusion that the payroll tax is borne entirely by wage earners. Even if labour supply is inelastic, some wages are set in the process of collective bargaining between unions and large firms. If the payroll tax results in a higher gross wage in the bargaining process, firms may find themselves faced with higher costs. Higher costs, in turn, either reduce profits to owners or are passed on to consumers in the form of higher product prices.

THE INCIDENCE OF CORPORATE PROFITS TAXES

Another tax that requires careful analysis is the corporate profits tax that is levied by the federal government, as well as by all provinces. The *corporate profits tax* or *corporate income tax,* is a tax on the profits of firms that are organized as corporations. The owners of partnerships and proprietorships do not pay this tax; rather, they report their firms' income directly on their individual income tax returns.

Thus, we can think of the corporate tax as a tax on *capital income,* or profits, in one sector of the economy. For the sake of simplicity we will assume that there are only two sectors of the economy, corporate and noncorporate, and only two factors of production, labour and capital. Owners of capital receive profits, and workers (labour) are paid a wage.

Like the payroll tax, the corporate tax may affect households on the sources or the uses side of the income equation. The tax may affect profits earned by owners of capital, wages earned by workers, or prices of corporate and noncorporate products. Once again, the key question is how large these changes are likely to be.

When first imposed, the corporate profits tax initially reduces net (after-tax) profits in the corporate sector. Assuming that the economy was in long-run equilibrium before the tax was levied, firms in both the corporate and noncorporate sectors were earning a *normal rate of return;* there was no reason to expect higher profits in one sector than in the other. All of a sudden, firms in the corporate sector become significantly less profitable as a result of the tax.

In response to these lower profits, capital investment begins to favour the nontaxed sector because after-tax profits are higher there. Firms in the taxed sector contract in size or (in some cases) go out of business, while firms in the nontaxed sector expand and new firms enter its various industries. As this happens, the flow of capital from the taxed to the nontaxed sector reduces the profit rate in the nontaxed sector: more competition springs up, and product prices are driven down. Some of the tax burden now shifts to capital income earners in the noncorporate sector, who end up earning lower profits.

As capital flows out of the corporate sector in response to lower after-tax profits, the profit rate in that sector rises somewhat because fewer firms means less supply, which means higher prices, and so forth. Presumably, capital will continue to favour the nontaxed sector until the after-tax profit rates in the two sectors are equal. Thus, even though the tax is imposed on just one sector, it eventually depresses profits in all sectors equally.

Under these circumstances, the products of corporations will probably become more expensive and products of proprietorships and partnerships will probably become less expensive. But because almost everyone buys both corporate and noncorporate products, these *excise effects* (that is, effects on the prices of products) are likely to have a minimal impact on the distribution of the tax burden; in essence, the price increases in the corporate sector and the price decreases in the noncorporate sector cancel each other out.

Finally, what effect does the imposition of a corporate income tax have on labour? Wages could actually rise or fall, but the effect is not likely to be large. Taxed firms will have an incentive to substitute labour for capital because capital income is now taxed. This could benefit labour by driving up wages. In addition, the contracting sector will use less labour *and* capital, but if the taxed sector is capital-intensive, the bulk of the effect will be felt by capital; its price will fall more than the price of labour.

■ **The Burden of the Corporate Tax**   The ultimate burden of the corporate tax appears to depend on several factors: the relative capital/labour intensity of the two sectors, the ease with which capital and labour can be substituted in the two sectors, and elasticities of demand for the products of each sector. In 1962, Arnold Harberger of the University of Chicago analyzed this problem rigorously and concluded that:

> Owners of corporations, proprietorships, and partnerships all bear the burden of the corporate tax in rough proportion to profits, even though it is directly levied only on corporations.

He also found that wage effects of the corporate tax were small and that excise effects, as we noted above, probably cancel each other out.[6]

Although most economists accept Harberger's view of the corporate tax, there are arguments against it. For example, a profits tax on a monopoly firm earning above-normal profits is *not* shifted to other sectors unless the tax drives profits below the competitive level.

---

[6]*Arnold Harberger, "The Incidence of the Corporate Income Tax,"* Journal of Political Economy *vol. LXX (June 1962).*

Table 18.7

Estimated Incidence of Corporate Income Taxes in Canada, 1988

Income	Tax as a % of Income
Less than $10 000	0.05
$10 000–$20 000	0.06
$20 000–$30 000	0.07
$30 000–$40 000	0.07
$40 000–$50 000	0.07
$50 000–$60 000	0.07
$60 000–$70 000	0.07
$70 000–$80 000	0.07
$80 000–$90 000	0.07
$90 000–$100 000	0.07
$100 000–$150 000	0.07
$150 000–$300 000	4.0
Over $300 000	12.0

Source: Frank Vermaeten, W. Irwin Gillespie, and Arndt Vermaeten, "Tax Incidence in Canada," *Canadian Tax Journal* vol. 42, no. 2 (1994): pp. 348–416.

You might be tempted to conclude that because monopolists can control market price, they will simply pass on the profits tax in higher prices to consumers of monopoly products. But theory predicts just the opposite: that the tax burden will remain with the monopolist.

Remember that monopolists are constrained by market demand. That is, they choose the combination of price and output that is consistent with market demand and that maximizes profit. If a proportion of that profit is taxed, the choice of price and quantity will not change. Why not? Quite simply, if you behave so as to maximize profit, and then I come and take half of your profit, you maximize your half by maximizing the whole, which is exactly what you would do in the absence of the tax. Thus, your price and output do not change, the tax is not shifted, and you end up paying the tax. In the long run, capital will not leave the taxed monopoly sector, as it did in the competitive case. Even with the tax, the monopolist is earning higher profits than are possible elsewhere.

The great debate about whom the corporate tax hurts illustrates the advantage of broad-based direct taxes over narrow-based indirect taxes. Because it is levied on an institution, the corporate tax is indirect, and therefore it is always shifted. Furthermore, it taxes only one factor (capital) in only one part of the economy (the corporate sector). The income tax, in contrast, taxes all forms of income in all sectors of the economy, and it is virtually impossible to shift. It is difficult to argue that a tax is a good tax if we can't be sure who ultimately ends up paying it.

Table 18.7 presents an estimate of the actual incidence of the Canadian corporate income tax in 1988. The burden of the corporate income tax is clearly progressive, because profits and capital income make up a much bigger part of the incomes of high-income households.

THE OVERALL INCIDENCE OF TAXES IN CANADA: EMPIRICAL EVIDENCE

A complete treatment of tax incidence, one that includes an analysis of each individual tax, would take more space than we have here. Many researchers have done complete analyses under varying assumptions about incidence, and in most cases their results are similar:

> Provincial and local taxes (with sales taxes playing a big role) seem as a group to be mildly regressive. Federal taxes, dominated by the personal income tax but increasingly affected by the regressive payroll tax, are mildly progressive. The overall system is mildly progressive.

Excess Burdens and the Principle of Neutrality

You have seen that when households and firms make decisions in the presence of a tax that differ from those they would make in its absence, the burden of the tax can be shifted from those for whom it was originally intended. Now we can take the same logic one step further:

> When taxes distort economic decisions, they impose burdens on society that in aggregate exceed the revenue collected by the government.

excess burden *The amount by which the burden of a tax exceeds the total revenue collected. Also called* dead weight losses.

The amount by which the burden of a tax exceeds the revenue collected by the government is called the **excess burden** of the tax. The *total burden* of a tax is the sum of the revenue collected from the tax and the excess burden created by the tax. Because excess burdens are a form of waste, or lost value, tax policy should be written with an eye toward minimizing them. (Excess burdens are also sometimes called *dead weight losses.*)

The size of the excess burden imposed by a tax depends on the extent to which economic decisions are distorted. Thus, the general principle that emerges from the analysis of excess burdens is the **principle of neutrality.** That is,

principle of neutrality *All else equal, taxes that are neutral with respect to economic decisions (that is, taxes that do not distort economic decisions) are generally preferable to taxes that distort economic decisions. Taxes that are not neutral impose excess burdens.*

> *Ceteris paribus* or all else equal,[7] a tax that is neutral with respect to economic decisions is preferred to one that distorts economic decisions.

In practice, all taxes change behaviour and distort economic choices. A product-specific excise tax raises the price of the taxed item, and people can avoid the tax by buying substitutes. An income tax distorts the choice between present and future consumption and between work and leisure. The corporate tax influences investment and production decisions—investment is diverted away from the corporate sector, and firms may be induced to substitute labour for capital.

How Do Excess Burdens Arise?

The idea that a tax can impose an extra cost, or excess burden, by distorting choices can be illustrated by a simple numerical example. Consider a competitive industry that produces an output, *X*, using the technology shown in Figure 18.3. Using technology A, firms can produce one unit of output with seven units of capital (*K*) and three units of labour (*L*). Using technology B, the production of one unit of output requires four units of capital and seven units of labour. A is thus the more capital-intensive technology.

If we assume that labour and capital each cost $2 per unit, it costs $20 to produce each unit of output with technology A and $22 with technology B. Thus, firms will choose technology A. Because we assume competition, output price will be driven to cost of production, and the price of output will in the long run be driven to $20 per unit.

Now let us narrow our focus to the distortion of technology choice that is brought about by the imposition of a tax. We assume that demand for the good in question is perfectly inelastic at 1000 units of output. That is, regardless of price, households will buy 1000 units of product. A price of $20 per unit means consumers pay a total of $20 000 for 1000 units of *X*.

Now suppose that the government comes along and levies a tax of 50% on capital. This has the effect of raising the price of capital, P_K, to $3. Figure 18.4 shows what would happen to the unit cost of production after the tax is imposed. With capital now more expensive, the firm switches to the more labour-intensive

	Input requirements per unit of output *X*		Per unit cost of *X* $= K(P_K) + L(P_L)$	
Technology	*K*	*L*	$P_K = \$2$, $P_L = \$2$	
A	7	3	$20	Least cost
B	4	7	$22	

FIGURE 18.3

Firms Choose the Technology That Minimizes the Cost of Production

If the industry is competitive, long-run equilibrium price will be $20 per unit of *X*. If 1000 units of *X* are sold, consumers will pay a total of $20 000 for *X*.

[7]*The phrase* ceteris paribus *(all else equal) is important. In judging the merits of a tax or a change in tax policy, the degree of neutrality is only one criterion among many, and it often comes into conflict with others. For example, tax A may impose a larger excess burden than tax B, but society may deem B more equitable.*

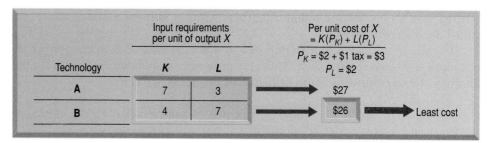

Technology	Input requirements per unit of output X		Per unit cost of X $= K(P_K) + L(P_L)$ $P_K = \$2 + \$1 \text{ tax} = \$3$ $P_L = \$2$
	K	L	
A	7	3	$27
B	4	7	$26 → Least cost

FIGURE 18.4

Imposition of a Tax on Capital Distorts the Choice of Technology

If the industry is competitive, price will be $26 per unit of X when a tax of $1 per unit of capital is imposed. If technology B is used, and if we assume that total sales remain at 1000 units, total tax collections will be 1000 × 4 × $1 = $4000. But consumers will pay a total of $26 000 for the good—$6000 more than before the tax. Thus, there is an excess burden of $2000.

technology B. With the tax in place, X can be produced at a unit cost of $27 per unit using technology A but for $26 per unit using technology B.

If we assume that demand is inelastic, buyers continue to buy 1000 units of X regardless of its price. (We shall ignore any distortions of consumer choices that might result from the imposition of the tax.) Recall that the tax is 50%, or $1 per unit of capital used. Because it takes four units of capital to produce each unit of output, firms—which are now using technology B—will pay a total tax to the government of $4 per unit of output produced. With 1000 units of output produced and sold, total tax collections amount to $4000.

But if you look carefully, you will see that the burden of the tax exceeds $4000. After the tax, consumers will be paying $26 per unit for the good. Twenty-six dollars is now the unit cost of producing the good using the best available technology in the presence of the capital tax. Thus, consumers will pay $26 000 for 1000 units of the good. This represents an increase of $6000 over the previous total of $20 000. The revenue raised from the tax is $4000, but its total burden is $6000. Thus, there is an *excess burden* of $2000.

How did this excess burden arise? Look back at Figure 18.3. You can see that technology B is less efficient than technology A (unit costs of production are $2 higher per unit using technology B). But the tax on capital has caused firms to switch to this less efficient, labour-intensive mode of production. The result is a waste of $2 per unit of output. The total burden of the tax is equal to the revenue collected plus the loss due to the wasteful choice of technology, and the excess burden is $2 per unit times 1000 units, or $2000.

The same principle holds for taxes that distort consumption decisions. Suppose that I prefer to consume bundle X to bundle Y when there is no tax but choose bundle Y when there is a tax in place. Not only do I pay the tax, I also end up with a bundle of goods that is worth less than the bundle I would have chosen had the tax not been levied. Again, we have the burden of an extra cost.

In general:

> The larger the distortion that a tax causes in behaviour, the larger the excess burden of the tax. Taxes levied on broad bases tend to distort choices less and impose smaller excess burdens than taxes on more sharply defined bases.

This follows from our discussion earlier in this chapter: the more partial the tax, the easier it is to avoid. An important part of the logic behind proposals for a "flat tax" is that a broader base and a lower rate reduce the distorting effects of the tax system and minimize excess burdens. For a discussion of recent "flat tax" proposals, see the Issues and Controversies box on pages 468–469 titled "Progressivity: Should the Tax System Redistribute Income?"

THE PRINCIPLE OF SECOND BEST

Now that we have established the connection between taxes that distort decisions and excess burdens, we can add more complexity to our earlier discussions. Although it may seem that distorting taxes always create excess burdens, this is not necessarily the case. In fact, a distorting tax is sometimes actually desirable when other distortions already exist in the economy. This is called the **principle of second best**.

> At least two kinds of circumstances favour nonneutral (that is, distorting) taxes: the presence of externalities and the presence of other distorting taxes.

principle of second best *The fact that a tax distorts an economic decision does not always imply that such a tax imposes an excess burden. If previously existing distortions exist, such a tax may actually improve efficiency.*

We already examined externalities at some length in Chapter 16. If some activity by a firm or household imposes costs on society that are not considered by decision makers, then firms and households are likely to make economically inefficient choices. Pollution is the classic example of an externality, but there are thousands of others. An efficient allocation of resources can be restored if a tax is imposed on the externality-generating activity that is exactly equal to the value of the damages caused by it. Such a tax forces the decision maker to consider the full economic cost of the decision.

Because taxing for externalities changes decisions that would otherwise be made, it does in a sense "distort" economic decisions. But its purpose is to force decision makers to consider real costs that they would otherwise ignore. In the case of pollution, for example, the distortion caused by a tax is desirable. Instead of causing an excess burden, it results in an efficiency gain. (Review Chapter 16 if this is not clear in your mind.)

A distorting tax can also improve economic welfare when there are other taxes present that already distort decisions. Suppose, for example, that there were only three goods, X, Y, and Z. Suppose further that there was a 5% excise tax on both Y and Z. The taxes on Y and Z distort consumer decisions away from those goods and toward X. Imposing a similar tax on X reduces the distortion of the existing system of taxes. When consumers face equal taxes on all goods, they cannot avoid the tax by changing what they buy. Thus, the distortion caused by imposing a tax on X corrects for a pre-existing distortion—the taxes on Y and Z.

Let's return to the example described earlier in Figures 18.3 and 18.4. Imposing the tax of 50% on the use of capital generated revenues of $4000 but imposed a burden of $6000 on consumers. A distortion now exists. But consider what would happen if the government now imposed an additional tax of 50%, or $1 per unit, on labour. Such a tax would push our firm back toward the more efficient technology A. In fact, the labour tax will generate a total revenue of $6000, but the burden it imposes on consumers would be only $4000. (It is a good idea for you to work these figures out yourself.)

■ **Optimal Taxation** The idea that taxes work together to affect behaviour has led tax theorists to search for optimal taxation systems. Knowing how people will respond to taxes would allow us to design a system that would minimize the overall excess burden. For example, if we know the elasticity of demand for all traded goods, we can devise an optimal system of excise taxes that are heaviest on those

Economists evaluating taxation typically focus on four criteria: (1) efficiency—a "good" tax system raises any given amount of tax revenue with the minimal adverse consequences for efficiency in the allocation of resources; (2) equity—a "good" tax system should raise revenue in a way which people consider "fair"; (3) administrative costs—a "good" tax system raises revenue with minimal expenditure on administration by government and individual firms and taxpayers; and (4) political accountability—under a "good" tax system, people are able to keep politicians accountable. Unfortunately, these criteria often conflict and trade-offs are necessary.

In the last few years the idea of a flat tax has become extremely popular with certain groups in Canada. A flat tax involves a single tax rate applied to all income. Most deductions, exemptions, and credits are eliminated and the tax return form is dramatically simplified. The following article by John Geddes of the *Financial Post* examines the flat tax concept. The piece is an example of critical analysis of an argument. Although Geddes

does find fault with the flat tax idea, the goal of critical analysis is to carefully analyze an argument and arrive at a reasonable judgment about its worth or merit. Critical analysis can and often does yield very favourable judgments. Read through the article once sympathetically, noting the arguments made and judgments drawn by Geddes. Then read it again, but this time critically, and arrive at your own judgments. Take the evaluative criteria listed in the first paragraph into account when conducting your critical analysis. If you are interested in an accessible, detailed, and sympathetic discussion of the flat tax concept, read Robert E. Hall and Alvin

Rabushka, *The Flat Tax* (Hoover Institution Press: Stanford, 1985).

The concept of a flat tax, like the notion of a flat Earth, is a triumph of simplicity over reality. True believers in either share a tendency to dismiss their critics for over-complicating matters.

But it is a complex universe we live in, where planets are spherical and tax systems are as unwieldy as the social and political forces that shape them. When flat tax advocates wave off as irrelevant the policy pressures that caused the Income Tax Act to swell to

goods with relatively inelastic demands and lightest on those goods with relatively elastic demands.

Of course, it is impossible to collect all the information required to implement the optimal tax systems that have been suggested. This point brings us full circle, and we end up where we started, with the *principle of neutrality:* all else equal, taxes that are neutral with respect to economic decisions are generally preferable to taxes that distort economic decisions. Taxes that are not neutral impose excess burdens.

OPTIONAL MATERIAL

Measuring Excess Burdens

It is possible to measure the size of excess burdens if we know something about more than 1400 pages today from just 20 in 1917, they ignore the most critical elements of any tax reform discussion....

The main selling point of all flat tax schemes is supposed to be clarity. Proponents gush about shrinking the income tax return to the size of a postage stamp by getting rid of loopholes and deductions. Sounds good. So why are the flat taxers on both sides of the border unwilling to let their plans succeed or fail on that basis?... [F]lat tax advocates admit that levelling rates will only win over voters if combined with across-the-board tax cuts.

Well, if the presumed outcome is a lighter burden for everyone, you could sell a tax reform based on hair colour or average local snowfall. A more revealing and realistic test of any proposed change is how it compares with the status quo when the assumption is that it must bring in the same amount of revenue....

[T]he flat tax debate turns out not to be about simplification after all. The underlying issues are how much revenue governments need to collect, and to what extent the tax system should be used to redistribute income. And it is these core questions—not the increasingly superficial argument over ending complexity—that increasingly defines the fundamental divide between liberals and conservatives.

In Canada, most liberals, including Finance Minister Paul Martin, contend that tax hauls cannot fall by much until the deficit and debt fight has been won. Most conservatives, such as those now ruling Ontario, and many Reform MPs accept the supply-side economics tenet that tax cuts designed to stimulate growth should be offered in tandem with fiscal restraint.

Wealth redistribution is even more contentious. Liberals have watched the ability of government to spend directly on social programs [become] severely eroded; they are now eyeing the tax system to see if it can be used more effectively for the same ends. Martin said in a recent interview that tax reform aimed at "fairness" is the next big policy issue facing his department.

The inclination toward greater progressivity is derided as "social engineering" by conservatives such as those designing Reform's alternative tax policy. They generally believe taxation should raise necessary revenues, not shift wealth among income groups.

If the argument between left and right over the need for spending cuts is all but over, on tax policy the ideological divide is widening. It is the new battleground. But don't be distracted by the flat tax fuss. Who pays and how much matters far more than the length of the return they fill out.

Source: John Geddes, "Flat Tax Debate Is Not About Simplification After All: Ideological Divide on Tax Policy Widening," *Financial Post* vol. 90, no. 4 (January 27/29, 1996), p. 20.

how people respond to price changes. Look at the demand curve in Figure 18.5 on the next page. The product in question originally sold for a price, P_0, equal to marginal cost (which, for the sake of simplicity, we assume is constant). As you recall, when input prices are determined in competitive markets, marginal cost reflects the real value of the resources used in producing the product.

To measure the total burden of the tax we need to recall the notion of consumer surplus from Chapter 6. At any price, some people pay less for a product than it is worth to them. All we reveal when we buy a product is that it is worth *at least* the price being charged. For example, if only one unit of product X were auctioned, someone would pay a price close to D in Figure 18.5. By paying only P_0, that person received a "surplus" equal to $(D - P_0)$. (For a review of consumer surplus and how it is measured, see Chapter 6.)

Now consider what happens when an excise tax raises the price of X from P_0

to $P_1 = P_0 + T$, where T is the tax per unit of X. First, the government collects revenue. The amount of revenue collected is equal to T times the number of units of X purchased (X_1). If you look carefully at Figure 18.5, you can see that $T \times X_1$ is equal to the area of rectangle P_1ABP_0. Second, since consumers must now pay a price of P_1, the consumer surplus generated in the market is reduced from the area of triangle DCP_0 to the area of the smaller triangle DAP_1. The excess burden is equal to the original (pre-tax) consumer surplus *minus* the after-tax surplus *minus* the total taxes collected by the government.

In other words, the original value of consumer surplus (triangle DCP_0) has been broken up into three parts: the area of triangle DAP_1 that is still consumer surplus; the area of rectangle P_1ABP_0 that is tax revenue collected by the government; and the area of triangle ACB that is lost. Thus, the area ACB is an approximate measure of the excess burden of the tax. The total burden of the tax is the sum of the revenue collected and the excess burden: the area of P_1ACP_0.

EXCESS BURDENS AND THE DEGREE OF DISTORTION

The size of the excess burden that results from a decision-distorting tax depends on the degree to which decisions change in response to that tax. In the case of an excise tax, consumer behaviour is reflected in elasticity of demand:

> The more elastic the demand curve, the greater is the distortion caused by any given tax rate.

Figure 18.6 on the next page shows how the size of the consumer response determines the size of the excess burden. At price P_0, the quantity demanded by consumers is X_0. Now suppose that the government imposes a tax of $\$T$ per unit of X. The two demand curves (D_1 and D_2) illustrate two possible responses by consumers. The change in quantity demanded along D_1 (from X_0 to X_1) is greater than the change in quantity demanded along D_2 (from X_0 to X_2). In other words, the response of consumers illustrated by D_1 is more elastic than the response of consumers along D_2.

The excess burdens that would result from the tax under the two alternative

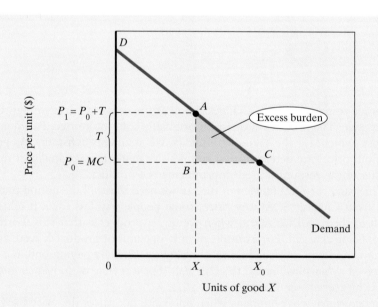

FIGURE 18.5

The Excess Burden of a Distorting Excise Tax

A tax that alters economic decisions imposes a burden that exceeds the amount of taxes collected. An excise tax that raises the price of a good above marginal cost drives some consumers to buy less desirable substitutes, reducing consumer surplus.

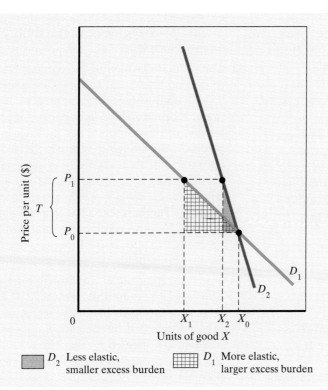

FIGURE 18.6

The Size of the Excess Burden of a Distorting Excise Tax Depends on the Elasticity of Demand

The size of the excess burden from a distorting tax depends on the degree to which decisions or behaviours change in response to it.

D_2 Less elastic, smaller excess burden

D_1 More elastic, larger excess burden

assumptions about demand elasticity are approximately equal to the areas of the shaded triangles in Figure 18.6. As you can see, where demand is more responsive (more elastic), the excess burden is larger.

If demand were perfectly inelastic, no distortion would occur, and there would be no excess burden. The tax would simply transfer part of the surplus being earned by consumers to the government. That is why some economists favour uniform land taxes over other taxes. Because land is in perfectly inelastic supply, a uniform tax on all land uses distorts economic decisions less than taxes levied on other factors of production that are in variable supply.

Summary

The Economics of Taxation

1. Public finance is one of the major subfields of applied economics. A major interest within this subfield is the economics of taxation.

2. Taxes are ultimately paid by people. Taxes may be imposed on transactions, institutions, property, and all kinds of other things, but in the final analysis, taxes are paid by individuals or households.

3. The *base* of a tax is the measure or value upon which the tax is levied. The *rate structure* of a tax determines the portion of the base that must be paid in tax.

4. A tax whose burden is a constant proportion of income for all households is a *proportional tax*. A tax that exacts a higher proportion of income from higher-income households is a *progressive tax*. A tax that exacts a lower proportion of income from higher-income households is a *regressive tax*. In Canada, income taxes are progressive, and sales and excise taxes are regressive.

5. Your average tax rate is the total amount of tax you pay divided by your total income. Your marginal tax rate is the tax rate that you pay on any additional income that you've earned. Marginal tax rates have the most influence on behaviour.

6. There is much disagreement over what constitutes a fair tax system. One theory contends that people should bear tax burdens in proportion to the benefits that they receive from government expenditures. This is the *benefits-received principle.* Another contends that people should bear tax burdens in line with their ability to pay. This *ability-to-pay principle* has dominated Canadian tax policy.

7. The three leading candidates for best tax base are income, consumption, and wealth.

Tax Incidence: Who Pays?

8. As a result of behavioural changes and market adjustments, tax burdens are often not borne by those initially responsible for paying them. When we speak of the *incidence of a tax,* we are referring to the ultimate distribution of its burden.

9. Taxes change behaviour, and changes in behaviour can affect supply and demand in markets, causing prices to change. When prices change in input markets or in output markets, some people may be made better off and some may be made worse off. These final changes determine the ultimate burden of a tax.

10. *Tax shifting* occurs when households can alter their behaviour and do something to avoid paying a tax. In general, broad-based taxes are less likely to be shifted and more likely to stick where they are levied than are partial taxes.

11. When labour supply is more elastic, firms bear the bulk of a tax imposed on labour. When labour supply is more inelastic, workers bear the bulk of the tax burden. Because the elasticity of labour supply in Canada is close to zero, most economists conclude that most of the payroll tax is probably borne by workers.

12. The payroll tax is regressive for two reasons. First, most of the tax does not apply to wages and salaries above a specified maximum. Second, wages and salaries fall as a percentage of total income as we move up the income scale. Those with higher incomes earn a larger portion of their incomes from profits, dividends, rents, and so forth, and these kinds of income are not subject to the payroll tax.

13. The ultimate burden of the corporate tax appears to depend on several factors. One generally accepted study shows that the owners of corporations, proprietorships, and partnerships all bear the burden of the corporate tax in rough proportion to profits, even though it is directly levied only on corporations; that wage effects are small; and that excise effects are roughly neutral. However, there is still much debate about whom the corporate tax "hurts." The burden of the corporate tax is progressive, because profits and capital income make up a much bigger part of the incomes of high-income households.

14. Taken together under a reasonable set of assumptions about tax shifting, provincial and local taxes seem as a group to be mildly regressive. Federal taxes, dominated by the personal income tax but increasingly affected by the regressive payroll tax, are mildly progressive. The overall system is mildly progressive.

Excess Burdens and the Principle of Neutrality

15. When taxes distort economic decisions, they impose burdens that in aggregate exceed the revenue collected by the government. The amount by which the burden of a tax exceeds the revenue collected by the government is called the *excess burden.* The size of excess burdens depends on the degree to which economic decisions are changed by the tax. The *principle of neutrality* holds that the most efficient taxes are broad-based taxes that do not distort economic decisions.

16. The *principle of second best* holds that a tax that distorts economic decisions does not necessarily impose an excess burden. If previously existing distortions or externalities exist, such a tax may actually improve efficiency.

(Optional) Measuring Excess Burdens

17. The excess burden imposed by a tax is equal to the pre-tax consumer surplus minus the after-tax consumer surplus minus the total taxes collected by the government. The more elastic the demand curve, the greater is the distortion caused by any given tax rate.

ability-to-pay principle 454

benefits-received principle 454

excess burden 464

principle of neutrality 465

principle of second best 467

progressive tax 451

proportional tax 451

regressive tax 451

sources side/uses side 458

tax base 451

tax incidence 458

tax rate structure 451

tax shifting 459

1. If the Canadian government were to cut taxes, it could either reduce income tax rates or reduce the Goods and Services Tax (GST) rate. What arguments can you make for and against each of these options?

2. The tax calculation in Table 18.3 was based on the existence of a tax credit equal to 17% of the basic personal amount of $6456. Suppose that instead of receiving this credit the individual is allowed to exempt $6456 of his or her income from taxation. Calculate the tax payable. Is this individual better off with the credit or the exemption? Now consider someone earning $18 000 per year. Is this person better off with a credit or an exemption?

3. Suppose that a citizens' group in Atlantic Canada has the following statement in its charter:

"Our goal is to ensure that large, powerful corporations pay their fair share of taxes in this country."

To implement this goal, the group has recommended and lobbied for an increase in the corporation income tax and a reduction in the individual income tax. Would you support such a petition? Explain your logic.

4. "Taxes imposed on necessities that have low demand elasticities impose large excess burdens because consumers can't avoid buying them." Do you agree or disagree? Explain.

5. For each of the following, do you agree or disagree? Why?
    a. "Economic theory predicts unequivocally that a payroll tax reduction will increase the supply of labour."
    b. "Corporate income taxes levied on a monopolist are likely to be regressive, because the monopoly can simply pass on its burden to consumers."
    c. "All nonneutral taxes are undesirable."

6. In calculating total faculty compensation, the administration of Doughnut University includes employer contributions to the Canada Pension Plan as a benefit to faculty. After all, these contributions will generate future pensions for faculty. However, the Canadian Association of University Professors argues that, far from being a benefit, the employer contribution is simply a tax and that its burden actually falls on the faculty even though it is paid by the university. Discuss both sides of this debate.

7. Developing countries rarely have sophisticated income tax schemes like that in Canada. The primary means of raising revenues in many developing countries is through commodity taxes. What problems do you see with taxing particular goods in these countries? (*Hint:* Think about elasticities of demand.)

8. Suppose a special tax were introduced that used the value of one's automobile as the tax base. Each person would pay taxes equal to 10% of the value of his or her car. Would the tax be proportional, regressive, or progressive? What assumptions do you make in answering this question? What distortions do you think would appear in the economy if such a tax were introduced?

9. You are given the following information on a proposed "restaurant meals tax" in the Republic of Olympus. Assume that Olympus collects no other specific excise taxes, and that all other government revenues come from a neutral lump-sum tax. (A lump-sum tax is a tax of a fixed sum paid by all people, regardless of their circumstances.) Assume further that the burden of the tax is fully borne by consumers.

    Now consider the following data:
    - Meals consumed before the tax: 12 million
    - Meals consumed after the tax: 10 million
    - Average price per meal: $15 (not including the tax)
    - Tax rate: 10%

    Estimate the size of the excess burden of the tax. What is the excess burden as a percentage of revenues collected from the tax?

19

The Economics of Labour Markets and Labour Unions

In July 1997, over 14.4 million people in the Canadian labour force of 15.8 million held jobs. Somehow 14.4 million people sorted themselves into thousands of different occupations and jobs, performing an enormous variety of tasks in exchange for wages that ranged from a few dollars an hour to millions of dollars a year. Some had little or no formal education; others had invested many years and thousands of dollars in education and training. Some worked only part time; others held more than one job. Some large employers hired hundreds of people each year into well-defined jobs with specific job descriptions. Small firms may have hired only one or two people every few years for very loosely defined jobs. And, of course, many people worked for themselves.

This chapter, the second of several chapters designed to survey some of the subfields of applied economics, addresses a number of important questions. How do people and jobs get matched? How are wage rates determined? Under what circumstances do people get trained? When do firms hire? What happens when people lose their jobs? These questions, by and large, are answered in what we refer to collectively as "the labour market," but in fact there are many labour markets. There is a market for professional basketball players, a market for lawyers, a market for carpenters, and a market for unskilled workers. Each market operates under a different set of rules and through a different set of institutions, but the basic forces that drive all of them are the same.

The importance of the labour market to the economy should not be underestimated. Indeed, perhaps the most dramatic of all the changes currently underway in the republics of the former Soviet Union and Eastern Europe is the introduction of a labour market. Under the central planning systems that dominated Eastern Europe before 1989, national planning agencies determined the economies' staffing needs. Training programs were then designed to meet those needs, and people were channelled through the training programs into jobs. The introduction of a labour market into these systems means that the responsibility for finding a job is left to workers and the responsibility for finding workers is left to firms. Firms can exercise choice in hiring and firing. Presumably, employment and advancement in the Eastern European economies will begin to depend more on productivity.

Several earlier chapters have touched on the economics of labour markets. In Chapter 6 we looked at some of the decisions that lie behind the labour supply curve. In Chapter 10 we discussed the factors that determine the demand for labour. In Chapter 17 we listed several reasons for the inequality of wages. After a quick review, this chapter discusses the workings of labour markets in a more systematic fashion.

In the final part of the chapter, we take up the topic of labour unions. Labour unions have existed for about 200 years now, and their effects are the subject of considerable controversy. Do unions succeed in raising wages? Do they create unemployment? What is their impact on productivity? Almost everyone has a strong opinion about unions. Some say they are responsible for many of our economic woes; others believe that they are the only hope for economic justice.

Competitive Labour Markets: A Review

A brief review of a few key concepts is in order before we begin to examine the theory of labour markets. (You may also wish to review Chapter 10 at this point.)

■ **Marginal Revenue Product and the Demand for Labour** Remember that firms make several decisions simultaneously. They decide how much to produce, they choose among alternative techniques of production, and they decide how much of each input to demand. If they have market power, they also decide what price to charge. In making these decisions, they use information from product output markets, from input markets, and from their knowledge of technology.

The concept of marginal revenue product (MRP) is central to an understanding of the demand for labour. The **marginal revenue product of labour (MRP_L)** is the additional revenue that a firm would take in by hiring one additional unit of labour, *ceteris paribus*. Because labour is presumed to be productive, hiring more yields more product. The product produced by one marginal unit of labour is called the *marginal physical product of labour* or simply *marginal product of labour*. To be turned into revenue, that product must be sold. Product prices are determined in output markets, and purely competitive firms take them as given. Thus, for perfectly competitive firms the added revenue from hiring one more unit of labour is the marginal product of labour (MP_L) *times the price of output*: $MP_L \times P_X$.[1]

Figure 19.1 on the next page graphs a firm's decision to hire in a competitive labour market. The market-determined wage rate is W^*. The firm can hire all the labour it wants at that wage. Thus, we can think of W^* as the marginal cost of a unit of labour. Firms will hire as long as the marginal gains in revenue from hiring additional units of labour (MRP_L) equal or exceed W^*. When labour is the only

marginal revenue product of labour (MRP_L) *The additional revenue that a firm will take in by hiring one additional unit of labour, ceteris paribus. For perfectly competitive firms, the marginal revenue product of labour is equal to the marginal physical product of labour times the price of output.*

[1]*For firms in imperfect markets where output is set by the firm, marginal revenue is equal to marginal physical product times marginal revenue—MRP$_L$ = MP$_L$ × MR. MRP$_L$ is still the revenue gained by hiring an additional unit of labour.*

FIGURE 19.1

Demand for Labour in Competitive Markets Depends on Labour's Productivity

Competitive firms will hire labour as long as marginal revenue product of labour ($MRP_L = MP_L \times P_X$) equals or exceeds the market wage, W^*. When labour is the only variable factor of production, the marginal revenue product curve is the demand curve for labour.

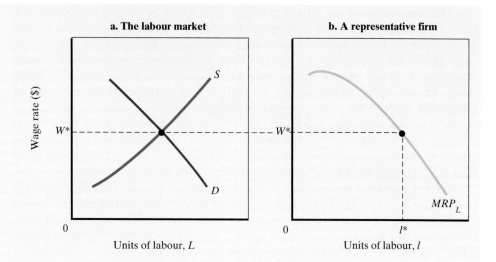

a. The labour market

b. A representative firm

variable input, the *MRP* curve is the firm's demand curve for labour. When more than one factor of production can vary, the demand curve is more complicated but essentially the same. (These points are explained fully in Chapter 10.)

The point is that:

> Demand for labour depends on what labour can produce and how much its product sells for in output markets. The *physical* product of labour is technologically determined. Given the state of the technology, machinery, and other equipment available, and the level of effort required to produce something, there is a limit to what one unit of labour can produce. The *revenue* product of labour depends on the market value of its product; if no one wants to buy a product, that product has no market value.

■ **The Supply of Labour**   Households supply labour. In any given labour market, the supply of labour depends on some factors that households control and some that they do not.

First, each household member must decide whether to work. The alternatives to working for a wage are either working for no pay or enjoying one's leisure. In this regard, households face a trade-off. Working yields a wage as well as some nonpecuniary rewards and/or costs—you may like your working environment and derive satisfaction from being creative or productive, or you may hate your job because it is dull or dangerous. The opportunity cost of working is either the value of what can be produced using the same time *or* the value of leisure. If you are not in the labour force working for a wage, you can paint your house, raise children, or sleep in the sun. All these alternatives have a value that must be weighed in a decision to take a job.

Beyond this basic decision to work or not to work, a more complicated set of choices and constraints comes into play. Not everyone can supply his or her labour in every market. A 50-kilogram man would probably not offer his services to the Canadian Football League as a football player. A carpenter with no medical training would be breaking the law if she sold herself as a surgeon. Each market requires its own set of skills that workers either are born with or must acquire.

■ **Human Capital**   The stock of knowledge, skills, and talents that human beings possess by nature or through education and training is called **human capital**. When

human capital *The stock of knowledge, skills, and talents that people possess; it can be inborn or acquired through education and training.*

people who have special skills or knowledge earn higher wages, a part of their wage can be thought of as a return on human capital.

Both households and firms invest in human capital. The principal form of human capital investment financed primarily by households is education. When parents send their children to school, they are investing in human capital that they hope will pay dividends later on. The principal form of human capital investment financed primarily by firms is **on-the-job training.** Presumably, training workers raises their productivity and yields dividends to the firms that provide such training.

Governments also invest in human capital. Federal and provincial governments have sponsored and subsidized numerous training programs over the years. As well, Canadian governments have created a public elementary and secondary education system, subsidized universities, and provided millions of dollars in student financial aid. Some argue that public health expenditures are also essentially human capital investment. A healthy labour force is a prerequisite for a productive labour force.

on-the-job training *The principal form of human capital investment financed primarily by firms.*

■ **The Equilibrium Wage**   Wage rates in competitive markets are determined by supply and demand:

> If quantity of labour demanded exceeds quantity of labour supplied, wages should rise until the quantity demanded and the quantity supplied are equal. The resulting higher wages should then reduce the quantity of labour demanded and increase the quantity of labour supplied.

Figure 19.2a shows excess demand for labour; as you can see, the initial wage of W_0 rises until the market clears at W^*. When an excess supply of labour exists, we would expect to see market wages fall. At W_0 in Figure 19.2b, quantity supplied exceeds quantity demanded; this situation creates a downward pressure on wages. If wages fall, quantity demanded will increase and quantity supplied will fall until equilibrium is restored at W^*.

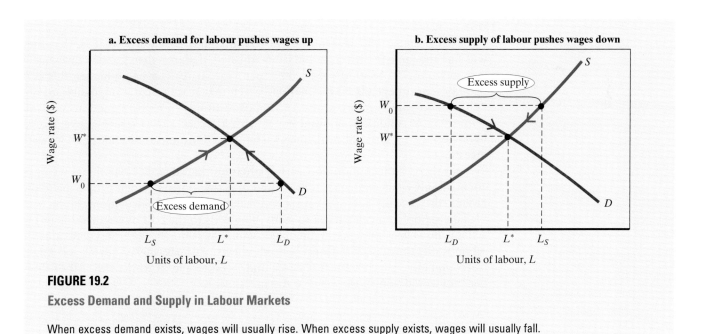

FIGURE 19.2

Excess Demand and Supply in Labour Markets

When excess demand exists, wages will usually rise. When excess supply exists, wages will usually fall.

Disequilibria sometimes persist, however. Minimum wage laws may prevent wages from falling in response to a surplus. Union contracts may hold wages above the equilibrium level. Even in competitive markets, some prices are slow to adjust in response to surpluses.

The Labour Market in Action

So far we have discussed the labour market only in the abstract. A better way to grasp the basic economic logic of labour markets is to work through a number of concrete examples of the theory as it applies in everyday decisions.

■ **Investing in Human Capital: Should I Go to School?** Carrie graduated from the University of Manitoba with a Bachelor of Arts degree two years ago. Currently she works as a technical assistant in a small firm that trains people to work with personal computers. She likes the job, but she feels trapped; there isn't any room for her to move up in the company without more training. She makes $7.50 per hour.

A technical school located near Carrie's home is offering a one-year program leading to a certificate of proficiency in two computer languages. With this training, which would move her up a notch in the labour market, she is all but assured of a job paying $9.50 per hour. But tuition at the school is $5000, and students must attend full time. If going to school full time for a year means that Carrie must give up her job, she will incur an opportunity cost of $12 000 in take-home pay ($15 000 less taxes of $3000) in addition to the $5000 tuition. If the books and materials that she needs for the program cost $1000, the full cost of a year's training is $18 000. Carrie must decide if the investment is worth making.

Carrie is considering an investment in human capital. The training will increase her productivity and thus her wages in the future. Figure 19.3 on the next page shows some simple calculations. If we assume that Carrie works 40 hours per week and 50 weeks per year, her gross wages will increase by $4000 each year when she graduates from school. To determine the *net* return, we must remember to subtract taxes. Suppose her marginal tax rate (that is, the rate applicable to marginal dollars of income) is about 25%.[2] After taxes, then, Carrie's income will be $3000 a year higher if she gets the training.

If we assume that these flows will continue into the future—that is, that they will stay the same in "real," or inflation-adjusted, dollars—then Carrie's investment will yield 16.7% ($3000 ÷ $18 000) per year in real terms. Whether this is a "good" return depends on the market. Given that it is currently impossible to obtain a secure rate of return above 16.7%, education is currently a good investment. But if market conditions allowed her to earn a secure rate of return above 16.7% by investing in a physical or financial asset, the education would not be the "best" investment.

But there is much more to Carrie's situation than this. For one thing, we have counted only costs and benefits measured in actual dollars. When people make decisions, they usually add other costs and benefits into their calculations. Some people hate school and can't stand to study; this adds to the cost of the investment. At school, however, students might make valuable contacts, and they can use the school's placement service to get job interviews. And the higher-paying job might offer intangible psychological rewards and nicer people to work with. All of these benefits would add to the yield of the investment.

---

[2]*Notice that Carrie's average tax rate is only 20%. She is currently paying a total of $3000 in taxes on an income of $15 000. What matters when we calculate her gains from the new job at the margin is her marginal tax rate, which is 25%. (Review Chapter 18 if you are unsure why this is so.)*

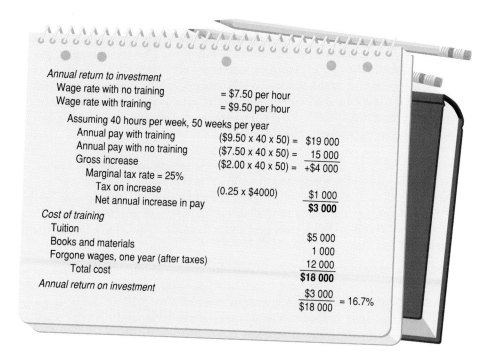

Annual return to investment
Wage rate with no training = $7.50 per hour
Wage rate with training = $9.50 per hour
Assuming 40 hours per week, 50 weeks per year
Annual pay with training ($9.50 x 40 x 50) = $19 000
Annual pay with no training ($7.50 x 40 x 50) = 15 000
Gross increase ($2.00 x 40 x 50) = +$4 000
Marginal tax rate = 25%
Tax on increase (0.25 x $4000) $1 000
Net annual increase in pay $3 000
Cost of training
Tuition $5 000
Books and materials 1 000
Forgone wages, one year (after taxes) 12 000
Total cost $18 000
Annual return on investment $3 000 / $18 000 = 16.7%

Often these "utility" gains and losses dominate the pecuniary costs and benefits. Someone might decide to pursue a Ph.D. in classics even if the probability of landing a good faculty position in the field were very low. The yield on such an investment would lie entirely in psychological rewards.

Taxes and financial aid affect the yields of different courses of action and also have an impact on decisions. For example, a $5000 tuition scholarship would reduce the cost of Carrie's investment considerably—to $13 000. This raises the yield on the investment to 23% ($3000 ÷ $13 000) and might well tip the balance in favour of school.

A cut in taxes would have the conflicting effects of increasing the cost of the training while increasing the net benefits. Carrie would sacrifice more take-home pay (higher forgone earnings) to attend school, but she would get to keep more of the $4000 annual wage increase in the foreseeable future. The net effect will probably be to increase the return on an investment made now.

Carrie's calculations provide a hypothetical illustration of the use of rates of return on human capital in discussions of human capital. But few if any students actually undertake these calculations. Did you estimate an expected rate of return when you chose to attend university? Not likely. However, potential economic gains almost certainly played some role in your decision. You knew that university graduates generally earn better incomes and face lower unemployment rates than do people who have not attended university. Parents, teachers, guidance counsellors, and career advisers seemed to think it was in your best interests to attend university and strongly urged you to do so. Your own observations and information you picked up from newspapers and television seemed to support their arguments. But did you make a mistake and overestimate the advantages? After all, tales of the problems faced by university graduates are well known. It is not easy to get a job even with a degree. A general university degree does not seem practical enough. Perhaps community or technical college training in job-specific skills would have been a better investment.

It should be comforting to find that a university education still offers very attractive rates of return on investment. Recent studies by François Vaillancourt at the Université de Montréal, and Vaughan Dickson, William Milne, and David Murrell at the University of New Brunswick found that for the average Canadian university graduate the rate of return on university education was more than 10%.[3] Given that demand for highly educated labour appears to be increasing relative to the demand for less educated labour, the rate of return is likely higher today than it was at the time these studies were undertaken.[4] Although university graduates are not having an easy time finding work, it is a much more difficult task for those who never attended university.

A recent study by Robert C. Allen at the University of British Columbia suggests that the arguments for technical training may also be overstated.[5] The general skills developed in university programs, including traditional liberal arts and science programs, are rewarded in the labour market, and graduates generally experience lower unemployment rates and seem to enjoy significantly higher lifetime incomes.

■ **What Does McDonald's Pay?** At two locations about 40 minutes apart, McDonald's hires workers at very different wage rates. At one franchise, a small sign on the counter reads "Help wanted, full or part time." If you ask about a job, you will find that only one part-time opening is available, and that the wage rate offered is the minimum wage, $5.50 per hour. At the other location, a large sign says "Full-time or part-time positions available, day or night shifts, excellent benefits and $7.50 per hour." There are six positions available at this location.

Why would one restaurant pay wages significantly higher than an identical restaurant with identical jobs in the same metropolitan area? Quite simply, because the franchise owner finds that she has no applicants—and thus no workers—at lower wages. Even at the higher wage rates, she has a very difficult time keeping her positions filled.

Clearly, the two restaurants are buying labour in different labour markets. If people could get from one point to another at no cost, such wage differences would disappear. But there are costs. Neither of these restaurants is accessible by public transportation. Thus, to take a job at one of them, you must live nearby or have a car. Fast-food restaurants like McDonald's draw much of their labour from the supply of high school students who want to work part time. Most of them don't have cars. The high-wage franchise is on a major highway at some distance from local high schools and residential areas; the low-wage franchise is in the centre of town.

There are probably other factors that affect the available labour supplies at the two locations as well. Suppose, for example, that the average income of the four towns surrounding the high-wage franchise is 50% higher than the average income of the four towns surrounding the low-wage franchise. To the extent that the labour supply is made up of students, parents' income may well have an effect.

[3]François Vaillancourt, "Private and Public Monetary Returns to Schooling in Canada, 1985," Economic Council of Canada Working Paper (Ottawa: Minister of Supply and Services, 1992), and Vaughan Dickson, William J. Milne, and David Murrell, "Who Should Pay for University Education?" Canadian Public Policy vol. 22, no. 4 (December 1996): pp. 315–329.
[4]This argument is advanced in Craig Riddell, "Human Capital Formation in Canada: Recent Developments and Policy Responses," in Keith G. Banting and Charles M. Beach (eds.), Labour Market Polarization and Social Policy Reform (Kingston: Queen's University School for Policy Studies, 1995), p. 146.
[5]Robert C. Allen, "The Economic Benefits of Post-Secondary Training and Education in B.C.: An Outcomes Assessment," UBC Department of Economics Discussion Paper No. 96–13, March 1996.

Higher-income families may spend some of their money buying leisure for their children, while many lower-income families expect older children to contribute to the family income.

This example illustrates three important points:

> First, labour supply depends on a number of factors, including wage rates, nonlabour income, and wealth. Second, individual firms have very little control over the market wage; firms are forced to pay the wage that is determined by the market. Finally, because people cannot get from one place to another free of charge, and because most people do not reside at their workplaces— as capital does—there is an important spatial dimension to labour markets.

Different supply and demand conditions can and do prevail at different geographical locations. This is true across regions as well as within cities. Labour markets in different regions of the country are very different.

■ **The Importance of Individual Preferences**   David was a highly paid young lawyer with a major Edmonton law firm. Three years ago he was made a partner, and his share of the firm's earnings last year was over $150 000. This year he resigned, sold his condominium, and moved to Banff where he bought a small restaurant and a cabin near the edge of the national park. The best he can hope to earn from the restaurant is about $20 000 per year, and even that is an optimistic forecast.

Were David's decisions irrational? If we add up the dollars and calculate the monetary gains and losses, as we did for Carrie, we can see that David is giving up a great deal. But economic theory in no way suggests that such decisions are irrational. David made his decision to accept a lower income in exchange for a number of things from which he derives utility. The hectic life of a big city may have been a significant cost to him. The beauty of Banff and the climate may be invaluable benefits. He may like to ski, or he might simply have wanted to buy more leisure time.

The critical point is that:

> Preferences play a very important role in the decisions we make about labour supply and in the decisions we make about what to consume.

As you saw at the beginning of this chapter, there are 14.4 million jobholders in Canada. Every one of them has a unique set of talents and preferences. Every one of them has made a different set of decisions about investing in human capital. Some go to university and some do not. Some stay in high school and some do not. Those differences help to explain the way people end up being sorted across jobs.

■ **A Word of Caution**   Do not assume that the importance of individual preferences and choices makes generalization about labour market behaviour impossible. An enormous amount of empirical work has documented that labour behaves in predictable ways in response to incentives. The manager of the McDonald's franchise in the high-wage area got the desired response by raising wages, not by lowering them. People with high nonwage incomes do supply less labour than people with low nonwage incomes.

Let us now turn to a more detailed discussion of several important public policy issues that involve the labour market.

Labour Markets and Public Policy

The government influences the operation of the market in a variety of ways. This section examines a number of important current public policy issues that affect the labour market. Specifically, we examine the effects of minimum wage legislation, tax policy, welfare programs, and employment insurance.

THE MINIMUM WAGE CONTROVERSY

One strategy for reducing poverty that has been used for almost 100 years in many countries is the **minimum wage.** A minimum wage is the lowest wage that firms are permitted to pay workers. In Canada, both federal and provincial governments have minimum wage laws covering workers in their respective jurisdictions. The minimum wage in Ontario in 1997 was set at $6.85 an hour. For someone working 35 hours per week for the full 50 weeks of the year the minimum wage yields an income of $12 400 per year.

Minimum wage legislation is intended to help the working poor by forcing employers to pay at least "a living wage." But since 1975 the average minimum wage in Canada has fallen from approximately 50% of the average manufacturing wage to approximately 38% of the average manufacturing wage.[6] Many social policy activists argue that $12 000 a year is far from a living wage and that minimum wages should be increased significantly, perhaps back to 1975 levels in real terms.

But is minimum wage legislation an efficient and equitable way of addressing poverty? Indeed, does the minimum wage even reduce poverty? Critics of minimum wage legislation argue that minimum wage legislation interferes with the smooth functioning of the labour market and creates unemployment. Thus, it is argued, minimum wage legislation will increase the incomes of some workers and reduce the incomes of others. On the other hand, proponents of minimum wage increases argue that minimum wage legislation can increase the incomes of the poorest workers and alleviate poverty without creating much unemployment.

These arguments can best be understood with a simple supply and demand diagram. Figure 19.4 shows hypothetical demand and supply curves for unskilled labour. The equilibrium wage rate is $5.00. At that wage, the quantity of unskilled labour supplied and the quantity of unskilled labour demanded are equal. Now suppose that a law is passed setting a minimum wage of $6.85. At that wage rate, the quantity of labour supplied increases from the equilibrium level, L^*, to L_S. At the same time, the higher wage reduces the quantity of labour demanded by firms, from L^* to L_D. As a result, firms lay off $L^* - L_D$ workers.

It is true that those workers who remain on payrolls receive higher wages. With the minimum wage in effect, unskilled workers receive $6.85 per hour instead of $5.00. But is it worth it? Some gain while others (those who had been employed at the equilibrium wage) lose.

About one-third of all minimum wage workers in Canada are teenagers and a very high unemployment rate among young people is often cited as evidence that the unemployment problem caused by the minimum wage is significant. In 1996, the unemployment rate for those aged 15–24 was over 16% compared to an average unemployment rate for those 25 and over of just over 9%. But proponents of minimum wages argue that such data do not prove that minimum wages increase unemployment since there are numerous other factors at work. Moreover, they argue that both the demand for and supply of labour are relatively inelastic with respect to the wage rate, and that minimum wages have a small effect on

---

[6]*Dwayne Benjamin, "Do Minimum Wages Really Matter?" Policy Options vol. 17, no. 6 (July/August 1996): p. 38.*

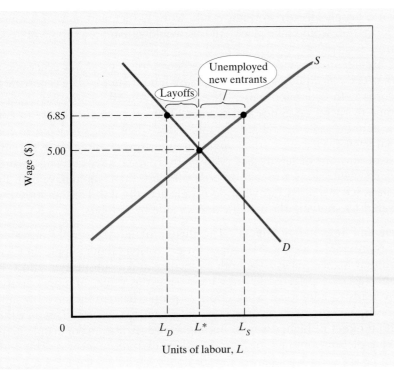

FIGURE 19.4

Effect of Minimum Wage Legislation

If the equilibrium wage in the market for unskilled labour is below the legislated minimum wage, the result is likely to be unemployment. The higher wage will attract new entrants to the labour force (quantity supplied will increase from L^* to L_S), but firms will hire fewer workers (quantity demanded will drop from L^* to L_D).

unemployment. (Try to reproduce Figure 19.4 and the analysis based on it assuming both demand and supply are inelastic.)

Recent empirical research has been generally supportive of the arguments of those who suggest that minimum wages have a small impact on unemployment.[7] Thus most minimum wage workers gain from a minimum wage increase and only a few lose their jobs. But are minimum wage workers poor? If minimum wage legislation is to be an efficient antipoverty strategy it must target benefits to the poor. Not all minimum wage earners are poor. Indeed, a significant portion of the teenagers benefiting from the minimum wage are not from poor families. Thus there may be better ways to deal with the problem of poverty.

In sum, given the significant decline in the real minimum wage over the last 20 or so years and new empirical evidence that suggests minimum wages have a relatively small impact on employment, it seems possible to conclude that Canadian minimum wage legislation does not have a large effect on Canadian unemployment rates. But whether further increases in the minimum wage are appropriate as an antipoverty strategy is still very much a subject of ongoing debate. (For an interesting controversy over minimum wage legislation, see the Issues and Controversies box on page 486 titled "A Minimum Wage for Babysitters.")

TAXES AND LABOUR SUPPLY

One of the basic beliefs of conservatives, which is echoed in the policy platforms of the Progressive Conservative government in Ontario and the Reform Party of Canada, is that high rates of taxation are the root of Canada's economic problems. High taxes reduce the incentive to work, save, and invest, it is said. If tax rates were decreased (thus increasing take-home pay), it is argued, more people would

---

[7]*See David Card and Alan Krueger,* Myth and Measurement: The New Economics of the Minimum Wage *(Princeton: Princeton University Press, 1995) for a review of the empirical literature.*

go to work, people already working would work harder, and more investment and capital formation would take place. All this would expand the supply of goods and services.

The arguments are widely accepted as "common sense." Yet economic theory shows that tax cuts could increase or *decrease* labour supply. The economic theory also accords with "common sense." If taxes are reduced, people have more after-tax income to spend on goods and services. Thus, they *might* choose to consume the same amount as before the tax cut and reduce their hours of work to consume additional leisure. Of course, they *might* choose to work more since the opportunity cost of an hour of leisure has risen (with a larger after-tax wage people lose more goods when they opt to take an hour off work than would have been the case before the wage increase). But what do people actually do? This question can only be answered by studying the actual choices made by workers.

■ **Income and Substitution Effects**   The theory of labour supply introduced in Chapter 6 provides a technical language for discussing labour supply. In Chapter 6 we noted that higher wages have both an income and a substitution effect. Higher wages increase the price of leisure. Increasing the price, or opportunity cost, of leisure leads to additional work effort as people face an incentive to substitute other goods, bought with income from working, for leisure. This is called the **substitution effect of higher wages.** But higher wages also make people better off. By working the same number of hours, workers earn more income. This added income can be spent on any combination of goods, including leisure. Because I have a higher income, I may decide to consume more leisure; the result is that I actually work less. This is the **income effect of higher wages.**

> The income and substitution effects of higher wages work in opposite directions. If the income effect is larger than the substitution effect, higher net wages will actually reduce the supply of labour.

■ **Wages and Elasticity of Labour Supply**   Because economic theory does not predict how people react to higher wages and because people's reactions to wage changes are so important in public policy, significant resources have been devoted to discovering how people actually react to such changes. There have even been large-scale social experiments that have allowed economic researchers to hold almost everything else equal and isolate the impact of higher wages on behaviour. One such experiment was conducted in Manitoba in the 1970s.

These studies focus on three elasticities of labour supply: the total wage elasticity; the income elasticity; and the substitution elasticity. The total labour supply elasticity measures the change (in percentage) in labour supply that results from a 1% increase in the net wage. The total labour supply elasticity can be decomposed (broken into parts) into an income elasticity, which isolates the income effect of the wage increase, and the substitution elasticity, which isolates the substitution effect of the wage increase.

Derek Hum and Wayne Simpson at the University of Manitoba produced a set of the elasticity estimates from the Manitoba experiment, which are shown in Table 19.1. A range of estimates is reported to reflect the use of sensitivity analysis. The researchers used a variety of techniques and assumptions to produce their estimates and reported a range rather than a single number to indicate that the elasticity

substitution effect of higher wages *Consuming an additional hour of leisure means sacrificing the wages that would be earned by working. Thus, when the wage rate rises, leisure becomes a more expensive commodity, and households may "buy" less of it. This means working more.*

income effect of higher wages *When wages rise, people are better off. If leisure is a normal good, they may decide to consume more of it and to work less.*

Table 19.1	Estimates of Labour Supply Elasticities		
	Total Wage Elasticity	Income Elasticity	Substitution Elasticity
Men	−0.1 to 0.3	0 to −0.1	0 to 0.3
Married women	−0.2 to 0	0 to −0.2	0
Unmarried women	−0.2 to 0.8	0 to −0.2	0 to 0.8

Source: Derek Hum and Wayne Simpson, *Income Maintenance, Work Effort, and the Canadian Mincome Experiment,* A Study Prepared for the Economic Council of Canada (Ottawa: Minister of Supply and Services, 1991), p. 90.

estimate depends on the technique used as well as statistical error. The estimates of the total wage elasticity for men generally fell between −0.1 and 0.3. Thus the overall impact of an increase in wages on labour supply is very small. An estimated elasticity of −0.1 means that a 10% increase in the wage will reduce labour supply by 1%. In other words, the labour supply curve actually bends back as the wage increases. An estimated labour supply of 0.3 means that a 10% increase in the wage will increase labour supply by 3%. In this case the labour supply curve has a positive slope but is very "steep." But most importantly, both estimates are close to zero, indicating that tax changes have a small impact on labour supply.

The range of elasticity estimates for married women suggests married women will decrease the amount of labour they supply when wages rise but, as was the case with men, the labour supply response is relatively small. Although the range of estimates of the labour supply for unmarried women is larger than that for men or married women, the general conclusion that higher wages have a relatively small impact continues to hold.

The results of the Manitoba experiment are remarkably consistent with most estimates of labour supply elasticities. Labour supply appears inelastic. Moreover, both the income and substitution effects are small.

Interestingly, tax reforms can be designed to increase labour supply by cutting marginal tax rates but expanding the tax base at the same time. (Recall from Chapter 18 that the income tax base is the amount of income that is subject to taxation.) Such a change in the tax system makes leisure more expensive relative to other goods, but it does not provide households with more income to buy leisure. There is thus a substitution effect but no income effect to counteract it.

WELFARE AND LABOUR SUPPLY

There has always been some worry that, by providing a "guaranteed" minimum standard of living, welfare programs available to those at the bottom of the income distribution give potential workers a disincentive to enter the labour force and go to work. Are such worries justified?

When we examined the incentive effects of taxes (Chapter 18), we discovered that income and substitution effects work in opposite directions. Imposing a tax reduces income. If people think of leisure as a good, they will choose to buy less of it and will instead tend to work more when a tax is imposed. But it is also true that imposing a tax or increasing marginal tax rates reduces the opportunity cost, or price, of leisure. With leisure less expensive at the margin, people will tend to buy more of it and work less. Because the two effects counteract each other, theory cannot tell us whether taxes will increase or decrease the supply of labour.

Minimum wage legislation in Canada does not cover all workers. For example, both teenage and adult babysitters are generally exempt from minimum wage laws. Why? In the case of teenage babysitters the argument for the exemption is clear. A market exchange between a teenage babysitter and parents wanting a night out is seen as mutually beneficial. The babysitter gains desired spending money, the parents gain a night out. Moreover, the parents of the babysitter typically believe that babysitting is a worthwhile learning experience that helps develop responsibility and provides valuable skills in dealing with young children.

If imposing a minimum wage on teenage babysitters were expected to have little effect on demand, the extension of minimum wage legislation would just redistribute income from parents to the babysitter. But many believe that extending the minimum wage to cover teenage babysitters would result in a significant drop in demand for babysitting services.

The case for exempting adult babysitters is less clear. These babysitters typically work full time and in most respects are much like other workers covered by minimum wage legislation. Indeed, the government of Saskatchewan concluded that they are very much like other workers and it extended the Saskatchewan minimum wage law to cover this class of worker. The resulting outcry is documented in the following Canadian Press Newswire article:

Saskatchewan parents have a new worry to add to the sometimes painful problem of finding babysitters—finding the legislated $5.60 an hour to pay them. One single mother is headed back to welfare after quitting her job because she couldn't afford care for her

The extension of minimum wage legislation to cover babysitting services is a controversial topic, which can be subject to economic analysis using the tools developed in this book.

three children. A couple in Saskatoon faces a $4,000 bill for babysitter back pay. And parents across the province are concerned after learning recently that Saskatchewan's NDP government changed the law almost two years ago to classify as employers all parents who hire care-givers at home for their children.

That means parents have to pay people who come into their homes to care for their children the provincial minimum wage of $5.60 an hour—plus overtime, statutory holiday pay, vacation pay and pay in lieu of notice if wrongfully fired.

Parents say the move makes it prohibitively expensive to hire babysitters, who more traditionally earn $2 or $3 an hour. "I ended up having to quit my job—I had to quit it because I couldn't afford to pay

a sitter," said Sandra Ginter, who left her job at a car rental firm at the Saskatoon airport last week to look after three daughters aged five, two, and five months. Ginter originally hired a sitter so she could return to work from welfare...

But Labour Minister Bob Mitchell ruled out relaxing the law. "The people who take care of young children are doing a pretty important service and it's hard to understand why somebody that's pumping gas in a service station would be entitled to more than someone who's looking after your kids," Mitchell said Tuesday. Ginter said she sees Mitchell's point, but wants him to view the problem from her perspective.

Source: "Parents Pay As Babysitters Get Minimum Wage in Saskatchewan," Canadian Press Newswire, December 17, 1996.

Unlike taxes, however,

> Income maintenance programs produce income and substitution effects that work in the same direction. Theory predicts that both effects will reduce work effort and labour supply. Nearly all income maintenance programs are targeted to households with low incomes. Because households with higher incomes are ineligible, households that increase their incomes by working will lose some or all of their income maintenance benefits. The system, then, imposes an *implicit tax* on income from labour earned by those who are eligible for welfare.

Because of the number of income tested programs, such as social assistance and public housing, this implicit tax on earnings can be quite high. If you earn $3000 and lose $2000 worth of benefits, your implicit tax rate would be 66%. For some people, the loss of benefits has been estimated at over 100% of marginal income earned.

When we think of loss of benefits as an implicit tax, we come to the conclusion that income and substitution effects do not offset each other when an income maintenance program is involved. Labour supply is likely to be lower in the presence of the program. Income maintenance programs obviously provide income, some of which is "spent" on leisure. Withdrawing benefits as income rises also reduces the opportunity cost of leisure. Suppose, for example, that for every dollar of income I earn, I lose $0.50 in benefits. If the hourly wage available is $4.00, then consuming an extra hour of leisure would cost me only $2.00 ($4.00 × 0.50); I give up $4.00 in income but retain $2.00 in benefits. Thus, the substitution effect also leads to a decrease in labour supply.

However, the estimates of both income and substitution elasticities reported in Table 19.1 suggest that the impact of income maintenance programs is quite small. Hum and Simpson note the following in their review of elasticity estimates and presentation of results from the Manitoba experiment:

> Our conclusions are guarded but reassuring. First, we believe there is a hint of an emerging consensus on the likely range of behaviour. Much of this consensus has been achieved only in recent years and after 20 years of intensive research. Second, our research leads us to believe that the labour supply response to changes in the tax-transfer system, such as those involved in income maintenance programs, will be small. Although precise measurement of labour supply response is a very difficult problem, and one that economists have not yet mastered, we have narrowed the range of reasonable estimates to those that indicate that individuals and families are likely to be fairly insensitive to changes in the tax-transfer system facing them.[8]

This is an important conclusion. If the conclusion is correct, it means that social assistance recipients have not dramatically reduced their labour supply to take advantage of the "welfare system." Effective implicit tax rates can be quite high, in some cases over 100%. If people continue to choose work over social assistance (and many do), there must be significant nonpecuniary rewards associated with holding a job.

---

[8]*Derek Hum and Wayne Simpson,* Income Maintenance, Work Effort, and the Canadian Mincome Experiment, *A Study Prepared for the Economic Council of Canada (Ottawa: Minister of Supply and Services, 1991), p. xvi.*

One important fact about the labour market is that the flow of workers into and out of the labour force is continuous. Some enter school, some graduate, others are promoted. As the population ages, some retire. Some people quit jobs, some are fired, and some take leaves or drop out of the labour force temporarily. At the same time, some firms expand and must hire new workers, changes in technology generate needs for new skills and make others obsolete, and some firms fall on hard times and must lay people off.

This constant flux results in a continuous process of sorting available workers among available jobs. New entrants into the labour force expend time and effort searching for the best possible jobs; firms send out recruiters to schools or raid competing firms, often bringing in candidates from long distances. But no matter how well these systems work:

> The distribution of skills and abilities among the available workforce never corresponds exactly to the skills and abilities currently in demand.

Some people find it puzzling that the newspaper is full of available job listings while the headlines of the same paper lament very high unemployment rates. In February 1997, when 1.5 million people were unemployed, the classified ads carried pages and pages of available jobs. The problem is that the skills and abilities of available job seekers often do not match firms' needs. And, of course, unemployment also has a regional dimension. Not only do the skills demanded not always match the skills supplied, the location of jobs (labour demand) does not always correspond to the location of job seekers. In February 1997, over 20% of the labour force in Newfoundland was out of work, while in Saskatchewan the unemployment rate was under 7 percent.

A person who is entering the labour force for the first time or who is considering a job change must carefully sift through the set of jobs that might be available given his or her skills, experience, ability, and location. People, even those without highly specialized skills, might have hundreds of possibilities open to them. The problem is finding out about them. Job searching is a process of gathering data. By making phone calls, applying, being rejected, or perhaps even turning down job offers, job hunters find out about what is available and what they can expect. The **job search** is thus an extended process of information gathering.

job search *The process of gathering information about job availability and job characteristics.*

To be counted as unemployed by Statistics Canada, one must be actively looking for a job. If a person stops looking, he or she is no longer considered a part of the labour force and thus is no longer technically "unemployed." This is why full-time homemakers and students are not counted as unemployed. Because workers without jobs who are seeking work are unemployed, the efficiency of the search process can have a significant impact on the amount of measured unemployment.

Thinking about the job search as an information-gathering process is revealing. We all want the best available job, the one that matches our abilities and aspirations and pays the highest possible wage. For many people, there are readily available jobs that are not desirable; every university graduate could get a job working the counter at Burger Baby's, but most have higher expectations.

In theory:

> Job hunting by an individual should continue as long as the expected gains from continuing the search exceed the costs of doing so.

The opportunity costs of search are those things that are lost by continuing the search, the most important of which are *forgone earnings* and *time*. Other costs include transportation, dressing for interviews, paper, postage, and telephone bills. The potential benefits from continued search depend on the job seeker's expectations. As the person gathers more and more information, expectations should become more and more accurate.

Both the government and the marketplace have responded to the problem of providing information to job hunters. In recent years, employment agencies have become more and more common. Many employers are making use of "headhunters," specialized firms that quietly and confidentially gather information from people interested in senior positions, people who are currently employed and do not want it known that they are looking to change jobs. This keeps costs low, both to the potential applicant and to society. Acutely aware of the unemployment problem, the government also sponsors a number of programs to help match jobs and workers. Canada Employment Centres play an especially important role in providing information on available jobs to job seekers.

The government can have other impacts on the search process. Consider, for example, the Employment Insurance program. Being laid off or spending an extended period of time unemployed—that is, actively looking for a job—can be a devastating experience. During periods of unemployment, suicide rates increase, the crime rate increases, and other indicators of "pain" appear in the economy. To alleviate some of this pain, Canada has a system—Employment Insurance—that pays benefits to workers who lose their jobs.

Employment Insurance benefits reduce the cost of job search, and some researchers have argued that this results in inefficiency. With the costs of looking for a job reduced, people have an incentive to prolong the process. Prolonged job search can drain tax revenues, artificially increase the unemployment rate, and keep productive workers off the job. On the other hand, some researchers argue that a longer search results in a better match between workers and jobs, thereby decreasing unemployment rates and increasing productivity in the long run.

Wage and Income Differentials in Canada

We have already said that the labour market is not one market—it is made up of many separate, but often closely related, markets. Nonetheless, a general sorting process is always going on. As a result, different occupational groups end up earning different wages, and the distribution of income reflects these differences. As you recall from Chapter 17, wages differ across jobs for two basic reasons: differences in jobs and differences in workers.

Some jobs are more desirable than others. Some jobs, like those in coal mining or heavy construction, involve higher levels of risk than others. *Ceteris paribus*, jobs that are more desirable and less risky tend to pay less than jobs that are less desirable and more risky. These wage differences are called **compensating differentials**.

In competitive markets, equilibrium wages are equal to the productivity of the marginal worker. And the product of a highly skilled machine operator is clearly worth more than that of an unskilled labourer. An unskilled labourer working on a routine set of tasks adds little to the final value of a product compared to the value added by a skilled machinist working with complex capital equipment. Workers who supply their labour in markets that demand unusual or highly developed skills can expect to earn higher wages, *ceteris paribus*.

But wages are determined by the forces of supply *and* demand. At most major North American universities, you must have a Ph.D. to be appointed to the humanities faculty. The training and skills required are quite high. But because there are few positions relative to the number of qualified applicants, wages for humanities

compensating differentials
Differences in wages that result from differences in working conditions. Risky jobs usually pay higher wages, and highly desirable jobs usually pay lower wages.

professors have remained low. In contrast, many computer software companies have had difficulty filling open positions. As a result, programmers' salaries have increased significantly in recent years.

EARNINGS AND OCCUPATIONAL SEGREGATION

Tables 19.2 and 19.3 present some data on trends in the Canadian labour market and on actual wage rate and income differentials. During the last three and a half decades, the labour force has changed significantly. For example, in 1961 only 29% of all women were in the labour force. This figure is now approaching 60%. Male labour-force participation has dropped slightly, largely due to reductions in the normal retirement age.

Table 19.3 gives a very rough breakdown of occupations in Canada. An examination of the number of workers shows evidence of **occupational segregation** by sex. In 1993, about 80% of all workers employed in clerical occupations were women, while only 18% of all workers in manufacturing jobs were women. Over 40% of all workers in managerial/administrative jobs were women in 1993, up significantly from less than 30% in 1982. Women also earn substantially lower wages than men in virtually every category, and on average, women employed full time earn about 73% as much as the average man.

LABOUR MARKET DISCRIMINATION, CROWDING, AND INEFFICIENCY

The above data make it clear that women and men are not randomly distributed across occupations. They also show that women, on average, earn significantly less than men. One possible explanation for these observations is gender discrimination in the labour market.

Labour market discrimination occurs when one group of workers receives inferior treatment from employers because of some characteristic irrelevant to job performance. Inferior treatment may involve being systematically barred from certain occupations, receiving lower wages, or inability to win promotion or obtain training.

Suppose that women (the same argument can be made for any group experiencing discrimination) were systematically barred from a number of occupations. To simplify our example, let's call the occupations reserved for men sector X, and the rest of the economy sector Y. Since women are excluded from X, the supply of labour in sector X is reduced, and wages are higher than they would otherwise be. At the same time, women must *crowd* into the occupations reserved for them. Such crowding increases the supply of labour in sector Y and pushes wages down. Thus, occupational segregation resulting from discrimination is sufficient to cause a wage differential if the number of restricted jobs is significant.

But there is more to the story than wage differentials. Occupational discrimination also results in a net loss of welfare in the economy. To understand this argument, you need to recall that the demand for labour depends on the productivity of that labour. When extra workers are crowded into sector Y, wages fall. Because wages are lower, more workers will be hired. (Recall that workers will be hired as long as the value of their product at the margin exceeds the going wage.) With more workers working at a lower wage, the marginal product of workers in Y will end up lower than it otherwise would be.

The opposite situation occurs in sector X. With fewer workers supplying their labour in the reserved sector, wages remain high. The marginal product of workers in X, then, remains high. Now consider what would happen if we transferred one worker at a time from sector Y to sector X. If we assume that the discrimination was unrelated to job qualifications, workers will be moving from a sector in which their productivity was low at the margin to a sector where it is high. Thus,

occupational segregation *The concentration of men and women in certain occupations.*

labour market discrimination *Occurs when one group of workers receives inferior treatment from employers because of some characteristic irrelevant to job performance.*

Table 19.2

Labour Force Participation Rates

	Men	*Women*
1961	81.0	29.0
1971	76.0	40.0
1981	78.6	51.0
1986	77.1	55.1
1991	76.3	58.7
1996	71.2	56.8

Sources: Penny Basset, "Declining Female Labour Force Participation," *Perspectives on Labour and Income* vol. 6, no. 2 (Summer 1994): p. 36; and Statistics Canada, *The Labour Force*, Cat. no. 75-001E.

Table 19.3	Earnings Difference by Sex and Selected Occupations		
	Women as a % of Total Employment		Women's Earnings as a % of Men's Earnings
	1982	1993	1993
Managerial/administrative	29.2	42.2	64.8
Natural sciences	14.6	18.0	73.6
Social sciences/religion	42.8	56.2	60.0
Teaching	59.3	65.8	78.8
Clerical	79.0	80.2	68.4
Service	54.5	56.8	72.6
Manufacturing	18.4	18.2	60.4

Source: Statistics Canada, *Women in the Labour Force, 1994,* Cat. no. 75-507E.

the value of the product gained in sector X is greater than the value of the product lost in sector Y. There is thus a net gain in value. *Ending discrimination, then, should increase national income.* The logic behind this argument is simple:

> If workers vary in their talents in ways unrelated to sex, race, or other attributes, rules or behaviours that force one group into specific occupations are clearly inefficient.

Critics of discrimination theory argue that competition should put an end to discrimination rather quickly. If women (or any other group that is discriminated against) were more productive than the current wage would suggest, some firms would hire them into the restricted occupations, thus driving those who persist in their discrimination out of business.

Those who defend the discrimination and crowding theory rejoin that the pure-competition scenario is naive and unrealistic. They argue that the link between productivity and wages is difficult to establish, and that those in positions of power (often men) have both the incentive and the ability to maintain discriminatory practices over long periods of time.

A lively and emotional debate among labour economists that has ended up in the courts in recent years is the controversy over *comparable worth*. The basic argument is that women are systematically paid less than men for work of equal, or at least comparable, value. This controversy is discussed in Chapter 17.

Labour Unions

Thus far we have focused on the behaviour of firms and workers in competitive labour markets. This is by no means the whole story, however. A substantial number of workers are employed under contracts negotiated between their employers and their labour unions. In 1997, 38% of the labour force in Canada belonged to unions. The bargaining that takes place between firms' representatives and those of workers' unions does not necessarily produce the same outcome as the operation of an unregulated, competitive labour market.

Nearly all eligible workers in a number of major industries, including automobile manufacturing, mining, steel, and the public service, belong to unions. Moreover, the wages and working conditions of many nonunion workers are indirectly affected by unions who set standards that nonunion employers must meet to retain workers and pre-empt unionization of their own workplaces. But workers in many other industries (perhaps the most significant of which are the high-tech industries) have not been influenced by unions. In total, almost two of every five nonagricultural workers in Canada belong to a union.

We begin our discussion of labour unions with a brief history of the labour movement in Canada. The purpose of this historical discussion is twofold: (1) to identify clearly why workers opt to join unions, and (2) to identify certain critical institutional features of industrial relations in Canada. We then turn to economic theory and an analysis of the potential effects of an organized labour force on the economy. Finally, we present some issues and controversies concerning what is known about the actual effects of unions.

THE CANADIAN UNION MOVEMENT

■ **Early Unions in Canada**   The first unions in Canada emerged in Nova Scotia and New Brunswick around 1812. The early unions were local and associated with specific trades. They not only bargained with employers over wages, but also provided a social support system for members. There were no workers' compensation, employment insurance, or pension plans at the time; the unions and the churches had almost complete responsibility for what we would now call social service provision.

In the 1850s and 1860s, international unions made an appearance in Canada. U.S. unions came to Canada in part because Canadian workers recognized the potential advantages of having experienced and relatively well-financed representation. However, U.S. unions also came to Canada out of their own self-interest. American workers believed that Canadian workers posed a potential threat in that low Canadian wages could endanger American jobs. The concern of American workers should not come as a surprise given that one of the central goals of the union movement is to reduce competition among workers, especially competition that allows employers to play one worker against another as a strategy to increase profits. Like the earliest Canadian unions, the international unions tended to specialize along craft lines with different U.S. unions representing different skilled trades. There might be one union for journeymen shoemakers, another for iron moulders, still another for cigarmakers, etc.

In 1869 a new type of labour union emerged. The *Knights of Labor*, which included both skilled and unskilled workers, attempted to organize all workers into one great union. Their objective was not only to provide social support and to bargain with employers. They also sought more fundamental changes to the capitalist system. They were extremely popular for a time, reputedly attracting as many as 60 000 members in Canada at their peak in 1886. But after 1886 the Knights of Labor declined in importance.

The **Knights of Labor** did, however, establish several precedents, which the union movement follows to this day. Bargaining with employers, social protection, and political action have all become important functions of the union movement. Moreover, certain structural characteristics of the union movement in Canada today date from our experience with the Knights of Labor. For example:

- Bargaining is considered a local matter. This means that negotiations take place between individual employers (even individual plants) and workers belonging to a union local.
- Locals are relatively autonomous in their operation. The local is typically affiliated with a larger union (possibly an international union) that supplies specialized assistance when needed and perhaps financial support in the event of a strike.
- The larger union is in turn affiliated with a broader organization representing many workers. The broader organization, or federation of unions, deals

Knights of Labor *One of the earliest successful labour organizations in Canada. It recruited both skilled and unskilled labourers. Founded in 1869, the power of the Knights declined after 1886.*

with political matters since the voice of workers carries more weight when it is expressed collectively.

■ **Collective Bargaining** The role of unions in the political arena, although important, is less important than their local role in representing workers in the workplace. The most visible impact of unions is the strike. A strike is an organized withdrawal of labour services by a union to put pressure on an employer to agree to workers' demands. Prior to 1943 strikes occurred for a variety of reasons. Employers did not have to recognize the existence of the union or even to negotiate with the union. Although some employers were willing to work with unions, many faced strikes because unions were forced to exert pressure to get recognition. Before World War II strikes also occurred as a result of disputes arising out of the day-to-day management of an organization. For example, firing a popular worker might result in a strike. Of course strikes also occurred as workers fought for higher wages.

In 1943 the government of Canada issued an order of the Privy Council Office, **PC 1003**, which was to have a profound impact on the nature of industrial relations in this country over the next 50 years. PC 1003 attempted to balance the interests of workers and business owners by: (1) offering business owners restrictions on a union's right to strike and (2) by offering workers a set of rules that would govern employers' response to unions. After PC 1003, an employer would, by law, have to negotiate with a union representing its workers, provided the union established that a significant proportion of workers voluntarily agreed to have the union enter into negotiations on their behalf. But if the union could not establish that such agreement with its members had been reached, the employer could ignore the union and rely on the labour market to set wages and working conditions and the union could, by law, do nothing in response. This process whereby union members agree to let union leaders negotiate on their behalf is known as **collective bargaining.** As a result of PC 1003, there are workplaces in Canada where wages and working conditions are subject to collective bargaining, and others where wages and working conditions are determined in the labour market or in negotiations between the employer and individual workers.

In workplaces where unions have gained legal recognition, collective bargaining generates a contract or collective agreement that governs working conditions and pay in that workplace. The contract is in force for a fixed period of time (generally one to three years) and thus must be renegotiated at regular intervals. Since strikes are illegal when a collective agreement is in force, strikes over day-to-day operations are rare (and always illegal). A special legal system—the grievance arbitration system—exists to handle disputes over violations of a collective agreement that is in force.

In the period immediately prior to the expiration of the collective agreement the union and the employer must enter into negotiations to produce a new collective agreement. Almost all negotiations generate a new collective agreement without a strike or lockout (a lockout occurs when the employer attempts to get the union to agree to its terms by "locking the workers out" of the establishment). But on rare occasions employers and employees cannot come to an agreement on their own. When this happens the parties have to accept the intervention of a government-appointed mediator or conciliator who tries to get the parties together. If conciliation is unsuccessful the parties are in a position to call either a strike or a lockout. Given that a strike or lockout is damaging to both parties, turning to these weapons of last resort is uncommon. But the existence of these weapons provides incentives for both employers and unions to resolve their differences in negotiations.

PC 1003 *A law that forced employers to negotiate with a union, provided the union could establish that a majority of workers wished the union to act as their representative in negotiations with an employer.*

collective bargaining *The process by which union leaders bargain with management as the representatives of all union employees.*

■ **Political Activity of the Union Movement** In addition to negotiating with employers at the local level, unions also attempt to influence government policy. Unions have an obvious interest in the laws that govern the collective bargaining process since changes in these laws can affect the relative bargaining power of unions. For example, a law that prohibits employers from hiring new workers to do the jobs of those on strike—popularly known as anti-scab legislation—can increase the relative bargaining strength of a union by increasing the cost an employer incurs as a result of a strike. Not surprisingly, employers also attempt to influence government policy in hopes of reducing the relative bargaining strength of unions. As a consequence, unions often engage in political activity to defend their interests.

Unions not only try to shape legislation affecting collective bargaining, but they also attempt to influence government economic and social policy. Taxes, employment policy, education and training, income security, health care policy, and pensions all have a significant effect on the well-being of workers. Unions, as representatives of the workers' interests, are active in the political arena whenever government policies have important implications for the well-being of workers.

The political activity of unions in Canada is not generally initiated at the local level. Instead most political activity is initiated by federations of unions representing large numbers of workers. The largest national federation of labour organizations in Canada is the **Canadian Labour Congress (CLC)**. It represents approximately 60% of unionized workers in Canada. The CLC focuses on federal government policy and has traditionally supported the New Democratic Party of Canada. There are also provincial federations of labour, which focus on provincial government policy.

■ **The Strength of the Union Movement in Canada Today** In recent years in the United States, the proportion of workers belonging to a union has fallen dramatically. Traditionally Canadian industrial relations have been heavily influenced by developments south of the border and so one would expect to see a corresponding decline in union membership in Canada. But this has not happened here, at least not yet. The proportion of workers belonging to unions in Canada reached a peak in the mid 1980s, a time when unions in the U.S. were in decline. Although the proportion has fallen slightly in recent years, unions remain an important force in our economy. (For a look at labour unions in other countries, see the Global Perspective box on the opposite page.)

ECONOMIC EFFECTS OF LABOUR UNIONS

One way to analyze union power is to think of a union as a monopolistic seller of labour in a market. If there were many buyers, the union's situation would be very similar to that of a pure monopolist selling in output markets: the union would restrict the supply of labour and charge a wage rate above the competitive equilibrium wage rate. But wages may not be the only concern of unions. Other objectives might include keeping all of their members employed or improving working conditions.

■ **Unions as Monopolies** Let us assume for a moment that a union is the only seller of labour in some market. Let us also suppose that, as an initial condition, union membership is less than the number of workers that would be employed if the market were competitively organized and that the union's objective is to maximize its members' wages and keep them all employed. In Figure 19.5 on page 496, if there were 2200 union members, the union would set a wage of $8, corresponding to the relevant point on the demand curve for labour. This is above the competitive wage rate of $6. At $8, 4200 labourers are working or available for work, but firms will hire only 2200 of them. There would thus be an excess supply of workers,

Canadian Labour Congress (CLC) *The largest national federation of labour organizations in Canada. The CLC was created in 1956 and represents approximately 60% of unionized workers in Canada.*

Global Perspective

Labour Unions around the World

The characteristics and histories of labour unions vary significantly from country to country. In Canada, over 37% of the labour force belongs to a union and the number of union members is growing at about the same rate as the labour force as a whole. In contrast, union membership in the United States has been in decline since peaking in the late 1950s. In 1954, over 35% of employed workers in the U.S. belonged to a union; today, fewer than 16% of U.S. workers belong to a labour union. But union membership has not been declining in other parts of the world. In fact, membership is steady or growing in many countries including Sweden, Denmark, and Germany. Union membership is highest in Sweden and Denmark, where only 1 in 10 workers is not in a union.

In the United States, the roles and functions of unions are very similar to those found in Canada. The prime function of U.S. unions is to negotiate contracts and bargain on behalf of workers. Negotiations typically occur at the local level and relationships between unions and firms tend to be adversarial, sometimes violent. Labour federations pursue limited political goals. The U.S. equivalent of the Canadian Labour Congress, the AFL-CIO (American Federation of Labor–Congress of Industrial Organizations), has historically supported the Democratic Party. The U.S. government's role in the industrial relations system involves establishing and enforcing "rules of the game." The National Labor Relations Board oversees collective bargaining to make sure the basic rules are followed.

In countries outside North America, the government is much more involved in unions, and firms and unions cooperate to a much greater extent. Often, union goals are political as well as economic. For example, in the United Kingdom, where almost half of all wage and salary

The strength of labour unions varies from country to country. In the United States, labour union membership has been declining since the 1950s. But in other countries, such as Poland and the Czech Republic, unions have been an important source of social change. Here, Czech coal miners gather to demonstrate their loyalty to their union.

workers are union members, the unions are officially affiliated with the Labour Party and are actively involved in all aspects of politics.

In Japan, unions and firms are highly cooperative. Large companies like Toyota and Hitachi have what are called *enterprise unions*. Each enterprise union represents only one company's workers, so its loyalty is not divided among different companies. The Japanese tradition of lifelong employment goes some way toward explaining the relationships that exist between firms and unions and their cooperative focus on firms' long-term prosperity.

The system of labour relations in Germany is called *industrial democracy*. German law requires all corporations to involve workers in the decision-making process. *Works councils* are made up of managers and workers who are jointly responsible for work rules and many operational decisions. In addition, between one-third and one-half of all boards of directors of German corporations have worker representatives as members, a system known as *codetermination*.

Bargaining in Germany is done across industries and, as in Japan, a spirit of cooperation exists between workers and managers.

In Sweden and in Denmark, almost all workers belong to unions. Unions are actually involved in setting wage levels nationally. In Sweden, unions are represented on many governmental commissions, where they represent workers.

Unfortunately, there are signs that the labour relations systems in both Germany and Japan are in danger. Recent recessions in both countries have put pressure on employment practices and are eroding the traditionally close cooperation between management and workers. In Germany, high labour costs and the economic costs of reunification are forcing companies to drive a harder bargain with unions. And in Japan, a closer look at lifetime employment policies shows that they have always been restricted to the largest companies, apply only to men, and end at age 55. Moreover, in recent years companies that have had such policies have been scaling them back.

FIGURE 19.5

A Competitive Labour Market and a Monopoly Union

If the union imposes a wage of $8, demand for labour will be limited to 2200 workers. But there will be a labour supply of 4200 workers. Thus, many will not be able to find jobs. But if union membership is 2200, all the unemployed would be nonunion workers.

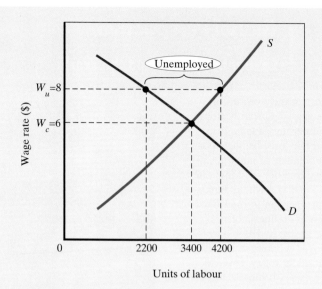

or unemployment, in this market equal to the difference between 4200 and 2200 (= 2000), but the unemployed would all be nonunion workers.

For the $8 wage to hold, the union would have to restrict membership, because increasing the number of union members would also mean decreasing the wages that union members receive. (This is implied by the downward-sloping demand curve, of course.) Restriction of union membership is a common practice. Some unions simply refuse to admit new members; others have long apprenticeship programs that must be completed before a worker is admitted. Unions have also been accused of using racial and gender barriers to restrict membership.

> Union power in a competitive labour market is likely to be inefficient. Pushing up wages reduces labour demand and can actually cause unemployment and restrictions on union membership.

You can see the trade-off in Figure 19.5. If wages were set lower than $8, more workers would be employed. If union membership were greater than 2200, the leadership would have to make a tough decision. They could get more members into jobs, but only by accepting a lower wage for everyone or by somehow increasing demand for their members' services.

Over the years, unions have shown great concern for keeping members in jobs. The preferred route has been to increase demand for workers rather than to take pay cuts. Unions have used many techniques for shifting the demand curve to the right. Union contracts now include provisions for job security, especially for those with seniority. Some contracts have clauses that preserve jobs even when it is inefficient to do so. The most often-cited example of this widely used and widely criticized policy, called **featherbedding**, involves the coal shovellers that trains had to carry for years after they were all powered by diesel engines rather than by coal.

featherbedding *The common union practice of preserving jobs even when it is inefficient to do so.*

Unions have actively sought protective trade measures such as tariffs (taxes on imports) and quotas to prevent foreign producers from cutting into the demand for domestic, union-made goods. Parking your new Toyota in the parking lot of a General Motors plant in Oshawa would certainly not make you popular with your fellow union members. Some unions have even gone so far as to advertise union-produced products.

■ **Empirical Evidence: Do Unions Raise Wages?**   The answer to this question, not surprisingly, is yes:

> An overwhelming number of studies using very different sets of data and techniques have found that unions have succeeded in raising wages.

Modern cross-sectional studies using sophisticated statistical techniques to control for characteristics of union and nonunion workers have found that unions have succeeded in increasing wages of their members by between 10% and 25%. Studies have also found that wages tend to be more equally distributed in union firms than they are in nonunionized firms.

■ **Costs and Benefits of Unions**   The picture of unions that has emerged from our discussion so far is not very positive. The monopoly model leads us to the same unflattering conclusions. First, unions raise wages above the competitive level, which leads to unemployment and the underuse of labour. Second, union work rules and featherbedding reduce productivity. Third, unions create inequities by forcing wage differentials between similar workers. And finally, unions may discriminate to limit membership and hold down labour supply.

However, unions are much more than monopolies attempting to redistribute income from the rest of society to their members. They are also political organizations committed to redistributing power from those who own and control capital to those who must supply labour to achieve the quality of life they desire. In particular, unions help ensure that managers cannot arbitrarily dismiss workers without "just cause"; they keep management accountable for health and safety in the workplace; and they generally work to improve the quality of life in the work world at large. Also, through political action, the union movement has attempted to improve the quality of life of low-wage workers by relentlessly supporting social programs. A commitment to equality is also evident in the fact that the distribution of earnings in unionized firms tends to be more equal than in nonunionized firms. Thus unions also contribute to equality.

Moreover, it is possible that unions actually have a positive effect on the allocation of resources. This position was recently advanced by two Harvard University economists, Richard Freeman and James Medoff, who argue that unions raise productivity. They claim union members have lower quit rates, remain more loyal to the firm, maintain higher morale, and are more likely to cooperate on the job. By communicating with management they help to put efficient policies into effect. They collect information on workers' preferences that leads to more efficient design of benefit packages and better personnel administration.[9] Also, unions have been very active in the training of workers and there is substantial evidence to suggest unions have a positive impact on human capital formation.

It is also possible that unions can raise employment. This can happen when workers face monopsonistic or oligopsonistic labour markets (as in one-industry towns, for example). Such a case is examined in the optional section below.

Freeman and Medoff present a very convincing argument supported with a great deal of data. Their conclusions have not been universally accepted, however, and there is still significant debate over the impact of unionization.

---

[9]*Richard Freeman and James Medoff,* What Do Unions Do? *(New York: Basic Books, 1984).*

Union Power versus Monopsony Power

In Chapter 13, we examined *monopsony,* a market structure in which there is just one buyer. To maximize profits, a single buyer of labour—a monopsonist—that could control part of the labour market would lower wages and hire fewer workers.

Recall that in competitive markets, firms can hire all the labour they need at the market-determined wage rate. Since every firm in competition is small relative to the market, no single firm has any control over the wage rate. A profit-maximizing competitive firm will hire labour as long as the marginal revenue product of labour (MRP_L) is equal to or greater than the market wage rate; the equilibrium condition for a competitive firm is $W = MRP_L$. In competition, the market demand curve is simply the sum of all the marginal revenue product curves of all the firms demanding labour.

In Figure 19.6, the red curve is the market demand curve for labour (the sum of the firms' MRP_L curves). The equilibrium market wage rate is determined by the interaction of competitive demanders and the supply of labour (the lower blue curve in Figure 19.6). Thus, if the market were organized competitively, the equilibrium wage rate would be W_c.

But now suppose that instead of many firms demanding labour, there is only one firm demanding labour (a *monopsonist*). This changes our analysis significantly. Under competition, firms can hire all the labour they want at the market wage. But now the large firm faces the *market* labour supply curve. This means that the more labour the firm decides to hire, the higher is the wage that the firm must pay. At lower wages, less labour is supplied.

The upper blue curve in Figure 19.6 is called the *marginal factor cost* curve for labour (MFC_L). (See Chapter 13 for a review of this concept.) It represents the added cost of hiring an additional unit of labour. The supply of labour curve (S) shows the wage that must be paid to attract each level of labour supply. Marginal

FIGURE 19.6

A Profit-Maximizing Monopsonist

A profit-maximizing monopsonist would pay a wage, W_m, below the competitive level, W_c.

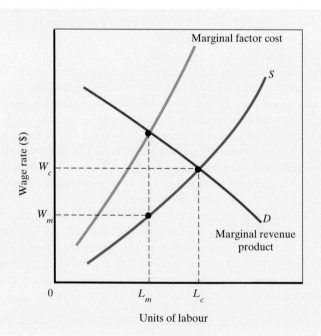

factor cost at every level of output is *higher* than the wage because to attract added workers at the margin, the wage paid to *all* workers must be raised. For example, suppose that at a wage of $5, six units of labour are supplied, and that at a wage of $6, seven units of labour are supplied. Hiring six units of labour costs $30 (6 units $\times$ $5), while hiring seven units of labour costs $42 (7 units $\times$ $6). The marginal factor cost of the seventh unit of labour is thus $12 ($42 − $30), which is higher than the $6 wage rate.

A profit-maximizing firm that is the only buyer of labour in a market (i.e., our monopsonist) will hire labour as long as the marginal revenue product of labour (MRP_L) equals or exceeds the marginal factor cost (MFC_L). Thus, in Figure 19.6, the optimal quantity of labour is L_m (the point at which $MRP_L = MFC_L$), and the wage paid to workers is W_m (the lowest wage required to attract L_m units of labour). In essence, monopsony power leads to lower wages and fewer jobs than would be the case under competitive conditions.

When a monopsonist faces a monopolistic *seller* of labour such as a union, the story is different. The union, of course, tries to impose a wage rate above the going wage, W_c. The monopsonist wants to pay a wage below W_c. The final result depends on the relative bargaining strengths of the union and the firm. In a sense, the union in this model exists to resist and exercise *countervailing power* on the buying side of the labour market. Indeed, many of the most highly unionized markets are in concentrated monopsonist-like industries such as steel and automobiles.

Although union power in a competitive market is likely to be inefficient, unions may actually drive wages closer to their efficient levels in markets where the buying side is highly concentrated.

Summary

Competitive Labour Markets: A Review

1. Demand for labour in competitive markets depends on labour's productivity. Firms will hire labour as long as the *marginal revenue product* equals or exceeds the market wage. The marginal revenue product of labour depends on the market value of its product; if no one wants to buy a product, that product has no market value.

2. Households supply labour. The supply of labour depends on some factors that households control and some that they do not. The alternatives to working for a wage are working for no pay or enjoying one's leisure. Labour supply decisions depend to a large extent on preferences for work and leisure.

3. The stock of knowledge, skills, and talents that human beings possess by nature or through education and training is called *human capital*. The principal form of human capital investment financed primarily by households is education. The principal form of human capital investment financed primarily by firms is *on-the-job training*. Governments invest heavily in human capital.

4. Wages in competitive markets are determined by supply and demand. When excess supply exists in a labour market, we can usually expect to see wages fall, but sometimes disequilibria persist.

The Labour Market in Action

5. Labour supply depends on a number of factors, including wage rates, tax rates, nonlabour income, and wealth. Individual firms have very little control over the market wage; firms are forced to pay the wage that is determined by the market. Because people cannot get from one point to another free of charge and because most people do not reside at their workplaces—as capital does—there is an important spatial dimension to labour markets.

6. Personal preferences play a very important role in the decisions that households make about labour supply and in the decisions they make about what to consume.

Labour Markets and Public Policy

7. The *minimum wage* is the lowest wage that firms

are permitted to pay workers by law. Opponents argue that minimum wage legislation interferes with the smooth functioning of the labour market and creates unemployment. Proponents argue that the minimum wage has been successful in raising the wages of the poorest workers and alleviating poverty without creating much unemployment. The current (1997) provincial and territorial minimum wages range from $5 to $7 per hour.

8. Unlike taxes, income maintenance programs produce income and substitution effects that work in the same direction. Both effects will reduce work effort and labour supply. Because households on welfare lose some or all of their benefits by working, the system imposes an implicit tax on any income that those households earn.

9. The distribution of skills and abilities among the available workforce never corresponds exactly to the skills and abilities currently in demand.

10. *Job searching* is a process of gathering data. In theory, job hunting should continue as long as the expected gains from continuing to search exceed the costs of doing so.

11. Employment Insurance benefits reduce the cost of the job search. When the costs of looking for a job are reduced, people have an incentive to prolong the process. This may drain tax revenues, artificially increase the unemployment rate, and keep productive workers off the job. Or it may decrease unemployment rates and increase productivity in the long run by ensuring a better match of workers and jobs.

Wage and Income Differentials in Canada

12. *Ceteris paribus*, jobs that are more desirable and less risky tend to pay less than jobs that are less desirable and more risky. These wage differences are called *compensating differentials*.

13. Recent data show evidence of *occupational segregation* by sex. Women are concentrated in clerical,

teaching, and service positions; men are concentrated in the natural sciences, manufacturing, and senior executive positions.

14. *Labour market discrimination* occurs when one group of workers receives inferior treatment from employers because of some characteristic irrelevant to job performance. Inferior treatment may involve being systematically barred from certain occupations, receiving lower wages, or being unable to win promotion or obtain training. If workers vary in their talents in ways unrelated to sex, race, or other attributes, rules or behaviours that force one group into specific occupations are inefficient.

Labour Unions

15. Unions are an important force in the economy and in Canadian society. About 38% of the Canadian labour force is represented by unions.

16. Union power in a competitive labour market is likely to be inefficient. Pushing up wages reduces labour demand and can cause unemployment and restrictions on union membership.

17. An overwhelming number of studies have found that unions have succeeded in raising wages. Modern cross-sectional studies find that unions have raised wages by 10% to 25%.

18. One school of thought holds that unions lead to unemployment, the underuse of labour, lower productivity, and artificial wage differentials. Another school argues that unions raise productivity because union members have lower turnover, maintain higher morale, and are more likely to cooperate on the job.

(Optional) Union Power versus Monopsony Power

19. Although union power in a competitive labour market is likely to be inefficient, unions may actually drive wages closer to their efficient levels in markets where the buying side is highly concentrated.

Canadian Labour Congress (CLC) 494

collective bargaining 493

compensating differentials 489

featherbedding 496

human capital 476

income effect of higher wages 484

job search 488

Knights of Labor 492

labour market discrimination 490

marginal revenue product of
labour (MRP_L) 475

minimum wage 482

occupational segregation 490

on-the-job training 477

PC 1003 493

substitution effect of higher wages
484

Problem Set

1. In January of 1996, the average hourly earnings of private production workers in Canada were $15.50. Suppose in that same month, a proposal were advanced to increase the minimum wage to $8 in every province. Opponents argue that such an increase would lead to additional unemployment. If the minimum wage is *below* the average wage even after the increase, how could the increase lead to unemployment?

2. In January of 1996, Statistics Canada reported that the number of persons classified as employed (working for a wage) increased by 34 000 to 15 244 000. At the same time the unemployment rate increased from 9.5% to 9.6%. How could the unemployment rate rise when the number of employed actually increased?

3. Draw a diagram to illustrate each of the following situations:
   a. A labour supply curve for a group of households for whom the income effect of a wage increase is stronger than the substitution effect.
   b. The effect of a general increase in the productivity of labour (an overall rise in the marginal product of labour).
   c. The effect of a union contract that succeeds in raising wage rates above the competitive equilibrium.
   d. The effect of a minimum wage above equilibrium in a competitive labour market.

4. Justine is considering returning to school to get an MBA. She currently makes $30 000 and pays $9000 in taxes (30%). Tuition at the school of her choice is $15 000 per year, and the program requires two years to complete. She must attend full time and would receive no financial aid.
   a. What is the total monetary cost of acquiring an MBA?
   b. What other information might you need to get a better picture of the full cost of acquiring an MBA? (*Hint:* What about summers?)

c. If the degree would raise Justine's expected after-tax wage by $5000 per year in real terms for a long time, what is the rate of return on investment in an MBA for Justine? What if the increase were $15 000?
   d. To make a final decision, what other factors might Justine want to consider?

5. Explain how Employment Insurance benefits could lead to unemployment. If evidence were found to support this claim, should we repeal or abandon the employment insurance system altogether? Explain your answer.

6. Explain how the functioning of income tested programs such as welfare acts as a tax on the poor that can have an effect on their work effort.

*7. The Canadian Brotherhood of Widget Makers has 15 000 members. Today all are employed at a wage rate of $15 per hour. The union is considering a push to raise wages by $1.50 per hour. A union economist has pointed out that evidence for the industry suggests a labour demand elasticity of −1. What is the potential cost of a new wage contract that accepts the 10% hike? What further contract provisions might you suggest to reduce or eliminate these potential losses?

8. In many developing countries, the government sector pays a much higher wage for workers than the private sector does. This practice has been widely criticized on the grounds that it creates unemployment as people queue for government jobs in the cities rather than staying in the countryside working for market-determined wages. Using supply and demand curves, show how this situation could lead to higher wages and less employment in the private sector job market.

9. What factors are important in determining a person's wages? Connect these factors to explanations of why some groups (e.g., women, teenagers) earn less than others.

20

Current Problems in Applied Microeconomics: Health Care and Immigration

In this chapter, we use microeconomic theory to examine two important Canadian public policy issues: health care and immigration. Our goal is to show how relatively simple economic concepts can be used to illuminate important public policy debates. As these two issues are extraordinarily complex, it is impossible to cover all aspects of the policy debates surrounding them. It is, however, possible to illustrate how economic theory can be employed in policy analysis. The discussion of health care illustrates how economics provides not a set of definitive answers, but rather, a way of thinking about issues. The discussion of immigration emphasizes the importance of empirical evidence in policy debates.

Economic Analysis of Health Care Policy

The Production Possibility Frontier and Health Policy

To discuss any microeconomic policy issue we must begin with the most basic analytical device in economics: the production possibility frontier (ppf) curve. Figure 20.1 shows a production possibility frontier curve with health on the horizontal axis and all other goods and services on the vertical axis. The ppf shows all combinations of health and other goods that could be produced if resources were fully employed and if all health care and all other goods were produced at least cost.

One of the first things to note about use of the production possibility frontier is that it is applied at a high level of abstraction. It is assumed that health is produced with scarce resources. But the precise meaning of health is left undefined. We could try to be very precise, but it is unnecessary at this stage. Also, no attempt is made to define the relationship between resource use and health beyond assuming that more resources, if efficiently employed, will produce more health. Human health is a product of a complex set of factors including genetics, the presence of environmental pollutants, lifestyle choices, nutrition, work, and family environment, as well as the diagnosis and treatment of illness in the formal health care system. Health scientists know very little about how the "factors of production" in this "health production function" interact to produce health. Nonetheless, the production possibility frontier and the "health production function," despite their high level of abstraction, can be used to organize an analysis of health issues and direct attention to important unanswered questions for future health research.

It is also noteworthy that the production possibility frontier is independent of institutional arrangements. In other words, it is based only on what is possible given fixed amounts of scarce resources and a given state of knowledge about how to produce. Thus, there are no presumptions about market or nonmarket institutions in the construct. Ultimately, these institutions are critical in any discussion of health, but they make their appearance as one moves from the abstract to the concrete.

The first question the production possibility frontier focuses attention on is: are we currently on the production possibility frontier? If not, we can obtain more health and more other goods and services by reorganizing production in a way that fully employs resources and produces at least cost. This is illustrated in Figure 20.1 in which a society at point A can move to any point between B and C and obtain more of both products.

How can we determine if we are on the production possibility frontier? Ideally we would want to know the "health production function," which describes all possible ways of producing the current level of health in Canadian society. We could use this to determine if the current level of health is being produced with the least expensive technique. Alas, we know little about the health production function and so we cannot use this approach. It is possible, however, to look for specific cases of waste in the system, such as excessive use of tests, pharmaceuticals, and surgery,

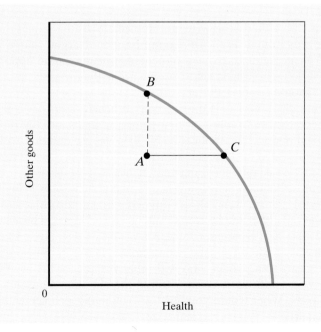

FIGURE 20.1

Inefficiency in the Production of Health

If resources are used inefficiently, as at point *A*, it is possible to obtain better health and more other goods by efficiently organizing the system. But if the health system is organized efficiently, as at a point such as *B*, the only way to secure more health is to give up some other goods.

or unnecessarily long hospital stays. Thus, we can say something despite not knowing the details of the "health production function." As well, we can look critically at the way current and alternative institutions work to deliver health and determine if these institutions produce the information and incentives needed to generate an efficient outcome.

Although the concept of the "health production function" cannot be used directly in determining if we are on the production possibility frontier, it is still a valuable concept. Specifically, it encourages us to adopt a holistic approach to the study of health by emphasizing the fact that health can be produced in many different ways and that factor substitution is possible. For example, it is possible, in principle, to reduce resources going to medical care (one factor in the production of health) and still improve health by using resources to reduce environmental pollutants, improve nutrition and work and family environments, and/or change lifestyle choices (other factors in the production of health). Production functions and the principle of substitution are powerful tools in thinking about any policy.

The second question the production possibility frontier focuses our attention on is: what is the opportunity cost of better health? We cannot have everything we would like. Better health is a good thing. But so too are education, travel, the arts, etc. If we are on (or once we move to) the production possibility frontier, choices must be made and those choices inevitably involve opportunity costs. Moreover, if we must accept current production techniques as given even if they are inefficient, we will find ourselves on a *constrained production possibility frontier* that shows all combinations of health and other goods that we can possibly attain given current resources and current production techniques. Society must choose among these alternatives. Choosing better health involves an opportunity cost in moving from a point such as C on the constrained production possibility frontier in Figure 20.2 to a point such as D.

By emphasizing opportunity costs the production possibility frontier forces us to deal with a difficult ethical problem that must be faced in any economic analysis of health and health care: the problem of putting a value on human health and life. Once we are on the frontier we cannot have more health without accepting less of something else. In other words, human life has an opportunity cost and thus a price that people must decide if they are willing to pay. Suppose moving from point C to point D in Figure 20.2 involves the use of resources to put an artificial heart in a patient who would otherwise face immediate death. Should the resources be used to save this human life? An economist would argue that this decision should be based on a careful assessment of benefits (the maximum opportunity cost people are willing to incur) and costs. If people are willing to give up at least what is required, they should support the operation.

Basing life and death decisions on this type of benefit and cost analysis makes many people uncomfortable. Indeed, at first glance, it seems morally reprehensible. Yet on closer examination, the application of this way of thinking to health care decisions can be shown to have many virtues.

One argument for cost/benefit analysis in health care is that in a world of scarcity choices must be made (choosing not to make a choice is actually a choice for the status quo). Thus, every choice involves an opportunity cost, and the "right" choice can only be made by comparing gains and losses. This can be starkly illustrated in a simple health example. Suppose you have been given $10 million to spend on human health care. You face two options: (1) use the $10 million to provide an artificial heart to a patient who will otherwise die, or (2) use the $10 million to improve water and waste treatment and thereby save thousands of lives in a developing country. What would you do? Can you make a choice without weighing costs and benefits?

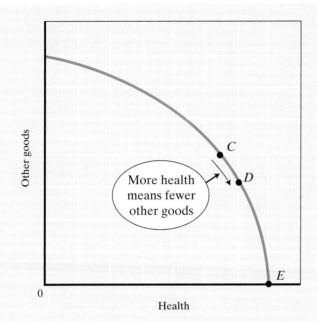

FIGURE 20.2

The Opportunity Cost of Better Health

A society could, in theory, produce at a point such as *E* at which all resources are devoted to health.

A second argument for cost/benefit analysis is that we, as individuals and as a society, implicitly do these types of calculations, but without thinking sufficiently about them. For example, when asked to put a value on human life many would argue that human life has infinite value. But this implies that a life should always be saved provided the opportunity cost is less than infinity. By this logic almost all of society's resources should be devoted to health so that we end up at point E in Figure 20.2. No society behaves in this way. Moreover, placing infinite value on human life would also involve each individual devoting most of his or her own income to preserving health and increasing life expectancy. As few, if any, individuals do this, their behaviour thus suggests that the value they place on their own health is less than infinite.

Valuing human life is necessary in the abstract world of the production possibility frontier if one is to choose among the points on the ppf. It is also necessary in the reality of Canadian society. We must decide whether we are willing to incur the cost of better health; we must decide if we want to use resources to provide a heart transplant to save the life of one person or whether to use those same resources to improve water and sewage treatment in a developing country to save thousands of lives, etc. Economists cannot make these choices for society, but they can identify the alternatives and thus the opportunity costs.

The final important issue emphasized by the production possibility frontier is the potential role of new knowledge in pushing out the frontier over time, thus allowing society to obtain better health and more goods. Medical research is one important source of new knowledge that potentially can generate better health. But other forms of new knowledge can also be important. Indeed, decreases in infant mortality and increases in life expectancy in this century probably owe more to improvements in water and waste treatment, better nutrition, public health (immunization), and improved refrigeration techniques than to advances in "high-tech" medical knowledge. The importance of the holistic approach to health suggested by the "health production function" cannot be over-emphasized, especially given that the debate over health in Canada has tended to focus on medical and hospital care.

In summary, the production possibility frontier is the starting point for all microeconomic analysis of policy, including health and health care policy. It is, however, only a starting point, helping the analyst identify issues and suggesting areas for further thinking and research.

THE COMPETITIVE MARKET MODEL AND HEALTH CARE POLICY

A frequently employed second step in microeconomic analysis is to use the competitive market model as a benchmark to determine if there is any chance that market institutions could generate an outcome that is both equitable and efficient without government. Under certain conditions, the competitive market model will generate production at minimum cost, an efficient mix of output, and an efficient distribution of output. In other words, when these conditions hold, a society can reach the production possibility frontier and arrive at a mix and distribution of output at which, without government action, no member of society can be made better off without someone else being made worse off.

Like the production possibility frontier, the competitive model is applied at a high level of abstraction. It is a world created by the economist, which allows systematic thinking about policy issues. We will assume that everyone in this world starts with the same income, that everyone in this world possesses knowledge about the health effects of different patterns of expenditure, that producers of goods and services (including goods and services affecting health) maximize profits, and that competitive conditions prevail.

Because they are attempting to maximize profit, producers of health products will produce as long as the marginal cost is less than the additional revenue gained from production of an additional unit of the good or service. At the same time, consumers of health products must compare the opportunity cost of buying each unit of health-related product with what they are willing to pay. They will buy provided what they are willing to pay exceeds the opportunity cost.

In the competitive model, competition ensures that a single price emerges for each product and that each producer and each consumer takes this price as given. Significantly, this price is just the opportunity cost for the consumer and the marginal revenue of the producer. Thus the producers have an incentive (potential profits) to produce health products to the point at which marginal cost is just equal to the maximum people are willing to pay and consumers have an incentive to purchase exactly what is produced. This is illustrated in Figure 20.3, which uses a demand curve to show the maximum consumers are willing to pay for each unit and a supply curve to show the minimum cost incurred to produce each unit.

The outcome in the competitive model is a point on the production possibility frontier since profit-maximizing firms have an incentive to produce at minimum cost. The mix and distribution of goods produced will depend on the preferences of consumers. If consumers have different preferences, some will opt to spend income on travel, entertainment, etc., and die at a younger age, and others will forgo these luxuries and invest in a longer, healthier life. Society as a whole doesn't have to worry about the problem of valuing human life—that problem is left to each individual.

The competitive model outlined above is not the "real world." First, we know incomes are not distributed equally. Thus differences in health will not just reflect differences in preferences but also differences in ability to pay. Second, the efficiency of competitive market outcomes is based on a set of assumptions that do not hold in real-world markets. In the model, markets are assumed to be competitive, there is perfect information, property rights are clearly defined and enforceable, and there are no external costs or benefits. These conditions do not hold in real markets for health care.

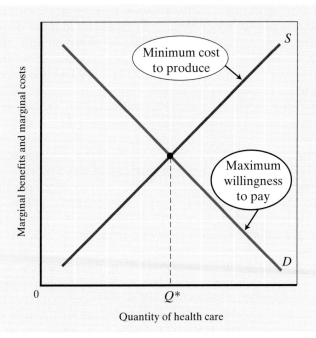

FIGURE 20.3

Health Care Production and Consumption under Perfect Competition

People are willing to pay enough to cover the cost of additional health care up to quantity Q^*. Beyond that point it costs more to provide health care than people are willing to pay. In the pure competitive model, Q^* will emerge from profit-maximizing behaviour by providers and utility-maximizing behaviour by consumers.

MARKET FAILURES AND INEQUITIES IN HEALTH AND HEALTH CARE

The third stage in our economic analysis of health and health care involves looking for market failures and inequities. In many respects health and health care goods and services are much like most other goods and services produced by the private sector of the Canadian economy. Basically, health care is a **private good.** People can be excluded from its benefits if they do not pay. The primary beneficiary of the services provided is the patient, and while it is not the current practice in Canada, in principle, people can be excluded from health care benefits if they do not pay (unlike the case of goods such as radio signals or national defence). In some countries, such as the United States, most physicians are in private practice or work for private hospitals or health maintenance organizations (HMOs),[1] many of which are in business to make a profit. In these countries, health care costs are largely determined in markets by the interaction of supply and demand. Just as in any other market, labour costs (such as physicians' salaries) and capital costs interact with technology to determine costs of production, and willingness and ability to pay play a role in determining demand.

private good *A product produced by firms for sale to individual households. People can be excluded from the benefits of a private good if they do not pay for it.*

However, a number of characteristics of the market for health and health care services suggest possible inequities and inefficiencies in a market health care system. First, asymmetric (imperfect) information, fee-for-service reimbursement, externalities, imperfect market structure, and high transactions costs all suggest that the market may operate inefficiently.[2] Second, the fact that a free market system may leave many citizens unable to access health care services is thought by many to be inequitable.

■ **Asymmetric Information** For markets to be efficient, buyers must have complete information on product quality and price. Yet health care markets are typically

---

[1] *A health maintenance organization or HMO is a private sector managed-care plan that provides comprehensive medical services for members for a flat fee. Companies often set up HMOs for their employees as an alternative to traditional private health insurance. HMOs are often profit-maximizing organizations.*

[2] *For a review of externalities and imperfect information, see Chapter 16. For a review of ineffiency and imperfect market structures, see Chapter 12.*

asymmetric information *A situation in which the participants in an economic transaction have different information about the transaction.*

adverse selection *An imperfect-information problem that can occur when a buyer or seller enters into an exchange with another party who has more information.*

moral hazard *Arises when one party to a contract passes the cost of his or her behaviour on to the other party to the contract.*

deductible *An annual out-of-pocket expenditure that an insurance policy holder must make before the insurance plan makes any reimbursement.*

copayment *A fixed amount of money that an insured person pays for each visit to a doctor's office.*

characterized by **asymmetric information,** a situation in which the participants in an economic transaction have different information about the transaction. Most of us know little about medicine. It takes years of education and on-the-job training to become a licensed physician. In addition, the practice of medicine has become increasingly specialized, and the gap between a doctor's knowledge and her patient's knowledge has increased. Virtually all information on product quality and price rests with the supplier—essentially, with the physician. In a market health care system, the appropriate services to "buy" are chosen by the very person who supplies them! A used-car salesperson would love to be able to tell potential customers what they need to buy and have them actually buy it in deference to the used-car salesperson's expert opinion. But few used-car buyers are willing to defer to the used-car salesperson's expert opinion. On the other hand, people often will unquestioningly follow a physician's advice. Clearly, when suppliers control information needed to make effective demand decisions, the opportunity for waste and abuse exists. A number of studies exist that document substantial use of expensive yet inappropriate or ineffective medical procedures.

Asymmetric information may also result in the problem of **adverse selection,** which was discussed in Chapter 16. Adverse selection happens when insurance buyers know more about their health than the insurer does. Suppose, for example, that there are only two types of people: sick people and well people. If insurers could not tell the difference between the two groups, they would charge the average cost of providing health care coverage. By doing so, they would charge the sick much less than the expected costs of coverage. The sick would be more likely to buy health insurance, while some of the well would buy no insurance. Since a larger percentage of the insured are now sick, premiums would rise, further discouraging the well from buying insurance. This process would continue until only the sick are insured at very high prices—clearly not an ideal situation. Thus asymmetric information may lead to a need for government involvement.

■ **Fee-for-Service Reimbursement** If health care meant going to a doctor's office a couple of times per year, we would not worry about having insurance. But most people know that the costs of a serious illness can be catastrophic. In the United States, spending a week in a hospital and having a serious operation can cost well over $100 000. A serious head injury could leave even a high-income family destitute.

As a consequence, people want insurance. Even in the private health care system in the United States, over 63% of the population is covered by insurance provided by profit-maximizing insurance companies. The private insurance contract involves members of the population paying the insurance company money (the insurance premium) if they are well and receiving money sufficient to cover medical expenses if they become sick.

Coverage by public or private insurance leads to a number of problems. First, full coverage creates a **moral hazard** problem. If patients do not bear the costs of health care, they have an incentive to overuse medical services. In other words, since the price of a visit to a physician is zero, people will tend to go to the doctor too often. The increase in utilization will depend on the elasticity of demand for physicians' services. Most private insurance contracts incorporate a **deductible** (an annual out-of-pocket expenditure that an insurance policy holder must make before the plan makes any reimbursement) and a **copayment** (a fixed amount of money that an insured person pays for each visit to a doctor's office) to ensure that at least a small price is paid.

The moral hazard problem is unlikely to result in the average person overusing the system. Visits to the doctor involve real and often large opportunity costs (time lost, increased risk of contracting infectious diseases, etc.) and very few people go to a doctor without good reason. However, moral hazard is a potential problem of physicians. Patients have very little control over their use of health care services. They cannot decide what types of prescription drugs they need, they cannot check themselves into a hospital, they cannot order laboratory tests themselves, etc. These important utilization decisions are made, with almost complete control, by the patients' physicians. The physicians are thus the **gatekeepers** in the medical system in Canada. But if the cost to both physicians and patients is zero, one would expect that physicians will overuse the system. For example, if there is even a remote chance that a test will provide positive health benefits, physicians are likely to order the test. They have no incentive to weigh the cost of the test against the expected benefits.

A second problem with insurance is that the method of reimbursement may lead providers to oversupply services. Traditionally, health care providers have been reimbursed on a **fee-for-service** basis. As long as the price paid by the insurer is greater than the marginal cost of production, providers have an incentive to oversupply. This system makes the problem of asymmetric information more serious. Suppliers have not only all the information needed to make an informed choice about what services a patient needs, but also a big incentive to oversupply.

Private insurance schemes typically involve a third potential problem, **experience rating.** In the United States, the fact that those who get very sick are very costly to the insurance companies has led insurance companies to link premiums to an individual's current health status or to the probability that the individual will become sick. Private insurance companies, which are in business to make money, will not insure people at all if certain pre-existing conditions (such as heart disease, cancer, or AIDS) exist when the application is filed. Since most injuries and illness do not result from the behaviour of the insured, experience rating does not for the most part improve the efficiency of health care provision. In a sense, experience rating defeats the purpose of insurance, which is to spread risk so that no single household must face the full cost of an illness.

■ **Externalities**   As we saw in Chapter 16, an externality exists when the actions or decisions of one person or a group impose a cost or bestow a benefit on some second or third parties. The result is usually inefficient. The most often-used example is pollution. One way of "internalizing" externalities is to tax activities that generate public harms and subsidize activities that generate public benefits.

Health care may in fact produce positive externalities. Clearly, public health is improved when individuals receive proper immunizations and when communicable diseases are treated in a timely fashion. In addition, poor health may lead to negative externalities. Poor health leads to lower productivity, and lower productivity leads to lower wages. Poverty, dependence on social assistance, and homelessness may all be linked to some extent to health.

■ **Imperfect Structure and Market Power**   Drug and biotechnology companies spend millions of dollars on research and development to create drugs and discover procedures that will cure diseases and save lives. Their incentive to conduct R&D is provided by the patent system, which protects the producers of new drugs, equipment, and procedures for a limited number of years. This monopoly power has led to extraordinarily high prices for some patented prescription drugs and equipment over the years.

As we discussed in Chapter 13, there are two sides to this story. A patent system is necessary to provide the private sector with an incentive to engage in research and development. However, our society must decide if patent protection should be decreased or eliminated when the product of research is a life-saving drug

gatekeepers *The capacity in which doctors in Canada act when they prescribe drugs, check patients into hospitals, order diagnostic tests, etc.*

fee-for-service reimbursement *A program in which insurance companies reimburse health care providers for the services they've rendered.*

experience rating *The insurance company practice of charging individuals or groups of individuals premiums that are linked to their current state of health or to the probability that they will become sick.*

that can be produced at a low cost. Many have called for more funds for publicly sponsored research the results of which would be available as a public good.

Another example of imperfect market structure can be found in the labour market. The supply of physicians in Canada is restricted by admissions standards at Canadian medical schools, by provincial licensing practices, and by provincial-government-imposed limits on the number of physicians allowed to practise in a province. It is sometimes argued that these restrictions on supply keep physicians' incomes high.

However, some economists argue that supply restrictions are desirable. They point out that asymmetric information allows doctors to determine the level of utilization of medical services and thus the physicians' income. As a consequence, they argue that an increase in the supply of physicians will not lead to competition and lower prices but instead will lead to an increase in the utilization of physicians' services. There is some evidence that suggests that an increase in the number of physicians results in physicians calling patients back more frequently for second and third appointments and increased referrals to other doctors. Thus an increase in supply can result in a **supplier-induced increase in demand.**

■ **Transactions Costs**   Whenever we buy or sell goods in a market system, some resources are used to complete the transaction. For example, when you buy food at the local grocery store the purchase price must cover the cost of the cash registers, checkout clerks, pricing clerks, and sales supervisors. In general, these **transactions costs** are relatively small and thus use few resources. But in many private insurance programs, transactions costs are relatively high and they are especially high in health insurance. Administrative costs are often more than 20% of benefits paid out in private insurance plans versus only 10% in public insurance schemes.[3] Thus, private provision can waste resources. In 1985 in the largely private U.S. health care sector, the processing of claims and other administrative tasks cost 0.59% of GDP versus only 0.11% in the Canadian health care system.[4]

■ **Equity**   Although there are numerous inefficiencies that can potentially arise in a pure market health system, the biggest concern seems to be equity. Many view health care as a commodity that is fundamentally different from other goods and services. Indeed, some argue that health care is a basic right that all citizens should have, regardless of their ability to pay. Several theories of distribution we discussed in Chapter 17 lend potential support to the idea of government involvement in providing universal coverage. Voters may well understand that health care produces positive externalities and therefore they will support programs out of self-interest. In addition, those who subscribe to the idea of Rawlsian justice would argue that a just set of rules (determined by members of society before they know the circumstances that their life will lead them to) would declare a set of basic entitlements for all that would include medical care.

The Canadian Health Care System: An Overview

Over $70 billion (about 10% of all Canadian income) is spent on hospital care, health care services (provided by physicians, nurses, chiropractors, physiotherapists, naturopaths, practitioners of homeopathy, etc.), diagnostic services (laboratory testing), and prescribed pharmaceuticals. This makes the health care industry one of the most important sectors in our economy. It is an extremely complex

supplier-induced demand
Demand that, due to asymmetric information, is determined largely by the supplier, rather than the consumer of the commodity.

transactions costs *In a market system, the resources that are used to complete a transaction.*

---

[3]*Joseph E. Stiglitz*, Economics of the Public Sector, *second edition (New York: W.W. Norton & Co., 1988), pp. 126–127.*
[4]*R.G. Evans et al., "Controlling Health Expenditures—the Canadian Reality,"* New England Journal of Medicine *320 (1989): pp. 571–577.*

sector, involving a unique mix of government and market institutions with over 70% of health care spending funded by government. Government covers the costs of hospital care and most diagnostic services, it pays for most physician services provided to patients, and it closely regulates the pharmaceutical industry by offering patent protection and issuing final approval on the introduction of new drugs. Government does not, however, cover visits to alternative medical practitioners, most drug purchases, or a variety of "nonessential" services. Figure 20.4 illustrates the distribution of government health expenditures.

Prior to World War II, health care in Canada was entirely provided and financed by the private sector. Those needing health care were responsible for covering their own costs, and a variety of private health insurance schemes existed for those who could afford to purchase coverage. But these plans did not cover the full cost of health care and even those who had purchased insurance faced severe financial problems when hit with a serious illness. Only the very wealthy could afford to get sick. Charitable organizations often helped the poor, and doctors frequently offered their services free of charge to ease the financial burden imposed by illness.

The substantial government role in the health care sector evolved in the post–World War II period. In 1947, Saskatchewan introduced a public health insurance scheme covering hospitalization. By 1955 five provinces (Saskatchewan, British Columbia, Newfoundland, Alberta, and Ontario) had public hospital insurance programs in place. Health was considered an area of exclusive provincial jurisdiction and the federal government did not play a role in the system until 1957, when it passed the Hospital Insurance and Diagnostic Services Act. This piece of legislation committed the federal government to covering one-half of the costs of hospital insurance contingent upon the provincial plans meeting the following conditions: (1) comprehensiveness; (2) accessibility; (3) universal coverage; (4) public administration; and (5) portability of benefits. The act sidestepped the issue of constitutional jurisdiction by offering the provinces funds as a "gift" provided the provinces met the conditions listed above. The "gift" enticed the remaining provinces to introduce hospital insurance plans and a relatively uniform Canada-wide system of hospital insurance developed.

In 1961, Saskatchewan again took the lead by extending its insurance system to cover medical services provided by physicians outside of hospitals. The legislation

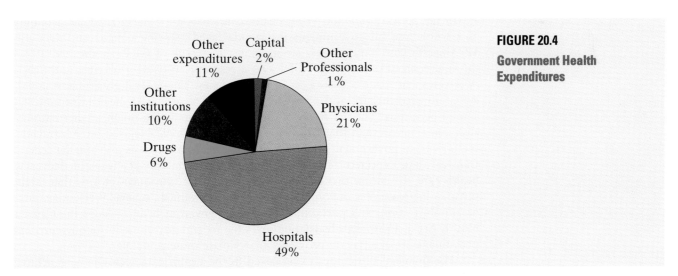

FIGURE 20.4

Government Health Expenditures

Source: Health Canada, *Government Health Expenditures By Category, 1994* (Ottawa: Minister of Supply and Services, 1996).

was vehemently opposed by the doctors of Saskatchewan; they argued that the market provided the best means to allocate medical services and that government involvement would jeopardize freedom of choice and thus the special relationship between doctor and patient. Over 90% of doctors in Saskatchewan went on strike in an attempt to block the legislation. But in the end, the government won. In 1966, the government of Canada introduced the Medical Care Act which, similar to the earlier Hospital Insurance and Diagnostic Service Act (which had covered hospital insurance only), offered to cover one-half of the costs of provincial medical insurance programs provided that the five conditions in the 1957 legislation were met. The provinces quickly responded by introducing their own plans, creating the Canada-wide system that is popularly known as medicare.

In 1977, the federal government abandoned the **cost-sharing** approach of the Hospital Insurance and Diagnostic Services Act and the Medical Care Act. New legislation, the Federal-Provincial Fiscal Arrangements and Established Program Financing Act, provided a **block grant** to each provincial government based on the province's population. Under this legislation, the federal government covered part of the transfer directly in cash and part by providing the provinces additional **tax room.** The transfer of tax room involved the federal government reducing tax rates and the provinces increasing tax rates (keeping overall tax rates constant) as a way of providing the provinces with additional money to spend on health care. In 1977, roughly half the transfer was in cash, half in additional tax room.

The new approach to funding health care had two important implications. First, it eliminated any links between the size of the transfer and the province's expenditure on health care. If health care costs grew faster than the transfer, the provinces would face increased difficulty paying for the program. But if health care costs grew more slowly than the transfer, the provinces would enjoy a windfall gain. Thus the new arrangement introduced new incentives for the provinces to control health care costs. Second, the relative size of the cash transfer was expected to decline over time as economic growth generated rapidly growing tax revenues from the new tax room available to the provinces. The federal government had hoped that strong public support for the Canadian public health care system would keep individual provinces from undermining the basic principles of comprehensiveness, accessibility, universality, public administration, and portability. But the federal government realized that the reduction in the size of the cash transfer would reduce its ability to penalize provinces that did not adhere to these principles.

In the period following 1977, health care costs grew faster than the economy as a whole and all governments in Canada faced growing deficits and debt. (In 1975 health care expenditures stood at just over 7% of GDP. By the mid 1990s this had risen to over 10% of GDP.) As a response to fiscal problems, both levels of government made adjustments in their policies. The federal government unilaterally adjusted the size of the transfer in support of provincial health insurance on several occasions. The net result of these adjustments was a much smaller national cash contribution than that called for in the original 1977 legislation. Meanwhile, the provincial governments, faced with rising health care costs and smaller federal transfers than expected, began to search for new and cheaper ways of delivering health care. To ensure that the provinces would not introduce reforms that might threaten the principles of comprehensiveness, accessibility, universal coverage, public administration, and portability, the federal government introduced the Canada Health Act in 1984. This legislation gives the federal government the power to impose financial penalties on provinces that violate these principles.

The financial difficulties experienced in the health care sector have generated many calls for reform. Some argue that Canada should abandon the universal, publicly administered system, and allow the free market to work in the health care

cost-shared transfer *A financial arrangement between federal and provincial governments whereby each government covers a share of the cost of providing a program.*

block grant *A financial arrangement whereby one level of government gives a block of money to another to cover part of the cost of a program. The size of the transfer does not depend on program cost.*

tax room *An arrangement to transfer money from one government to another in which one government reduces tax rates and thus tax revenue, and the other government increases tax rates and thus tax revenue.*

Table 20.1	Indicators of Health Status: Canada and the United States, 1990

	Life Expectancy at Birth		Infant Mortality (per 1000 live births)	
Canada	Males	73.7	Canada	7
	Females	80.6		
United States	Males	71.6	United States	10
	Females	78.6		

Source: Cyril Nair, Razaul Karim, and Christine Nyers, "Health Care and Health Status: A Canada–United States Statistical Comparison," in Statistics Canada, *Health Reports* vol. 4, no. 2 (Ottawa: Minister of Supply and Services, 1992): pp. 175–184.

sector. The Canadian Medical Association (CMA) debated this approach in 1996 and seriously considered advocating a two-tier system, with a publicly administered health care system for those with low incomes and a private system for those with high incomes. The CMA's position is motivated, in part, by doctors' inability to deliver the type of health care they would like to due to long waiting lists for important medical procedures and, in part, by their concern with restrictions placed on the growth of physicians' incomes. The CMA also fears increased government involvement in the actual practice of medicine, with governments assuming control over diagnosis and treatment, thus undermining the traditional doctor–patient relationship. Others, including a significant number of physicians, vehemently oppose the use of the market system to solve problems in the health care system. They argue that the Canadian health care system produces better health outcomes than more market-based health care systems and at a much lower cost. Figure 20.5 and Table 20.1 show that Canadians enjoy better health and lower relative costs than the Americans with their more market-oriented health system.

The federal and provincial governments remain committed to a publicly

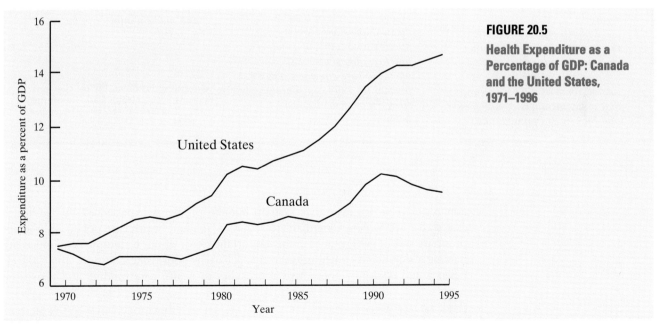

FIGURE 20.5

Health Expenditure as a Percentage of GDP: Canada and the United States, 1971–1996

Source: Health Canada, *National Health Expenditures in Canada, 1975–1996* (Ottawa: Health Canada, 1997).

In the 1992 presidential election in the United States, Bill Clinton listed health reform as his number-one priority. The largely private U.S. health care system was the most expensive in the world, yet it insured a smaller fraction of its population than other industrialized countries and it ranked relatively poorly on indicators of health outcomes such as life expectancy and infant mortality. In October 1993, President Clinton sent the U.S. Congress a 1324-page bill, which promised to completely restructure the U.S. health care system. The bill failed to pass, but over the same period the market was generating significant changes in the U.S. health care system. The following article from *The New York Times* outlines some of the important changes.

In the two years that Congress wrangled over health care before quashing proposals for fundamental change, private market forces were acting on their own to transform the country's medical system dramatically.

Indeed, cost cutting, intensive competition and the growing role of large profit seeking corporations in health care escalated some of the very trends that many members of Congress said they most opposed, like limitations on the choice of doctors. Among the milestones American health care reached without fanfare during 1993 and 1994 were these:

■ A MAJORITY *of privately insured Americans were enrolled in managed-care plans that limit choice of doctors and treatments. Sixty-five percent of workers at medium and large companies were in such plans by 1994.*

■ FOR-PROFIT *health maintenance organizations grew so fast that they overtook nonprofit H.M.O.'s as the dominant force in managed care. Today the majority of all people enrolled in H.M.O.'s, the most common and stringent form of managed care, are in plans run by for-profit companies.*

■ AT LEAST *three-fourths of all doctors signed contracts, covering at least some of their patients, to cut their fees and accept oversight of their medical decisions. Among doctors who work in group practices, the share of such managed-care contracts was 89 percent by 1993, up sharply from 56 percent the year before.*

Run for decades more like a collection of cottage industries than a system that now accounts for one-seventh of the economy, medical care is increasingly the domain of big business, offering a rich new playing field for Wall Street. Mergers and acquisitions of hospitals; clinics; doctor groups with their patient lists; medical laboratories, and other patient-care services, have totaled $20 billion this year, up from just $6 billion in 1992. Combined with the $22 billion in pharmaceutical deals, health care mergers surpassed in value those of any other industry for 1994, according to the Securities Data Company, a research firm in Newark.

But this restructuring has done nothing to ease the plight of the uninsured, whose numbers keep climbing, and it is also raising profound new questions about how quality care and medical ethics can be guarded.

Source: Erik Eckholm, "While Congress Remains Silent, Health Care Transforms Itself," *The New York Times*, December 18, 1994, p. 1.

administered health insurance system, but the problems experienced by the health care sector are forcing Canadians to rethink Canadian health care policy and the appropriate role of government in this important sector of our economy. Economists are making a significant contribution to this debate by addressing questions about the efficiency and equity of alternative approaches to health care funding and provision.

EFFICIENCY AND EQUITY OF THE CANADIAN HEALTH CARE SYSTEM

The Canadian health care system is much like that in the United States: doctors sell their services to patients who have freedom to choose which doctor to see. Doctors are gatekeepers to the hospital/diagnostic services system. However, in Canada, insurance is provided by government instead of private insurance companies. The public insurance is paid for largely out of general tax revenues and all Canadians are covered. The public insurance system in Canada addresses some of the inefficiencies and inequities of the private market system, but certainly not all. Moreover, the Canadian public system may generate its own inefficiencies and inequities. (For a discussion of some recent developments in the U.S. health care system, see the Global Perspective box on the opposite page.)

Because all Canadians are covered by the public health insurance system, many might conclude that the Canadian public system is more equitable than a private system. In the United States, at least 35 million people have no insurance whatsoever and as many as 50 million more have inadequate insurance.[5] Also, there is no experience rating in the Canadian public insurance system, thus the insurance package made available may be considered superior to any that would be offered under a free market system. Finally, universality eliminates adverse selection problems, addresses most potential externalities, and keeps transactions costs low.

However, in many respects the Canadian public insurance system is similar to a private system and is vulnerable to the same inefficiencies: doctors are paid on a fee-for-service basis; there is still asymmetric information; the public system does not reduce moral hazard; and doctors exercise significant control over supply.

The Canadian public insurance system might also introduce some inefficiencies not present in a private market system. The moral hazard problem faced by both patients and doctors in the Canadian public insurance plan is potentially more serious than in a private insurance system since there are no deductibles or co-payments. In addition, provincial governments, faced with pressure from a public concerned with rising tax rates, have taken a number of steps to control cost, steps that can introduce inefficiencies and inequities.

Governments in Canada have attempted to control costs in a number of ways. First, they have placed limits on expenditures on new medical technologies and hospital facilities. As a consequence, facilities are relatively scarce and it is not always possible to secure immediate treatment with the state-of-the-art technologies. Even if individuals are willing to pay more to secure what they consider better health care, they are unable to do so, except by travelling to the United States, where health care is provided using a market system. Second, governments have attempted to control costs by restricting the growth in doctors' incomes and by limiting the number of doctors able to secure billing numbers (a billing number is necessary for the doctor to receive payment from the government for services provided to a patient). Consequently, many doctors have moved to the United States to practise. This costs Canada some good doctors and limits the choices available to patients. Moreover, denying some doctors the option to practise in the location of their choosing could be judged inequitable. (See the Issues and Controversies box "Shifting Costs in Canadian Health Care" on the next page for more about cost control in Canadian health care.)

Where Do We Go from Here?

The debate over Canadian health care will continue into the next century. There are some who believe that Canadian governments should permit a private market in health care services to emerge to supplement the public system. This would allow those who can afford it to secure faster treatment with better technology if they are

---

[5]*Michael Rachlis and Carol Kushner,* Strong Medicine: How to Save Canada's Health Care System *(Toronto: HarperCollins Publishing, 1994), p. 196.*

Issues and Controversies

Shifting Costs in Canadian Health Care

The shifting, or "downloading," of some health care costs from government to individual citizens is one of the most controversial attempts at solving government deficit and debt problems. To reduce their own spending, governments will cut their spending on a program or service—for example, by removing certain drugs from those covered by government drug plans—and shift the responsibility for payment directly onto the individuals who use that program. In the case of drug benefit plans, since citizens still need these drugs, their direct spending for these goods increases. The reduction in government spending does not necessarily equal the increase in spending by the individual citizens. Indeed, the cost to society (bear in mind that the citizens are society and that they either pay for drugs directly in the market or indirectly through taxes) for the same amount of drugs may increase, decrease, or remain the same as a result of the downloading. Thus, it is not clear that such reductions in government spending are efficient.

It is clear, however, that downloading does have implications for the distribution of well-being in society. The user of the drug must now pay its full cost while taxpayers escape responsibility. Thus, it is possible that downloading can result in a less efficient and less equitable use of society's scarce resources. This is not always necessarily going to be the case, but it is important to be aware of the possibility.

As the following excerpt makes clear, recent developments in the Canadian health care system open new opportunities for cost shifting.

In the medicare health arena, given today's fiscal climate, one must expect the provincial ministries of health to strip their health programs to the bare

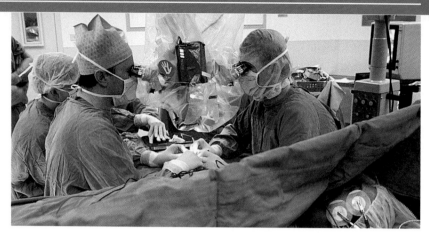

Rising health care costs are causing significant changes in the way health care is produced and financed.

minimum required by the Canada Health Act, with the resulting deletion of all remaining seniors' drug plans, the remaining children's dental plans in Quebec, paramedical and ambulance services, and many others. Even one reading of the Canada Health Act is frightening because of the latitude available for further cost cutting. Essentially, the Act requires the provinces to provide a medicare plan that covers services that are "medically necessary" or "medically required." Under the Constitution Act, each province has the authority and power to define those terms.

A recent court case in Prince Edward Island supported the province's application for a "conditional access" clause. Under this clause, P.E.I. would only pay for the medical services provided if certain listed conditions have been met. For provinces trying to shrink their covered services, conditional access sets up quite a cost-shifting opportunity.

Let's take this a step fur-

ther. It may be suggested that conditional access could be applied so as to restrict a smoker from ever receiving a lung transplant or alcoholics from receiving a liver transplant. Personal health risks that are voluntarily assumed by a resident of a province could restrict his or her access to subsidized care. Injuries sustained in school sports and such weekend recreational activities as skiing, tennis, and horseback riding could put citizens at risk of not being covered by the state.

While the Canada Health Act opens the door to these possibilities, the P.E.I. court case confirms it in case law.

The examples given in this article range from ambulance services to lung transplants to smokers. Think about the efficiency and equity implications in each case. Do concepts like moral hazard help when thinking about the cases?

Source: "Shifting the Burden: It is Time Government Stopped Shifting Health Care Costs Onto the Backs of Employers and Met to Discuss a Co-sharing Alternative," *Benefits Canada* vol. 21, no. 1 (January 1997): pp. 41, 43.

willing to cover the cost. It is argued that this would result in a more efficient outcome since such mutually beneficial transactions are not possible under the public insurance system.

Others argue that any privatization is likely to undermine the public system. Those taking this position argue that any private provision will result in one system for the relatively affluent and another for the relatively poor. Moreover, they argue that the relatively affluent will be less willing to support the public system when a private system exists. These individuals generally favour maintaining the Canadian system as is.

Still others argue that the government should play a much larger role in the health care system. Those taking this position believe that governments should limit the control of doctors in the system by increasing the importance of nurses and other medical practitioners (increasing competition between service providers), by prohibiting doctors from ordering tests and procedures for which the costs exceed the known benefits, and by putting many doctors on salary. This type of reform is opposed by most doctors, who believe that it is their role to examine each patient as an individual and to recommend the course of action that they, based on accumulated expertise, consider best regardless of cost. Those in favour of increased control over doctors argue that research has shown that many tests and procedures prescribed by doctors offer no benefits to the average patient but use significant amounts of society's resources and increase doctors' incomes.[6] Moreover, they believe that reforms can generate better health for Canadians at lower cost without compromising universality.

Economics contributes to the debate by emphasizing opportunity costs, by continually reminding people of the importance of weighing costs against benefits, and by identifying market and political failures that affect resource allocation in our society. But it cannot provide a final answer. Each position has its merits and there are always trade-offs that must be made in any debate about policy. The progress we make in dealing with health care issues over the next few years will be a good test of whether representative democracy can deal with an issue of such complexity when no easy answers exist.

The Economics of Immigration

People from all over the world want to come to Canada to build a better life for themselves and their families. But Canada only allows a small fraction of the people who would like to come to this country to actually enter. Should we allow all who want to to come in? Or are restrictions justified? And, if restrictions are justified, what types of restrictions are best?

Immigration is a controversial topic. One of the sources of controversy in discussions about immigration policy is that it raises difficult moral questions. Most Canadians are either immigrants or can trace their roots to immigrants. What gives us the moral right to restrict others from entering the country? This is an especially difficult question given that Canadian standards of living are higher than those in most other parts of the world. Indeed, the gap is so great that people will take extraordinary risks to get into this country. In 1992, over 500 Romanians were caught inside cargo containers destined for Canada at the port of Antwerp in

---

[6] *Specific examples of overuse include the very high rate of surgical (Caesarean section) deliveries in Canada (approximately one in five births in 1989). The benefit of surgical delivery is supposed to be better health for both baby and mother. The cost is the cost of the surgery and hospitalization. Yet only 7% of deliveries in the Netherlands are by Casearean, and both mothers and babies do just as well as in Canada. Thus the costs seem to outweigh the benefits in many surgical deliveries in Canada.*

Table 20.2
Immigration in Canada

Years	Immigration (thousands)
1861–1871	260
1871–1881	350
1881–1891	680
1891–1901	250
1901–1911	1550
1911–1921	1400
1921–1931	1200
1931–1941	149
1941–1951	548
1951–1961	1543
1961–1971	1429
1971–1981	1429
1981–1991	1977
1991–1996	1588

Sources: 1861–1991: Statistics Canada, *Canada Yearbook, 1994,* Cat. no. 11-402E/1994; 1991–1995: Statistics Canada, *Canadian Economic Observer: Historical Supplement, 1995/96,* Cat. no. 11-210-XPB; 1996: Statistics Canada, *Canadian Social Trends* no. 45 (Summer 1997), Cat. no. 11-008-XPE.

Belgium.[7] Stowaways such as these risk their lives hiding in what amounts to a cold, dark, iron box that sits on the deck of a ship, in desperate hope of securing a new life in this country.

The debate over immigration is complicated by social and political concerns over the effect of immigrants on the traditions and heritage of Canadians. The ability to set immigration policy is considered one of the most basic rights of nation states because nation states around the world want to be able to ensure some sort of collective identity or purpose. Canada has officially adopted a policy of multiculturalism and is at least formally committed to creating a multicultural community. However, this official commitment is not unanimously endorsed by Canadians. French Canadians are particularly concerned about the effect of immigration on their traditions and heritage, and on their political power in this multicultural society. English Canadians are also concerned that high levels of immigration will undermine their traditions and heritage.

Economics cannot answer the difficult moral, social, and political questions that arise in discussions of immigration. Economics can, however, address other questions that necessarily arise in such discussions. What effect does immigration have on the Canadian economy? Does it reduce incomes of Canadians already in the country? Do immigrants take jobs from Canadians? Are immigrants a drain on the public treasury?

A BRIEF HISTORY OF IMMIGRATION INTO CANADA

Although Canada is largely a country of immigrants, net migration in any given year has been of relatively minor significance in contributing to the rate of growth in the Canadian population. For example, it is estimated that only 10 000 people immigrated from France during the French regime (1600–1763). Yet in the 1991 Census, over 8.4 million Canadians indicated that they had French origins. Still, in certain periods Canada has experienced high rates of immigration.

Table 20.2 presents data on immigration in the post-Confederation period. The table illustrates significant variation in immigration over time. This variation was due in part to economic conditions in Canada and in part to changes in Canadian government policy.

In the second half of the nineteenth century there were few government-imposed restrictions on immigration. But economic conditions in Canada, especially relative to those in the United States, were not very attractive. Indeed, between 1861 and 1901 the number of Canadians leaving this country exceeded the number of immigrants. This changed dramatically after 1901. The Canadian government, interested in developing the Prairies, launched a vigorous immigration campaign to attract new immigrants to Canada. At the same time, the Canadian economy boomed. Over one and a half million people immigrated to Canada in the first decade of this century. This amounted to almost 25% of the average Canadian population in that decade. In 1911 alone over 331 000 people entered Canada.

This influx of immigrants generated a backlash. A piece of legislation introduced in 1910 placed entry barriers on immigrants likely to go to larger urban centres and, in particular, on "those belonging to nationalities unlikely to assimilate and who consequently prevent the build up of a united nation of people of similar customs and ideals."[8] In 1923, the pro-European, especially pro-British, policy was strengthened by legislation that kept out all Chinese immigrants.

---

[7]Sunday Morning [radio program]. July 25, 1993. Produced by CBC Radio.
[8]Department of Manpower and Immigration, The Immigration Program, Vol. 2, Report of the Canadian Immigration and Population Study (Ottawa: Information Canada, 1974), pp. 7–8, quoted in Wayne W. McVery Jr. and Warren E. Kalbach, Canadian Population (Nelson Canada: Toronto, 1995), p. 85.

The flow of immigrants slowed to a trickle during the Great Depression and World War II, but following the war immigration increased again to levels experienced at the turn of the century. In 1967, the official policy of favouring certain nationalities was eliminated. In addition, immigration policy opened up a number of ways to secure entry to Canada. The typical approach was based on a formula known as the "point system." Under the point system, applicants were awarded points based on education, language skills, and occupation (with applicants receiving points based on labour force needs). Entry was granted if the applicant accumulated sufficient points. A second track to secure entry was by means of the family reunification program; a blood relative could sponsor an immigrant provided the immigrant was of good health and character. Finally, refugees were granted entry on humanitarian grounds.

The elimination of pro-European biases in legislation and more liberal administrative practices increased the numbers of non-European immigrants tremendously. Applicants from Africa, the Caribbean, and especially Asian countries increased dramatically. In 1955, 82% of immigrants were European and only 3.3% originated in Asia; by 1975, Europeans accounted for 38% of immigrants and Asians for over 25%. In 1995, European immigrants had fallen to 19.7% of the total and Asian immigrants had risen to over 60%.

In the 1990s, Canada has been accepting over 200 000 new immigrants per year, despite almost unprecedented levels of unemployment. Declining fertility rates in Canada are being consciously countered by higher levels of immigration to keep Canadian population growth rates near historic levels. Although the current Liberal government (in its Red Book policy proposals in the 1993 election) promised to set annual immigration at about 1% of the Canadian population, it has actually opted to pursue a slightly less open policy. In fact, the Liberals have introduced a substantial immigration processing fee and reduced their immigration targets by 50 000. They seem to believe that attitudes toward immigration are polarizing in Canada and that this is a potentially divisive issue.

ECONOMIC ARGUMENTS FOR FREE IMMIGRATION

Should a country permit completely free immigration into its borders? The argument for free immigration is that it increases world output. Labour flows across borders in response to wage differentials. Consider the case of the Caribbean and Canada. Low-wage workers in the Caribbean migrate to Canada because wages are higher in Canada. If markets are basically competitive, wages reflect the workers' productivity. In other words, because Canada has more capital and uses more advanced technology than the Caribbean, the productivity of labour is higher in Canada than in the Caribbean. Thus, the same labour produces more total output after immigration, and world output rises.[9]

Now consider the case of France and Italy. If a labour shortage develops in France because the demand for French wine increases, French wages will rise and attract workers from other European countries. If at the same time the demand for leather goods produced in Italy drops off, Italian wages will fall, and Italian workers will move to France, where their productivity is higher.

The argument for the free movement of labour among nations is exactly the same as the argument for the free movement of labour among the sectors of the domestic economy. Suppose an economy produces only two goods, X and Y. If demand for good X picks up, the demand for labour used to produce X rises as the marginal revenue product of labour employed in the production of X increases. Labour will move out of the production of good Y if and only if its

---

[9]For a review of how the labour market works, see Chapters 10 and 19.

productivity is higher in X in terms of the value of output. This movement ensures efficiency. Recall the simple definition that an efficient economy is one that produces what people want at least cost.

Those who favour a looser policy toward immigrants believe that immigrants do not displace Canadian workers but rather take jobs that Canadians do not want. Immigrants produce things that Canadians need. In addition, the Canadian economy has absorbed wave after wave of immigrants with continued income and employment growth.

THE ARGUMENT AGAINST FREE IMMIGRATION

No economist disputes the idea that the distribution of income is likely to change among countries and among groups within each country in response to immigration. Consider the case of low-wage immigrant workers. Equilibrium wages in the market for unskilled workers will rise in the country of origin and fall in the country of destination.

The argument in favour of free immigration assumes that all workers get jobs. However, the popular impression is certainly that immigrants (who often work for relatively low wages) take jobs away from low-income Canadians and drive up unemployment rates. In addition, many believe that immigrants end up on welfare rolls and become a burden to taxpayers. Opponents also point to crime in ethnic neighbourhoods and rivalries among ethnic groups as evidence of further costs to society.

THE EVIDENCE: THE NET COSTS OF IMMIGRATION

To determine whether the benefits of immigration outweigh the costs, we must ask two important questions. To what extent does immigration reduce domestic wages and increase unemployment? And, do immigrants impose a net burden on taxpayers?

A number of recent studies have found that immigration has a very small effect on wages and unemployment. Perhaps the most influential recent study was conducted by Canadian-born economist David Card, who currently teaches at Princeton University.[10] Card examined wages and employment opportunities in the Miami metropolitan area during and after the Mariel boat lift in 1981. Almost overnight, about 125 000 Cubans arrived in Florida and increased the labour force in Miami by over 7%. Card looked at trends in wages and unemployment among Miami workers between 1980 and 1985 and found virtually no effect. In addition, the data he examined mirrored the experience of workers in Los Angeles, Houston, Atlanta, and similar cities that were not hit by the same shock.

Work with Canadian data generates similar conclusions.[11] A study of the early 1980s in Canada by Ather Akbari of St. Mary's University and Don J. DeVoretz of Simon Fraser University found that job displacement occurred in a limited number of industries, but the authors were unable to detect any displacement for the economy as a whole. A study of the relationship between unemployment and immigration in Canada was carried out by William Marr and Pierre Siklos of Wilfrid Laurier University over the period from 1926 to 1992. Marr and Siklos were unable to identify a relationship between immigration and unemployment in the period up to 1962, but they were able to conclude that immigration had a small effect on unemployment after 1962.

---

[10]David Card, "The Impact of the Mariel Boat Lift on the Miami Labour Market," Industrial and Labour Relations Review, January 1990, pp. 245–257.
[11]The next two paragraphs draw heavily on Don J. DeVoretz, "New Issues, New Evidence, and New Immigration Policies for the Twenty First Century," in Don J. DeVoretz (ed.), Diminishing Returns (C.D. Howe Institute: Toronto, 1995), pp. 1–30.

Immigration into Canada has been high in the 1990s. The evidence seems to suggest immigration does not have large effects on the Canadian economy.

On the issue of immigration's effects on governments' costs and revenues, the evidence suggests that immigrants have a positive effect. It is clear that earlier generations of immigrants have had a positive effect on both the economy as a whole and on government budgets. A recent study by Akbari examines the effect of immigrants on government spending and taxes and he finds that, as of 1990, immigrants continue to add more in revenue than they receive in government expenditures.[12] Another study by Susanna Lui-Gurr finds only 2.7% of social assistance recipients in British Columbia in 1989 were foreign born despite the fact that immigrants made up 22% of the province's population.[13]

But it has also been argued that the mix of immigrants has changed significantly in recent years with over 50% securing entry under the family reunification program. These immigrants have, on average, less education and lower skills than previous immigrants, and there is concern that past experience is not necessarily a useful indicator of what is happening at the present, especially given high rates of unemployment. But, because families of immigrants under the family reunification program must post a bond that will cover the cost of any welfare use by sponsored immigrants in the first 10 years after arrival, any potential burden on taxpayers is reduced.

IS IMMIGRATION GOOD OR BAD?

Immigration is another of those economic issues in which no right answer clearly emerges. The evidence on the effects of immigration is mixed and theory gives us arguments on both sides of the issue. Only time will tell if recent immigrants will assimilate as well as past waves. In the meantime, immigration will remain an important issue in Canada.

---

[12]Ather H. Akbari, "The Impact of Immigrants on Canada's Treasury, circa 1990," in Don J. DeVoretz, Diminishing Returns, pp. 113–127.
[13]Susanna Lui-Gurr, "The British Columbia Experience with Immigrants and Welfare Dependency, 1989," in Don J. DeVoretz, Diminishing Returns, pp. 128–145.

Summary

The Economics of Health Care Reform

1. Canadians spend almost 10% of GDP on health care. This makes health care one of our most important industries.

2. Like everything, better health has an opportunity cost since improving health status involves using resources available to society in a different way. Economists contribute to the health care debate in Canada by emphasizing the importance of opportunity costs.

3. Several efficiency- and equity-related factors appear to favour government involvement in providing health care services. As a result of *asymmetric information* and *fee-for-service reimbursement* programs, health care providers have an incentive to oversupply expensive services. Such oversupply is clearly inefficient from society's point of view. In addition, poor health can be considered a negative externality that imposes costs on society. Market power allows companies to charge very high prices for drugs and technology they've developed—prices that the working poor and the uninsured cannot afford to pay. Finally, many view health care as a basic right that should be provided to all citizens, regardless of their ability to pay.

4. Compared to the more market oriented health care systems in the United States, the Canadian system produces better health care at a lower cost. However, the Canadian system does involve longer waiting lists and less freedom for those willing to pay to choose the care they consider best.

5. Reform proposals range from advocacy of a two-tier system with government insurance covering only the poor, to a system in which government exercises considerable control over the practice of medicine.

The Economics of Immigration

6. In recent years Canada has admitted almost a quarter of a million new immigrants per year. This is high by historical standards and has stimulated debate over the impact of immigration on the Canadian economy.

7. The argument for free immigration is that it increases world output. Those who favour free immigration also point out that Canada has absorbed many waves of immigrants while maintaining virtually full employment. Those who argue against free immigration believe that immigrants take jobs away from low-income Canadians and end up on welfare rolls.

Review Terms and Concepts

adverse selection 508

asymmetric information 508

block grant 512

copayment 508

cost-shared transfer 512

deductible 508

experience rating 509

fee-for-service reimbursement 509

gatekeepers 509

moral hazard 508

private good 507

supplier-induced demand 510

transactions costs 510

tax room 512

1. Write a brief essay outlining the advantages and disadvantages of market provision of health care.

2. What is the likely effect of a policy making people pay $5.00 for every time they visit the emergency department of a hospital? Explain your answer briefly.

3. The Global Perspective box in this chapter documents the rise in the use of managed-care providers of health care services in the United States. What sets a managed-care plan apart from other providers? Why do you suppose that managed-care providers emerged in the marketplace in the U.S.? What are the disadvantages of managed care?

4. Suppose you have been given $1 million to spend on human health. You face two options: (1) use the $1 million to provide an artificial heart to a patient who will otherwise die; or (2) use the $1 million to improve water and waste treatment and thereby save thousands of lives in a developing country. What is the right thing to do?

5. The potential exists for patients to overuse Canada's health care system. Why?

6. Illness (as measured by visits to physicians per 10 000 people) tends to be higher in areas where there are more physicians (as a percentage of the population). One explanation is that physicians locate in areas where there is more sickness. Thus, illness determines the number of physicians. Another explanation is that causation runs the other way, with high numbers of physicians "causing" high use of physician services. Explain this second hypothesis using the concepts of assymetric information and supplier-induced demand.

7. Cigarette smoking is known to increase risk of disease. How might one reduce smoking by changing the health insurance system?

8. Doctors are committed to providing the best possible health care for their patients. They are also gatekeepers to the medical system. Explain how this combination can result in inefficient resource use in the health care sector.

9. In the early 1980s the Mariel boat lift brought 120 000 Cubans to Miami. This represented a 7% increase in the workforce of the Miami metropolitan area. However, work by David Card found no impact on employment or wages in Miami. How can you explain this finding? Does your answer depend on whether you think of a metropolitan area as a closed economy or an open economy? Does Card's research mean that immigration has no impact on wages?

Radical Reform of the Canadian Health Care System

The rising cost of Canadian health care between 1970 and 1990 generated an important debate over the future of Canadian health care policy. On the one hand, there are those who would prefer to see more market provision in health care as a way of drawing new funds into the system. On the other hand, there are those who do not want to tamper with the existing system but who want governments to spend more on health.

There is, however, a third, more radical approach that is being proposed by a number of health care analysts and interest groups. Although these parties disagree on some of the details, they are united in their call for a fundamental restructuring of the health care sector in Canada. Such restructuring entails five key components: (1) retain government as the single payer; (2) combine primary care, acute care, and long-term care systems; (3) change who does what in health care; (4) change the method of payment; (5) improve efficiency of hospital use.

Retain Government as the Single Payer

Retaining government as the single payer is advocated to control costs. The following excerpt from an article in *Maclean's Magazine* indicates why some argue this is important:

> It is fashionable and often practical to talk about privatizing many services that governments provide. So it is perhaps inevitable that the

notion has spread to medicare.... The problem, however, is that governments do not provide health care: they buy it from providers such as doctors who bargain as a unit. And those providers, in turn, have a captive market. Consider the system: the usual market rules do not apply. Most medical service is available to everyone who needs it. The user cannot be priced out of the market. The user often does not even know if he or she really needs the service: that is the job of the provider. In such circumstances, when it is difficult to curb the patient's demand for service, most health care experts say that it is more useful to control the suppliers. And, they say, that means governments should preserve their hold on the purse strings as much as possible—because only a single payer has the power to counterbalance the demands of a powerful provider such as a provincial doctors' association. A single buyer is also in a better position to encourage internal competition among such suppliers as drug companies.

> If governments relinquish their control, health care experts warn that costs could increase dramatically—as they have in the mainly private American system. That would penalize users—and it

would divert resources away from other goals, such as education. "Most of the advocates of privatization are saying that we have got to get more money into the system," says University of British Columbia economist Robert Evans. "But that is essentially saying 'Abandon the target of cost control, and let's keep this system expanding.' If you want to try to manage your system more tightly so as to live within your constrained means, then you have to stay with a single payer."

Combine Primary Care, Acute Care, and Long-Term Care Systems

The current health care system focuses on acute care—the treatment of those who are already sick. Advocates of reform argue that primary care (including disease prevention, health promotion, and community-based care) should be integrated into the overall health care system. They argue that the goal of the system should be to keep people healthy rather than just treating people when they are sick.

Change Who Does What in Health Care

Physicians play the role of gatekeepers in the current system and they are paid on a fee-for-service basis. Nurses claim they are capable of taking over many services now performed by doctors and they argue that they can perform these services at a much lower cost. The typical visit to a doctor's office involves one of a small number of ailments that are relatively easy to diagnose and treat (strep throat, ear infections, the flu, etc.). These could easily be handled by nurses if they were allowed to diagnose and prescribe appropriate treatment. In cases where the nurse was unable to identify the problem the patient would be referred to a physician with the appropriate expertise. "A 1980 study by the California-based Kaiser-Permanente Health Services Research Centre, for example, concluded that nurse practitioners could do 63 per cent of doctors' work—at 38 per cent of the cost."

Change the Method of Payment

This same study also suggested that health care providers should be put on salary rather than fee-for-service. A fee-for-service payment system "awards more money to doctors who spin patients through their offices, inflating their billings by performing multiple services instead of providing nurturing care." It also encourages doctors to protect their gatekeeping role since rationally allocating roles in the health care system, say by giving nurses a bigger part, will reduce visits to a doctor and thus the doctor's income.

Improve Efficiency of Hospital Use

The cost of a hospital stay exceeds $500 per night. Hospitals are designed for acute care patients yet sometimes "patients who belonged in nursing homes were [in 1984] occupying 20 per cent of acute-care beds." Since neither doctors nor patients directly pay for a decision to extend the length of a hospital visit, patients often stay in hospital even though the cost to society exceeds any value of health benefits to the individual. In recent years governments have forced hospitals to deal with this problem by closing hospital beds. The hospital administrators, faced with a scarcity of beds, are unable to keep people in hospital too long. But there are few substitutes available for hospitals. It is inappropriate simply to send patients home if it is possible to provide some form of care outside the hospital that offers health benefits that exceed the costs. But the current system does not provide these alternative forms of care. Reformers argue that it is possible to design an integrated system that deals with this problem if the incentives are right.

The centrepiece of the radical reformers' proposals is known as the comprehensive health organization/capitation model (CHO). In this approach a team of salaried health care providers—physicians, nurses, dietitians, social workers, etc.—are assigned a group of citizens and they are responsible for the health of these citizens, including primary health, acute health care (diagnostic testing, hospitalization, and specialist medical procedures), and long-term care. Government provides a single annual payment based on the number of citizens enrolled and a number of risk factors (including age, sex, and health status) rather than on the cost of services performed. The comprehensive health organization gets to keep the difference between the annual government payment and the cost of providing its services. Advocates of this model believe that providers will have an incentive to integrate primary and acute health care, to assign tasks in a way that reflects both benefits and costs of provision, to cost-effectively ration hospital use, and to consider both costs and benefits when choosing diagnostic tests and treatment.

The comprehensive health organization/capitation also involves governments collecting information on the performance of the teams of health care providers and making it available to all citizens. Armed with this information, citizens are able to voice any concerns at meetings of the organizations or if need be move to another organization that performs better.

Questions for Analytical Thinking

1. Doctors are obligated by the Hippocratic Oath to deliver the best health care possible. Economists on the other hand are interested in opportunity costs, trade-offs, and the allocation of scarce resources among competing ends. As a consequence, doctors and economists are likely to look at the health care system differently, and their views are likely to come into conflict. Explain why the views of doctors and economists are likely to conflict when discussing cost control in the health care sector.

2. If, as some people argue, the value of human life is infinite, there should be no limits on health care spending. Do you believe the value of human life is infinite? Defend your position paying special attention to the concept of opportunity cost.

3. It is sometimes argued that the fiscal problems of government are the source of problems in the health care sector. Government cannot afford to pay more so it is necessary to privatize parts of the system to ensure the continued health of the health care sector. But don't Canadians pay one way or the other (through taxes or through market prices)? Those opposed to privatization argue that

Canadians do indeed pay one way or the other and that what we need is a government-run system that delivers the desired level of health care most cheaply. Do you agree or disagree with this position? Defend your arguments.

4. Doctors argue that a fee-for-service system is necessary to maintain a special relationship that must exist between patient and doctor. Under the fee-for-service system a doctor bears full responsibility for each patient's health and has the freedom to choose the treatment the doctor considers most appropriate for that individual. Doctors argue that putting them on salary destroys this relationship. Under a salaried payment they will be accountable to their employer (the government?) and will have to respond to considerations other than the health of the patient. How does the incentive structure change when doctors are switched from fee-for-service to salary? Identify gains and losses.

5. The health maintenance organization or HMO is very similar to the comprehensive health organization (CHO). As the Issues and Controversies box in this chapter showed, HMOs are increasingly important in the U.S. private health care system. Why might the market generate this type of health care organization? Although CHOs and HMOs provide incentives to control costs, the same incentives might also result in poorer health care. Why?

Source: Maclean's (Toronto Edition) vol. 108, no. 31 (July 31, 1995): pp 10–15. Video Resource: "Medicare plus Armstrong plus Wilson plus British Health," *The National Magazine,* August 20, 1996

21

International Trade, Comparative Advantage, and Protectionism

International trade is extremely important to the Canadian economy. Canada's imports of goods and services from the rest of the world have a value of about 35% of Canadian GDP and exports are about 38%. Canada's volume of trade (1996 exports and imports of $307 billion and $281 billion, respectively) ranks it among the 10 largest trading countries in the world. Although the United States may be the world's largest trader, U.S. imports represent only about 13% of that country's GDP. This is one of the principal differences between the Canadian and U.S. economies.

Canada trades with virtually every country in the world. Our greatest volume of trade is with the United States, which has been the source of about three-quarters of Canada's goods imports since the end of World War II. Declining in importance over the years has been the United Kingdom, which furnished over 13% of Canada's goods and services imports in 1946 and only 3% in 1996. Canada's export markets have also changed substantially in the postwar period: in 1946, the United States purchased 40% of our goods exports and the United Kingdom 26%; in 1996, these figures stood at 81% and 2%, respectively. Japan is now Canada's second largest trading partner, currently purchasing about 5% of Canadian goods exports and providing about 3% of our goods imports.

What types of goods is Canada trading? Table 21.1 on page 528 lists some of the most important goods exports and imports in 1996 and shows the percentage of total exports or imports accounted for by each. It is probably not surprising that Canada exports lumber and imports coffee. What is perhaps less well known is the high volume of trade Canada has in motor vehicles and parts, both as exports and imports. This is primarily the result of the 1965 Canada–United States Automotive Products Trade Agreement (APTA), popularly known as the auto pact. The auto pact removed tariffs and other trade barriers on manufacturers' trade in motor vehicles and parts between the two countries to promote more efficient production on both sides of the border. But whether the trade be in auto parts with the United States, fruit with South America, grain with China, or financial services with the European Union, the inextricable connection among the economies of the world has had a profound impact on the discipline of economics and is the basis for one of its most important insights:

> All economies, regardless of their size, depend to some extent on other economies and are affected by events outside their borders.

As a means of getting you more fully acquainted with the international economy, this chapter discusses the economics of international trade. First, we examine Canada's trade surpluses and trade deficits. Next, we explore the basic logic of trade. Why should Canada or any other country engage in international trade? Finally, we address the controversial issue of protectionism. Should a country provide certain industries with protection in the form of import quotas, tariffs, or subsidies?

The International Economy: Trade Surpluses and Deficits

trade surplus *The situation when a country exports more than it imports.*

trade deficit *The situation when a country imports more than it exports.*

In recent years, Canada has exported more than it has imported. When a country exports more than it imports, it runs a **trade surplus.** When a country imports more than it exports, as Canada did in the late 1980s, it runs a **trade deficit.** Canada generally runs a trade surplus for goods and a trade deficit for services. Table 21.2 shows the Canadian balance of trade for goods and for goods and services combined for selected years since 1946.

Table 21.1		Canada's Major Exports and Imports in 1996	
Major Goods Exports	*Percentage of Total Goods Exports*	*Major Goods Imports*	*Percentage of Total Goods Imports*
Automobiles	12.8	Motor vehicle parts	13.1
Motor vehicle parts	5.9	Automobiles	6.0
Trucks	4.6	Office machines and equipment	5.7
Lumber	4.6	Trucks	3.1
Newsprint	2.7	Crude petroleum	2.9
Natural gas	2.5	Apparel and footwear	2.1
Wood pulp	2.4	Fruits and vegetables	1.7
Wheat	1.8	Cocoa, coffee, and tea	0.9
Major Services Exports	*Percentage of Total Services Exports*	*Major Services Imports*	*Percentage of Total Services Imports*
Business services	36.2	Business services	40.0
Travel*	30.8	Travel*	31.5

*Note: Exports of travel services are the expenditures of nonresidents of Canada travelling in Canada; imports of travel services are the expenditures of Canadian residents travelling abroad.

Source: Adapted from Statistics Canada, CANSIM Database, series D70011–D70016, D70029–D70034, D397916–D397981, D399374–D399440.

Trade deficits can be a source of political controversy in countries that experience them. Especially in times of recession, when domestic jobs are being lost, the reaction against the importation of cheaper foreign-made goods can be quite severe. A natural response to try to protect domestic jobs is to call for governments to impose taxes and restrictions on imports (as Canada did on the importation of Japanese automobiles in the early 1980s) to make them more expensive and less available. As you might guess, this argument is not a new one. For hundreds of years, industries have petitioned governments for protection, and societies have debated the pros and cons of free and open trade. For the last century and a half, the principal argument used against protection has been the theory of comparative advantage, which we first discussed in Chapter 2.

The Economic Basis for Trade: Comparative Advantage

Perhaps the best-known debate on the issue of free trade took place in the British Parliament during the early years of the nineteenth century. At that time, the landed gentry—the landowners—controlled Parliament. For a number of years, imports and exports of grain had been subject to a set of tariffs, subsidies, and restrictions collectively called the **Corn Laws**. Designed to discourage imports of grain and encourage exports, the Corn Laws' purpose was to keep the price of food high. The landlords' incomes, of course, depended on the prices they got for what their land produced. The Corn Laws thus clearly worked to the advantage of those in power.

With the Industrial Revolution, a class of wealthy industrial capitalists began to emerge. The industrial sector had to pay workers at least enough to live on, and a living wage depended to a great extent on the price of food. Tariffs on grain imports and export subsidies that kept grain and food prices high increased the wages that capitalists had to pay, and these high wage payments cut into their profits. The political battle raged for years. But as time went by, the power of the landowners in the House of Lords was significantly reduced. When the conflict ended in 1846, the Corn Laws were repealed.

Participating in this battle on the side of repeal was David Ricardo, a businessman, economist, member of Parliament, and one of the fathers of modern economics. Ricardo's principal work, *Principles of Political Economy and Taxation*, was published in 1817, two years before he entered Parliament. Ricardo's **theory of comparative advantage**, which he used to argue against the Corn Laws, claimed that trade enables countries to specialize in producing the products that they produce best. According to the theory:

> Specialization and free trade will benefit all trading partners (real wages will rise), even those that may be absolutely less efficient producers.

This basic argument remains at the heart of free-trade debates even today.

■ **Specialization and Trade: The Two-Person Case**   Perhaps the easiest way to understand the theory of comparative advantage is to examine a simple two-person society. Recall Ivan and Colleen, who were stranded on a deserted island in Chapter 2. Suppose that they have only two basic tasks to accomplish each week: gathering food to eat and cutting logs that will be used in constructing a house. If Colleen could cut more logs than Ivan in a day and Ivan could gather more berries and fruits, specialization would clearly benefit both of them.

But suppose that Ivan is slow and somewhat clumsy and that Colleen is better at both cutting logs *and* gathering food. Ricardo's point is that it still pays for them

Table 21.2

Canada's Balance of Trade (Exports minus Imports), 1946–1996 (Millions of Dollars)

	Goods	Goods and Services
1946	571	606
1956	−728	−1 013
1966	266	−147
1976	1 559	−1 027
1986	9 943	4 749
1987	1 221	4 914
1988	8 917	2 925
1989	6 059	−2 177
1990	8 696	−2 306
1991	3 616	−7 958
1992	6 201	−6 066
1993	9 323	−3 164
1994	14 936	4 423
1995	28 390	19 034
1996	34 525	25 176

Source: Adapted from Statistics Canada, CANSIM Database, Series D71003 and D71005.

Corn Laws *The tariffs, subsidies, and restrictions enacted by the British Parliament in the early nineteenth century to discourage imports and encourage exports of grain.*

theory of comparative advantage *Ricardo's theory that specialization and free trade will benefit all trading partners (real wages will rise), even those that may be absolutely less efficient producers.*

to specialize. They can produce more in total by specializing than they can by sharing the work equally. (It may be helpful to review the discussion of comparative advantage in Chapter 2 before proceeding.)

ABSOLUTE ADVANTAGE VERSUS COMPARATIVE ADVANTAGE

absolute advantage *The advantage in the production of a product enjoyed by one country over another when it uses fewer resources to produce that product than the other country does.*

A country is said to enjoy an **absolute advantage** over another country in the production of a product if it uses fewer resources to produce that product than the other country does. For example, suppose that country A and country B produce wheat, but that A's climate is more suited to wheat and its labour is more productive. Country A will therefore produce more wheat per hectare than country B and use less labour in growing it and bringing it to market. Country A thus enjoys an absolute advantage over country B in the production of wheat.

■ **Gains from Mutual Absolute Advantage** To illustrate Ricardo's logic in more detail, let's start with a very simple case. Suppose that Australia and New Zealand each have a fixed amount of land and do not trade with the rest of the world. Suppose further that there are only two goods—wheat, used to produce bread, and cotton, used to produce clothing. This kind of two-country/two-good world does not exist, of course, but its operations can be generalized to many countries and many goods.

Before we proceed, we have to make some assumptions about the preferences of the people living in New Zealand and those living in Australia. If the citizens of both countries go around naked, there is no need to produce cotton at all; all the land can be used to produce wheat. For the sake of simplicity, however, let us assume that people in both countries have similar preferences with respect to food and clothing: the populations of both countries use both cotton and wheat. We will also assume that preferences for food and clothing are such that both countries consume equal amounts of wheat and cotton.

Finally, we shall assume that each country has only 100 hectares of land for planting and that land yields are those given in Table 21.3. Notice that New Zealand can produce three times the wheat that Australia can on one hectare of land, and that Australia can produce three times the cotton that New Zealand can in the same space. New Zealand thus has an absolute advantage in the production of wheat, and Australia has an absolute advantage in the production of cotton. In cases like this, we say that the two countries have *mutual absolute advantage*.

If there is no trade and each country divides its land to obtain equal units of cotton and wheat production, each country produces 150 tonnes of wheat and 150 bales of cotton. New Zealand puts 75 hectares into cotton but only 25 hectares into wheat, while Australia does the reverse. (See Table 21.4.)

We can organize the same information in a somewhat different way if we construct separate production possibility frontiers for each country. In Figure 21.1, which presents the positions of the two countries before trade, each country is constrained by its own resources and productivity. If Australia put all its land into cotton, it would produce 600 bales of cotton (100 hectares × 6 bales/hectare) and no wheat; if it put all its land into wheat, it would produce 200 tonnes of wheat (100 hectares × 2 tonnes/hectare) and no cotton.

Table 21.3	Yield per Hectare of Wheat and Cotton		
		New Zealand	*Australia*
Wheat		6 tonnes	2 tonnes
Cotton		2 bales	6 bales

Table 21.4	Total Production of Wheat and Cotton Assuming No Trade, Mutual Absolute Advantage, and 100 Available Hectares	
	New Zealand	*Australia*
Wheat	25 hectares × 6 tonnes/hectare 150 tonnes	75 hectares × 2 tonnes/hectare 150 tonnes
Cotton	75 hectares × 2 bales/hectare 150 bales	25 hectares × 6 bales/hectare 150 bales

But let us consider some intermediate cases. Suppose Australia put 99 hectares into wheat and 1 hectare into cotton. It would produce 198 tonnes of wheat and 6 bales of cotton. Now suppose it switched another hectare from wheat to cotton so that it had 98 hectares of wheat and 2 hectares of cotton. You can see it would produce 196 tonnes of wheat and 12 bales of cotton. You can also see that Australia always faces a constant trade-off in production: at any time, it can switch 1 hectare from wheat to cotton, and get 6 more bales of cotton but lose 2 tonnes of wheat. In terms of Figure 21.1, this is what makes the production possibility frontier a straight line. At any point on the frontier, 6 bales of cotton can be obtained for the sacrifice of 2 tonnes of wheat—this ratio never changes, so the slope never changes and the line is straight. (The constant slope of the curve is equal to the gain in cotton divided by the loss in wheat, which is 6 bales divided by −2 tonnes, which equals −3 bales/tonne.)

FIGURE 21.1

Production Possibility Frontiers for Australia and New Zealand before Trade

Without trade, countries are constrained by their own resources and productivity.

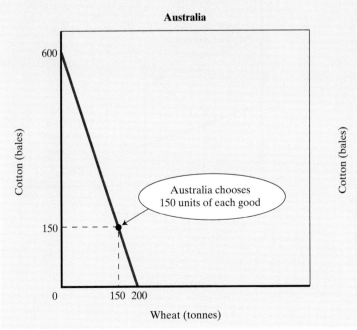
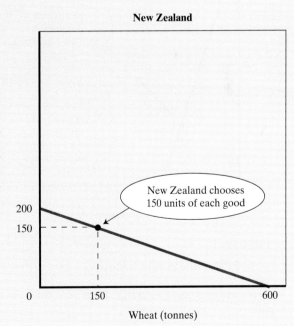

Table 21.5

Table 21.5   **Production and Consumption of Wheat and Cotton after Specialization**

| | PRODUCTION | | | CONSUMPTION | |
	New Zealand	Australia		New Zealand	Australia
Wheat	100 hectares × 6 tonnes/hectare 600 tonnes	0 hectares 0 tonnes	Wheat	300 tonnes	300 tonnes
Cotton	0 hectares 0 bales	100 hectares × 6 bales/hectare 600 bales	Cotton	300 bales	300 bales

If you have any doubts about this, take a piece of paper and graph out Australia's production possibility curve to confirm the frontier is a straight line. The key reason the line is straight is that we are assuming that all land is the same and there is no land that is better for one crop or the other. Hence switching a hectare from one crop to the other always involves the same gains and losses.

Now turn to New Zealand. You should be able to see that New Zealand's maximum production of cotton is 200 bales, its maximum production of wheat is 600 tonnes and that again the production possibility frontier is a straight line, although this time with a slope of 1 bale divided by −3 tonnes, which equals −1/3 bales/tonne.

For both countries, the production possibility frontier represents all the combinations of goods that can be produced given the countries' resources and state of technology. Without trade, each country must pick a point along its own production

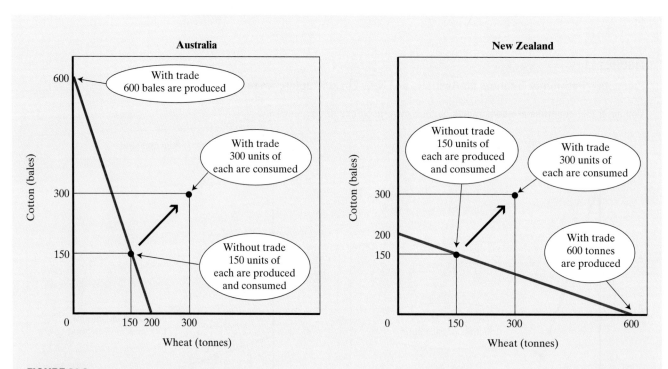

FIGURE 21.2

Expanded Possibilities after Trade

Trade enables both countries to move out beyond their own resource constraints—beyond their individual production possibility frontiers.

possibility curve and both produce and consume at that point. We have assumed each country would consume 150 tonnes and 150 bales and have marked that point on the curves.

Because both countries have an absolute advantage in the production of one product, it is reasonable to expect that specialization and trade will benefit both countries. Clearly, Australia should produce cotton and New Zealand should produce wheat. Transferring all land to wheat production in New Zealand yields a total of 600 tonnes; transferring all land to cotton production in Australia yields 600 bales. An agreement to trade 300 tonnes of wheat for 300 bales of cotton would double both wheat and cotton consumption in both countries. (Remember, before trade both countries produced 150 tonnes of wheat and 150 bales of cotton. After trade, each country will have 300 tonnes of wheat and 300 bales of cotton to consume. Final production and trade figures are given in Figure 21.2 and Table 21.5.) Thus,

> Trade enables both countries to move out beyond their previous resource and productivity constraints.

The advantages of specialization and trade seem obvious when one country is technologically superior at producing one product and another country is technologically superior at producing another product. Now, however, let us turn to the case in which one country has an absolute advantage in the production of *both* goods.

■ **Gains from Trade When One Country Has an Advantage in Both Goods**   Now suppose the yields changed to those given in Table 21.6. In this new case, New Zealand has a considerable absolute advantage in the production of both cotton and wheat, with one hectare of land yielding six times as much wheat and twice as much cotton as one hectare in Australia. Ricardo would argue that *specialization and trade are still mutually beneficial.*

Assume again that preferences for food and clothing imply consumption of equal units of cotton and wheat in both countries. With no trade, New Zealand would divide its 100 available hectares evenly, or 50/50, between the two crops. The result would be 300 bales of cotton and 300 tonnes of wheat. Australia would divide its land into 75 hectares wheat and 25 hectares cotton. Table 21.7 on the next page shows that final production in Australia would be 75 bales of cotton and 75 tonnes of wheat. (Remember, we are assuming that, in each country, people consume equal amounts of cotton and wheat.) Once again, before any trade takes place each country is constrained by its own domestic production possibility curve.

Now imagine that we are at a meeting of trade representatives of both countries. As a special adviser, David Ricardo is asked to demonstrate that trade can benefit both countries. The professor divides his demonstration into three stages, which you can follow in Table 21.8.

In stage 1, Australia transfers all its land into cotton production. When it does, it will have no wheat at all and 300 bales of cotton. New Zealand cannot completely specialize in wheat because it needs at least 300 bales of cotton and thus

Table 21.6	Yield per Hectare of Wheat and Cotton	
	New Zealand	*Australia*
Wheat	6 tonnes	1 tonne
Cotton	6 bales	3 bales

Chapter 21: Trade, Comparative Advantage, and Protectionism | **533**

Table 21.7	Total Production of Wheat and Cotton Assuming No Trade and 100 Available Hectares	
	New Zealand	**Australia**
Wheat	50 hectares × 6 tonnes/hectare 300 tonnes	75 hectares × 1 tonne-/hectare 75 tonnes
Cotton	50 hectares × 6 bales/hectare 300 bales	25 hectares × 3 bales/hectare 75 bales

will not be able to get enough cotton from Australia. This is because we are assuming that each country wants to consume equal amounts of cotton and wheat. Thus, in stage 2, New Zealand transfers 25 hectares out of cotton and into wheat. Now New Zealand has 25 hectares in cotton that produce 150 bales and 75 hectares in wheat that produce 450 tonnes.

Finally, the two countries trade. We assume that New Zealand ships 100 tonnes of wheat to Australia in exchange for 200 bales of cotton. After the trade, New Zealand has 350 bales of cotton and 350 tonnes of wheat; Australia has 100 bales of cotton and 100 tonnes of wheat. Both countries are better off than they were before the trade (review Table 21.7), and both have moved beyond their own production possibility frontiers.

■ **Why Does Ricardo's Plan Work?** To understand why Ricardo's scheme works, first let us define comparative advantage. A country enjoys **comparative advantage** in the production of a good if that good can be produced at lower cost *in terms of other goods*. The real cost of producing cotton is the wheat that must be sacrificed to produce it. *When we think of cost this way, it is less costly to produce cotton in Australia than to produce it in New Zealand, even though a hectare of land produces more cotton in New Zealand.* Consider the "cost" of three bales of cotton in the two countries. In terms of opportunity cost, three bales of cotton in New Zealand cost three tonnes of wheat; in Australia, however, three bales of cotton cost only one tonne of wheat. Because three bales are produced by one hectare of

comparative advantage *The advantage in the production of a product enjoyed by one country over another when that product can be produced at lower cost in terms of other goods than it could be in the other country.*

Table 21.8	Realizing a Gain from Trade When One Country Has a Double Absolute Advantage					
	STAGE 1			**STAGE 2**		
	New Zealand	**Australia**		**New Zealand**	**Australia**	
Wheat	50 hectares × 6 tonnes/hectare 300 tonnes	0 hectares 0 tonnes	Wheat	75 hectares × 6 tonnes/hectare 450 tonnes	0 hectares 0 tonnes	
Cotton	50 hectares × 6 bales/hectare 300 bales	100 hectares × 3 bales/hectare 300 bales	Cotton	25 hectares × 6 bales/hectare 150 bales	100 hectares × 3 bales/hectare 300 bales	

		STAGE 3		
		New Zealand		**Australia**
Wheat		350 tonnes	100 tonnes (trade) ———→ (after trade)	100 tonnes
Cotton		350 bales	200 bales (trade) ←——— (after trade)	100 bales

Australian land, to get three bales an Australian must transfer one hectare of land from wheat to cotton production. And because a hectare of land produces a tonne of wheat, losing one hectare to cotton implies the loss of one tonne of wheat. Thus, *Australia has a comparative advantage in cotton production* because its opportunity cost, in terms of wheat, is lower than New Zealand's. This situation is illustrated in Figure 21.3.

Conversely, New Zealand has a comparative advantage in wheat production. A unit of wheat in New Zealand costs one unit of cotton; a unit of wheat in Australia costs three units of cotton.

> When countries specialize in producing those goods in which they have a comparative advantage, they maximize their combined output and allocate their resources more efficiently.

TERMS OF TRADE

Ricardo might suggest a number of options open to the trading partners. The one we just examined benefited both partners; in percentage terms, Australia made out slightly better. Other deals might have been more advantageous to New Zealand.

The ratio at which a country can trade domestic products for imported products is called the **terms of trade.** The terms of the trade determine how the gains from trade are distributed among the trading partners. In the case we just considered, the agreed-upon terms of trade were one tonne of wheat for two bales of cotton. Such terms of trade benefit New Zealand, which can now get two bales of cotton for each tonne of wheat. If it were to transfer its own land from wheat to cotton, it would get only one. The same terms of trade benefit Australia, which can now get one tonne of wheat for two bales of cotton. A direct transfer of its own land would force it to give up three bales of cotton for one tonne of wheat.

If the terms of trade changed to three bales of cotton for every tonne of wheat, only New Zealand would benefit. In fact, at those terms of trade *all* the gains from

terms of trade *The ratio at which a country can trade domestic products for imported products.*

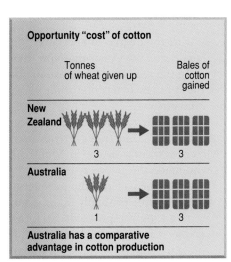

FIGURE 21.3

Comparative Advantage Means Lower Opportunity Cost

The real cost of cotton is the wheat that must be sacrificed to obtain it. The cost of three bales of cotton in New Zealand is three tonnes of wheat (one-half hectare of land must be transferred from wheat to cotton—refer to Table 21.6). But the cost of three bales of cotton in Australia is only one tonne of wheat (one hectare of land must be transferred). Thus, Australia has a comparative advantage over New Zealand in the production of cotton, and New Zealand has a comparative advantage over Australia in wheat production.

trade would flow to New Zealand. Such terms do not benefit Australia at all because the opportunity cost of producing wheat domestically is *exactly the same* as the trade cost: one tonne of wheat costs three bales of cotton. If the terms of trade went the other way—one bale of cotton for each tonne of wheat—only Australia would benefit. New Zealand gains nothing, because it can already substitute cotton for wheat at that ratio. To get a tonne of wheat domestically, however, Australia must give up three bales of cotton, and one-for-one terms of trade would make wheat much less costly for Australia.

Clearly, both parties must have something to gain for trade to take place. In this case, you can see that both Australia and New Zealand will gain when the terms of trade are set between 1:1 and 3:1, cotton to wheat.

EXCHANGE RATES

While the previous example makes most of our basic points, let us now take a few steps toward a more realistic model. First, we should remind ourselves that while we discuss trade as if the country Australia trades with the country New Zealand, we do not mean that this is intergovernmental trade, but rather, that individual households and firms in one country trade with individual households and firms in the other. Private households decide whether to buy Toyotas or Chevrolets, and private firms decide whether to buy machine tools made in Canada or machine tools made in Taiwan, raw steel produced in Germany or raw steel produced in Hamilton.

> When trade is free (that is, unimpeded by government-instituted barriers), patterns of trade and trade flows result from the independent decisions of thousands of importers and exporters and millions of private households and firms.

Second, we have assumed so far that production possibility frontiers are straight lines so that to produce three extra bales of cotton in Australia *always* means the sacrifice of one tonne of wheat. It would seem more likely that there is at least some land that is good for wheat and almost useless for cotton. Hence in a more realistic example, Australia probably would not specialize completely in cotton because that would involve growing cotton on land for which it is not well suited. More generally, it is unlikely a country will ever specialize completely in a single good. For the most part, we can just focus on the direction of trade and not concern ourselves with the degree of specialization.

Finally, in the Australia/New Zealand case, trade was by barter, cotton for wheat. In the real world, almost all goods are put on the market with money prices and these prices determine trade flows. Of course different money is used in different countries.

Before a citizen of one country can buy a product made in, or sold by, someone in another country, a currency swap must take place. Consider Marc, who buys a Mercedes from a dealer in Montreal. He pays in dollars, but the German workers who made the car receive their salaries in deutsche marks. Somewhere between the buyer of the car and the producer, a currency exchange must be made. The regional distributor probably takes payment in dollars and converts them into marks before remitting the proceeds back to Germany.

To buy a foreign-produced good, then, I in effect have to buy foreign currency. The price of Marc's Mercedes in dollars depends on both the price of the car stated in deutsche marks and the price of deutsche marks. You probably know the ins and outs of currency exchange very well if you have ever travelled in another country. In March of 1997, a dollar exchanged for 4.2 French francs, making each franc worth $0.238. Now suppose that you are in France, and you see a nice bottle of

Bordeaux wine for 120 francs. How can you figure out whether you want to buy it? You know what dollars will buy you in Canada, so you have to convert the price into dollars. Since each franc will cost you $0.238, 120 francs is worth 120 × 0.238, or $28.56.

The relative attractiveness of foreign goods to Canadian buyers, and of Canadian goods to foreign buyers, depends in part on **exchange rates,** the ratio at which two currencies are traded for each other. If the rate at which dollars could be converted into francs suddenly jumped to 10 francs for every dollar, that same bottle of wine would cost only $12.

Of course the price of goods in domestic currency (for example, the price of the wine in francs) also influences trade patterns. But the prices of many goods do not change frequently, while the exchange rate for most currencies changes every minute on the foreign exchange market. So to keep things as simple as possible, in the following discussion we will focus on the impact of different values of the exchange rate *assuming that the domestic prices of goods do not change.* This allows us a simple way of studying how trade flows change when the prices of the goods of one country change relative to the prices of the goods of another country.

How is the exchange rate itself determined? You will likely have learned or will learn something about this elsewhere in your study of macroeconomics. For now, we note only that the exchange rates depend on such factors as the price level, interest rates, trade flows, and current and projected government fiscal and monetary policies. What is important to know here is that the exchange rate will almost always be at a level that allows for two-way trade so that each country has some level of exports and imports.[1] Here, however, we can show that:

> For any pair of countries, and given domestic prices, there is a range of exchange rates that can lead automatically to both countries realizing the gains from specialization and comparative advantage.

■ Trade and Exchange Rates in a Two-Country/Two-Good World First consider a new simple two-country/two-good example. Suppose that Canada and the United States produce only two goods—lumber and cloth. Table 21.9 gives the current prices of both goods as domestic buyers see them. In Canada both goods are C$5 per metre. In the United States, lumber is US$4 per metre, and the price of cloth is US$3 per metre.

Now suppose that Canadian and U.S. buyers have the option of buying at home or importing to meet their needs. The options they ultimately choose will depend on the exchange rate. For the time being, we will ignore transportation costs between countries and assume that Canadian and U.S. products are of equal quality.

Let us start with the assumption that the exchange rate is 1 Canadian dollar equals 50 U.S. cents, that is C$1 = US$0.50. Table 21.10 on the next page gives all the prices for lumber and cloth in Canadian dollars, using this exchange rate. As US$4 is worth C$8, the Canadian-dollar price of U.S. lumber is C$8 per metre and similarly U.S. cloth is C$6 per metre. Since both of these products cost only C$5 per metre in Canada, no Canadian will purchase the more expensive U.S. products. But note that Americans will also want to purchase from Canada. Since

exchange rate *The ratio at which two currencies are traded for each other. The price of one currency in terms of another.*

[1] *If Canada only exported, we would in effect be giving up goods in return for foreign currency. But we would expect that at least eventually this accumulated foreign currency would be used to import goods. Similarly, if Canada only imported, we would be acquiring goods by paying with Canadian currency. Eventually foreigners would want to use that currency to buy Canadian goods and Canada would export. Hence, at least in the long run, we cannot export without importing and we cannot import without exporting, and we can expect the exchange rate to adjust so that is so.*

Table 21.9

Domestic Prices of Lumber (per Metre) and Cloth (per Metre) in Canada and the United States

	Canada	United States
Lumber	C$5	US$4
Cloth	C$5	US$3

Table 21.10

Canadian-Dollar Prices of Lumber (per Metre) and Cloth (per Metre) in Canada and the United States if C$1 = US$0.50 (or US$1 = C$2)

	Canada	United States
Lumber	C$5	US$4 = C$8
Cloth	C$5	US$3 = C$6

Table 21.11

Canadian-Dollar Prices of Lumber (per Metre) and Cloth (per Metre) in Canada and the United States if C$1 = US$1

	Canada	United States
Lumber	C$5	US$4 = C$4
Cloth	C$5	US$3 = C$3

Table 21.12

Canadian-Dollar Prices of Lumber (per Metre) and Cloth (per Metre) in Canada and the United States if C$1 = US$0.80 (or US$1 = C$1.25)

	Canada	United States
Lumber	C$5	US$4 = C$5
Cloth	C$5	US$3 = C$3.75

C$5 = US$2.50, the U.S.-dollar price of both Canadian products is US$2.50 per metre, a bargain compared to U.S. domestic prices of US$4 and US$3. American buyers will convert U.S. dollars to Canadian dollars and purchase both products from Canada. The United States will import both products and Canada will import nothing.

Now consider Table 21.11 in which the exchange rate is C$1 = US$1, or one-for-one. As US$4 now equals C$4 and US$3 now equals C$3, the Canadian-dollar prices of both goods are lower in the United States; so Canadian buyers will want to convert Canadian dollars into U.S. dollars and purchase from the United States. Americans will have no interest in Canadian products because at this exchange rate the U.S.-dollar prices of both Canadian products are US$5 and these exceed the U.S.-dollar prices of their own goods. At this exchange rate, Canada imports both goods.

It is easy to provide more examples at different exchange rates. So far we have shown that at C$1 = US$0.50 and C$1 = US$1, we get trade flowing in only one direction. In Table 21.12 we consider a case with an exchange rate in between: C$1 = US$0.80 (or equivalently US$1 = C$1.25). First notice that Canada will import cloth from the United States because the Canadian-dollar price of U.S. cloth is C$3.75 per metre, lower than the Canadian-dollar price of Canadian cloth. U.S. buyers will also find that American cloth is cheaper and not buy in Canada. At this same exchange rate, however, lumber is the same price in both countries and hence there likely will be no trade in lumber.

But suppose the exchange rate falls just slightly, so that the Canadian dollar is worth US$0.79. While U.S. cloth is still cheaper for both Canadians and Americans, U.S. lumber is now more expensive for Canadians. At this exchange rate, the U.S.-dollar price of $4 per metre converts to C$5.06 (4/0.79 is approximately 5.06). Since the domestic price in Canada is C$5 per metre, Canadians will buy Canadian lumber. But that price will also look good to U.S. buyers. In their currency, C$5 is now US$3.95 (5 × 0.79 = 3.95) and US$3.95 per metre is less than the U.S. price. Therefore, as the exchange rate falls from C$1 = US$0.80, trade begins to flow in both directions. The United States will import lumber and Canada will import cloth.

If you examine Table 21.13 carefully, you will see that in fact trade flows in both directions as long as the exchange rate for the Canadian dollar settles between US$0.60 and US$0.80. Stated the other way around, trade will flow in both directions as long as the price of a U.S. dollar is between C$1.25 and C$1.67.

■ **Exchange Rates and Comparative Advantage** Let us continue our example. If the Canadian dollar is between US$0.60 and US$0.80, the countries will automatically adjust and comparative advantage will be realized. At these exchange rates, Canadian buyers begin buying all their cloth in the United States. The Canadian cloth industry finds itself in trouble. Mills close and Canadian workers begin to lobby for tariff protection against American cloth. At the same time, the Canadian lumber industry does well, fuelled by strong export demand from the United States. Thus the lumber-producing sector expands. Resources, including capital and labour, are attracted into lumber production.

The opposite occurs in the United States. The U.S. lumber industry suffers losses as export demand dries up and Americans turn to cheaper Canadian imports. U.S. lumber companies turn to their government and ask for protection from cheap Canadian lumber. But cloth producers in the United States are happy. Not only are they supplying 100% of the domestically demanded cloth, but they are selling to Canadian buyers as well. Thus the cloth industry expands and the lumber industry contracts. Resources flow into cloth production.

With this expansion-and-contraction scenario in mind, let us look again at our

Table 21.13	Trade Flows Determined by Exchange Rates		
Exchange Rate	**Price of US$**	**Result**	
C$1 = US$1	C$1.00	Canada imports lumber and cloth	
C$1 = US$0.80	C$1.25	Canada imports cloth	
C$1 = US$0.79	C$1.27	Canada imports cloth; U.S. imports lumber	
C$1 = US$0.61	C$1.64	Canada imports cloth; U.S. imports lumber	
C$1 = US$0.60	C$1.67	U.S. imports lumber	
C$1 = US$0.50	C$2.00	U.S. imports lumber and cloth	

original definition of comparative advantage. If we assume that prices reflect resource use and that resources can be transferred from sector to sector, we can calculate the opportunity cost of cloth and lumber in both countries. In Canada, the production of a metre of cloth consumes the same level of resources that the production of a metre of lumber consumes. Assuming that resources can be transferred, the opportunity cost of a metre of cloth is one metre of lumber. (Refer again to Table 21.9.) In the U.S., however, a metre of cloth uses resources costing US$3, while a metre of lumber costs US$4. Thus to produce a metre of cloth means the sacrifice of only three-quarters of a metre of lumber. Because the opportunity cost of a metre of cloth (in terms of lumber) is lower in the United States, we say that the U.S. has a comparative advantage in cloth production.

Conversely, consider the opportunity cost of lumber in the two countries. Increasing lumber production in the United States requires the sacrifice of four-thirds, or one and a third, metres of cloth for every metre of lumber—producing a metre of lumber uses US$4 worth of resources, while producing a metre of cloth requires only US$3 worth of resources. But each metre of lumber production in Canada requires the sacrifice of only one metre of cloth. Because the opportunity cost of lumber is lower in Canada, Canada has a comparative advantage in the production of lumber.

In short:

> If exchange rates end up in the right ranges, the free market will drive each country to shift resources into those sectors in which it enjoys a comparative advantage. Only those products in which a country has a comparative advantage will be competitive in world markets.

The Sources of Comparative Advantage

You have now seen that specialization and trade can benefit all trading partners, even those that may be inefficient producers in an absolute sense. If markets are competitive, and if foreign exchange markets are linked to goods-and-services exchange, countries will specialize in producing those products in which they have a comparative advantage.

So far, however, we have said nothing about the sources of comparative advantage. What determines whether a country has a comparative advantage in heavy manufacturing or in agriculture? What explains the actual trade flows observed around the world? Various theories and empirical work on international trade have provided a number of partial answers to these questions. Most economists look to **factor endowments**—that is, to the quantity and quality of labour, land, and

factor endowments *The quantity and quality of labour, land, and natural resources of a country.*

natural resources—as the principal sources of comparative advantage. Factor endowments seem to explain a significant portion of actual world trade patterns.

THE HECKSCHER-OHLIN THEOREM

Eli Heckscher and Bertil Ohlin, two Swedish economists who wrote in the first half of this century, expanded and elaborated on Ricardo's theory of comparative advantage. The **Heckscher-Ohlin theorem** ties the theory of comparative advantage to factor endowments. It assumes that products can be produced using differing proportions of inputs and that inputs are mobile between sectors in each economy, but that factors are not mobile *between* economies. According to the Heckscher-Ohlin theorem:

> A country has a comparative advantage in the production of a product if that country is relatively well endowed with inputs used intensively in the production of that product.

Heckscher-Ohlin theorem *A theory that explains the existence of a country's comparative advantage by its factor endowments: a country has a comparative advantage in the production of a product if that country is relatively well endowed with inputs used intensively in the production of that product.*

This idea is quite simple. A country with a lot of good fertile land per person is likely to have a comparative advantage in agriculture. A country with a large amount of labour but little capital is likely to have a comparative advantage in labour-intensive goods.

After an extensive study, American economist Edward Leamer of the University of California at Los Angeles has concluded that a relatively short list of factors accounts for a surprisingly large portion of world trade patterns. Natural resources, knowledge capital, physical capital, land, and skilled and unskilled labour, Leamer believes, explain "a large amount of the variability of net exports across countries."[2]

OTHER EXPLANATIONS FOR OBSERVED TRADE FLOWS

Comparative advantage is not the only reason that countries trade, of course. It does not explain why many countries both import and export the same kinds of goods. Canada, for example, both exports and imports automobiles as we saw in Table 21.1.

Another explanation for international trade is that, just as industries within a country differentiate their products to capture a domestic market, so too do they differentiate their products to please the wide variety of tastes that exists worldwide. The Japanese automobile industry, for example, began producing small, fuel-efficient cars long before North American automobile makers did. In doing so, they developed expertise in creating products that attracted a devoted following and that elicited considerable brand loyalty. BMWs, made only in Germany, and Volvos, made only in Sweden, also have their champions in many countries. Just as product differentiation is a natural response to diverse preferences within an economy, it is also a natural response to diverse preferences across economies.

This idea is not inconsistent with the theory of comparative advantage. If the Japanese have developed skills and knowledge that gave them an edge in the production of fuel-efficient cars, that knowledge can be thought of as a very specific kind of capital not currently available to other producers. The Volvo company invested in a form of intangible capital that we call *goodwill*. That goodwill, which may come from establishing a reputation for safety and quality over the years, is one source of the comparative advantage that keeps Volvos selling on the international market. Some economists distinguish between gains from *acquired comparative advantages* and those from *natural comparative advantages*.

---

[2]*Edward E. Leamer*, Sources of International Comparative Advantage: Theory and Evidence *(Cambridge, Mass.: MIT Press, 1984), p. 187.*

Acquired comparative advantage may in some cases require R&D expenditures that only make sense if the company is producing for the world market. This is one instance of an economy of scale. Relatively few countries make computer chips, for example. To illustrate another type of economy of scale: it may be cost efficient to build a television plant big enough (and hence serve a market big enough) so that each size of television screen can have its own production line, thereby avoiding having to stop the line periodically to start making a different size. Hence economies of scale may be another source of the gains from specialization in trade.

Trade Barriers: Tariffs, Export Subsidies, and Quotas

Trade barriers—also called *obstacles to trade*—take many forms, the three most common of which are tariffs, export subsidies, and quotas. All of these are forms of **protection** by which some sector of the economy is shielded from foreign competition.

A **tariff** is a tax on imports. Tariffs vary by product and country of origin. According to the World Trade Organization, most Canadian import tariffs average about 6.6% on manufactured goods, 18% on processed textiles, and almost 34% on food, beverages, and tobacco. For some agricultural products such as milk, tariffs are over 300% for imports in excess of a quota. However, partly because Canada has many special trade arrangements such as those with the United States and Mexico, tariffs only represent in total about 1.6% of the cost of imports, and this percentage is expected to fall further.

Export subsidies—government payments made to domestic firms to encourage exports—can also act as a barrier to trade. One of the provisions of the Corn Laws that stimulated Ricardo's musings in the nineteenth century was an export subsidy that was automatically paid to farmers by the British government when the price of grain fell below a specified level. This subsidy tended to encourage British exports and to reduce the price of world grain. Foreign farmers who were not subsidized were driven out of the international marketplace by the artificially low prices.

Farm subsidies remain very much a part of the international trade landscape today. Many countries, especially those in Europe, continue to appease their farmers by heavily subsidizing exports of agricultural products. In fact, the political power of the farm lobby in many countries has had an important effect on international trade negotiations aimed at reducing trade barriers.

Closely related to subsidies is the practice of **dumping**. Dumping takes place when a firm or an industry sells products on the world market at prices *below* the cost of production. The charge has been levied against several specific Japanese industries, including automobiles, consumer electronics, and silicon computer chips.

Some dumping reflects subsidization by other countries. At other times it may be an attempt by an individual company to dominate a world market. After the lower prices of the dumped goods have succeeded in driving out all the competition, the dumping company can exploit its position by raising the price of its product. Many countries, including Canada, have trade laws that contain antidumping measures. The Canadian Anti-Dumping and Countervailing Directorate, a federal agency, examines many complaints of dumping every year and has the power to impose a duty on the good in question to raise its market price in Canada. In 1995 it ruled that sugar was being dumped on the Canadian market by a number of countries, and therefore in some cases it set punitive duties as high as 179% of the export price. More recent cases have involved bacteriological cultures, dry pasta, and fresh garlic.

protection *The practice of shielding a sector of the economy from foreign competition.*

tariff *A tax on imports.*

export subsidies *Government payments made to domestic firms to encourage exports.*

dumping *Takes place when a firm or industry sells products on the world market at prices below the cost of production.*

quota *A limit on the quantity of imports.*

A **quota** is a limit on the quantity of imports. Quotas can be mandatory or voluntary, and they may be legislated or negotiated with foreign governments. In the best-known voluntary quota, or "voluntary restraint," negotiated with the Japanese government in 1981, Japan agreed to reduce the number of automobiles it exported to Canada. Other quotas in Canada apply primarily in the agricultural sector.

■ **World Trade and the World Trade Organization** Just as the British Corn Laws influenced the economies of the world in the nineteenth century, so in turn did the U.S. **Smoot-Hawley tariff** in the twentieth century. This piece of tariff legislation, which pushed the average tariff rate in the United States to 60%, was passed in 1930 and set off an international trade war when the United States' trading partners retaliated with tariffs of their own. For example, in the same year, Canada passed the (short-lived) Dunning tariff, which gave preferential treatment to Britain. Many economists point to the decline in trade that followed Smoot-Hawley as one of the causes of the worldwide depression of the 1930s.[3]

Smoot-Hawley tariff *The U.S. tariff law of the 1930s that set the highest tariffs in U.S. history (60%). It set off an international trade war and caused the decline in trade that is often considered a cause of the worldwide depression of the 1930s.*

In 1947, Canada and 22 other countries agreed to reduce barriers to trade and established an organization to promote trade liberalization. The **General Agreement on Tariffs and Trade (GATT)** was first considered an interim arrangement, but it continued until 1995. The "Final Act" of the GATT was the Uruguay Round of multilateral trade negotiations that began in Punta del Este, Uruguay, in 1986 and concluded on December 15, 1993. Negotiations took several years longer than anticipated when the United States and the European Union could not come to an agreement on agricultural policy.

General Agreement on Tariffs and Trade (GATT) *An international agreement signed by Canada and 22 other countries in 1947 to promote the liberalization of foreign trade. Replaced by the World Trade Organization (WTO).*

The Uruguay Round involved over 100 countries, among them a huge number of developing countries. Previously, the GATT had been considered by many developing nations to be a "rich man's club." The Uruguay Round, with its broad involvement by so many countries, reflected a significant change in the world trade arena. Negotiations moved beyond the traditional GATT mandate of reducing tariffs and included reductions of nontariff barriers such as quotas. In addition, while the GATT had previously governed trade only in goods, the Final Act also covered trade in services, an increasingly large component of world trade. Finally, the Uruguay Round developed rules for trade-related intellectual property, such as patents, trademarks, and copyrights.

With so many sweeping changes, it was felt that the framework of the GATT had served its purpose, and it was time for an organizational restructuring. As a result, the GATT was abolished and the **World Trade Organization (WTO)** was established on January 1, 1995, the same day the Uruguay Round changes went into effect. As with the GATT, the WTO is headquartered in Geneva, Switzerland. Membership stands at over 120 countries, and several other countries have been granted observer status with a view to becoming full members in the future.

World Trade Organization (WTO) *The body responsible for governing world trade. Entered into force January 1, 1995, replacing the General Agreement on Tariffs and Trade (GATT). See the WTO's website for more information: www.wto.org*

As a member of the WTO, Canada must abide by the reductions in tariffs and other trade barriers negotiated in the Uruguay Round. These are likely to be the most difficult in the area of agricultural trade. Agriculture is a highly protected industry in Canada, and Canada must reduce agricultural tariffs and export subsidies by 36% over a six-year period. Manufacturing tariffs, most of which are not especially high, must be approximately halved. Existing high tariffs on textiles and clothing must be reduced by an average of 20% and a significant number of nontariff barriers to trade in those goods must be eliminated.

economic integration *Occurs when two or more countries join to form a free trade zone.*

■ **Economic Integration: The European Union (EU)** **Economic integration** occurs when two or more countries join to form a free trade zone. In 1958, six European countries formed a customs union. Over the years, membership in the union grew, as did the economic ties among the countries. In 1991, the European Community

---

[3]*See especially Charles Kindleberger,* The World in Depression 1929–1939 *(London: Allen Lane, 1973).*

(EC, or the Common Market) went a step further and began the process of forming the largest free trade zone in the world. The economic integration process began in December of that year, when its 12 existing members (the United Kingdom, Belgium, France, Germany, Italy, the Netherlands, Luxembourg, Denmark, Greece, Ireland, Spain, and Portugal) signed the Maastricht Treaty. The treaty called for the end to border controls, a common currency (to be called the Euro), an end to all tariffs, and the coordination of monetary and even political affairs. In 1995, Austria, Finland, and Sweden became members of this **European Union (EU)**, as the EC is now called, bringing the number of member countries to 15.

On January 1, 1993, all tariffs and trade barriers were dropped among the member countries. Border checkpoints were closed in early 1995. Citizens can now travel among member countries without passports. The most difficult step will be the adoption of a common currency. The goal is to have it in place by 1999, but most think it will take longer, and not all members will initially be part of the currency union. Many economists believe that the advantages of free trade within the bloc, a reunited Germany, and the ability to work well as a bloc will make the EU one of the most powerful players in the international marketplace in the coming decades.

■ **Economic Integration: NAFTA** In 1988, Canada (under Prime Minister Brian Mulroney) and the United States (under President Ronald Reagan) signed the **Canada–U.S. Free Trade Agreement** to remove all barriers to trade, including tariffs and quotas, between the two countries over a 10-year period.

In addition, in 1992, Canada, the United States, and Mexico signed the **North American Free Trade Agreement (NAFTA),** in which the three countries agreed to establish all of North America as a free trade zone. NAFTA came into effect on January 1, 1994. The North American free trade area includes 360 million people and a total output of over $7 trillion—a larger output than that of the European Union. The agreement will eliminate all tariffs over a 10- to 15-year period and remove restrictions on most investments. (For more information, see the Global Perspective box on the next page titled "Free Trade in Canada.")

Free Trade or Protection?

As we pointed out earlier in this chapter, one of the great economic debates of all time revolves around free trade versus protection. The arguments in favour of each are summarized briefly in the following discussion.

THE CASE FOR FREE TRADE

Let us begin with three short but powerful arguments in favour of free trade. First, international trade can improve the level of competition within an economy. For example, if automobile imports to North America were prohibited, many would guess that the prices of automobiles sold by the North American "Big Three" producers would increase.

Second, suppose Canada decided to put a new tariff on the imports of some product, say U.S. wine. It is probable that the United States would retaliate by putting a new tariff on Canadian beer. Canada could retaliate for the retaliation with a new tariff on U.S. strawberries, but soon there would be a U.S. tariff on Canadian apples in response. In short, even if protection were desirable, it is difficult to protect one's own industries without other countries protecting their industries. As Canada is both a relatively small economy (at least relative to its major trading partner) and a net exporter, it is hard to see it winning very many trade wars.

Third, there is a particular problem concerning tariffs on intermediate goods that

European Union (EU) *The European trading bloc composed of Austria, Belgium, Denmark, Finland, France, Germany, Greece, Ireland, Italy, Luxembourg, the Netherlands, Portugal, Spain, Sweden, and the United Kingdom.*

Canada–U.S. Free Trade Agreement *An agreement, which came into effect January 1, 1989, in which Canada and the United States agreed to eliminate all barriers to trade between the two countries over a 10-year period.*

North American Free Trade Agreement (NAFTA) *An agreement signed by Canada, the United States, and Mexico, in which the three countries agreed to establish all of North America as a free trade zone.*

The idea of free trade in Canada, especially with the United States, is not new. The Reciprocity Treaty of 1854–1866 allowed free trade in natural products between British North America and the U.S. and permitted each party to fish in the other's waters. More recently, the 1965 auto pact, mentioned earlier in this chapter, established free trade (for manufacturers satisfying certain conditions) in one sector of the economy. The auto pact and subsequent free-trade agreements do not pertain directly to consumers. Thus, for example, a Canadian cannot easily buy a car in the United States and bring it back into Canada.

The Canada–U.S. Free Trade Agreement, which came into effect January 1, 1989, was seen by many in Canada as a way of safeguarding access to U.S. markets. As Britain joined the other European countries in forming the European Union, and the United States (which was a large enough trader to stand on its own if it so chose) appeared to be growing more protectionist, Canada was finding itself increasingly alone.

Supporters of the trade agreement with the U.S. argued that a reduction in Canadian tariffs on American goods would allow Canadians to purchase lower-cost American goods more cheaply than domestically produced goods. Inefficient Canadian industries would be eliminated, allowing investment and resources to be concentrated in industries in which Canada could compete internationally, aided by the economies of scale achieved by building plants large enough to serve the combined Canadian and American market rather than the Canadian market alone. But there was nonetheless quite vocal opposition to the idea. Many Canadians argued that Canadian culture and political sover-

eignty would be imperilled by closer association with their powerful neighbour. Some felt that the deal as written did not provide sufficient guarantees for access to the American market. Most opposition, however, centred on the fear that those who lost jobs in the eliminated industries would not easily, if ever, find jobs in the Canadian industries that were supposed to expand. (Some proponents of the agreement tried to assuage these fears by also supporting special adjustment assistance for those who lost jobs because of the deal. However, when the agreement was signed, no new assistance programs were implemented.) Despite the opposition, the Conservative government of Brian Mulroney, which supported the Canada–U.S. agreement, won re-election in 1988.

Subsequent proposals to include Mexico in the agreement were met with some reservation, both in Canada and in the U.S. The economic recession in Canada that began in the early 1990s was blamed by many on the Canada–U.S. agree-

ment, and there were those in both countries who argued that domestic jobs would be lost to the much less expensive Mexican labour force. (You should think about these arguments in light of what you have learned in this chapter.) As well, Canada seemed to have little economic reason for seeking a trade union with Mexico, as Canada–Mexico trade was very small. However, the two major U.S. presidential candidates in the campaign of 1992 supported the idea and the North American Free Trade Agreement among the three countries came into effect on January 1, 1994.

Canada's trade with Mexico has increased substantially since NAFTA began. Canada's exports to Mexico by the end of 1996 were nearly 50% higher than at the end of 1993 and imports from Mexico were over 60% higher over the same period. In addition, the idea of an economic union throughout the Americas seems to be attracting further interest. For example, in 1996 Canada signed a free trade agreement with Chile.

are used as inputs for further manufacturing. For example, in the United States there is a substantial tariff on fine European cloth used in making expensive men's suits. Canadian manufacturers, primarily located in the Montreal area, do not pay such a tariff if the cloth is used in suits for export. Because such suits enter the United States without tariff under NAFTA, there has been a sharp increase in Canadian suit exports to the United States to the detriment of American manufacturers. A country's tariffs and quotas on intermediate goods may tend to hurt the domestic industries that use those goods.

Now let us consider the more intricate argument for free trade, that of comparative advantage. Trade has potential benefits for all countries. A good is not imported unless its net price to buyers is below that of the domestically produced alternative. When Americans in our earlier example found Canadian lumber less expensive than their own, they bought it, yet they continued to pay the same price for homemade cloth. Canadians bought less expensive American cloth, but they continued to buy domestic lumber at the same lower price. Under these conditions, *both Canadians and Americans ended up paying less and consuming more.*

At the same time, resources (including labour) move out of cloth production and into lumber production in Canada. In the United States, resources (including labour) move out of lumber production and into cloth production. Thus, the resources in both countries are more efficiently used. Tariffs, export subsidies, and quotas, which interfere with the free movement of goods and services around the world, reduce or eliminate the gains of comparative advantage.

We can use supply and demand curves to illustrate this point. We continue to use cloth, or more broadly textiles, in our example but make the more realistic assumption that instead of all Canadian cloth being produced at $5 per metre, different amounts of textiles will be produced, depending on the price. That is, we say there is a domestic supply curve for textiles. Suppose that Figure 21.4a on page 546 shows such domestic supply along with domestic demand and we assume that in the absence of trade, the market clears at a price of $4.20 (now working entirely in Canadian dollars). At equilibrium, 450 million metres of textiles are produced and consumed.

We also change our previous two-country example to recognize that Canada does not only import from the United States but, particularly for a product such as textiles, from other countries around the world, especially European and Asia-Pacific countries. The world market sets a world price. Because Canada is a small consumer and producer, Canadian demand and supply have essentially no effect on that price. Let us assume that the world price is $2 per metre. Assuming again no quality difference, no domestic producer will be able to charge more than $2. If there are no barriers to trade, the world price sets the price in Canada. As the price in Canada falls from $4.20 to $2, the quantity demanded by consumers increases from 450 million metres to 700 million metres, but the quantity supplied by domestic producers drops from 450 million metres to 200 million metres. The difference, 500 million metres, is the quantity of textiles imported.

The argument for free trade holds that each country should specialize in producing the goods and services in which it enjoys a comparative advantage. Clearly, if foreign producers can produce textiles at a much lower price than domestic producers, they have a comparative advantage. As the world price of textiles falls to $2, domestic (Canadian) supply drops and resources are transferred to other sectors. These other sectors, which may be export industries or domestic industries, are not shown in Figure 21.4a. It is clear, however, that the allocation of resources is more efficient at a price of $2. Why should Canadians produce what foreign producers can produce at a lower cost? Canadian resources should move into the production of the things Canada produces best.

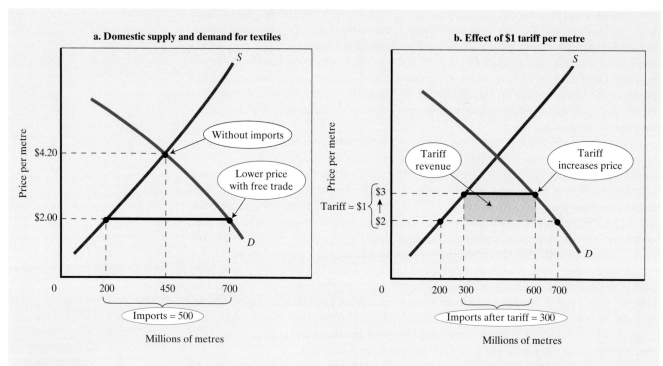

a. Domestic supply and demand for textiles

Price per metre

$4.20

$2.00

Without imports

Lower price
with free trade

Imports = 500

0   200   450   700

Millions of metres

S

D

b. Effect of $1 tariff per metre

Price per metre

Tariff
revenue

Tariff
increases price

$3

Tariff = $1

$2

Imports after tariff = 300

0   200 300   600 700

Millions of metres

S

D

FIGURE 21.4

The Gains from Trade and Losses from the Imposition of a Tariff

A tariff of $1 per metre increases the market price facing consumers from $2 per metre to $3 per metre. The government collects revenues equal to the grey shaded area. The loss of efficiency has two components. First, consumers must pay a higher price for goods that could be produced at lower cost. Second, marginal producers are drawn into textiles and away from other goods, resulting in inefficient domestic production.

Now consider what happens to the domestic price of textiles when a trade barrier is imposed. Figure 21.4b shows the effect of a set tariff of $1 per metre imposed on imported textiles. The tariff raises the domestic price of textiles to $2 + $1 = $3. The result is that some of the gains from trade are lost. First, consumers are forced to pay a higher price for the same good; the quantity of textiles demanded drops from 700 million metres under free trade to 600 million metres because some consumers simply are not willing to pay the higher price.

At the same time, the higher price of textiles draws into textile production some marginal domestic producers who could not make a profit at $2. (Remember, domestic producers do not pay a tariff.) As the price rises to $3, the quantity supplied by producers rises from 200 million metres to 300 million metres. The overall result is a decrease in imports from 500 million metres to 300 million metres.

Finally, the imposition of the tariff means that the government collects revenue equal to the shaded grey area in Figure 21.4b. This shaded area is simply equal to the tariff rate per metre, ($1), times the number of metres that are imported after the tariff is in place (300 million metres). Thus, receipts from the tariff are $300 million.

What is the final result of the tariff? The answer should be clear. Domestic producers that were receiving revenues of only $2 per metre before the tariff was imposed now receive a higher price and earn higher profits. But these higher profits are achieved at a loss of efficiency. All of this leads us to conclude that:

Trade barriers prevent a country from reaping the benefits of specialization, push it to adopt relatively inefficient production techniques, and force consumers to pay higher prices for protected products than they would otherwise pay.

THE CASE FOR PROTECTION

Arguments can also be made in favour of tariffs and quotas, of course. The most frequently heard of these are described below.

■ **Protection Saves Jobs** The main argument for protection is that foreign competition costs Canadians their jobs. When Canadians buy Volvos, Canadian-made cars go unsold. This leads to layoffs in the domestic auto industry. When Canadians buy Japanese or German steel, steelworkers in Hamilton lose their jobs. When Canadians buy textiles from Korea or Taiwan, the millworkers in Quebec lose their jobs.

It is true that when we buy goods from foreign producers, domestic producers do suffer. But workers laid off in the contracting sectors may be ultimately re-employed in other expanding sectors. Foreign competition in textiles, for example, has clearly meant the loss of jobs in that industry. Many textile workers in Southern Ontario lost their jobs as the textile mills there closed down. But with the expansion of the high-tech computer industry in the Waterloo area as well as the opening of an automobile plant in the Cambridge region, many jobs have also been created in Southern Ontario.

Nevertheless, the adjustment process is far from costless. The knowledge that some other industry, perhaps in some other part of the country, may be expanding is of little comfort to the person whose skills become obsolete or whose pension benefits are lost when his or her company abruptly closes a plant or goes bankrupt. The social and personal problems brought about by industry-specific unemployment, obsolete skills, and bankruptcy as a result of foreign competition are significant.

This does reflect a real shortcoming in our model. We assumed full employment of resources. So, for example, we argued that the problem with putting a tariff on textiles was that it would draw firms and individuals into the textile industry to produce textiles at $3 per metre when others in the world could produce them for $2 per metre. The implication was that the workers in Canada would be better employed in some other industry, but what if the alternative is that they remain unemployed?

These problems can be addressed in two ways. (1) Canada could institute trade barriers. This would invite retaliation by other countries and cause the loss of the gains from free trade. Canadian consumers would then find themselves having to pay $3 per metre for textiles to save domestic jobs even though these textiles can be produced more efficiently at $2 per metre elsewhere. Or, (2) Canada could take a long-term view and accept the transitional costs of unemployment in the textile industry and decide not to produce domestically something that can be produced more cheaply elsewhere. Perhaps the victims of free trade could be helped by retraining, or income or relocation assistance. Still, the costs of free trade are very likely to be borne disproportionately by the textile workers who lose their jobs. It is obvious that moves toward freer trade will have lower cost if the macroeconomy can otherwise be managed so that it is close to full employment.

■ Some Countries Engage in Unfair Trade Practices   Attempts by Canadian firms to monopolize an industry are illegal under the Competition Act. If a strong company decided to drive the competition out of the market by setting prices below cost, it would be aggressively prosecuted. But, the argument goes, if we won't allow a Canadian firm to engage in predatory pricing or monopolize an industry or market, can we stand by and let a German firm or a Japanese firm do so in the name of free trade? This is a legitimate argument and one that has gained significant favour in recent years. How should we respond when a large international company or a country behaves strategically against a domestic firm or industry? Free trade may be the best solution when everybody plays by the rules, but sometimes retaliation is necessary.

■ Cheap Foreign Labour Makes Competition Unfair   Let us say that a particular country gained its "comparative advantage" in textiles by paying its workers low wages. How can Canadian domestic companies compete with foreign companies that pay wages that are less than a quarter of domestic wages?

First, we need to remember that while Canadian textile workers and companies may complain about competing with cheap foreign labour, other Canadians gain from being able to purchase cheaper foreign cloth. But, second, if Canadian firms cannot produce textiles as cheaply as foreign firms, this is a signal that labour and other resources are not being used efficiently. The reason that Canadian workers earn higher wages is that they are more productive: Canada has more capital per worker, and its workers are better trained. But the return to this higher productivity is only fully realized if workers are in industries in which they can produce goods at a lower price than they can be produced in other countries. A low-wage country will never produce everything, but instead, wages and possibly exchange rates will adjust so that the low-wage country produces the goods in which it has a *comparative advantage* and Canada produces the goods in which it has a comparative advantage. We would expect the low-wage country to produce goods (for example, cotton textiles) that require a lot of cheap, low-productivity labour and the natural resources available in those countries, and Canada to produce goods (for example, computer software, nickel) that require high-productivity labour, more capital, and Canadian resources.

Protected by the government, Japan's politically powerful farmers tie up very valuable land like these farms. Efficiency requires that land should be allocated to its most valuable use.

■ Protection Safeguards National Independence and Security   Beyond the argument of saving jobs, certain sectors of the economy may appeal for protection in the name of national independence and security. Many Canadians, remembering the rationing and food shortages during World War II, argue for the protection of the agricultural sector. Similar arguments were made for protection of the oil and gas industries in the wake of the Arab oil embargo of the 1970s. In the event of war or other international disruptions, Canada would not want to depend on foreign countries for products as vital as food or energy. Even if we acknowledge another country's comparative advantage, we may want to protect our own resources. Some also argue that promoting east–west economic relations among Canadians, rather than north–south Canada–U.S. trade, helps protect Canada's sense of nationhood. (See the Application box titled "Trade and Borders.")

Closely related to the argument above is the claim that countries, particularly small or developing countries, may come to rely too heavily on one or more trading

Application

Trade and Borders

While there continues to be discussion of lowering barriers to interprovincial trade in Canada (barriers which, for example, have led the major brewers to locate breweries in almost every province rather than having more consolidated operations), the most recent evidence suggests that provincial trade barriers are very low relative to national trade barriers. In a study published in the *American Economic Review*, John McCallum, formerly of McGill University and now senior vice president and chief economist of the Royal Bank of Canada, found that even though Canada–U.S. trade barriers may seem small, the border has nonetheless very large implications for trade.

Dr. McCallum developed a model that would predict trade flows among the provinces of Canada and the states of the United States if all that mattered were provincial and state output levels and distances and there were no trade barriers at all. For ex-

ample, the Prairie provinces are probably more likely to trade with Ontario than with the Atlantic provinces because Ontario is closer and because the Ontario economy is bigger. He then compared the predictions of that model with actual trade flows.

The results were that actual trade between provinces is much higher than predicted and trade between provinces and states much lower. For example, if the national border did not matter, the model would predict that Ontario should export 10 times more to California than to British Columbia, because the distances are about the same and California's economy is about 10 times larger than British Columbia's. In fact, Ontario exports three times more to B.C. than it does to California. As another example, the model would predict that if the national border did not affect trade, for both the Atlantic and the Prairie provinces no more than 25% of their North American trade would

be with other provinces and 75% would be with the United States. In fact, 60% of such trade is with other provinces and only 40% is with the U.S.

This does not mean that interprovincial trade barriers have no effects, but it does remind us how important interprovincial trade is. Dr. McCallum used the (latest-available) 1988 data and hence was not able to capture the effects of NAFTA, but concludes from examination of other evidence that the effects on interprovincial trade (p. 621) "of continental free trade could turn out to be relatively modest, or if not modest, at least gradual." East–west trade continues to be an important feature of the Canadian economy.

Source: John McCallum, "National Borders Matter: Canada–U.S. Regional Trade Patterns," *American Economic Review* (June 1995): pp. 615–623.

partners for many items. If Canada comes to rely on a major power for food or energy or some important raw material, it may be difficult for Canada to remain politically independent. Some critics of free trade argue that the developed countries have engaged in trade with the developing countries in a way that creates these kinds of dependencies.

■ **Protection Safeguards Infant Industries** Young industries in a given country may have a difficult time competing with established industries in other countries. And in a dynamic world, a protected **infant industry** might mature into a strong one worldwide because of an acquired, but real, comparative advantage. If such an industry is undercut and driven out of world markets at the beginning of its life, that comparative advantage might never develop.

Yet efforts to protect infant industries can backfire. Suppose that after protection has been imposed, it gradually becomes clear that such an industry will never be able to match world prices and withstand foreign competition. By that time, the industry might nonetheless have grown to employ a significant number of employees. Elimination of protection at that stage might cause great disruption. Indeed, it might be politically impossible to remove the protective measures. Even if the industry does

infant industry *A young industry that may need temporary protection from competition from the established industries of other countries in order to develop an acquired comparative advantage.*

achieve sufficient efficiency to stand on its own, its firms and workers may resist the elimination of protection, preferring instead to preserve high domestic prices and the resulting higher profits and/or wages. Real resources will be used up in lobbying for protection and real costs will be imposed upon the political system. Industry participants may never admit that the infant industry has grown up.

The infant industry argument is one example of an argument for protection, sometimes called strategic trade policy, in which the government tries to pick successful industries and promote their development by protection or subsidy. Besides the attempt to acquire a comparative advantage by allowing time for the development of expertise and technology (sometimes called "learning by doing"), it is sometimes argued that in high fixed-cost industries in which ultimately there will be only a few highly profitable firms, a government subsidy may make the difference between success and failure, and a successful firm will be able to repay the subsidy.

The classic international example is probably the Japanese automobile industry, which received extensive tariff protection in its early years and has clearly been a success. More recently, the Japanese government provided developmental subsidies in a number of high-tech industries such as semiconductors, and it is less clear that the gains in terms of profits and employment will offset the costs. In Canada, federal government subsidies through Atomic Energy of Canada Limited have led to the development of the CANDU nuclear reactor, which is widely acknowledged as having some technological advantages over its competitors; but, nonetheless, the only international sales have been at extremely concessionary terms and the program has not come close to financial success. In a similar way a number of provincial governments have been involved in what is in effect strategic trade policy, with some famous failures such as the subsidization of the now-bankrupt Bricklin sports car plant in New Brunswick. The problem is that picking winners is difficult.

An Economic Consensus

Critical to our study of international economics is the important debate between free traders and protectionists. On one side is the theory of comparative advantage, formalized by David Ricardo in the early part of the nineteenth century. According to this view, all countries benefit from specialization and trade. The gains from trade are real, and they can be large; free international trade raises real incomes and improves the standard of living.

On the other side of the debate are the protectionists, who point to the loss of jobs and argue for the protection of workers from foreign competition. But, although foreign competition can cause job loss in specific sectors, it is unlikely to cause net job loss in an economy, and workers may be absorbed over time into expanding sectors. This is particularly true in a net exporting country like Canada.

> Moves toward free trade will have victims, particularly in times of high unemployment. But while economists disagree about many things, the majority believe the long-term gains resulting from free trade offset the costs of transition.

1. All economies, regardless of their size, depend to some extent on other economies and are affected by events outside their borders.

The International Economy: Trade Surpluses and Deficits

2. Currently, Canada exports more than it imports—in other words, it runs a *trade surplus.* In the late 1980s, Canada imported more than it exported—a *trade deficit.*

The Economic Basis for Trade: Comparative Advantage

3. The *theory of comparative advantage,* dating to the writings of David Ricardo in the nineteenth century, holds that specialization and free trade will benefit all trading partners, even those that may be absolutely less efficient producers.

4. A country enjoys an *absolute advantage* over another country in the production of a product if it uses fewer resources to produce that product than the other country does. A country has a *comparative advantage* in the production of a product if that product can be produced at a lower cost in terms of other goods.

5. Trade enables countries to move out beyond their previous resource and productivity constraints. When countries specialize in producing those goods in which they have a comparative advantage, they maximize their combined output and allocate their resources more efficiently.

6. When trade is free, patterns of trade and trade flows result from the independent decisions of thousands of importers and exporters and millions of private households and firms.

7. The relative attractiveness of foreign goods to Canadian buyers and of Canadian goods to foreign buyers depends in part on *exchange rates,* the ratios at which two currencies are traded for each other.

8. For any pair of countries, there is a range of exchange rates that will lead automatically to both countries realizing the gains from specialization and comparative advantage.

9. If exchange rates end up in the right range (that is, in a range that facilitates the flow of goods between countries), the free market will drive each country to shift resources into those sectors in which it enjoys a comparative advantage. Only those products in which a country has a comparative advantage will be competitive in world markets.

The Sources of Comparative Advantage

10. The *Heckscher-Ohlin theorem* looks to relative *factor endowments* to explain comparative advantage and trade flows. According to the theorem, a country has a comparative advantage in the production of a product if that country is relatively well endowed with the inputs that are used intensively in the production of that product.

11. A relatively short list of inputs—natural resources, knowledge capital, physical capital, land, and skilled and unskilled labour—explains a surprisingly large portion of world trade patterns. But the simple version of the theory of comparative advantage cannot explain why many countries import and export the same goods.

12. Some theories argue that comparative advantage can be acquired. Just as industries within a country differentiate their products to capture a domestic market, so too do they differentiate their products to please the wide variety of tastes that exists worldwide. This theory is not inconsistent with the theory of comparative advantage.

Trade Barriers: Tariffs, Export Subsidies, and Quotas

13. Trade barriers take many forms, the three most common of which are *tariffs, export subsidies,* and *quotas.* All of these are forms of *protection* by which some sector of the economy is shielded from foreign competition.

14. Although Canada historically has been a high-tariff country, the general movement is now away from tariffs and quotas. The World Trade Organization, of which Canada is a member, replaced the General Agreement on Tariffs and Trade (GATT) in 1995; its purpose is to reduce barriers to world trade and keep them down. Also important are the *Canada–U.S. Free Trade Agreement,* which came into effect January 1, 1989, and the *North American Free Trade Agreement,* signed by Canada, the United States, and Mexico, which came into effect on January 1, 1994.

15. The *European Union (EU)* is a free trade bloc

composed of 15 countries: Austria, Belgium, Denmark, Finland, France, Germany, Greece, Ireland, Italy, Luxembourg, the Netherlands, Portugal, Spain, Sweden, and the United Kingdom. Many economists believe that the advantages of free trade within the bloc, a reunited Germany, and the ability to work well as a bloc will make the EU one of the most powerful players in the international marketplace in the coming decades.

Free Trade or Protection?

16. A country that follows a free trade policy will improve competition in its domestic markets, prevent retaliatory trade restrictions by other countries, and help certain domestic industries by reducing the costs of their imported inputs. Moreover, trade barriers prevent a country from reaping the benefits of specialization, push it to adopt relatively inefficient production techniques, and force consumers to pay higher prices for protected products than they would otherwise pay.

17. The case for protection rests on a number of propositions, one of which is that foreign competition results in a loss of domestic jobs. But workers laid off in the contracting sectors may ultimately be reemployed in other expanding sectors. This adjustment process is far from costless, however.

18. Other arguments for protection hold that cheap foreign labour makes competition unfair; that some countries engage in unfair trade practices; that it safeguards national independence and security; and that it protects *infant industries*. Despite these arguments, however, most economists favour free trade.

Review Terms and Concepts

absolute advantage 530

Canada–U.S. Free Trade Agreement 543

comparative advantage 534

Corn Laws 529

dumping 541

economic integration 542

European Union (EU) 543

exchange rate 537

export subsidies 541

factor endowments 539

General Agreement on Tariffs and Trade (GATT) 542

Heckscher-Ohlin theorem 540

infant industry 549

North American Free Trade Agreement (NAFTA) 543

protection 541

quota 542

Smoot-Hawley tariff 542

tariff 541

terms of trade 535

theory of comparative advantage 529

trade deficit 528

trade surplus 528

World Trade Organization (WTO) 542

Problem Set

1. Canada imported $12.9 billion worth of "food, feeds, beverages and tobacco" in 1996 and exported $18.1 billion worth.

   a. Name some of the imported items that you are aware of in this category. Also name some of the exported items.

   b. Canada is said to have a comparative advantage in the production of agricultural goods. How would you go about testing this proposition? What data would you need?

   c. Are the numbers above consistent with the theory of comparative advantage? Suppose you had a more detailed breakdown of which items Canada imports and which it exports. What would you look for?

   d. What other theories of international trade might explain why the same goods are imported and exported?

2. The following table gives 1996 figures for tonne yield per hectare in Manitoba and Saskatchewan:

	WHEAT	CANOLA
Manitoba	2.5	1.7
Saskatchewan	2.3	1.4

Source: Adapted from Statistics Canada, Field Crop Reporting Series, November 1996, Cat. no. 22-002.

   a. If we assume that farmers in Manitoba and Saskatchewan use the same amount of labour, capital, and fertilizer, which province has an absolute advantage in wheat production? Canola production?

   b. If we transfer land out of wheat into canola, how many tonnes of wheat do we give up in Manitoba per additional tonne of canola produced? In Saskatchewan?

   c. Which province has a comparative advantage in wheat production? In canola production?

The following table gives the distribution of land planted for each province in millions of hectares in 1996:

	TOTAL HECTARES SEEDED	WHEAT	CANOLA
Manitoba	4.7	1.8 (38%)	0.6 (13%)
Saskatchewan	14.8	7.6 (52%)	1.6 (11%)

Source: Adapted from Statistics Canada, Field Crop Reporting Series, November 1996, Cat. no. 22-002.

   Are these data consistent with your answer to part c? Explain.

3. The North American Free Trade Agreement (NAFTA) took effect on January 1, 1994. The Final Act of the Uruguay Round of the General Agreement on Tariffs and Trade (GATT) took effect on January 1, 1995. Both were ratified over very strong political opposition from lobby groups. Using newspaper articles and periodicals at the time, write a short report about the opposition to each of these agreements. Who opposed them? Can you offer an explanation for their opposition? What logic did the Canadian government rely on in supporting these measures?

4. The provinces and territories of Canada may be viewed as separate economies, each specializing in the products it produces best and trading with each other.

   a. What product or products does your province or territory specialize in?

   b. Can you identify the source of the comparative advantage that lies behind the production of one or more of these products (a natural resource, plentiful cheap labour, a skilled labour force, etc.)?

   c. Do you think that the theory of comparative advantage and the Heckscher-Ohlin theorem help to explain why your region specializes in the way that it does?

5. Export subsidies have been proposed to prop up food prices and help struggling family farmers. Would you favour such subsidies?

6. Germany and France produce white and red wines. Current domestic prices for each are given in the following table:

	GERMANY	FRANCE
White wine	5 DM	10 francs
Red wine	10 DM	15 francs

Suppose that the exchange rate is 1 deutsche mark = 1 franc.

   a. If the price ratios within each country reflect resource use, which country has a comparative advantage in the production of red wine? White wine?

   b. Assume that there are no other trading partners and that the only motive for holding foreign currency is to buy foreign goods. Will the current exchange rate lead to trade flows in both directions between the two countries?

   c. What adjustments might you expect in the exchange rate? Be specific.

   d. What would you predict about trade flows between Germany and France in the long run?

7. The goal of the European Union (EU) is to remove all trade barriers within its member countries and to become one "common market" with one uniform currency. Explain the likely benefits and costs to the EU's member countries. Should Canada be concerned about the EU? Why or why not?

22

Economic Growth in Developing Countries

Our primary focus in this text has been on economic issues facing Canada. Cuts to social programs, slow economic growth in recent years, and worries about the debt are familiar to Canadians. But the economics we have been studying also applies to other countries. Welfare reform is a big issue in the Netherlands, Japan is facing major fiscal deficits, and the German central bank has been wrestling with slow economic growth. We can analyze these and other issues in the Netherlands, Japan, and Germany with some confidence because these countries have so much in common with Canada. In spite of differences in languages and cultures, all these countries have modern industrialized economies that rely heavily on markets to allocate resources. But what about the economic problems facing Somalia or Haiti? Can we apply the same economic principles that we have been studying to these less developed countries (sometimes called LDCs)?

Most economists think that the answer is yes. All economic analysis deals with the basic problem of making choices under conditions of scarcity, and the problem of satisfying their citizens' wants and needs is certainly as real for Somalia and Haiti as it is for the Netherlands, Germany, and Japan. The universality of scarcity is what makes economic analysis relevant to all nations, regardless of their level of material well-being or ruling political ideology.

The basic tools of supply and demand, theories about consumers and firms, and theories about the structure of markets all contribute to an understanding of the economic problems confronting the world's developing nations. However, these nations often face economic problems quite different from those faced by richer, more developed countries. In the developing nations, the economist may have to worry about chronic food shortages, explosive population growth, and hyperinflations that reach triple, and even quadruple, digits. Canada and other industrialized economies rarely encounter such difficulties.

The instruments of economic management also vary from country to country. Canada has well-developed financial market institutions and a strong central bank (the Bank of Canada) through which the government can control the macroeconomy to some extent. But even limited intervention is impossible in some of the developing countries. In Canada, tax laws can be changed to stimulate saving, to encourage particular kinds of investments, or to redistribute income. In most developing countries, there are neither meaningful personal income taxes nor effective tax policies.

But even though economic problems and the policy instruments available to tackle them vary across countries, economic thinking about these problems can often be transferred quite easily from one setting to another. In this chapter we discuss several of the economic problems specific to developing countries in an attempt to capture some of the insights that economic analysis can offer.

Life in the Developing Countries: Population and Poverty

By the year 2000, the population of the world will reach over 6.1 billion people. Most of the world's more than 200 countries belong to the developing world, in which about three-quarters of the world's population lives.

In the early 1960s, the countries of the world could be assigned rather easily to categories. The *developed countries* included most of Europe, North America, Japan, Australia, and New Zealand; the *developing countries* included the rest of the world. The developing nations were often referred to as the "Third World" to distinguish them from the Western industrialized nations (the "First World") and the former socialist bloc of Eastern European nations (the "Second World").

Today, however, the world does not divide into three neat parts. Rapid economic progress has brought some developing nations closer to developed economies. Countries such as Argentina and Korea, while still considered to be "developing," are often referred to as middle-income, or newly industrialized, countries. Meanwhile, other countries, such as much of sub-Saharan Africa and some of South Asia, have stagnated and fallen so far behind the economic advances of the rest of the world that a new designation, the "Fourth World," has been coined. It is not clear yet where the republics of the former Soviet Union and other formerly Communist countries of Eastern Europe will end up. Production has fallen sharply in many of them. For example, between 1989 and 1992 industrial production fell 47.3% in Albania, 46% in Bulgaria, and 44% in the former East Germany. Between 1990 and 1994, real GDP in Russia fell nearly 50% and one estimate puts 1995 per capita GDP in Russia at around US$2500. Some of the new republics now have more in common with developing countries than with developed countries.

While the countries of the developing world exhibit considerable diversity, both in their standards of living and in their particular experiences of growth, marked differences continue to separate them from the developed countries. To begin with, the developed countries have a higher average level of material well-being. By material well-being, we mean the amounts of food, clothing, shelter, and other commodities consumed by the average person. One very crude way to illustrate these differences across countries is to compare gross national product (GNP) per capita. (GNP is very much like GDP, but it is usually used for these kinds of comparisons because it only includes the production of a country's residents and not that of foreign factors of production.)

Other characteristics of economic development we can examine include improvements in basic health and education. The degree of political and economic freedom enjoyed by individual citizens might also be part of a comprehensive definition of what it means to be a developed nation. Some of these criteria are easier to quantify than others; Table 22.1 presents data for different types of economies according to some of the more easily measured indexes of development. As you can see, high-income economies enjoy higher standards of living according to whatever indicator of development is chosen.

Behind these statistics lies the reality of the very difficult life facing the people of the developing world. For most, meagre incomes provide only the basic necessities of life. Most meals are the same, consisting of the region's food staple—typically rice, wheat, or corn. Shelter is primitive. Many people share a small room, usually with an earthen floor and no sanitary facilities. The great majority of the population lives in rural areas where agricultural work is hard and extremely time-consuming. Productivity (output produced per worker) is low because household plots are small and only the crudest of farm implements are available. Low productivity means that farm output per person is at levels barely sufficient to feed a farmer's own family, with nothing left over to sell to others. School-age children may receive some formal education, but illiteracy remains chronic for young and old alike. Infant mortality runs 10 times higher than in high-income countries. Although parasitic infections are common and debilitating, there is only one

Table 22.1	Indicators of Economic Development				
COUNTRY GROUP	**RANGE OF GNP PER CAPITA IN COUNTRY GROUP, 1995 (US$)**	**LIFE EXPECTANCY, 1995 (YEARS)**	**INFANT MORTALITY, 1995 (DEATHS BEFORE AGE ONE PER 1000 BIRTHS)**	**SECONDARY SCHOOL ENROLMENT, 1993 (NUMBER ENROLLED AS PERCENTAGE OF RELEVANT AGE GROUP)**	**PERCENTAGE OF POPULATION IN URBAN AREAS, 1995**
		Male *Female*			
Low-income (e.g., China, Ethiopia, Haiti, India)	765 or less	62 64	69	42 (1992)	29
Lower middle-income (e.g., Guatemala, Poland, Philippines, Thailand)	766–3034	64 70	41	64	56
Upper middle-income (e.g., Argentina, Brazil, Mexico, South Africa)	3035–9385	66 73	35	55	73
High-income (e.g., Canada, Germany, New Zealand, United States)	9386 or greater	74 81	7	97	78

Sources: World Bank, *World Development Report, 1996,* and *World Development Indicators, 1997.* Note that all numbers, except for Range of GNP per Capita, refer to weighted averages for each country group, where the weights equal the populations of each country in a specific country group.

physician per 5000 people. In addition, many developing countries are engaged in civil and external warfare.

Life in the developing nations is a continual struggle against the circumstances of poverty, and prospects for dramatic improvements in living standards for most people are dim. However, as with all generalizations, there are important exceptions. Some countries are better off than others, and in any given country an elite group always lives in considerable luxury. Just as in any advanced economy, income is distributed in a fashion that allows a small percentage of households to consume a disproportionately large share of national income. Income distribution in developing countries is often so skewed that the richest households surpass the living standards of many high-income families in the advanced economies. Table 22.2 on the next page presents some data on the distribution of income in some developing countries. We can see that in Kenya, for example, the poorest one-fifth of the population (bottom 20%) gets 3.4% of total Kenyan income, but the richest one-fifth (top 20%) gets 62.1%.

Civil wars in the African nation of Angola have posed major obstacles to economic development. Homes and other valuable capital in that country are constantly being damaged or destroyed by wartime activities.

Clearly, poverty—not affluence—dominates the developing world. Recent studies suggest that 40% of the people of the developing nations have annual incomes insufficient to provide for adequate nutrition.

> While the developed countries account for only about one-quarter of the world's population, they are estimated to consume three-quarters of the world's output. This leaves the developing countries with about three-fourths of the world's people, but only one-quarter of the world's income. The simple result is that most of our planet's population is poor.

In Canada, the poorest one-fifth (bottom 20%) of families receives just under 5% of total income, while the richest one-fifth receives about 44% of the income. But the inequality in the world distribution of income is much greater. When we look at the population of the world, the poorest one-fifth of families receives about 0.5% of the total world income and the richest one-fifth receives 79% of world income!

Economic Development: Sources and Strategies

Economists have been trying to understand the process of economic growth and development since the days of Adam Smith and David Ricardo in the eighteenth and nineteenth centuries, but the study of development economics as it applies to the developing countries has a much shorter history. The geopolitical struggles that followed World War II brought increased attention to the developing countries and their economic problems. During this period, the central question

Table 22.2

	Canada	Sri Lanka	Kenya	Brazil	Pakistan	Indonesia
Per Capita GNP 1995	US$19 380	US$700	US$280	US$3640	US$460	US$980
Bottom 20%	4.7	8.9	3.4	2.1	8.4	8.7
Second 20%	10.2	13.1	6.7	4.9	12.9	12.3
Third 20%	16.7	16.9	10.7	8.9	16.9	16.3
Fourth 20%	24.8	21.7	17.0	16.8	22.2	22.1
Top 20%	43.6	39.3	62.1	67.5	39.7	40.7

Income Distribution in Some Developing Countries

Sources: World Bank, *World Development Indicators, 1997,* Tables 1.1 and 2.6; Statistics Canada, *Income Distributions By Size in Canada, 1994;* Cat. no. 13–207.

of the new field of development economics was simply, why are some countries poor and others rich? If economists could understand the barriers to economic growth that prevent countries from developing and the prerequisites that would help them to develop, then they could prescribe suitable strategies for achieving economic advancement.

THE SOURCES OF ECONOMIC DEVELOPMENT

While a general theory of economic development applicable to all countries has not emerged and probably never will, some basic factors that limit a poor country's economic growth have been suggested. These include insufficient capital formation, a shortage of human resources and entrepreneurial ability, a lack of social overhead capital, and the constraints imposed by dependency on the already developed nations.

■ **Capital Formation** One explanation for low levels of output in developing countries is the absence of sufficient quantities of necessary inputs. Developing countries have diverse resource endowments—Congo, for instance, is abundant in natural resources, while Bangladesh is resource poor. Almost all developing nations have a scarcity of physical capital relative to other resources, especially labour. The small stock of physical capital (including factories, machinery, farm equipment, and other types of productive capital) constrains labour's productivity and holds back national output.

But citing capital shortages as the cause of low productivity does not really explain much. To get to the heart of the matter, we need to know why capital is in such short supply in developing countries. Many explanations have been offered. One, the **vicious-circle-of-poverty hypothesis,** suggests that a poor country must consume most of its income just to maintain its already low standard of living. Just like a poor family, a poor nation finds that the opportunity cost of forgoing current consumption (that is, saving instead of consuming) is too high. Consuming most of national income implies limited saving, and this in turn implies low levels of investment. Without investment, the capital stock does not grow, income remains low, and the vicious circle is complete. Poverty becomes self-perpetuating.

The difficulty with the vicious-circle argument is that if it were true, no country could ever develop. For example, Japanese GDP per capita at the turn of the century was well below that of many of today's developing nations. If the vicious-circle explanation were completely correct, Japan could never have grown into the industrial power it is today. The vicious-circle argument fails to recognize that every country has some surplus above consumption needs that is

vicious-circle-of-poverty hypothesis *Suggests that poverty is self-perpetuating because poor countries are unable to save and invest enough to accumulate the capital stock that would help them grow.*

available for investment. Often this surplus is most visible in the conspicuous-consumption habits of the nation's richest families. In short:

> Poverty alone cannot explain capital shortages, nor is poverty necessarily self-perpetuating.

In a developing economy, scarcity of capital may have more to do with a lack of incentives for citizens to save and invest productively than with any absolute scarcity of income available for capital accumulation. The inherent riskiness and uncertainty that surround a developing country's economy and its political system (including the frequency of internal war) tend to reduce incentives to invest in any activity, especially those that require long periods of time to yield a return. Many of the rich in developing countries take their savings and invest them in developed countries rather than risk holding them in what is often an unstable political climate (itself often due to the social and economic divisions within the country). Savings transferred to the developed countries do not lead to physical capital growth in the developing countries. The term **capital flight** is often used to refer to the fact that capital (domestic savings) often leaves developing countries in search of higher rates of return elsewhere. In addition, a range of government policies in the developing nations—including price ceilings, import controls, and even outright appropriation of private property—tend to discourage investment activity. In many cases, governments are controlled by an elite often involving the military and are unlikely to set policies in the broader social interest.

capital flight *The tendency for capital to leave developing countries in search of higher rates of return elsewhere.*

Whatever the causes of capital shortages, it is clear that the absence of productive capital prevents income from rising in any economy. The availability of capital is a necessary, but not a *sufficient,* condition for economic growth. The Third World landscape is littered with idle factories and abandoned machinery. Clearly, other ingredients are required to achieve economic progress.

■ **Human Resources and Entrepreneurial Ability** Capital is not the only factor of production required to produce output. Labour is an equally important input. But the quantity of available labour rarely constrains a developing economy. In most developing countries, rapid population growth for several decades has resulted in rapidly expanding labour supplies. The *quality* of available labour, however, may pose a serious constraint on the growth of income. Or, to put it another way, the shortage of *human capital*—the stock of knowledge and skill embodied in the workforce—may act as a barrier to economic growth.

Human capital may be developed in a number of ways. Because malnutrition and the lack of basic health care can substantially reduce labour productivity, programs to improve nutrition and health represent one kind of human capital investment that can lead to increased productivity and higher incomes. The more familiar forms of human capital investment, including formal education and on-the-job training, may also play an important role. Basic literacy, as well as specialized training in farm management, for example, can yield high returns to both the individual worker and the economy. Education has grown to become the largest category of government expenditure in many developing nations, in part because of the belief that human resources are the ultimate determinant of economic advance.

Those lucky enough to get an education often leave developing countries because they can do better financially in the developed world. Just as financial capital seeks the highest and safest return, so does human capital. Students from developing countries, many of whom were supported by their governments, graduate

brain drain *The tendency for talented people from developing countries to become educated in a developed country and remain there after graduation.*

every year from North American and European colleges and universities as engineers, doctors, scientists, economists, and the like. After graduation, these people face a difficult choice: to remain in North America or Europe and earn a high salary or to return home and accept a job at a much lower salary. Many people choose not to return home. This **brain drain** siphons off many of the most talented minds from developing countries.[1] But the brain drain is in part just a consequence of extending somewhat more equal opportunity to some of the world's poor. In any case, arguments about the brain drain are not very relevant to the consideration of basic literacy and skills programs.

Another frequently cited barrier to economic development is the apparent shortage of entrepreneurial activity in developing nations. Innovative entrepreneurs who are willing to take risks are an essential human resource in any economy. In a developing country, new techniques of production rarely need to be invented, since they can usually be adapted from the technology already developed by the technologically advanced countries. But entrepreneurs who are willing and able to organize and carry out economic activity appear to be in short supply. Family and political ties often seem to be more important than ability when it comes to securing positions of authority. Whatever the explanation:

> Development cannot proceed without human resources capable of initiating and managing economic activity.

■ **Social Overhead Capital** Anyone who has spent time in a developing nation knows how difficult it can be to send a letter, make a local phone call, or travel within the country itself. Add to this list of obstacles problems with water supplies, frequent electrical power outages—in areas where electricity is available at all—and often ineffective mosquito and pest control, and you soon realize how deficient even the simplest, most basic government-provided goods and services can be. In politically unstable areas, military spending is often high, to the detriment of spending on basic health and education.

In any economy, Third World or otherwise, the government has considerable opportunity and responsibility for involvement where conditions encourage natural monopoly (as in the utilities industries) and where public goods (such as roads and pest control) must be provided. In a developing economy, the government must place particular emphasis on creating a basic infrastructure—roads, power generation, irrigation systems. There are often good reasons why such projects, referred to as **social overhead capital,** cannot successfully be undertaken by the private sector. First, many of these projects operate with economies of scale, which means that they can be efficient only if they are very large. In that case, they may be simply too large for any private company, or even a group of such companies, to carry out.

social overhead capital *Basic infrastructure projects such as roads, power generation, and irrigation systems.*

Second, many socially useful projects cannot be undertaken by the private sector because there is no way for private agents to capture enough of the returns to make such projects profitable. For example, consider the control of malaria by draining swamps. A private firm that tried to enter the business and charge neighbouring individuals might find a reluctance to pay, the so-called free-rider problem. Why should I pay if your purchase will also protect me? Why should you pay if my purchase will also protect you?

---

[1] *It is sometimes argued that there is also a brain drain from Canada to the United States, or within regions of Canada.*

The governments of developing countries can do important and useful things to encourage development, but many of their efforts must be concentrated in areas that the private sector would never touch. If government action in these realms is not forthcoming, economic development may be curtailed by a lack of social overhead capital.

■ **Dependency Theories** In trying to understand why some countries are rich and others poor, one position, **dependency theory**, holds that the poverty of the developing countries is due to the "dependence" of the developing world on nations that are already developed. (A *dependent country* is one whose economy is dependent on the development and expansion of another country's economy.) During the colonial period, European powers dominated much of the political and economic life of what is today the developing world. By not developing basic physical infrastructure or local human capital, by draining mineral wealth from the colonies, and by playing upon ethnic differences among the inhabitants as a means of maintaining power, the colonial powers created countries that had become helpless and economically dependent by the time they achieved political independence.

Some economists contend that economic dependency is maintained today, even though colonialism is long past, through the structure of international trade relations. Developed economies provide important markets for the exports of developing countries and often are their only sources of critical inputs. Industrialized economies also influence world interest rates, capital flows, and exchange rates. Through their economic power, it is argued, industrialized nations often determine to their own advantage (and the disadvantage of others) the relative prices and conditions under which the international exchange of goods takes place.

The unequal relationship between rich and poor nations in world markets works to the detriment of the developing world. This has led many Third World leaders to call for a *new international economic order.* Such an arrangement would require agreements between developed and developing countries that would increase the gains that accrue to the developing world from international exchange. Plans for such a set of agreements have been widely discussed in the developing world. But because of divisions among the developing nations and a lack of cooperation from most developed countries there has been virtually no progress in reaching any sort of accord.

dependency theory *The theory that the poverty of the developing countries is due to the "dependence" of the developing world on countries that are already developed; it suggests that even after the end of colonialism, this dependence is maintained because developed countries are able to use their economic power to determine to their own advantage (and to the disadvantage of others) the relative prices and conditions under which the international exchange of goods takes place.*

STRATEGIES FOR ECONOMIC DEVELOPMENT

Just as no single theory appears to explain lack of economic advancement, so too is it unlikely that one development strategy will succeed in all countries. In fact, many alternative development strategies have been proposed over the past 30 or 40 years. Although these strategies have been very different, they all share the recognition that a developing economy faces certain basic trade-offs. An insufficient amount of both human and physical resources dictates that choices must be made. Some of the basic trade-offs that underlie any development strategy include those between agriculture and industry, exports and import substitution, and central planning and free markets.

■ **Agriculture or Industry?** Most Third World countries began to gain political independence just after World War II. The tradition of promoting industrialization as the solution to the problems of the developing world dates from this time. The early five-year development plans of India called for promoting manufacturing; the current government in Ethiopia (an extremely poor country) has similar intentions.

Industry has several apparent attractions over agriculture. Perhaps most important, one of the primary characteristics of more developed economies is their structural transition away from agriculture. As Table 22.3 shows, agriculture's share in GDP declines substantially as per capita incomes increase.

Many countries have pursued industry at the expense of agriculture. In many cases, however, industrialization has not brought the benefits that were expected. Experience suggests that simply trying to replicate the structure of developed economies does not in itself guarantee, or even promote, successful development.

Since the early 1970s, the agricultural sector has received considerably more attention. Agricultural strategies have had numerous benefits. Although some agricultural projects (such as the building of major dams and irrigation networks) are very capital intensive, many others (such as services to help teach better farming techniques and small-scale fertilizer programs) have low capital and import requirements. Programs like these can affect large numbers of households, and because their benefits are directed at rural areas, they are most likely to help a country's poorest families.

Experience over the last three decades suggests that some balance between these approaches leads to the best outcome—that is, it is important and effective to pay attention to both industry and agriculture. The Chinese have referred to this dual approach to development as "walking on two legs."

■ Exports or Import Substitution?

As developing countries expand their industrial activities, they must decide what type of trade strategy to pursue. The choice usually boils down to one of two major alternatives: import substitution or export promotion.

import substitution *An industrial trade strategy that favours developing local industries that can manufacture goods to replace imports.*

Import substitution is an industrial trade strategy that favours developing local industries that can manufacture goods to replace imports. For example, if fertilizer is currently imported, import substitution calls for establishment of a domestic fertilizer industry to produce replacements for fertilizer imports. This strategy gained prominence throughout South America in the 1950s. At that time, most developing countries exported agricultural and mineral products, goods that faced uncertain and often unstable international markets. Furthermore, the *terms of trade* for these nations—the ratio of export to import prices—seemed to be on a long-run decline.[2] A decline in a country's terms of trade means that its imports of manufactured goods become relatively expensive in the domestic market, while its exports—mostly primary goods such as rubber, grains, and oil—become relatively inexpensive in the world market.

Under these conditions, the call for import-substitution policies was understandable. Special government actions, including tariff and quota protection and subsidized imports of machinery, were set up to encourage new domestic industries. Multinational corporations were also invited into many countries to begin domestic operations.

Most economists believe that import-substitution strategies have failed almost everywhere they have been tried. With domestic industries sheltered from international competition by high tariffs (often as high as 200%), major economic inefficiencies were created. For example, Peru has a population of about 24 million, only

---

[2]*It now appears that the terms of trade for Third World countries as a group were not actually on a long-run decline. Of course, the prices of commodities have changed, with some doing very well and others doing quite poorly. During the 1950s, however, many policy makers believed that the purchasing power of developing-country exports was in a permanent slump.*

Table 22.3	The Share of Agriculture in Selected Developing Economies, 1995	
COUNTRY	PER CAPITA INCOME (US$)	AGRICULTURE (AS A PERCENTAGE OF GROSS DOMESTIC PRODUCT)
Uganda	$240	50
Pakistan	$460	26
China	$620	21
Colombia	$1910	14
Thailand	$2740	11
South Africa	$3160	5

Source: World Bank, *World Development Indicators, 1997*, Tables 1.1 and 4.2.

a tiny fraction of whom could ever afford to buy an automobile. Yet at one time the country had five different automobile manufacturers, each of which produced only a few thousand cars per year. Since there are substantial economies of scale in automobile production, the cost per car was much higher than it needed to be, and valuable resources that could have been devoted to higher productivity activities were squandered producing cars.

Furthermore, policies designed to promote import substitution often encouraged capital-intensive production methods, which limited the creation of jobs and hurt export activities. Obviously, a country like Peru could not export automobiles, since it could produce them only at a cost far greater than their price on the world market. Worse still, import-substitution policies encouraged the use of expensive domestic products, such as tractors and fertilizer, instead of lower-cost imports. These policies thus served to tax the very sectors that might have successfully competed in world markets. To the extent that the Peruvian sugar industry had to rely on domestically produced, high-cost fertilizer, for example, its ability to compete in international markets was reduced, because its production costs were artificially raised.

As an alternative to import substitution, some nations have pursued strategies of export promotion. **Export promotion** is simply the policy of encouraging exports. As an industrial market economy, Japan is a striking example to the developing world of the economic success that exports can provide. With an average annual per capita real GDP growth rate of roughly 6% per year since 1960, Japan's achievements are in part based on industrial production oriented toward foreign consumers.

Several countries in the developing world have attempted to emulate Japan's success. Starting around 1970, Hong Kong, Singapore, Korea, and Taiwan (sometimes called the "four little dragons" between the two big dragons, China and Japan) all began to pursue export promotion of manufactured goods. Today their growth rates have surpassed even Japan's. Other nations, including Brazil, Colombia, and Turkey, have also had some success at pursuing a more outward-looking trade policy.

■ **Central Planning or the Market?**   As part of its strategy for achieving economic development, a country must decide how its economy will be directed. Its basic choices lie between a market-oriented economic system and a centrally planned one.

In the 1950s and into the 1960s, development strategies that called for national planning commanded wide support. The rapid economic growth of the Soviet Union, a centrally planned economy, provided a historical example of the

export promotion *A trade policy designed to encourage exports.*

speed with which a less developed agrarian country could be transformed into a modern industrial power. (The often appalling costs of this strategy—namely violation of human rights and environmental damage—were less widely known.) In addition, the underdevelopment of many commodity and asset markets in the Third World led many experts to believe that market forces could not direct an economy reliably and that major government intervention was therefore necessary.

Today, planning takes many forms in the developing countries. In a few extreme cases, central planning has replaced market-based outcomes with direct, administratively determined controls over such economic variables as prices, output, and employment. In other situations, national planning amounts to little more than the formulation of general 5- or 10-year goals that serve as rough blueprints for a nation's economic future.

The economic appeal of planning lies theoretically in its ability to channel savings into productive investment and to coordinate economic activities that private actors in the economy might not otherwise undertake. The reality of central planning, however, is that it is technically difficult, highly politicized, and a nightmare to administer. Given the scarcity of human resources and the unstable political environment in many developing countries, planning itself—let alone the execution of the plan—becomes a formidable task.

The failure of many central planning efforts has brought increasing calls for less government intervention and more market orientation in developing economies. The elimination of price controls, privatization of state-run enterprises, and reductions in import restraints are examples of market-oriented reforms that are frequently recommended by such international agencies as the **International Monetary Fund,** whose primary goals are to stabilize international exchange rates and to lend money to countries that have problems financing their international transactions, and the **World Bank,** which lends money to individual countries for projects that promote economic development.

Members' contributions to both organizations are determined by the size of their economies. Only 20% of the World Bank's funding comes from contributions; the other 80% comes from retained earnings and investments in capital markets. Throughout the developing world, a recognition of the value of market forces in determining the allocation of scarce resources appears to be increasing. Nonetheless, government still has a major role to play. In the decades ahead, the governments of developing countries will need to determine those situations in which planning is superior to the market and those in which the market is superior to planning.

GROWTH VERSUS DEVELOPMENT: THE POLICY CYCLE

Until now, we have used the words "growth" and "development" as though they meant essentially the same thing. But this may not always be the case. One can easily imagine instances in which a country has achieved higher levels of income (growth) with little or no benefit accruing to most of its citizens (development). Thus, one central question in evaluating alternative strategies for achieving economic development is whether economic growth necessarily brings about economic development.

In the past, most development strategies were aimed at increasing the growth rate of income per capita. Many still are, based on the theory that benefits of economic growth will "trickle down" to all members of society. If this theory is correct, then growth should promote development.

By the early 1970s, however, the relationship between growth and development

<aside>
International Monetary Fund *An international agency whose primary goals are to stabilize international exchange rates and to lend money to countries that have problems financing their international transactions. Web address: www.imf.org*

World Bank *An international agency that lends money to individual countries for projects that promote economic development. Web address: www.worldbank.org*
</aside>

was being questioned more and more. A major study by the World Bank in 1974 concluded that

> it is now clear that more than a decade of rapid growth in underdeveloped countries has been of little or no benefit to perhaps a third of their population. . . . Paradoxically, while growth policies have succeeded beyond the expectations of the first development decade, the very idea of aggregate growth as a social objective has increasingly been called into question.

The World Bank study indicated that increases in GDP per capita did not guarantee significant improvements in such development indicators as nutrition, health, and education. Although GDP per capita did indeed rise, its benefits trickled down to only a small minority of the population. This realization prompted a call for new development strategies that would directly address the problems of poverty. Such new strategies favoured agriculture over industry, called for domestic redistribution of income and wealth (especially land), and encouraged programs to satisfy such basic needs as food and shelter.

In the late 1970s and early 1980s, the international macroeconomic crises of high oil prices, worldwide recession, and Third World debt forced attention away from programs designed to eliminate poverty directly. Then, during the 1980s and 1990s, the World Bank began demanding "structural adjustment" in the developing countries as a prerequisite for sending aid to them. **Structural adjustment** programs entail reducing the size of the public sector through privatization and/or expenditure reductions, substantially cutting budget deficits, reining in inflation, and encouraging private saving and investment with tax reforms. The hope was that saving and investment would increase enough to increase growth more than cuts in education and social overhead capital would reduce it. In any case, distributional consequences took a back seat.

Aid from the developed to the developing countries has become increasingly problematic, especially as the countries of the developed world struggle with their own economies. For example, in recent years, Canada has been reducing its level of aid to other countries. How much foreign aid does Canada provide and how is it used? For the answers to these questions, see the Global Perspective box on page 567 titled "Canadian Foreign Aid."

structural adjustment *A series of programs in developing countries designed to (1) reduce the size of their public sectors through privatization and/or expenditure reductions, (2) decrease their budget deficits, (3) control inflation, and (4) encourage private saving and investment through tax reform.*

Issues in Economic Development

Every developing country has a cultural, political, and economic history all its own and therefore confronts a unique set of problems. Still, it is possible to discuss common economic issues that each nation must face in its own particular way. These issues include rapid population growth, food shortages, agricultural output and pricing policies, and the Third World debt problem.

POPULATION GROWTH

The populations of the developing countries are estimated to be growing at a rate of about 1.7% per year. (Compare this with a population growth rate of only 0.5% per year in the industrial market economies.) If the Third World's population growth rate remains at 1.7%, it will take only 41 years for the population of the Third World to double from its 1990 level of 4.1 billion to over 8 billion by the year 2031. It will take the industrialized countries 139 years to double their populations. What is so immediately alarming about these numbers is that, given the developing countries' current economic problems, it is hard to imagine how they can possibly absorb so many more people in such a relatively short period.

Concern over world population growth is not new. The Reverend Thomas Malthus (who would one day become England's first professor of political economy) expressed his fears about the population increases he observed 200 years ago. Malthus believed that populations grow geometrically (that is, at a constant growth rate; thus the absolute size of the increase each year gets larger and larger), but that food supplies grow much more slowly because of the diminishing marginal productivity of land.[3] These two phenomena led Malthus to predict the increasing impoverishment of the world's people unless population growth could be slowed.

Malthus's fears for Europe and America proved unfounded, because he neither anticipated the technological changes that revolutionized agricultural productivity nor the eventual decrease in population growth rates in Europe and North America. But Malthus's prediction may have been right, only premature. Do the circumstances in the developing world now fit his predictions? While some contemporary observers believe that the Malthusian view is correct and that the earth's population will eventually grow to a level that the world's resources will be unable to support, others argue that technological change and demographic transitions (to slower population growth rates) will permit further increases in global welfare.

■ **The Consequences of Rapid Population Growth** Surprisingly, we know far less about the economic consequences of rapid population growth than you might expect. Conventional wisdom warns of dire economic consequences from the developing countries' "population explosion," but these predictions are difficult to substantiate with the available evidence. The rapid economic growth of North America, for example, was accompanied by relatively rapid population growth by historical standards. Nor has any slowing of population growth been necessary for the economic progress achieved by many of the newly industrialized countries. Nonetheless, population expansion in many of today's poorest nations is of a magnitude unprecedented in world history, as Figure 22.1 on page 568 clearly shows. From the year 1 A.D. until the mid-1600s, populations grew slowly, at rates of only about 0.04% per year. Since then, and especially since 1950, rates have skyrocketed. Today, populations are growing at rates of up to 4% per year in parts of the developing world.

Because growth rates like these have never occurred before the twentieth century, no one knows what impact they will have on future economic development. But a basic economic concern is that such rapid population growth may limit investment and restrain increases in labour productivity and income. Rapid population growth changes the age composition of a population, generating many dependent children relative to the number of productive working adults. Such a situation may diminish saving rates, and hence investment, as the immediate consumption needs of the young take priority over saving for the future.

Even if low saving rates are not a necessary consequence of rapid population growth, other economic problems remain. The ability to improve human capital through a broad range of programs, from infant nutrition to formal secondary education, may be severely limited if the population explosion continues. Such programs are most often the responsibility of the state, and governments that are already weak cannot be expected to improve their services under the burden of

---

[3]*The law of diminishing marginal productivity says that with a fixed amount of some resource (land), additions of more and more of a variable resource (labour) will produce smaller and smaller gains in output.*

Global Perspective

Canadian Foreign Aid

On a per capita basis, Canada is one of the more generous aid donors among the G-7 countries. However, the Scandinavian countries of Denmark, Norway, and Sweden are by far the largest per capita foreign aid donors in the world. The Netherlands also provides a high per capita level of aid. Table 1 shows that Official Development Assistance in 1993 amounted to US$83 per person in Canada, compared to US$258 per person in Denmark.

All Canadian government-provided aid is in the form of grants and contributions, and serves to fund projects from the provision of low-cost housing in Thailand to helping girls stay in school in Africa. One on-going project in particular has met with great success, and involves supplementing iodine-deficient diets among children to prevent such problems as neurological damage and dwarfism. In 1996, Canada spent $5.5 million on this program, which the United Nations Children's Emergency Fund (UNICEF) estimates helped save four million children from handicaps caused by iodine deficiencies.

Canada has an agreement with the U.N. that sets a target for Canada's foreign aid donations at

Table 1

Per Capita Provision of Foreign Aid, Selected Countries, 1993

COUNTRY	OFFICIAL DEVELOPMENT ASSISTANCE (US$)	PRIVATE VOLUNTARY AID (US$)
Denmark	258	9
Norway	234	30
Sweden	203	15
Netherlands	165	18
France*	137	3
Japan*	90	1
Germany*	86	10
Canada*	83	10
Italy*	52	1
United Kingdom*	50	8
United States*	38	10

*denotes G-7 countries.

Source: U.S. Bureau of the Census, *Statistical Abstract of the United States, 1996,* Table 1375. Military flows are excluded.

0.7% of GNP. However, reduced government spending in Canada has lowered the actual level of provision and it is estimated that Canada's aid spending will be less than half of this target before the end of the century, its lowest level (as a fraction of GNP) in over 30 years. It is unlikely that private aid in Canada or in any donor country would be able to compensate for significant reductions in

government-sponsored aid. As can be seen in Table 1, private aid is a small fraction of official assistance in virtually all donor countries.

Sources: Canadian International Development Agency (CIDA), *Meeting Basic Human Needs: A Major Contribution to Poverty Reduction (Backgrounder),* February 1997 (from CIDA's web site at www.acdi-cida.gc.ca); U.S. Bureau of the Census, *Statistical Abstract of the United States, 1996,* Table 1375.

population pressures that rapidly increase demands for all kinds of public goods and services.

For example, the population growth rate of the northwest African country of Mali is projected by the World Bank to be 3.0% from 1995 to 2010. This is one of the highest growth rates in the world, and it means that Mali's 1995 population of 10 million will grow to 15 million by 2010, a 50% increase in only 15 years. This is a daunting prospect, and it is hard to imagine how in so little time Mali will be able to provide its population with the physical and human capital needed to maintain, let alone improve, already low standards of living.

■ **Causes of Rapid Population Growth** Population growth is determined by the rela-

FIGURE 22.1

The Growth of World Population, Projected to 2020 A.D.

For thousands of years, population grew slowly. From 1 A.D. until the mid-1600s, population grew at about 0.04% per year. Since the Industrial Revolution, population growth has occurred at an unprecedented rate.

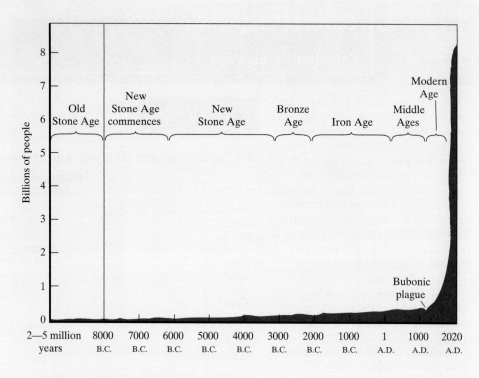

fertility rate *The birth rate. Equal to the number of births per year divided by the population multiplied by 100.*

mortality rate *The death rate. Equal to the number of deaths per year divided by the population multiplied by 100.*

natural rate of population increase *The difference between the birth rate and the death rate. It does not take migration into account.*

tionship between births and deaths—that is, between **fertility rates** and **mortality rates**. The **natural rate of population increase** is defined as the difference between the birth rate and the death rate. If the birth rate is 4%, for example, and the death rate is 3%, the population is growing at a rate of 1% per year.

Historically, low rates of population growth were maintained because of high mortality rates despite high levels of fertility. That is, families had many children, but average life expectancies were low, and many children died young. In Europe and North America, improvements in nutrition, in public health programs (especially those concerned with drinking water and sanitation services), and in medical practices have led to a drop in the mortality rate and hence to more rapid population growth. Eventually fertility rates also fell, returning population growth to a low and stable rate, as you can see in Figure 22.2a on page 569.

Public health programs and improved nutrition over the past 30 years have brought about precipitous declines in mortality rates in the developing nations also. But fertility rates have not declined as quickly, and the result has been high natural rates of population growth (Figure 22.2b). Reduced population growth depends to some extent on decreased birth rates, but attempts to lower fertility rates must take account of how different cultures feel and behave with regard to fertility.

Family planning and modern forms of birth control are important mechanisms for decreasing fertility, but by themselves such programs have had rather limited success in most countries where they have been tried. If family planning strategies are to be successful, they must make sense to the people who are supposed to benefit from them. The planners of such strategies must therefore understand why families in developing countries have so many children.

To a great extent, in developing countries people want large families because they believe they need them. Economists have attempted to understand fertility

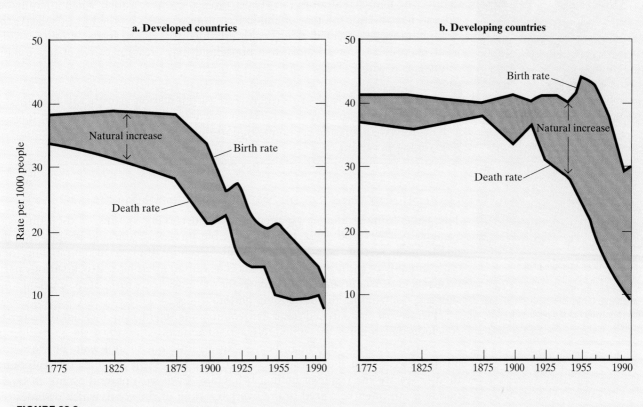

FIGURE 22.2

The Natural Rate of Population Increase, 1775–1990

patterns in the developing countries by focusing on the determinants of the demand for children. In agrarian societies, children are important sources of farm labour, and they may thus make significant contributions to household income. In societies without public old-age support programs, children may also provide a vital source of income for parents when they become too old to support themselves. With the high value of children enhanced by high rates of infant mortality, it is no wonder that families try to have many children to ensure that a sufficient number will survive into adulthood.

Cultural and religious values also affect the number of children families want to have, but the economic incentives to have large families are extremely powerful. Only when the relationship between the costs and benefits of having children changes will fertility rates decline. Expanding the opportunities for women in an economy increases the opportunity costs of child rearing (by giving women a more highly valued alternative to raising children) and often leads to lower birth rates. Government incentives for smaller families, such as subsidized education for families with fewer than three children, can have a similar effect. In general, rising incomes appear to decrease fertility rates, indicating that economic development itself reduces population growth rates.

Economic theories of population growth suggest that fertility decisions made by poor families should not be viewed as uninformed and uncontrolled. An individual family may find that having many children is a rational strategy for economic

Several African countries have come to rely on foreign support to provide food for their people. Here, members of the French Red Cross distribute grains and other foodstuffs to the people of Rwanda.

survival given the conditions in which it finds itself. This does not mean, however, that having many children is a net benefit to society as a whole. When a family decides to have a large number of children, it imposes costs on the rest of society; the children must be educated, their health provided for, and so forth. In other words, what makes sense for an individual household may create negative effects for the country as a whole. Thus:

> Any country that wants to slow its rate of population growth will probably find it necessary to have in place economic incentives for fewer children (perhaps by expanding the economic opportunities for women) as well as family planning programs.

FOOD SHORTAGES: ACTS OF NATURE OR HUMAN MISTAKES?

Television footage and newspaper photos portraying victims of the famine in Somalia in 1991 and 1992 burned indelible images of starving people into the minds of the rest of the world. This event forcefully dramatized the ongoing food crisis in many of the developing nations. The famines that have struck various parts of Africa and Asia in this century represent the most acute form of the chronic food shortage confronting the developing nations.

Pictures of the parched Somalian countryside might lead a casual observer to conclude that famines are ultimately acts of nature. After all, if the rains do not come or the locusts do, human beings can do little but sit and wait. But this simplistic view of food shortages fails to recognize the extent to which contemporary food crises are the result of human behaviour. Even such natural events as severe flooding can often be traced to the overharvesting of firewood, which denudes the landscape, increases soil erosion, and exacerbates spring floods.

Human behaviour is indeed a very strong factor in the inadequate distribution of available food to those who need it. India now grows enough grain to feed its vast population, for example, but malnutrition remains widespread because many people cannot afford to buy it. Other parts of the distribution problem involve poor storage facilities and transportation and communication barriers that prevent supplies from reaching those in need. World and domestic politics also heavily influence where, how, and whether food is available. During the Ethiopian famine in 1988, for example, the Ethiopian government blocked relief agencies from delivering food and medical supplies to an area controlled by rebels. Similar events occurred when the United Nations attempted to aid Somalia in 1992. War between the Hutu and the Tutsis in Rwanda in 1994 led to mass exodus into Zaire, loss of crops, and starvation. In the summer of 1997, an inability to resolve its political and security disputes with Japan, South Korea, and the United States slowed food aid to a starving North Korea.

While food shortages are recognized chronic problems, developing countries often pursue farm policies that actually discourage agricultural production. Agricultural production in sub-Saharan Africa today is lower than it was 20 years ago. Economists believe that misguided agricultural policies are responsible for much of this decline.

AGRICULTURAL OUTPUT AND PRICING POLICIES

Few governments in either industrialized or developing countries have permitted market forces alone to determine agricultural prices. In Canada, the United States, and much of Europe, farm subsidies often encourage production that results in food surpluses rather than shortages. Some developing countries follow similar policies, maintaining high farm prices both to increase agricultural production and to maintain farm incomes. However, many developing countries follow a different route, offering farmers low prices for their output.

To appreciate the motives behind different pricing policies, you need to understand several things about the structure of agricultural markets in many developing countries. Often the government is the primary purchaser of both basic foodstuffs and export crops. The governments of some developing countries buy farm output and sell it to urban residents at government-controlled prices. By setting the prices they pay to farmers at low levels, the government can afford to sell basic foodstuffs to urban consumers at low prices. Governments often find this an attractive course of action because the direct political influence of the relatively small urban population typically far outweighs the influence of the majority who live in the countryside. Because most city dwellers spend about half their incomes on food, low consumer prices bolster the real incomes of the urban residents and help keep them content. Urban food riots have been common in developing nations over the years, and whether a government is allowed to exist may hinge on its food-pricing strategy.

While we can easily appreciate the political motives behind food pricing, policies that set artificially low prices have significant pitfalls. Farmers react to these prices—often set so low that farmers cannot cover their production costs—by reducing the amount of output they produce. In the city, meanwhile, excess demand for food at the artificially low ceiling prices imposed by the government may promote the emergence of black markets.

Many developing economies that have followed low agricultural pricing policies have experienced exactly these results. Until recently, for example, Mexico kept corn prices low in order to hold down the price of tortillas, the staple in the diet of much of Mexico's urban population. As a result, corn production fell as farmers switched to crops whose prices the government did not control. Domestic corn shortages became widespread, and corn had to be imported to meet urban demand.

■ **Agricultural Output: The Supply Side**   About 3% of Canada's population lives on farms. Yet this small fraction of the population is able to produce enough food for Canada's own needs and have enough left over to make Canada a substantial net exporter of agricultural products. In most developing economies, a single farmer can provide barely enough food to feed his or her own family. While differences in agricultural pricing policies account for a part of this gap, other factors are also at work. Traditionally, low agricultural productivity in the developing world was blamed on the ignorance and laziness of farmers. Today's more enlightened view traces the problem to a shortage of inputs, including land, fertilizer, irrigation, machinery, new seed varieties, and agricultural extension services (which provide credit and technical advice to farmers).

Modern agricultural science has created a so-called **Green Revolution** (not to be confused with the "environmental revolution") based on new, high-yield varieties of wheat, rice, and other crops. Using new, faster growing varieties instead of the single-crop plants they have relied upon for centuries, some farmers can now grow three crops of rice a year. In Mexico, under ideal conditions, "miracle" wheat has produced over seven tonnes per hectare, compared with traditional varieties that yield less than one tonne per hectare.

If the Green Revolution suggests that science can, in principle, solve world food shortages, the often disappointing history of developing countries' experiments with scientific agriculture offers a less optimistic outlook. Economic factors have greatly limited the adoption of Green Revolution techniques in developing countries. New seeds are expensive, and their cultivation requires the presence of many

Green Revolution *The agricultural breakthroughs of modern science, such as the development of new, high-yield crop varieties.*

The Green Revolution holds promise for developing countries looking to farm their land more productively. Here, Professor Wim VanCotthem of the University of Gand in Belgium demonstrates a new technique he devised to irrigate the arid zones of West Africa.

complementary inputs, including fertilizers and irrigation. With poorly developed rural credit markets, farmers often face interest rates so high that new technologies, regardless of their promise of higher crop yields, are out of reach or ultimately unprofitable. Although the reluctance of farmers to adopt new agricultural techniques has often been blamed on superstition or lack of education, such decisions typically reflect a rational choice. Given the costs and benefits of new inputs and the inherent riskiness of any new method of cultivation, it is not surprising that it has been difficult to get farmers in the developing countries to accept the advances of the Green Revolution.

Farmers in developing countries are also constrained by the amount of land they have to work. In some countries, high population density in the rural areas requires highly labour-intensive cultivation. In other countries, poor distribution of land decreases agricultural output. Throughout Latin America, for example, it is estimated that less than 2% of all landowners control almost 75% of the land under cultivation. Improved crop yields often follow land reforms that redistribute holdings, because owner households are often more productive than tenant farmers. Land reform has had positive effects on output in countries with economic systems as diverse as those of South Korea and the People's Republic of China.

In sum:

> Although acts of nature will always threaten agricultural production, human actions, especially policies designed to support the agricultural sector, can have a major impact on reducing the food problems of the developing world.

THIRD WORLD DEBT

In the 1970s, development experts worried about many crises facing the developing world, but the debt crisis was not among them. Within a decade, this situation changed dramatically. The financial plight of countries such as Brazil, Mexico, and the Philippines had become front-page news. What alarmed those familiar with the debt situation was not only its potential impact on the developing countries, but a belief that it threatened the economic welfare of the developed countries as well.

Between 1970 and 1984, developing countries borrowed so much money from other countries, primarily the United States, that their combined debt increased by 1000%, to almost US$700 billion. As recession took hold in the economically advanced countries during the early 1980s, growth in the exports of the debtor countries slowed, and many found they could no longer pay back the money they owed. Part of the problem was that some of the borrowing had not been for sound investment with economic returns but instead had been for ill-advised megaprojects or military spending. Also, interest rates rose sharply during the early 1980s, largely due to tight monetary policy in the United States.

As the situation continued to deteriorate, many feared that debtor nations might simply repudiate their debts outright and default on their outstanding loans. When *default* (nonpayment) occurs with domestic loans, some collateral is usually available to cover all or part of the remaining debt. For loans to another country, however, such collateral is virtually impossible to secure. Given their extensive involvement with Third World borrowers, Western banks did not want to set in motion a pattern of international default. Nor did borrowers want to default. Leaders of the developing countries recognized that to default might result in the denial of access to developed-country banking facilities and to markets in the industrial countries. Such results would likely pose major obstacles to further development efforts.

Various countries rescheduled their debt as an interim solution. Under a **debt rescheduling** agreement, banks and borrowers negotiate a new schedule for the repayment of existing debt, often with some of the debt written off and with repayment periods extended. In return, borrowing countries are expected to sign an agreement with the International Monetary Fund to revamp their economic policies to provide incentives for higher export earnings and lower imports. This kind of agreement is often referred to as a **stabilization program,** and it usually requires painful austerity measures such as currency devaluations, a reduction in government expenditures, and an increase in tax revenues.

By the early 1990s, the debt crisis was not over but it had lessened somewhat, largely as a result of reduced interest rates. The international economy subsequently revived somewhat, helping some countries to increase their export earnings. Other countries have benefited from new domestic policies. Still other countries, however, continue to face debt burdens that are unmanageable in the short run. Table 22.4 presents figures for a selected group of countries in 1995.

The big news in recent years has been Mexico's monetary and debt situation. Mexico's total external debt in 1992, $113 billion, was second only to Brazil's. Following approval of the North American Free Trade Agreement (NAFTA), there was great optimism about Mexico, and massive amounts of capital flowed to Mexico to take advantage of the relatively high interest rates available on Mexican debt. As a result, Mexico's total external debt increased dramatically. Though the flow of capital pushed up the value of the peso during 1993 and early 1994, by mid-1994 investors had become nervous about the possibility of a decline in the peso's value and began to pull out of Mexico. The peso's value finally collapsed in early 1995, and the Mexican government's inability to get investors to buy Mexican bonds pushed it to the brink of defaulting on its obligations. A loan guarantee of $37 billion from the International Monetary Fund and the United States at least temporarily restored confidence and may have saved Mexico the embarrassment of a default in 1995.

debt rescheduling *An agreement between banks and borrowers through which a new schedule of repayments of the debt is negotiated; often some of the debt is written off and the repayment period is extended.*

stabilization program *An agreement between a borrower country and the International Monetary Fund in which the country agrees to revamp its economic policies to provide incentives for higher export earnings and lower imports.*

Table 22.4	Total (Public and Private) External Debt for Selected Countries, 1995 (Billions of U.S. Dollars)	
COUNTRY	**TOTAL EXTERNAL DEBT**	**TOTAL EXTERNAL DEBT AS A PERCENTAGE OF GDP**
Mexico	165.7	67.2
Brazil	159.1	22.9
Russian Federation	120.5	34.9
India	93.8	22.6
Thailand	56.8	35.3
Poland	42.3	30.5
Egypt	34.1	55.6
Peru	30.8	52.2
Sudan	17.6	244.1
Nicaragua	9.3	520.3

Source: World Bank, *World Development Indicators, 1997,* Tables 4.23 and 4.24.

One of the major economic lessons of recent years is that proper management of foreign capital in developing countries is essential. Much foreign borrowing was wasted on projects that had little chance of generating the returns necessary to pay back their initial costs. In other cases, domestic policies that used debt as a substitute for adjusting to new economic circumstances proved to be harmful in the long run. And, overall, much of the optimism about the prospects of the developing economies was inappropriate. Whatever else we may have learned from these mistakes, the debt crisis underscored the growing interdependence of all economies—rich and poor, large and small.

Summary

1. The economic problems facing the developing countries are often quite different from those confronting industrialized nations. The policy options available to governments may also differ. Nonetheless, the tools of economic analysis are as useful in understanding the economies of less developed countries as in understanding the Canadian economy.

Life in the Developing Countries: Population and Poverty

2. The central reality of life in the developing countries is poverty. Although there is considerable diversity across the developing nations, most of the people in most developing countries are extremely poor by Canadian standards.

Economic Development: Sources and Strategies

3. Almost all developing countries have a scarcity of physical capital relative to other resources, especially labour. The *vicious-circle-of-poverty hypothesis* argues that poor countries cannot escape from poverty because they cannot afford to postpone consumption (that is, to save) in order to make investments. In its crude form, the hypothesis is wrong inasmuch as some prosperous countries were at one time poorer than many developing countries are today. However, it is often difficult to mobilize savings efficiently in many developing nations.

4. Human capital—the stock of education and skills embodied in the workforce—plays a vital role in economic development.

5. Developing countries are often burdened by inadequate *social overhead capital,* ranging from poor public health and sanitation facilities to inadequate roads,

telephones, and court systems. Such social overhead capital is often expensive to provide, and many governments are simply not in a position to undertake many useful projects because they are too costly.

6. *Dependency theory* argues that the reason for the poverty of the developing countries is the relationship between the advanced industrial nations and the developing countries, a relationship designed by the former to work to their own advantage at the expense of the latter.

7. Because developed economies are characterized by a large share of output and employment in the industrial sector, many developing countries seem to believe that development and industrialization are synonymous. In many cases, developing countries have pursued industry at the expense of agriculture, with mixed results. Recent evidence suggests that some balance between industry and agriculture leads to the best outcome.

8. *Import substitution* policies, a trade strategy that favours developing local industries that can manufacture goods to replace imports, were once very common in the developing countries. In general, such policies have not succeeded as well as those promoting open, export-oriented economies.

9. The failure of many central planning efforts has brought increasing calls for less government intervention and more market orientation in developing economies.

Issues in Economic Development

10. Rapid population growth is characteristic of many developing countries. Large families can be economically rational for parents who need support in their old age, or because children offer an important source of labour. But the fact that parents find

it in their interests to have large families does not mean that having many children is a net benefit to society as whole. Rapid population growth can put a strain on already overburdened public services, such as education and health.

11. Food shortages in developing countries are not simply the result of bad weather. Public policies that depress the prices of agricultural goods, thereby lowering farmers' incentives to produce, are common throughout the developing countries, and human behaviour is very much behind the inadequate distribution of available food to those who need it. While acts of nature will always threaten agricultural production, human actions, especially policies designed to support the agricultural sector, can have a major impact on reducing the food problems of the developing world.

12. Between 1970 and 1984 the debts of the developing countries grew tenfold. As recession took hold in the advanced countries during the early 1980s, growth in the exports of the debtor countries slowed, and many found they could no longer pay back money they owed. The prospect of loan defaults by Third World nations threatened the entire international financial system and transformed the debt crisis into a global problem. While Third World debt has not been in the press as much lately, the problem is still serious in many countries.

Review Terms and Concepts

brain drain 560

capital flight 559

debt rescheduling 573

dependency theory 561

export promotion 563

fertility rate 568

Green Revolution 571

import substitution 562

International Monetary Fund 564

mortality rate 568

natural rate of population
increase 568

social overhead capital 560

stabilization program 573

structural adjustment 565

vicious-circle-of-poverty
hypothesis 558

World Bank 564

Problem Set

1. Argentina and Mexico experienced excellent growth during the early 1990s but fell on hard times in 1995. Argentina's banking system nearly collapsed, while a precipitous decline in the value of the Mexican peso was at the centre of Mexico's difficulties. Choose either Mexico or Argentina, and using an index to the popular press such as the *Canadian Index,* write a chronology of events starting in mid-1994. Using what you have learned in economics, what explanations can you offer for what happened? Were the problems that arose problems of mismanagement by governments, or were they the result of the way the markets worked (or failed to work)? What lessons have we learned?

2. The GDP of any country can be divided into two kinds of goods: capital goods and consumption goods. The proportion of national output devoted to capital goods determines, to some extent, the nation's growth rate.

   a. Explain how capital accumulation leads to economic growth.

   b. Briefly describe how a market economy determines how much investment will be undertaken each period.

   c. "Consumption versus investment is a more painful conflict to resolve for developing countries." Comment.

   d. If you were the benevolent dictator of a developing country, what plans would you implement to increase per capita GDP?

3. "The main reason developing countries are poor is that they don't have enough capital. If we give them machinery, or build factories for them, we can greatly improve their situation." Comment.

4. "Poor countries are trapped in a vicious circle of poverty. For output to grow, they must accumulate capital. To accumulate capital, they must save (consume less than they produce). But because they are poor, they have little or no extra output available for savings—it must all go to feed and clothe the present generation. Thus they are doomed to stay poor forever." Comment on each step in this argument.

5. If children are an "investment in the future," why do some developing countries offer incentives to households that limit the size of their families? Why are these incentives often ignored?

6. If you were in charge of economic policy for a developing country and wanted to promote rapid economic growth, would you choose to favour industry over agriculture? What about exports versus import substitution? In each case, briefly explain your reasoning. How do you explain the fact that many countries choose industry and a protectionist import-substitution policy?

7. "All we need to do is to promote rapid growth of per capita incomes in the developing countries and the poverty problems will take care of themselves." Comment.

8. "Famines are acts of God, resulting from bad weather or other natural disasters. There is nothing we can do about them except to send food relief after they occur." Explain why this position is inaccurate. Concentrate on agricultural pricing policies and distributional issues.

Economies in Transition and Alternative Economic Systems

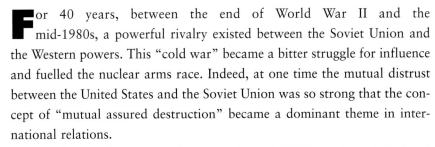

For 40 years, between the end of World War II and the mid-1980s, a powerful rivalry existed between the Soviet Union and the Western powers. This "cold war" became a bitter struggle for influence and fuelled the nuclear arms race. Indeed, at one time the mutual distrust between the United States and the Soviet Union was so strong that the concept of "mutual assured destruction" became a dominant theme in international relations.

But the world began to change in the mid-1980s as the political and economic structures of the Soviet Union and the Eastern European Communist countries started to crumble. In 1989, relatively peaceful revolutions took place in rapid succession in Poland, Hungary, and Czechoslovakia (now divided into the Czech and Slovak republics). A bloody revolution in Romania toppled Nicolae Ceauşescu, who had ruled autocratically for 24 years. The Berlin Wall, which had separated the two halves of Germany since 1961, was knocked down and the country reunited. Then, in August 1991, after a failed coup attempt by hard-line Communists, the Soviet Union itself began to come apart. By the end of 1991, the Soviet Union had dissolved into 15 independent states, the largest of which is the Russian Federation. Ten of these 15 republics formed the Commonwealth of Independent States (CIS) in December 1991. The Cold War was over.

Why do we reflect on historical political rivalries in an economics text? There are two reasons. First, the 40-year struggle between the West and the Soviet Union was fundamentally a struggle between two economic systems: market-based capitalism (the Western system) and centrally planned socialism (the Soviet system). Second, the Cold War ended so abruptly in the late 1980s because the Soviet and Eastern European economies virtually collapsed during that period. In a sense, one could say that 1991 was the year that the market triumphed.

But what now? The independent states of the former Soviet Union and the other former Communist economies of Eastern Europe are struggling to make the transition from centrally planned socialism to some form of market-based capitalism. In some countries, such as Serbia and Bosnia-Herzegovina, economic reforms have taken a back seat to bitter and violent ethnic and political rivalries that have been simmering for decades. In other countries, like Poland and Russia, the biggest issue continues to be economic transformation.

The success or failure of this transition from centrally planned socialism to market-based capitalism will determine the course of history, yet it has no historical precedent. Although many countries have made the transition from a market-based system to a centrally planned system, the opposite has never occurred. Undoubtedly, the process has been and will continue to be painful and filled with ups and downs. Between 1989 and 1992, industrial production fell more than 40% in countries like the former East Germany, Albania, Poland, and Romania. In Russia, production decreased about 30%. In all these countries, fairly prosperous people suddenly found themselves with annual real incomes closer to those of people in developing countries. For many people, the issue became survival: how to get enough food and fuel to get through the winter.

By 1995, things had turned around, and while much uncertainty and many problems remained, output was rising in much of Eastern and Central Europe. A growing sense of optimism seemed to be spreading slowly. The biggest success story was in the former East Germany, where real output in 1994 grew by over 9%, the fastest growth rate of any region of Europe. A construction boom, rapid development of infrastructure, low inflation, and rising exports all contributed to the region's success. But East Germany's situation was unique because it was absorbed by a prosperous, fully developed, and modern West Germany that made development in the East its primary goal.

The countries of Central Europe, including Hungary, Poland, the Czech Republic, Bulgaria, and Romania, also achieved basic macroeconomic stability and began to grow in 1993 and 1994. Poland enjoyed the most rapid economic growth in the group (around 4.5%). Fuelled by foreign investment, privatization, and entrepreneurship, the Polish private sector by 1992 accounted for well over one-third of the nation's total output, although many problems persist. (For more details, see the Global Perspective box titled "The Challenges to Private Enterprise in Poland.") Russia and the former countries of the Soviet Union have achieved less since reforms began. Nonetheless, conditions have improved and prospects for success are greater than they were only a few years ago. From 1990 to 1996, Russian real GDP fell continuously, with reductions ranging from 4% to 15% per year. But by 1997, the World Bank was predicting small but positive real growth.

In this chapter, we focus on the ongoing debate over economic reform. What can be done to make the transition from socialism to capitalism successful? In what sequence should changes be made? How quickly can market institutions be established? How much help from the rest of the world will be required?

To understand the transformation process, it is necessary to begin with some history. From what are these countries making a transition? Our chapter starts with a discussion of alternative economic systems, the vision of communism, and a brief description of the economic structure of the former Soviet Union. We then turn to

Global Perspective

The Challenges to Private Enterprise in Poland

Since 1991 the private sectors of most of the countries of the former Soviet Union and the formerly Communist countries of Central and Eastern Europe have expanded dramatically. Outside of the former East Germany, Poland's private sector has expanded the most, and it now accounts for well over a third of the economy's production.

This private expansion comes from four sources:

- **FIRST,** thousands of entrepreneurs have started new businesses. It is estimated that more than 2 million Polish entrepreneurs have formed businesses, and small business in Poland is growing at about 10% per year.

- **SECOND,** foreign investment is flowing into the region, although not at the pace once anticipated.

- **THIRD,** "spontaneous privatizations," initiated by managers of state-owned enterprises, have converted many firms to private ownership without a great deal of state participation. The earliest forms of spontaneous privatization in Russia took the form of managers setting up parallel private firms opposite or even inside state-owned enterprises. The new private firm would buy the product of the state-owned enterprise at a controlled price and then resell it at the market price.

- **FOURTH,** most countries have been selling off state-owned private enterprises directly or indirectly to private shareholders.

Because the process of selling off state-owned assets has been slow, much of the economic action has occurred in small entrepreneurial businesses. But as *The Wall Street Journal* has reported, 95% of the new entrepreneurial businesses in Poland are "mom and pop" proprietorships. In

95% of the new entrepreneurial businesses in Poland are small "mom and pop" proprietorships.

such businesses, the potential for generating serious job growth or raising the country's standard of living is not great. Even the 5% of larger start-ups face serious difficulties:

KRAKOW, Poland—At first, making money in capitalist Poland was easy: All you did was buy low and sell high.

Qumak International remembers those days fondly. Customers were begging the Krakow company to import computers from Singapore. Its profits were fat. Its revenues quadrupled to $8 million last year [1994] from $2 million in 1990. Its founders expected to "earn a lot of money and build a big and strong company," says Krzysztof Pyzik, its president.

They were in for a surprise. Now struggling to break even amid growing competition, Qumak has eliminated 20 of its 100 jobs. It has left the personal-computer market to focus on potentially more lucrative

business computers. And it says revenue could plunge 25% this year [1995]. . . .

Mr. Pyzik's predicament is one facing millions of East European entrepreneurs. After an initial burst of capitalist energy, they are being slowed by cash shortages, high interest rates and foreign competition. They still lack the managerial skills required to turn small trading operations into large, stable businesses that can make products, create jobs and underpin an entire economy. Often alumni of state companies, they have little experience dealing with inflation, load payments, inventories and accounts receivable.*

Sources: *Dana Milbank, "Polish entrepreneurs Revitalize Economy but Battle Huge Odds," *The Wall Street Journal*, March 31, 1995, p. 1; Olivier Jean Blanchard, Kenneth A. Froot, and Jeffrey D. Sachs (eds.), *The Transition in Eastern Europe* (Chicago: University of Chicago Press, 1994).

the current debate over the transition process, focusing on the experiences of Poland and Russia. We end the chapter by examining a different kind of economic transformation that has been ongoing for some time in China and discussing the performance of the Japanese economy since World War II.

Political Systems and Economic Systems: Socialism, Capitalism, and Communism

Every society has both a political system and an economic system. Unfortunately, the political and economic dimensions of a society are often confused.

The terms "democracy" and "dictatorship" refer to *political* systems. A *democracy* is a system of government in which ultimate power rests with the people, who make governmental decisions either directly through voting or indirectly through representatives. A *dictatorship* is a political system in which ultimate power is concentrated in either a small elite group or a single person.

Historically, two major alternative *economic* systems have existed: socialism and capitalism. A **socialist economy** is one in which most capital—factories, equipment, buildings, railroads, and so forth—is owned by the government rather than by private citizens. *Social ownership* is another term that is often used to describe this kind of system. A **capitalist economy** is one in which most capital is privately owned. Beyond these systems is a purely theoretical economic system called *communism*.

Communism is an economic system in which the people control the means of production (land and capital) directly, without the intervention of a government or state. In the world envisioned by communists, the state would wither away and society would plan the economy in much the same way that a collective would. In fact, although some countries still consider themselves communist—including China, North Korea, Cuba, and Tanzania—economic planning is done by the government in all of them. Thus:

> In terms of comparing economies today, the real distinction is between centrally planned socialism and capitalism, not between capitalism and communism.

No pure socialist economies and no pure capitalist economies exist. Even the Soviet Union, which was basically socialist, had a large private sector. Fully one-quarter of agricultural output in what was the USSR was legally produced on private plots and sold, and in a large "second economy" private citizens provided goods and services to each other, sometimes in violation of the law. Canada is what is known as a mixed capitalist economy. This means that most production occurs in the private sector but that there are a number of government enterprises in the economy as well, such as Canada Post or the Canadian Broadcasting Corporation (CBC). Public ownership is the exception in Canada and private ownership was the exception in the Soviet Union.

Whether particular kinds of political systems tend to be associated with particular kinds of economic systems is hotly debated. Canada and Japan are examples of countries with essentially capitalist economic systems and essentially democratic political institutions. China and North Korea have basically socialist economies with political power highly concentrated in a single political party. These observations do not imply that all capitalist countries have democratic political institutions, however, or that all socialist countries are subject to totalitarian party rule.

socialist economy *An economy in which most capital is owned by the government rather than by private citizens. Also called* social ownership.

capitalist economy *An economy in which most capital is privately owned.*

communism *An economic system in which the people control the means of production (capital and land) directly, without the intervention of a government or state.*

Many countries—Indonesia and Taiwan, for example–have basically capitalist economies without democratic political systems. Many other countries that are much closer to the socialist end of the economic spectrum also maintain strong democratic traditions. France and Sweden are examples of democratic countries that support certain strong socialist institutions.

Nonetheless, Austrian economist Friedrich Hayek argues that democratic freedom requires economic freedom:

> Economic reforms and government coercion are the road to serfdom. . . . Personal and economic freedoms are inseparable. Once you start down the road to government regulation and planning of the economy, the freedom to speak minds and select political leaders will be jeopardized.[1]

Some counter Hayek's argument by claiming that social reform and active government involvement in the economy are the only ways to prevent the rise of a totalitarian state. They argue that free and unregulated markets lead to inequality and the accumulation of economic power. Accumulated economic power, in turn, leads to political power that is inevitably used in the interests of the wealthy few, not in the interests of all.

CENTRAL PLANNING VERSUS THE MARKET

In addition to the degree to which capital is owned by private citizens rather than the government, economic systems also differ significantly in the extent to which economic decisions are made through central planning rather than through a market system. In some socialist economies, the allocation of resources, the mix of output, and the distribution of output are determined centrally according to a plan. The former Soviet Union, for example, generated one-year and five-year plans laying out specific production targets in virtually every sector of the economy. In market economies, decisions are made independently by buyers and sellers responding to market signals. Producers produce only what they expect to sell. Labour is attracted to and away from various occupations by wages that are determined by the forces of supply and demand.

Just as there are no pure capitalist and no pure socialist economies, there are no pure market economies and no pure planned economies. Even in the former Soviet Union markets existed and determined, to a large extent, the allocation of resources. The market supply of many commodities is regulated in Canada, primarily in the agricultural sector.

Generally, socialist economies favour central planning over market allocation, while capitalist economies rely to a much greater extent on the market. Nonetheless, some variety exists. The former Yugoslavia, for example, was a socialist country that made extensive use of the market. While ownership of capital and land rested with the government, individual firms determined their own output levels and prices and made their own investment plans. Yugoslavian firms borrowed from banks to finance investments and paid interest on their loans. This type of system, which combines government ownership with market allocation, is often referred to as a **market-socialist economy**.

market-socialist economy *An economy that combines government ownership with market allocation.*

The Economic Theories of Karl Marx

The conflict between economic systems has taken place on two levels. On the one hand, there are alternative economic *theories* that lead to dramatically different conclusions about the relative merits of market-capitalist and planned socialist

---

[1]*Friedrich Hayek,* The Road to Serfdom *(Chicago: University of Chicago Press, 1944).*

systems. On the other hand, the actual *performance* of these differently organized economies must be considered.

The events of the early 1990s in Eastern Europe provide strong evidence that central planning has come up a big loser on the basis of performance. Why, then, should we spend time studying the theoretical underpinnings of communism and socialism? There are at least three reasons. First, for over 70 years in the Soviet Union, and for over 40 years in most parts of Eastern Europe and China, socialist ideology was dominant. Until very recently, about one-third of the world's population lived in countries whose economies were based on socialist and communist philosophies. Second, even though the economies of the republics of the former Soviet Union and the economies of Eastern Europe are moving rapidly toward a market-based system, a number of other countries remain firmly committed to the ideas of centrally planned socialism. Finally, to understand the capitalist system, one must understand the criticisms that have been levelled against it.

■ **Marxian Economics: An Overview** Perhaps no single modern thinker has had a greater impact on the world in the twentieth century than Karl Marx, whose work is the basis of the communist ideology. Stated simply, Marxian economic analysis concludes that the capitalist system is morally wrong and doomed to ultimate failure.

The most common misconception about Marx's work is that it contains a blueprint for the operation of a socialist or communist economy. In fact, Marx did not write much about socialism; he wrote about capitalism. Published mostly after his death in 1883, his major work, the three-volume *Das Kapital*, is an extensive analysis of how capitalist economies function and how they are likely to develop over time. *The Communist Manifesto* (written with Friedrich Engels and published in 1848) and his other writings contain only a rough sketch of the socialist and communist societies that Marx predicted would ultimately replace capitalism.

Ironically, Marx's economics is based on the work of Adam Smith and David Ricardo, two economists who were staunch defenders of capitalism. But Marx uses the economics of Smith and Ricardo in a novel way. Instead of looking at capitalism from the perspective of human beings as consumers, Marx adopts the perspective of human beings as workers. Work, according to Marx, is the creative activity of humankind which allows human beings to reach their full potential. But under a capitalist system work becomes a means to an end: a source of profit to employers and a source of consumer goods for workers. One of Marx's main ethical objections to capitalism is that it degrades work and prevents people from realizing their full potential.

■ **Asymmetries of Power in Marx's Economic Theory** In contrast to the theory advanced in the rest of this text, Marx's theory claims that the capitalists and workers do not meet in the labour market as equals. This claim is based on two arguments. First, capitalists enjoy access to wealth through ownership of society's **means of production**, Marx's term for land and capital. But individual workers have no way to make a living except by selling their labour power. Thus workers are forced to sell their capacity to work to capitalists if they are to survive. Capitalists, on the other hand, can survive by consuming their wealth. Second, Marx argues that unemployment is endemic to capitalism. This further strengthens the hand of the capitalist since the workers' choice is not between work and leisure but between work and unemployment. Thus Marx argues that there is an asymmetry of power in the labour market which allows capitalists to keep wages lower than they otherwise would be and to impose dehumanizing working conditions.

In the theory adopted in the rest of this text, competition may result in some equalization of power in the labour market. Capitalists compete for workers who can choose to work for the capitalist who offers the best terms and conditions of employment. According to this theory, competition results in improved wages and

means of production *Marx's term for land and capital.*

working conditions. In contrast, Marx's theory suggests that the existence of unemployment allows capitalists to compete by reorganizing production processes to get the maximum work from workers at the lowest wage. Thus the very process which results in lower prices for consumers also results, according to Marx, in deteriorating working conditions and worker alienation. **Alienation** is a term used by Marx to describe a condition of workers under capitalism in which they lose a sense of meaning or purpose in life because their main life activity—work—is under the control of their employer.

■ The Nature of Profit: The Marxian View

Like the theories of his predecessors Smith and Ricardo, Marx begins his treatment of profit by focusing on the ability of capitalist society to produce a **surplus** of goods and services above and beyond what is needed to keep the labour force clothed and fed at at least a subsistence level and beyond what is needed to replace capital goods and services consumed in the production process. This surplus can provide profits for the capitalists or improve the living standards of the workers. The distribution of surplus—and thus the share of this surplus which ends up as profit—depends, in Marx's theory, on the relative strengths of workers and capitalists.

Marx argued that unemployment keeps the workers in a weak bargaining position and thus allows capitalists to claim a relatively large share of the surplus as profit. Marx admits that in periods of rapid economic growth, labour demand grows faster than labour supply, increasing the wages of workers and reducing profits. But he argues that this trend will not persist indefinitely. Captialists will respond to higher wages by replacing workers with capital and to lower profits by reducing levels of production and labour demand. Thus unemployment rises, restoring the bargaining strength of capitalists.

In summary, Marx sees profit as determined by the ability of a society to produce a surplus (which is based on the skills and knowledge of workers and the nature of the means of production with which they work) and the ability of those who own the means of production to capture part of that surplus. Unemployment keeps workers from acquiring the bargaining strength needed to capture the entire surplus. Moreover, implicit in Marx is the view that profit is unjust since profit is claimed by the capitalist based on ownership of capital goods and services and not on the basis of any real contibrution of the capitalist to the production of surplus.

■ The Nature of Profit: The Neoclassical View

The bulk of this text has presented mainstream, or neoclassical, economic theory. At this point we should reflect briefly on the nature of profit in that model, because it is so different from the Marxian notion of profit.

Neoclassical economics views both capital and labour as productive factors of production which are bought and sold in perfectly competitive markets. If you have one worker digging a hole and you want a bigger hole faster, you can accomplish your goal by hiring a second worker or by giving the first worker a better shovel. Add labour and you get more product; add capital and you also get more product. According to neoclassical theory, every factor of production in a competitive market economy ends up being paid in accordance with the market value of its product. Profit-maximizing firms hire labour and capital as long as both contribute more to the final value of a product than they cost.

In sum:

> Neoclassical theory views profit as the legitimate return to capital. Marx, however, saw profit as unjustly expropriated by nonproductive capitalists who own the means of production and thus are able to exploit labour.

alienation *A term used by Marx to describe a condition of workers under capitalism in which they lose a sense of meaning or purpose in life, because their main life activity—work—is under the control of their employer.*

surplus *In the Marxian sense, the output of goods and services in excess of what is necessary to: (1) keep the labour force clothed and fed at at least a subsistence level and (2) replace capital goods and services consumed in the production process.*

■ Marx's Predictions Marx concluded that capitalism was doomed. The essence of his argument was that the rate of profit has a natural tendency to fall over time. With the rate of profit falling, capitalists increase their exploitation of workers, pushing them deeper and deeper into misery. At the same time, the ups and downs of business cycles become more and more extreme. Ultimately, Marx believed, workers would rise up and overthrow the repressive capitalist system.

The theory that capitalism would ultimately collapse under its own weight was part of Marx's longer view of history. Capitalism had emerged naturally from a previous stage (*feudalism*) which had emerged from an even earlier stage (*ancient slavery*), and so forth. In the economic evolutionary process, Marx believed, capitalism would come to be replaced by socialism, which ultimately would be replaced by communism.

At each stage of economic evolution, Marx said, a set of rules called the *social relations of production* defines the economic system. Contradictions and conflicts inevitably arise at each stage, and these problems are ultimately resolved in the establishment of a new set of social relations. The conflicts in capitalism include alienation, increasing exploitation, misery (or, as Marx called it, "emiserization"), and deeper and deeper business cycles.

It is clear that Marx was eager for the demise of capitalism. He advocated strong and powerful labour unions for two reasons. First, unions would push wages above subsistence and transfer some surplus value back to workers. Second, unions were a way of raising the consciousness of workers about their condition. Only through class consciousness, Marx believed, would workers be empowered to throw off the shackles of capitalism.

At the heart of Marx's ideas is the argument that private ownership and profit are unfair and unethical. Even if it could be demonstrated that the incentives provided by the institution of private property result in faster economic growth or improved material living standards, one still could reject capitalism on moral grounds, on ideological grounds, or on both.

Table 23.1

Per Capita Income (Rubles)

	1861	1913
Russia	71	119
U.K.	323	580
France	150	303
Germany	175	374
U.S.	450	1033
Norway	166	659
Italy	183	261

Note: Comparable Canadian data are not available but authors' calculations based on data in Urquhart and Buckley suggest that Canadian per capita GNP was about 80% of U.S. levels in 1913.

Sources: Paul Gregory and Robert Stuart, *Soviet Economic Structure and Performance,* second edition (New York: Harper & Row, 1981), p. 20; M.C. Urquhart and K.A.H. Buckley (eds.), *Historical Statistics of Canada,* first edition (Toronto: Macmillan, 1965).

Economies in Transition: The Experiences of Russia and Eastern Europe

The Eastern European countries' transitions to market systems were in large measure the result of the economic failures of centrally planned socialism, which had ultimately failed to "deliver the goods." To understand the failure of the Eastern European socialist economies and the difficult process of transition that lies ahead for them, students of economics must be aware of these countries' economic histories. In this section, we briefly describe the Soviet system as it existed for nearly 75 years and the changes taking place today. Although the transformation process is well under way, it will be some time before the process of dismantling the old system is complete.

THE SOVIET UNION: HISTORY AND REFORM

Marx believed that socialist revolution would occur in advanced capitalist states where a repressive industrial society would push workers to unite and rise up against their industrialist masters. The Russian nation in 1913 had experienced the beginnings of modern economic growth, but it could hardly have been called an advanced capitalist system. It still lagged far behind the other industrial countries of the world, as shown in Table 23.1.

When the Bolsheviks took power after the October Revolution in 1917, they found themselves without the advanced industrial base that Marx had envisioned and with no real blueprint for running a socialist or communist state. Marx's writings provided only the broadest guidelines. Undaunted, the new government immediately abolished private land ownership and ordered that the land be distributed to those who worked on it. It also established worker control of industry and nationalized the banks. Sweeping nationalization of industry began in June 1918. Money, private trade, and wage differentials were abolished. All decisions were made centrally.

The headlong rush into uncharted waters was too much too soon, and between 1921 and 1928 Soviet leaders retreated from their initial hard line back toward a market orientation. The **New Economic Policy** of the period was characterized by decentralization. Most smaller industrial enterprises were denationalized, although the peasants remained in control of agriculture. State control of production was replaced by market links between consumers and industry and between industry and agriculture.

The relative merits and demerits of these two periods, 1917–1921 and 1921–1928, were debated at length among the Soviet leadership. Finally, in 1928, the Soviet Union settled on an economic structure that lasted into the 1980s: comprehensive central planning and collectivization of agriculture. In 1928, under the leadership of Joseph Stalin, the first of many **five-year plans** was approved. The plan emphasized rapid industrialization and the production of industrial capital; in fact, the plan called for a doubling of the fixed capital stock of the Soviet Union in five years. Consumer goods were to be produced only when all other needs of the new industrial structure had been met.

The industrialization program depended on a steady flow of food and agricultural raw materials from the countryside, and that did not come easily. As a result, Stalin relied more and more on coercion. In 1929 the land holdings of the peasants were organized into collective farms that were obligated to deliver state-ordered quotas of farm products. Repression was severe, and millions of peasants perished.[2]

No serious debate about economic matters took place in the Soviet Union until after Stalin's death in 1953. In 1965 official reforms were introduced by the government of Alexei Kosygin. More recently, Mikhail Gorbachev announced a series of reforms in 1986 and more dramatic reforms in 1987, but the structure of the economy was not changed fundamentally on either of these occasions.

In 1991, Boris Yeltsin became president of the Russian Federation and the champion of reform. Yeltsin deregulated most prices, began the privatization process, and attempted to stabilize the macroeconomy. A new "economic constitution" in the form of revised laws to establish property rights and stimulate economic activity went into effect in 1995. By early 1997, it was estimated that three-quarters of the Russian economy had been privatized and that the near hyperinflation of earlier years had come under control. But things were not going well across the board. Organized crime was becoming a huge force as privatization and desperation provided a new incentive for criminal activity. In addition, oil production continued to fall, and agricultural reform remained problematic.

■ Economic Performance The Soviet-Stalinist strategy was to achieve high rates of growth by forcing high rates of capital accumulation through the central plans. This worked for many years. While estimates of production for the former Soviet Union vary, the highest rates of growth in Soviet output were undoubtedly during the 1950s. Official Soviet statistics put the real annual growth rate during that decade at over 10%, an extraordinary rate at which real output would double

New Economic Policy *The Soviet economic policy in effect between 1921 and 1928; characterized by decentralization and a retreat to a market orientation.*

five-year plans *Plans developed in the Soviet Union that provided general guidelines and directions for the next five years.*

---

[2] *George Orwell's novel* Animal Farm *is a parable of this period in Soviet history.*

every seven years. Even the more conservative figures of the U.S. Central Intelligence Agency, shown in Table 23.2, estimate the Soviet growth rate at 5.7%, nearly 25% above the Canadian average for the decade.

In 1955, Soviet output per capita stood at just under half the level in Canada and this situation continued until approximately 1970. But while both economies grew during the 1970s and 1980s, Canadian growth rates were typically higher. Even though growth slowed in Canada in the early 1990s, real growth in Russia was sharply negative so that by 1995 the gap was very large. Russia, while having five times the population of Canada, had just more than half the total output: Russian per capita GDP that year was only about $3500 compared to Canadian per capita GDP of $26 000.

■ **Gorbachev and _Perestroika_** In March 1985, Mikhail Gorbachev became general secretary of the Soviet Communist Party and almost immediately began to press for reforms that had an enormous impact on the world. In 1990, Gorbachev won the Nobel Peace Prize for ending the Cold War and was named "Man of the Decade" by _Time_ magazine. Yet despite his enormous popularity around the world and his political successes, one prize continued to elude Gorbachev: improved economic performance in the Soviet Union.

Gorbachev's reforms fell into two broad categories: _glasnost_ ("openness") and _perestroika_ ("restructuring"). _Glasnost_ led to the almost completely open discussion of virtually every aspect of political and economic reform in the Soviet Union. It also led to a new set of political institutions, including an end to the power monopoly of the Communist Party[3] and more free elections. Glasnost was relatively easy to achieve, but the establishment of new economic structures—the key element of Gorbachev's _perestroika_—proved much more difficult.

The initial goal of _perestroika_ was to increase workers' responsibilities and discipline by attacking corruption and alcoholism. In these arenas, Gorbachev met with some success. Numerous bureau chiefs were replaced, alcoholism was reduced through strict law enforcement, absenteeism declined, and productivity increased. Then, in 1986, the focus of reform shifted to the performance of agriculture. In that year, Gorbachev announced a major restructuring of the agricultural sector that gave local farm units and the farmers significant new freedoms. Local farm units, for example, were allowed to use the market to dispose of any surplus over five-year-plan levels. Payments to state and collective farm workers were tied to productivity and profits, and local directors were given much more authority over management and investment decisions.

In June 1987, Gorbachev announced yet another series of reforms. The package included some surprising changes. First, price subsidies were to be drastically reduced or eliminated, even on such staple items as meat, bread, dairy products, and housing. Second, all limits on what workers could earn were to be removed, and salaries were to be tied directly to performance. Third, the decision-making

---

[3]_For many years, membership in and loyalty to the Communist Party were the ticket to the good life in the Soviet Union. Under the_ nomenklatura _party patronage system, Communist Party leaders received power and privilege in exchange for loyalty to the party. In addition to determining the staffing of government and industrial posts (a practice that led to a good deal of favouritism and nepotism), party members also enjoyed the right to shop at special state-run stores. These stores stocked luxury items that were not available to the general public. Travel privileges, admissions to the best colleges and universities, larger apartments, and bigger cars also went to members of the_ nomenklatura. _In 1990, the Central Committee of the Soviet Communist Party approved a proposal by President Gorbachev calling for an end to the party's constitutional guarantee of power and thus an end to the_ nomenklatura. _After the failed August 1991 coup, the Communist Party was completely dismantled._

Table 23.2	Economic Growth in the Soviet Union/Russian Federation and Canada, 1950–1995		

	ANNUAL AVERAGE RATE OF GROWTH		
	U.S.S.R. Net Material Product (U.S.S.R., Official Figures)	U.S.S.R./Russian Real GDP*	Canada Real GDP
1950–1960	10.3	5.7	4.6
1960–1970	7.1	5.1	5.2
1970–1975	5.7	3.7	5.2
1975–1980	4.3	2.7	3.9
1980–1985	—	3.2	2.9
1985–1990	—	2.1	2.9
1990–1994	—	−14.7	1.3
1995	—	−4.0	2.3

Note: *Up to 1980, figures are U.S.S.R. GNP growth rates as estimated by the U.S. Central Intelligence Agency and given in Bergson. Later figures are World Bank GDP growth rates for the area corresponding to the Russian Federation.

Sources: Abram Bergson, "Gorbachev Calls for Intensive Growth," *Challenge,* November–December 1985, pp. 11–14; The World Bank, *Trends in Developing Economies,* various years; adaptation of Statistics Canada, CANSIM Database, Series D14442.

authority of the farms and enterprises was to be greatly expanded. Central plans were to contain far less detail than in previous years. At the same time, Gorbachev called for sharp increases in small-scale family farming and for a "competitive atmosphere" among enterprises to ensure that goods were sold to consumers at the lowest possible prices that would still cover costs of production.

Perhaps the most radical of the 1987 reforms, however, was that job security, a sacred tenet of the Soviet system, would be reduced. For the first time, enterprises could actually fire workers, and unproductive enterprises could be shut down.

■ **Economic Crisis and Collapse** Although many of Gorbachev's ideas seemed promising, the situation in the Soviet Union deteriorated sharply after 1987. The attempted transition from central planning to a partly free-market system caused major problems. Growth of output slowed to a crawl in 1989 and 1990, and in 1991 the economic system collapsed. Industrial production dropped sharply, food shortages grew worse, inflation became a serious problem, and external debt increased rapidly. It proved difficult to transfer resources from the military to other uses, partly because, at least from the perspective of many Soviets, there had been no lessening of the external military threat.

Gorbachev ran out of time in August 1991 as the struggle between the hardliners and the radical reformers came to a head. The hard-liners took Gorbachev prisoner and assumed control of the government. The coup lasted only three days. People took to the streets of Moscow and resisted the tanks, the Soviet army refused to obey orders, and the hard-liners were out.

But the end was near for both Gorbachev and the Soviet Union. In December of 1991, the Soviet Union was dissolved, 10 of the former Soviet republics formed the Commonwealth of Independent States (CIS), and Boris Yeltsin became president of the Russian Federation as Gorbachev became part of history. From the beginning, Yeltsin showed himself to be a reformer committed to converting the

In Ukraine and in other transitional economies, less formal markets are one way to reduce fixed costs and avoid government regulation and taxation.

Russian economy rapidly into a market system while maintaining hard-won political freedoms for the people. His reform plan called for deregulating prices, privatizing public enterprises, and stabilizing the macroeconomy.

The Transition to a Market Economy

The reforms under way in the Russian Federation and in the other formerly Communist countries of Eastern Europe have taken shape very slowly and amid a great deal of debate about how best to proceed. It is important to remember that there is absolutely no historical precedent to provide lessons. Despite this lack of precedent, however, there is substantial agreement among economists about what needs to be done. Specifically:

> Economists generally agree on six basic requirements for a successful transition from socialism to a market-based system: (1) macroeconomic stabilization; (2) deregulation of prices and liberalization of trade; (3) privatization of state-owned enterprises and development of new private industry; (4) the establishment of market-supporting institutions, such as property and contract laws, accounting systems, and so forth; (5) a social safety net to deal with unemployment and poverty; and (6) external assistance.

We discuss each of these components in the sections that follow. While we focus on the experience of the Russian Federation, keep in mind that these principles apply to all economies in transition.

■ **Macroeconomic Stabilization**   Virtually every one of the countries in transition has had a problem with inflation, but nowhere has it been worse than in Russia.

As economic conditions worsened, the government found itself with serious budget problems. As revenue flows slowed and expenditure commitments increased, large budget deficits resulted. At the same time, each of the new republics established its own central bank. Each central bank began issuing "ruble credits" to keep important enterprises afloat and to pay the government's bills. The issuance of these credits, which were generally accepted as a means of payment throughout the country, led to a dramatic expansion of the money supply.

Almost from the beginning, the expanded money supply meant that too much money was chasing too few goods. This situation was made worse by government-controlled prices set substantially below market-clearing levels. The combination of monetary expansion and price control was deadly. Government-run shops that sold goods at controlled prices were empty. People waited in line for days and often became violent when their efforts to buy goods at low official prices were thwarted. At the same time, suppliers found that they could charge much higher prices for their products on the black market—which grew bigger by the day, further exacerbating the shortage of goods at government shops. Over time, the ruble became worth less and less as black market prices continued to rise ever more rapidly. As a result, Russia found itself with consumer price inflation of over 1300% in 1992.

To achieve a properly functioning market system, prices must be stabilized. To do so, the government must find a way to move toward a balanced budget and to bring the supply of money under control. Russian inflation had fallen to around 15% by mid 1997. Nonetheless the cumulative effect of recent inflations led to the announcement in the summer of 1997 of a conversion program under which 1000 old rubles would equal one new ruble.

■ **Deregulation of Prices and Liberalization of Trade** To move successfully from central planning to a market system, individual prices must be deregulated. A system of freely moving prices forms the backbone of a market system. When people want more of a good than is currently being produced, its price will rise. This higher price increases producers' profits and provides an incentive for existing firms to expand production and for new firms to enter the industry. Conversely, if an industry is producing a good for which there is no market or a good that people no longer want in the same quantity, the result will be excess supply and the price of that good will fall. This reduces profits or creates losses, providing an incentive for some existing firms to cut back on production and for others to go out of business. In short, an unregulated price mechanism ensures an efficient allocation of resources across industries provided markets are competitive. Until prices are deregulated, this mechanism cannot function.

Trade barriers must also be removed. To achieve a successful transition, reform-minded countries must be able to import capital, technology, and ideas from abroad. In addition, it makes no sense to continue to subsidize industries that cannot be competitive on world markets. If it is cheaper to buy steel from an efficient Canadian steel mill than to produce it in a subsidized antiquated Russian mill, the Russian mill should be modernized or shut down. Ultimately, as the theory of comparative advantage suggests, liberalized trade will push each country to produce those products that it produces best.

Deregulating prices and eliminating subsidies can bring serious political problems. Many products in Russia and the rest of the socialist world were priced below market-clearing levels for equity reasons. Housing, food, and clothing were considered by many to be entitlements. Making them more expensive, at least relative to their prices in previous times, is not likely to be popular. In addition, forcing inefficient firms to operate without subsidies will lead many to go out of business, and jobs will be lost. So while price deregulation and trade liberalization are necessary, they are very difficult politically.

tragedy of the commons *The idea that collective ownership may not provide the proper private incentives for efficiency because individuals do not bear the full costs of their own decisions but do enjoy the full benefits.*

■ **Privatization** One problem with a system of central ownership is a lack of accountability. Under a system of private ownership, owners reap the rewards of their successes and suffer the consequences of their failures. Private ownership provides a strong incentive for efficient operation, innovation, and hard work that is lacking when ownership is centralized and profits are distributed to the people.

The classic story used to illustrate this point is called the **tragedy of the commons.** Suppose that an agricultural community has 4000 hectares of grazing land. If the land were held in common so that all farmers had unlimited rights to graze their animals, each farmer would have an incentive to overgraze. He or she would reap the full benefits from grazing additional calves while the costs of grazing the calves would be borne collectively. The system provides no incentive to manage the land efficiently. Similarly, if the efficiency and benefits of my hard work and managerial skills accrue to others or to the state, what incentive do I have to work hard or to be efficient?

One solution to the tragedy of the commons attempted in eighteenth-century Britain was to divide up the land into private holdings. Today, many economists argue, the solution to the incentive problem encountered in state-owned enterprises is to privatize them and let the owners compete.

In addition to increasing accountability, privatization means creating a climate in which new enterprises can flourish. If there is market demand for a product not currently being produced, individual entrepreneurs should be free to set up a business and make a profit. During the last months of the Soviet Union's existence, private enterprises such as taxi services, car repair services, restaurants, and even hotels began to spring up all over the country.

Like deregulation of prices, privatization is difficult politically. Privatization means that many protected enterprises will go out of business because they cannot compete at world prices. Going out of business means a loss of jobs, at least temporarily. Germany's form of privatization in the former East Germany often included payments to the new owners of the enterprises in return for job guarantees, but the total cost was $250 billion, a level of resources few other countries have.

■ **Market-Supporting Institutions** In the early 1990s firms from the West raced to Eastern Europe in search of markets and investment opportunities and immediately became aware of a major obstacle. The institutions that make the market function relatively smoothly in Western economies did not exist in Eastern Europe.

For example, the capital market, which most economists argue channels private saving into mostly productive capital investment in developed capitalist economies, is made up of hundreds of different institutions. The banking system, venture capital funds, the stock market, the bond market, the commodity exchanges, brokerage houses, investment banks, and the like have all developed over a period of hundreds of years, and they will not simply be replicated overnight in the formerly Communist world.

Many market-supporting institutions are so basic that Canadians take them for granted. The institution of private property, for example, is a set of rights that must be protected by laws that the government must be willing to enforce. Suppose that the French hotel chain Novotel decides to build a new hotel in Moscow. Novotel must first acquire land. Then it will construct a building based on the expectation of renting rooms to customers. These investments are made with the expectation that the owner has a right to use them and a right to the profits that they produce. For such investments to be undertaken, these rights must be guaranteed by a set of property laws. This is equally true for large business firms and for Russian entrepreneurs who want to start their own enterprises.

Similarly, the law must provide for the enforcement of contracts. In Canada, a huge body of law determines what happens to you if you break a formal promise made in good faith. Businesses exist on promises to produce and promises to pay. Without recourse to the law when a contract is breached, contracts will not be entered into, goods will not be manufactured, and services will not be provided.

Another seemingly simple matter that turns out to be quite complex is the establishment of a set of accounting principles. In Canada, the rules of the accounting game are embodied in a set of Generally Accepted Accounting Principles (GAAP) that carry the force of law. Companies are required to keep track of their receipts, expenditures, and liabilities so that their performance can be observed and evaluated by shareholders, taxing authorities, and others who have an interest in the company. If you have ever taken a course in accounting, you know how detailed these rules have become. Imagine trying to do business in a country operating under hundreds of different sets of rules and you can imagine what has been happening in Russia.

Another institution worthy of mention is insurance. Whenever a venture undertakes a high-risk activity, it buys insurance to protect itself. Several years ago, Amnesty International (a nonprofit organization that works to protect civil liberties around the world) sponsored a worldwide concert tour with a number of well-known rock bands and performers. The most difficult part of organizing the tour was obtaining insurance for the artists and their equipment when they played in the then-Communist countries of Eastern Europe.

■ **Social Safety Net** In a centrally planned socialist economy, the labour market does not function freely. Everyone who wants a job is guaranteed one somewhere. The number of jobs is determined by a central plan to match the number of workers. Thus, in centrally planned economies, there is essentially no such thing as unemployment. This, it has been argued, is one of the great advantages of a planned system. In addition, a central planning system provides basic housing, food, and clothing at very affordable levels for all. With no unemployment and necessities available at very low prices, there is no need for unemployment insurance, welfare, or other social programs.

Transition to a free labour market and liberalization of prices means that some workers will end up unemployed and everyone will pay higher prices for necessities. Indeed, during the early phases of the transition process, unemployment will be high. Inefficient state-owned enterprises will go out of business; some sectors will contract while others expand. As more and more people experience unemployment, popular support for reform is likely to drop unless some sort of social safety net is erected to ease the transition. This social safety net might include unemployment insurance, aid for the poor, and food and housing assistance. The experiences of the developed world have shown that such programs are expensive.

■ **External Assistance** Very few believe that the transition to a market system can be achieved without outside support and some outside financing. Knowledge of and experience with capitalist institutions that exist in Canada, the United States, Western Europe, and Japan are of vital interest to the Eastern European nations. The basic skills of accounting, management, and enterprise development can be taught to those in Eastern Europe, and many argue that it is in everyone's best interest to do so.

There is little agreement about the extent of *financial* support that should be given, however. Financial aid, many argue, will help Russia stabilize its macroeconomy and buy desperately needed goods from abroad. However, critics argue that pouring money into Russia now is like pouring it into a black hole. No matter how much money we donate, they say, it will have little impact on the ultimate success or failure of the reforms.

Although economists generally agree on what the former socialist economies need to do, much debate exists about the sequence and timing of specific reforms.

The popular press describes the debate as one between those who believe in "shock therapy" (sometimes called the "Big Bang" approach) and those who prefer a more gradual approach. Advocates of **shock therapy** believe that the economies in transition should proceed immediately on all fronts. That is, they should stop printing money, deregulate prices and liberalize trade, privatize, develop market institutions, build a social safety net, and acquire external aid—all as quickly as possible. The pain will be severe, the argument goes, but in the end it will be forgotten as the transition raises living standards. Advocates of a *gradualist* approach believe the best course of action is to build up market institutions first, gradually decontrol prices, and privatize only the most efficient government enterprises first.

Those who favour moving quickly point to the apparent success of Poland, which moved quite rapidly through the first phases of reform. Russia's experience during the first years of its transition have demonstrated that, at least in that country, change must be to some extent gradual. In theory, stabilization and price liberalization can be achieved instantaneously. But to enjoy the benefits of liberalization, a good deal of privatization must have taken place—and that will take more time. As one analyst has said, privatization means "selling assets with no value to people with no money." Some estimates suggest that as many as half of Russian state-owned enterprises are incapable of making a profit at world prices. Simply cutting them loose would create chaos. In a sense, Russia has no choice but to move slowly.

shock therapy *The approach to transition from socialism to market capitalism that advocates rapid deregulation of prices, liberalization of trade, and privatization.*

Alternative Economic Systems

We now turn to a discussion of two alternative economic systems: that of China and that of Japan.

THE PEOPLE'S REPUBLIC OF CHINA

Continuing around the globe eastward from the Russian Federation lies China, the world's most populous country. With 1.2 billion people, mainland China accounts for one out of every five people in the world.

China remains a country in which political dissent is not tolerated and the economic system remains communist but in which private enterprise is permitted and even encouraged. This seemingly incongruous system is performing, at least for now, as well as any economy in the world. China, like Russia, is an enormously important power in the world, and understanding its history and the nature of its economic institutions is an essential part of understanding economics.

Compared to Canada, the People's Republic of China is very populous and very poor. Per capita income in China is about 3% of per capita income in Canada. The history of the People's Republic, established after the Communist victory in the revolution of 1949, has been marked by wild gyrations of policy and some extraordinary economic experiments.

■ **Socialization under Mao Zedong** Soon after gaining power, the Chinese Communists, under the leadership of Chairman Mao Zedong, became involved in the Korean War and found themselves heavily dependent on the Soviet Union. Not surprisingly, then, the early structure of the Chinese economic system was built on the Soviet-Stalinist model. China's first five-year plan, from 1953 to 1957, focused on developing capital-intensive heavy industries. Agriculture was collectivized, household farming was eliminated, and compulsory output quotas were put in place.

In 1958 China departed sharply from the Soviet model and launched a new economic strategy called the **Great Leap Forward**. The focus of production shifted from large-scale, capital-intensive industry to small-scale, labour-intensive industry scattered across the countryside. In addition, material incentives were reduced and replaced by the motivating power of revolutionary ideology and inspiration. Although initially successful, the strategy ultimately failed. In the early 1960s, output fell below 1958 levels. Between 1961 and 1965, material incentives were restored and a period of relative calm followed.

During the late 1960s and 1970s, economic development in China suffered a heavy blow from the **Great Proletarian Cultural Revolution** that began in 1966. For almost a decade, the rule was ideological purity. The faithful—which included almost everyone—denounced those who favoured material incentives and reform, and scientists, engineers, managers, and scholars whose views were out of favour were sent to the countryside to work in the fields. The universities were essentially closed down. Untrained revolutionary *cadres* (small groups of leaders) replaced trained specialists in almost all jobs, and the economy suffered terribly. Most estimates place per capita income and consumption in the late 1970s at levels only slightly above the levels of 1956–1957.[4]

■ The Reforms of Deng Xiaoping

When Chairman Mao died in September 1976, the Cultural Revolution formally ended. In the meantime, China watched as its once poor neighbours—Japan, South Korea, Taiwan, and Singapore—enjoyed extraordinary growth and prosperity.

In December 1978, the Chinese Central Committee, under the leadership of Deng Xiaoping, announced sweeping reforms. These early reforms focused on agriculture, and they signalled the beginning of profound changes in the Chinese economy that would continue over the next 10 years.

Prior to 1978, each agricultural commune had distributed the harvest equally among its members. Incentives were purely collective, with everything done for the glory of the revolution. Because the cadres often overstated harvests, the state raised local delivery quotas, leaving the farmers with barely enough to go around. The new system begun under Deng Xiaoping gave individual families, through a 15-year family contract, formal rights to the land that they worked. Families were also given the rights to dispose of any surpluses and to hire out part of the family labour force to enterprises outside the family plot. Deng gave the Chinese farmers permission to enrich themselves, and they did.

The results were extraordinary. Output of grain and other basic necessities, such as cotton, increased substantially. More importantly, rural industry grew dramatically, employing over 20% of the rural labour force by 1985. From 1978 through 1983, wheat production increased at an annual rate of 8.6%, rice at 4.3%, and cotton at 16.4%. From 1981 to 1984, the growth rate of all agricultural output reached 11.0% annually. In 1984 China actually became an exporter of food, despite a population of over one billion. Farmers' income more than doubled in less than a decade, and private consumption and housing construction increased sharply.[5]

Similar reforms were implemented in Chinese industry on an experimental basis. Initially, enterprises were able to retain 15% to 25% of any profits over and above those specified by the plan. By 1984, Chinese enterprises across the country were retaining over 85% of increased profits. As with agricultural reform, the goals of industrial reform were to increase the role of the producing

Great Leap Forward *The economic strategy in the People's Republic of China that began in 1958 when it departed from the Soviet model and shifted from large-scale, capital-intensive industry to small-scale, labour-intensive industry scattered across the countryside. Material incentives were reduced and replaced by the motivating power of revolutionary ideology and inspiration.*

Great Proletarian Cultural Revolution *(1966–1976) A period of ideological purity in the People's Republic of China. Material incentives and reforms were denounced and highly trained specialists were sent to work in the fields. The effect of the Cultural Revolution on the Chinese economy was catastrophic.*

---

[4]See Nicholas Lardy, "Agricultural Reform," *Journal of International Affairs*, *Winter 1986.*
[5]"*China: Economic Performance in 1985, A Report to the Subcommittee on Economic Resources, Competitiveness and Security of the Joint Economic Committee,*" The Central Intelligence Agency, Washington, D.C.: March 17, 1986 (mimeo), p. 2.

unit, to increase individual incentives, and to reduce the role of the state and the central planners.

The most significant element of all these reforms, however, was the movement by the Chinese government to support the expansion of enterprise rights. In the spirit of the Soviet New Economic Policy of the 1920s, the Chinese are actively encouraging small private trade and manufacturing. Today there is an increasingly important Chinese private sector competing with state stores in style, service, quality, and even price. By 1986, 480 000 "new economic associations" were employing 4.2 million people.[6] China is also now encouraging foreign investment. Initially only joint ventures with the government were permitted, but now foreigners retain 100% ownership in several projects.

■ **China after Tiananmen Square** Despite the economic advances that China has made in the last decades, there is a great deal of political unrest in the country. In May 1989, thousands of university students openly challenged the authority of the government by occupying Tiananmen Square in Beijing. Many went on hunger strikes to protest China's lack of democracy. The "democracy movement" was crushed on June 3, 1989, when the government cleared the square with troops and tanks as the world watched in horror.

The events of 1989 turned the tide of world opinion against the Chinese and at least temporarily slowed the movement toward economic reform. A number of joint ventures were cancelled, and the amount of direct aid flowing into China was reduced. But even before Tiananmen Square, Chinese economic reforms were beginning to encounter difficulty.

In 1988, China experienced serious inflation for the first time. By late 1988, prices were rising in historically unprecedented amounts, nearly 30% per year. In September, the government began implementing an austerity program that included strict price controls, reduced state investment, and reduced imports. The rate of inflation had dropped by 1989, but output of goods and services in China fell in 1989 and grew only slightly in 1990.

The years 1991–1995 saw a dramatic turnaround for China. While the current Communist government has retained power and maintained a hard line on the political front, economic freedoms have been extended into every sphere. Private enterprise continues to be encouraged (see the Global Perspective box on page 595). A stock market was established and stock prices have boomed dramatically. Hundreds of billions of dollars in foreign investment are now flowing into China from Western as well as Asian countries. In 1997, Britain returned Hong Kong to China with Hong Kong retaining its capitalist system. That same year Deng died and was succeeded by Jiang Zemin, with little change in overall policy.

Recent estimates put China's growth rate at about 10% per year. There has been a real estate boom in Shanghai, where a middle-class home is now more expensive than a comparable house in Canada. Problems and challenges remain. First, many fear that food shortages are imminent. While the Chinese population has continued to grow, the country's expanding industrial and housing sectors have led to a declining amount of land under cultivation. (In fact, China contains 20% of the world's population but only 7% of the world's arable land.) Second, over 50 000 state-owned enterprises continue to operate, although the process of selling these enterprises to foreign investors and allowing them to go into a form of bankruptcy continues. However, the recurrence of inflation in the mid 1990s has since come under control. In early 1995, inflation was running at 22% annually, but by mid 1997 it was less than 3%.

---

[6]Beijing Review, no. 25 (June 23, 1986).

Global Perspective

China: Free Enterprise in a Communist Country

The following excerpt from a *New York Times* article summarizes one aspect of a rapidly changing China:

QIAOTOU, China—For a glimpse into China's economic revolution, it is useful to stroll down the main street of this humble little town. . . [which] has propelled itself over the last dozen years into the button capital of the world.

Each year, the privately run factories of Qiaotou produce about 12 billion buttons. . . . This button boom, amounting to two buttons annually per inhabitant on earth, has transformed rice paddies into factory districts, and peasants into tycoons.

One of them is Zhan Yusheng, a 27-year-old who began making buttons in his home 10 years ago. Today he owns a button factory with 100 employees, and last year he had sales of nearly $200,000.

"Now we need to upgrade our quality and produce more high-quality buttons," said Chen Jianlin, Qiaotou's Communist Party secretary. "Then we can expand on the international market.". . . Mr. Chen sees his mission primarily as promoting private enterprise.

"My most important job is building up the economy," Mr. Chen said as he sipped tea at the conference table in his office. "People here say: 'If you push the economy along, you're

Each year, the privately run factories of Qiaotou, China, produce about 12 billion buttons, primarily of the inexpensive kind found on discount-priced clothing.

a good leader. Otherwise, you're not.'"

While his salary is only $20 a month, about a third as much as the 20,000 migrant workers employed in Qiaotou's factories, . . . the party covers most of his expenses, supplies him with a house, a chauffered Audi, a phone with international direct dialing, a beeper, and a Mastercard.

"A lot of people here now carry credit cards when they travel," Mr. Chen said, beaming as he passed around his Mastercard for inspection. "Credit cards are very convenient and you don't have to carry so much cash."

Source: Nicholas D. Kristof, "Free Enterprise Encouraged," *The New York Times*, January 18, 1993.

JAPAN

No discussion of alternative economic systems would be complete without a few words on Japan. No country in history has accomplished what the Japanese economy has during the post–World War II period. Japan's economic progress over the last several decades is, with good reason, called the "Japanese economic miracle."

In the early 1950s, per capita GDP in Japan was about 20% of Canadian per capita GDP; by 1970, this figure stood at around 60%. Between 1951 and 1973, real output in Japan grew at an average annual rate of over 10%—in just over two decades, a seven-and-a-half-fold increase. Since the mid 1970s, economic growth in Japan has slowed from the dramatic pace of previous years, but it remained strong until 1992. Japan's level of GDP per capita is now greater than Canada's (although bear in mind that GDP by itself is not a measure of economic welfare).

What led to the Japanese "miracle"? Was it simply a matter of culture? Japan is a very disciplined society with a strong work ethic and a long tradition of co-operation. But although cultural differences may be part of the story, there is far more to it than that.

In some ways, Japan's is essentially a free market capitalist economy. No industrialized country in the world has a smaller public sector, and none has a more "pro-business" government. But Japan's government nonetheless intervenes substantially to promote growth, and much of the economy is controlled by a relatively small number of firms whose behaviour is far from competitive.

To explain Japan's success more specifically, analysts point to four major factors[7]: (1) very high rates of saving and investment, (2) a highly trained labour force, (3) rapid absorption and effective utilization of technology, much of it imported, and (4) a pro-growth government policy. Of these, perhaps the single most important cause of Japan's growth has been its incredible rate of investment. Between 1951 and 1973, the capital stock of Japan grew by more than 9% per year, and for a substantial period of time investment approached 40% of output. Virtually all of Japan's investment was financed with domestic saving. As shown in Table 23.3, Japan's rate of saving by households has been among the highest in the world.

Until recent years, rates of return on new investment in Japan were high. But today Japan faces a new problem. As the interest rate figures in Table 23.3 indicate, Japan's high rates of investment have virtually exhausted the investment opportunities in the country and pushed rates of return on saving to very low levels. The saving rate has remained high, however, and this has led many Japanese citizens to look abroad for a place to put their savings as real returns are much higher in other countries than in Japan.

The second factor contributing to Japan's economic success is the quality of the Japanese labour force. As early as 1950, Japan had an education level comparable to that of many Western countries, despite a much lower level of economic development. Most Japanese workers were employed in jobs that demanded extremely low productivity relative to the education and training of those holding them. As the country's capital stock grew, workers moved easily into higher productivity jobs.

Japan also consciously adopted the most advanced industrial technologies in the world. Much of the knowledge necessary to do this was available in technical journals or obtainable in the educational institutions of other countries, and some came embodied in machinery and equipment imported into Japan. The Japanese were extremely effective at improving upon and commercializing what they imported. By importing technology, Japan did not have to develop it on its own; and, until recently, Japan devoted a smaller portion of its output to research and development than did other industrialized countries such as Canada and the United States.

There is disagreement among economists about the importance of government as an instrument of growth in the economy of Japan. It is clear that the

---

[7]See Hugh Patrick and Henry Rosovsky, "Japan's Economic Performance: An Overview," in Asia's New Giant, Hugh Patrick and Henry Rosovsky (eds.), The Brookings Institution, 1976.

main source of growth has been the private sector but that the government has played a supportive role. For example, after World War II, the Japanese government, through the **Ministry of Trade and Industry (MITI),** used tariffs and quotas to protect and subsidize a number of key industries, including coal, steel, electric power, and shipbuilding. During the 1960s, chemicals and machinery were added to the list. In the mid 1980s, the government and the private sector launched a partnership designed to develop and market the next generation of computers. MITI also helps some sectors of the economy plan orderly reductions in capacity. In short, the Japanese government is actively involved in the allocation process and has much to say about which industries will grow and which will not.

Ministry of Trade and Industry (MITI) *The agency of the Japanese government responsible for industrial policy. It uses tariffs and subsidies to protect and support key industries and helps some sectors plan orderly reductions in capacity.*

■ **Japan in the 1990s** The enormous success of the Japanese economy led to seemingly unbounded optimism at the end of the 1980s. Spurred by the profitability of Japanese firms, the market prices of Japanese stocks raced to unprecedented levels. At the same time, Japanese land values boomed. At one point, land in Tokyo was trading for as much as $50 000 per square metre. At that price, a modest 10 metre by 30 metre plot of land, on which you could build an average-sized house in Canada, was worth $15 million!

Then, in 1992, the Japanese stock market experienced major losses and land prices began to fall. During 1992 and 1993, Japan slipped into a recession, which continued into 1994, and real GDP fell (and unemployment went up to a level of about 3%). People in Japan began referring to the 1980s as the period of the "bubble economy." Late 1994 saw a return to growth, but 1995 brought new economic challenges, including a devastating earthquake in the city of Kobe as well as a tremendous increase in the value of the yen. Real GDP growth was expected to be about 2% for 1997, with unemployment remaining at over 3%.

Despite these setbacks, Japan remains an enormous economic power and a vital Canadian trading partner. As the economy becomes even more globalized in the coming years, it will be essential to understand more fully the successes and failures of Japanese industrial policy.

Table 23.3	Household Saving and Real Interest Rates, Selected Countries, 1985–1995		
	1985	**1990**	**1995**
Household saving*			
Japan	15.6	12.1	13.0
Canada	13.3	9.7	7.0
United Kingdom	10.7	8.1	11.0
United States	7.1	5.2	4.9
Real interest rates**			
Japan	4.6	4.6	1.3
Canada	5.6	8.2	4.8
United Kingdom	6.1	5.3	3.3
United States	4.0	2.1	2.7

Notes: *Expressed as a percentage of nominal household disposable income.
    **Short-term interest rate less percentage increase in consumer prices.

Source: OECD, *Economic Outlook,* December 1996, Annex tables 16, 36, and 58.
    ©(1996) (Economic Outlook). Reproduced by permission of the OECD.

Conclusion

This chapter has introduced very briefly the structure, history, and performance of several different economic systems. It has also discussed the enormous problems of transforming a socialist economy into a market-based economy. So brief a description and analysis, we acknowledge, must be somewhat frustrating. After all, many volumes have been written on these topics. But a study of basic economics without such a "tour," however hasty, would be incomplete.

Studying alternative economic systems is a fitting way to conclude an introduction to economics. One of the themes running through this book has been the role of government in a market economy. We have tried to present a balanced description of how economies function, both in theory and in the real world. Throughout, we have focused on the potential benefits and problems associated with public sector involvement. Eastern Europe, Russia, China, and Japan present very different perspectives on the interaction between the private and public sectors.

Concluding with this chapter is also, we hope, an enticement to further study. This is an exciting time in the world's economic history. Never before have systems changed so dramatically in such a short time. Many believe that the reforms in China, Eastern Europe, and Russia have brought the world much closer together and that the time is ripe for a significant reduction in world political tensions. Others believe that the problems of transition are so difficult that the whole process will disintegrate into chaos. Only time will tell.

Summary

Political Systems and Economic Systems: Socialism, Capitalism, and Communism

1. A *socialist economy* is one in which most capital is owned by the government rather than by private citizens. A *capitalist economy* is one in which most capital is privately owned. *Communism* is a theoretical economic system in which the people directly control the means of production (capital and land) without the intervention of a government or state.

2. Economies differ in the extent to which decisions are made through central planning rather than through a market system. Generally, socialist economies favour central planning over market allocation, and capitalist economies rely to a much greater extent on the market. Nonetheless, there are markets in all societies, and planning takes place in all economies.

The Economic Theories of Karl Marx

3. According to Marxian thought, private ownership and profit are both unfair and unethical. Profits accrue to nonproductive capitalists, who are able to exploit labour by virtue of their ownership of the means of production (land and capital). Unemployment also strengthens the bargaining position of capitalists.

4. Marx predicted that falling rates of profit, increasing exploitation, and deeper business cycles would eventually cause capitalism to collapse.

5. Neoclassical economics sees profit as a return to a productive factor (capital) just as wages are the return to another productive factor (labour).

Economies in Transition: The Experiences of Russia and Eastern Europe

6. When the Bolsheviks took power in Russia after the October Revolution in 1917, they found themselves without the advanced industrial base that Marx had envisioned and with no real blueprint for running a socialist or communist state. Marx had written mainly about capitalism, not socialism.

7. In 1928, the Soviet Union settled into comprehensive central planning and collectivization of agriculture, an economic structure that lasted into the 1980s. Virtually all productive assets, including most land and capital, were publicly owned. There was no formal private business sector, no market for capital goods, and no income from property.

8. The Soviet Union grew rapidly through the mid 1970s. During the 1950s, the Soviet Union's economy was growing faster than that of Canada, although Soviet GNP per capita was about half of

Canada's. The late 1970s saw things begin to deteriorate. Dramatic reforms were finally introduced by Mikhail Gorbachev after his rise to power in 1985. Nonetheless, the Soviet economy collapsed in 1991. The Soviet Union was dissolved, and the new president of the Russian Federation, Boris Yeltsin, was left to start the difficult task of transition to a market system.

9. Economists generally agree on six requirements for a successful transition from socialism to a market-based system: (1) macroeconomic stabilization, (2) deregulation of prices and liberalization of trade, (3) privatization, (4) the establishment of market-supporting institutions, (5) a social safety net, and (6) external assistance.

10. Much debate exists about the sequence and timing of specific reforms. The idea of *shock therapy* is to proceed immediately on all six fronts, including rapid deregulation of prices and privatization. The gradualist approach is to build up market institutions first, gradually decontrol prices, and privatize only the most efficient government enterprises first.

Alternative Economic Systems

11. China, the most populous country in the world, became communist following the revolution of 1949. In its early years under Chairman Mao Zedong, China organized under the Soviet model of central planning and rapid capital accumulation in heavy industry. In 1958, China departed sharply from the Soviet model, shifting instead to emphasis on small-scale, labour-intensive industry scattered around the countryside.

12. In 1978, Deng Xiaoping instituted sweeping reforms in the organization of the Chinese economy, particularly in agriculture. These reforms moved China away from central planning toward a system driven by market incentives.

13. China remains a country in which political dissent is not tolerated and the economic system remains communist, but one in which private enterprise is permitted and even encouraged. In the last several years the country has enjoyed rapid growth and substantial outside investment. However, a fear of food shortages remains and more than 50 000 state-owned enterprises continue to operate.

14. No country in history has accomplished what the Japanese economy has during the postwar period. Analysts point to four major factors to explain Japan's success: (1) a very high rate of saving and investment, (2) a highly trained labour force, (3) rapid absorption and effective utilization of technology, much of it imported, and (4) a pro-growth government policy. Despite some setbacks in the 1990s, Japan remains an important economic power.

Review Terms and Concepts

alienation 583

capitalist economy 580

communism 580

five-year plans 585

Great Leap Forward 593

Great Proletarian Cultural Revolution 593

market-socialist economy 581

means of production 582

Ministry of Trade and Industry (MITI) 597

New Economic Policy 585

shock therapy 592

socialist economy 580

surplus 583

tragedy of the commons 590

Problem Set

1. Choose one of the transitional economies of Central Europe (Poland, Hungary, Bulgaria, the Czech and Slovak republics, or Romania) or one of the 10 countries of the Commonwealth of Independent States (Armenia, Azerbaijan, Ukraine, Uzbekistan, Russia, etc.). Write a brief paper on how the transition to a market economy has proceeded. Has the economy (prices, employment, etc.) stabilized? Has there been economic growth? How far has privatization progressed? What problems have been encountered? (A good source of information would be a chronological index such as the *Canadian Index*.)

2. "The difference between Canada and the Soviet Union is that Canada has a capitalist economic system and the Soviet Union had a totalitarian government." Explain how this comparison confuses the economic and political aspects of the two societies. What words describe the former economic system of the Soviet Union?

3. What is the "tragedy of the commons"? Suppose that all workers in a factory are paid the same wage and have no chance of being fired. Use the logic of the "tragedy of the commons" to predict the result. How would you expect workers to behave?

4. You are assigned the task of debating the strengths of a socialist economy (regardless of your own viewpoint). Outline the points that you would make in the debate. Be sure to define socialism carefully in your presentation.

5. Explain why Karl Marx thought profit was unjustified. Contrast the Marxian view with the neoclassical view of profit.

6. Do you agree or disagree with the following statements? Explain your answers.
   a. Over time, the Chinese have shifted from a decentralized approach to economic development to a more centrally planned system. Since the events of 1989 in Tiananmen Square, there has been a severe crackdown on private businesses.
   b. Both Japan and the Soviet Union grew rapidly during the 1950s and 1960s. Growth in the Soviet Union occurred entirely due to government control of the economy. In Japan, growth was entirely the result of market forces.
   c. Although economists generally agree that transition from socialism to a market-based system must proceed rapidly, there is little agreement about what must be done to make the transition successful.

7. The distribution of income in a capitalist economy is likely to be more unequal than it is in a socialist economy. Why is this so? Is there a tension between the goal of limiting inequality and the goal of motivating risk taking and hard work? Explain your answer in detail.

8. "There is no doubt that a centrally planned socialist system has the potential to grow faster than a market-oriented capitalist system." Do you agree or disagree?

9. In the 1990s the world witnessed the rapid decline of several Eastern European governments (East Germany, Poland, and Romania, to name just a few). Poland immediately began moving its socialist economy toward a capitalist economy. Some of the effects of this transition have been increased unemployment and price inflation. Can you explain why? (*Hint:* Focus on differences between socialist and capitalist systems regarding the determination of prices and production levels.)

Politics and Trade

Since 1990, an array of international agreements and new international organizations have brought the world toward closer trading ties and economic cooperation. One such agreement is the Maastricht Treaty, which moved the countries of the European Union (EU) even closer economically—so much closer, in fact, that there are plans for a common currency. One can view the North American Free Trade Agreement (NAFTA) among Canada, the United States, and Mexico partly as a reaction to these closer ties among the members of the EU. In addition, as Asia includes the fastest growing economies in the world—such as South Korea, Taiwan, Singapore, and Thailand—Canadian policy has tried to promote trade with Asia through membership in the Asia-Pacific Economic Cooperation (APEC) forum (APEC includes the United States, Japan, and 15 other countries besides Canada). The Canadian government has also sponsored the "Team Canada" trade missions of federal and provincial political leaders led by Prime Minister Jean Chrétien, first to China in 1994 and then to India and three other countries in 1996.

Because some of the Asian nations, as well as Mexico and other Latin American countries, have very different political and social systems than Canada, these trade initiatives have revived interest in the perennial policy issue as to whether Canada should trade at all with countries that have poor human rights records, low environmental standards, or other characteristics that Canadians would

Many economists argue that trade with developed economies such as Canada will eventually help the disadvantaged in developing countries such as Vietnam by creating jobs in firms that sell their output on Canadian markets.

generally not like to promote in the world context. On the 1996 Team

Canada trip to India, for example, Craig Kielberger, a 13-year-old boy from Thornhill, Ontario, followed the prime minister's entourage and gained national publicity in Canada with his protests against the use of child labour in India and elsewhere, arguing that Canada should do more to ensure that the products of child labour were not imported into Canada. Many critics of NAFTA argued that Canada should not sign until Mexico was forced to adopt environmental standards similar to those in Canada. Others suggest we should not promote trade with countries whose unrestrictive labour laws allow firms to "exploit" their workers. Mexican wages, for example, are typically only 10% to 30% of *minimum* legal wages in Canada.

The main principle of international law in such matters is that nations should not be subject to international interference in internal matters, though this principle is not always honoured. The principle was articulated in the Treaty of Westphalia in the seventeenth century. Extending it to today, it would suggest, for example, that a country should not attempt to force a trading partner to increase its minimum wage. This is consistent with the economic argument that the Mexican workers who take jobs with wages and working conditions that look poor to Canadians must be doing so because they feel it is in their best interest, since the alternative is worse. On the other hand, the Treaty of Westphalia principle would not rule out Canada using trade measures to pressure Mexico to enforce environmental standards to the extent that pollution in Mexico may eventually affect Canada. Many Canadians believe there are some situations in which

trade should be ruled out on moral grounds, even if the exact situations are not well defined.

If Canada does decide to impose trade restrictions, would they be effective? United Nations trade sanctions, which Canada supported strongly, appeared to play a major role in ending apartheid in South Africa. But Canada is not important enough economically to have much impact on its own. For example, should Canada take a stand against human rights abuses in East Timor in Indonesia by not trading or investing in that area, knowing full well that other countries will simply take its place? This may be a moral question about which economics has little to say. Recent Canadian governments have argued, however, that trade is a way of keeping channels of communication open, and that in the end this will promote the cause of human rights. While most Canadians would not regard South Korea as a democratic ideal, it is far closer to it than North Korea, which has had a much lower level of international economic contact.

Questions for Analytical Thinking

1. The suggestion above is that if workers have chosen jobs that pay poorly, it probably means the alternative is worse and that a trade policy that eliminates those jobs will likely worsen their situation. Does this logic necessarily apply to child labour? If the goal were to reduce the use of child labour, what sort of policy would you advocate?

2. The economic arguments for free trade typically suggest that even

if Canada is not able to reduce trade barriers elsewhere, it should go ahead and reduce its own trade barriers so that Canadian consumers will be able to buy goods as cheaply as possible and Canadian resources will be used most efficiently. (This is sometimes called the "Adam Smith principle": Never make at home something that you can purchase more cheaply elsewhere.) But government policy often seems to be "mercantilist," that is, it aims at increasing exports and restricting imports. This seems to some to reflect the interests of some producers over the broader interests of consumers and taxpayers. If trade theory is correct in saying that the gains from free trade to consumers exceed the losses to producers, what does this say about the political system in situations in which there are broadly distributed gains but highly concentrated losses?

3. The comparative advantage argument for free trade assumes that goods prices reflect all costs. Suppose some Mexican farms use a pesticide that causes serious local environmental damage but does not affect the produce. Who gains and who loses if production is increased to export to Canada? Do the gains necessarily outweigh the losses?

Sources: Paul Krugman, "What Should Trade Negotiators Negotiate About?" *Journal of Economic Literature* (March 1997): pp. 113–120; APEC Secretariat home page: www.apecsec.org.sg/

Video Resource: "International Trade: Selling Canada," *News in Review,* March 1996

Microeconomics on the Internet

The home page for this book may be found on the Prentice Hall Canada website, at **http://www. phcanada.com**. This site has home pages for a large number of books in a variety of subjects plus methods to access a number of Prentice Hall surveys and trivia quizzes. Our home page includes many things, among which are links to many websites that first-year students may find useful. Here are a few of the websites included there, with a brief descriptions. All of these sites are free.

Perhaps the most important site for Canadian data is the Statistics Canada website, **http://www.statcan.ca**. This site has the latest Statistics Canada data in its "Daily News" feature, plus census information, the latest economic indicators for both Canada and all the provinces, an annual data section where detailed economic information is available, a section on government finances, and much more.

Another very useful site for Canadian economics students is the federal government Department of Finance at **http://www.fin.gc.ca**. Not only is there information on federal government budgets and speeches by the minister of finance, but there are also links to many other pages including Canadian and international banks and other financial institutions, stock exchanges, provincial, national and international economic organizations, pages for all the provincial departments of finance (with provincial government budgets), and sites where there s tax and budgetary information for many other countries.

Two other federal government sites worth special mention to students studying microeconomics are those of Industry Canada at **http://www.ic.gc.ca** and Human Resources and Development Canada (HRDC) at **http://www.hrdc-drhc.cg.ca**. The former calls its websites "Strategis" and, for example, has extensive information on individual businesses and industries and government regulations such as those governing bankruptcy, consumer product safety, competition, and patents. There is extensive data on interprovincial trade and links to sites with international trade data. The HRDC site has extensive information on programs such as Employment Insurance and the Canada Pension Plan.

The sites of major international organizations include those of the World Bank (**http://www. worldbank.org**), the International Monetary Fund (**http://www.imf.org**), and the World Trade Organization (**http://www.wto.org**). All describe their organiztions in detail and have links to many other national and international organizations.

There are a number of useful links at Canadian universities and many departments maintain pages with a good set of outside links. One useful university site is **http://pacific.commerce.ubc.ca**, maintained by Professor Werner Antweiler of the University of British Columbia. During Canadian elections you might find the "Election Stock Market" interesting—participants (and you can join if you wish) invest their money in shares whose value is determined on election day by how many seats a particular party wins. So, for example, if the Liberals win 55% of the vote, a "Liberal share" will be worth 55¢. There is electronic trading before the election—the trick as always is to try to buy low and sell high. There are also pages at this site devoted to competition policy, the Canadian tax system, and the Canadian Economics Association.

Finally, one of the most comprehensive overall sites is "NetEc" at **http://netec.wustl.edu** at the University of Washington at St. Louis. From here you can link to three other well-known pages: "WebEc" (maintained by Lauri Saarinen of the University of Helsinki); "Resources for Economists on the Internet" (maintained by Professor Bill Goffe of the University of Southern Mississippi); and "EDIRC," a page listing all the economics organizations in the world (maintained by Professor Christian Zimmermann of the University of Quebec at Montreal). There is also a page for jokes about economists (which are an acquired taste).

Concise Dictionary of Economic Terminology

ability-to-pay principle A theory of taxation that holds that citizens should bear tax burdens in line with their ability to pay taxes.

absolute advantage The advantage in the production of a product enjoyed by one country over another when it uses fewer resources to produce that product than the other country does.

abuse of dominant position Any policy pursued by the dominant firm in an industry to limit competition.

adverse selection An imperfect-information problem that can occur when a buyer or seller enters into an exchange with another party who has more information.

alienation A term used by Marx to describe a condition of workers under capitalism in which they lose a sense of meaning or purpose in life because their main life activity—work—is under the control of their employer.

asymmetric information A situation in which the participants in an economic transaction have different information about the transaction.

average-cost pricing Setting price to cover average cost per unit including a fair return.

average fixed cost (*AFC*) Total fixed cost divided by the number of units of output; a per unit measure of fixed costs.

average product The average amount produced by each unit of a variable factor of production.

average total cost (*ATC*) Total cost divided by the number of units of output.

average variable cost (*AVC*) Total variable cost divided by the number of units of output.

Averch-Johnson effect The tendency for regulated monopolies to build more capital than they need. Usually occurs when allowed rates of return are set by a regulatory agency at some percentage of fixed capital stocks.

barrier to entry Something that prevents new firms from entering and competing in an industry.

benefits-received principle A theory of fairness that holds that taxpayers should contribute to government (in the form of taxes) in proportion to the benefits that they receive from public expenditures.

black market A market in which illegal trading takes place at market-determined prices.

block grant A financial arrangement whereby one level of government gives a block of money to another to cover part of the cost of a program. The size of the transfer does not depend on program cost.

brain drain The tendency for talented people from developing countries to become educated in a developed country and remain there after graduation.

breaking even The situation in which a firm is earning exactly a normal profit rate.

budget constraint The limits imposed on household choices by income, wealth, and product prices.

Canada–U.S. Free Trade Agreement An agreement, which came into effect January 1, 1989, in which Canada and the United States agreed to eliminate all barriers to trade between the two countries over a 10-year period.

Canadian Labour Congress (CLC) The largest national federation of labour organizations in Canada. The CLC was created in 1956 and represents approximately 60% of unionized workers in Canada.

capital Things that have already been produced that are in turn used to produce other goods and services.

capital flight The tendency for capital to leave developing countries in search of higher rates of return elsewhere.

capital income Income earned on savings that have been put to use through financial capital markets.

capital market The input/factor market in which households supply their savings, for interest or for claims to future profits, to firms that demand funds in order to buy capital goods.

capital stock The current market value of a firm's plant, equipment, inventories, and intangible assets.

capital-intensive technology Technology that relies heavily on capital rather than human labour.

capitalist economy An economy in which most capital is privately owned.

cartel A group of firms that gets together and makes joint price and output decisions in order to maximize joint profits.

ceteris paribus Literally, "all else equal." Used to analyze the relationship between two variables while the values of other variables are held unchanged.

choice set or opportunity set The set of options that is defined and limited by a budget constraint.

Coase theorem Under certain conditions, when externalities are present, private parties can arrive at the efficient solution without government involvement.

collective bargaining The process by which union leaders bargain with management as the representatives of all union employees.

collusion The act of working with other producers in an effort to limit competition and increase joint profits.

command economy An economy in which a central authority or agency draws up a plan that establishes what will be produced and when, sets production goals, and makes rules for distribution.

communism An economic system in which the people control the means of production (capital and land) directly, without the intervention of a government or state.

comparative advantage The advantage in the production of a product enjoyed by one country over another when that product can be produced at lower cost in terms of other goods than it could be in the other country.

compensating differentials Differences in wages that result from differences in working conditions. Risky jobs usually pay higher wages; highly desirable jobs usually pay lower wages.

complementary inputs Factors of production that can be used together to enhance each other.

complements, complementary goods Goods that "go together"; a decrease in the price of one results in an increase in demand for the other, and vice versa.

constant returns to scale An increase in a firm's scale of production has no effect on average costs per unit produced.

consumer goods Goods produced for present consumption.

consumer sovereignty The idea that consumers ultimately dictate what will be produced (or not produced) by choosing what to purchase (and what not to purchase).

consumer surplus The difference between the maximum amount a person is willing to pay for a good and its current market price.

copayment A fixed amount of money that an insured person pays for each visit to a doctor's office.

Corn Laws The tariffs, subsidies, and restrictions enacted by the British Parliament in the early nineteenth century to discourage imports and encourage exports of grain.

corporate income taxes Taxes levied on the net incomes of corporations.

corporation A form of business organization resting on a legal charter that establishes the corporation as an entity separate from its owners. Owners hold shares and are liable for the firm's debts only up to the limit of their investment, or share, in the firm.

cost-benefit analysis The formal technique by which the benefits of a public project are weighed against its costs.

cost-shared transfer A financial arrangement between federal and provincial governments whereby each government covers a share of the cost of providing a program.

Cournot model A model of a two-firm industry (duopoly) in which a series of output-adjustment decisions leads to a final level of output that is between that which would prevail if the market were organized competitively and that which would be set by a monopoly.

cross-price elasticity of demand A measure of the response of the quantity of one good demanded to a change in the price of another good.

crown corporation A corporation owned and operated by government.

debt rescheduling An agreement between banks and borrowers through which a new schedule of repayments of the debt is negotiated; often some of the debt is written off and the repayment period is extended.

decreasing returns to scale, or diseconomies of scale An increase in a firm's scale of production leads to higher average costs per unit produced.

deductible An annual out-of-pocket expenditure that an insurance policy holder must make before the insurance plan makes any reimbursement.

demand curve A graph illustrating how much of a given product a household would be willing to buy at different prices.

demand determined price The price of a good that is in fixed supply; it is determined exclusively by what firms and households are willing to pay for the good.

demand schedule A table showing how much of a given product a household would be willing to buy at different prices.

demogrant A transfer payment that depends only on a demographic characteristic (such as age) and that does not change as income changes.

dependency theory The theory that the poverty of the developing countries is due to the "dependence" of the developing world on countries that are already developed; it suggests that even after the end of colonialism, this dependence is maintained because developed countries are able to use their economic power to determine to their own advantage (and to the disadvantage of others) the relative prices and conditions under which the international exchange of goods takes place.

depreciation The amount by which an asset's value falls in a given period.

derived demand The demand for resources (inputs) that is dependent on the demand for the outputs those resources can be used to produce.

descriptive economics The compilation of data that describe phenomena and facts.

diamond/water paradox A paradox stating that (1) the things with the greatest value in use frequently have little or no value in exchange, and (2) the things with the greatest value in exchange frequently have little or no value in use.

dividends The portion of a corporation's profits that the firm pays out each period to shareholders. Also called *distributed profits*.

dominant strategy In game theory, a strategy that is best no matter what the opposition does.

drop-in-the-bucket problem A problem intrinsic to public goods: The good or service is usually so costly that its provision generally does not depend on whether or not any single person pays.

dumping Takes place when a firm or industry sells products on the world market at prices below the cost of production.

economic costs The full costs of production including (1) a normal rate of return on investment and (2) the opportunity cost of each factor of production.

economic growth An increase in the total output of an economy. It occurs when a society acquires new resources or when it learns to produce more using existing resources. Defined by some economists as an increase of real GDP per capita.

economic income The amount of money a household can spend during a given time period without increasing or decreasing its net assets. Wages, salaries, dividends, interest income, transfer payments, rents, and so forth are sources of economic income.

economic integration Occurs when two or more countries join to form a free-trade zone.

economic problem Given scarce resources, how exactly do large, complex societies go about answering the three basic economic questions?

economic profits, or excess profits Profits over and above the normal rate of return on investment.

economic theory A statement or set of related statements about cause and effect, action and reaction.

economics The study of how individuals and societies choose to use the scarce resources that nature and previous generations have provided.

efficiency The condition in which the economy is producing what people want at least possible cost.

elastic demand A demand relationship in which the percentage change in quantity demanded is larger in absolute value than the percentage change in price (a demand elasticity with an absolute value greater than one).

elasticity A general concept that can be used to quantify the response in one variable when another variable changes.

elasticity of labour supply A measure of the response of labour supplied to a change in the price of labour. Can be positive or negative.

elasticity of supply A measure of the response of quantity of a good supplied to a change in price of that good. Likely to be positive in output markets.

empirical economics The collection and use of data to test economic theories.

entrepreneur A person who organizes, manages, and assumes the risks of a firm, taking a new idea or a new product and turning it into a successful business.

equilibrium The condition that exists when quantity supplied and quantity demanded are equal. At equilibrium, there is no tendency for price to change. In the macroeconomic goods market, equilibrium occurs when planned aggregate expenditure is equal to aggregate output.

equity Fairness.

European Union (EU) The European trading bloc composed of Austria, Belgium, Denmark, Finland, France, Germany, Greece, Ireland, Italy, Luxembourg, the Netherlands, Portugal, Spain, Sweden, and the United Kingdom.

excess burden The amount by which the burden of a tax exceeds the total revenue collected. Also called *dead weight losses*.

excess demand The condition that exists when quantity demanded exceeds quantity supplied at the current price.

excess supply The condition that exists when quantity supplied exceeds quantity demanded at the current price.

exchange rate The ratio at which two currencies are traded for each other; the price of one currency in terms of another.

excise taxes Taxes on specific commodities.

exclusive dealing A policy of supplying a product only if the purchaser agrees not to buy similar products from competitors.

expected rate of return The annual rate of return that a firm expects to obtain through a capital investment.

experience rating The insurance-company practice of charging individuals or groups of individuals premiums that are linked to their current state of health or to the probability that they will become sick.

export promotion A trade policy designed to encourage exports.

export subsidies Government payments made to domestic firms to encourage exports.

externality A cost or benefit resulting from some activity or transaction that is imposed or bestowed upon parties outside the activity or transaction. Sometimes called *spillovers* or *neighbourhood effects*.

factor endowments The quantity and quality of labour, land, and natural resources of a country.

factor substitution effect The tendency of firms to substitute away from a factor whose price has risen and toward a factor whose price has fallen.

factors of production The inputs into the production process. Land, labour, and capital are the three key factors of production.

fallacy of composition The belief that what is true for a part is necessarily true for the whole.

favoured customers Those who receive special treatment from dealers during crises.

featherbedding The common union practice of preserving jobs even when it is inefficient to do so.

fee-for-service reimbursement A program in which insurance companies reimburse health care providers for the services they've rendered.

fertility rate The birth rate. Equal to the number of births per year divided by the population multiplied by 100.

financial capital market The complex set of institutions in which suppliers of capital (households that save) and the demand for capital (business firms wanting to invest) interact.

firm An organization that transforms resources (inputs) into products (outputs). Firms are the primary producing units in a market economy.

five-year plans Plans developed in the Soviet Union that provided general guidelines and directions for the next five years.

fixed cost Any cost that a firm bears in the short run that does not depend on its level of output. These costs are incurred even if the firm is producing nothing. There are no fixed costs in the long run.

free entry The condition that exists when there are no barriers to prevent new firms from competing for profits in a profitable industry.

free exit The condition that exists when firms can simply stop producing their product and leave a market. Firms incur no additional costs by exiting the industry.

free-rider problem A problem intrinsic to public goods: Because people can enjoy the benefits of public goods whether they pay for them or not, they are usually unwilling to pay for them.

game theory Analyzes oligopolistic behaviour as a complex series of strategic moves and reactive countermoves among rival firms. In game theory, firms are assumed to anticipate rival reactions.

gatekeepers The capacity in which doctors in Canada act when they prescribe drugs, check patients into hospitals, order diagnostic tests, etc.

General Agreement on Tariffs and Trade (GATT) An international agreement signed by Canada and 22 other countries in 1947 to promote the liberalization of foreign trade. Replaced by the World Trade Organization (WTO).

general equilibrium The condition that exists when all markets in an economy are in simultaneous equilibrium.

Gini coefficient A commonly used measure of inequality of income derived from a Lorenz Curve. It can range from zero to a maximum of one.

government failure Occurs when the government becomes the tool of the rent seeker and the allocation of resources is made even less efficient by the intervention of government.

government franchise A monopoly by virtue of government directive.

government interest payments Cash payments made by the government to those who own government bonds.

government purchases of goods and services Expenditures by federal, provincial, and local governments for final goods and labour.

government transfer payments Cash payments made by the government directly to households for which no current services are received. They include Old Age Security benefits, Employment Insurance, and welfare payments.

Great Leap Forward The economic strategy in the People's Republic of China that began in 1958 when it departed from the Soviet model and shifted from large-scale, capital-intensive industry to small-scale, labour-intensive industry scattered across the countryside. Material incentives were reduced and replaced by the motivating power of revolutionary ideology and inspiration.

Great Proletarian Cultural Revolution (1966–1976) A period of ideological purity in the People's Republic of China. Material incentives and reforms were denounced and highly-trained specialists were sent to work in the fields. The effect of the Cultural Revolution on the Chinese economy was catastrophic.

Green Revolution The agricultural breakthroughs of modern science, such as the development of new, high-yield crop varieties.

gross domestic product (GDP) The total market value of all final goods and services produced within a given period by factors of production located within a country.

Heckscher-Ohlin theorem A theory that explains the existence of a country's comparative advantage by its factor endowments: A country has a comparative advantage in the production of a product if that country is relatively well endowed with inputs used intensively in the production of that product.

homogeneous products Undifferentiated products; products that are identical to, or indistinguishable from, one another.

households The consuming units in an economy.

human capital A form of intangible capital that includes the skills and other knowledge that workers have or acquire through education and training and that yields valuable services to a firm over time.

imperfect competition An industry in which single firms have some control over price and competition. Imperfectly competitive industries give rise to an inefficient allocation of resources.

imperfect information The absence of full knowledge regarding product characteristics, available prices, and so forth.

import substitution An industrial trade strategy that favours developing local industries that can manufacture goods to replace imports.

impossibility theorem A proposition demonstrated by Kenneth Arrow showing that no system of aggregating individual preferences into social decisions will always yield consistent, nonarbitrary results.

income The sum of all a household's wages, salaries, profits, interest payments, rents, and other forms of earnings in a given period of time. It is a flow measure.

income effect of higher wages When wages rise, people are better off. If leisure is a normal good, they may decide to consume more of it and to work less.

income elasticity of demand Measures the responsiveness of demand with respect to changes in income.

income tested transfer A transfer that changes continuously as income changes.

increasing returns to scale, or economies of scale An increase in a firm's scale of production leads to lower average costs per unit produced.

inductive reasoning The process of observing regular patterns from raw data and drawing generalizations from them.

Industrial Revolution The period in England during the late eighteenth and early nineteenth centuries in which new manufacturing technologies and improved transportation gave rise to the modern factory system and a massive movement of the population from the countryside to the cities.

industry All the firms that produce a similar product. The boundaries of a "product" can be drawn very widely ("agricultural products"), less widely ("dairy products"), or very narrowly ("cheese"). The term *industry* can be used interchangeably with the term *market*.

inelastic demand Demand that responds somewhat, but not a great deal, to changes in price. Inelastic demand always has a numerical value between zero and minus one.

infant industry A young industry that may need temporary protection from competition from the established industries of other countries in order to develop an acquired comparative advantage.

inferior goods Goods for which demand falls when income rises.

injunction A court order forbidding the continuation of behaviour that leads to damages.

input or factor markets The markets in which the resources used to produce products are exchanged.

intangible capital Nonmaterial things that contribute to the output of future goods and services.

interest The fee that a borrower pays to a lender for the use of his or her funds. Almost always expressed as an annual rate.

International Monetary Fund An international agency whose primary goals are to stabilize international exchange rates and to lend money to countries that have problems financing their international transactions.

international sector From any one country's perspective, the economies of the rest of the world.

investment The process of using resources to produce new capital. Although capital is measured at a given point in time (a stock), investment is measured over a period of time (a flow). The flow of investment increases the stock of capital.

job search The process of gathering information about job availability and job characteristics.

kinked demand curve model A model of oligopoly in which the demand curve facing each individual firm has a "kink" in it. The kink follows from the assumption that competitive firms will follow suit if a single firm cuts price but will not follow suit if a single firm raises price.

Knights of Labor One of the earliest successful labour organizations in Canada. It recruited both skilled and unskilled labourers. Founded in 1869, the power of the Knights declined after 1886.

labour market The input/factor market in which households supply work for wages to firms that demand labour.

labour market discrimination Occurs when one group of workers receives inferior treatment from employers because of some characteristic irrelevant to job performance.

labour supply curve A diagram that shows the quantity of labour supplied as a function of the wage rate. Its shape depends on how households react to changes in the wage rate.

labour-intensive technology Technology that relies heavily on human labour rather than capital.

laissez-faire economy Literally from the French: "allow [them] to do." An economy in which individual people and firms pursue their own self-interests without any central direction or regulation.

land market The input/factor market in which households supply land or other real property in exchange for rent.

law of demand The negative relationship between price and quantity demanded: As price rises, quantity demanded decreases. As price falls, quantity demanded increases.

law of diminishing marginal utility The more of any one good consumed in a given period, the less satisfaction (utility) generated by consuming each additional (marginal) unit of the same good.

law of diminishing returns When additional units of a variable input are added to fixed inputs after a certain point, the marginal product of the variable input declines.

law of supply The positive relationship between price and quantity of a good supplied: An increase in market price will lead to an increase in quantity supplied, and a decrease in market price will lead to a decrease in quantity supplied.

liability rules Laws that require A to compensate B for damages imposed.

logrolling Occurs when elected representatives trade votes, agreeing to help each other get certain pieces of legislation passed.

long run That period of time for which there are no fixed factors of production. Firms can increase or decrease scale of operation, and new firms can enter and existing firms can exit the industry.

long-run average cost curve (*LRAC*) A graph that shows the different scales on which a firm can choose to operate in the long run.

long-run competitive equilibrium When $P = SRMC = SRAC = LRAC$ and economic profits are zero.

Lorenz Curve A widely used graph of the distribution of income, with cumulative percentage of families plotted along the horizontal axis and cumulative percentage of income plotted along the vertical axis.

low income cutoffs The income levels used by Statistics Canada to determine the incidence of low income in Canada.

macroeconomics The branch of economics that deals with the economy as a whole. Macroeconomics focuses on the determinants of total national income, deals with aggregates such as aggregate consumption and investment, and looks at the overall level of prices rather than individual prices.

marginal cost (*MC*) The increase in total cost that results from producing one more unit of output. Marginal costs reflect changes in variable costs.

marginal damage cost (*MDC*) The additional harm done by increasing the level of an externality-producing activity by one unit. If producing product X pollutes the water in a river, *MDC* is the additional cost imposed by the added pollution that results from increasing output by one unit of X per period.

marginal factor cost (*MFC*) The additional cost of using one more unit of a given factor of production.

marginal private cost (*MPC*) The amount that a consumer pays to consume an additional unit of a particular good.

marginal product The additional output that can be produced by adding one more unit of a specific input, *ceteris paribus*.

marginal product of labour (*MP*$_L$) The additional output produced by one additional unit of labour.

marginal productivity theory of income distribution At equilibrium, all factors of production end up receiving rewards determined by their productivity as measured by marginal revenue product.

marginal revenue (*MR*) The additional revenue that a firm takes in when it increases output by one additional unit. In perfect competition, $P = MR$.

marginal revenue product (*MRP*) The additional revenue a firm earns by employing one additional unit of input, *ceteris paribus*.

marginal revenue product of labour (*MRP*$_L$) The additional revenue that a firm will take in by hiring one additional unit of labour, *ceteris paribus*. For perfectly competitive firms, the marginal revenue product of labour is equal to the marginal physical product of labour multiplied by the price of output.

marginal social cost (*MSC*) The total cost to society of producing an additional unit of a good or service. *MSC* is equal to the sum of the marginal costs of producing the product and the correctly measured damage costs involved in the process of production.

marginal utility (*MU*) The additional satisfaction gained by the consumption or use of *one more* unit of something.

market The institution through which buyers and sellers interact and engage in exchange.

market demand The sum of all the quantities of a good or service demanded per period by all the households buying in the market for that good or service.

market failure Occurs when resources are misallocated, or allocated inefficiently. The result is waste or lost value.

market organization The way an industry is structured. Structure is defined by how many firms there are in an industry, whether products are differentiated or are virtually the same, whether or not firms in the industry can control prices or wages, and whether or not competing firms can enter and leave the industry freely.

market power An imperfectly competitive firm's ability to raise price without losing all demand for its product.

market supply The sum of all that is supplied each period by all producers of a single product.

market-socialist economy An economy that combines government ownership with market allocation.

maximin strategy In game theory, a strategy chosen to maximize the minimum gain that can be earned.

means of production Marx's term for land and capital.

merger The combining of two or more companies into a single company.

microeconomics The branch of economics that deals with the functioning of individual industries and the behaviour of individual decision-making units—business firms and households.

midpoint formula A more precise way of calculating percentages using the value halfway between P_1 and P_2 for the base in calculating the percentage change in price, and the value halfway between Q_1 and Q_2 as the base for calculating the percentage change in quantity demanded.

minimum wage The lowest wage that firms are permitted to pay workers.

Ministry of Trade and Industry (MITI) The agency of the Japanese government responsible for industrial policy. It uses tariffs and subsidies to protect and support key industries and helps some sectors plan orderly reductions in capacity.

misleading advertising and deceptive marketing practices Occur when firms attempt to capture customers by providing inaccurate information about product availability, quality, and price.

model A formal statement of a theory. Usually a mathematical statement of a presumed relationship between two or more variables.

money income The measure of income used by Statistics Canada. Because it excludes capital gains, noncash transfer payments, and many fringe benefits, it is less inclusive than economic income.

monopolistic competition An industry structure (or market organization) in which many firms compete, producing similar but slightly differentiated products. There are close substitutes for the product of any given firm. Monopolistic competitors have some control over price. Price and quality competition follow from product differentiation. Entry and exit are relatively easy, and success invites new competitors.

monopoly An industry structure (or market organization) in which there is only one large firm that produces a product for which there are no close substitutes. Monopolists can set prices but are subject to market discipline. For a monopoly to continue to exist, something must prevent potential competitors from entering the industry and competing for profits.

monopsony A market in which there is only one buyer for a good or service.

moral hazard Arises when one party to a contract passes the cost of his or her behaviour on to the other party to the contract.

mortality rate The death rate. Equal to the number of deaths per year divided by the population multiplied by 100.

movement along a demand curve What happens when a change in price causes quantity demanded to change.

Nash equilibrium In game theory, the result of all players playing their best strategy given what their competitors are doing.

natural monopoly An industry that realizes such large economies of scale in producing its product that single-firm production of that good or service is most efficient.

natural rate of population increase The difference between the birth rate and the death rate. It does not take migration into account.

net income The profits of a firm.

New Economic Policy The Soviet economic policy in effect between 1921 and 1928; characterized by decentralization and a retreat to a market orientation.

nonexcludable A characteristic of most public goods: Once a good is produced, no one can be excluded from enjoying its benefits.

nonrival in consumption A characteristic of public goods: One person's enjoyment of the benefits of a public good does not interfere with another's consumption of it.

normal goods Goods for which demand goes up when income is higher and for which demand goes down when income is lower.

normal rate of profit, or normal rate of return A rate of profit that is just sufficient to keep owners and investors satisfied. For relatively risk-free firms, it should be nearly the same as the interest rate on risk-free government bonds.

normative economics An approach to economics that analyzes outcomes of economic behaviour, evaluates them as good or bad, and may prescribe courses of action. Also called policy economics.

North American Free Trade Agreement (NAFTA) An agreement signed by Canada, the United States and Mexico in which the three countries agreed to establish all of North America as a free-trade zone.

occupational segregation The concentration of men and women in certain occupations.

Ockham's razor The principle that irrelevant detail should be cut away.

oligopoly An industry structure (or market organization) with a small number of (usually) large firms producing products that range from highly differentiated (automobiles) to standardized (copper). In general, entry of new firms into an oligopolistic industry is difficult but possible.

on-the-job training The principal form of human capital investment financed primarily by firms.

operating profit (or loss) or net operating revenue Total revenue minus total variable cost ($TR - TVC$).

opportunity cost That which we give up, or forgo, when we make a choice or a decision.

optimal level of provision for public goods The level at which resources are drawn from the production of other goods and services only to the extent that people want the public good and are willing to pay for it. At this level, society's willingness to pay per unit is equal to the marginal cost of producing the good.

optimal method of production The production method that minimizes cost.

optimal scale of plant The scale of plant that minimizes cost.

outputs Usable products.

PC 1003 A law that forced employers to negotiate with a union, provided the union could establish that a majority of workers wished the union to act as their representative in negotiations with an employer.

Pareto efficiency or Pareto optimality A condition in which no change is possible that will make some members of society better off without making some other members of society worse off.

partial equilibrium analysis The process of examining the equilibrium conditions in individual markets and for households and firms separately.

partnership A form of business organization in which there is more than one proprietor. The owners are responsible jointly and separately for the firm's obligations.

patent A barrier to entry that grants exclusive use of the patented product or process to the inventor.

payroll taxes Taxes levied at a flat rate on wages and salaries. Proceeds support various government-administered social-benefit programs, including the social security system and the unemployment benefits system.

perfect competition An industry structure (or market organization) in which there are many firms, each small relative to the industry, producing virtually identical products and in which no firm is large enough to have any control over prices. In perfectly competitive industries, new competitors can freely enter and exit the market.

perfect knowledge The assumption that households possess a knowledge of the qualities and prices of everything available in the market and that firms have all available information regarding wage rates, capital costs, and output prices.

perfect substitutes Identical products.

perfectly contestable market A market in which entry and exit are costless.

perfectly elastic demand Demand in which quantity demanded drops to zero at the slightest increase in price.

perfectly inelastic demand Demand in which quantity demanded does not respond at all to a change in price.

physical, or tangible, capital Material things used as inputs in the production of future goods and services. The major categories of physical capital are nonresidential structures, durable equipment, residential structures, and inventories.

positive economics An approach to economics that seeks to understand behaviour and the operation of systems without making judgments. It describes what exists and how it works.

post hoc, ergo propter hoc Literally, "after this (in time), therefore because of this." A common error made in thinking about causation: If Event A happens before Event B happens, it is not necessarily true that A caused B.

predatory pricing A strategy whereby a firms sells at a price below cost to drive competitors out of business. The goal is to absorb losses in the short run to reduce competition thereby opening up an opportunity to make economic profits in the long run.

price The amount that a product sells for per unit. It reflects what society is willing to pay.

price ceiling A maximum price that sellers may charge for a good, usually set by government.

price elasticity of demand The ratio of the percentage change in quantity demanded to the percentage change in price.

price leadership A form of oligopoly in which one dominant firm sets prices and all the smaller firms in the industry follow its pricing policy.

price rationing The process by which the market system allocates goods and services to consumers when quantity demanded exceeds quantity supplied.

principle of neutrality All else equal, taxes that are neutral with respect to economic decisions (that is, taxes that do not distort economic decisions) are generally preferable to taxes that distort economic decisions. Taxes that are not neutral impose excess burdens.

principle of second best The fact that a tax distorts an economic decision does not always imply that such a tax imposes an excess burden. If previously existing distortions exist, such a tax may actually improve efficiency.

private good A product produced by firms for sale to individual households. People can be excluded from the benefits of a private good if they do not pay for it.

private sector Includes all independently owned profit-making firms, nonprofit organizations, and households; all the decision-making units in the economy that are not part of the government.

privatization The transfer of government business to the private sector.

producers Those people or groups of people, whether private or public, who transform resources into usable products.

product or output markets The markets in which goods and services are exchanged.

product differentiation A strategy that firms use to achieve market power. Accomplished by producing products that have distinct positive identities in consumers' minds.

production The process by which resources are transformed into useful forms.

production function or total product function A numerical or mathematical expression of a relationship between inputs and outputs. It shows units of total product as a function of units of inputs.

production possibility frontier (ppf) A graph that shows all the combinations of goods and services that can be produced if all of society's resources are used efficiently.

production technology The relationship between inputs and outputs.

productivity of an input The amount of output produced per unit of an input.

profit The difference between total revenues and total costs.

progressive tax A tax whose burden, expressed as a percentage of income, increases as income increases.

property income Income from the ownership of real property and financial holdings. It takes the form of profits, interest, dividends, and rents.

proportional tax A tax whose burden is the same proportion of income for all households.

proprietorship A form of business organization in which a person simply sets up to provide goods or services at a profit. In a proprietorship, the proprietor (or owner) is the firm. The assets and liabilities of the firm are the owner's assets and liabilities.

protection The practice of shielding a sector of the economy from foreign competition.

public choice theory An economic theory that proceeds on the assumption that the public officials who set economic policies and regulate the players act in their own self-interest, just as firms do.

public, or social, goods Goods or services that bestow collective benefits on members of society; they are, in a sense, collectively consumed. Generally, no one can be excluded from enjoying their benefits. The classic example is national defence.

public sector Includes all agencies at all levels of government—federal, state, and local.

pure monopoly An industry with a single firm that produces a product for which there are no close substitutes and in which significant barriers to entry prevent other firms from entering the industry to compete for profits.

pure rent The return to any factor of production that is in fixed supply.

quantity demanded The amount (number of units) of a product that a household would buy in a given period if it could buy all it wanted at the current market price.

quantity supplied The amount of a particular product that a firm would be willing and able to offer for sale at a particular price during a given time period.

queuing A nonprice rationing mechanism that uses waiting in line as a means of distributing goods and services.

quota A limit on the quantity of imports.

ration coupons Tickets or coupons that entitle individual persons to purchase a certain amount of a given product per month.

Rawlsian justice A theory of distributional justice that concludes that the social contract emerging from the "original position" would call for an income distribution that would maximize the well-being of the worst-off member of society.

refusal to supply A policy of not selling a product to another firm as part of a strategy to increase market share by eliminating that firm as a competitor.

regressive tax A tax whose burden, expressed as a percentage of income, falls as income increases.

rent-seeking behaviour Actions taken by households or firms to preserve extranormal profits.

resale price maintenance A policy of forcing retailers to sell a product at a price fixed by the manufacturer.

resources or inputs Anything provided by nature or previous generations that can be used directly or indirectly to satisfy human wants.

retained earnings The profits that a corporation keeps, usually for the purchase of capital assets. Also called *undistributed profits*.

revenue, or total revenue Receipts from the sale of a product ($P \times Q$).

shares of stock Financial instruments that give to the holder a share in the firm's ownership and therefore the right to share in the firm's profits.

shift of a demand curve The change that takes place in a demand curve when a new relationship between quantity demanded of a good and the price of that good is brought about by a change in the original conditions.

shock therapy The approach to transition from socialism to market capitalism that advocates rapid deregulation of prices, liberalization of trade, and privatization.

short run The period of time for which two conditions hold: The firm is operating under a fixed scale (fixed factor) of production and firms can neither enter nor exit an industry.

short-run industry supply curve The sum of marginal cost curves (above *AVC*) of all the firms in an industry.

shut-down point The lowest point on the average variable cost curve. When price falls below the minimum point on *AVC*, total revenue is insufficient to cover variable costs and the firm will shut down and bear losses equal to fixed costs.

Smoot-Hawley tariff The U.S. tariff law of the 1930s, which set the highest tariffs in U.S. history (60%). It set off an international trade war that is often considered a cause of the worldwide depression of the 1930s.

social capital, or infrastructure Capital that provides services to the public. Most social capital takes the form of public works (roads and bridges) and public services (police and fire protection).

social choice The problem of deciding what society wants. The process of adding up individual preferences to make a choice for society as a whole.

social overhead capital Basic infrastructure projects such as roads, power generation, and irrigation systems.

socialist economy An economy in which most capital is owned by the government rather than by private citizens. Also called social ownership.

sources side/uses side The impact of a tax may be felt on one or the other or on both sides of the income equation. A tax may cause net income to fall (damage on the sources side), or it may cause prices of goods and services to rise so that income buys less (damage on the uses side).

spreading overhead The process of dividing total fixed costs by more units of output. Average fixed cost declines as q rises.

stability A condition in which output is steady or growing, with low inflation and full employment of resources.

stabilization program An agreement between a borrower country and the International Monetary Fund in which the country agrees to revamp its economic policies to provide incentives for higher export earnings and lower imports.

structural adjustment A series of programs in developing countries designed to (1) reduce the size of their public sectors through privatization and/or expenditure reductions, (2) decrease their budget deficits, (3) control inflation, and (4) encourage private saving and investment through tax reform.

substitutable inputs Factors of production that can be used in place of one another.

substitutes Goods that can serve as replacements for one another; when the price of one increases, demand for the other goes up.

substitution effect of higher wages Consuming an additional hour of leisure means sacrificing the wages that would be earned by working. Thus, when the wage rate rises, leisure becomes a more expensive commodity, and households may "buy" less of it. This means working more.

supplier-induced demand Demand that, due to asymmetric information, is determined largely by the supplier, rather than the consumer of the commodity.

supply curve A graph illustrating how much of a product a firm will supply at different prices.

supply schedule A table showing how much of a product firms will supply at different prices.

surplus In the Marxian sense, output of goods and services in excess of what is necessary to 1) keep the labour force clothed and fed at least at a subsistence level and 2) replace capital goods and services consumed in the production process.

tacit collusion *Collusion* occurs when price- and quantity-fixing agreements among producers are explicit. *Tacit collusion* occurs when such agreements are implicit.

tariff A tax on imports.

tax base The measure or value upon which a tax is levied.

tax incidence The ultimate distribution of a tax's burden.

tax rate structure The percentage of a tax base that must be paid in taxes—25% of income, for example.

tax room An arrangement to transfer money from one government to another whereby one government reduces tax rates and thus tax revenue, and the other government increases tax rates and thus tax revenue.

tax shifting Occurs when households can alter their behaviour and do something to avoid paying a tax.

technological change The introduction of new methods of production or new products intended to increase the productivity of existing inputs or to raise marginal products.

terms of trade The ratio at which a country can trade domestic products for imported products.

theory of comparative advantage Ricardo's theory that specialization and free trade will benefit all trading partners (real wages will rise), even those that may be absolutely less efficient producers.

three basic questions The questions that all societies must answer: (1) What will be produced? (2) How will it be produced? (3) Who will get what is produced?

Tiebout hypothesis An efficient mix of public goods is produced when local land/housing prices and taxes come to reflect consumer preferences just as they do in the market for private goods.

tied selling A policy of supplying a product only if the purchaser agrees to buy other products from the supplier.

total cost (*TC*) Fixed costs plus variable costs.

total fixed costs (*TFC*), or overhead The total of all costs that do not change with output, even if output is zero.

total revenue (*TR*) The total amount that a firm takes in from the sale of its product: the price per unit multiplied by the quantity of output the firm decides to produce ($P \times q$).

total utility The total amount of satisfaction obtained from consumption of a good or service.

total variable cost (*TVC*) The total of all costs that depend on or vary with output in the short run.

total variable cost curve A graph that shows the relationship between total variable cost and the level of a firm's output.

trade deficit The situation when a country imports more than it exports.

trade surplus The situation when a country exports more than it imports.

tragedy of the commons The idea that collective ownership may not provide the proper private incentives for efficiency because individuals do not bear the full costs of their own decisions but do enjoy the full benefits.

transactions costs In a market system, the resources that are used to complete a transaction.

transfer payments Cash payments made by the government to people who do not supply goods, services, or labour in exchange for these payments. They include Old Age Security benefits and Employment Insurance.

unitary elasticity A demand relationship in which the percentage change in quantity of a product demanded is the same as the percentage change in price (a demand elasticity of −1).

utilitarian justice The idea that "a dollar in the hand of a rich person buys less than a dollar in the hand of a poor person." If the marginal utility of income declines with income, transferring income from the rich to the poor will increase total utility.

utility The basis of choice. The satisfaction, or reward, a product yields relative to its alternatives.

utility possibilities frontier A graphical representation of a two-person world that shows all points at which A's utility can be increased only if B's utility is decreased.

variable A measure that can change from time to time or from observation to observation.

variable cost Any cost that a firm bears that depends on the level of production chosen.

vicious-circle-of-poverty hypothesis Suggests that poverty is self-perpetuating because poor countries are unable to save and invest enough to accumulate the capital stock that would help them grow.

voting paradox A simple demonstration of how majority-rule voting can lead to seemingly contradictory and inconsistent results. A commonly cited illustration of the kind of inconsistency described in the impossibility theorem.

wealth or net worth The total value of what a household owns minus what it owes. It is a stock measure.

World Bank An international agency that lends money to individual countries for projects that promote economic development.

World Trade Organization (WTO) The body responsible for governing world trade. Entered into force January 1, 1995, replacing the General Agreement on Tariffs and Trade (GATT).

Solutions to Even-Numbered Problems

Chapter 1:

2. a, c, and f are examples of positive economics. b, d, and e are examples of normative economics because they make value judgments about the outcomes.

4. Total tax if 200 students are used = 200 students × 10 days × 5 hours per day × $5 per hour = $50 000. This would mean a tax of $5 per person ($50 000 ÷ 10 000 citizens).

Total tax if 400 students are used = 400 students × 10 days × 5 hours per day × $5 per hour = $100 000. This would mean a tax of $10 per person.

By paying an additional $5 in tax (i.e., $10 instead of $5), people avoid standing in line for an hour. If time is valued at $10 per hour, every citizen gains value of $5 when the waiting time is eliminated ($10 in benefits from reduced waiting time minus $5 in additional taxes). Moving from 200 to 400 students makes all citizens better off, and since the students are willing to work for $5, no one is worse off! Thus, switching to 400 students from 200 students would be efficient. One could argue that it is also fair because everyone is paying an equal amount, and because everyone gains from the higher tax in proportion to what he or she pays.

6. Equity is "fairness" in distributing burdens and benefits. Building the bridge would certainly be fair if those who used it and gained from its existence also paid the cost of building it.

Appendix:

2. The slopes are as follows:

a. −2

b. −4

c. 6

d. −1/500 or −0.002

Chapter 2:

2. Both land and capital are inputs, but capital is something that is produced by human beings. Trees growing wild are like land; they are not produced by human beings. However, an orchard that is planted by human beings can be classified as capital. It took time, labour, and perhaps machinery to plant the orchard and to prune the trees.

4. **a.** A straight-line ppf curve intersecting the *Y* axis at 1000 units of luxury goods and intersecting the *X* axis at 500 units of necessity goods. These are the limits of production if all resources are used to produce only one good.

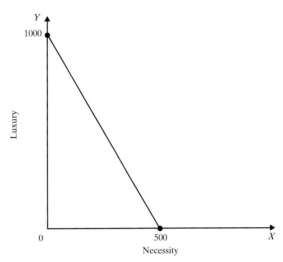

b. Unemployment or underemployment of labour would put the society inside the ppf. Full employment would move the society to some point on the ppf.

c. Answers will vary, but the decision should be based on the relative value of necessities and luxuries, and the degree of concern that all fellow citizens have enough necessities.

d. If left to the free market, prices would (at least ideally) be determined by market forces; incomes would be determined by a combination of ability, effort, and inheritance. It would be up to each individual to find a job and determine how to spend the income.

6. Answers will vary.

Chapter 3:

2. **a.** This, along with a variety of other information, can be found in the *Canada Yearbook*, an annual publication of Statistics Canada. It will be in your library.

b. The biggest functions of local government are education, police, sewers and sanitation, roads, and fire protection.

c. People in different places may have different preferences or demands for assigning a function to local government as opposed to provincial or federal government.

4. Unions and Canadian nationalists were the key opponents to NAFTA. Unions feared job losses since it would be cheaper to produce goods in Mexico. Canadian nationalists lamented the loss of political sovereignty and the reduction in our ability to use tariffs to pursue Canadian political objectives. Advocates of NAFTA argued that prices of goods and services in Canada would fall (benefiting Canadian consumers) as a result of specialization according to comparative advantage (see Chapter 2), exploitation of economies of scale (Chapter 9), and reductions in monopoly power (Chapters 13 and 14).

6. Government expenditure as a percentage of GDP increased between 1980 and 1994. Government purchases of goods and services have fallen as a percentage of GDP in the two decades since 1970.

8. Disagree. Change the word *corporations* to *sole proprietorships* and the statement is true.

10. No matter how much the firm produces, it is so small relative to the total market that its output has no effect on the market price. Therefore, the firm must be a "price taker"; it accepts the market-determined price charged by all other firms as a given that it cannot influence.

12. Government spending could increase while taxes are decreasing due to deficit spending (borrowing). Government spending could increase while government employment is decreasing if government is purchasing goods and services from the private sector that it formerly produced itself.

Chapter 4:

2. a. A simple demand shift: same diagram for both cities.

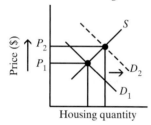

b. Rightward shift of supply with new development; leftward shift of demand with falling incomes: same diagram for both cities.

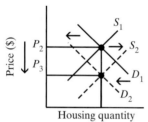

4. a. This sequence confuses changes in demand (shifts of the demand curve) with changes in quantity demanded (movements along a demand curve). First, a demand *shift* does cause price to rise. As price rises, the *quantity supplied* increases along the supply curve, and the *quantity demanded* declines along the demand curve as the market moves to re-establish equilibrium. Nothing here suggests that demand shifts back down.

b. This sequence confuses a change in price (per unit) with a change in total spending on meat. When price falls, the *quantity demanded* increases along the demand curve. Thus, the total amount spent (price × quantity demanded) depends on whether quantity demanded goes up by more than price per unit falls. Total spending could increase if demand responds strongly to the lower price.

6. The advertising campaign, if successful, will result in a reduction in demand (a shift in the demand curve to the left). The impact,

other things being equal, will be to lower tobacco sales and lower tobacco prices. This is shown in the diagram below as a new equilibrium at point *B*.

The marketing board fixes the amount of tobacco grown at a level below that which would be grown if tobacco growers were free from the marketing board restrictions. The fixed supply is shown by the new supply curve S_2 in the diagram below. The impact of the marketing board, other things held unchanged, is to reduce tobacco sales and increase prices. This is shown by the new equilibrium at point *C*. (Note that the change identified is from point *A*, where there is no marketing board and no advertising campaign, to point *C*, where there is a marketing board and no advertising campaign.)

In combination, the two policies reduce tobacco consumption, but it is impossible to predict whether tobacco prices will rise, fall, or remain constant. The combined impact of the policies is captured by the equilibrium point *D*. Notice that tobacco prices are the same as at point *A*, thus this is just one possible outcome. Try to identify conditions required for tobacco prices to rise and to fall.

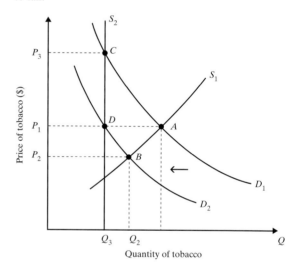

8. a.

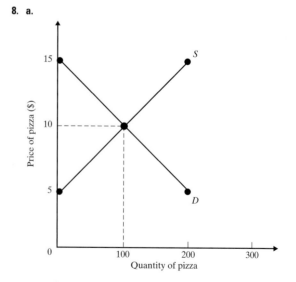

b. $Q_d = Q_s \rightarrow 300 - 20P = 20P - 100 \rightarrow P = \$10$. Substitute $P = \$10$ into either the demand or supply equation to get $Q = 100$.

c. With $P = \$15$, producers would want to supply $20(15) - 100 = 200$ pizzas, but consumers would want to buy $300 - 20(15) = 0$ pizzas. There would be an excess supply of pizzas, which would bring the price down. As the price decreased, quantity supplied would decrease while quantity demanded would increase until both were equal at a price of $10 and quantity of 100.

d. The new market demand for pizzas would be $Q_d = 600 - 40P$.

e. $Q_d = Q_s \rightarrow 600 - 40P = 20P - 100 \rightarrow P = 700/60 = \$11.66$. Substitute $P = \$11.67$ into either the demand or supply equation to get $Q = 133.2$.

Chapter 5:

2. Answers will vary. But scalping—regardless of its morality—helps to eliminate shortages by creating a "market" where the price can rise to its equilibrium value. Anyone willing to pay the equilibrium price should be able to obtain a ticket. Also, by allowing price rationing to work somewhat, scalping reduces the need for waiting in line, and so results in less wasted time.

4. The subsidy does increase the "cost" of planting . . . there is now an opportunity cost. (By planting, the farmers will have to give up the subsidy.) The subsidy will clearly lead to fewer hectares of production and higher farm prices. In effect, it shifts the supply curve to the left.

6. Absolutely not. This statement confuses a shift of demand with change in quantity demanded along a demand curve. The demand for blue jeans shifted up, causing price to rise.

8. a. $\% \Delta Q \div \% \Delta P = 0.2$.
Thus $\%\Delta P = \%\Delta Q \div 0.2 = 10\% \div 0.2 = 50\%$.

b. A price ceiling at US$1.40 per gallon would create a shortage of gasoline. The result might be long lines at gas stations and perhaps a black market in gasoline.

Chapter 6:

2. a., b., and c.

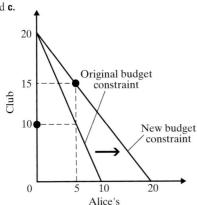

10 lunches at the club, and 5 at Alice's cost a total of $(10)(\$5) + (5)(\$10) = \$100$. This is within the budget constraint.

d. This is tricky. The price of eating at Alice's went down, but consumption did not change. Since the opportunity cost went down, the substitution effect would suggest that Professor Smith would consume more. That didn't happen, thus it must have been counteracted by a negative income effect. That is, he was better off, yet he spent all the added purchasing power at the club. A good with a negative income effect is an inferior good.

4. a. and b.

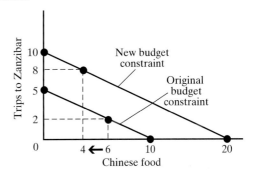

c. Zanzibar is a normal good; Chinese food is an inferior good. As income rises, Zanzibar consumption rises but Chinese food consumption falls.

d. The entire effect is due to an income effect. Mei is clearly better off, but the *opportunity costs* haven't changed because the prices have not changed! The cost of a Zanzibar trip in terms of meals sacrificed has not changed.

6. Personal responses—answers will vary.

8. Virtually any good—when consumed in too great a quantity—will have a negative marginal utility, since having more of it crowds one's living quarters and it must be gotten rid of, which takes time and trouble. (Imagine having 12 couches in your apartment.) Consuming another unit of a good with negative marginal utility will make total utility decrease. A utility-maximizing consumer would never knowingly purchase additional units of such a good.

Appendix:

2. $I/P_{x1} = 100$ and $I = 100$, thus $P_{x1} = \$1.00$ (Point A on demand curve).

$I/P_{x2} = 200$ and $I = 100$, thus $P_{x2} = \$0.50$ (Point B on demand curve).

$I/P_{x3} = 300$ and $I = 100$, thus $P_{x3} = \$0.33$ (Point C on demand curve).

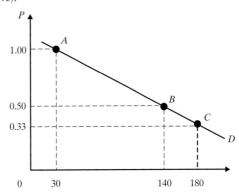

4. a. We know that $P_A A + P_N N = 100 \rightarrow 5N + 10A = 100$. We also know that $MU_N/MU_A = A/N = P_N/P_A = 5/10 \rightarrow N = 2A$. Substituting, we find that $5(2A) + 10A = 100 \rightarrow A = 5; N = 10$.

  b. If $P_N = 10$, $N = 5$ and if $P_N = 2$, $N = 25$.

  c. Answers will vary, but graph should show an indifference curve tangent to a budget constraint drawn for $P_A = \$10$ and P_N equal to one of the prices given in the answer to **b.**

Chapter 7:

2. The size of the theatre is the fixed factor. Decisions include how to divide up the tickets, what price to charge, what shows to put on, what kind of stage sets to use. All are constrained by the scale of the theatre. In the long run you might be able to raise money and build or acquire a bigger theatre. There is no fixed factor in the long run; you can think big!

4. a. The marginal product decreases as a single variable factor increases, holding all other factors constant.

  b. The table does exhibit diminishing returns because the marginal product of labour falls as labour increases:

L	TP	MP
0	0	—
1	5	5
2	9	4
3	12	3
4	14	2
5	15	1

6. The addition of capital (tractors, combines, etc.) and the application of new technology (nitrous fertilizers) raise the productivity of labour, just as the new grill discussed in the chapter raised the productivity of workers. Capital is also a substitute input for labour.

Appendix:

2. At A, $MP_L/MP_K > P_L/P_K$ because the slope of the isoquant is greater than the slope of the isocost. That means that $MP_L/P_L > MP_K/P_K$; thus the firm can cut costs by hiring more labour and less capital. At B, $MP_L/MP_K < P_L/P_K$ because the slope of the isoquant is less than the slope of the isocost. That means that $MP_K/P_K > MP_L/P_L$; thus the firm can cut costs by hiring more capital and less labour.

Chapter 8:

2. a. False. MC may be rising, but if it is below AC, then AC will still be falling.

  b. False. At the level of output where ATC is minimized, if $P > MC$, the firm should increase production even if this decision raises ATC. As long as $P > MC$, a competitive firm will increase its profits by increasing production (with one exception, as explained in Ch. 9).

  c. False. AFC = Total fixed cost/Output = TFC/q. As q rises, fixed cost remains constant, so AFC must decrease.

4. a. Marginal cost is a constant $1 from one unit of output up to 100 units since the most efficient machine will be used. From the 101st unit to the 300th unit, MC is constant at $2. From the 301st unit to the 800th unit, MC is constant at $3.

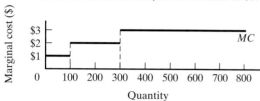

Total cost is $100 at zero units of output and rises by $1 per unit up to a total of $200 at 100 units of output. From 101 units of output up to 300 units, total cost increases by $2 per unit up to a total of $600. After that it rises at $3 per unit to a total of $2100 at 800 units of output.

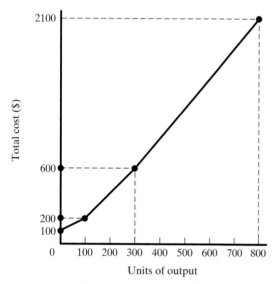

  b. At a price of $2.50, the company should produce 300 books. $TR = \$750$, $TC = \$600$, so profit = $150.

6. a. The table gives the marginal product from each day's efforts: 100, 80, 60, and 40 kilograms.

  b. Marginal cost of a kilogram of fish is the change in cost divided by the change in q. During prime season, each day brings in 100 kilograms of fish at a cost of 6000 levs, or $MC = 6000/100 = 60$ levs. During month 7, it's $6000/80 = MC = 75$ levs. During month 8, it's $6000/60 = MC = 100$ levs. During the rest of the year it's $6000/40 = 150$ levs.

  c. Produce as long as price, which is marginal revenue (80 levs), is greater than MC. Thus, the boat should be in the water fishing during prime season and month 7, but should not fish during month 8 or during the rest of the year.

Chapter 9:

2. One could make a case that some economies probably exist in all seven, but the case is much stronger in electric power (needs a big power plant or dam) and aircraft manufacturing (requires a big assembly line and a great deal of cooperation).

Home Building: Home building is usually done by small independent contractors, although there are some large contractors who produce thousands of homes each year. They do quantity buying and use mass-produced parts.

Higher education: This one is tricky. While big schools have bigger classes and fewer professors per student, they produce a different product than smaller schools do.

It is hard to find economies of much significance in *software development, vegetable farming,* and *accounting.* Although some firms in those industries are large, many are quite small and quite competitive.

4. a. and **b.**

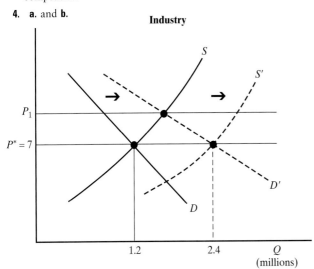

Industry

c. In the short run, demand shifts from D to D', and price rises to P_1. Firms are making profits, and they raise output to q_1.

In the long run, new firms enter the industry and existing firms expand their operations. Supply shifts from S to S', and price falls back to $7. (The new production level will be 18 000 for a given firm only if no new firms enter.)

6. a. Not true. A firm will never sell its output for less than the *marginal* cost of producing it, but may indeed sell at less than *average* total cost, as long as it can earn an operating profit.

b. Not true. The short-run marginal cost curve assumes at least one input is fixed. The long-run average cost curve allows all

inputs to vary. For example, the short-run *MC* curve for each fixed level of capital could be U-shaped, and yet the *LRAC* curve could be flat (constant returns to scale).

Appendix:

2. See the story on pages 242–243 and Figure 9A.2 on p. 243 for an increasing-cost industry.

Chapter 10:

2.

WORKERS	KILOGRAMS	MP	MRP
0	0	—	—
1	40	40	$80
2	70	30	$60
3	90	20	$40
4	100	10	$20
5	105	5	$10
6	102	−3	−$6

The firm should hire workers as long as MRP > W. When W = $30, the firm should hire 3 workers. If W increases to $50, the firm should cut back to only 2 workers, since the MRP of the third worker ($40) is now less than the cost of hiring him/her ($50).

4. a. Demand curve for construction workers shifts leftward; wage decreases; employment decreases.

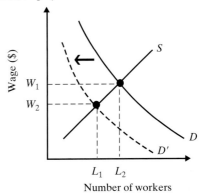

b. and **c.** Demand curve for construction workers shifts rightward; wage increases; employment increases.

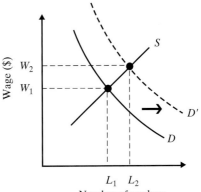

6. Investment tax credits reduce the cost of capital relative to the cost of labour. To the extent that capital is a substitute for labour, these credits can lead to layoffs and slower employment growth.

Chapter 11:

2. No. The total capital cost of the station is $1 million. With revenues of $420 000 and costs of $360 000, profit is just $60 000, which is a 6% yield on an investment of $1 million. If I can get 7.5% by investing in perfectly safe government securities, why buy a gas station?

4. a. Laura is saving. Stefan is dissaving. There is no investment going on; assets are simply being exchanged.

   b. Saving of $1000. (Also investment of $1000 if BCE uses this money to purchase new capital.)

   c. Investment of $350 million by Toronto developer. The savers are the bank's depositors.

   d. Dissaving (negative saving) of $5000 by grandmother. No investment. Saving is being done by whoever is financing the bond dealer.

   e. Saving by Tom of $10 000. Investment of $10 000 by Mexican government.

6. Savings can be borrowed by business firms, which can purchase new technology, engage in research to develop new technology, expand existing plants, or build new plants. Savings can be borrowed by individuals, who can invest in human capital (university education, professional school, technical training) or purchase newly constructed houses.

   Investment is what enables a country's average standard of living to grow. With more capital, labour is more productive, output is greater, and real incomes rise. But investment requires that productive resources be diverted from consumer goods. Thus, investment requires a sacrifice of current consumption.

8. Stockholders have put up $100 000 and receive dividends of $30 000. With an interest rate of 10%, $10 000 of this is the normal rate of return. The other $20 000 is economic profit, earned by the stockholders.

Appendix:

2. Disagree. The bridge cannot be justified on efficiency grounds, because simply investing the $25 000 000 in the financial markets would generate a stream of income worth more to citizens than the benefits from the bridge. However, at substantially lower interest rates, the PDV of the benefits would be higher, and might exceed $25 000 000. In that case, the bridge should be built.

Chapter 12:

2. a. First, calculate *MP* and $P \times MP$:

WORKERS	LOAVES OF BREAD	MP	$P \times MP$
0	0	—	—
1	15	15	210
2	30	15	210
3	42	12	168
4	52	10	140
5	60	8	112
6	66	6	84
7	70	4	56

At a wage of 119 koruna per hour, 4 workers should be hired. The fifth worker would produce less value in an hour (112 koruna) than his/her wage.

b. When the price of bread rises to 20 koruna, the last column must be recalculated:

WORKERS	$P \times MP$
0	—
1	300
2	300
3	240
4	200
5	160
6	120
7	80

Now, 6 workers should be hired.

c. If the wage rises to 125 koruna per hour, assuming bread still costs 20 koruna, only 5 workers should be hired. (If bread still costs 14 koruna, as in the first example, only 4 workers would be hired.)

d. Yes, the allocation of labour would be efficient, because each firm would hire labour until the wage were equal to the value of the marginal product of output. If all firms paid the same wage, they would all have the same marginal product of labour, and no reallocation of labour could increase total output.

4. The cost of chicken is likely to go up. Substitutes for chicken include fish, turkey, and perhaps pork and beef. In each of these markets, the demand curve will shift rightward, and both equilibrium price and equilibrium quantity will rise. Complements might include rice and canned and packaged chicken gravy. The demand curves for these goods would shift leftward, causing both equilibrium price and quantity to decrease. In the market for farmland, we might see more hectares devoted to substitutes when the anchovies disappear, because the demand for substitutes will increase, as will its equilibrium price.

6. Demand for G shifts left (from D_0 to D_1), driving down the price of G from P_0 to P_1 and creating losses in the short run for firms in G. Demand for S shifts to the right, causing the price of S to rise from P_0 to P_1 and creating short-run profits for firms in S. In the long run, firms exit G, shifting the supply curve left (from S_0 to S_1), driving the price of G back up to P_0 and eliminating the losses. At the same time firms will enter S, shifting the supply curve to the right (from S_0 to S_1) and driving price back down to P_0 to eliminate profits. In the long run, employment will expand in S and shrink in G. (Supply and demand curves are shown at the top of the opposite page).

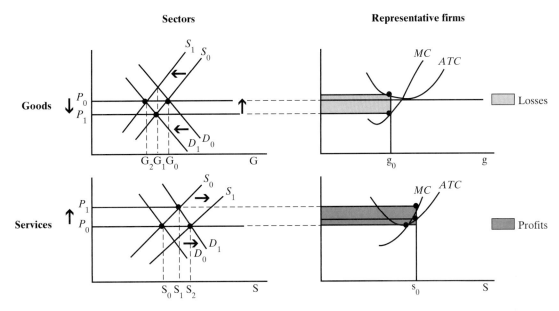

Sectors

Goods

S_1 S_0

P_0
P_1

D_1 D_0

$G_2 G_1 G_0$ G

Services

P_1
P_0

S_0
S_1

D_1
D_0

$S_0 S_1 S_2$ S

Representative firms

MC ATC

Losses

g_0 g

MC ATC

Profits

s_0 S

Chapter 13:

2. A competitive firm can sell all the output it wants without having any impact on market price. For each additional unit sold, its revenue will rise by the market price. Hence, *MR* is the same at all levels of output.

Each time a monopolist increases output by one unit, the market price falls. The additional revenue the monopolist receives is actually less than the price, because consumers who were already buying the output get a price break too. *MR* is thus lower than price, and as output increases, both price and *MR* decline.

4. a. and **b.**

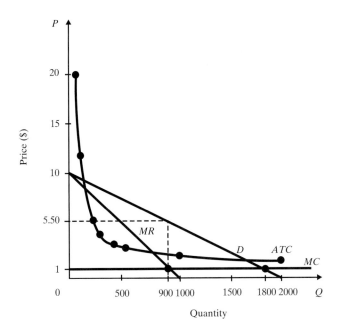

c. Profit-maximizing output is 900; profit-maximizing price is $5.50.

d. Efficient price would be $1, where the demand curve intersects the marginal cost curve. At this price, $Q = 1800$.

e. Long-run output would be zero, because losses would cause the monopoly to exit the industry.

f. Alternatively, regulators could require the monopoly to charge a price equal to marginal cost and then subsidize the monopoly's loss.

Chapter 14:

2. a. Monopolistic competition: free entry, lots of firms, product differentiation, close substitutability.

b. As new establishments open, demand curves for existing firms shift left. Price of admission falls and profits drop to zero at the tangency of demand and *ATC* (see Figure 14.3).

4. Both A's and B's potential losses are minimized by cheating. To minimize the maximum loss, A should cheat, because it yields higher profit regardless of what B does. The same is true for B. If A cheats, so will B, and if B cheats, so will A. Most likely outcome: both will cheat.

6. a. 30 units.

b. $P = \$14$.

c. $TR = 30 \times \$14 = \$420$.

$TC = \$9 \times 30 = \$270$.

Profit $= \$420 - \$270 = \$150$.

d. In the long run, entry will shift the demand and marginal revenue curves leftward until normal profit is earned at the profit-maximizing output level. This occurs when the demand curve is tangent to the *ATC* curve.

8. a. Both have dominant strategies in Game 1—charge the low price. Neither has a dominant strategy in Game 2.

b. You might try tit-for-tat (match the competitor's move) to signal the opposition that if she prices high, you might do so also.

c. If you are risk averse, you would probably swerve to guarantee a gain of 3. This minimizes your losses from the worst thing that can happen to you (a maximin strategy).

Chapter 15:

2. One would have to establish that the intent was to restrict competition or observe that the aggressive firm is making losses in the short term and economic profits in the long term.

4. Yes, it would be allowed. Competition exists just 80 kilometres away.

6. $TR = \$0.105 \times 89.3$ million $= \$9\ 376\ 500$.

$TC = \$0.048 \times 89.3$ million $+ \$1\ 500\ 000 = \$5\ 786\ 400$.

Profit $= TR - TC = \$3\ 590\ 100$.

Rate of profit $=$ Profit/Invested capital $=$
$\$3\ 590\ 100/\$45\ 000\ 000 = 0.0798$, or 7.98%. You would recommend a rate hike.

If the "fair rate of return" is 10%, then the utility should be permitted to earn a profit of $\$4\ 500\ 000$ (which is 10% of its invested capital). The utility will have to earn revenue of $\$4\ 500\ 000 + \$5\ 786\ 400 = \$10\ 286\ 000$. Since 89.3 million kW·h will be demanded, the charge per kW·h must be $\$10\ 286\ 000/89\ 300\ 000 = \$0.115$ per kW·h. So the utility should be permitted to hike its rate from $\$0.105$ per kW·h to $\$0.115$ per kW·h, an increase of one cent per kW·h.

8. The answer to this question is based on work in Chapter 13 (pages 331–334) and Figure 13.8. A monopoly firm will restrict output to maximize profits. Breaking up the monopoly results in lower prices and higher levels of output. This will have two effects. First, income will be redistributed from the owners of the monopoly (lower profits) to the current consumers (through lower prices). Second, there will be a gain to society since consumers are willing to pay more for the additional output than it cost to produce it. This second effect represents a more efficient allocation of resources.

10. Like any group of consumers, students would like to be able to purchase products, including their university education, at a low or even zero price. But since scarce resources are used to produce education, a zero price or any price set lower than average cost necessarily implies forcing someone else to pay all or at least part of the cost. Students might argue that they are poor and therefore deserve free tuition and that the rich should pay based on some concept of equity. Alternatively, they might argue, based on analysis in this chapter, that universities collude when setting prices, and that the resulting prices are above the average cost of producing education. As a consequence, government should regulate prices to assure the price is not set higher than average cost.

Arguments against regulation of tuition fees include: (1) universities do not seem to collude but instead act as monopolistic competitors by competing on price and by differentiating their products; (2) competition results in an outcome which is more efficient than that which would emerge with regulation; (3) university education is already heavily subsidized and prices are well below average cost; and (4) students actually have high lifetime incomes and are not poor.

The discussion of externalities, public goods and other market failures in the next chapter will provide other possible reasons for government inolvement in university education.

Chapter 16:

2. a. With private goods, we each get to choose what quantity of each good we want. If I don't like a good, I don't buy it. But with public goods, we all get the same level of output. We all breathe better air if it is cleaned up, and we all get the same amount of national defence. When public goods are produced locally we have more choice (see discussion of the Tiebout hypothesis).

b. Representative democracy is not guaranteed to produce the socially optimal mix of public goods. Some problems are logrolling, a poorly informed electorate, poor incentives for people to become informed and vote, and the fact that votes are limited to *bundles* of public goods. Also, Arrow's theorem implies that there is no consistent, nonarbitrary way to agree on what the socially optimal mix is. The voting paradox is an example of why majority voting does not provide a consistent social choice mechanism.

c. An example might be a bureaucrat who is motivated just to increase the power, prestige, and budget of her bureau. This might lead to bloated bureaucracies. Clearly there has been great pressure in recent years to keep politicians and bureaucrats honest.

4. a. *Elementary and secondary education:* Private aspects—substantial benefits accrue to the individual, and those who do not pay could, in theory, be excluded from receiving them. Also rivalry, in that there is a limited number of students one teacher can effectively teach. Public aspects—there are substantial benefits to the public at large (more informed voting, more socialized behaviour). It is impossible to limit these benefits to those who pay.

b. *Higher education:* Same as above, but here even more of the benefits accrue to the individual, and the costs are often borne by those who benefit.

c. *Medical care:* Private aspects—most of the benefits of good health are enjoyed by the individual, and in theory we could exclude those who won't or can't pay. Also, high degree of rivalry. Public aspects—substantial public benefits when communicable diseases are reduced or public health is improved.

d. *Air traffic control:* Private aspects—there is certainly rivalry, as shown by the congested skies over urban airports and the ulcers suffered by overworked air traffic controllers. Public aspects—all air traffic in a given area must be controlled from a single set of controllers. Competing firms would not be able to supply this service effectively. Also, substantial benefits to the public at large, which are nonexcludable (e.g., reduced probability of a plane crashing into one's home).

6. a. People disagree about this. There are private aspects of housing for the poor: excludability and rivalry. There may also be substantial benefits for society at large when everyone has a place to sleep at night.

b. Disagree. An unregulated market economy tends to *under*produce public goods, because nonexcludability and the free-rider problem prevent the private sector from charging for these goods.

8. Most economists would argue that the patent system is, on balance, a good thing. True, patent holders—as monopolies—charge a higher-than-efficient price for the technology. But without such monopolies, the new technologies would not have been developed in the first place. Still, government involvement in research may be justified on several grounds. It might be better to have the government fund the research and make the results widely available than to encourage research via patents that impart monopoly control over new ideas. Also, patents may not be sufficient to keep new technology from being imitated once developed. In this case, the private sector has little incentive to develop the new technology.

10. a. *Imperfect information:* impossible to verify who is faking. Also, *moral hazard:* less reason to avoid injury due to benefits received.

b. *Adverse selection:* disproportionate number of damaged computers will be sold.

c. *Imperfect information:* difficult to know how well a company's system will work until after it is in place. Hard to evaluate competing bids.

d. *Adverse selection:* The worst drivers will buy more insurance, forcing up rates and causing better drivers to choose between subsidizing bad drivers or doing without insurance. Also, *moral hazard:* less reason to avoid collisions if insurance company will bear the costs.

Chapter 17:

2. There are two ways this might be justified. First, if the rich acquired their riches through a sequence of voluntary exchanges, one could conclude that the outcome was fair and just because the process that generated it is fair and just. Second, if taxing the rich to give to the poor reduces total income by an amount large enough to leave the poor worse off, one could argue, following Rawls, that the original situation (with some people very rich) is just and fair.

4. Disagree. The statement ignores different working conditions, differing vacations, and differing time available for other income opportunities (writing books, consulting). Also, choices reveal preferences for various jobs. Academic jobs must yield more utility to some or no one would be an academic.

6. Answers will vary. Cost-of-living differences would imply that they should be different. The concept of "horizontal equity" (equal treatment of equals) would argue for similar benefits after adjusting for cost-of-living differences. On the other hand, it may well be true that people tend to move to higher-benefit areas and away from low-benefit areas.

8. Answers will vary. Philosophical arguments might include the importance of shelter to human survival and dignity, and the values of a humanitarian society. Practical arguments might stress the public goods aspects of reducing homelessness—we all benefit from reduced homelessness, whether we contribute to the effort or not.

Chapter 18:

2. The individual earning $70 000 per year owed $13 007.26 when the personal amount was treated as a tax credit (see Table 18.3). If instead the basic personal amount is treated as a deduction, it is subtracted from total income to yield taxable income ($70 000

− $5000 − $6456 = $59 544). Calculating the federal tax yields $12 829.56 and subtracting CPP and EI credits gives us federal tax owed, which is $12 622.54. The $70 000-per-year income earner gains $384.72 if the basic personal amount is treated as a deduction rather than as a credit. If you complete the calculations for the individual earning $18 000, you find it makes no difference for after-tax income. Thus the use of credits results in a more progressive income tax system.

4. Disagree. Excess burdens come about because of distortions in behaviour. If a good has a low demand elasticity, the tax will have ve a relatively small effect on quantity demanded, and the excess burden will be relatively small.

6. If one thinks of the employer contribution to the CPP as a payment for future pensions, it would be correct to list it as part of employee compensation. However, Parliament could always change the law so that those entitlements aren't received, and faculty may prefer to receive cash rather than future benefits; to this extent, the full value of the payroll tax should not be counted as compensation. Also, it must be pointed out that the imposition of the tax does not raise overall employee compensation. If it really is just another form of compensation, wages will simply fall by the amount of the tax. To the extent that it is a tax because workers prefer to be compensated in a different way, if the supply of labour is inelastic, workers will bear the burden of the tax and their compensation will be reduced.

8. If the cost of one's car is proportional to one's income, then the tax would be proportional. If high-income people spend a smaller (larger) *percentage* of their income on cars, then the tax would be regressive (progressive). The tax would distort by discouraging automobile ownership (especially ownership of expensive cars) but might also correct for existing externalities (congestion, air pollution, noise).

Chapter 19:

2. The unemployment rate is the number of unemployed as a fraction of the labour force. To be in the labour force, one has to have a job or be looking for a job. In essence, the labour force is the supply of labour. If the labour force expands by more than the number of employed expands, the unemployment rate rises!

4. a. Total money cost = two years' forgone salary + 2 years' tuition = $21 000 + $21 000 + $15 000 + $15 000 = $72 000 (ignoring discounting of the second year's costs).

b. Loss of seniority in present job; possible summer employment to partially offset lost annual income of $21 000; loss of work experience; etc.

c. Rate of return = $5000/$72 000 = 0.069 or 6.9%. With increase in net wage of $15 000, rate of return = $15 000/$72 000 = 0.208 or 20.8%.

d. Justine should look at the interest rate and see if she could earn a higher rate of return by investing her money in a financial asset. She should also consider the nonmonetary rewards of a job that requires an MBA, and how much she would enjoy (or dislike) business school.

6. When you work, you lose some of your income. Thus, when I earn a dollar, I don't get to keep a full dollar. The existence of taxes affects the opportunity cost of leisure and thus can impact work effort.

8.

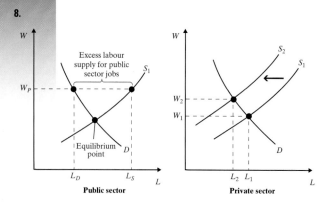

Public sector — Private sector

Chapter 20:

2. A $5.00 fee is unlikely to have a large impact on use by those who have a real emergency. Demand for emergency treatment in the event of a real emergency is highly inelastic. However, even in this case, demand may not be perfectly inelastic. Those who are very price sensitive—the very poor, street people, etc.—may delay visits to emergency rooms.

   It is important to recognize that not all demand for emergency treatment arises from real emergencies. Some people use emergency/outpatient facilities because they are more convenient than visits to a family doctor or because they believe some minor ailment is a real emergency. But even in this case a $5.00 fee is unlikely to have a significant impact on demand.

   Thus the fee is unlikely to have much impact on utilization or costs. If it has any effect, it is likely to be on those who are very price sensitive, especially those with very low incomes. It will generate additional revenue for the health care system, but this tax imposed explicitly on the sick might not be considered "fair."

4. An economist cannot answer this question since it involves putting a value on human life. There are many possible answers, each of which depends on the ethical perspective of the decision maker. For example, if the decision maker believes all human beings are equally deserving of having their life saved and that the value of each life is less than infinity, the funds should be spent on the water and waste treatment facility since this results in the maximum number of lives saved. On the other hand, if the artificial heart transplant recipient is considered more valuable (in the subjective judgment of the decision maker) than the thousands in the developing country, the resources should go to the transplant operation.

6. If illness (as measured by incidences of illness rather than by visits to the physician) is equally common in all areas, doctors locating to areas with relatively high physician–population ratios will find their incomes are lower (fewer patients) if they behave in the same way as physicians in areas with few physicians. But if they behave differently, say by calling back patients for second or third visits, they can make up for the lost income. They can do this because patients have less information than doctors and therefore place their trust in the doctors' judgment. The ability of physicians to determine utilization is known as supplier-induced demand.

8. Doctors will look at the expected benefits from an intervention and they will not consider the cost. One would expect them to prescribe services even if marginal cost exceeds the marginal benefit.

Chapter 21:

2. a. Manitoba would have an absolute advantage in both wheat and canola.

   b. In Manitoba, taking one hectare out of wheat and moving it into canola sacrifices 2.5 tonnes of wheat for 1.7 tonnes of canola. This is 2.5/1.7 = 1.47 tonnes of wheat for each tonne of canola. In Saskatchewan, the sacrifice is 2.3/1.4 = 1.64 tonnes of wheat for each tonne of canola.

   c. Based on the calculations in **b.** above, Saskatchewan has a comparative advantage in wheat, and Manitoba has a comparative advantage in canola.

   d. Yes, the data are consistent with the conclusions in **c.** above. While each province grows more wheat than canola, a higher fraction of land in Saskatchewan is in wheat and a (slightly) higher fraction of land in Manitoba is in canola. Although neither province completely "specializes," each province seems to be devoting more of its resources to producing the good in which it has a comparative advantage.

4. Answers will vary.

6. a. The opportunity cost of a bottle of red wine is 1.5 bottles of white in France and 2 bottles of white in Germany. France, therefore, has a comparative advantage in red wine.

   The opportunity cost of a bottle of white wine is 0.66 bottles of red in France and 0.5 bottles of white in Germany. Germany, therefore, has a comparative advantage in white wine.

   b. No. At the current exchange rate, both white and red wine are cheaper in Germany. French citizens will want to import both types of wine from Germany, but Germans will not want to import French wine.

   c. In this situation, we would expect the price of the franc to decrease until French red wine became attractive to Germans while German white wine was still attractive to the French. (An exchange rate between 1.5 and 2 francs per mark would accomplish this.)

   d. In the long run, we would expect exchange rates to adjust until the French are exporting red wine to Germany, and the Germans are exporting white wine to France.

Chapter 22:

2. a. Capital increases the productivity of labour. A given-sized labour force can produce more output, and output per capita rises.

   b. In a market economy, individual household savings decisions determine the pool of aggregate savings. Aggregate savings, in turn, is the amount made available for firms to purchase capital. Savings are matched to investment projects in financial markets, where the interest rate adjusts to equate total desired investment with total desired savings.

   c. In developing countries, a greater fraction of output is needed just to ensure the current population's survival. An increase in investment—which requires a decrease in current consumption—cuts dangerously close to this survival level of consumption, and at a minimum causes more discomfort than it would in developed countries.

d. Answers will vary. Market-oriented economists would stress increased incentives for private investment (political stability, lower government budget deficit, and perhaps loans from abroad). Planning-oriented economists might stress government-directed projects, taxes on luxury goods, and capital controls designed to prevent capital flight to developed countries.

4. It is true that poor countries must accumulate capital in order to grow, but many poor countries do indeed have extra output available for savings. The problem is often that the available savings goes abroad (capital flight). Increased political stability and a more stable investment climate would help investment in the domestic economy. In addition, poor countries can get loans and other assistance from developed countries to help them accumulate capital.

6. A country should work to develop both its agricultural and its industrial sectors. Development of the agricultural sector can have high payoffs because it often requires little capital investment and directly benefits the poorest (rural) segment of society. Experience has shown that import substitution is a poor development policy. Its disadvantages include lessened competition in the domestic market, fewer jobs created, and expensive inputs for domestic industries.

Many countries favour industry as a more direct route to growth in the capital stock, and also to emulate the production pattern of already developed countries. Import substitution is attractive because it lessens dependence on unstable foreign demand for exports.

8. Many recent famines have resulted from government policies. In some cases, keeping farm prices artificially low has led to a decrease in production. In other cases, a failure to invest in a distributional infrastructure has led to famine in outlying rural areas.

Chapter 23:

2. The speaker confuses political systems with economic systems.

The Soviet economic system was one of socialism (government ownership of land and capital) and central planning (government direction of resource allocation). Totalitarianism is a political—not an economic—system in which the ruler exercises authoritarian control without the consent of those governed.

4. Socialism is an economic system in which the "means of production" (land and capital) are owned and controlled by government. The possible strengths: rapid growth from planned capital accumulation, internalization of external costs, more fair distribution of income (because no property income).

6. a. Disagree. Exactly the opposite has occurred. Since 1958, China has moved toward a decentralized industrial base. Since Tiananmen Square, China has cracked down on political dissent but it has encouraged private enterprise.

b. Disagree. No economy is completely free of either government intervention or market forces. While the economies of the Soviet Union and Japan in the 1950s and 1960s may have differed in the relative role of each factor, both of them had some degree of influence. An important part of Soviet growth was the large rate of capital accumulation forced by the central plan, but the private sector was also important, particularly in agriculture. In Japan, while private sector saving and investment was a very significant factor, so was the public education system and (perhaps arguably) the coordinating role of the Ministry of Trade and Industry.

c. Disagree. The opposite is true. Economists agree about the six components of transition, but disagree about the sequencing and speed.

8. Disagree. While it is true that central planners can control resource allocation, central planning requires keen and virtuous planners to ensure that scarce resources flow to where they are needed most. In a capitalist market economy, the self-interest of resource owners steers resources to those sectors where they are needed most—that is, those sectors offering the highest rate of return.

Index

Photo Credits